SPARKNOTES
101

Shakespeare

PUBLISHER: Daniel Weiss
EDITORIAL DIRECTOR: Laurie Barnett
MANAGING EDITOR: Vincent Janoski

SERIES EDITOR: Emma Chastain
CONTRIBUTING EDITOR: Anna Medvedovsky
DESIGN: Daniel Williams

This edition published by Spark Publishing

Spark Publishing
A Division of SparkNotes LLC
120 Fifth Avenue, 8th Floor
New York, NY 10011

ISBN 1-4114-0027-5

Please submit comments and questions or report errors to www.sparknotes.com/errors

Printed and bound in the United States

CONTENTS

THE HISTORY PLAYS 363

A VERY BRIEF INTRODUCTION TO SHAKESPEARE'S SONNETS 503

GLOSSARY 545

TAKING THE BITE OUT OF THE BARD

We know this is tough stuff, and we're here to help.

Don't be daunted by the size of the book you're holding in your hand. *SparkNotes 101: Shakespeare* is the size of an elephant because it covers every single play Shakespeare wrote—from the legendary (*Hamlet*) to the obscure (*King John*), as well as twenty of Shakespeare's most frequently studied sonnets. Each entry includes:

- *Quick plot overview*
- *Scene-by-scene summary*
- *Character list*
- *Themes, motifs, symbols, and quotations*

We're there for you through thick and thin—from *All's Well that Ends Well* to *The Winter's Tale*, from "To be or not to be" to "Now die, die, die, die, die."

WILLIAM SHAKESPEARE: AN OVERVIEW OF THE BARD

William Shakespeare, the most influential writer in all of English literature, was born in 1564 to a successful middle-class glovemaker in Stratford-upon-Avon, England. Shakespeare's formal education did not progress beyond grammar school. In 1582, he married an older woman, Anne Hathaway; this union with Anne produced three children. Around 1590, Shakespeare left his family behind and traveled to London to work as an actor and playwright. He quickly earned public and critical acclaim, and eventually became the most popular playwright in England and part-owner of the Globe Theater. Shakespeare's career bridged the reigns of Elizabeth I (ruled 1558–1603) and James I (ruled 1603–1625), and he was a favorite of both monarchs. James paid Shakespeare's company a great compliment by giving its members the title of King's Men. Shakespeare retired to Stratford a wealthy and renowned man and died in 1616 at the age of fifty-two. At the time of Shakespeare's death, literary luminaries such as Ben Jonson hailed his works as timeless.

Shakespeare's works were collected and printed in various editions in the century following his death, and by the early eighteenth century, his reputation as the greatest poet ever to write in English was well established. The unprecedented regard in which Shakespeare's works were held led to a fierce curiosity about his life, but many details of Shakespeare's personal history are unknown or shrouded in mystery. Some people have concluded from this lack of information and from Shakespeare's modest education that someone else actually wrote Shakespeare's plays—Francis Bacon and the Earl of Oxford are the two most popular candidates—but the support for this claim is overwhelmingly circumstantial, and many scholars do not take this theory seriously.

Scholars generally consider Shakespeare the author of the thirty-eight plays (two of them possibly collaborations), and 154 sonnets that bear his name. The legacy of this body of work is immense. A number of Shakespeare's plays have transcended even the category of brilliance, influencing the very course of Western literature and culture.

SHAKESPEARE'S GENRES

Shakespeare's plays can be divided into three major categories: comedies, tragedies, and histories. He wrote most of the comedies in the beginning of his career. These lighthearted plays concern love, exclude death, and almost always end with a marriage. Among Shakespeare's most famous plays are his tragedies, most of which he wrote later in his career. The tragedies usually end with the deaths of many or all of the main characters. In his history plays, Shakespeare fictionalizes the lives of historical English rulers. (For a detailed explanation see "The History Plays.") Beyond the three major genres, problem plays and romances are the two most commonly identified genres. Critics disagree about which plays belong to which categories, and most major editions of Shakespeare categorize the plays slightly differently. The list below follows conventional groupings, and we have noted those plays whose categorizations are most controversial.

In this book, Shakespeare's plays are organized alphabetically, except for the history plays, which are organized in order of historical events.

Histories
    2 Henry VI
    3 Henry VI
    1 Henry VI
    Richard III
    Richard II
    King John
    1 Henry IV
    2 Henry IV
    Henry V
    Henry VIII*

Comedies (13 = 10 + 3)
    The Two Gentlemen of Verona
    The Taming of the Shrew
    The Comedy of Errors
    Love's Labour's Lost
    A Midsummer Night's Dream
    The Merchant of Venice
    The Merry Wives of Windsor
    Much Ado About Nothing
    As You Like It
    Twelfth Night
    Troilus and Cressida†
    Measure for Measure†
    All's Well That Ends Well†

Tragedies (10)
    Titus Andronicus
    Romeo and Juliet
    Julius Caesar
    Hamlet
    Othello
    Timon of Athens
    King Lear
    Macbeth
    Antony and Cleopatra
    Coriolanus

Romances (5)
    Pericles, Prince of Tyre
    The Winter's Tale
    Cymbeline
    The Tempest
    The Two Noble Kinsmen

*sometimes identified as a romance
† sometimes identified as problem plays

TRAGEDIES, COMEDIES, AND ROMANCES

ALL'S WELL THAT ENDS WELL

Helena manages to marry Bertram, but he does not agree to be a true husband to her until she tricks him into sleeping with her.

ALL'S WELL THAT ENDS WELL IN CONTEXT

The date of composition of *All's Well that Ends Well* is uncertain. The earliest known version appears in the Folio of 1623, seven years after Shakespeare's death, so other clues must be sought in order to date the work. The composition is usually attributed to the period between 1601 and 1606, around the same time as Shakespeare's other "problem plays": *Troilus and Cressida* and *Measure for Measure*. All three share a dark, bitter wit and an unpleasant view of human relations; all three contrast sharply in mood with earlier, sunnier comedies such as *Twelfth Night* and *As You Like It*. The darker sensibility of the problem plays, and *All's Well that Ends Well* in particular, is attributed to the coarse pragmatism of sexual relations and the difficulties of rejoicing about a "happy ending" that unites ill-suited couples such as Helena and Bertram.

A minority of scholars suggests that *All's Well that Ends Well* was composed earlier, and they associate its text with a "lost play" called *Love's Labour Won*, which is listed in a 1598 catalogue of Shakespeare's plays but has never been seen mentioned elsewhere. These scholars argue that the plot of *All's Well* matches the title of this hypothetical work: Helena "labors" to gain her love, and wins. *All's Well*, they suggest, is a reworked version of *Love's Labour Won* that Shakespeare published at a later date.

The story of the plot is less murky: it is derived, more or less directly, from the ninth story of the third day of Boccaccio's *Decameron*, a classic of early Renaissance literature, written between 1348 and 1358. The work and the story in question were translated into English in the mid-sixteenth century by William Painter as *The Palace of Pleasure*, and it was this version that Shakespeare probably drew upon. In typical fashion, Shakespeare altered and reshaped the original text to create a richer story, adding characters such as Lafew, the countess of Roussillon, and Parolles while keeping essential elements like the bed-trick and the Florentine war.

The critical reception of *All's Well* has always been mixed. Both critics and audiences bristle at the match between Helena and Bertram. Its reputation has revived significantly in recent years, but it remains an unpopular and little-performed play.

ALL'S WELL THAT ENDS WELL: KEY FACTS

Full title: All's Well that Ends Well

Time and place written: 1604 (?); London

Date of first performance: 1604–1605 (?)

Genre: Comedy; problem play

Setting (time): Early seventeenth century

Setting (place): France

Protagonist: Helena

Major conflict: Helena seeks to win the love and acceptance of her husband Bertram.

ALL'S WELL THAT ENDS WELL: CHARACTER LIST

Clown The countess's servant and messenger. The clown enjoys coarse, sexual humor.

Diana A young Florentine virgin whom Bertram attempts to seduce. Diana helps Helena trick Bertram into sleeping with Helena, his lawful wife.

Widow	Diana's mother.

First Lord (Dumaine) and Second Lord (Dumaine) Two brothers. The lords are genial French noblemen who serve in the Florentine army and befriend Bertram. Together with Bertram, they plot to expose Parolles for what he is.

Duke of Florence The ruler of Florence, whose army includes several volunteer French lords, including Bertram, Parolles, and the brothers Dumaine.

King of France The ruler of France and Bertram's liege. Deathly ill at the start of the play, the king is miraculously cured by Helena with her father's medicine. The king appreciates Helena, and is appalled by Bertram's behavior.

Helena The play's heroine. The orphan daughter of a great doctor, Helena becomes the ward of the countess of Roussillon and falls in love with the countess's son Bertram. She is a resourceful and determined woman, not easily discouraged by setbacks.

Lafew An old French nobleman who offers advice to the king and is friendly with the countess. He is wise and discerning, perceiving both Helena's worth and Parolles' worthlessness.

Mariana A Florentine woman.

Parolles Bertram's companion. A coward, liar, and braggart, Parolles is eventually exposed and disgraced.

Count Bertram of Roussillon The countess's only son. Bertram is a handsome, well-liked young man. An excellent soldier, Bertram treats Helena miserably: he marries her at the king's urging, and then quickly abandons her.

Countess of Roussillon Bertram's mother, Helena's guardian, and the mistress of Roussillon. A wise, discerning old woman, the countess supports Helena and condemns Bertram's behavior.

Steward The countess's servant.

ALL'S WELL THAT ENDS WELL: PLOT OVERVIEW

Helena, the orphan daughter of a famous physician, is hopelessly in love with Count Bertram of Roussillon, son of Helena's guardian, the countess of Roussillon. Using her father's medicine, Helena cures the king of France from a fatal illness. In return, the king allows her to marry Bertram. Appalled by the match, Bertram flees with his scoundrel friend Parolles to fight in the army of the duke of Florence. He sends Helena a letter saying that he will never be her husband until she can get his family ring from off his finger and become pregnant with his child. Despondent, Helena travels to Florence, where she discovers that Bertram is trying to seduce Diana, the daughter of a widow. To help Helena, Diana procures Bertram's ring as a token of his love, and trades places with Helena when Bertram comes to sleep with her. Meanwhile, Bertram's two friends, the brothers Dumaine, expose Parolles as a coward and a villain. With the Florentine war over, Bertram returns to France. Helena follows, and reveals that she has satisfied Bertram's conditions: she has his ring, and is pregnant with his child. Bertram agrees to be a good husband.

ALL'S WELL THAT ENDS WELL: SCENE SUMMARY

ACT I

Helena plans to use her late father's medicines to cure the king of France from a fatal illness, hoping to win the hand of her guardian's son, Count Bertram.

I.I Location: Roussillon. The count's palace

Helena, daughter of a great deceased doctor and ward of the countess of Roussillon, is secretly in love with the countess's son Bertram.

Helena has been the ward of the wise, kindly, elderly countess of Roussillon since the death of Helena's father, a famous doctor. The countess's husband has also recently died, and her son Count Bertram, a brave and handsome but callow young man, is sent to serve the king of France whom, we learn, is dying. Helena is in love with Bertram, but hopelessly, since he is a nobleman and she a commoner. As Bertram departs for the king's court, she banters with Parolles, an unsavory liar and coward who has managed to gain Bertram's trust. Parolles recommends that Helena find herself a husband and lose her virginity soon. During their conversation, Helena comes up with a plan for getting Bertram to marry her.

I.II   Location: Paris. The king's palace

Bertram arrives at the court of the king of France, who suffers from a fatal illness.

The king of France has decided to stay out of a war between Austria and Florence with the caveat that any French nobleman who wants to may go fight. Bertram arrives, and the king greets him. The king laments the loss of both Bertram's father and Helena's father, saying only a doctor as great as Helena's father could save the king's life now.

I.III   Location: Roussillon. The count's palace

Helena confesses to the countess that she loves Bertram and resolves to try to cure the king of France.

The countess chats with the coarse, bawdy clown who once served her husband. Her steward joins them and informs the countess that he overheard Helena declaring her love for Bertram. The countess sends for Helena immediately. After much dissembling, Helena admits that she is in love with the countess's son, and then immediately declares her plan to go see the king of France and try to cure him using the medical knowledge that she learned from her father. The countess expresses doubt that the king and the royal doctors will accept the help of a young woman, but gives her blessing and sends Helena on her way.

ACT II

Helena cures the king and marries Bertram, but Bertram departs for the Florentine wars without consummating the marriage.

II.I   Location: Paris. The king's palace

French noblemen leave to fight in Florence; the king promises Helena that if her father's medicine cures him, she may marry whomever she wishes.

The king of France bids farewell to a party of noblemen bound for the war in Florence, declaring that he may well be dead by the time they return. Two brothers, the First and Second Lords Dumaine, urge Bertram to come with them to fight, but Bertram says regretfully that the king has commanded him to remain at court. Parolles boasts of his own prowess in battle and suggests that Bertram sneak away. Parolles wishes the two Lords Dumaine good luck and the blessings of Mars, the god of war.

The king converses with old Lafew, who has recently come from Roussillon. Lafew tells his sovereign that a female doctor (Helena, of course) has recently arrived promising a cure for his ailment. Helena is ushered in, and tells the king that on his deathbed her father gave her a powerful medicine, and that she has brought it to save the king's life. The king thanks her for her offer, but says that there is no point in trying, since his doctors insist that the disease is incurable. Helena responds that there is no harm in making an attempt, and then boldly promises that the medicine will restore his health within two days. She goes further, saying that if she fails, she may be executed, but if she succeeds, she asks permission to choose whomever she desires as a husband. The king agrees to the bargain, and promises to try the medicine immediately.

II.II   Location: Roussillon. The count's palace

The countess sends Helena a message with the clown.

The countess, after letting her clown jest with her for a time, sends him to the king's court with a message for Helena.

II.III Location: Paris. The king's palace

The king is cured, and Bertram reluctantly marries Helena.

Parolles and Lafew remark on the amazing success of Helena's cure that has restored the king to good health. True to his word, the king assembles five stalwart young noblemen as potential mates, but Helena passes over them all and selects Bertram. Bertram is taken aback and declares that she is too far beneath him for the marriage to work. The king rebukes him, saying that inner worth is more important than noble birth, and promises to raise Helena to a higher rank. When Bertram still refuses to agree to the match, his monarch threatens to disfavor him. Bertram unhappily agrees, and the couple is immediately led to the altar. Left behind, Lafew and Parolles argue over the relative worth of the new husband and wife. Lafew criticizes Bertram's conduct, and Parolles takes offense and tries to pick a fight, but then backs away, saying that Lafew is too old for a duel. Lafew sees through Parolles' bluster and calls him a coward. Bertram returns, newly married, and tells Parolles that he will never consummate the marriage: he plans to send Helena home to his mother and then run away to war.

II.IV Location: Paris. The king's palace

Helena finds out that Bertram plans to depart, leaving their marriage unconsummated.

Helena receives the countess's greetings from the clown and inquires after her health. Parolles joins them and informs Helena that pressing business calls Bertram away, so their marriage must remain unconsummated for the present. She should prepare to return home and then come bid him goodbye.

II.V Location: Paris. The king's palace

Accompanied by Parolles, Bertram takes his leave of Helena.

Lafew warns Bertram that Parolles is not the great soldier that he claims to be, but Bertram pays no attention to him. Helena comes to her husband, who apologizes for his hasty departure. She asks him for a parting kiss but he refuses and rides off, accompanied only by Parolles.

ACT III

Unhappy that Bertram has rejected her, Helena travels to Florence and plots to sleep with him without his knowledge.

III.I Location: Florence. The duke's palace

French noblemen arrive in Florence to support the duke in war.

The duke of Florence expresses his regret that the king of France has refused to support him in battle. The First and Second Lords Dumaine, recently arrived from France, remind the duke that many young French nobles will come to fight for Florence nonetheless.

III.II Location: Roussillon. The count's palace

In a letter, Bertram announces to Helena that he will effectively never be a true husband to her; she resolves to leave home.

Helena has returned home. The countess reads Bertram's letter, in which he declares his intention to remain abroad rather than endure his marriage. The two Lords Dumaine arrive with another letter for Helena from Bertram. He announces that he will not be a real husband to her until she wears his ring (which he never takes off) and bears his child (impossible, since he has not slept with her); in other words, never. Brokenhearted, she resolves to leave Roussillon, since her presence keeps Bertram away from home, and seek refuge elsewhere.

III.III Location: Florence

The duke of Florence gives Bertram a promotion: he is now general of the duke's cavalry.

III.IV Location: Roussillon. The count's palace

The countess discovers that Helena has left and blames Bertram for mistreating her.

The countess discovers Helena's letter declaring her intention to make a pilgrimage to a monastery. The countess curses Bertram's folly and orders letters sent immediately to Bertram, hoping that he will hurry home. She hopes that Helena will eventually return as well, and that a reconciliation can be effected.

III.V Location: Florence

Helena meets the widow, whose daughter (Diana) Bertram has been trying to seduce.

Helena overhears a conversation between an old widow, her daughter Diana, and their neighbor Mariana. Bertram, who rides by with the duke of Florence's army, has been trying to seduce Diana. Helena joins the discussion. The widow advises Diana to stay chaste. The three Florentine women have heard that Bertram has a wife he detests, but do not know that Helena is that wife. The widow invites Helena to stay with her.

III.VI Location: Florence. The duke of Florence's camp

The two Lords Dumaine devise a plan to expose Parolles to Bertram as a bragging coward.

The two Lords Dumaine advise Bertram not to put his faith in Parolles, who is a boastful coward with no military experience and no loyalty. To expose Parolles, they devise a plan: they will goad Parolles into attempting to retrieve the regiment's drum, lost on the battlefield to the regiment's disgrace. Then, disguised as enemy soldiers, they will "capture" him, blindfold him, and interrogate him, thus demonstrating to Bertram how quickly Parolles turns traitor if his life is threatened. Bertram and the Dumaines encounter Parolles, and the Dumaines use reverse psychology to provoke Parolles to boastfully swear to recapture the drum. Once Parolles is gone, the two Lords Dumaine laugh, saying that Parolles is a coward and will do no such thing. Bertram is skeptical, but invites the second lord to accompany him to meet Diana, whom he still plans to bed.

III.VII Location: Florence. The widow's house

Helena plots to trick Bertram into sleeping with her, thinking that she is Diana.

Helena has revealed her identity to the widow, and gives her a purse of gold to get her help in a scheme which Helena hopes will fulfill her husband's conditions: Diana will obtain Bertram's ring as a token of his love and invite him to her bedchamber, where Bertram will obliviously sleep with Helena instead of Diana. The widow agrees, and sends Helena to secure Diana's cooperation.

ACT IV

Helena tricks Bertram into sleeping with her; the two Lords Dumaine expose Parolles as a coward.

IV.I Location: Near the duke of Florence's camp

The two Lords Dumaine pretend to be enemy soldiers and capture Parolles.

The two Lords Dumaine wait with a party of their men to capture the unfortunate Parolles. They decide to disguise their voices by speaking nonsense, and pick a soldier whose voice is unfamiliar to their victim to act as "interpreter." Parolles comes along soon enough, debating with himself how to make it look like he attempted to recover the drum without exposing himself to any danger. He considers giving himself a flesh wound or ripping his clothes, and then wishes aloud that he had one of the enemy's drums, so he could pretend to have taken it. Then, screaming nonsense words, the group of soldiers falls upon him, binds him and blindfolds him. The ruse works: he believes himself to be captured by the enemy.

IV.II Location: Florence. The widow's house

Diana obtains Bertram's ring and invites him to see her alone later that night.

Bertram professes his love for Diana, trying to get her to sleep with him. After much prodding, she agrees to allow him to come to her bedroom late that night, but she demands the ring of his finger as a token of his love. He reluctantly gives it, telling her that the ring is an heirloom passed down "from many ancestors." In return, she makes him wear a ring of hers. (This ring was a gift to Helena from the king of France.) Bertram departs, looking forward to a pleasurable evening.

IV.III Location: The duke of Florence's camp

The two Lords Dumaine humiliate Parolles and expose him to Bertram as a coward.

Back at the camp, the two Lords Dumaine discuss Bertram's conduct. His mother's letter condemning his behavior has arrived, and so has the false news that Helena has died in a monastery (a rumor spread by Helena herself). When Bertram returns from visiting Diana's bedroom, where he has been successfully duped into having sex with Helena, the Lords Dumaine take him to watch Parolles' "interrogation." The "interpreter" threatens Parolles with torture unless he tells all the secrets of his army. Parolles, terrified, complies, and then goes on to give extremely unflattering descriptions of Bertram and both of the Lords Dumaine. The soldiers search Parolles' bags and find a letter addressed to Diana, offering her money if she sleeps with Bertram. The soldiers declare that they will kill Parolles anyway. Completely undone, Parolles weeps and begs for his life. Amid much laughter, the blindfold is removed. Parolles is left a disgraced man, but resolves to get on with his life.

IV.IV Location: Florence. The widow's house

Helena has succeeded in tricking Bertram and departs for the king's court in Marseilles.

The bed-switch has succeeded: Bertram has slept with Helena unawares, thinking that she is Diana. Helena thanks the widow and Diana profusely for their assistance, and then invites them to accompany her to see the king in Marseilles. There, Helena plans to find her husband and reveal how she has fulfilled his conditions.

IV.V Location: Roussillon. The count's palace

The war over, Bertram returns home, believing Helena dead.

The war has ended with a truce. The countess laments Helena's death to Lafew, who proposes that Bertram be betrothed to *his* daughter. The countess assents, and the clown comes in to announce that Bertram has returned home.

ACT V

Before the king, Helena reveals her tricks and Bertram promises to be a good husband.

V.I Location: Marseilles

Accompanied by the widow and Diana, Helena hurries to join the king in Roussillon.

Helena arrives to discover that the king of France has removed his court to Roussillon, and hurries after him, accompanied by the widow and Diana.

V.II Location: Roussillon. The count's palace

Lafew feeds Parolles, now a vagabond.

Parolles has come to Roussillon as a beggar. Lafew takes pity on him and gives him a meal.

V.III Location: Roussillon. The count's palace

Helena reveals that she is pregnant with Bertram's baby; Bertram repents and promises to be a good husband.

The king prepares to announce Bertram's engagement to Lafew's daughter when he notices the ring that he gave to Helena on Bertram's finger. Reluctant to explain about his dalliance with Diana, Bertram tells the king a vague story about someone throwing the ring to him in Florence. No one believes him, and the king furiously threatens to throw Bertram in prison, believing that Bertram stole the ring from Helena. Just then Diana is ushered in. She and the widow tell the story of how Bertram seduced her. Parolles, called as a witness, confirms it. Diana declares that she gave the ring to Bertram, but refuses to explain where she got it. The king's anger briefly turns on Diana, but the widow brings in Helena, who explains the entire deception and tells Bertram that she has met his conditions: she has his ring, and is pregnant with his child. Bertram, repentant, agrees to be a good husband and love Helena. The king promises Diana her choice of husband. Lafew weeps, everyone rejoices, and all ends happily.

THEMES, MOTIFS, & SYMBOLS IN *ALL'S WELL THAT ENDS WELL*

THEMES

ENDS JUSTIFY MEANS   Many of the play's characters resort to manipulation to get what they want. Indeed, the very title of the play suggests that the ends justify the means: if it has ended well, it can't have been all bad. Diana insists that trickery is a fine way to punish a would-be seducer: "I think't no sin / To cozen him that would unjustly win" (IV.ii.76–77). The brothers Dumaine trick Parolles to expose him as a coward. Most impressively, Helena tricks Bertram twice, first into marrying him and then, more egregiously, into impregnating her. Indeed, some critics have suggested that Helena's merciless pursuit lands her the husband that she deserves: a petty, idle womanizer. The play's quasi-happy ending fits this morally ambiguous play. As First Lord Dumaine asserts, "The web of our life is of a mingled yarn, good and ill together" (IV.iii.69–70).

WOMEN AS CUNNING AND RESOURCEFUL   Helena and Diana emerge as the victors of the play by winning the right to choose a husband. Helena in particular goes to great lengths to orchestrate her life. Her strength as a character is enhanced by her miraculous power to cure the king's illness. By the end, she has overcome great odds and won all her battles.

SEXUAL UNRESTRAINT   *All's Well* repeatedly suggests that sex cannot be restrained by law and marriage. Parolles asserts of chastity, "'Tis against the rule of nature" (I.i.127), because every human being is the child of a woman who is not a virgin. He tries, only half-jokingly, to persuade Helena to give up her virginity. Bertram too tries to separate sex from marriage, refusing to sleep with his wife Helena, but works to seduce Diana.

MOTIFS

YOUTH AND OLD AGE   Although the main characters of *All's Well* are young, they are surrounded by a number of mature older characters, all close to death. There are no characters in the middle of life's

9

journey; no married characters with young children, for example. The countess, the king, Lafew, and the widow all inhabit the play as reminders of imminent death. Indeed, the near-death of the king in the beginning of the play spurs the plot into action.

TRAVEL The play's action constantly moves around, from Roussillon, to Paris, to Florence, and back. Helena, Diana, and the widow even make a seemingly gratuitous stop in Marseilles in search of the king on the way from Florence to Roussillon. Most of the travel is undertaken by young characters in pursuit of fortune: Bertram seeks glory and Helena seeks Bertram.

SYMBOLS

THE RING Here, as elsewhere, rings symbolize trust and commitment in human relationships. Bertram implicitly acknowledges the symbolic power of rings when he insists that Helena must procure his family ring in order to become his wife. Similarly, the king gives Helena a ring as a token of his gratitude.

PAROLLES' CLOTHES Shakespeare repeatedly brings up Parolles and fanciful clothes. One character mentions his elaborate shoulder pads, and another compares his crisscrossed scarf to the lattice of a window. Parolles is thus a fop; a dandy who cares more about striking a pose than doing great deeds. Parolles' garb, the outward finery that disguises his body, symbolizes his behavior: his showy boasting hides his true cowardice.

The preference for appearance over truth echoes the rest of the play. For example, Helena gets Bertram's commitment to their marriage using deceit.

IMPORTANT QUOTATIONS FROM *ALL'S WELL THAT ENDS WELL*

1. *Our remedies oft in ourselves do lie*
   Which we ascribe to heaven.

Location: I.i.199–200
Speaker: Helena
Context: Helena resolves to take matters into her own hands to win the right to marry Bertram

Many of Shakespeare's characters struggle to decide that they can or should control their own destinies. Here, Helena makes an emphatic proclamation that she, rather than God, bears the responsibility for fixing her unhappiness. The "remedies" (solutions to her problems) recall the literal medicines with which she cures the sick king, the first step in her scheme to marry Bertram.

2. *Then I confess,*
   Here on my knee, before high heaven and you,
   That before you and next unto high heaven
   I love your son.
   My friends were poor but honest; so' 's my love.

Location: I.iii.175–178
Speaker: Helena to the countess
Context: Pressed by the countess, Helena confesses that she is in love with Bertram.

Helena confesses her love in simple and direct phrases such as "Here on my knee," and "I love your son." Her unadorned language is a reminder of the fact that Helena is a commoner by birth and unaccustomed to fancy courtly speech. It also suggests that her love is similarly direct and simple. The line "I love your son" is six syllables too short for Shakespeare's usual pentameter. This difficult phrase stands as naked and vulnerable as Helena does in proclaiming her love.

3. *Here, take her hand,*
   Proud, scornful boy, unworthy this good gift,
   That dost in vile misprision shackle up
   My love and her desert.

Location: II.iii.146–149
Speaker: he king to Bertram
Context: The king pressures Bertram to marry Helena.

The king's language reverses the natural social hierarchy: Bertram is a nobleman, but he is "unworthy" of the commoner Helena. His words testify to the extraordinary devotion that Helena inspires in everyone she meets (except Bertram). At the same time, the king's command raises the same questions that have made audiences uncomfortable with the plot and outcome of *All's Well*. Even after Bertram can be pressured to marry Helena, can he be pressured into being a good husband? Moreover, the king may claim that Helena deserves Bertram's love, but audiences and critics have long held that Bertram does not deserve hers. These questions remain unresolved at the end, complicating the ostensibly happy ending.

4. *Who knows himself a braggart,*
   Let him fear this, for it will come to pass
   That every braggart shall be found an ass.
   Rust, sword; cool, blushes; and Parolles live
   Safest in shame; being fooled, by fool'ry thrive.
   There's place and means for every man alive.
   I'll after them.

Location: IV.iii.311–317
Speaker: Parolles
Context: Disgraced by the two Lords Dumaine, Parolles resolves to live life as an openly unsavory character.

Parolles quickly acquiesces to his new life as a ruined man. He sees a place in the world "for every man alive," even rogues like him. Self-aware yet unself-conscious, Parolles, like other Shakespearean villains such as *King Lear's* Edmund, *Othello's* Iago, and *Richard III's* title character, knows that he is "bad" and does not plan to reform. For Parolles, shame and disgrace are a relief because they mean he need no longer pretend to be honest, and can be openly dishonest.

5. *If she, my liege, can make me know this clearly*
   I'll love her dearly, ever ever dearly.

Location: V.iii.312–313
Speaker: Bertram
Context: Bertram promises the king that he will be a good husband to Helena if she proves that she has fulfilled his seemingly impossible conditions.

Bertram's final promise to love Helena has troubled many readers. His sudden change of heart is prompted at least in part by his honor: Helena has technically fulfilled the condition that he had flippantly set. Though it is Helena who asks Bertram if he will make a commitment to her as his wife, his answer is addressed to the king. Moreover, his vow to love her "dearly, ever ever dearly" protests too much. As the critic Harold Bloom wryly notes, Bertram utters one "ever" too many.

ANTONY AND CLEOPATRA

Mark Antony's love for the exotic Cleopatra brings about his downfall at the hands of Octavius Caesar.

ANTONY AND CLEOPATRA IN CONTEXT

Scholars believe that Shakespeare wrote *Antony and Cleopatra* in 1606, immediately after *Macbeth*, and that the play is one of his last great tragedies. Shakespeare's most geographically sweeping play, *Antony and Cleopatra* is set across the whole Roman Empire, its backdrop the well-documented history of Octavius Caesar, Marc Antony, and Cleopatra. Shakespeare's primary source for *Antony and Cleopatra* was Plutarch's text *Life of Marcus Antonius*, included in his *Lives of the Noble Grecians and Romans*, which was translated into English by Sir Thomas North in 1579. North's language was so rich that Shakespeare incorporated large, relatively unchanged excerpts of it into his text. The plot of the play also remains close to North's history, although secondary characters such as Enobarbus and Charmian are largely Shakespearean creations.

The action of the story takes place roughly two years after the events of *Julius Caesar*, which begins with Caesar triumphant over his rival Pompey the Great, the father of *Antony and Cleopatra*'s Pompey. Caesar seeks to be crowned king, but is assassinated by Cassius and Brutus, who hope to preserve the Roman Republic. Cassius and Brutus are defeated in turn by Mark Antony and Caesar's nephew and heir Octavius Caesar. These two join Marcus Aemilius Lepidus to create a triumvirate (three-man government) over the Roman Empire.

The action of *Antony and Cleopatra*, which historically took place over a ten-year span, has been compressed to fit the needs of the stage. Antony is much older than he was in *Julius Caesar*, and his political instincts are waning. Only a minor character in *Julius Caesar*, Octavius Caesar here comes into his own as the man who will rise to become the first Roman emperor. Most of the political battles and machinations depicted are historically accurate, as is the romance of the title characters.

ANTONY AND CLEOPATRA: KEY FACTS

Full title: The Tragedy of Antony and Cleopatra	
Time and place written: 1606–1607; London	
First publication: First Folio (1623)	
Genre: Tragedy	
Setting (time): 40–30 B.C.	
Setting (place): Egypt, Rome, and elsewhere in the Roman Empire	
Protagonist: Mark Antony	
Major conflict: Torn between his Roman official duties and desire for his Egyptian lover Antony becomes embroiled in a war with Octavius Caesar.	

ANTONY AND CLEOPATRA: CHARACTER LIST

Agrippa One of Octavius Caesar's officers. Agrippa leads the retreat from Antony's unexpectedly powerful forces.
Mark Antony A once-fierce and feared soldier who rules the Roman Empire along with Octavius Caesar and Lepidus. When the play opens, Antony has neglected his duties as a ruler in order to live in Egypt, where he carries on a highly visible love affair with Cleopatra. His loyalty is divided between the Western and Eastern worlds. He is torn between the sense of duty and the desire to seek pleasure;

between reason and passion. While he feels the need to reaffirm the honor that has made him a celebrated Roman hero, he is also madly in love with Cleopatra.

Octavius Caesar The nephew and adopted son of Julius Caesar. Octavius rules the Roman Empire with Antony and Lepidus. Relations between Caesar and Antony are strained throughout the play, for the young triumvir believes that Antony squanders his time and neglects his duties while in Egypt. Ambitious and extremely pragmatic, Octavius lacks Antony's military might as a general, but his careful and stoic reasoning enables him to avoid Antony's tendency toward heroic or romantic folly. Destined to be the first Roman emperor (later renamed Caesar Augustus), he symbolizes "Western" values in the play, which stand opposed to the exotic lures of Cleopatra's "East."

Camidius A general in Antony's army. After the battle in which Antony follows Cleopatra's lead and flees, Camidius surrenders and defects to Caesar's side.

Charmian Cleopatra's attendant.

Cleopatra The queen of Egypt and Antony's lover. A highly attractive woman who once seduced Julius Caesar, Cleopatra delights in the thought that she has caught Antony like a fish. In matters of love, as in all things, Cleopatra favors high drama: her emotions are as volatile as they are theatrical, and regardless of whether her audience is her handmaid or the emperor of Rome, she always offers a top-notch performance. Although she tends to make a spectacle of her emotions, one cannot doubt the genuine nature of her love for Antony. Shakespeare makes clear that the queen *does* love the general, even if her loyalty is sometimes misplaced.

Clown An Egyptian who brings a basket of figs containing poisonous snakes to Cleopatra.

Decretas One of Antony's soldiers.

Diomedes Cleopatra's servant. She employs Diomedes to bring Antony the message that she has not committed suicide and is still alive.

Dolabella One of Octavius Caesar's men. Dolabella is assigned to guard the captive Cleopatra.

Enobarbus Antony's most loyal supporter. Worldly and cynical, Enobarbus is friendly with the subordinates of both Pompey and Caesar, yet stays faithful to his master even after Antony makes grave political and military missteps. He abandons Antony only when the general appears to be completely finished.

Eros An attendant serving Antony. Eros's love for his master compels him to refuse Antony's order that Eros kill him.

Iras Cleopatra's attendant.

Marcus Aemilius Lepidus The third member of the triumvirate and the weakest, both politically and personally. Lepidus's rather desperate attempts to keep the peace between Caesar and Antony fail when Caesar imprisons him after the defeat of Pompey.

Menas An ambitious young soldier under Pompey. During the dinner party that Pompey hosts for the triumvirate, Menas asks for permission to kill Caesar, Antony, and Lepidus, which would result in the control of the world falling into his master's hands.

Octavia Octavius Caesar's sister. Octavia marries Antony in order to cement an alliance between the two triumvirs. She is a victim of Antony's deception, and her meekness, purity, and submission make her the paradigm of Roman womanhood, and Cleopatra's polar opposite.

Pompey The son of a great general who was one of Julius Caesar's partners in power. Pompey is young and popular with the Roman people, and he possesses enough military might to stand as a legitimate threat to the triumvirs. He fancies himself honorable for refusing to allow one of his men to kill the unsuspecting Caesar, Antony, and Lepidus when they are his guests.

Proculeius One of Caesar's soldiers, who proves untrustworthy.

Scarus A brave young soldier serving under Antony. Scarus garners fantastic wounds in the battle against Caesar's army, and begs for the opportunity to win more.

Seleucus Cleopatra's treasurer. He betrays her to Caesar.

Soothsayer An Egyptian fortuneteller who follows Antony to Rome and predicts that his fortune will always pale in comparison to Caesar's.

Ventidius A Roman soldier under Antony's command. Ventidius leads the legions to victory against the kingdom of Parthia. Although a competent fighter, he cautiously decides not to push his troops further into battle, for fear that winning too much glory would sour his relationship with Antony.

ANTONY AND CLEOPATRA: PLOT OVERVIEW

Mark Antony, a Roman general, is torn between his official duties as one of the three triumvirs of the Roman Empire and his life of pleasure with his lover, the exotic Egyptian Queen Cleopatra. Despite Cleopatra's jealous fits, Antony returns to Rome when he hears that his wife Fulvia has died and that the rebel Pompey threatens the Roman Empire. Antony reconciles with his disgruntled fellow triumvir Octavius Caesar, and marries Octavia to cement their renewed alliance. Caesar, Antony, and Lepidus (the third triumvir) negotiate peace with Pompey. Antony and Octavia leave for Athens. While he is gone, Caesar moves to seize exclusive power of the Empire, waging war against Pompey and betraying Lepidus. Antony sends Octavia to Rome to make peace, and returns to Egypt and Cleopatra. There he raises an army to fight Caesar.

Antony fights Caesar at sea with the Egyptian fleet, but when Cleopatra's ship flees the battle, Antony shames himself by fleeing after her. Enobarbus, Antony's close friend, deserts to Caesar's side, but dies of grief and shame. Antony scores a surprise victory in the next battle on land, but in the next sea battle, the Egyptian fleet once again deserts Antony, defecting to join the more powerful Caesar. Caesar has won. Cleopatra hides herself in a monument and broadcasts that she has committed suicide. Hearing that she is dead, Antony tries to kill himself. Wounded, he is taken to see Cleopatra, with whom he dies. Rather than face shame as Caesar's trophy prisoner in Rome, Cleopatra kills herself. Caesar orders that Antony and Cleopatra be buried together.

ANTONY AND CLEOPATRA: SCENE SUMMARY

ACT I

Mark Antony returns to Rome to bury his wife and defend the empire after a long stay in Egypt with his lover Cleopatra.

I.I   Location: Alexandria. Cleopatra's palace

In love with Cleopatra, Mark Antony has neglected his duties in the Roman Empire.

Roman soldiers discuss their general Mark Antony, who has fallen in love with the Egyptian queen Cleopatra and forsaken his official duties as one of the triumvirs (three rulers) of the Roman Empire. Antony and Cleopatra enter, grandly speaking of love. A messenger from Rome arrives with news for Antony. Antony does not want to listen to the message, but Cleopatra disagrees. She teases that Antony may be ignoring a message from his wife Fulvia or from his young fellow triumvir Octavius Caesar. Antony refuses to hear the message, and leaves with Cleopatra, claiming that Rome means nothing to him anymore. Antony's soldiers despair at Antony's flippant attitude toward Caesar and the empire.

I.II   Location: Alexandria. Cleopatra's palace

His wife dead and his power in the Roman Empire threatened, Antony decides to return to Rome.

Charmian and Iras, Cleopatra's attendants, ask a soothsayer (fortune-teller) to reveal their futures. The soothsayer tells them that their pasts will prove better than their futures and that they shall outlive Cleopatra. Cleopatra comes in, complaining that Antony has been preoccupied with Rome recently. She sends for Antony, but leaves as he approaches to avoid seeing him. A messenger reports to Antony that his brother Lucius and wife Fulvia have lost in battle against Caesar. The messenger hesitantly suggests that this loss would never have happened if Antony had been in Rome. A second messenger arrives and announces that Fulvia is dead.

Aggrieved by Fulvia's death and concerned about Pompey, who threatens Rome from the sea, Antony decides to return to Rome.

I.III Location: Alexandria. Cleopatra's palace

Antony swears his love and takes his leave of Cleopatra.

Cleopatra summons Antony and laments that he does not love her enough. Antony tells her about Fulvia's death and the volatile political situation in Rome. They argue about the depth of his feelings until Antony finally departs.

I.IV Location: Rome

Caesar and Lepidus plan to raise an army to defend Rome against Pompey's mounting threat.

The triumvirs Octavius Caesar and Lepidus argue about whether Antony is responsible for the weaknesses that have led him to abandon his responsibilities as a statesman. A messenger announces that Pompey's forces are gathering strength. Caesar laments that Antony, a valiant soldier, is not with them. Caesar and Lepidus resolve to raise an army against Pompey.

I.V Location: Alexandria. Cleopatra's palace

Cleopatra misses Antony.

Cleopatra bemoans Antony's absence. Her servant Alexas brings her a pearl, which Antony had sent as a token of his love before leaving Egypt. Cleopatra quizzes Alexas about how happy Antony appeared. She plans to send him a message every day.

ACT II

Despite internal tensions, the triumvirate negotiates a bloodless peace with Pompey.

II.I Location: Sicily

Pompey assesses his position against Rome.

Pompey assesses his military position against Rome. He controls the sea and he is popular with Romans. A messenger announces that Antony has returned to Rome, and Pompey predicts that Antony and Caesar will shelf their mutual enmity to defend the Empire.

II.II Location: Rome

Antony agrees to marry Caesar's sister Octavia to seal their alliance against Pompey.

Antony and Caesar meet to discuss the situation in Rome. Caesar is annoyed at Fulvia's and Lucius's rebellion against him and at Antony's failure to support Rome with his army. One of Caesar's companions suggests that Caesar and Antony put aside their conflicts to face Pompey. At the suggestion of Agrippa, another of Caesar's companions, Antony and Caesar agree to cement their alliance with Antony's marriage to Caesar's sister Octavia.

With everyone gone, Antony's follower, Enobarbus, tells Agrippa about the good life in Egypt and about the beautiful Cleopatra. Antony, he says, will never leave her.

II.III Location: Rome

Warned by the soothsayer that his fortunes cannot rise near Caesar's, Antony thinks of returning east.

Antony says goodbye to Octavia, who departs with Caesar. In comes the soothsayer, who predicts that Antony will return to Egypt. Because Caesar will have a brighter future than Antony, the soothsayer adds, Antony should keep his distance lest he be overshadowed. Antony dismisses the soothsayer and resigns himself to returning to the east, where his "pleasure lies" (II.iii.38). He sends his follower Ventidius on a military campaign to Pathia, in the east.

II.IV Location: Rome

Caesar's allies prepare to meet Pompey's army.

Lepidus orders Caesar's followers Maecenas and Agrippa to gather their armies at Mount Misenum, where they will meet Pompey's army.

II.V Location: Alexandria. Cleopatra's palace

Cleopatra is enraged to find out that Antony has married Octavia.

Cleopatra amuses herself with her eunuch Mardian and Charmian. A messenger from Rome hesitantly announces that Antony has married Octavia. Enraged, Cleopatra strikes the messenger, then sends him to report what Octavia is like.

II.VI Location: Mount Misenum

Pompey and the triumvirs negotiate and resolve their conflict.

The triumvirate's forces are prepared for battle, and Pompey meets with Caesar, Lepidus, and Antony. The triumvirs offer Pompey rule over Sicily and Sardinia if he agrees to rid the sea of pirates and to send tribute to Rome. After Antony promises to thank Pompey for giving refuge to his mother in Sicily, the men make peace.

The triumvirs join Pompey in a feast on Pompey's ship. Enobarbus and Pompey's ambitious follower Menas stay behind and discuss Antony and their careers.

II.VII Location: Pompey's ship

Pompey and the triumvirs celebrate their peace settlement.

Servants discuss Pompey's dinner and Lepidus's drunkenness. Pompey and the triumvirs enter. Lepidus babbles about crocodiles which, according to popular belief, formed spontaneously out of the river mud. In private, Menas suggests that Pompey kill the three triumvirs while they are drunk aboard his ship. Pompey feels honor-bound not to carry out this plan, but wishes that Menas had done it without telling him. Disappointed, Menas vows to leave Pompey. Pompey and the triumvirs continue their revelry.

ACT III

Antony and Cleopatra lose to Caesar when Antony shamefully follows Cleopatra's retreat.

III.I Location: Syria

Victorious in his Parthian campaign, Ventidius halts his advance to avoid Antony's competitive displeasure.

Ventidius has defeated the Parthians and killed the king's son. One of his soldiers urges him to push on, but Ventidius fears Antony's displeasure at his too-great success. He halts his army and sends news to Antony.

III.II Location: Rome

Antony and Octavia leave Rome for Athens.

Preparations for Antony and Octavia's departure to Athens are underway. Agrippa and Enobarbus mock Lepidus who, as the weakest triumvir, desperately tries to remain in favor with both Antony and Caesar. Caesar tenderly says goodbye to his sister and urges Antony not to mistreat her. Antony and Octavia depart.

III.III   Location: Alexandria. Cleopatra's palace

Cleopatra's messenger brings a report on Octavia.

Cleopatra is pleased to hear that Octavia is not as vivacious as she is. She rewards the messenger and apologizes for hitting him earlier. She looks forward to Antony's return.

III.IV   Location: Athens

At Octavia's suggestion, Antony sends her to Rome to make peace between himself and Caesar.

Antony is concerned that Caesar has broken the peace treaty with Pompey and belittled Antony in public. Octavia pleads with Antony to keep peace with Caesar so as not to make her choose between her husband and her brother. Antony agrees to send her to Rome to smooth relations with Caesar.

III.V   Location: Alexandria

Caesar has imprisoned Lepidus and defeated Pompey.

Antony has returned to Egypt. Enobarbus and Antony's follower Eros discuss the latest developments. Caesar has defeated Pompey's army and killed Pompey. Caesar has also imprisoned Lepidus, alleging that Lepidus is a traitor. Antony's navy prepares to sail back to Italy.

III.VI   Location: Rome

The rift between Antony and Caesar widens as they prepare to go war.

Caesar rails against Antony, who has given Cleopatra power over much of the Middle East. Neither Caesar nor Antony has shared with each other the lands each of them has recently conquered. Octavia arrives. Caesar laments that she has such a small retinue, and tells her that Antony has returned to Egypt and plans to wage war against Rome. Octavia is heartbroken.

III.VII   Location: Actium (Greece). Antony's camp

Antony's generals are displeased that Antony plans to fight Caesar at sea with Cleopatra's fleet.

Cleopatra is angered by Enobarbus's suggestion that her presence in battle will be a distraction to Antony. Despite the objections of Enobarbus and Antony's general Camidius, who think their army's strength lies on land, Antony plans to use Cleopatra's fleet to fight Caesar at sea. Camidius complains that because of Antony they are all "women's men," ruled by Cleopatra (III.vii.70). He leaves to prepare the land defenses.

III.VIII   Location: Actium. Antony's camp

Caesar orders his foot army to hold off its attack until the sea battle ends.

III.IX   Location: Actium. Antony's camp

Antony instructs Enobarbus to set their squadrons on a hillside in order to see the battle at sea.

III.X   Location: Actium

Antony has lost the sea battle by following Cleopatra when her ships deserted.

Enobarbus describes the sea battle: Antony's forces had the upper hand until Cleopatra's ship deserted and Antony followed her. In the confusion, Caesar won. Antony's soldiers are disgusted by Antony's shameful desertion. Camidius follows others and defects with his army to Caesar's side.

III.XI   Location: near Actium

Antony and Cleopatra reconcile after Antony's shameful defeat.

Antony wallows in shame and self-hatred. He urges his servants to desert him. Cleopatra enters to find Antony alone. She tries to comfort Antony, but he laments how he has fallen from his former glory. He asks her why she led him to infamy and she begs his forgiveness. She never dreamed that he would follow her retreat. He responds that his heart was tied to her ship. He forgives her and remarks that her kiss repays him for his shame.

III.XII   Location: Alexandria. Caesar's camp

Caesar sends Thidias to persuade Cleopatra to betray Antony.

Antony's ambassador arrives to see Caesar with Antony and Cleopatra's requests. Antony asks to be allowed to live in Egypt or, if not, Athens. Cleopatra asks that Egypt be passed on to her heirs. Caesar dismisses Antony's requests, but says that he will consider Cleopatra's provided that she execute or exile Antony. Caesar sends his supporter Thidias to persuade Cleopatra to agree.

III.XIII   Location: Alexandria. Cleopatra's palace

Antony orders Caesar's ambassador Thidias whipped, and Enobarbus deserts Antony.

Enobarbus tells Cleopatra that the defeat was Antony's fault, not hers. After hearing Caesar's response to his request, Antony declares that he will challenge Caesar to single combat. Enobarbus thinks about his loyalties. Thidias arrives and gives Cleopatra Caesar's terms: he will show her mercy if she gives him Antony. Antony walks in as she is swearing allegiance to Caesar. Furious, Antony orders Thidias whipped. He rails at Cleopatra, but she mollifies him. Antony's fleet has reassembled, and much of his land forces remain intact, ready to attack Caesar again. Enobarbus decides to desert Antony.

ACT IV

After another battle with Caesar, Antony mortally wounds himself, thinking that Cleopatra is dead.

IV.I   Location: Alexandria. Caesar's camp

Caesar prepares to crush Antony.

Caesar laughs at Antony's challenge. Caesar's supporter Maecenas thinks that Caesar should fight Antony now because Antony will be weakened by his rage. Caesar prepares his army.

IV.II   Location: Alexandria. Cleopatra's palace

Antony plans to fight Caesar the next day.

Enobarbus brings word that Caesar has refused Antony's challenge. Antony declares that he will go to battle the next day, whatever the odds. He thanks his servants and warns them that this may be his last night. They weep. Antony leads them off to a feast.

IV.III   Location: Alexandria. Cleopatra's palace

Antony's soldiers think that they hear an omen: Antony's god deserting him.

That night, Antony's soldiers hear strange underground music from somewhere underground. They whisper that it is the music of Hercules, the god after whom Antony modeled his life, who now abandons him.

IV.IV   Location: Alexandria. Cleopatra's palace

Antony leads his men into battle.

The next day, Eros and Cleopatra arm Antony for battle. Antony feels confident about the battle. His troops are ready. Antony kisses Cleopatra goodbye and leads his men into battle.

IV.V   Location: Alexandria. Antony's camp

Antony receives the news that Enobarbus has deserted him with melancholy.

Antony finds out that Enobarbus, his most trusted friend, has deserted him. Antony orders that the valuable possessions that Enobarbus left behind be sent to him with "gentle adieus and greetings" (IV.v.14–17).

IV.VI   Location: Alexandria. Caesar's camp

Caesar begins the battle; Enobarbus wants to die.

Certain of victory, Caesar orders Agrippa to begin the battle. Caesar orders that the front lines be staffed with Antony's former allies who have deserted him. Enobarbus receives the treasure. Overcome with guilt, he leaves to seek out a "ditch wherein to die" (IV.vi.39).

IV.VII   Location: Alexandria. Caesar's army

Agrippa calls for retreat, for Antony's forces have exceeded his expectations.

IV.VIII   Location: Alexandria. Antony's army

Antony's army wins the battle for Alexandria.

Antony's men win the battle and retake Alexandria with a fierce display of force. Scarus, who has been wounded, longs to continue fighting.

IV.IX   Location: Alexandria. Antony's army

Antony, his army, and Cleopatra rejoice in the victory.

Antony returns from war, vowing to destroy Caesar's army completely the following day. He praises his soldiers for their valor and declares his love for Cleopatra. On Antony's request, Cleopatra honors Scarus. Antony leads Cleopatra and his troops in a triumphant march through the streets.

IV.X   Location: Alexandria. Caesar's army

Enobarbus dies of grief and shame.

Caesar's sentries discuss the coming battle as Enobarbus berates himself nearby. He collapses, and the sentries discover that he has died.

IV.XI   Location: Alexandria. Antony's camp

Antony is ready to meet Caesar's attack, which Antony determines will come by sea.

IV.XII   Location: Alexandria. Caesar's camp

Caesar holds his armies back, preparing to attack Antony at sea.

IV.XIII   Location: near Alexandria

Antony watches Cleopatra's ships defect to Caesar's side during the naval battle.

Antony and Scarus watch the naval battle. Scarus privately considers Cleopatra's fleet weak. Antony watches the Egyptian fleet betray him and defect to Caesar. In horror, he commands Scarus to order his army to flee. Alone, Antony says that Cleopatra is a deadly enchantress. When she approaches, he threatens to kill her.

IV.XIV   Location: Alexandria. Cleopatra's palace

Cleopatra sends Mardian to tell Antony that she has killed herself.

Cleopatra tells her maids about Antony's murderous rage. Charmian suggests that Cleopatra send Antony word that she has killed herself, to quell his anger. Cleopatra sends Mardian with the message.

IV.XV   Location: Alexandria

Thinking that Cleopatra is dead, Antony kills himself.

Antony arms himself to kill Cleopatra. Mardian arrives and reports (falsely) that Cleopatra is dead. Overcome with remorse, Antony asks Eros to kill him so that he can join Cleopatra in death. Eros refuses and when Antony persists, kills himself instead. Antony falls on his own sword, but does not die yet. Cleopatra's servant Diomedes arrives and reports that she is still alive. It is too late. Antony, dying, asks to be brought to Cleopatra.

IV.XVI   Location: the monument

Antony and Cleopatra bid adieu, and he dies.

Cleopatra and her maids are above. Diomedes appears below with Antony's dying body. Antony and Cleopatra call to each other. He asks her to come down so that he can embrace her, but she refuses, saying that she is afraid to be captured by Caesar. Instead, she asks the soldiers to heave Antony up to her. She kisses him. Antony advises her to ask for Caesar's mercy, and trust Caesar's friend Proculeius. Antony recalls his own glory and says he will die "a Roman by a Roman / Valiantly vanquished" (IV.xvi.59–60). He dies. Cleopatra laments. She plans to bury him and seek to die herself.

ACT V

Cleopatra finds Caesar charming, and kills herself rather than become a prisoner.

V.I   Location: Alexandria. Caesar's camp

Caesar finds out that Antony has committed suicide and makes plans to keep Cleopatra in Rome.

Caesar sends his man Dolabella to demand Antony's surrender. Decretas, one of Antony's men, enters with Antony's sword and asks to be allowed to serve Caesar because Antony has committed suicide. Caesar remarks that the passing of so great a man ought to be marked by great tumult and mourning. Antony's death is the end of half the world (V.i.18). Cleopatra's messenger arrives to ask what Caesar intends for her. Caesar dispatches him back with promises of honor and kindness. He neglects to tell her that he intends to keep her in Rome to mark his triumph. He sends some of his men, led by Proculeius, to ensure that Cleopatra does not commit suicide.

V.II   Location: the monument

Rather than be shamed as Caesar's trophy prisoner in Rome, Cleopatra kills herself with poisonous asps.

Cleopatra tells Proculeius that she hopes Caesar will allow her sons to rule Egypt. Proculeius answers with encouragement. At the same time, his soldiers, who have slipped into the monument, move to seize Cleopatra. She draws her dagger, but Proculeius disarms her before she can kill herself. She vows never to be paraded through Rome as Caesar's trophy.

Dolabella arrives to take over for Proculeius, and she pressures him to reveal whether Caesar plans to display her as his prisoner. Caesar arrives and promises to treat Cleopatra well and spare Cleopatra's children if she stays alive. She gives Caesar a scroll that, she says, gives all her treasure to him, but her treasurer Seleucus tells Caesar otherwise. Caesar leaves, and Cleopatra tells Iras and Charmian that although he is charming with words, she does not trust him. Dolabella admits to her that Caesar means to convey her to Rome.

Cleopatra resolves to kill herself rather than be shamed. She orders Charmian and Iras to dress her in her finest royal garments. She lets in a clown who brings her a basket of figs with asps (poisonous snakes). She kisses Iras and Charmian goodbye. Iras falls dead. Cleopatra presses one asp to her breast and another to her arm, and dies. As the guards rush in, Charmian too kills herself with an asp. Dolabella and Caesar enter, and Caesar orders Cleopatra to be buried next to Antony in a public funeral.

ANALYSIS OF MAJOR CHARACTERS IN *ANTONY AND CLEOPATRA*

MARK ANTONY

Throughout the play, Antony is torn between his love for Cleopatra and his duties to the Roman Empire. In I.i, he engages Cleopatra in a conversation about the nature and depth of their love, dismissing the duties he has neglected for her sake: "Let Rome in Tiber melt, and the wide arch / Of the ranged empire fall" (I.i.35–36). In the very next scene, however, Antony worries that he is about to "lose [him]self in dotage" (I.ii.106) and fears that the death of his wife is only one of the ills that his "idleness doth hatch" (I.ii.119). The geographical poles that draw him in opposite directions—West and East, Rome and Egypt—represent deep-seated conflicts between his reason and emotion, his sense of duty and his desire, his obligations to the state and his private needs.

Bound to his honor, Antony sees himself as a Roman hero first and foremost. He often recalls the golden days of his own heroism, but his current behavior has imperiled his honor, the Roman hero's defining characteristic: "If I lose my honor, / I lose myself. Better I were not yours[, Octavia] / Than yours so branchless" (III.iv.22–24). Rather than amend his identity to accommodate his desires as well as his duties, Antony takes his own life, an act that cements him as "a Roman by a Roman / Valiantly vanquished" (IV.xvi.59–60).

CLEOPATRA

Cleopatra is both a decadent exotic foreigner and a noble ruler. Philo and Demetrius declare her Cleopatra a lustful "gipsy" (I.i.10), which is a frequently repeated description. She is labeled a "wrangling queen" (I.i.50), a "slave" (I.iv.19), an "Egyptian dish" (II.vi.123), and a "whore" (III.vi.67). She is called "Salt Cleopatra" (II.i.21) and an enchantress who has made Antony "the noble ruin of her magic" (III.x.18).

The Romans who characterize Cleopatra in these terms are threatened by her beauty and open sexuality. This sexuality is awe-inspiring. Enobarbus describes her in famously glowing terms in II.ii. As Antony describes Cleopatra, she is a woman "[w]hom everything becomes—to chide, to laugh / To weep" (I.i.51–52). It is this ability to be all things to all men, to embody everything at once—beauty and ugliness, virtue and vice—that Cleopatra stands to lose when she is taken prisoner by Caesar. By parading her through the streets of Rome as his trophy, he intends to reduce her character to a single, base element. He effectively plans to immortalize her as a whore.

OCTAVIUS CAESAR

Octavius Caesar is both a menacing adversary for Antony and a rigid representation of Roman law and order. He is not a two-dimensional villain, and his frustrations with the ever-neglectful Antony seem justified. He is not a particularly likeable character. His treatment of Lepidus, for instance, betrays the cruel underside of Caesar's aggressive ambitions. Still, he is complicated; he is, in other words, convincingly human. Indeed, his complex relationship with Antony is our best evidence for the fullness of Caesar's character. For much of the play, Caesar's goal is to destroy Antony. When he achieves this desired end, however, he mourns the loss of a great soldier and musters enough compassion to be not only fair-minded but also fair-hearted, commanding that Antony and Cleopatra be buried beside one another.

THEMES, MOTIFS, & SYMBOLS IN *ANTONY AND CLEOPATRA*

THEMES

THE STRUGGLE BETWEEN REASON AND EMOTION   The play is more concerned with the battle between reason and emotion than the triumph of one over the other, and this battle is waged most forcefully in Antony's character. Antony vacillates between Western and Eastern sensibilities, feeling pulled by both his duty to the empire and his desire for pleasure, his want of military glory and his passion for Cleopatra. Soon after his nonchalant dismissal of Caesar's messenger, the empire, and his duty to it, he chastises himself for his neglect and commits to return to Rome, lest he "lose [him]self in dotage" (I.ii.106). By "dotage," he means fond foolishness.

As the play progresses, Antony continues to inhabit conflicting identities that play out the struggle between reason and emotion. As his Roman allies, even the ever-faithful Enobarbus, abandon him, Antony feels that he has, indeed, lost himself in dotage, and he determines to rescue his noble identity by taking his own life. In the end, Antony is ruled by passion as much as by reason. Likewise, in the play, reason cannot ever fully conquer passion, nor can passion wholly undo reason.

THE CLASH BETWEEN EAST AND WEST   The Western and Eastern poles of the play are characterized by those who inhabit them: Caesar embodies the stoic duty of the West, while Cleopatra, in all her theatrical grandeur, represents the free-flowing passions of the East. In the play, West meets East and conquers it, regardless of the Roman Empire's triumph over Egypt. Cleopatra's suicide suggests that something of the East's spirit—the freedoms and passions that are not represented in the play's conception of the West—cannot be subsumed by Caesar's victory. The play suggests that the East will live on as a visible and unconquerable counterpoint to the West, bound as inseparably and eternally as Antony and Cleopatra are in their tomb.

FEMALE SEXUALITY AS THREATENING   Throughout the play, the male characters rail against the power of female sexuality. Caesar and his men condemn Antony for the weakness that makes him bow to Cleopatra, but they clearly lay the blame for his downfall on her. On the rare occasion that the Romans do not refer to her as a whore, they describe her as an enchantress whose beauty casts a dangerous spell over men. As Enobarbus notes, Cleopatra possesses the power to warp the minds and judgment of all men, even "holy priests" who "[b]less her" when she acts like a whore (II.ii.244–245).

The unapologetic openness of Cleopatra's sexuality stands to threaten the Romans, but they are equally obsessed with the powers of Octavia's sexuality. Caesar's sister, who in beauty and temperament stands as Cleopatra's opposite, is nevertheless considered to possess power enough to mend the triumvir's damaged relationship: Caesar and Antony expect that she will serve to "knit [their] hearts / With an unslipping knot" (II.ii.132–133). In this way, women are saddled with both the responsibility for men's political alliances and the blame for their personal failures.

MOTIFS

EXTRAVAGANT DECLARATIONS OF LOVE In I.i, Antony and Cleopatra argue whether their love for one another can be measured and articulated:

> *Cleopatra: [to Antony]* If it be love indeed, tell me how much.
> *Antony:* There's beggary in the love that can be reckoned.
> *Cleopatra:* I'll set a bourn how far to be beloved.
> *Antony:* Then must thou needs find out new heaven, new earth.
> (I.i.14–17)

This exchange sets the tone for the way that love will be discussed and understood throughout the play. Cleopatra expresses the expectation that love should be declared or demonstrated grandly. She wants to hear and see exactly how much Antony loves her. Love, in *Antony and Cleopatra*, is not comprised of private intimacies, as it is in *Romeo and Juliet*. Instead, love belongs in the public arena. In the lines quoted above, Cleopatra claims that she will set the boundaries of her lover's affections and Antony responds that to do so, she will need to discover uncharted territories. By likening their love to the discovery and claim of "new heaven, new earth," the couple links private emotions to affairs of state. Love, in other words, becomes an extension of politics, with the annexation of another's heart analogous to the conquering of a foreign land.

PUBLIC DISPLAYS OF AFFECTION In *Antony and Cleopatra*, public displays of affection function as expressions of political allegiance and power. Caesar, for example, laments that Octavia arrives in Rome without the fanfare of a proper entourage because it betrays her weakness: without an accompanying army of horses, guardsmen, and trumpeters, she cannot possibly be recognized as Caesar's sister or Antony's wife. The connection between public display and power is one that the characters, especially Caesar and Cleopatra, understand well. After Antony's death, their battle of wills revolves around Caesar's desire to exhibit the Egyptian queen on the streets of Rome as a sign of his triumph. Cleopatra refuses such an end, choosing instead to take her own life. Even this act is meant as a public performance, however: decked in her grandest royal robes and playing the part of the tragic lover, Cleopatra intends her last act to be as much a defiance of Caesar's power as a gesture of romantic devotion.

SYMBOLS

CLEOPATRA'S FLEEING SHIPS Cleopatra's fleeing ships appear twice in the play. Antony twice does battle with Caesar at sea, and both times his navy is betrayed by Cleopatra's retreat. The ships stand as a reminder of the inconstancy of character. One cannot be sure of Cleopatra's allegiance: it is uncertain whether she flees out of fear or because she realizes it would be politically savvy to align herself with Caesar. Her fleeing ships are an effective symbol of her changeability.

THE ASPS The asps that Cleopatra applies to her skin are a prop in her final and most magnificent performance. As she lifts one snake, then another to her breast, they become her children and she a common wet nurse: "Dost thou not see my baby at my breast, / That sucks the nurse asleep?" (V.ii.300–301). The domestic nature of the image contributes to Cleopatra's final metamorphosis, in death, into Antony's wife. She assures him, "Husband, I come" (V.ii.278).

IMPORTANT QUOTATIONS FROM *ANTONY AND CLEOPATRA*

---

1. *Let's grant it is not*
   Amiss to tumble on the bed of Ptolemy,
   To give a kingdom for a mirth, to sit
   And keep the turn of tippling with a slave,
   To reel the streets at noon, and stand the buffet
   With knaves that smells of sweat. Say this becomes him—

> As his composure must be rare indeed
> Whom these things cannot blemish—yet must Antony
> No way excuse his foils when we do bear
> So great a weight in his lightness. If he filled
> His vacancy with his voluptuousness,
> Full surfeits and the dryness of his bones
> Call on him for' t. But to confound such time
> That drums him from his sport, and speaks as loud
> As his own state and ours—'tis to be chid
> As we rate boys who, being mature in knowledge,
> Pawn their experience to the present pleasure,
> And so rebel to judgment.

Location: I.iv.16–33
Speaker: Caesar to Lepidus
Context: Caesar criticizes Antony for staying in Egypt and neglecting his official Roman duties.

Caesar's speech defines the Western sensibilities against which Cleopatra's Egypt is judged and by which Antony is ultimately measured. As Caesar dismisses Antony's passion for Cleopatra as boyish irresponsibility, he asserts the Roman expectation of duty over pleasure, reason over emotion. These competing worlds and worldviews provide the framework for understanding the coming clashes between Caesar and Antony, Antony and Cleopatra, and Cleopatra and Caesar.

> 2. Upon her landing Antony sent to her,
> Invited her to supper. She replied
> It should be better he became her guest,
> Which she entreated. Our courteous Antony,
> Whom ne'er the word of 'No' woman heard speak,
> Being barbered ten times o'er, goes to the feast,
> And for his ordinary pays his heart
> For what his eyes eat only.
> I saw her once
> Hop forty paces through the public street,
> And having lost her breath, she spoke and panted,
> That she did make defect perfection,
> And breathless, pour forth breath.
> Age cannot wither her, nor custom stale
> Her infinite variety. Other women cloy
> The appetites they feed, but she makes hungry
> Where most she satisfies. For vilest things
> Become themselves in her, that the holy priests
> Bless her when she is riggish.

Location: II.ii.225–245
Speaker: Enobarbus to the men on Pompey's ship
Context: Enobarbus has described Cleopatra floating down the Nile on her gilded barge and goes on to tell how she and Antony met.

According to Enobarbus, Antony fell under Cleopatra's spell immediately. Whatever power Antony had in relation to Cleopatra, he surrenders it almost immediately. In fact, he surrenders it before the two even meet: "She replied / It should be better he became her guest," and Antony agreed. In addition to demonstrating Cleopatra's power over Antony, this passage describes Cleopatra's talent for performance. Her performance in "the public street" makes "defect"—her inability to breathe—"perfection." Whether sitting stately on her "burnished throne" (II.ii.197) or hopping "forty paces," Cleopatra never loses her ability to quicken the breath of her onlookers or persuade the "holy priests" to bless what they would certainly, in others, condemn.

---

3. *You take from me a great part of myself.*
   Use me well in 't.—Sister, prove such a wife
   As my thoughts make thee, and as my farthest bond
   Shall pass on thy aproof.—Most noble Antony,
   Let not the piece of virtue which is set
   Betwixt us as the cement of our love
   To keep it builded, be the ram to batter
   The fortress of it; for better might we
   Have loved without this mean if on both parts
   This be not cherished.

Location: III.ii.24–33
Speaker: Caesar to Antony and Octavia
Context: Caesar offers his sister Octavia to Antony as his bride.

Caesar's plan to marry his sister to Antony in order to cement their alliance attests to the power that men ascribe to women and female sexuality in this play. What men consider the wrong kind of female sexuality, as embodied proudly and openly by Cleopatra, stands as a threat to men, their reason, and sense of duty. What they consider the right kind, however, as represented by the modest "piece of virtue" Octavia, promises to be "the cement" of Caesar's love for Antony. Caesar's language here is particularly important: the words he chooses to describe Antony's union to Octavia and, by extension, his reunion with Caesar, belong to the vocabulary of builders: "the *cement* of our love / To keep it *builded*, be the ram to batter / The *fortress* of it." This language makes an explicit connection between the private realm of love and the public realm of the state, a connection that causes Caesar more than a little anxiety throughout the play.

---

4. *Sometimes we see a cloud that's dragonish,*
   A vapour sometime like a bear or lion,
   A towered citadel, a pendent rock,
   A forked mountain, or blue promontory
   With trees upon't that nod unto the world
   And mock our eyes with air. Thou hast seen these signs;
   They are black vesper's pageants.
   That which is now a horse even with a thought
   The rack disdains, and makes it indistinct
   As water is in water.
   Here I am Antony,
   Yet cannot hold this visible shape, my knave.
   I made these wars for Egypt, and the Queen—
   Whose heart I thought I had, for she had mine,
   Which whilst it was mine had annexed unto't
   A million more, now lost—she, Eros, has
   Packed cards with Caesar, and false-played my glory
   Unto an enemy's triumph.
   Nay, weep not, gentle Eros. There is left us
   Ourselves to end ourselves.

Location: IV.xv.3–22
Speaker: Antony
Context: When Cleopatra's ships abandon Antony in battle for the second time, he faces the greatest defeat of his military career.

As a Roman, Antony has a rigid perception of himself: he must live within the narrowly defined confines of the victor and hero or not live at all. Here, he complains to his trusted attendant, Eros, about the shifting of his identity. He feels himself helplessly changing, morphing from one man to another like a cloud that turns from a dragon, to a bear, to a lion as it moves across the sky. He tries desperately to cling to himself, saying "Here I am Antony," but laments he "cannot hold this visible shape." Left without military might or Cleopatra, Antony loses his sense of who he is. Rather than amend his identity to incorporate this loss; rather than become an Antony conquered, he chooses to end his life. In the end, he clings to the image of himself as the unvanquished hero in order to achieve this last task: "[t]here is left us / Ourselves to end ourselves."

---

5. *Nay, 'tis most certain, Iras. Saucy lictors*
   Will catch at us like strumpets, and scald rhymers
   Ballad us out o' tune. The quick comedians
   Extemporally will stage us, and present
   Our Alexandrian revels. Antony
   Shall be brought drunken forth, and I shall see
   Some squeaking Cleopatra boy my greatness
   I' th' posture of a whore.

Location: V.ii.210–217
Speaker: Cleopatra
Context: With Antony dead, Cleopatra convinces her servant women that suicide is her best course.

Cleopatra conjures up a horrific image of the humiliation that awaits her as Caesar's trophy, employing the vocabulary of the theater, fearing that "quick comedians / Extemporally will stage us." She imagines that Antony will be played as a drunk, and a squeaking boy will portray her as a whore. Throughout the play, Cleopatra is a consummate actress. We are never quite sure how much of her emotion is genuine and how much theatrical fireworks. Because of this acting, Cleopatra's refusal to let either Antony or herself be portrayed in such a way is especially significant. To Cleopatra, the Roman understanding of her character and her relationship with Antony is a gross and unacceptable wrong. It does not mesh with the grandness of her self-perception. Rather than being a queen of the order of Isis, she will go down in history "[i]' th' posture of a whore." Just as Antony cannot allow his self-image to expand to include defeat, Cleopatra refuses to allow her image to be stripped to its basest parts.

AS YOU LIKE IT

Exiled from a corrupt court, Rosalind and Orlando flee into the forest, where they fall in love and their problems are resolved.

AS YOU LIKE IT IN CONTEXT

As You Like It was most likely written around 1598–1600, during the last years of Elizabeth's reign. The play belongs to the literary tradition known as pastoral. With roots in the literature of ancient Greece, the pastoral came into its own in Roman antiquity with Virgil's Eclogues, and continued as a vital literary mode through Shakespeare's time and long after. Typically, a pastoral story involves exiles from urban or court life, who flee to the refuge of the countryside, where they often disguise themselves as shepherds in order to converse with other shepherds on a range of established topics, from the relative merits of life at court versus life in the country, to the relationship between nature and art. The most fundamental concern of the pastoral mode is comparing the worth of the natural world, represented by the relatively untouched countryside, to the world built by humans, which contains the joys of art and the city as well as the injustices of rigid social hierarchies. Pastoral literature, then, has great potential to serve as a forum for social criticism and can even inspire social reform.

As You Like It develops many of the traditional features and concerns of the pastoral genre. This comedy examines the cruelties and corruption of court life and gleefully pokes holes in one of humankind's greatest artifices: the conventions of romantic love. The play's investment in pastoral traditions leads to an indulgence in rather simple rivalries: court versus country, realism versus romance, reason versus mindlessness, nature versus fortune, young versus old, and those who are born into nobility versus those who acquire their social standing. But rather than settle these scores by coming down on one side or the other, *As You Like It* offers up a world of myriad choices and endless possibilities. In the world of this play, no one thing need cancel out another. In this way, the play manages to offer both social critique and social affirmation. It is a play that at all times stresses the complexity of things, and the simultaneous pleasures and pains of being human.

AS YOU LIKE IT: KEY FACTS

Full title: As You Like It

Time and place written: 1598–1600; London, England

Date of first publication: 1623 (First Folio)

Genre: Comedy; pastoral

Setting (time): Sixteenth century

Setting (place): France, primarily the fictional Forest of Arden

Protagonist: Rosalind

Major conflict: Rosalind and Orlando fall in love, but Rosalind is unjustly banished from Duke Frederick's court; Orlando is both denied his birthright by his jealous brother Oliver and forced to flee from the vindictive Duke Frederick.

AS YOU LIKE IT: CHARACTER LIST

Adam   The elderly former servant of Sir Rowland de Bois. Having witnessed Orlando's hardships, Adam offers not only to accompany his young master into exile, but to fund their journey with the whole of his modest life's savings. He is a model of loyalty and devoted service.

Lord Amiens   A faithful lord who accompanies Duke Senior into exile in the Forest of Arden. Lord Amiens is rather jolly and loves to sing.

Audrey   A simpleminded goatherd who agrees to marry Touchstone.

Celia The daughter of Duke Frederick, and Rosalind's dearest friend. Celia's devotion to Rosalind is unmatched, as evidenced by her decision to follow her cousin into exile. To make the trip, Celia assumes the disguise of a simple shepherdess and calls herself Aliena. As elucidated by her extreme love of Rosalind and her immediate devotion to Oliver, whom she marries at the end of the play, Celia possesses a loving heart but is prone to deep, almost excessive emotions.

Charles A professional wrestler in Duke Frederick's court. Charles demonstrates both his caring nature and his political savvy when he asks Oliver to intercede in his upcoming fight with Orlando: he does not want to injure the young man and thereby lose favor among the nobles who support him. Charles's concern for Orlando proves unwarranted when Orlando beats him senseless.

Corin An old shepherd. Corin attempts to counsel his friend Silvius in the ways of love, but Silvius refuses to listen.

Duke Frederick The brother of Duke Senior and the usurper of his throne. Duke Frederick's cruel nature and volatile temper are displayed when he banishes his niece, Rosalind, from court without reason. That Celia, his own daughter, cannot mitigate his unfounded anger demonstrates the intensity of the duke's hatefulness. Frederick mounts an army against his exiled brother but aborts his vengeful mission after he meets an old religious man on the road to the Forest of Arden. He immediately changes his ways, dedicating himself to a monastic life and returning the crown to his brother, thus testifying to the ease and elegance with which humans can sometimes change for the better.

Duke Senior The father of Rosalind and the rightful ruler of the dukedom in which the play is set. Having been banished by his usurping brother, Frederick, Duke Senior now lives in exile in the Forest of Arden with a number of loyal men, including Lord Amiens and Jaques. We have the sense that Senior did not put up much of a fight to keep his dukedom, for he seems to make the most of whatever life gives him. Content in the forest, where he claims to learn as much from stones and brooks as he would in a church or library, Duke Senior proves to be a kind and fair-minded ruler.

Jaques A faithful lord who accompanies Duke Senior into exile in the Forest of Arden. Jaques is an example of a stock figure in Elizabethan comedy, the man possessed of a hopelessly melancholy disposition. Much like a referee in a football game, he stands on the sidelines, watching and judging the actions of the other characters without ever fully participating. Given his inability to participate in life, it is fitting that Jaques alone refuses to follow Duke Senior and the other courtiers back to court, and instead resolves to assume a solitary and contemplative life in a monastery.

Oliver The oldest son of Sir Rowland de Bois and sole inheritor of the de Bois estate. Oliver is a loveless young man who begrudges his brother, Orlando, a gentleman's education. He admits to hating Orlando without cause or reason and goes to great lengths to ensure his brother's downfall. When Duke Frederick employs Oliver to find his missing brother, Oliver finds himself living in despair in the Forest of Arden, where Orlando saves his life. This display of undeserved generosity prompts Oliver to change into a better, more loving person. His transformation is evidenced by his love for the disguised Celia, whom he takes to be a simple shepherdess.

Orlando The youngest son of Sir Rowland de Bois and younger brother of Oliver. Orlando is an attractive young man who, under his brother's neglectful care, has languished without a gentleman's education or training. Regardless, he considers himself to have great potential, and his victorious battle with Charles proves him right. Orlando cares for the aging Adam in the Forest of Arden and later risks his life to save Oliver from a hungry lioness, proving himself a proper gentleman. He is a fitting hero for the play and, though he proves no match for her wit or poetry, the most obvious romantic match for Rosalind.

Phoebe A young shepherdess who disdains the affections of Silvius. She falls in love with Ganymede, who is really Rosalind in disguise, but Rosalind tricks Phoebe into marrying Silvius.

Rosalind The daughter of Duke Senior. Rosalind, considered one of Shakespeare's most delightful heroines, is independent-minded, strong-willed, good-hearted, and terribly clever. Rather than slink off into defeated exile, Rosalind resourcefully uses her trip to the Forest of Arden as an opportunity to take control of her own destiny. When she disguises herself as Ganymede, a handsome young man, and offers herself as a tutor in the ways of love to her beloved Orlando, Rosalind's talents and charms are on full display. Only Rosalind, for instance, is both aware of the foolishness of romantic love *and* delighted to be in love. She teaches those around her to think, feel, and love better than they have previously, and she ensures that the courtiers returning from Arden are far gentler than those who fled there.

Sir Rowland de Bois The father of Oliver and Orlando, friend of Duke Senior, and enemy of Duke Frederick. Upon Sir Rowland's death, the vast majority of his estate was handed over to Oliver according to the custom of primogeniture.

Silvius A young, suffering shepherd who is desperately in love with the disdainful Phoebe. Conforming to the model of Petrarchan love, Silvius prostrates himself before a woman who refuses to return his affections. In the end, however, he wins the object of his desire.

Touchstone A clown in Duke Frederick's court who accompanies Rosalind and Celia in their flight to Arden. Although Touchstone's job as fool is to criticize the behavior and point out the folly of those around him, Touchstone fails to do so with even a fraction of Rosalind's grace. Next to his mistress, the clown seems hopelessly vulgar and narrow-minded. Almost every line he speaks echoes with bawdy innuendo.

William A young country boy who is in love with Audrey.

AS YOU LIKE IT: PLOT OVERVIEW

Sir Rowland de Bois, recently dead, left the vast majority of his estate to his eldest son Oliver. Against Sir Rowland's wishes, Oliver has not provided for his youngest brother Orlando's education. Moreover, Oliver plots with the court wrestler Charles to harm Orlando during the upcoming wrestling match. At the court, Duke Senior's throne has been usurped by his younger brother Duke Frederick. Duke Senior has fled to the Forest of Arden, where he lives a life of hunting and leisure with a band of loyal followers. Duke Senior's daughter Rosalind has remained at Duke Frederick's court as companion to Duke Frederick's daughter Celia.

Orlando defeats Charles at the court wrestling match. He meets Rosalind and each falls secretly in love with the other. However, when Orlando returns home, he finds out that Oliver has plotted against his life. Orlando and his father's old servant Adam leave for the forest. Meanwhile, Duke Frederick banishes Rosalind from the court. Celia cannot bear to part from her, and the two flee together accompanied by the court jester Touchstone. Rosalind disguises herself as a young man named Ganymede, and Celia dresses as a shepherdess and calls herself Aliena. Duke Frederick is furious to discover his daughter's disappearance. He guesses that Orlando has something to do with it, and sends Oliver into the forest to find Orlando.

In the forest, Orlando meets and joins the band of Duke Senior, who was Orlando's father's dear friend. Celia and Rosalind purchase a modest cottage. Rosalind runs into the lovesick Orlando, who has been covering the trees with love poems to Rosalind. Rosalind, as Ganymede, says that she can help cure Orlando of his infatuation if he pretends that Ganymede is Rosalind and comes to woo her every day. Orlando agrees, and the love lessons begin. Rosalind falls more in love with Orlando.

Rosalind watches the shepherdess Phoebe cruelly reject the lovesick shepherd Silvius. When Rosalind-as-Ganymede intervenes, Phoebe falls hopelessly in love with Ganymede. Meanwhile, Touchstone romances a goatherd named Audrey.

One day, Orlando fails to show up for his tutorial with Ganymede. Oliver appears and describes how Orlando stumbled upon him in the forest and saved him from being devoured by a hungry lioness. Oliver and Celia-as-Aliena fall instantly in love and agree to marry.

Phoebe becomes increasingly insistent in her pursuit of Ganymede, and Orlando grows tired of pretending that a boy is his dear Rosalind. Rosalind decides to end the charade. She promises that Ganymede will wed Phoebe, if Ganymede will ever marry a woman, and she makes everyone pledge to meet the next day at the wedding. They all agree.

On the day of the wedding, Rosalind gathers everyone, and makes Phoebe promise that if she does not marry Ganymede, she will marry Silvius. Rosalind and Celia reveal their true identities. Hymen, the god of marriage, marries the four couples—Rosalind and Orlando, Celia and Oliver, Phoebe and Silvius, and Audrey and Touchstone. The wedding party receives news that Duke Frederick has repented and returned the dukedom to Duke Senior. The revelers continue the celebration, planning to return to the court.

AS YOU LIKE IT: SCENE SUMMARY

ACT I

Both Orlando and Rosalind, accompanied by Celia, plan to flee to the Forest of Arden to escape the wrath of Celia's father, the usurper Duke Frederick.

I.I   Location: Oliver's estate

Oliver has inherited his father's estate, and now plots to bring down his poor younger brother Orlando.

Orlando, the youngest son of the recently deceased Sir Rowland de Bois, describes his unfortunate state of affairs to Adam, Sir Rowland's loyal former servant. From his father, Orlando inherited only a paltry sum; Orlando's eldest brother Oliver inherited almost everything from their father's estate. Moreover, Oliver has disregarded their father's wish that Orlando receive a decent education. Oliver enters and the hostility between the two brothers escalates into violence. Adam tries to pacify them in vain. Orlando, who is stronger than Oliver, refuses to let go of Oliver's throat until Oliver promises to give Orlando part of the inheritance. In a rage, Oliver dismisses Orlando and Adam.

Oliver meets with Charles, the wrestler from the duke's court. Charles tells Oliver the latest news: Duke Senior's younger brother Frederick has usurped power, and Duke Senior has fled with a small retinue to the Forest of Arden. Duke Senior's daughter Rosalind has remained at court, companion to her cousin and Duke Frederick's daughter Celia. Charles asks Oliver for help: he has heard rumors that Orlando plans to enter the court wrestling match incognito. Charles has a reputation to maintain, and worries that he will maim Orlando. He has come to ask Oliver to intervene on Orlando's behalf. Oliver convinces Charles that Orlando is a deceitful scoundrel who will cheat in the match, perhaps with poison. Charles promises to repay Orlando in kind. Oliver is pleased.

I.II   Location: Duke Frederick's court

Orlando defeats Charles, falls in love with Rosalind, and flees the court to escape Duke Frederick's wrath.

Celia attempts to cheer up Rosalind, who is sad because her father, Duke Senior, has been banished. Celia promises to bequeath the dukedom to Rosalind after she inherits it from her father, Duke Frederick. Celia and Rosalind's witty discussion of "Fortune" and "Nature" is interrupted by Touchstone, the court jester. Le Beau, a dapper young courtier, also arrives and intrigues them with news of an upcoming wrestling match involving the famous Charles.

Duke Frederick and his court enter for the match. At Duke Frederick's request, Rosalind and Celia attempt to dissuade Orlando, the challenger, from wrestling with Charles. Orlando insists that he has nothing to lose. Orlando and Charles wrestle, and Orlando quickly defeats Charles. Duke Frederick finds out that Orlando is the youngest son of Sir Rowland de Bois with regret: he and Sir Rowland were enemies. Rosalind admits to Orlando how much Duke Senior had admired Sir Rowland. Orlando and Rosalind are smitten with each other, but do not confess their feelings.

After everyone leaves, Le Beau warns Orlando that Duke Frederick may wish him harm. Orlando resolves to flee.

I.III   Location: Duke Frederick's court

Duke Frederick banishes Rosalind, and she and Celia resolve to disguise themselves and flee to seek Rosalind's father in the forest.

Rosalind confesses to Celia her strong feelings for Orlando. Duke Frederick approaches, condemns Rosalind as a traitor, and demands that Rosalind leave the court on pain of death. Both Rosalind and Celia plead with Duke Frederick on Rosalind's behalf, but he remains firm. He suggests to Celia that with the comely Rosalind gone, Celia herself will seem more attractive. Celia resolves to leave with Rosalind, and together they decide to seek out Duke Senior in the Forest of Arden. For safety, they will disguise themselves: Celia as a shepherdess named Aliena, and Rosalind, who is "more than common tall," as a young man named Ganymede. The two convince Touchstone to accompany them.

ACT II

Two groups of travelers—Orlando's and Rosalind's—find refuge in the Forest of Arden.

II.I   Location: Forest of Arden. Duke Senior's camp

Duke Senior and his companions enjoy life in the Forest of Arden.

The banished Duke Senior expounds on the wonders of life in the forest. The woods provide Duke Senior with everything he needs: conversation, education, spiritual edification. Lord Amiens agrees. The duke suggests that they hunt some venison, but remarks that he always mourns the fate of the deer. One of his companions mentions that the melancholy Jaques was recently seen weeping over a wounded deer. Duke Senior, who likes arguing with Jaques, asks to be taken to see him.

II.II   Location: Duke Frederick's court

Duke Frederick hopes to find Rosalind and Celia by finding Orlando.

Duke Frederick is enraged to discover that Rosalind, Celia, and Touchstone have disappeared. An attendant lord suggests that Celia and Rosalind have taken a liking to Orlando, and may be with him. Duke Frederick orders that Oliver be recruited to find Orlando.

II.III   Location: Oliver's estate

Orlando and Adam flee Oliver's estate.

Old Adam greets Orlando and begs him not to enter Oliver's house: Oliver has heard about Orlando's triumph at the wrestling match, and plans to set fire to the place where Orlando sleeps. Adam suggests that the two of them take to the road with his modest life savings. Touched, Orlando agrees.

II.IV   Location: Forest of Arden

Rosalind and Celia encounter shepherds and find a place to stay in the forest.

Exhausted, Rosalind, Celia, and Touchstone arrive in the forest. Their rest is interrupted by two shepherds: old Corin and young Silvius are discussing Silvius's hopeless love for the shepherdess Phoebe. After Silvius wanders off, Rosalind, Celia, and Touchstone approach Corin and ask where they might find shelter. Corin suggests that his master's property is up for sale, and Rosalind and Celia decide to buy it.

II.V   Location: Forest of Arden. Duke Senior's camp

Duke Senior's lords sing and prepare for dinner.

Amiens, Jaques, and others prepare for Duke Senior's dinner. Amiens leads the others in a song about "winter and rough weather" (II.v.8). Jaques, who can "suck melancholy out of a song as a weasel sucks eggs" (II.v.11–12), adds his own verse about fools who abandon their wealth and take to the forest.

II.VI   Location: Forest of Arden

Orlando and Adam arrive in the forest.

Orlando and Adam arrive in the forest, exhausted and starving. Orlando carries Adam to shelter before setting off to hunt.

II.VII   Location: Forest of Arden. Duke Senior's camp

Orlando and Adam join Duke Senior for dinner.

Jaques has not shown up for dinner. A lord reports that for once Jaques has been seen in good spirits. Jaques arrives and tells a merry story about running into a fool—Touchstone. Duke Senior and Jaques playfully argue about criticizing others. Orlando barges in, draws his sword, and rudely demands food. Duke Senior invites him to the banquet, and Orlando leaves to fetch Adam. Duke Senior comments on all the unhappiness of the world. Jaques remarks that "all the world's a stage, and all the men and women merely players" (II.vii.138–39). All humans pass through the stages of infancy, childhood, and adulthood. All humans experience love and seek honor, but all eventually succumb to the debility of old age. Orlando returns with Adam and all begin to eat. Duke Senior is happy to welcome Orlando when he realizes that Orlando is Sir Rowland's son.

ACT III

Rosalind-as-Ganymede promises to cure Orlando of his love for Rosalind, and becomes the object of Phoebe's love.

III.I   Location: Duke Frederick's court

Duke Frederick confiscates Oliver's property until Oliver finds Orlando.

III.II   Location: Forest of Arden

Rosalind, disguised as Ganymede, promises to cure Orlando of his infatuation with Rosalind.

Orlando has been composing love poems for Rosalind and hanging them on every tree. Corin and Touchstone enter, deep in discussion about the relative merits of court and country life. Rosalind enters, disguised as Ganymede. She reads one of Orlando's poems aloud. Touchstone makes fun of Orlando's verse, but Rosalind rebukes Touchstone for his meddling. Celia enters as Aliena. She reads another of Orlando's verses. Rosalind and Celia agree that the poems are terrible, but Rosalind is thrilled when Celia tells her that they were written by Orlando.

Orlando and Jaques enter, and Celia and Rosalind hide to eavesdrop on their conversation. Jaques dislikes Orlando's sentimentality, while Orlando scoffs at Jaques's melancholy. Jaques walks off. Rosalind decides to confront Orlando, and Orlando, who sees her as Ganymede, confesses that he is the lovesick author of the verses. He asks her for help. She promises to cure him of his infatuation if he woos her (Ganymede) as though Ganymede were Rosalind. Orlando agrees.

III.III   Location: Forest of Arden

Touchstone plans to marry Audrey in a church.

Touchstone and Audrey, a goatherd, wander through the forest. Jaques follows them, eavesdropping. Touchstone courts Audrey and arranges to marry her. Sir Oliver Martext, a nearby vicar, arrives to officiate. Jaques offers to give Audrey away, but convinces Touchstone to get married in a church. Jaques, Touchstone, and Audrey leave the bewildered vicar alone in the forest.

III.IV   Location: Forest of Arden

Orlando stands Rosalind up.

Rosalind is distraught because Orlando has failed to show up for his morning appointment with Ganymede. Celia, who thinks that Orlando is no great lover, tries to comfort her. Corin arrives and invites Rosalind and Celia to come watch Silvius woo Phoebe.

III.V   Location:

Phoebe rejects Silvius's advances and falls in love with Ganymede.

Silvius pleads with Phoebe not to reject him. Corin enters with Rosalind and Celia, both still disguised. Phoebe cruelly mocks Silvius's hyperbolic words. Rosalind steps forward and scolds Phoebe who, as no great beauty, should feel lucky to have Silvius. Phoebe is instantly attracted to Rosalind-as-Ganymede. Rosalind mocks her further, and leaves with Celia. Phoebe employs Silvius to help her woo Ganymede.

ACT IV

Rosalind falls more in love with Orlando; Orlando and Oliver are reconciled.

IV.I   Location: Forest of Arden

As Orlando pretends to woo Rosalind-as-Ganymede, she falls more in love with him.

Jaques approaches the disguised Rosalind. She skillfully criticizes him for his melancholy, and he departs.
   Orlando arrives an hour late for his lesson in love. As agreed, he addresses Ganymede as Rosalind, and asks her to forgive his tardiness. Rosalind berates him, but eventually relents and allows him to woo her. She teaches him when to kiss and what to do if the kiss is denied. Orlando claims that he will die if she refuses his affections, but she insists that no man in history has ever died for love.
   Rosalind then asks Celia-as-Aliena to play a priest and marry them. She warns Orlando that women often become unpleasant after marriage. He doesn't believe her, but leaves to dine with Duke Senior, promising to return in two hours.
   Rosalind tells Celia that her love for Orlando has only grown.

IV.II   Location: Forest of Arden. Duke Senior's camp

Duke Senior's followers kill a deer and sing about cuckoldry.

Jaques and other lords kill a deer and plan to present it to Duke Senior. At Jaques's request, the lords mark the occasion by singing a song about cuckoldry, which is symbolized by horns.

IV.III   Location: Forest of Arden.

Orlando has been wounded saving Oliver's life.

Two hours have passed, but Orlando has not yet returned. Silvius delivers a love letter from Phoebe to Rosalind-as-Ganymede. She reads it aloud and Silvius is hurt by how romantic it turns out to be. Rosalind sends him back to Phoebe with a message: Ganymede will never love Phoebe unless Phoebe loves Silvius.
   Oliver enters, looking for Ganymede and Aliena. He gives Rosalind-as-Ganymede a bloody handkerchief from Orlando and tells them a lengthy story: soon after leaving Ganymede, Orlando stumbled upon a sleeping ragged man under attack by a snake. As Orlando scared away the snake, a hungry lioness emerged from the underbrush. Orlando recognized the ragged man as Oliver. Because Orlando's nobler nature would not allow him to let Oliver die, Orlando fought the lion, injuring his shoulder but saving Oliver's life. Orlando's kindness transformed Oliver into a new man, and he and Orlando resolved their former differences. Orlando brought Oliver to see Duke Senior. Weak from loss of blood, Orlando sent Oliver to find Ganymede, and fainted. Upon hearing this story, Rosalind faints. Celia and Oliver revive

her. Oliver is surprised at Rosalind's weakness of spirit, though she assures him that she was only pretending.

ACT V

Four couples, including Orlando and Rosalind, are married; Duke Frederick returns the dukedom to Duke Senior.

V.I   Location: Forest of Arden

Touchstone mocks William, who loves Audrey.

Touchstone and Audrey wander through the forest discussing their postponed marriage. Touchstone mentions the youth in love with Audrey. Just then William, the simpleminded youth in question, appears. Touchstone quizzes William and completely confuses him before sending him away. Corin arrives to fetch Touchstone and Audrey on Rosalind's behalf.

V.II   Location: Forest of Arden

Rosalind promises Orlando, Phoebe, and Silvius that they will all marry tomorrow, when Oliver weds Celia-as-Aliena.

Orlando finds it hard to believe that Oliver has fallen in love with Aliena so quickly. Oliver pledges to turn over their father's estate to Orlando once he and Aliena are married. Orlando orders preparations for a wedding the next day. Oliver leaves just as Rosalind arrives, disguised as Ganymede. Orlando confesses that he misses his Rosalind and is tired of wooing Ganymede instead of Rosalind. Rosalind promises Orlando that he will marry as he desires when Oliver marries Aliena.

Phoebe and Silvius appear. Phoebe accuses Ganymede of "ungentleness" (V.ii.67). Phoebe and Silvius take turns professing love for Ganymede and Phoebe, respectively, until Rosalind shuts them up. She promises that Ganymede will marry Phoebe tomorrow if Ganymede will ever marry a woman and makes everyone promise to meet the next day at the wedding.

V.III   Location: Forest of Arden

Duke Senior's pages sing a song about love and springtime.

Touchstone and Audrey look forward to their marriage the next day. They meet two of Duke Senior's pages and Touchstone asks for a song. The pages sing of springtime and blossoming love. Touchstone proclaims the song foolish.

V.IV   Location: Forest of Arden

Four couples are married, and everyone except Jaques plans to return to court.

The next day, everyone—Duke Senior and his retinue, Jaques, Oliver, Orlando, and Celia-as-Aliena—gathers for the miracle of multiple marriages. Rosalind enters as Ganymede, followed by Silvius and Phoebe. She reminds all parties of their agreements: Duke Senior will allow Orlando to marry Rosalind if she appears. Phoebe will marry Ganymede unless she refuses to, in which case she will marry Silvius. Rosalind and Celia disappear into the forest.

Duke Senior notes how much Ganymede resembles Rosalind, and Orlando agrees. Touchstone and Audrey join the party, and Touchstone tells a funny story about a quarrel he had. Rosalind and Celia return in their proper attire, accompanied by Hymen, the god of marriage. Phoebe, realizing that Ganymede is a woman, agrees to marry Silvius. Hymen marries the happy couples: Orlando and Rosalind, Oliver and Celia, Phoebe and Silvius, and Touchstone and Audrey.

Halfway through the festivities, Jaques de Bois, the middle brother of Oliver and Orlando, arrives and announces that Duke Frederick had mounted an army to destroy Duke Senior, but a forest priest converted him to a peace-loving life. Duke Frederick has abdicated his throne to his brother and moved to a monastery. All rejoice, happy to be able to return to the court. Only Jaques decides not to return: like Duke Frederick, he plans a solitary and contemplative existence in a monastery. The revelers dance as everyone except Rosalind exits.

EPILOGUE

Rosalind asks the audience for applause.

Rosalind asks the audience to overlook the fact that a woman is performing the epilogue. She asks the women to like the play "for the love [they] bear to men," and the men "for the love [they] bear to women" (Epilogue, 12–15). She asks for applause as she curtsies.

ANALYSIS OF MAJOR CHARACTERS IN *AS YOU LIKE IT*

ROSALIND

Rosalind dominates *As You Like It.* So fully realized is she in the complexity of her emotions, the subtlety of her thought, and the fullness of her character that no one else in the play matches up to her. Fully aware of people's foolishnesses, including her own she, unlike Jaques, nevertheless always wholly participates in life. She may chastise Silvius for his irrational devotion to Phoebe, and still come undone when her lover is tardy and faint at the sight of his blood.

Rosalind is a particular favorite among feminist critics, who admire her ability to subvert the limitations that society imposes on her as a woman. With boldness and imagination, she disguises herself as a young man in order to woo the man she loves and instruct him in how to be a more accomplished, attentive lover. These are lessons she would not be able to deliver as a woman. There is endless comic appeal in Rosalind's lampooning of the conventions of both male and female behavior, but an Elizabethan audience might have felt a certain amount of anxiety faced with her boldness. In the end, Rosalind dispenses with her charades and with her own character. Her emergence as an actor in the Epilogue assures theatergoers that they, like the Arden foresters, are about to exit an enchanted realm and return to the familiar world they left behind.

ORLANDO

According to his brother, Orlando is unschooled yet somehow learned, full of noble purposes, and loved by people of all ranks as if he had enchanted them (I.i.141–144). Orlando has a brave and generous spirit, though he does not possess Rosalind's wit and insight. As his love tutorial shows, he relies on commonplace clichés in matters of love, declaring that without the fair Rosalind he would die. He does have a decent wit, however, as he demonstrates when he argues with Jaques, suggesting that Jaques should seek out a fool who wanders about the forest: "He is drowned in the brook. Look but in, and you shall see him," meaning that Jaques will see a fool in his own reflection (III.ii.262–263). But next to Rosalind, Orlando's imagination burns less brightly. This upstaging is no fault of Orlando's, given the fullness of Rosalind's character. Shakespeare clearly intends his audience to delight in the match. Time and again, Orlando performs tasks that reveal his nobility and demonstrate why he is so well-loved: he travels with the ancient Adam and makes a fool out of himself to secure the old man food; he risks his life to save the brother who has plotted against him; he cannot help but violate the many trees of Arden with testaments of his love for Rosalind.

JAQUES

Jaques lacks the keenness of insight of Shakespeare's most accomplished jesters: he is not as penetrating as *Twelfth Night*'s Feste or *King Lear*'s fool. His faculties as a critic of the goings-on around him are considerably diminished in comparison to Rosalind, who understands so much more and conveys her understanding with superior grace and charm. Rosalind criticizes in order to transform the world, to make Orlando a more reasonable husband and Phoebe a less disdainful lover. In contrast, Jaques is content to stew in his own melancholy. It is appropriate that Jaques decides not to return to court. While the other characters merrily revel, Jaques determines that he will follow the reformed Duke Frederick into the monastery, where he believes the converts have much to teach him. Jaques's refusal to resume life in the dukedom not only confirms our impression of his character, but also resonates with larger issues in the play. As the title promises, everyone gets just what he or she wants. At the same time, a world so complex and full of so many competing forces cannot stand united.

THEMES, MOTIFS, & SYMBOLS IN *AS YOU LIKE IT*

THEMES

LOVE AS DELIGHTFUL *As You Like It* spoofs many of the conventions of poetry and literature dealing with love, such as the idea that love is a disease that brings suffering and torment to the lover, or the assumption that the male lover is the slave or servant of his mistress. These ideas are central features of the courtly love tradition, which greatly influenced European literature for hundreds of years before Shakespeare's time. *As You Like It* breaks with the courtly love tradition by portraying love as a force for happiness and fulfillment, and ridicules those who revel in their own suffering. While Orlando's metrically incompetent poems conform to the notion that he should "live and die [Rosalind's] slave," these sentiments are roundly ridiculed (III.ii.142). When Rosalind famously insists that "[m]en have died from time to time, and worms have eaten them, but not for love," she argues against the notion that love concerns the perfect, mythic, or unattainable (IV.i.91–92). Unlike Jaques and Touchstone, both of whom have keen eyes and biting tongues trained on the follies of romance, Rosalind does not mean to disparage love. On the contrary, she seeks to teach a version of love that not only can survive in the real world, but can bring delight as well.

THE CAPACITY OF HUMANS TO CHANGE Physically, emotionally, or spiritually, those who enter the Forest of Arden are often remarkably different when they leave. The most dramatic and unmistakable change, of course, occurs when Rosalind assumes the disguise of Ganymede. As a young man, Rosalind demonstrates how vulnerable to change men and women truly are. Orlando, of course, is putty in her hands. More impressive, however, is her ability to manipulate Phoebe's affections, which move from Ganymede to the once despised Silvius with amazing speed. Moreover, the *As You Like It* characters do not struggle to become more pliant. Rather, their changes are instantaneous. Oliver, for instance, learns to love both his brother Orlando and a disguised Celia within moments of setting foot in the forest. Furthermore, the vengeful and ambitious Duke Frederick abandons all thoughts of fratricide after a single conversation with a religious old man. Certainly, these transformations have much to do with the restorative, almost magical effects of life in the forest, but the consequences of the changes also matter in the real world: the government that rules the French duchy, for example, will be more just under the rightful ruler Duke Senior, while the class structures inherent in court life promise to be somewhat less rigid after the courtiers' sojourn in the forest. These social reforms are a clear improvement and result from the more private reforms of the play's characters.

CITY LIFE VERSUS COUNTRY LIFE Pastoral literature thrives on the contrast between life in the city and life in the country. Often, it suggests that the oppressions of the city can be remedied by a trip into the country's therapeutic woods and fields, and that a person's sense of balance and rightness can be restored by conversations with uncorrupted shepherds and shepherdesses. This type of restoration, in turn, enables one to return to the city a better person, capable of making the most of urban life. Although Shakespeare tests the bounds of these conventions—his shepherdess Audrey, for instance, is neither articulate nor pure—he begins *As You Like It* by establishing the city/country dichotomy on which the pastoral mood depends. In I.i, Orlando rails against the injustices of life with Oliver and complains that he "know[s] no wise remedy how to avoid it" (I.i.20–21). Later in that scene, as Charles relates the whereabouts of Duke Senior and his followers, the remedy is clear: "in the forest of Arden … many young gentlemen … fleet the time carelessly, as they did in the golden world" (I.i.99–103). Indeed, many are healed in the forest. The lovesick are coupled with their lovers and the usurped duke returns to his throne. But Shakespeare reminds us that life in Arden is a temporary affair. As the characters prepare to return to life at court, the play does not laud country over city or vice versa, but instead suggests a delicate and necessary balance between the two. The simplicity of the forest provides shelter from the strains of the court, but it also creates the need for urban style and sophistication: one would not do, or even matter, without the other.

MOTIFS

HOMOEROTICISM   Like many of Shakespeare's plays and poems, *As You Like It* explores different kinds of love between members of the same sex. Celia and Rosalind, for instance, are such close friends that they are almost like sisters, and the profound intimacy of their relationship seems at times more intense than that of ordinary friends. Everybody, male and female, seems to love Ganymede, the beautiful boy who looks like a woman because he is really Rosalind in disguise. The name Rosalind chooses for her alter ego, Ganymede, traditionally belonged to a beautiful boy who became one of Jove's lovers, and carries strong homosexual connotations. Even though Orlando is supposed to be in love with Rosalind, he seems to enjoy the idea of acting out his romance with the beautiful young boy Ganymede. Phoebe too is more attracted to the feminine Ganymede than to the real male, Silvius.

In drawing on the motif of homoeroticism, *As You Like It* is influenced by the pastoral tradition, which typically contains elements of same-sex love. In the Forest of Arden, as in pastoral literature, homoerotic relationships are not necessarily antithetical to heterosexual couplings, as modern readers tend to assume. Instead, homosexual and heterosexual love exist on a continuum across which, as the title of the play suggests, one can move as one likes.

EXILE   Many of the characters live in exile. Some, like Duke Senior, Rosalind, and Orlando, have been forcibly removed or threatened from their homes. Others have voluntarily abandoned their positions in sympathy. These include Celia, Adam, and Duke Senior's loyal band of lords. It is, then, rather remarkable that the play ends with four weddings, ceremonies that unite individuals into couples and usher these couples into the community. The community that sings and dances its way through Arden at the close of V.iv is the same community that will return to the dukedom in order to rule and be ruled. This event, where the poor dance in the company of royalty, suggests a utopian world in which wrongs can be righted and hurts healed. The sense of restoration with which the play ends depends upon the formation of a community of exiles in politics and love coming together to soothe their various wounds.

SYMBOLS

THE SLAIN DEER   In IV.ii, Jaques and other lords in Duke Senior's party kill a deer. Jaques proposes to "set the deer's horns upon [the hunter's] head for a branch of victory" (IV.ii.4–5). To an Elizabethan audience, however, the slain deer would have signaled more than just an accomplished archer. As the song that follows the lord's return to camp makes clear, the deer placed atop the hunter's head is a symbol of cuckoldry, commonly represented by a man with horns atop his head. Allusions to the cuckolded man run throughout the play, betraying one of the dominant anxieties of the age—that women are sexually uncontrollable—and pointing out the schism between ideal and imperfect love.

GANYMEDE   Rosalind's choice of alternative identities is significant. Ganymede is the cupbearer and beloved of Jove and is a standard symbol of homosexual love. In the context of the play, her choice of an alter ego contributes to a continuum of sexual possibilities.

IMPORTANT QUOTATIONS FROM *AS YOU LIKE IT*

1. *Now, my co-mates and brothers in exile,*
   Hath not old custom made this life more sweet
   Than that of painted pomp? Are not these woods
   More free from peril than the envious court?
   Here feel we not the penalty of Adam,
   The seasons' difference, as the icy fang
   And churlish chiding of the winter's wind,
   Which when it bites and blows upon my body
   Even till I shrink with cold, I smile, and say
   'This is no flattery. These are counselors
   That feelingly persuade me what I am.'

Sweet are the uses of adversity
Which, like the toad, ugly and venomous,
Wears yet a precious jewel in his head;
And this our life, exempt from public haunt,
Finds tongues in trees, books in the running brooks,
Sermons in stones, and good in everything.

Location: II.i.1–17
Speaker: Duke Senior to his companions
Context: Duke Senior rhapsodizes about natural life in the Forest of Arden.

With great economy, Shakespeare draws a dividing line between the "painted pomp" of court, with its perils great enough to drive the duke and his followers into exile, and the safe and restorative Forest of Arden (II.i.3). The woods are romanticized, as they typically are in pastoral literature, and the mood is set for the remainder of the play. Although perils may present themselves, they remain distant and, in the end, there truly is "good in everything" (II.ii.17). This passage, more than any other in the play, presents the conceits of the pastoral mode. Here, the corruptions of life at court are left behind in order to learn the simple and valuable lessons of the country. Shakespeare highlights the educational, edifying, and enlightening nature of this foray into the woods by employing language that invokes the classroom, the library, and the church: in the trees, brooks, and stones surrounding him, the duke finds tongues, books, and sermons. As is his wont, Shakespeare goes on to complicate the literary conventions upon which he depends. His shepherds and shepherdesses, for instance, ultimately prove too lovesick or dim-witted to dole out the kind of wisdom the pastoral form demands of them, but for now, Shakespeare merely sets up the opposition between city and country that provides the necessary tension to drive his story forward.

---

2. As I do live by food, I met a fool,
    Who laid him down and basked him in the sun,
    And railed on Lady Fortune in good terms,
    In good set terms, and yet a motley fool.
    'Good morrow, fool,' quoth I. 'No, sir,' quoth he,
    'Call me not fool till heaven hath sent me fortune.'
    And then he drew a dial from his poke,
    And looking on it with lack-lustre eye
    Says very wisely 'It is ten o'clock.'
    'Thus we may see', quoth he, 'how the world wags.
    'Tis but an hour ago since it was nine,
    And after one hour more 'twill be eleven.
    And so from hour to hour we ripe and ripe,
    And then from hour to hour we rot and rot;
    And thereby hangs a tale.'

Location: II.vii.14–28
Speaker: Jaques
Context: Jaques tells about how he ran into Touchstone, who entertained him with his nihilistic musings.

In this passage, melancholy Jaques displays an uncharacteristic burst of delight. While wandering through the forest, he relates, he met a fool who entertained him with rather nihilistic musings on the passage of time and man's life. According to Touchstone, time ensures nothing other than man's own decay: "from hour to hour we rot and rot" (II.vii.27). That this speech appeals to Jaques says much about his character: he delights not only in the depressing, but also in the rancid. Practically all of Touchstone's lines contain some bawdy innuendo, and these are no exception. Here, by punning the word "hour" with "whore," he transforms the general notion of man's decay into the unpleasant specifics of a man dying from venereal disease. Touchstone appropriately, if distastefully, confirms this hidden meaning by ending his speech with the words "thereby hangs a tale"—"tale" was Elizabethan slang for penis (II.vii.28).

---

3. *No, faith; die by attorney. The poor world is almost six thousand years old, and in all this time there was not any man died in his own person, videlicet, in a love-cause. Troilus had his brains dashed out with a Grecian club, yet he did what he could to die before, and he is one of the patterns of love. Leander, he would have lived many a fair year though Hero had turned nun if it had not been for a hot midsummer night, for, good youth, he went but forth to wash him in the Hellespont and, being taken with the cramp, was drowned; and the foolish chroniclers of that age found it was Hero of Sestos. But these are all lies. Men have died from time to time, and worms have eaten them, but not for love.*

Location: IV.i.81–92
Speaker: Rosalind to Orlando
Context: Rosalind disagrees with Orlando, insisting that men do not die out of unrequited love.

Rosalind's insistence that "[m]en have died from time to time, and worms have eaten them, but not for love" is one of the most recognizable lines from the play and perhaps the wisest (IV.i.91–92). Here, Rosalind takes on one of the most dominant interpretations of romantic love, an understanding that is sustained by mythology and praised in literature, and insists on its unreality. She holds to light the stories of Troilus and Leander, both immortal lovers, in order to expose their falsity. Men are, according to Rosalind, much more likely to die by being hit with a club or drowning than in a fatal case of heartbreak. Rosalind does not mean to deny the existence of love; on the contrary, she delights in loving Orlando. Instead, her criticism comes from an unwillingness to let affection cloud or warp her sense of reality. By casting aside the conventions of the standard, and usually tragic, romance, Rosalind advocates a kind of love that belongs to—and can survive in—the real world that she inhabits.

---

4. *O sir, we quarrel in print, by the book, as you have books for good manners. I will name you the degrees. The first, the Retort Courteous; the second, the Quip Modest; the third, the Reply Churlish; the fourth, the Reproof Valiant; the fifth, the Countercheck Quarrelsome; the sixth, the Lie with Circumstance; the seventh, the Lie Direct. All these you may avoid but the Lie Direct; and you may avoid that, too, with an 'if'. I knew when seven justices could not take up a quarrel, but when the parties were met themselves, one of them thought but of an 'if', as 'If you said so, then I said so', and they shook hands and swore brothers. Your 'if' is the only peacemaker; much virtue in 'if'.*

Location: V.iv.81–92
Speaker: Touchstone
Context: Touchstone describes a recent argument of his.

Touchstone's anatomy of the quarrel, as this speech might be called, is a deftly comic moment that skewers all behavior that is "by the book," whether it be rules for engaging an enemy or a lover (V.iv.81). The end of the speech, in which Touchstone turns his attentions to the powers of the word "if," is particularly fine and fitting. "If" points to the potential of events in possible worlds. "If" allows slights to be forgiven, wounds to be salved, and promising opportunities to be taken. Notably, within a dozen lines of this speech, Duke Senior, Orlando, and Phoebe each usher in a new stage of life with a simple sentence that begins with that simple word.

---

5. *It is not the fashion to see the lady the epilogue; but it is no more unhandsome than to see the lord the prologue. If it be true that good wine needs no bush, 'tis true that a good play needs no epilogue. Yet to good wine they do use good bushes, and good plays prove the better by the help of good epilogues. What a case am I in then, that am neither a good epilogue nor cannot insinuate with you in the behalf of a good play! I am not furnished like a beggar, therefore to beg will not become me. My way is to conjure you; and I'll begin with the women. I charge you, O women, for the love you bear to men, to like as much*

of this play as please you. And I charge you, O men, for the love you bear to women—as I perceive by your simpering none of you hates them—that between you and the women the play may please. If I were a woman I would kiss as many of you as had beards that pleased me, complexions that liked me, and breaths that I defied not. And I am sure, as many as have good beards, or good faces, or sweet breaths will for my kind offer, when I make curtsy, bid me farewell.

Location: Epilogue (entire)
Speaker: Rosalind
Context: Rosalind asks the audience for applause.

The epilogue was a standard component of Elizabethan drama. One actor remains onstage after the play has ended to ask the audience for applause. As Rosalind herself notes, it is odd that she has been chosen to deliver the epilogue, as that task is usually assigned to a male character. By the time she addresses the audience directly, Rosalind has discarded her Ganymede disguise. She is again a woman and has married a man. Finally, we must remember that women were forbidden to perform onstage in Shakespeare's England. Rosalind would have been played by a man, which further obscures the boundaries of gender. She is a man who pretends to be a woman who pretends to be a man who pretends to be a woman to win the love of a man. When the actor solicits the approval of the men in the audience, he says, "If I were a woman I would kiss as many of you as had beards that pleased me," returning us to the dizzying intermingling of homosexual and heterosexual affections that govern life in the Forest of Arden (Epilogue, 14–16). The theater, like Arden, is an escape from reality where the wonderful, sometimes overwhelming complexities of human life can be witnessed, contemplated, enjoyed, and studied.

THE COMEDY OF ERRORS

Antipholus of Syracuse and his servant Dromio visit Ephesus, where they are repeatedly mistaken for their twin brothers, Antipholus of Epheseus and his servant Dromio.

THE COMEDY OF ERRORS IN CONTEXT

Scholars generally agree that *The Comedy of Errors* is one of Shakespeare's early plays, perhaps his first. Its emphasis on slapstick comedy over verbal humor has led many critics to call it an "apprentice comedy." It was first performed on December 28, 1594, at the Gray's Inn Christmas Revels, for an audience largely composed of lawyers and law students.

As with many of his plays, Shakespeare drew on classical sources for the plot of *The Comedy of Errors*. The bare bones of the story come the Roman comedy *Menaechmi*, by the dramatist Plautus (c.254–184 B.C.). Shakespeare probably read the play in the original Latin, but may have seen the first English translation that circulated in 1594, a year before its official publication. He made a number of changes to the original story, adding a second set of identical twins (the Dromios), expanding Adriana's character, giving her a sister, and including a back-story involving Egeon and Emilia. *The Comedy of Errors* also draws on a number of other sources. The scene in which Antipholus of Ephesus is locked out of his house resembles a scene in another Plautine work, *Amphitruo*, in which a master is kept out of his own house while the God Jupiter impersonates him. The general tone of *The Comedy of Errors* resembles Italian comedy of the time, and the shrewish wife is a characteristic figure in English comedy. The play has always been very popular with audiences, if somewhat less so with critics. In this century, Rodgers and Hart borrowed the plot of *The Comedy of Errors* for a musical called *The Boys from Syracuse*.

THE COMEDY OF ERRORS: KEY FACTS

Full title: The Comedy of Errors

Author: William Shakespeare

Time and place written: Around 1592–1594; London

Date of first performance: 1594

Genre: Comedy

Setting (time): Ancient times

Setting (place): Ephesus, Greece

Protagonist: Antipholus of Syracuse and Antipholus of Ephesus

Major conflict: A great deal of confusion results because Antipholus of Syracuse and Antipholus of Epheseus are constantly mistaken for each other.

THE COMEDY OF ERRORS: CHARACTER LIST

Abbess (Emilia) The long-lost wife of Egeon and the mother of the two Antipholi.

Adriana The wife of Antipholus of Ephesus. Adriana is a fierce, jealous woman.

Angelo A goldsmith in Syracuse and a friend to Antipholus of Ephesus.

Antipholus of Ephesus The twin brother of Antipholus of Syracuse, the son of Egeon, and the husband of Adriana. The Ephesian Antipholus is a well-respected merchant in Ephesus.

Antipholus of Syracuse The twin brother of Antipholus of Ephesus and the son of Egeon. The Syracusan Antipholus has been traveling the world with his slave, Dromio of Syracuse, trying to find his long-lost brother and mother.

Balthasar A merchant in Syracuse.

Courtesan An expensive prostitute and friend of Antipholus of Ephesus.

Dromio of Ephesus The bumbling, comical slave of Antipholus of Ephesus. The Ephesian Dromio is the Syracusan Dromio's twin brother.

Dromio of Syracuse The bumbling, comical slave of Antipholus of Syracuse. The Syracusan Dromio is the twin brother of the Ephesian Dromio.

Egeon A Syracusan merchant. Egeon is Emilia's husband and the father of the two Antipholi. Like his Syracusan son, he is searching for the missing half of his family.

Luciana Adriana's unmarried sister. Luciana is the object of Antipholus of Syracuse's affections.

Merchant of Ephesus An Ephesian friend of Antipholus of Syracuse.

Nell (known as "Luce" in some editions) Antipholus of Ephesus's prodigiously fat maid. Nell is married to Dromio of Ephesus.

Doctor Pinch A schoolteacher, conjurer, and would-be exorcist.

Second Merchant A tradesman to whom Angelo owes money.

Solinus The Duke of Ephesus. Solinus is a just but merciful ruler.

THE COMEDY OF ERRORS: PLOT OVERVIEW

Egeon, a merchant of Syracuse, is condemned to death in the city of Ephesus for violating the ban against travel between the two rival cities. As he is led to his execution, he tells the Ephesian duke, Solinus, that he has come to Syracuse in search of his wife and one of his identical twin sons, from whom he was separated twenty-five years ago in a shipwreck. His remaining twin son is also traveling the world in search of the missing half of their family. The twins are identical, and each has an identical twin slave (both slaves are named Dromio, although the duke does not know this). The story so moves the duke that he grants Egeon a day to raise the thousand-mark ransom he needs to save his life.

Unbeknownst to Egeon, his son, Antipholus of Syracuse, and Antipholus's slave Dromio are visiting Ephesus, where Antipholus's missing twin, known as Antipholus of Ephesus, is a prosperous citizen. Adriana, Antipholus of Ephesus's wife, mistakes Antipholus of Syracuse for her husband and drags him home for dinner, leaving Dromio of Syracuse to guard the door and admit no one. Antipholus of Ephesus soon arrives home with his slave Dromio of Ephesus and is refused entry to his own house.

Antipholus of Syracuse has fallen in love with Luciana, Adriana's sister, who is appalled by the advances of the man she thinks is her brother-in-law. The confusion increases when a gold chain ordered by the Ephesian Antipholus is given to the Syracusan Antipholus. Because he never received the chain, Antipholus of Ephesus refuses to pay for it and is arrested for debt. His wife thinks he has gone mad and orders him bound and held in a cellar room. Antipholus of Syracuse and his slave decide to flee the city, which they believe is enchanted. Adriana and the debt officer menace them, so they seek refuge in a nearby abbey.

Adriana begs the duke to intervene and remove her "husband" from the abbey into her custody. Her real husband has broken loose and now comes to the duke and levels charges against his wife. The situation is finally resolved by the abbess, Emilia, who brings out the Syracusan set of twins and reveals herself to be Egeon's long-lost wife. Antipholus of Ephesus reconciles with Adriana, Egeon is pardoned by the Duke and reunited with his spouse, Antipholus of Syracuse resumes his romantic pursuit of Luciana, and all ends happily with the two Dromios embracing.

THE COMEDY OF ERRORS: SCENE SUMMARY

ACT I

We learn that Antipholus of Syracuse and his twin brother, Antipholus of Ephesus, were separated at birth; Antipholus of Syracuse arrives in Ephesus.

ACT I, SCENE I   Location: Ephesus

Egeon tells the duke of Ephesus how he lost his wife and one of his twin sons after a shipwreck.

Solinus, the duke of Ephesus, leads a merchant named Egeon to his execution. Egeon talks to the duke, and we learn that he is a native of Syracuse, Ephesus's great commercial rival. Because of strife between the two cities, any Syracusan caught in Ephesus must pay a fee of a thousand marks, a price that Egeon cannot afford, or face execution. Seeming resigned to his death, he declares that the execution will bring an end to his "woes." Curious, the duke asks him to explain why he is traveling in Ephesus.

Egeon says that he married and prospered, trading with the neighboring city of Epidamnum. Eventually his representative in Epidamnum died, leaving his business in disarray, and Egeon was forced to travel there to set his affairs in order. His pregnant wife went with him and gave birth to identical twin sons in Epidamnum. A poor woman staying in the same inn also gave birth to identical boys, and Egeon bought her newborns, intending to bring them up as slaves for his sons.

On the return journey to Ephesus, their ship was broken apart by a storm, and the sailors abandoned Egeon and his family on the wreckage. Egeon's wife tied herself to one of the masts with one son and one slave, and Egeon tied himself to another mast with the other son and the other slave. They floated for a while. The sea grew calm, and soon two ships came toward them—one from Corinth and one from Epidaurus. Before the ships reached them, they ran into a rock that split the wreckage in two, carrying Egeon in one direction and his wife in the other. The Corinthian ship rescued Egeon and his son, but they were unable to catch up to the Epidaurian ship, which had picked up his wife and his other son and carried them away.

Egeon says the son who remained with him recently took his slave and set off into the world to find his brother and mother. Egeon himself followed suit, and his wanderings eventually led him to Ephesus, where he was willing to brave arrest and execution in the hopes of finding the missing half of his family.

The duke finds Egeon's story deeply moving, and although he cannot violate his city's laws, he offers Egeon a day of liberty to find someone to ransom his life. Egeon still despairs, because the task seems hopeless, but he sets off to search for assistance.

ACT I, SCENE II   Location: a street in Ephesus

Dromio E. mistakes Antipholus S. for his master, Antipholus E., and orders him home to dinner.

Egeon's son, Antipholus of Syracuse, is also in Ephesus, although neither he nor his father is aware of the other's presence. A friendly merchant warns Antipholus about the law concerning Syracusans and advises him to pretend to be from another city in order to avoid arrest. Antipholus thanks him and sends his servant, Dromio of Syracuse, to the Centaur Inn with their money (a thousand gold marks) and luggage. Left alone, he thinks about his fruitless quest for his brother and mother. But although no one knows it, Antipholus of Syracuse's missing brother is actually a prosperous citizen of Ephesus. Antipholus of Ephesus is married to a woman named Adriana and is a great favorite of Duke Solinus's.

As Antipholus of Syracuse muses, Dromio of Ephesus, Antipholus of Ephesus's servant, appears. Mistaking Antipholus S. for Antipholus E., Dromio E. demands that his master come home to dinner. Antipholus S., in turn, mistakes Dromio E. for his own servant. Their misunderstanding leads to an argument. Dromio E. tells Antipholus S. that his wife is impatient with him, while Antipholus S. demands to know what has become of their money and belongings. The master slaps the slave, and Dromio E. flees, leaving Antipholus S. to remark that Ephesus is reportedly full of sorcerers and that one must have bewitched his slave. Fearing for the safety of his possessions, he hurries off in the direction of the Centaur Inn.

ACT II

Adriana mistakes Antipholus of Syracuse for her husband and brings him home for dinner.

ACT II, SCENE I   Location: in front of Antipholus E.'s house

Dromio of Ephesus reports that his master is behaving strangely, and Adriana assumes he has taken a mistress.

Adriana, Antipholus E.'s wife, talks to her sister, Luciana. Adriana is anxious for her husband and his slave to return. Luciana rebukes her for being impatient, saying that a dutiful wife should be a docile servant to her husband. Adriana tells Luciana that she doesn't know what she's talking about—once she is married, she will have a different point of view. Dromio of Ephesus returns and reports his master's bizarre behavior (Antipholus S., whom Dromio mistook for Antipholus E.), saying that Antipholus is mad and will talk of nothing but his gold. Furious, Adriana threatens to beat him unless he brings her husband back, and Dromio reluctantly goes out again. Once he is gone, Adriana tells Luciana that Antipholus must have taken a lover—that is the only explanation for his absence and peculiar behavior.

ACT II, SCENE II Location: a street in Ephesus

Adriana mistakes Antipholus S. for her husband and brings him to her house.

Antipholus S. goes to the inn and finds that his slave brought his money and luggage there after all. Confused, he wanders the city until he encounters Dromio S., who has no memory of telling him to come home to dinner. Antipholus S. grows angry with him, but the slave manages to defuse the situation by telling a long, involved joke about baldness.

While the master and slave joke around, Adriana and Luciana come upon them, mistaking them for Antipholus E. and his Dromio. Adriana accuses the man she believes to be her husband of infidelity and rebukes him for violating his own promise of love and their marriage bed. Antipholus S., confused, says that he has never met her. Enraged, Adriana drags her perplexed "husband" home to dinner, bringing Dromio S. with them. The confused Antipholus S. decides to play along until he understands the situation better. They go into Antipholus E.'s house, and Dromio S. is left below to guard the door during dinner.

ACT III

Because they think that he is already inside, Antipholus of Ephesus's family members will not let him in; the goldsmith, mistaking Antipholus of Syracuse for Antipholus of Ephesus, gives him a gold chain.

ACT III, SCENE I Location: outside the house of Antipholus of Ephesus

Antipholus E. cannot enter his own house.

Antipholus E. returns from the marketplace accompanied by Dromio E., Angelo the goldsmith, and Balthasar the merchant. He asks the other businessmen to give Adriana an excuse for his tardiness and mentions that his slave is behaving oddly. When he knocks at the gate, Dromio S. refuses to let him in. Antipholus E. pounds and shouts furiously, bringing Nell, his maid, to the door. Adriana comes to the door too. Since both believe that Antipholus E. is already inside, they refuse to admit him. In a rage, Antipholus is about to break down the door, but Balthasar dissuades him, telling him that doing so would reflect badly on his wife's honor, and that Adriana must have a good reason for keeping him out. Still seething, Antipholus E. leads his friends away, resolving to dine with a courtesan at the Porcupine Inn. He asks Angelo to fetch a gold chain, recently made, that he had promised to his wife. Antipholus now plans to give it to the courtesan instead.

ACT III, SCENE II Location: outside the house of Antipholus of Ephesus

Antipholus of Syracuse appalls Luciana by confessing that he loves her; mistaking Antipholus of Syracuse for Antipholus of Ephesus, the goldsmith gives him the gold chain.

Alone with Antipholus S., Luciana rebukes the man she believes to be her brother-in-law for treating Adriana badly. If he must betray his wife, she says, he should at least do it secretly. Antipholus S. insists that he is not Adriana's husband and then professes his love for Luciana. Appalled, she flees to find her sister.

Dromio S. joins his master and says that the kitchen maid, Nell, mistook him for her husband (Dromio E.). Dromio S. describes Nell as a prodigiously fat, ugly, and fearsome woman, and he and his master have a good laugh at her expense. Antipholus S. tells his slave that he intends to depart from Ephesus immediately, and sends him to the harbor to book passage. Once Dromio is gone, Antipholus S. resolves to resist the temptation of the beautiful Luciana and leave the city, since "none but witches do inhabit here" (III.ii.154). Angelo the goldsmith comes in and mistakes Antipholus S. for Antipholus E. He gives him the gold chain that Antipholus E. ordered, promising to stop by later to collect payment.

ACT IV

Antipholus of Ephesus goes to jail for refusing to pay Angelo for the gold chain and eventually everyone thinks he has gone mad.

ACT IV, SCENE I   Location: a street in Ephesus

Antipholus of Ephesus refuses to pay Angelo for the gold chain, so Angelo has him arrested.

Angelo is in debt to a second merchant, who threatens to arrest him. Angelo promises to collect the sum from Antipholus E., whom he sees walking down the street with Dromio E. Antipholus E. sends his slave off to buy rope with which he plans to beat his wife and servants for locking him out of the house.

Angelo asks for payment for the gold chain. Antipholus E., who never received the chain, refuses to pay, so Angelo has him arrested. Dromio S. returns from the harbor and mistakes Antipholus E. for his master, telling him which ships are ready to sail. Cursing, Antipholus E. orders him to be silent and sends him to Adriana to fetch bail money.

ACT IV, SCENE II   Location: outside the house of Antipholus of Ephesus

Luciana tells Adriana about Antipholus E.'s advances; Adriana gives Dromio S. money to bail her husband out of jail.

Luciana has told Adriana that the man she thinks is Antipholus of Ephesus declared his love for her. She says she is entirely innocent in the affair. Adriana curses Antipholus furiously but admits that she still loves him. Dromio S. dashes in to report that Antipholus has been arrested and needs money. Adriana sends Luciana to fetch it and then orders Dromio to hurry and save her husband from prison.

ACT IV, SCENE III   Location: Ephesus

The courtesan asks Antipholus S. for the ring he borrowed from her; he does not know what she is talking about.

Antipholus S., exploring the city, remarks that people he has never met are greeting him, thanking him for favors, showing him goods he has ordered, and so on. Dromio S. dashes up to him, carrying the gold that Adriana sent to free Antipholus E. from jail. Antipholus S. has no idea why his servant is bringing him money. He asks Dromio whether there are ships in the harbor on which they can book passage out of Ephesus.

The courtesan, at whose home Antipholus E. ate dinner, comes along and asks Antipholus S. for the ring he borrowed from her during the meal. He and Dromio decide that she is a witch and flee. The courtesan, convinced that Antipholus is mad, resolves to go to Adriana's home, tell her that her husband has stolen the ring, and demand repayment.

ACT IV, SCENE IV   Location: Ephesus

Officers tie up Antipholus of Syracuse and Dromio of Syracuse, deeming them mad.

Dromio E. encounters Antipholus E. in an officer's custody. Antipholus E. demands to know where the bail money is. Dromio E., baffled, replies that he has brought the rope's end that Antipholus E. sent him to buy. Antipholus flies into a rage and tries to assault his slave. The appearance of Adriana, Luciana, the courtesan, and a schoolteacher named Doctor Pinch brings him up short. The women plan to have the doctor use exorcism to cure Antipholus's supposed madness. Antipholus protests and argues with Adriana. She claims he dined at home, while her husband, backed up by Dromio, tells her that he was shut out of his own house. Pinch says both master and slave are mad. They are bound and taken to Adriana's house.

Adriana promises the officer she will pay all her husband's debts. He tells her that Antipholus owes money to Angelo the goldsmith for a gold chain. Neither the courtesan nor Adriana has seen the chain. Antipholus S. and Dromio S. rush in with drawn swords, and everyone else flees, mistaking them for Antipholus E. and Dromio E., who, they assume, have escaped from Pinch. Remarking that even witches are afraid of swords, Antipholus S. orders his slave to take their belongings on board a ship.

ACT V

The abbess tells Egeon that she is his long-lost wife and that the Antipholi are their twin sons.

ACT V, SCENE I Location: in front of a religious house

The abbess clears up all the confusion, explaining that she is the twins' mother.

Angelo and the second merchant discuss Antipholus E.'s claim that he never received the gold chain from Angelo. They encounter Dromio S. and Antipholus S., who is wearing the gold chain. After Angelo and Antipholus S. exchange harsh words, Antipholus and the second merchant draw their swords. Adriana, Luciana, and the courtesan enter, and Antipholus and Dromio flee into a nearby abbey. The abbess comes out and demands to know what is going on. Adriana describes her husband's madness, but the abbess blames Adriana's jealousy for driving Antipholus mad and denies everyone entry to her house, saying that she will cure the man herself.

It is now five o'clock. Duke Solinus appears, leading Egeon to his execution. Adriana, seeing the duke, appeals to him for aid in removing her husband from the abbey. The duke, remembering promises that he made to Adriana when she married Antipholus, agrees to mediate. Just then a messenger comes in with news

that Antipholus E. and Dromio E. have escaped Pinch's clutches. Adriana calls him a liar, saying that her husband is in the abbey. Antipholus E. himself rushes in, accompanied by his slave and demanding that the duke grant him justice against his wife, who has locked him out of the house, allowed him to be arrested, and placed him in the hands of Pinch. After a flurry of charges and countercharges, the duke summons the abbess, hoping that she can untangle the mess.

Egeon mistakes Antipholus E. for the son he brought up and greets him happily. Antipholus E. is confused. He says that he has never seen his father in his life, and that he has always been a citizen of Ephesus. The abbess enters, bringing with her Antipholus S. and Dromio S., which causes general consternation. The abbess greets Egeon and says that she is his long-lost wife, Emilia, and that the identical Antipholi are their twin sons. The courtesan gets her ring back, for the jeweler receives payment for the chain, and the duke refuses an offer of payment for Egeon's life, pardoning the old man. The entire company goes inside the abbey for a celebratory feast. The two Dromios exit last, hand in hand, "like brother and brother" (V.i.426).

THEMES, MOTIFS & SYMBOLS IN *THE COMEDY OF ERRORS*

THEMES

THE INSTABILITY OF IDENTITY Much of the humor in *The Comedy of Errors* comes from the implications of mistaken identities, silly situations in which a husband does not recognize his wife, or a master does not recognize his servant. This brand of comedy has led critics to classify *The Comedy of Errors* as a farce, a work in which the playwright does not aim for depth of character or psychological nuance. But while the identity confusion in *The Comedy of Errors* can be interpreted as a plot device used to get laughs out of the audience, some critics understand it as a device with serious philosophical implications. Antipholus of Syracuse comes to Ephesus on a serious existential quest: "So I, to find a mother and a brother, / In quest of them, unhappy, lose myself" (I.ii.39–40). He dislikes himself and longs to leave his personality behind by diving into the search for his family. The instability of Antipholus's identity stems not just from the confusion his appearance causes, but also from his inner conflicts.

THE FRAGILITY OF HUMAN RELATIONS Shakespeare suggests that everyday relations with friends and family are balanced precariously on the perceptions of others. Daily life for Antipholus of Ephesus is solidly predictable before the arrival of his look-alike from Syracuse. He has stable, amicable relationships with his wife, servants, and local merchants and shopkeepers. His double's appearance in town throws his orderly life into chaos. He brutally beats the man he believes to be his servant, he finds his apparently happy marriage devolving into a morass of suspicions, jealousies, and spousal violence, and he quarrels with merchants. Once Antipholus of Ephesus's friends and family perceive that he is acting poorly, his relationships collapse with alarming speed.

THE SEARCH FOR WHOLENESS When Antipholus of Syracuse arrives in Ephesus to seek out the missing half of his family, he describes his search not just as a quest for two individuals, but as a quest for personal wholeness. He says he cannot enjoy personal happiness, or "mine own content" (I.ii.33), until he locates his long-lost brother. He does not simply want to find his sibling; he needs to find him in order to be happy. Antipholus's search for a whole self suggests a powerful myth that goes back at least to Plato's *Symposium*, in which Plato writes that every human is searching for his "other half" from which he was separated long ago. The Syracusan Antipholus is more aware of the spiritual pain that results from separation from his other half, while the Ephesian Antipholus is more concerned with his everyday business.

MOTIFS

WITCHCRAFT Ephesus, the setting of *The Comedy of Errors*, has a long association with witchcraft and deception: it was the city in which St. Paul preached Christianity to a local population famous for its practice of pagan magic. Both Antipholus of Syracuse and Dromio of Syracuse blame strange events on Ephesus's witches and "dark-working sorcerers that change the mind" (I.ii.99). Although what seems like magic is actually the result of mistaken identity, some mystical force does seem to have brought the long-lost twins together. Though the spiritual quest of Antipholus of Syracuse has nothing to do with black magic, it does produce chaos in Ephesus just as a sorcerer's spell would, ultimately leading to an unlikely, if not miraculous, family reunion.

MARRIAGE PROBLEMS Even before the identity confusion begins, Adriana reveals anxieties about her domestic life. In conversation with her sister, Luciana, she objects to the idea that men should be freer than women, asking, "Why should their liberty be more than ours?"(II.i.10). Later, Antipholus of Ephesus plans to tie up Adriana with rope, a severe punishment for an annoying but minor crime. The speed with which Adriana becomes convinced that Antipholus is cheating on her and Antipholus starts threatening violence suggests that the twin confusion does not so much create trouble in the marriage as expose what was lying dormant.

SYMBOLS

THE CHAIN The gold chain for which Antipholus of Ephesus refuses to pay symbolizes the web that binds a person to others. Antipholus's gold chain symbolizes his connection to the goldsmith and the merchant who owes him money, as well as to the debt officer who arrests him. It also connects him to his wife, for whom he originally intended the chain, and to the courtesan, to whom Antipholus decides to give the chain after he grows angry with his wife. The social network the chain symbolizes can be comforting or imprisoning. Dromio says his master was arrested not on a legal bond, "but on a stronger thing— / A chain, a chain" (IV.ii.50–51). The chain of Antipholus's relationships is inescapable, and leads to his arrest.

THE SHIPWRECK Unlike the shipwrecks in other Shakespearean dramas such as *The Tempest* or *Twelfth Night*, the shipwreck in *The Comedy of Errors* occurred in the distant past and seems more like a mythological event than a physical one. The broken-up ship suggests the deep losses that the Antipholi and Dromios suffer.

IMPORTANT QUOTATIONS FROM *THE COMEDY OF ERRORS*

Proceed, Solinus, to procure my fall,
And by the doom of death end woes and all.

Location: I.i.1–2
Speaker: Egeon to Solinus
Context: Egeon prepares to be executed.

These first lines are typical of *The Comedy of Errors*, whose lighthearted farce is tempered by dark undercurrents. The play opens with a man headed to his own execution and speaking of life as a series of "woes." Although amusing identity confusion fills the scenes that follow, the play also features masters beating their servants, a man threatening to tie up his wife with rope, and main characters who descend into near-madness and violence.

Christian references also occur in these first lines. Egeon speaks of his "fall," a reference to the fall of Adam, who sinned and then encountered death. Like Adam, Egeon is a criminal father punished by the "doom of death."

They say this town is full of cozenage,
As nimble jugglers that deceive the eye,
Dark-working sorcerers that change the mind,
Soul-killing witches that deform the body,
Disguised cheaters, prating mountebanks,
And many such-like libertines of sin.

Location: I.ii.97–102
Speaker: Antipholus of Syracuse
Context: Antipholus of Syracuse has mistaken Dromio of Ephesus for his own slave.

Antipholus of Syracuse's reference to the mysticism and magic of Ephesus would have been familiar to Shakespeare's Elizabethan audience, who was conversant in Saint Paul's Epistle to the Ephesians in the New Testament. In the Epistle, Paul preaches the gospel of Christ to the locals, who practice the pagan arts of sorcery. In Christian terms, the Ephesians are unspiritual pagans, or "natural men" not yet transformed into spiritual men by baptism. But in *The Comedy of Errors*, the Ephesians are not exotic magicians, but normal, even dull, people.

Call thyself sister, sweet, for I am thee.
Thee will I love, and with thee lead my life.
Thou hast no husband yet, nor I no wife.
Give me thy hand.

Location: III.ii.66–69
Speaker: Antipholus of Syracuse to Luciana
Context: Antipholus of Syracuse tells Luciana he loves her.

Antipholus of Syracuse's confession of love to Luciana is partly another comic consequence of the confusion over the twins. The Syracusan's misfortune in falling in love with the sister-in-law of his twin plays with the taboo of adultery, although it is entirely innocent. The confession also suggests that in matters of love, the loss of identity can lead to a happy outcome. Antipholus insists that he is Luciana, citing his similarity to her as one reason they should love each other.

Be patient, for I will not let him stir
Till I have used the approved means I have,
With wholesome syrups, drugs, and holy prayers
To make of him a formal man again.
It is a branch and parcel of mine oath,
A charitable duty of my order.

Location: V.i.103–108
Speaker: the abbess to Adriana
Context: The abbess refuses to hand over Antipholus of Syracuse.

The abbess's determination to make Antipholus of Syracuse a "formal," or whole, man just before she reveals that he is the twin of Antipholus of Ephesus suggests that the twins are two divided halves of one human being. The abbess says that making Antipholus normal is her duty as a religious woman. She plans to treat both body and soul, using drugs and prayers, as if his physical and spiritual halves have been separated and must be rejoined.

We came into the world like brother and brother,
And now let's go hand in hand, not one before another.

Location: V.i.426–427
Speaker: Dromio of Ephesus to Dromio of Syracuse
Context: The twin slaves prepare to leave the stage.

Dromio insists on walking side by side with his newfound twin brother, creating a visual image that reflects the play's conceit that human nature has two equal sides, as represented by the two sets of twins. The Ephesian, or natural, side of humanity consists of family life and work, while the Syracusan, or spiritual, side consists of profound, incomprehensibly strong connections with others. Dromio's desire to walk side by side with his brother suggests that neither of these sides of human nature is more valuable than the other.

CORIOLANUS

Prevented from becoming a consul by his pride and hasty words, Coriolanus avenges himself on Rome by attacking it with the Volscians, who eventually assassinate him.

CORIOLANUS IN CONTEXT

Coriolanus was the next-to-last tragedy that Shakespeare composed, following on the heels of *Othello*, *King Lear*, *Macbeth*, and *Antony and Cleopatra*, all of which Shakespeare probably wrote between 1604 and 1606. Like *Antony and Cleopatra*, it is a Roman play, but unlike that play (and *Julius Caesar*), *Coriolanus* is set not in the Imperial Rome of the first century A.D., but more than four centuries earlier, when Rome was one Italian city among many and fighting for survival. The semi-historical action is set in the aftermath of the fall of Tarquin, the last king of Rome. It focuses on the struggle between the plebeians, or common people, and the patricians, or aristocrats, during Rome's transition from monarchy to republic.

Shakespeare's interest in Roman history typified the general Renaissance fascination with the classical world. Renaissance playwrights and political philosophers consistently turned to Greece and Rome for inspiration. The source for *Coriolanus*'s plot is likely the "Life of Caius Martius Coriolanus," written in the first decade A.D. by the celebrated biographer Plutarch and first translated into English in 1579 by Sir Thomas North. Other sources may include Livy's *History of Rome*. A number of scholars have also argued that one of Shakespeare's intentions with *Coriolanus* was to comment on current politics. Early seventeenth century London was rent by an ongoing struggle between King James and Parliament, which Shakespeare's portrayal of the patrician-plebeian conflict may reflect.

Although the limited appeal of its characters and the limited scope of the play have prevented *Coriolanus* from becoming a universal favorite, the play's political messages have provided a lasting source of debate. Liberals and conservatives alike have taken to the play with equal gusto at various points in history; directors have staged it both as a pro-fascist and pro-communist piece, depending upon their inclinations.

CORIOLANUS: KEY FACTS

Full Title: The Tragedy of Coriolanus

Author: William Shakespeare

Time and place written: 1607–1609; London

Date of first performance: Uncertain; probably 1609 or 1610

Genre: Tragedy

Setting (time): The early days of the Roman republic: late fifth century B.C.

Setting (place): Rome

Protagonist: Coriolanus

Antagonist: Brutus, Sicinius, and the Roman plebeians

Major conflict: Coriolanus's pride angers the plebeians and results in his exile.

CORIOLANUS: CHARACTER LIST

Tullus Aufidius A general of the Volscians, Rome's enemy. Tullus Aufidius is Coriolanus's great rival in warfare, but he is not quite Coriolanus's equal.

Brutus One of the tribunes elected by the plebeians to serve as their representative in government. A clever politician, Brutus regards Coriolanus as a great danger to the plebeians and the Roman state and works to keep him out of power.

Cominius A patrician and a former consul. Cominius is a friend of Coriolanus's and one of the generals who leads the Roman army against the Volscians.

Coriolanus (Caius Martius) The protagonist of the play. He receives the name "Coriolanus" after leading the Roman armies to victory against the Volscian city of Corioles. Brave, fearsome in battle, and extremely honorable, Coriolanus is also proud, immature, inflexible, and snobbish. These faults lead to his downfall.

Titus Lartius An old Roman nobleman. Titus Lartius is appointed, along with Cominius, general against the Volscians.

Menenius A Roman patrician and a friend of Coriolanus's. Menenius uses his wit and clever tongue to avoid conflict.

Sicinius A Roman tribune, a clever politician, and Brutus's ally in the struggle against Coriolanus.

Valeria A Roman noblewoman. Valeria is close friends with Virgilia and Volumnia.

Virgilia Coriolanus's loyal wife.

Volumnia Coriolanus's mother. Volumnia is devoted to her son. She raised him to be a warrior and delights in his military exploits. Coriolanus often allows his iron-willed mother to dominate him.

Young Martius Coriolanus and Virgilia's son.

CORIOLANUS: PLOT OVERVIEW

A famine has plagued ancient Rome. The plebeians, or common people, demand the right to set their own price for the city's grain supply. In response to their protests, the patricians, or ruling aristocracy, grant the plebeians five tribunes, or representatives. This decision infuriates the proud patrician soldier Caius Martius, who holds the lower classes in contempt. War breaks out with a neighboring Italian tribe, the Volscians, who Martius's great rival, Tullus Aufidius, leads. In the campaign that follows, the Volscians meet with defeat, and the Romans take the Italian city of Corioles, thanks to the heroism of Caius Martius. In recognition of his great deeds, he receives the name Coriolanus.

Coriolanus enjoys a hero's welcome when he returns to Rome, and the Senate offers to make him consul. In order to gain this office, he must go out and plead for plebeians' votes, a task he undertakes reluctantly. At first, the common people agree to give him their votes, but later they reverse their decision under the influence of two clever tribunes, Brutus and Sicinius, who consider Coriolanus an enemy of the people. This reversal drives the proud Coriolanus into a fury, and he speaks out impulsively against the very idea of popular rule. Brutus and Sicinius, seizing on his hasty words, declare him a traitor to the Roman state and drive him into exile.

Craving revenge against Rome, Coriolanus goes to his Volscian enemy, Aufidius, in the city of Antium, and makes peace with him. Aufidius is planning a new campaign against the Romans and welcomes Coriolanus's assistance, although he soon finds himself overshadowed by his new ally. The Volscian army marches on Rome, throwing the city into a panic. Rome's armies are helpless to stop the advance, and soon Aufidius and Coriolanus are encamped outside the city walls. Two of Coriolanus's oldest friends come to plead for mercy, but Coriolanus refuses to hear them. Yet when his beloved mother, Volumnia, begs him to make peace, he relents. The Romans hail Volumnia the savior of the city. Meanwhile, Coriolanus and the Volsces return to Antium, where the residents hail Coriolanus as a hero. Aufidius, feeling slighted, declares that Coriolanus's failure to take Rome amounts to treachery. In the ensuing argument, some of Aufidius's men assassinate Coriolanus.

CORIOLANUS: SCENE SUMMARY

ACT I

After acquitting himself brilliantly in battle against the Volsces, Caius Martius is renamed Coriolanus.

ACT I, SCENE I   Location: Rome

The rioting plebeians win two representatives, and the Volsces declare war against Rome.

The plebeians are rioting against their rulers, the patricians, whom they accuse of hoarding grain while the common people starve. The plebeians say they will not accept the price of grain set by the Senate (the governing body, run by the patricians) and demand the right to set the price themselves. They single out Caius Martius, a patrician general and war hero, as the "chief enemy to the people" (I.i.5–6). As the plebeians make their way to the Capitol, Menenius, a patrician and a friend of Martius's, intercepts them and tells the mob that the patricians have their best interests at heart. He compares the role of the Senate in Rome to the role of the stomach in the human body: just as the stomach serves as a storehouse and collecting place for all the nutrients and then dispenses them throughout the rest of the body, the patricians collect and dispense grain to the entire city.

As Menenius and the rioters argue, Caius Martius himself comes and delivers a general curse to the mob, calling them dogs and cowards. He tells Menenius that the Senate has agreed to allow the plebeians to elect five tribunes to advocate for their interests in the Roman state. A messenger dashes in, bringing word that the Volsces, one of Rome's enemies among the Italian tribes, are arming for war. Martius declares that the war will be good for their city and notes that the Volsces are led by a great general, Tullus Aufidius, whom he respects as a worthy adversary. A group of senators orders Cominius (who is the consul, or chief magistrate of Rome, for the year) and Titus Lartius (another patrician) to command the impending war. Martius will act as a lieutenant under Cominius. The crowd disperses, and the senators return to the Capitol to prepare for the campaign.

The plebeians have already elected their tribunes. Two of them, Sicinius and Brutus, have been watching Martius and now comment on how proud and domineering he is. Sicinius wonders how Martius will bear being under the command of Cominius, but Brutus points out that as second-in-command, Martius will escape blame if things go badly and receive all the credit if things go well.

ACT I, SCENE II Location: the Volscian city of Corioles

The Volscian senators refuse to listen to Tullus Aufidius.

Tullus Aufidius, about to depart for his attack on Rome, tells the senators of Corioles that the Romans are already prepared for his offensive. The senators doubt this. They advise Aufidius to take his army into the field as planned and return to Corioles only if the Romans arrive and besiege the city.

ACT I, SCENE III Location: the house of Caius Martius in Rome

Volumnia and Virgilia talk about Caius Martius.

Volumnia and Virgilia, Caius Martius's mother and wife, sit sewing together. Volumnia tells her daughter-in-law that she raised Martius to be a great soldier and takes more enjoyment from his victories than she would from a husband's embrace. She hopes he will crush the Volscians and Tullus Aufidius in the coming war and speaks of the beauty of bloody wounds. Valeria, another Roman noblewoman, visits the two women. They all discuss Virgilia and Martius's son, who takes after his father in his appetite for physical activity and fighting. Valeria tells them the news from the battlefield: Cominius has taken part of the Roman army to meet Aufidius's forces in the field, and Titus Lartius and Martius are leading the rest of the army in a siege against Corioles.

ACT I, SCENE IV Location: Corioles

The Volscians fend off the Romans.

The Volscian senators come to the walls of their city to parley with Martius and Lartius. Warning the Romans that Aufidius's army will soon return to rescue their city, they send out a few remaining troops against the besiegers. The Volscians drive the Romans back to their trenches.

ACT I, SCENE V Location: the outskirts of Corioles, and then the city proper

Under Martius's command, the Romans invade Corioles.

Martius, cursing his men for their cowardice, leads them back, all the way up to gates of the city. In the course of the battle, he is cut off from his troops and trapped within the walls of Corioles. Lartius assumes that he is dead. Martius single-handedly holds off the Volscians, forces the gate open again, and allows the Roman army to surge in and seize the city.

ACT I, SCENE VI (THROUGH XI)   Location: Corioles

Martius defeats Aufidius and his men on the battlefield and is renamed Coriolanus.

The Romans ravage Corioles. Martius, wounded and bleeding, takes part of the army to join up with Cominius's forces, who are fighting with Aufidius's men. Cominius has not yet heard the news of Corioles's fall, so the sight of the bloody Martius makes him wonder if the Romans have been defeated. Martius assures him that Corioles is in Roman hands and then leads Cominius's forces against Aufidius's men, seeking out Aufidius to engage him in one-on-one combat. Martius drives Aufidius and several other Volscians back while the Roman forces pursue their triumph. Although he has led the victories over the city and the battlefield, Martius selflessly refuses any share of the spoils, leaving them all to his men, who cheer him. Cominius insists that he deserves a new name, Coriolanus, for his valor in the taking of Corioles. The beaten Aufidius curses his Roman nemesis, who has now defeated him five times, and sends messengers to lobby for peace.

ACT II

The senators want to make Coriolanus consul, so he reluctantly seeks out the approval of the plebeians.

ACT II, SCENE I   Location: Rome

Brutus and Sicinius fret over Coriolanus's increased power, but decide he will undermine himself.

Brutus and Sicinius converse with Menenius as they await news from the battlefield. The two tribunes criticize Caius Martius, calling him a proud man and an enemy of the common people of Rome. Menenius says they should look to their own faults before criticizing others, since they themselves are "unmeriting, proud, violent, testy magistrates, alias fools, as any in Rome (II.i.39–41)." Brutus and Sicinius point out that Menenius is hardly a perfect public servant. He is better known as a wit and a gossip than as a great politician.

Volumnia, Virgilia, and Valeria arrive with news of Martius' victory. While Volumnia describes the wounds her son received in this campaign, Menenius gives thanks that his friend is alive and that Rome is victorious over the Volscians. Surrounded by his soldiers, Martius—now Coriolanus—enters Rome and greets his wife and mother. Then, accompanied by Cominius, Titus Lartius, and Menenius, he makes his way to the Capitol to greet the Senate.

Brutus and Sicinius worry that Coriolanus will be made consul in gratitude for his victories and that once he gains power he will eliminate their offices. They comfort themselves with the knowledge that the proud general is unlikely to go out in the marketplace and gain the votes of the common people, which every aspiring consul must do. Indeed, his contempt for the lower classes will likely destroy the popularity that he has won with his battlefield exploits. The two tribunes make their way to the Capitol.

ACT II, SCENE II   Location: the Capitol

The senators urge Coriolanus to drum up votes so that he can be made Consul.

Two officers are setting down cushions for the senators and discussing the likelihood of Coriolanus becoming consul. The senators come in and seat themselves. Cominius rises to recount Coriolanus's exploits against the Volscians. Coriolanus, embarrassed by the adulation, leaves the chamber while Cominius describes the battle and Coriolanus's great feats. Amazed by the account of Coriolanus's valor, the senators recall him and declare that they are eager to make him consul. They advise him to dress himself in the toga of candidacy and go to the marketplace at once, where he must gain the people's votes by describing his exploits and showing his scars. Coriolanus begs permission to avoid this custom, since he finds it demeaning, but the senators insist that he must do it. Observing his reluctance and disdain for the common people, Brutus and Sicinius plot to stir up resentment against him.

ACT II, SCENE III   Location: the marketplace

The citizens approve of Coriolanus but then retract their approval at the urging of Brutus and Sicinius.

A group of citizens discusses Coriolanus's candidacy, saying that if he uses the scars of battle in his appeal to them, they will probably make him consul. Coriolanus comes in accompanied by Menenius, who encourages him and then leaves. Coriolanus struggles to talk to the small groups of citizens and cannot conceal his arrogance, but by calling attention to his military service, he manages to convince many people to vote for him. Brutus and Sicinius reluctantly acknowledge that he has passed the test, and Menenius leads him back to the Capitol.

When Coriolanus has gone, the plebeians remark on his arrogance, and Brutus and Sicinius demand to know why they voted for such an arrogant patrician. The plebeians decide to retract their approval of Coriolanus. Elated, Brutus and Sicinius tell the crowds to gather their friends and go to the Capitol. To protect themselves, the two tribunes advise the crowds to say that they only voted for Coriolanus because the tribunes told them to and that they have come to their senses and want the vote declared invalid.

ACT III

Despite attempts to rein in his temper, Coriolanus angers the plebeians by denouncing their role in government, and they banish him.

ACT III, SCENE I   Location: the Capitol

When Coriolanus hears that the plebeians do not support his bid for consul, he is enraged and denounces them.

Titus Lartius tells Coriolanus that Tullus Aufidius has raised a new army. Coriolanus worries that the Volsces will attack Rome despite the newly signed peace treaty, but Lartius assures him that the Volsces been broken and will not fight again. The two tribunes arrive and tell the assembled senators that the people of Rome will not accept Coriolanus as consul. Furious, Coriolanus accuses Brutus and Sicinius of rallying the plebeians against him. He denigrates the common people, warning his fellow patricians that allowing the rabble to hold power will ultimately lead to the downfall of the Senate. Menenius urges Coriolanus to return to the market and beg the people's pardon, but Coriolanus refuses and continues to denounce the plebeians. He also denounces the patricians for ever having agreed to allow the plebeians a share in Rome's governance. Brutus and Sicinius accuse Coriolanus of treason and call in a crowd of plebeians to seize him. He raves at them, and the two tribunes declare that he must be executed. Coriolanus draws his sword, and the senators come to his aid. Coriolanus and the senators drive away the mob of plebeians, along with the two tribunes, and Coriolanus flees to a senator's house. The mob returns with renewed strength, but Menenius convinces the people to allow him to reason with Coriolanus. He says he will bring Coriolanus to the market place for a public airing of grievances.

ACT III, SCENE II   Location: Coriolanus's house

Coriolanus grudgingly agrees to beg the plebeians' pardon.

Coriolanus tells a group of Roman nobles that he has no intention of changing his character to suit the desires of the mob. Volumnia comes in and berates him for his stubbornness. Menenius arrives with the senators and advises Coriolanus to go the marketplace and make peace with the people. If he recants what he said about the plebeians and their tribunes, perhaps they will allow him to be consul. Coriolanus refuses, but his mother advises him to act humbly, even if he is only feigning humility. Eventually Coriolanus relents and agrees to make peace with the plebeians.

ACT III, SCENE III Location: the marketplace

The plebeians banish Coriolanus.

Brutus and Sicinius plan to bait Coriolanus into losing his temper. The war hero enters the marketplace, accompanied by Menenius and Cominius, and declares that he will submit to the will of the people. But when Sicinius accuses him of planning to tyrannize the Roman state, Coriolanus loses his temper and launches into a tirade against the tribunes and plebeians. As his friends watch helplessly, Sicinius and Brutus, supported by the entire populace, declare that Coriolanus must leave Rome forever. Coriolanus says he will go gladly.

ACT IV

Coriolanus allies himself with Aufidius and the Volsces and marches on Rome.

ACT IV, SCENE I Location: Rome's gates

Coriolanus leaves Rome.

Coriolanus prepares to leave the city, pausing only to bid farewell to his wife, Virgilia, and to his mother and friends. Volumnia weeps and curses the city for casting him out. Cominius offers to accompany him for a time, but Coriolanus refuses and departs.

ACT IV, SCENE II Location: Rome's gates

Brutus and Sicinius snipe at Volumnia.

Brutus and Sicinius dismiss the people and try to avoid Volumnia, Virgilia, and Menenius, who are returning from bidding farewell to Coriolanus. Volumnia spots the two tribunes and denounces them, saying they have exiled the best man in Rome. Brutus and Sicinius tell her she has lost her wits.

ACT IV, SCENE III Location: a road outside Rome

Two spies talk about Coriolanus's banishment.

A Roman in the pay of the Volscians meets up with another Volscian spy and reports that Coriolanus has been banished. The two men agree that this will give Tullus Aufidius an excellent chance to take revenge on Rome for the defeats he has suffered.

ACT IV, SCENE IV Location: Antium

Coriolanus announces that he is now an enemy of Rome.

Coriolanus comes to the city of Antium, where Aufidius is staying. He informs the audience that he plans to ally himself with Aufidius against his native city and become Rome's greatest enemy.

ACT IV, SCENE V Location: Antium

Coriolanus allies himself with Aufidius.

Coriolanus asks for admission to Tullus Aufidius's house. One of the servants fetches his master. Aufidius does not recognize Coriolanus either, so Coriolanus identifies himself and says that he has come to offer his friendship to Aufidius and to support to the Volscian cause, or to be killed—it matters little to him. Aufidius, overcome with emotion, embraces him and welcomes him in, promising him the opportunity to exact revenge on the Romans. The two generals dine together. One of the servants brings word to his fellows that there will soon be war with Rome.

ACT IV, SCENE VI Location: Rome

After getting word of Coriolanus's impending attack on Rome, Brutus and Sicinius begin to feel their position weakening.

Brutus and Sicinius congratulate each other on the ease with which they disposed of the troublesome Coriolanus. They tell Menenius that the city is better off without him. A messenger brings word that Aufidius and the Volscians are preparing to make war on Rome again. Brutus refuses to believe it, but a second messenger brings even worse news: Coriolanus himself is leading the Volscian army. Menenius and Cominius tell the tribunes that this catastrophe is their fault. Brutus and Sicinius protest, but the plebeians, panicked by the tidings, begin to say that they were wrong to banish Coriolanus. The two tribunes, fearing for their own position, depart for the Capitol.

ACT IV, SCENE VII Location: the Volscian camp

Aufidius worries about Coriolanus's growing power.

Aufidius is beginning to have second thoughts about his alliance with his former adversary. His soldiers have become begun to show more devotion to Coriolanus than to him. He assumes that Rome will fall to Coriolanus and plots a way to dispose of Coriolanus once the city has been taken.

ACT V

Volumnia convinces Coriolanus to call off his attack on Rome, a reversal Aufidius uses to convince the Voscians to kill Coriolanus.

ACT V, SCENE I Location: the border of Rome

Romans try and fail to call off Coriolanus.

Coriolanus arrives on the borders of the city with his army. Cominius goes out to plead with his old friend for mercy, but to the great despair of Romans, Coriolanus turns him away. Brutus and Sicinius plead with Menenius to appeal to Coriolanus, and the old patrician reluctantly agrees. However, Cominius tells the tribunes that there is no hope—Coriolanus is immovable.

ACT V, SCENE II Location: the Volscian camp

Menenius cannot move Coriolanus.

Sentries refuse to allow Menenius to see their generals. Eventually Coriolanus and Tullus Aufidius emerge, but Menenius's pleas do not move them. The guards mock Menenius and he is sent away.

ACT V, SCENE III Location: the Volscian camp

Under pressure from his mother, Coriolanus agrees to call off his attack on Rome.

Aufidius remarks that he is impressed with Coriolanus's fortitude in the face of pleas from his oldest friends. Coriolanus says that henceforth he will accept no more embassies from Rome. But a shout goes up, and Virgilia, Volumnia, Valeria, and Young Martius, Coriolanus's son, arrive from Rome. Coriolanus vows to steel his heart against them but allows them to approach. Volumnia kneels before him and begs him to make peace. She tells him that she will block his path to Rome: "thou shalt no sooner / March to assault thy country than to tread … on they mother's womb / That brought thee to this world." (V.iii.123–26) Young Martius pledges that when he has grown older, he will fight against his father. Moved, Coriolanus starts to leave, but his mother stops him and again asks him to make an honorable peace, one that rewards Romans and Volscians alike, rather than destroy his native city. When Coriolanus does not reply, Volumnia makes ready to return to Rome and "die among our neighbors (V.iii.174)." But Coriolanus is convinced. He pledges to make peace immediately. Seeing this, Aufidius tells the audience that he now has an opportunity to eliminate the Roman general.

ACT V, SCENES IV AND V   Location: Rome

The Romans learn that Volumnia has saved them.

Menenius, unaware of Coriolanus's change of heart, tells Sicinius that all is lost and that the tribunes have doomed their city with their folly. Just then a messenger arrives with news that the women have suc-ceeded in their mission and Rome is saved. The Romans celebrate and welcome Volumnia home as the savior of her city.

ACT V, SCENE VI   Location: Antium

The Volscians kill Coriolanus.

Aufidius and a band of conspirators prepare to dispose of the returning Coriolanus, who is being given a hero's welcome by the people of the city. When Coriolanus arrives and is greeted by Antium's senators, Aufidius denounces him, accusing him of betraying the Volscan army by giving in to the Roman women and failing to take Rome. Coriolanus loses his temper and curses Aufidius, whose conspirators are now turning the people against Coriolanus, reminding them that he once led Roman armies against them. As Aufidius shouts and the senators try to intervene, the conspirators stab Coriolanus, who falls dead. Declaring Coriolanus a great and noble man, the Senate orders a hero's burial for him. Now remorseful, Aufidius joins his men in carrying Coriolanus's body through the city.

THEMES, MOTIFS & SYMBOLS IN *CORIOLANUS*

THEMES

THE DUBIOUS THREAT OF TYRANNY   Brutus plays on the sensitivities of the plebeians, who as members of a newly established republic are understandably worried that Coriolanus's pride points to a lust for power. Brutus connives to make the Roman plebeians exile Coriolanus by representing him as a tyrant obsessed with gaining absolute power. He instructs Sicinius to publicly accuse Coriolanus of tyr-anny: "In this point charge him home: that he affects / Tyrannical power" (III.iii.1–2). Brutus wants to portray Coriolanus as a power-mad man determined to wrest control of the state from the people and consolidate it in his own hands. Coriolanus unwittingly plays into Brutus's hands, constantly losing his temper and making unfortunate, offensive speeches. But as Brutus and Sicinius know, Coriolanus does not really long to rule Rome as a tyrant. His tyrannical tendencies are less a real political danger than a shortcoming that lesser men can use to take him down. He is not a likeable man, but this does not make him an evil one. He is a snob who is uncomfortable around the lower classes, and he does believe that the aristocrats should rule alone, but he has no coherent plan or even desire to wrest power away from the plebeians. Coriolanus seems more interested in fighting than in governing either well or badly.

THE TRUE NATURE OF THE HERO   Traditionally, artists represent war heroes as ideals of mas-culinity and bravery. But in his character Coriolanus, Shakespeare creates a cynical portrait of the mili-tary hero. He begins by demonstrating the reason military men are lionized: at the beginning of the play, Coriolanus boldly risks everything in battle, winning the hearts of his men with his courage and leader-ship. But, Shakespeare suggests, perfection in battle does not equal kindness, thoughtfulness, good sense, or generosity. Far from the ideal of masculinity, Coriolanus is a limited man created by his mother and cramped by his military identity. He has virtually none of the capability for self-reflection that makes Shakespeare's other heroes so sympathetic. Coriolanus has only a single, very brief monologue, giving the impression of a man incapable of deep private thoughts. We never see him interacting with his fam-ily, showing affection to his wife, or teaching his son. His preoccupation with war leaves him with no time for those who love him, other than the mother who turned him into a fighter. When Coriolanus willingly renounces wife, mother, child, and fatherland for the sake of pride, he reveals the shallow nature of his human connections.

MOTHER AS LOVER AND CREATOR Coriolanus has a bleak and disturbing relationship with his mother. His father is dead, and his wife and son matter little to him. Volumnia is the central figure in his life. As in a standard love story in which the lovers adore, misunderstand, quarrel, and reconcile, Coriolanus passes from veneration of his formidable mother, to dismay when she seems to betray him, to rejection of her, to a final return to her embrace. Volumnia takes all the credit for turning her son into a war machine. She is less a pleased, controlling mother than a satisfied creator whose project has turned out well. She says, "Thou art my warrior. / I holp to frame thee" (V.iii.63–4), laying claim to Coriolanus as if he were a piece of her property, something she has manufactured and claimed. As Volumnia tells Virgilia, she always wanted to raise Coriolanus to be a hero, and encouraged him to play in dangerous situations.

MOTIFS

PLEBEIANS As the bedrock of the Roman city-state, the Roman plebeians—non-aristocratic citizens entitled to vote for their leader in the newly formed Roman republic—are politically and socially important. But Shakespeare emphasizes not their key role in fending off tyranny, or their sturdiness and hard work, but rather their self-involvement, vanity, and baseness. We may condemn Coriolanus's snobbery, but Shakespeare forces us to see the masses through his judgmental eyes. At the same time, he suggests that the plebeians' childish requests—make a speech, show us your wounds, ask us to like you—are inevitable, and that Coriolanus's furious responses to them are silly. The people may be tricked by fine words into exiling Coriolanus, but it is Coriolanus's fault that the people dislike him in the first place.

THE BODY Images of the body occur repeatedly in *Coriolanus*. Battles and preparations for battles make up most of the action, which summons up images of blood and wounds and reduces the men to their physical capacity to be fighting machines. Fighting an enemy resembles lovemaking in its passion and its total use of the body. When Coriolanus befriends his former enemy Aufidius, Aufidius says he has often dreamed of holding Coriolanus's neck in his fist as they wrestle on the ground. The image is a homoerotic one that emphasizes the close connection between the two kinds of bodily engagement.

Body imagery is also used politically. The senators defend themselves to the angry commoners at the beginning of the play by portraying themselves as the "belly" of the city, taking in grain in order to feed the rest of the organism. When Brutus and Sicinius contemplate exiling Coriolanus, they compare him to a foot infected with gangrene that must be cut off. Coriolanus rejects the idea that Rome is a body politic with leaders at its head. He dislikes the idea of sharing any kind of relationship with the commoners, and considers his body, even his symbolic body, his own.

SYMBOLS

WOUNDS For the city, the Senate, and Volumnia, Coriolanus's twenty-seven battle wounds symbolize his military prowess. Each wound stands for an occasion on which he placed himself in harm's way for the sake of his homeland. The wounds also symbolize the success of Volumnia's plans. By incurring battle injuries, Coriolanus follows the wishes of Volumnia, who proudly admits she raised her son to seek danger and win fame. Coriolanus's wounds are also mutilations that eat away at his identity. After the siege of Corioles, Coriolanus is so covered with blood that he jokes that people will not see him blush beneath the gore. The joke suggests that his warrior wounds are obscuring his humanity.

CORIOLES The city of Corioles symbolizes the totality of Coriolanus's martial success. His stunning victory in conquering that city, effectively ending the threat from Aufidius's Volscian forces, reveals the extent of his military prowess. Rome commemorates the victory by naming the man responsible for it after Corioles. But the city becomes a more ambiguous symbol of victory after Coriolanus's defection to the enemy camp. It changes from a conquest to a home. Coriolanus's name no longer means "the man who won Corioles," but rather "the man who chose to live in Corioles." The symbol of enmity becomes a symbol of affiliation. The shift in symbolism suggests Coriolanus's shaky civic pride. He is a great warrior, but not necessarily a Roman hero. He loves winning, but his pride is personal, not civic.

IMPORTANT QUOTATIONS IN *CORIOLANUS*

When yet he was but tenderbodied and the only son of my womb, when youth with his comeliness plucked all gaze his way, when for a day of kings' entreaties a mother should not sell him an hour from her beholding, I…was pleased to let him seek danger where he was like to find fame.

Location: I.iii.5–11
Speaker: Volumnia to Virgilia
Context: Volumnia responds to Virgilia's sadness.

Volummia's speech defines her role as both doting mother and cold-hearted creator. She describes Coriolanus lovingly as a "tenderbodied" boy, the "only son of [her] womb," but she proudly admits that she enjoyed letting him find danger. Fame, the reward for seeking danger, may motivate Volumnia. She seems less devoted to her son than to the glory she hopes he will win for himself and, by association, for her.

Pray now, no more. My mother,
Who has a charter to extol her blood,
When she does praise me grieves me. I have done
As you have done, that's what I can; induced
As you have been, that's for my country.

Location: I.x.13–17
Speaker: Martius (Coriolanus) to the Roman soldiers
Context: Lartius begins to praise Martius, who cuts him off.

After the successful siege of Corioles, Martius responds to his fellow Romans' praise with noble modesty. He claims to be embarrassed by the tributes, saying that he has done nothing more than his civic duty, just as any other Roman would have done. But his insistence that "[he has] done / As you have done" might be sarcastic. Martius rarely shows any appreciation or gratitude for what his fellow soldiers have done. Instead, he spends a great deal of time chastising them for their cowardice and ineptitude. When he refers to what they have done, he really means what they should have done, or would have done if they were as courageous as he. Martius pays lip service to the notion that every Roman citizen does his best, but his praise is laced with contempt.

You have been a scourge to her [Rome's] enemies, you have been a rod to her friends. You have not, indeed, loved the common people.

Location: II.iii.83–85
Speaker: Fourth Citizen to Coriolanus
Context: Tensions mount in Rome as Coriolanus rests on his military triumphs.

From the battlefield where he rails against the common soldiers to the podium where he insults the populace, Coriolanus gives Romans ample evidence that he does not love the common people. In response, the common people turn against him, as the Fourth Citizen does here. They believe that he is a "scourge" to their enemies not because he is a faithful Roman who loves his people and wants to defend them, but because he is an undiscriminating menace who hurts everyone, friend and foe alike.

The people are the city.

Location: III.i.199
Speaker: the citizens to Sicinius
Context: Coriolanus has insulted the people.

Corolianus is incensed by the belief that "the people are the city," a belief the people accept as fact. He envisages Rome as a grander, worthier place than the one suggested by living, breathing Romans who trudge through the city streets and clamor for a voice in government. Coriolanus willingly risks his life to defend the abstract Rome, but he despises most of its real inhabitants. The inconsistency in his attitude toward Rome—loving it as symbol, scorning it as a reality—sets in motion the chain of events that ends in his death. The idea that a city or country is its people would have had special relevance at the time *Coriolanus* was first performed. In the 1610s, a wave of popular riots spread through the western counties of England, including Stratford-upon-Avon, Shakespeare's hometown. The issue was popular representation in the capital, and the grievance was that the rich leaders were forgetting their poor constituencies, hoarding grain to raise prices.

Wife, mother, child, I know not. My affairs
Are servanted to others. Though I owe
My revenge properly, my remission lies
In Volscian breasts. That we have been familiar,
Ingrate forgetfulness shall poison rather
Than pity note how much.

Location: V.ii.78–83
Speaker: Coriolanus to Menenius
Context: Menenius has come to beg Coriolanus not to attack Rome.

When Coriolanus is expelled from Rome, he turns against not only his countrymen, but his family. As a son raised by his mother to be a hero of Rome, he must turn his back on his mother when he turns his back on Rome. Line 82 may mean that Coriolanus will turn against Rome with "ingrate forgetfulness," or it may mean that Rome has turned against Coriolanus. It may also refer to Volumnia's ingratitude toward Coriolanus, or his toward her.

CYMBELINE

Believing that his wife Imogen is unfaithful, Posthumus tries to have her killed, but she saves herself by disguising herself as a boy.

CYMBELINE IN CONTEXT

Cymbeline is one of Shakespeare's final plays, composed and performed around 1609 or 1610. Given the play's capacity for spectacular scenic effects, actors probably performed it on the indoor Blackfriars stage rather than at the more famous outdoor stage of the Globe. *Cymbeline* is, like *Pericles*, *The Winter's Tale*, and *The Tempest*, a genre-defying later play critics usually refer to as a romance or tragicomedy. Unlike Shakespeare's histories and tragedies, these plays end happily, but they also emphasize the danger and power of evil in the world, and the constant threat of death. The plot of *Cymbeline* echoes a number of Shakespeare's tragedies. Imogen maintains her virtuousness despite the king's unchecked rage, a steadfastness that echoes the relationship between Lear and Cordelia in *King Lear*. Iachimo plays a role similar to that of Iago in *Othello* by stealing Imogen's bracelet (just as Iago steals Desdemona's handkerchief and presents it to Othello), tricking Posthumus into thinking his wife is an adulteress. Imogen takes a sleeping potion just as Juliet does in *Romeo and Juliet*.

There is no clear source for *Cymbeline*. The titular king and his sons Guiderius and Arviragus are quasi-historical figures possibly drawn from Raphael Holinshed's *Chronicles of England, Scotland, and Ireland*, a resource Shakespeare employed for several of his history plays. According to Holinshed, Cymbeline ruled in Britain around the time of Christ. (The same source was used for the title character in *King Lear*, another play set in pre-Christian Britain.) The Iachimo plot, in which a character attempts to seduce a virtuous wife, may have its roots in the *Decameron*, a collection of stories by the Renaissance author Boccaccio. However, the bulk of the plot and most of the characters are original products of Shakespeare's creation.

CYMBELINE: KEY FACTS

Full Title: Cymbeline, King of Britain
Time and place written: 1609–1610, London (uncertain)
Date of first performance: 1610 (uncertain)
Genre: Romance or tragicomedy
Setting (time): Ancient times
Setting (place): Britain, Rome
Protagonist: Imogen
Major conflict: Imogen's enduring virtue triumphs over the evils that would thwart proper order.

CYMBELINE: CHARACTER LIST

Arviragus   Cymbeline's younger son and Imogen's brother. Arviragus was kidnapped and raised by Belarius under the name "Cadwal."

Belarius   A British nobleman. To revenge himself on Cymbeline, who banished him unjustly, Belarius kidnapped Cymbeline's infant sons and raised them as his own under the name "Morgan."

Caius Lucius   The Roman ambassador to Britain and, later, the general of the Roman invasion force.

Cloten   The Queen's son. Cloten, who is an arrogant, clumsy fool, was betrothed to Imogen before her secret wedding to Posthumus.

Cornelius   A doctor at Cymbeline's court.

Cymbeline   The king of Britain and Imogen's father. A wise and gracious monarch, Cymbeline is led astray by the machinations of his wicked queen.

Guiderius Cymbeline's eldest son and Imogen's brother. Guiderius was kidnapped and raised by Belarius under the name "Polydore."

Iachimo A clever and dishonest Italian gentleman. Iachimo makes a wager with Posthumus that he can seduce Imogen, and when his attempt at seduction fails, he resorts to trickery to make Posthumus believe that he has succeeded.

Imogen (called Innogen in some editions) Cymbeline's daughter. Imogen, the British princess, is wise, beautiful, and resourceful. She displeases her father by choosing to marry the low-born Posthumus instead of Cymbeline's oafish stepson, Cloten.

Philario (called Filario in some editions) An Italian gentleman. Posthumus stays at Philario's home during his exile from Britain.

Philarmonus A soothsayer in the service of Caius Lucius.

Pisanio Posthumus's loyal servant. When Pisanio's master goes into exile, Pisanio is left behind in Britain and acts as a servant to Imogen and the queen.

Posthumus An orphaned gentleman. Cymbeline adopts and raises Posthumus, who marries Imogen in secret. Although Posthumus is deeply in love with Imogen, he is nevertheless willing to think the worst of her when she is accused of infidelity.

Queen Cymbeline's wife and Imogen's stepmother. A villainous woman, the queen will stop at nothing to see her son Cloten married to Imogen.

CYMBELINE: PLOT OVERVIEW

Imogen, the daughter of the British king Cymbeline, goes against her father's wishes and marries Posthumus, a low-born gentleman, instead of Cloten, Cymbeline's oafish stepson. Cymbeline sends Posthumus into exile in Italy. There, Posthumus makes a bet with Iachimo, a smooth-tongued Italian, that Iachimo cannot seduce Imogen. Iachimo goes to Britain, where he fails to seduce Imogen. He hides in her bedroom to observe her as she sleeps, and steals her bracelet. He convinces Posthumus that he won the wager by showing him the bracelet and accurately describing Imogen's chambers and a mole on her left breast. Posthumus orders his servant Pisanio to murder Imogen. When Pisanio encounters Imogen, however, he convinces her to disguise herself as a boy and search for Posthumus.

Imogen gets lost in the wilderness in Wales. She discovers a cave in which an English nobleman named Belarius is hiding. After Cymbeline unjustly banished Belarius years ago, Belarius kidnapped Cymbeline's two infant sons, Guiderius and Arviragus, and renamed them Polydore and Cadwal. He has raised them as his own. Cloten appears, searching for Imogen. He is dressed in Posthumus's clothes and plans on using the guise to rape her, but he ends up dying in a duel with Guiderius. Feeling ill, Imogen drinks a potion that Pisanio had given to her. However, unbeknownst to Pisanio, this potion is from Cymbeline's evil wife and is meant to kill Imogen. Rather than killing her, however, the potion merely puts Imogen into a deathlike sleep.

While Imogen sleeps, a Roman army invades England because Cymbeline has not paid the customary tribute to Rome. Imogen awakes and sees the dead body of Cloten, mistaking it for Posthumus and falling into despair. She then hires herself out to the Roman army as a page. Posthumus and Iachimo arrive as conscripts in the Roman. Posthumus, overwhelmed with guilt that he ordered Imogen's death, switches sides and fights for the Britons. Then, to inflict punishment on himself, he lets himself be taken prisoner as a Roman after the Britons win the battle. Cymbeline calls the prisoners before him, and all the confusion is resolved. Iachimo confesses his lie, and Posthumus and Imogen reunite. Belarius returns his adopted sons to their birth father, Cymbeline, and England makes peace with Rome.

CYMBELINE: SCENE SUMMARY

ACT I

In defiance of her father, who wanted her to marry his stepson, Cloten, Imogen has married Posthumus; Cymbeline banishes Posthumus; the queen tries to poison Pisanio; Iachimo tries to seduce Imogen.

I.I Location: Britain. Cymbeline's garden

The queen promises to be kind to Imogen; Cymbeline berates his daughter for marrying the low-born Posthumus when he wanted her to marry the queen's son, Cloten; Posthumus is banished, leaving his servant Pisanio to care for Imogen.

Two noblemen discuss the recent events of King Cymbeline's court. Cymbeline's daughter, Imogen, was betrothed to Cloten, the son of Cymbeline's new queen. However, Imogen secretly married Posthumus, an Italian-born orphan who was raised as Cymbeline's ward. Infuriated by their disobedience, Cymbeline banished Posthumus and imprisoned Imogen. Imogen is effectively Cymbeline's only child because his two sons, Guiderius and Arviragus, were kidnapped years ago.

The queen meets with Posthumus and Imogen and she promises to be kind to them, not "evil-eyed" as most stepmothers would be in such circumstances. She swears she will try to convince Cymbeline to relent, and then allows the couple to take one last walk together around the garden before Posthumus goes into exile. When her stepmother has gone, Imogen says she sees through the queen, whose kindness is all an act. The lovers agree to be faithful to one another and exchange love-tokens—a ring and a bracelet—and promise to wear them forever. As they speak, Cymbeline enters with his court, and Posthumus departs in haste. Cymbeline berates his daughter for her conduct. She defends herself vigorously, but he orders her locked away, despite the queen's protests. Pisanio, Posthumus's servant, enters, bringing word that as his master departed, Cloten assaulted him. Bystanders separated them before anyone was hurt. Pisanio offers his services to Imogen, saying Posthumus wished him to her during his exile.

I.II Location: Cymbeline's court

Cloten boasts to two lords of the court, who consider him a total fool.

Cloten boasts to two lords that he would have cut Posthumus to pieces had they been allowed to fight. The lords flatter him to his face, but their conversation with each other makes it clear that they consider the queen's son a strutting fool and a poor swordsman who would have had no chance against Posthumus.

I.III Location: Cymbeline's palace

Pisanio assures Imogen that Posthumus will miss her.

Pisanio tells Imogen how much Posthumus will miss her. He promises they will hear from him soon. Imogen goes to attend to the queen.

I.IV Location: Philario's house in Rome

Iachimo bets Posthumus that he, Iachimo, can seduce Imogen.

Posthumus has gone into exile in Italy, in the home of his friend Philario. There he debates with a large company of men from around Europe on the respective virtue of their countries' women. One man, Iachimo, declares there is no woman who cannot be seduced. Posthumus angrily disagrees, citing Imogen as an invulnerable woman who would never betray him with another man. Iachimo says he will take this as a challenge and go to England to seduce Imogen. He convinces Posthumus to make a bet with him: if Imogen sleeps with Iachimo, Posthumus will give him his ring. If Imogen refuses, Iachimo will pay Posthumus 10,000 ducats.

I.V Location: Cymbeline's palace

The queen tries to poison Pisanio, not knowing that what she thinks is poison is actually just a sleeping potion.

The queen has ordered a doctor named Cornelius to prepare a deadly poison, which she claims will be used for scientific purposes. But Cornelius is suspicious of her and, as he tells the audience, opts not to give her poison and instead concocts a sleeping potion that will create the appearance of death. When

Cornelius has gone, the queen gives the potion, which she thinks is a deadly poison, to Pisanio. She tells him she is giving him a soothing medicine. The queen believes that by killing Pisanio, who champions his master, Posthumus, she will have an easier time convincing Imogen to marry Cloten.

I.VI Location: Cymbeline's palace

Iachimo tries and fails to seduce Imogen.

Iachimo arrives in Britain and goes to see Imogen on the pretext of delivering a letter from Posthumus. He compliments her grace and beauty. When Imogen asks about Posthumus, Iachimo tells her that Posthumus has all but forgotten her and is enjoying himself—that is, he implies, he is enjoying himself by sleeping around. Iachimo attempts to play on Imogen's injured feelings by suggesting that she should revenge herself on the unfaithful Posthumus by being unfaithful herself. Imogen is taken aback. She rebuffs Iachimo and says she does not believe his malicious stories about her husband's conduct. Iachimo quickly admits that it was all a lie and says he only attempted to seduce her because he loves Posthumus so much and wanted to test Imogen to make certain he had a faithful and worthy wife. After begging her pardon profusely, Iachimo offers to carry her letters to her husband. He also asks her permission to use her chambers as a storage place for a large trunk containing his valuables. Imogen grants his request.

ACT II

Hidden inside a trunk, Iachimo sneaks into Imogen's bedroom, where he observes her carefully and steals a bracelet; he goes back to Italy and convinces Posthumus that he slept with Imogen.

II.I Location: Cymbeline's court

Two lords make fun of Cloten and express sympathy for Imogen.

Cloten complains about his poor luck in a game of bowling while the two lords who attend on him make fun of him behind his back. When he has gone, one of them remarks on how peculiar it is that such a crafty mother should have such a foolish son. This lord then expresses his sympathy for Imogen, who has a cowed father, a scheming stepmother, and an admirer worth less than Posthumus's farts. The lord says he hopes that she will weather her bad luck and find happiness with her husband.

II.II Location: Imogen's room

Iachimo observes Imogen and her bedroom, and steals a bracelet from her wrist.

Imogen goes to bed. After she has fallen asleep, Iachimo's trunk, which has been stored in her room, opens, and Iachimo himself slips out of it. He watches Imogen as she sleeps and then makes careful note of all the furnishings in her bedchamber, as well as a birthmark on her left breast. Iachimo slips from Imogen's wrist the bracelet that Posthumus gave to her and puts it into the trunk.

II.III Location: Cymbeline's palace

Cloten tries to woo Imogen but succeeds only in quarreling with her; Imogen notices that her bracelet is missing.

The next morning, Cloten orders musicians to play under Imogen's window, in the hopes of winning her heart. While the musicians play, Cymbeline and the queen pass by. They advise Cloten to be persistent and promise that Imogen will forget Posthumus eventually. A messenger comes in, bringing word that ambassadors from Rome have arrived. The royal couple goes to greet the Romans, asking Cloten to join them once he has bid Imogen good morning.

Cloten knocks on Imogen's door. When one of her ladies-in-waiting comes out, he clumsily attempts to bribe her. Imogen appears and treats Cloten coldly, telling him she will never accept him as a husband. Cloten says she is being disobedient to her father for the sake of Posthumus, whom he calls a second-rate, low-born fool. Imogen retorts that Cloten is far inferior to Posthumus—indeed, that he is not fit to be Posthumus's servant. She says she treasures Posthumus's most humble piece of clothing far more than she cares for every hair on Cloten's head. This insult cuts Cloten to the quick, and he swears that he will be revenged on Posthumus. Imogen, after snapping that she is tortured by a fool, stops paying attention to Cloten. She has noticed that her bracelet is missing and orders Pisanio to have her servants look for it, since Posthumous gave it to her.

II.IV   Location: Philario's house

Iachimo goes back to Italy and tells Posthumus he won the bet.

Iachimo has returned to Italy and goes to Philario's house, where Philario and Posthumus are discussing the prospects of war between Rome and Britain over the tribute that Cymbeline owes the Romans. ("Tribute" here means the money one nation gives another in exchange for a promise of non-aggression.) Iachimo bears letters from Imogen and declares that he won the bet. Posthumus refuses to believe him, but Iachimo describes Imogen's bedroom in detail and displays the bracelet as a token of his triumph. Posthumus, heartbroken, curses his wife. Philario tries to calm him, pointing out that this is not perfect proof: the bracelet might have been stolen. But when Iachimo adds the detail of the tiny mole on Imogen's breast, Posthumus is convinced. He turns over the ring that he wagered and storms out.

II.V   Location: Philario's house

Posthumus curses women.

Posthumus curses the treachery of women, saying all men are bastards. He imagines Iachimo mounting Imogen and crying out in pleasure. Posthumus says man's sins come from the "woman's part" (II.v.20) in him.

ACT III

Disobeying Posthumus's orders to kill Imogen, Pisanio dresses Imogen as a boy and fakes her death; Cloten, discovering Imogen's absence, vows to kill Posthumus and rape Imogen; Imogen takes shelter in the cave where her long-lost brothers live, although she does not know their true identity; Italy prepares to attack Britain.

III.I   Location: Cymbeline's palace

Cymbeline refuses to pay a tribute to Italy.

Cymbeline, the queen, and Cloten meet with Caius Lucius, the Roman ambassador. Rome demands the continuation of a tribute that was begun in Julius Caesar's time. Britain pays this tribute in exchange for Rome's promise not to invade. Supported by his wife and stepson, Cymbeline refuses to pay the tribute, declaring that Britain is an independent isle and will remain so. Lucius says, regretfully, that in that case a state of war must exist between Rome and Britain.

III.II   Location: Cymbeline's palace

Pisanio gets orders from Posthumus to lead Imogen away from the palace and kill her.

Pisanio has received a letter from Posthumus accusing Imogen of infidelity and asking his servant to lead her away and murder her. Pisanio is horrified and cannot believe what he is being asked to do. Nevertheless, he begins to carry out his master's orders. He gives Imogen another letter, also from Posthumus, in which Posthumus asks her to meet him at Milford Haven, on the coast of Wales. Imogen is transported with joy at the thought of seeing him again and immediately makes preparations to slip away from her father's palace.

III.III   Location: a cave in Wales

In a soliloquy, Belarius explains that the two boys who think they are his sons are actually the sons of Cymbeline.

An old shepherd named Belarius tells his two sons, Guiderius and Arviragus, about the wonders of nature. The young men are restless because they have never been allowed to leave their wilderness home and see the wider world, but Belarius insists there is nothing in the city but treachery and wickedness. He says he was once a nobleman in Cymbeline's court but was banished for crimes he did not commit. When his sons exit, Belarius tells the audience that the boys are actually Cymbeline's sons. Belarius kidnapped them when they were very young in order to avenge his unjust exile. They are ignorant of their true identity, and they believe that Belarius's name is Morgan and that they themselves are named Polydore and Cadwal.

III.IV   Location: Milford Haven, Wales

Pisanio tells Imogen she should fake her own death in order to make Posthumus feel guilty, and advises her to disguise herself as a boy.

Imogen, seeing no sign of her husband, becomes perturbed. Pisanio reveals the deception and he shows Imogen Posthumus's letter accusing her of infidelity. Imogen weeps, cursing her husband for not trusting her. She begs Pisanio to follow his master's orders and kill her, since her life is no longer worth living, but Pisanio refuses. Imogen asks why he bothered to bring her to Milford Haven if he did not plan to kill her. Pisanio says that by making it look like they followed through with the plan, they may instill guilt in Posthumus and restore his love for Imogen. Pisanio thinks Posthumus must have been deceived by some villain into thinking Imogen was unfaithful. Perhaps the villain will also become contrite upon hearing of Imogen's death, and turn himself in. Pisanio suggests that Imogen disguise herself as a boy, with clothes that he has brought for this purpose, and enter the service of Caius Lucius, who will soon be leaving England from the Milford Haven port. Imogen can then make her way to Italy, where Posthumus resides. Imogen agrees to this plan and changes clothes. As a parting gift, Pisanio presents Imogen with the potion the queen gave him, telling her what he believes to be true, that the potion is a soothing cordial that will help her if she grows sick on the voyage.

III.V   Location: Cymbeline's court

Imogen's flight is discovered; Cloten plans to kill Posthumus and rape Imogen.

Cymbeline, accompanied by the queen and Cloten, bids farewell to Caius Lucius. The king sends a messenger to fetch Imogen, but the messenger returns saying that her bedroom door is locked, and she has not been seen for days. Worried, Cymbeline goes to see for himself. Cloten follows. After a moment, Cloten returns with word of Imogen's flight. The queen goes to comfort Cymbeline, and Cloten is left alone to fume and plot revenge on Imogen and Posthumus. Pisanio comes in, returning from Milford Haven, and Cloten accosts him, demanding to know where Imogen has gone. Pisanio, deciding that Imogen has had enough time to make her getaway, sends Cloten to the sea coast on what he knows will be a wild goose chase. Cloten, convinced he will catch Imogen and Posthumus, takes one of Posthumus's garments with him—the same garments Imogen claimed to prefer to Cloten. He plans to kill Posthumus and rape Imogen while wearing Posthumus's clothes.

III.VI   Location: Belarius's cave

Imogen-as-Fidele takes shelter in Belarius's cave.

Imogen, disguised as a boy, has gotten lost in the Welsh wilderness. She seeks shelter in the same cave where Guiderius, Arviragus, and Belarius live. Shortly afterward, the three men come home after a day of hunting. They find Imogen-as-boy in their cave, eating their food. Imogen-as-boy apologizes, offers to pay for the meat, and introduces herself as "Fidele." Guiderius and Arviragus, unaware that the boy Fidele is actually their sister, nonetheless feel a strange kinship with their guest, and Imogen reciprocates the feeling.

III.VII   Location: a street in Rome

A Roman army prepares to go to Britain.

A Roman army commanded by Caius Lucius gets ready to sail for Britain.

ACT IV

Guiderius kills Cloten, and Imogen mistakes his corpse for Posthumus; the queen falls ill; Guiderius and Arviragus insist on joining Cymbeline's forces.

IV.I   Location: near Belarius's cave

Cloten arrives in Wales.

Cloten arrives at Milford Haven. He complains that there is no reason Imogen should love Posthumus instead of him. He knows Cymbeline will be a bit angry when Cloten kills Posthumus and rapes Imogene, but he has confidence his mother will sort things out.

IV.II   Location: Belarius's cave

Guiderius chops off Cloten's head; he and his family think Imogen-as-Fidele is dead, although she has only taken the sleeping potion; they put her in the forest next to the corpse, which Imogen assumes is Posthumus's; Imogen-as-Fidele volunteers to be Caius Lucius's page.

Imogen has fallen ill. While her hosts go out to hunt, she takes the potion that Pisanio gave her, believing it to be medicine. In the forest, Cloten, dressed in Posthumus's clothing, encounters Guiderius, Arviragus, and Belarius. He rudely challenges them to fight. Guiderius duels with Cloten and kills him, cutting off his head. Belarius recognizes Cloten from his days at court and panics, but his sons are elated. Arviragus goes to wake Fidele, only to find Fidele seemingly dead. Dismayed and grief-stricken, Belarius and his adoptive sons lay her body in the woods, sing a prayer over her, and then depart, after setting Cloten's headless body down beside her.

After a time, Imogen awakes. Seeing the headless corpse dressed in Posthumus's clothes, she assumes the dead man is her husband. Realizing that the medicine she drank was a sleeping potion and believing that Pisanio gave it to her knowingly, she now thinks that Pisanio must have killed Posthumus. Stricken with grief, Imogen lies on top of the corpse.

The Roman army has landed. Caius Lucius and his men come upon Imogen and Cloten. At first they think both of them are dead, but Imogen gets up, identifies herself as Fidele, and offers herself as a servant to the Roman commander. Caius Lucius accepts this offer and employs Fidele as his page.

IV.III   Location: Cymbeline's court

The queen falls ill, and Rome threatens invasion.

The disappearance of Cloten has made the queen ill. Cymbeline threatens Pisanio with torture in an attempt to find out where Imogen is. The Roman invasion of Britain looms ahead, and Cymbeline must prepare his army.

IV.IV   Location: Belarius's cave

Guiderius and Arviragus insist on going to aid Cymbeline's forces.

Guiderius, Arviragus, and Belarius hear armies moving through the wilderness. Belarius wants to lie low, since he is afraid that some of the Britons may recognize him from his days at court, but his adoptive sons are eager to fight. They insist on going down to assist Cymbeline's forces.

ACT V

Britain wins the battle, with a great deal of help from Posthumus, Belarius, Guiderius, and Arviragus; all of the confusion is cleared up, and everyone is happily reunited.

V.I Location: the Roman camp

Posthumus returns to Britain as an Italian soldier, but decides to fight on Britain's side.

Posthumus returns to Britain. As an Italian resident, he has been conscripted into the Roman forces. He has received a bloody handkerchief from Pisanio, ostensibly a token of Imogen's death, and he is overcome with remorse. He says he has killed Britain's princess and does not want to wound the country further. Posthumus takes off his Roman uniform and dresses himself as a British peasant for the battle.

V.II Location: the battlefield

Iachimo fights with the disguised Posthumus.

Iachimo, fighting on the side of the Romans, loses his sword in a duel with the disguised Posthumus. Left alone, he expresses remorse for lying about Imogen's faithlessness.

V.III Location: the battlefield

Belarius, Guiderius, and Arviragus save Cymbeline.

The battle goes badly for the British until the sudden arrival of Belarius, Guiderius, and Arviragus, who save Cymbeline from capture and turn the tide.

V.IV Location: the battlefield

Britain wins.

The Romans lose the battle, and Caius Lucius becomes a prisoner.

V.V Location: the battlefield

Posthumus is imprisoned; the spirits of Posthumus's ancestors ask Jupiter to help Posthumus, who wakes and is summoned before Cymbeline.

Although Posthumus fought for the victorious Britons, he wants to punish himself for his supposed murder of Imogen, so he has quickly changed back into Roman garb in order to be taken prisoner. He is thrown into a British stockade, where he falls asleep. While Posthumus sleeps, a group of spirits ascends from the netherworld and gathers around him. They are Posthumus's dead ancestors. They plead with Jupiter, the king of the gods, to take pity on their descendant and restore his fortunes. After a time, Jupiter himself arrives from the heavens, surrounded in thunder and lightning and riding on an eagle's back. He berates the spirits for troubling him, but grudgingly agrees to make Posthumus happy. The supernatural creatures depart, and Posthumus awakens, feeling refreshed. He finds a written oracle on the ground beside him, which he is unable to interpret. The jailer comes to take him to be hanged, but then a messenger arrives, summoning Posthumus to come before Cymbeline.

V.VI Location: the British camp

Iachimo confesses, Imogen and Posthumus are reunited, and Cymbeline recovers his sons.

Cymbeline summons Guiderius, Arviragus, and Belarius to reward them for their valor in battle. He regrets that the unknown peasant who fought so well for Britain cannot be found. Cymbeline knights Belarius and the two young men (his own sons, though only Belarius knows it) in gratitude for their service.

Just then, Cornelius comes in, bringing word that the queen has died of her fever. Before she died, Cornelius says, she confessed that she never loved Cymbeline and planned to gradually poison him so that her son, Cloten, would be made king. Cymbeline is amazed. He says she managed to deceive him completely, a success he attributes to her great beauty.

The Roman prisoners, including Caius Lucius, Iachimo, and Posthumus come in together, with Imogen-as-Fidele following at the rear. The Roman general asks that Cymbeline treat them mercifully. He also asks that his servant, a British boy (Imogen in disguise), be ransomed and freed. Imogen-as-Fidele is brought before her father, who does not recognize her but orders her freed and offers her any privilege within his power to grant. She asks to speak with him in private. They talk alone and then return. Imogen-as-Fidele asks Iachimo to step forward and demands to know where he got the ring that encircles his finger. Iachimo, feeling pangs of remorse, confesses that he tricked Posthumus into thinking he had won a bet. Iachimo describes how he gained entrance to Imogen's bedroom. Hearing this, Posthumus attempts to assault Iachimo, but Imogen hastily reveals her true identity, stripping off her boy's disguise. The reunited couple embraces.

The characters piece together the story of how Imogen came to the cave, how she only appeared dead after taking the queen's potion, and how Cloten met his death. Cymbeline declares that Guiderius must die for killing a prince, but Belarius hastily reveals himself as the banished courtier and tells the king that Guiderius and Arviragus are Cymbeline's long-lost sons. Cymbeline, overcome with happiness, forgives Belarius and welcomes him back to court.

Iachimo offers his life to Posthumus as payment for his sins, but Posthumus graciously forgives him. Philarmonus, Caius Lucius's soothsayer, comes forward and interprets the prophecy that Posthumus found beside him that morning to mean that Imogen will be reunited with her husband and Cymbeline's two sons will return. Cymbeline promises to free the Romans, allow them to return home unpunished, and he even promises to resume paying the tribute. Rejoicing, the entire company exits together to have a great feast and offer sacrifices to the gods.

THEMES, MOTIFS, & SYMBOLS IN *CYMBELINE*

THEMES

BRITAIN'S FOREIGN RELATIONS Alongside a lighthearted romance about a princess who wins her true love and finds her long-lost brothers, *Cymbeline* is an exploration of world affairs and Britain's place in them. Shakespeare emphasizes international relations most simply by using "Britain" instead of "England," a word that is never spoken in the play. Partly Shakespeare is showing respect to the Scottish king James I, who sought to unify the British kingdom. But he is also moving beyond the narrower English patriotism of his earlier plays to portray Britain from a broader perspective that takes into account England's relations not just with Scotland and Wales, but also with mainland Europe.

Some characters in *Cymbeline* advocate a jingoistic, warlike isolation for Britain. For example, Cymbeline stops paying tribute to Rome, which had claimed possession of Britain since Caesar invaded the island a few decades earlier. Cloten boldly affirms that "there is no more such Caesars"(III.i.36) in Rome, and claims Britain is stronger than it was when Rome conquered it. Like Cymbeline, Cloten trumpets the cause of British independence. But these characters' objectionable personalities make their opinions suspect—Cymbeline has been hoodwinked by his wife, and Cloten is an evil idiot.

By the end of the play, Shakespeare has provoked the greatest sympathy for those characters who pass for foreigners, such as Imogen and Posthumus. Imogen and Posthumus are able to step outside their British identities, seeing things from a foreign point of view and eventually striking a friendly accord with foreign powers. Shakespeare condones Imogen's and Posthumus's brand of inclusiveness, ending the play with a peaceful alliance symbolized by Cymbeline's decision to restore tribute payments to Rome and to fly the Roman and British banners side by side.

LOVE ACROSS SOCIAL CLASSES In the early seventeenth century, when *Cymbeline* was written, social boundaries were gradually blurring. Many British aristocrats grew impoverished, robbed of inheritances by the tradition of primogeniture, which gave the whole estate exclusively to the eldest son and neglected the other siblings. Meanwhile, the urban middle class grew increasingly wealthy. When riches ceased to function as a reliable marker of high class, marriages between titled aristocrats and untitled commoners ceased to seem unthinkable. The union of the royal Imogen with the lowly Posthumus reflects changing seventeenth-century society much more than it does the first century A.D., in which the play is set, when such a mixed-class marriage would have been unimaginable.

Cymbeline frequently refers to humans as inconsequential bits of dust, so that a marriage between an aristocrat and a commoner is nothing more than a union of "clay and clay" (IV.ii.4) that has no cosmic significance. The song about golden lads and girls coming "to dust" like chimney-sweepers (IV.ii.264) reinforces the view that class distinctions are silly in a life where everyone is equally insignificant.

The idea that love can obliterate social divisions does not go unchallenged. The king is outraged by it, and exiles Posthumus because of it. Cloten rants that Imogen has insulted him by favoring the "low Posthumus" (III.v.76) over a noble. But Cymbeline and Cloten are unfortunate men, and Imogen's marriage to Posthumus is sanctified in the end, suggesting that Shakespeare approves of the match between a commoner and a princess.

THE DEGRADATION OF WOMEN *Cymbeline* contains a passage that has been described as the most misogynistic in all of Shakespeare's work: Posthumus's venomous denunciation of all women, which he delivers after Iachimo convinces him of his wife's infidelity. In his fury, Posthumus asks why women exist at all, and whether it is possible to have a world in which males reproduce without them: "Is there no way for men to be, but women / Must be half-workers?" (II.v.1–2). His hatred of women is cast as partly justified by the presence of the play's only maternal figure, the murderous and deceitful queen.

The pure, good Imogen might seem to undermine the case for degrading women in *Cymbeline*. Victorian readers in particular tended to exalt Imogen as the ideal of femininity. Still, her importance in the play dwindles considerably as the story unfolds. In Act I, she is the heir apparent to the British throne, a potentially important ruler on the order of Elizabeth I, who inherited the throne from her father Henry VIII in 1558. By the end of the play, Imogen has surrendered the throne to her long-lost brothers and faded into a quiet, happy, domestic life with Posthumus. Shakespeare does not degrade Imogen by placing her in the domestic sphere, but he does demote her from future monarch to simple housewife. In a play in which the only other powerful woman is evil and manipulative, Imogen's removal from political power is troubling.

MOTIFS

TESTS OF LOVE *Cymbeline* features love—both romantic love and familial love—stretched nearly to its breaking point as lovers are forced to put their devotion to the test. The obstacles faced by the lovers in *Cymbeline* lead to separation and anger, but never a total loss of love. Imogen's actions never suggest that her love for her father is diminished in any way. Similarly, Posthumus confesses that he still loves Imogen even after he believes she has betrayed him and has plotted to kill her. The love tests in *Cymbeline* never endanger love itself. Cymbeline and Imogen survive the test of their familial love, just as Imogen and Posthumus survive the test of their romantic love. Posthumus puts aside his angry conviction that Imogen has cheated on him, and Imogen forgives Posthumus for plotting to kill her.

BRITAIN'S PLACE IN THE WORLD *Cymbeline* is, in part, a tribute to the British kingdom and the British character. The major climax of the play occurs in Wales, the legendary seat of King Arthur's British throne. There, the future rulers of Britain—Guiderius and Arviragus—magically emerge from the Welsh wilderness as if they have grown up from British soil. These rulers illustrate a national ideal. They are simple but innately noble, and far removed from courtly corruptions. But despite its patriotism, *Cymbeline* is not provincial or limited. While characters like Cloten voice the anti-European view that Britain should show its superiority by cutting off ties with the rest of the world, wiser and more sympathetic characters like Imogen support a more cosmopolitan view that the British crown is not infallible or all-important. She asks, "Hath Britain all the sun that shines?" (III.iv.136).

SYMBOLS

WALES Wales has a symbolic importance in British national mythology that has persisted in modern times. King Arthur's heroic and uncorrupted court was said to have been located in Wales, and the title of the heir apparent of the British throne has long been "the Prince of Wales." If London symbolizes the cosmopolitan and worldly side of Britain, Wales can be said to symbolize its purity and heroism. Because Imogen's brothers Arviragus and Guiderius grew up and are discovered in Wales, some of the mystique of that country attaches to them. They have lived in a state of nature in which their strength and fortitude are continuously exercised, and yet they are more civilized than the members of the British court. When Arviragus and Guiderius reclaim the throne at the end of the play, it is as if the court of Britain has been improved and purified by the spirit of Wales.

IACHIMO'S FORCED ENTRY Iachimo's violation of Imogen's private space symbolizes the invasion of Britain and the defiling of its native purity by a disreputable, disloyal foreign schemer. The tapestry hanging on Imogen's bedroom wall illustrates the story of Antony and Cleopatra—a love affair in which the participants represented two empires. Like Antony and Cleopatra, Imogen and Iachimo stand for England and a foreign country, the other. When Iachimo rudely scans Imogen's bedroom for information to be used against her later, Shakespeare intends his actions to seem typical of a crafty, villainous European taking advantage of an innocent Briton.

IMPORTANT QUOTATIONS FROM *CYMBELINE*

---

1. No, be assured you shall not find me, daughter,
    After the slander of most stepmothers,
    Evil-eyed unto you.

Location: I.i.71–73
Speaker: the queen to Imogen
Context: The conniving queen consoles Imogen after Cymbeline banishes Posthumus.

The queen's first speech introduces the themes of divided families, falsity, and betrayal, all of which will be central to *Cymbeline*. Although the queen says, "be assured," Imogen has every reason not to trust her stepmother's assertion of goodwill. The queen's familiarity in addressing Imogen as "daughter" rings exaggerated and forced.

---

2. Is there no way for men to be, but women
    Must be half-workers? We are bastards all,
    And that most venerable man which I
    Did call my father was I know not where
    When I was stamped.

Location: II.v.1–5
Speaker: Posthumus, in a soliloquy
Context: Believing his wife Imogen is an adulteress, the angry Posthumus curses all women.

Posthumus, exiled in Italy, reacts with dismayed horror to the idea that Imogen has betrayed him by sleeping with Iachimo. His denunciation, not just of Imogen in particular, but of women in general, has been called one of the most misogynistic passages in all of Shakespeare's work. Posthumus accuses all women, including his mother, of being whores who father illegitimate children.

---

3. I love her therefore; but

Disdaining me, and throwing favours on
The low Posthumus, slanders so her judgement
That what's else rare is choked...

Location: III.v.74–78
Speaker: Cloten, in a soliloquy
Context: Cloten expresses outrage that Imogen loves a commoner instead of him.

Cloten's outrage at Imogen's lack of love for him is nearly endearing. With painful simplicity, he declares, "I love her therefore." His protestations of love, on this and several other occasions, are awkward and sincere. Cloten is a clod, as his name suggests, but his affection for Imogen is real, and not solely the product of power hunger. Yet despite Cloten's sincerity, his vanity and narrow-mindedness make him the play's most unsympathetic character. With total imperceptiveness, he declares that Imogen's disdain for him shows very bad judgment on her part. He never wonders whether his own shortcomings have anything to do with her feelings. Cloten can only perceive Imogen's tenderness toward Posthumus as her "throwing favours" on him, as if she is condescending to him rather than returning his love. Typically for him, Cloten dismisses Posthumus as a shockingly "low" man.

---

4. *These are kind creatures. Gods, what lies I have heard!*
   Our courtiers say all's savage but at court.
   Experience, O thou disprov'st report!
   Th'imperious seas breeds monsters...

Location: IV.ii.32–35
Speaker: Imogen, in an aside
Context: Imogen meets her brothers (though neither party knows the men's true identity), and remarks on their surprising nobility.

Imogen is surprised to discover that the Welsh countryside contains not hostile "savages," as everyone at court told her, but kindly and generous men like Guiderius and Arviragus. She immediately contrasts the pompous, insular life she has known at the British court with the pastoral peace of Wales. She says the court "breeds monsters," evil wretches like the queen and her wicked son Cloten, and traitors like Iachimo. By contrast, the displaced royals in the countryside are noble and good, just as the royals of legend were purported to be.

---

5. *Set we forward, let*
   A Roman and a British ensign wave
   Friendly together. So through Lud's town march,
   And in the temple of great Jupiter
   Our peace we'll ratify, seal it with feasts.

Location: V.vi.479–483
Speaker: Cymbeline to the assemblage of Roman and British courtiers
Context: At the conclusion of the play, Cymbeline declares peace with the Romans and renews his payments of tribute.

Cymbeline's proclamation of friendship between Britain and Rome has puzzled some critics and readers. Cymbeline cut off tributes to Rome and soundly defeated the Roman forces in battle, so it seems counter-intuitive that he should suddenly reaffirm friendship with his former declared enemy. His willingness to continue paying tribute further complicates the matter. Still, Cymbeline's gesture of friendship is a statement of alliance, not subservience. He will not subordinate the British banner to the Roman one, but declares that both will "wave / Friendly together," on an equal footing. This allied equality is cultural as well as military and political, as we see in Cymbeline's references to the Roman god

Jupiter and the mythical founder of London, King Lud. The culture clash ends not in one culture vanquishing the other, but in multicultural harmony. Scholars have pointed out that Shakespeare's patron King James I, a Catholic, was eager to restore good relations between Britain and Rome, despite the skepticism of many Britons who mistrusted Roman Catholicism. In this sense, *Cymbeline*'s conclusion is an idealized portrait of James I's aspirations.

HAMLET

Charged by his father's ghost to kill his uncle, the new King Claudius, Prince Hamlet struggles with doubt and alienation in Denmark's corrupt court.

HAMLET IN CONTEXT

Written in the first years of the seventeenth century, *Hamlet* was probably first performed in July 1602. It was first published in printed form in 1603, and appeared in an enlarged edition in 1604. As was common practice during the sixteenth and seventeenth centuries, Shakespeare borrowed for his plays ideas and stories from earlier literary works. The story of Hamlet probably came from several sources, potentially including a twelfth-century Latin history of Denmark compiled by Saxo Grammaticus and a prose work by the French writer François de Belleforest, entitled *Histoires Tragiques*.

The raw material that Shakespeare appropriated in writing Hamlet is the story of a Danish prince whose uncle murders the prince's father, marries his mother, and claims the throne. The prince pretends to be feeble-minded to throw his uncle off guard, and then manages to kill his uncle in revenge. Shakespeare altered the emphasis of this story: his Hamlet struggles with existential questions and delays taking action because he is never sure that his uncle is actually guilty. Many of the play's questions are never answered: Did Gertrude help Claudius murder her husband? Does Hamlet love Ophelia? Is the ghost telling the truth? At the same time, the stakes are enormous: the actions of these characters bring disaster upon an entire kingdom.

By changing the focus of his story, Shakespeare transformed an unremarkable revenge story into a play whose problems resonate with the most fundamental concerns of the Renaissance, a cultural phenomenon marked by a new interest in the human experience and an enormous optimism about the potential scope of human understanding. Hamlet's famous speech in Act II, "What a piece of work is a man! How noble in reason, how infinite in faculty, in form and moving how express and admirable, in action how like an angel, in apprehension how like a god—the beauty of the world, the paragon of animals!" (II.ii.293–297) is directly based upon one of the major texts of the Italian humanists, Pico della Mirandola's *Oration on the Dignity of Man*. Humanists initially sought to cultivate reason in order to understand how to act in a way that would benefit society as a whole. As the Renaissance spread throughout Europe during the sixteenth and seventeenth centuries, some humanists turned to studying the limitations of human understanding. For example, Michel de Montaigne maintained that human beings could never hope to understand the realities hiding behind the masks of the world. This is the world of *Hamlet*: Hamlet is charged with correcting an injustice that he can never know completely. His is a common dilemma. The play as a whole demonstrates how difficult it is to know other people and to understand their guilt or innocence, their motivations, their feelings, their mental states. *Hamlet* is, fundamentally, a play about the difficulty of living in that world.

HAMLET: KEY FACTS

Full title: The Tragedy of Hamlet, Prince of Denmark

Date of first publication: 1603 (a pirated quarto edition)

Genre: Tragedy; revenge tragedy

Setting (time): Late middle ages

Setting (place): Denmark

Protagonist: Hamlet

Major conflict: Hamlet struggles with doubts and difficulties as he considers killing his uncle Claudius to avenge his father's death.

CHARACTERS IN *HAMLET*

Bernardo and Marcellus Officers. It is Bernardo and Marcellus who first see the ghost walking the ramparts of Elsinore.

Claudius The King of Denmark, Hamlet's uncle, King Hamlet's brother, and the play's antagonist. Claudius is a calculating, ambitious politician driven by his sexual appetites and his lust for power. He sincerely loves Gertrude.

Fortinbras The young Prince of Norway. Fortinbras's father, King Fortinbras of Norway, was killed by Hamlet's father, King Hamlet of Denmark. A foil for Hamlet, Fortinbras seeks to avenge his father's honor by conquering Denmark.

Francisco A soldier and guardsman at Elsinore.

Queen Gertrude Hamlet's mother. After the death of King Hamlet, Gertrude marries Claudius. Gertrude loves Hamlet, but she seeks the good life more energetically than she does truth. Hamlet feels that Gertrude has betrayed his father and, by extension, him.

The Ghost The spirit of King Hamlet, Hamlet's recently deceased father. The ghost claims to have been murdered by Claudius and calls upon Hamlet for revenge. The question of what the ghost is or where it comes from is never definitively resolved.

Hamlet, Prince of Denmark The play's protagonist. Hamlet is the son of Gertrude and the late King Hamlet, and the nephew of Claudius. Thirty years old at the start of the play, Hamlet is melancholy, bitter, and cynical, full of hatred for Claudius's scheming and disgust for Gertrude's sexuality. A reflective young man who has studied at the University of Wittenberg, Hamlet is often indecisive and hesitant, but at other times prone to rash and impulsive acts.

Horatio Hamlet's close friend. Horatio, who is a classmate of Hamlet's at the University in Wittenberg, is loyal and helpful to Hamlet throughout the play. He is the only major character to survive past the last act.

Laertes Polonius's son and Ophelia's brother. Passionate and quick to action, Laertes is a foil for the reflective Hamlet. Laertes spends much of the play in France.

Ophelia Polonius's daughter, Laertes's sister, and Hamlet's sometime love. A sweet and innocent young girl, Ophelia obeys both Polonius and Laertes. Ophelia is smart and loving, but madness and death overtake her.

Osric The foolish courtier who summons Hamlet to his duel with Laertes.

Polonius The Lord Chamberlain of Claudius's court, and the father of Laertes and Ophelia. Polonius is a pompous, conniving old man.

Reynaldo Polonius's servant. Reynaldo is sent to France to check up on and spy on Laertes.

Rosencrantz and Guildenstern Bumbling courtiers and former friends of Hamlet's from Wittenberg. They are summoned by Claudius and Gertrude to discover the cause of Hamlet's strange behavior.

Voltimand and Cornelius Courtiers sent to Norway to prevent Fortinbras's attack.

HAMLET: PLOT OVERVIEW

Prince Hamlet of Denmark is visited by the ghost of King Hamlet, his recently deceased father. The ghost reveals that his own brother Claudius killed him. Claudius has married Queen Gertrude and taken the throne. Hamlet vows to revenge his father's murder, but he wants more proof that what the ghost says is true. To keep Claudius from detecting his plans, Hamlet begins to behave as if he is insane, which worries Claudius and Gertrude. Polonius, the lord chamberlain, suggests that Hamlet is lovesick for Polonius's daughter, Ophelia, but when they test this suggestion, Hamlet spurns Ophelia.

To test whether Claudius is guilty, Hamlet arranges for actors to reenact Claudius killing old King Hamlet as the ghost had described it to him. Claudius leaps to his feet and leaves the room at the moment of the murder, which Hamlet interprets as proof of his guilt. Hamlet goes to kill Claudius, but when he sees Claudius praying he decides to kill him later. Hamlet angrily confronts his mother Gertrude in her bedroom and stabs Polonius, who is hiding behind a curtain, thinking that Polonius is Claudius. Claudius orders Hamlet sent to England, and entrusts the courtiers Rosencrantz and Guildenstern to deliver a letter asking the king of England to put Hamlet to death at once.

Ophelia goes mad after her father's death and drowns in a river. Her brother Laertes returns from France to avenge Polonius's and Ophelia's deaths, which Claudius blames on Hamlet. Hamlet returns to Denmark after pirates attack his ship, and Claudius arranges a fencing match between Laertes and Hamlet in which he poisons both Laertes' sword and a cup that he intends to give Hamlet. Laertes wounds Hamlet, but then is poisoned by his own sword; Gertrude drinks out of the poisoned cup; Hamlet kills Claudius; and then Hamlet dies from his poisoned wound. Prince Fortinbras of Norway, whose father had been killed by Hamlet's father, arrives to rule Denmark.

HAMLET: SCENE SUMMARY

ACT I

The ghost of the dead king demands that his son Hamlet kill Claudius, the current king and Hamlet's uncle.

I.I Location: Denmark. Outside Elsinore Castle

The Elsinore Castle watchmen and Horatio resolve to tell Prince Hamlet about the ghost of his father, the dead King Hamlet, which has been haunting the castle at night.

On a dark winter night an officer named Bernardo comes to relieve the watchman Francisco. They cannot see each other in the darkness, but finally recognize each other by voice. Cold, tired, and apprehensive from his many hours of guarding the castle, Francisco thanks Bernardo and goes home. Just before Francisco leaves, Bernardo is joined by Marcellus, another watchman, and Horatio, Prince Hamlet's childhood friend. Bernardo and Marcellus have urged Horatio to stand watch with them because they believe they have something shocking to show him. In hushed tones, Bernardo and Marcellus discuss the apparition they have seen for the past two nights, and which they now hope to show Horatio: the ghost of the recently deceased King Hamlet, which they claim has appeared before them on the castle ramparts in the late hours of the night.

Horatio is skeptical, but then the ghost suddenly appears before the men and, just as suddenly, vanishes. Terrified, Horatio acknowledges that the specter does indeed resemble the dead king of Denmark. It even wears the armor King Hamlet wore when he battled against the armies of Norway, and the same frown he wore when he fought against the Poles. Horatio declares that the ghost must bring warning of impending misfortune for Denmark, perhaps in the form of a military attack. He recounts the story of King Hamlet's conquest of certain lands once belonging to Norway, saying that Fortinbras, the young prince of Norway, now seeks to reconquer those forfeited lands.

The ghost materializes for a second time and Horatio tries to speak to it. The ghost remains silent, however, and disappears again just as the cock crows at the first hint of dawn. Horatio suggests that they tell Prince Hamlet, the dead king's son, about the apparition. He believes that though the ghost did not speak to him, if it is really the ghost of King Hamlet, it will not refuse to speak to his beloved son.

I.II Location: Denmark. Elsinore Castle

At his mother Gertrude's urgings during a public ceremony, Hamlet reluctantly agrees to stay in Denmark.

The next morning, the new King Claudius of Denmark gives a speech to his courtiers explaining his recent marriage to Queen Gertrude, the widow of the dead King Hamlet, who was Claudius's brother and the mother of Prince Hamlet. Claudius says that he mourns his brother but has chosen to balance Denmark's mourning with the delight of his marriage. He mentions that young Fortinbras of Norway has written to him, rashly demanding the surrender of the lands the dead King Hamlet won from Fortinbras's father, and dispatches Cornelius and Voltimand with a message for the king of Norway, Fortinbras's elderly uncle.

Claudius then turns to Laertes, the son of the lord chamberlain, Polonius. Laertes expresses his desire to return to France, where he was staying before his return to Denmark for Claudius's coronation. Polonius gives his son permission, and Claudius jovially grants Laertes his consent as well.

Turning to Prince Hamlet, Claudius asks why "the clouds still hang" (I.ii.66) upon him. (Hamlet is still wearing black mourning clothes.) Gertrude urges him to cast off his "nightly color" (I.ii.68), but he replies bitterly that his inner sorrow is much greater than his dour appearance might suggest. Affecting a tone of fatherly advice, Claudius declares that all fathers die, and all sons must lose their fathers. When a son loses a father, he is duty-bound to mourn, but to mourn for too long is unmanly and inappropriate. Claudius urges Hamlet to think of him as a father and reminds him that Hamlet stands in line to succeed to the throne upon his death.

With this in mind, Claudius says that he does not wish for Hamlet to return to school at Wittenberg (where he had been studying before old King Hamlet's death), as Hamlet has asked to do. Gertrude too professes a desire for Hamlet to remain close to her. Hamlet stiffly agrees to obey. Claudius claims to be so pleased by Hamlet's decision to stay that he will celebrate with festivities and cannon fire, an old custom called "the king's rouse." Ordering Gertrude to follow him, he escorts her from the room, and the court follows.

Alone, Hamlet exclaims that he wishes he could die; that he could evaporate and cease to exist. He wishes bitterly that God had not made suicide a sin. Anguished, he laments his father's death and his mother Gertrude's too-hasty marriage to his uncle Claudius. He remembers how deeply in love his parents seemed, and he curses the thought that now, not yet two months after his father's death, his mother has married his father's far inferior brother.

Hamlet quiets suddenly as Horatio strides into the room, followed by Marcellus and Bernardo. Horatio was a close friend of Hamlet at the university in Wittenberg and Hamlet, happy to see him, asks why he has left the school to travel to Denmark. Horatio says that he came to see King Hamlet's funeral, to which Hamlet curtly replies that Horatio came to see his mother's wedding. Horatio agrees that the one followed closely on the heels of the other. He then tells Hamlet that he, Marcellus, and Bernardo have seen what appears to be his father's ghost. Stunned, Hamlet agrees to keep watch with them that night, in the hope that he will be able to speak to the apparition.

I.III Location: Denmark. Polonius's house

Laertes, the son of royal adviser Polonius, leaves for France; Polonius forbids his daughter Ophelia to see Hamlet, who has been courting her.

Laertes prepares to leave for France. Bidding his sister Ophelia farewell, he cautions her against falling in love with Hamlet who is, according to Laertes, too far above her by birth to be able to love her honorably. Hamlet is responsible not only for his own feelings, but for his position in the state, so it may be impossible for him to marry her. Ophelia agrees to keep Laertes' advice as a "watchman" close to her heart, but urges him not to give her advice that he does not practice himself. Laertes reassures her that he will take care of himself.

Polonius enters to bid his son farewell. He tells Laertes that he must hurry to his ship but then delays him by giving him a great deal of advice about how to behave with integrity and practicality. Polonius admonishes Laertes to keep his thoughts to himself, restrain himself from acting on rash desires, and treat people with familiarity but not with vulgarity. He advises him to hold on to his old friends but be slow to embrace new friends; to be slow to quarrel but to fight boldly if the need arises; to listen more than he talks; to dress richly but not gaudily; to refrain from borrowing or lending money; and finally, to be true to himself above all things.

Laertes leaves, bidding farewell to Ophelia once more. Alone with his daughter, Polonius asks Ophelia what Laertes told her before he left. Ophelia says that it was "something touching the Lord Hamlet" (I.ii.89). Polonius asks her about her relationship with Hamlet. She tells him that Hamlet claims to love her. Polonius sternly echoes Laertes' advice, and forbids Ophelia to associate with Hamlet anymore. He tells her that Hamlet has deceived her in swearing his love, and that she should see through his false vows and rebuff his affections. Ophelia pledges to obey.

I.IV Location: Denmark. Outside Elsinore Castle

Hamlet sees the ghost of his father and follows it.

That night, Hamlet keeps watch outside the castle with Horatio and Marcellus, waiting in the cold for the ghost to appear. Shortly after midnight, trumpets and gunfire sound from the castle, and Hamlet explains that the new king is spending the night carousing, as is the Danish custom. Disgusted, Hamlet declares that this sort of custom is better broken than kept, saying that the king's revelry makes Denmark a laughingstock among other nations and lessens the Danes' otherwise impressive achievements. Then the ghost appears and Hamlet calls out to it. The ghost beckons Hamlet to follow it out into the night. His companions urge him not to follow, begging him to consider that the ghost might lead him toward harm.

Hamlet himself is unsure whether the ghost is truly his father's spirit or an evil demon, but he declares that he cares nothing for his life and that, if his soul is immortal, the ghost can do nothing to harm his soul. He follows after the apparition and disappears into the darkness. Horatio and Marcellus, stunned, declare that the event bodes ill for the nation. Horatio proclaims that heaven will oversee the outcome of Hamlet's encounter with the ghost, but Marcellus says that they should follow and try to protect him themselves. After a moment, Horatio and Marcellus follow after Hamlet and the ghost.

I.V Location: Denmark. Outside Elsinore Castle

The ghost demands that Hamlet kill Claudius to avenge the death of Hamlet's father; Hamlet decides to pretend to be mad.

The ghost speaks to Hamlet, claiming to be his father's spirit come to rouse Hamlet to revenge his death, a "foul and most unnatural murder" (I.v.25). Hamlet is appalled at the revelation that his father has been murdered, and the ghost tells him that as he slept in his garden, a villain poured poison into his ear. That villain is Claudius, the very man who now wears his crown. Hamlet's worst fears about his uncle are confirmed. "O my prophetic soul!" he cries (I.v.40). The ghost exhorts Hamlet to seek revenge, telling him that Claudius has corrupted Denmark and corrupted Gertrude, having taken her from the pure love of her first marriage and seduced her in the foul lust of their incestuous union. But the ghost urges Hamlet not to act against his mother in any way, telling him to "leave her to heaven" and to the pangs of her own conscience (I.v.86).

As dawn breaks, the ghost disappears. Intensely moved, Hamlet swears to remember and obey the ghost. Horatio and Marcellus arrive upon the scene and frantically ask Hamlet what has happened. Shaken and extremely agitated, he refuses to tell them and insists that they swear upon his sword not to reveal what they have seen. He tells them further that he may pretend to be a madman, and he makes them swear not to give the slightest hint that they know anything about his motives. Three times the ghost's voice echoes from beneath the ground, proclaiming, "Swear." Horatio and Marcellus take the oath upon Hamlet's sword, and the three men exit toward the castle. As they leave, Hamlet bemoans the responsibility he now carries: "The time is out of joint: O cursed spite / That ever I was born to set it right!" (I.v.189–190).

ACT II

Hamlet pretends to be crazy, hesitates to kill Claudius, and increasingly feels alienated from everyone else.

II.I Location: Denmark. Polonius's house

Ophelia tells Polonius that Hamlet has accosted her, acting crazy.

Polonius dispatches his servant Reynaldo to France with money and letters for Laertes. In addition, Polonius orders Reynaldo to inquire about and spy on Laertes' personal life. He gives him explicit directions as to how to pursue his investigations and then sends him on his way. As Reynaldo leaves, Ophelia enters, visibly upset. She tells Polonius that Hamlet, unkempt and wild-eyed, has accosted her. Hamlet grabbed her, held her, and sighed heavily, but did not speak to her. Polonius says that Hamlet must be mad with his love for Ophelia, for she has distanced herself from him ever since Polonius ordered her to do so. Polonius speculates that this lovesickness might be the cause of Hamlet's moodiness, and he hurries out to tell Claudius of his idea.

II.II Location: Denmark. Elsinore Castle

Hamlet feels betrayed by his school friends and worries Gertrude and Claudius with his crazy behavior.

Claudius and Gertrude welcome Rosencrantz and Guildenstern, two of Hamlet's friends from Wittenberg. Increasingly concerned about Hamlet's erratic behavior and his apparent inability to recover from his father's death, Claudius and Gertrude have summoned Rosencrantz and Guildenstern to Elsinore in the hope that they might be able to cheer Hamlet out of his melancholy, or at least discover why he's in a funk. Rosencrantz and Guildenstern agree to investigate, and the queen orders attendants to take them to her "too much changèd" son (II.ii.36).

Polonius enters, announcing the return of the ambassadors whom Claudius sent to Norway. Voltimand and Cornelius enter and describe what took place with the aged and ailing king of Norway: the king rebuked Fortinbras for attempting to make war on Denmark, and Fortinbras swore he would never again attack the Danes. The Norwegian king, overjoyed, bequeathed upon Fortinbras a large annuity, and urged him to use the army he had assembled to attack the Poles instead of the Danes. He has therefore sent a request back to Claudius that Prince Fortinbras's armies be allowed safe passage through Denmark on their way to attack the Poles. Relieved to have averted a war with Fortinbras's army, Claudius declares that he will see to this business later. Voltimand and Cornelius leave.

Polonius declares, after a wordy preamble, that Hamlet is mad with love for Ophelia. He shows Claudius and Gertrude the letters and love poems Hamlet has given to Ophelia and proposes a plan to test his theory. Hamlet often walks alone through the lobby of the castle and, at such a time, they could hide behind an arras (a curtain or wall hanging) while Ophelia confronts Hamlet, allowing them to see for themselves whether Hamlet's madness really emanates from his love for her. Claudius agrees to try Polonius's plan. Gertrude notices that Hamlet approaches, reading from a book as he walks, and Polonius says that he will speak to Hamlet. Gertrude and Claudius exit.

Polonius attempts to converse with Hamlet, who appears insane. He calls the old man a "fishmonger" and answers his questions irrationally. But many of Hamlet's seemingly lunatic statements hide barbed observations about Polonius's pomposity and his old age. Polonius comments that while Hamlet is clearly mad, his replies are often "pregnant" with meaning (II.ii.206). He hurries away, determined to arrange the meeting between Hamlet and Ophelia.

As Polonius leaves, Rosencrantz and Guildenstern enter and Hamlet seems pleased to see them. They discuss Hamlet's unhappiness about recent affairs in Denmark. Hamlet asks why they have come. Sheepishly, the two men claim they have come merely to visit Hamlet, but he sternly declares that he knows that Claudius and Gertrude sent for them. They confess this to be true, and Hamlet says that he knows why: because he has lost all of his joy and descended into a state of melancholy in which everything (and everyone) appears sterile and worthless.

Rosencrantz smiles and says he wonders how Hamlet will receive a theatrical troupe that is currently traveling toward the castle. The trumpets blow, announcing the arrival of the actors (or "players"). Hamlet tells his friends they are welcome to stay at Elsinore, but that his "uncle-father and aunt-mother" are deceived in his madness. He is mad only some of the time and at other times is sane.

Polonius enters to announce the arrival of the players, who follow him into the room. Hamlet welcomes them and entreats one of them to give him a speech about the fall of Troy and the death of the Trojan king and queen, Priam and Hecuba. Impressed with the player's speech, Hamlet orders Polonius to see them escorted to guestrooms. He announces that the next night they will hear "The Murder of Gonzago" performed, with an additional short speech that he will write himself. Hamlet leaves Rosencrantz and Guildenstern and now stands alone in the room.

He immediately begins cursing himself, bitterly commenting that the player who gave the speech was able to summon a depth of feeling and expression for long-dead figures who mean nothing to him, while Hamlet is unable to take action even with his far more powerful motives. He resolves to devise a trap for Claudius, forcing the king to watch a play whose plot closely resembles the murder of Hamlet's father. If the king is guilty, he thinks, he will surely show some visible sign of guilt when he sees his sin reenacted on stage. Then, Hamlet reasons, he will obtain definitive proof of Claudius's guilt. "The play's the thing," he declares, "wherein I'll catch the conscience of the king" (II.ii.581–582).

ACT III

Reeling from Claudius's violent reaction to a play about the murder of Hamlet's father, Hamlet mistakenly kills Polonius.

III.I   Location: Denmark. Elsinore Castle

Hamlet contemplates suicide and then spurns Ophelia when he suspects that she has betrayed him.

Rosencrantz and Guildenstern report to Claudius and Gertrude that they have been unable to learn the cause of Hamlet's melancholy. They tell Claudius and Gertrude about Hamlet's enthusiasm for the players. Encouraged, Gertrude and Claudius agree that they will see the play that evening. Rosencrantz and Guildenstern leave and Claudius orders Gertrude to leave as well, saying that he and Polonius intend to spy on Hamlet's confrontation with Ophelia. Gertrude exits and Polonius directs Ophelia to walk around the lobby. Polonius hears Hamlet coming, and he and the king hide.

Hamlet enters, speaking thoughtfully and agonizingly to himself about the question of whether to commit suicide to end the pain of experience: "To be, or not to be: that is the question" (III.i.58). He says that the miseries of life are such that no one would willingly bear them, except that they are afraid of "something after death" (III.i.80). Because we do not know what to expect in the afterlife, we would rather "bear those ills we have," Hamlet says, "than fly to others that we know not of" (III.i.83–84). In mid-thought, Hamlet sees Ophelia approaching. Having received her orders from Polonius, she tells him that she wishes to return the tokens of love he has given her. Angrily, Hamlet denies having given her anything. He laments the dishonesty of beauty and claims both to have loved Ophelia once and never to have loved her at all. Bitterly commenting on the wretchedness of humankind, he urges Ophelia to enter a nunnery (also Elizabethan slang for "brothel") rather than become a "breeder of sinners" (III.i.122–23). He criticizes women for making men behave like monsters and for contributing to the world's dishonesty by painting their faces to appear more beautiful than they are. Working himself into a rage, Hamlet denounces Ophelia, women, and humankind in general, saying that he wishes to end all marriages. As he storms out, Ophelia mourns the "noble mind" that has now lapsed into apparent madness (III.i.149).

Claudius and Polonius emerge from behind the tapestry. Claudius says that Hamlet's strange behavior has clearly not been caused by love for Ophelia and that his speech does not seem like the speech of insanity. He says that he fears that melancholy sits on something dangerous in Hamlet's soul like a bird sits on her egg, and that he fears what will happen when it hatches. He declares that he will send Hamlet to England, in the hope that a change of scenery might help him get over his troubles. Polonius agrees that this is a good idea, but he still believes that Hamlet's agitation comes from loving Ophelia. He asks Claudius to send Hamlet to Gertrude's chamber after the play, where Polonius can hide again and watch unseen. He hopes to learn whether Hamlet is really mad with love. Claudius agrees, saying that "[m]adness in great ones" must be carefully watched (III.i.187).

III.II   Location: Denmark. Elsinore Castle

Hamlet decides that Claudius is indeed guilty of murder by watching Claudius's reaction to a staged reenactment of the crime.

Hamlet anxiously lectures the players on how to act the parts he has written for them. Polonius shuffles by with Rosencrantz and Guildenstern, and Hamlet dispatches them to hurry the players in their preparations. Horatio enters and Hamlet, pleased to see him, praises him heartily, expressing his affection for and high opinion of Horatio's mind and manner, especially Horatio's qualities of self-control and reserve. Having told Horatio the ghost's claim that Claudius murdered King Hamlet, he now asks him to watch Claudius carefully during the play so that they might compare their impressions of his behavior afterward. Horatio agrees, saying that if Claudius shows any signs of guilt, he will detect them.

The trumpets play a Danish march as the audience of lords and ladies begins streaming into the room. Hamlet warns Horatio that he will begin to act strangely. Sure enough, when Claudius asks how he is, his response seems quite insane: "Excellent, i' faith; of the chameleon's dish: I eat the air, promise-crammed" (III.ii.84–86). Hamlet asks Polonius about his history as an actor and torments Ophelia with a string of erotic puns.

The players enter and act out a dumbshow (a brief, silent version of the play to come). In the dumbshow, a king and queen display their love. The queen leaves the king to sleep, and while he is sleeping, a man murders him by pouring poison into his ear. The murderer tries to seduce the queen, who gradually accepts his advances.

The players begin to enact the play in full, and we learn that the man who kills the king is the king's nephew. Throughout, Hamlet keeps up a running commentary on the characters and their actions, and continues to tease Ophelia with oblique sexual references. When the murderer pours the poison into the sleeping king's ear, Claudius rises and cries out for light. Chaos ensues as the play comes to a sudden halt, the torches are lit, and the king flees the room, followed by the audience. When the scene quiets, Hamlet is left alone with Horatio.

Hamlet and Horatio agree that the king's behavior was telling. Now extremely excited, Hamlet continues to act frantic and scatterbrained, speaking glibly and inventing little poems. Rosencrantz and Guildenstern arrive to tell Hamlet that he is wanted in his mother's chambers. Rosencrantz asks again about the cause of Hamlet's "distemper," and Hamlet angrily accuses the pair of trying to play him as if he were a musical pipe. Polonius enters to escort Hamlet to the queen. Hamlet says he will go to her in a moment and asks for a moment alone. He steels himself to speak to his mother, resolving to be brutally honest with her but not to lose control of himself: "I will speak daggers to her, but use none" (III.ii.366).

III.III   Location: Denmark. Elsewhere in Elsinore Castle

Hamlet almost kills Claudius as Claudius prays for forgiveness for his crime.

Badly shaken by the play, Claudius asks Rosencrantz and Guildenstern to escort Hamlet on a voyage to England and to depart immediately. They agree and leave to make preparations. Polonius enters and reminds the king of his plan to hide in Gertrude's room and observe Hamlet's confrontation with her. He promises to tell Claudius all that he learns. When Polonius leaves, Claudius is alone, and he immediately expresses his guilt and grief over his sin. A brother's murder, he says, is the oldest sin and "hath the primal eldest curse upon't" (III.iii.37). He longs to ask for forgiveness, but says that he is unprepared to give up that which he gained by committing the murder: namely, the crown and the queen. He falls to his knees and begins to pray.

Hamlet slips quietly into the room and steels himself to kill the unseeing Claudius. But suddenly it occurs to him that if he kills Claudius while he is praying, he will end Claudius's life at a moment of penance, sending Claudius's soul to heaven. This is hardly an adequate revenge, Hamlet thinks, especially since Claudius, by killing Hamlet's father before he had time to make his last confession, ensured that Hamlet's father would not go to heaven. Hamlet decides to wait, resolving to kill Claudius when the king is sinning by being drunk, angry, or lustful. He leaves. Claudius rises and declares that he has been unable to pray sincerely: "My words fly up, my thoughts remain below" (III.iii.96).

III.IV   Location: Gertrude's chamber

In confrontation with Gertrude, Hamlet kills Polonius, who is hiding behind a curtain.

Gertrude and Polonius wait for Hamlet's arrival. Polonius plans to hide in order to eavesdrop on Gertrude's confrontation with Hamlet, in the hope that doing so will enable him to determine the cause of Hamlet's bizarre and threatening behavior. Polonius urges Gertrude to be harsh with Hamlet when he arrives, saying that she should chastise him for his recent behavior. Gertrude agrees and Polonius hides behind an arras, or tapestry.

Hamlet storms into the room and asks his mother why she has sent for him. She says that he has offended his father—meaning his stepfather, Claudius. He interrupts her and says that she has offended his father—meaning the dead King Hamlet, by marrying Claudius. Hamlet accosts her with an almost violent intensity and declares his intention to make her fully aware of the profundity of her sin. Fearing for her life, Gertrude cries out. From behind the arras, Polonius calls out for help. Hamlet, realizing that someone is behind the arras and suspecting that it might be Claudius, cries, "How now! a rat?" (III.iv.22). He draws his sword and stabs it through the tapestry, killing the unseen Polonius. Gertrude asks what Hamlet has done and he replies, "Nay, I know not: / Is it the king?" (III.iv.24). Gertrude says his action was a "rash and bloody" deed, and Hamlet replies that it was almost as rash and bloody as murdering a king and marrying his brother (III.iv.26–28). Disbelieving, the queen exclaims, "As kill a king!" and Hamlet replies that she heard him correctly (III.iv.29).

Hamlet lifts the arras and discovers Polonius's body. He is disappointed and bids Polonius farewell, calling him an "intruding fool" (III.iv.30). He turns to his mother, declaring that he will wring her heart. He shows her a picture of the dead King Hamlet and a picture of the current King Claudius, bitterly comments on the superiority of his father to his uncle, and asks her furiously what has driven her to marry a rotten man such as Claudius. She pleads with him to stop, saying that he has turned her eyes onto her soul and that she does not like what she sees there. Hamlet continues to denounce her and rail against Claudius until suddenly, the ghost of his father again appears before him.

Hamlet speaks to the ghost, but Gertrude is unable to see it and believes him to be mad. The ghost intones that it has come to remind Hamlet of his purpose, that Hamlet has not yet killed Claudius and must achieve his revenge. Noting that Gertrude is amazed and unable to see him, the ghost asks Hamlet to intercede with her. Hamlet describes the ghost, but Gertrude sees nothing and in a moment the ghost disappears. Hamlet tries desperately to convince Gertrude that he is not mad but has merely feigned madness all along, and he urges her to forsake Claudius and regain her good conscience. He urges her as well not to reveal to Claudius that his madness has been an act. Gertrude, still shaken from Hamlet's furious condemnation of her, agrees to keep his secret. He bids her goodnight, but before he leaves he points to Polonius's corpse and declares that heaven has "punished me with this, and this with me" (III.iv.158). Hamlet reminds his mother that he must sail to England with Rosencrantz and Guildenstern, whom he says he will regard with suspicion, as though they were poisonous snakes, since he assumes that their loyalties are with Claudius, not with him. Dragging Polonius's body behind him, Hamlet leaves his mother's room.

ACT IV

Claudius sends Hamlet to England, but Hamlet manages to return, resolved to kill Claudius.

IV.I Location: Elsinore Castle

Gertrude betrays Hamlet and tells Claudius that Hamlet has killed Polonius.

Frantic after her confrontation with Hamlet, Gertrude hurries to Claudius, who is conferring with Rosencrantz and Guildenstern. She asks to speak to Claudius alone. When Rosencrantz and Guildenstern exit, she tells Claudius about her encounter with Hamlet. She says that he is as mad as the sea during a violent storm. She also tells Claudius that Hamlet has killed Polonius. Aghast, Claudius notes that had he been concealed behind the arras, Hamlet would have killed him. Claudius wonders aloud how he will be able to handle this public crisis without damaging his hold on Denmark. He tells Gertrude that they must ship Hamlet to England at once and find a way to explain Hamlet's misdeed to the court and to the people. He calls Rosencrantz and Guildenstern, tells them about the murder, and sends them to find Hamlet.

IV.II Location: elsewhere in Elsinore Castle

Hamlet's school friends take Hamlet to see Claudius.

Hamlet has just finished disposing of Polonius's body, commenting that the corpse has been "safely stowed" (IV.ii.1). Rosencrantz and Guildenstern appear and ask what he has done with the body. Hamlet refuses to give them a straight answer, instead saying, "The body is with the king, but the king is not with the body" (IV.ii.25–26). Feigning offense at being questioned, he accuses them of being spies in the service of Claudius. He calls Rosencrantz a "sponge . . . that soaks up the king's countenance, his rewards, his authorities," and warns him that "when he needs what you have gleaned, it is but squeezing you, and, sponge, you shall be dry again" (IV.ii.11–19). At last he agrees to allow Rosencrantz and Guildenstern to escort him to Claudius.

IV.III Location: Elsinore Castle

Claudius confronts Hamlet and sends him to England with a sealed order requesting that Hamlet be put to death.

Claudius speaks to a group of attendants, telling them of Polonius's death and his intention to send Hamlet to England. Rosencrantz and Guildenstern appear with Hamlet, who is under guard. Pressed by Claudius to reveal the location of Polonius's body, Hamlet is by turns inane, coy, and clever, saying that Polonius is being eaten by worms, and that the king could send a messenger to find Polonius in heaven or seek him in hell himself. Finally, Hamlet reveals that Polonius's body is under the stairs near the castle lobby, and the king dispatches his attendants to look there. The king tells Hamlet that he must leave at once for England and Hamlet enthusiastically agrees. He exits and Claudius sends Rosencrantz and Guildenstern to ensure that he boards the ship at once. Alone with his thoughts, Claudius states his hope that England will obey the sealed orders he has sent with Rosencrantz and Guildenstern. The orders call for Prince Hamlet to be put to death.

IV.IV Location: Denmark. A plain

On the way to England, Hamlet encounters the army of Fortinbras of Norway on its way to war, and resolves to stop wallowing and start acting.

Young Prince Fortinbras marches at the head of his army, traveling through Denmark on the way to attack Poland. Fortinbras orders his captain to go and ask the king of Denmark for permission to travel through his lands. On his way, the captain encounters Hamlet, Rosencrantz, and Guildenstern on their way to the ship bound for England. The captain informs them that the Norwegian army rides to fight the Poles. Hamlet asks about the basis of the conflict, and the man tells him that the armies will fight over "a little patch of land / That hath in it no profit but the name" (IV.iv.98–99). Astonished by the thought that a bloody war could be fought over something so insignificant, Hamlet marvels that human beings are able to act so violently and purposefully for so little gain. By comparison, Hamlet has a great deal to gain from seeking his own bloody revenge on Claudius, and yet he still delays and fails to act toward his purpose. Disgusted with himself for having failed to gain his revenge on Claudius, Hamlet declares that from this moment on, his thoughts will be bloody.

IV.V Location: Elsinore Castle

Ophelia has gone mad; Laertes returns from France demanding revenge for his father Polonius's death.

Gertrude does not wish to see Ophelia, but one of the servants says that grief has made Ophelia disordered and incoherent. Horatio concurs. Ophelia enters. Adorned with flowers and singing strange songs, she seems to have gone mad. Claudius enters and hears Ophelia's ravings, such as, "They say the owl was a baker's daughter" (IV.v.42). He says that Ophelia's grief stems from her father's death, and that the people have been suspicious and disturbed by the death as well: "muddied, / Thick and unwholesome in their thoughts and whispers / For good Polonius' death" (IV.v.77–79). He also mentions that Laertes has secretly sailed back from France.

A loud noise echoes somewhere in the castle. Claudius calls for his guards and a gentleman enters to warn the king that Laertes has come with a mob of commoners. The mob calls Laertes "lord," according to the gentlemen, and the people whisper that "Laertes shall be king" (IV.v.102–106). A furious Laertes storms into the hall, fuming in his desire to avenge his father's death. Claudius attempts to soothe him by frankly acknowledging that Polonius is dead. Gertrude nervously adds that Claudius is innocent in it. When Ophelia reenters, obviously insane, Laertes is plunged again into rage. Claudius claims that he is not responsible for Polonius's death and says that Laertes' desire for revenge is a credit to him, so long as he seeks revenge upon the proper person. Claudius convinces Laertes to hear his version of events, which he says will answer all his questions. Laertes agrees and Claudius seconds his desire to achieve justice in the aftermath of Polonius's death: "Where th' offence is, let the great axe fall" (IV.v.213).

IV.VI   Location: elsewhere in Elsinore Castle

In a letter to Horatio, Hamlet explains that he has returned to Denmark.

Horatio is introduced to a pair of sailors bearing a letter for him from Hamlet. In the letter, Hamlet says that his ship was captured by pirates who have returned him to Denmark. He asks Horatio to escort the sailors to the king and queen, for they have messages for them as well. He also says that he has much to tell of Rosencrantz and Guildenstern. Horatio takes the sailors to Claudius and then follows them to find Hamlet, who is in the countryside near the castle.

IV.VII   Location: Elsinore Castle

Claudius sweet-talks Laertes into a plot to kill Hamlet; in her madness, Ophelia has drowned.

Claudius and a calmer Laertes discuss Polonius's death. Claudius explains that he acted as he did—burying Polonius secretly and not punishing Hamlet for the murder—because both the common people and Gertrude love Hamlet very much. As a king and as a husband, he did not wish to upset either of them. A messenger enters with the letter from Hamlet to Claudius, which informs the king that Hamlet will return tomorrow. Laertes is pleased that Hamlet has come back to Denmark, since it means that his revenge will not be delayed.

Claudius agrees that Laertes deserves to be revenged upon Hamlet and he is disposed to encourage Laertes to kill Hamlet, since Hamlet's erratic behavior has made him a threat to Claudius's reign. The devious king begins to think of a way for Laertes to ensure his revenge without creating any appearance of foul play. He recalls that Hamlet has been jealous in the past of Laertes' prowess with a sword, which was recently praised before all the court by a Frenchman who had seen him in combat. Claudius speculates that if Hamlet could be tempted into a duel with Laertes, it might provide Laertes with the chance to kill him. Laertes agrees, and they settle on a plan. Laertes will use a sharpened sword rather than the customary dull fencing blade. Laertes also proposes to poison his sword, so that even a scratch from it will kill Hamlet. Claudius concocts a backup plan as well, proposing that if Hamlet succeeds in the duel, Claudius will offer him a poisoned cup of wine to drink from in celebration.

Gertrude enters with tragic news. Ophelia, mad with grief, has drowned in the river. Anguished to have lost his sister so soon after his father's death, Laertes flees the room. Claudius summons Gertrude to follow. He tells her it was nearly impossible to quiet Laertes' rage, and worries that the news of Ophelia's death will reawaken it.

ACT V

Denmark is purged of corruption as Claudius's treachery is exposed and everybody—Claudius, Gertrude, Laertes, and Hamlet—dies.

V.I   Location: Denmark. A churchyard

Hamlet meets a gravedigger and picks a fight with Laertes at Ophelia's funeral.

In the churchyard, two gravediggers shovel out a grave for Ophelia. They argue whether Ophelia should be buried in the churchyard, since her death looks like a suicide. According to religious doctrine, suicides may not receive Christian burial. The first gravedigger, who speaks cleverly and mischievously, asks the second gravedigger a riddle: "What is he that builds stronger than either the mason, the shipwright, or the carpenter?" (V.i.46–47). The second gravedigger answers that it must be the gallows-maker, for his frame outlasts a thousand tenants. The first gravedigger corrects him, saying that it is the gravedigger, for his "houses" will last until doomsday.

Hamlet and Horatio enter at a distance and watch the gravediggers work. Hamlet looks with wonder at the skulls they excavate to make room for the fresh grave and speculates darkly about what occupations the owners of these skulls served in life: "Why may not that be the skull of a lawyer? Where be his quiddities now … ?" (V.i.90–91). Hamlet asks the gravedigger whose grave he digs and the gravedigger spars with him verbally, first claiming that the grave is his own, since he is digging it, then that the grave belongs to no man and no woman, because men and women are living things and the occupant of the grave will be dead. At last he admits that it belongs to one "that was a woman sir; but, rest her soul, she's dead" (V.i.146). The gravedigger, who does not recognize Hamlet as the prince, tells him that he has been a gravedigger since King Hamlet defeated the elder Fortinbras in battle, the very day on which young Prince Hamlet was born. Hamlet picks up a skull, and the gravedigger tells him that the skull belonged to Yorick, King Hamlet's jester. Hamlet tells Horatio that as a child he knew Yorick and is appalled at the sight of the skull. He realizes forcefully that all men will eventually become dust, even great men like Alexander the Great and Julius Caesar. Hamlet imagines that Julius Caesar has disintegrated and is now part of the dust used to patch up a wall.

Suddenly, the funeral procession for Ophelia enters the churchyard, including Claudius, Gertrude, Laertes, and many mourning courtiers. Hamlet, wondering who has died, notices that the funeral rites seem "maimed," indicating that the dead man or woman took his or her own life (V.i.242). He and Horatio hide as the procession approaches the grave. As Ophelia is laid in the earth, Hamlet realizes it is she who has died. At the same moment, Laertes becomes infuriated with the priest, who says that to give Ophelia a proper Christian burial would profane the dead. Laertes leaps into Ophelia's grave to hold her once again in his arms. Grief-stricken and outraged, Hamlet bursts upon the company, declaring in agonized fury his own love for Ophelia. He leaps into the grave and fights with Laertes, saying that "forty thousand brothers / Could not, with all their quantity of love, / make up my sum" (V.i.254–256). Hamlet cries that he would do things for Ophelia that Laertes could not dream of. He would eat a crocodile for her; he would be buried alive with her. The combatants are pulled apart by the funeral company. Gertrude and Claudius declare that Hamlet is mad. Hamlet storms off, and Horatio follows. Claudius urges Laertes to be patient and to remember their plan for revenge.

V.II Location: Elsinore Castle

Denmark is purged of corruption as everyone dies; Gertrude drinks poison intended for Hamlet, Hamlet finally kills Claudius, and Hamlet and Laertes kill each other in a fencing match.

The next day, Hamlet tells Horatio how he plotted to overcome Claudius's scheme to have him murdered in England. He replaced the sealed letter carried by the unsuspecting Rosencrantz and Guildenstern, which called for Hamlet's execution, with one calling for the execution of the bearers of the letter—Rosencrantz and Guildenstern themselves. He tells Horatio that he has no sympathy for Rosencrantz and Guildenstern, who betrayed him and catered to Claudius, but that he feels sorry for having behaved with such hostility toward Laertes. In Laertes' desire to avenge his father's death, he says, he sees the mirror image of his own desire and he promises to seek Laertes' good favor.

Their conversation is interrupted by Osric, a foolish courtier. Osric tries to flatter Hamlet by agreeing with everything Hamlet says, even when he contradicts himself. In the space of seconds, Osric agrees first that it is cold, then that it is hot. He has come to tell them that Claudius wants Hamlet to fence with Laertes and that the king has made a wager with Laertes that Hamlet will win. Then Osric begins to praise Laertes effusively, though Hamlet and Horatio are unable to determine what point he is trying to make with his overly elaborate proclamations. Finally, a lord enters and asks Hamlet if he is ready to come to the match, as the king and queen are expecting him. Against Horatio's advice, Hamlet agrees to fight, saying that "all's ill here about my heart," but that one must be ready for death, since it will come no matter what one does (V.ii.222). The court marches into the hall and Hamlet asks Laertes for forgiveness, claiming that it was his madness, not his own will, that murdered Polonius. Laertes says that he will not forgive Hamlet until an elder, an expert in the fine points of honor, has advised him in the matter. But in the meantime, he says, he will accept Hamlet's offer of love.

They select their foils (blunted swords used in fencing), and Claudius says that if Hamlet wins the first or second hit, he will drink to Hamlet's health, then throw into the cup a valuable gem (actually the poison) and give the wine to Hamlet. The duel begins. Hamlet strikes Laertes but declines to drink from the cup, saying that he will play another hit first. He hits Laertes again, and Gertrude rises to drink from the cup. Claudius tells her not to drink, but she does so anyway. In an aside, Claudius murmurs, "It is the poison'd cup: it is too late" (V.ii.235). Laertes remarks under his breath that to wound Hamlet with the poisoned sword is almost against his conscience. But they fight again, and Laertes scores a hit against Hamlet, drawing blood. Scuffling, they manage to exchange swords, and Hamlet wounds Laertes with Laertes' own blade.

Gertrude falls. Laertes, poisoned by his own sword, declares, "I am justly kill'd with my own treachery" (V.ii.318). Gertrude moans that the cup must have been poisoned, calls out to Hamlet, and dies. Laertes tells Hamlet that he, too, has been slain, by his own poisoned sword, and that the king is to blame both for the poison on the sword and for the poison in the cup. Hamlet, in a fury, runs Claudius through with the poisoned sword and forces him to drink down the rest of the poisoned wine. Claudius dies crying out for help. Hamlet tells Horatio that he is dying and exchanges a last forgiveness with Laertes, who dies after absolving Hamlet.

The sound of marching echoes through the hall and a shot rings out nearby. Osric declares that Fortinbras has come in conquest from Poland and now fires a volley to the English ambassadors. Hamlet tells Horatio again that he is dying, and urges his friend not to commit suicide in light of all the tragedies, but instead to stay alive and tell his story. He says that he wishes Fortinbras to be made king of Denmark. Then he dies.

Fortinbras marches into the room accompanied by the English ambassadors, who announce that Rosencrantz and Guildenstern are dead. Horatio says that he will tell everyone assembled the story that led to the gruesome scene now on display. Fortinbras orders for Hamlet to be carried away like a soldier.

ANALYSIS OF MAJOR CHARACTERS IN *HAMLET*

HAMLET

Hamlet, an enigmatic, intelligent man, has fascinated audiences and readers for centuries. Neither the characters in the play nor the readers of it can agree on Hamlet's personality, veracity, or intentions. Hamlet himself tells the other characters that there is more to him than meets the eye, but he is not forthcoming about his true nature. When he speaks, he sounds as if he is leaving out something important, maybe something even he is not aware of. The ability to write soliloquies and dialogues that create this effect is one of Shakespeare's most impressive achievements.

Hamlet, whose studies at university are interrupted by his father's death, is very philosophical and contemplative. He is particularly drawn to difficult questions or questions that cannot be answered with any certainty. Faced with solid evidence that his uncle murdered his father, evidence that most people would accept as proof, Hamlet becomes obsessed with irrefutably proving his uncle's guilt before trying to act. He is also plagued by questions about the afterlife, about the wisdom of suicide, and about what happens to bodies after death, among other things.

Although he is thoughtful to the point of obsession, Hamlet is also rash and impulsive. When he does act, it is with surprising swiftness and little or no premeditation, as when he stabs Polonius through a curtain without even checking to see who he is trying to kill. We do not know whether Hamlet is truly mad or feigning madness, but in either case he steps easily into the role of a madman, behaving erratically and upsetting the other characters with his wild speech and pointed innuendos.

Hamlet is also melancholy and discontented with the state of affairs in Denmark, in his own family, and in the world at large. He is angry and disappointed with his mother for marrying his uncle so quickly and he casts off Ophelia, a woman he once claimed to love, in the harshest terms. His words often indicate his disgust with and distrust of women in general. At a number of points in the play, he contemplates his own death and the option of suicide.

CLAUDIUS

Hamlet's antagonist is a shrewd, lustful king who contrasts sharply with the other male characters in the play. Whereas most of the other important men in *Hamlet* are preoccupied with ideas of justice, revenge, and moral balance, Claudius is most concerned with maintaining power, perhaps because of the criminal way in which he seized it. Claudius is tormented by the knowledge that he murdered his brother in order to attain the throne.

The old King Hamlet is remembered as a stern warrior, but Claudius is a politician whose main weapon is his ability to manipulate others through his skillful use of language. Claudius killed Hamlet's father by pouring poison in his ear, and his speech is compared to this same method of murder. Claudius loves Gertrude, but he may have married her as a strategic move, to ensure that Hamlet did not make a successful claim to the throne after the death of King Hamlet. As the play progresses, Claudius's mounting fear of Hamlet's insanity makes him increasingly preoccupied with himself and his safety. When Gertrude tells him that Hamlet has killed Polonius, for example, Claudius remarks that he would have been in danger had he been in the room, a comment he later repeats to Laertes. Claudius's craftiness undoes him in the end. In Act V, scene ii, rather than allowing Laertes only two methods of killing Hamlet (the sharpened sword and the poisoned blade), Claudius insists on a third (the poisoned goblet). When Gertrude inadvertently drinks the poison and dies, Hamlet is at last able to bring himself to kill Claudius.

GERTRUDE

Many of Gertrude's actions and feelings are hard to read. We do not know whether she was involved with Claudius before the death of her husband, whether she loved her husband, whether she knew about Claudius's plan to commit the murder, whether she married Claudius simply to keep her high station in Denmark, whether she believes Hamlet when he insists that he is not mad, or whether she intentionally betrays Hamlet to Claudius.

These questions can be answered in numerous ways, depending upon one's reading of the play. We do know that Gertrude craves affection and has a strong instinct for self-preservation. Hamlet's most famous comment about Gertrude is his furious condemnation of women in general: "Frailty, thy name is woman!" (I.ii.146). This comment is as much indicative of Hamlet's agonized state of mind as of anything else, but Gertrude does seem morally frail. Instead of thinking critically about her situation, she makes instinctive choices that seem safe, as when she immediately runs to Claudius after her confrontation with Hamlet. She is at her best in social situations (I.ii and V.ii), when her natural grace and charm suggest a rich, rounded personality.

THEMES, MOTIFS, & SYMBOLS IN *HAMLET*

THEMES

THE IMPOSSIBILITY OF CERTAINTY What separates *Hamlet* from other revenge plays is that the action we expect to see, particularly from Hamlet himself, is continually postponed while Hamlet tries to obtain more certain knowledge about what he is doing. He questions that which the people around him take for granted: that ghosts exist; that the ghost of Hamlet's father is what it appears to be and not a lying fiend; that the ghost has reliable knowledge about its own death. Hamlet also wonders how we know for certain the facts about a crime that has no witnesses. He wonders if he can know the state of Claudius's soul by watching his behavior or know the facts of what Claudius did by observing the state of his soul. He wonders if our actions will have their intended consequences, and if we can know anything about the afterlife. His refusal to leap to conclusions about these questions paralyzes him.

THE COMPLEXITY OF ACTION In *Hamlet*, the difficulty of taking reasonable, effective action is complicated by rational considerations, such as the need for certainty. It is also complicated by emotional, ethical, and psychological factors. Hamlet seems to question whether it is even possible to act in a controlled, purposeful way. When he does act, he does so blindly, recklessly, and violently. The other characters think much less about the philosophy of action, and act without first worrying about whether it is possible to act effectively—but the fact that all of their actions miscarry might mean that Hamlet is right to worry. By taking bold action, Claudius gets a queen and a crown, but his conscience torments him and he is beset by threats to his authority. In the end, his power grab results in his death. Laertes resolves that nothing will distract him from acting out his revenge, but he is easily influenced and manipulated into serving Claudius's ends, and his poisoned rapier is turned upon himself.

DEATH In the aftermath of his father's murder, Hamlet is obsessed with the idea of death, and over the course of the play he considers death from many perspectives. He ponders both the spiritual aftermath of death and the physical remainders of the dead, such as Yorick's skull and the decaying corpses in the cemetery. Hamlet often thinks about his own death, wondering whether or not suicide is a morally legitimate action in an unbearably painful world. Hamlet's grief and misery pain him so much that he frequently longs for death to end his suffering, but he fears that if he commits suicide he will be consigned to eternal suffering in hell. (Christianity prohibits suicide.) In his famous "To be or not to be" soliloquy

(III.i), Hamlet concludes that no one would choose to endure the pain of life if he or she were not afraid of what will come after death, and that it is this fear of what happens after we die that makes us worry about complex moral considerations and prevents us from taking action.

MOTIFS

INCEST AND INCESTUOUS DESIRE Hamlet and the ghost frequently refer to incest in connection with Gertrude and Claudius, who used to be siblings-in-law. A subtle hint of incestuous desire can be found in Laertes' relationship with Ophelia: Laertes sometimes speaks to his sister in suggestively sexual terms and, at her funeral, leaps into her grave to hold her in his arms. The strongest overtones of incestuous desire are present in the relationship between Hamlet and Gertrude. Hamlet is fixated on Gertrude's sex life with Claudius and preoccupied with her in general, storming into her bedroom and lecturing her on the disgusting nature of female sexuality.

EARS AND HEARING In *Hamlet*, language is slippery. Words are used to communicate facts, but they can also be used to distort the truth, manipulate other people, and further corrupt quests for power. Claudius, the shrewd politician, is the most obvious example of a man who manipulates words to enhance his own power. The sinister uses of words are represented by images of ears and hearing, from Claudius's murder of the king by pouring poison into his ear to Hamlet's claim to Horatio that "I have words to speak in thine ear will make thee dumb" (IV.vi.21). The ghost points to the poison poured in the king's ear by Claudius as a symbol of the corrosive effect of Claudius's dishonesty on the health of Denmark. Declaring that the story that he was killed by a snake is a lie, he says that "the whole ear of Denmark" is "rankly abused" (I.v.36–38).

SYMBOLS

YORICK'S SKULL In *Hamlet*, physical objects are rarely used to represent thematic ideas. One important exception is Yorick's skull, which Hamlet discovers in the graveyard in the first scene of Act V. The skull makes Hamlet think about the inevitability of death and bodily disintegration. He reveals his fascination with the physical consequences of death, tracing the skull's mouth and saying, "Here hung those lips that I have kissed I know not how oft" (V.i.174–75). Physical decomposition after death is an image that recurs throughout the play. Hamlet frequently alludes to the eventual decay of every human body: Polonius will be eaten by worms, even kings are eaten by worms, and dust from the decayed body of Alexander the Great might be used to plug a hole in a beer barrel.

ROT In *Hamlet*, the welfare of the royal family affects the health of the state as a whole. The play's early scenes explore the general anxiety and dread that surround the transfer of power from one ruler to the next. Throughout the play, characters draw explicit connections between the moral legitimacy of a ruler and the health of the nation. Denmark is frequently described as a physical body made ill by the moral corruption of Claudius and Gertrude, and many observers interpret the presence of the ghost as a supernatural omen indicating that "[s]omething is rotten in the state of Denmark" (I.iv.67). The dead King Hamlet is portrayed as a strong, forthright ruler under whose guard the state was in good health, while Claudius, a wicked politician, is portrayed as a power-hungry man who has corrupted and compromised Denmark. At the end of the play, the upright Fortinbras's rise to power suggests that Denmark will be strengthened once again.

IMPORTANT QUOTATIONS FROM *HAMLET*

1. O that this too too solid flesh would melt,
   Thaw, and resolve itself into a dew!
   Or that the Everlasting had not fixed
   His canon 'gainst self-slaughter! O God! O God!
   How weary, stale, flat, and unprofitable
   Seem to me all the uses of this world!

Fie on 't! O fie! 'tis an unweeded garden,
That grows to seed; things rank and gross in nature
Possess it merely. That it should come to this!
But two months dead!—nay, not so much, not two:
So excellent a king; that was, to this,
Hyperion to a satyr; so loving to my mother,
That he might not beteem the winds of heaven
Visit her face too roughly. Heaven and earth!
Must I remember? Why, she would hang on him
As if increase of appetite had grown
By what it fed on: and yet, within a month,—
Let me not think on 't,—Frailty, thy name is woman!—
A little month; or ere those shoes were old
With which she followed my poor father's body
Like Niobe, all tears;—why she, even she,—
O God! a beast that wants discourse of reason,
Would have mourned longer,—married with mine uncle,
My father's brother; but no more like my father
Than I to Hercules: within a month;
Ere yet the salt of most unrighteous tears
Had left the flushing in her galled eyes,
She married:—O, most wicked speed, to post
With such dexterity to incestuous sheets!
It is not, nor it cannot come to good;
But break my heart,—for I must hold my tongue.

Location: I.ii.129–158

Speaker: Hamlet

Context: Hamlet has agreed to remain in Denmark instead of continuing his studies at Wittenberg; angst-ridden, he contemplates his father's death and his mother's swift remarriage.

In this soliloquy, Hamlet considers suicide. The world is "weary, stale, flat, and unprofitable," so he desires his flesh to "melt" and wishes that God had not made "self-slaughter" (suicide) a sin. In other words, suicide seems like a desirable alternative to life in a painful world, but religion forbids it. Hamlet goes on to describe the causes of his pain, specifically his intense disgust at his mother's marriage to Claudius. He describes the haste of their marriage, noting that the shoes his mother wore to his father's funeral were not worn out before her marriage to Claudius. He compares Claudius and his father, saying his father was "so excellent a king" while Claudius is a bestial "satyr." He blames his mother for remarrying so quickly, saying she leaped into "incestuous sheets," and blames all women for being fickle and unfaithful. ("Frailty, thy name is woman!") The marriage, he thinks, is a bad omen for Denmark.

---

2. Give thy thoughts no tongue,
  Nor any unproportioned thought his act.
  Be thou familiar, but by no means vulgar.
  Those friends thou hast, and their adoption tried,
  Grapple them unto thy soul with hoops of steel;
  But do not dull thy palm with entertainment
  Of each new-hatched, unfledged comrade. Beware
  Of entrance to a quarrel; but, being in,
  Bear 't that the opposed may beware of thee.
  Give every man thine ear, but few thy voice:
  Take each man's censure, but reserve thy judgment.
  Costly thy habit as thy purse can buy,
  But not expressed in fancy; rich, not gaudy:

For the apparel oft proclaims the man;
And they in France of the best rank and station
Are most select and generous chief in that.
Neither a borrower nor a lender be:
For loan oft loses both itself and friend;
And borrowing dulls the edge of husbandry.
This above all: to thine own self be true;
And it must follow, as the night the day,
Thou canst not then be false to any man.

Location: I.iii.59-80
Speaker: Polonius to Laertes
Context: Polonius gives his son Laertes advice about how to live before Laertes leaves for France.

Polonius's advice amounts to a list of clichés: keep your thoughts to yourself; do not act rashly; treat people with familiarity but not excessively so; hold on to old friends and be slow to trust new ones; avoid fighting but fight boldly if it is unavoidable; be a good listener; accept criticism but do not be judgmental; maintain a proper appearance; do not borrow or lend money; and be true to yourself. Polonius's unexceptional fatherly advice shows how ordinary Laertes' relationship with his father is compared to Hamlet's.

---

3. *Something is rotten in the state of Denmark.*

Location: I.iv.67
Speaker: Marcellus
Context: Marcellus and Horatio debate whether or not to follow Hamlet and the ghost into the dark night.

Marcellus's line refers both to the idea that the ghost is a bad omen for Denmark, and to the larger theme of the connection between the moral legitimacy of a ruler and the health of the state. The ghost is a visible symptom of the rottenness of Denmark brought about by Claudius's crime.

---

4. *I have of late, — but wherefore I know not, — lost all my mirth, forgone all custom of exercises; and indeed, it goes so heavily with my disposition that this goodly frame, the earth, seems to me a sterile promontory; this most excellent canopy, the air, look you, this brave o'erhanging firmament, this majestical roof fretted with golden fire, — why, it appears no other thing to me than a foul and pestilent congregation of vapors. What a piece of work is man! How noble in reason! how infinite in faculties! in form and moving, how express and admirable! in action how like an angel! in apprehension, how like a god! the beauty of the world! the paragon of animals! And yet, to me, what is this quintessence of dust?*

Location: II.ii.287–298
Speaker: Hamlet to Rosencrantz and Guildenstern
Context: Hamlet explains why Gertrude and Claudius have sent for Rosencrantz and Guildenstern to cheer him up.

Hamlet's explanation of the melancholy that has afflicted him since his father's death is essentially a rhetorical exercise, building up an elaborate and glorified picture of the earth and humanity before declaring it all merely a "quintessence of dust." Hamlet examines the earth, the air, and the sun, and rejects them as "a sterile promontory" and "a foul and pestilent congregation of vapors." He then describes human beings from several perspectives, each one glorifying them more than the last. Human reason is noble, human abilities infinite, human movements fast and admirable, human actions angelic, and human understanding godlike. But to Hamlet, humankind is merely dust—a recurring thought that reaches its height in Hamlet's speech over Yorick's skull. It is telling that Hamlet describes humankind as more impressive in "apprehension" (that is, in understanding) than in action. Hamlet himself is more prone to thinking and apprehending than to acting, which is why he delays so long before seeking his revenge on Claudius.

---

5. *To be, or not to be: that is the question:*
Whether 'tis nobler in the mind to suffer
The slings and arrows of outrageous fortune
Or to take arms against a sea of troubles,
And by opposing end them? — To die, — to sleep, —
No more; and by a sleep to say we end
The heartache, and the thousand natural shocks
That flesh is heir to, — 'tis a consummation
Devoutly to be wished. To die, — to sleep; —
To sleep: perchance to dream: — ay, there's the rub;
For in that sleep of death what dreams may come,
When we have shuffled off this mortal coil,
Must give us pause: there's the respect
That makes calamity of so long life;
For who would bear the whips and scorns of time,
The oppressor's wrong, the proud man's contumely,
The pangs of despised love, the law's delay,
The insolence of office, and the spurns
That patient merit of the unworthy takes,
When he himself might his quietus make
With a bare bodkin? who would these fardels bear,
To grunt and sweat under a weary life,
But that the dread of something after death, —
The undiscovered country, from whose bourn
No traveler returns, — puzzles the will,
And makes us rather bear those ills we have
Than fly to others that we know not of?
Thus conscience does make cowards of us all;
And thus the native hue of resolution
Is sicklied o'er with the pale cast of thought;
And enterprises of great pith and moment,
With this regard, their currents turn awry,
And lose the name of action.

Location: III.i.58–90
Speaker: Hamlet
Context: Tormented by his sense of his responsibility to avenge his father's death, Hamlet contemplates why people do not commit suicide.

In the most famous speech of the English language, Hamlet examines the moral legitimacy of suicide in an unbearably painful world. He first debates the possibility of committing suicide as a logical problem: "To be, or not to be" — that is, to live or not to live. He then weighs the moral ramifications of living and dying. Is it nobler to passively suffer life, with its "slings and arrows of outrageous fortune," or to try to put an end to suffering? He compares death to sleep and thinks of death as an end to suffering, pain, and uncertainty, "[t]he heartache, and the thousand natural shocks / That flesh is heir to." He decides that suicide is a desirable course of action, "a consummation / Devoutly to be wished." But as signaled by the religious word "devoutly," there is more to the question — namely, what will happen in the afterlife. Hamlet reconfigures his metaphor of death as sleep to include the possibility of dreaming. He says that the dreams that may come in the sleep of death are daunting, that they "must give us pause." The possibility of nightmares lead us to hesitate before committing suicide, as does the possibility that dreams will not exist at all, because consciousness will not exist after death.

Hamlet decides that it is the impossibility of knowing what happens after death that prevents humans from killing themselves to end the pain of life. He outlines a long list of the miseries of experience, ranging from lovesickness to hard work to political oppression, and asks who would choose to bear those miseries if he could bring himself peace with a knife. He answers his own question, saying no one would choose to live if not for "the dread of something after death," which makes people submit to the suffering of their lives rather than choose another state of existence which might be even more miserable. The dread of the afterlife that our consciousnesses allow, Hamlet concludes, makes action impossible.

Hamlet's speech connects many of the play's main themes, including Hamlet's obsession with death and suicide, the impossibility of knowledge in a spiritually ambiguous universe, and the tension between thought and action. The speech also illuminates Hamlet's thought processes: his relentless intellect works furiously to find a logical solution to his misery. Religion has proved inadequate to spur him on to action. Here, Hamlet turns to a logical philosophical inquiry and finds it equally frustrating.

JULIUS CAESAR

Brutus helps murder Caesar to protect Roman liberty, but Mark Antony casts doubt on Brutus's motives, drives him out of Rome, and hunts him down.

JULIUS CAESAR IN CONTEXT

Julius Caesar takes place in ancient Rome in 44 B.C., when Rome was the center of an empire stretching from Britain to North Africa and from Persia to Spain. As the empire grew stronger, the dangers threatening its existence increased: Rome suffered from constant infighting between ambitious military leaders and the weak senators to whom they supposedly owed allegiance. The empire also suffered from a sharp division between citizens, who were represented in the senate, and plebeian masses, who were increasingly underrepresented. A succession of men aspired to rule Rome, Julius Caesar among them. Fearful of Caesar's growing power, a group of conspirators assassinated him. The assassination failed to put an end to Rome's power struggles, and civil war erupted. The plot of *Julius Caesar* includes the events leading up to the assassination of Caesar as well as much of the subsequent war.

Shakespeare's English contemporaries, who were well versed in ancient Greek and Roman history, probably detected parallels between *Julius Caesar*'s portrayal of Rome's shift from republicanism to imperialism and their own country's trend toward consolidated monarchal power. In 1599, when the play first appeared on a stage, Queen Elizabeth I had held the throne for nearly forty years, consolidating her power at the expense of the aristocracy and the House of Commons. She was sixty-six years old, so her reign seemed likely to end soon, but she had no heirs (neither did Julius Caesar). Many feared that her death would plunge England into the kind of chaos that had plagued England during the fifteenth-century Wars of the Roses. In an age when censorship would have limited direct commentary on these worries, Shakespeare perhaps intended the story of Caesar to imply what he could not say outright.

As his chief source in writing *Julius Caesar*, Shakespeare probably used Thomas North's translation of Plutarch's *Lives of the Noble Greeks and Romans*, written in the first century A.D.. Plutarch, who believed that great men propelled history, saw the role of the biographer as inseparable from the role of the historian. Shakespeare followed Plutarch's lead by emphasizing how the actions of Rome's leaders, rather than class conflicts or larger political movements, determined history. However, he also concedes that the leaders' power depends on the fickle favor of the populace.

Contemporary accounts tell us that *Julius Caesar*, Shakespeare's shortest play, was first performed in 1599. It was probably the first play performed in the Globe Theater, the playhouse that was erected around that time in order to accommodate Shakespeare's increasingly successful theater company. The first authoritative text of the play did not appear until the 1623 First Folio edition. The elaborate stage directions suggest that this text was derived from the company's promptbook rather than Shakespeare's manuscript.

JULIUS CAESAR: KEY FACTS

Full title: The Tragedy of Julius Caesar	
Time and place written: 1599; London	
Date of first publication: Published in the First Folio of 1623	
Genre: Tragic drama, historical drama	
Setting (time): 44 B.C.	
Setting (place): Ancient Rome	
Protagonist: Brutus	
Major conflict: Brutus attempts to think only of the public good, but his actions lead to bloodshed and civil war.	

CHARACTERS IN *JULIUS CAESAR*

Antony A friend of Caesar's. Antony is a masterful public speaker, taking an audience of fervent Brutus supporters and convincing them to condemn Brutus as a traitor. Antony's desire to exclude Lepidus from power hints at his own ambitious nature.

Brutus A supporter of the republic. Brutus's inflexible sense of honor makes it easy for Caesar's enemies to manipulate him into believing that Caesar must die in order to preserve the republic. While the other conspirators act out of envy and rivalry, Brutus acts because he loves Caesar but truly believes that his death will benefit Rome. Because he puts matters of state above personal loyalties, Brutus epitomizes Roman virtue.

Julius Caesar A great Roman general and senator. Caesar does not exhibit the hunger for tyranny of which his enemies accuse him. Still, he cannot separate his public life from his private life, and he allows himself to be seduced by the populace's adoration.

Calpurnia Caesar's wife. Calpurnia believes in omens and portents.

Casca A public figure opposed to Caesar's rise to power. Casca believes that Caesar's repeated refusals of the crown are an act designed to lull the populace into believing that he has no personal ambition.

Cassius A talented general and longtime acquaintance of Caesar's. Cassius is sly, envious, impulsive, and unscrupulous. He tricks Brutus into believing that Caesar must die for the good of Rome.

Cicero A Roman senator renowned for his oratorical skill.

Decius A member of the conspiracy against Caesar.

Flavius A tribune (an official elected by the people to protect their rights). Flavius condemns the plebeians for their fickleness in cheering Caesar, when once they cheered Caesar's enemy, Pompey.

Lepidus The third member of Antony's and Octavius's coalition. Antony has a low opinion of Lepidus, but Octavius thinks he is loyal.

Murellus A tribune who condemns the plebeians for their fickleness in cheering Caesar.

Octavius Caesar's adopted son and appointed successor. By following Caesar's example, Octavius emerges as a figure of authority.

Portia Brutus's wife. Portia is accustomed to being Brutus's confidante and worries when Brutus will not tell her what is troubling him. When Antony and Octavius gain power, Portia kills herself out of grief.

JULIUS CAESAR: PLOT OVERVIEW

Two tribunes, Flavius and Murellus, find scores of Roman citizens wandering the streets, neglecting their work in order to watch Julius Caesar's triumphal parade. Caesar has defeated the Roman general Pompey, his archrival, in battle. The tribunes scold the citizens for abandoning their duties and remove decorations from Caesar's statues. Caesar enters with his entourage, including the military and political figures Brutus, Cassius, and Antony. A Soothsayer calls out to Caesar to "beware the Ides of March," but Caesar ignores him and proceeds with his victory celebration (I.ii.19 and I.ii.25).

Cassius and Brutus, both longtime intimates of Caesar and each other, converse. Cassius tells Brutus that he has seemed distant lately; Brutus replies that he has been at war with himself. Cassius states that he wishes Brutus could see himself as others see him, for then Brutus would realize how honored and respected he is. Brutus says that he fears that the people want Caesar to become king, which would overturn the republic. Cassius concurs that people treat Caesar like a god though he is merely a man, no better than Brutus or Cassius. Cassius recalls incidents of Caesar's physical weakness and marvels that this fallible man has become so powerful. He blames his and Brutus's lack of will for allowing Caesar's rise to power: surely the rise of such a man cannot be the work of fate. Brutus considers Cassius's words as Caesar returns. Upon seeing Cassius, Caesar tells Antony that he deeply distrusts Cassius.

Caesar departs, and another politician, Casca, tells Brutus and Cassius that, during the celebration, Antony offered the crown to Caesar three times and the people cheered, but Caesar refused it each time. He reports that Caesar then fell to the ground and had some kind of seizure before the crowd; his demonstration of weakness, however, did not alter the plebeians' devotion to him. Brutus goes home to consider Cassius's words regarding Caesar's poor qualifications to rule, while Cassius hatches a plot to draw Brutus into a conspiracy against Caesar.

That night, Rome is plagued with violent weather and a variety of bad omens and portents. Brutus finds letters in his house apparently written by Roman citizens worried that Caesar has become too powerful. The letters have in fact been forged and planted by Cassius, who knows that if Brutus believes it is the people's will, he will support a plot to remove Caesar from power. A committed supporter of the republic, Brutus fears the possibility of a dictator-led empire, worrying that the populace would lose its voice. Cassius arrives at Brutus's home with his conspirators, and Brutus, who has already been won over by the letters, takes control of the meeting. The men agree to lure Caesar from his house and kill him. Cassius wants to kill Antony too, for Antony will surely try to hinder their plans, but Brutus disagrees, believing that too many deaths will render their plot too bloody and dishonor them. Having agreed to spare Antony, the conspirators depart. Portia, Brutus's wife, observes that Brutus appears preoccupied. She pleads with him to confide in her, but he rebuffs her.

Caesar prepares to go to the Senate. His wife, Calpurnia, begs him not to go, describing recent nightmares she has had in which a statue of Caesar streamed with blood and smiling men bathed their hands in the blood. Caesar refuses to yield to fear and insists on going about his daily business. Finally, Calpurnia convinces him to stay home—if not out of caution, then as a favor to her. But Decius, one of the conspirators, then arrives and convinces Caesar that Calpurnia has misinterpreted her dreams and the recent omens. Caesar departs for the Senate in the company of the conspirators.

As Caesar proceeds through the streets toward the Senate, the Soothsayer again tries but fails to get his attention. The citizen Artemidorus hands him a letter warning him about the conspirators, but Caesar refuses to read it, saying that his closest personal concerns are his last priority. At the Senate, the conspirators speak to Caesar, bowing at his feet and encircling him. One by one, they stab him to death. When Caesar sees his dear friend Brutus among his murderers, he gives up his struggle and dies.

The murderers bathe their hands and swords in Caesar's blood, thus bringing Calpurnia's premonition to fruition. Antony, having been led away on a false pretext, returns and pledges allegiance to Brutus but weeps over Caesar's body. He shakes hands with the conspirators, thus marking them all as guilty while appearing to make a gesture of conciliation. When Antony asks why they killed Caesar, Brutus replies that he will explain their purpose in a funeral oration. Antony asks to be allowed to speak over the body as well; Brutus grants his permission, though Cassius remains suspicious of Antony. The conspirators depart, and Antony, alone now, swears that Caesar's death shall be avenged.

Brutus and Cassius go to the Forum to speak to the public. Cassius exits to address another part of the crowd. Brutus declares to the masses that though he loved Caesar, he loves Rome more, and Caesar's ambition posed a danger to Roman liberty. The speech placates the crowd. Antony appears with Caesar's body, and Brutus departs after turning the pulpit over to Antony. Repeatedly referring to Brutus as "an honorable man," Antony's speech becomes increasingly sarcastic; questioning the claims that Brutus made in his speech that Caesar acted only out of ambition, Antony points out that Caesar brought much wealth and glory to Rome, and three times turned down offers of the crown. Antony then produces Caesar's will but announces that he will not read it for it would upset the people inordinately. The crowd nevertheless begs him to read the will, so he descends from the pulpit to stand next to Caesar's body. He describes Caesar's horrible death and shows Caesar's wounded body to the crowd. He then reads Caesar's will, which bequeaths a sum of money to every citizen and orders that his private gardens be made public. The crowd becomes enraged that this generous man lies dead; calling Brutus and Cassius traitors, the masses set off to drive them from the city.

Meanwhile, Caesar's adopted son and appointed successor, Octavius, arrives in Rome and forms a three-person coalition with Antony and Lepidus. They prepare to fight Cassius and Brutus, who have gone into exile and are raising armies outside the city. At the conspirators' camp, Brutus and Cassius have a heated argument regarding matters of money and honor, but they ultimately reconcile. Brutus reveals that he is sick with grief, for in his absence Portia has killed herself. The two continue to prepare for battle with Antony and Octavius. That night, the ghost of Caesar appears to Brutus, announcing that Brutus will meet him again on the battlefield.

Octavius and Antony march their army toward Brutus and Cassius. Antony tells Octavius where to attack, but Octavius says that he will make his own orders; he is already asserting his authority as the heir of Caesar and the next ruler of Rome. The opposing generals meet on the battlefield and exchange insults before beginning combat.

Cassius witnesses his own men fleeing and hears that Brutus's men are not performing effectively. Cassius sends one of his men, Pindarus, to see how matters are progressing. From afar, Pindarus sees one of their leaders, Cassius's best friend, Titinius, being surrounded by cheering troops and concludes that he has been captured. Cassius despairs and orders Pindarus to kill him with his own sword. He dies proclaiming that Caesar is avenged. Titinius himself then arrives–the men encircling him were actually his comrades, cheering a victory he had earned. Titinius sees Cassius's corpse and, mourning the death of his friend, kills himself.

Brutus learns of the deaths of Cassius and Titinius with a heavy heart, and prepares to take on the Romans again. When his army loses, doom appears imminent. Brutus asks one of his men to hold his sword while he impales himself on it. Finally, Caesar can rest satisfied, he says as he dies. Octavius and Antony arrive. Antony speaks over Brutus's body, calling him the noblest Roman of all. While the other conspirators acted out of envy and ambition, he observes, Brutus genuinely believed that he acted for the benefit of Rome. Octavius orders that Brutus be buried in the most honorable way. The men then depart to celebrate their victory.

THEMES AND SYMBOLS IN *JULIUS CAESAR*

THEMES

FATE VERSUS FREE WILL Cassius refuses to believe that Caesar's rising power is fated, calling a belief in fate nothing more than passivity or cowardice. As he tells Brutus, "The fault, dear Brutus, is not in our stars, / But in ourselves, that we are underlings" (I.ii.140–142). He blames the situation on his own and Brutus's passivity, not on a predestined plan. In contrast, Caesar purports to believe in fate. He wonders why men fear death, since they can do nothing to control the hour of their own deaths. He believes that certain events lie beyond human control, and that to realize this is to free one's self from fear. Both men get to maintain their worldviews to the last. Cassius takes control of his life, assassinating Caesar and feeling he has changed the course of Roman history. Caesar dies after a series of portents, probably feeling that his death was fated.

THE DANGER OF NEGLECTING THE PRIVATE SELF Part of the play's tragedy stems from the characters' neglect of private feelings and loyalties in favor of what they believe to be the public good. Brutus rebuffs his wife, Portia, when she pleads with him to confide in her. Believing himself to be acting on the people's will, he murders Caesar without consulting her. Brutus puts aside his personal loyalty to Caesar and kills him out of loyalty to the public. Cassius also focuses exclusively on his public life. Caesar's neglect of his private life indirectly leads to his death. Although he briefly agrees to stay home in order to please Calpurnia, who has dreamed of his murder, he gives way to ambition after Decius tells him that the senators plan to offer him the crown. When Caesar stops seeing the difference between his omnipotent, immortal public image and his vulnerable human body, he makes himself vulnerable.

MISINTERPRETATIONS AND MISREADINGS Misinterpretation fills the play, often revealing what characters desire or fear. As Cicero says, "Men may construe things after their fashion, / Clean from the purpose of the things themselves" (I.iii.34–35). The night before Caesar's assassination, Cassius misreads the many portents. He believes they signify the danger that Caesar's impending coronation would bring to the state, when really they warn of the destruction that Cassius is about to wreak on Rome. Cassius encourages Brutus to misinterpret, forging letters that Brutus wrongly believes are authentic pleas from the Roman people. Misinterpretation causes Cassius's death. Pindarus's erroneous conclusion that Titinius has been captured by the enemy causes Cassius to kill himself.

SYMBOLS

OMENS AND PORTENTS Until Caesar's death, each omen and nightmare seems to signal Caesar's impending demise. These portents may simply announce what is fated to occur, or they may be warnings about what might occur if the characters do not take active steps to change their behavior.

WOMEN AND WIVES Calpurnia and Portia function not as sympathetic personalities or sources of insight or poetry but as symbols of the private, domestic realm. Both women ask their husbands to confide in them, to trust them, to combat danger by paying attention to the home. Caesar and Brutus rebuff their wives, actively turning away from the domestic realm.

IMPORTANT QUOTATIONS FROM *JULIUS CAESAR*

1. *He was my friend, faithful and just to me.*
   But Brutus says he was ambitious,
   And Brutus is an honourable man.
   When that the poor have cried, Caesar hath wept.
   Yet Brutus says he was ambitious,
   And Brutus is an honourable man.
   I thrice presented him a kingly crown,
   Which he did thrice refuse. Was this ambition?
   Yet Brutus says he was ambitious,
   And sure he is an honourable man.

Location: III.ii.82–96
Speaker: Antony to the Romans
Context: Antony gives Caesar's funeral oration.

Antony's funeral oration is a rhetorical tour de force, damning the conspirators while appearing to praise them. Antony's rhetoric is the verbal equivalent of his action in the previous scene, when he shook hands with each of the murderers in turn, smearing Caesar's blood among all of them and marking them as guilty while appearing to make a gesture of reconciliation. The funeral oration draws power from repetition. Antony alternates memories of Caesar's friendship and kindness with Brutus's claim that Caesar was "ambitious," making Brutus's claim appear increasingly ridiculous. Antony repeatedly declares that Brutus "is an honourable man," layering on sarcasm until the meaning of the sentiment has been turned on its head. Without showing the crowd what he is doing, Antony incites it to bloodthirsty mutiny.

2. *We at the height are ready to decline.*
   There is a tide in the affairs of men
   Which, taken at the flood, leads on to fortune;
   Omitted, all the voyage of their life
   Is bound in shallows and in miseries.
   On such a full sea are we now afloat,
   And we must take the current when it serves,
   Or lose our ventures.

Location: IV.ii.269-276
Speaker: Brutus to Cassius
Context: Brutus tries to convince Cassius that the time is right to engage Octavius and Antony in battle.

Brutus speaks of a metaphorical "tide" in the lives of human beings: by taking advantage of the high tide, one may float out to sea and travel far. If one misses this chance, the "voyage" will be confined to the shallows. Brutus conceives of life as influenced by both fate and free will: we cannot control fate, just as we cannot control the tide, but we can control our reaction to fate, just as we can choose to swim out with the high tide or stay in the shallows. Brutus assumes that we can tell when the tide is high, but characters repeatedly fail to register fate's opportunities and warnings, neglecting to choose correctly because they don't realize a choice exists.

3. *I could be well moved if I were as you.*
   If I could pray to move, prayers would move me

But I am constant as the Northern Star,
Of whose true fixed and resting quality
There is no fellow in the firmament.
The skies are painted with unnumbered sparks;
They are all fire, and every one doth shine;
But there's but one in all doth hold his place.

Location: III.i.58–65
Speaker: Caesar to the senators
Context: Metellus has asked Caesar to pardon his banished brother, Publius Cimber.

---

4. *[My horse] is a creature that I teach to fight,*
   To wind, to stop, to run directly on,
   His corporal motion governed by my spirit;
   And in some taste is Lepidus but so.
   He must be taught, and trained, and bid go forth—
   A barren-spirited fellow, one that feeds
   On objects, arts, and imitations,
   Which, out of use and staled by other men,
   Begin his fashion. Do not talk of him
   But as a property.

Location: IV.i.31–40
Speaker: Antony to Octavius
Context: Antony and Octavius make plans to retake Rome.

KING JOHN

Challenged from many sides, King John makes and breaks unpredictable alliances with the French, the pope, and his own nobles.

KING JOHN IN CONTEXT

King John presents a perspective on English history radically different from that of Shakespeare's earliest history plays, which portrayed the internal conflicts among the English nobles during the fifteenth-century War of the Roses. Unlike these other plays, *King John* attributes little meaning or significance to the king's reign. The play depicts history as a series of unpredictable events, in which seemingly decisive moments become insignificant episodes in a haphazard universe.

Some critics suggest that the dynastic struggle in *King John* was meant to comment on the contemporary sixteenth-century debate. King John's claim to the throne was based on the will of Richard the Lionhearted, the previous king and John's eldest brother. At the same time, the right of primogeniture supports the claim of Arthur, son of John and Richard's middle brother Geoffrey. The parallels to Queen Elizabeth's situation are numerous: her father Henry VIII named her his heir, and her challenger Mary, Queen of Scots, was the descendant of Henry VIII's eldest sister. The pope excommunicated both John and Elizabeth, and John and Elizabeth's father Henry VIII seized Catholic monastic treasures after declaring independence from the Catholic Church. Foreign powers supported both Arthur and Mary— Arthur by France, Mary by Spain. Like John, Elizabeth reluctantly ordered her challenger executed. Like Arthur's death, Mary's death precipitated a foreign invasion. Like the French forces, the Spanish Armada was destroyed at sea. Such a list of parallels may oversimplify both theater and history, but it also evokes *King John*'s most important problems: the struggle for power with the pope, the threat of invasion, and the issue of illegitimate rule.

Critics believe that Shakespeare based his play on an earlier anonymous play entitled *The Troublesome Reign of John, King of England* (1591). Both this play and *King John* relied on Raphael Holinshed's *Chronicles of England, Scotland, and Ireland* (1587), which Shakespeare drew on extensively throughout the 1590s for his history plays. In the Elizabethan era, John was seen as a proto-Protestant king who had stood up to the Catholic Church, but Shakespeare toned down John's temporary resistance to the pope. John emerges as a supporter of neither the Protestants nor the Catholics. He weakens the Catholic Church by pillaging the monasteries, but eventually gives in to Rome.

KING JOHN: KEY FACTS

Full Title: The Life and Death of King John

Time and place written: 1596; London

Date of first publication: 1623 (First Folio)

Genre: History play; allegory

Setting (time): Thirteenth century

Setting (place): England

Protagonist: The Bastard; King John

Antagonist: King Philip of France; Louis the Dauphin; Cardinal Pandolf

Major conflict: The French, the pope, and the dissatisfied English noblemen all threaten King John's reign.

CHARACTERS IN *KING JOHN*

THE ENGLISH AND ALLIES

Arthur, Duke of Brittany John's young nephew, and the rightful heir to the throne, and Constance's son. Pushed by Constance and backed by the French King Philip, Arthur becomes a meek pawn in the game of royal succession. Arthur himself just wants to be a peaceful shepherd. Arthur's innocent nature prompts his jailer Hubert to spare his life, but Arthur dies when he leaps off the castle walls trying to escape.

Philip the Bastard The illegitimate son of the former King Richard the Lionhearted (King John's eldest brother). The Bastard disavows his rightful inheritance in favor of his younger half-brother in order to become a knight and fight the French. He persistently favors war over truce. As other English noblemen desert, the Bastard remains King John's most loyal supporter. Throughout, he comments on the action, interpreting and analyzing scenes.

Lord Bigot, Pembroke, and Salisbury English noblemen. They defect to the French after Arthur's death but return to the English after they discover that Louis plans to kill them. Salisbury functions as their leader and spokesman.

Blanche Daughter of the King of Spain and John's niece. To cement the shaky alliance between the French and the English, Blanche is married to Louis. She is caught in the middle of the conflict when the French declare war on the English again.

Constance Arthur's mother, who champions his right to the throne and secures French support. She dies after the English capture Arthur.

Eleanor John's mother and staunchest supporter. She dies in France after the battle of Angiers; her death greatly disheartens John.

Essex An English nobleman.

Falconbridge The Bastard's younger half-brother, and the late Robert Falconbridge's legitimate son. He and the Bastard argue over Robert Falconbridge's estate until the Bastard concedes it.

Lady Falconbridge Mother of the Bastard and Falconbridge, and the late Robert Falconbridge's wife. King Richard the Lionhearted, the Bastard's biological father seduced her.

Hubert John's supporter. Hubert is an ugly man. John asks Hubert to kill Arthur, but Hubert, touched by Arthur's innocence, spares his life.

Prince Henry John's son and heir to the throne. At the end of the play, Henry becomes King Henry III.

King John of England The ruler of England. John took the throne because the previous king, his eldest brother Richard the Lionhearted, named him his heir. Legally the throne should have passed to Arthur, the son of John and Richard's deceased middle brother. Throughout the play, the French attack John, the pope challenges him, and his noblemen desert him. He dies after being poisoned by a monk who is angry that John ordered the monasteries plundered after breaking with Rome.

THE FRENCH AND ALLIES

Duke of Austria A French ally the bastard kills in battle.

Chatillon A French messenger.

Louis King Philip's son and the heir (Dauphin) to the French throne. Louis is married to Lady Blanche to cement the tenuous French-English truce, but heads to war when Pandolph pressures Philip. Though he continues his war after Pandolf asks him to pull back, he ultimately allows Pandolf to broker a peace after his reinforcements perish at sea and the English lords desert him.

Count Melun A French nobleman. Mortally wounded in battle, Melun tips off the defecting English lords that Louis plans to behead them if the French win the battle.

King Philip of France The ruler of France, and Louis's father. Philip champions Arthur's claim to the throne and threatens war unless King John abdicates. Philip changes his mind and makes a tenuous peace with the English in exchange for a lucrative marriage for Louis. He changes his mind again when Cardinal Pandolf demands that Philip oppose the English on behalf of the Pope.

THE CATHOLIC CHURCH

Cardinal Pandolf The pope's emissary. Pandolf excommunicates John when John refuses to bow to Church authority, and pressures Philip of France to wage war on the English. Later, he fails to call off the French offensive even after John pledges allegiance to the pope. He eventually succeeds in negotiating peace between the French and the English after both lose many of their soldiers.

KING JOHN: PLOT OVERVIEW

King John's right to the English throne is shaky: Arthur, the young son of John's older brother, has a better claim. King Philip of France threatens war unless John abdicates in Arthur's favor. John heads to battle, supported by the bastard son of the former King Richard the Lionhearted. The English and French battle to a stalemate over the English-controlled town of Angiers. Just as the two armies are about to join forces to destroy Angiers before battling each other, the townspeople propose a truce cemented by a marriage between John's niece Blanche and Philip's son Louis. The bastard is amazed at the absurd progression of events. Just after Louis and Blanche marry, the pope's emissary Cardinal Pandolf, arrives. Pandolf excommunicates John for disobeying the Church, and convinces Philip to make war on England once again. In battle, John captures Arthur and returns to England, where he orders his follower Hubert to assassinate Arthur. Moved by Arthur's innocence, Hubert allows him to escape, but Arthur falls from the castle wall and dies anyway. Outraged by Arthur's death, the English nobles turn against King John and welcome the French invaders. John swears allegiance to the pope, but Cardinal Pandolph fails to persuade Philip to call off his armies. The battle goes badly for the French, and the English nobles come back to John's side. Cardinal Pandolf finally brokers peace between the French and the English. An angry monk poisons John, and he dies. John's son Henry inherits the throne. The Bastard remarks that England cannot be conquered unless she is first weakened by internal strife.

KING JOHN: SCENE SUMMARY

ACT I

England and France go to war because the French King Philip wants the English King John to abdicate in favor of John's nephew Arthur.

I.I Location: London. King John's Northampton palace

King Philip of France supports Arthur's right to the English throne over King John's; John plans to wage war on France, aided by the bastard son of Richard the Lionhearted.

King John of England, his mother Queen Eleanor, and the lords Pembroke, Essex, and Salisbury greet Chatillon, a messenger from France. Chatillon reports that King Philip of France declares that John is not the legitimate King of England. If John does not abdicate in favor of his young nephew Arthur, Philip will declare war. Arthur is the son of John's deceased elder brother, so primogeniture supports his claim to the throne. John refuses to give up his throne and sends Chatillon back to France under threat of violence.

Queen Eleanor suggests that Arthur's troublesome mother Constance must have orchestrated France's involvement in the question of succession. John says that he needs unequivocal possession of the throne to protect England from future conflicts. Eleanor agrees and hints that John's right to the throne is questionable.

A sheriff brings in Falconbridge and Philip the Bastard, two men who want King John to resolve their conflict. They explain that they were both raised as sons of the deceased Robert Falconbridge. The bastard is older. Falconbridge claims that the Bastard is not their father's biological son, but rather the son of the former King Richard the Lionhearted, who spent time at their estate while Robert Falconbridge was away in Germany. The Bastard agrees that he looks nothing like Robert Falconbridge. Falconbridge further claims that his father willed the estate to him, although he is the younger son. John argues that Robert Falconbridge's will does not matter: the Bastard was raised as Robert Falconbridge's eldest son, and so must inherit the property.

Queen Eleanor interrupts and tells the Bastard that he has a choice: he can either claim to be the bastard son of the great Richard the Lionhearted, or inherit the Falconbridge property. She invites him to leave the estate to Falconbridge and follow her attack on France. The bastard agrees, and King John knights him Sir Richard Plantagenet, after Richard the Lionhearted.

Alone, the Bastard contemplates his change of fortune. As a knight, he expects great things, but he must also beware false flattery. Lady Falconbridge, who is Robert Falconbridge's widow and the Bastard's mother, enters to scold Falconbridge for accusing her of having cheated on her husband. The bastard tells her that he has renounced the Falconbridge lands, and asks her about his real father. After hedging, she admits that his father was Richard the Lionhearted, who had seduced her while her husband was away. The Bastard assures her that he could not wish for a better father, and promises to staunchly defend her reputation from anyone who accuses her of sin.

ACT II

Instead of meeting in battle, the French and the English make a weak truce.

II.I Location: English territories in France. Before the walls of Angiers

Their armies in stalemate before Angiers, the French and the English cement a weak truce with a royal marriage.

King Philip of France walks with the Dauphin Louis (the heir to the French throne), Constance, Arthur, and the Duke of Austria. Arthur and Constance thank Austria for joining them against England. Philip urges his men to ready themselves for an attack on Angiers if the town doesn't swear allegiance to Arthur. Chatillon warns Philip that the English approach with a mighty army led by King John and the bastard son of Richard the Lionhearted. Eleanor and Lady Blanche, daughter of the King of Spain, accompany them.

John, Eleanor, Blanche, the Bastard, and Pembroke enter. John offers to hold off his army if Philip accepts his right to the throne. Philip too offers peace if John abdicates in favor of Arthur. When asked, Philip says that heaven has made him guardian of Arthur's rights to the throne.

Eleanor calls Arthur a bastard. Arthur's mother Constance accuses Eleanor of adultery in turn. Austria and the Bastard also exchange insults. Philip interrupts the arguments, and outlines Arthur's claims, which include full possession of English lands in Ireland and France. Eleanor tries to lure Arthur away from the French, but Constance mocks Arthur to keep him in line. Arthur, a sweet-tempered boy, weeps and wishes he were not in the middle of the argument. Constance and Eleanor exchange insults again. Constance again insists that John is a bastard.

Philip silences them again and suggests asking the citizens of Angiers to make a choice. John addresses the people of Angiers and demands that the citizens open their gates to him, on pain of destruction. Philip demands that the citizens open the gates for Arthur. The citizens agree that they are English subjects, but refuse to open the gates until either John or Arthur proves his definitive right to the throne. The citizens stand firm as John and Philip both threaten to destroy the city, so John and Philip urge their armies to battle.

Two heralds, one French and one English, arrive and narrate the bloody battle. The citizens of Angiers note that the French and English armies are equally matched, and resolve to keep the doors closed until one side wins the battle. Philip and John return and appeal to the citizens again, to no avail.

The Bastard comments that the citizens of Angiers are watching the battle from their walls, as though it were a play. He urges John and Philip to make a temporary truce and punish the citizens for their insolence. Once they destroy Angiers, they can break their alliance and continue to fight each other. Both John and Philip agree, but the citizens suggest another idea: Lady Blanche (who is King John's niece) would be a wonderful match for the Dauphin Louis. Such a marriage would unite in truce the three kingdoms of Spain, France, and England. The Bastard is privately surprised that the citizens' proposal has trumped his call to war .

Eleanor advises John to agree to the match because it would enable him to keep his crown. John offers the French several English territories in France as a dowry for Blanche. Louis announces that Blanche transfixes him, and the bastard wryly comments on Louis's swift enrapturement. Blanche also consents to the match: she and Louis join hands and kiss. Philip asks the citizens of Angiers to open their gates. He and Louis remark that Constance has disappeared, probably because she is upset by the truce. John promises to cheer Constance up by giving Arthur a dukedom.

Alone, the Bastard contemplates the madness of kings. In order to prevent Arthur from taking the throne, John has given part of his lands away to Louis. Philip too arrived to make war on England and help Arthur, but left with something else entirely. Greed has converted an honorable war into a vile and weak peace. The Bastard himself is torn. On the one hand, he is still poor and will rail against the rich, but on the other hand, wealth is a good thing. Even kings are willing to sacrifice their honor for gain. The Bastard resolves to worship gain as well.

II.II Location: The French camp outside Angiers

Arthur's mother Constance grieves that the French-English alliance has destroyed Arthur's hopes for the English throne.

Salisbury informs Constance that King John and King Philip have made a truce. Constance is furious that Philip has broken his alliance with her. After Louis marries Blanche, France will get territories that rightfully belong to Arthur. She curses Salisbury, and Arthur tries to soothe her. She tells Arthur that she wishes that he had been born malformed, because then she would not love him or think that he deserves a crown. Instead, Arthur has been blessed by nature, if not by fortune. Both fortune and France are now on John's side. Constance laments her great grief.

ACT III

Incited by the pope's emissary, the French wage war against the English; John takes Arthur prisoner.

III.I Location: Near Angiers. The French camp

On the day of the marriage alliance, Cardinal Pandolf excommunicates John from the Catholic Church, and Philip of France is compelled to wage war against England again.

It is Blanche and Louis's wedding day. King John, King Philip, Eleanor, the Bastard, Constance, and Austria are all in attendance. Philip proclaims that the day will become an annual festival. Constance grumbles about her and Arthur's misfortune. Philip and Austria both try to calm her, but she accuses Philip of betrayal and curses Austria.

Cardinal Pandolf arrives. On behalf of the pope, Pandolf asks John why he has prevented the pope's nominee from becoming Archbishop of Canterbury (the most powerful post of the Catholic hierarchy in England). John replies that the pope has no power over him. Philip warns John against blaspheming, but John declares his independence from the Church. Pandolf announces that he will excommunicate John. Delighted, Constance asks Pandolf to curse John, but he mildly rebuffs her. Pandolf demands that Philip break with John. Constance, Eleanor, the Bastard, and Austria all urge Philip with their own agendas. Perplexed, Philip remains silent throughout the discussion. Pandolf threatens to excommunicate Philip too unless Philip agrees to oppose John and wage war on England, but Philip asks Pandolf to be reasonable: he has just made peace with King John and cemented the alliance with a marriage. How could he now break this new alliance? Pandolf will not be swayed. He reminds Philip that his primary oath is always to the Church. All later allegiances are secondary.

Blanche, despondent, doesn't want her wedding day to become a day of war. She begs Louis not wage war against her Uncle John. Constance begs Louis for his support against England, especially since the Church sanctions it. Finally, when Pandolf threatens to curse Philip, Philip drops John's hand. John and his party make threats, and Blanche mourns her allegiance to both sides of the conflict. The two warring nations once again depart to prepare for battle.

III.II Location: Near Angiers. A battlefield

In battle, John takes Arthur prisoner.

The battle breaks out. The Bastard emerges from the fray with Austria's head. John enters with Arthur as prisoner. He asks Hubert, one of his men, to guard Arthur, and leaves to check on Eleanor.

III.III   Location: Near Angiers. A battlefield

John puts Arthur in his servant Hubert's care, and suggests that Hubert should kill Arthur.

England has won the battle of Angiers. John instructs Eleanor to remain in France and oversee the English territories. He consoles the captive Arthur, telling him that his grandmother Eleanor and his uncle John will treat him lovingly in England. John sends the Bastard ahead to England, to appropriate the wealth of the Catholic Church.

John takes Hubert aside and thanks him for his loyal service. John first tells him that he wants to ask Hubert something, but then changes his mind. He tries to ask Hubert again, but stops himself. Hubert assures John that he loves him well enough to do anything he asks. John points at Arthur and calls Arthur a serpent standing in his way. Hubert promises to keep Arthur out of John's way, but John suggests that the grave might be the best place for him. Hubert promises that Arthur will not live. Pleased, John bids farewell to Eleanor and sets off for England.

III.IV   Location: Near Angiers. The French camp

With France defeated at the battle of Angiers and Arthur captured, Constance despairs, but Pandolf predicts that John will have many problems in England.

Philip speaks to Louis and Pandolf, summarizing the French losses: Angiers is lost and Arthur is captured. Constance enters, disheveled and distracted. She chastises Philip for his short-lived truce with John, and calls mournfully for her own death. Philip tries but fails to soothe her. Pandolf suggests that she suffers from madness, not sorrow, but Constance disagrees. She used to be a queen, mother of heirs to the English throne, but now she is nothing, and her son Arthur is gone. Indeed, if she were mad she could forget Arthur, but her sanity forces her to contemplate suicide. Philip urges her to pull herself together, but when she remembers Arthur, she despairs and leaves. Philip follows.

Louis unburdens himself to Pandolf, but Pandolf urges him to ride out the misfortune and prophesies discord in England. John may have Arthur, Pandolf suggests, but doesn't have popular support, and will be forced to defend his kingdom time and time again. Pandolf also predicts that John will kill Arthur, and reasons that Louis and Blanche will be able to make a claim for the English throne. When Louis continues to despair, Pandolf says that after John kills Arthur the appalled English will turn against their King John and embrace Louis. The people of England will also be outraged when John plunders the Catholic monasteries. Pandolf urges Louis to plan another assault with King Philip.

ACT IV

Arthur escapes from prison but dies anyway; outraged English lords defect to the French side.

IV.I.   Location: England. A prison

Moved by Arthur's innocence, Hubert spares Arthur's life and secretly lets him out of prison.

Hubert tells executioners to hide and stay ready. He calls in Arthur. Arthur laments his noble birth. If he had been born a simple shepherd, he would not be involved in dynastic wars. Hubert is moved by Arthur's innocence. He shows Arthur an order to blind Arthur with hot iron. Arthur asks Hubert whether Hubert plans to do it, considering how close they have become. Hubert tells him that he must.

Hubert calls the executioners. Frightened, Arthur tells Hubert that he will submit to his punishment without struggle. Hubert sends away the executioners and tells Arthur to prepare himself. Arthur begs Hubert to spare his life. Even hot iron will cool when it comes in contact with his innocent tears, and

Arthur asks if Hubert could be more hard-hearted than iron. Finally, Hubert relents and promises not to hurt Arthur, making Arthur promise not to let John know that he is still alive.

IV.II Location: England. King John's court

Threatened by England's indignation at Arthur's death and the approach of a French army, John is delighted to hear that Arthur is still alive.

John has just had a second coronation ceremony, which his lords Pembroke and Salisbury have found wasteful and ridiculous. John defends himself, but promises to do as they advise in the future. They ask that Arthur be released. The people want it, and Arthur poses little threat. John agrees. Hubert enters. While John and Hubert speak in private, Pembroke and Salisbury confer. They have heard that Hubert was hired to assassinate Arthur, and fear the worst. John returns and explains that Arthur has died. Salisbury and Pembroke are displeased and suggest that Arthur was murdered. They depart to attend to Arthur's burial.

John comments that death has only hurt his reign. His nobles are furious, which weakens his power. A messenger reports the approach of a huge French army. John wonders why Eleanor failed to warn him about the mobilization of the French, but the messenger reports that both Eleanor and Constance are dead. John is upset.

The Bastard arrives to report on his mission to seize monastic properties. He has been successful, but has heard unpleasant rumors that many people have been having visions and strange dreams. The Bastard introduces John to a citizen who predicts that John will abdicate before the next holiday. John charges Hubert to imprison and then hang the citizen.

John and the Bastard discuss the approaching French army and the displeased English nobles. John sends the Bastard to mollify and win over the nobles. Hubert returns and reports that people have seen an unsettling vision: four moons fixed in the sky with another moon circling around them. The people mourn Arthur's death and make dreadful prophesies.

John accuses Hubert of convincing him to murder Arthur. Hubert denies it and shows John the order to kill Arthur, in John's own handwriting. John insists that it is Hubert's ugliness that made him even consider a deed as ugly as murder. He bemoans his situation. His lords and his people are discontented, and France threatens his country. Hubert interrupts him to report that Arthur still lives. Despite his ugliness, Hubert says, his heart is too pure to kill a child. John is delighted, apologizes for his harsh words, and orders Hubert to announce that Arthur lives.

IV.III Location: Outside King John's castle

Trying to escape, Arthur falls to his death; outraged, English nobles plan to defect to the French side.

Arthur stands on the walls of the castle in disguise, planning to jump off the wall. Even if he dies, no one will recognize the body. He jumps and dies.

Salisbury and Pembroke enter with Lord Bigot, discussing their upcoming meeting with Louis. The Bastard comes to convince them to be loyal to King John. They refuse, and exchange barbed comments. Suddenly Salisbury notices Arthur's body. The lords are horrified, and outraged that John would have ordered Arthur killed in so barbaric a manner.

Hubert enters and announces that Arthur is alive. Salisbury accuses him of murder and draws his sword. The Bastard tries to keep the peace, but Bigot demands to know who killed Arthur. Hubert says that he saw Arthur alive recently. The lords do not believe him, and leave to join the French forces.

The Bastard tells Hubert that he will certainly be damned if he knew of the plan to kill Arthur thus. Hubert insists that Arthur was alive when he left him. The Bastard tells Hubert to carry Arthur's body away, thinking that he cannot tell truth from lies. He sees Arthur in Hubert's arms and wonders at how easily Hubert lifts and carries the hopes of England. Expecting much turmoil, the Bastard leaves to join King John.

ACT V

The English nobles return to the English side; the Pope's emissary manages to broker peace; King John dies absurdly, and the throne passes to his son Henry.

V.I Location: London. King John's court

King John swears allegiance to the Catholic Church in return for help negotiating with the approaching French army.

Cardinal Pandolf ceremoniously crowns King John in the name of the pope. John urges Pandolf to keep his end of the bargain and convince the French to give up their attack. Pandolf departs.

The Bastard enters to report on the French offensive: aided by English nobles, the French have entered London. John wonders why the English nobles did not remain on his side after they found out that Arthur was alive. The Bastard tells him that Arthur is dead. John falters, but the Bastard urges him to be strong in the face of his problems. John tells the Bastard about his deal with Pandolf. Upset by John's new pacifism, the Bastard urges John to fight the French. John agrees, and puts the Bastard in command of the English army.

V.II Location: Suffolk. St. Edmundsbury

Cardinal Pandolf fails to persuade the French to call off their attack.

Louis of France marches with English noblemen Salisbury, Pembroke, and Lord Bigot, as well as the French Count Melun. Louis wants the English lords to put down their allegiance to him in writing, but Salisbury assures him that they will be loyal. Salisbury mourns the sadness of being forced to make war on his own country. Louis compliments Salisbury on his noble sentiments and urges him onward to a successful fight.

Pandolf enters. He announces that John has reconciled with the Church, and orders Louis to withdraw his army. Louis refuses, saying that he will not bow to anyone else's commands. Pandolf and the Church may have started this war, Louis adds, but he will finish it. Louis also reminds Pandolf that the war is in defense of Arthur's claim to the throne.

The Bastard enters and announces to Louis that John has prepared an enormous army that will crush the tiny French forces. Moreover, the Bastard tells the English lords that their wives are on the English side. Louis calls for battle, and the Bastard threatens Louis with death.

V.III Location: The battlefield

The French reinforcements have been destroyed.

John, distraught, runs into Hubert. A messenger reports that the French army's expected reinforcements have been wrecked at sea. Feeling weak, John leaves to seek the Bastard.

V.IV Location: Elsewhere on the battlefield

The defecting English noblemen find out that the French plan to betray them, and so decide to return to the English side.

Salisbury, Pembroke, and Bigot meet on the field, astonished that King John's forces have proven so powerful. The French Count Melun enters, wounded. He urges the English lords to return to King John and plead for mercy. Even if the French win the battle, Louis has ordered the English lords beheaded. The English are incredulous, but Melun insists that because he is dying, he has no reason to lie. Salisbury believes him, and urges Pembroke and Bigot to return to John.

V.V Location: Elsewhere on the battlefield

The battle is going very badly for the French.

Louis enters, remarking on the strength of the English army. A messenger arrives with news: Melun is dead, the English lords have deserted back to the English side, and the reinforcements from France have been shipwrecked off the English shore. Louis is dismayed: his chances for victory are now very slim indeed.

V.VI Location: Lincolnshire. Swineshead Abbey

An angry monk has poisoned King John.

With the outcome of the war still uncertain, Hubert and the Bastard encounter each other in the darkness. Hubert reports that King John's food taster, a monk angered by the plunder of the monasteries, has poisoned him. Hubert adds that the English lords have begged forgiveness and returned to the English side. The Bastard tells Hubert that during the night, his soldiers drowned in the rising tide on the flatlands. The Bastard alone escaped. He asks Hubert to convey him to see John before John dies.

V.VII Location: Lincolnshire. Swineshead Abbey

Cardinal Pandolf has brokered a peace with the French; John's son Henry inherits the throne.

Pembroke reports to Prince Henry, Salisbury, and Bigot that King John can still speak. Henry laments the sickness of John, who has lost his mind but retained his bodily health. John is brought in, babbling. The Bastard arrives and reports that the French forces approach unimpeded because the Bastard's forces have drowned.

King John dies. The Bastard swears to avenge John's death and urges the lords to assemble their forces to repel the French from England. Salisbury reports that Cardinal Pandolf has brokered a peace with the French. The Bastard wants to attack anyway, but Salisbury insists that the peace agreement has been made.

The Bastard and the other lords swear allegiance to the new King Henry. The Bastard speaks of the suffering that they have endured. He remarks that England has never been defeated except when her enemies were helped by internal strife.

THEMES, MOTIFS, & SYMBOLS IN *KING JOHN*

THEMES

HISTORY AS ABSURD AND RANDOM *King John* suggests that historical events happen at random, not guided by any grand plan. Developments that initially seem important prove trivial, and insignificant accidents determine the course of events. The French and English stalemate in battle, but then decide to call a temporary truce to raze the insolent town of Angiers. Equally abruptly, they decide to spare the town and strike a political deal sealed with a marriage. Private lives progress just as haphazardly. The Bastard initially pursues his rights as heir to the Falconbridge fortune, only to forgo his inheritance to seek valor in battle. Hubert allows Arthur to escape—a seemingly important development—but Arthur ironically falls to his death anyway.

The perspective of history that Shakespeare presents in *King John* differs substantially from that of his other history plays. In the Henriad (*Richard II, 1 Henry IV, 2 Henry IV,* and *Henry V*), Shakespeare questions the idea of a divine right of kings. Richard II is the legitimate king but an ineffectual ruler; Henry IV usurps the throne but then does his best to govern his country through a difficult period; and Henry V is a great ruler worried about the legitimacy of his throne. The *Henry VI* trilogy and *Richard III* show the will of heaven as revealed on Earth when England sinks into and emerges triumphant from years of civil war. In contrast, *King John* is far less preoccupied with the idea of a divine will. King John never frets over his questionable legitimacy, and protects the crown from Arthur, the rightful heir. He is more concerned with holding on to the throne.

THE SUFFERING OF THE INNOCENT *King John* takes place in an unjust world in which innocent people suffer. The young Arthur is sentenced to blinding and death, although King John has a difficult time deciding whether getting rid of Arthur is politically practical. The town of Angiers only too narrowly avoids complete and undeserved destruction. By a cruel twist of fate, France's reinforcements are shipwrecked. Similarly, English soldiers die in an unexpected flood. The play's developments, including the infliction of suffering, are prompted by absurd, meaningless whims.

THE MONARCH AS IGNOBLE The title character of *King John* lives an ignoble life and dies an ignoble death. He prepares for war with the French twice, and both times a roundabout solution renders war unnecessary. At Angiers, John and Philip form an alliance through marriage. Later, Pandolf brokers a peace treaty with Louis. Shakespeare devotes much stage time to John's orders to plunder the Catholic monasteries after his break with the Church. At the end, an embittered monk poisons John, and he dies an absurd death. In contrast to other kings, including the poetic Richard II, the pious Henry VI, the strong Henry V, and the brilliantly eloquent Richard III, John is Shakespeare's pettiest and least glorious monarch.

MOTIFS

POWERFUL MOTHERS Both John and Arthur are supported and spurred on by their strong mothers, a fact thrown into relief when Eleanor and Constance trade insults at the battle of Angiers. Dowager Queen Eleanor's blessing is John's strongest claim to the throne. Arthur, as a child, appears all the more weak next to the strong-willed Constance. Indeed, both John and Arthur fade away and die soon after their mothers do. *King John* gives a portrait of two forceful women who propel their sons to political prominence and achieve great power through them.

ILLEGITIMACY Two sets of characters in *King John* clash over inheritance: Falconbridge against the Bastard and John against Arthur. Though Arthur is the more legitimate heir to the throne, he is a weak child. Shakespeare forces us to favor the petty, less legitimate John. Similarly, the Bastard is a more valorous and stronger figure than his legitimate half-brother Falconbridge. Indeed, the Bastard embraces his illegitimacy because it associates him with the great King Richard the Lionhearted. Some critics have suggested that the Bastard is an abstract personification of amorality, the descendant of the Vice figure from medieval morality plays. At the same time, the Bastard, through his asides, emerges as the play's most sympathetic figure. Shakespeare's depiction of illegitimacy in *King John* differs radically from that of other plays. The bastards in *King Lear* (Edmund) and *Richard III* (Richard) are villains whose wickedness is associated with the illegitimacy of their birth. In *King John*, however, the illegitimates come across as more capable than their legitimate counterparts.

SYMBOLS

THE CLOSED GATES OF ANGIERS The closed gates of the French town of Angiers serve as a potent symbol of the popular voice. While most of the play concerns the petty maneuvers of aristocrats, II.i shows commoners who refuse admittance to both John and Philip, preferring to wait out the storm until the powerful monarchs have settled their own dispute. The closed gates are a reminder that kingship affects vast numbers of people. That the citizens refuse to choose between John and Arthur suggests that, for the commoners, there is little difference between them.

ARTHUR'S FALL Arthur's absurd death is a symbol of the ultimate meaninglessness of both death and life in *King John*. Both Eleanor's and Constance's deaths are anticlimactic. John's death, a result of being poisoned by a monk, is small and ridiculous. In giving John such a ludicrous and undignified death, Shakespeare refuses to give John's life higher meaning. Arthur's death is the most helplessly absurd and ironic of all: he is released from prison only to fall off a wall by accident. The events of the play tumble as accidentally as Arthur.

IMPORTANT QUOTATIONS FROM *KING JOHN*

1. *If old Sir Robert did beget us both*
   And were our father, and this son like him,
   O old Sir Robert, father, on my knee
   I give heaven thanks I was not like to thee.

Location: I.i.80–83
Speaker: The Bastard to King John
Context: The Bastard insults Falconbridge.

The Bastard's struggle with his half-brother Falconbridge for their father's inheritance echoes John's struggle with Arthur for the throne. Here the Bastard mocks filial deference by thanking the deceased Robert Falconbridge "on my knee" for the fact that he does not resemble him. The Bastard's spirit and wit makes him a compelling hero.

2. *Thou monstrous injurer of heaven and earth!*
   Call not me slanderer. Thou and thine usurp
   The dominations, royalties, and rights
   Of this oppressèd boy. This is thy eld'st son's son,
   Infortunate in nothing but in thee.
   Thy sins are visited in this poor child . . .

Location: II.i.174–179
Speaker: Constance to Eleanor
Context: During the argument outside Angiers, Constance accuses Eleanor of adultery.

Constance suggests that John is illegitimate, accusing Eleanor of adultery. She goes on to imply that Eleanor's sins implicate Arthur, who is Eleanor's grandson. In *King John*, the innocent often suffer without reason.

3. *Is it my fault I was Geoffrey's son?*
   No, indeed is 't not, and I would to God
   I were you son, so you would love me, Hubert.

Location: IV.i.22–24
Speaker: Arthur to Hubert
Context: Arthur begs Hubert not to kill him.

Arthur's simple words and language show him to be an innocent and naïve boy. He suffers in prison through no fault of his own. An accident of birth has made him a contender for the English throne. His question ("Is it my fault . . .") emphasizes *King John*'s perspective that history is neither just nor rational. No more than a child, Arthur longs for love and peace and dreams of life as a shepherd. But *King John* depicts a loveless, ruthlessly ambitious world. Just before death, Arthur compares love to a prophet briefly envisioning a better world, which is a vision as ephemeral as Arthur.

4. *What surety of the world, what hope, what stay,*

When this was now a king and now clay?

Location: V.vii.68–9
Speaker: Prince Henry
Context: Prince Henry laments the death of his father, King John.

In Shakespeare's time, the monarch was a symbol of the cosmic order. Accordingly, Prince Henry here calls King John the "surety of the world"—a guarantee of the world's well-being. Henry's grief is both private and public. He mourns King John as a son and as a fellow human being, but is also aware of the significance of John's death, which is a loss of "hope" and "stay" for the whole country.

---

5. *This England never did, nor never shall,*
   Lie at the proud foot of a conqueror
   But when it first did help to wound itself.
   Now these her princes are come home again,
   Come the three corners of the world in arms
   And we shall shock them. Naught shall make us rue
   If England to itself do rest but true.

Location: V.vii.112–118
Speaker: The Bastard
Context: In his last soliloquy, the Bastard proclaims that it is only domestic discord that makes England vulnerable to foreign enemies.

Like Shakespeare's other history plays, *King John* ends with restored order: England's "princes," the defecting noblemen, have returned home, and the French attack has been curtailed. The irony of the bastard's suggestion that England can resist her enemies so long as she stands united rests in how much disharmony the English aristocracy has exhibited throughout the play. With these words, Shakespeare foreshadows the bloody civil wars that he portrays in the other history plays—the six *Henrys* and the two *Richards*.

KING LEAR

King Lear divides Britain between his daughters, who bring ruin to the kingdom.

KING LEAR IN CONTEXT

King Lear, which Shakespeare wrote around 1605, is usually ranked with *Hamlet* as one of Shakespeare's greatest plays. *King Lear* dramatizes events from the eighth century B.C., but the parallel stories of Lear's and Gloucester's sufferings at the hands of their own children reflect anxieties that would have resonated with current events of Shakespeare's day. One event that may have influenced this play is a lawsuit that occurred not long before *King Lear* was written, in which the eldest of three sisters tried to have her elderly father, Sir Brian Annesley, declared insane so that she could take control of his property. Annesley's youngest daughter, Cordell, successfully defended her father against her sister. Another relevant story concerned William Allen, a mayor of London, who divided his wealth among his daughters and subsequently suffered poor treatment at their hands. Finally, *King Lear* relates to the 1603 transfer of power from Elizabeth I to James I. Elizabeth had produced no male heir, and people worried that uncertainty over her successor would lead to a dynastic struggle along the lines of the fifteenth-century Wars of the Roses.

KING LEAR: KEY FACTS

Full title: The Tragedy of King Lear	
Time and place written: England; 1604–1605	
Date of first publication: 1623 in First Folio	
Genre: Tragedy	
Setting (time): Eighth century B.C.	
Setting (place): England	
Protagonist: King Lear	
Major conflict: Lear unjustly exiles Cordelia and suffers at the hands of his older daughters; Edmund tricks his father because he wants land and respect.	

KING LEAR: CHARACTER LIST

Albany   The husband of Lear's daughter Goneril. Albany is good at heart, and eventually he denounces the cruelty of Goneril, Regan, and Cornwall; yet he is indecisive and obtuse.

Cordelia   Lear's youngest daughter. Cordelia remains loyal to Lear despite his cruelty to her, and is patient with her brutal sisters. Despite her obvious virtues, Cordelia's reticence makes her motivations difficult to read.

Cornwall   The husband of Lear's daughter Regan. Cornwall is domineering, cruel, and violent. With his wife and sister-in-law Goneril, he persecutes Lear and Gloucester.

Edgar   Gloucester's older, legitimate son. Edgar plays many different roles, from a gullible fool easily tricked by his brother, to a mad beggar, to an armored champion.

Edmund   Gloucester's younger, illegitimate son. Edmund resents his status as a bastard and schemes to usurp Gloucester's title and possessions from Edgar. Almost all of his schemes are successful, and he harms almost everyone around him.

Fool   Lear's jester. The fool uses double-talk and seemingly frivolous songs to give Lear important advice.

Gloucester   A nobleman loyal to King Lear. Gloucester has one legitimate son, Edgar, and one bastard son, Edmund. Like Lear, Gloucester trusts the wrong child. He is weak and ineffectual in the early acts, but he later proves himself capable of great bravery.

Goneril   Lear's ruthless oldest daughter and the wife of the duke of Albany. Goneril is jealous, treacherous, and amoral. She challenges Lear's authority, boldly initiates an affair with Edmund, and wrests military power away from her husband.

Kent   A nobleman loyal to King Lear. Kent spends most of the play disguised as "Caius," a peasant, so that he can continue to serve Lear even after Lear banishes him. Kent is extremely loyal, but his blunt outspokenness gets him in trouble.

King Lear   The protagonist of the play. Lear, the aging king of Britain, is used to absolute power and flattery and he does not respond well when people contradict him. At the beginning of the play, Lear prioritizes the appearance of love over actual devotion and wishes to maintain the power of a king while casting off a king's responsibilities. Nevertheless, he inspires loyalty in subjects such as Gloucester, Kent, Cordelia, and Edgar, all of whom risk their lives for him.

Oswald   The steward, or chief servant, in Goneril's house. Oswald aids Goneril in her conspiracies.

Regan   Lear's middle daughter and the wife of the duke of Cornwall. Like Goneril, Regan is ruthless and aggressive. When they are not egging each other on to further acts of cruelty, Regan and Goneril compete for Edmund.

KING LEAR: PLOT OVERVIEW

Lear, the aging king of Britain, decides to step down and divide his kingdom between his three daughters. Because his youngest daughter, Cordelia, refuses to flatter him, he disowns her and gives the kingdom to his older daughters, Goneril and Regan. When Goneril and Regan subsequently abuse Lear, he begins to go insane and wanders out onto a heath, or field, during a dangerous thunderstorm. Meanwhile, an elderly nobleman named Gloucester also experiences family problems. His illegitimate son, Edmund, tricks him into believing that his legitimate son, Edgar, is trying to kill him. Fleeing the manhunt that his father has set for him, Edgar disguises himself as a crazy beggar, calls himself "Poor Tom," and heads out onto the heath. When the loyal Gloucester realizes that Lear's daughters have turned against their father, he decides to help Lear in spite of the danger.

Regan and her husband, Cornwall, discover Gloucester helping Lear, accuse him of treason, blind him, and turn him out to wander the countryside. His disguised son, Edgar, finds him and leads him toward the city of Dover, where Lear has also been brought. In Dover, a French army lands as part of an invasion led by Cordelia to save her father. Edmund becomes romantically entangled with both Goneril and Regan, and Goneril and Edmund conspire to kill Albany, Goneril's husband. The despairing Gloucester tries to commit suicide, but Edgar saves him by leading him off an imaginary cliff and convincing him that his survival means it is not yet time for him to die. The English troops reach Dover and, led by Edmund, defeat Cordelia's army. Lear and Cordelia are captured. Edgar duels with Edmund and kills him. Gloucester's heart breaks at being reconciled with Edgar, and he dies. Goneril poisons Regan out of jealousy over Edmund and then kills herself. Cordelia is executed on Edmund's earlier orders, and Lear dies of grief.

KING LEAR: SCENE SUMMARY

ACT I

Angry about Cordelia's refusal to flatter him, Lear divides his kingdom between Goneril and Regan, who immediately turn against him; Edmund tricks Gloucester into thinking that Edgar is trying to kill Gloucester.

I.I   Location: King Lear's throne room

When Cordelia refuses to flatter him, Lear disowns her and divides his kingdom between Goneril and Regan.

Two noblemen, Gloucester and Kent, discuss the fact that King Lear is about to divide his kingdom. Gloucester introduces his son, Edmund, explaining that Edmund is a bastard being raised away from home. Still, he loves his son dearly. Lear, the ruler of Britain, enters his throne room and announces his plan to divide the kingdom among his three daughters. He intends to give up the responsibilities of government and spend his old age visiting his children. He tells his daughters that he will give the greatest share of his kingdom to the daughter who loves him most.

Lear's scheming older daughters, Goneril and Regan, respond to his test with flattery, telling him in wildly overblown terms that they love him more than anything else. But Cordelia, Lear's youngest (and favorite) daughter, refuses to speak. When pressed, she says that she cannot "heave her heart into her mouth," that she loves him exactly as much as a daughter should love her father, and that her sisters would not have husbands if they loved their father as much as they say (I.i.90–91). Lear flies into a rage, disowns Cordelia, and divides his kingdom between Goneril and Regan.

The earl of Kent, a nobleman who has served Lear faithfully for many years, is the only courtier who questions the king's actions. Kent tells Lear he is insane to reward the flattery of his older daughters and disown Cordelia, who loves him more than her sisters do. Lear banishes Kent from the kingdom, telling him he must be gone within six days.

The king of France and duke of Burgundy are at Lear's court waiting for Lear to decide which one of them will marry Cordelia. Lear calls them in and tells them that Cordelia no longer has any title or land. Burgundy withdraws his offer of marriage, but France is impressed by Cordelia's honesty and decides to make her his queen.

Goneril and Regan scheme together in secrecy. Although they recognize that they now have complete power over the kingdom, they agree that they must reduce their father's remaining authority.

I.II Location: Gloucester's house

Edmund tricks Gloucester into thinking that Edgar is trying to murder him.

Edmund delivers a soliloquy expressing his dissatisfaction with society's attitude toward bastards. He bitterly resents his legitimate half-brother, Edgar, who will inherit their father's estate. He resolves to do away with Edgar and seize the privileges that society has denied him.

Edmund begins his campaign to discredit Edgar by forging a letter in which Edgar appears to plot the death of their father, Gloucester. Edmund makes a show of hiding this letter from his father, so Gloucester demands to read it. Edmund answers his father with careful lies, manipulating Gloucester into thinking that his legitimate son, Edgar, has been scheming to kill him in order to hasten his inheritance of Gloucester's wealth and lands. Later, Edmund tells Edgar that Gloucester is very angry with him and that Edgar should avoid him as much as possible and carry a sword with him at all times.

I.III Location: Albany's castle

Goneril plans a confrontation with her father, who is staying with her.

Lear is spending the first portion of his retirement at Goneril's home. Goneril complains to her steward, Oswald, that Lear's knights are becoming "riotous" and that Lear himself is an obnoxious guest (I.iii.6). Seeking to provoke a confrontation, she orders her servants to behave rudely toward Lear and his attendants.

I.IV Location: Albany's castle

Lear takes Kent, disguised as Caius, into his service; Goneril insults Lear, forcing him to leave her house.

Disguised as a simple peasant, Kent appears in Goneril's castle, calling himself Caius. In conversation with Lear, Caius emphasizes his plainspoken-ness and honesty, and Lear accepts him into service. Lear's servants and knights notice that Goneril's servants no longer obey their commands. When Lear asks Oswald where Goneril is, Oswald rudely leaves the room without replying. Oswald soon returns, but his disrespectful replies to Lear's questions induce Lear to strike him. Kent steps in to aid Lear and trips Oswald.

The fool arrives and, in a series of puns and double entendres, tells Lear that he has made a great mistake in handing over his power to Goneril and Regan. After a long delay, Goneril arrives to speak with

Lear. She tells him that his servants and knights have been so disorderly that he will have to send some of them away whether he likes it or not.

Lear is shocked, but Goneril insists that Lear send away half of his one hundred knights. Enraged, Lear repents ever handing his power over to Goneril. He curses his daughter, asking nature to make her childless. Surprised by his own tears, he calls for his horses. He says he will stay with Regan, whom he believes will give him the respect that he deserves. When Lear has gone, Goneril argues with her husband, Albany, who is upset that she has treated Lear so harshly. She says that she has written a letter to Regan, who is also determined not to house Lear's hundred knights.

I.V Location: Albany's castle

Lear leaves for Regan's house.

Lear sends Kent to deliver a message to Gloucester. The fool needles Lear about his bad decisions, predicting that Regan will treat Lear no better than Goneril did. Lear calls on heaven to keep him from going mad. Lear and his attendants leave for Regan's castle.

ACT II

Edgar flees at Edmund's insistence, eventually disguising himself as a beggar; Edmund pretends that Edgar has tried to kill him; Goneril and Regan insult Lear so greatly that he runs outside into a threatening storm.

II.I Location: Gloucester's castle

Edmund convinces Edgar to flee and then pretends that Edgar has tried to kill him; Cornwall and Regan come to Gloucester's house.

Gloucester's servant Curan tells Edmund that he has informed Gloucester that the duke of Cornwall and his wife, Regan, are coming to the castle that night. Curan also mentions vague rumors about trouble brewing between the duke of Cornwall and the duke of Albany.

Edmund is delighted to hear of Cornwall's visit, realizing that he can make use of him in his scheme to get rid of Edgar. Edmund calls to Edgar, who has been hiding, and tells him that Cornwall is angry with him for being on Albany's side of their disagreement. Edgar has no idea what Edmund is talking about. Edmund also tells Edgar that Gloucester has discovered his hiding place and that he ought to flee the house immediately under cover of night. When he hears Gloucester coming, Edmund draws his sword and pretends to fight with Edgar, while Edgar runs away. Edmund cuts his arm with his sword and lies to Gloucester, telling him that Edgar wanted him to join in the plot against Gloucester's life and then tried to kill him when he refused. The unhappy Gloucester praises Edmund and vows to pursue Edgar, sending men out to search for him.

Cornwall and Regan arrive at Gloucester's house. They believe Edmund's lies about Edgar, and Regan asks if Edgar is one of the disorderly knights that attend Lear. Edmund says he is, and Regan speculates that these knights put Edgar up to the idea of killing Gloucester. Regan asks Gloucester for his advice in answering letters from Lear and Goneril.

II.II Location: outside Gloucester's castle

Kent, disguised, fights with Oswald and is put in the stocks.

Kent, disguised as Caius, meets Oswald, the chief steward of Goneril's household. Oswald does not recognize Kent from their scuffle in Act I, scene iv. Kent-as-Caius insults Oswald, describing him as cowardly, vain, boastful, overdressed, servile, and groveling. Oswald still says that he does not know the man before him. Kent-as-Caius draws his sword and attacks him.

Oswald's cries for help bring Cornwall, Regan, and Gloucester. They ask for an explanation, but Kent-as-Caius replies rudely. Cornwall orders him put in the stocks, a wooden device that shackles a person's ankles and renders him immobile. Gloucester objects that this humiliating punishment of Lear's messenger will be seen as disrespectful of Lear himself and that the former king will take offense. But Cornwall and Regan say the messenger deserves this treatment for assaulting Goneril's servant, and put him in the stocks.

After everyone leaves, Kent reads a letter that he has received from Cordelia in which she promises to find some way, from her current position in France, to help improve conditions in Britain. Unhappy and resigned, Kent dozes off in the stocks.

II.III Location: outside Gloucester's castle

Edgar, on the run from his pursuers, disguises himself as a beggar named Tom.

As Kent, disguised as Caius, sleeps in the stocks, Edgar enters. He has escaped the manhunt so far, but is afraid he will soon be caught. Stripping off his fine clothing and covering himself with dirt, he turns himself into "poor Tom," saying he will pretend to be one of the beggars who have been released from insane asylums and wander the countryside seeking food and shelter (II.iii.20).

II.IV Location: Gloucester's castle

Goneril and Regan insult Lear, refusing to house him unless he gets rid of all his servants; Lear heads outsid, and his daughters lock the doors behind him.

Lear, accompanied by the fool and a knight, arrives at Gloucester's castle. Lear spies Kent, disguised as Caius, in the stocks and is shocked that anyone would treat one of his servants so badly. When Kent, disguised as Caius, tells Lear that Regan and Cornwall put him there, Lear cannot believe it and demands to speak with them. Regan and Cornwall refuse to speak with Lear, claiming they are sick and weary from traveling. Lear has difficulty controlling his emotions, but he finally says sickness can make people behave strangely. When Regan and Cornwall eventually appear, Lear starts to tell Regan about Goneril's "sharp-toothed unkindness" toward him (II.iv.128). Regan suggests that Goneril may have been justified in her actions, that Lear is old and unreasonable, and that he should return to Goneril and beg her forgiveness.

On his knees, Lear begs Regan to shelter him, but she refuses. He curses Goneril, who arrives at Gloucester's castle, much to Lear's dismay. Regan, who knew that Goneril was coming, takes her sister's hand and allies herself with Goneril against their father. They both tell Lear that he is getting old and weak and that he must give up half of his men if he wants to stay with either of his daughters.

Lear, confused, says that he and his hundred men will stay with Regan. Regan says she will allow him only twenty-five men. Lear turns back to Goneril, saying he will come down to fifty men if he can stay with her. But Goneril is no longer willing to allow him even that many. A moment later, both Goneril and Regan refuse to allow Lear any servants.

Outraged, Lear curses his daughters and heads outside, where a wild storm is brewing. Gloucester begs Goneril and Regan to bring Lear back inside, but the daughters say it is best to leave him alone. They order the doors shut and locked, leaving their father outside in the threatening storm.

ACT III

Lear wanders the heath; Edmund betrays his father to Cornwall; Goneril and Cornwall gouge out Gloucester's eyes.

III.I Location: the heath

Kent, in disguise, tells one of Lear's knights that trouble is brewing between Albany and Cornwall, and sends the knight to Cordelia.

A storm rages on the heath. Kent, disguised as Caius, seeking Lear in vain, runs into one of Lear's knights and learns that Lear is somewhere in the area, accompanied only by his fool. Kent gives the knight secret information: he has heard that there is unrest between Albany and Cornwall and that there are spies for the French in the English courts. Kent tells the knight to go to Dover, the city in England nearest to

France, where he may find friends who will help Lear's cause. He gives the knight a ring and orders him to give it to Cordelia, who will understand it as a sign that Kent has sent the knight. Kent-as-Caius leaves to search for Lear.

III.II   Location: the heath

Lear wanders the heath with the fool, cursing Goneril and Regan, until Kent-as-Caius persuades him to take shelter in a hovel.

Lear wanders around in the storm, cursing the weather and challenging it to do its worst. He seems irrational, his thoughts wandering from idea to idea but always returning to his two cruel daughters. The fool, who accompanies Lear, urges him to humble himself before his daughters and seek shelter indoors, but Lear ignores him. Kent, disguised as Caius, finds Lear and the fool and urges them to take shelter inside a nearby hovel. Lear finally agrees and follows Kent-as-Caius. The fool makes a strange and confusing prophecy.

III.III   Location: Gloucester's castle

Gloucester tells Edmund of his sympathy to Lear and the coming invasion of the French; Edmund immediately plans to betray his father to Cornwall, whom he hopes will put Gloucester to death.

Gloucester speaks with Edmund. The loyal Gloucester says he was uncomfortable when Regan, Goneril, and Cornwall shut Lear out in the storm. When he asked them if he could go out and help Lear, they became angry, took possession of his castle, and ordered him never to speak to Lear or plead on his behalf.

Gloucester tells Edmund that he has received news of a conflict between Albany and Cornwall. He also informs him that a French army will soon invade. Part of the army has already landed in England. Gloucester feels he must take Lear's side and plans to seek him out in the storm. He tells Edmund that there is a letter with news of the French army locked in his room, and asks his son to go distract the duke of Cornwall while Gloucester searches for Lear. He says it is imperative that Cornwall not notice his absence, or Gloucester might die.

Gloucester leaves and Edmund rejoices at the opportunity that has presented itself. He plans to betray his father immediately, going to Cornwall to tell him about Gloucester's plans to help Lear and the location of the traitorous letter from the French. Edmund expects to inherit his father's title, land, and fortune as soon as Gloucester is put to death.

III.IV   Location: a hovel on the heath

Kent-as-Caius takes Lear to a hovel where Edgar-as-Tom happens to be hiding; Gloucester finds Lear and convinces him to go back to the castle.

Kent, disguised as Caius, leads Lear through the storm to the hovel. He tries to get him to go inside but Lear resists, saying his mental anguish drowns out the storm. He sends his fool inside to take shelter and then kneels and prays. He reflects that, as king, he did not take adequate care of the wretched and homeless, who have scant protection from storms such as this one.

The fool runs out of the hovel claiming that there is a spirit inside. The spirit turns out to be Edgar, who is disguised as Tom O'Bedlam. Edgar-as-Tom pretends to be mad, complaining that he is being chased by a devil and fiends are inhabiting his body. Lear, whose grip on reality is loosening, sees nothing strange about these statements. He sympathizes with Edgar-as-Tom, asking him whether bad daughters have ruined him too.

Lear asks Edgar-as-Tom what he used to be before he went mad. Edgar-as-Tom says he was once a wealthy courtier who spent his days having sex with many women and drinking wine. Observing Edgar-as-Tom's nakedness, Lear tears off his own clothes in sympathy.

Gloucester, carrying a torch, comes looking for the king. He is unimpressed by Lear's companions and tries to bring Lear back inside the castle with him, despite the possibility of provoking Regan and

Goneril's anger. Kent-as-Caius and Gloucester finally convince Lear to go with Gloucester, but Lear insists on bringing the disguised Edgar with him.

III.V Location: Gloucester's castle

Edmund betrays his father to Cornwall, who rewards Edmund by making him Earl of Gloucester.

Cornwall vows revenge against Gloucester, whom Edmund has betrayed by showing Cornwall a letter that proves Gloucester's secret support of a French invasion. Edmund pretends to be horrified at the discovery of his father's intentions. The powerful Cornwall, now his ally, confers upon Edmund the title of earl of Gloucester. Cornwall sends Edmund to find Gloucester. Edmund reasons that if he can catch his father in the act of helping Lear, Cornwall's suspicions will be confirmed.

III.VI Location: near Gloucester's castle

Lear holds an imaginary trial for Goneril and Regan; Gloucester hears of a plot against Lear's life and asks Kent, disguised as Caius, to take Lear to Dover.

Gloucester, Kent-as-Caius, Lear, and the fool take shelter in a small building on Gloucester's property. Gloucester leaves to find provisions for the king. Lear, whose mind is wandering ever more widely, holds a mock trial of his wicked daughters. Edgar-as-Tom, Kent-as-Caius, and the fool preside. Both Edgar-as-Tom and the fool speak like madmen, and the trial is an exercise in hallucination and eccentricity.

Gloucester hurries back in to tell Kent-as-Caius that he has overheard a plot to kill Lear. Gloucester begs Kent-as-Caius to take Lear toward Dover, in the south of England, where allies will be waiting for him. Gloucester, Kent-as-Caius, and the fool leave. Edgar remains behind for a moment and speaks in his own, undisguised voice about how much less important his own suffering seems in comparison to Lear's.

III.VII Location: Gloucester's castle

Goneril and Cornwall gouge out Gloucester's eyes, incurring the wrath of their servants, one of whom attacks Cornwall; they also tell Gloucester that his son Edmund betrayed him.

Cornwall gives Goneril the treasonous letter concerning the French army at Dover and tells her to show it to her husband, Albany. Cornwall sends his servants to apprehend Gloucester and orders Edmund to go with Goneril to Albany's palace so that Edmund will not have to witness the violent punishment of his father.

Oswald brings word that Gloucester has helped Lear escape to Dover. Gloucester is found and brought before Regan and Cornwall. They tie him up like a thief, insult him, and pull his white beard. Cornwall remarks to himself that he cannot put Gloucester to death without holding a formal trial, but he can punish him brutally and get away with it.

Admitting that he helped Lear escape, Gloucester swears that he will see Lear's wrongs avenged. Cornwall replies, "See 't shalt thou never," and proceeds to dig out one of Gloucester's eyes, throw it on the floor, and step on it (III.vii.68). Gloucester screams and Regan demands that Cornwall put out the other eye too.

One of Cornwall's servants steps in, saying he cannot stand by and let this outrage happen. Cornwall draws his sword. The servant wounds Cornwall, but Regan grabs a sword from another servant and kills the first servant before he can injure Cornwall further. Irate, the wounded Cornwall gouges out Gloucester's remaining eye.

Gloucester calls out for his son Edmund to help him, but Regan triumphantly tells him it was Edmund who betrayed him. Gloucester, realizing immediately that Edgar is his truly loyal son, laments his folly and prays to the gods to help Edgar. Regan and Cornwall order that Gloucester be thrown out of the house to "smell / His way to Dover" (III.vii.96–97). Cornwall, realizing that his wound is bleeding heavily, exits with Regan's help.

Left alone with Gloucester, Cornwall's and Regan's servants express their shock and horror at what has just happened. They decide to treat Gloucester's bleeding face and hand him over to the mad beggar to lead Gloucester where he will.

ACT IV

Edgar, in disguise, pretends to help Gloucester commit suicide in order to save Gloucester's life, and kills Oswald when he tries to attack Gloucester; Albany condemns Goneril for mistreating her father and Gloucester; Goneril and Regan vie for Edmund's affections; Cordelia is reunited with the partially-mad Lear and forgives him for banishing her.

IV.I Location: outside Gloucester's Castle

Edgar, disguised as Tom, runs into Gloucester on the heath.

Edgar, disguised as Tom, talks to himself on the heath, reflecting that his situation is not as bad as it could be. Then he runs into his father, now blinded. Gloucester is led by an old man who has been a tenant of both Gloucester and Gloucester's father for eighty years. Edgar hears Gloucester tell the old man that if he could only touch his son Edgar again, it would be worth more to him than his lost eyesight. But Edgar chooses to remain disguised as Poor Tom rather than reveal himself to his father. Gloucester asks the old man to bring some clothing to cover Edgar-as-Tom, and he asks Edgar-as-Tom to lead him to the top of the highest cliff in Dover.

IV.II Location: outside Albany's castle

Goneril learns that her husband, Albany, has turned against her, and starts flirting with Edmund; Albany, horrified by Goneril's and Edmund's deeds, decides to harm Edmund and help Gloucester.

Goneril and Edmund arrive at Goneril's home. Goneril expresses surprise that her husband, Albany, did not meet them on the way. Oswald tells her that Albany is displeased with Goneril's and Regan's actions, glad to hear that the French army has landed, and sorry to hear that Goneril is returning home. Goneril realizes that Albany is no longer her ally. She criticizes his cowardice and resolves to assert greater control over his military forces. She directs Edmund to return to Cornwall's house and raise Cornwall's troops for the fight against the French. She informs him that she will seize her husband's power and promises to send Oswald with messages. She kisses Edmund goodbye, hinting that she wants to become his mistress.

As Edmund leaves, Albany enters. He harshly criticizes Goneril. He has not yet learned about Gloucester's blinding, but he is outraged that Lear has been driven mad by Goneril and Regan's abuse. Goneril angrily insults Albany, accusing him of cowardice. She tells him that he ought to be preparing to fight against the French invaders. Albany calls her monstrous and condemns the evil that she has done to Lear.

A messenger arrives and says Cornwall has died from the wound he received while putting out Gloucester's eyes. Albany is horrified to hear of Gloucester's blinding and interprets Cornwall's death as divine retribution. Goneril is pleased that Cornwall's death makes Regan less powerful, but she worries that now Regan will pursue Edmund herself. Goneril leaves to answer her sister's letters.

Albany demands to know where Edmund was when his father was being blinded. When he hears that it was Edmund who betrayed Gloucester and that Edmund left the house specifically so that Cornwall could punish Gloucester, Albany resolves to take revenge upon Edmund and help Gloucester.

IV.III Location: the French camp near Dover

Kent, disguised as Caius, learns that Cordelia, who is the French queen, is in charge of the French army and that Albany's and the late Cornwall's armies are on the march.

Kent, disguised as Caius, speaks with a gentleman in the French camp near Dover. The gentleman tells Kent-as-Caius that the king of France landed with his troops but quickly departed to deal with a problem at home. Kent's letters have been brought to Cordelia, who is now the queen of France and who has been left in charge of the army. Kent-as-Caius questions the gentleman about Cordelia's reaction to the letters, and the gentleman gives a moving account of Cordelia's sorrow upon reading about her father's mistreatment. Kent-as-Caius tells the gentleman that Lear, who now fluctuates between sanity and madness, has also arrived safely in Dover. Lear refuses to see Cordelia because he is ashamed of the way he treated her. The gentleman informs Kent-as-Caius that the armies of both Albany and the late Cornwall are on the march.

IV.IV   Location: the French camp

Cordelia sends her soldiers to find Lear and asks a doctor whether he can recover his sanity.

Cordelia enters, leading her soldiers. Lear has hidden from her in the cornfields, draping himself in weeds and flowers and singing madly to himself. Cordelia sends one hundred of her soldiers to find Lear and bring him back. She consults with a doctor about Lear's chances of regaining sanity. The doctor tells her that what Lear most needs is sleep. A messenger brings Cordelia the news that the British armies of Cornwall and Albany are marching toward them. Cordelia's army is ready to fight.

IV.V   Location: Gloucester's castle

Regan tells Oswald that she wants Edmund for herself, and promises him a reward if he kills Gloucester.

Oswald tells Regan that Albany's army has set out, although Albany has been dragging his feet about the expedition. It seems that Goneril is a "better soldier" than Albany (IV.v.4). Regan is extremely curious about the letter that Oswald carries from Goneril to Edmund, but Oswald refuses to show it to her. Regan guesses that the letter concerns Goneril's love affair with Edmund, and she tells Oswald plainly that she wants Edmund for herself. Regan says she has already spoken with Edmund about this possibility. It would be more appropriate for Edmund to get involved with her, a widow, than with Goneril, a married woman. She gives Oswald a token or a letter (the text doesn't specify which) to deliver to Edmund and promises Oswald a reward if he can find and kill Gloucester.

IV.VI   Location: near Dover

Gloucester tries to commit suicide and believes the assertion of Edgar, who is disguised as a gentleman, that the gods do not want him to die yet; Oswald tries to kill Gloucester, but Edgar, disguised as a peasant from the west, defends his father and kills Oswald.

Edgar, disguised as Tom, leads Gloucester toward Dover. Edgar-as-Tom pretends to take Gloucester to the cliff, telling him that they are going up steep ground and that they can hear the sea. He tells Gloucester that they are at the top of the cliff and that looking down from the great height gives him vertigo. He waits quietly nearby as Gloucester prays to the gods to forgive him. Gloucester can no longer bear his suffering and intends to commit suicide. He falls to the ground in a faint.

Edgar wakes Gloucester up. He now pretends to be an ordinary gentleman, although he still does not tell Gloucester that he is his son. Edgar-as-gentleman says he saw Gloucester fall all the way from the cliffs and that it is a miracle he is still alive. He says the gods must not want Gloucester to die just yet. Edgar-as-gentleman also informs Gloucester that he saw the creature who had been with him at the top of the cliff and that this creature was not a human being but a devil. Gloucester accepts Edgar's explanation that the gods have preserved him and resolves to endure his sufferings patiently.

Lear, wandering across the plain, stumbles upon Edgar and Gloucester. He is wearing a crown of wild flowers and is clearly mad. He babbles to Edgar and Gloucester, speaking irrationally but with a strange perceptiveness. He recognizes Gloucester, alluding to Gloucester's sin and source of shame—his adultery. Lear pardons Gloucester for this crime. Adultery makes him think of copulation and then womankind, and he thunders against women and sexuality in general. Lear's disgust makes him incoherent. He deserts iambic pentameter and spits out the words "Fie, fie, fie! pah! pah!" (IV.vi.126). Cordelia's men enter. Relieved to find Lear at last, they try to take him into custody. Lear runs away and Cordelia's men follow him.

Oswald comes across Edgar-as-gentleman and Gloucester on the plain. He does not recognize Edgar, but he plans to kill Gloucester and collect the reward from Regan. Edgar adopts yet another persona, imitating the dialect of a peasant from the west of England. He defends Gloucester and kills Oswald with a cudgel. As he dies, Oswald entrusts Edgar with his letters.

Gloucester is disappointed that his assailant did not succeed in killing him. Edgar reads Goneril's letter to Edmund in which she urges Edmund to kill Albany if he gets the opportunity, so that Edmund and Goneril can be together. Edgar is outraged. He decides to keep the letter and show it to Albany when the time is right. Meanwhile, he buries Oswald nearby and leads Gloucester off to temporary safety.

IV.VII Location: the French camp near Dover

Cordelia sees Lear, who does not quite recognize her, and forgives him for banishing her.

Cordelia speaks with Kent. She knows his real identity, but he wants to keep it secret from everyone else. Lear, who has been sleeping, is brought in to Cordelia. He only partially recognizes her. He says he knows that he is senile and not in his right mind, and he assumes that Cordelia hates him and wants to kill him just as her sisters do. Cordelia tells her father that she forgives him for banishing her.

The news of Cornwall's death is repeated in the camp, and we learn that Edmund is now leading Cornwall's troops.

ACT V

Lear's forces are defeated; Gloucester dies of shock and happiness when Edgar reveals himself; Goneril fatally poisons Regan and kills herself; Cordelia is hanged; Edmund dies; Lear dies; Albany invites Edgar and Kent to rule with him.

V.I Location: the British camp near Dover

Albany says he will fight alongside Edmund, Goneril, and Regan; Edgar, in disguise, gives Albany a compromising letter from Goneril; Edmund announces that he has sworn his love to both Goneril and Regan.

Regan asks Edmund if he loves Goneril and if he has had sex with her. Edmund responds in the negative to both questions. Regan expresses jealousy of her sister and beseeches Edmund not to have an affair with her.

Goneril and Albany enter with their troops. Albany says he has heard that the invading French army has been joined by Lear and unnamed others who may have legitimate grievances against the present government. Despite his sympathy with Lear and these other dissidents, Albany says he intends to fight alongside Edmund, Regan, and Goneril to repel the foreign invasion. Goneril and Regan spar over Edmund. Neither sister is willing to leave the other alone with him. The three exit together.

Albany begins to leave, but Edgar, now disguised as an ordinary peasant, stops him. He gives Albany the letter he took from Oswald's body—the letter in which Goneril's involvement with Edmund is revealed and Goneril asks Edmund to kill Albany. Edgar-as-peasant tells Albany to read the letter and says that if Albany wins the upcoming battle, he can sound a trumpet and Edgar will provide a champion to defend the claims made in the letter.

Edgar-as-peasant vanishes and Edmund returns. Edmund tells Albany that the battle is almost upon them, and Albany leaves. Alone, Edmund addresses the audience, stating that he has sworn his love to both Regan and Goneril. He debates what he should do, reflecting that choosing either one would anger the other. He decides to put off the decision until after the battle, observing that if Albany survives it, Goneril can take care of killing him herself. He says if the British win the battle and he captures Lear and Cordelia, he will show them no mercy.

V.II Location: near the battle

Edgar, in disguise, tells Gloucester that Lear's side has lost, and Cordelia and Lear have been captured.

The battle begins. Edgar, disguised as a peasant, leads Gloucester to the shelter of a tree and goes into battle to fight on Lear's side. He soon returns, shouting that Lear's side has lost and that Lear and Cordelia have been captured. Gloucester says he will stay where he is and wait to be captured or killed, but Edgar says one's death occurs at a predestined time. Persuaded, Gloucester goes with Edgar.

V.III Location: the British camp near Dover

> *Edgar defeats Edmund in combat and says that when he revealed himself to Gloucester, Gloucester died; Goneril fatally poisons Regan and kills herself; Cordelia is hanged on Edmund's orders, even though Edmund repents and tries to reverse his orders; Edmund dies; Lear dies; Albany invites Edgar and Kent to rule with him.*

Edmund leads in Lear and Cordelia as his prisoners. Cordelia expects to confront Regan and Goneril, but Lear vehemently refuses to do so. He says he and Cordelia should go to prison where they will live alone together like birds in a cage, hearing about the outside world but observed by no one. Edmund sends them away, giving the captain who guards them a note with instructions about what to do with them. The captain agrees to follow Edmund's orders.

Albany enters with Goneril and Regan. He praises Edmund for his brave fighting on the British side and orders him to produce Lear and Cordelia. Edmund lies to Albany, claiming that he sent Lear and Cordelia far away because he feared that they would excite the sympathy of the British forces and create a mutiny. Albany rebukes him for getting above his place, but Regan interrupts to announce that she plans to make Edmund her husband. Goneril tells Regan that Edmund will not marry her. Regan feels sick.

Albany intervenes, arresting Edmund on a charge of treason. Albany challenges Edmund to a trial by combat and he sounds the trumpet to summon his champion. While Regan, who is worsening, is helped to Albany's tent, Edgar appears in full armor to accuse Edmund of treason and face him in single combat. Edgar defeats Edmund and Albany tells him to leave Edmund alive for questioning. Goneril tries to help the wounded Edmund, but Albany brings out the treacherous letter to show that he knows of her conspiracy against him. Goneril rushes off in desperation.

Edgar takes off his helmet and reveals his identity. He reconciles with Albany and tells the company how he disguised himself as a mad beggar and led Gloucester through the countryside. He adds that he revealed himself to his father only as he was preparing to fight Edmund and that Gloucester, torn between joy and grief, died.

A gentleman rushes in carrying a bloody knife. He announces that Goneril has committed suicide, fatally poisoning Regan before she died. The two bodies are carried in and laid out.

Kent enters and asks where Lear is. Albany recalls with horror that Lear and Cordelia are still imprisoned and demands that Edmund say where they are. Edmund repents and decides to do good before his death. He tells the others that he ordered Cordelia hanged. He sends a messenger to try to stop the execution.

Lear enters, carrying the dead Cordelia in his arms. The messenger arrived too late. Slipping in and out of sanity, Lear grieves over Cordelia's body. Kent speaks to Lear, but Lear barely recognizes him. A messenger enters and reveals that Edmund has also died. Lear asks Edgar to loosen Cordelia's buttons so she can breathe. Lear dies.

Albany restores power and titles to Edgar and Kent, inviting them to rule with him. Kent, feeling himself near death, refuses, but Edgar seems to accept. The few survivors exit as a funeral march plays.

ANALYSIS OF MAJOR CHARACTERS IN *KING LEAR*

KING LEAR At the beginning of the play, Lear values appearances over reality. He wants to be treated as a king and to enjoy the title, but he does not want to fulfill a king's governing obligations. He wants his daughters to make a flattering public display of their love for him, but he is not interested how much they truly love him. He does not ask "which of you doth love us most," but rather, "which of you shall we say doth love us most?" (I.i.49). He values Goneril's and Regan's fawning over Cordelia's sincere sense of filial love. Critics debate how much Lear develops as a character over the course of the play. He does not recover his sanity completely, but he does recognize his weakness and insignificance as a creature in the natural world, and he does become more humble and caring. By the end of the play, Lear cherishes

Cordelia above everything else, to the point that he would rather live in prison with her than rule as a king again.

CORDELIA Cordelia's chief characteristics are devotion, kindness, beauty, and honesty. Her honesty is so searing and stubborn, however, that it sometimes seems perverse. Her refusal to take part in Lear's love test at the beginning of the play is honorable, but almost self-destructive. Cordelia is offstage for most of the middle section of the play, but her virtue is implicitly contrasted to the cruelties of Goneril and Regan and the madness of Lear. Characters also speak of her while she is offstage, describing her beauty in religious terms. Rumors of Cordelia's return to Britain begin to surface almost immediately, and once she lands at Dover the action of the play moves toward her as all the characters converge on the coast. Cordelia's reunion with Lear is a fleeting moment of familial happiness that makes the devastating conclusion of *King Lear* even harder to bear. Cordelia, the personification of kindness and virtue, becomes a literal sacrifice to the heartlessness of an unjust world.

EDMUND Of all of the play's villains, Edmund is the most complex and sympathetic. He is a consummate schemer, a Machiavellian character eager to seize any opportunity and do anything to achieve his goals. His ambition is motivated not only by a desire for land and power, but also by a craving to be recognized as a legitimate person. His serial treachery is not merely self-interested; it is a conscious rebellion against the social order that has denied him, a bastard child, the same status as Gloucester's legitimate son, Edgar. "Now, gods, stand up for bastards," Edmund commands, but he does not require divine aid—his own initiative serves him (I.ii.22). Edmund is such a cold and capable villain that it is entertaining to watch him work. Only at the close of the play does he show a flicker of weakness. Mortally wounded, he sees that both Goneril and Regan have died for him, and whispers, "Yet Edmund was beloved" (V.iii.238). After this ambiguous statement, he seems to repent of his villainy and admits to having ordered Cordelia's death. His peculiar change of heart is rare among Shakespearean villains.

THEMES, MOTIFS, & SYMBOLS IN *KING LEAR*

THEMES

THE UNLIKELIHOOD OF JUSTICE *King Lear* is a brutal play filled with human cruelty and awful, seemingly meaningless disasters. The play's succession of terrible events makes the characters wonder whether there is any possibility of justice or whether the world is fundamentally indifferent, even hostile, to humankind. Gloucester believes "As flies to wanton boys are we to the gods; / They kill us for their sport" (IV.i.37–38). He thinks it is foolish to imagine that some benevolent force cares for humans or is even kind enough to be indifferent to them. Rather, he believes the world is governed by malevolent beings which kill us for fun. In contrast, Edgar believes that "the gods are just," and people get what they deserve (V.iii.169). The play suggests that Edgar's opinion is naïve: the wicked may die in the end, but so do the good.

AUTHORITY VERSUS CHAOS *King Lear* is about political authority as much as it is about family strife. Lear is not only a father but also a king, and when he gives away his authority to the unworthy Goneril and Regan, he delivers not only himself and his family but all of Britain into chaos. As the two wicked sisters indulge their appetites for power and Edmund begins his ascension, the kingdom descends into civil strife and it is clear Lear has destroyed not only his own authority, but all authority in Britain. The stable, hierarchal order that Lear initially represents falls apart and disorder engulfs the realm.

THE POSSIBILITY OF RECONCILIATION Darkness and unhappiness pervade *King Lear*, but the play's central relationship dramatically embodies true, self-sacrificing love. Rather than despising Lear for banishing her, Cordelia remains devoted, even from afar, and eventually brings an army from a foreign country to rescue her father from his tormentors. Lear learns a lesson in humility and eventually reunites with Cordelia and experiences the balm of her forgiving love. He comes to understand the sincerity and depth of Cordelia's love for him, which makes him understand how gravely he wronged her when he accused her of not loving him. Cordelia's reconciliation with Lear suggests that love can flourish, if only briefly.

MOTIFS

MADNESS   Insanity, a central motif in the play, is associated with both disorder and wisdom. When Lear goes mad, the turmoil in his mind echoes the chaos that has descended upon his kingdom. His madness also strips him of his royal pretensions, an experience that eventually leads to wisdom and humility. The fool cloaks his sometimes-wise counsel in a seemingly mad babble. Edgar's feigned insanity contains nuggets of wisdom for the king to mine. Edgar is also hardened by his time as a beggar, which prepares him to defeat Edmund at the close of the play.

BETRAYAL   The play's constant familial betrayals have varying political consequences for the betrayers. Lear's betrayal of Cordelia leads to madness and weakness, but Goneril and Regan's betrayal of Lear raises them to power in Britain, as does Edmund's betrayal of Edgar and Gloucester. However, the betrayers who succeed politically inevitably turn on one another. Goneril and Regan fall out when they both become attracted to Edmund, and their jealousy leads to mutual destruction.

SYMBOLS

THE STORM   As Lear wanders on a desolate heath in Act III, a terrible storm rages overhead. The storm is partly a physical, turbulent symbol of Lear's inner turmoil and mounting madness. It also symbolizes the awesome power of nature, which forces the powerless king to recognize his own human frailty and to feel humble for the first time. The storm may also symbolize a divine presence, as if nature itself is angry about the events in the play. Finally, the storm symbolizes Britain's political disarray.

BLINDNESS   Gloucester's physical blindness symbolizes the metaphorical blindness of Gloucester and Lear. Both men have loyal children and disloyal children, both are blind to the truth, and both end up banishing the loyal children and making the wicked children their heirs. Only when Gloucester has lost the use of his eyes and Lear has gone mad does each understand his error.

IMPORTANT QUOTATIONS FROM *KING LEAR*

1. *Unhappy that I am, I cannot heave*
   My heart into my mouth. I love your majesty
   According to my bond; no more nor less.

Location: I.i.90–92
Speaker: Cordelia to King Lear
Context: Lear has asked his daughters to tell him how much they love him before he divides his kingdom among them.

In contrast to the empty flattery of Goneril and Regan, Cordelia offers her father a truthful, unembellished account of her love for him. She loves him "according to [her] bond." That is, she understands and unquestioningly accepts her duty to love him as a father and king. Although Cordelia loves Lear much more than her sisters do, she cannot "heave" her heart into her mouth. Her integrity prevents her from making a false declaration in order to gain her father's wealth. Lear's rage at what he perceives to be Cordelia's lack of affection sets the tragedy in motion and establishes Cordelia's virtue and stubborn insistence on truthfulness.

2. *Thou, nature, art my goddess; to thy law*
   My services are bound. Wherefore should I
   Stand in the plague of custom, and permit
   The curiosity of nations to deprive me,
   For that I am some twelve or fourteen moonshines
   Lag of a brother? Why bastard? wherefore base?

> *Legitimate Edgar, I must have your land.*
> *Our father's love is to the bastard Edmund*
> *As to the legitimate. Fine word—"legitimate"!*
> *Well, my legitimate, if this letter speed,*
> *And my invention thrive, Edmund the base*
> *Shall top the legitimate. I grow; I prosper.*
> *Now, gods, stand up for bastards!*

Location: I.ii.1–22
Speaker: Edmund
Context: Edmund is about to trick his father into believing that Edgar is plotting against him.

Deprived by his bastard birth of the respect and rank that he believes are rightfully his, Edmund focuses his entire existence on raising himself up by his bootstraps, forging personal prosperity by betraying and lying to his relatives. The repeated use of the epithet "legitimate" in this passage reveals Edmund's obsession with his brother's enviable status as their father's rightful heir. Edmund characterizes the social order as a "plague of custom" that he refuses to respect, invoking "nature" as an unregulated, anarchic place where a person of low birth could achieve his goals. He wants recognition more than anything else—perhaps, it is suggested later, because of the familial love that has been denied him.

---

3. *O, reason not the need! Our basest beggars*
   Are in the poorest thing superfluous.
   Allow not nature more than nature needs,
   Man's life's as cheap as beast's . . .
   You heavens, give me that patience, patience I need!
   If it be you that stir these daughters' hearts
   Against their father, fool me not so much
   To bear it tamely; touch me with noble anger,
   And let not women's weapons, water-drops,
   Stain my man's cheeks! No, you unnatural hags,
   No, I'll not weep.
   I have full cause of weeping, but this heart
   Shall break into a hundred thousand flaws,
   Or ere I'll weep. O fool, I shall go mad!

Location: II.iv.259–281
Speaker: King Lear to Goneril and Regan
Context: The cruelties of his daughters have shattered Lear.

Lear rages against Goneril and Regan, telling them that their attempts to take away his knights and servants strike at his heart. "O, reason not the need!" he cries, forbidding them to ask why he needs servants. He says humans would be no different from animals if they did not need more than the fundamental necessities of life to be happy. Lear needs knights and attendants not only because of the service that they provide him, but because their presence identifies him as a king and an important man. Goneril and Regan, in stripping Lear of the trappings of power, are stripping him of his self-respect. They are also driving him mad, as the last line of this quotation indicates, since Learn cannot bear the idea that his daughters have lied to him and betrayed him. Despite his attempt to assert his authority, Lear is powerless. All he can do is to vent his rage.

---

4. *As flies to wanton boys are we to the gods;*

They kill us for their sport.

Location: IV.i.37–38
Speaker: earl of Gloucester
Context: Cornwall and Regan have gouged out Gloucester's eyes.

Gloucester wanders on the heath, gripped by profound despair. He voices one of the play's key themes: the question of whether justice exists in the universe. Gloucester believes that it does not. Even a godless universe would be better than what he believes exists: a universe ruled by capricious, cruel beings which reward cruelty and enjoy the sight of suffering humans. In many ways, the events of the play bear out Gloucester's understanding of the world, as the good die along with the wicked, and no reason is offered for the unbearable suffering of the characters.

---

5. *Howl, howl, howl, howl! O, you are men of stones:*
   Had I your tongues and eyes, I'd use them so
   That heaven's vault should crack. She's gone forever!
   I know when one is dead, and when one lives;
   She's dead as earth.

Location: V.iii.256–260
Speaker: King Lear
Context: Lear emerges from prison carrying Cordelia's body.

Lear believes that "heaven's vault should crack" at his daughter's death—but no sign comes to confirm that Cordelia's death is an abomination. Instead, it is a pointless death that means nothing.

LOVE'S LABOUR'S LOST

A king and his lords swear to avoid women, but cannot keep their oaths.

LOVE'S LABOUR'S LOST IN CONTEXT

Published in 1598, *Love's Labour's Lost* is one of Shakespeare's earlier plays, which he probably wrote from 1594–1595. It appeared as a comedy in Shakespeare's *First Folio*. The play, a witty exploration of love, ends happily but atypically, with the couples reconciling but not marrying. Berowne notes this unusual twist on the comedy genre, saying it proves how much life differs from fiction: "Our wooing doth not end like an old play. / Jack hath not Jill. These ladies' courtesy / Might well have made our sport a comedy" (V.ii.851–53).

LOVE'S LABOUR'S LOST: KEY FACTS

Full title: Love's Labour's Lost

Time and place written: 1594–1595; London

Date of first performance: 1595

Genre: Comedy

Setting (time): Unspecified

Setting (place): The kingdom of Navarre, in southwest France

Protagonist: Berowne

Major conflict: The men try and fail to resist women.

LOVE'S LABOUR'S LOST: CHARACTER LIST

Berowne, Longaville, Dumaine (Biron and Longueville in the Norton edition) Three lords. They join the king in his oath of scholarship and fall in love with Rosaline, Maria, and Katherine, respectively.

Boyet A lord attending on the princess. Boyet serves as a messenger to the king's court and exchanges jokes with the lords.

Costard The fool.

Don Armado A Spaniard. Don Armado catches Costard and Jaquenetta in the forest and falls in love with Jaquenetta.

Dull A constable. Dull provides a contrast to Sir Nathaniel's and Holofernes' scholarliness.

Ferdinand, King of Navarre The king. Ferdinand, a scholar, has sworn an oath to study without indulging in bodily pleasures, the most tempting of which turns out to be receiving women at his court.

Jaquenetta A country wench. Don Armado falls in love with Jaquenetta.

Mercadé (Marcade in some editions) A lord attending on the princess.

Moth (Mote in the Norton edition) Don Armado's page.

Princess of France She pays a visit to the king of Navarre and, along with some of her attendants, plays a game of wits with the king and his lords.

Rosaline, Maria, Katherine Three ladies attending the princess. These three catch the fancy of the king's lords.

Sir Nathaniel, Holofernes A curate and schoolmaster, respectively. Sir Nathaniel and Holofernes provide learned commentary on the letters of the other characters and coordinate the masque of the Nine Worthies.

LOVE'S LABOUR'S LOST: PLOT SUMMARY

The King of Navarre and his three lords, Berowne, Longaville, and Dumaine, swear an oath to study, fast, and resist contact with women for three years. They receive a letter from Don Armado, a Spaniard visiting the king's court, who writes that he has caught Costard, a fool, and Jaquenetta, a country wench, consorting in the park. The king announces Costard's sentence, and he and the lords go off to begin their oath.

Don Armado confesses to Moth, his page, that he has fallen in love with Jaquenetta. He writes her a letter and asks Costard to deliver it. The princess of France arrives to visit the king, but because of the king's oath, he cannot receive her and her party at his court. Instead, he and his lords must visit them at their camp outside the castle. The three lords fall in love with the three ladies, and the king falls in love with the princess. Berowne gives Costard a letter to deliver to Rosaline, but Costard accidentally switches it with the letter from Don Armado to Jaquenetta. When he gives Berowne's letter to Jaquenetta, she brings it to the learned Holofernes and Sir Nathaniel to read for her. They tell her that the letter was meant for someone else and she should deliver it to the king.

Berowne watches the king from a hiding spot as he reads aloud a poem about his love for the princess. Longaville enters, and the king hides. He and Berowne observe Longaville reading aloud about his love for Maria. Dumaine enters, Longaville hides, and with the king and Berowne sees Dumaine reading an ode he has written to Katherine. Longaville emerges and tells Dumaine that he is not alone in love. The king then emerges and scolds the two men for breaking their oath. Berowne emerges and reveals that the king is in love as well. Jaquenetta arrives and gives Berowne the letter, which he rips up. However, Dumaine picks up a piece of the letter with Berowne's name on it, and Berowne confesses that he is in love too. The four men decide to court their women.

The king and his lords arrive at the princess's pavilion disguised as Muscovites. The women, who were warned about the disguises, disguise themselves so that the men confuse them. After the men leave and reappear as themselves, the women reveal their prank. They all watch a show of the Nine Worthies performed by Don Armado, Sir Nathaniel, and Holofernes. A messenger arrives to tell the princess that her father has died, and she prepares to return to France. The women tell their suitors to seek them again in a year, and the play ends with their departure.

LOVE'S LABOUR'S LOST: SCENE SUMMARY

ACT I

The king and his friends swear an oath to give up their fun in favor of study, but Don Armado immediately falls in love with a wench.

I.I Location: the king's courtyard

The king and his friends swear an oath to study only and give up everything fun; the king punishes Costard for fooling around with Jaquenetta.

The King of Navarre and his three lords, Berowne, Longaville, and Dumaine, discuss the founding of their *academe*, or academy. The king reflects on the goal of their scholarship, which is primarily fame. He asks the three lords to sign their names to an oath that swears their commitment to the academe for three years. Longaville and Dumaine agree, but Berowne worries about the strictness of the oath. He calls the requirements for fasting, little sleep, and the avoidance of women "barren tasks, too hard to keep, / Not to see ladies, study, fast, not sleep" (I.i.47–48). He argues this point with the king, but finally agrees to sign the oath. Berowne reads the text of the decrees, which begin, "[I]f any man be seen to talk with a woman within the term of three years, he shall endure such public shame as the rest of the court can possible devise" (I.i.128–130). He points out that the king is going to break this article himself, since the daughter of the French king is about to pay a visit to their court. The king says that this decree must be rejected "on mere necessity" (I.i.146). Berowne says that he does not mind subscribing to a decree that can be rejected, and signs the document.

The constable Dull enters with a letter and the fool, Costard. He says he has a letter from Don Armado, and Costard tells them that the letter concerns himself and Jaquenetta. The king reads the letter, which says that Armado has caught Costard consorting with Jaquenetta and has sent him to the king to receive a punishment. Costard tries to escape with clever wordplay, but he fails and is sentenced to a week of eating only bran and water.

I.II Location: the king's courtyard

Don Armado confesses that he is in love with Jaquenetta.

Don Armado confesses to his page, Moth, that he has fallen in love with Jaquenetta. He asks Moth to comfort him by telling him of other great men that have been in love, and Moth mentions Hercules and Samson. Dull returns with Costard and Jaquenetta and tells Armado that the king has sent Costard to serve his sentence. Armado tells Jaquenetta that he loves her, but she departs with Dull. Armado sends Costard with Moth to prison. Left alone, he laments that he is too much in love to resist Jaquenetta. He then begins to write.

ACT II

The princess of France arrives with her ladies.

II.I Location: the king's courtyard

The princess of France arrives with her ladies, and the king houses them in a field rather than break his oath.

The princess of France arrives with her entourage. She sends Boyet, one of her attendants, to the king to announce their arrival, since she has heard the king's vow that "[n]o woman may approach his silent court" (II.i.24). The princess asks her attendants about the other men with whom the king shares his oath. Maria describes Lord Longaville, Katherine mentions Dumaine, and Rosaline mentions Berowne.

Boyet returns and informs the princess that the king intends to "lodge you in the field" (II.i.85) rather than break his oath and allow women in his house. The king enters with his lords and tells the princess that he cannot bring her to the court because of his oath. They conduct some business. The princess hands the king a paper, and they discuss the payment of 100,000 crowns and the control of Aquitaine. The king leaves, saying he will return the next day to visit the women. Before they leave, Dumaine, Longaville, and Berowne ask Boyet for the name of the woman they fancy. When they have gone, Boyet tells the princess that he believes the king is in love with her.

ACT III

Armado and Berowne entrust Costard with letters to the women they love.

III.I Location: the king's courtyard

Costard agrees to deliver letters to Jaquenetta and Rosaline.

Armado asks Moth to bring Costard to him to deliver a letter. Moth returns with Costard, who has broken his shin, and the three discuss riddles and morals. Armado tells Costard that will set him free if he agrees to will deliver a letter to Jaquenetta. Costard agrees, so Armado gives him money and leaves with Moth. Berowne enters and asks Costard to deliver a letter to Rosaline for him. Costard agrees, so Berowne gives him money and exits. After Costard leaves, Berowne laments his love for Rosaline.

ACT IV

After a mix-up of letters and a great deal of eavesdropping, it emerges that the king and his friends are all in love.

IV.I   Location: the king's courtyard

Costard accidentally gives the princess the letter meant for Jaquenetta.

The princess and her party go into the woods on a hunt. Costard finds them and gives the princess a letter, telling her it is for Rosaline from Berowne. However, Costard has switched the letters by mistake and given the princess the letter intended for Jaquenetta. Boyet reads the letter, which is signed "Don Armado," and the princess tells Costard that he has delivered the letter mistakenly.

IV.II   Location: the king's courtyard

Costard accidentally gives Jaquenetta the letter meant for Rosaline.

Holofernes, Sir Nathaniel, and Dull discuss the hunt they have just witnessed. They argue about whether the deer the princess killed was a pricket (a two-year-old deer), and Holofernes presents "an extemporal epitaph on the death of the deer" (IV.ii.46–47). Jaquenetta and Costard arrive. Jaquenetta asks Holofernes and Nathaniel to read the letter that Costard has delivered to her. She believes this to be a letter from Don Armado, but as Holofernes reads, it turns out to be the letter from Berowne to Rosaline. Nathaniel reads the letter aloud, and he and Holofernes give a critique of its poetry. They inform Jaquenetta and Costard that the letter was actually written by Berowne—one of the king's lords—and ask them to bring the letter to the king.

IV.III   Location: the king's courtyard

It emerges that the king and his men are all in love.

Berowne enters with a poem to Rosaline. He hears someone else coming and hides. The king enters in a love-induced swoon and reads from a poem he has written. Berowne is surprised to learn that the king is also in love. The king hears Longaville approaching and hides. Longaville enters, speaks of his love for Maria, and begins to read from a poem he has written. He hides when he hears someone approaching. Dumaine enters, moaning longingly for Kate. He reads an ode that he has written and laments that his friends do not share his suffering.

Longaville comes out of hiding to chide Dumaine. The king advances and reveals that he has heard Longaville speak of his love for Maria. He scolds the two lords for breaking their oath and asks, "What will Berowne say when that he shall hear / Faith so infringèd, which such zeal did swear?" (IV.iii.141–142). Berowne advances and asks the king what right he has to criticize his friends, when he himself is in love. Berowne reprimands the three men for breaking their oath and says that an honest man like himself is put in a bad position when he has to spend time with such dishonest friends.

Jaquenetta and Costard enter with the letter, telling the king it amounts to treason. He gives Berowne the letter to read. Berowne, recognizing it as his own verses to Rosaline, tears it up. Dumaine finds a piece of the letter with Berowne's name on it, and Berowne confesses that he, too, is in love. The four men begin to argue about which of their loves is the most beautiful.

The king realizes that they are all in love and so have all broken their oath. He asks Berowne to prove, somehow, that their love does not contradict the oath. Berowne delivers a long speech arguing that to look at a woman is the best way to learn beauty. He says that their scholarship oath actually led them further away from true study. The king seems to accept this argument, and they decide to woo the women.

ACT V

Some of the men put on a show of the Nine Worthies; before they leave, the women tell the men to behave well and then seek them out in a year.

V.I Location: the king's courtyard

Holofernes, Nathaniel, Don Armado and others plan to put on a show of the Nine Worthies for the entertainment of the princess and her party.

Holofernes and Nathaniel discuss Don Armado, with whom Nathaniel has been conversing. They mock his inferior intellect, criticizing his pronunciation of English. Armado, Moth, and Costard enter. Armado tells the learned men that the king has asked him to prepare "some delightful ostentation, or show, or pageant, or antick or firework" (V.i.94–95) to entertain the princess and her party. He asks Holofernes and Nathaniel for their help in planning this entertainment, and Holofernes suggests presenting a show of the Nine Worthies. Holofernes says he will play three of the roles himself. They go off to plan their show.

V.II Location: the king's courtyard

The women reveal the tricks they have played on the men; the princess learns of her father's death; the women order the men to seclude themselves for a year.

The princess shows her women a jewel the king has sent her, and the four women discuss love. Katherine says that her sister died of love. Rosaline tells them that she has received a letter from Berowne with verses and a picture of her. Katherine has received a letter and a pair of gloves from Dumaine, and Maria has received a letter and some pearls from Longaville.

Boyet arrives and tells the women that the king and his companions are on their way, dressed as Muscovites, to court their respective loves. The princess tells her ladies to mask themselves and switch their possessions so that the men will get confused and woo the wrong women. The men enter, and Moth makes a speech, which is interrupted by Boyet and corrected by Berowne. Rosaline, pretending to be the princess, asks what the strangers want. The king tells her they want to converse with the women. Each man appeals to the woman he thinks is his lady, and each pair goes off to talk in private. Rosaline tells them it is time to go, and the men leave. Each woman reveals that her respective man has pledged his love to her, and they happily note how gullible the men are.

The women realize that the men will return, so they switch back to their rightful possessions. The men arrive, dressed as themselves, and the king offers to bring the women to his court. The princess tells him she does not want him to break his oath. She says a group of Russians has recently visited them, and Rosaline complains that the Russians were fools. The women reveal that they knew their visitors were the men dressed up as Russians.

The king confesses to the ruse, and the princess asks him what he told his lady. She warns him that he has to keep his oath, and he says he will. She then asks Rosaline what the Russian told her, and she repeats the king's words. He says he knew the princess by the jewel on her sleeve, and the men realize the trick that the women played on them. Berowne says that they have perjured themselves once again.

Costard enters and asks the king if he would like the Worthies to begin their show. Berowne tells them to prepare. Costard enters as Pompey, and Boyet mocks him during his speech. Berowne professes to admire Boyet's mocking. The princess thanks him, and Nathaniel enters as Alexander. Boyet and Berowne mock him, but the princess encourages him to continue. Berowne tells Pompey to take Alexander away, and Nathaniel exits. Holofernes and Moth enter as Judas Maccabeus and Hercules, respectively. Holofernes delivers a speech about Hercules, and Moth exits. Boyet, Berowne, Longaville, and Dumaine all mock Holofernes, and he complains that "[t]his is not generous, not gentle, not humble" (V.ii.617) and leaves. Armado enters as Hector and begins his speech after the princess encourages him. While he is speaking, Costard enters and tells Armado that Jaquenetta is pregnant. Armado threatens to kill Costard, and Costard says that if he does, he will get a whipping for impregnating Jaquenetta and hanged for killing Pompey. Armado challenges Costard, and the rivals prepare to fight.

A messenger named Mercadé enters and tells the princess that he has news of her father. Even before he relates the news, the princess guesses that her father is dead. Berowne sends the Worthies away. The princess thanks the king and his lords for their entertainment and tells the king that they will leave that night. He begs her to stay, and the men again appeal to their women for love. The princess tells the king that he should become a hermit for twelve months and then seek her again, and Katherine and Maria tell Dumaine and Longaville to do similarly. Rosaline tells Berowne that he must spend one year using his wit to make the sick smile. He says the task is impossible, but agrees to it when she insists.

As the women are about to depart, Armado enters and asks the king if they can perform the song that would have been sung at the conclusion of their play. The king gives permission, and the cast of the play re-enters and performs a song about winter and spring.

THEMES, MOTIFS & SYMBOLS IN *LOVE'S LABOUR'S LOST*

THEMES

THE ABUSE OF LANGUAGE Many critics consider *Love's Labor's Lost* the most verbally scintillating of all of Shakespeare's plays. Nearly every line is packed with puns, wordplay, and metaphors. The king and his men define wit as the combination of intelligence and facility with language. The king and his three friends put on constant shows of wit. As the play opens, their apparent devotion to the goals of study, dramatized by the king's formal, classical first speech, testifies to their desire to put their verbal powers to good use, pursuing high ideals of fame and wisdom rather than more worldly goals. The king and courtiers will use their wit not in the service of courtly flirtation and seduction, but for reading and philosophizing.

Yet almost immediately, the men break their vow and use their facility with language for worldly purposes. They try to flirt and seduce instead of read and philosophize, but their language skills are less sharply honed than they thought. In the end, their attempts to seduce the women with language fail. When the king says "All hail" and the princess pretends he is referring to a hailstorm (V.ii.340), she undercuts his royal grandeur and makes him look silly.

Misuse of language is not confined to the noblemen. Don Armado prays to the "god of rhyme" to help him seduce Jaquenetta (I.ii.162), associating the skillful use of language with divinity and asking that divinity to help him find sexual success. When Costard defends himself before the king's charges of fooling around with Jaquenetta, he uses language in the service of evasion and trickery. He tries to claim that the king ruled against the company of "wenches" in particular, while Jaquenetta is a damsel. Costard uses language in the service of wrongdoing, avoiding a harsh but just punishment.

THE LEVELING OF CLASS DISTINCTIONS Like many Shakespearean romances, the cast of characters in *Love's Labor's Lost* includes representatives from all across the social spectrum, from King Ferdinand and the French Princess to the country bumpkins Jaquenetta and Costard. Shakespeare does mine the gap between high and low class for humor—for example, the lower-class characters misuse and mispronounce words that the upper-class characters handle with ease—but in general, he suggests that the gap between high and low is a small one. The upper classes are no more disciplined or true to their word than the lower classes are. They feel superior when the lowly Costard is "taken with a wench" in the first scene, but eventually they all long for women. They make lyrical, idealistic speeches about wisdom and self-control, but they are just as susceptible to the allures of the flesh as the uneducated country folk are. At the end of the play, the aristocrats promise to stay away from their women for only a year, but the lowly Armado vows chastity for a full three years.

Both high and low earn Shakespeare's mockery by pretending to be what they are not. The aristocrats snicker at the commoners' poor performances in the Show of the Nine Worthies, but Shakespeare portrays their own performances in the Muscovite pageant as ridiculous and unconvincing. Shakespeare suggests that a better grasp of vocabulary and syntax may be the only thing separating the nobles from the peasants.

MEN'S SUBJECTION TO ROMANTIC LOVE In *Love's Labor's Lost*, men's power and autonomy wither as the men fall prey to romantic love. At the beginning of the play, the men are in full command. The king and his courtiers, all noble, rich, intelligent, and powerful, speak grandly about their own fame and grace, which they confidently anticipate. By the end of the play, they have broken their most cherished oaths, acted like idiots, dressed up in disguises that fool nobody, and used all of their intelligence and passion in the service of women who leave them. As great as the noblemen's power is, the power of romantic love is greater.

At the outset, the king and his friends view women as objects they can do without—a luxury that is difficult to give up, but a dispensable luxury. They assume their lives will be improved without women, reinforcing the idea, inherited from ancient Greece, that women and the passions they arouse keep men from wisdom and intellectual achievement. As Don Armado says of Jaquenetta, women are "the weaker vessel" (I.i.256). But by the end of the play, women have subdued men. The men have abandoned their former oaths and beg their departing lovers to stay with them longer. The tables have turned, and the women are now the ones in the powerful position of withholding love, as the men were in the first act. The princess's hunt symbolizes the rising power of women. The hunt, a typically masculine activity, and the image of a woman wielding a weapon, suggest that the males are now the prey. Indeed, the princess bags a male deer.

MOTIFS

DEATH Reminders of death, which recur in the last act of *Love's Labour's Lost*, destabilize the lively spirits that characterize the play. The first hint of death comes when Rosaline refers to the demise of Katherine's sister, who died because of love. The sister's lover "made her melancholy, sad, and heavy,/ And so she died" (V.ii.14–15). Rosaline describes the death not as a tragedy, but as a sad fact: love can often give way to death. The news of the princess's father's demise suggests that death is present, if only unconsciously, in the minds of the characters. To us this bulletin comes as a total shock, but the princess seems ready for it even before the messenger speaks. Before he finishes his sentence, the princess delivers the blow herself, declaring her father "Dead, for my life" (V.ii.703).

TEMPTATION The men see love, and the women who excite love in men, as a dangerous tempta- tion. The king proposes a three-year renunciation of women for the pursuit of wisdom and study, suggest- ing that men are more virtuous and accomplished without the temptation of women. Longaville echoes the classical Greek notion of passions as debased, and the Christian notion of the body as corrupter of the mind and soul, when he declares that "Fat paunches have lean pates" (I.i.26). By this he means that fall- ing prey to the temptations of the flesh, such as food or sex, will starve one's higher mental faculties. Shakespeare's recurring allusions to Christianity in this play make the temptations of the flesh appear serious: giving in is not just a matter of neglecting the mind, but of neglecting the soul. But while the men understand the risks, they succumb to temptation almost instantly. Armado denounces love in harsh terms, saying "love is a devil," but in the very next line he refers to Biblical examples of strong men who fall prey to love's temptations: "Yet was Samson so tempted, and he had an excellent strength. Yet was Solomon so seduced, and he had a very good wit" (I.ii.154–6). His quick change is typical of the other men's willingness to put aside worries and succumb to temptation.

SYMBOLS

THE MUSCOVITE COSTUMES Unlike other costumes in Shakespearean comedy (in *Twelfth Night* or *As You Like It*, for example), the Russian costumes the men don during the masque are unsuc- cessful and even ludicrous. The outlandish Russian costumes symbolize the men's doomed attempts to impress women with false shows of brilliance. Shakespeare contrasts the men's ineffectual costumes with the women's highly effective ones. The women are well aware than the Russians are not Russian, but the men do not see that the women have switched identities. The women even use the men's Muscovite dis- guises against them, complaining about the courtiers to the courtiers themselves: "Let us complain to them what fools were here," says Rosaline, "Disguised like Muscovites in shapeless gear" (V.ii.302–303). The interaction is typical. Throughout the play, the men's tricks not only fail to give them the upper hand, they provide an occasion for the women to undercut them.

THE WRITTEN WORD The written word symbolizes human striving for satisfaction and the disap- pointment that results from using empty words. The king and his courtiers repeatedly use the written word as a tool with which to satisfy their desires. At first they try to quench their thirst for fame by study- ing written works of philosophy and scholarship, vowing that they will find fame as bookworms. After the arrival of the women, the men's goals become more sexual than scholarly, but their dependence on the written word persists. The courtiers use overblown literary language that they borrow from books as a means of sweeping the women off their feet, and their most intense efforts at communication with the women are through sonnets, written poems. Writing symbolizes all the intellectual and spiritual "labor" that men use to get what they want.

Ultimately, however, words are empty. Most of the key letters get lost in the mail, never arriving at their destinations or having little effect if they finally do. Nathaniel unknowingly sums up the dissatisfying nature of writing when he insults Dull's ignorance of books. He says Dull "hath never fed of the dainties that are bred in a book. / He hath not eat paper, as it were, he hath not drunk ink" (IV.ii.21–2). Nathaniel implies that literate people like the courtiers do eat paper and drink ink, and in saying this he unwittingly points out that courtiers have an unsatisfying diet.

IMPORTANT QUOTATIONS FROM *LOVE'S LABOUR'S LOST*

1. Katherine: *Therefore I'll darkly end the argument.*
   Rosaline: *Look what you do, you do it still i'th'dark.*
   Katherine: *So do not you, for you are a light wench.*
   Rosaline: *Indeed I weigh not you, and therefore light.*
   Katherine: *You weigh me not? O, that's you care not for me.*

Location: V.ii.23–27
Speaker: Katherine and Rosaline
Context: Katherine and Rosaline playfully quarrel after Katherine tells Rosaline that she will live a long time because she has a light heart.

This passage is typical of *Love's Labour's Lost* exuberantly witty repartee. In it, words change their meanings with dazzling speed: "dark" means first "serious" and then "not lit," while "light" changes from "sexually uninhibited" to "not heavy." The women entertain themselves by shifting meanings this way. They are having light, purposeless fun. Purposelessness characterizes language and love in *Love's Labour's Lost*. Much of the charm of its witticisms comes from their superfluity. Language shines and shimmers for its own sake, without any real use or purpose. Unlike the traditional courtly use of fancy rhetoric to impress others, Shakespeare's characters speak wittily even when they have no need at all to impress anyone. The king's courtiers amuse themselves with sophisticated language, and they are all of the same social stature and can gain nothing by impressing each other. In this quotation, Rosaline and Katherine speak cleverly for no reason but entertainment. They are not trying to look good for the Englishmen or snag husbands by showing off their intelligence. Wit is its own justification.

2. *Therefore, brave conquerors—for so you are,*
   That war against your own affections
   And the huge army of the world's desires—
   Our late edict shall strongly stand in force.
   Navarre shall be the wonder of the world.

Location: I.i.8–12
Speaker: King Ferdinand to his friends
Context: The king congratulates his friends on their decision to study.

The king's first lines radiate a noble idealism that makes us expect heroic behavior. His style is classical, formal, and to the point: he proudly announces that his edict will stand, and that the world will admire Navarre for renouncing sex. He avoids the metaphors and figures of speech that fill the rest of *Love's Labour's Lost*, expressing himself straightforwardly just as he plans to live chastely. This style of speech is misleading, however. The king's and courtiers' behavior fails to conform to their idealistic self-image. They may feel like "brave conquerors" of their own passions, but it soon becomes clear that they are losers in the struggle for chastity and self-discipline. Even the king's opening lines contain a hint of the failure to come. Between the dashes, the king gets defensive, insisting that his friends are warriors, even though they are not traditional ones. He also lets figurative language slip into his speech, describing his friends as an "army."

3. *I will hereupon confess I am in love; and as it is base for a soldier to love, so am I in love with a base wench. If drawing my sword against the humour of affection would deliver me from the reprobate thought of it, I would take desire prisoner and ransom him to any French courtier for a new-devised curtsy.*

Location: I.ii.53–58
Speaker: Don Armado to Moth
Context: Armado tells Moth that he loves Jaquenetta.

Don Armado's silly and affected confession of love for Jaquenetta shows his lowly, uneducated status. He speaks in prose, while the aristocrats speak in verse, and he uses awkward and outlandish figures of speech that courtiers like Berowne would try to avoid. But Armado's speech also reveals his similarities to the aristocrats. He echoes the king's opening speech, denouncing the degrading effects of erotic passion. He condemns himself for being in love, just as the king expressed contempt for desire. Armado also uses a military metaphor to describe his relation to love—declaring that he would draw his sword against "affection" if he could—just as the king referred to the "war against your own affections" (I.i.9). By showing Armado echoing the king, Shakespeare suggests that a king and a lowly man react similarly when they find themselves battling love.

---

4. *Good Lord Boyet, my beauty, though but mean,*
   Needs not the painted flourish of your praise.
   Beauty is bought by judgement of the eye,
   Not uttered by base sale of chapmen's tongues.
   I am less proud to hear you tell my worth
   Than you much willing to be counted wise
   In spending your wit in the praise of mine.

Location: II.i.13–19
Speaker: the princess to Boyet
Context: Boyet has praised the princess's beauty in courtly language.

The princess's rejoinder to Boyet sums up the women's attitudes toward men's attempts at seduction in *Love's Labour's Lost.* Women see through men's grandiloquent speeches, playing along but not giving in. The princess resists men's language, insulting Boyet's words by comparing them to "chapmen's tongues," or salesmen always on the make. The princess believes that some things should not be dirtied by language and its lies, beauty among them. Beauty is understood by the eye alone and cannot be "uttered." The princess also manages to accuse Boyet—and by extension, all the other men who praise her unduly—of selfishness. While men may seem to be focused on the women they praise so highly, in fact they are most interested in showing off. They use feminine beauty mainly as an opportunity to flaunt their verbal prowess.

---

5. *Our wooing doth not end like an old play.*
   Jack hath not Jill. These ladies' courtesy
   Might well have made our sport a comedy.

Location: V.ii.851–852
Speaker: Berowne to his friends
Context: The women have left the men.

Berowne's remarks on the unexpected result of his and his friends' wooing could be taken as a commentary on the play as a whole. In its ambiguous ending, *Love's Labour's Lost* departs from Shakespeare's other romances and from the long tradition of dramas about love dating back to the Roman New Comedy. In general, comedies end in marriage. The story of the king and his friends, as Berowne notes, does not end as such "old play[s]" do.

MACBETH

Inspired by a witches prophecy, Macbeth murders his way to the throne of Scotland, but his conscience plagues him and his fellow lords rise up against him.

MACBETH IN CONTEXT

Shakespeare's shortest and bloodiest tragedy, *Macbeth* tells the story of Macbeth, a brave Scottish general who receives a prophecy from a trio of sinister witches that one day he will become king of Scotland. Consumed with ambitious thoughts and spurred to action by his wife, Macbeth murders King Duncan and seizes the throne for himself. He begins his reign wracked with guilt and fear and soon becomes a tyrannical ruler, as he is forced to commit more and more murders to protect himself from enmity and suspicion. The bloodbath swiftly propels Macbeth and Lady Macbeth to arrogance, madness, and death.

Macbeth was most likely written in 1606, early in the reign of James I, who had been James VI of Scotland before he succeeded to the English throne in 1603. James was a patron of Shakespeare's acting company, and of all the plays Shakespeare wrote under James's reign, *Macbeth* most clearly reflects the playwright's close relationship with the sovereign. In focusing on Macbeth, a figure from Scottish history, Shakespeare paid homage to his king's Scottish lineage. Additionally, the witches' prophecy that Banquo will found a line of kings is a clear nod to James's family's claim to have descended from the historical Banquo. In a larger sense, the theme of bad versus good kingship, embodied by Macbeth and Duncan, respectively, would have resonated at the royal court where James was busy developing his English version of the theory of divine right.

Macbeth is not Shakespeare's most complex play, but it is certainly one of his most powerful and emotionally intense. Whereas Shakespeare's other major tragedies, such as *Hamlet* and *Othello*, fastidiously explore the intellectual predicaments faced by their subjects, and the fine nuances of their subjects' characters, *Macbeth* tumbles madly from its opening to its conclusion. It is a sharp, jagged sketch of theme and character that has shocked and fascinated audiences for nearly four hundred years.

MACBETH: KEY FACTS

Full title: Macbeth
Time and place written: 1606; England
Date of first publication: 1623 (First Folio)
Genre: Tragedy
Setting (time): Eleventh century
Setting (place): Scotland and, briefly, England
Protagonist: Macbeth
Major conflict: Ambitious Macbeth struggles with his conscience before and after he murders Duncan; evil (Macbeth and Lady Macbeth) struggles with good (Malcolm and Macduff).

MACBETH: CHARACTER LIST

Banquo The brave, noble general whose children, according to the witches' prophecy, will inherit the Scottish throne. Like Macbeth, Banquo thinks ambitious thoughts, but he does not translate those thoughts into action. In a sense, Banquo's character stands as a rebuke to Macbeth, since he represents the path Macbeth chose not to take: a path in which ambition need not lead to betrayal and murder. Appropriately, it is Banquo's ghost—not Duncan's—that haunts Macbeth. In addition to embodying Macbeth's guilt over killing Banquo, the ghost also reminds Macbeth that he did not react as well as Banquo did to the witches' prophecy.

Donalbain Duncan's son and Malcolm's younger brother.

King Duncan The good king of Scotland whom Macbeth murders in order to attain the crown. Duncan is the model of a virtuous, benevolent, and farsighted ruler. His death symbolizes the destruction of an order in Scotland that can be restored only when Duncan's line, in the person of Malcolm, once more occupies the throne.

Fleance Banquo's son. Fleance survives Macbeth's attempt to murder him, and at the end of the play his whereabouts are unknown. Presumably, he may rule Scotland one day, fulfilling the witches' prophecy that Banquo's sons will sit on the Scottish throne.

Hecate The goddess of witchcraft. Hecate helps the three witches work their mischief on Macbeth.

Lennox A Scottish nobleman.

Macbeth The main character in the play. Macbeth, a Scottish general and the Thane of Glamis, is led to wicked by the prophecies of the three witches. Macbeth is a brave soldier and a powerful man, but he is not a virtuous one. He has ambitions to the throne and is easily tempted into murder in order to fulfill them. Once he commits his first crime and is crowned king of Scotland, he embarks on further atrocities with increasing ease. His response to every problem is violence and murder. Ultimately, Macbeth lacks the skills necessary to rule without being a tyrant, and is better suited to the battlefield than to political intrigue. Unlike Shakespeare's great villains, such as Richard III and *Othello*'s Iago, Macbeth is never truly comfortable in his role as a criminal.

Lady Macbeth Macbeth's wife. Lady Macbeth is a deeply ambitious woman who lusts for power and position. Early in the play she seems to be the stronger and more ruthless of the two, as she urges her husband to kill Duncan and seize the crown. After the bloodshed begins, however, Lady Macbeth falls victim to guilt and madness to an even greater degree than her husband. Her conscience affects her to such an extent that eventually she commits suicide. Shakespeare suggests that she and Macbeth are deeply in love, and many of Lady Macbeth's speeches imply that her influence over her husband is primarily sexual. Their joint alienation from the world, occasioned by their partnership in crime, strengthens their already strong attachment.

Macduff A Scottish nobleman hostile to Macbeth's kingship from the start. Eventually Macduff becomes a leader of the crusade to unseat Macbeth. The crusade's mission is to place the rightful king, Malcolm, on the throne, but Macduff also desires vengeance for Macbeth's murder of Macduff's wife and young son.

Lady Macduff Macduff's wife. The scene in her castle provides our only glimpse of a domestic realm other than Macbeth and Lady Macbeth's. Lady Macduff and her home serve as contrasts to Lady Macbeth and the hellish world of Inverness.

Malcolm The son of Duncan, whose restoration to the throne signals Scotland's return to order following Macbeth's reign of terror. Initially weak and uncertain of his own power, as when he and Donalbain flee Scotland after their father's murder, Malcolm becomes a serious challenge to Macbeth with Macduff's aid and the support of England.

The Murderers A group of ruffians ordered by Macbeth to murder Banquo, Fleance (whom they fail to kill), and Macduff's wife and children.

Porter The drunken doorman of Macbeth's castle.

Ross A Scottish nobleman.

The Three Witches Three "black and midnight hags" who plot mischief against Macbeth using charms, spells, and prophecies. The witches' predictions prompt Macbeth to murder Duncan, order the deaths of Banquo and his son, and blindly believe in his own immortality. The play leaves the witches' true identity unclear. Aside from the fact that they are servants of Hecate, we know little about their place in the cosmos. In some ways they resemble the mythological Fates, who impersonally weave the threads of human destiny. The witches take a perverse delight in using their knowledge of the future to toy with and destroy human beings.

MACBETH: PLOT OVERVIEW

At a military camp, King Duncan of Scotland is pleased to hear that his generals Macbeth and Banquo have defeated the Irish and the Norwegian armies. On their way back to court, Macbeth and Banquo encounter three witches who predict that Macbeth will be king and that Banquo's heirs will be kings after him. Macbeth, spurred on by his ambitious wife Lady Macbeth, decides to make the prophecy come true while Duncan visits Inverness, Macbeth's castle. Despite doubts and visions of a bloody dagger, Macbeth kills Duncan in his sleep and frames two chamberlains for the murder.

Macbeth becomes king. Fearful of the witches' prophecy that Banquo's heirs will seize the throne, Macbeth hires a group of murderers to kill Banquo and his son Fleance, but Fleance escapes. At a feast, Banquo's ghost appears to Macbeth, and Macbeth frightens his guests by raving at it. Meanwhile, Duncan's son Malcolm, together with his friend Macduff, has been petitioning the English King Edward for help against the "tyrant" Macbeth. Frightened, Macbeth visits the witches at their cavern who present him with further prophecies: he must beware Macduff, he cannot be harmed by any man born of woman, and he will be safe until Birnam Wood comes to Dunsinane Castle. Macbeth seizes Macduff's castle and has Lady Macduff and her children murdered. Macduff and Malcolm invade Scotland with the English army. Meanwhile, Lady Macbeth has been sleepwalking and lamenting imaginary bloodstains on her hands. Before the battle, Macbeth receives news that she has killed herself. The witches' warnings prove prophetic: the army advances on Dunsinane shielded by boughs cut from Birnam wood, and Macduff was not born of woman but delivered by cesarean section. Macduff kills Macbeth, and Malcolm becomes king of Scotland.

MACBETH: SCENE SUMMARY

ACT I

After the witches' prophecy that Macbeth will become king, Lady Macbeth convinces him to take matters into his own hands and kill the current King Duncan.

I.I Location: a moor

Three witches plot to meet Macbeth after the battle.

Thunder and lightning crash above a Scottish moor. Three haggard female witches appear out of the storm. In eerie, chanting tones, they make plans to meet with Macbeth upon the heath after the battle.

I.II Location: King Duncan's camp near his palace at Forres

King Duncan receives news that Macbeth and Banquo have fought valiantly in a recent battle.

The Scots, led by King Duncan, are at war with Irish invaders, led by the rebel Macdonald. A bloody captain, wounded helping Duncan's son Malcolm escape capture, tells Duncan that the Scots have emerged victorious. Scottish generals Macbeth and Banquo fought with great courage and Macbeth slew the traitorous Macdonald. The Thane of Ross arrives to tell Duncan that the traitorous thane of Cawdor has been defeated and the Norwegian army repelled. Duncan condemns the thane of Cawdor to death, and bestows Cawdor's title on the brave Macbeth. Ross leaves to deliver the news to Macbeth.

I.III Location: a heath

The witches prophecy that Macbeth will become king.

Thunder rolls and the three witches appear and tell rhymes about what they have been doing. A drum beats, and Macbeth and Banquo enter on their way to Forres. They notice the witches and recoil in horror. The witches hail Macbeth as thane of Glamis, thane of Cawdor, and "king that shall be." Macbeth is baffled and intrigued; he is indeed thane of Glamis, but has not yet heard Duncan proclaim him thane of Cawdor. The witches turn to Banquo. In riddles, they call Banquo "lesser than Macbeth, and greater" (I.iii.63), and then tell him that although he will not be king, his children will be kings. Macbeth presses the witches for more information, but they vanish into thin air.

In disbelief, Macbeth and Banquo discuss the strange encounter. Their conversation is interrupted by the arrival of Ross and Angus. Ross tells Macbeth that he is now thane of Cawdor, as the former thane is to be executed for treason. Macbeth, amazed that one of the witches' prophecies has come true, ignores his companions and speaks to himself, wondering whether he will become king and whether he will have to perform a dark deed in order to gain the crown. As they group departs for Forres, Macbeth whispers to Banquo that they should speak about the witches later.

I.IV Location: Forres. Duncan's palace

Duncan pronounces Malcolm heir to his throne.

Malcolm reports to Duncan, his father, that Cawdor repented for his treason before he was executed. Macbeth and Banquo enter with Ross and Angus. Duncan thanks Macbeth and Banquo for their heroism and proclaims Malcolm the heir to his throne. Macbeth notes to himself that Malcolm now stands between him and the crown. Macbeth departs home to make preparations for Duncan to dine at his castle that evening.

I.V Location: Inverness (Macbeth's castle)

Lady Macbeth resolves to use violence to eliminate Duncan so that Macbeth can become king.

Lady Macbeth reads to herself a letter from Macbeth in which he tells about his encounter with the witches and about his new title as thane of Cawdor. Lady Macbeth murmurs that she fears that Macbeth is too full of "th' milk of human kindness" (I.v.15) to carry out his ambitions. A messenger informs her that Macbeth is on his way and that King Duncan is arriving later that evening. Lady Macbeth appeals to spirits to "unsex me here, / And fill me from the crown to the toe top-full / Of direst cruelty" (I.v.39–41). She resolves to be less feminine and help Macbeth seize the crown. She greets Macbeth as he arrives, and promises him that she will devise a plan to get rid of Duncan that night.

I.VI Location: outside Inverness

Duncan arrives at Macbeth's castle.

Duncan, the Scottish lords, and their attendants arrive at the castle. Lady Macbeth greets him hospitably, and leads them inside.

I.VII Location: Inverness

Lady Macbeth taunts Macbeth into committing to killing Duncan.

As the evening's feast is prepared, Macbeth, alone, ponders whether he should assassinate Duncan. He would risk eternal damnation if he could be sure that his earthly life would not end terribly. On the other hand, Duncan is his kinsman, ruler, and guest, as well as a virtuous king. Lady Macbeth enters and tells Macbeth that the king has been asking for him during dinner. Macbeth tells her that he has resolved not to kill Duncan. Lady Macbeth, outraged, calls him a coward and questions his manhood. Then she tells him her plan: she will give Duncan's chamberlains wine to make them drunk, and after they (Macbeth and Lady Macbeth) kill Duncan, they will smear his blood on the sleeping chamberlains and frame them for the murder. Astonished at the brilliance and daring of her plan, Macbeth tells his wife she should bear male children only. He agrees to proceed.

ACT II

With Lady Macbeth's help, Macbeth kills Duncan and takes the throne.

II.I Location: Inverness

On his way to kill Duncan, Macbeth has a vision of a bloody dagger.

Banquo tells his son Fleance that he has been having trouble sleeping. Macbeth enters. Banquo tells him that Duncan is asleep. Banquo also tells Macbeth that he has had bad dreams about the witches, but they decide to speak of them later. Banquo and Fleance leave. Alone in the darkened hall, Macbeth has a vision of a bloody dagger floating in the air before him, its handle pointing toward his hand and its tip aiming at Duncan. Though spooked, Macbeth still resolves to do his bloody work. A bell tolls as Lady Macbeth's signal that the chamberlains are asleep, and Macbeth strides toward Duncan's chamber.

II.II Location: Inverness. Outside Duncan's rooms

Supported by Lady Macbeth, Macbeth kills Duncan.

Lady Macbeth enters as Macbeth leaves. She imagines Macbeth killing the king. Had Duncan not resembled her father, she notes, she would have killed him herself. Macbeth emerges, his hands covered in blood, and says that the deed is done. Badly shaken, he tells her that he heard the chamberlains awake and say their prayers before going back to sleep. Although he tried, he could not bring himself to say "amen" with them. He thought he heard a voice cry out, "Sleep no more, / Macbeth does murder sleep" (II.ii.33–34). Lady Macbeth becomes angry when she notices that Macbeth forgot to leave the bloody daggers with the sleeping chamberlains. He refuses to return to the room, so she takes the daggers herself. As she leaves, Macbeth hears a mysterious knocking. Lady Macbeth returns and takes him back to their bedchamber, where he can wash the blood off his hands.

II.III Location: Inverness

Early in the morning, Macduff discovers that Duncan has been murdered.

A drunken porter stumbles to answer the knocking, grumbling comically about the noise. Macduff and Lennox enter. The porter says that he was up late carousing and rambles on humorously about the effects of alcohol, which "provokes and unprovokes" lechery: alcohol facilitates arousal but makes men impotent (II.iii.27). Macbeth enters, and Macduff asks to see Duncan. Macbeth stiltedly says that Duncan is still asleep. As Macduff enters the king's chamber, Lennox describes the storms that raged the previous night. With a cry of "O horror, horror, horror!" (II.iii.59), Macduff rushes out and announces that the king has been murdered. General chaos ensues. As Macbeth and Lennox emerge from the bedroom, Duncan's sons Malcolm and Donalbain arrive and hear that Duncan has been murdered, most likely by his chamberlains. Macbeth declares that in his rage he has killed the chamberlains.

Macduff is suspicious of Macbeth, but Lady Macbeth faints and must be attended to. Banquo and Macbeth call for a meeting of the lords. Malcolm and Donalbain fear for their lives and resolve to flee in secret: Malcolm to England and Donalbain to Ireland.

II.IV Location: outside Inverness

While the natural behaves unnaturally, Macbeth is to be crowned king.

Ross and an old man discuss the strange and ominous events of the past few days: it has been dark during the day, an owl has killed a falcon, and Duncan's beautiful horses have eaten one another. Macduff emerges from the castle and tells Ross that the lords have chosen Macbeth to be king. Because Malcolm and Donalbain have fled the scene, it is suspected that they were involved in the murder. Macduff returns home to Fife, and Ross goes to Scone for Macbeth's coronation.

ACT III

Macbeth has Banquo killed, but Macduff and Malcolm are preparing to invade Scotland with an English army.

III.I Location: Forres. Royal palace

Macbeth plots to kill Banquo and Fleance.

Banquo thinks about the weird sisters' prophecies. Macbeth has become king, and Banquo wonders if that means that Banquo's sons will be kings. Macbeth and Lady Macbeth enter as king and queen. They invite Banquo to their feast that evening. Banquo accepts, and says that he will go for a ride in the afternoon. Macbeth says to Banquo that Malcolm and Donalbain may be plotting against his crown.

Macbeth dismisses his court and orders the men waiting for him to be invited in. Alone, Macbeth muses that Banquo is the only person whom he fears. If Banquo's sons take over the throne after Macbeth, as the witches had predicted, the murder of Duncan will have been pointless. The two hired murderers come in. Macbeth inspires them to want to kill Banquo, and they promise to kill both Banquo and Fleance.

III.II   Location: Forres. Royal palace

Macbeth and Lady Macbeth, both uneasy, discuss Banquo's upcoming murder.

In despair, Lady Macbeth sends for her husband. Macbeth enters and tells his wife that he too is discontented. He tells her about "a deed of dreadful note" (III.ii.45) that he has planned for Banquo and Fleance and urges her to be friendly with Banquo during the feast to lull him into a false sense of security.

III.III   Location: Forres. Park outside the royal palace

Macbeth's murderers kills Banquo, but Fleance escapes.

At dusk, the two murderers, joined by a third, wait for Banquo. Banquo and Fleance approach on their horses and dismount. The murderers kill Banquo, but Fleance manages to escape in the darkness. The murderers leave to report to Macbeth.

III.IV   Location: Forres. Royal palace banquet hall

At a royal banquet, Macbeth is tormented by Banquo's ghost.

Macbeth and Lady Macbeth enter, followed by the court. One of the murderers comes up to speak to Macbeth, and privately tells him that Banquo is dead but that Fleance has escaped. This news angers Macbeth. Returning to head of the table, Macbeth sees Banquo's ghost, invisible to everyone else. Horror-struck, Macbeth speaks to the ghost, confusing the guests. Lady Macbeth makes excuses for Macbeth, and urges the guests to ignore his behavior. Privately, she berates Macbeth. The ghost disappears, and Macbeth recovers. As he offers a toast, however, Banquo's specter reappears. and shocks Macbeth into further outbursts. Lady Macbeth sends the alarmed guests out of the room as the ghost vanishes again. Macbeth tells Lady Macbeth that Macduff may be plotting against him. He adds that he will visit the witches again tomorrow and ask them for more information. He is committed to doing whatever is necessary to keep his throne. They retire to bed.

III.III   Location: a heath

The witches prepare to receive Macbeth the next day.

The witches meet with Hecate, the goddess of witchcraft. She says that the next day, when Macbeth arrives, they should summon spirits to "draw him on to his confusion" (III.v.29).

III.VI   Location: Scotland

Macduff and Malcolm have been preparing for war against the tyrant Macbeth.

Lennox and another lord discuss the situation. Banquo's murder has been officially blamed on Fleance, but they both suspect that the "tyrant" Macbeth killed Duncan and Banquo. The lord tells Lennox that Macduff has gone to England to join Malcolm in asking King Edward for aid. Macbeth too prepares for war.

ACT IV

Warned by the witches against Macduff, Macbeth murders Macduff's wife and children, and Macduff vows to take revenge, with the help of an English army.

IV.I Location: a dark cavern

The witches tell Macbeth to beware Macduff.

Hecate and the witches prepare spells around their cauldron. Macbeth enters and asks them to reveal to him the truth of their prophecies. The witches summon horrible apparitions: first, a floating head warns him to beware Macduff, and then a bloody child tells him that "none of woman born / shall harm Macbeth" (IV.i.96–97). Next, a crowned child carrying a tree tells him that he is safe until Birnam Wood moves to Dunsinane Hill. Finally, a procession of eight crowned kings walks by, followed by Banquo's ghost. Refusing to tell Macbeth what the maddening final image means, the witches vanish. Lennox enters and tells Macbeth that Macduff has fled to England. Macbeth resolves to send murderers to Macduff's castle.

IV.II Location: Macduff's castle

Macduff's castle is attacked by Macbeth's murderers.

Lady Macduff feels betrayed that her husband has fled without telling her why. Lady Macduff complains about Macduff to her perceptive little son. A messenger rushes in and urges her to flee. A group of murderers then enters. They stab Macduff's son and chase Lady Macduff.

IV.III Location: England. Outside King Edward's palace

Malcolm and Macduff plan to return to Scotland at the head of an English army.

Malcolm tests Macduff's loyalty by berating himself and wondering whether he is fit to be king. Hearing Malcolm describe himself as lustful, greedy, and violent, Macduff finally agrees that Malcolm is not fit to govern, thereby passing Malcolm's test of loyalty. Malcolm retracts his supposed shortcomings and embraces Macduff as an ally. Malcolm mentions to Macduff that King Edward of England has a miraculous power to cure disease.

Ross enters, recently arrived from Scotland. He tells Macduff that his wife and children are well, but that the country is in terrible shape. Malcolm says that he will return to Scotland with ten thousand soldiers lent him by King Edward. Ross breaks down and confesses that Macbeth has murdered Macduff's wife and children. Macduff is crushed with grief, and Malcolm urges him to turn his grief to anger.

ACT V

Lady Macbeth dies, Macduff kills Macbeth, and Malcolm becomes king.

V.I Location: Dunsinane Castle

Lady Macbeth descends into madness, crippled by guilt over the murders she and Macbeth have committed.

At night, a doctor and a gentlewoman discuss Lady Macbeth's strange habit of sleepwalking. Suddenly, Lady Macbeth enters in a trance with a candle in her hand. She sees blood on her hands and claims that nothing will ever wash it off.

V.II Location: Dunsinane. Outside the castle

Malcolm approaches with the English army.

Scottish lords discuss the military situation: Malcolm approaches with the English army, and the Scottish army will join up with them near Birnam Wood. Macbeth has fortified Dunsinane Castle in a mad rage.

V.III   Location: Dunsinane Castle

Macbeth arms himself in preparation for the battle.

Macbeth calls his servant Seyton, who confirms that an army of ten thousand Englishmen approaches. Macbeth puts on his armor even though the battle is far off. The doctor tells Macbeth that Lady Macbeth is troubled by "thick-coming fancies" (V.iii.40). Macbeth orders him to cure her of her delusions.

V.IV   Location: the country near Birnam Wood

Malcolm's army will approach Dunsinane carrying tree boughs to disguise their number.

Malcolm and the English lord Siward decide to disguise the number of their troops by having each soldier carry a bough from Birnam Wood as they approach the castle.

V.V   Location: Dunsinane Castle

Lady Macbeth dies, and Macbeth resolves to die fighting.

Macbeth boasts that the castle will repel the enemy, and blusteringly orders that banners be hung. Seyton appears to tell Macbeth that the queen is dead. Macbeth numbly speaks about the pointlessness of life: life is "a tale / Told by an idiot, full of sound and fury, / Signifying nothing" (V.v.25–27). A messenger enters with astonishing news: the trees of Birnam Wood are advancing toward Dunsinane. With terror Macbeth recalls the witches' prophecy: he will not be vanquished till Birnam Wood moves to Dunsinane. He resolves to die fighting.

V.VI   Location: outside Dunsinane Castle

The battle commences.

Malcolm orders the English soldiers to throw down their boughs and draw their swords.

V.VII   Location: battlefield outside Dunsinane Castle

Macbeth insolently slays Siward's son.

Macbeth fights vigorously, unafraid to die because no man born of woman can harm him. He slays Siward's son and disappears in the fray.

V.VIII   Location: battlefield outside Dunsinane Castle

Macduff searches for Macbeth, whom he longs to kill personally.

V.IX   Location: battlefield outside Dunsinane Castle

Malcolm and Siward enter Dunsinane Castle.

V.X   Location: battlefield outside Dunsinane Castle

Macbeth fights Macduff, and finds out that Macduff was technically not "of woman born."

Macbeth encounters Macduff and they fight. When Macbeth insists that he is invincible because of the witches' prophecy, Macduff tells Macbeth that he was "from his mother's womb / Untimely ripped" (V.x.15–16)—that is, his mother had a Caesarean birth. They exit fighting.

V.XI   Location: Dunsinane Castle

Macduff has killed Macbeth, and Malcolm becomes king of Scotland.

Malcolm and Siward have captured Dunsinane Castle. Ross tells Siward that his son is dead. Macduff emerges with Macbeth's head in his hand and proclaims Malcolm king of Scotland. Malcolm declares that Scottish nobles will now be known as earls rather than thanes, according to the English system. Malcolm curses Macbeth and invites all to see him crowned at Scone.

ANALYSIS OF MAJOR CHARACTERS IN *MACBETH*

MACBETH

Before he kills Duncan, Macbeth is plagued by worry and almost aborts the crime. It takes Lady Macbeth's steely sense of purpose to push him into the deed. After the murder, however, her powerful personality begins to disintegrate, leaving Macbeth increasingly alone. He fluctuates between fits of fevered action, in which he plots a series of murders to secure his throne, and moments of terrible guilt (as when Banquo's ghost appears) and absolute pessimism (after his wife's death, when he seems to succumb to despair). These fluctuations reflect the tragic tension within Macbeth: he is at once too ambitious to allow his conscience to stop him from murdering his way to the top and too conscientious to be happy with himself as a murderer. As things fall apart for him at the end of the play, he seems almost relieved. With the English army at his gates, he can finally return to life as a warrior, and he displays a kind of reckless bravado as his enemies surround him and drag him down. In part, this stems from his fatal confidence in the witches' prophecies, but it also seems to derive from the fact that he has returned to the arena where he has been most successful and where his internal turmoil need not affect him—namely, the battlefield. Unlike many of Shakespeare's other tragic heroes, Macbeth never seems to contemplate suicide: "Why should I play the Roman fool," he asks, "and die / On mine own sword?" (V.x.1–2). Instead, he goes down fighting, bringing the play full circle: it begins with Macbeth winning on the battlefield and ends with him dying in combat.

LADY MACBETH

Lady Macbeth is one of Shakespeare's most famous and frightening female characters. When we first see her, she is already plotting Duncan's murder, and she is stronger, more ruthless, and more ambitious than her husband. She seems fully aware of this and knows that she will have to push Macbeth into committing murder. At one point, she wishes that she were not a woman so that she could do it herself. This theme of the relationship between gender and power is the key to Lady Macbeth's character: her husband implies that she is a masculine soul inhabiting a female body, which seems to link masculinity to ambition and violence. Shakespeare, however, seems to use her—and the witches—to undercut Macbeth's idea that "undaunted mettle should compose / Nothing but males" (I.vii.73–74). These crafty women use the *female* method of manipulation in order to achieve power and further their supposedly male ambitions. Women, the play implies, can be as ambitious and cruel as men, yet social constraints deny them the means to pursue these ambitions on their own.

Afterward the murder, Lady Macbeth begins a slow slide into madness. Just as ambition affects her more strongly than Macbeth before the crime, so does guilt plague her more strongly afterward. By the close of the play, she has been reduced to sleepwalking through the castle, desperately trying to wash away an invisible bloodstain. Once the sense of guilt comes home to roost, Lady Macbeth's sensitivity becomes a weakness and she is unable to cope. Significantly, she (apparently) kills herself, signaling her total inability to deal with the legacy of their crimes.

THE THREE WITCHES

Throughout the play, the witches—referred to as the "weird sisters" by many of the characters—lurk like dark thoughts and unconscious temptations to evil. In part, the mischief they cause stems from their supernatural powers, but mainly it is the result of their understanding of the weaknesses of their specific interlocutors. They play upon Macbeth's ambition like puppeteers. The witches bear a striking and obviously intentional resemblance to the Fates, female characters in both Norse and Greek mythologies who weave a fabric of human lives and then cut the threads to end them. Some of their prophecies seem self-fulfilling. For example, it is doubtful that Macbeth would have murdered his king without the push given by the witches' predictions. In other cases, though, their prophecies are just remarkably accurate readings of the future. It is hard to see Birnam Wood's arrival in Dunsinane as self-fulfilling in any way. The play offers no easy answers. Instead, Shakespeare keeps the witches well outside the limits of human comprehension. They embody an unreasoning, instinctive evil.

THEMES, MOTIFS, & SYMBOLS IN *MACBETH*

THEMES

UNCHECKED AMBITION AS A CORRUPTING FORCE   The destruction wrought when ambition goes unchecked by moral constraints, which is the main theme of *Macbeth*, finds its most powerful expression in the play's two main characters. Macbeth is a courageous Scottish general who is not naturally inclined to commit evil deeds, yet deeply desires power and advancement. He kills Duncan against his better judgment and afterward stews in guilt and paranoia. Toward the end of the play he descends into a kind of frantic, boastful madness. Lady Macbeth, in contrast, pursues her goals with greater determination than her husband, yet has more difficulty withstanding the repercussions of her immoral acts. One of Shakespeare's most forcefully drawn female characters, she spurs her husband mercilessly to kill Duncan and urges him to be strong in the murder's aftermath, but she is eventually driven to distraction by the very violence she has demanded. In each case, ambition—helped along by the malign prophecies of the witches—is what drives the couple to commit ever more terrible atrocities. The problem, the play suggests, is that once one decides to use violence to further one's quest for power, it is difficult to stop. There are always potential threats to the throne—Banquo, Fleance, Macduff—and it is always tempting to use violent means to dispose of them.

THE RELATIONSHIP BETWEEN CRUELTY AND MASCULINITY   Both   Macbeth   and Lady Macbeth equate masculinity with naked aggression, and whenever they converse about manhood, violence soon follows. Lady Macbeth manipulates her husband by questioning his manhood, wishes that she herself could be "unsexed," and does not contradict Macbeth when he says that a woman like her should give birth only to boys. Using tactics his wife would condone, Macbeth provokes the murderers he hires to kill Banquo by questioning their manhood.

At the same time, women are a clear source of evil in the play. The witches' prophecies spark Macbeth's ambitions and then encourage his violent behavior, and Lady Macbeth provides the brains and the will behind her husband's plotting. *Macbeth* traces the root of chaos and evil to women, which has led some critics to argue that this is Shakespeare's most misogynistic play.

KINGSHIP VERSUS TYRANNY   In the play, Duncan is always referred to as a "king," while Macbeth soon becomes known as a "tyrant." The difference between the two types of rulers is expressed in a conversation that occurs in scene IV.iii, when Macduff meets Malcolm in England. In order to test Macduff's loyalty to Scotland, Malcolm pretends that he would make an even worse king than Macbeth. He tells Macduff of his reproachable qualities, such as a thirst for personal power and a violent temperament, both of which characterize Macbeth perfectly. On the other hand, Malcolm says that the right virtues for a king are "justice, verity, temp'rance, stableness, / Bounty, perseverance, mercy, [and] lowliness" (IV.iii.92–93). The model king, then, offers the kingdom an embodiment of order and justice, but also comfort and affection. Under him, subjects are rewarded according to their merits, as when Duncan makes Macbeth Thane of Cawdor after Macbeth's victory over the invaders. Most important, a good king is loyal to Scotland above himself. Macbeth, by contrast, brings only chaos to Scotland, as symbolized by the bad weather and bizarre supernatural events. He offers no real justice, only a habit of capriciously murdering those he sees as a threat. As the embodiment of tyranny, he must be overcome by Malcolm so that Scotland can have a true king once more.

MOTIFS

HALLUCINATIONS Visions and hallucinations recur throughout the play and serve as reminders of Macbeth and Lady Macbeth's joint culpability for the growing body count. When he is about to kill Duncan, Macbeth sees a dagger floating in the air. Covered with blood and pointed toward the king's chamber, the dagger represents the bloody course on which Macbeth is about to embark. Later, he sees Banquo's ghost sitting in a chair at a feast, pricking his conscience by mutely reminding him that he murdered his former friend. The seemingly hardheaded Lady Macbeth also eventually gives way to visions, as she sleepwalks and believes that her hands are stained with blood that cannot be washed away by any amount of water. In each case, it is ambiguous whether the vision is real or purely hallucinatory, but in both cases, the Macbeths read them uniformly as supernatural signs of their guilt.

PROPHECY Prophecy sets *Macbeth*'s plot in motion, specifically the witches' prophecy that Macbeth will become first thane of Cawdor and then king. The weird sisters make a number of other prophecies: they tell us that Banquo's heirs will be kings, Macbeth should beware Macduff, Macbeth is safe till Birnam Wood comes to Dunsinane, and no man born of woman can harm Macbeth. Save for the prophecy about Banquo's heirs, all of these predictions are fulfilled within the course of the play. Still, it is left deliberately ambiguous whether some of them are self-fulfilling. For example, we do not know whether Macbeth wills himself to be king or is fated to be king. Additionally, as the Birnam Wood and "born of woman" prophecies make clear, the prophecies must be interpreted as riddles, since they do not always mean what they seem to mean.

SYMBOLS

BLOOD Blood is everywhere in *Macbeth*, beginning with the opening battle between the Scots and the Norwegian invaders, which is described in harrowing terms by the wounded captain in scene I.ii. Once Macbeth and Lady Macbeth embark upon their murderous journey, blood comes to symbolize their guilt, and they begin to feel that their crimes have stained them and they cannot be washed clean: "Will all great Neptune's ocean wash this blood / Clean from my hand?" (II.ii.58–59). Macbeth cries after he has killed Duncan, even as his wife scolds him and says that a little water will clean up the mess. Later, though, she comes to share his horrified sense of being stained: "Out, damned spot; out, I say … who would have thought the old man to have had so much blood in him?" (V.i.30–34) she asks as she wanders through the halls of their castle near the close of the play. Blood symbolizes the guilt that sits like a permanent stain on the consciences of both Macbeth and Lady Macbeth.

WEATHER Macbeth's grotesque murder spree is accompanied by a number of unnatural occurrences in the natural realm. This link between weather and behavior is a common one in Shakespearean tragedies. From the thunder and lightning that accompany the witches' appearances to the terrible storms that rage on the night of Duncan's murder, these violations of the natural order reflect corruption in the moral and political orders.

IMPORTANT QUOTATIONS FROM *MACBETH*

---

1. *The raven himself is hoarse*
   That croaks the fatal entrance of Duncan
   Under my battlements. Come, you spirits
   That tend on mortal thoughts, unsex me here,
   And fill me from the crown to the toe top-full
   Of direst cruelty. Make thick my blood,
   Stop up th' access and passage to remorse,
   That no compunctious visitings of nature

Shake my fell purpose, nor keep peace between
Th' effect and it. Come to my woman's breasts,
And take my milk for gall, you murd'ring ministers,
Wherever in your sightless substances
You wait on nature's mischief. Come, thick night,
And pall thee in the dunnest smoke of hell,
That my keen knife see not the wound it makes,
Nor heaven peep through the blanket of the dark,
To cry 'Hold, hold!'

Location: I.v.36-52
Speaker: Lady Macbeth
Context: Lady Macbeth appeals to evil spirits to give her masculine courage so that she can help Macbeth murder King Duncan.

Lady Macbeth's strength of purpose is contrasted with her husband's tendency to waver. This speech shows the audience that Lady Macbeth is the real steel behind Macbeth and that her ambition will be strong enough to drive her husband forward. At the same time, the language of this speech touches on the theme of masculinity. As she prepares to commit murder, Lady Macbeth says "unsex me here / … / … Come to my woman's breasts, / And take my milk for gall." The language suggests that her womanhood, represented by breasts and milk, usually symbols of nurture, impedes her from performing acts of violence and cruelty, which she associates with manliness. Later, this sense of the relationship between masculinity and violence will be deepened when Macbeth is unwilling to go through with the murders and his wife tells him, in effect, that he needs to be a man and get on with it.

2. *If it were done when 'tis done, then 'twere well*
   It were done quickly. If th' assassination
   Could trammel up the consequence, and catch
   With his surcease success: that but this blow
   Might be the be-all and the end-all, here,
   But here upon this bank and shoal of time,
   We'd jump the life to come. But in these cases
   We still have judgment here, that we but teach
   Bloody instructions which, being taught, return
   To plague th' inventor. This even-handed justice
   Commends th' ingredience of our poisoned chalice
   To our own lips. He's here in double trust:
   First, as I am his kinsman and his subject,
   Strong both against the deed; then, as his host,
   Who should against his murderer shut the door,
   Not bear the knife myself. Besides, this Duncan
   Hath borne his faculties so meek, hath been
   So clear in his great office, that his virtues
   Will plead like angels, trumpet-tongued against
   The deep damnation of his taking-off,
   And pity, like a naked new-born babe,
   Striding the blast, or heaven's cherubin, horsed
   Upon the sightless couriers of the air,
   Shall blow the horrid deed in every eye
   That tears shall drown the wind. I have no spur
   To prick the sides of my intent, but only
   Vaulting ambition which o'erleaps itself

And falls on th' other.

Location: I.vii.1-28
Speaker: Macbeth
Context: Macbeth debates whether or not to kill Duncan.

Macbeth's fear that "[w]e still have judgement here, that we but teach / Bloody instructions which, being taught, return / To plague th' inventor," foreshadows the way that his deeds will eventually come back to haunt him. The imagery in this speech is dark. We hear of "bloody instructions," "deep damnation," and a "poisoned chalice." This imagery suggests that Macbeth is aware of how the murder would open the door to a dark and sinful world. At the same time, he admits that his only reason for committing murder, "ambition," suddenly seems an insufficient justification for the act. The destruction that comes from unchecked ambition will continue to be explored as one of the play's themes. As the soliloquy ends, Macbeth seems to resolve not to kill Duncan, but this resolve only lasts until Lady Macbeth returns to convince him, by sheer strength of will, to go ahead with their plot.

---

3. *Whence is that knocking?—*
   How is 't with me, when every noise appalls me?
   What hands are here! Ha, they pluck out mine eyes.
   Will all great Neptune's ocean wash this blood
   Clean from my hand? No, this my hand will rather
   The multitudinous seas incarnadine,
   Making the green one red.

Location: II.ii.55-61
Speaker: Macbeth
Context: Having just murdered Duncan, Macbeth is startled by a knock at his door.

The mysterious knocking on Macbeth's gate promises doom. Indeed, the person knocking is Macduff, who will indeed eventually destroy Macbeth. The enormity of Macbeth's crime has awakened in him a powerful sense of guilt that will hound him throughout the play. Blood—specifically Duncan's blood—serves as the symbol of that guilt, and until his death Macbeth will be haunted by the sense that "all great Neptune's ocean" cannot cleanse him; that there is enough blood on his hands to turn the entire sea red. Lady Macbeth's response to this speech will be her prosaic remark, "A little water clears us of this deed" (II.ii.65). By the end of the play, however, she shares Macbeth's sense that Duncan's murder has irreparably stained them with blood.

---

4. *Out, damned spot; out, I say. One, two,—why, then 'tis time to do't. Hell is murky. Fie, my lord, fie, a*
   soldier and afeard? What need we fear who knows it when none can call our power to account? Yet who
   would have thought the old man to have had so much blood in him?

Location: V.i.30-34
Speaker: Lady Macbeth
Context: Lady Macbeth is sleepwalking and sees Duncan's blood on her hands on the eve of Macbeth's last battle.

Earlier in the play, Lady Macbeth possessed a stronger resolve and sense of purpose than her husband, and was the driving force behind their plot to kill Duncan. When Macbeth believed his hand was irreversibly bloodstained earlier in the play, Lady Macbeth told him, "A little water clears us of this deed" (II.ii.65). Now, however, she too sees blood. She is completely undone by guilt and descends into madness. It may be a reflection of her mental and emotional state that she is not speaking in verse. This is one of the few moments in the play when a major character—save for the witches, who speak in four-foot couplets—strays from iambic pentameter. Lady Macbeth's inability to sleep was foreshadowed in the voice that her husband thought he heard while killing the king. This voice cried out that Macbeth was murdering sleep. Here, Lady Macbeths' delusion that there is a bloodstain on her hand furthers the play's use of blood as a symbol of guilt. "What need we fear who knows it when none can call our power to account?" she asks, asserting that as long as her own and her husband's power is secure, the murders they committed cannot harm them. But her guilty state and her mounting madness show how hollow her words are. So, too, does the army outside her castle. "Hell is murky," she says, implying that she already knows that darkness intimately. The pair, in their destructive power, have created their own hell, where they are tormented by guilt and insanity.

---

5. She should have died hereafter.
    There would have been a time for such a word.
    Tomorrow, and tomorrow, and tomorrow
    Creeps in this petty pace from day to day
    To the last syllable of recorded time.
    And all our yesterdays have lighted fools
    The way to dusty death. Out, out, brief candle.
    Life's but a walking shadow, a poor player
    That struts and frets his hour upon the stage,
    And then is heard no more. It is a tale
    Told by an idiot, full of sound and fury,
    Signifying nothing.

Location: V.v.16-27
Speaker: Macbeth
Context: Macbeth has learned that Lady Macbeth is dead.

Macbeth's oddly muted response to his wife's death quickly segues into an expression of pessimism and despair that is one of Shakespeare's most famous speeches. Macbeth insists that there is no meaning or purpose in life. Rather, life "is a tale / Told by an idiot, full of sound and fury, / Signifying nothing." One can easily understand how, with his wife dead and armies marching against him, Macbeth succumbs to such pessimism. But there is also a defensive and self-justifying quality to his words. If everything is meaningless, then Macbeth's crimes are less horrific, because, like everything else, they too "signify nothing."

Macbeth's statement that "[l]ife's but a poor player / That struts and frets his hour upon the stage" can be read as Shakespeare's somewhat deflating reminder of the illusionary nature of the theater. After all, Macbeth is only a "player" himself, an actor strutting on an Elizabethan stage and playing a king. In any play, there is a conspiracy of sorts between the audience and the actors, as both pretend to accept the play's reality. Macbeth's comment calls attention to this conspiracy and partially explodes it. His nihilism embraces not only his own life but the entire play. If we take his words to heart, the play, too, can be seen as an event "full of sound and fury, / Signifying nothing."

MEASURE FOR MEASURE

Angelo enforces a strict code of sexual morals in Vienna, but then tries to force the chaste Isabella to have sex with him.

MEASURE FOR MEASURE IN CONTEXT

In recent years, *Measure for Measure* has been most often classified as a problem play, a category that includes *All's Well that Ends Well*, *Troilus and Cressida*, and *The Winter's Tale*. All of these plays involve deeply flawed yet sympathetic main characters who do unequivocally reprehensible things (Angelo in *Measure*, Bertram in *All's Well*, Leontes in *Winter's Tale*, Cressida in *Troilus*). All of the plays feature a keen awareness of nearing death and problematic, qualified endings. The three forced marriages at the end of *Measure for Measure* — Angelo and Mariana's, the duke and Isabella's, and Lucio and his lover's — have troubled many readers, especially since Isabella, who had planned on becoming a nun, is never given the opportunity to agree.

The plot is constructed around a series of secret identities and substitutions. The duke disguises himself as a friar and advises two other deceptions: the substitution of Mariana for Isabella in Angelo's bed and the substitution of a dead pirate's head for Claudio's. The resolution of the play depends on the unraveling of all the layers of intrigue created by the duke, who functions as master of ceremonies throughout.

MEASURE FOR MEASURE: KEY FACTS

Full title: Measure for Measure

Time and place written: 1604; London

Date of first performance: 1604

Genre: Comedy

Setting (time): Sixteenth century

Setting (place): Vienna

Protagonist: Isabella; Angelo; Duke

Major conflict: Angelo promises Isabella that he will spare her brother's life if she has sex with him

MEASURE FOR MEASURE: CHARACTER LIST

Lord Angelo The merciless nobleman whom the duke leaves in charge of Vienna. He tries to enforce a strict code of sexual morals, but then hypocritically pressures Isabella to have sex with him.

Barnardine A long-term prisoner in the jail. Barnardine is sentenced to be executed at the same time as Claudio. The duke eventually decides that even Barnardine's life deserves to be spared.

Claudio Isabella's brother. Claudio is sentenced to death for impregnating his common-law bride, Juliet.

Elbow A dim-witted constable charged with making arrests. His malapropisms provide comic relief.

Escalus A wise lord who advises Angelo to be more merciful. He is loyal to the duke but does not dare defy Angelo.

Isabella The play's protagonist. Isabella, Claudio's sister, is a virtuous young nun-in-training. She refuses to have sex with Angelo to save her brother's life.

Juliet Claudio's lover. She is pregnant with his baby.

Lucio Claudio's bachelor friend. Lucio is a flamboyant "fantastic" who provides much of the play's comedic content.

Mariana Angelo's former fiancée. He called off the wedding after Mariana lost her dowry in the ship-wreck that killed her brother.

Mistress Overdone The madam of a Vienna brothel.

Pompey A clown who works for Mistress Overdone.

Provost The keeper of the prison where Claudio is held.

Vincentio, the duke of Vienna The kind-hearted ruler of Vienna. Concerned about Vienna's depravity, the duke contrives to leave the stricter Angelo in charge of Vienna while he himself observes the pro-ceedings disguised as a friar.

MEASURE FOR MEASURE: PLOT OVERVIEW

The Duke of Vienna decides that he has allowed his subjects to become too lax in obeying the law, so he pretends to go on a journey and appoints Angelo in his place, knowing that Angelo will be very strict. Angelo cracks down on vice and sex crimes, arresting a man named Claudio for impregnating his fiancée Juliet before they are married. To set an example, Angelo condemns Claudio to death. Claudio's devoutly religious sister Isabella pleads with Angelo to show mercy, and Angelo, overcome with lust for her, offers to release Claudio if she has sex with him. She refuses, but Claudio urges her to reconsider her decision and save his life. The duke, who remains in Vienna disguised as a friar, intervenes and tells Isa-bella to agree to Angelo's request. The duke says that he will send Mariana, a woman Angelo jilted when she lost her money in a shipwreck, in Isabella's place. Angelo has sex with Mariana, thinking she is Isa-bella, but the next morning he orders Claudio executed anyway. The duke sends Angelo the head of a drunken pirate, making him believe it is Claudio's. The duke returns and takes back his power. Isabella comes forward and complains how Angelo has treated her. The duke pretends to disbelieve her at first, but when he reveals that he was there in disguise all along, Angelo has to admit his wrongs. Claudio and Angelo are pardoned, Angelo will marry Mariana, and the duke asks Isabella to marry him.

MEASURE FOR MEASURE: SCENE SUMMARY

ACT I

Left in charge by the duke of Vienna, Angelo passes strict laws and sentences Claudio to death for having sex with his fiancée.

I.I Location: Vienna. The duke's palace

The duke leaves Angelo in charge of Vienna while he is away.

The duke calls Lord Angelo to leave him temporarily in charge of Vienna, while he (the duke) goes on a journey. Angelo modestly refuses, asking the duke to test his skill as a ruler in some smaller way first. The duke replies that his mind is already made up, and that he must leave right away.

I.II Location: Vienna. A street

In accordance with Angelo's strict new laws regulating sexual morality, Claudio has been arrested for having sex with his common-law fiancée.

Some time later, Lucio discusses recent events with two gentlemen soldiers. They joke about the duke's trip to see the king of Hungary, and the war between Hungary and Vienna. The gentlemen disapprove of the proposed peace treaty, because peace is against their nature as soldiers.

They are making jokes about venereal disease when the brothel madam, Mistress Overdone, approaches. She tells them that Claudio has been arrested for fornication. His common-law fiancée Juliet is now pregnant. Lucio and the gentlemen leave to find out what is going on.

Pompey the clown enters and tells Mistress Overdone about a new proclamation shutting down all brothels in the suburban red-light district. Brothels in the city proper, like Mistress Overdone's, may still stay open, thanks to the political influence of a wealthy investor, but Mistress Overdone worries about her business. They leave just as Claudio approaches, led by the provost.

Claudio asks the provost why he is being taken to prison, and the provost replies that he is following Angelo's orders. Lucio asks Claudio what he has done, and Claudio replies that he has taken too many liberties and is being punished. Lucio tries to guess Claudio's crime—murder? lechery? Claudio replies that Lucio has guessed correctly. Lucio is surprised that sex should be so harshly punished.

Claudio responds that his intentions are honorable. He plans to marry Juliet but her family disapproves, so they have been waiting for a good time to announce their engagement. Claudio guesses that Angelo has passed such strict laws in order to assert his power. Claudio asks Lucio to find Isabella, Claudio's sister, who has recently joined a convent, and ask her to appeal on Claudio's behalf.

I.III Location: a monastery

The duke plans to disguise himself as a friar to observe how Angelo rules Vienna.

The duke asks Friar Thomas to let him hide in the monastery. He explains that for the past fourteen years, the people of Vienna have flagrantly disobeyed city laws with impunity. According to the duke, when the government does not enforce its own laws it loses all authority, and "the baby beats the nurse" (I.iii.30). In other words, the people regulate the government instead of the other way around. It would be unfair of the duke to all of a sudden begin punishing people for breaking laws, so he has asked Angelo to take over. However, to observe Angelo's actions in disguise, he would like to borrow one of Friar Thomas's friar robes.

I.IV Location: a convent

Lucio urges Claudio's sister Isabella to beg Angelo for Claudio's life.

Isabella learns about the rules of the nunnery that she plans to join. A man—Lucio—approaches, and Isabella is asked to answer the door: she has not been sworn in yet and so is still allowed to speak to men. Lucio tells Isabella that Claudio has impregnated his "friend." Isabella does not understand Lucio at first, but then guesses that Claudio's friend is her friend Juliet. Isabella asks why Claudio and Juliet do not simply marry. Lucio explains that the duke has given Angelo control of Vienna. Angelo, a logical and unemotional man, wants to make an example out of Claudio and execute him. Lucio urges Isabella to visit Angelo and use all of her feminine charms to beg for mercy. Isabella plans to leave immediately.

ACT II

Angelo promises to spare Claudio's life if Claudio's chaste sister Isabella consents to have sex with him.

II.I Location: Vienna. Court of law

Escalus advocates mercy, but Angelo is resolved to have Claudio executed the next morning.

Angelo tells Escalus that they must be firm in their sentencing. Escalus disagrees. Just as it is better to prune at the tree than to cut it down, he says, it is better to pressure people to reform than to execute them. As an example, Escalus asks Angelo whether he could ever sin like Claudio has sinned. Angelo responds firmly: "'Tis one thing to be tempted, Escalus, another thing to fall" (II.i.17). The law must punish harshly, Angelo argues, and if he himself should ever transgress, he should be treated harshly too. Angelo calls in the provost and reminds him that Claudio must be executed before nine o'clock the next morning.

Constable Elbow enters with Pompey and Froth, presenting them as two "notorious benefactors"— meaning malefactors. Eventually, we figure out that Pompey and Froth were found in a brothel. Froth confesses that he works for Mistress Overdone, and Escalus warns him that prostitution is illegal. Escalus questions Elbow about other constables. Privately, Escalus mourns Claudio's fate, but thinks that there is nothing to be done.

II.II Location: Vienna. Court of law

Isabella pleads with Angelo for Claudio's life, and Angelo, confused by how much he desires her, tells her to come back tomorrow.

The provost tries to convince Angelo to spare Claudio's life. He mentions Juliet's baby, which will be born fatherless if Claudio is executed.

A servant announces Isabella's arrival. She prefaces her plea by saying that she too abhors fornication, and that she is sorry to have to beg for Claudio's pardon. Yet she asks Angelo to condemn Claudio's fault instead of him. Angelo argues that people must be punished for their crimes. Isabella acquiesces, exclaiming, "O just but severe law!" (II.ii.42). She has resigned herself to mourning Claudio's death. Lucio whispers to her that she should not give up so easily, encouraging her to plead with more warmth.

She tries again, and again Lucio tells her that she is too cold. Angelo tells her that she is wasting her time and should leave. He says he would condemn his relatives the same way. Finally, Lucio sees that Angelo is wavering. Angelo tells Isabella to come back tomorrow.

Alone, Angelo ponders how much he desires Isabella. He tries to figure out why, wondering if it is because she is so chaste.

II.III Location: the prison

The duke encounters Claudio's fiancée returning from visiting Claudio.

The duke, disguised as a friar, visits the prison. Juliet enters and, when he asks her, tells him that she repents for her sin, but that she loves the man who impregnated her (Claudio). The duke tells her that she has sinned more than Claudio. He plans to visit Claudio, who must die tomorrow. Juliet is full of sorrow.

II.IV Location: Vienna. Court of law

Angelo tells Isabella that he will spare Claudio's life if she has sex with him.

Angelo is in emotional turmoil. On the one hand, laws must be followed and fornication is despicable, but on the other hand, he desires Isabella. She is announced.

Angelo tells Isabella that her brother will die unless she gives up her virginity. Isabella does not understand his implication, and he clarifies: would she be willing to sin to save Claudio's life? She again misunderstands, and Angelo asks his question again, more explicitly. Isabella answers that she would rather die than give up her chastity. Angelo replies that Claudio must then die and Isabella agrees. She believes it is better for Claudio to die than for her to tarnish her soul with sin. Angelo tells her that she is cruel. Angelo tells Isabella that he loves her. She replies that love does not excuse fornication. After all, Claudio is sentenced to die for love. Isabella realizes that his proposition is in earnest. She threatens to expose him, but he insists that no one will believe her given his impeccable reputation. He tells her that Claudio's death will be long and painful unless she consents to sleep with him. He gives her until the next day to decide and leaves.

In turmoil, Isabella resolves to visit Claudio and prepare him for death, sure that he will agree her chastity is worth more than his life.

ACT III

The duke plans to save Claudio by tricking Angelo into having sex with his jilted fiancée Mariana instead of with Isabella.

III.I Location: the prison

Claudio breaks down and asks Isabella to sleep with Angelo and save his life, but the duke has a better idea.

Claudio tells the duke (who is still disguised as a friar) that he hopes to live but is ready to die. The duke says that death, in many ways, may be easier and simpler than life, which is marred with so many complexities. He says it is strange how much humans fear death. Claudio thanks him. Isabella enters and asks to speak to Claudio. In private, the duke asks the provost to take him somewhere where he can overhear Isabella and Claudio's conversation.

Claudio asks Isabella about her conversation with Angelo. Isabella tells Claudio that he will die. When pressed, she vaguely tells him that the only way to stay his sentence is for her to lose her honor. He presses her further, but she hesitates to tell him about Angelo's proposition. Only when Claudio says that he is prepared to die if he must does she reveal to him that Angelo has promised to free him if she sleeps with Angelo.

Claudio initially expresses his disgust and says that he is ready to die, but then hesitates, saying, "Death is a fearful thing" (III.i.117). He tells her about his horror of death, and finally openly asks her to sleep with Angelo and save him. Isabella grows angry and calls him a coward, adding that his sinful sex with Juliet is a reflection of his ignoble nature.

The duke, who has heard this exchange, comes out of his hiding place. He privately tells Claudio that Angelo was only testing Isabella's virtue. Angelo would have executed Claudio either way. Claudio goes to apologize to Isabella.

Later, the duke speaks to Isabella alone, and tells her that he has a plan for saving Claudio without tarnishing her honor. He tells her about Mariana, Angelo's former fiancée. Angelo broke off their engagement when Mariana's dowry was lost in a shipwreck. The duke tells Isabella to consent to sleep with Angelo, but then send Mariana in her place. Angelo will be forced to marry Mariana, and Claudio will be freed.

III.II Location: outside the prison

The duke, disguised, runs into Lucio and Escalus.

The duke, disguised, runs into Constable Elbow with Pompey. Pompey is a pimp and a pickpocket, and will be sent to jail. Lucio, a friend of Pompey's, approaches and learns that Pompey is to be imprisoned, but refuses to pay Pompey's bail. Lucio asks the disguised duke about the duke's whereabouts. Angelo has been too strict about lechery, Lucio complains. The duke likes women and would have been more lenient. The duke-as-friar argues with Lucio and threatens to report Lucio to the duke. Lucio says he suspects that the duke has a reason to be circumspect. (Some productions imply that Lucio recognizes the duke through his disguise at this point.)

Lucio leaves. Escalus enters with the provost and Mistress Overdone, and tells the provost to send Mistress Overdone to prison for running a brothel. The duke asks Escalus about Angelo, whom Escalus describes as temperate and unyielding, as always.

Alone, the duke speaks about how Angelo will be tricked into paying for his sins.

ACT IV

Angelo sleeps with Mariana, but orders Claudio's execution anyway; the duke, disguised, prevents it.

IV.I Location: Mariana's house

Isabella makes plans to trick Angelo with Mariana.

Isabella tells the duke that she has agreed to have sex with Angelo, who has given her two keys along with instructions to meet him in a garden. Angelo showed her the way twice. She told Angelo that she will not be able to stay long for fear of suspicion.

The duke introduces Mariana to Isabella and tells them to discuss their plans together on their own. They go for a walk, and when they return they have agreed on the plan. Isabella tells Mariana to be sure to remind Angelo about Claudio before leaving. The duke assures Mariana that sleeping with Angelo is not a sin because she is his fiancée.

IV.II Location: the prison

The duke schemes to delay Claudio's execution and send Angelo another prisoner's head instead.

The provost asks Pompey for help executing Claudio and Barnardine, another prisoner, in exchange for a commuted sentence. Pompey agrees, and the provost introduces him to Abhorson, the executioner. Abhorson is not optimistic about Pompey's execution skills, but tells him to be ready at four o'clock the next day.

The duke arrives disguised, and the provost asks if there is any hope of saving Claudio. The duke replies that a pardon may arrive before morning, because Mariana-as-Isabella has slept with Angelo, as planned. A messenger arrives—not with a pardon, but with instructions to execute Claudio by four o'clock and send Claudio's head to Angelo by five. Barnardine is to be executed in the afternoon.

The provost explains that Barnardine is a Bohemian who has been in prison for nine years. He has not repented, and has not seemed perturbed by news of his impending execution. The duke asks the provost to delay Claudio's execution for four days, and to send Barnardine's head to Angelo instead of Claudio's. To trick Angelo, the provost should shave Barnardine's head and beard.

IV.III Location: the prison

The duke tells Isabella that Claudio has been executed.

Pompey compares the prison with Mistress Overdone's brothel: many of the same people frequent both places. Abhorson enters and tells Pompey to fetch Barnardine. Barnardine tells them that he has been drinking all night and does not want to die today.

The provost tells the duke that Ragazine, a notorious pirate of about Claudio's age, died in prison the night before, and that they can use his head instead of Barnardine's. The duke feels lucky, and tells the provost to hide both Barnardine and Claudio and send Ragazine's head to Angelo immediately.

Isabella enters and asks about the pardon. The duke tells her that Claudio has been executed. She should wait for the duke's return before accusing Angelo of injustice. He gives her a letter to take to Friar Peter.

Lucio enters and tells Isabella that if the duke had been in Vienna, Claudio would not have died. Isabella exits and Lucio brings up the duke's relations with women again. The disguised duke refuses to talk about it. Lucio tells him that he, Lucio, also was once accused of impregnating a woman, but he denied it because he did not want to marry her.

IV.IV Location: Vienna. A public place

In a letter to Angelo, the duke announces his imminent return.

Angelo and Escalus discuss the duke's letter. He has asked to be met at the gates, which confuses them. Moreover, the duke orders anyone with a complaint against Angelo to present it on the public street. Escalus leaves and Angelo hopes to himself that Isabella will be too shy to lodge a public complaint. He says that he ordered Claudio executed because he was worried that Claudio might get back at him for sleeping with Isabella.

IV.V Location: outside Vienna

The duke makes final preparations to return.

The duke, dressed as himself, arrives with Friar Peter. He tells Friar Peter to deliver some letters and to fetch and alert some of the duke's companions.

IV.VI Location: Vienna. A public place

Isabella prepares to make a public complaint against Angelo.

Isabella has received letters with instructions from the duke-as-friar. She is nervous about accusing Angelo in public, but Mariana tells her to obey the duke-as-friar's request. Friar Peter arrives to tell them that he will take them to stand near the duke.

ACT V

All secrets are revealed; Angelo will marry Mariana and the duke will marry Isabella.

V.I Location: Vienna. A public place near the city gates

The duke reasserts his power, pardons Claudio and Angelo, forces Angelo to marry Mariana, and asks Isabella to marry him.

The duke, dressed as himself, greets Angelo and Escalus. Friar Peter enters with Isabella and tells her to speak to the duke. She begs him for justice, and refuses to speak to Angelo when the duke suggests it. She calls Angelo a murderer, hypocrite, "adulterous thief," and "virgin-violator," and the duke calls her insane and sends her away. She asks him to reconsider, and the duke agrees to hear her story. She explains how Claudio was sentenced to death, and how Angelo promised to spare him if she had sexual intercourse with him. The duke claims not to believe her.

Isabella says that Friar Lodowick (the man the duke is pretending to be) could support her story. The duke demands to see him. Friar Peter comes forth and says that Isabella is lying, and that Friar Lodowick is indisposed and has sent him, Friar Peter, in his place. On the duke's orders, Isabella is led away by guards. Mariana enters, veiled, as a witness.

Despite the duke's request, Mariana refuses to show her face. Only her husband has the authority to request to see her face. At the same time, Mariana says that she is not married, is not a maid, and is not a widow. She explains that her marriage was consummated without her husband's knowledge and that Angelo is her husband.

Mariana lifts her veil and says that she had sex with Angelo on Tuesday night. Angelo confesses that he was engaged to her five years earlier, but has not seen her since. The duke leaves with Friar Peter, saying that he will see Friar Lodowick, and leaves Escalus to hear testimony in his place.

The duke returns as Friar Lodowick, and demands to see the duke. Lucio claims that he has heard Friar Lodowick slander the duke. The duke, as Friar Lodowick, argues with him. During the course of the argument, Lucio pulls off the duke's hood, revealing his identity.

Angelo confesses to his crime and asks for a death sentence. The duke sentences him to marry Mariana instead. But when Isabella accuses Angelo of killing Claudio, he sentences Angelo to death to pay for Claudio's death. Mariana begs the duke to spare Angelo's life. At Mariana's request, Isabella too asks the duke to pardon Angelo.

The duke asks the provost why Claudio was executed earlier than planned. The provost explains that someone (the duke-as-friar) wanted to save Barnardine. Barnardine is brought in, along with a muffled Claudio. The duke pardons Barnardine. The provost unveils Claudio. The duke pardons Angelo and Claudio, then he asks Isabella to marry him. Finally, he sentences Lucio to marry his pregnant lover (mentioned in III.ii).

THEMES, MOTIFS, & SYMBOLS IN *MEASURE FOR MEASURE*

THEMES

THE VALUE OF MODERATION *Measure for Measure* suggests that too much of anything is a bad thing. Both modesty and sex are good, but too much modesty makes would-be nun Isabella into a harsh and unyielding monster of virtue, and too much sexual liberty in Vienna brings venereal disease and prostitution. Too much freedom leads to depravity and must be reigned in, but laws too harsh cannot be sustained either: Angelo succumbs to the very sin of lechery that he condemns. It is Angelo's extremism that leads him both to coldly condemn Claudio and to desire to sleep with Isabella in secret. By the end of the play, all the moral extremists have been brought closer to the human center of moderation.

Claudio the libertine must marry Juliet; Isabella the virgin must marry the duke; Angelo the merciless law-enforcer must marry Mariana. Indeed, Claudio suggests that the moderation comes naturally after too much nonrestraint: "As surfeit is the father of much fast, / So every scope, by the immoderate use, / Turns to restraint" (I.ii.106–7).

MERCY *Measure for Measure* argues that law without mercy is cruel and inhuman. Punishments must fit crimes, "measure . . . for measure." Angelo's laws and principles may be just (however much modern audiences may disagree), but the play condemns relentless application of any principle without regard for extenuating circumstance. Indeed, Isabella argues that mercy is desirable on both human and religious terms: "neither heaven nor man grieve at the mercy" (II.ii.51). Shakespeare manipulates us into favoring mercy by presenting Claudio as a sympathetic, if bumbling, character.

PUBLIC LEGISLATION OF PRIVATE MORALITY *Measure for Measure* explores what happens when sexual mores are strictly legislated by the state. The idea has been suggested since ancient times. In the *Republic*, Plato advocated strict regulation of sex for his utopian society. The play suggests that some regulation may be necessary to curtail the spread of prostitution and venereal disease, but Angelo's too-strict approach is a clear failure. His regulations to put an end to all out-of-wedlock sexual relations only relegate sex to a shameful, hidden sphere.

MOTIFS

SUBSTITUTION The plot of *Measure for Measure* is driven by a series of substitutions and replacements. Mariana replaces Isabella in Angelo's bed, and Ragazine's head is sent to Angelo instead of Claudio's. More generally, Angelo replaces the duke as ruler of Vienna. More subtly, Angelo is forced into Claudio's place when he desires to sleep with a woman out of wedlock.

PROSTITUTION Prostitution combines the two traditionally sinful desires of lust and greed. Its presence signals Vienna as a depraved city. Mistress Overdone's brothel and its extreme sexual license is the counterpoint to Isabella's convent and its extreme abstinence. Angelo pressures the chaste Isabella to buy her brother's freedom with her body by becoming, in effect, a prostitute. Ironically, Isabella and Mistress Overdone share similar traits. The prostitute and the nun, the whore and the virgin, have both escaped marriage as a traditional institution.

SYMBOLS

PREGNANCY Juliet, Elbow's wife and Lucio's girlfriend are pregnant in the play. Their pregnancies are prohibited by men's laws and focus attention on the role of women in a male-dominated world. The play's women create life while the play's men legislate to squelch life. The pregnancies symbolize the conflict between human desire and social legislation. Moreover, the multiple mentions of pregnancy represent messy, real-world concerns characteristic of Shakespeare's problem plays. Unlike the lighthearted comedies such as *As You Like It*, or even tragedies such as *Romeo and Juliet*, *Measure for Measure* shows a world in which love and sex come with practical, unexalted consequences.

MARIANA'S VEIL In V.i, Mariana enters in a veil which she refuses to take off even when the duke asks her. She responds that she will only take it off when her husband asks her. The veil represents power, for the woman's right to remain secretive and hidden is trumped only by her husband's right over her. At the same time, Mariana uses her veil to trick Angelo into marrying her. She is similarly disguised ("veiled") when Angelo sleeps with her.

IMPORTANT QUOTATIONS FROM *MEASURE FOR MEASURE*

1. *Some rise by sin, and some by virtue fall.*

Location: II.i.45
Speaker: Escalus
Context: Escalus has just heard that Claudio will be sentenced to death.

Escalus's response reveals him acquiesced to the common injustices of the world. In an ideal world, such as the world envisioned by the strict moralist Angelo, virtue is rewarded and sin is punished. But in the messy world of *Measure for Measure* bad things may happen to good people.

2. *O, 'tis excellent*
   To have a giant's strength, but it is tyrannous
   To use it as a giant.

Location: II.ii.110
Speaker: Isabella to Angelo
Context: Isabella tries to convince Angelo to spare her brother's life.

Isabella's pleas are based in abstract moral theorizing. Her requests are objective rather than personal, intellectual rather than emotional, cold rather than warm. Lucio urges her to implore and cajole with warmth and emotion, but it is her detachment and intelligence that reach Angelo. Her statement echoes the main theme of the play: brute force must be tempered with human compassion.

3. *What's this? What's this? Is this her fault or mine?*
   The tempter or the tempted, who sins most, ha?
   Not she; nor doth she tempt; but it is I
   That, lying by the violet in the sun,
   Do, as the carrion does, not as the flower,
   Corrupt with virtuous season…
   O, fie, fie, fie!
   What doest thou, or what art thou, Angelo?
   Dost thou desire her foully for those things
   That make her good?

Location: II.ii.170
Speaker: Angelo
Context: Angelo realizes that he desires Isabella

Angelo's syntax dramatizes his turmoil. Torn between his virtue and his desire for Isabella, he questions himself and his identity: "What art thou, Angelo?" His use of natural imagery, even if it is a disgusting reference to carrion flesh, suggests that human sexuality is a similarly natural impulse.

4. *Were I under the terms of death,*
   Th' impression of keen whips I'd wear as rubies,
   And strip myself to death, as to a bed
   That longing have been sick for, ere I'd yield

My body up to shame.

Location: II.iv.100–04
Speaker: Isabella to Angelo
Context: Isabella refuses to sleep with Angelo, even to save her brother Claudio's life.

Isabella staunchly defends her chastity, but uses startlingly sexual vocabulary in her description of her flesh with red whip marks and her body tied to death like it would be tied to a bed. Her imagery suggests that extreme chastity and extreme sexuality are psychologically closer to each other than to moderation.

---

5. *The very mercy of the law cries out*
   Most audible, even from his proper tongue,
   'An Angelo for Claudio, death for death.'
   Haste still pays haste, and leisure answers leisure,
   Like doth quit like, and measure still for measure.

Location: V.i.399–403
Speaker: Duke
Context: The duke argues that since Claudio was sentenced to death for sexual unrestraint, so Angelo should be too.

The play takes its title from this passage, which comes at the dramatic and moral climax. The passage itself refers to the Biblical "with what measure ye mete, it shall be measured to you again" (Matthew 7:2–3). Angelo measured out a severe punishment for Claudio, and therefore must be measured the same punishment himself. Indeed, the duke's language—"Angelo for Claudio, death for death"—evokes the play's motif of substitution. At the same time, the glibness of the duke's rhyming couplet as he condemns Angelo to death has troubled many readers.

THE MERRY WIVES OF WINDSOR

Falstaff tries to seduce two married women, but they turn the tables on him and shame him.

THE MERRY WIVES OF WINDSOR IN CONTEXT

Probably written in 1597–1598, *The Merry Wives of Windsor*, which takes place in a provincial English town, is Shakespeare's most middle-class play in setting, subject matter, and outlook. It is also one of his most farcical works, loaded with physical gags and linguistic jokes. The play's main plot closely resembles *Il Pecorone*, a 1558 Italian play by Ser Giovanni Fiorentino. This plot and the primary subplot also draw on ancient Roman comedy and medieval farce. Though *The Merry Wives of Windsor* does include characters both above and below the middle class, as well as culturally stereotyped foreigners, in general the play insists on the assimilating power of the middle class.

According to theatrical legend, Queen Elizabeth saw *1 Henry IV* and liked the character of *Falstaff* so much that she asked Shakespeare to write another play about him, supposedly giving him only fourteen days to complete it. Shakespeare may have put aside *2 Henry IV* to complete *Merry Wives*. Several characters from the Henry plays appear in *Merry Wives*, including Pistol, Nim, Bardolph, Mistress Quickly, and Shallow. The first performance of *Merry Wives* is said to have occurred in London on April 23, 1597, at a feast of the Order of the Garter, an aristocratic fraternity. Queen Elizabeth is said to have been in attendance.

The text of *Merry Wives* survives in two different versions, one in the First Quarto (1602) and another in the First Folio (1623). The Folio is printed from a manuscript that was based on either a playhouse promptbook or an authorial manuscript, and has a close connection with the first performance of the play. The Quarto is most likely a reconstruction from memory by actors who performed in the first performances. Half the length of the Folio version, the Quarto is probably a poorly remembered account, or a version trimmed down for provincial performances. Modern editions are based on the Folio edition, though stage directions and certain passages from the Quarto have been integrated into modern editions.

THE MERRY WIVES OF WINDSOR: KEY FACTS

Full title: The Merry Wives of Windsor

Time and place written: 1597–1598, London (uncertain)

Date of first performance: 1597–1598 (uncertain)

Genre: Comedy

Setting (time): Sixteenth century

Setting (place): Windsor, England

Protagonist: Anne Page, Mistress Page, and Ford

Major conflict: Mistresses Page and Ford reject Falstaff's advances

THE MERRY WIVES OF WINDSOR: CHARACTER LIST

Bardolph   One of Falstaff's men. Bardolph takes over as the bartender of the Garter Inn in order to pay for Falstaff's entourage's room and board.

Caius   The local doctor. Caius is Mistress Quickly's master. He is French, so he suffers humiliation because of his accent and broken English. He hopes to marry Anne Page.

Sir Hugh Evans   The local clergyman. The other English citizens find Evans's Welsh accent very amusing and constantly make fun of him.

Falstaff A knight, a scoundrel, and occasionally a thief. Falstaff, who appears in several of Shakespeare's plays, is boisterous, lively, cowardly, funny, and mischievous. He is out of his element in the country-side, where *The Merry Wives of Windsor* takes place.

Fenton One of Anne Page's suitors. Fenton is high-born but poor, and his interest in Anne is purely financial at first, although eventually he falls in love with her.

Ford Mistress Ford's husband. Ford is very jealous of his wife and dons a disguise to thwart Falstaff's plans to seduce her.

Mistress Ford Ford's husband and Mistress Page's friend. Mistress Ford hopes to root out her husband's oppressive jealousy by proving that she is entirely faithful to him.

Host The host of the Garter Inn.

Nim One of Falstaff's men. Nim wants to stay honest and refuses to deliver Falstaff's seductive letters to Mistress Page and Mistress Ford. He and Pistol decide to let the husbands know of Falstaff's scheme.

Anne Page The daughter of Page and Mistress Page. An array of idiots, including Caius and Slender, seek Anne's hand in marriage, but Anne manages to trick her parents and elope with a man of her choosing.

Page Mistress Page's husband. Page is not jealous of his wife, so Falstaff's plan does not threaten him.

Mistress Page Page's husband, Mistress Ford's friend, and Anne's mother. Like her husband, Mistress Page plans for her daughter's marriage without consulting her daughter.

Pistol One of Falstaff's men. Pistol wants to stay honest. He and Nim decide to let the husbands know of Falstaff's scheme.

Mistress Quickly Caius's servant. Mistress Quickly delivers messages for Mistress Page, Mistress Ford, and all three of Anne Page's suitors. She prefers Fenton and supports his suit most enthusiastically. Mistress Quickly chronically misunderstands or mishears other people, mistakenly believing she is hearing sexually charged conversations.

Shallow An officer of the law. Shallow is a foolish man. He urges Slender to try to seduce Anne Page.

Simple Slender's servant.

Slender The third suitor for Anne Page's hand. Slender speaks nothing but nonsense to Anne. Page favors him as a good match for his daughter.

THE MERRY WIVES OF WINDSOR: PLOT OVERVIEW

Sir John Falstaff attempts to seduce two wealthy married women, Mistress Ford and Mistress Page, in order to try to get money from them. The women are offended and decide to get revenge on Falstaff by pretending to desire him and then playing tricks on him. Mistress Ford's husband, Ford, is extremely jeal-ous, a trait the two women use to their advantage. Each time Falstaff comes to meet with Mistress Ford, Ford arrives instead of his wife, and Falstaff is dunked in a river and beaten. To cure Ford of his jealousy, the wives tell Ford about the game they have been playing. The wives agree to meet Falstaff in the woods and then arrange to have the town's children dress as fairies to terrify and pester him, exposing him in front of the whole town.

Meanwhile, the unmarried men of Windsor compete for the chance to marry the Pages' daughter, Anne Page. Mistress Page wants her daughter to marry Caius, a French doctor, while Page wants her to marry a fool named Slender. Each parent tries to persuade Anne to disguise herself and elope with one of these men during the confusion with the children in the woods, but Anne instead elopes with Fenton, the man she loves.

THE MERRY WIVES OF WINDSOR: SCENE SUMMARY

ACT I

Three suitors decide they love Anne Page; Falstaff determines to seduce Mistress Page and Mistress Ford for financial gain.

I.I Location: outside Page's house

Falstaff admits to various crimes and Shallow proposes to Anne on Slender's behalf.

Justice Shallow walks along with Master Slender and Sir Hugh Evans. Shallow is angry at Sir John Falstaff and says he will bring him before the court. Evans, a man of the church, misunderstands and thinks he can help bring Falstaff before a church council. He says they should focus their attentions on trying to arrange a marriage between Slender and Anne Page. They approach Master Page's house. Page enters and thanks Shallow for his gift of venison. Shallow asks if Falstaff is at Page's house, and Page says he is. Shallow says Falstaff wronged him, and Page says Falstaff admits it.

Falstaff enters with his friends Bardolph, Nim, and Pistol. Shallow accuses Falstaff of beating his men and killing his deer. Falstaff admits it. Slender accuses Falstaff of beating him, and Evans accuses Falstaff's men of stealing Slender's wallet. The men deny it, saying Slender was too drunk to know what happened to his wallet. Slender says he will never again drink with men who are not good and honest.

Anne Page enters to serve the men wine, but Page says they will all go inside. Mistress Page and Mistress Ford enter, greet Falstaff, and go inside with the others to dine. Slender sits alone, wishing he had his book of love poems. His servant Simple enters and Slender asks him where his book is. Shallow and Evans emerge from Page's house, and Evans says he has proposed to Anne on Slender's behalf. Shallow asks Slender if he can love and marry Anne, and Slender says he can, remarking that even if love does not exist at first, it will come once he and Anne get to know each other.

Anne enters to call the men to dinner. Slender says he is not hungry and won't go in. He tries to make conversation with Anne but fails miserably. Page enters and encourages Slender to come inside. Slender insists that he is not hungry, but goes inside.

I.II Location: outside Page's house

Evans sends Simple to find Mistress Quickly.

Evans leaves the Pages' house and sends Simple to Doctor Caius's house to ask for Mistress Quickly, Caius's servant. He asks Simple to give Mistress Quickly a letter in which he asks for her help in convincing Anne Page to marry Slender.

I.III Location: a room at the Garter Inn

Falstaff reveals his plan to seduce the Mistresses Ford and Page to Nim and Pistol, who react with distaste.

Falstaff, Bardolph, Nim, and Pistol enter the Garter Inn and call for the inn's host. The host agrees to house Falstaff for a sum of money and for Bardolph's services as a bartender. Falstaff says he is glad to have Bardolph off his hands. He tells Pistol and Nim that he plans to seduce Mistress Ford. He likes her good-natured attitude and he hears she controls her husband's cash. He has written two letters, one to Mistress Ford and the other to Mistress Page, whom he also hopes to seduce and hit up for money. Falstaff asks Pistol and Nim to deliver his letters to the ladies but they refuse, saying they prefer to behave respectably. Falstaff leaves to find a willing messenger, and Pistol and Nim scorn Falstaff's base behavior. They plan to go to Ford and Page to reveal Falstaff's plan.

I.IV Location: Doctor Caius's house

Despite her real beliefs, Mistress Quickly assures all of Anne's suitors that Anne loves only them.

Mistress Quickly awaits the return of her master, Doctor Caius. Simple tells her about Evans's request for help, and Mistress Quickly agrees that Anne Page would do well to marry Slender. She promises to urge Anne to make the match. Caius approaches, so Mistress Quickly hides Simple in a closet. Caius looks for his equipment in preparation for a visit to the court. When he looks in the closet, he finds Simple. Quickly explains that Simple has come on an errand from Evans, and Simple confirms that Evans sent him to ask Quickly to put in a good word for Slender with Anne. Upset, Caius writes a note. While he writes, Quickly whispers to Simple that Caius is in love with Anne Page too.

Caius hands his letter to Simple and announces that he will challenge Evans to a fight. He sends Simple to deliver the letter. Caius scolds Quickly, who had told him she could convince Anne to marry him. Quickly insists that Anne does love him. Caius departs for court, and Quickly comments to herself that she doubts Anne loves either Caius or Slender.

Master Fenton comes in and asks Quickly about Anne. Quickly swears that Anne loves him and says they spoke of him at length. Fenton says he will visit her that day and departs. Quickly says she is sure Anne does not love Fenton either.

ACT II

Page is wrongly convinced that his wife plans to cheat on him and assumes a disguise, planning to catch her in the act; Evans does not show up to fight Caius.

II.I Location: outside Page's house

Mistresses Page and Ford react to Falstaff's love letters with disgust; their husbands learn of Falstaff's designs, and Ford plans to assume a disguise to find out if his wife is unfaithful.

Mistress Page reads her letter from Falstaff aloud. He writes that they are similar in their equally advanced age, sense of merriment, and love of wine. Mistress Page is astonished that such a fat old knight would try to play the young suitor, especially since he hardly knows her. She wonders how she can take revenge on him. Mistress Ford enters with her own letter from Falstaff. They realize that the two letters are identical. Mistress Page suggests leading him on until he has to pawn his horses to raise money to court them. Mistress Ford agrees, although she does not want to engage in any bad behavior that will sully their honor. She says it is good that her husband didn't see the letter, which would have inflamed his already irrational jealousy.

Ford and Page enter with Pistol and Nim, and the women withdraw to discuss their plans. Pistol and Nim tell the men that Falstaff is after their wives. Nim says they have tired of Falstaff's lying and have decided to use this opportunity to revenge themselves on him for past wrongs. Pistol and Nim depart, leaving Ford and Page to rage against Falstaff.

Mistresses Ford and Page approach their husbands and speak with them. Mistress Quickly enters, and the ladies realize that she can be their messenger to Falstaff. The women go inside together. Page and Ford wonder if Pistol and Nim were speaking the truth. Page doubts it, but he says if it were true, his wife would give Falstaff a piece of her mind. Ford says he does not mistrust his wife, but he would not want her to be anywhere near Falstaff.

The host of the Garter enters followed by Shallow, who invites them all to watch Evans and Caius fight. Ford takes the host aside and tells him that he is not angry at Falstaff, but that he wants to have access to him under a false name. He offers to pay the host to introduce him as Brooke. The host agrees. The others depart. Alone, Ford calls Page a fool for trusting his wife. With his new disguise, he plans to find out how Falstaff has progressed with Mistress Ford.

II.II Location: a room at the Garter Inn

Disguised as a man named Brooke, Ford pays Falstaff to woo Mistress Page, saying that if she sleeps with Falstaff, she will have to sleep with him too.

Falstaff refuses to lend Pistol any money, telling Pistol he has already gotten him out of trouble. Falstaff says he gets cash by lying and cheating, while Pistol is poor because he insists on behaving honorably. Mistress Quickly arrives and draws Falstaff aside. She tells him that Mistress Ford has had many noble suitors over the years, yet she chooses Falstaff. She also reports that Ford will be out of the house between ten and eleven the next day. Quickly mentions Ford's extreme jealousy and repeats the hour when Falstaff may visit. She adds that Mistress Page sends word that her husband is often at home, but that she hopes a time may come when Falstaff may visit her, and wants him to send her a letter. Falstaff sends his regards to the women and Quickly departs.

Bardolph enters with news that a man named Brooke wants to speak to Falstaff. Ford enters, disguised as Brooke, and offers money to Falstaff in return for help in wooing Mistress Ford for himself. He says he has loved her for a long time but has failed to get her attention. She has always behaved honestly, but he hopes there are cracks in her virtue. He compliments Falstaff's power over women. Falstaff asks Ford if he really wants him to seduce her, and Ford explains that if she falls for Falstaff first, then she can no longer use her honesty as an excuse to scorn him.

Falstaff accepts Ford's money and tells him that he already has a plan to visit her between ten and eleven the next morning. Ford asks him if he knows what Ford looks like, and Falstaff says he does not. He urges Ford to come to him the next day to hear about his visit with Mistress Ford and then departs. Alone, Ford speaks angrily of his wife, who has already made a date with Falstaff. He says he cannot trust his wife to control herself. He can hardly wait for the next morning when he can avenge himself on Falstaff, catch his wife in the act, and prove to Page that his jealousy is not misplaced.

II.III Location: a field near Windsor

Evans does not show up to fight Caius, who agrees to go back to Windsor and woo Anne along the way.

Caius waits for Evans to arrive. The host of the Garter, along with Shallow, Page, and Slender, comes to see the fight, but Evans is not there. Shallow says that Evans is smart to have stayed away, since to fight Caius would go against both men's professions. As a clergyman, Evans heals souls, and as a doctor, Caius heals bodies. Shallow says that he has come to try to convince Caius to forget the fight. The host insults Caius by using words Caius does not know. When Caius asks what the host is saying, he lies and says his insults are actually honorable, valorous words. Caius believes him and uses the words incorrectly. The host promises to bring Caius back to Windsor by a route that will pass a farmhouse where Anne is feasting. Caius is delighted and goes with the host.

ACT III

Evans and Caius realize that the host has played a joke on them; Anne decides she loves Fenton, the suitor of whom both her parents disapprove; Mistresses Page and Ford trick Falstaff and Master Ford.

III.I Location: a field near Frogmore

Evans and Caius realize that the host and his friends have encouraged them to fight for their own amusement.

Evans wanders through the fields with Simple, looking for Caius. Simple has misdirected him, so the search is fruitless. Evans sends Simple off to find Caius and sits down to read his book of poems and luxuriate in melancholy. Simple reappears and takes Evans to Shallow, Slender, and Page. Shallow says that Caius is nearby.

The host enters with Caius, and Evans and Caius face off. Shallow and Page disarm the two men. Speaking quietly to each other, Evans and Caius explain their mutual suspicion that the others encouraged them to fight in order to make fun of them. They agree the host has plotted against them. The host speaks, urging the two men to make peace. The spectators exit, and Caius and Evans are left alone to plot their revenge.

III.II Location: a street in Windsor

Page tells Slender that he supports Slender's suit of Anne, but that his wife supports Caius's.

Ford meets Mistress Page and Falstaff's boy-servant. Mistress Page says that she is on her way to see Mistress Ford. After she leaves, Ford says that Page is a fool to think that his wife is honest, since she is now on her way to his wife's house with a messenger from Falstaff. The clock strikes ten, and Ford prepares to trap Falstaff. Page, Shallow, Slender, the host, Evans, and Caius enter. Ford invites them all to come to his house. The group has been discussing a match between Slender and Anne Page. Page tells Slender that he supports him, but his wife supports Caius. The host asks about Fenton, of whom Page does not approve as a husband for his daughter, Anne. Ford invites them to dine at his house and Caius, Evans, and Page join him.

III.III   Location: Ford's house

Mistresses Ford and Page trick Falstaff and Master Ford, having Falstaff thrown into the river and convincing Ford that his wife is cheating on him.

Mistresses Ford and Page prepare for Falstaff's arrival. They order two of Ford's servants to be ready with a large laundry basket, which they will carry to the Thames and throw in the water. Falstaff's boy-servant announces his arrival and Mistress Page hides. Falstaff enters. He tells Mistress Ford he wishes her husband were dead so he could marry her and make her a lady. She says that she would make a plain lady. Falstaff says that he does not have the skill with words that young wooers do.

A servant announces that Mistress Page is at the door. Falstaff hides, and Mistress Page rushes in with news that her husband is coming with officers of Windsor to search for a gentleman he believes is in his house at Mistress Ford's invitation. Mistress Ford says no gentleman is present. Mistress Page says she would be in trouble if there were. Mistress Ford admits that a man is in her house and says she must find a way to hide him quickly. Mistress Page suggests hiding him in the laundry basket and having the servants carry the basket out.

Falstaff emerges and says he will consent to be smuggled out. Mistress Page pretends to be surprised to see him. She asks him if he wrote love letters to her recently. He whispers that he loves her, then he climbs into the basket. Mistresses Ford and Page pile dirty clothes on top of him and order two servants to carry the basket away. They are poised to leave when Ford, Page, Caius, and Evans enter.

The servants depart with the basket. Ford and the other men look around the house but do not find anyone. Mistress Ford and Page agree that they don't know whom they enjoy fooling more, Falstaff or Ford. They think that Ford was convinced that Falstaff would be there, and criticize his jealousy. They plan to play more tricks on Falstaff to draw out the root of Ford's jealous behavior.

The men return, and Mistress Page tells Ford that he wrongs Mistress Ford by distrusting her. Evans and Caius agree that Mistress Ford seems to be honest. Page proposes hunting the next day. Caius and Evans agree and reaffirm their plot against the host.

III.IV   Location: Page's house

Anne wants to marry Fenton, but her parents disapprove.

Fenton and Anne Page meet outside her house. He tells her that her father does not want them to marry because Fenton has no money, although he is high-born, and Master Page suspects that Fenton only wants Anne's substantial dowry. He admits that Page's wealth first drew him to Anne, but in wooing her, he has found her to be worth more than money. Anne urges him to seek her father's favor.

They draw to the side as Slender enters with Shallow and Mistress Quickly. Quickly calls to Anne, saying Slender wants to talk to her. Anne tells Fenton that Slender is her father's choice, but she does not like him at all. Anne approaches Slender and Shallow. Slender begins telling an irrelevant joke, so Shallow jumps in, telling Anne that Slender loves her. Shallow speaks for Slender while Slender says foolish things, so Anne asks Shallow to let Slender speak for himself. Slender mumbles idiotically, and Anne asks him what he wants of her. He says Page and Shallow have made the arrangements, and he will not mind if things don't work out.

Master and Mistress Page enter. Page demands to know why Fenton is hanging around. He tells Fenton that he will never have his daughter and goes into the house with Shallow and Slender. Quickly urges Fenton to speak to Mistress Page. He tells Mistress Page that he loves Anne, and Anne asks her mother not to make her marry Slender. Mistress Page says she won't, but she favors Caius. Anne is unsatisfied. They go into the house.

Fenton thanks Quickly for her aid and gives her money. Alone, Quickly considers her duplicity. Although she has promised to help all three of Anne's suitors, she particularly likes Fenton and will give him extra aid. Quickly says she must go speak to Falstaff at the command of Mistress Page and Mistress Ford.

III.V Location: a room at the Garter Inn

Falstaff tells Ford, disguised as Brooke, of his adventures with Mistress Ford.

Falstaff orders Bardolph to make him some warm wine and moans about his bad luck. He has just dragged himself out of the Thames after the servants dropped him in with Mistress Ford's laundry. Mistress Quickly enters with reports from Mistress Ford. Falstaff says that he is fed up with her, but Quickly explains that Miss Ford's servants misunderstood her orders about what to do with the laundry. Quickly says that Mistress Ford wants Falstaff to visit her between eight and nine that evening. Falstaff agrees to go, and Quickly goes to deliver the message.

Ford enters disguised as Brooke. He asks how Falstaff did with Mistress Ford. Falstaff says he had just begun to woo Mistress Ford when her husband arrived. He gives a melodramatic account of his flight in a laundry basket, saying he was filled with fear and horror as he hid in the basket and then flew through the air and into the river. Brooke asks if Falstaff will give up on Mistress Ford now, but Falstaff says he has another date with her and rushes out to keep it. Ford is astonished to think that Falstaff was in his house when he arrived that morning, and enraged that he is on his way back. He declares he will go to his house and find him this time.

ACT IV

Mistresses Page and Ford again trick Falstaff and eventually tell their husbands what they have been up to, plotting with them to humiliate Falstaff; the host realizes the three Germans have tricked him; Fenton schemes to marry Anne.

IV.I Location: a street

Evans quizzes William Page on his schoolwork.

Mistress Page, Mistress Quickly, and William Page enter. The two women wonder if Falstaff has arrived at Mistress Ford's yet. Mistress Page says she must take her son to school, but Evans, the schoolteacher, enters and says he has cancelled school that day. Mistress Page expresses concern that her son has not been learning much at school, so Evans asks him a few questions. As Evans quizzes William about Latin conjugations and declensions, mangling most of the words with his Welsh accent, the uneducated Mistress Quickly interprets the words she cannot understand as sexualized slang.

IV.II Location: Ford's house

Mistresses Ford and Page trick Master Ford and Falstaff again, dressing Falstaff in women's clothing and convincing Ford that his wife is still cheating on him.

Falstaff arrives at Mistress Ford's house and tells her he is glad to have a second chance. Mistress Page arrives and Falstaff hides. Mistress Page speaks of Ford's jealousy and says it is good that Falstaff is not there, since Ford is on his way to the house in a rage. Mistress Ford admits Falstaff is there and wonders what to do with him. Falstaff emerges and says he refuses to hide in the laundry basket again. Mistress Ford suggests he wear some clothes belonging to her maid's aunt, a fat lady whose clothing will fit Falstaff.

While Falstaff puts on the dress, Mistress Ford reveals that her husband hates the maid's aunt and threatened to beat her if she came to his house again. Mistress Page explains that Ford really is coming. They decide to parade the laundry basket past Ford so he will waste time looking through it. Mistress Page says their actions will prove that wives can be merry and honest at the same time.

Mistress Ford's servants enter with the laundry basket. Ford, Page, Caius, Evans, and Shallow enter. Ford demands that the servants put down the laundry basket and then searches it. Ford's companions urge him not to act so rashly, saying his wife is clearly honest. Mistress Ford enters, and Ford angrily asks her if she is honest or if he suspects her without cause. She says she is honest, and Ford sarcastically applauds her for lying so boldly. Finding nothing in the laundry, Page and Shallow tell Ford that he is just jealous and paranoid.

Mistress Page and the disguised Falstaff enter. Ford flies into a rage, saying that he forbid the old lady to come to his house, especially since she is said to be a witch. He beats Falstaff and chases him out. Evans notes that the old lady had a rather thick beard, and Ford realizes his mistake. He and the other men bolt out of the house after Falstaff.

The two women discuss their successful campaign. They are sure they have scared the lust out of Falstaff. They debate telling their husbands about their schemes in order to convince them that they have been honorable, but they agree that Falstaff should be publicly humiliated first.

IV.III Location: a room at the Garter Inn

The host allows the German guests to borrow three of his horses.

Bardolph asks the host if the German guests may borrow three of the host's horses so they can ride to court to meet their duke. The host reluctantly gives permission.

IV.IV Location: Ford's house

Mistresses Page and Ford confess their deception to their husbands and with them plot to embarrass Falstaff in public.

Ford, Page, Mistress Ford, Mistress Page, and Evans talk. The women have told their husbands about their plots against Falstaff, and Ford asks his wife to forgive him. He says he will never doubt her again. Page suggests continuing with the sport and planning a public humiliation of Falstaff. Mistress Page recalls an old tale about ghostly Herne the hunter, a vicious spirit known to visit a particular oak tree at midnight in winter. Many people are still afraid to walk by Herne's oak tree at night.

Mistress Ford understands what Mistress Page is suggesting. She says they should get Falstaff to go to the oak tree disguised as Herne. Then their sons and daughters will come out of hiding, all dressed up as elves and goblins, to encircle Falstaff and pinch him. They will ask Falstaff leading questions and get him to reveal why he came to the woods at that time. When he admits his dishonorable intentions, they can mock him openly in Windsor.

The men like this plan, especially Page, who imagines that he can use the ensuing confusion as an opportunity for Slender to elope with Anne Page. Ford says that he will go to Falstaff disguised as Brooke to find out if he plans to accept the third invitation from Mistress Ford. Evans goes off to prepare the children's costumes. Mistress Page decides she can conveniently get Caius to elope with Anne when they are all in disguise.

IV.V Location: a room at the Garter Inn

The host realizes the Germans have stolen his horses.

The host enters the inn with Simple. Simple wants to see Falstaff, but he thought he saw a fat woman going to his room and does not want to interrupt. Worried that Falstaff is being robbed, Simple and the host go to Falstaff's room. Falstaff says the fat woman is gone. Simple and the host ask if the old lady made any predictions about them. Falstaff makes up ambiguous replies that reveal nothing.

Bardolph enters, covered with mud. He says that the Germans ran off and stole the host's horses. Evans enters and tells the host that he has heard reports of three German men stealing horses in neighboring towns. Caius enters and announces that the duke of Germany, of whom the Germans spoke, does not exist. The host realizes that someone has tricked him and he has lost three horses. Falstaff comments that the whole world seems to be having bad luck. He has had bad luck and been beaten besides. Mistress Quickly enters with a message from Mistresses Ford and Page. She says that Mistress Ford was beaten and is upset at Falstaff's misfortune. Quickly says she has news and asks Falstaff to speak to her in private.

IV.VI Location: another room at the Garter Inn

Fenton asks the host to help him marry Anne Page.

Fenton asks the host to help him. He just received a letter from Anne Page, the woman he loves. The letter tells of a plot to trick Falstaff. Her father has commanded her to dress in white as a fairy queen and to elope with Slender once confusion arises. Meanwhile, her mother has ordered her to dress in green, wear a mask, and elope with Caius. The host asks which of her parents she means to deceive, and Fenton says she means to deceive both. He asks the host to help him find a vicar to marry him to Anne that evening.

ACT V

Falstaff is tricked; Fenton and Anne marry.

V.I Location: a room at the Garter Inn

Falstaff tells Ford, disguised as Brooke, of his misadventures with Mistress Ford.

Falstaff tells Mistress Quickly he will keep his third appointment with Mistress Ford and disguise himself as Herne. Quickly departs and Ford, disguised as Brooke, enters. Falstaff tells Brooke that things will be decided that evening in the park at midnight. Brooke asks Falstaff about the previous day's adventure with Mistress Ford. Falstaff says he had to disguise himself as a woman, and Mistress Ford's insane husband beat him. Now he wants revenge on Ford.

V.II Location: Windsor Park

Page, Shallow, and Slender prepare to trick Falstaff.

Page, Shallow, and Slender prepare for the evening's events. Page reminds Slender that his daughter will be wearing white.

V.III Location: a street in Windsor

Mistress Ford, Mistress Page, and Caius prepare to trick Falstaff.

Mistress Ford, Mistress Page, and Caius prepare for the ruse. Mistress Page tells Caius that her daughter is wearing green and sends him to look for her. She admits that her husband will be unhappy about the marriage between Anne Page and Caius, but says she does not mind. The women look forward to frightening and mocking Falstaff later that night. They head to Herne's oak.

V.IV Location: Windsor Park

The children prepare to trick Falstaff.

Evans leads the children, all in disguise, to their hiding spot near the oak.

V.V Location: another part of Windsor Park

Mistress Quickly and the others succeed in tricking Falstaff; Fentone and Anne announce their marriage.

Falstaff arrives at Herne's oak disguised as Herne with large horns on his head. He thinks about the Greek gods, who disguised themselves as animals to seduce women. Mistresses Ford and Page enter. Falstaff embraces Mistress Ford and is delighted to see that Mistress Page is there too. They hear a noise and the ladies flee. Evans enters with many children in disguise, Mistress Quickly disguised as the fairy queen, and Anne Page disguised as a fairy. Shouting to each other, they speak of magic and the supernatural. Terrified, Falstaff falls to the ground and hides his face.

Mistress Quickly speaks eloquently of fairies and potions, flowers and gems. Evans says he smells a man. Quickly says they will test him by setting him on fire. If he burns, then they will know he is corrupt.

They burn Falstaff with candles, and Quickly declares him corrupt. The children chant as they encircle Falstaff and pinch him.

Caius sneaks off with a boy wearing a white outfit, and Slender steals away with a boy wearing green. Fenton and Anne run off together. Finally, all the children in disguise run away. Falstaff gets up and tries to run away, but Ford and Page appear with their wives. Page tells Falstaff they have caught him in the act of trying to seduce their wives. Ford reveals to Falstaff that he was Brooke, and says he plans to take Falstaff's horses in return for the money he lent Falstaff. Falstaff realizes that they have made a fool of him. He says he suspected the fairies were not real.

Evans tells Falstaff the fairies won't pinch him if he serves God instead of his desires. Evans advises Ford to leave behind his jealousies. Ford says he will not distrust his wife until Evans can speak good English. Falstaff is upset at receiving a scolding from Evans, a man who mangles his native language so badly. Mistress Page asks Falstaff if he really thought they would have consented to lose their honor for him: an unattractive, drunken old man. Falstaff admits that he is defeated and says they can do what they want with him. Ford says they will take him to Windsor and make him pay back his debts.

But Page invites him to a feast at his house in honor of his daughter's wedding. Just then, Slender enters. He arrived at the country church only to discover he had eloped with a boy. Page scolds him for not finding his daughter. Mistress Page says it is her fault because she made Anne wear green for Caius. Caius enters and announces he has married a boy. Fenton enters with Anne. Anne's parents ask her why she disobeyed them, but Fenton explains that they should be ashamed for trying to marry her to men she did not love. He and Anne have been in love for a long time, he explains, and now the tie is finalized. Ford tells Page and his wife that love has guided the turn of events, so they should be glad. Falstaff says he is delighted that the evening, designed to humiliate him, did not turn out quite the way Page and his wife planned. Page embraces Fenton and Mistress Page welcomes him. As they depart for the feast, Ford comments to Falstaff that his promise to Brooke will come true, for Brooke will get to seduce Mistress Ford.

THEMES, MOTIFS, & SYMBOLS IN *THE MERRY WIVES OF WINDSOR*

THEMES

THE TRIUMPH OF THE MIDDLE CLASS Unlike most of Shakespeare's other comedies, in which the key players are aristocrats and the marginal figures of comic relief are lower-class people, the main characters in *The Merry Wives of Windsor* are of the middle class. The strong and interesting main characters are untitled commoners, while the representatives of the upper classes are either pathetic, like Falstaff, or sweetly pitiable, like Fenton. Members of the middle classes know what they want and know how to get it, while the aristocrats bumble around helplessly. The surest sign of the triumph of the middle class over the aristocracy is the noblemen's passivity toward the powerful autonomy of the housewives. Falstaff thinks of himself as clever and sexy, but he is no match for the aggressive trickery of Mistress Page and Mistress Ford. The disparity between his swaggering confidence and the women's quietly superior power makes Falstaff a figure of fun. Fenton is a sympathetic character, but not a powerful one. His noble stature does not impress the Page parents, who would rather find a wealthy husband for their daughter. Fenton wins Anne only because she happens to love him, not because he mounts a successful campaign to woo her.

THE DANGER OF SEEKING WEAK WOMEN Shakespeare's comedies are often populated by intelligent and self-confident women, but *The Merry Wives of Windsor* is one of the few comedies in which those women are married. Mistresses Page and Ford fend off con artists, control their husbands, and run their homes frugally. Shakespeare suggests that men who object to powerful wives such as these will come to grief. Men looking for a weak trophy wife or her money—like Falstaff, Slender, and Caius—find only disappointment. Falstaff is outsmarted by his two intended victims, and Slender and Caius nearly marry boys. In contrast, Fenton, who appreciates the strength of the Page women, succeeds in his suit. Though he first woos Anne to get at her money, he comes to love her, even though she is as smart and strong-willed as he.

THE ACCEPTABILITY OF DECEIT In *The Merry Wives of Windsor*, deceit is often the moral choice. The middle-class characters in the play, who consider honorable behavior very important, do not perceive any difficulty with simultaneously deceiving and acting honorably. Mistress Page, who says she will do anything to punish Falstaff as long as it is not dishonorable ("I will consent to act any villainy against him that may not sully the chariness of our honesty" II.i.86–87), is one of the great deceivers in the play. According to the Windsor wives' moral code, the proper response to a trickster who tries to take advantage of you is not to condemn him for his sin, but to fight fire with fire and outdo him in trickery. In *Merry Wives*, trickery is light-hearted and even compassionate, since it saves the wrongdoer from the harsher punishment he deserves. The wives deceive Falstaff, first teaching him a lesson and then forgiving him. The play ends with a repentant Falstaff heading off to dinner with the women who have tricked him.

MOTIFS

SEXUAL HUMOR The Frenchman Caius and the Welshman Evans are easy targets for the other characters in the play because of their difficulty speaking or pronouncing English. Their struggles with language are also the occasion for sexual humor. In trying to impress Anne Page with courtly, refined language, they often refer to sex unintentionally. Similarly, Mistress Quickly often makes obscene mistakes or hears sexual content where none exists. During Evans's Latin lesson, for instance, she misconstrues the "vocative" case (pronounced by Evans as "focative") as a reference to sex.

CROSS-DRESSING Although women often don men's clothing in Shakespearean plays, it is much rarer that men don women's clothing. In *The Merry Wives of Windsor*, cross-dressing degrades the men who do it. Falstaff is forced to dress like a woman in order to hide from Master Page, a necessity that marks his subordination to another man. Slender and Caius are also degraded by female dress—though not their own—when they nearly marry boys dressed up like girls. In *Merry Wives*, women use drag to trick men into insulting positions, calling their masculine power into question.

SYMBOLS

THE LAUNDRY BASKET The basket in which the mistresses smuggle Falstaff stands for the prosaic atmosphere of the play. Laundry baskets and similarly humble objects do not crop up in comedies like *As You Like It* or *Much Ado About Nothing*, because these plays do not pretend to be solidly grounded in everyday life. Their main characters are aristocrats who never need to do laundry. The main characters in *Merry Wives*, in contrast, are ordinary, middle-class women who must do their own chores. The laundry basket also symbolizes Falstaff's degrading comeuppance. As a knight, Falstaff considers himself far above trivialities like laundry, but as a lowlife trickster he deserves to be covered in dirty clothes and tossed into the Thames.

MISTRESS FORD'S KERCHIEF When Falstaff attempts to woo Mistress Ford by telling her that her beauty merits an aristocratic lady's extravagant hat, she dismisses his suggestion, telling him that her plain kerchief is good enough for her: "my brows become nothing else" (III.iii.49). Mistress Ford's satisfaction with her kerchief, the standard headwear worn by middle-class wives in Shakespeare's day, symbolizes her contentment with her social standing. The frugal, rich Mistress Ford could afford one of the fanciful hats that Falstaff imagines her wearing, but she is not interested in showing off her wealth or imitating the aristocracy.

IMPORTANT QUOTATIONS FROM *THE MERRY WIVES OF WINDSOR*

---

1. *If there be no great love in the beginning, yet heaven may decrease it upon better acquaintance, when we are married and have more occasion to know one another. I hope, upon familiarity will grow more contempt.*

Location: I.i.206–210
Speaker: Slender to Shallow
Context: Shallow has asked Slender if he can love Anne Page

Slender expresses his willingness to marry Anne Page in his usual inept way. He means to say that heaven may "increase" their love and that familiarity may breed "content," but he bungles the words, accidentally saying "decrease" and "contempt." Shakespeare associates the gold-digging characters, like Slender, with unskilled speech. What Slender says is closer to the truth than what he means: if they married, Slender and Anne probably would dislike each other more and more as time passed. Slender's intended meaning is also disheartening. He means to say that perhaps he could learn to like Anne—an unromantic admission that he is willing to risk marriage to a woman he does not know simply because she comes with a hefty dowry.

---

2. *Pistol: [drawing his sword] Why, then the world's mine oyster,*
   Which I with sword will open.
   Falstaff: Not a penny.

Location: II.ii.4–5
Speaker: Pistol and Falstaff
Context: Pistol has asked Falstaff for a loan

Angry that Falstaff has refused to lend him money, Pistol threatens violence. Falstaff is unimpressed, curtly telling Pistol, "Not a penny." Falstaff's bored reaction is comical, as is the juxtaposition of high and low styles of speech and the melodrama of Pistol's response. He characterizes himself as a hero opening the world with a sword—a vision more suited to a tragedy about a king than to a comedy involving a minor character who wants a small loan. The image of Pistol opening the twin halves of an oyster shell with his sword has strong sexual connotations typical of Falstaff and his gang. They believe they can overpower women and convince them to commit adultery, when in fact the women rebuff the men as easily and calmly as Falstaff brushes off Pistol's threats.

---

3. *O, what a world of vile ill-favour'd faults*
   Looks handsome in three hundred pounds a year!

Location: III.iv.31–32
Speaker: Anne to Fenton
Context: Mistress Quickly has told Anne that Slender wants to speak to her

Anne's words to Fenton are savvy and cynical. She knows that her father cares about how much money her suitors have, not about how much Anne likes them. She thinks her father is turning a blind eye to Slender's "world of vile ill-favour'd faults" because Slender is moderately well-off. Her choice of words emphasizes how little money it takes to make a bad man look good: Slender has a "world" of faults, but it only takes "three hundred pounds" to turn him into an attractive potential son-in-law for her father.

---

4. *Pardon me, wife. Henceforth do what thou wilt.*
   I rather will suspect the sun with cold
   Than thee with wantonness. Now doth thy honour stand,
   In him that was of late an heretic,
   As firm as faith.

Location: IV.iv.5–9
Speaker: Ford to Mistress Ford
Context: Mistress Ford has explained her deception

After indulging his jealous rage for most of the play, in this passage Ford finally admits that he has treated his wife unfairly. Ford's speaking style mixes the plain talk of the London middle classes with courtly, poetic rhetoric. The first line is straightforward and literal, communicating Ford's apology and relinquishment of power without embellishment. But in the next lines, Ford uses metaphorical language, comparing his wife to the sun and her honor to a religion that he briefly abandoned.

---

5. *Well, I will muse no further. Master Fenton,*
   Heaven give you many, many merry days!
   Good husband, let us every one go home,
   And laugh this sport o'er by a country fire,
   Sir John and all.

Location: V.v.216–220
Speaker: Mistress Page to Fenton and Master Page
Context: Fenton and Anne have announced their marriage

Mistress Page's last speech is cheerful and loving, even though she has just found out that her daughter has married a penniless man. Although Mistress Page wanted Anne to marry Caius, she seems sincere in her wish that heaven grant Fenton "many, many merry days!" Mistress Page is scheming and manipulative, but she means well and does want her daughter to be happy. The speech also stresses the simple comforts of middle-class life. Mistress Page considers simply laughing by the fire the best possible ending to the day's activities.

A MIDSUMMER NIGHT'S DREAM

After a bewildering night in a fairy-haunted forest, three couples are united in marriage.

A MIDSUMMER NIGHT'S DREAM IN CONTEXT

Written in the mid-1590s, probably shortly before Shakespeare began *Romeo and Juliet*, A *Midsummer Night's Dream* is one of Shakespeare's strangest and most delightful plays. The range of references in the play is among its most extraordinary attributes: Shakespeare draws on sources as various as Greek mythology (He loosely bases Theseus, for instance, on the Greek hero of the same name, and the play is peppered with references to Greek gods and goddesses); English country fairy lore (the character of Puck, or Robin Goodfellow, was a popular figure in sixteenth-century stories); and the theatrical practices of Shakespeare's London (the craftsmen's play refers to and parodies many conventions of English Renaissance theater, such as men playing the roles of women). The characters recall diverse texts: Titania comes from Ovid's *Metamorphoses*, and Shakespeare may have taken Oberon from the medieval romance *Huan of Bordeaux*, which Lord Berners translated into English in the mid-1530s. Unlike the plots of many of Shakespeare's plays, however, the storyline of *A Midsummer Night's Dream* seems to be the original product of the playwright's imagination, not a variation on a story already in existence.

A MIDSUMMER NIGHT'S DREAM: KEY FACTS

Full title: A *Midsummer Night's Dream*

Time and place written: London; 1594 or 1595

Date of first publication: 1600

Genre: Comedy; fantasy; romance; farce

Setting (time): Combines elements of Ancient Greece with elements of Renaissance England

Setting (place): Athens and the forest outside its walls

Protagonist: Puck

Major conflict: Couples are mismatched and frustrated.

A MIDSUMMER NIGHT'S DREAM: CHARACTER LIST

ATHENIANS

Demetrius A young man of Athens. Demetrius is initially in love with Hermia and ultimately in love with Helena. His obstinate pursuit of Hermia throws love out of balance among the quartet of Athenian youths.

Egeus Hermia's father. Egeus has given Demetrius permission to marry Hermia, but Hermia refuses to marry him because she is in love with Lysander. Egeus insists that Hermia either respect his wishes or be held accountable to Athenian law.

Helena A young woman of Athens. Helena is in love with Demetrius, who abandoned her for her friend Hermia. Helena lacks confidence in her looks.

Hermia Egeus's daughter. Hermia, a young woman of Athens, is in love with Lysander. Self-conscious about her short stature, Hermia suspects that Helena has attracted Lysander and Demetrius with her height.

Hippolyta The legendary queen of the Amazons. Hippolyta is engaged to Theseus. Like him, she symbolizes order.

Lysander A young man of Athens. Lysander is in love with Hermia, but Hermia's father wants her to marry Demetrius. In the forest, Lysander becomes the victim of misapplied magic and wakes up in love with Helena.

Philostrate Theseus's master of the revels. Philostrate is responsible for organizing the entertainment for the duke's marriage celebration.

Theseus The heroic duke of Athens. Theseus, who is engaged to Hippolyta, represents power and order. He appears only at the beginning and end of the story.

FAIRIES AND THEIR COMPANIONS

Oberon The king of the fairies. Oberon wants to take revenge on Titania, his wife, because she refuses to relinquish control of a young Indian prince whom he wants for a knight. His vengefulness leads him to send Puck to obtain the love-potion flower that creates so much confusion.

Peaseblossom, Cobweb, Mote, and Mustardseed Fairies. Titania orders them to attend to Bottom after she falls in love with him.

Puck Oberon's jester. Puck, also known as Robin Goodfellow, is a mischievous fairy who delights in playing pranks on mortals. His antics propel the plot.

Titania The beautiful queen of the fairies. Titania is married to Oberon.

PARTICIPANTS IN THE CRAFTSMEN'S PLAY

Nick Bottom An overconfident weaver. Bottom plays Pyramus in the craftsmen's play for Theseus's marriage celebration. He is full of advice and confidence but frequently makes silly mistakes and misuses language. He is nonchalant about the beautiful Titania's love for him and unaware that Puck has transformed his head into an ass's head.

Francis Flute A bellows-mender. Francis Flute plays Thisbe, a young girl in love, in the craftsmen's play for Theseus's marriage celebration.

Tom Snout A tinker. Tom Snout plays Pyramus's father in the craftsmen's play. He ends up playing the part of Wall, dividing the two lovers.

Snug A joiner. Snug plays the lion in the craftsmen's play. He worries that his roaring will frighten the ladies in the audience.

Robin Starveling A tailor. Robin Starveling plays Thisbe's mother in the craftsmen's play. He ends up playing the part of Moonshine.

Peter Quince A carpenter and the nominal leader of the craftsmen's play. The abundantly confident Bottom often shoves Quince aside.

A MIDSUMMER NIGHT'S DREAM: PLOT OVERVIEW

As Theseus, the Duke of Athens, prepares for his wedding celebration, a nobleman named Egeus marches in and asks for Theseus's help in forcing his daughter, Hermia, to marry a young man named Demetrius. Hermia loves another young man, Lysander, and plans to elope with him. She tells her friend Helena about the plan. Demetrius dumped Helena when he fell in love with Hermia. In the hopes of winning back Demetrius's love, Helena tells him that Hermia is planning to elope with Lysander. That night, Demetrius follows Hermia and Lysander into the woods. Helena follows Demetrius.

In the woods, the fairy king and queen, Oberon and Titania, quarrel with one another. Oberon tells his servant Puck to sprinkle love juice in Titania's eyes when she sleeps so that she will fall in love with the first creature she sees upon awakening. He also tells Puck to spread some love juice on Demetrius's eyes so that he will love Helena. Puck mistakes Lysander for Demetrius and accidentally makes Lysander fall in love with Helena. When Puck corrects his mistake, Demetrius and Lysander fight over Helena, who thinks they are mocking her.

Meanwhile, a group of clownish Athenian craftsmen are in the woods rehearsing a play for Theseus's wedding. Puck transforms the head of one of the craftsmen, Bottom, into the head of an ass, and causes Titania to fall in love with him. Eventually, Oberon is satisfied with his revenge, and Puck undoes his potions. In the morning, Demetrius realizes he loves Helena, and Hermia realizes she loves Lysander. The couples are married with Theseus. Bottom and his group put on a hilarious play at the wedding.

A MIDSUMMER NIGHT'S DREAM: SCENE SUMMARY

ACT I

Hermia plans to elope with Lysander, despite her father's objections; Helena pines for Demetrius; the laborers plan a play.

I.I Location: the Duke Theseus's palace

Egeus complains to Theseus that Hermia refuses to marry Demetrius; Hermia and Lysander plan to elope; Helena decides to tell Demetrius about the elopement so he will love her.

Theseus, Duke of Athens, and Hippolyta, his fiancée, discuss their wedding, which will take place in four days under the new moon. Impatient for the event and in a celebratory mood, Theseus orders Philostrate, his master of the revels, to "stir up the Athenian youth to merriments" and devise entertainments with which the couple can pass the time until their wedding (I.i.12). Philostrate takes his leave, and Theseus promises Hippolyta that though he wooed her with his sword (Hippolyta, Queen of the Amazons, presumably met Theseus in combat), he will wed her "with pomp, with triumph, and with reveling" (I.i.19).

Egeus, a citizen of Athens, comes into the room, followed by his daughter Hermia and the Athenian youths Lysander and Demetrius. Egeus has come to see Theseus with a complaint against his daughter: although Egeus has promised Hermia in marriage to Demetrius, who loves her, Lysander has won Hermia's heart, and Hermia refuses to obey her father and marry Demetrius. Egeus demands that Hermia be punished if she fails to comply with his demands. Theseus speaks sharply to Hermia, telling her to expect to be sent to a nunnery or put to death. Lysander interrupts, accusing Demetrius of being fickle in love, saying that he was once engaged to Hermia's friend Helena but abandoned her after he met Hermia. Theseus admits he has heard this story, and he takes Egeus and Demetrius aside to discuss it. He orders Hermia to take the time remaining before his marriage to Hippolyta to make up her mind. Theseus, Hippolyta, Egeus, and Demetrius depart, leaving Hermia alone with Lysander.

Hermia and Lysander discuss the trials that those who are in love must face: "The course of true love never did run smooth," Lysander says (I.i.134). He proposes a plan: he has a wealthy, childless aunt who lives seven leagues from Athens and who dotes on Lysander like a son. Hermia and Lysander could marry at her house. Because the manor is outside of Athens, they would be free from Athenian law. Hermia is overjoyed, and they agree to travel to the house the following night.

Helena enters the room. She is lovesick and deeply melancholy because Demetrius no longer loves her. Hermia and Lysander confide their plan to her and wish her luck with Demetrius. They depart to prepare for the following night's journey. Helena remarks to herself that she envies their happiness. She thinks up a plan: if she tells Demetrius of the elopement that Lysander and Hermia are planning, he will follow them to the woods to try to stop them. If she then follows him into the woods, she might have a chance to win back his love.

I.II Location: Athens

Peter Quince and his friends make plans to put on a play.

A group of common laborers meets at Peter Quince's house to rehearse a play that the men hope to perform for the grand celebration preceding the wedding of Theseus and Hippolyta. Quince, a carpenter, tries to conduct the meeting, but the talkative weaver Nick Bottom continually interrupts him with advice and direction. Quince tells the group what play they will perform: *The Most Lamentable Comedy and Most Cruel Death of Pyramus and Thisbe*, which tells the story of two lovers, separated by their parents' feud, who speak to each other at night through a hole in a wall. In the play, a lion surprises Thisbe one night and tatters her mantle before she escapes. When Pyramus finds the shredded garment, he assumes that the lion has killed Thisbe. Stricken with grief, he commits suicide. When Thisbe finds Pyramus's bloody corpse, she too commits suicide. Quince assigns parts: Bottom is to play Pyramus; Francis Flute, Thisbe; Robin Starveling, Thisbe's mother; Tom Snout, Pyramus's father; Quince himself, Thisbe's father; and Snug, the lion.

As Quince doles out the parts, Bottom often interrupts, announcing that he should be the one to play the assigned part. He says that his ability to speak in a woman's voice would make him a wonderful Thisbe and that his ability to roar would make him a wonderful lion. Quince eventually convinces Bottom that Pyramus is the part for him, by virtue of the fact that Pyramus is supposed to be very handsome. Snug worries that he will be unable to learn the lion's part, but Quince reassures him that it will be very easy to learn, since the lion speaks no words and only growls and roars. This worries the craftsmen, who reason that if the lion frightens any of the noble ladies in the audience, they will all face execution. They are only common laborers, and do not want to risk upsetting powerful people. Bottom says he could roar as sweetly as a nightingale so as not to frighten anyone, but Quince again convinces him that he can only play Pyramus. The group disperses, agreeing to meet in the woods the following night to rehearse their play.

ACT II

After quarreling with Titania, Oberon plans to exact his revenge by putting a love potion on her eyes. Puck attempts to put the love potion on Demetrius, but accidentally anoints Lysander, who wakes up and falls in love with Helena.

II.I Location: the forest

Titania and Oberon quarrel over Theseus and Hippolyta's impending marriage, and over the Indian prince; Oberon plans to take revenge on Titania by making her fall in love with a foolish creature.

Two fairies, one a servant of Titania, the other a servant of Oberon, meet by chance in a glade. Oberon's servant tells Titania's to keep Titania out of Oberon's sight, because the two are very angry with each other. Titania has taken a little Indian prince as her attendant, and the boy is so beautiful that Oberon wants to make him his knight. But Titania refuses to give the boy up.

Titania's servant is delighted to recognize Oberon's servant as Robin Goodfellow, better known as Puck, a mischievous sprite notorious for his pranks and jests. Puck admits his identity and describes some of the tricks he plays on mortals.

Oberon interrupts the two when he enters from one side of the glade, followed by a train of attendants. At the same moment, Titania enters from the other side of the glade, followed by her own train. The two fairy royals confront one another, each questioning the other's motive for coming so near Athens just before the marriage of Theseus and Hippolyta. Titania accuses Oberon of loving Hippolyta and wishing to bless the marriage; Oberon accuses Titania of loving Theseus. The conversation turns to the little Indian boy, whom Oberon again asks Titania to give him. Titania says that the boy's mother was a devotee of hers before she died, and Titania wants to keep the boy near her in honor of his mother's memory. She invites Oberon to dance with her in a fairy round and see her nightly revels, but Oberon declines, saying they will be at odds until she gives him the boy.

Titania storms off, and Oberon vows to take revenge on her before the night is out. He sends Puck to find a white and purple flower called love-in-idleness, which Cupid once hit with an arrow. He says that the flower's juice, if rubbed on a sleeper's eyelids, will cause the sleeper to fall in love with the first living thing he or she sees upon waking. Oberon announces that he will use this juice on Titania, hoping that she will fall in love with some ridiculous creature. He will then refuse to reverse the juice's effect until she yields the Indian prince to him.

II.II Location: a glade in the forest

Oberon puts the love potion on Titania's eyes and orders Puck to put some on Demetrius's eyes; by accident, Puck anoints Lysander's eyes, and Lysander wakes up and falls in love with Helena.

As Puck flies off to seek the flower, Demetrius and Helena pass through the glade. Oberon makes himself invisible so that he can watch and hear them. Demetrius harangues Helena, saying he does not love her, does not want to see her, and wishes she would stop following him. He curses Lysander and Hermia, whom he is pursuing. He wants to prevent their marriage and slay Lysander. Helena repeatedly declares her adoration for Demetrius, who repeatedly insults her. They exit the grove, with Helena following closely behind Demetrius. Oberon materializes. He declares that before the night is out, Demetrius will be the one chasing Helena.

Puck appears, carrying the flower whose juice will serve as the love potion. Oberon takes the flower and says he knows of a fragrant stream bank surrounded with flowers where Titania often sleeps. Before hurrying away to anoint Titania's eyelids with the flower's juice, Oberon orders Puck to look for an Athenian youth being pursued by a lady and to put some of the juice on the disdainful youth's eyelids, so that when he wakes he will fall in love with the lady. He tells Puck he will know the youth by his Athenian garb. Puck agrees to carry out his master's wishes.

After her dancing and revelry, Titania falls asleep by the stream bank. Oberon creeps up and squeezes the flower's juice onto her eyelids, chanting a spell. Oberon departs, and Lysander and Hermia wander into the glade. Lysander admits that he has forgotten the way to his aunt's house and says they should sleep in the forest until morning, when they can find their way by daylight. Lysander wants to sleep close to Hermia, but she insists that they sleep apart, to respect custom and propriety. At some distance from each other, they fall asleep.

Puck enters, complaining that he has looked everywhere but cannot find an Athenian youth and pursuing lady. He is relieved when he finally happens upon the sleeping Lysander and Hermia, assuming that they are the Athenians of whom Oberon spoke. Noticing that the two are sleeping apart, Puck surmises that the youth refused to let Hermia come closer to him. Puck spreads the potion on Lysander's eyelids and departs.

Helena pursues Demetrius through the glade. He insults her again and insists that she stop following him. Although Helena says she is afraid of the dark, Demetrius storms off without her. Helena bemoans her unrequited love. She sees the sleeping Lysander and wakes him up. The potion takes effect, and Lysander falls deeply in love with Helena. He begins to praise her beauty and to declare his undying passion for her. Helena reminds him that he loves Hermia, but Lysander says Hermia is nothing to him. Helena thinks Lysander is making fun of her, and she grows angry. She leaves in a huff, and Lysander follows her. Hermia soon wakes and is shocked to find Lysander gone. She stumbles into the woods to find him.

ACT III

Due to the love potion, Titania falls in love with Bottom, and Lysander and Demetrius fall in love with Helena, who thinks they are mocking her by pretending to love her.

III.I Location: a grove in the forest

The craftsmen rehearse; Puck changes Bottom's head into an ass's head; the potion makes Titania fall in love with Bottom.

The craftsmen meet in the woods at the appointed time to rehearse their play. Since they will be performing in front of a large group of nobles, and since they are worried about the delicacy of noble ladies, Bottom wants to change certain elements of the play. He fears that Pyramus's suicide and the lion's roaring will frighten the ladies and lead to the actors' executions. The other men share Bottom's concern and decide to write a prologue explaining that the lion is not really a lion nor the sword really a sword and assuring the ladies that no one will really die. They also decide that, to clarify the fact that the story takes place at night and that Pyramus and Thisbe are separated by a wall, one man must play the wall and another the moonlight.

As the craftsmen rehearse, Puck enters and marvels at the sight of the "hempen homespuns" trying to act (III.i.65). When Bottom steps aside, temporarily out of view of the other craftsmen, Puck transforms Bottom's head into that of an ass. When the ass-headed Bottom reenters the scene, the other men are terrified and run for their lives. Delighting in the mischief, Puck chases after them. Bottom, perplexed, remains behind.

In the same grove, the sleeping Titania wakes. When she sees Bottom, the flower juice on her eyelids works its magic, and she falls deeply and instantly in love with the ass-headed Bottom. She insists that he remain with her, embraces him, and appoints a group of fairies—Peaseblossom, Cobweb, Mote, and Mustardseed—to see to his every wish. Bottom takes these events in stride, having no notion that he has the head of an ass. He comments that his friends have acted like asses in leaving him, and introduces himself to the fairies. Titania looks on him with undisguised love as he follows her to her forest bower.

III.II Location: the forest

Oberon squeezes love potion on the eyes of Demetrius, who wakes and falls in love with Helena; Hermia grows furious at Helena, who thinks everyone is mocking her.

In another part of the forest, Puck tells Oberon about Titania and Bottom. Oberon is delighted that his plan is working so well. Hermia, having run into Demetrius after losing Lysander, enters the clearing with Demetrius. Puck is surprised to see her with a different man than the one he enchanted. Oberon is surprised to see the man he ordered Puck to enchant with a different woman. He realizes that a mistake has occurred and says he and Puck will have to remedy it.

Hermia presses Demetrius about Lysander's whereabouts, fearing him dead, but Demetrius does not know where Lysander has gone and is bitter and reproachful that Hermia would rather be with Lysander than with him. Hermia grows angrier and angrier, and Demetrius decides it is pointless to follow her. He lies down and falls asleep, and Hermia storms away to find Lysander.

Oberon sends Puck to find Helena and squeezes the flower juice onto Demetrius's eyelids. Puck returns, saying that Helena is close behind him. Helena enters with Lysander still pledging his undying love to her. Helena still thinks he is mocking her, and is angry and hurt. Their bickering wakes Demetrius, who sees Helena and immediately falls in love with her. Demetrius joins Lysander in declaring his love for Helena. Lysander says Demetrius does not really love Helena; Demetrius says that Lysander is truly in love with Hermia. Helena believes that they are both mocking her.

Hermia reenters, having heard Lysander from a distance. When she learns that her beloved Lysander now claims to love Helena, as does Demetrius, she is appalled and incredulous. Helena assumes Hermia is involved in the joke that she believes the men are playing on her, and she chides Hermia furiously for treating their friendship so lightly.

Lysander and Demetrius are ready to fight one another for Helena's love. As they lunge at one another, Hermia holds Lysander back, provoking his scorn and disgust: "I will shake thee from me like a serpent" (III.ii.262). Hermia begins to suspect that Helena has somehow stolen Lysander's love from her. She decides that Helena must have used her height to lure Lysander. Furious with Helena, Hermia threatens to scratch out her eyes. Helena says Hermia was always much quicker than she to fight. Demetrius and Lysander vow to protect Helena from Hermia, but they quickly become angry with each other and storm off into the forest to have a duel. Helena runs away from Hermia. Hermia, reaffirming her amazement at the turn of events, departs.

Oberon dispatches Puck to prevent Lysander and Demetrius from fighting. He says they must resolve this confusion by morning. Puck flies through the forest hurling insults in the voices of both Lysander and Demetrius, confusing the would-be combatants until they are hopelessly lost.

III.III Location: a glade in the forest

As the Athenians sleep in the glade, Puck squeezes the potion onto Lysander's eyelids.

All four of the young Athenian lovers wander back separately into the glade and fall asleep. Puck squeezes the herb onto Lysander's eyelids to remedy the mistaken effects of the love potion, declaring that in the morning all will be well.

ACT IV

Everyone returns to normal; Bottom pleases his friends by showing up alive.

IV.I Location: a glade in the forest

Pleased with his revenge and in possession of the Indian prince, Oberon restores Titania to normal; Puck restores Bottom's human head; the Athenian youths wake up to find that Demetrius and Helena love each other, as do Lysander and Hermia.

As the Athenian lovers lie asleep in the grove, Titania enters with Bottom, who still has the head of an ass, and their fairy attendants. Titania tells Bottom to lie down with his head in her lap so that she may twine roses into his hair and kiss his "fair large ears" (IV.i.4). Bottom orders Peaseblossom to scratch his head and sends Cobweb to find him some honey. Titania asks Bottom if he is hungry, and he says he has a strange appetite for hay. Titania suggests sending a fairy to fetch him nuts from a squirrel's hoard, but Bottom says he would rather have a handful of dried peas. Yawning, he declares that he is very tired. Titania tells him to sleep in her arms and sends the fairies away. Gazing at Bottom's head, she cries, "O how I love thee, how I dote on thee!" (IV.i.42) They fall asleep.

Puck and Oberon enter the glade and comment on the success of Oberon's revenge. Oberon says he saw Titania earlier in the woods and taunted her about her love for the ass-headed Bottom. When Titania begged him to stop mocking her, he asked for and received the Indian child. Satisfied, Oberon bends over the sleeping Titania and speaks the charm to undo the love potion. Titania wakes and is amazed to find that she is sleeping with the ass-headed Bottom. Oberon calls for music and takes his queen away to dance. Titania says she hears the morning lark, and they exit. Puck speaks a charm over Bottom to restore his normal head and then follows after his master.

As dawn breaks, Theseus, his attendants, Hippolyta, and Egeus enter. They are startled to find the Athenian youths sleeping in the glade. They wake them and demand to know what happened. The youths are only partly able to recall the events of the previous night, which seem as insubstantial as a dream. They only know that Demetrius and Helena love each other, as do Lysander and Hermia. Theseus orders them to follow him to the temple for a great wedding feast. As they leave, Bottom wakes. He says he has had a wondrous dream and that he will have Peter Quince write a ballad about it to perform at the end of their play.

IV.II   Location: Quince's house

The craftsmen, who are worried about Bottom and feel they cannot perform the play without him, are overjoyed when he suddenly returns.

The craftsmen sit around worrying about Bottom, who is missing. They last saw him shortly before the appearance of the ass-headed monster in the forest and are worried that he fell prey to this terrifying creature. Starveling suspects that the fairies have cast some enchantment on Bottom. Flute asks whether they will go through with the play if Bottom does not return from the woods, and Peter Quince says that to do so would be impossible, as Bottom is the only man in Athens capable of portraying Pyramus. The craftsmen agree that their friend is the wittiest, most intelligent, and best person in all of Athens.

Snug enters with an alarming piece of news: Theseus has been married, along with "two or three lords and ladies" (presumably Lysander, Hermia, Demetrius, and Helena), and the newlyweds are eager to see a play (IV.ii.16). Flute laments Bottom's absence, noting that Bottom would certainly have won a great deal of money from the admiring duke for his portrayal of Pyramus.

Just then, Bottom bursts triumphantly into the room and asks why everyone looks so sad. The men are overjoyed to see him. He declares that he has an amazing story to tell them about his adventure in the forest. Quince asks to hear it, but Bottom says there is no time: they must don their costumes and go straight to the duke's palace to perform their play. As they leave, Bottom tells them not to eat onions or garlic before the play, as they must be prepared to "utter sweet breath" (IV.ii.36).

ACT V

The craftsmen put on their play, and Oberon and Titania bless all in the palace.

V.I   Location: Duke Theseus's palace

The craftsmen put on their play.

Theseus speaks with Hippolyta about the story the Athenian youths told them concerning the magical, romantic mix-ups of the previous night. Theseus says that he does not believe the story, adding that darkness and love have a way of exciting the imagination. But Hippolyta says that if their story is not true, it is strange that all of the lovers managed to narrate the events in exactly the same way.

The youths enter and Theseus greets them heartily. He says they should pass the time before bed with a performance, and summons Egeus (or, in some editions of A *Midsummer Night's Dream*, Philostrate) to read him a list of plays, each of which Theseus deems unacceptable. Egeus tells him of the Pyramus and Thisbe story that the common craftsmen have prepared. He says the play is terrible in every respect, and urges Theseus not to see it. Theseus says that if the craftsmen's intentions are dutiful, there will be something of merit in the play no matter how poor the performance.

The lords and ladies take their seats, and Quince enters to present a prologue, which he delivers haltingly. His strange pauses give the words unintended meaning, so that he says, "Our true intent is. All for your delight / We are not here. That you should here repent you," though he means to say, "Our true intent is all for your delight. / We are not here that you should here repent you" (V.i.114–115). The other players enter, including two characters performing the roles of Wall and Moonshine. They act out a clumsy version of the story, during which the noblemen and women joke among themselves about the actors' strange speeches and mistakes. Bottom, in particular, makes many perplexing statements while playing Pyramus, such as "I see a voice ... I can hear my Thisbe's face" (V.i.190–191). Pyramus and Thisbe meet at, and speak across, the actor playing Wall, who holds up his fingers to indicate a chink. Snug, as the lion, enters and pours forth a speech explaining to the ladies that he is not really a lion. He roars, scaring Thisbe away, and clumsily rends her mantle. Finding the bloody mantle, Pyramus duly commits suicide. Thisbe does likewise when she finds Pyramus dead. After the conclusion of the play, during which Bottom pretends to kill himself, with a cry of "die, die, die, die, die," Bottom asks if the audience would like an epilogue or a bergamask dance. Theseus says they will see the dance. Bottom and Flute perform the dance, and the whole group exits for bed.

V. EPILOGUE

Oberon and Titania bless the palace and its occupants, and Puck asks for applause.

Puck says now that night has fallen, the fairies will come to the castle. He has been "sent with broom before / To sweep the dust behind the door" (V.ii.19–20). Oberon and Titania enter and bless the palace and its occupants with a fairy song, so that the lovers will always be true to one another, their children will be beautiful, and no harm will ever visit Theseus and Hippolyta. Oberon and Titania leave, and Puck makes a final address to the audience. He says that if the play has offended, the audience should remember it simply as a dream. He wishes the audience members good night and asks them to give him their hands in applause if they are kind friends.

ANALYSIS OF MAJOR CHARACTERS IN *A MIDSUMMER NIGHT'S DREAM*

PUCK

Though there is little character development in A *Midsummer Night's Dream* and no true protagonist, critics generally point to Puck as the most important character in the play. The mischievous, quick-witted sprite sets many of the play's events in motion with his magic, by means of both deliberate pranks on the human characters (transforming Bottom's head into that of an ass, for example) and unfortunate mistakes (such as smearing the love potion on Lysander's eyelids instead of Demetrius's). More important, Puck's capricious spirit, magical fancy, fun-loving humor, and lovely, evocative language permeate the play's atmosphere. Puck embodies the wild contrasts that dominate the play, like the implicit comparison between the rough, earthy craftsmen and the delicate, graceful fairies. Puck is graceful but not so saccharine as the other fairies; good-hearted but capable of cruel tricks; a fairy but a strange-looking "hobgoblin" (II.i.40).

NICK BOTTOM

The comedy of the overconfident weaver Nick Bottom is hilariously overt. Bottom dominates his fellow craftsmen actors with an extraordinary belief in his own abilities and his comical incompetence. He thinks he is perfect for every part in the play, but he is a terrible actor and frequently makes rhetorical and grammatical mistakes. Bottom is unaware of his own absurdity. His speeches are overdramatic and self-aggrandizing, and he believes that everyone takes him as seriously as he does himself. His self-importance reaches its pinnacle after Puck transforms Bottom's head into that of an ass. When Titania, whose eyes have been anointed with a love potion, falls in love with the now ass-headed Bottom, Bottom is not surprised. He thinks it is natural that a beautiful, magical fairy queen has fallen in love with him and believes that all of the trappings of her affection, including the servants who attend him, are his proper due.

HELENA

Helena, the young woman lovesick for Demetrius, is perhaps the most fully drawn character aside from Puck and Bottom. Among the quartet of Athenian lovers, Helena is the one who thinks most about the nature of love, perhaps because she is initially left out of the love triangle involving Lysander, Hermia, and Demetrius. Utterly faithful to Demetrius despite her recognition of his shortcomings, Helena sets out to win his love by telling him about Lysander's and Hermia's plan to elope into the forest. Once Helena enters the forest, many of her traits are amplified by the confusion that the love potion creates. Compared to the other lovers, she is extremely unsure of herself, worrying about her appearance and believing that Lysander is mocking her when he declares his love for her.

THEMES, MOTIFS & SYMBOLS IN *A MIDSUMMER NIGHT'S DREAM*

THEMES

IMBALANCE IN RELATIONSHIPS   "The course of true love never did run smooth," comments Lysander, articulating one of A *Midsummer Night's Dream's* most important themes: the difficulty of love (I.i.134). Love is almost always out of balance in the play. Disparity or inequality interferes with the harmony of nearly every relationship. The prime instance of this imbalance is the uneven love among the four young Athenians: Hermia loves Lysander, Lysander loves Hermia, Helena loves Demetrius, and Demetrius loves Hermia. In a numeric imbalance, two men love the same woman, leaving one woman with too many suitors and one with too few. As the audience knows, the happy outcome will be achieved when the lovers' tangle resolves itself into symmetrical pairings. In the relationship between Titania and Oberon, an imbalance arises because Oberon's desire for Titania's Indian boy eclipses his love for her. Later, Titania's passion for the ass-headed Bottom is an imbalance of appearance and nature: Titania is beautiful and graceful, Bottom clumsy and grotesque.

THE USE OF MAGIC   The fairies' magic, which brings about many of the most bizarre and hilarious situations in the play, enhances the play's fantastical atmosphere. Shakespeare uses magic both to suggest the almost supernatural power of love, as symbolized by the love potion, and to create a surreal world. Although the misuse of magic causes chaos, as when Puck mistakenly applies the love potion to Lysander's eyelids, magic ultimately resolves the play's tensions by balancing the love among the quartet of Athenian youths.

THE ILLOGICAL, COMFORTING QUALITY OF DREAMS   Shakespeare is interested in the illogical quality of dreams, in the way events in dreams occur without explanation, time loses its normal flow, and the impossible occurs as a matter of course. He recreates the effect of dreams with the nonsensical, illogical intervention of the fairies in the magical forest. Shakespeare also examines the way we look at our lives through the filter of dreams. Characters in the play often attempt to explain the bizarre events that take place in the forest by blaming them on dreams. When Bottom cannot fathom the magic that has transpired, he says, "I have had a dream, past the wit of man to say what / dream it was. Man is but an ass if he go about t'expound this dream." At the end of the play, Puck tells the audience that if they have been offended by the play, they should remember it as nothing more than a dream.

MOTIFS

CONTRAST   Shakespeare frames A *Midsummer Night's Dream* around groups of opposites and doubles. Nearly every characteristic in the play has an opposite: Helena is tall, Hermia is short; Puck plays pranks, Bottom is the victim of pranks; Titania is beautiful, Bottom is grotesque. The three main groups of characters contrast with one another: the fairies are graceful and magical, while the craftsmen are clumsy and earthy; the craftsmen are merry, while the lovers are overly serious. Contrast is also the defining visual characteristic of A *Midsummer Night's Dream*. The play's most indelible image is of the beautiful, delicate Titania weaving flowers into the hair of the ass-headed Bottom. The juxtaposition of extraordinary differences is the most important component of the play's surreal atmosphere.

SYMBOLS

THESEUS AND HIPPOLYTA   Theseus and Hippolyta bookend A *Midsummer Night's Dream*, appearing in the daylight at the beginning and the end of the play's main action. They disappear for the duration of the action, leaving in the middle of Act I, scene i and not reappearing until Act IV, as the sun is coming up to end the magical night in the forest. Shakespeare uses Theseus and Hippolyta, the ruler of Athens and his warrior bride, to represent order and stability. They contrast with the uncertainty, instability, and darkness that characterize most of the play. Whereas an important element of the dream realm is that one is not in control of one's environment, Theseus and Hippolyta are always entirely in control of theirs. Their reappearance in the daylight signifies the end of the dream state of the previous night and a return to rationality.

THE CRAFTSMEN'S PLAY   The play-within-a-play that takes up most of Act V, scene i represents, in condensed form, many of the important ideas and themes of the main plot. With their bumbling performances, the actors accidentally satirize the melodramatic Athenian lovers and give the play a purely joyful, comedic ending. Pyramus and Thisbe face parental disapproval in the play-within-a-play, just as Hermia and Lysander do. The theme of romantic confusion enhanced by the darkness of night comes up in the play, just as the Athenian lovers experience intense misery because of the mix-ups caused by the fairies' meddling. The craftsmen's play is a kind of symbol for A *Midsummer Night's Dream* itself: it is a story involving powerful emotions that is made hilarious by its comical presentation.

IMPORTANT QUOTATIONS FROM *A MIDSUMMER'S NIGHT DREAM*

---

1. *Ay me, for aught that I could ever read,*
   Could ever hear by tale or history,
   The course of true love never did run smooth.

Location: I.i.132–134
Speaker: Lysander to Hermia
Context: Hermia despairs about the difficulties facing their relationship

Lysander tries to soothe Hermia, who is worried that Egeus, her father, has forbidden them to marry and that Theseus has threatened her with death if she disobeys her father. Lysander tells Hermia that as long as there has been true love, seemingly insurmountable difficulties have cropped up to challenge it. He goes on to list a number of these difficulties, many of which later appear in the play: differences in birth or age ("misgrafted in respect of years"), difficulties caused by friends, and "war, death, or sickness," which make love seem "swift as a shadow, short as any dream" (I.i.137, I.i.142–144). The passage introduces the play's theme of love's difficulties and foreshadows the problems that lie ahead for Lysander and Hermia.

---

2. *Through Athens I am thought as fair as she.*
   But what of that? Demetrius thinks not so.
   He will not know what all but he do know.
   And as he errs, doting on Hermia's eyes,
   So I, admiring of his qualities.
   Things base and vile, holding no quantity,

Love can transpose to form and dignity.
Love looks not with the eyes, but with the mind,
And therefore is winged Cupid painted blind.

Location: I.i.227–235
Speaker: Helena
Context: Helena thinks about her merits compared to Hermia's

In these lines, Helena articulates the play's general presentation of love as an erratic, inexplicable, and exceptionally powerful force. Distressed by the fact that her beloved Demetrius loves Hermia and not her, Helena says that although she is as beautiful as Hermia, Demetrius cannot see her beauty. Helena says she dotes on Demetrius, even though not all of his qualities are admirable, in the same way that Demetrius dotes on Hermia. She believes that love has the power to transform "base and vile" qualities into "form and dignity"—that is, even ugliness and bad behavior can seem attractive to someone in love. This is the case, Helena argues, because "love looks not with the eyes, but with the mind." That is, love depends not on an objective assessment of appearance but rather on an individual perception of the beloved. These lines prefigure aspects of the play's examination of love, such as Titania's passion for the ass-headed Bottom, which epitomizes the transformation of the "base and vile" into "form and dignity."

---

3. *Lord, what fools these mortals be!*

Location: III.ii.115
Speaker: Puck
Context: the four Athenians have been behaving outlandishly

Puck makes this declaration of amazement at the ludicrous behavior of the young Athenians. This line is one of the most famous in A *Midsummer Night's Dream* for its pithy humor, but it is also thematically important. It captures the exaggerated silliness of the lovers' behavior, and it marks the contrast between the human lovers, completely absorbed in their emotions, and the magical fairies, impish and never too serious.

---

4. *I have had a most rare vision. I have had a dream past the wit of man to say what dream it was. Man is but an ass if he go about t'expound this dream. Methought I was—there is no man can tell what. Methought I was, and methought I had—but man is but a patched fool if he will offer to say what methought I had. The eye of man hath not heard, the ear of man hath not seen, man's hand is not able to taste, his tongue to conceive, nor his heart to report what my dream was. I will get Peter Quince to write a ballad of this dream. It shall be called 'Bottom's Dream,' because it hath no bottom.*

Location: IV.i.199–209
Speaker: Bottom
Context: Bottom has had an adventure with Titania

Bottom makes this bombastic speech after waking up after his adventure with Titania. His human head restored, he believes that his experience as an ass-headed monster beloved by the beautiful fairy queen was merely a bizarre dream. He says dramatically that his dream is beyond human comprehension. Then, contradicting himself, he says that he will ask Quince to write a ballad about it. These lines offer humorous commentary on dreams; they also exemplify what is so lovable and amusing about Bottom. His overabundant self-confidence makes him think that no one could possibly understand his dream, but his tremendous self-regard makes him want his dream, which no mortal can understand, to be immortalized in a poem written by his friend. He makes many melodramatic rhetorical mistakes, suggesting that eyes hear, ears see, hands taste, tongues think, and hearts speak.

5. *If we shadows have offended,*
   Think but this, and all is mended:
   That you have but slumbered here,
   While these visions did appear;
   And this weak and idle theme,
   No more yielding but a dream,
   Gentles, do not reprehend.
   If you pardon, we will mend.

Location: V.epilogue.1-8
Speaker: Puck to the audience
Context: Puck concludes the play

In these lines, Puck extends the theme of dreams beyond the world of the play and asks the audience to question the reality of its experiences. Just as many of the characters (Bottom and Theseus among them) believe that the magical events of the play's action were merely a dream, Puck tells the crowd that if the play has offended them, they too should remember it simply as a dream—"That you have but slumbered here, / While these visions did appear." The speech extends the dreamlike atmosphere of A *Midsummer Night's Dream* and casts the play as a magical dream in which the audience partakes.

MUCH ADO ABOUT NOTHING

Believing that his fiancée Hero is unfaithful, Claudio publicly shames her before recognizing his mistake and marrying her; longtime rivals Beatrice and Benedick are tricked into admitting that they love each other.

MUCH ADO ABOUT NOTHING IN CONTEXT

One of Shakespeare's best comedies, *Much Ado About Nothing* combines elements of robust humor with more serious meditations on honor, shame, and court politics. It was likely written in 1598–99, as Shakespeare approached the middle of his career. Like *As You Like It* and *Twelfth Night*, *Much Ado* touches upon darker concerns but ends joyfully with multiple marriages and no deaths.

Although characters do not die in Shakespearean comedies, *Much Ado* treats death as part of the natural cycle of life. Indeed, death is vividly present here: for several scenes, many characters believe that Hero has died. The play's central crisis has troubled many readers and audience members. The play deals with anger, betrayal, grief, and despair, and ties up these strong emotions quickly and, some have thought, flippantly.

Many critics have noted that the plot of *Much Ado About Nothing* shares important elements with the plot of *Romeo and Juliet*. *Much Ado* is also similar to a late Shakespearean romance, or "problem play," *The Winter's Tale*. Like Hero, *The Winter's Tale's* Hermione stages a false death only to come back to life once her beloved has repented.

Although the trials of the young lovers Hero and Claudio fuel the main storyline, it is the courtship between the older, wiser Benedick and Beatrice that makes *Much Ado* so memorable. Benedick and Beatrice argue with delightful wit, and Shakespeare develops their journey from antagonism to sincere affection with both rich humor and compassion. Beatrice and Benedick have a back story and are more mature than many of Shakespeare's lovers, but they prove to be childishly competitive amateurs in love.

MUCH ADO ABOUT NOTHING: KEY FACTS

Full Title: Much Ado About Nothing

Time and place written: 1598; England

Date of first publication: 1600

Genre: Comedy

Setting (time): 1500s

Setting (place): The Sicilian town of Messina, on and around Governor Leonato's estate

Protagonist: Claudio, Hero, Beatrice, and Benedick

Major conflict: Don John makes Hero appear to be unfaithful to Claudio; Beatrice and Benedick's rivalry blinds them to the fact that they love each other; Claudio and Benedick fear marriage as an entrapment

MUCH ADO ABOUT NOTHING: CHARACTER LIST

Antonio Leonato's elderly brother, and Hero and Beatrice's uncle.

Balthasar A musician and servant in Leonato's household. Balthasar flirts with Margaret at the masked party and helps Leonato, Claudio, and Don Pedro trick Benedick into falling in love with Beatrice. Balthasar sings the song, "Sigh no more, ladies, sigh no more," which is about accepting men's infidelity as natural.

Beatrice Leonato's niece and Hero's cousin. Generous and loving, Beatrice has a very sharp tongue and frequently mocks others with elaborately tooled jokes and puns. She has been waging a spirited war of wits with Benedick, but insists that she will never marry.

Benedick An aristocrat-soldier who fights under his friend Don Pedro, and Claudio's friend. Witty and spirited, Benedick carries on a "merry war" of wits with Beatrice, but swears that he will never fall in love or marry.

Borachio Don John's servant and accomplice, and Margaret's lover. Borachio conspires with Don John to trick Claudio and Don Pedro into thinking that Hero is unfaithful to Claudio. *Borachio* means "drunkard" in Italian, which is perhaps a subtle direction to the actor.

Claudio A young soldier who has won great acclaim fighting under Don Pedro during the recent wars. Claudio falls in love with Hero upon his return to Messina. His suspicious nature makes him quick to believe evil rumors and hasty to despair and seek revenge.

Conrad One of Don John's intimate associates, entirely devoted to Don John. Several recent productions have suggested that Conrad is Don John's male lover, an appealing choice for a director since this relationship would Don John's feelings of being a social outcast and therefore motivates his desire for revenge.

Dogberry The constable in charge of the watchmen of Messina. Dogberry is very sincere and takes his job seriously, but he has a habit of using exactly the wrong word to convey his meaning. Dogberry is one of the few "middling sort," or middle-class characters in the play though his desire to speak formally and elaborately as the noblemen do becomes an occasion for parody.

Hero The beautiful young daughter of Leonato and the cousin of Beatrice. Hero is lovely, gentle, and kind. She falls in love with Claudio, and when Don John slanders her and Claudio rashly takes revenge, she suffers terribly.

Don John (the Bastard) The illegitimate brother of Don Pedro. Don John is melancholy and sullen by nature, and he creates a dark scheme to ruin the happiness of Hero and Claudio. He is the villain of the play. His evil actions are likely motivated by his envy of his brother's social authority.

Leonato A respected, well-to-do, elderly noble at whose home, in Messina, Italy, the action is set. Leonato is the father of Hero and the uncle of Beatrice. As governor of Messina, he is second in social power only to Don Pedro.

Margaret Hero's serving woman. Margaret unwittingly helps Borachio and Don John deceive Claudio into thinking that Hero is unfaithful. Unlike Ursula, Hero's other lady-in-waiting, Margaret is lower class. Though she is honest, she does have some dealings with the villainous world of Don John: her lover is the mistrustful and easily bribed Borachio. Also unlike Ursula, Margaret loves to flout decorum, especially with bawdy jokes and teasing.

Don Pedro, Prince of Aragon Leonato's longtime friend. Don Pedro is also close to the soldiers who have been fighting under him: the younger Benedick and the very young Claudio. Don Pedro is generous, courteous, intelligent, and loving to his friends, but he is also quick to believe evil of others and hasty to take revenge. He is the most politically and socially powerful character in the play.

Ursula One of Hero's waiting women.

Verges Dogberry's deputy.

MUCH ADO ABOUT NOTHING: PLOT OVERVIEW

Leonato, the governor of idyllic Messina, shares his household with his daughter Hero, his clever niece Beatrice, and his elderly brother Antonio. As the play begins, Leonato prepares to welcome Don Pedro's army returning from battle. Don Pedro's company includes the young, brave Claudio and the witty Benedick, and Don Pedro's bitter illegitimate brother Don John.

At Leonato's house, Claudio falls in love with Hero. Benedick and Beatrice resume their long-standing war of witty insults. At a masked ball, Don Pedro arranges Claudio and Hero's betrothal. To pass time until the wedding, the lovers and their friends trick Beatrice and Benedick into secretly falling in love with each other.

Don John, who hates Claudio for being the new upstart favorite, makes trouble. He arranges for his companion Borachio to make love to Hero's servant Margaret on Hero's balcony while Don Pedro and Claudio look on. Claudio and Don Pedro mistake Margaret for Hero, according to Don John's plan. The enraged Claudio humiliates Hero by publicly denouncing her on the day of their wedding and abandoning her at the altar. Hero's stricken family decides to conceal her and announce that she has died of shock and grief. In the aftermath of the scandal, Benedick and Beatrice finally confess their love to each other. Fortunately, the night watchmen overhear Borachio bragging about his crime and arrest him. Everyone learns that Hero is innocent. Claudio, who believes she is dead, grieves for her.

To atone for Hero's death, Leonato asks Claudio to marry Leonato's "niece," who turns out to be Hero in disguise. Benedick and Beatrice too agree to get married. Don John is captured. The double wedding is celebrated with music and dance.

MUCH ADO ABOUT NOTHING: *SCENE SUMMARY*

ACT I

Don Pedro plans to woo Hero on Claudio's behalf; Don John plots to make trouble for Claudio.

I.I   Location: outside Leonato's house

Don Pedro, whose army has arrived to stay with Leonato, plans to help his brave soldier Claudio woo Leonato's daughter Hero.

Leonato, the governor of the Italian town of Messina, prepares to welcome home the army of Don Pedro of Aragon, returning from battle. The messenger who announces the army's imminent arrival tells of a brave young soldier named Claudio who has distinguished himself in battle. Leonato's niece Beatrice cleverly mocks and insults another of Don Pedro's soldiers, Signor Benedick. The messenger tries to defend Benedick as an honorable and virtuous man, but Leonato explains that Beatrice and Benedick carry on a "merry war" of wits with one another, trading jibes whenever they meet.

Don Pedro, Claudio, and Benedick arrive and are joyfully welcomed. Also accompanying Don Pedro is his quiet, sullen, illegitimate brother Don John, "the bastard." While Leonato and Don Pedro have a private talk, Beatrice and Benedick insult each other's looks, intelligence, and personality in an extremely fast-paced exchange of barbs.

Don Pedro and his officers will stay with Leonato for a month. Everyone except Claudio and Benedick leaves for the house. Claudio shyly tells Benedick that he has fallen in love with Leonato's daughter Hero. Benedick teases Claudio for wanting to become a tame husband. But when Don Pedro returns to look for his friends, Benedick tells him Claudio's secret, and Don Pedro approves highly of the match. Don Pedro proposes a trick for the evening's costume ball: Don Pedro will disguise himself as Claudio and declare his love to Hero. He will then negotiate the match with Leonato. The three friends head off excitedly to get ready for the ball.

I.II   Location: Leonato's house

Misinformed, Leonato will tell Hero that Don Pedro plans to woo her that night.

Leonato runs into his elder brother Antonio, who tells him that his servant has overheard Don Pedro and Claudio's conversation: Don Pedro plans to woo Hero at that night's ball. (We know that the servant has made a mistake: Don Pedro plans to woo Hero on Claudio's behalf.) Leonato plans to warn Hero so that she can think about her response, should this rumor prove true.

I.III   Location: elsewhere in Leonato's house

Don John and his servants plot to make trouble for Claudio.

In conversation with his servant Conrad, Don John explains that it is in his nature to always look angry and melancholy. Conrad reminds Don John that Don John and Don Pedro have only recently started being on good terms again, and if Don John wants the protection of his powerful brother he ought to be more cheerful. Don John bitterly bristles at having to stay in Don Pedro's favor. Borachio, another of Don John's servants, tells Don John that he has heard rumors of the planned match between Claudio and Hero. (Borachio has overhead the same conversation as Antonio's servant, but has interpreted it correctly.) Don John decides to make trouble for Claudio, whom he hates for being so well loved and respected. Conrad and Borachio swear to help him.

ACT II

Claudio and Hero are engaged; Don John plots to ruin Hero's reputation; Benedick is tricked into thinking that Beatrice is in love with him.

II.I Location: a hall in Leonato's house

At the masked ball, Claudio and Hero become engaged, despite Don John's plotting.

Waiting for the masked ball to begin, Hero and Beatrice discuss their idea of the perfect man, who is a happy combination of the taciturn Don John and the garrulous Benedick. The conversation leads to Beatrice's plans to marry, and she laughingly claims that she never will. The other partygoers enter and the men put on masks. Supposedly, the women now cannot tell who the men are. The music begins and the dancers pair off. Don Pedro's musician, Balthasar, and Antonio dance with Margaret and Ursula, Hero's servants. Don Pedro dances and flirts with Hero. Benedick dances with Beatrice, who does not— or pretends not to—recognize him. She makes fun of Benedick to her dancing partner.

Don John has seen Don Pedro with Hero, and decides to make Claudio jealous. Pretending not to recognize Claudio behind his mask, Don John addresses Claudio as if he were Benedick, and mentions to him that contrary to the plan, Don Pedro is courting Hero for himself and will marry her that very night. Angry and miserable, Claudio rushes out when the real Benedick comes in. Don Pedro comes in with Hero and Leonato. True to his word, Don Pedro has wooed and won Hero for Claudio. Benedick, bitter about the nasty things Beatrice said to him during the dance, leaves as Beatrice approaches with Claudio. Claudio is overwhelmed when he finds out that Hero has agreed to marry him. In private, he and Hero make their promises to each other.

When Beatrice makes a half-serious remark about her lack of a husband, Don Pedro offers himself to her. Beatrice declines with a fancy conceit. With Beatrice and Benedick gone, Leonato and Claudio discuss plans. The wedding will take place on Monday, a week away. In the meantime, Don Pedro comes up with a diversion: together, they will get Beatrice and Benedick to stop arguing and fall in love with each other.

II.II Location: Leonato's house

Don John and his servants plot to convince Claudio that Hero has been unfaithful.

Borachio comes up with a plan to upset Claudio and Hero's marriage. Borachio will convince his lover, Hero's servant Margaret, to dress up in Hero's clothing on the night before the wedding. At the same time, Don John will go to Claudio and Don Pedro and tell them that Hero has been unfaithful to Claudio. To prove his accusation, Don John will lead Don Pedro and Claudio to hide and watch under Hero's window, where they will see Borachio making love to Margaret. The watchers will think that Margaret is Hero, and her reputation will be ruined. Don John is very pleased with the plan.

II.III Location: Leonato's garden

Benedick's friends trick him into thinking that Beatrice is in love with him.

Benedick wanders around the garden, wondering aloud how intelligent men such as Claudio can fall in love given that love makes men into idiots. Suddenly, he hears Don Pedro, Claudio, and Leonato approaching and hides to eavesdrop. Don Pedro and Claudio speak loudly for Benedick's benefit. They talk about how Beatrice has fallen passionately in love with Benedick. She dares not tell Benedick, they say, for fear that he would mock her. They all agree that Benedick is unworthy of so fine a woman as Beatrice, and would be a fool to turn her away. Then they go in for dinner.

Benedick, amazed, decides to "take pity" upon the beautiful, witty, and virtuous Beatrice and love her in return. Beatrice comes in to fetch Benedick for dinner. She is scornful to him, but he is unusually courteous to her. Benedick interprets her confused and suspicious words as hidden words of love, and runs off to have a little portrait of her made for him.

ACT III

Don John makes Hero look like a whore; night watchmen arrest Don John's accomplices; Beatrice is tricked into thinking that Benedick loves her.

III.I   Location: Leonato's garden

Hero and her servingwomen trick Beatrice into thinking that Benedick is in love with her.

Hero and her servingwomen, Margaret and Ursula, prepare to trick Beatrice into believing that Benedick loves her, just as Don Pedro, Leonato, and Claudio have tricked Benedick in II.iii. Margaret lures Beatrice into the garden to eavesdrop on Hero and Ursula's conversation. In a loud voice, Hero tells Ursula that she just found out that Benedick is in love with Beatrice. Hero can't tell Beatrice about it because Beatrice would just mock both Hero and Benedick. That's why it's better, she says, to let poor Benedick waste away silently from unrequited love than expose him to Beatrice's scorn. Ursula disagrees: Benedick is one of the cleverest and handsomest men in Italy, and Beatrice is too smart to reject him. They leave so that Hero can try on her wedding dress.

Shocked, Beatrice, like Benedick, decides to cast off her scorn and pride and "take pity" on the worthy Benedick by loving him in return.

III.II   Location: Leonato's house

Don John tells Claudio and Don Pedro that Hero is a whore, and offers to prove it that night.

Don Pedro, Claudio, and Leonato tease Benedick about his frequent protestations that he will remain a bachelor. When Benedick announces that he has changed, the others tease him about being in love. Subdued, Benedick ignores them and speaks aside to Leonato.

Don John approaches Claudio and Don Pedro. He tells them that Hero is a whore, and offers proof if they come with him to watch at Hero's window that night. Claudio, suspicious, resolves that if he finds out that she has been unfaithful, he will disgrace her publicly at their wedding the next day. Don Pedro vows to help. The three leave together, full of dark thoughts.

III.III   Location: A street outside Leonato's house

Having overheard how Hero was framed, Messina watchmen arrest Borachio and Conrad.

The Messina night watchmen, led by the earnest yet ridiculous Dogberry and his deputy Verges, discuss the night's assignments. Under Dogberry, the watch is courteous but ineffective. For example, they shouldn't catch thieves because honest men should not have too much to do with dishonest men.

Dogberry and Verges depart, and the remaining watchmen prepare to go to sleep. Borachio and Conrad come in. Not noticing the watchmen. Borachio tells Conrad what has happened that night: according to plan, Don Pedro and Claudio saw Borachio making love to Margaret in Hero's clothing, and now think that Hero has been sleeping around. Heartbroken and betrayed, Claudio vowed to take revenge on Hero by publicly humiliating her at the wedding ceremony the next day. The watchmen, who have heard this exchange, arrest Borachio and Conrade for "lechery" (meaning treachery), and haul them away for questioning.

III.IV   Location: Hero's suite

Hero prepares for her wedding.

On her wedding day, Hero wakes up early and sends Ursula to wake Beatrice. Margaret and Hero argue about what she should wear. Hero is excited, but has a foreboding of disaster. When Beatrice arrives, Margaret subtly teases her about wanting to marry Benedick. Claudio and the wedding party arrive to take Hero to church.

III.V   Location: outside the church

Just before the wedding, Leonato has no time to listen to the watchmen's stories.

Just outside the church, Dogberry and Verges catch up to Leonato. They try to explain that they have caught two criminals, but in so bumbling a fashion that Leonato defers their business. Dogberry and Verges head off to question the prisoners on their own. Leonato enters the church for his daughter's wedding.

ACT IV

Fooled into thinking that Hero has been unfaithful, Claudio denounces her at the altar and refuses to marry her.

IV.I   Location: the church

On their wedding day, Claudio publicly accuses Hero of being a whore, and her father and friends decide to conceal her and announce that she has died of shame.

During the wedding ceremony, Claudio publicly calls Hero a whore. Leonato asks for an explanation, and Claudio says that the previous night he, together with Don Pedro and Don John, watched Hero "tal[k]" (IV.i.82) with a vile man who claimed to have had sex with her many times. Don Pedro and Don John corroborate Claudio's accusations. Leonato cries out for a dagger to commit suicide. Hero faints. As Benedick and Beatrice rush to help her, Claudio, Don Pedro, and Don John leave. Weeping, Leonato wants Hero to die rather than live in shame, but Beatrice is convinced that Hero has been slandered.

Friar Francis steps in. He says that the shocked expression on Hero's face proves her innocence. Hero comes to and insists that she is a virgin. Benedick realizes that the treacherous Don John must be behind the scandal. Friar Francis suggests telling everyone that Hero has died of shock and grief, and waiting for her accusers to regret their unfair accusations. Perhaps the treachery will expose itself. In the meantime, Hero will stay out of sight. In the worst-case scenario, she can later be sent to a convent to become a nun. Leonato agrees, aggrieved.

Everyone but Benedick and Beatrice depart. Benedick tries to comfort Beatrice, and suddenly confesses his love for her. Surprised, she replies in kind. But when Benedick says that he will do anything for Beatrice, she asks him to kill his friend Claudio. Benedick refuses, but Beatrice savagely denounces Claudio, saying that if she were a man she would kill him herself. After her diatribe, Benedick agrees to challenge Claudio for Hero and for Beatrice.

IV.II   Location: a prison

Under interrogation, Borachio confesses that Don John paid him to frame Hero.

Dogberry, Verges, and the other watchmen interrogate Borachio and Conrad. Borachio confesses that Don John paid him to pretend to make love to Hero and then lie about it to Claudio and Don Pedro. When they hear about what has happened at the wedding, the watchmen take the captives to Leonato's house.

ACT V

Claudio realizes that Hero was innocent; to atone for his mistake he marries Leonato's niece, who turns out to be Hero in disguise.

V.I   Location: Leonato's house

Claudio realizes that Hero was innocent and agrees to marry Leonato's (fictitious) niece to make up for ruining Hero.

In vain, Antonio tries to cheer Leonato. Don Pedro and Claudio enter. As they try to leave, Leonato pursues and accuses them of lying and causing Hero's death. He challenges Claudio to a duel. Claudio and Don Pedro are embarrassed because Leonato is old, and pretend to ignore the challenges. Leonato and Antonio leave.

Benedick enters, and Claudio and Don Pedro welcome him and ask him to cheer them up with his wit. But Benedick quietly challenges Claudio to a duel. When Don Pedro and Claudio keep trying to joke with him, Benedick tells them that he can no longer be their companion. He also tells them that Don John has fled the city. After Benedick leaves, Claudio and Don Pedro slowly realize that he was serious and guess correctly that he has challenged Claudio out of love for Beatrice.

Dogberry, Verges, and other watchmen arrive with the captured villains Conrad and Borachio. Dogberry announces that Borachio has confessed to treachery and lying. Borachio confesses again. Claudio and Don Pedro realize that Hero was innocent, and that their mistaken accusations have caused her death.

Leonato and Antonio return, and Claudio and Don Pedro beg Leonato's forgiveness. Leonato orders Claudio to publicly clear Hero's name and to write her an epitaph (a poem honoring her in death) to sing at her tomb. He tells Claudio that his brother Antonio has a daughter who is very much like Hero, and asks Claudio to marry her in Hero's place. Claudio accepts these terms. Leonato orders that Borachio be carted away for further interrogation.

V.II   Location: near Leonato's house

Benedick and Beatrice, in love, find out that Hero has been exculpated.

Benedick asks Margaret to call Beatrice to him. Alone, he laments his inability to write a love sonnet for Beatrice. Beatrice arrives, and the two lovers flirt and tease each other with gentle insults but also with great affection, as they now seem always to have done. Benedick tells Beatrice that he awaits Claudio's answer to his challenge.

Ursula runs in to tell them that the scheme against Hero has come to light. Benedick and Beatrice follow Ursula in to the house.

V.III   Location: Hero's tomb

Claudio honors Hero with an epitaph.

Claudio has written an epitaph celebrating Hero's innocence and grieving the slander that (he believes) has led to her death. He reads the epitaph and hangs it on the tomb, promising to come back every year. Everyone leaves to prepare for Claudio's wedding to the (supposed) Hero look-alike.

V.IV   Location: the church

At his wedding, Claudio discovers that Hero is alive, and the two couples—Claudio and Hero, Beatrice and Benedick—celebrate their weddings.

As the preparations for the wedding proceed, we learn that Margaret never realized that she was taking part in Don John's treachery. Benedick is relieved that he does not need to duel with his friend Claudio. In private, he asks Leonato for his permission to marry Beatrice. Don Pedro and Claudio enter, and Antonio goes off to fetch the masked women. Don Pedro and Claudio tease Benedick about his love for Beatrice and about his yet-unannounced wedding. Hero, Beatrice, Margaret, and Ursula enter, all masked. Claudio vows to marry the masked woman whom he believes to be Leonato's mysterious niece. Hero takes off her mask. Leonato and Hero tell the shocked Claudio that now that Hero's name has been cleared, she can figuratively come back to life and be his wife.

Benedick stops the ceremony and publicly asks Beatrice whether she loves him. Beatrice denies that she loves him. He, in turn, denies loving her. They agree that they are only good friends. But Claudio and Hero laugh and announce that they are lying, and both whip out scribbled, half-finished love poems that they have found, one from Benedick to Beatrice and another from Beatrice to Benedick. Caught red-handed, Beatrice and Benedick agree to marry. Benedick silences Beatrice by kissing her. He laughs off Claudio and Don Pedro's teasing. He says that he is determined to be married. He and Claudio reassert their friendship, and Benedick calls for a dance before the double wedding.

A messenger rushes in to inform everyone that Don John has been arrested fleeing Messina, and is now in the Messina prison. Benedick tells Don Pedro that they can think about fine tortures for Don John tomorrow. Benedick calls for music and a celebratory dance.

ANALYSIS OF MAJOR CHARACTERS IN *MUCH ADO ABOUT NOTHING*

BEATRICE

Beatrice and her cousin Hero are in many ways opposites. Whereas Hero is polite, quiet, respectful, and gentle, Beatrice is feisty, cynical, witty, and sharp. Beatrice keeps up a "merry war" of wits with Benedick of Padua. The text suggests that she was once in love with Benedick, but that he led her on and their relationship ended. Now when they meet, the two constantly compete to outdo one another with clever insults.

Beatrice is one of Shakespeare's strong female characters. She refuses to marry because she has not discovered the perfect, equal partner and because she is unwilling to eschew her liberty and submit to the will of a controlling husband. When Hero has been humiliated and accused of violating her chastity, Beatrice explodes with fury at Claudio for mistreating her cousin. In her frustration and rage, Beatrice rebels against the unequal status of women: "O that I were a man for his sake! Or that I had any friend would be a man for my sake!" she passionately exclaims. "I cannot be a man with wishing, therefore I will die a woman with grieving" (IV.i.312–318).

BENEDICK

Benedick is the willful lord, recently returned from fighting in the wars, who vows that he will never marry. He engages with Beatrice in a competition to outwit, outsmart, and out-insult the other. Benedick is one of the most histrionic characters in the play. He constantly performs for the benefit of others, indulging in witty hyperbole to express his feelings. He delivers a perfect example of his inflated rhetoric when Beatrice enters during the masked ball. Turning to his companions, Benedick bids Don Pedro to send him to the farthest corners of the earth rather than make him spend one minute more with his nemesis: "Will your grace command me any service to the world's end? I will go on the slightest errand now to the Antipodes that you can devise to send me on. I will fetch you a toothpicker from the furthest inch of Asia … do you any embassage to the pigmies, rather than hold three words' conference with this harpy" (II.i.229–235).

DON PEDRO, PRINCE OF ARAGON

Don Pedro is the most powerful and the most elusive of the play's main characters. His friends Benedick and Claudio depend on his patronage and must defer to him in judgment. Unlike his bastard brother, the villain Don John, Don Pedro usually uses his authority for good. It is his idea, for instance, to convince Beatrice and Benedick that each is in love with the other and by doing so bring the two competitors together. He orchestrates the whole plot and plays the role of director in this comedy of wit and manners.

Don Pedro is the only one of the three gallants not to end up with a wife at the end. Benedick laughingly jokes in the final scene that Don Pedro, the melancholy prince, must "get thee a wife" in order to enjoy true happiness (V.iv.117). Don Pedro may be sad because his proposal to Beatrice at the masked ball was sincere. Perhaps he is in love with Beatrice. The text gives no conclusive explanation.

THEMES, MOTIFS, & SYMBOLS IN *MUCH ADO ABOUT NOTHING*

THEMES

COURTLY GRACE The dense, metaphor-laden speech of *Much Ado*'s characters in many ways represents the ideal that Renaissance courtiers strove for in their social interactions. Courtiers were expected to speak in highly contrived language but to make their clever performances seem effortless. The most famous model for this kind of behavior is Baldassare Castiglione's sixteenth-century manual *The Courtier*, translated into English from Italian by Thomas Hoby in 1561. According to this work, the ideal courtier masks his effort and appears to project elegance and natural grace by means of what Castiglione calls *sprezzatura*, the illusion of effortlessness. Benedick, Claudio, and Don Pedro all produce the kind of witty banter that courtiers used to attract attention and approval in noble households.

At the same time, the play pokes fun at the fanciful language of love that courtiers used. When Claudio falls in love, he tries to be the perfect courtier by using intricate language. Benedick notes that Claudio's "words are a very fantastical banquet, just so many strange dishes" (II.iii.18–19). When Claudio believes that Don Pedro has deceived him and wooed Hero for himself, Claudio, who owes his current popularity to Don Pedro, does not drop his polite civility. Beatrice jokes that Claudio is "civil as an orange" (II.i.256), punning on the Seville orange, a bitter fruit. Claudio remains polite and nearly silent even though he is upset, wishing "Don Pedro joy of [Hero]" (II.i.170).

DECEPTION AS A MEANS TO AN END Several deliberate deceptions, both malevolent and benign, drive the play's plot. Hero is disgraced because Don John dupes Claudio and Don Pedro. Her counterfeited death paves the way for her redemption and reconciliation with Claudio. In the more light-hearted subplot, Beatrice and Benedick are fooled into thinking that each is loved, and the deception helps them fall in love. Deceit in *Much Ado* is not an inherenty evil. Rather, it is a tool to be used for good or bad results.

It is often difficult to distinguish good deception from bad. When Claudio announces his desire to woo Hero, Don Pedro takes it upon himself to woo her for Claudio, a "good" deception that turns sour when, at Don John's instigation, Claudio begins to mistrust Don Pedro's true intentions. The play's characters are caught up in the illusions that they have created for one another just as we, the audience, temporary believe in the illusions of the theater. Benedick and Beatrice flirt caustically at the masked ball, each possibly aware of the other's presence yet pretending not to know the person hiding behind the mask. Likewise, when Claudio has shamed and rejected Hero, Leonato and his household announce that Hero has died in order to punish Claudio for his mistake. When Claudio returns, penitent, to accept the hand of "Leonato's niece" (Hero in disguise), Leonato forces him to wed blindly. The group of masked women, one of whom is the bride, points to the fact that the social institution of marriage has little to do with love. Claudio's confused question "Which is the lady I must seize upon?" (V.iv.53) highlights his readiness to marry one of a group of unknowns. He marries not only to atone for Hero's death, but also to regain Leonato's favor. Yet again deceit functions as a means to an end.

LOST HONOR In Shakespeare's time, a woman's honor was based upon her virginity and modest behavior. A woman known to have had sexual relations before marriage lost her good reputation forever. Moreover, her lost honor tainted her whole family. When Leonato believes Claudio's accusations, he initially wants to obliterate Hero entirely: "Hence from her, let her die" (IV.i.153). He speaks of Hero's loss of honor as an indelible stain from which he cannot distance himself: "O she is fallen / Into a pit of ink, that the wide sea / Hath drops too few to wash her clean again" (IV.i.138–140).

MOTIFS

OVERHEARING AND OVER-SEEING The plot hinges on several instances of overhearing and unseen observation. When the women manipulate Beatrice into believing that Benedick adores her, they conceal themselves in the orchard so that Beatrice can better overhear their conversation. Each line the women speak is a carefully placed note for Beatrice to take up and ponder. The same is true of the scheme to convince Benedick of Beatrice's passion.

Don John's plot to undo Claudio also hinges on observing unnoticed: in order for Claudio to believe that Hero is unchaste and unfaithful, he must be brought to her window to witness Margaret (whom he takes to be Hero) bidding farewell to Borachio in the semidarkness. Later, Dogberry, Verges, and the rest of the comical night watchmen discover and arrest Don John because they overhear the story that frames Hero. At the end of the play, over-seeing unites Beatrice and Benedick: Hero and Claudio reveal love sonnets written by Beatrice and Benedick, textual evidence to prove their love for each another.

WAR IMAGERY   Images of war recur throughout the play to describe verbal arguments and confrontations. Leonato describes Beatrice and Benedick's rivalry as a "merry war": "They never meet but there's a skirmish of wit between them" (I.i.50–51). Beatrice carries on this martial imagery when describing how, when she won the last duel with Benedick, "four of his five wits went halting off" (I.i.53). Beatrice and Benedick's witty repartee resembles the blows and parries of a well-executed fencing match. Later, Leonato accuses Claudio of killing Hero with words: "Thy slander hath gone through and through her heart" (V.i.68). In the same scene, Benedick challenges Claudio to a duel to the death.

SYMBOLS

TAMING WILD ANIMALS   In Beatrice and Benedick's courtship, tamed wild animals represent the two wild souls finally "tamed" and able to submit themselves to the shackles of love and marriage. Beatrice vows to submit to Benedick's love by "[t]aming my wild heart to thy loving hand" (III.i.113). She uses falconry terms to suggest that Benedick will become her master. Similarly, Claudio and Don Pedro compare Benedick to a wild animal in teasing him about his aversion to marriage: "In time the savage bull doth bear the yoke"—that is, in time even the savage Benedick will surrender to being tamed by marriage (I.i.213; see also Quotations 1). At end of the play, Claudio returns to the image on Benedick as a bull:

> Tush, fear not, man, we'll tip thy horns with gold,
> And all Europa shall rejoice at thee
> As once Europa did at lusty Jove
> When he would play the noble beast in love.
> (V.iv.44–47)

Claudio changes Benedick from a laboring farm animal, a bull straining under a yoke, to a wild god, empowered by his bestial form to take sexual possession of his lady. Claudio alludes to the classical myth in which Zeus takes the form of a bull to carry off and seduce the human Europa. This second bull represents the other side of the marriage coin: the bull of bestial male sexuality.

HERO'S DEATH   When Claudio accuses Hero in the church, she faints and collapses, apparently lifeless. Leonato further pushes her into a literal death when he renounces her: "Hence from her, let her die" (IV.i.153). In a symbolic sense, Hero—and Hero's honor—has died. After he realizes his mistake, Claudio performs the rites of mourning and hires a choir to sing a dirge at Hero's tomb. Her honor dead, Hero must be reborn, pure again, in order for Claudio to marry her. Hero's false death functions both as a charade to induce remorse in Claudio and as a social ritual to cleanse her name of infamy.

IMPORTANT QUOTATIONS FROM *MUCH ADO ABOUT NOTHING*

1. *The savage bull may, but if ever the sensible Benedick bear it, pluck off the bull's horns and set them in my forehead, and let me be vilely painted, and in such great letters as they write 'Here is good horse to hire' let them signify under my sign 'Here you may see Benedick, the married man.'*

Location: I.i.215–219
Speaker: Benedick to Claudio and Don Pedro
Context: Benedick mocks the old adage that even the wildest people eventually settle down and marry.

Benedick imagines a fantastical scene: if the sensible Benedick ever married, he may as well get the horns of a wild bull and have writing branded on his forehead. Cuckolds (husbands of adulterous wives) were traditionally represented with horns on their heads. Benedick uses the image to suggest that any woman he marries will certainly cheat on him. Claudio and Don Pedro continue to tease Benedick with bull imagery throughout the play.

---

2. *What should I do with him—dress him in my apparel and make him my waiting gentlewoman? He that hath a beard is more than a youth, and he that hath no beard is less than a man; and he that is more than a youth is not for me, and he that is less than a man, I am not for him.*

Location: II.i.28–32
Speaker: Beatrice
Context: Beatrice jokingly explains why she can never marry

Beatrice claims that there is no perfect match for her: every man is either too old or too young to satisfy her desires. Beatrice's joke about dressing up a beardless youth as a woman has a secondary meaning for Elizabethan audiences. In Shakespeare's time, the actor playing Beatrice would have been a prepubescent boy doing exactly that. Indeed, beardless adolescents, youths on the cusp of manhood, held special allure for both men and women in Renaissance literature and culture. *Much Ado* toys with Beatrice's desire for a man both with and without a beard: during the course of the play, Benedick shaves off his beard once he falls in love with her.

---

3. *They say the lady is fair. 'Tis a truth, I can bear them witness. And virtuous—'tis so, I cannot reprove it. And wise, but for loving me. By my troth, it is no addition to her wit—nor no great argument of her folly, for I will be horribly in love with her.*

Location: II.iii.204–208
Speaker: Benedick (soliloquy)
Context: Benedick weighs Beatrice's virtues after overhearing Claudio, Leonato, and Don Pedro discussing Beatrice's (fabricated) love for him.

Benedick concludes that he should return Beatrice's supposed love: "I will be horribly in love with her" (II.iii.208). The line is comical. It is preposterous to fall "horribly" in love with someone after weighing her virtues. The word "horrible" recalls Beatrice and Benedick's "merry war" of wits, and demonstrates that Benedick will not be outdone by Beatrice, even in love.

---

4. *O Hero! What a Hero hadst thou been*
   If half thy outward graces had been placed
   About thy thoughts and counsels of thy heart!
   But fare thee well, most foul, most fair, farewell
   Thou pure impiety and impious purity.
   For thee I'll lock up all the gates of love,
   And on my eyelids shall conjecture hang
   To turn all beauty into thoughts of harm,
   And never shall it more be gracious.

Location: IV.i.98–106
Speaker: Claudio
Context: Claudio has publicly rebuked Hero at their wedding, believing her to have been unchaste and unfaithful to him.

Claudio's lines are full of wordplay and double meanings. The word "Hero" appears twice in the first line, denoting first Hero, Leonato's daughter, and then a hero, an idealized conqueror of Claudio's heart. Hero has lost her heroic qualities. "Fare thee well most foul, most fair, farewell" plays with repetition and opposites: the sound of the word "fair" repeats three times in the space of one line, underscoring Claudio's despair at (mistakenly) discovering that Hero's outward beauty, or "fairness," conceals a "foul" spirit.

Both the combination of "fair" and "foul" in the same line and "pure impiety and impious purity" in the following line are examples of antithesis (the combination of paradoxical opposites for emphasis), a rhetorical technique for which Shakespeare is famous. Shakespeare's characters resort to antithesis usually only at the height of passion. Claudio's use of these particular opposites demonstrate that he is livid with rage and frustration at Hero's seemingly fair exterior, and her false and foul interior.

---

5. *Dost thou not suspect my place? Dost thou not suspect my years? O that he were here to write me down an ass! But masters, remember that I am an ass. Though it be not written down, yet forget not that I am an ass. No, thou villain, thou art full of piety, as shall be proved upon thee by good witness. I am a wise fellow, and which is more, an officer, and which is more, a householder, and which is more, as pretty a piece of flesh as any is in Messina, and one that knows the law, go to ... and one that hath two gowns, and everything handsome about him. Bring him away. O that I had been writ down an ass!*

Location: IV.ii.67–78
Speaker: Dogberry
Context: Dogberry, who brought Borachio and Conrad before the sexton, responds after Conrad calls him an "ass"

This indignant comic speech is littered with malapropisms: "suspect" instead of "respect" and "piety" instead of "impiety." Dogberry's determined insistence that he be "writ down an ass" is comical. Instead of asking that the sexton note that Conrad has insulted him, Dogberry insists that the sexton write down that he (Dogberry) is "an ass," contributing to Conrad's insult. Shakespeare sets up a contrast between the villainous nobleman Conrad and the well-intentioned, if uneducated, commoner Dogberry.

OTHELLO

The Moor general Othello kills his wife Desdemona out of jealousy after Iago lies to him that she has been unfaithful.

OTHELLO IN CONTEXT

Othello was first performed by the King's Men at the court of King James I on November 1, 1604. Written during Shakespeare's great tragic period, which also included the composition of *Hamlet* (1600), *King Lear* (1604–5), *Macbeth* (1606), and *Antony and Cleopatra* (1606–7), *Othello* is set against the backdrop of the wars between Venice and Turkey that raged in the latter part of the sixteenth century. Cyprus, which is the setting for most of the action, was a Venetian outpost attacked by the Turks in 1570 and conquered the following year. Shakespeare's information on the Venetian-Turkish conflict probably derives from *The History of the Turks* by Richard Knolles, which was published in England in the autumn of 1603. The story of *Othello* is also derived from an Italian prose tale written in 1565 by Giovanni Battista Giraldi Cinzio (usually referred to as Cinthio). The original story contains the bare bones of Shakespeare's plot: a Moorish general is deceived by his ensign into believing his wife is unfaithful. To Cinthio's story Shakespeare added supporting characters such as the rich young dupe Roderigo and the outraged and grief-stricken Brabanzio, Desdemona's father. Shakespeare compressed the action into the space of a few days and set it against the backdrop of military conflict. And, most memorably, he turned the ensign, a minor villain, into the arch-villain Iago.

The question of Othello's exact race is open to some debate. The word "Moor" now refers to the Islamic Arabic inhabitants of North Africa who conquered Spain in the eighth century, but the term was used rather broadly in Shakespeare's time and was sometimes applied to Africans from other regions. George Abbott, for example, in his *A Brief Description of the Whole World* of 1599, made distinctions between "blackish Moors" and "black Negroes." A 1600 translation of John Leo's *The History and Description of Africa* distinguishes "white or tawny Moors" of the Mediterranean coast of Africa from the "Negroes or black Moors" of the south. Othello's darkness or blackness is alluded to many times in the play, but Shakespeare and other Elizabethans frequently described brunette or darker-than-average Europeans as black. The opposition of black and white imagery that runs throughout *Othello* is certainly a marker of difference between Othello and his European peers, but the difference is never quite so racially specific as a modern reader might imagine it to be.

While Moor characters abound on the Elizabethan and Jacobean stage, none are given so major or heroic a role as Othello. Perhaps the most vividly stereotypical black character of the period is Aaron, the villain of Shakespeare's early play *Titus Andronicus*. The antithesis of Othello, Aaron is lecherous, cunning, and vicious. His final words are: "If one good deed in all my life I did / I do repent it to my very soul" (*Titus Andronicus*, V.iii.188–189). Othello, by contrast, is a noble figure of great authority, respected and admired by the duke and senate of Venice as well as by those who serve him, such as Cassio, Montano, and Lodovico. Only Iago voices an explicitly stereotypical view of Othello, depicting him from the beginning as an animalistic, barbarous, foolish outsider.

OTHELLO: KEY FACTS

Full title: The Tragedy of Othello, the Moor of Venice	
Time and place written: Between 1601 and 1604; England	
Date of first publication: 1622	
Genre: Tragedy	
Setting (time): Late sixteenth century, during the wars between Venice and Turkey	
Setting (place): Act I: Venice; Acts II–V: Cyprus	
Protagonist: Othello	
Major conflict: Iago's lies convince Othello that his wife Desdemona has been unfaithful.	

OTHELLO: CHARACTER LIST

Bianca A courtesan, or prostitute, in Cyprus. Bianca's favorite customer is Cassio, who teases her with promises of marriage.

Brabanzio Desdemona's father and Othello's friend. Brabanzio is a blustering and self-important Venetian senator. He feels betrayed when Othello marries Desdemona in secret.

Clown Othello's servant. A minor character, the clown reflects and distorts the action and words of the main plots: his puns on the word "lie" in III.iv, for example, anticipate Othello's confusion of two meanings of that word (recline, prevaricate) in IV.i.

Desdemona Brabanzio's daughter and Othello's wife. Meek, virtuous, and self-possessed, Desdemona is able to defend her marriage in court, jest bawdily with Iago, and respond with dignity to Othello's jealousy.

Duke of Venice The ruler of Venice. The duke holds Othello in great esteem. He reconciles Othello and Brabanzio in I.iii, and then sends Othello to Cyprus.

Emilia Iago's wife and Desdemona's attendant. Cynical and worldly Emilia is devoted to Desdemona and distrusts Iago.

Graziano Brabanzio's kinsman. Graziano accompanies Lodovico to Cyprus, bringing news that Brabanzio is dead.

Iago Othello's twenty-eight-year-old ensign (also "ancient" and "standard-bearer") and the play's villain. Iago's motivations for ruining Othello are unclear. Although he claims to be angry that he was passed over for promotion to lieutenant, and hints that Othello slept with his wife Emilia. Iago takes an obsessive, aesthetic delight in manipulating people.

Lodovico Brabanzio's kinsman, who brings a message from the duke of Venice to Cyprus.

Michael Cassio Othello's lieutenant. Cassio is young and inexperienced, but truly devoted to Othello. Iago resents Cassio's high position and uses Cassio's youth, good looks, and friendship with Desdemona to play on Othello's insecurities about Desdemona's fidelity.

Montano The former governor of Cyprus, before Othello.

Othello The play's protagonist, a Moor general of Venetian troops, and Desdemona's husband. An eloquent and physically powerful figure, Othello is respected by all those who know him but feels insecure because of his age, his race, and his rough soldier lifestyle. Iago uses Othello's "free and open nature" (I.iii.381) to twist Othello's love for Desdemona into a destructive jealousy.

Roderigo Desdemona's jealous suitor. Young, rich, and foolish, Roderigo pays Iago for help winning Desdemona's hand and becomes an instrument of Iago's machinations.

OTHELLO: PLOT OVERVIEW

Iago, a military officer of Venice, bitterly resents his master Othello, the Moor general of the Venetian army. Othello has just eloped with Desdemona, the daughter of senator Brabanzio. Iago tries to stir up trouble for Othello by rousing Brabanzio against Othello, but Brabanzio can do nothing because the duke needs Othello to go fight the Turks. Desdemona insists on going with Othello. The Turkish fleet is scattered in a storm, and Iago, Othello, and Desdemona arrive in Cyprus.

Iago's next plot is to make Othello insane with jealousy by convincing him that Desdemona is unfaithful. Iago pits Roderigo, a Venetian in love with Desdemona, against Michael Cassio, the lieutenant Othello promoted over Iago. Roderigo picks a fight with Cassio during a victory celebration, causing Cassio to lose his position for brawling. Iago plants the suspicion in Othello's mind that Cassio is sleeping with Desdemona. When Desdemona pleads on Cassio's behalf, her actions appear to confirm Othello's suspicions. Iago's wife Emilia finds Desdemona's handkerchief and gives it to Iago, who plants it in Cassio's room. When Othello sees Cassio with the handkerchief, he sees it as concrete proof of Desdemona's unfaithfulness and swears revenge against both of them. Iago attacks Cassio and murders Roderigo in an alley. Othello murders Desdemona by smothering her with a pillow. Emilia realizes what Iago has done and reveals Iago's crimes to Othello, who kills himself. Iago is arrested and led off to be tortured.

OTHELLO: SCENE SUMMARY

ACT I

Othello has married Desdemona and sails to Cyprus on assignment; Iago hates him and plots his downfall.

I.I   Location: Venice. A street outside Brabanzio's home

Iago incites Roderigo to rouse Brabanzio and tell him that his daughter Desdemona has eloped with the Moor Othello.

Wealthy Roderigo, who has been paying Iago to help him woo Desdemona, has discovered that Desdemona has secretly married the Moor general Othello. Iago, who is Othello's ensign, assures Roderigo that he too hates Othello, in large part because Othello recently promoted Michael Cassio, and not Iago, to the post of lieutenant. Iago incites Roderigo to make trouble for Othello by rousing Desdemona's family. Iago and Roderigo shout to wake up Brabanzio, Desdemona's father, a Venetian senator. At first Brabanzio does not believe them, but Iago graphically describes that Othello and Desdemona are "making the beast with two backs" (I.i.118)—that is, having sex—and Brabanzio, angered, descends from his apartments. Iago rushes off to join Othello before Brabanzio can see him, and Brabanzio and Roderigo head to Othello's house.

I.II   Location: Venice. A street outside Othello's home

Othello is summoned to the duke of Venice, and Brabanzio decides to plead his case there, too.

Iago warns Othello that Brabanzio is on his way, enraged. A party of officers of the Venetian court, led by Cassio, arrives to summon Othello to the duke of Venice about a matter concerning Cyprus (a Mediterranean island part of present-day Greece, but then under Venetian control). Before Cassio and his men leave, Brabanzio arrives with his retinue and Roderigo. Othello prevents a brawl between his and Brabanzio's followers and Brabanzio agrees to follow Othello to the duke to plead his case.

I.III   Location: Venice. A council chamber

The duke upholds Othello and Desdemona's marriage, and sends Othello to defend Cyprus from the Turks.

The duke's meeting with his senators about the Turks' imminent invasion of Cyprus is interrupted by two messengers: the first reports that the Turks have turned toward Rhodes instead, the second that the Turks have turned back toward Cyprus. Brabanzio, Othello, Cassio, Iago, Roderigo, and others arrive. Brabanzio accuses Othello of having used magic to woo Desdemona, and demands justice. Othello admits that he married Desdemona, but claims that he wooed Desdemona with stories of his harrowing adventures.

Desdemona enters, and Brabanzio asks her to choose between him and Othello. She confirms that she married Othello of her own free will and her primary loyalty must now be with Othello. Brabanzio reluctantly acquiesces. The duke sends Othello to Cyprus to defend the island from the Turks. Desdemona will accompany Othello a little later. Everyone except Roderigo and Iago leaves the court.

Roderigo is despondent, but Iago mocks and cheers him, repeating "put money in thy purse." Iago promises to work everything out if Roderigo follows him and Othello to Cyprus. Roderigo leaves and Iago, alone, declares his hatred for Othello, in part because he suspects that Othello has slept with Iago's wife Emilia. He lays out his plan to cheat Roderigo out of money, and to convince Othello that Cassio has slept with Desdemona, thereby bringing about Othello's downfall.

ACT II

The night that all arrive in Cyprus, Iago arranges for Othello to dismiss his lieutenant Cassio for disgraceful behavior.

II.I   Location: Cyprus. The port

All arrive in Cyprus, and Iago convinces Roderigo to quarrel with Cassio that evening.

Montano, the Cyprian governor, is informed that most of the Turkish fleet has perished in the recent tempest. The recently arrived Cassio has brought this news. A new ship arrives, with Desdemona, Emilia, Iago, and Roderigo. Othello's ship has yet to come, but has been sighted. Cassio and Desdemona tease Emilia about being a chatterbox, and Iago takes the opportunity to criticize women as deceptive and hypocritical. Cassio takes Desdemona away to speak with her privately about Othello's arrival. Iago notes Cassio taking her by the hand, and plans to use this gesture against Cassio.

Othello arrives, and all but Roderigo and Iago head to the castle to celebrate the drowning of the Turks. Iago insists that even when Desdemona grows tired of the brutish Othello, she will turn to Cassio before Roderigo, and encourages Roderigo to start a quarrel with Cassio that evening. Alone, Iago explains that ideally, he would seduce Desdemona himself, in part to get back at Othello for sleeping with Emilia. But if he can't, he will ruin Othello by making him think Desdemona has been unfaithful with Cassio.

II.II   Location: Cyprus

Othello plans festivities for the evening.

A herald announces Othello's plan for revelry, in celebration of Cyprus's safety from the Turks and his marriage to Desdemona.

II.III   Location: Cyprus

Iago gets Cassio drunk until Cassio disgraces himself by stabbing Montano; Othello dismisses Cassio from service; Iago makes more devious plans.

Othello leaves Cassio on guard during the revels, reminding him to practice self-restraint during the celebration. Othello and Desdemona leave to consummate their marriage. Iago enters and convinces Cassio to take a drink.

Once Cassio leaves to fetch the revelers, Iago tells us his plan: Roderigo and three other Cypriots, all of whom are drunk, will join Iago and Cassio on guard duty. Amid all the drunkards, Iago will lead Cassio into doing something disgraceful. Cassio returns, already drinking, with Montano and his attendants. Soon drunk, Cassio wanders offstage, assuring his friends that he isn't drunk. With Cassio gone, Iago tells Montano that while Cassio is a wonderful soldier, he fears that Cassio may have too much responsibility for someone with such a serious drinking problem. Roderigo enters, and Iago points him in Cassio's direction. As Montano continues to suggest that something be said to Othello of Cassio's drinking problem, Cassio chases Roderigo across the stage, threatening to beat him. Montano steps in to prevent the fight and is attacked by Cassio. Iago orders Roderigo to leave and "cry a mutiny" (II.iii.140). As Montano and others attempt to hold Cassio down, Cassio stabs Montano. An alarm bell is rung, and Othello arrives with armed attendants.

Othello demands to know what happened, but both Iago and Cassio claim to have forgotten how the struggle began. Montano insists that he is in too much pain to speak and insists that Iago tell the story. At first Iago feigns reluctance to incriminate Cassio. He emphasizes the fact that Cassio was chasing after another man (Roderigo) when the fight between Cassio and Montano began and suggests that this unknown man must have done something to upset Cassio. Othello falls into Iago's trap: convinced that Iago is trying to protect Cassio, Othello dismisses Cassio from his service.

Othello leads Desdemona, who has been awakened by the commotion, back to bed. Iago and Cassio remain behind, and Cassio laments the permanent damage now done to his reputation by a quarrel whose cause he cannot even remember. Iago suggests that Cassio appeal to Desdemona, because she commands Othello's attention and goodwill.

When Cassio leaves, Iago jokes about the irony of the fact that his so-called villainy involves counseling Cassio to a course of action that would actually help him. Desdemona really is generous, and Othello does dote on her. But, Iago reminds us, his most evil actions look like good actions. Now that Cassio will be spending time with Desdemona, Iago will find it easier to convince Othello that Desdemona is having an affair with Cassio.

Roderigo enters, upset that he has been beaten and angry because Iago's plans have led nowhere so far. Iago counsels Roderigo to be patient and assures Roderigo that everything is going according to plan. Alone again, Iago finishes outlining his plan: he will convince Emilia to speak to Desdemona on Cassio's behalf, and will arrange for Othello to witness Cassio's entreaties to Desdemona.

ACT III

Desdemona makes appeals to Othello on Cassio's behalf, which Iago uses to convince Othello that Cassio and Desdemona are having an affair.

III.I Location: Cyprus. Before Othello's house

At Iago's suggestion, Cassio tries to ask Desdemona to speak to Othello on his behalf.

Cassio sends musicians to play music beneath Othello's window. Othello sends his clownish servant to tell the musicians to go away. Cassio asks the clown to entreat Emilia to come speak with him, so that he can ask her for access to Desdemona. When the clown leaves, Iago enters and tells Cassio that he will send for Emilia as well as arrange for Cassio to have a chance to speak to Desdemona privately. After Iago exits, Emilia enters and tells Cassio that Othello and Desdemona have been discussing his case. Desdemona has pleaded for Cassio, but Othello is worries that Montano is too popular for him to reappoint Cassio. Emilia allows Cassio to come in and tells him to wait for Desdemona.

III.II Location: Cyprus

Iago has taken Othello away to give Cassio an opportunity to speak to Desdemona.

Iago, Othello, and a gentleman walk together at the citadel. Othello gives Iago some letters to deliver and decides to take a look at the town's fortification.

III.III Location: Cyprus. Othello's house

Iago makes subtle insinuations until Othello is convinced that Cassio is sleeping with Desdemona and vows revenge; Iago acquires a handkerchief that Desdemona has misplaced.

Desdemona, Cassio, and Emilia enter mid-conversation. Desdemona has just vowed to do everything she can on Cassio's behalf when Othello and Iago enter. Cassio quickly departs, protesting to Desdemona that he feels too uneasy to do himself any good. Othello asks whether it was Cassio he saw leaving the room, and Iago responds that surely Cassio would not behave like a guilty man at Othello's approach.

Desdemona entreats Othello to forgive Cassio and reinstate him as lieutenant. Othello assures her that he will speak to Cassio, but answers evasively when she tries to set a meeting time. She criticizes Othello for responding to her request so grudgingly and hesitantly, and he tells her that he will deny her nothing but wishes to be left to himself for a little while.

Alone with Othello, Iago begins to insinuate that Cassio and Desdemona are having an affair. He reminds Othello that Cassio served as Othello and Desdemona's go-between during their courtship. Othello asks Iago whether he believes Cassio to be honest, and Iago feigns reluctance to answer. Iago plants in Othello's mind thoughts of adultery, cuckoldry, and hypocrisy, until Othello screams at Iago to speak his mind. Iago suggests that Othello observe his wife closely when she is with Cassio.

Othello tells Iago to have Emilia watch Desdemona when she is with Cassio. Iago appears to recoil from his accusations and suggests that Othello leave the matter alone, but he has already made his point. Alone, Othello muses that his wife no longer loves him, probably because he is too old for her, because he is black, and because he doesn't have the manners of a courtier.

Desdemona and Emilia enter to inform Othello that he is expected at dinner. Othello says that he has a pain in his forehead, and Desdemona offers to bind his head with her handkerchief. Othello pushes her handkerchief away, telling her that it is too small. The handkerchief drops to the floor, where it remains as Othello and Desdemona exit. Emilia, staying behind, picks up the handkerchief, remarking that Iago has asked her to steal it at least a hundred times. Iago enters, and Emilia teases him with the promise of a surprise. He is ecstatic when she gives it to him, and sends her away.

As Iago gleefully plots to plant the handkerchief in Cassio's room, Othello enters and flies into a rage at him. Othello declares that his soul is in torment, and that it would be better to be deceived completely than to suspect without proof. He demands that Iago bring him actual evidence ("ocular proof") that Desdemona is a whore. Iago protests that evidence of a sexual affair is impossible to find, but promises to provide circumstantial evidence. First, he tells Othello that while Cassio and Iago were sharing a bed, Cassio called out Desdemona's name in his sleep, wrung Iago's hand, kissed him hard on the lips, and threw his leg over Iago's thigh. This story enrages Othello, and Iago reminds him that it was only Cassio's dream. Iago then claims to have witnessed Cassio wiping his beard with the handkerchief Othello gave Desdemona as her first gift. Furious, Othello cries out for blood. He kneels and vows to heaven that he will take his revenge on Desdemona and Cassio, and Iago kneels with him, vowing to help execute Othello's vengeance. Othello promotes Iago to lieutenant.

III.IV   Location: near Othello's house

Tormented by Iago's lies, Othello demands that Desdemona produce her handkerchief; Cassio finds it planted in his room and gives to his courtesan.

Desdemona sends the clown to tell Cassio that she has asked Othello to forgive him. He leaves, and she wonders to Emilia where her handkerchief might be. Othello enters and tells Desdemona to give him her hand. She does so, and he chastises her for its moistness (a suggestion of sexual promiscuity). He then asks her to lend him her handkerchief. When Desdemona cannot produce the handkerchief, he explains its history. An Egyptian sorceress gave it to his mother and told her that it would make her desirable and keep Othello's father loyal, but if she lost it or gave it away, Othello's father would leave her. Othello's mother gave him the magic handkerchief on her deathbed, instructing him to give it to the woman he desired to marry. Desdemona is unsettled by the story and says that she has the handkerchief, but not with her. Othello does not believe her and vehemently demands that she show it to him. To change the subject, she brings up Cassio's plight.

After Othello storms off, Emilia laments the fickleness of men. Cassio and Iago enter, and Cassio immediately continues with his suit to Desdemona for help. Desdemona tells Cassio that his timing is unfortunate, as Othello is in a bad humor, and Iago promises to go soothe his master. Emilia speculates that Othello is jealous, but Desdemona maintains her conviction that Othello is upset by some political matter. She tells Cassio to wait while she goes to find Othello and bring him to talk with his former lieutenant.

While Cassio waits, Bianca, a prostitute, enters. She reprimands him for not visiting her more frequently, and he apologizes, saying that he is under stress. He asks her to copy the embroidery of a handkerchief he recently found in his room onto another handkerchief. Bianca accuses him of making her copy the embroidery of a love gift from some other woman, but Cassio tells her she is being silly. They make a plan to meet later that evening.

ACT IV

Iago contrives to provide Othello with "proof" that Cassio and Desdemona are having an affair.

IV.I   Location: Cyprus

In a jealous rage, Othello has an epileptic fit; Iago arranges for him to overhear and misinterpret Cassio's sexual jokes; Othello sees Cassio's courtesan with the handkerchief.

Othello and Iago enter in mid-conversation. Iago goads Othello by arguing that it is no crime for a woman to be naked with a man, if nothing happens. Iago then remarks that if he were to give his wife a handkerchief, it would be hers to do as she wished with it. These persistent insinuations of Desdemona's unfaithfulness work Othello into an incoherent frenzy. He focuses obsessively on the handkerchief and keeps pumping Iago for information about Cassio's comments to Iago. Finally, Iago says that Cassio has told him he has lain with Desdemona, and Othello "[f]alls down in a trance" (IV.i.41 SD).

Cassio enters, and Iago mentions that Othello has fallen into his second fit of epilepsy in two days. He warns Cassio to stay out of the way but tells him that he would like to speak once Othello has gone. Othello comes out of his trance, and Iago explains that Cassio stopped by and that he has arranged to speak with the ex-lieutenant. Iago orders Othello to hide nearby and observe Cassio's face during their conversation. Iago explains that he will make Cassio retell the story of where, when, how, and how often he has slept with Desdemona, and when he intends to do so again. When Othello withdraws, Iago informs the audience of his actual intention. He will joke with Cassio about the prostitute Bianca, so that Cassio will laugh as he tells the story of Bianca's pursuit of him. Othello will be driven mad, thinking that Cassio is joking with Iago about Desdemona.

The plan works: Cassio laughs uproariously as he tells Iago the details of Bianca's love for him, and even makes gestures in an attempt to depict her sexual advances. Just as Cassio says that he no longer wishes to see Bianca, she herself enters with the handkerchief and again accuses Cassio of giving her a love token given to him by another woman. Bianca tells Cassio that if he doesn't show up for supper with her that evening, he will never be welcome to come back again. Othello has recognized his handkerchief and, coming out of hiding when Cassio and Bianca are gone, wonders how he should murder his former lieutenant. Othello goes on to lament his hardheartedness and love for Desdemona, but Iago reminds him of his purpose. Othello has trouble reconciling his wife's delicacy, class, beauty, and allure with her adulterous actions. He suggests that he will poison his wife, but Iago advises him to strangle her in the bed that she contaminated through her infidelity. Iago also promises to arrange Cassio's death.

Desdemona enters with Lodovico, who has come from Venice with a message from the duke. Lodovico irritates Othello by inquiring about Cassio, and Desdemona irritates Othello by answering Lodovico's inquiries. The contents of the letter also upset Othello. He has been called back to Venice, with orders to leave Cassio as his replacement in Cyprus. When Desdemona hears the news that she will be leaving Cyprus, she expresses her happiness, whereupon Othello strikes her. Lodovico is horrified by Othello's loss of self-control, and asks Othello to call back Desdemona, who has left the stage. Othello does so, only to accuse her of being a false and promiscuous woman. He tells Lodovico that he will obey the duke's orders, commands Desdemona to leave, and storms off. Lodovico cannot believe that the Othello he has just seen is the same self-controlled man he once knew. He wonders whether Othello is mad, but Iago refuses to answer Lodovico's questions, telling him that he must see for himself.

IV.II Location: Cyprus

Othello openly accuses Desdemona of infidelity; Iago incites Roderigo to kill Cassio.

Othello interrogates Emilia about Desdemona's behavior, but Emilia insists that Desdemona has done nothing suspicious. Othello tells Emilia to summon Desdemona. When they come in, Othello sends Emilia to guard the door. Alone with Desdemona, Othello weeps and proclaims that he could have borne any affliction other than the pollution of the "fountain" from which his future children are to flow (IV.ii.61). When Desdemona fervently denies being unfaithful, Othello sarcastically replies that he begs her pardon: he took her for the "cunning whore of Venice" who married Othello (IV.ii.93). Othello storms out of the room, and Emilia comes in to comfort her mistress. Desdemona tells Emilia to lay her wedding sheets on the bed for that night.

At Desdemona's request, Emilia brings in Iago, and Desdemona tries to find out from him why Othello has been treating her like a whore. Emilia says to her husband that Othello must have been deceived by some villain—the same sort of villain who made Iago suspect Emilia of sleeping with Othello. Iago assures Desdemona that Othello is merely upset by some official business. A trumpet flourish calls Emilia and Desdemona away to dinner.

Roderigo enters, furious at Iago. He threatens to demand back the jewels that Iago was supposed to have delivered to Desdemona from him. Iago proceeds to convince Roderigo to kill Cassio. He says that Othello is being reassigned to Mauritania, in Africa, and Cassio is taking his place. The only way to keep Desdemona here is to prevent Othello's departure by killing Cassio.

IV.III Location: Cyprus

A melancholy Desdemona talks with her servant about adultery as she prepares for bed.

After dinner, Othello proposes to walk with Lodovico, and sends Desdemona to bed. Desdemona prepares for bed. She asks Emilia to use her wedding sheets as a funeral shroud should Desdemona die. As Emilia helps Desdemona undress, Desdemona sings a song called "Willow," about a woman whose love left her. She says she learned the song from her mother's maid, Barbary, who died singing the song after she had been deserted by her lover. The song makes Desdemona think about adultery. She asks Emilia whether she would cheat on her husband "for all the world" (IV.iii.62). Emilia says that she would not deceive her husband for jewels or rich clothes, but that the whole world is a huge prize and would outweigh the offense. This leads Emilia to speak about the fact that women have appetites for sex and infidelity just as men do, and that men who deceive their wives have only themselves to blame if their wives cheat on them. Desdemona replies that she prefers to answer bad deeds with good deeds rather than with more bad deeds. She readies herself for bed.

ACT V

Othello kills Desdemona; when he learns that Iago has been lying about her infidelity, he kills himself.

V.I Location: Cyprus. Outside Bianca's brothel

Roderigo wounds Cassio; in the commotion, Iago kills Roderigo.

Iago and Roderigo wait outside the brothel in which Cassio visits Bianca, waiting to ambush Cassio. Iago then withdraws himself. Cassio enters, and Roderigo stabs at him but fails to pierce Cassio's armor. Cassio stabs and wounds Roderigo. Iago darts out in the commotion, stabs Cassio in the leg, and exits. Not knowing who has stabbed him, Cassio falls. At this moment, Othello enters. Hearing Cassio's cries, Othello believes that Iago has killed him to avenge his (Othello's) honor. Inspired, Othello returns to his bedroom to kill Desdemona.

Lodovico and Graziano enter and hear Cassio's and Roderigo's cries. They can see nothing because of the darkness, and they are wary of helping the crying men in case it is a trap. Iago enters carrying a light. He first pretends to discover Cassio, who begs him for help, and then stumbles upon Roderigo, whom Iago stabs without hesitation. Graziano and Ludovico are still unable to see Iago, and they are unaware of what he is doing. Finally, the three men come face-to-face, and they question Cassio about his injuries.

Bianca enters and begins to cry out when she sees the wounded Cassio. Iago questions Cassio about his assailant, but Cassio can provide no explanation for what has happened. Iago suggests that Roderigo is to blame. Cassio says that he does not know Roderigo. Attendants carry off Cassio and Roderigo's corpse. Emilia enters, and Iago tells her what has happened, adding the explanation, "This is the fruits of whoring" (V.i.118). He and Emilia chastise Bianca, at whose house Cassio had dined that evening. Iago takes Bianca under arrest and sends Emilia to tell Othello and Desdemona what has happened. Iago ends the scene with an aside: "This is the night / That either makes me or fordoes me quite" (V.i.130–131).

V.II Location: Desdemona's chambers

Othello smothers Desdemona, then kills himself when he learns that Desdemona was faithful and Iago was lying.

Holding a candle, Othello stands over the sleeping Desdemona and prepares to kill her. He bends down to kiss her once before he does the deed, she wakes, and he tells her to prepare to die. Growing frightened, Desdemona asks her husband why he means to kill her, and Othello responds that she has been unfaithful to him with Cassio. He has seen the proof in the handkerchief. Othello refuses to believe Desdemona's denial of the charge, saying that Cassio has confessed but will speak no more, since he has been killed by Iago. Desdemona begins to weep for Cassio, which only drives Othello into a greater rage. He begins wrestling with her as she begs to be allowed to live just a little longer, but finally manages to smother her. Emilia calls from outside the door, and Othello confuses her cries with Desdemona's and smothers Desdemona again.

Othello draws closed the bed curtains and lets Emilia in. Emilia informs Othello that Cassio has killed Roderigo, but Cassio himself is still alive. Just then, Desdemona cries out that she has been murdered. She stays alive long enough to tell Emilia that it is her (Desdemona's) own fault that she is dead. She dies. Othello triumphantly admits to Emilia that he killed Desdemona, and when she asks him why, Othello tells her that Iago opened his eyes to Desdemona's infidelity. Emilia calls out for help, bringing Montano, Graziano, and Iago to the scene.

As Emilia makes accusations, Othello begins to realize that Iago has been lying to him and falls weeping upon Desdemona's bed. Graziano mentions that Brabanzio is dead and says it is good that he has not lived to see Desdemona smothered by Othello. Othello mentions the handkerchief and Cassio's "confession." Iago tries to stop Emilia from talking, but Graziano prevents him, and Emilia explains how she found the handkerchief and gave it to Iago. Othello tries to kill Iago, but Montano disarms him. In the commotion, Iago stabs Emilia and flees. Montano and Graziano pursue him. Othello searches for another sword. Dying, Emilia's sings "Willow" again. She tells Othello that Desdemona was chaste and loved him.

Graziano returns to find Othello armed and defiant. Montano, Lodovico, and Cassio arrive, with Iago as prisoner. Othello wounds Iago, but Lodovico orders Othello disarmed. Iago refuses to talk. Lodovico produces a letter found in Roderigo's pocket. The letter reveals all of Iago's lies. When Othello asks, Cassio tells him that he found the handkerchief in his room.

Lodovico tells Othello that he will be tried in Venice. Othello asks his captors, "When you shall these unlucky deeds relate, / Speak of me as I am" (V.ii.350–351). He reminds them of a time in Aleppo when he served the Venetian state and slew a malignant Turk. "I took by the throat the circumcised dog / And smote him thus," (V.ii.364–365) he says, and stabs himself with a third, hidden, dagger. He falls down next to Desdemona's body.

Lodovico leaves Graziano in charge of Cyprus, charges Montano with Iago's execution, and prepares to leave for Venice.

ANALYSIS OF MAJOR CHARACTERS IN *OTHELLO*

OTHELLO

Beginning with the opening lines of the play, Othello remains at a distance from much of the action that concerns and affects him. Roderigo and Iago refer ambiguously to a "he" or "him" for much of the first scene. When they begin to specify whom they are talking about, especially once they stand beneath Brabanzio's window, they do so with racial epithets, not names. These include "the Moor" (I.i.57), "the thick-lips" (I.i.66), "an old black ram" (I.i.88), and "a Barbary horse" (I.i.113). Although Othello appears at the beginning of the second scene, we do not hear his name until well into I.iii.48. Othello's ship is the last to arrive in Cyprus in II.i. Othello stands apart while Cassio and Iago supposedly discuss Desdemona in IV.i. As an outsider, he is easy prey for Iago.

At the same time, Othello's skill as a soldier makes him an integral part of Venetian civic society. He is in great demand by the duke and the senate. The senate "sent about three several quests" to look for him (I.ii.46). The Venetian government trusts Othello to give him command of Cyprus, and as he dies, he reminds the Venetians of the "service" (V.ii.348) he has done their state.

Nevertheless, even those who consider Othello their social and civic peer—such as Desdemona and Brabanzio—are drawn to him in part because of his exotic, foreign qualities. Othello admits as much when he tells the duke about his friendship with Brabanzio: "[Desdemona's] father loved me, oft invited me, / Still questioned me the story of my life / From year to year" (I.iii.127–129). Othello is careful to present himself as an outsider. In spite of his obvious eloquence, he protests, "Rude am I in my speech, / And little blessed with the soft phrase of peace" (I.iii.81–82). His eloquence suffers under pressure from Iago's manipulations, but in the final moments of the play, Othello regains his composure and once again seduces both his onstage and offstage audiences with his words. It is Othello's willingness to torment himself as a permanent outsider that makes him into a tragic figure.

IAGO

Possibly the most heinous villain in Shakespeare, Iago is fascinating for his most terrible characteristic: his utter lack of convincing motivation for his actions. In the first scene, he claims to be angry at Othello for having passed him over for the position of lieutenant (I.i.7–32). At the end of Act I, scene iii, Iago says he thinks Othello may have slept with his wife, Emilia: "It is thought abroad that 'twixt my sheets / He has done my office" (I.iii.369–370). Iago mentions this suspicion again at the end of Act II, scene i, explaining that he lusts after Desdemona because he wants to get even with Othello "wife for wife" (II.i.286). None of these claims seems to adequately explain Iago's deep hatred of Othello, and Iago's lack of motivation, or his inability or unwillingness to express his true motivation, makes his actions all the more terrifying. He is willing to take revenge on anyone—including Othello, Desdemona, Cassio, Roderigo, even Emilia—at the slightest provocation and enjoys the pain and damage he causes.

Iago is often funny, especially in his scenes with the foolish Roderigo, which serve as a showcase of Iago's manipulative abilities. He seems almost to wink at the audience as he revels in his own skill. As entertained spectators, we find ourselves on Iago's side when he is with Roderigo, but the interactions between the two also reveal a streak of cowardice in Iago—a cowardice that becomes manifest in the final scene, when Iago kills his own wife (V.ii.231–242).

Iago's murder of Emilia could also stem from the general hatred of women that he displays. Some readers have suggested that Iago's true, underlying motive for persecuting Othello is his homosexual love for the general. He certainly seems to take great pleasure in preventing Othello from enjoying marital happiness, and he expresses his love for Othello frequently and effusively.

It is Iago's talent for understanding and manipulating the desires of those around him that makes him both a powerful and a compelling figure. Iago is able to take the handkerchief from Emilia and know that he can deflect her questions; he is able to tell Othello of the handkerchief and know that Othello will not doubt him; he is able to tell the audience, "And what's he then that says I play the villain," and know that it will laugh as though he were a clown (II.iii.310). Though the most inveterate liar, Iago inspires in all of the play's characters the trait that is most lethal to Othello: trust.

DESDEMONA

The play depicts Desdemona both as a bold, independent personality and as a self-effacing, faithful wife. She delivers her first speech with authority: "My noble father, / I do perceive here a divided duty" (I.iii.179–180); and reacts with terse fury after Othello strikes her: "I have not deserved this" (IV.i.236). In II.i, she jests bawdily with Iago, and displays the same chiding, mischievous wit in III.iii.61–84, as she attempts to persuade Othello to forgive Cassio. At the same time, Desdemona submissively blames herself for Othello's violence. In response to Emilia's question, "O, who hath done this deed?" Desdemona's final words are, "Nobody, I myself. Farewell. / Commend me to my kind lord. O, farewell" (V.ii.133–134).

The contradictions in Desdemona's character parallel Desdemona's confusion as she is forced to defend her fidelity to Othello soon after defending their marriage to Brabanzio. She dies smothered by a pillow in a bed covered in her wedding sheets, literally suffocated beneath the demands put on her fidelity. Desdemona herself eerily prepares for her death. She asks Emilia to put her wedding sheets on the bed, and mentions that she would like to be buried in them. Like the audience, Desdemona is powerless to stop Othello's jealousy. That she forgives Othello (V.ii.133) helps the audience to forgive him as well.

THEMES, MOTIFS, & SYMBOLS IN *OTHELLO*

THEMES

HONOR IN WAR AS METAPHOR FOR HONOR IN LOVE Othello's career as a soldier affects his married life from the earliest moments. Asking "fit disposition" (I.iii.234) for his wife after being ordered to Cyprus, Othello notes that "the tyrant custom ... / Hath made the flinty and steel couch of war / My thrice-driven bed of down" (I.iii.227–229). He has become used to the most uncomfortable of accommodations. Desdemona is not perturbed by Othello's lifestyle—not by the uncomfortable sleeping quarters, not by threats of tempests and enemy ships, not by the nighttime drunken brawl of II.iii. She is indeed Othello's "fair warrior." For Othello, the military is a ticket into Venetian society. (Historically, mercenary Moors were commonplace in Shakespeare's time.) His tales of military success win him Desdemona's love, and Othello predicates his success in love on his success as a soldier.

With the Turks drowned, Othello is left without anything to do and begins to confuse his identity as a lover with his identity as a soldier. Convinced that Desdemona is unfaithful, he mourns first his "tranquil mind" and then continues:

> Farewell the plumed troops and the big wars
> That make ambition virtue! O, farewell,
> Farewell the neighing steed and the shrill trump,
> The spirit-stirring drum, th'ear piercing fife,
> The royal banner, and all quality,
> Pride, pomp, and circumstance of glorious war!
> (III.iii.353–359)

Entirely preoccupied with his identity as a soldier, Othello mourns the trappings of war, not happy marriage. At the same time, critics and audiences alike have found comfort and nobility in Othello's final speech and the anecdote of the "malignant and ... turbaned Turk" (V.ii.362), even though there as elsewhere, Othello depends on his identity as a soldier to glorify himself in the public's memory.

THE DANGERS OF ISOLATION The action of *Othello* moves from the metropolis of Venice to the island of Cyprus. Protected by military fortifications as well as by the surrounding sea, Cyprus faces little threat from external forces. Once in Cyprus, Othello, Iago, Desdemona, Emilia, and Roderigo have nothing to do but prey upon one another. Isolation from others enables many of the play's narrative devices: Iago frequently speaks in soliloquies; Othello stands apart while Iago talks with Cassio in IV.i. and is briefly left alone onstage with Emilia's and Desdemona's bodies in V.ii; Roderigo interacts with no one except Iago; Othello is isolated from others because of his physical stature and the color of his skin. Iago is an expert at manipulating the distance between characters, isolating his victims until they succumb to their own obsessions. Isolated himself, Iago falls prey to his own obsession with revenge. The play suggests that self-isolation as an act of self-preservation ultimately leads to self-destruction. Indeed, self-isolation brings about the deaths of Roderigo, Iago, Othello, and even Emilia.

MOTIFS

SIGHT AND BLINDNESS Desdemona explains that she decided never to be separated from Othello when she "saw Othello's visage in his mind, / And to his honors and his valiant parts / Did I my soul and fortunes consecrate" (I.iii.250–52). In his face she saw not his black skin, but his mind and spirit. Desdemona's declaration is one of many references to various kinds of sight in the play. Earlier in I.iii, a senator suggests that the Turkish retreat to Rhodes is "a pageant / To keep us in false gaze" (I.iii.19–20). Act II begins with people staring out to sea, waiting for the arrival of ships, friendly or otherwise. Othello, though he demands "ocular proof" (III.iii.365), is frequently convinced by things he does not see: he accuses Desdemona and Cassio based on Iago's stories only. After Othello's suicide in the final scene, Lodovico tells Iago, "Look on the tragic loading of this bed. / This is thy work. The object poisons sight. / Let it be hid" (V.ii.373–375).

PLANTS Iago is strangely preoccupied with plants. His speeches to Roderigo in particular make extensive and elaborate use of vegetable metaphors and conceits: "Our bodies are our gardens, to which our wills are gardeners; so that if we will plant nettles or sow lettuce, set hyssop and weed up thyme . . . the power and corrigible authority of this lies in our wills" (I.iii.317–322); "Though other things grow fair against the sun, / Yet fruits that blossom first will first be ripe" (II.iii.349–350); "And then, sir, would he gripe and wring my hand, / Cry 'O sweet creature!', then kiss me hard, / As if he plucked kisses up by the roots, / That grew upon my lips" (III.iii.425–428). This example best explains how the plant metaphor functions: the play portrays its characters as the product of certain inevitable, natural forces, which, if left unchecked, will grow wild. Iago understands these natural forces particularly well: he is, according to his own metaphor, a good "gardener," both of himself and of others.

Many of Iago's botanical references concern poison: "I'll pour this pestilence into his ear" (II.iii.330); "The Moor already changes with my poison. / Dangerous conceits are in their natures poisons, / . . . / ...

Not poppy nor mandragora / Nor all the drowsy syrups of the world / Shall ever medicine thee to that sweet sleep" (III.iii.329–36). Iago cultivates his "conceits" so that they become lethal poisons and then plants their seeds in the minds of others.

ANIMALS Iago calls Othello a "Barbary horse," an "old black ram," and also tells Brabanzio that his daughter and Othello are "making the beast with two backs" (I.i.117–118). In I.iii, Iago tells Roderigo, "Ere I would say I would drown myself for the love of a guinea-hen, I would change my humanity with a baboon" (I.iii.312–313). He then remarks that drowning is for "cats and blind puppies" (I.iii.330–331). Cassio laments that, when drunk, he is "by and by a fool, and presently a beast!" (II.iii.284–285). Othello tells Iago, "Exchange me for a goat / When I shall turn the business of my soul / To such exsufflicate and blowed surmises" (III.iii.184–186). He later says that "[a] horned man's a monster and a beast" (IV.i.59). Even Emilia, in the final scene, says that she will "play the swan, / And die in music" (V.ii.254–255). These references to animals add to the impression that the laws of nature, rather than those of society, are the primary forces governing the characters in this play.

SYMBOLS

THE HANDKERCHIEF For Desdemona, the handkerchief represents Othello's love. Iago manipulates Othello into seeing the handkerchief as a symbol of Desdemona's faith and chastity. Later he uses it as evidence of her infidelity. Othello tells Desdemona that it was woven by a two-hundred-year-old sibyl (female prophet) using silk from sacred worms and dye extracted from the hearts of mummified virgins. He claims that his mother used it to keep his father faithful to her. To Othello, therefore, the handkerchief represents marital fidelity. The pattern of strawberries (dyed with virgins' blood) on a white background strongly suggests the bloodstains left on the sheets on a virgin's wedding night, so the handkerchief implicitly suggests a guarantee of virginity as well as fidelity.

THE SONG "WILLOW" As she prepares for bed in Act V, Desdemona sings a song about a woman who is betrayed by her lover. She was taught the song by her mother's maid, Barbary, who suffered a misfortune similar to that of the woman in the song. She even died singing "Willow." The song's lyrics suggest that both men and women are unfaithful to one another. To Desdemona, the song represents a melancholy resignation that she has been alienated from Othello's affections.

IMPORTANT QUOTATIONS FROM *OTHELLO*

---

1. *Were I the Moor I would not be Iago.*
   In following him I follow but myself;
   Heaven is my judge, not I for love and duty,
   But seeming so for my peculiar end.
   For when my outward action doth demonstrate
   The native act and figure of my heart
   In compliment extern, 'tis not long after
   But I will wear my heart upon my sleeve
   For daws to peck at. I am not what I am.

Location: I.i.57–65
Speaker: Iago to Roderigo
Context: Iago explains why he serves Othello even though he hates him.

Iago explains that he serves Othello not out of "love" or "duty," but because he feels he can exploit and dupe him and get revenge on Othello for sleeping with Emilia (as Iago suspects). Iago finds that people who are what they seem are foolish. They "wear their heart upon [their] sleeve" so that birds can peck on it. This speech exemplifies Iago's cryptic and elliptical manner of speaking. Phrases such as "Were I the Moor I would not be Iago" and "I am not what I am" confuse more than they explain. The riddles that Iago's words create are emblematic of Iago's power throughout the play. His smallest sentences ("Think, my lord?" in III.iii.109) or gestures (beckoning Othello closer in IV.i) open up whole worlds of interpretation.

---

2. *My noble father,*
   I do perceive here a divided duty.
   To you I am bound for life and education.
   My life and education both do learn me
   How to respect you. You are the lord of my duty,
   I am hitherto your daughter. But here's my husband,
   And so much duty as my mother showed
   To you, preferring you before your father,
   So much I challenge that I may profess
   Due to the Moor my lord.

Location: I.iii.179–188
Speaker: Desdemona to Brabanzio
Context: Desdemona announces in public that although she respects her father Brabanzio, her primary allegiance must be to her husband Othello.

This speech, Desdemona's first, shows her thoughtfulness. She does not insist on her loyalty to Othello at the expense of respect for Brabanzio, but rather acknowledges that her duty is "divided." These words establish Desdemona as a woman of courage and conviction. Her ability to separate different degrees and kinds of affection later prompts her to try to help Cassio, inadvertently fueling Othello's jealousy. Again and again, Desdemona speaks clearly and truthfully but Othello, poisoned by Iago's manipulation of language and emotions, is blinded to her honesty.

---

3. *Haply for I am black,*
   And have not those soft parts of conversation
   That chamberers have; or for I am declined
   Into the vale of years—yet that's not much—
   She's gone. I am abused, and my relief
   Must be to loathe her. O curse of marriage,
   That we can call these delicate creatures ours
   And not their appetites! I had rather be a toad
   And live upon the vapor of a dungeon
   Than keep a corner in the thing I love
   For others' uses. Yet 'tis the plague of great ones;
   Prerogatived are they less than the base.
   'Tis destiny unshunnable, like death.

Location: III.iii.267–279
Speaker: Othello
Context: Convinced by Iago that Desdemona has been unfaithful, Othello laments his lot.

In Act I, Othello belies his claim that he is "rude" in speech by delivering a lengthy and convincing speech about winning Desdemona's love with his wonderful storytelling (I.iii.81). Here he returns to his insecurities. Perhaps he has lost Desdemona because he is inarticulate and barbaric, lacking "those soft parts of conversation / That chamberers have." He also, for the first time, refers to his race or his age. Convinced by a mere one hundred lines of text that Desdemona has abandoned him, he calls her a mere "creature" of "appetite" and imagines himself as a "toad" in a "dungeon." This ugly imagery anticipates his speech in IV.ii, where he compares Desdemona to a "cistern for foul toads / To knot and gender in," and says that she is as honest "as summer flies are in the shambles [slaughterhouses], / That quicken even with blowing" (IV.ii.63–64, 68–69). Othello's only comfort is that cuckoldry is "the plague of great ones," a fate as inescapable as death.

---

4. *I am glad I have found this napkin.*
    This was her first remembrance from the Moor,
    My wayward husband hath a hundred times
    Wooed me to steal it, but she so loves the token—
    For he conjured her she should ever keep it—
    That she reserves it evermore about her
    To kiss and talk to. I'll ha' the work ta'en out,
    And give 't Iago. What he will do with it,
    Heaven knows, not I.
    I nothing, but to please his fantasy.

Location: III.iii.294–303
Speaker: Emilia
Context: Emilia finds Desdemona's handkerchief

This speech ushers in *Othello*'s "handkerchief plot." An insignificant event—the dropping of a handkerchief—becomes the means by which Othello, Desdemona, Cassio, Roderigo, Emilia, and Iago are all undone. Emilia's speech explains that handkerchief's significance: as Othello's first love token to Desdemona, it represents their oldest and purest feelings for each other. Her remark that Iago "hath a hundred times / Wooed me to steal it" tips us off that the handkerchief will play a prominent role in the tragic sequence of events. Emilia considers the handkerchief a trifle, "light as air," and keeps silent about its whereabouts even after Desdemona begins to suffer for its absence. Many critics have found Emilia's silence a great implausibility. It is yet another manifestation of Iago's extraordinary power to make those around him see only what they want to see.

---

5. *Then must you speak*
    Of one that loved not wisely but too well,
    Of one not easily jealous but, being wrought,
    Perplexed in the extreme; of one whose hand,
    Like the base Indian, threw a pearl away
    Richer than all his tribe; of one whose subdued eyes,
    Albeit unused to the melting mood,
    Drop tears as fast as the Arabian trees
    Their medicinable gum. Set you down this,
    And say besides that in Aleppo once,
    Where a malignant and a turbaned Turk
    Beat a Venetian and traduced the state,
    I took by th' throat the circumcised dog
    And smote him thus.

Location: V.ii.352–365
Speaker: Othello
Context: Confronted with Desdemona's innocence, Othello asks his jailers to tell his story and kills himself.

In this farewell speech, Othello reaffirms his position simultaneously both inside and excluded from Venetian society. The smooth eloquence of the speech and its references to "Arabian trees," "Aleppo," and a "malignant and a turbaned Turk" remind us of Othello's monologue in I.iii.127–168 and of his tales of adventure and war that wooed Desdemona. No longer inarticulate with grief as he was when he cries, "O fool! fool! fool!" (V.ii.332), Othello has regained his calm, his dignity, and our respect. He reminds us once again of his famous martial prowess. At the same time, however, by killing himself as he is describing the killing of a Turk, Othello implicitly identifies himself with a people who pose a military (and a psychological) threat to Venice, acknowledging the fact that he is and will always remain an outsider. His suicide is a kind of martyrdom, a last act of service to the state, as he kills the only foe he has left to conquer: himself.

PERICLES

In a series of adventures, Pericles loses his wife and daughter, but years later all three are reunited.

PERICLES IN CONTEXT

Pericles, probably written in 1607–1608, came late in Shakespeare's career, but in its plot and devices harks back to some of his earliest work, such as *The Comedy of Errors*. Both plays are set in the Mediterranean, both depend on shipwreck to drive the plot, and both tell the story of family separated and reunited. At the same time, the mythical tone of *Pericles* is very different from the zany comedy of *The Comedy of Errors*. *Pericles* is Shakespeare's first romance. His later romances include *The Tempest*, *The Winter's Tale*, and *Cymbeline*. These plays all explore the possibility of redemption for a hero who has suffered a great loss.

In terms of location, *Pericles* is one of Shakespeare's most widely-ranging plays. It is set in six different cities, as well as at sea. The shifts in location give rise to an unusually large cast of characters, an episodic adventure plot, and thematic emphasis on the sea that connects these destinations. Like many romances, *Pericles* is the story of a quest; a wandering that concludes with Pericles' reunion with his wife and daughter. Moreover, the eastern Mediterranean setting endows *Pericles* with an epic quality. Pericles moves in the ancient world, near the cradle of civilization, among legendary cities.

The most direct source for *Pericles* is the work of the fourteenth-century poet John Gower, who appears as the chorus. His *Confessio Amantis*, completed in 1390, includes a story about Apollonius of Tyre, a prince who faces many challenges and setbacks before achieving redemption. The authorship of *Pericles* has long been debated. It is likely that a playwright named George Wilkins wrote most of the first nine scenes and Shakespeare wrote most of the remaining thirteen. Dual authorship explains the stylistic differences between the two parts of the play. The language of the first half more closely resembles John Gower's fourteenth-century English than Shakespeare's language. Though the play is written in iambic pentameter, the first section has more rhyming couplets, whereas the second has more instances of enjambment (phrases split over two lines), a Shakespearean characteristic. Structurally, the actions of the first half of the play repeat themselves in the second half, giving more support to the dual-author theory. To add to the difficulty, there is no definitive *Pericles* source text: all editions are cobbled from reported texts, such as the 1609 quarto that comes from an actor's promptbook.

PERICLES: KEY FACTS

Full title: Pericles, Prince of Tyre

Time and place written: 1607–1608; London

Date of first publication: 1609 (Henry Gosson's Quarto)

Genre: Romance; comedy

Setting (time): Antiquity (end of the first millennium B.C.)

Setting (place): The eastern Mediterranean: Antioch, Tyre, Tarsus, Pentapolis, Ephesus, Mytilene, and at sea

Protagonist: Pericles

Antagonist: Antiochus; fate

Major conflict: Pericles loses his wife Thaisa and daughter Marina at the hands of fate

PERICLES: CHARACTER LIST

Aeschines Pericles' advisor.

Antiochus King of Antioch. After his wife's death, Antiochus enters into an incestuous relationship with his daughter. He makes her potential suitors agree to a test: either they answer a riddle or lose their lives. The action of the play begins with Pericles' arrival to try for Antiochus's daughter's hand.

Antiochus's daughter   The princess of Antioch. Antiochus's daughter has an incestuous relationship with her father. The play begins with Pericles' attempt to win her hand.

Bawd   A brothel madam. Together with Pander, Bawd purchases Marina from pirates and unsuccessfully tries to convince her to become a prostitute.

Boult   Servant to Pander and Bawd. Boult too falls under Marina's spell of virtue and offers to help her find a more honorable place to work.

Cerimon   A kindly Ephesus physician. A model of charity, Cerimon miraculously brings Thaisa back from the brink of death and helps her become a priestess.

Cleon   Governor of Tarsus and Dionyza's husband. Pericles saves Tarsus from famine when he flees Tyre to protect Tyre from Antiochus's attack. Later, Cleon pledges to take care of Marina, but Dionyza plots to kill her. Cleon claims to have been unaware of Dionyza's scheme, but is punished along with Dionyza at the end.

Diana   Goddess of chastity, the moon, and the hunt in Greek mythology. Diana appears to Pericles and urges Pericles and Marina to go to Ephesus, prompting their reunion with Thaisa.

Dionyza   Cleon's wife. Dionyza pledges to care for Marina, but is jealous when her own daughter grows up less beautiful and gracious, so plots to have Marina killed. Both Dionyza and Cleon are punished at the end.

Three Fishermen   Pentapolis laborers who meet Pericles and fish his armor out of the sea. The fishermen impress Pericles with their folk wisdom about the world of the sea and the world of man.

Helicanus   Pericles' advisor, who rules Tyre in his absence. Though the lords of Tyre want to crown him king, Helicanus is loyal to Pericles, and he refuses.

John Gower   The play's narrator. Gower introduces each act and concludes the play, sometimes with dumbshows (pantomimed performances of action about to come). The historical John Gower was a fourteenth-century English poet who wrote the *Confessio Amantis*, part of which inspired the story of *Pericles*.

Leonine   A murderer hired by Dionyza to kill Marina. Leonine fails when Marina is captured by pirates. Dionyza poisons him to keep him silent.

Lychordia   Thaisa's nurse. Later, Lychordia is Marina's nurse in Tarsus.

Lysimachus   Governor of Mytilene. Lysimachus comes to Marina's brothel, but she convinces him not to take her virginity. Impressed with her grace, he suggests that she talk to the grief-stricken Pericles when Pericles arrives in Mytilene. Lysimachus is betrothed to Marina at the end.

Marina   Pericles and Thaisa's daughter. Born at sea during a storm, Marina is raised by Cleon and Dionyza in Tarsus. A model of beauty, grace, and chastity, Marina suffers a series of adventures. She becomes famous for her virtue in Mytilene, and is reunited with Pericles when she is summoned to heal his woes.

Pander   A pimp. Pander buys Marina from the pirates for his brothel.

Pericles   The prince of Tyre; Thaisa's husband and Marina's father. Pericles wins Thaisa with his virtue and jousting skills, but loses her in a storm. He suffers the vicissitudes of fate with patience and virtue, and is rewarded at the end and reunited with Thaisa and Marina.

Philemon   Cerimon's assistant.

Simonides   King of Pentapolis and Thaisa's father. Impressed with Pericles' jousting skill, Simonides tests Pericles by insulting his honor before blessing Pericles' marriage to Thaisa.

Thaisa   Simonides' daughter, Pericles' wife, and Marina's mother. She apparently dies in childbirth at sea, but is revived by Cerimon. Believing Pericles dead, Thaisa becomes a priestess at Diana's temple in Ephesus.

Thaliart   The villain hired by Antiochus to kill Pericles.

PERICLES: PLOT OVERVIEW

King Antiochus of Antioch has offered his daughter to anyone who can solve a riddle, but the penalty for guessing wrongly is death. Pericles, the prince of Tyre, solves the riddle, but the answer reveals that Antiochus and his daughter have an incestuous relationship. Afraid of retribution from Antiochus, Pericles flees for his life. He cannot remain in Tyre because Antiochus may wage war against Tyre in order to kill him, so he travels. He brings food to the starving nation of Tarsus, earning the gratitude of Cleon and Dionyza. He is shipwrecked in Pentapolis, where he weds King Simonides' daughter Thaisa after winning a jousting tournament. On their way back to Tyre, Pericles and Thaisa are caught in a storm. Thaisa dies in childbirth, and her body is thrown overboard to save the ship.

Thaisa washes up in Ephesus, where a doctor manages to revive her. She becomes a priestess of the goddess Diana. Pericles leaves his daughter Marina with Creon and Dionyza of Tarsus, but when Marina grows up, the jealous Dionyza tries to murder her. Marina is saved and captured by pirates who sell her into prostitution in Mytilene. Marina protects her virginity by converting the men who come to her to a life of virtue, and eventually finds work in a respectable house. Pericles believes Marina dead and arrives in Mytilene very depressed. Marina is summoned to heal him, and they are reunited. Marina is betrothed to the governor of Mytilene. Following Pericles' dream, Marina and Pericles go to Diana's temple in Ephesus, where they reunite with Thaisa as well.

PERICLES: SCENE SUMMARY

ACT I

Prince Pericles of Tyre flees to Tarsus to escape the wrath of King Antiochus of Antioch.

I.PROLOGUE Location:

Gower gives background for the play: King Antiochus forces his daughter's suitors to answer a riddle or die.

Gower announces that he has assumed a human form to tell an interesting story. The story is set in the Syrian city of Antioch, ruled by King Antiochus. After the queen died, Antiochus took a liking to his attractive daughter and began an incestuous relationship with her. Antiochus wanted to keep his daughter for himself, so whenever young princes approached him for her hand, he forced them to agree to answer a difficult riddle or forfeit their lives. Many have already tried and died.

I.I Location: Antioch. Antiochus's palace

In trying to win Antiochus's daughter's hand, Pericles figures out Antiochus's horrible secret; Pericles flees and Antiochus sends a murderer after him.

King Antiochus asks Pericles, the prince of Tyre, whether he understands the consequences if he fails to answer the riddle. Pericles assures him that he does. Antiochus's daughter enters, and Pericles describes her virtues: "Her face the book of praises, where is read / Nothing but curious pleasures" (I.i.58–59). Antiochus reminds Pericles of the other princes who tried the riddle and died, but Pericles says that he is ready to die if he must. Frustrated at Pericles' willingness to throw away his life, since his willingness means that Pericles might figure out the riddle and expose the incestuous relationship, Antiochus hurls the written riddle on the floor. Antiochus's daughter wishes Pericles well.

Pericles reads the riddle and figures it out at once: it is from the point of view of Antiochus's daughter, who is both daughter and lover to her father. Pericles is horrified to have figured out the Antioch court's terrible secret, and tells Antiochus that he knows the truth, but it is a truth better kept concealed. Antiochus understands that Pericles has solved the riddle, but will not confess it. Because he gives no answer to the riddle, Pericles is doomed to die in forty days.

Left alone, Pericles expresses his disgust at Antiochus and his daughter's relationship. He realizes that his life is in danger, especially now that he knows the truth, and determines to flee Antioch. Pericles exits.

Antiochus enters and admits that he wants to kill Pericles before Pericles can tell his secret to the world. Antiochus gives Thaliart, a murderous royal servant, gold to kill Pericles, but news arrives that Pericles has fled. Antiochus sends Thaliart to find and destroy Pericles. Antiochus concludes, saying he will not be calm until Pericles is dead.

I.II Location: Tyre. Pericles' palace

Pericles' advisor Helicanus recommends that Pericles leave Tyre until Antiochus no longer wants to kill him.

Pericles is overwhelmed by melancholy: he is worried that King Antiochus will not trust him to remain silent and will try to kill him. If Antiochus invades Tyre and threatens war, Pericles thinks that he and his people will surely lose. Several lords enter with Pericles' advisor Helicanus, who scolds Pericles for languishing in gloom and offers to give him advice. Pericles sends the lords away and tells Helicanus about his trip to Antioch, the discovery of incest at the Antioch court, his own flight, and his concern about Tyre's well-being. Helicanus urges Pericles to leave Tyre in Helicanus's hands until Antiochus's anger has passed. Pericles agrees and decides to depart for Tarsus.

I.III Location: Tyre. The palace

Antiochus's hired murderer finds out that Pericles has left Tyre, and plans to report that Pericles perished at sea.

Thaliart arrives, intending to kill Pericles. He realizes that if he kills Pericles he will be hanged in Tyre, but if he does not, Antiochus will hang him at home. Thaliart overhears Helicanus speaking to an advisor named Aeschines about Pericles' departure. Thaliart introduces himself to the court as Antiochus's messenger. Since Pericles is gone, he will take his message back to Antioch. Thaliart plans to tell Antiochus that Pericles has perished at sea.

I.IV Location: Tarsus

Pericles takes refuge in Tarsus, saving the city from famine.

Cleon, governor of Tarsus, enters with his wife Dionyza. Cleon and Dionyza try and fail to distract each other from their sorrow by telling sad stories. Instead they relate their misfortune: for several years, a terrible famine has devastated Tarsus, decimating the city's former riches. One of Cleon's lords reports that a ship (Pericles' ship) has been spotted off the coast. Cleon suspects that one of his neighbors has come to conquer his weakened nation. His lord tells him that the ship displays a white flag of peace, but Cleon has doubts.

Pericles enters and allays Cleon's fears: his ship is full of corn to feed the Tarsus hungry. Pericles asks only for refuge in Tarsus in exchange. Cleon welcomes him and his men.

ACT II

On his way home, Pericles is shipwrecked in Pentapolis, where he marries the king's daughter Thaisa.

II.PROLOGUE

On his way home to Tyre, Pericles is shipwrecked on a foreign shore.

Gower reviews the action of Act I, juxtaposing the bad King Antiochus and the good Prince Pericles. A dumbshow presents Pericles receiving a letter and showing it to Cleon. Gower explains that this was Helicanus sending word to Pericles about Thaliart's arrival in Tyre and recommending Pericles' return. While sailing home, Pericles suffers a shipwreck and is cast on a foreign shore.

II.I Location: Pentapolis. The seashore

Pentapolis fishermen help Pericles recover his armor and find his way to the court of King Simonides.

Several fishermen and their master talk about how bigger fish eat the smaller fish in the sea, just like men do on land. Pericles overhears them, and is impressed with their understanding of the human condition through the sea metaphor. He comes forward and asks them for help, saying that he is not used to begging. The fishermen ask him if he can fish. He says no and faints. The fishermen's master helps Pericles up and tells him that he is in the peaceful city of Pentapolis, ruled by King Simonides. Moreover, the next day, many knights will joust for the hand of Simonides' daughter in honor of her birthday.

The fishermen pull Pericles' armor out of the sea. Pericles is happy, because his dead father bequeathed the armor to him. Pericles asks the fishermen to give it back to him so that can participate in the tournament for Simonides' daughter. The fishermen ask him to remember their kindness, give him the armor, and take him to the court.

II.II Location: Pentapolis. The tournament ground

Pericles looks bedraggled as he competes in the tournament for the hand of King Simonides' daughter Thaisa.

King Simonides and his daughter Thaisa watch the jousting tournament. Each knight passes by in turn, showing off his coat of arms, each with a motto in Latin or Italian. King Simonides reads each motto aloud, translates it, and makes a comment. Pericles is the sixth knight. His armor is rusty and he has no gaudy trappings. King Simonides reads Pericles' motto—"I live in this hope"—as one of his lords mocks Pericles' rusty outfit. King Simonides scolds the lords for judging Pericles solely on the basis of his appearance.

II.III Location: Pentapolis. A banquet hall in King Simonides' palace

Pericles has won the tournament, and catches the eye of both Thaisa and Simonides.

King Simonides, Thaisa, Pericles, and other knights enter to a prepared banquet. Simonides and Thaisa congratulate Pericles on winning the tournament, and Thaisa gives him the wreath of victory. At dinner, both Simonides and Thaisa are so taken with Pericles that they lose their appetite. Pericles compares Simonides' court to his own father's glorious reign, and remarks how different his life is outside of Tyre: here no one knows that he is a prince, so he must take things as they come.

Simonides sends Thaisa to ask Pericles about his parentage, so as to dispel Pericles' melancholy. He tells her that he is the shipwrecked prince of Tyre. Thaisa repeats Pericles' story to Simonides, who pities Pericles' misfortune and offers his help. Dancing follows the banquet, and then the knights go to bed to prepare to woo Thaisa the next day.

II.IV Location: Tyre. Pericles' palace

Antiochus and his daughter have perished for their sins, but the lords of Tyre are restless without Pericles.

Helicanus and Aeschines discuss how Antiochus and his daughter were magically burnt to a crisp in a heavenly fire that punished them for their sins. Helicanus says that justice has been done. Several lords enter. They want to crown Helicanus because Pericles has been gone for so long. Helicanus resists, and recommends that they wait twelve months before making any decisions. The lords leave to seek out Pericles.

II.IV Location: Pentapolis. King Simonides's palace

[Note: This scene is absent from many editions of Pericles.] Pericles plays music in private.

A gentleman shows Pericles his lodgings. Pericles asks for a musical instrument, which he plays while he sings to himself.

II.V Location: Pentapolis. King Simonides's palace

Simonides tests both Pericles' honor and Thaisa's love for Pericles before allowing them to get married.

The next day, King Simonides tells his knights that Thaisa has written him a letter announcing that she does not want to be married. The knights leave. Alone, Simonides reveals that Thaisa's letter announces that she wants to marry Pericles. When Pericles enters, Simonides commends his singing the night before and asks him what he thinks of Thaisa. Simonides shows him Thaisa's letter, and Pericles immediately thinks that he has offended Simonides. Simonides plays along. He calls Pericles a traitor and accuses him of bewitching Thaisa. Offended, Pericles says that he came to the court in search of honor, and intends to defend it with his sword.

Thaisa enters, and Pericles asks her to tell Simonides that Pericles never said a word of love to her. Thaisa, who is in love with Pericles, is confused, but then Simonides takes her aside to ask her if she is sure that she wants to marry Pericles, especially since they know nothing about him. Thaisa responds that Pericles is virtuous even if he's not a nobleman, and that she is in love with him and won't be controlled. Simonides threatens to banish Pericles, but Thaisa defends him. Simonides threatens to punish her by making her marry Pericles. He clasps their hands together, they kiss, and are thus married. Simonides, Pericles, and Thaisa are all happy with the match.

ACT III

Pericles believes Thaisa dead and leaves his newborn daughter Marina in Tarsus; Thaisa believes Pericles dead and becomes a priestess in Ephesus.

III.PROLOGUE

Pericles sets off for Tyre with his pregnant wife Thaisa.

Gower announces that Thaisa is now pregnant, and introduces a dumbshow. In Pentapolis, Pericles hears that Antiochus and his daughter are dead. Moreover, Pericles hears that the Tyre lords plan to crown Helicanus. Pericles prepares to return home to reclaim his throne and prevent a mutiny. He, the pregnant Thaisa, and Thaisa's old nurse board a ship for Tyre. At sea, the ship is threatened by a tempest.

III.I Location: a ship at sea

Pronounced dead in childbirth during a storm, Thaisa is tossed overboard in a chest.

Pericles bemoans his fate. This is his second storm at sea. Lychordia comes out with an infant baby and tells Pericles that Thaisa has died in childbirth. Pericles rails at the gods. Lychordia says that his baby's life will surely be calm and peaceful, unlike her birth in a storm. The shipmaster declares that Thaisa's body must be tossed overboard, following a sailor's superstition that the sea will not be calm until the dead are off the ship.

Pericles speaks over Thaisa's body. He regrets that he cannot give her a proper burial. The shipmaster gives him a chest for the body, into which Pericles also puts jewels, spices and a letter. The shipmaster says the boat is near Tarsus. Pericles orders the ship to dock, intending to leave his baby with Cleon because he thinks it will not survive until Tyre.

III.II Location: Ephesus. Cerimon's house

The doctor Cerimon finds Thaisa's body and revives her.

Cerimon, a kindly doctor, and his helper Philemon provide fire and food to those suffering from the wicked storm. Two gentlemen enter and discuss Cerimon's reputation for his charity. Philemon enters with a chest discovered floating in the sea. Inside, Cerimon and Philemon find Thaisa's body, along with a note asking whoever finds the chest to give Thaisa, a king's daughter, a proper burial. Cerimon determines that Thaisa is not yet dead. He gives her medicines. She stirs and wakes.

III.III Location: Tarsus. Cleon's house

Pericles names his baby Marina and leaves her with Cleon, governor of Tarsus.

Pericles tells Cleon and Dionyza about his misfortune. He asks Cleon and Dionyza to take care of his daughter, whom he has named Marina. Cleon, eager to repay Pericles for saving Tarsus from famine, promises to raise her as a noblewoman. Pericles leaves, swearing not to cut his hair until Marina marries.

III.IV Location: Ephesus. Cerimon's house

Thaisa, believing Pericles dead, decides to become a chaste priestess.

Cerimon tells Thaisa about the jewels and the letter that lay in the chest along with her body. She recognizes Pericles' writing and believes that she will never see him again. She decides to become a priestess, one of the goddess Diana's vestal virgins. Cerimon offers to help her.

ACT IV

Pirates steal Marina and sell her to a brothel; Pericles and Thaisa marry.

IV.PROLOGUE

Marina grows up so perfect that Cleon's wife Dionyza hires a murderer to kill her.

Years pass. Pericles is king of Tyre, Thaisa is a priestess in Ephesus, and Marina grows up in Tarsus. Dionyza resents Marina's grace and beauty because they obscure Dionyza's own daughter's virtues. Dionyza makes plans to murder Marina so that her daughter will look better. After Marina's nurse Lychordia dies, Dionyza hires the murderer Leonine.

IV.I Location: Tarsus. The seashore

The murderer is prevented from killing Marina by pirates, who steal her away.

Dionyza makes Leonine swear never to reveal who ordered Marina's death. Marina enters to strew flowers on Lychordia's grave. Dionyza notes how pale she is, and suggests that she take a walk along the sea with Leonine. Marina reluctantly agrees.
   As they walk, Marina speaks of the tempest in which she was born, and what Lychorida had told her of her father. Leonine tells her to say her prayers because he will kill her. Marina asks why Dionyza would have her killed, but Leonine says that he does not know why. He only knows that he must kill her. Marina begs him to spare her life.
   Suddenly, pirates arrive. They wound Leonine and take Marina. Leonine decides to tell Dionyza that he has killed Marina and thrown her in the sea.

IV.II Location: Mytilene. A brothel

The pirates sell Marina to a brothel.

Pander, a pimp, and Bawd, a madam, send their servant Boult to the market to look for women for their brothel. Pander and Bawd discuss retiring, since prostitution is a bad vocation.
   Boult returns with the pirates and Marina. Pander decides to buy her. Marina wishes that Leonine had killed her. Bawd tells her that she will lead a life of pleasure and receive gifts from all the gentlemen. Since she is a virgin, Bawd has Boult advertise Marina in the marketplace.
   Bawd tells Marina to stop crying or else they won't like her. Bawd promises Boult that he will be allowed to sleep with Marina too, and sends him off to advertise her more thoroughly. Marina swears to the goddess Diana that she will stay a virgin.

IV.III Location: Tarsus. Cleon's house

Cleon has found out that Dionyza has killed Marina.

Cleon wishes that Dionyza had not killed Marina. Dionyza has poisoned Leonine to keep her plot secret. Cleon asks Dionyza what she will say when Pericles asks about his daughter, and Dionyza responds, "That she is dead." Since the murderer is dead, nobody will ever suspect her unless Cleon turns her in. Dionyza reminds Cleon that Marina had been stealing all of their daughter's suitors. And as for Pericles, she suggests they mourn Marina properly and build her a monument. Cleon calls Dionyza a harpy. Dionyza laughs at him for being so scared of the gods.

IV.IV Location: Tarsus. Marina's tomb

Pericles hears that Marina is dead and resolves never to cut his hair again.

Gower announces that Pericles is on his way to Tarsus with Helicanus to see Marina. Another dumb-show: Pericles arrives in Tarsus, where Cleon and Dionyza show him Marina's tomb. Pericles puts on sackcloth and swears never to wash his face or cut his hair again. Gower reads Marina's epitaph, which declares that she was a good, virtuous person.

IV.V Location: Mytilene. In front of and inside the brothel

Marina has been preaching virtue to the brothel visitors.

[Note: some editions break this scene into two scenes at the point where the action shifts inside]
Two gentlemen emerge from the brothel, remarking on the divinity they have heard preached within. They determine to be virtuous and go looking for religious entertainment.

Pander and Bawd are annoyed that Marina is bad for business: she makes anyone who meets her want to be virtuous. Someone must take her virginity, or their brothel will go bust. Lysimachus, the governor of Myteline in disguise, enters. Bawd offers him Marina. Marina is brought out and Bawd assures her that Lysimachus is an honorable man, but Marina seems skeptical.

Left alone with Marina, Lysimachus finds her a clever conversationalist. He asks her how long she has been in the business. She misunderstands him, and answers that she has always been in the business of being honorable. He explains that he is the governor, and has the power to punish or overlook corruption as he sees fit, and he is drawn to her beauty. Marina, touched by his seemingly honorable nature, asks him to govern himself as he was born to govern, and not to take her honor from her. She asks him not to deface her honor. Impressed by her impassioned pleas, he admits that his impure intentions have been cleansed by her words. He gives her gold, and leaves.

Pander and Bawd return to discover that Marina has talked Lysimachus into being virtuous too. They send Boult to rape her, so that she can at last be useful to the brothel. Alone with her, Boult too is swayed by her insistence that to take her honor is the worst thing anyone could do to her. She tells him that she can become a teacher, or make money in other honest ways. Boult promises to do what he can to help her.

ACT V

Pericles, Marina, and Thaisa are reunited.

V.PROLOGUE

Pericles arrives in Mytilene.

Gower says that Marina has been sold to an honest work house. She thrives, sewing and teaching. She gives her extra money to Bawd. Meanwhile, Pericles has been at sea, and arrives in Mytilene. Lysimachus sets out to meet Pericles on his ship.

V.I Location: off the Mytilene coast. Pericles' ship

Pericles snaps out of his depression when he is reunited with Marina.

Helicanus explains to Lysimachus that Pericles has not said a word in three months. Lysimachus tries to speak to him, but Pericles won't respond. Lysimachus tells them that there is an amazing woman in Mytilene (Marina) who may be able to convince Pericles to speak. He sends one of his men to get Marina.

Marina arrives, and Lysimachus comments on her beauty. He sends her to talk to Pericles. Marina tells Pericles that she too has endured great grief: she was born a princess, but now works as a servant. Pericles speaks to her, remarking that she reminds him of Thaisa. He asks her to tell him about her parents, adding that if her story is anywhere near as awful as his own, he will deem himself weak to have given in to his suffering.

She tells him that her name is Marina. Pericles interrupts her, thinking that she mocks him. She tells him that she was born at sea, her father is a king, and her mother died in childbirth. Pericles thinks that he is dreaming. Marina tells him about Cleon and Dionyza plotting her death in Tarsus, about the pirates' fortuitous intervention. Finally, she says that her father is King Pericles. Pericles tells Marina that he is Pericles, and asks her mother's name. She names Thaisa, and Pericles is overjoyed.

Left alone, Pericles sleeps and is visited by the goddess Diana. She tells Pericles to visit her temple in Ephesus and recount the story of how he lost his wife and daughter and rediscovered Marina. When he wakes, Pericles sets sail for Ephesus. Before leaving, he promises Marina to Lysimachus.

V.II Location: off the Mytilene coast

Guided by Pericles' vision of the goddess Diana, Pericles and Marina go to Ephesus.

Gower tells about Pericles in Mytilene, where Lysimachus was betrothed to Marina. They plan to wed after Marina and Pericles return from Ephesus.

V.III Location: Ephesus. Diana's temple

Pericles and Marina are reunited with Thaisa.

Pericles explains his story: he married Thaisa at Pentapolis but Thaisa died in childbirth at sea. Their daughter Marina lived at Tarsus until Cleon ordered her killed. Pericles himself arrived in Mytilene, where Marina miraculously arrived on his ship.

Thaisa, in attendance as a priestess, hears his story and faints. Cerimon tells Pericles about how he found Thaisa in a chest and revived her.

When Thaisa recovers, she, Pericles, and Marina are reunited. Pericles promises that he will give daily offerings to Diana. When Marina is married, he can finally cut his hair. Thaisa tells Pericles that she has heard about the death of her father Simonides. Pericles decides that he and Thaisa should see their daughter married and then live in Pentapolis, leaving Tyre for Marina and Lysimachus.

V.EPILOGUE Location: Ephesus. Diana's temple

Gower concludes that corruption is punished but virtue is ultimately rewarded.

Gower reminds us that the monstrously corrupt Antiochus received his just reward. On the other hand, Pericles, Thaisa, and Marina were assailed with terrible misfortune, but they preserved with virtue intact, and thus are rewarded with joy at last. Helicanus, he notes, is a figure of truth, faith, and loyalty, and Cerimon of charity. As for Cleon and Dionyza, once the story of their evil deed had spread, Tarsus revolted and burned them to death in their palace. The play ends.

THEMES, MOTIFS, & SYMBOLS IN *PERICLES*

THEMES

JUST DESSERTS In the play, good or bad fortune corresponds to good or bad virtue. Antiochus and his daughter have a corrupt, incestuous relationship, and so are burnt to a crisp. Cleon and Dionyza are killed by their own citizens when their treachery is made known. Pericles, Thaisa, and Marina manage to keep their virtues throughout their tribulations, and so find themselves happily reunited at the end, against all odds.

In Shakespearean comedies, the good end well and the bad end badly, but the characters' destinies are determined by they way they play off one another. *Pericles* is a romance, and the fates of its characters are determined by divine forces. Thus Antiochus and his daughter are killed by a bolt of fire come down from heaven. Creon and Dionyza too die in a fire, which is a traditional symbol of divine intervention. (Indeed, Gower notes, "The gods for murder seemed so content / To punish [them]" (V.Epilogue.15–16)). Similarly, Pericles' final reunion with Thaisa is brought about by the goddess Diana, who comes to him in a dream. In *Pericles*, the *deus ex machina*—an otherwise impossible happy ending brought about by a supernatural force—is literal.

CHASTITY AS A VIRTUE *Pericles* places a premium on chastity in women. In this case, chastity is not abstention from sex, but appropriate sexual behavior. A woman should have sex only within the bonds of marriage, in moderation, and without excessive pleasure. In Act IV, Marina defends her virginity with a religious fervor. Thinking her husband dead, Marina's mother Thaisa chooses to become a nun in the temple of Diana, the goddess of chastity. Both Marina and Thaisa are rewarded for their chastity and reunited with Pericles and their family. In contrast, the daughter of Antiochus, who indulges in an incestuous relationship with her father, is punished by a bolt of fire come down from heaven.

This emphasis on chastity is couched in long-standing tradition. Until recently, women were often seen as irrational beings with insatiable sexual impulses in Western culture and literature. Many works, to this day, have played on the juxtaposition of the virgin and the whore: the former praised for her innocence, the latter despised for her dangerous lust.

THE POSSIBILITY OF REDEMPTION Shakespearean romances—*Pericles, Cymbeline, The Tempest*, and *The Winter's Tale*—all involve a hero who regains what he had long thought lost. The different Shakespearean genres—comedies (which end in marriage), tragedies (which end in death), and romances (which end in rediscovery)—represent the different perspectives on human destiny. Romances explore the possibility of redemption. Pericles regains his family through both patient suffering and fantastic strokes of luck. Like the biblical Job, Pericles suffers losses in order to be able to appreciate what he has more fully. At the same time, fate and luck play an enormous role: Marina is rescued from her would-be murderer by pirates, Thaisa survives a near-fatal childbirth, Pericles comes to Mytilene to find Marina by coincidence and is sent to Ephesus to find Thaisa by divine providence. Throughout, Pericles accepts his fate, believing that what will happen will happen. It is this resignation to fate that is rewarded. The gods reward those who, like Pericles, Thaisa, and Marina, accept their actions without complaint.

MOTIFS

FATHER-DAUGHTER LOVE *Pericles* shows us three father-daughter pairs: Antiochus and his daughter, engaged in an incestuous relationship; Pericles' father-in-law Simonides and Pericles' bride Thaisa; and Pericles and Marina. These pairings contrast to show us what is proper and improper.

Antiochus and his daughter's depraved love is juxtaposed with the healthy relationship between Simonides and Thaisa. Pericles' participation in competitions to win the daughters, in quick succession, reinforces the parallels between these two pairs. Pericles' relationship with his daughter is shown in a more transcendent light. Their reunion is the emotional high point of the play: Marina, to whom Pericles gives life, returns the favor and gives him a new desire to live. At the moment of reunion, he exclaims, "O, come hither, Thou that beget'st him that did thee beget" (V.i.181–182). This line alludes to the Christian holy family. Mary, like all humans, is a child of God. In giving birth to Jesus, she also gives birth to God. This parallel suggests that Marina and Pericles' relationship is touched with the divine.

DOUBLED ACTION   Much of the play's action is doubled: Pericles competes in two tournaments in search of a wife; he suffers two disasters at sea; he believes both wife and daughter dead; both Pericles and Marina flee plots to murder them; both Cleon and Dionyza, and Antiochus and his daughter, burn to death for their evil deeds. Indeed, Pericles' redemption at the end of the play is a repetition of previous events: Pericles finds a wife and gains a daughter in the middle of the play, and then finds the wife and gains the daughter again at the end. Those acquainted with sorrow are all the better equipped to appreciate happiness. Pericles' reunion with Thaisa and Marina is sweeter for the suffering he has endured.

SYMBOLS

THE SEA   All of *Pericles* takes place in port cities or on the open sea. Marina is born at sea and named for the sea. The hand of fate acts through the sea: Pericles suffers two tempests and Marina is saved from death by pirates. For a seafaring nation such as Elizabethan England, the sea represents fortune, both good and bad. Prosperity came from across the sea, but sea journeys were inherently dangerous.

The sea also symbolizes birth, because it evokes both amniotic fluid (the liquid in which a fetus is suspended in the womb) and the primordial soup from which human ancestors emerged. Born at sea, Marina comes to land to bring spiritual or emotional rebirth to those she encounters. Wind and Storm

In the play, storms represent the cataclysmic hand of fate. The first of the play's two storms casts Pericles on the shore near Pentapolis, where he meets his wife Thaisa. During the second, Thaisa gives birth and appears to die. The characters see their lives as metaphorical storms, tossing them around without their control. Marina, mourning her bad luck, remarks, "This world to me is but a ceaseless storm, / Whirring me from my friends" (IV.i.71–72). Upon hearing that Marina is dead, Pericles "bears / A tempest, which his mortal vessel tears, And yet he rides it out" (IV.iv.29–31).

Wind imagery, on the other hand, suggests more subtly shifting fortunes. Just before Leonine tries to murder Marina, they note that the wind is blowing from the southwest, whereas during Marina's birth the wind blew from the north. Marina's destiny has changed: born a princess, she finds herself the helpless victim of a murder plot. The violent winds that blew as Marina was born foreshadow the dramatic shifts in fortune over the course of her life.

IMPORTANT QUOTATIONS FROM *PERICLES*

---

1. *O you gods!*
   Why do you make us love your goodly gifts,
   And snatch them straight away? We here below
   Recall not what we give, and therein may
   Use honour with you.

Location: III.i.22–26
Speaker: Pericles
Context: Pericles grieves for Thaisa's death in childbirth

Act III, scene i, in which Marina is born and Thaisa apparently dies, marks the beginning of Pericles' long journey through grief and patience towards redemption. His initial reaction to Thaisa's death is dismay and outrage. He distinguishes between the behavior of gods toward humans and the behavior of humans toward gods. In making prayers and offerings to the gods, humans give without hesitation and never take back their sacrifices. The gods, on the other hand, give and take away at will: Pericles' wife dies soon after their marriage, on the brink of returning home and giving birth. In his grief Pericles appeals to the gods, but does not condemn them. It is this patience that earns him his redemption at the end.

---

2. *This world to me is but a ceaseless storm,*

Whirring me from my friends.

Location: IV.i.71–72
Speaker: Marina
Context: Marina grieves her misfortune in having been separated from her parents

Here, Marina recognizes the symbolic significance of her birth at sea in a storm. In the play, storms signal overwhelming and incomprehensible actions of fate. The sea represents the vicissitudes of fortune. Moreover, traditional astrology believes that the circumstances of a person's birth determine that person's life. Like the storm that enables her birth and separates her from her parents, Marina's life is characterized by dramatic shifts. Her acceptance of her shifting fate is a manifestation of her virtue, which is rewarded by the reunions at the end of the play.

---

3. *He bears*
   A tempest, which his mortal vessel tears,
   And yet he rides it out.

Location: IV.iv.29–31
Speaker: Gower
Context: Gower describes Pericles' grief upon being told of Marina's death

Grieving for Marina's death, Pericles vows never to bathe, shave, or cut his hair. Gower explains that Pericles' bad luck is like a storm. His body, "his mortal vessel," is like a ship torn apart by the storm. At the same time, Gower explains, this storm does not sink Pericles: he somehow manages to ride it out. The sea holds crucial symbolic value in *Pericles*. In these lines, Gower makes a direct connection between the literal sea journeys that Pericles undertakes and the metaphorical journey of Pericles' life. His life is a series of dramatic shifts and changes in fortune, and yet he "rides it out." In a real sea-storm, sailors ride out the storm by slacking the sails to prevent them from catching the wind. Similarly, Pericles endures and survives through his suffering by going slack and not resisting the winds of fate. Indeed, he literally takes to the sea.

---

4. *Called Marina*
   For I was born at sea.

Location: V.i.143–144
Speaker: Marina
Context: an astonished Pericles has asked Marina how she came by her name

Pericles' first inkling that the woman who has compelled him to speak may be his daughter comes when he learns her name. She replies that she was named Marina because she was born at sea. As a character, Marina is in many ways associated with the sea. Her name comes from the Latin root for "sea." The sea symbolizes birth, and Marina is born, at sea, to give her life to her parents. Moreover, the sea and its shifting tides are associated with the moon. Diana, the goddess of the moon, is also the goddess of chastity to whom Marina prays. Lastly, the sea is associated with shifting fortunes. Marina's birth at sea has characterized her whole life. Her shifting fortunes and her separation from Pericles provide the emotional arc of the play.

---

5. *O, come hither,*
   Thou that beget'st him that did thee beget;
   Thou that wast born at sea, buried at Tarsus,

And found at sea again!

Location: V.i.181–184
Speaker: Pericles
Context: Pericles, finally assured that Marina is indeed his daughter, rejoices in their reunion.

Pericles' reunion with Marina is one of the most poignant Shakespearean scenes. This line constitutes this scene's climax. Pericles, who conceived Marina (and so begot her), is given new life (begotten) by Marina in turn. Although *Pericles*, populated by pagan gods and inscrutable shifts in fortune, is not an overwhelmingly Christian play, the paradoxical idea of begetting someone who begot you alludes to the relationship between Mary and Jesus. As human, Mary is a child of God. As Jesus' mother, she is the mother of God. Not only does Marina's name resemble Mary's, but both are also associated with virginity and virtue. Finally, when Pericles speaks about her being born, buried, and reborn, Marina associates him with Jesus, who was resurrected after death.

ROMEO AND JULIET

Romeo and Juliet, children of rival families, marry in secret but die tragically, reconciling their families.

ROMEO AND JULIET IN CONTEXT

Shakespeare did not invent the story of *Romeo and Juliet*. He did not, in fact, even introduce the story into the English language. A poet named Arthur Brooks first brought the story of *Romeus and Juliet* to an English-speaking audience in a long and plodding poem—an adaptation of adaptations that stretched across nearly a hundred years and two languages. Many of the details of Shakespeare's plot are lifted directly from Brooks's poem, including the meeting of Romeo and Juliet at the ball, their secret marriage, Romeo's fight with Tybalt, the sleeping potion, and the timing of the lovers' eventual suicides.

Despite its many sources, Shakespeare's play distinguishes itself from its predecessors in several important respects: the subtlety and originality of its characterization (Shakespeare almost wholly created Mercutio); the intense pace of its action, compressed into four frenetic days; a powerful enrichment of the story's thematic aspects; and above all, an extraordinary use of language.

Romeo and Juliet is also similar in plot and themes to the story of Pyramus and Thisbe, which appears in Ovid's *Metamorphoses*. Shakespeare was certainly aware of the Pyramus and Thisbe story: *Romeo and Juliet* contains a reference to Thisbe. Moreover, the story of Pyramus and Thisbe is presented as the comically awful play-within-a-play put on by Bottom and his friends in *A Midsummer Night's Dream*—a play Shakespeare wrote around the same time he was composing *Romeo and Juliet*. Indeed, one can look at the play-within-a-play in *A Midsummer Night's Dream* as parodying the very story that Shakespeare seeks to tell in *Romeo and Juliet*. Shakespeare wrote *Romeo and Juliet* in full knowledge that the story he was telling was old, clichéd, and an easy target for parody. In writing *Romeo and Juliet*, Shakespeare, then, implicitly set the task of telling a love story despite the considerable forces he knew were stacked against its success. Through the incomparable intensity of his language Shakespeare succeeded in this effort, writing a play that is universally accepted in Western culture as the preeminent, archetypal story of tragic love.

ROMEO AND JULIET: KEY FACTS

Full title: The Most Excellent and Lamentable Tragedy of Romeo and Juliet

Time and place written: Mid-1590s; London, England

Date of first publication: 1597 (First Quarto, incomplete and likely unauthorized); 1599 (Second Quarto)

Genre: Tragedy

Setting (time): Renaissance (fourteenth or fifteenth century)

Setting (place): Italy: Verona and Mantua

Protagonist: Romeo; Juliet

Major conflict: Lovers Romeo and Juliet struggle to be together despite their families' feud

ROMEO AND JULIET: CHARACTER LIST

THE CAPULETS

Capulet The patriarch of the Capulet family, father of Juliet, husband of Lady Capulet, and enemy—for unexplained reasons—of Montague. He truly loves his daughter, though he is not well acquainted with Juliet's thoughts or feelings, and seems to think that what is best for her is a "good" match with Paris. Often prudent, he commands respect and propriety, but he is liable to fly into a rage when either is lacking.

Lady Capulet Juliet's mother, Capulet's wife. A woman who herself married young (by her own estimation she gave birth to Juliet at close to the age of fourteen), she is eager to see her daughter marry Paris. She is an ineffectual mother, relying on the nurse for moral and pragmatic support.

Juliet The daughter of Capulet and Lady Capulet. A beautiful thirteen-year-old girl, Juliet begins the play as a naïve child who has thought little about love and marriage, but she grows up quickly upon falling in love with Romeo, the son of her family's great enemy. Because she is a girl in an aristocratic family, she has none of the freedom Romeo has to roam around the city, climb over walls in the middle of the night, or get into swordfights. Nevertheless, she shows amazing courage in trusting her entire life and future to Romeo, even refusing to believe the worst reports about him after he kills her cousin Tybalt. Juliet's closest friend and confidant is her nurse, though she's willing to shut the nurse out of her life the moment the nurse turns against Romeo.

The Nurse Juliet's nurse, the woman who breast-fed Juliet when she was a baby and who has cared for Juliet her entire life. A vulgar, long-winded, and sentimental character, the nurse provides comic relief with her frequently inappropriate remarks and speeches. But until a disagreement near the play's end, the nurse is Juliet's faithful confidante and loyal intermediary in Juliet's affair with Romeo. She provides a contrast with Juliet, given that her view of love is earthy and sexual, whereas Juliet is idealistic and intense. The nurse believes in love and wants Juliet to have a nice-looking husband, but the idea that Juliet would want to sacrifice herself for love is incomprehensible to her.

Peter A Capulet servant who invites guests to Capulet's feast and escorts the nurse to meet with Romeo. He is illiterate and a bad singer.

Sampson and Gregory Two servants who, like their master, hate the Montagues. At the outset of the play, they successfully provoke some Montague men into a fight.

Tybalt Juliet's cousin on her mother's side. Vain, fashionable, supremely aware of courtesy and the lack of it, he becomes aggressive, violent, and quick to draw his sword when he feels his pride has been injured. Once drawn, his sword is something to be feared. He loathes the Montagues.

THE MONTAGUES

Abram Montague's servant, who fights with Sampson and Gregory in the first scene of the play.

Balthasar Romeo's dedicated servant. He brings Romeo the news of Juliet's death, unaware that her death is a ruse.

Benvolio Montague's nephew, Romeo's cousin and thoughtful friend. He makes a genuine effort to defuse violent scenes in public places, though Mercutio accuses him of having a nasty temper in private. He spends most of the play trying to help Romeo get his mind off Rosaline, even after Romeo has fallen in love with Juliet.

Montague Romeo's father, the patriarch of the Montague clan and bitter enemy of Capulet. At the beginning of the play, he is chiefly concerned about Romeo's melancholy.

Lady Montague Romeo's mother, Montague's wife. She dies of grief after Romeo is exiled from Verona.

Romeo The son and heir of Montague and Lady Montague. Romeo is handsome, intelligent, and sensitive. Though impulsive and immature, his idealism and passion make him an extremely likable character. He lives in the middle of a violent feud between his family and the Capulets, but he is not at all interested in violence. His only interest is love. At the beginning of the play he is madly in love with a woman named Rosaline, but the instant he lays eyes on Juliet, he falls in love with her and forgets Rosaline. Thus, Shakespeare gives us every reason to question how real Romeo's new love is, but Romeo goes to extremes to prove the seriousness of his feelings. He secretly marries Juliet, the daughter of his father's worst enemy, he happily takes abuse from Tybalt, and he would rather die than live without his beloved. Romeo is also an affectionate and devoted friend to Benvolio, Mercutio, and Friar Lawrence.

ADDITIONAL CHARACTERS

The Apothecary An apothecary in Mantua. Had he been wealthier, he might have been able to afford to value his morals more than money, and refused to sell poison to Romeo.

The Chorus A character developed in Greek drama, whose function is to comment on the play's plot and themes.

Friar Lawrence A Franciscan friar, friend to both Romeo and Juliet. Kind, civic-minded, a proponent of moderation, and always ready with a plan, Friar Lawrence secretly marries the impassioned lovers in hopes that the union might eventually bring peace to Verona. As well as being a Catholic holy man, Friar Lawrence is also an expert in the use of seemingly mystical potions and herbs.

Friar John A Franciscan friar charged by Friar Lawrence with taking the news of Juliet's false death to Romeo in Mantua. Friar John is held up by a quarantine, and the message never reaches Romeo.

Mercutio A kinsman to Prince Escalus, and Romeo's close friend. One of the most extraordinary characters in all of Shakespeare's plays, Mercutio overflows with imagination, wit, and at times a strange, biting satire and brooding fervor. Mercutio loves wordplay, especially sexual double entendres. He can be quite hotheaded, and hates people who are affected, pretentious, or obsessed with the latest fashions. He finds Romeo's romanticized ideas about love tiresome, and tries to convince Romeo to view love as a simple matter of sexual appetite.

Paris A kinsman of Prince Escalus, and the suitor of Juliet most preferred by Capulet. Once Capulet has promised him he can marry Juliet, he behaves very presumptuously toward her, acting as if they are already married.

Prince Escalus The prince of Verona and a kinsman of Mercutio and Paris. As the seat of political power in Verona, he is concerned about maintaining the public peace at all costs

Rosaline The woman with whom Romeo is infatuated at the beginning of the play. Rosaline never appears onstage, but it is said by other characters that she is very beautiful and has sworn to live a life of chastity.

ROMEO AND JULIET: PLOT OVERVIEW

The houses of Montague and Capulet are engaged in a violent feud. After yet another outbreak of fighting, Prince Escalus of Verona threatens death to anyone who breaks the peace. Montague's lovesick son Romeo sneaks into a masked ball at the Capulets' house and falls in love at first sight with Capulet's daughter Juliet. Juliet falls in love with Romeo just as quickly. That night, they profess their love at her balcony. The next day, they are married secretly by Friar Lawrence, who hopes that their union will end the feud.

Later that sweltering day, Juliet's cousin Tybalt, who had recognized Romeo as an intruder at the ball, challenges Romeo. Romeo refuses to be provoked, but when Tybalt kills Romeo's friend Mercutio, Romeo kills Tybalt in a rage. Prince Escalus banishes Romeo from Verona, but Romeo spends one last night with Juliet to consummate their marriage.

Juliet's father plans to marry her to Paris, a relative of Prince Escalus. She seeks Friar Lawrence's help, and he tells her to take a potion that will make her appear to be dead so that Romeo can pick her up from her tomb when she awakes and whisk her away. She takes the potion, fools her family, and is placed in the tomb. Romeo doesn't get Friar Lawrence's message, and only hears that Juliet has died. He procures poison, goes to Juliet's tomb at night, kills Paris when Paris challenges him, and dies by Juliet's side by drinking poison. Juliet wakes up, and finding Romeo dead, kills herself with his dagger. Friar Lawrence reveals the whole story. The Capulets and the Montagues forget their feud in grief.

ROMEO AND JULIET: SCENE SUMMARY

PROLOGUE

The Chorus summarizes the action of the play.

The Chorus summarizes the play in a fourteen-line sonnet: the children of two feuding Verona households will fall in unlucky love. The quarrel between their families will end with their deaths.

ACT I

Romeo and Juliet, of rival families, meet and fall in love.

I.I Location: Verona. A street

Prince Escalus forbids further brawls between the Capulets and the Montagues on pain of death; Romeo suffers from unrequited love.

Sampson and Gregory, two Capulet servants, provoke two Montague servants into a fight when Sampson "bites" his thumb—that is, flicks his thumb past his upper teeth. Benvolio, a Montague, arrives and draws his sword in an attempt to stop the brawl. Tybalt, a Capulet, sees Benvolio's drawn sword and attacks Benvolio. The brawl spreads. A group of citizens with clubs attempt to beat down the combatants. Montague and Capulet enter, and only their wives prevent them from attacking each another.

Prince Escalus arrives and puts a stop to the fighting. He declares that the violence between the two families has gone on for too long, and forbids further fighting on pain of death. Capulet exits with him, the brawlers disperse, and Benvolio is left alone with Montague and Lady Montague. Benvolio describes how the brawl began, and tells Montague and Lady Montague that he glimpsed their son Romeo earlier that morning, in a troubled mood. The Montagues are concerned. Benvolio sees Romeo approaching and promises to find out what is the matter. The Montagues quickly depart.

Romeo reveals to Benvolio that he suffers from unrequited love for the chaste Rosaline. Benvolio counsels Romeo to seek other women, but Romeo departs disconsolate.

I.II Location: Verona. Another street

Capulet plans a masquerade feast for the evening.

Capulet and Paris discuss Paris's desire to marry Capulet's daughter Juliet. Capulet's only reservation is that Juliet, not quite fourteen, may be too young. Nevertheless, he invites Paris to his masquerade feast so that Paris can begin to woo Juliet. Capulet dispatches his servant Peter to invite a list of people to the feast.

Peter is illiterate and asks Romeo and Benvolio, who happen by, to read the list to him. Rosaline is one of the guests. Benvolio and Romeo decide to go to the feast in secret. Benvolio hopes that Romeo will see other Verona beauties, but Romeo wants only to see Rosaline.

I.III Location: Capulet's house

Lady Capulet asks Juliet to think about marrying Paris.

Lady Capulet calls the nurse to help her find Juliet. When Juliet arrives, Lady Capulet first dismisses and then calls back the nurse. The nurse launches into a long story about how, as a little girl, Juliet unwittingly said something that could be interpreted as a sexual joke. Lady Capulet tries to change the subject, but the nurse cannot stop laughing. Embarrassed, Juliet finally quiets her nurse.

Lady Capulet asks Juliet about marriage. She herself, Lady Capulet says, was already a mother by the time she was Juliet's age. She encourages Juliet to think about Paris, who has expressed an interest in her. Juliet dutifully agrees to check Paris out at the feast. A servant announces that the feast has begun.

I.IV Location: Verona. A street

On the way to the Capulet feast, Mercutio entertains his friends with a tale about Queen Mab.

Romeo, Benvolio, and their friend Mercutio, all masked, have gathered with a group of masqueraded friends to crash Capulet's feast. Mercutio makes fun of Romeo and his melancholy. When Romeo mentions that he saw in a dream that the feast will lead to something bad, Mercutio tells about the fairy Queen Mab, who visits people in their dreams. The speech begins as a flight of fancy, but Mercutio becomes entranced by it and a bitter, fervent strain creeps in. Romeo breaks in and calms Mercutio down. Despite Romeo's continuing premonitions, the friends continue to the feast.

I.V Location: Capulet's house. Great hall

At the feast, Romeo and Juliet meet, kiss, and fall in love.

All is a-bustle. Capulet makes his rounds through groups of guests, joking with them and encouraging all to dance. From across the room, Romeo sees Juliet, and declares that he has never known love until that moment. Tybalt overhears and recognizes Romeo's voice, and sends a servant to fetch his rapier. Capulet overhears Tybalt and reprimands him, insisting that his feast not be spoiled by brawls. Tybalt vows to himself that he will not let this indignity pass.

Romeo approaches Juliet and touches her hand. He convinces her to let him kiss her, as though she were a saint and he a pilgrim seeking to be absolved of his sins. Juliet kisses him back again. The nurse arrives to fetch Juliet to see Lady Capulet. Romeo asks the nurse who Juliet is, and is devastated to learn that she is a Capulet. As feast breaks up, Benvolio leads Romeo away.

Juliet, also struck with Romeo, sends the nurse to discover who Romeo is. The nurse returns with the news: his name is Romeo, and he is a Montague. In anguish because she loves her family's enemy, Juliet follows her nurse out.

ACT II

Romeo and Juliet meet at Juliet's balcony at night, and secretly marry the next day.

II.PROLOGUE

The Chorus summarizes the situation: Romeo and Juliet, of rival families, are in love.

The Chorus tells that their families' hatred makes it difficult for Romeo and Juliet to meet, but love gives them strength and determination.

II.I Location: outside the Capulet estate

Romeo ditches his friends to look for Juliet.

After the feast, Romeo climbs over a wall into the Capulet orchard. Benvolio and Mercutio enter, looking for Romeo. Exasperated that he is hiding, Mercutio mocks Romeo's love for Rosaline. They leave without him.

II.II Location: Capulet's orchard

Romeo and Juliet—she on her balcony, he beneath—pledge their love to each other.

Romeo sees Juliet appear on her balcony. He compares her to the morning sun, far more beautiful than the moon it banishes. He almost speaks to her, but decides against it. Unaware that Romeo is below, Juliet muses to herself. She asks why Romeo must be Romeo—a Montague, her family's enemy. If he refused his Montague name, she would give herself to him. Romeo startles her by responding to her plea. They profess their love for each other. Juliet goes inside for a moment when her nurse calls her. When she reappears, she tells Romeo that she will send someone the next day. If he intends to wed her, he should make plans. Juliet withdraws again. She reappears once more, and they say goodnight.

II.III Location: Friar Lawrence's cell

Friar Lawrence agrees to marry Romeo and Juliet in secret.

Early in the morning, Friar Lawrence gathers various weeds, herbs, and flowers. Romeo enters, and tells him that he has fallen in love with Juliet and has come to ask him to marry them that very day. Though skeptical at how quickly Romeo has forgotten Rosaline, Friar Lawrence agrees. He hopes that their marriage might end the feud between the Montagues and Capulets.

II.IV Location: Verona. A street

Romeo sends Juliet a message with the nurse: they will be married in the afternoon.

Later that morning, Mercutio and Benvolio converse about Romeo: he did not come home the previous night, and Tybalt has challenged him to a duel. Mercutio describes Tybalt as a master swordsman and a vain "fashionmonger." Romeo arrives, and he and Mercutio exchange intricate, clever jokes with sexual overtones.

The nurse enters with Peter, looking for Romeo. Mercutio teases and infuriates her. Benvolio and Mercutio leave for dinner at the Montagues' house. Romeo asks the nurse to tell Juliet to go to confession at Friar Lawrence's cell that afternoon. There they will be married. The nurse agrees to deliver the message, and to set up a cloth ladder at Juliet's window for Romeo that night.

II.V Location: Juliet's chamber

The nurse tells Juliet that Romeo will marry her at Friar Lawrence's cell that day.

Juliet impatiently waits for the nurse, whom she sent to meet Romeo three hours earlier. At last the nurse returns, and Juliet anxiously presses her for news. The nurse first claims to be too tired and out of breath to talk, but then relents and tells Juliet that Romeo will marry her at Friar Lawrence's cell that day.

II.VI Location: Friar Lawrence's cell

Friar Lawrence counsels Romeo.

Romeo and Friar Lawrence wait for Juliet. Friar Lawrence counsels Romeo to love moderately, for "violent delights have violent ends" (II.v.9). Juliet arrives, and they leave to perform the ceremony.

ACT III

Romeo kills Tybalt and is exiled from Verona.

III.I Location: Verona. A street

Romeo is exiled from Verona for killing Tybalt, who killed Mercutio.

Benvolio tells Mercutio that he fears a brawl in such boiling weather. Tybalt enters with a group of cronies. He and Mercutio taunt each other. When Romeo arrives, Tybalt tries to provoke him, but Romeo, who has just married Tybalt's cousin Juliet, refuses to be provoked. Mercutio, angered by Romeo's submissiveness, provokes Tybalt, and the two fight. In an attempt to restore peace, Romeo throws himself between the combatants. Tybalt stabs Mercutio under Romeo's arm. As Mercutio falls, Tybalt and his men hurry away. Mercutio dies, cursing both the Montagues and the Capulets: "A plague o' both your houses" (III.i.87). Enraged, Romeo declares that his love for Juliet has made him effeminate. When Tybalt, still angry, storms back onto the scene, Romeo draws his sword. They fight, and Romeo kills Tybalt. As a group of outraged citizens approaches, Romeo flees, at Benvolio's urging. Prince Escalus arrives on the scene. Benvolio explains what happened, and Prince Escalus exiles Romeo on pain of death.

III.II Location: Juliet's chamber

The nurse tells Juliet about Tybalt's death and Romeo's banishment.

Juliet longs for night to fall so that Romeo will come to her. The nurse rushes in and tells her that Romeo killed Tybalt and has been exiled. Juliet first curses nature for putting "the spirit of a fiend" in Romeo's "sweet flesh" (III.ii.81–82), but then rushes to Romeo's defense when the nurse curses Romeo, too. The nurse promises to sneak Romeo into Juliet's room for their wedding night.

III.III Location: Friar Lawrence's cell

Friar Lawrence and the nurse calm the despondent Romeo down.

Friar Lawrence announces to Romeo that he has been banished from Verona. Romeo collapses to the floor in grief. The nurse arrives and tells Romeo that Juliet still loves him. Friar Lawrence devises a plan: Romeo and Juliet will spend the night together, but Romeo will leave Verona before morning. He will stay in Mantua until the friar can announce their marriage.

III.IV Location: Capulet's house

Capulet decides to marry Juliet to Paris in three days.

In conversation with Paris, Capulet decides that because of the recent tragedy of Tybalt's death, he has not had the chance to speak with Juliet about Paris properly. Capulet promises Juliet to Paris, and the wedding is planned for Thursday, three days hence.

III.V Location: Juliet's chamber

Romeo leaves Juliet after their wedding night; Capulet announces that Juliet must marry Paris in two days' time.

Romeo and Juliet have spent the night together. Before dawn, Romeo prepares to leave. Juliet first urges him to stay because she thinks the day is not yet near, but when he mentions that he will be put to death if he is discovered, she tells him that he must flee. The nurse enters to warn Juliet that Lady Capulet approaches. Romeo and Juliet tearfully part. Romeo climbs out the window. They both think that the other is pale, as though dead. He hurries away.

Lady Capulet enters. Misinterpreting that Juliet's tears are for Tybalt, she condemns Romeo. Juliet answers her in double entendres—Lady Capulet thinks that Juliet longs for Romeo's death, but we know that Juliet longs for Romeo. Lady Capulet tells Juliet that Capulet has arranged for her to be married on Thursday. Juliet is appalled. Capulet enters the chamber. Enraged to hear that Juliet refuses to marry Paris, he threatens to disown her. Lady Capulet refuses to intercede on Juliet's behalf, and she and Capulet storm away.

When Juliet asks her nurse for advice, the nurse suggests she marry Paris. Though disgusted by her nurse's disloyalty, Juliet pretends to agree, and tells her she is going to Friar Lawrence to make confession. If Friar Lawrence cannot help, Juliet muses to herself, she can always kill herself.

ACT IV

On Friar Lawrence's advice, Juliet takes a potion so as to appear dead on the morning of her wedding.

IV.I Location: Friar Lawrence's cell

Friar Lawrence proposes a plan: Juliet will avoid marrying Paris by taking a potion that will make her look dead.

Friar Lawrence speaks to Paris about his impending marriage to Juliet. Paris says that Capulet wants to marry Juliet to distract her from grieving for Tybalt. Juliet enters, and Paris speaks to her very courteously, if arrogantly. Juliet responds with indifference. Once Friar Lawrence ushers Paris away, Juliet begs for Friar Lawrence's help, saying that she would rather kill herself than marry Paris. The friar proposes a plan: Juliet will consent to marry Paris. Then, on the night before the wedding, she will drink a sleeping potion that will make her appear dead. The friar will send to Mantua for Romeo, who will retrieve her from the Capulet tomb before she wakes up. Juliet consents, and Friar Lawrence gives her the sleeping potion.

IV.II Location: Capulet's house

Juliet apologizes to her parents and agrees to marry Paris.

Juliet returns home, where Capulet and Lady Capulet are preparing for the wedding. She surprises her parents by repenting her disobedience and cheerfully agreeing to marry Paris. Capulet moves the wedding up to Wednesday, the next day.

IV.III Location: Juliet's chamber

Terrified of the consequences, Juliet drinks the sleeping potion.

Juliet asks both the nurse and Lady Capulet to let her spend the night alone. Alone, she prepares to drink the sleeping potion. She is terrified. The potion may kill her, or she may awaken in the tomb early and go mad with fear. She drinks to Romeo.

IV.IV Location: Juliet's chamber

In the morning, Juliet is discovered dead.

The next morning, the day of the wedding, Capulet sends the nurse to rouse Juliet. The nurse finds Juliet dead and begins to wail, soon joined by both Lady Capulet and Capulet. Paris arrives with Friar Lawrence and a group of musicians for the wedding. Friar Lawrence urges them all to cease lamentation and prepare for the funeral. They all exit.

Peter enters and asks the musicians to play a happy tune to cheer him up. They think it inappropriate, and Peter and the musicians insult one another. The musicians decide to wait for the funeral lunch.

ACT V

Romeo and Juliet both kill themselves thinking the other dead; the Montagues and the Capulets reconcile in tragedy.

V.I Location: Mantua

Romeo hears of Juliet's death and purchases poison.

Romeo describes his dream: Juliet found him dead, but breathed life into his body by kissing him. Romeo's servant Balthasar arrives from Verona and tells Romeo that Juliet has died. Romeo writes a letter to his father Montague, and plans to return to Verona that night. Balthasar is afraid to return to Verona for fear that Romeo may do something rash, but Romeo insists.

Alone, Romeo resolves to "lie with Juliet" that night. He finds an impoverished apothecary (a druggist), and offers him much money for poison. Although selling poison is illegal in Mantua, the apothecary needs the money and consents. Again alone, Romeo vows to kill himself at Juliet's tomb.

V.II Location: Friar Lawrence's cell

Friar Lawrence finds out that Romeo has not heard about Juliet's false death.

Friar John, whom Friar Lawrence had sent to Mantua with a letter for Romeo, explains to Friar Lawrence that he could not reach Mantua because there was an outbreak of the plague and he was quarantined on the way. Friar Lawrence realizes that he will have to fetch Juliet from the tomb when she wakes up. He sends another letter to Romeo, planning to keep Juliet in his cell until Romeo arrives.

V.III   Location: Capulet's tomb

Romeo kills Paris and then drinks poison at Juliet's body; Juliet wakes to find Romeo dead and stabs herself; the Montagues and the Capulets are finally united in tragedy.

Paris enters with a page bearing a torch. He orders the page to withdraw and scatters flowers on Juliet's grave. The page whistles to warn him that someone approaches, and Paris withdraws into the darkness. Romeo, carrying a crowbar, enters with Balthasar. He sends Balthasar away and gives him a letter for Montague to be delivered in the morning. Balthasar withdraws, but mistrusting Romeo's intentions, lingers to observe.

Still hidden, Paris recognizes Romeo as Tybalt's murderer. Thinking that Romeo has come to deface the Capulet tomb, Paris accosts Romeo. They fight. Paris's page runs off to alert the civil watch. Romeo kills Paris. Dying, Paris asks to be laid near Juliet in the tomb, and Romeo consents. Romeo finds Juliet still fresh and beautiful in her tomb. He kisses Juliet, drinks the poison, kisses Juliet again, and dies.

Friar Lawrence approaches, and Balthasar tells him that Romeo is in the tomb. Troubled, Friar Lawrence enters to find Paris and Romeo both dead. At that moment Juliet wakes. Friar Lawrence hears the arriving watch and tells Juliet that both Romeo and Paris are dead, and that she must leave with him. She refuses, and Friar Lawrence leaves without her. Juliet sees Romeo dead, and surmises that he has taken poison. Hearing the watch approach, Juliet kills herself with Romeo's dagger and falls upon his body.

The watchmen detain Balthasar and Friar Lawrence. Prince Escalus and the Capulets enter. Romeo, Juliet, and Paris—all dead—are discovered in the tomb. Montague arrives. Lady Montague has died of grief for Romeo's exile. Friar Lawrence reveals to all the story of Romeo and Juliet's secret marriage and its consequences. Romeo's letter to Montague, which Balthasar gives to Prince Escalus, confirms Friar Lawrence's story. Prince Escalus scolds the Capulets and Montagues, and they clasp hands and agree to put their vendetta behind them. Montague vows to build a golden statue of Juliet, and Capulet promises to raise Romeo's likeness in gold beside hers.

ANALYSIS OF MAJOR CHARACTERS IN *ROMEO AND JULIET*

JULIET

Juliet's development from a wide-eyed girl into a self-assured, loyal, and capable woman is one of Shakespeare's early triumphs of characterization. It also marks one of his most confident and rounded treatments of a female character.

Though Juliet begins the play a naïve, sheltered child, she gives glimpses of her determination, strength, and sober-mindedness from her earliest scenes. At her mother's request, she promises to consider Paris as a possible husband, but only to the precise degree her mother has stated. Juliet will accede to her mother's wishes, but she will not go out of her way to fall in love with Paris.

Though Juliet loves Romeo, she is able to see and criticize his rash decisions and his tendency to romanticize things. After Romeo kills Tybalt and is banished, Juliet does not follow him blindly. She makes a logical and heartfelt decision that her loyalty and love for Romeo must be her guiding priorities. She cuts herself loose from her prior social moorings to her nurse, her parents, and her social position in order to try to rejoin her husband. When she wakes in the tomb to find Romeo dead, she kills herself not out of weakness, but out of loyalty and love. Indeed, her method of suicide requires more nerve than Romeo's easy poison.

ROMEO

Despite the fact that the epithet "Romeo" has become synonymous with "lover," Romeo's relation to love is not so simple. At the beginning of the play, Romeo's Rosaline-induced histrionics seem rather juvenile. Romeo is a great reader of love poetry, and the portrayal of his love for Rosaline suggests that he loves, as he kisses, "by th' book"—that is, according to the rules and without originality. The love he shares with Juliet is far deeper, more authentic and unique than his puppy love for Rosaline. Romeo's love matures over the course of the play from the shallow desire to be in love to a profound and intense passion.

Romeo's deep capacity for love is merely a part of his larger capacity for intense feeling of all kinds. Romeo lacks the capacity for moderation. Love compels him to sneak into the garden of his enemy's daughter, risking death simply to catch a glimpse of her. Anger compels him to kill his wife's cousin in a reckless duel to avenge the death of his friend. Despair compels him to suicide upon hearing of Juliet's death. Such extreme behavior dominates Romeo's character throughout the play and contributes to the ultimate tragedy that befalls the lovers.

MERCUTIO

With a lightning-quick wit and a clever mind, Mercutio is a scene stealer and one of the most memorable characters in all of Shakespeare's works. Though he constantly puns, jokes, and teases—sometimes in fun, sometimes with bitterness—Mercutio is not a mere jester or prankster. With his wild words, Mercutio punctures the romantic sentiments and blind self-love that exist within the play. He mocks Romeo's self-indulgence just as he ridicules Tybalt's hauteur and adherence to fashion. The critic Stephen Greenblatt describes Mercutio as a force within the play that functions to deflate the possibility of romantic love and the power of tragic fate. Unlike the other characters who blame their deaths on fate, Mercutio dies cursing all Montagues and Capulets. Mercutio believes that specific people are responsible for his death rather than some external impersonal force.

THEMES, MOTIFS, & SYMBOLS IN *ROMEO AND JULIET*

THEMES

THE POWER OF LOVE In *Romeo and Juliet,* love is a violent, ecstatic, overpowering force that supersedes all other values, loyalties, and emotions. In the course of the play, the young lovers are driven to defy their entire social world: families ("Deny thy father and refuse thy name," Juliet asks, "Or if thou wilt not, be but sworn my love, / And I'll no longer be a Capulet"); friends (Romeo abandons Mercutio and Benvolio after the feast in order to go to Juliet's garden); and ruler (Romeo returns to Verona for Juliet's sake after being exiled by the prince on pain of death in II.i.76–78). Love in *Romeo and Juliet* is a brutal, powerful emotion that captures individuals and catapults them against their world and, at times, against themselves.

Love's strength and power is evidenced by the way descriptions of love consistently fail to capture its entirety. At times love is described in the terms of religion, as in the fourteen lines when Romeo and Juliet first meet. At others it is described as a sort of magic: "Alike bewitchèd by the charm of looks" (II.Prologue.6). Juliet, perhaps, most perfectly describes her love for Romeo by refusing to describe it: "But my true love is grown to such excess / I cannot sum up some of half my wealth" (III.i.33–34). Love, in other words, resists any single metaphor because it is too powerful to be so easily contained or understood.

LOVE LEADS TO VIOLENCE Romeo and Juliet's love is linked with death from the moment of its inception: Tybalt notices that Romeo has crashed the feast and determines to kill him just as Romeo catches sight of Juliet and falls instantly in love with her. From that point on, love seems to push the lovers closer to violence, not farther from it. Romeo and Juliet are plagued with thoughts of suicide and a willingness to experience it: in III.iii, Romeo brandishes a knife in Friar Lawrence's cell and threatens to kill himself after he has been banished from Verona and his love. Juliet also pulls a knife in order to take her own life in Friar Lawrence's presence just three scenes later. After Capulet decides that Juliet will marry Paris, Juliet says, "If all else fail, myself have power to die" (III.v.242). Finally, each imagines that the other looks dead the morning after their first, and only, sexual experience ("Methinks I see thee," Juliet says, " … as one dead in the bottom of a tomb" (III.v.242; III.v.55–56). This theme continues until its inevitable conclusion: double suicide. This tragic choice is the highest, most potent expression of love that Romeo and Juliet can make. It is only through death that they can preserve their love, and their love is so profound that they are willing to end their lives in its defense. In the play, love emerges as an amoral thing, leading as much to destruction as to happiness.

THE TENSION BETWEEN SELF AND SOCIETY Much of *Romeo and Juliet* involves the lovers' struggles against public and social institutions that either explicitly or implicitly oppose their love. Such structures range from the concrete to the abstract: families and the placement of familial power in the father; law and the desire for public order; religion; and the social importance placed on masculine honor. These institutions often come into conflict with each other. The importance of honor, for example, time and again results in brawls that disturb the public peace.

Romeo and Juliet may be viewed as a battle between the responsibilities and actions demanded by social institutions and those demanded by the private desires of the individual. Romeo and Juliet's appreciation of night, with its darkness and privacy, and their renunciation of their names, with the attendant loss of obligation, make sense in the context of individuals who wish to escape the public world. But the lovers cannot stop the night from becoming day, and Romeo cannot cease being a Montague simply because he wants to, because the rest of the world will not let him. The lovers' suicides can be understood as the ultimate night; the ultimate privacy.

MOTIFS

LIGHT AND DARK IMAGERY One of the play's most consistent visual motifs is the contrast between light and dark, often in terms of night and day imagery. This contrast is not given a particular metaphoric meaning. Light is not always good, and dark is not always evil. On the contrary, light and dark are used to provide a sensory contrast and to hint at opposed alternatives. One of the more important instances of this motif is Romeo's lengthy meditation on the sun and the moon during the balcony scene, in which Juliet, metaphorically described as the sun, is seen as banishing the "envious moon" and transforming the night into day (II.i.46). A similar blurring of night and day occurs in the early morning hours after the lovers' only night together. Romeo, forced to leave for exile in the morning, and Juliet, not wanting him to leave her room, both try to pretend that it is still night and that the light is actually darkness: "More light and light, more dark and dark our woes" (III.v.36).

MULTIPLE PERSPECTIVES Shakespeare includes numerous speeches and scenes in Romeo and Juliet that hint at alternative ways to evaluate the play. Shakespeare uses two main devices in this regard: Mercutio and servants. Mercutio consistently skewers the viewpoints of all the other characters in play: he sees Romeo's devotion to love as a sort of blindness that robs Romeo from himself. Similarly, he sees Tybalt's devotion to honor as blind and stupid. His punning and the Queen Mab speech can be interpreted as undercutting virtually every passion evident in the play. Mercutio serves as a critic of the delusions of righteousness and grandeur held by the characters around him.

Where Mercutio is a nobleman who openly criticizes other nobles, the views offered by servants in the play are less explicit. There is the nurse who lost her baby and husband, the servant Peter who cannot read, the musicians who care about their lost wages and their lunches, and the apothecary who cannot afford to make the moral choice. The lower classes present a second tragic world to counter that of the nobility. The nobles' world is full of grand tragic gestures. The servants' world, in contrast, is characterized by simple needs, and by early deaths brought about by disease and poverty rather than dueling and grand passions. Where the nobility almost seem to revel in their capacity for drama, the servants' lives are such that they cannot afford tragedy of the epic kind.

SYMBOLS

THUMB-BITING In I.i, the buffoonish Samson begins a brawl between the Montagues and Capulets by flicking his thumbnail from behind his upper teeth, an insulting gesture known as biting the thumb. He engages in this juvenile and vulgar display because he wants to get into a fight with the Montagues but doesn't want to be accused of starting the fight by making an explicit insult. Because of his timidity, he settles for being annoying rather than challenging. Biting the thumb, a silly gesture, represents the foolishness of the Capulet-Montague feud.

QUEEN MAB In I.iv, Mercutio delivers a dazzling speech about the fairy Queen Mab, who rides through the night on her tiny wagon bringing dreams to sleepers. The dreams she brings do not bring out the best sides of the dreamers. Rather, they confirm their vices—greed, violence, lust. The description of Mab and her carriage goes to extravagant lengths to emphasize how tiny and insubstantial she and her accoutrements are. Queen Mab and her carriage symbolize the power of waking fantasies, daydreams, and desires. Through the Queen Mab imagery, Mercutio suggests that all desires and fantasies are as nonsensical and fragile as Mab. This point of view contrasts starkly with that of Romeo and Juliet, who see their love as real and ennobling.

IMPORTANT QUOTATIONS FROM *ROMEO AND JULIET*

1. *But soft, what light through yonder window breaks?*
   It is the east, and Juliet is the sun.
   Arise, fair sun, and kill the envious moon,
   Who is already sick and pale with grief
   That thou, her maid, art far more fair than she . . .
   The brightness of her cheek would shame those stars
   As daylight doth a lamp; her eye in heaven
   Would through the airy region stream so bright
   That birds would sing and think it were not night.

Location: II.i.44-64
Speaker: Romeo
Context: After Capulet's dance, Romeo hides in the Capulet orchard and glimpses Juliet at her window.

Juliet's beauty makes Romeo imagine that she is the sun, transforming the darkness into daylight. Romeo likewise personifies the moon, calling it "sick and pale with grief" at the fact that Juliet, the sun, is far brighter and more beautiful. Romeo then compares Juliet to the stars, claiming that she eclipses the stars as daylight overpowers a lamp—her eyes alone shine so bright that they will convince the birds to sing at night as if it were day. The passage introduces one of the play's most beautiful and famous sequences, and plays with the light/dark imagery that peppers the play.

2. *O Romeo, Romeo,*
   Wherefore art thou Romeo?
   Deny thy father and refuse thy name,
   Or if thou wilt not, be but sworn my love,
   And I'll no longer be a Capulet.

Location: II.i.74–78
Speaker: Juliet
Context: Unaware that Romeo is hiding in the orchard, Juliet declares her love for him.

Juliet asks why (wherefore) Romeo must be Romeo—why he must be a Montague, the son of her family's greatest enemy. Still unaware of Romeo's presence, she asks him to deny his family for her love. She adds, however, that if he will not, she will deny her family in order to be with him if he merely tells her that he loves her.

The tension between social and family identity (represented by one's name) and personal identity is one of the important themes explored in the play. Juliet thinks of Romeo in individual terms, and thus her love for him overrides her family's hatred for the Montague name. She says that if Romeo were not called "Romeo" or "Montague," he would still be the person she loves. "What's in a name?" she asks. "That which we call a rose / By any other word would smell as sweet" (II.i.85–86).

3. *O, then I see Queen Mab hath been with you . . .*
   She is the fairies' midwife, and she comes
   In shape no bigger than an agate stone
   On the forefinger of an alderman,
   Drawn with a team of little atomi

Athwart men's noses as they lie asleep.

Location: I.iv.53–59
Speaker: Mercutio
Context: Mercutio tries to mock Romeo into coming to the Capulet feast.

Mercutio's famous Queen Mab speech has some interesting thematic implications. The main point of the passage is that the dreams Queen Mab brings are directly related to the person who dreams them — lovers dream of love, soldiers of war, etc. But in the process of making this rather prosaic point, Mercutio falls into a sort of wild bitterness in which he seems to see dreams as destructive and delusional.

---

4. *From forth the fatal loins of these two foes*
   A pair of star-crossed lovers take their life,
   Whose misadventured piteous overthrows
   Doth with their death bury their parents' strife …

Location: Prologue.5–8
Speaker: Chorus
Context: the Chorus summarizes the action of the play

O, I am fortune's fool!

Location: III.i.131
Speaker: Romeo
Context: Romeo has just killed Tybalt, hours after marrying Tybalt's cousin Juliet

---

Then I defy you, stars!

Location: V.i.24
Speaker: Romeo
Context: Romeo has been misinformed that Juliet is dead.

This trio of quotes advances the theme of fate as it plays out through the story. The Chorus's remark that Romeo and Juliet are "star-crossed" and fated to "take their li[ves]" informs the audience that the lovers are destined to die tragically. Romeo's "O, I am fortune's fool!" illustrates the fact that Romeo sees himself as subject to the whims of fate. When he cries out "Then I defy you, stars," after learning of Juliet's death, he declares himself openly opposed to the destiny that so grieves him. Sadly, in "defying" fate he actually brings it about. Romeo's suicide prompts Juliet to kill herself, thereby ironically fulfilling the lovers' tragic destiny.

THE MERCHANT OF VENICE

Shylock tries to use the law to butcher the merchant Antonio, but the resourceful Portia disguises herself as a legal scholar and saves Antonio.

THE MERCHANT OF VENICE IN CONTEXT

The Merchant of Venice was probably written in either 1596 or 1597, after Shakespeare had written such plays as *Romeo and Juliet* and *Richard III*, but before he penned the great tragedies of his later years. Its basic plot outline, which features a merchant, a poor suitor, a fair lady, and a villainous Jew, is found in a number of contemporary Italian story collections. Shakespeare borrowed several details, such the choice of chests that Portia inflicts on all her suitors, from preexisting sources. *The Merchant of Venice's* Italian setting and marriage plot are typical of Shakespeare's earlier comedies, but the characters of Portia, Shakespeare's first great heroine, and Shylock, an unforgettable villain, mark a new level of achievement for Shakespeare.

Shylock is one of literature's most memorable villains, but many readers and playgoers have also found him a compelling and sympathetic figure. The question of whether or not Shakespeare endorses the anti-Semitism of the Christian characters in the play has been much debated. Jews in Shakespeare's England were a marginalized group, and portrayals of Jews as villains and fools were common. For example, Christopher Marlowe's *The Jew of Malta*, a bloody farce about a murderous Jewish villain, was a great popular success. Shakespeare certainly draws on this anti-Semitic tradition in portraying Shylock, exploiting Jewish stereotypes for comic effect. But Shylock is a more complex character than the Jew in Marlowe's play, and Shakespeare makes it clear that his hatred is born of the mistreatment he has suffered in a Christian society.

THE MERCHANT OF VENICE: KEY FACTS

Full title: The Comical History of the Merchant of Venice, or Otherwise Called the Jew of Venice

Time and place written: 1598; London, England

Date of first publication: 1600 (in quarto)

Genre: Comedy

Setting (time): Sixteenth century

Setting (place): Venice and Belmont, Italy

Protagonist: Bassanio

Major conflict: Antonio defaults on a loan from Shylock.

THE MERCHANT OF VENICE: CHARACTER LIST

Antonio   A merchant. Antonio's love for his friend Bassanio prompts him to sign a contract with Shylock and almost lose his life. Antonio is often inexplicably melancholy. As Shylock points out, he dislikes all Jews. However, Antonio's friends love him, and he does show mercy to Shylock.

Bassanio   A kinsman and dear friend of Antonio's. Bassanio's love for the wealthy Portia leads him to borrow money from Shylock with Antonio as his guarantor. Bassanio is an ineffectual businessman but a worthy suitor.

Balthasar   Portia's servant.

Doctor Bellario   A wealthy Paduan lawyer and Portia's cousin. Doctor Bellario never appears in the play, but he sends Portia the letters of introduction she needs to make her appearance in court.

The Duke of Venice   The ruler of Venice. The duke presides over Antonio's trial.

Graziano   A friend of Bassanio's. A coarse young man, Graziano is Shylock's most vocal and insulting critic during the trial. Graziano falls in love with and eventually weds Portia's lady-in-waiting, Nerissa.

Jessica   Shylock's daughter. Jessica hates life in her father's house and elopes with a young Christian gentleman, Lorenzo. The play's characters question the fate of her soul, wondering if her marriage can overcome the fact that she was born a Jew.

Lancelot Gobbo   Bassanio's servant. A comical, clownish, punning figure, Lancelot leaves Shylock's service in order to work for Bassanio.

Lorenzo   A friend of Bassanio's and Antonio's. Lorenzo is in love with Shylock's daughter, Jessica, with whom he elopes to Belmont.

Nerissa   Portia's lady-in-waiting and confidante. Nerissa marries Graziano and escorts Portia to Venice by disguising herself as a law clerk.

Old Gobbo   Lancelot's father. Old Gobbo is a servant in Venice.

Portia   A wealthy heiress from Belmont. Portia's beauty is matched only by her intelligence. Bound by a clause in her father's will that forces her to marry whichever suitor chooses correctly from among three chests, Portia is nonetheless able to marry her true love, Bassanio. Portia, in the disguise of a young law clerk, saves Antonio from Shylock.

The Prince of Aragon   An arrogant Spanish nobleman. The prince attempts to win Portia's hand, but makes an unwise choice of chests.

The Prince of Morocco   A Moorish prince. The prince seeks Portia's hand in marriage, asking her to ignore his dark countenance. He picks the wrong chest.

Salerio   A Venetian gentleman and friend to Antonio, Bassanio, and Lorenzo. Salerio escorts the newlyweds Jessica and Lorenzo to Belmont, and returns with Bassanio and Graziano for Antonio's trial. He is often almost indistinguishable from his companion Solanio.

Solanio   A Venetian gentleman. Solanio is a frequent companion to Salerio.

Shylock   A Jewish moneylender. Angered by his mistreatment at the hands of Venice's Christians, particularly Antonio, Shylock schemes to take revenge by demanding a pound of Antonio's flesh in payment for a debt.

Tubal   One of Shylock's friends.

THE MERCHANT OF VENICE: PLOT OVERVIEW

Bassanio, a nobleman of Venice, wants to marry Portia, a wealthy heiress of Belmont, but he needs money so he can go to Belmont in style. Antonio, a wealthy merchant of Venice who loves Bassanio, agrees to guarantee a large loan from Shylock, the Jewish moneylender. Shylock hates Antonio because Antonio has abused him, so he makes Antonio guarantee a pound of his flesh if the money is not paid on time. Bassanio goes to Belmont and wins Portia by successfully passing a test in which he has to choose between three chests. Immediately thereafter, he receives word that Antonio has lost all of his ships at sea and cannot repay the loan.

He returns to Venice with Portia's money, but Shylock insists on having his pound of flesh. Portia disguises herself as a legal scholar and argues in court that Shylock can have the flesh but must not spill any blood. Moreover, Shylock is found guilty of conspiring against the life of a Venetian and must forfeit his land. He is allowed to keep most of his money on the condition that he convert to Christianity and leave all of his money to his daughter, Jessica, and Lorenzo, the Christian man she secretly married.

THE MERCHANT OF VENICE: SCENE SUMMARY

ACT I

Antonio guarantees a loan for Bassanio, agreeing to give Shylock a pound of his own flesh if the loan is late; Portia complains about her disagreeable suitors and the stipulation of her father's will.

I.I Location: a street in Venice

Antonio agrees to guarantee a loan that his friend Bassanio needs in order to woo the wealthy Portia.

Antonio, a Venetian merchant, complains to his friends, Salerio and Solanio, that a sadness has overtaken him and dulled his faculties, although he does not know why. Salerio and Solanio suggest that his sadness must be due to his commercial investments, for Antonio has dispatched several trade ships to various ports. Salerio says it is impossible for Antonio not to feel sad at the thought of the perilous ocean sinking his entire investment, but Antonio says his business ventures do not depend on the safe passage of any one ship. Solanio declares that Antonio must be in love, but Antonio dismisses the suggestion.

The three men encounter Bassanio, Antonio's kinsman, walking with two friends named Lorenzo and Graziano. Salerio and Solanio bid Antonio farewell and depart. When Graziano notices Antonio's unhappiness and suggests that the merchant worries too much about business, Antonio says he is but a player on a stage, destined to play a sad part. Graziano warns Antonio against becoming the type of man who affects a solemn demeanor in order to gain a reputation as a wise man. He takes his leave with Lorenzo. Bassanio jokes that Graziano does not have much to say. Antonio asks Bassanio to tell him about the clandestine love that Bassanio is harboring. Bassanio admits that although he already owes Antonio a substantial sum of money from his earlier, more extravagant days, he has fallen in love with Portia, a rich heiress from Belmont, and hopes to win her heart by holding his own with her other wealthy and powerful suitors. In order to woo Portia, Bassanio needs to borrow more money from Antonio. Antonio says he cannot give Bassanio another loan, because all his money is tied up in his present business ventures, but he offers to guarantee any loan Bassanio can get.

I.II Location: Portia's house in Belmont

Portia complains about her various unpleasant suitors and the fact that any man who wants to marry her must choose the correct chest from three chests.

Portia complains to her lady-in-waiting, Nerissa, that she is weary of the world. Her deceased father's will stipulates that she cannot choose her husband for herself. Instead, Portia's various suitors must choose between three chests, one of gold, one of silver, and one of lead, in the hopes of selecting the one that contains her portrait. The man who guesses correctly will win Portia's hand in marriage, but those who guess incorrectly must swear never to marry anyone. Nerissa lists the suitors who have come to guess—a Neapolitan prince, a Palatine count, a French nobleman, an English baron, a Scottish lord, and the nephew of the duke of Saxony—and Portia criticizes their many hilarious faults. She says the Neapolitan prince is too fond of his horse, the Palatine count is too serious, the Englishman lacks any knowledge of Italian or the other languages Portia speaks, and the German suitor is a drunk. Each of these suitors has left without even attempting a guess for fear of the penalty for guessing wrong. This relieves Portia. Both she and Nerissa remember Bassanio, who has visited once before, as the suitor most worthy of praise. A servant enters to tell Portia that the Prince of Morocco will arrive soon, which annoys Portia.

I.III Location: a street in Venice

Antonio agrees to give Shylock a pound of his own flesh if the loan is not repaid on time.

Shylock, a Jewish moneylender, agrees to loan Bassanio three thousand ducats for a term of three months. Bassanio assures Shylock that Antonio will guarantee the loan, but Shylock is doubtful because Antonio's wealth is currently invested in business ventures that may fail. In the end, however, Shylock decides that Antonio's guarantee of the loan is sufficient assurance, and asks to speak with him. When Antonio arrives, Shylock, in an aside, confesses his hatred for Antonio. Shylock says that Antonio is a Christian who lends money without interest, which makes it more difficult to practice usury, in which money is lent out at exorbitant interest rates. Shylock is also incensed by Antonio's frequent public denunciations of Shylock. Antonio makes it clear to Shylock that he is not in the habit of borrowing or lending money, but has decided to make an exception on behalf of his friend Bassanio. As they talk, Antonio chastises the business of usury, which Shylock defends as a way to thrive.

As he calculates the interest on Bassanio's loan, Shylock remembers the many times that Antonio has cursed him, calling him a "misbeliever, cut-throat, dog / And spit upon [his] Jewish gaberdine" (I.iii.107–108). Antonio responds that he is likely to insult Shylock again, and insists that Shylock lend him the money as an enemy. Such an arrangement, Antonio claims, will make it easier for Shylock to exact a harsh penalty if the loan is not repaid. Assuring Antonio that he means to be friends, Shylock offers to make the loan without interest. Instead, he suggests, seemingly in jest, that Antonio should forfeit a pound of his own flesh if the loan is not repaid in due time. Bassanio warns Antonio against entering such an agreement, but Antonio assures him he will have no trouble repaying the debt, since his ships will soon bring him wealth far exceeding the value of the loan. Shylock attempts to dismiss Bassanio's suspicions, asking what profit he stands to make by procuring a pound of Antonio's flesh.

As Shylock heads off to the notary's office to sign the bond, Antonio remarks on Shylock's newfound generosity: "The Hebrew will turn Christian; he grows kind" (I.iii.174). Bassanio remains suspicious of the arrangement, but Antonio reminds him that his ships will arrive within the next two months.

ACT II

Lancelot leaves Shylock's employ to serve Bassanio; two princes try and fail to win Portia's hand; Jessica runs away from Shylock and elopes with Lorenzo, enraging Shylock.

II.I Location: Portia's Home, Belmont

The Prince of Morocco arrives to woo Portia.

The Prince of Morocco arrives to seek Portia's hand in marriage. He asks Portia not to judge him by his dark complexion, assuring her that he is as good as any European man. Portia reminds the prince that her own tastes do not matter, since the chest-picking process puts all the suitors on the same level. With a lengthy proclamation of his own bravery and heroism, the prince asks Portia to lead him to the chests. She reminds him that the penalty for guessing incorrectly is that he must remain unmarried forever. The prince accepts this stipulation, and Portia leads him off to dinner.

II.II Location: A street in Venice

Lancelot leaves Shylock to serve Bassanio; Bassanio agrees to take Graziano to Belmont with him.

Lancelot Gobbo, a servant of Shylock's, struggles to decide whether or not he should run away from his master. Part of him, which he calls "[t]he fiend … at mine elbow," wants to leave, while his conscience reminds him of his honest nature and urges him to stay (II.ii.2). Although Lancelot has no specific complaints, he seems troubled by the fact that his master is Jewish, or, as Lancelot puts it, "a kind of devil" (II.ii.19). Just when Lancelot determines to run away, his father, Old Gobbo, enters. The old man is blind, and he asks how to get to Shylock's house, where he hopes to find young Lancelot. Because his father does not recognize him, Lancelot decides to play a prank on him—he gives the old man confusing directions and reports that Lancelot is dead.

Lancelot soon reveals the deception, but Old Gobbo doubts that the man before him is his son. Lancelot convinces his father of his identity. He confesses to his father that he is leaving Shylock's employment in the hopes of serving Bassanio. Just then, Bassanio enters and the two plead with him to accept Lancelot as his servant. Bassanio takes several moments to understand their bumbling proposition, but he accepts the offer. Bassanio then meets Graziano, who asks to accompany him to Belmont. Bassanio agrees on the condition that Graziano tame his wild behavior. Graziano promises to behave, and the two men plan a night of merriment to celebrate their departure.

II.III Location: Shylock's house

Shylock bids Lancelot a sad farewell.

Shylock's daughter, Jessica, bids good-bye to Lancelot. She tells him that his presence made life with her father more bearable. Jessica gives Lancelot a letter to carry to Bassanio's friend Lorenzo, and Lancelot leaves, almost too tearful to say good-bye. Jessica, left alone, confesses that although she feels guilty for being ashamed of her father, she is only his daughter by blood, not by actions. She hopes to escape Shylock by marrying Lorenzo and converting to Christianity.

II.IV Location: a street in Venice

Lorenzo and his friends discuss the plan for getting Jessica away from Shylock.

Graziano, Lorenzo, Salerio, and Solanio discuss the plan to unite Lorenzo with Jessica. Graziano frets that they are not well-prepared, but Lorenzo assures the men that they have enough time to gather the necessary disguises and torchbearers. As they talk, Lancelot enters bearing Jessica's letter. Lorenzo recognizes the writing, lovingly exclaiming that the hand that penned the message is "whiter than the paper it writ on" (II.iv.13). Lorenzo tells Lancelot to return to Shylock's house and secretly assure Jessica that Lorenzo will not let her down. Lancelot departs, and Lorenzo orders his friends to prepare for the night's festivities. Salerio and Solanio leave. Lorenzo tells Graziano that Jessica will escape from Shylock's house by disguising herself as Lorenzo's torchbearer. Lorenzo gives Graziano the letter and asks Graziano to read it, then leaves, excited.

II.V Location: Shylock's house

Shylock asks Jessica to keep the doors locked and not to look outside.

Shylock warns Lancelot that Bassanio will not be as lenient a master as Shylock himself has been, and Lancelot will no longer be at liberty to overeat and oversleep. Shylock calls for Jessica and tells her he has been summoned for dinner. Worried by a premonition that trouble is brewing, Shylock asks Jessica to keep the doors locked and not look out at the revelry taking place in the streets. Lancelot whispers to Jessica that she must disobey her father and look out the window for the Christian who "will be worth a Jewës eye" (II.v.41). Shylock asks Jessica about her furtive conversation with Lancelot. He says that Lancelot is kind, but he eats and sleeps too much to be a worthwhile servant. After Shylock has left to see Bassanio, Jessica bids him farewell. She thinks that if all goes according to plan, Shylock will soon have lost a daughter, and she a father.

II.VI Location: outside Shylock's house

Jessica, dressed as a page, joins Lorenzo and the others.

As planned, Graziano and Salerio meet in front of Shylock's house. They are anxious because Lorenzo is late, and they think that lovers tend to be early. The garrulous Graziano expounds on Salerio's theory that love is at its best when the lover chases the object of his affection, and that once the lover captures his lady and consummates the relationship, he tends to tire and lose interest. Lorenzo joins them, apologizes for his tardiness, and calls up to Jessica, who appears on the balcony dressed as a page. Jessica tosses him a chest of gold and jewels. She descends and exits with Lorenzo and Salerio. Antonio enters to report that Bassanio is sailing for Belmont immediately. Graziano is obliged to leave the festivities and join Bassanio at once.

II.VII Location: Portia's house

The Prince of Morocco wrongly chooses the gold chest.

Portia shows the Prince of Morocco to the chests, where he will attempt to win her hand by guessing which one contains her portrait. The first chest, made of gold, is inscribed with the words, "Who chooseth me shall gain what many men desire" (II.vii.37). The second, made of silver, reads, "Who chooseth me shall get as much as he deserves" (II.vii.23). The third, a heavy leaden chest, declares, "Who chooseth me must give and hazard all he hath" (II.vii.16). After much pondering, the prince chooses the gold chest, reasoning that only the most precious metal could house the picture of such a beautiful woman. He opens the chest to reveal a skull with a scroll in its eye socket. After reading a short poem chastising him for the folly of his choice, the prince makes a hasty departure. Portia is glad to see him go and hopes that "[a]ll of his complexion choose me so" (II.viii.79).

II.VIII   Location: a street in Venice

Solanio describes Shylock's rage and the disaster that is rumored to have struck Antonio's fleet.

Solanio describes how enraged Shylock was when he learned of Jessica's elopement. Shylock, Solanio tells Salerio, railed against the loss of his daughter and his ducats and shouted a loud, urgent appeal for justice and the law to prevail. Solanio hopes that Antonio is able to pay his debt, but Salerio reminds him of rumors that the long-awaited ships have capsized in the English Channel. The two men remember how Antonio told Bassanio not to allow thoughts of debt or danger to interfere with his courtship of Portia.

II.IX   Location: Portia's house

The Prince of Aragon wrongly picks the silver chest.

The Prince of Aragon is in Belmont to try his luck at winning Portia's hand in marriage. When brought to the chests, he selects the silver one, confident that he "shall get as much as he deserves" (II.ix.35). Inside, he finds a portrait of a blinking idiot, and a poem that condemns him as a fool. Soon after he departs, a messenger arrives to tell Portia that a promising young Venetian, who seems like the perfect suitor, has come to Belmont to try his luck at the chest game. Hoping that it is Bassanio, Portia and Nerissa go out to greet the new suitor.

ACT III

Bassanio marries Portia; Nerissa marries Granziano; Antonio loses all of his ships and is imprisoned; Portia and Nerissa plan to dress up as young men and go to Venice.

III.I   Location: Venice

Shylock curses Jessica, but cheers up when he hears that Antonio is almost certainly ruined.

Salerio and Solanio discuss the rumors that yet another of Antonio's ships has been wrecked. They are joined by Shylock, who accuses them of helping Jessica escape. The two Venetians proudly take credit for their role in Jessica's elopement. Shylock curses his daughter's rebellion, to which Salerio responds, "There is more difference between thy flesh and hers than between jet and ivory" (III.i.32–33). Salerio asks Shylock whether he can confirm the rumors of Antonio's lost vessels. Shylock replies that Antonio will soon be bankrupt and swears to collect his bond. Salerio doubts Shylock's resolve, wondering what the old man will do with a pound of flesh. Shylock replies that Antonio's flesh will at least feed his revenge. In a short monologue, Shylock says Antonio has mistreated him solely because Shylock is a Jew, but now Shylock is determined to apply the lessons of hatred and revenge that Christian intolerance has taught him so well.

Salerio and Solanio head off to meet with Antonio, just as Tubal, a Jewish friend of Shylock's, enters. Tubal announces that he cannot find Jessica. Shylock rants against his daughter. He wishes her dead as he bemoans his losses. He is especially embittered when Tubal reports that Jessica has taken a ring given to Shylock in his bachelor days by a woman named Leah, presumably Jessica's mother. Jessica has traded that ring for a monkey. Shylock's spirits brighten, however, when Tubal reports that Antonio's ships have run into trouble and that Antonio's creditors are certain Antonio is ruined.

III.II   Location: Portia's house

Bassanio chooses the right chest and wins Portia's hand; Nerissa and Granziano announce that they are in love; Antonio writes that he has lost all of his ships.

Portia begs Bassanio to delay choosing between the chests for a day or two, because if Bassanio chooses incorrectly she will lose his company. Bassanio insists on choosing immediately in order to avoid prolonging the torment of living without Portia as his wife. Portia orders music played while her love makes his choice. She compares Bassanio to the Greek hero and demigod Hercules. Like the suitors who have come before him, Bassanio carefully examines the three chests and puzzles over their inscriptions. He rejects the gold chest, saying that "[t]he world is still deceived with ornament" (III.ii.74), while the silver he deems a "pale and common drudge / 'Tween man and man" (III.ii.103–104). After much debate, Bassanio picks the lead chest, which he opens to reveal Portia's portrait, along with a poem congratulating him on his choice and confirming that he has won Portia's hand.

The happy couple promises each other love and devotion, and Portia gives Bassanio a ring that he must never part with, as his removal of it will signify the end of his love for her. Nerissa and Graziano congratulate them and confess that they too have fallen in love with each other. They suggest a double wedding. Lorenzo and Jessica arrive in the midst of this rejoicing, along with Salerio, who gives a letter to Bassanio. In the letter, Antonio writes that all of his ships are lost, and that Shylock plans to collect his pound of flesh. The news provokes a fit of guilt in Bassanio. Portia offers to pay twenty times the sum, but Jessica worries that her father is more interested in revenge than in money. Bassanio reads the letter from Antonio out loud. In the letter, Antonio asks only for a brief reunion before he dies. Portia urges Bassanio to rush to his friend's aid, and Bassanio leaves for Venice.

III.III Location: the Venetian prison

Shylock takes Antonio to prison.

Shylock escorts the bankrupt Antonio to prison. Antonio pleads with Shylock to listen to him, but Shylock refuses. Remembering the many times Antonio called him a dog, Shylock advises Antonio to beware of his bite. Convinced that the duke will grant him justice, Shylock insists that he will have his bond and tells the jailer not to bother speaking to him of mercy. Solanio declares Shylock the worst of men, and Antonio reasons that Shylock hates him for bailing out many of Shylock's debtors. Solanio attempts to comfort Antonio by saying the duke will never allow such a ridiculous contract to stand, but Antonio is not convinced. Venice, Antonio says, is a wealthy trading city with a great reputation for upholding the law, and if the duke breaks that law, Venice's economy may suffer. As Solanio departs, Antonio prays desperately that Bassanio will arrive to "see me pay his debt, and then I care not" (III.iii.36).

III.IV Location: Portia's house

Portia says that she and Nerissa will dress up as young men and visit their husbands in disguise.

Lorenzo assures Portia that Antonio is worthy of all the help she is sending him, and that if Portia only knew the depths of Antonio's love and goodness, she would be proud of her efforts to save him. Portia says she has never regretted doing a good deed, and she could never deny help to anyone so close to Bassanio. Indeed, Antonio and Bassanio are so inseparable that Portia believes saving her husband's friend is no different than saving her own husband (she and Bassanio are now married). She has sworn to live in prayer and contemplation until Bassanio returns to her, and announces that she and Nerissa will go to a nearby monastery. Lorenzo and Jessica will rule the estate in her absence.

Portia sends her servant, Balthasar, to Padua. There, Portia's cousin, Doctor Bellario, will provide Balthasar with certain documents and clothing. Balthasar will take the ferry to Venice, where Portia will be waiting for him him. After Balthasar departs, Portia informs Nerissa that the two of them will dress as young men and pay an incognito visit to their new husbands. When Nerissa asks why, Portia promises to explain on the coach ride to Venice.

III.V Location: Portia's house

Lancelot worries about Jessica's soul; Jessica tells Lorenzo she considers Portia nearly perfect.

Quoting the adage that the sins of the father shall be delivered upon the children, Lancelot says he fears for Jessica's soul. When Jessica claims that she will be saved by her marriage to Lorenzo, Lancelot complains that the conversion of the Jews, who do not eat pork, will have disastrous consequences on the price of bacon. Lorenzo enters and chastises Lancelot for impregnating a Moorish servant. Lancelot delivers a dazzling series of puns in reply and departs to prepare for dinner. When Lorenzo asks Jessica what she thinks of Portia, she responds that the woman is without match, nearly perfect in all respects. Lorenzo jokes that he is as good a spouse as Portia, and leads the way to dinner.

ACT IV

Portia, disguised as a lawyer, saves Antonio from Shylock; she and Nerissa trick their husbands.

IV.I Location: the Venetian courthouse

Portia, disguised as a lawyer, saves Antonio from Shylock; she demands the ring she gave Bassanio as payment, and Bassanio eventually agrees to give it to her.

The court convenes for Antonio's trial. The Duke of Venice greets Antonio and expresses pity for him, calling Shylock an inhuman monster. Antonio says he knows the duke has done all that he can to lawfully counter Shylock's malicious intentions, and that since nothing else can be done, Antonio will respond to Shylock's rage "with a quietness of spirit" (IV.i.11). The duke summons Shylock into the courtroom and addresses him, saying he believes that Shylock only wants to frighten Antonio by extending the drama this far. No one, the duke says, believes that Shylock actually means to inflict such a horrible penalty on Antonio, who has already suffered the loss of his ships. Shylock reiterates his intentions and says that should the court deny him his right, the city's very laws and freedoms will be nullified. Shylock offers no explanation for his insistence other than to say that certain hatreds, like certain passions, are lodged deep in a person's heart. Shylock hates Antonio, and for him that is reason enough.

Bassanio, who has arrived from Belmont, attempts to argue with Shylock, but Antonio tells him his efforts are for naught. Hatred and predation, Antonio says, come as naturally to some men as they do to the wolf. Bassanio offers Shylock six thousand ducats, twice the amount of the original loan, but Shylock turns down the offer, saying he would not forfeit his bond for six times that sum. When the duke asks Shylock how he expects to be shown mercy when he offers none, Shylock says he has no need for mercy, because he has done nothing wrong. Just as the slave-owning Christians of Venice would refuse to set their human property free, Shylock will not relinquish the pound of flesh that belongs to him.

The duke says he has sent messages to the learned lawyer, Doctor Bellario, asking him to come and decide on the matter. News comes that a messenger has arrived from Bellario, and Salerio runs off to fetch him. Bassanio tries, without much success, to cheer the despairing Antonio. Nerissa enters, disguised as a lawyer's clerk, and gives the duke a letter from Bellario. Shylock whets his knife, anticipating a judgment in his favor, and Graziano says he has the soul of a wolf. Shylock ignores these slurs and states resolutely, "I stand here for law" (IV.i.141). The duke alludes to the fact that Bellario's letter mentions a learned young lawyer named Balthasar, and orders Nerissa-as-clerk to admit the young man to the court. The duke then reads the letter in its entirety. In it, Bellario writes that he is ill and cannot come to court, but that he has sent the learned young Balthasar to judge in his stead.

Portia enters, disguised as Balthasar. The duke greets her and asks whether she is familiar with the circumstances of the case. Portia says she knows the case well, and the duke calls Shylock and Antonio before her. Portia asks Antonio if he admits to owing Shylock money. When Antonio says he does, Portia concludes that the Jew must be merciful. Shylock asks why he must show mercy, and Portia says "[t]he quality of mercy is not strained," but is a blessing both to those who provide and to those who receive it (IV.i.179). Because mercy is an attribute of God, Portia reasons, humans approach the divine when they exercise it. Shylock brushes aside her speech and reiterates his demands for justice and revenge.

Portia asks whether Antonio is able to pay the money, and Bassanio offers Shylock twice the sum owed. If need be, Bassanio says, he is willing to pay the bond ten times over, or with his own life. Bassanio begs the court to bend the law slightly in order to exonerate Antonio, reasoning that such a small infraction is a little wrong for a great right. But Portia says the laws of Venice must stand. Shylock joyfully praises Portia's wisdom and gives her the bond for inspection. She looks it over, declares it legal and binding, and bids Shylock to be merciful. Shylock remains deaf to reason, however, and Portia tells Antonio to prepare himself for the knife. She orders Shylock to have a surgeon on hand to prevent the merchant from bleeding to death, but Shylock refuses because the bond stipulates no such safeguard.

Antonio bids Bassanio farewell. He asks his friend not to grieve for him and tells Bassanio that he is happy to sacrifice his life, if only to prove his love. Both Bassanio and Graziano say they would give up their wives in order to save Antonio. In a pair of sarcastic asides, Portia and Nerissa mutter that Bassanio's and Graziano's wives are unlikely to appreciate such sentiments.

Shylock is on the verge of cutting into Antonio when Portia suddenly reminds him that the bond stipulates a pound of flesh only, and makes no allowances for blood. She urges Shylock to continue collecting his pound of flesh, but reminds him that if a drop of blood is spilled, then he will be guilty of conspiring against the life of a Venetian citizen and all his lands and goods will be confiscated by the state. Stunned, Shylock hastily backpedals, agreeing to accept three times the sum, but Portia is insistent, saying that Shylock must have the pound of flesh or nothing. When Shylock finds out that he cannot even take the original three thousand ducats in place of the pound of flesh, he drops the case. Portia reminds him of the penalty that noncitizens face when they threaten the life of a Venetian. In such a case, half of Shylock's property would go to the state, while the other half would go to the offended party—Antonio. Portia orders Shylock to beg for the duke's mercy.

The duke says he will show mercy. He spares Shylock's life and demands only a fine, rather than half of Shylock's estate. Shylock says they may as well take his life, as it is worthless without his estate. Antonio offers to return his share of Shylock's estate on the condition that Shylock convert to Christianity and bequeath all his goods to Jessica and Lorenzo upon his death. Shylock consents and departs, saying, "I am not well" (IV.i.392).

After Shylock leaves, the duke invites Portia, still in the disguise of a young lawyer, to dinner. Portia declines, saying that she must leave immediately for Padua. As she leaves, the duke tells Antonio to reward the young law clerk, since it was he who saved Antonio's life. Bassanio thanks Portia, who he does not recognize, and offers her the money he brought with him in order to pay off Shylock. Portia declines the gift and says that delivering Antonio from Shylock's clutches is payment enough. Bassanio insists that she take some token from him, and eventually she agrees. Portia asks Antonio for his gloves and Bassanio for his ring (which she herself gave Bassanio on the condition that he never part with it).

Bassanio pulls his hand away, calling the ring a trifle and saying he will not dishonor the judge by giving him such a lowly gift. Instead, Bassanio offers to find the most valuable ring in Venice. Portia remains firm and demands the trifle or nothing. When Bassanio admits that the ring was a gift from his wife, who made him promise never to part with it, Portia says the excuse is convenient and used by many men to hold onto possessions they would rather not lose. With that, she leaves. Antonio urges Bassanio to let the law clerk have the ring, saying he should value Antonio's love and the clerk's worth more than his wife's orders. Bassanio gives in and sends Graziano to run after Portia and present her with the ring. Antonio and Bassanio leave for Antonio's house to plan their trip to Belmont.

IV.II Location: a street in Venice

Nerissa heads to Shylock's house, planning to force Graziano to give his ring to her.

Portia sends Nerissa to Shylock's house to ensure that Shylock signs the deed that will leave his fortune to Lorenzo and Jessica. Portia observes that Lorenzo will be happy to have this document. Once they complete this task, the disguised women plan to leave for Belmont, which will ensure their arrival a full day before their husbands'. Graziano enters, offers Bassanio's ring to Portia, and invites her to dinner. Portia accepts the ring but declines the invitation. Portia asks Graziano to show Nerissa to Shylock's house. Before leaving, Nerissa tells Portia she will try to convince Graziano to part with his ring. The plan satisfies Portia, who imagines how Graziano and Bassanio will swear up and down that they gave their rings to men. She looks forward to embarrassing them. Nerissa turns to Graziano and asks him to lead her to Shylock's house.

ACT V

Portia and Nerissa reunite with their husbands, Lorenzo learns that he will inherit Shylock's money, and Antonio learns that some of his ships have survived.

V.I Location: Belmont

Portia and Nerissa chastise their husbands, but relent.

Jessica and Lorenzo compare themselves to famous lovers from classical literature, like Troilus and Cressida, Pyramus and Thisbe, and Dido and Aeneas. They are trading declarations of love when a messenger interrupts them. The messenger informs them that Portia will soon return from the monastery. Lancelot enters and announces that Bassanio will return to Belmont the next day. Lorenzo calls for music, and he and Jessica sit on a grassy bank beneath the stars. Lorenzo contemplates the music made by the movement of heavenly orbs, which mortal humans cannot hear while alive. The musicians arrive and begin to play, and Lorenzo decides that anyone who is not moved by music deserves the worst cruelties and betrayals.

Portia and Nerissa enter and hear the music before they reach the estate. Portia believes the night makes the music more beautiful, and the flickering candles lighting up her estate enchant her. She thinks the worth of things is determined largely by the context in which they are experienced. Lorenzo greets Portia, and she asks him not to mention her absence to her husband. Trumpets sound as Bassanio, Antonio, and Graziano arrive. Portia greets Bassanio, who introduces her to Antonio, who reports that he has been acquitted in the courts of Venice.

Graziano and Nerissa argue over the ring with which he promised never to part. Nerissa chastises her husband not for hurting her feelings, but for breaking his own promise. Graziano insists that he gave the ring to a lawyer's clerk as a fee. Portia criticizes him for parting with so precious a gift, saying that her own husband would never have parted with his ring. Graziano corrects her and reveals that Bassanio has, in fact, given his ring to the lawyer who saved Antonio. Portia declares that her husband's heart is as empty as his finger, and she promises never to visit his bed until he produces the ring.

Bassanio pleads with Portia to understand that he gave the ring to a worthy man to whom he was indebted, but Portia dismisses his reasoning, saying it is more likely that Bassanio gave the ring to another woman. Portia vows to be equally unfaithful, threatening to offer the same worthy man anything she owns, including her body or her husband's bed. Antonio intercedes on behalf of Bassanio and Graziano, asking the women to accept his soul should either Bassanio or Graziano prove unfaithful again. Portia and Nerissa relent, giving each of their husbands a ring and suggesting that they exercise more care in keeping these ones. Bassanio and Graziano recognize these as the same rings they gave to the lawyer and his clerk, and Portia and Nerissa claim they slept with the gentlemen in order to get back the rings. Before either Bassanio or Graziano can become too upset at being cuckolded, however, Portia reveals that she was the lawyer in Venice, and Nerissa her clerk. Antonio receives news that some of his ships have miraculously arrived in port, and Lorenzo is told that he will inherit Shylock's fortune. The company rejoices in its collective good fortune.

ANALYSIS OF MAJOR CHARACTERS IN *THE MERCHANT OF VENICE*

SHYLOCK

Critics disagree about whether Shylock is a bloodthirsty villain, a clownish Jewish stereotype, or a tragic figure whose sense of decency has been fractured by the persecution he endures. Shylock is the play's antagonist, and he is menacing enough to threaten the happiness of Venice's businessmen and young lovers. His attempt to murder Antonio is cold and calculated. But Shylock is also a product of his environment. Even while pursuing a pound of flesh, he often mentions the cruelty he has endured at Christian hands, which suggests that his nastiness is learned, not natural. In one of Shakespeare's most famous monologues, Shylock says that Jews are humans and that the cruelty of Venetian citizens has taught him how to be vengeful.

PORTIA

At the beginning of the play, Portia's potential for initiative and resourcefulness is quashed by her compulsion to follow her father's dying wishes. Rather than ignoring the stipulations of her father's will, she watches a stream of suitors pass her by. She is not interested in these particular suitors, but she is sad that she has no choice in the matter. When Bassanio arrives, Portia manages to do as she likes without technically disobeying her father. Portia defeats Shylock by applying a more rigid standard than Shylock himself, agreeing that his contract entitles him to his pound of flesh but does not allow for any loss of blood. Portia's effectiveness comes from her ability to ignore the spirit of the law while sticking to its letter.

ANTONIO

Antonio, the merchant of the play's title, emerges in Act I, scene i as a hopeless depressive, someone who cannot name the source of his melancholy. As the play progresses, he devolves into a self-pitying lump, unable to muster the energy required to ward off execution. Antonio never names the cause of his melancholy, but if a cause exists, the evidence points to love, despite his denial of this idea in Act I, scene i. The most likely object of Antonio's affection is Bassanio, who takes full advantage of the merchant's boundless fondness for him. Antonio has risked his entire fortune on overseas trading ventures, yet he agrees to guarantee the potentially lethal loan Bassanio secures from Shylock. In the context of his unrequited and presumably unconsummated relationship with Bassanio, Antonio's willingness to offer up a pound of his own flesh suggests a violent version of the rites of marriage, in which two partners become "one flesh."

Late in the play, Antonio's proclamations sound like the hyperbole and self-satisfaction of a doomed lover: "Pray God Bassanio come / To see me pay his debt, and then I care not" (III.iii.35–36). Antonio ends the play restored to wealth, but not delivered into love. Without a mate, he is indeed the "tainted wether"—or castrated ram—of the flock (IV.i.113).

THEMES, MOTIFS & SYMBOLS IN *THE MERCHANT OF VENICE*

THEMES

SELF-INTEREST VERSUS LOVE On the surface, the main difference between the Christian characters and Shylock appears to be that the Christians value human relationships over business ones, whereas Shylock is only interested in money. The Christian characters certainly view the difference this way. Merchants like Antonio lend money free of interest and put themselves at risk for those they love, whereas Shylock agonizes over the loss of his money and is reported to run through the streets crying, "O, my ducats! O, my daughter!" (II.viii.15), words that suggest he values his money at least as much as his daughter. However, upon closer inspection, this supposed difference between Christian and Jew breaks down. In Act III, scene i, Shylock seems more hurt by the fact that his daughter sold a ring that his dead wife gave to him than distraught over the loss of the ring's monetary value. In a different way, his relationship with his persecutors also matters to him more than money. He insists on pound of flesh rather than any amount of money, because vengeance is more important to him than wealth. Neither are the Christian characters always more interested in love than they are in money. Though Portia and Bassanio come to love one another, Bassanio seeks her hand in the first place because he is monstrously in debt and needs her money. Bassanio is anxious to view his relationship with Antonio as a matter of business rather than of love, which is why he asks Antonio to look at the loan as an investment, though Antonio insists that he lends him the money solely out of love. And while the Christian characters may talk more about mercy, love, and charity, they show none of those virtues in their dealings with Jews, whom they hate for no reason other than their religion.

THE DIVINE QUALITY OF MERCY The conflict between Shylock and the Christian characters comes to a head over the issue of mercy. The other characters acknowledge that the law is on Shylock's side, but they expect him to show mercy, which he refuses to do. When, during the trial, Shylock asks Portia what could possibly compel him to be merciful, Portia's long reply, beginning with the words, "[t]he quality of mercy is not strained," clarifies what is at stake in the argument (IV.i.179). She says human beings should be merciful because God is merciful: mercy is an attribute of God himself and therefore greater than power, majesty, or law. Portia's understanding of mercy is based on the way Christians in Shakespeare's time understood the difference between the Old and New Testaments. The Old Testament depicts a God who requires strict adherence to rules and harshly punishes those who stray. The New Testament, in contrast, emphasizes adherence to the spirit rather than the letter of the law, portraying a God who forgives and offers salvation to those who forgive others. When Portia warns Shylock against pursuing the law without regard for mercy, she is promoting what Elizabethan Christians would have seen as a pro-Christian, anti-Jewish agenda.

Once she has turned Shylock's greatest weapon—the law—against him, Portia has the opportunity practice the mercy she advocates. Instead, she backs Shylock into a corner, stripping him of his bond, his estate, and his dignity, and forcing him to kneel and beg for mercy. Antonio decides not to seize Shylock's goods as punishment for conspiring against him, an action that could be interpreted as merciful. But it may not be merciful to return to half Shylock's goods to him only to take away his religion and his profession. By forcing Shylock to convert, Antonio prevents him from practicing usury, which, according to Shylock's reports, was Antonio's primary reason for berating him and spitting on him in public. Antonio's compassion seems to stem as much from self-interest as from concern for his fellow man. Mercy, as delivered in *The Merchant of Venice*, is never as sweet, selfless, or full of grace as Portia suggests.

HATRED AS A CYCLICAL PHENOMENON Throughout the play, Shylock claims that he is simply applying the lessons taught to him by his Christian neighbors. This claim becomes an integral part of his character and his argument in court. In Shylock's first appearance, as he conspires to harm Antonio, he seems motivated by the insults and injuries Antonio has inflicted on him in the past. As the play continues, and Shylock unveils more of his reasoning, he continues to blame his behavior on years of conditioning. Responding to Salerio's query of what good the pound of flesh will do him, Shylock responds, "The villainy you teach me I will execute, and it shall go hard but I will better the instruction" (III.i.60–61). Not all of Shylock's actions can be blamed on his poor treatment at the hands of the Christians. Also, it is possible that Antonio understands that he is partly to blame for his own near-execution.

MOTIFS

THE LAW *The Merchant of Venice* explores laws and rules—the laws of the state of Venice and the rules stipulated in contracts and wills. Laws and rules can be manipulated for cruel or unjustifiable purposes, but they can also lead to good when executed by the right people. The game of chests that virtually imprisons Portia first seems like a questionable rule, but she is able to manipulate it so that it works exactly as she wants. By the time Bassanio picks the correct chest, the choice comes across as a more efficient indication of human nature than any person could come up with. A similar phenomenon occurs with Venetian law. Until Portia's arrival, Shylock is the law's strictest adherent, and it seems as if the city's adherence to contracts will result in tragedy. However, when Portia arrives and manipulates the law, the outcome is happy, at least to an Elizabethan audience: Antonio is rescued and Shylock forced to abandon his religion. Still, the fact that the trial is such a close call does raise the worrisome idea that people can misuse the law.

FILIAL PIETY Like Shakespeare's other comedies, *The Merchant of Venice* includes characters who treat filial piety lightly. Lancelot greets his blind, long-lost father by giving the old man confusing directions and telling him that his beloved son Lancelot is dead. This moment of impertinence or cruelty can be excused as essential to the comedy of the play, but it sets the stage for Jessica's more complex hatred of her father. Jessica can list no specific complaints when she explains her desire to leave Shylock's house, and in the one scene in which she appears with Shylock, he fusses over her in a way that some might see as tender. Jessica's behavior after leaving her father is questionable at best. Most notably, she trades her father's ring, given to him by her dead mother, for a monkey. The hurtful frivolity of this exchange, in which an heirloom is tossed away for the silliest of objects, puts us, at least temporarily, in Shylock's corner.

SYMBOLS

THE THREE CASKETS The contest for Portia's hand, in which suitors from various countries choose among a gold, a silver, and a lead chest, resembles the cultural and legal system of Venice in some respects. Like the Venice of the play, the chest contest presents the same opportunities and the same rules to men of various nations, ethnicities, and religions. Also like Venice, the hidden bias of the chest test is fundamentally Christian. To win Portia, Bassanio must ignore the gold chest, which bears the inscription, "Who chooseth me shall gain what many men desire" (II.vii.5), and the silver chest, which says, "Who chooseth me shall get as much as he deserves" (II.vii.7). The correct chest is lead and warns that the person who chooses it must give and risk everything he has. The contest combines a number of Christian teachings, such as the idea that desire is an unreliable guide and should be resisted, and the idea that human beings do not deserve God's grace but receive it in spite of themselves. Christianity teaches that appearances are often deceiving, and that people should not trust the evidence of their senses—hence the humble appearance of the lead chest. Faith and charity are the central values of Christianity, and these values are evoked by the lead chest's injunction to give all and risk all, as one does in making a leap of faith. Portia's father conceives of marriage as a union between people who risk everything for and give everything to each other. The contest suits Bassanio, who knows he does not deserve his good fortune but is willing to risk everything on a gamble.

THE POUND OF FLESH   The pound of flesh that Shylock seeks lends itself to multiple interpretations. It is a metaphor for two of the play's closest relationships, and also a symbol of Shylock's inflexible adherence to the law. The fact that Bassanio's debt is to be paid with Antonio's flesh shows that their friendship is so binding it has made them almost one. Jessica's departure strengthens Shylock's determination, as if he were seeking recompense for the loss of his own flesh and blood by collecting it from his enemy. Lastly, the pound of flesh is a constant reminder of the rigidity of Shylock's world, in which numerical calculations are used to evaluate even the most serious of situations. Shylock never explicitly demands that Antonio die, but instead, and more chillingly, asks for a pound of flesh in exchange for his three thousand ducats.

IMPORTANT QUOTATIONS FROM *THE MERCHANT OF VENICE*

1. *I am a Jew. Hath not a Jew eyes? Hath not a Jew hands, organs, dimensions, senses, affections, passions; fed with the same food, hurt with the same weapons, subject to the same diseases, healed by the same means, warmed and cooled by the same winter and summer as a Christian is? If you prick us do we not bleed? If you tickle us do we not laugh? If you poison us do we not die? And if you wrong us shall we not revenge? If we are like you in the rest, we will resemble you in that. If a Jew wrong a Christian, what is his humility? Revenge. If a Christian wrong a Jew, what should his sufferance be by Christian example? Why, revenge. The villainy you teach me I will execute, and it shall go hard but I will better the instruction.*

Location: III.i.49–61
Speaker: Shylock to Salanio and Salerio
Context: Shylock has blamed Antonio for persecuting him because he is a Jew

Shylock says that all people, even those who are not part of the majority culture, are human. A Jew, he reasons, is equipped with the same faculties as a Christian, and is therefore subject to the same pains and comforts and emotions. The speech, however, is not a celebration of shared experience or even an invitation for the Venetians to acknowledge their enemy's humanity. Instead of using reason to elevate himself above his Venetian tormenters, Shylock sinks to their level, vowing to behave as villainously as they have.

2. *What if my house be troubled with a rat,*
   And I be pleased to give ten thousand ducats
   To have it baned? What, are you answered yet?
   Some men there are love not a gaping pig,
   Some that are mad if they behold a cat,
   And others when the bagpipe sings i'th' nose
   Cannot contain their urine; for affection,
   Mistress of passion, sways it to the mood
   Of what it likes or loathes…
   So can I give no reason, nor I will not,
   More than a lodged hate and a certain loathing
   I bear Antonio, that I follow thus
   A losing suit against him. Are you answered?

Location: IV.i.43–61
Speaker: Shylock to the duke
Context: Antonio and Shylock have been summoned before the court

When the duke asks Shylock to show his adversary some mercy, Shylock responds by reasoning that he has no reason. He blames his hatred of Antonio on "affection, / Mistress of passion," who affects men's moods and actions in ways they cannot explain (IV.i.49–50). Just as certain people have inexplicable aversions to cats or certain strains of music or eating meat, Shylock has an illogical dislike for Antonio.

Shylock's language patterns in this speech reinforce our impression of his character. He frequently repeats himself, returning to the same imagery—the "gaping pig" (IV.i.53) and the "woolen bagpipe" (IV.i.55)—and bookending his speech with the simple question, "Are you answered?" (IV.i.61). Shylock's tightly controlled speech reflects the narrow and determined focus of his quest to satisfy his hatred.

The speech's prosaic imagery is typical of Shylock. Other characters speak in dreamily poetic language, evoking images of angels and waters scented with spice, but Shylock draws on the most mundane examples to prove his point. He suggests that Antonio is a rat, and that his dislike of Antonio is similar to the dislike some men feel toward pigs or cats. Shylock uses bodily functions to drive home his point, likening rage to urination. Also, Shylock's suggestion that a mere whim has made him hate Antonio makes him seem unpredictable, and fuels the perception that his actions are careless and cruel.

---

3. *You have among you many a purchased slave*
   Which, like your asses and your dogs and mules,
   You use in abject and in slavish parts
   Because you bought them. Shall I say to you
   'Let them be free, marry them to your heirs.
   Why sweat they under burdens? ... '
   You will answer
   'The slaves are ours.' So do I answer you.
   The pound of flesh which I demand of him
   Is dearly bought. 'Tis mine, and I will have it.

Location: IV.i.89–99
Speaker: Shylock to the Duke
Context: Shylock defends himself during his trial

In this speech, Shylock uses Venice's laws to justify his vengeful quest. Shylock has no interest in exposing the wrongfulness of owning or mistreating slaves. Such property rights simply happen to be established by Venetian laws, so Shylock uses them to appeal for equal protection. If Antonio and company can purchase human flesh to "use in abject and in slavish parts," Shylock reasons, then he can purchase part of the flesh of a Venetian citizen (IV.i.91). Unlike the Venetians, who are willing to bend or break the law to satisfy their wants, Shylock never strays from its letter in pursuit of his bond. His brand of abiding by the law, however, is gruesome.

---

4. *The quality of mercy is not strained.*
   It droppeth as the gentle rain from heaven
   Upon the place beneath ...
   It is enthronèd in the hearts of kings;
   It is an attribute to God himself,
   And earthly power doth then show likest God's
   When mercy seasons justice. Therefore, Jew,
   Though justice be thy plea, consider this:
   That in the course of justice none of us
   Should see salvation. We do pray for mercy,
   And that same prayer doth teach us all to render

The deeds of mercy.

Location: IV.i.179–197
Speaker: Portia to Shylock
Context: During Shylock's trial, Portia, disguised as a lawyer, tells Shylock why he must be merciful

Portia appeals to Shylock's methodical mind, making a reasonable rather than an emotional case for mercy. She states that forgiving the bond would benefit Shylock and elevate him to a godlike status. She also warns him that his quest for justice without mercy may result in his own damnation. Although well-measured and well-reasoned, Portia's speech also makes mercy a polarizing issue dividing Jews from Christians. Her frequent references to the divine are appeals to a Christian God, and mercy emerges as a marker of Christianity. Although it seems as if Portia is offering an appeal, in retrospect it is clear that her speech is an ultimatum, a final chance for Shylock to save himself before Portia crushes his legal arguments.

---

5. *The man that hath no music in himself,*
   Nor is not moved with concord of sweet sounds,
   Is fit for treasons, stategems, and spoils.
   The motions of his spirit are dull as night,
   And his affections dark as Erebus.

Location: V.i.82–86
Speaker: Lorenzo to Jessica
Context: Lorenzo and Jessica sit outside, looking at the stars

With Shylock stowed safely offstage, Shakespeare returns to comedy, lightening the mood with an exchange of rings that reunites the lovers, and with Antonio's lost ships brought back to port. Because Shylock has been such a powerful presence in the play, and because his decimation at the hands of the Venetians is profoundly disturbing, the comedy in Belmont never fully escapes the shadow of the trouble that precedes it. The lovers' happiness is probably little more than a passing moment. Even in ordering music to celebrate Portia's homecoming, Lorenzo reflects darkly that some men are not affected by music, and that these men are dark and dull.

THE TAMING OF THE SHREW

Petruccio tames his strong-willed wife, Katherine, by subjecting her to a grueling ordeal.

THE TAMING OF THE SHREW IN CONTEXT

The Taming of the Shrew, one of Shakespeare's earliest comedies, shares many essential characteristics with his other romantic comedies, such as *Much Ado About Nothing* and *A Midsummer Night's Dream*. These characteristics include lighthearted, slapstick humor, disguises and deception, and a happy ending. Like Shakespeare's other romantic comedies, *The Taming of the Shrew* focuses on courtship and marriage, but, unlike most of them, it devotes a great deal of attention to married life, not just wooing and weddings.

Renaissance England was preoccupied with questions of marriage because of Henry VIII. Angered that the pope would not grant him a divorce, Henry VIII separated England from the Catholic Church in 1534. Henry, like England's upper classes, sometimes suffered in marriages that were arranged for money, land, or power more than they were for love.

The figure of the "shrew" or "scold"—that is, a cantankerous or gossipy wife, who resists or undermines her husband's authority—was a stereotype of the day. A number of sermons, plays, and pamphlets of the time explained how husbands tamed their shrewish wives or how scolds were publicly punished by, for example, being repeatedly dunked in a river. Some of this literature took a diplomatic attitude toward women, but most of it was anti-woman. In some of it, parody and sincerity are difficult to distinguish between. Similar ambiguity exists in *The Taming of the Shrew*, which lampoons chauvinistic behavior while simultaneously reaffirming its social validity, and celebrates the quick wit and fiery spirit of its heroine while reveling in her humiliation.

THE TAMING OF THE SHREW: KEY FACTS

Full title: The Taming of the Shrew

Time and place written: Around 1592; London, England

Date of first publication: 1623

Genre: Romantic comedy

Setting (time): Unspecified, but presumably sometime during the Italian Renaissance

Setting (place): Padua, a city-state in Italy prominent during the Renaissance

Protagonist: Katherine, Petruccio

Major conflict: Petruccio's attempts to tame Katherine

THE TAMING OF THE SHREW: CHARACTER LIST

Baptista One of the wealthiest men in Padua, and Katherine's father. Baptista's daughters are very sought-after because of their substantial dowries. Baptista is good-natured, if a bit superficial.

Bianca Baptista's youngest daughter. Bianca is lovely, soft-spoken, sweet, and unassuming. She is Katherine's principal female foil. Baptista will not let Bianca marry before Katherine does.

Bixondello Lucentio's second servant. Bixondello assists his master and Tranio in carrying out their plot.

Christopher Sly The principal character in the play's brief Induction. Sly is a drunken tinker tricked by a mischievous nobleman into thinking that he is a lord.

Gremio and Hortensio   Two older gentlemen of Padua. Gremio and Hortensio are Bianca's suitors at the beginning of the play. Though they are rivals, they bond over their frustration and rejection. Hortensio ends up marrying a widow.

Grumio   Petruccio's servant and the fool of the play.

Lucentio   A young student from Pisa. The good-natured and intrepid Lucentio comes to Padua to study at the city's renowned university, but he is sidetracked when, meeting Bianca, he falls in love at first sight. By disguising himself as a classics instructor named Cambio, he gains access to Bianca and wins her love.

Katherine   The shrew of the play's title. Katherine, or Kate, is the daughter of Baptista Minola. She is sharp-tongued, quick-tempered, and prone to violence, particularly against anyone who tries to marry her. Her anger and rudeness disguise her insecurity and her jealousy of her sister, Bianca. Eventually she subjugates herself to her suitor, Petruccio.

Petruccio   A gentleman from Verona. Loud, boisterous, eccentric, quick-witted, and frequently drunk, Petruccio comes to Padua "to wive and thrive." His ideal wife is a woman with an enormous dowry, and he finds Kate the perfect fit. Disregarding everyone who warns him of her shrewishness, he eventually succeeds in winning Kate and curbing her tongue and temper with his own.

Tranio   Lucentio's servant. Tranio accompanies Lucentio from Pisa. Wry and comical, he plays an important part in his master's charade—he assumes Lucentio's identity and bargains with Baptista for Bianca's hand.

TAMING OF THE SHREW: PLOT OVERVIEW

In the English countryside, a lord finds a drunken tinker named Christopher Sly asleep in front of a tavern. The lord has Sly carried to his house, where the servants treat Sly as a lord. A troupe of actors puts on a play for Sly, which composes the main body of *The Taming of the Shrew*.

In the play, Lucentio, a young nobleman and scholar, arrives in Padua and falls in love with the beautiful Bianca. Bianca's father, Baptista, refuses to let her wed before her bad-tempered sister, Katherine, is married off. Lucentio disguises himself as a Latin tutor so he can get close to Bianca, while Lucentio's servant Tranio disguises himself as Lucentio to negotiate with Baptista for Bianca's hand.

Petruccio, a brash nobleman, arrives in Padua and resolves to marry Katherine for her money, despite her reputation as a shrew. After a tremendous duel of words, Petruccio obtains Katherine's unstated consent to marry him. Petruccio tames the wild Katherine by embarrassing and abusing her. On his insistence, he and Katherine leave their wedding before the reception. Petruccio then forbids Katherine to eat or sleep. Katherine ultimately satisfies Petruccio by agreeing with everything he says.

Disguised as Lucentio, Tranio persuades Baptista to agree to a marriage between Bianca and Lucentio by promising Bianca a huge sum of money. At the wedding banquet, Katherine's superior loyalty to Petruccio puts the other wives to shame.

THE TAMING OF THE SHREW: SCENE SUMMARY

INTRODUCTION.I

A lord decides to trick Christopher Sly, a drunken beggar, into thinking that he is a lord; he arranges for a troupe to put on a play at his house.

Outside an alehouse somewhere in the English countryside, a drunken tinker (a mender of pots) named Christopher Sly argues with the hostess over some glassware he has broken in his inebriated clumsiness. When the hostess leaves to get the local authorities, Sly passes out, and soon a lord returning from the hunt discovers him. This lord decides to have a bit of fun with the sleeping beggar and orders his servants to take Sly back to his house and treat him as if he were a lord—put him in a bed, place rings on his fingers, set a banquet for him, and so on. His huntsmen agree that this will be an excellent jest, and they take Sly offstage.

A troupe of players arrives and offers the lord their services. The lord welcomes them to spend the night at his home, but he warns them that they must not laugh at the strange behavior of the other lord for whom they will perform. Then the lord tells his serviceman to go to Bartholomew, the lord's pageboy, and instruct him to put on a lady's attire and play the part of Sly's wife. The lord wants the disguised Bartholomew to pretend to be overjoyed to see that Sly has recovered from his insanity and to say that Sly, in his madness, has insisted that he is a poor beggar for the past seven years.

INTRODUCTION.II

The lord and his servants convince Sly that he is a lord who has been mad for fifteen years.

Back at the house, the servants place Sly in the lord's bed, dressing him in fine clothes and jewelry, and the lord dresses himself as one of the servants. When Sly awakens, they present him with good wine and food and tell him that he is their master. He protests that he remembers being a poor tinker, but they say this memory is the result of a madness from which he has suffered for fifteen years. They plead and wail in feigned distress at his continued illness, but Sly remains skeptical. However, when his "wife" is mentioned, Sly is finally convinced. Overjoyed that their master's memory has returned, the servants try to entertain him. Sly attempts to dismiss the servants so that he can sleep with his wife (who is actually the disguised page, Bartholomew), but his wife explains apologetically that his physicians have ordered her to stay out of his bed for another night or two, lest his madness return. The players arrive to perform for the enjoyment of Sly and his wife. The play that they perform constitutes the rest of *The Taming of the Shrew*.

ACT I

Lucentio falls in love with Bianca; Petruccio decides to woo Katherine.

I.I Location: a street in Padua

Baptista says that no one can marry his gentle daughter, Bianca, until someone marries his hellion of a daughter, Katherine; Lucentio falls in love with Bianca and decides to pose as a tutor to get close to her.

A young man named Lucentio arrives in Padua with his manservant, Tranio. Lucentio was educated in Pisa and Florence and has come to Padua to further his studies at its famous university. As he tells Tranio, he is young and eager to learn new things. Tranio says they should not forget the pleasures of life in their academic pursuits. The noisy entrance of a group of people interrupts their discussion.

The group is composed of Baptista; his daughters, Katherine and Bianca; and Bianca's two suitors, older men named Hortensio and Gremio. Most of the noise comes from Katherine, who is screaming and cursing at everyone present. Baptista tells the suitors that they are free to court Katherine, but Bianca is off-limits, for he will not allow her to marry before Katherine does. The suitors say no one would ever marry a devil like Katherine. In return, Katherine threatens them with violence. Lucentio takes particular notice of Bianca, who behaves much more mildly than her sister. After Baptista leaves with his daughters, Hortensio and Gremio agree that they must look for someone to wed Katherine. However, they are not optimistic about their chances of finding a willing man. In the meantime, they say, they will also look for a schoolmaster for Bianca—Baptista had mentioned that he was looking for one, and they hope to please him by helping him.

The old men walk away, and Lucentio gushes to Tranio that he has fallen in love with Bianca and is determined to court her. Knowing that he cannot do so publicly, given Baptista's stance, he resolves to woo her in secret. He remembers that Hortensio and Gremio mentioned finding a schoolmaster, and he decides to disguise himself as a teacher in the hope that while tutoring Bianca he will be able to declare his love for her and win her heart. Tranio will pretend to be Lucentio and study at the university. Biondello, Lucentio's other servant, arrives and agrees to help with the deception.

At this point, the main story—which Shakespeare presents through a play for Christopher Sly—fades momentarily, and Sly reemerges. He declares that he is enjoying this entertainment, but he implies that he would prefer to be left alone with his wife.

I.II Location: a street in Padua

Petruccio grows determined to woo Katherine because of her large dowry; Tranio disguises himself as Lucentio and presents himself as another suitor of Bianca's.

A brash young man named Petruccio, newly arrived in Padua, goes with his servant Grumio to see Hortensio, whom he knows from Verona. Grumio and Petruccio have a comic misunderstanding at the door, but eventually Hortensio comes down to greet Petruccio and ask why he is in Padua. Petruccio says that after his father died, he set out to look for a wife, hoping to marry a rich man's daughter and thereby enlarge his family fortune. Hortensio, determined to find a potential suitor for Katherine so that he himself may marry Bianca, recognizes an opportunity and decides to convince Petruccio to marry Katherine. Being a friend, he first warns Petruccio about her, but Petruccio does not care about Katherine's behavior. He only cares that she has a rich father. Full of confidence, he tells Hortensio to lead him to the shrew. Hortensio plans to disguise himself as a schoolmaster so that he can court Bianca secretly.

Gremio and Lucentio enter on their way to Baptista's house, interrupting Hortensio and Petruccio. Lucentio has already disguised himself as a schoolmaster and has presented himself to Gremio, who gladly agreed to have him tutor Bianca. Gremio brags to Hortensio that he has found a schoolmaster for Bianca. Hortensio relays his own good news: Petruccio wishes to woo Katherine. Gremio can hardly believe it.

Tranio enters, disguised as Lucentio, with Biondello as his servant. He draws attention to himself, asking the suitors to direct him to the house of Baptista Minola, vaguely implying that he might be interested in one of the women there. Hortensio and Gremio have a hard time restraining their anger at the news that yet another man will be courting Bianca. (Lucentio has arranged for Tranio to make this entrance in order to distract Hortensio and Gremio and give him more time for his own wooing.) Tranio persuades the suitors that they can all be friends while they compete for Bianca, and he wins them over by offering to buy them a drink.

ACT II

By her silence, Katherine seems to agree to a marriage with Petruccio; Tranio, disguised as Lucentio, wins the promise of Bianca's hand.

II.1 Location: Baptista's house

After a verbal sparring match with Katherine, Petruccio insists that he will marry her the following Sunday; Tranio, disguised as Lucentio, pretends he is vastly wealthy, thereby getting Baptista to promise him Bianca.

Katherine chases Bianca, cursing at her in a fury. Katherine has tied Bianca's hands together and is trying to beat her, because Bianca will not tell her which of the suitors she prefers. When Baptista comes in to try to break up the fight, he only angers Katherine more by showing that he favors Bianca. Both sisters leave in a huff.

A group of gentlemen enters to see Baptista. The group includes Gremio, Lucentio (dressed as a schoolmaster), Petruccio, Hortensio (likewise dressed as a schoolmaster), Tranio (dressed as Lucentio), and Biondello (dressed as Lucentio's servant). The introductions begin in a fog of deception. Petruccio bluntly asks Baptista if he can see Katherine. In exchange, he offers a music instructor for her: the disguised Hortensio, whom he introduces as Licio. Baptista accepts the exchange, although he starts to tell Petruccio as kindly as possible that Petruccio must be crazy to want to see Katherine. Gremio, who cannot stand being upstaged, interrupts Baptista to present his own schoolmaster, the disguised Lucentio, whom he calls Cambio, a master of classical languages. Baptista accepts the gift and then hears from Tranio, who, pretending to be Lucentio, presents his own gift of books and a lute in exchange for permission to see and woo Bianca.

The two phony schoolmasters leave to instruct Bianca, while Petruccio presses Baptista for information about Katherine. After hearing that a substantial dowry will go to the man who wins Katherine, Petruccio assures Baptista of his abilities. Hortensio returns, his head now bleeding—apparently, when he attempted to teach Katherine how to play the lute, she took the instrument and smashed it over his head. Undaunted, Petruccio waits to meet Katherine. He decides to call her "Kate" and good-naturedly contradict everything she says.

Katherine tears into Petruccio immediately, but Petruccio's quick wit proves equal to hers. Katherine, who is accustomed to skewering the dim-witted men by whom she is surrounded, finds his aptitude for sparring highly frustrating. Katherine and Petruccio have a lengthy verbal duel, constructing a series of metaphors from the other's comments. Katherine's puns generally insult or threaten, but Petruccio twists them into sexual innuendo. Eventually, Katherine becomes so enraged that she hits Petruccio. Petruccio implacably continues the game, saying he will marry her whether or not she is willing: "will you, nill you, I will marry you" (II.i.263).

When Baptista, Gremio, and Tranio enter to check on Petruccio's progress, he claims he and Katherine have already agreed upon Sunday as the wedding day. Katherine, shocked, contradicts him, but he ignores her and insists to the other men that Katherine cannot keep her hands off him. Katherine remains silent after this remark, and when Petruccio again says they will marry on Sunday, she says nothing. They both leave.

After recovering from the shock of the hasty arrangement, Gremio and Tranio immediately move on to the matter of Bianca, who will be available after Sunday. Baptista says that whichever of the suitors can best ensure that Bianca will be provided for when she is a widow—in other words, whichever has the greatest wealth—may marry her. Because Tranio is claiming to be Lucentio, an unknown man in Padua, he can pretend that he has limitless funding: he simply guarantees ten times whatever Gremio offers. Baptista agrees to award Bianca to Lucentio as soon as Lucentio's father can back up Lucentio's claims of wealth. Tranio, confident of his ability to play the part of Lucentio, believes he can produce a convincing father for Lucentio as well.

ACT III

Lucentio and Hortensio tutor Bianca; Katherine and Petruccio get married.

III.I   Location: Baptista's house

Lucentio, disguised as Cambio, and Hortensio, disguised as Licio, tutor Bianca; Bianca appears to prefer Lucentio.

It is now Saturday, the day before Katherine is scheduled to wed Petruccio. Lucentio and Hortensio, in their respective disguises as Cambio and Licio, are battling for Bianca's exclusive attention. Bianca has begun to form a preference, and she declares she will hear her Latin lesson from Lucentio first, while Hortensio tunes his instrument.

During the Latin lesson, with Hortensio out of hearing range, Lucentio conveys his true intentions to Bianca through a mock translation of a Latin paragraph. She replies to him, using the same method, saying she distrusts him. Still, she does not hide the fact that she is taken with her young suitor. Hortensio tries to break in at intervals, but Bianca sends him off to tune again until she has finished her conversation with Lucentio.

Lucentio concludes, and Hortensio returns to try his hand at wooing Bianca. He gives her a sheet with a "gamut," or scale, of notes on it, with romantic words cleverly inserted to indicate his true intention. Lucentio was confident and coy, but Hortensio pleads: "show pity, or I die" (III.i.76). Bianca resists his overtures. A servant enters, calling on Bianca to prepare for her sister's wedding the next day.

Alone, Hortensio considers the signals he received from Bianca. He sees that Lucentio is infatuated with Bianca, and although he does not know what Bianca's intentions are, he suspects that his own chances might be slim. Preparing for the possibility of rejection, he tells himself that he will simply find another wife if Bianca is unwilling to marry him.

III.II   Location: outside Baptista's house

Petruccio arrives late and shabbily dressed for his wedding.

Everyone has gathered for the wedding of Katherine and Petruccio. The groom is late, and Baptista has begun to worry. Katherine wonders if Petruccio habitually woos women only to leave them standing at the altar. She runs off in tears, but Biondello rushes in to announce that the groom is on his way. He says that Petruccio is dressed in a ridiculous, shabby costume and is riding up the street on an old, broken-down horse riddled with diseases. Grumio rides at his side, similarly attired. When Petruccio finally arrives, the crowd sees that Biondello's description was accurate. Baptista begs Petruccio to change into a more fashionable outfit before marrying Katherine, but Petruccio refuses. He rides off to find Katherine. Most of the crowd follows.

III.III Location: outside Baptista's house

Petruccio behaves poorly at the ceremony and forces Katherine to leave with him before the wedding banquet begins.

Alone, Tranio and Lucentio briefly discuss the status of their plan to win Bianca. Tranio informs his master that they must find a father for him, and Lucentio suggests that the simplest solution may be to elope with Bianca. Gremio returns and reports that at the wedding ceremony, Petruccio swore at the altar, struck the priest, threw food, and, in general, was such an embarrassment that Gremio felt compelled to leave early. The rest of the company soon arrives, but before they can begin the wedding feast, Petruccio announces that he must leave at once and take Katherine with him, not even giving her time to receive congratulations from her friends and family. Katherine tries to draw the line, saying she will leave only when she wishes, but Petruccio says that she is now his wife and property. Pretending to defend her from jealous thieves, he exits quickly with her and Grumio. The rest of the party can only watch in amazement and laugh at the day's events, wondering how two such people could ever put up with each other. They resume the wedding feast, and Baptista moves to discuss the marriage of Bianca to Lucentio.

ACT IV

Petruccio annoys, starves, and bullies Katherine into submission; Tranio finds a pendant who will act as Lucentio's father; on the way to Padua, Katherine, Petruccio, and Hortensio run into Lucentio's real father.

IV.I Location: Petruccio's country house

Petruccio rages at his servants, then tells the audience that everything he does is to annoy Katherine.

Grumio complains that he has been sent ahead to ensure that the servants are preparing for the arrival of their master and his new wife, Katherine. Curtis, another servant, greets Grumio and hears his tale of the journey from Padua, on which Kate fell into the mud, Petruccio flew into a rage, and the horses ran away. Grumio orders Curtis to assemble all the other servants and make sure they are properly attired and on good behavior. Curtis calls for them, and a few arrive just as Petruccio and Kate return.

Petruccio flies into a rage, claiming that his servants are useless. They do their best, but nothing pleases him. At dinner, he claims that the meat is burned and pushes the whole meal off the table. Katherine, tired and hungry, pleads with him to be more patient with the servants. Petruccio tells her that he demands much of them for her benefit—his new bride will receive nothing short of perfection, he says. After taking Katherine off to bed without food, Petruccio returns to the stage alone and announces that everything he does is calculated to aggravate Kate and keep her wanting. He refers to her as a wild falcon that he must train to obey his call. He intends to prevent her from sleeping by making a fuss about the way the bed is made, just as he did with the food. This, he says, is the best way to "curb her mad and headstrong humour" (IV.i.190).

IV.II Location: Baptista's house

Tranio tricks a pedant into agreeing to pretend to be Tranio's (disguised as Lucentio) father.

Tranio (still disguised as Lucentio) and Lucentio (still disguised as the schoolmaster) are trying to wrap up their scheme to win Bianca for Lucentio. Hortensio, distraught at losing Bianca to his rival, tells Lucentio (Tranio in disguise) that he too has been defeated in his pursuit of Bianca. Tranio plays along, feigning surprise when he sees the real Lucentio and Bianca courting each other during their lesson. He pretends to be so angry that he decides to foreswear Bianca's charms, and he convinces Hortensio to do the same.

Tranio informs Bianca and Lucentio of these events after Hortensio leaves. Hortensio has decided to marry a wealthy widow instead of Bianca and is going to Petruccio's to attend "taming-school." He wants to see how Petruccio handles Katherine so that he can apply the lessons to his own marriage. Biondello rushes in with encouraging news: he has just seen a man entering Padua who would make a convincing fake father for Lucentio.

Tranio approaches the newcomer, who is a pedant schoolmaster from Mantua. Tranio comes up with a story to put the old man in his debt: he says the Duke of Padua has proclaimed that anyone from Mantua found in Padua shall be put to death. The pedant, frightened out of his wits, promises a favor to Tranio in exchange for protection. Tranio says it so happens he is in need of someone to act as his father (meaning Lucentio's father, Vincentio). The pedant agrees to help him.

IV.III   Location: Petruccio's country house

Petruccio deprives Katherine of food and sleep, dismisses her taste in clothing, and berates her for telling him what time it is.

Katherine has had little food or sleep for several days now. She begs Grumio to get her something to eat, but he refuses. Like his master, he claims that they are depriving her for her own benefit. Finally, Petruccio and Hortensio bring Katherine a meal, but she has little time to eat before Petruccio's tailor arrives. The tailor has prepared elegant and expensive clothes for their journey back to Baptista's house in Padua. Petruccio finds fault with everything that Kate likes, from the cap to the gown, and he blames the tailor for poor craftsmanship. The tailor tries to deflect the blame onto Grumio, but Petruccio and Grumio indignantly force him to leave. Petruccio secretly tells Hortensio to pull the tailor aside and tell him that he will be paid the following day, revealing that Petruccio is faking his anger at the tailor. Petruccio tells Katherine that they will leave at once for Padua in the clothes that they have on. He says they will arrive at noon. When Katherine tells Petruccio that noontime has already past, he angrily accuses her of contradicting him yet again. He says they will not go that day, and when they do go, "[i]t shall be what o'clock I say it is" (IV.iii.189).

IV.IV   Location: in front of Baptista's house

The pedant successfully passes himself off as Lucentio's father.

Tranio has outfitted the pedant as Vincentio. He rehearses with him to ensure that their stories match. When Baptista and Lucentio (still disguised as Cambio) enter, the pedant convinces Baptista that he is Lucentio's father and that he fully approves of the marriage between Bianca and his son. Baptista, the pedant, and Tranio then leave to discuss the financial details of the marriage.

IV.V   Location: in front of Baptista's house

Lucentio agrees to elope with Bianca.

Lucentio, disguised as Cambio, returns to the stage with Biondello, who informs him that Baptista has requested that Cambio bring Bianca to dinner. Biondello explains that he has personally arranged for a priest and witnesses to perform a hasty marriage in a church nearby. Lucentio agrees to elope with Bianca.

IV.VI   Location: a road

Petruccio finally subdues Katherine on the way to Padua.

Petruccio, Katherine, and Hortensio journey back to Padua. On the way, Petruccio continues trying to make Kate submit to his authority. It is midday, but Petruccio comments on how brightly the moon is shining. When Kate says the sun is shining, he refuses to continue the journey until she admits that it is the moon. Katherine agrees that it is the moon. Petruccio reverses his claim and says that it is in fact the sun. Hortensio persuades Petruccio that he has tamed Katherine, and they continue the journey.

They pass an old man on the same road to Padua, and Petruccio claims that the old man is a young maid. He entreats Kate to embrace the maid. Kate immediately obeys, but Petruccio says she is mistaken, for the maid is really an old man. Kate continues to play along.

The old man turns out to be Vincentio, the true father of Lucentio. He tells the trio that he has come to visit his son in Padua. Petruccio happily tells him of the marriage expected between Bianca and Lucentio and realizes that this will make Vincentio Petruccio's father-in-law. A bit confused, they all continue their journey to Padua together in order to sort things out there.

ACT V

Lucentio and Bianca marry; Katherine shocks everyone with her total subservience to Petruccio.

V.I Location: Padua

Lucentio and Bianca marry; Lucentio is forced to confess his deception when his real father arrives in Padua.

Biondello hurries Lucentio and Bianca to the church, where the priest is ready to marry them. Lucentio is no longer disguised as Cambio the schoolmaster. Petruccio's party and Vincentio knock on the door of Lucentio's house, where Tranio and the pedant are in their disguises. When the pedant answers, Vincentio says he is Lucentio's father, but the pedant claims to be Lucentio's true father and calls for the imposter's arrest. Just then, Biondello arrives. He turns white when he sees his old master, Vincentio, who recognizes him. Biondello pretends not to notice Vincentio as Baptista, Tranio, and the pedant come out of the house. Vincentio also recognizes Tranio in Lucentio's clothing, and he is further enraged when Tranio pretends not to know him.

The crowd turns against Vincentio and is preparing to escort him to jail when Lucentio and Bianca, newly married, arrive from the church. Biondello, Tranio, and the pedant run away from the scene, knowing the game is up. Lucentio can do nothing but beg his father's pardon and disclose the scheme to everyone present. He explains that his deception stemmed from his love for Bianca, which pacifies the two fathers somewhat. Nevertheless, they depart to seek some small revenge on the men who fooled them.

Katherine and Petruccio stand in amazement at the proceedings. They follow the rest to see the conclusion, but not before Petruccio demands one more thing of his wife. He asks her to kiss him, there in the middle of the street. Initially, Katherine refuses, saying she is ashamed to do so. But when Petruccio says they will go home, Kate kisses him. Petruccio finally seems satisfied with her.

V.II Location: Padua

Katherine proves herself the most obedient of wives.

Lucentio throws a banquet to celebrate the three recent marriages in Padua: Petruccio to Kate, Lucentio to Bianca, and Hortensio to the widow. As they sit around the table eating and chatting, Petruccio and the widow joke with each other, mostly at Hortensio's expense. Katherine joins in and begins to argue with the widow. The argument nearly becomes violent, with the men cheering them on to fight, but Bianca calms them, and the three wives go off together to talk.

The men chide Petruccio, thinking he has been stuck with a vicious shrew. Petruccio suggests a test to see which of the three new husbands has the most obedient wife. Each of them will send for his wife, and the one whose wife obeys first will be the winner. After placing a significant amount of money on the bet, Lucentio sends Biondello get Bianca. Biondello returns to tell them that Bianca is busy and will not come. Hortensio receives a similar response from the widow. Grumio goes back to get Katherine, and she returns at once. Everyone is surprised but Petruccio. Petruccio sends Katherine to bring in the other wives. Again, she obeys. Upon their return, Petruccio comments that he dislikes Kate's hat and tells her to throw it off. She obeys at once. Bianca and the widow, aghast at Katherine's subservience, are even more shocked when, at Petruccio's request, Katherine gives a speech on the duty that wives owe to their husbands.

In the speech, Kate reprimands the women for their angry dispositions, saying that it does not become them to behave this way, especially toward their husbands. A wife's duty to her husband, she says, is like the duty "the subject owes the prince," because the husband endures great pain and labor for her benefit (V.ii.159). She admits that once she was as haughty as Bianca and the widow are now, but that she has since changed her ways and most willingly obeys her husband. The other men admit complete defeat, and Petruccio leaves victorious. He and Katherine go to bed happily, and Hortensio and Lucentio remain behind to wonder at this miraculous change.

ANALYSIS OF MAJOR CHARACTERS IN *THE TAMING OF THE SHREW*

KATHERINE

At the beginning of the play, Katherine is a foul-tempered, sharp-tongued woman whom many people consider a shrew. She constantly insults and degrades the men around her, and she is prone to wild and sometimes physical displays of anger. Most of the play's characters believe Katherine to be inherently ill-tempered, but it is possible that her unpleasant behavior stems from unhappiness. Katherine may be unhappy because her father prefers her sister, or because she worries that she is undesirable, or because she thinks she may never win a husband, or because she hates the way men treat her. In many ways, Katherine feels out of place in her society. She is too intelligent and independent to passively obey her father and treat her intellectual inferiors with respect. At the same time, she knows that only by marrying will she find a secure and happy place in the world. A vicious circle ensues: the angrier Katherine becomes at the strictures of society, the less likely it is that she will be able to adapt to society, and the more her anger grows.

Despite Petruccio's fondness for humiliating and depriving Katherine, it is easy to understand why Katherine might marry a man like him. In their first conversation, Petruccio establishes himself as Katherine's intellectual and verbal equal, a different breed than the easily dominated men who bore Katherine. Petruccio constantly tries to convince Katherine that she has no real choice but to adapt to her social role as a wife. This argument must be attractive to Katherine on some level, since even if she dislikes the role of wife, playing it at least means she can command respect and consideration rather than suffer the universal revulsion she receives as a shrew. Having a social role, even if it is not ideal, must be less painful than continually rejecting any social role at all. Katherine might seem to become more passive by succumbing to Petruccio, but by the end of the play, she has gained a position and even an authoritative voice that she was previously lacking.

PETRUCCIO

Petruccio is a difficult character to decipher, and our interpretation of the play changes dramatically depending on how we interpret his actions. If he is nothing more than a vain, uncaring, greedy chauvinist who thinks of marriage as an act of domination, then the play becomes a dark comedy about the materialism and hunger for power that inspire people to get married. But if Petruccio is actually capable of loving Kate and wants to tame her merely to facilitate a happy marriage, then the play is an examination of the psychology of relationships.

Petruccio is unabashedly selfish, materialistic, and domineering, but he does love Katherine. He violently imposes his mastery on her, keeping her tired and hungry for some time after their marriage, but he frames this treatment in the language of love, saying that he wants Katherine to adapt to her rightful place in society and that he wants to make their marriage a happy one. Above all, Petruccio is a comic figure, an exaggerated personality who continually makes the audience laugh.

LUCENTIO

The intrepid, lovesick Lucentio is a foil for Petruccio. Lucentio has the sort of idyllic, poetic view of love that Petruccio dismisses. Lucentio is struck by love for Bianca at first sight, says he will die if he cannot win her heart, and indulges in romantic and fanciful schemes in order to be near her. Whereas *The Taming of the Shrew* presents marriage as a union defined by economic and social concerns, Lucentio maintains an impractical vision of courtly love. Petruccio's decision to marry is based on his self-proclaimed desire to win a fortune, but Lucentio's is based on romantic love. Petruccio devotes himself to taming his bride, but Lucentio submits to his. Petruccio stages his wedding as a public spectacle, but Lucentio elopes with Bianca.

The contrast between Lucentio and Petruccio distinguishes *The Taming of the Shrew* from other Elizabethan plays, which do not examine the post-wedding consequences of a romantic courtship. Once the practical business of being married begins, Lucentio's preoccupation with courtly love seems somewhat outmoded and ridiculous. In the end, it is Petruccio's disturbing, flamboyant pragmatism that produces a happy and functioning marriage. Lucentio's poetic instincts leave him humiliated when Bianca refuses to answer his summons.

THEMES, MOTIFS & SYMBOLS IN *THE TAMING OF THE SHREW*

THEMES

MARRIAGE AS AN ECONOMIC INSTITUTION   *The Taming of the Shrew* emphasizes how economic considerations determine who marries whom. The play tends to explore romantic relationships from a social perspective, surveying the institutions of courtship and marriage rather than the inner passions of lovers. Also, the play focuses on how courtship affects not just the lovers themselves, but their parents, their servants, and their friends. In general, while the husband and the wife are the primary players after the wedding, the main figures during the courtship are the future husband and the father of the future wife. Marriage becomes a transaction involving the transfer of money. Lucentio wins Bianca's heart, but he is given permission to marry her only after convincing Baptista that he is fabulously rich. Petruccio marries Katherine, but only because he wants her large dowry.

THE EFFECT OF SOCIAL ROLES ON INDIVIDUAL HAPPINESS   Each character in the play is expected to behave according to the dictates of his or her social position. Wealth, age, gender, profession, parentage, and education define those social positions, and family, friends, and society harshly enforce the rules governing them. Lucentio occupies the social role of the wealthy young student, Tranio that of the servant, and Bianca and Katherine that of eligible young upper-class women. Katherine wants nothing to do with her social role, and the impossibility of abandoning it makes her angry. By failing to live up to the behavioral expectations of her society, she incurs its cold disapproval, which results in her alienation and unhappiness. Besides Katherine, many other characters in *The Taming of the Shrew* attempt to circumvent or deny their socially defined roles. Lucentio transforms himself into a working-class Latin tutor, Tranio transforms himself into a wealthy young aristocrat, Christopher Sly finds himself transformed from a tinker into a lord, and so forth.

Compared with Katherine's serious anguish about her role, the other characters' attempts to subvert society seem like harmless fun. However, each transformation must be undone before conventional life can resume at the end of the play. A servant like Tranio may put on the clothes of a lord, but he is still a servant. Lucentio must reveal his subterfuge to his father and to Baptista. Katherine must adapt to her role as wife. Although the primary excitement of *The Taming of the Shrew* comes from the possibility of permeable social boundaries, the conventional order reestablishes itself in the end.

MOTIFS

DISGUISE   Disguise figures prominently in *The Taming of the Shrew*: Sly dresses as a lord, Lucentio dresses as a Latin tutor, Tranio dresses as Lucentio, Hortensio dresses as a music tutor, and the pedant dresses as Vincentio. These disguises enable the characters to transgress social and class barriers temporarily. They pose the question of whether clothes make the man—that is, whether a person can change his or her essence by changing his or her outward appearance. In *The Taming of the Shrew*, the answer is no. Despite convincing impersonations, class is always a matter of birth rather than behavior. Tranio, disguised as Lucentio, needs only to bump into Vincentio for his true identity to surface. As Petruccio implies on his wedding day, a garment is simply a garment, and the person beneath remains the same no matter what disguise is worn.

DOMESTICATION   As the word "taming" in the play's title indicates, domestication is the preoccupation of the plot. A great part of the action consists of Petruccio's attempts to cure Katherine of her hostility. Shakespeare frequently refers to Katherine as a wild animal that must be domesticated. Petruccio considers himself, as do his friends, to be a tamer who must train his wife. After the wedding, Petruccio and Katherine's relationship is defined by the rhetoric of domestication. Petruccio speaks of training Katherine like a "falcon" and says he plans to "kill a wife with kindness." Hortensio conceives of Petruccio's house as a place where other men may learn how to domesticate women, calling it a "taming-school."

SYMBOLS

PETRUCCIO'S WEDDING COSTUME   The ridiculous outfit Petruccio wears to his wedding with Katherine symbolizes his control over her. Simply by wearing the costume, he humiliates her. Despite her embarrassment, Katherine allows the ceremony to proceed, symbolically yielding to Petruccio's authority before the wedding even begins. The costume also symbolizes the relative unimportance of clothing. Petruccio declares that Katherine is marrying him, not his clothes, indicating that the man beneath the attire is more important and constant than the attire itself.

THE HABERDASHER'S CAP AND THE TAILOR'S GOWN   The cap and gown that Katherine likes and Petruccio denies her symbolize Petruccio's power over her. The outfit forces Katherine to recognize and comply with Petruccio's wishes.

IMPORTANT QUOTATIONS FROM *THE TAMING OF THE SHREW*

---

1. *Signor Hortensio, 'twixt such friends as we*
    Few words suffice; and therefore, if thou know
    One rich enough to be Petruccio's wife—
    As wealth is burden of my wooing dance—
    Be she as foul as was Florentius' love,
    As old as Sibyl, and as curst and shrewd
    As Socrates' Xanthippe or a worse,
    She moves me not—or not removes at least
    Affection's edge in me, were she as rough
    As are the swelling Adriatic seas.
    I come to wive it wealthily in Padua;
    If wealthily, then happily in Padua.

Location: I.ii.62–73
Speaker and interluctor: Petruccio to Hortensio
Context: Petruccio explains his determination to find a bride in Padua

Petruccio frankly states that he wants to marry for money. He equates wealth with a happy marriage. Apart from his prospective wife's wealth, Petruccio says that he does not care about any of her qualities. He says that he will marry a woman as "foul as was Florentius' love," referring to a story in which the knight Florent was forced to marry an old woman who saved his life. Petruccio's wife may be as "old as Sibyl," a mythic prophetess who lived forever, but continued to grow older and older. Or she may be as unpleasant as "Socrates' Xanthippe," a woman reputed to be a great shrew. This speech exemplifies Petruccio's brash, robust manner of speaking. He is unembarrassed by his materialism and selfishness, and he is straightforward in his acknowledgement that marriage is an economic agreement—something that everyone in the play knows but which only Petruccio discusses so frankly.

---

2. Petruccio: *Come, come, you wasp, i'faith you are too angry.*
    Katherine: *If I be waspish, best beware my sting.*
    Petruccio: *My remedy is then to pluck it out.*
    Katherine: *Ay, if the fool could find where it lies.*
    Petruccio: *Who knows not where a wasp does wear*

his sting? In his tail.
Katherine: *In his tongue.*
Petruccio: *Whose tongue?*
Katherine: *Yours, if you talk of tales, and so farewell.*
Petruccio: *What, with my tongue in your tail?*

Location: II.i.207–214
Speakers: Petruccio and Katherine
Context: Petruccio and Katherine, who have just met, banter

Petruccio's and Katherine's first conversation is an extraordinary display of verbal wit, with Petruccio making use of lurid sexual puns in order to undermine Katherine's standoffishness and anger. Other characters frequently compare Katherine to a dangerous wild animal, as Petruccio does here, calling her a wasp. Katherine angrily replies that if she is a wasp, he should watch out for her sting. Petruccio says he will simply pluck out her sting, rendering her harmless. In saying this, Petruccio challenges Katherine, acknowledging his intent to tame her. Katherine, disgusted, says that Petruccio is too much of a fool to know where a wasp's sting is. Katherine is referring to her sharp tongue, but Petruccio pretends that she made a sexual innuendo by saying that a wasp wears his sting in his tail. Katherine contradicts him, saying, "In his tongue." Katherine's metaphor implies that she will sting Petruccio with her wit, but Petruccio's metaphor implies that he will "pluck out" the stinger from Katherine's "tail," a reference to her genitals. When Petruccio asks "Whose tongue?" Katherine replies, "Yours, if you talk of tales," implying that if he continues to pursue her, she will sting him on his tongue. But Petruccio again gives her words sexual meaning, pretending to be surprised at the suggestion of "my tongue in your tail." This passage suggests not only the fiery conflict that instantly springs up between Petruccio and Katherine, but also the sexual attraction underlying it.

---

3. *Thus in plain terms: your father hath consented*
   That you shall be my wife, your dowry 'greed on,
   And will you, nill you, I will marry you.
   Now Kate, I am a husband for your turn,
   For by this light, whereby I see thy beauty—
   Thy beauty that doth make me like thee well—
   Thou must be married to no man but me,
   For I am he am born to tame you, Kate,
   And bring you from a wild Kate to a Kate
   Conformable as other household Kates.
   Here comes your father. Never make denial.
   I must and will have Katherine to my wife.

Location: II.i.261–272
Speaker: Petruccio to Katherine
Context: Petruccio informs Katherine that he is going to marry her

Shortly after meeting Katherine, Petruccio announces that since her father has agreed and the dowry has been settled, he will marry her whether she likes it or not ("will you, nill you, I will marry you"). Petruccio says "I am he am born to tame you, Kate," suggesting that Katherine is an animal and he is a tamer. Petruccio calls Katherine a "wild Kate"—a pun on "wildcat"—that he will "tame." This speech set the terms for Petruccio and Katherine's relationship. It also implicates Katherine in her fate. She is fully aware of Petruccio's intentions and implicitly consents to marry him by failing to protest when he falsely claims she has already agreed to do so.

---

4. *Then God be blessed, it is the blessed sun,*
   But sun it is not when you say it is not,

And the moon changes even as your mind.
What you will have it named, even that it is,
And so it shall be still for Katherine.

Location: IV.vi.19–23
Speaker: Katherine to Petruccio
Context: Petruccio has ordered Katherine to say that the sun is really the moon

Tired, hungry, and weary of their conflicts, Katherine at last relents and declares that, for all she cares, Petruccio can define reality for her from this point forward. She will believe, or at least say that she believes, that Petruccio controls even celestial events and objects. With this expression of defeat, Petruccio's victory over Katherine's spirit becomes inevitable.

---

5. *Thy husband is thy lord, thy life, thy keeper,*
   Thy head, thy sovereign, one that cares for thee,
   And for thy maintenance commits his body
   To painful labour both by sea and land,
   To watch the night in storms, the day in cold,
   Whilst thou liest warm at home, secure and safe,
   And craves no other tribute at thy hands
   But love, fair looks, and true obedience,
   Too little payment for so great a debt.
   My mind hath been as big as one of yours,
   My heart as great, my reason haply more,
   To bandy word for word and frown for frown;
   But now I see our lances are but straws,
   Our strength as weak, our weakness past compare,
   That seeming to be most which we indeed least are.
   Then vail your stomachs, for it is no boot,
   And place your hands below your husband's foot,
   In token of which duty, if he please,
   My hand is ready, may it do him ease.

Location: V.ii.140–183
Speaker: Katherine
Context: Katherine explains her new views on the wife's role

This speech, which stuns its hearers, indicates a shocking transformation of Katherine's opinions about marriage and men. The once shrewish Katherine now declares that Bianca and Hortensio's widow are ingrates for looking angrily at their husbands, whom Katherine describes as their lords, kings, and governors. She says that a woman's husband protects her and supports her, living a life of danger and responsibility while the woman is "warm at home, secure and safe." In return, she says, the husband asks only for his wife's kindness and obedience, a tiny payment for "so great a debt." A husband is to his wife as a prince is to his subject, and if a woman proves shrewish ("froward, peevish, sullen, sour"), then she is like a traitor to a just ruler.

Katherine says that women's bodies are soft and weak, and their inner selves should match them. She tells Bianca and the widow that she herself has been as proud and as headstrong as they are ("My mind hath been as big as one of yours, / My heart as great"), but now she understands that "our lances are but straws," meaning that women's weapons are insignificant. A woman should prepare herself to do anything for her husband, including, as Katherine does now, kneel before him and hold his foot. This speech summarizes the extent of Katherine's character development over the course of the play. She began by fighting against her social role, but now she offers a lengthy, seemingly sincere defense of it. The speech also summarizes the play's view of marital harmony, in which husbands provide peace, security, and comfort to their wives, and wives provide loyalty and obedience in return.

THE TEMPEST

Prospero, a powerful magician who used to be the duke of Milan, causes his enemies to wash up on his island, then uses his magic to reconcile with them and regain his dukedom.

THE TEMPEST IN CONTEXT

The Tempest probably was written in 1610–1611, and was first performed at court by the King's Men in the fall of 1611. It was performed again in the winter of 1612–1613 during the festivities in celebration of the marriage of King James's daughter Elizabeth. *The Tempest* is most likely the last play written entirely by Shakespeare, and it is remarkable for being one of only two plays by Shakespeare (the other being *Love's Labour's Lost*) whose plot is entirely original. The play does, however, draw on travel literature of its time—most notably the accounts of a tempest off the Bermudas that separated and nearly wrecked a fleet of colonial ships sailing from Plymouth to Virginia. The English colonial project seems to be on Shakespeare's mind throughout *The Tempest*, as almost every character, from the lord Gonzalo to the drunk Stefano, ponders how he would rule the island on which the play is set if he were its king. Shakespeare seems also to have drawn on Montaigne's essay "Of the Cannibals," which was translated into English in 1603. The name of Prospero's servant-monster, Caliban, may be an anagram or derivative of "Cannibal."

    The Tempest includes stage directions for a number of elaborate special effects. The many pageants and songs accompanied by ornately costumed figures or stage-magic—for example, the banquet in Act III, scene iii, and the wedding celebration for Ferdinand and Miranda in Act IV, scene i—give the play the feeling of a masque, a highly stylized form of dramatic, musical entertainment popular among the aristocracy of the sixteenth and seventeenth centuries. It is perhaps the tension between simple stage effects and elaborate and surprising ones that gives the play its eerie, dreamlike quality. *The Tempest* is rich and complex even though it is one of Shakespeare's shortest, most simply constructed plays.

    It is tempting to think of *The Tempest* as Shakespeare's farewell to the stage because one of its characters is a great magician giving up his art. Indeed, we can interpret Prospero's reference to the dissolution of "the great globe itself" (IV.i.153) as an allusion to Shakespeare's theatre. However, Shakespeare is known to have written at least two other plays after *The Tempest*: *The Two Noble Kinsmen* and *Henry VIII* in 1613, both possibly written with John Fletcher. A performance of the latter was, in fact, the occasion for the actual dissolution of the Globe. A cannon fired during the performance accidentally ignited the thatch, and the theater burned to the ground.

THE TEMPEST: KEY FACTS

Full title: The Tempest	
Time and place written: 1610–1611; England	
Date of first publication: 1623	
Genre: Romance	
Setting (time): The Renaissance	
Setting (place): An island in the Mediterranean Sea, probably off the coast of Italy	
Protagonist: Prospero	
Major conflict: Prospero seeks to use his magic to make Antonio and Alonso repent and restore him to his rightful place	

THE TEMPEST: CHARACTER LIST

Alonso The king of Naples and the father of Ferdinand. Alonso helped Antonio unseat Prospero twelve years before. He is acutely aware of the consequences of his actions, and blames the death of his son on his own decision to marry his daughter to the prince of Tunis. He also regrets his role in usurping Prospero.

Antonio   Prospero's brother. Antonio is power-hungry and foolish.

Ariel   Prospero's spirit helper. Most critics refer to Ariel as "he," but his gender and physical form are ambiguous. Rescued by Prospero from a long imprisonment at the hands of the witch Sycorax, Ariel is Prospero's servant until Prospero decides to release him. He is mischievous and ubiquitous, able to traverse the length of the island in an instant and change shape at will.

Boatswain   A shipman. The boatswain is vigorous and good-natured. He is competent and almost cheerful in the shipwreck scene, demanding practical help rather than weeping and prayer. He seems surprised but not stunned when he awakens from a long sleep at the end of the play.

Caliban   Another of Prospero's servants. Caliban, the son of the deceased witch Sycorax, acquainted Prospero with the island when Prospero arrived. Caliban believes that the island rightfully belongs to him and has been stolen by Prospero. His speech and behavior is sometimes coarse and brutal, as in his drunken scenes with Stefano and Trinculo, and sometimes eloquent and sensitive, as in his rebukes of Prospero and his description of the eerie beauty of the island.

Ferdinand   Alonso's son and heir. In some ways, Ferdinand is as pure and naïve as Miranda. He falls in love with her at first sight and happily submits to servitude in order to win her father's approval.

Gonzalo   An old, honest lord. Gonzalo helped Prospero and Miranda to escape after Antonio usurped Prospero's title. Gonzalo's speeches provide commentary on the events of the play.

Miranda   Prospero's daughter. Miranda was brought to the island at an early age and has never seen anyone other than her father and Caliban, although she dimly remembers being cared for by female servants as an infant. Miranda's perceptions of other people tend to be naïve and non-judgmental. She is compassionate, generous, and loyal to her father.

Prospero   The play's protagonist, and Miranda's father. Twelve years before the events of the play, Prospero was the duke of Milan. His brother, Antonio, in concert with Alonso, king of Naples, usurped him, forcing him to flee in a boat with his daughter. Prospero has spent twelve years on the island refining his magic.

Sebastian   Alonso's brother. Like Antonio, Sebastian is both aggressive and cowardly. He is easily persuaded to kill his brother, and he tells a ridiculous story about lions when Gonzalo catches him with his sword drawn.

Trinculo and Stefano   A jester and a drunken butler. Trinculo and Stefano are comic foils to the other, more powerful pairs of Prospero/Alonso and Antonio/Sebastian. Their drunken boasting and petty greed reflect and deflate the quarrels and power struggles of Prospero and the other noblemen.

THE TEMPEST: PLOT OVERVIEW

A storm strikes a ship carrying a party of Italian princes and noblemen returning from a wedding. On board the ship are: Alonso, the king of Naples; Alonso's brother, Sebastian, and son, Ferdinand; Antonio, the duke of Milan; and Gonzalo, an elderly courtier of Milan. The storm is the work of the magician Prospero, who was the duke of Milan until twelve years before, when his brother Antonio, with Alonso's help, overthrew him and put him out to sea with his daughter Miranda. Prospero and Miranda arrived on an island. Prospero freed a powerful spirit named Ariel from a tree and took him as a slave. He also educated and enslaved Caliban, the brutish offspring of a witch.

Prospero causes the ship's passengers to wash up onto his island. He has Ariel lead Ferdinand into Miranda's presence. Ferdinand and Miranda fall in love. Prospero plans to marry the two of them, but first he wants to test Ferdinand, so he imprisons him and sets him to work carrying logs. Elsewhere on the island, Antonio bemoans the loss of Ferdinand, and Gonzalo tries to comfort him while Antonio and Sebastian plot to kill their fellow castaways. Caliban offers himself as a slave to Trinculo and Stefano, Alonso's drunken jester and butler, and promises to teach them how to kill Prospero. Ariel keeps Prospero informed of everything that happens. Ariel leads Alonso and the other lords, who are tired and hungry, to a banquet set by spirits, then causes the banquet to vanish suddenly. Appearing as a harpy, Ariel chastises Alonso and Antonio for their treachery, and Alonso feels remorseful.

Prospero releases Ferdinand from servitude and gives Ferdinand and Miranda his blessing. He orders spirits to perform a wedding masque for them. Ariel tells Prospero how he used his music to lead Trinculo, Stefano, and Caliban into a filthy pond near Prospero's cell. Prospero and Ariel send spirits in the form of hounds to torment the threesome. Prospero brings Antonio, Alonso, and the other lords before him. He confronts Antonio and Alonso with their misdeeds and says he forgives them. Alonso apologizes and laments the loss of Ferdinand, whereupon Prospero draws aside a curtain to reveal Ferdinand and Miranda playing chess. The ship's crew, which had been in an enchanted sleep since the storm, appears, as do Trinculo, Stefano, and Caliban. Prospero invites the others to stay the night and listen to him explain the events of the past twelve years, after which they will return to Italy and Prospero will go back to being Duke of Milan.

THE TEMPEST: SCENE SUMMARY

ACT I

Prospero arranges a tempest to shipwreck his enemies on his island; he berates his slaves, Ariel and Caliban; Ferdinand and Miranda fall in love.

I.I Location: at sea

A tempest wracks a small ship carrying noblemen and the king.

A violent storm rages around a small ship at sea. The master of the ship calls for his boatswain to rouse the mariners to action and prevent the ship from running aground. Chaos ensues. Some mariners enter, followed by a group of nobles: Alonso, king of Naples; Sebastian, his brother; Antonio; Gonzalo; and others. We do not learn these men's names in this scene, nor do we learn yet that they have just come from Tunis, in Africa, where Alonso's daughter Claribel married the prince. As the boatswain and his crew take in the topsail and the topmast, Alonso and his party get in the way, and the boatswain tells them to get below-decks. Gonzalo reminds the boatswain that one of the passengers is of some importance, but the boatswain is unmoved. He will do what he has to in order to save the ship, regardless of who is aboard.

The lords go below, but three of them—Sebastian, Antonio, and Gonzalo—enter again only four lines later. Sebastian and Antonio curse the boatswain. Some mariners enter wet and crying. Gonzalo orders the mariners to pray for the king and the prince. There is a strange noise—perhaps the sound of thunder, splitting wood, or roaring water—and the cry of mariners. Antonio, Sebastian, and Gonzalo, preparing to sink to a watery grave, go in search of the king.

I.II Location: the island shore

Prospero explains Miranda's history to her; it comes out that he and Ariel arranged the shipwreck; Prospero scolds Ariel and berates Caliban; Miranda and Ferdinand fall in love, but Prospero decides to test Ferdinand.

Prospero and Miranda have witnessed the shipwreck. Miranda asks her father to make sure no one onboard comes to any harm. Prospero assures her that no one was hurt. He tells her it is time she learned who she is and where she comes from. Miranda seems curious, noting that Prospero has often started to tell her about herself but always stopped. Prospero begins telling his tale, interrupting himself three times to ask Miranda if she is listening to him. He tells her that he was once the duke of Milan and famous for his great intelligence.

Prospero explains that he gradually grew bored with politics and turned his attention more and more to his studies, neglecting his duties as duke. This gave his brother Antonio an opportunity to act on his ambition. Working with the king of Naples, Antonio usurped Prospero's dukedom. Antonio arranged for the king of Naples to pay him an annual tribute and pay homage to him as duke. Later, the king of Naples helped Antonio raise an army to march on Milan, driving Prospero out. Prospero and Miranda escaped death at the hands of the army in a rickety boat prepared for them by Prospero's loyal subjects. Gonzalo, an honest Neapolitan, provided them with food, clothing, and books from Prospero's library.

Prospero explains that sheer good luck has brought his former enemies to the island. Miranda suddenly grows very sleepy, perhaps because Prospero charms her with his magic. When she is asleep, Prospero calls forth a spirit, Ariel. Prospero and Ariel's conversation reveals that they were responsible for the storm that wrecked Prospero's enemies' ship. Ariel acted as the wind, the thunder, and the lightning. When everyone except the crew had abandoned the ship, Ariel did as Prospero requested and made sure everyone was brought safely to shore but dispersed around the island. Ariel reports that the king's son is alone. He also tells Prospero that the mariners and boatswain have been charmed to sleep in the ship, which has been brought safely to harbor. The rest of the fleet believes the ship was destroyed by the storm and has headed safely back to Naples.

Prospero thanks Ariel for his service. Ariel reminds Prospero that he promised to subtract one year from Ariel's agreed time of servitude if Ariel performed his services without complaint. Prospero chastises Ariel for his impudence. He reminds Ariel of where he came from and how Prospero rescued him. Ariel had been a servant of Sycorax, a witch banished from Algiers (Algeria) and sent to the island long ago. Ariel was too delicate to perform her horrible commands, so she imprisoned him in a "cloven pine" (I.ii.279). She did not free him before she died, and he might have remained imprisoned forever if Prospero had not rescued him. Prospero threatens to imprison Ariel for twelve years if does not stop complaining. Ariel promises to be more polite. Prospero commands him to take the form of a nymph of the sea and be invisible to all but Prospero. Ariel goes to do so. Prospero wakes Miranda, who does not realize that she fell asleep because of Prospero's enchantment.

Prospero calls to his servant Caliban, the son of Sycorax. Caliban appears and curses. Prospero promises to punish him by giving him cramps at night, and Caliban responds by chiding Prospero for imprisoning him on the island that once belonged to him alone. He reminds Prospero that he showed Prospero around when he first arrived. Prospero accuses Caliban of being ungrateful for all that he has taught and given him. He calls him a "lying slave" and reminds him of the effort he made to educate him (I.ii.347). Caliban's hereditary nature, he says, makes him unfit to live among civilized people. Caliban says he knows how to curse only because Prospero and Miranda taught him to speak. Prospero sends Caliban away, telling him to fetch more firewood and threatening him with cramps and aches if he refuses. Caliban obeys him.

Ariel, playing music and singing, enters, leading Ferdinand. Prospero tells Miranda to look at Ferdinand. Miranda, who has seen no humans in her life other than Prospero and Caliban, immediately falls in love. Ferdinand is smitten with Miranda. He reveals that he is the prince of Naples. Prospero is pleased that they are so taken with each other, but decides that they must not fall in love too quickly. He accuses Ferdinand of merely pretending to be the prince of Naples, and tells Ferdinand he is going to imprison him. Ferdinand draws his sword, but Prospero charms him so that he cannot move. Miranda asks her father to have mercy, but he silences her harshly. This man, he tells her, is a mere Caliban compared to other men. He says she simply doesn't know any better because she has never seen any other men. Prospero leads the charmed and helpless Ferdinand to his imprisonment. Secretly, he thanks the invisible Ariel for his help, sends him on another mysterious errand, and promises to free him soon.

ACT II

Antonio convinces Sebastian to make an attempt on Gonzalo's life, but Ariel wakes Gonzalo and saves him; after drinking Stefano's liquor, Caliban worships Stefano.

II.1   Location: the island

Alonso blames himself for Ferdinand's death; Antonio urges Sebastian to kill Gonzalo, but Ariel foils the scheme.

Alonso, Sebastian, Antonio, Gonzalo, and other shipwrecked lords search for Ferdinand on another part of the island. Alonso is despondent and unreceptive to the good-natured Gonzalo's attempts to cheer him up. Antonio and Sebastian childishly mock Gonzalo's suggestions that the island is a good place to be and that they are all lucky to have survived. Alonso finally openly expresses regret that he married away his daughter in Tunis. Francisco, a minor lord, pipes up that he saw Ferdinand swimming valiantly after the wreck, but this does not comfort Alonso. Sebastian tells his brother that he is indeed to blame for Ferdinand's death—if he had not married his daughter to an African (rather than a European), none of this would have happened.

Gonzalo tells the lords they are only making the situation worse and attempts to change the subject, discussing what he might do if he were the lord of the island. Antonio and Sebastian mock his utopian vision. Ariel enters playing "solemn music" (II.i.182, stage direction), and gradually everyone but Sebastian and Antonio falls asleep. Seeing the vulnerability of the sleeping men, Antonio tries to persuade Sebastian to kill his brother. He rationalizes this scheme by explaining that Claribel, who is now queen of Tunis, is too far from Naples to inherit the kingdom should her father die, and as a result, Sebastian would be the heir to the throne. Sebastian begins to warm to the idea, especially after Antonio tells him that usurping Prospero's dukedom was the best move he ever made. Sebastian wonders aloud whether he will be afflicted by conscience, but Antonio dismisses this worry. Sebastian is at last convinced, and the two men draw their swords. Sebastian seems to have second thoughts at the last moment and stops. While he and Antonio confer, Ariel enters, singing in Gonzalo's ear that a conspiracy is underway and that he should wake up. Gonzalo wakes and shouts "Preserve the king!" His exclamation wakes everyone else (II.i.303). Sebastian quickly concocts a story about hearing a loud noise that caused him and Antonio to draw their swords. Gonzalo is suspicious but does not challenge the lords. The group continues its search for Ferdinand.

II.II   Location: elsewhere on the island

Trinculo hides from the rain under a cloak with Caliban; Stefano enters and gives Caliban liquor, which inspires Caliban to worship Stefano.

Caliban enters with a load of wood. Thunder sounds in the background. Caliban curses and describes the torments that Prospero's spirits subject him to: they pinch, bite, and prick him, especially when he curses. Caliban sees Trinculo and imagines him to be one of the spirits. Hoping to avoid pinching, he lies down and covers himself with his cloak. Trinculo hears the thunder and looks about for some cover from the storm. The only thing he sees is the cloak-covered Caliban on the ground. He is not so much repulsed by Caliban as curious. He cannot decide whether Caliban is a "man or a fish" (II.ii.24). He thinks of a time when he traveled to England and saw freak shows there. Caliban, he thinks, would bring him a lot of money in England. Thunder sounds again and Trinculo decides that the best shelter in sight is beneath Caliban's cloak, so he joins the man-monster there.

Stefano enters singing and drinking. He hears Caliban cry out to Trinculo, "Do not torment me! O!" (II.ii.54). Hearing this and seeing the four legs sticking out from the cloak, Stefano thinks the two men are a four-legged monster with a fever. He decides to relieve this fever with a drink. Caliban continues to resist Trinculo, whom he still thinks is a spirit tormenting him. Trinculo recognizes Stefano's voice. Stefano assumes for a moment that the monster has two heads, and promises to pour liquor in both mouths. Trinculo calls out to Stefano, and Stefano pulls his friend out from under the cloak. While the two men discuss how they arrived safely on shore, Caliban enjoys the liquor and begs to worship Stefano. The men take advantage of Caliban's drunkenness, mocking him as a "most ridiculous monster" (II.ii.157) as he promises to lead them around and show them the isle.

ACT III

Miranda and Ferdinand get engaged; Caliban plots to kill Prospero; Ariel, in the form of a harpy, condemns the noblemen for leaving Prospero and his daughter to die.

III.I   Location: Ferdinand's cell

Miranda proposes to Ferdinand, who accepts; unbeknownst to the couple, Prospero watches the proposal.

Ferdinand takes over Caliban's duties and carries wood for Prospero. Unlike Caliban, Ferdinand is not angry. Instead, he enjoys his labors because they serve the woman he loves. As Ferdinand works and thinks of Miranda, she enters. Prospero also enters unseen by either lover. Miranda tells Ferdinand to take a break from his work or let her work for him. Ferdinand refuses to let her work for him but does rest. He asks Miranda her name. She tells him and he is pleased: "Miranda" comes from the same Latin word that gives English the word "admiration." Ferdinand's speech plays on the etymology: "Admired Miranda! / Indeed the top of admiration, worth / What's dearest to the world!" (III.i.37–39).

Ferdinand flatters Miranda, who says she has no idea of any woman's face but her own. She praises Ferdinand's face, but then stops herself, remembering her father's instructions that she should not speak to Ferdinand. Ferdinand assures Miranda that he is a prince and probably a king now, though he prays his father is not dead. Miranda seems unconcerned with Ferdinand's title, and asks only if he loves her. Ferdinand replies enthusiastically that he does, and Miranda proposes marriage. Ferdinand accepts and the two part. Prospero comes forth. He knew this would happen. He hastens to his book of magic to prepare for remaining business.

III.II   Location: elsewhere on the island

As Ariel secretly watches, Caliban plots to kill Prospero and install Stefano as king of the island.

Caliban, Trinculo, and Stefano continue to drink and wander around the island. Stefano now refers to Caliban as "servant monster" and repeatedly orders him to drink. Caliban seems happy to obey. The men begin to quarrel, mostly in jest. Stefano has now assumed the title of lord of the island and he promises to hang Trinculo if Trinculo mocks Caliban. Ariel, invisible, enters just as Caliban is telling the men that he is "subject to a tyrant, a sorcerer, that by his cunning hath cheated me of the island" (III.ii.40–41). Ariel begins to stir up trouble, calling out, "Thou liest" (III.ii.42). Caliban cannot see Ariel and thinks that Trinculo called him a liar. He threatens Trinculo, and Stefano tells Trinculo not to interrupt Caliban anymore. Trinculo protests that he said nothing. Drunkenly, they continue talking, and Caliban tells them of his desire to get revenge against Prospero. Ariel continues to interrupt now and then with the words, "Thou liest." Stefano finally hits Trinculo.

While Ariel looks on, Caliban plots against Prospero. The key, Caliban tells his friends, is to take Prospero's magic books. Once they have done this, they can kill Prospero and take his daughter. Stefano will become king of the island and Miranda will be his queen. Trinculo tells Stefano that he thinks this plan is a good idea, and Stefano apologizes for the previous quarreling. Caliban assures them that Prospero will be asleep within a half-hour.

Ariel plays a tune on his flute and tabor-drum. Stefano and Trinculo wonder what this noise is, but Caliban tells them it is nothing to fear. Stefano relishes the thought of possessing this island kingdom "where I shall have my music for nothing" (III.ii.139–140). The men decide to follow the music and then kill Prospero.

III.III   Location: the island

As Alonso and the other noblemen sit down to a magical banquet, Ariel appears and berates them for driving Prospero from Milan and leaving him to die.

Alonso, Sebastian, Antonio, Gonzalo, and their companion lords are exhausted. Alonso gives up all hope of finding his son. Antonio, still hoping to kill Alonso, whispers to Sebastian that Alonso's fatigue and desperation will give them the perfect opportunity to kill him later that evening.

"[S]olemn and strange music" fills the stage (III.iii.17, stage direction), and a procession of spirits in "several strange shapes" enters, bringing a banquet of food (III.iii.19, stage direction). The spirits dance around the table, invite the king and his party to eat, and dance away. Prospero enters, invisible to everyone but the audience. The men disagree at first about whether to eat, but Gonzalo persuades them it will be all right, noting that many travelers tell stories of unbelievable but true events. This, he says, might be such an event.

Just as the men are about to eat, thunder sounds, and Ariel enters in the shape of a harpy. He claps his wings on the table and the banquet vanishes. Ariel mocks the men for attempting to draw their swords, which have been enchanted to feel heavy. Calling himself an instrument of fate and destiny, Ariel accuses Alonso, Sebastian, and Antonio of driving Prospero from Milan and leaving him and his child at the mercy of the sea. For this sin, he tells them, the powers of nature and the sea have exacted revenge on Alonso by taking Ferdinand. Ariel vanishes, and the procession of spirits enters and removes the banquet table. Prospero, still invisible, applauds the work of his spirit and announces with satisfaction that his enemies are now in his control. He leaves them in their distracted state and goes to visit with Ferdinand and his daughter.

Alonso is desperate. He believes his son has died and runs to drown himself. Sebastian and Antonio decide to fight the spirits. Gonzalo tells the other, younger lords to run after Antonio, Sebastian, and Alonso to make sure that none of them do anything rash.

ACT IV

After a masque in celebration of Ferdinand and Miranda's engagement, Prospero foils the attempt on his life.

IV.I Location: Prospero's house

Prospero arranges a celebratory masque for Ferdinand and Miranda; Caliban tries to kill Prospero, but Prospero stops him.

Prospero gives his blessing to Ferdinand and Miranda and warns Ferdinand not to break Miranda's "virgin-knot" before the wedding has been solemnized (IV.i.15–17). Ferdinand promises he won't. Prospero calls in Ariel and asks him to summon spirits to perform a masque for Ferdinand and Miranda. Three spirits appear in the shapes of the mythological figures Iris (Juno's messenger and the goddess of the rainbow), Juno (queen of the gods), and Ceres (goddess of agriculture). This trio performs a masque celebrating the lovers' engagement. Juno wishes the couple honor and riches, and Ceres wishes them natural prosperity and plenty. The spectacle awes Ferdinand. He says he would like to live on the island forever, with Prospero as his father and Miranda as his wife. Juno and Ceres send Iris to fetch some nymphs and reapers to perform a country dance. Just as this dance begins, Prospero startles suddenly and then sends the spirits away. He has remembered that Caliban and the others are about to make an attempt on his life.

Prospero's anger alarms Ferdinand and Miranda, but he tells them he is upset as a result of his age, and a walk will soothe him. Prospero makes a short speech about the masque, saying that the world itself is as insubstantial as a play, and that human beings are "such stuff / As dreams are made on." Ferdinand and Miranda leave Prospero to himself and Prospero immediately summons Ariel, who seems to have made a mistake by not reminding Prospero of Caliban's plot before the beginning of the masque. Prospero asks Ariel to tell him again what happened. Ariel reports that he used his music to lead the men through rough and prickly briars and then into a filthy pond. Prospero thanks Ariel, and the two set a trap for the three would-be assassins.

Prospero and Ariel hang up an array of fine apparel for the men to attempt to steal, and then make themselves invisible. Caliban, Trinculo, and Stefano enter, wet from the filthy pond. The fine clothing immediately distracts Stefano and Trinculo. They want to steal it, but Caliban wants to stick to the plan and kill Prospero. Stefano and Trinculo ignore him. Soon after they touch the clothing, there is "[a] noise of hunters" (IV.i.251, stage direction). A pack of spirits in the shape of hounds drives out the thieves.

ACT V

Prospero takes back his dukedom, reveals the engagement of Ferdinand and Miranda, plans a return to Italy, frees Ariel, and delivers an epilogue.

V.I Location: the island

Prospero demands his dukedom back from Antonio, reveals Ferdinand to Alonso, plans to return to Italy with the others, and frees Ariel.

Ariel tells Prospero that the day has reached its "sixth hour" (6 P.M.), when Ariel is allowed to stop working. Prospero acknowledges Ariel's point and asks how the king and his followers are faring. Ariel tells him they are currently imprisoned in a grove, as Prospero ordered. Alonso, Antonio, and Sebastian are mad with fear, and Gonzalo is crying constantly. Prospero tells Ariel to go release the men. Alone, he says he will give up magic. He says he will perform his last task and then break his staff and drown his magic book.

Ariel enters with Alonso and his companions, who have been charmed and obediently stand in a circle. Prospero speaks to them, praising Gonzalo for his loyalty and scolding the others for their treachery. He sends Ariel to his cell to fetch the clothes he once wore as duke of Milan. Ariel goes and returns immediately to help his master to put on the garments. Prospero promises to give Ariel his freedom and sends him to fetch the boatswain and mariners from the wrecked ship. Ariel goes.

Prospero releases Alonso and his companions from their spell and speaks with them. He forgives Antonio but demands that Antonio return his dukedom. Antonio does not respond. In fact, he does not say a word for the remainder of the play except to note that Caliban is "no doubt marketable" (V.i.269). Alonso tells Prospero that Ferdinand is missing. Prospero tells Alonso that he, too, has lost a child in this last tempest. Prospero draws aside a curtain, revealing Ferdinand and Miranda playing a game of chess. Alonso is ecstatic. The sight of more humans impresses Miranda. Alonso embraces his son and future daughter-in-law and begs Miranda's forgiveness for the treacheries of twelve years ago. Prospero silences Alonso, saying the reconciliation is complete.

After arriving with the boatswain and mariners, Ariel is sent to fetch Caliban, Trinculo, and Stefano, which he speedily does. The three drunken thieves are sent to Prospero's cell to return the clothing they stole and to clean it in preparation for the evening's reveling. Prospero invites Alonso and his company to stay the night. He will tell them the tale of his last twelve years, and in the morning, they can all set out for Naples, where Miranda and Ferdinand will be married. After the wedding, Prospero will return to Milan, where he plans to contemplate the end of his life. The last charge Prospero gives to Ariel before setting him free is to make sure the trip home is made on "calm seas" with "auspicious gales" (V.i.318).

EPILOGUE

Location: the island

Prospero asks the audience to forgive him and set him free by clapping.

The other characters exit and Prospero delivers an epilogue. He describes the loss of his magical powers ("Now my charms are all o'erthrown") and says that as he imprisoned Ariel and Caliban, the audience has imprisoned him on the stage. He says the audience can release him by applauding, and asks them to remember that his only desire was to please them. He says that as his listeners would like to have their own crimes forgiven, they should forgive him and set him free.

ANALYSIS OF MAJOR CHARACTERS IN *THE TEMPEST*

PROSPERO

Prospero is one of Shakespeare's more enigmatic protagonists. He is a sympathetic character because he was wronged by his usurping brother, but his absolute power over the other characters and his overwrought speeches make him difficult to like. In our first glimpse of him, he appears puffed up and self-important, and his repeated insistence that Miranda pay attention suggests that his story is boring her, although once Prospero moves on to a subject other than his own pursuit of knowledge, Miranda's attention is riveted.

Prospero has many shortcomings beyond long-windedness. He lost his dukedom partly because he neglected everyday matters, giving his brother a chance to rise up against him. His possession and use of magical knowledge makes him extremely powerful and not entirely sympathetic. His punishments of Caliban are petty and vindictive. He is short-tempered and unfair to Ariel. He is unpleasant in his treatment of Ferdinand, leading him to his daughter and then imprisoning and enslaving him.

Despite his shortcomings as a man, however, Prospero is so powerful as to be almost beyond likeability or disagreeableness. He generates the plot of the play almost single-handedly, as his various schemes, spells, and manipulations unfold in a grand design and achieve the play's happy ending. Watching Prospero work in *The Tempest* is like watching a dramatist create a play, building a story from material at hand and developing a plot so that the resolution brings the world into line with his idea of goodness and justice. Many critics and readers of the play have interpreted Prospero as a surrogate for Shakespeare, a character who lets the audience watch the ambiguities and wonder of the creative endeavor.

Prospero's final speech, in which he likens himself to a playwright by asking the audience for applause, strengthens this reading of the play and makes the play's final scene a moving celebration of creativity, humanity, and art. In the final two acts of the play, Prospero is also redeemed as a man. His love for Miranda, his forgiveness of his enemies, and the legitimately happy ending his scheme creates all mitigate some of the undesirable means he has used to achieve his happy ending.

MIRANDA

Miranda, who is just under fifteen, is gentle, compassionate, and relatively passive. From her very first lines she displays a meek and emotional nature. "O, I have suffered / With those that I saw suffer!" she says of the shipwreck (I.ii.5–6), and hearing Prospero's tale of their narrow escape from Milan, she says "I, not rememb'ring how I cried out then, / Will cry it o'er again" (I.ii.133–134). When Prospero chooses Miranda's husband for her while she sleeps, she does not protest. After Prospero has given the lovers his blessing, he and Ferdinand talk with surprising frankness about Miranda's virginity and the pleasures of the marriage bed while Miranda stands quietly by. Prospero tells Ferdinand not to "break her virgin-knot" before the wedding night (IV.i.15), and Ferdinand replies that lust will not take away "the edge of that day's celebration" (IV.i.29). In the play's final scene, Miranda is presented, with Ferdinand, almost as a prop or piece of scenery as Prospero draws aside a curtain to reveal the pair playing chess.

But while Miranda is passive in many ways, she has at least two moments of surprising forthrightness and strength that complicate the impression that she is a naïve young girl. The first moment is in Act I, scene ii, in which Miranda and Prospero talk with Caliban. Prospero alludes to the fact that Caliban once tried to rape Miranda. When Caliban rudely agrees that he intended to violate her, Miranda responds with impressive vehemence, clearly appalled at Caliban's light attitude. She goes on to scold him for being ungrateful for her attempts to educate him: "When thou didst not, savage, / Know thine own meaning, but wouldst gabble like / A thing most brutish, I endowed thy purposes / With words that made them known" (358–361). These lines are so surprising coming from Miranda that many editors have amended the text and given them to Prospero. In Act III, scene i, comes the second surprising moment—Miranda's marriage proposal to Ferdinand: "I am your wife, if you will marry me; / If not, I'll die your maid" (III.i.83–84). This proposal comes shortly after Miranda has told herself to remember her "father's precepts" (III.i.58) forbidding conversation with Ferdinand, which suggests that Miranda might be so retiring because she wants to please her father. That is, her passivity might be a struggle for her, rather than a natural state.

CALIBAN

Prospero's dark, earthy slave, frequently referred to as a monster by the other characters, Caliban is the son of a witch-hag and the only real native of the island in the play. He is an extremely complex figure, and he mirrors or parodies several other characters in the play. In his first speech to Prospero, Caliban insists that Prospero stole the island from him. With this speech, Caliban suggests that he, like Prospero, has had his position usurped. Caliban's desire for sovereignty over the island also mirrors the lust for power that led Antonio to overthrow Prospero. And Caliban's conspiracy with Stefano and Trinculo to murder Prospero suggests Antonio and Sebastian's plot against Alonso, as well as Antonio and Alonso's original conspiracy against Prospero.

Caliban both parallels and is contrasted with Prospero's other servant, Ariel. While Ariel is "an airy spirit," Caliban is of the earth; his speeches metaphorically turn to "springs, brine pits" (I.ii.341), "bogs, fens, flats" (II.ii.2), or crabapples and pignuts (II.ii.159–160). While Ariel maintains his dignity and his freedom by serving Prospero willingly, Caliban achieves a different kind of dignity by refusing, if only sporadically, to cower before Prospero's intimidation. Caliban also parallels and contrasts with Ferdinand in certain ways. In Act II, scene ii, Caliban enters "with a burden of wood," and Ferdinand enters in Act III, scene i, "bearing a log." Both Caliban and Ferdinand profess an interest in untying Miranda's "virgin knot." Ferdinand plans to marry her, while Caliban has attempted to rape her. The glorified, romantic, almost ethereal love of Ferdinand for Miranda starkly contrasts with Caliban's desire to impregnate Miranda and people the island with Calibans.

Finally, and tragically, Caliban becomes a parody of himself. In his first speech to Prospero, he regretfully reminds the magician that he showed him all the ins and outs of the island when Prospero first arrived. Only a few scenes later, Caliban gets drunk and fawns before a new magical being in his life: Stefano and his bottle of liquor. Soon, Caliban begs to show Stefano the island and even asks to lick his shoe. Caliban repeats the mistakes he claims to curse.

Despite his savage demeanor and grotesque appearance, Caliban has a noble side that the audience is only allowed to glimpse briefly, and which Prospero and Miranda do not acknowledge at all. His beautiful speeches about his island home are some of the most affecting in the play, and suggest that he is unjustly enslaved by an oppressor who does not appreciate the land he has conquered. Caliban's dark appearance, forced servitude, and native residence on the island have led many readers to interpret him as a symbol of the native cultures occupied and suppressed by European colonial societies, which are represented by the power of Prospero. Whether or not one accepts this allegory, Caliban remains one of the most intriguing and ambiguous minor characters in all of Shakespeare.

THEMES, MOTIFS, & SYMBOLS IN *THE TEMPEST*

THEMES

THE ILLUSION OF JUSTICE *The Tempest* tells a fairly straightforward story about the usurpation of Prospero's throne by his brother, and Prospero's quest to reestablish justice by restoring himself to power. However, the ideal of justice that motivates Prospero is highly subjective. Prospero presents himself as a victim working to right the wrongs that have been done to him, but his ideas of justice and injustice are somewhat hypocritical: he is furious with his brother for taking over his power and domain, but he has no qualms about enslaving Ariel and Caliban on their own territory. Because Prospero is often sinister, and because the play offers no notion of higher order or justice to supersede Prospero's interpretation of events, *The Tempest* is morally ambiguous.

However, if we think of Prospero as an author creating a story, his sense of justice begins to seem, if not perfect, at least sympathetic, for authors have no choice but to impose their own morality on their fictional worlds. Like a writer, Prospero tries to show others the way he views the world. By using magic and tricks that echo the special effects and spectacles of the theater, Prospero gradually persuades the other characters and the audience of the rightness of his case. As he does so, the ambiguities surrounding his methods slowly resolve themselves. Prospero forgives his enemies, releases his slaves, and relinquishes his magic power. At the end of the play, he is only an old man whose work has given the audience pleasure. The establishment of Prospero's idea of justice becomes less a commentary on justice in life than on the nature of morality in art. Happy endings are possible, Shakespeare seems to say, because the creativity of artists can create them, even if the moral values that establish the happy ending originate from nowhere but the imagination of the artist.

THE DIFFICULTY OF DISTINGUISHING NATURE FROM NURTURE Upon seeing Ferdinand for the first time, Miranda says that he is "the third man that e'er I saw" (I.ii.449). The other two are, presumably, Prospero and Caliban. In their first conversation with Caliban, however, Miranda and Prospero say very little that suggests they consider Caliban a human. Miranda reminds Caliban that before she taught him language, he gabbled "like / A thing most brutish" (I.ii.59–60), and Prospero says that he gave Caliban "human care" (I.ii.349), implying that this was something Caliban did not deserve. Caliban's exact nature continues to be ambiguous later. In Act IV, scene i, Prospero refers to Caliban as a "devil, a born devil, on whose nature / Nurture can never stick" (IV.i.188–189). Miranda and Prospero think that their education has lifted Caliban from his brutish status, but they simultaneously think that his inherent brutishness can never be eradicated.

The audience is left to decide whether Caliban is inherently brutish or made brutish by oppression. Caliban claims he was kind to Prospero, but Prospero repaid that kindness by imprisoning him; Prospero claims he stopped being kind to Caliban after Caliban tried to rape Miranda. Our determination of who is telling the truth depends on our interpretation of Caliban's character. Caliban's behavior clarifies nothing. He alternates eloquent speeches with the most degrading kind of drunken, servile behavior.

THE ALLURE OF RULING A COLONY The nearly uninhabited island presents a sense of infinite possibility to almost everyone who lands there. In its isolation, Prospero has found it an ideal place to school his daughter. Sycorax, Caliban's mother, worked her magic there after she was exiled from Algeria. Caliban laments losing control of the island. As he attempts to comfort Alonso, Gonzalo imagines ruling over a utopian society on the island. Stefano imagines killing Prospero and ruling himself, saying to Caliban, "Monster, I will kill this man. His daughter and I will be King and Queen—save our graces!—and Trinculo and thyself shall be my viceroys" (III.ii.101–103). Stefano particularly looks forward to taking advantage of the spirits that make "noises" on the isle; they will provide music for his kingdom for free. All of these characters envision the island as a place where they could rule well.

Shakespeare does not support the ambitions of these would-be colonizers. Gonzalo's utopian vision is undercut by a sharp retort from the usually foolish Sebastian and Antonio. When Gonzalo says there would be no commerce or work or "sovereignty" in his society, Sebastian says sarcastically, "yet [Gonzalo] would be king on't," and Antonio adds, "The latter end of his commonwealth forgets the beginning" (II.i.156–157). Sebastian and Antonio criticize Gonzalo for suggesting that a society could be utterly free when a tyrant rules it. Their criticism is humorous in this context, but it applies in a serious way to Prospero's delusions.

MOTIFS

MASTERS AND SERVANTS   Nearly every scene in the play either explicitly or implicitly portrays a relationship between someone who possesses power and someone who is subject to that power: Prospero and Caliban, Prospero and Ariel, Alonso and his nobles, the nobles and Gonzalo, Prospero and Miranda, and so forth. These relationships can be generally positive (Prospero and Ariel), generally negative (Prospero and Caliban), and generally treacherous (Alonso and his nobles). The master-servant dynamic can turn sour or violent when the balance of power is threatened or disrupted. For instance, in the opening scene, the "servant" (the boatswain) is dismissive and angry toward his "masters" (the noblemen), whose ineptitude threatens to lead to a shipwreck.

WATER AND DROWNING   *The Tempest* is awash with references to water. The mariners enter "wet" in Act I, scene i, and Caliban, Stefano, and Trinculo enter "all wet" after being led by Ariel into a swampy lake (IV.i.193). Miranda's fear for the lives of the sailors in the "wild waters" (I.ii.2) causes her to weep. Alonso, believing himself responsible for his son's death, decides to drown himself. Prospero promises that once he has reconciled with his enemies, "deeper than did ever plummet sound / I'll drown my book" (V.i.56–57).

These are only a few of the references to water in the play. Occasionally, water references are used to compare characters. For example, the echo of Alonso's desire to drown himself in Prospero's promise to drown his book calls attention to the similarity of the sacrifices each man must make. Alonso must be willing to give up his life in order to become truly penitent and to be forgiven for his treachery against Prospero. Prospero must be willing to give up his magic and his power in order to rejoin civilization.

SYMBOLS

THE TEMPEST   The tempest that begins the play and puts all of Prospero's enemies at his disposal symbolizes the suffering Prospero endured, and the suffering he wants to inflict on others. All of those shipwrecked are put at the mercy of the sea, just as Prospero and his infant daughter were twelve years ago. The tempest also symbolizes Prospero's magic, and the frightening, potentially malevolent side of his power.

THE GAME OF CHESS   The chess game that Prospero arranges between Miranda and Ferdinand symbolizes the entire story he has created. The object of chess is to capture the king, which is what Prospero does by catching Alonso and reprimanding him for his treachery. Prospero manipulates people, even people he loves, like inanimate chess pieces, arranging things so that Alonso's son and Prospero's daughter marry, thus solidifying Prospero's hold on power (Alonso will have no interest in upsetting a dukedom to which his own son is heir).

Caught up in their game, Miranda and Ferdinand also symbolize something ominous about Prospero's power. For a few moments, they do not even notice the others staring at them, so perfect is the tableau that Prospero has arranged. "Sweet lord, you play me false," Miranda says, and Ferdinand assures her that he "would not for the world" do so (V.i.174–176). Miranda does not realize that her father is playing her as if she is a chess piece, and Ferdinand has nothing to do with it.

IMPORTANT QUOTATIONS FROM *THE TEMPEST*

1. *You taught me language, and my profit on't*
   Is I know how to curse. The red plague rid you
   For learning me your language!

Location: I.ii.366–368
Speaker: Caliban to Prospero and Miranda
Context: Miranda has scolded Caliban for his ingratitude

This speech articulates the vexed relationship between the colonized and the colonizer that lies at the heart of this play. The son of a witch, perhaps half-man and half-monster, his name a near-anagram of "cannibal," Caliban is an archetypal "savage" figure in a play that is concerned with colonization and the controlling of wild environments. Caliban and Prospero have different ways of interpreting their current relationship. Caliban sees Prospero as an oppressive force, while Prospero claims he has cared for and educated Caliban, or did until Caliban tried to rape Miranda. According to Prospero, Caliban is ungrateful for the help and civilization he has received. He and Miranda cannot understand why Caliban does not appreciate the gifts of language and self-knowledge. But for Caliban, self-knowledge is only a constant reminder of how he is different from Miranda and Prospero and how they have changed him from what he was and suggested that his natural self was wrong. Caliban's only hope for an identity separate from those who have invaded his home is to use what they have given him against them, as he does in this passage.

2. *There be some sports are painful, and their labour*
   Delight in them sets off. Some kinds of baseness
   Are nobly undergone, and most poor matters
   Point to rich ends. This my mean task
   Would be as heavy to me as odious, but
   The mistress which I serve quickens what's dead
   And makes my labours pleasures.

Location: III.i.1–7
Speaker: Ferdinand to Miranda
Context: Ferdinand expresses his willingness to perform the task Prospero has set him to, for her sake

Ferdinand joins in the spirit of *The Tempest*, which smiles on compromise and balance. Prospero must spend twelve years on an island in order to regain his dukedom; Alonso must think he has lost his son in order to be forgiven for his treachery; Ariel must serve Prospero in order to be set free; and Ferdinand must suffer Prospero's feigned wrath in order to reap true joy from his love for Miranda. As Ferdinand agrees to suffer in these lines, the structure of his speech suggests his desire for balance. He speaks of a series of antitheses—related but opposing ideas: "sports … painful" is followed by "labour … delights"; "baseness" and nobility; "poor matters" and "rich ends"; Miranda "quickens" (makes alive) what is "dead" in Ferdinand. Perhaps more than any other character in the play, Ferdinand is willing to let fate take its course, always believing that the good will balance the bad in the end. It is probably Ferdinand's balanced outlook that makes him such a sympathetic character, even though we see very little of him onstage.

3. *[I weep] at mine unworthiness, that dare not offer*
   What I desire to give, and much less take
   What I shall die to want. But this is trifling,
   And all the more it seeks to hide itself
   The bigger bulk it shows. Hence, bashful cunning,

And prompt me, plain and holy innocence.
I am your wife, if you will marry me.
If not, I'll die your maid. To be your fellow
You may deny me, but I'll be your servant
Whether you will or no.

Location: III.i.77–86
Speaker: Miranda to Ferdinand
Context: Miranda declares her undying love for Ferdinand

Miranda does not so much propose marriage as insist on it. This is one of two times in the play that Miranda seems to break out of the passivity she has developed under the influence of her father's magic. As in Act I, scene ii, when she scolds Caliban, here Miranda expresses her desires in forthright language. The naïve girl who can hardly hold still long enough to hear her father's long story in Act I, scene ii, and who is charmed asleep and awake as though she were a puppet, seems to turn into a stronger, more mature woman at this moment. Not only does Miranda make her intentions clear, she does so in boldly sexual language, using a metaphor that suggests both an erection and pregnancy (she compares her love to the "bigger bulk" trying to hide itself).

At the same time, the last three lines somewhat undercut the power of this speech. Miranda characterizes herself as a slave to her desires, pledging to follow Ferdinand no matter what the cost to her, and no matter what Ferdinand wants. This self-effacing language makes Miranda sound like Caliban, who uses similar words as he abases himself before Stefano.

---

4. *Be not afeard. The isle is full of noises,*
   Sounds, and sweet airs, that give delight and hurt not.
   Sometimes a thousand twangling instruments
   Will hum about mine ears, and sometime voices
   That, if I then had waked after long sleep
   Will make me sleep again; and then in dreaming
   The clouds methought would open and show riches
   Ready to drop upon me, that when I waked
   I cried to dream again.

Location: III.ii.130–138
Speaker: Caliban to Stefano and Trinculo
Context: Caliban explains the mysterious music

Though Caliban claims that the chief virtue of his newly learned language is that it allows him to curse, here he uses language in the most sensitive and beautiful fashion. This speech is generally considered one of the most poetic in the play, and that Shakespeare puts it in the mouth of the drunken man-monster suggests that Caliban has depths Prospero and Miranda do not see.

It is unclear whether the "noises" Caliban speaks of are the noises of the island itself or noises, like the music of the invisible Ariel, created by Prospero's magic. Caliban himself does not seem to know where these noises come from. His speech conveys the wondrous beauty of the island and the strength of his attachment to it, as well as a certain amount of respect and love for Prospero's magic, and for the possibility that he creates the "[s]ounds and sweet airs that give delight and hurt not."

---

5. *Our revels now are ended. These our actors,*
   As I foretold you, were all spirits, and
   Are melted into air, into thin air;
   And, like the baseless fabric of this vision,
   The cloud-capped towers, the gorgeous palaces,
   The solemn temples, the great globe itself,

Yea, all which it inherit, shall dissolve;
And, like this insubstantial pageant faded,
Leave not a rack behind. We are such stuff
As dreams are made on, and our little life
Is rounded with a sleep.

Location: IV.i.148-158
Speaker: Prospero
Context: Prospero has remembered the plot against his life

Prospero has been so swept up in his own visions, in the power of his own magic, that he forgot the plot against his life. From this point on, Prospero talks repeatedly of the "end" of his "labours" (IV.i.260), and of breaking his staff and drowning his magic book (V.i.54–57). In bringing his former enemies to the island, Prospero wants, among other things, to extricate himself from his position of near absolute power, from which everyday matters are forgettable. He looks forward to returning to Milan, where "every third thought shall be my grave" (V.i.315). It is with a sense of relief that he announces in the epilogue that he has given up his magic powers. Prospero's speech here emphasizes both the beauty of the world he has created for himself and the sadness of the fact that this world is without meaning, a kind of dream completely removed from anything substantial.

Prospero's mention of the "great globe," which to an audience in 1611 would have suggested the Globe Theatre, conflates the theatre and Prospero's island. When Prospero gives up his magic, the play will end and the audience, like Prospero, will return to real life.

TIMON OF ATHENS

When Timon goes bankrupt and discovers that his friends are false, he turns against Athens.

TIMON OF ATHENS IN CONTEXT

Shakespeare probably wrote *Timon of Athens* between 1605 and 1608. Apparently the play was never produced, perhaps because it was never finished, or perhaps because its subject matter was too controversial in the years after James I ascended to the English throne. *Timon* includes a sharp criticism of money management that Shakespeare's audience would have interpreted as a swipe at James's policies. In the early part of the seventeenth century, nobles competed to outdo one another in extravagant spending, even when they lacked the cash to pay for their purchases. James I himself was guilty of these poor spending habits. Like Shakespeare's Timon, a wealthy man who overspends and ends up borrowing from his friends to pay for the very gifts he has given them, James accrued enormous debt because he wanted to give his friends expensive gifts. Huge deficits in the royal bank were the result.

Timon of Athens chronicles the transformation of the money-lending industry. In the beginning of the play, as in the days before James I, friends make informal arrangements among themselves when they want to borrow or lend money. But as time goes on, the increasingly strained finances of the nobles make friendly understandings insufficiently binding. In *Timon*, as in James's England, usury (the practice of charging absurd interest rates on loans) becomes standard in borrowing and lending.

Like Shakespeare's earlier work, *The Merchant of Venice*, *Timon of Athens* is concerned with the relationship between friendship and money. Timon discovers how much friendship has to do with self-interest and how much impressive possessions heighten men's reputations. *Timon* has also been compared to *King Lear* because both plays address a great man's fall from power and authority, and his fierce, misanthropic reaction to his decline.

TIMON OF ATHENS: KEY FACTS

Full title: The Life of Timon of Athens

Time and place written: 1605–1608; probably London

Date of first publication: 1623

Genre: tragedy

Setting (time): Probably the 4th or 5th century B.C.

Setting (place): Athens, in Greece, and a cave near Athens

Protagonist: Timon

Major conflict: Timon loses his friends and respect when he loses his wealth.

TIMON OF ATHENS: CHARACTER LIST

Alcibiades An acquaintance of Timon's. When one of his friends is sentenced to death by the senators, Alcibiades protests, and the government banishes him. He promises to raise an army and conquer Athens. Timon eventually supports Alcibiades's cause.

Apemantus A philosopher and detractor of Timon's. Apemantus scorns Athenian citizens and scoffs at Timon's greetings. He thinks Timon's friends are flatterers and money-grubbers. Apemantus is delighted when Timon's luck changes. He follows Timon to the wilderness merely to remind him that his villainous friends refused to loan him money. Although Apemantus and Timon insult each other vigorously, they form a curious bond.

Bandits Thieves Timon encounters in the wilderness. When Timon offers them gold to destroy Athens and speaks longingly of the damage they could cause, his enthusiasm makes their own profession seem distasteful.

Flaminius One of Timon's servants.

Flavius Timon's steward. After Timon's downfall, Flavius decides to continue serving him and seeks him out in the wilderness. Flavius offers Timon all the money he has and weeps at Timon's downfall.

Fool A man who appears with Apemantus outside Timon's house while creditors's servants wait for their payments. The Fool draws a parallel between those who go to creditors and those who go to prostitutes.

Jeweler One of Timon's hangers-on. The jeweler provides the ostentatious jewelry that Timon gives as gifts to his friends.

Lucius One of Timon's friends. Lucius accepts Timon's gifts but refuses to give him a loan when he runs out of cash.

Lucullus One of Timon's friends. Lucullus accepts Timon's gifts but refuses to lend him money.

Painter One of Timon's hangers-on. The painter seeks out Timon after his fall, hearing that Timon found gold and hoping he can get into his good graces.

Poet One of Timon's hangers-on. Like the painter, the poet hears that Timon found gold in the wilderness and goes to seek him out.

Sempronius One of Timon's friends. Sempronius accepts Timon's gifts but refuses to give him a loan, claiming he is insulted that Timon only came to him after asking three other friends for money first.

Senators Members of the Athenian Senate. The senators try to defend Athens from Alcibiades, explaining that the city as a whole is not corrupt, and that the few bad eggs can be singled out and punished.

Servilius One of Timon's servants. Timon sends Servilius to ask for a loan from Timon's friends.

Timon The play's protagonist. After running through his money on gifts for friends, Timon goes bankrupt, and his friends will not lend him money. Convinced that humanity has turned against him, Timon declares his hatred for mankind and goes to the forest, where, to his dismay, he becomes a sought-after guru. Timon ends his days filled with vitriol.

Ventidius One of Timon's friends. Timon pays to get Ventidius out of prison, but Ventidius feels no obligation to help Timon in turn.

TIMON OF ATHENS: PLOT OVERVIEW

Timon, a rich citizen of Athens, is amazingly generous to his fellow citizens. When he runs out of money and gets into debt, his so-called friends turn on him and demand repayment. He throws a final banquet at which he serves stones and water and then he leaves Athens. Accompanied by his faithful servant Flavius, he goes to live in the woods, where he discovers a hidden supply of gold. Timon gives some of this gold to Alcibiades, an Athenian who was exiled from Athens and who plans to lead an army to destroy it. Two senators of Athens apologize to Timon and urge him to return, hoping his presence in Athens will dissuade Alcibiades from attacking, but Timon refuses. Alcibiades only punishes those Athenians who injured Timon or himself. When he hears that Timon has died, Alcibiades honors Timon, who was more admired in Athens than he believed.

TIMON OF ATHENS: SCENE SUMMARY

ACT I

A herd of sycophants and flatterers eagerly accepts Timon's gifts, and only Apemantus resists sweet-talking Timon; Flavius notes that Timon is in denial about his terrible financial situation.

I.I Location: Timon's house

Timon gets a friend out of jail by paying his debts, drives an easy bargain with an old man, and praises the work of a poet, a painter, and a jeweler; Apemantus scorns Timon's hangers-on.

A poet, a painter, a jeweler, and a merchant enter Timon's house in Athens. The jeweler shows off an impressive jewel he hopes to sell to Timon, and the painter and poet discuss commissioned works they have completed for Timon. The poet comments about the senators entering Timon's house, observing that Timon's large fortune and his generous nature draw all kinds of people, from the lowest flatterers to Apemantus, a man who is quicker to criticize than praise. The poet says that his latest work is about Timon, a man enthroned by Fortune, sitting atop a hill where all gaze at him adoringly. But, he says, fortune is fickle, and those who adore the man now blessed by fortune will later abandon him if he falls. The painter is impressed, but the poet says that it is easy to demonstrate the quick actions of fortune.

Timon and his attendants enter. A messenger tells Timon that his friend Ventidius has been imprisoned by creditors, and Timon decides to pay his debt in order to free him. An old Athenian enters and tells Timon that his servant Lucilius hangs around his house and charms his daughter. Timon negotiates with the old man for Lucilius to wed his daughter, offering cash to Lucilius to sweeten the deal. Lucilius says he owes Timon everything.

Timon accepts the poem and the painting and admires the jeweler's gem. Apemantus enters, and Timon greets him. But Apemantus says Timon should not expect a polite greeting from him until Timon is changed into his own dog, which is as unlikely as Timon's hangers-on changing into honest men. Timon asks Apemantus's opinion about the painting and the jewel, and Apemantus scorns both. He criticizes the poet, calling him a flatterer.

The arrival of Alcibiades is announced, and Timon welcomes him. Observing the scene, Apemantus scorns the fake courtesy of Timon's flatterers. Timon and Alcibiades exit, leaving Apemantus with several lords. They ask if Apemantus plans to attend Timon's feast, and he says he does, if only to watch flatterers at work. Apemantus exits, and the lords discuss Timon's seemingly inexhaustible bounty. His possessions seem to breed and multiply under his nearly magical touch.

I.II Location: Timon's house

Timon gives extravagant gifts to his friends, even though he is in debt and mortgaged to the hilt.

Timon and his friends and servants enter. Apemantus lags behind. Venditius, just released from prison, thanks Timon for paying his debts. He says he hopes to repay Timon someday, but Timon says he gave the money out of love, and he will not feel truly generous if he gets anything back.

Apemantus makes a snickering comment. Timon welcomes him, but again Apemantus reacts coldly. Timon sends Apemantus to a distant table by himself so his bad temper will not affect the rest of the party. Apemantus says he has come to the feast merely to observe. He scorns the food Timon proffers, saying he won't be paid to flatter Timon. He is horrified at the mob of senators and lords who eat up Timon's feast like birds of prey would eat Timon's flesh. Rather than notice the diminishment of his bounty, Timon urges them on. The other lords give thanks to the gods, but Apemantus says his own grace, saying he will never trust the oath or bond of anyone, and he prays for no one but himself.

Timon speaks to Alcibiades, asking him if he would rather be out in the field with his soldiers. Alcibiades says he would rather be at the feast. Apemantus scorns this flattery. A lord says he wishes Timon would have some difficulty so that his friends could help him for once. Timon says they help him by being his friends, and he was born to share his bounty with them.

A group of ladies disguised as Amazons enters and performs a dance for the feasters. Apemantus criticizes the dancers, calling them madwomen and depraved flatterers. The other lords join the ladies in dancing. After the women leave, Timon calls his servant Flavius to bring in a small casket. Flavius notes to himself that Timon's bounty is running out, but he cannot say anything to Timon about it. Flavius returns with the casket. From it Timon takes jewels, which he gives to all the lords.

Flavius asks Timon if he may speak to him about an important matter, but Timon puts him off. A servant enters and announces that nobles of the senate have come to visit. Another servant enters to say that Lord Lucius has sent Timon a gift, and a third servant announces that Lord Lucullus has sent gifts. To Flavius's dismay, Timon insists on paying back his friends for these gifts. Flavius privately notes that Timon is giving gifts from an empty coffer and refuses to listen to an account of his holdings. Timon is bankrupt and owes money on every gift. He has mortgaged all of his lands. Timon ruins himself faster by providing for friends than by struggling with enemies, declares Flavius.

Timon bestows an array of gifts on the lords in the room. He gives his horse to one lord and money to Alcibiades. The lords leave, saying they are greatly indebted to Timon. Apemantus stays behind, and Timon says he would give Apemantus a gift too if only Apemantus would be less sullen. Apemantus says in that case there would be no one to criticize Timon if he is bribed, and then Timon's downfall would come even faster. Timon says he will not listen to Apemantus and departs. Apemantus says he wishes men would listen to advice more readily than they listen to flattery.

ACT II

Timon's friends begin to ask Timon to repay money he owes them; Timon learns of his dire lack of funds from Flavius, but insists his friends will help him.

II.I Location: a senator's house

A senator marvels about Timon's unending flow of presents and decides to ask Timon to repay a loan he made him.

A senator speaks of Timon's unending bounty, expressing disbelief that he can be so generous without running out of cash. Timon seems to make money and goods multiply as if under some magical force. He cannot believe that Timon's financial situation can hold. In fact, Timon owes the senator money. The senator calls for Caphis and sends him to Timon's house to demand the repayment of his debt. He instructs Caphis not to take no for an answer.

II.II Location: in front of Timon's house

Three servants, acting on behalf of their masters, ask Timon to repay loans; Flavius succeeds in making Timon understand the gravity of his financial straits; Timon believes his friends will help him.

Flavius marvels at his master's spending. Timon takes no notice of his expenses, he says. No one was ever so careless in the project of being so kind. He knows Timon will refuse to hear anything about his expenses until something bad happens. Caphis, Varro's servant, enters with Isidore's servant. They realize they are all there to ask Timon for the money he owes their masters. Timon enters with Alcibiades, and the three servants make their case to Timon. Timon asks them to come back the next day, but they remind him he has repeatedly put them off. Timon asks Flavius why he is beset with people asking him for money. Flavius asks the servants to leave them alone briefly while he explains the situation to Timon.

Left to themselves, the servants notice the approach of Apemantus and a Fool, and look forward to some fun. The three servants riddle Apemantus and the Fool with absurd questions. The Fool finds out that the servants work for usurers, or moneylenders, and announces that he works for a prostitute. He tells a riddle about people who come to borrow money from usurers. These people are sad when they arrive at the usurer's, and happy when they leave. The servants agree that the Fool is capable of wisdom.

Flavius and Timon return, and Flavius dismisses the servants temporarily. Timon asks Flavius why he never told him about his expenses before. Flavius said he did, but Timon refused to listen. Timon orders his land to be sold, but Flavius says it has all been mortgaged already. Flavius says everyone loved Timon and his generosity, but now that the means to buy that praise and fondness are gone, perhaps his friends will go too. Flavius's suggestion shocks Timon. He calls for three servants, intending to prove to Flavius that he still has friends in Athens. He sends the servants to three of his friends, ordering them to ask for a loan on Timon's behalf.

Flavius says he already tried asking for loans from Timon's friends, but they refused to help. Timon does not believe it, but Flavius says all three answered in the same manner, saying they are sorry, it's a misfortune, but they're busy men. Timon says these men have a history of ingratitude, but his friend Ventidius, whom Timon just saved from prison and who recently inherited a large fortune, will be different. Timon asks Flavius to go to Ventidius and ask for a loan. Flavius says that it is the curse of generous people to assume that everyone else is generous too.

ACT III

Timon's friends refuse to lend him money; the government banishes Alcibiades for pleading a friend's case; Timon invites his friends to a feast of water and stones.

III.I Location: Lucullus's house

Lucullus refuses to lend money to Timon.

Flaminius, one of Timon's servants, arrives at Lucullus's house to ask for a loan. Lucullus is glad to see Flaminius, assuming he is bearing some gift from Timon. When Flaminius explains his errand, Lucullus says he has always enjoyed Timon's hospitality, but he often warned him that his holdings would run out. Now is not the time to make a loan based merely on friendship. He tries to bribe Flaminius with several coins, hoping that Flaminius will say he did not speak to Lucullus, but Flaminius hurls them back. Lucullus departs. Flaminius ponders the nature of friendship. Lucullus ate at Timon's table, yet now he won't pay him back. Flaminius wishes Lucullus ill.

III.II Location: an Athenian forum

Lucius refuses to lend money to Timon; a group of strangers remarks on Lucius's ingratitude.

Lucius, another of Timon's friends, enters, talking to several strangers. The strangers have heard rumors that Timon's finances are in bad shape, but Lucius finds it hard to believe. They have also heard that Timon asked Lucullus for money, and Lucullus refused him. Lucius admits he has received gifts from Timon too, though fewer than Lucullus has. He says he would never have denied Timon a loan if he had asked.

Servilius, Timon's servant, enters. Lucius too thinks Timon's servant has come to bring him a gift, but Servilius explains his mission is to ask for a loan. Lucius says unfortunately he has just spent all his money on a small investment and now has no ready cash. He sends his best wishes to Timon, but cannot send him any money. Servilius and Lucius depart, leaving the strangers to discuss the nature of friendship. They say Timon has been like a father to Lucius financially, yet Lucius refuses to lend Timon even a small percentage of what Timon has given him. Though they have never met Timon, the strangers agree he sounds like a man they would gladly help.

III.III Location: Sempronius's house

Sempronius, annoyed that Timon came to him last, refuses to lend him money.

Timon's third servant enters with Sempronius, another of Timon's friends. Sempronius is annoyed that Timon wants a loan, and says he should ask Lucullus or Lucius or even Ventidius. The servant explains that Timon has approached them all already, but they would give no money. Sempronius is even more annoyed when he hears that Timon has approached him after the other three. He wonders if he is Timon's last refuge. He feels disgraced to be so low on the totem pole, when he prided himself on being the first man to receive a gift from Timon. Feeling slighted, Sempronius refuses to make the loan and leaves. The servant calls Sempronius a villain.

III.IV Location: Timon's house

Despite their disgust for their masters' behavior, a group of servants asks Timon to repay their masters; Timon reacts with horrified anger.

A group of servants sent from Timon's creditors gathers outside his house, waiting for him to emerge. They greet one another and remark on how strange it is that one of the servants' masters wants money from Timon even while he wears enormous jewels recently given him by Timon. The servants find it odd that Timon's friends should demand their money back when they still enjoy Timon's gifts. The servants know their lords have sucked up Timon's bounty and now have no gratitude for the generosity he showed them in days past.

Flaminius and Flavius enter, and the servants demand to know the whereabouts of Timon. Flavius asks them why they didn't bring out their bills of debt when their lords were enjoying the bounty of Timon's table, instead of presenting them when Timon's luck has turned. Flavius angrily departs. Servilius enters and explains that Timon has fallen ill.

But Timon bursts from the house in a rage. He shouts angrily that he has always been free. Why should he now be confined to his house? Why now is mankind so cruel to him? Each of the creditors' servants present their bills, swarming around him. Timon is horrified and rushes back inside the house. The servants wonder if their masters should give up on collecting their money.

III.V Location: Timon's house

Timon tells Flavius to invite everyone to a feast.

Timon thinks of a plan. He orders Flavius to organize another feast. Flavius says no money remains for a feast, but Timon tells him not to worry. He sends Flavius out to invite everyone.

III.VI Location: the Senate

After vigorously speaking out on behalf of a friend, the government banishes Alcibiades from Athens.

Several senators discuss the fate of a man. Alcibiades enters and pleads for the release of his friend, an honorable man who acted foolishly out of passion. One senator says Alcibiades speaks as if he wants to make manslaughter legal. This senator says that revenge is not noble. Learning to bear slights and suffering is. Alcibiades announces he will speak as a soldier and asks if bearing suffering is valorous, does that mean prisoners are wiser than those who judge them? His friend may have acted rashly, but Alcibiades suggests everyone does sometimes.

The senators say Alcibiades's efforts are in vain. Alcibiades insists that his friend's service to Athens on the battlefield should be sufficient payment for his freedom. The senators condemn Alcibiades's friend to death. Though Alcibiades begs them to reconsider, the senators are now angry, and they banish Alcibiades.

Alcibiades, alone, is enraged. He has fought hard for Athens, only to be banished. He says he is nearly glad to leave the city, for now he can gather his troops and strike at Athens. Soldiers should not endure such wrongs, he declares.

III.VII Location: Timon's house

Timon invites his former friends to a feast, where he serves them water and stones and berates them.

Many of Timon's friends come to his house, including Lucullus, Lucius, Sempronius, and others. The lords discuss Timon's alleged fate, agreeing he must have been merely testing them when he asked for a loan in days previous. They all claim to be sad that they couldn't help him. Timon enters, and several lords apologize for the impossibility of loaning him money. He brushes off their apologies and urges them all to be seated. The lords gossip about the banishment of Alcibiades.

Timon speaks some words over the covered dishes. He says the gods should give enough that they are praised, but always hold something back. He urges the gods to give to men only enough so that they do not have to borrow from one another, for if later the gods needed to borrow from men, the men would forsake them. Timon asks that the meat he will serve be more beloved than the man who serves it, that any gathering have its fair share of villains, and that the people of Athens be ready for destruction. As for his present friends, he does not bless them, because they are nothing to him, and he welcomes them to nothing.

Once the dishes are uncovered, the guests realize they are full of steaming water and stones. Timon shouts that this is his last feast, and he will wash off his guests' flattery and villainy with the feast's water. He curses all the lords. When one lord tries to leave, Timon begins beating up his guests. He declares that he hates all men and all humanity, and leaves. The astonished lords are convinced that Timon has gone mad. One day he gives them jewels, says one lord, and the next day stones.

ACT IV

IV.I Location: outside Athens

Timon curses Athens and its residents.

Timon stands outside the wall of Athens and curses the city. He wishes death, destruction, plague, and misfortune upon the city's residents. He tears off his clothes and turns to the hills, where he expects to "find / Th' unkindest beast more kinder than mankind" (IV.i.35–6).

IV.II Location: Timon's house

Flavius decides to keep serving Timon.

Flavius and several servants discuss what has happened. They are amazed that such a great house has fallen. The servants sadly prepare to leave. Flavius divides his money among them, and they all swear to greet one another kindly should they meet again in the future. Alone, Flavius says anyone would want to be free from wealth if wealth inevitably leads to misery and false friendship. He mourns for Timon, whose own kindness was his downfall. Flavius decides to continue to serve Timon, and heads off to find him.

IV.III Location: outside Athens

Timon rages against humankind, finds gold, gives some to Alcibiades to fund his invasion of Athens, quarrels with Apemantus, talks to some thieves, and turns away Flavius despite Flavius's kindness.

Timon comes out of his cave and considers the sun and the earth. He hopes the sun breeds plagues, and that all of nature will turn against itself. He rages against flatterers, saying all things of men are devious and villainous. He abhors society and hopes it comes to destruction.

As Timon digs for roots, he finds gold. Astonished at his discovery, Timon speaks of the awful power of wealth. He says that gold, "this yellow slave" (IV.iii.34), makes or breaks religion, turns thieves into senators, and convinces aged widows to wed again. He tells the earth to hide the gold. He keeps some of the treasure and reburies the rest.

Alcibiades enters with a prostitute on each arm. He does not recognize Timon at first. Timon introduces himself as Misanthropos, a hater of mankind. Then Alcibiades recognizes Timon and asks how he changed so much. Alcibiades offers his friendship, but Timon turns it down, saying no man can be a genuine friend. Alcibiades says he would like to help Timon. He has only a little gold, but he offers Timon some of it. Timon turns it down. Alcibiades promises to help him when he has sacked Athens.

Timon perks up at the mention of an assault on Athens. He gives Alcibiades gold to support his campaign, urging him to kill everyone, even old men, virgins, children, women, and priests. Alcibiades takes the gold, but hesitates at taking his advice. The prostitutes ask Timon for gold, and he gives it to them, urging them to continue practicing their profession and spreading illness among their patrons. Alcibiades and the prostitutes prepare to depart for Athens, and Timon says he hopes he never sees Alcibiades again. Alcibiades is surprised, saying he never harmed Timon. Timon shoos him away.

Timon continues digging in the ground for edible roots. Apemantus comes along, and Timon curses him. Apemantus notes that Timon's recent change in fortune has altered him, while his former flatterers still live in silk-lined comfort, forgetting Timon ever existed. Apemantus says it is only fair that Timon has sunk to this, for he frittered away his money on villainous rascals. Timon tells Apemantus to leave, but Apemantus says he loves Timon more now than ever before. He says he only intends to vex Timon.

Apemantus says Timon has become a beggar by his own compulsion. Timon says Apemantus's experiences have been different, since he was never in fortune's favor. Timon is like an oak whose leaves have blown off in one blast of wintry air, and now must nakedly bear misfortune. He says it is hard for him because he has never suffered before, but Apemantus is used to suffering. Why does Apemantus hate mankind, Timon asks, when men have never flattered him? If Apemantus curses anyone, it should be his father, who left him to be raised by a beggar woman. Timon urges Apemantus to leave.

Apemantus asks Timon if he is done ranting and offers him food. Timon asks Apemantus if anyone ever loved him, and Apemantus says only he himself has. Timon asks what Apemantus would do with the world. Apemantus says he would give it to the beasts, but Timon says that would not help him, since every beast is subject to another beast. Apemantus says Athens has already become a forest of beasts.

Timon and Apemantus insult each other, and Timon throws a rock at Apemantus to try to get him to leave. Timon considers his epitaph, hoping his death will be imminent. He looks on his gold, remarks on its power to influence the actions of men, and hopes it will reduce mankind to the behavior of low beasts.

But Apemantus predicts throngs will soon arrive to seek the gold. Apemantus sees bandits approaching, and leaves at last.

The thieves speak among themselves, wondering how to get the gold from Timon. They approach Timon, saying they are soldiers. Although Timon suspects they are thieves, he gives them gold and urges them to steal money and take lives. He says the sun robs the sea, the moon robs the sun, the sea steals its tides from the moon, and the earth steals its fertility from excrement. Everything and everyone is a thief. Timon commands the bandits to go to Athens, break into shops, and steal as much as he has given them.

The thieves are so struck by Timon's speech that they almost want to reform. They realize Timon gives them this advice because he hates mankind, not because he is truly enthusiastic about thievery. But they decide to head to Athens before giving up their trade, and exit.

Flavius arrives, speaking sadly about his fallen master. When they meet, Flavius asks if Timon recognizes him. Timon says he has forgotten all men, so Flavius says he was once Timon's poor honest servant. Timon says he had no honest men around him. Flavius insists his grief is honest. Timon sees that he is crying and softens.

Flavius offers his money to Timon. Timon is astonished. The kindness of his servant is nearly enough to make him change his mind about abandoning mankind. He says there is one honest man among the villains of the world, and that man is but a servant. Still, he says, Flavius is more honest than he is wise, for he could have found a much better job by betraying Timon. Timon asks Flavius if he expects to earn extravagant interest on his kindness. Flavius insists that what he offers is real kindness and love. He wants to make Timon comfortable in the wilderness. He says his only wish is to get rich so that he could make Timon rich again.

Timon gives Flavius money on the condition that he lives apart from mankind and never gives anything to even the skinniest beggar. Flavius begs to be allowed to stay, but Timon sends him away.

ACT V

Turning down the request of the senators, Timon refuses to return to Athens and dies in the forest; Alcibiades agrees not to attack Athens.

V.I Location: Timon's home in the woods

The poet and painter visit Timon, trying to get in his good graces.

The poet and painter head toward Timon's home in the wilderness. They have heard that Timon is rich with gold and suspect that his apparent bankruptcy was just a trial for his friends. The two artists plan to be extremely kind to him and get on his good side. Neither man has any artwork to present to Timon, but they are convinced that the promise of future work is as good as the work itself.

Timon sees the two men and mutters derisively about them to himself, saying they are flatterers and bad artists. He approaches them, and they fawn over him. He asks them if they are honest. They say they have come to offer their services, but Timon asks if they heard he had gold. They admit they did, but say they did not come for it. He tells them they have one fault: they trust a rotten man who deceives them (meaning they trust each other). He tells them to go in opposite directions to search for the villain who pursues them—and sends them off to chase each other.

V.II Location: Timon's home in the woods

Timon turns away the two senators who ask him to return to Athens.

Two senators go with Flavius to Timon's cave, saying they have promised the Athenians that they will talk with Timon. They arrive at the cave and call to Timon, who emerges and curses them. The senators say they have come to beg Timon to return to Athens. Apparently the people of the republic have reconsidered Timon's fate and decided they were unfair to him. In apology, they want to offer him great wealth and love. Timon curses the senators. The senators say that if Timon comes to Athens, they will make him a leader, and he can help defend the city against Alcibiades. But Timon is uninterested. He says he does not care if Alcibiades sacks Athens and kills everyone from the youngest child to the oldest citizen.

The senators see they have come in vain. Timon says he does love his country and doesn't rejoice in its ruin. He tells the senators to commend him to the citizens of Athens and to pass on this advice about how to avoid Alcibiades' wrath: anyone who wants to save himself from the misery of Alcibiades' attack, says Timon, should come hang himself on a tree near Timon's cave. Timon tells the senators to go away and tell the Athenians that Timon has died. Henceforth his grave will be their oracle. He curses humanity again and withdraws to his cave. The senators leave.

V.III   Location: outside Athens

Senators discuss the importance, and impossibility, of getting Timon to return to Athens.

Two more senators discuss the fate of Athens and Timon. A messenger has heard that Alcibiades wants to work with Timon against Athens. The senators agree that it is more important than ever to lure Timon back to Athens. But the senators who spoke to Timon enter and declare Timon a lost cause.

V.IV   Location: the woods

A soldier finds a grave in the woods and assumes it is Timon's.

A soldier in the woods looks for Timon. He comes upon a gravestone, but he cannot read the writing on the stone. He takes a rubbing of the words to his superiors. He leaves believing Timon to be dead.

V.V   Location: Timon's tomb

Alcibiades agrees to call off his attack on Athens as long as the senators allow him to punish his and Timon's enemies; he says Timon was well-respected.

Alcibiades and his forces approach Athens. Several senators enter, and Alcibiades tells them that the time when he would crouch under the shadow of their power is past. The senators say they have tried to soothe Alcibiades's wrongs with gestures greater than his grievances. They have also tried to woo Timon back to Athens. They were not all unkind, and they do not deserve war. The senators say that the people who raised the walls of Athens are not the same ones who slighted Alcibiades, and those who caused Alcibiades's banishment are no longer living. They welcome him to march into the city, but ask him to kill only some citizens, not all, since not all of the citizens have offended Alcibiades. They ask Alcibiades to enter the city with friendliness and to throw down his glove as a gesture of kindness, which he does.

Alcibiades says that if the senators send out his and Timon's enemies for punishment, he will harm no one else. The soldier enters with the rubbing from the grave. Alcibiades reads the epitaph, which says that here lies Timon, "who alive / All living man did hate" (V.v.75–76). Alcibiades says that though he scorned humanity, Timon was well-respected. He hopes Timon's faults may be forgiven. He enters the city with hopes for peace.

THEMES, MOTIFS, & SYMBOLS IN *TIMON OF ATHENS*

THEMES

THE RAPIDITY OF DESCENT   Timon undergoes a remarkable transformation over the course of the play. He begins as a wealthy, important member of society, and he ends up a half-starved, half-naked beggar who dies of no apparent cause except the loss of his will to live. Timon loses first his money, then his friends, then his home, then his clothes, then perhaps his sanity, ultimately becoming a bitter hermit in a cave. Shakespeare strips away layer after layer of Timon's persona, exposing behind the successful society man a hateful, lonely creature.

Timon does not fall as other characters in tragedy tend to do. Unlike Macbeth or King Lear, for example, he does not gradually descend from the greatest heights to the lowest depths over the course of several acts. His downfall is sudden and immediate. The universal love Timon displays at the beginning of the play and the universal hate he displays at the end may seem worlds apart, but in fact they are closely connected, which is why he can switch between them so quickly. Timon has extreme ideas and is disposed to see humanity in black and white terms. When he decides that humans are fundamentally good, he takes to this idea completely and uncritically. When he discovers a flaw in this idea, he reverses it completely and uncritically. The all-encompassing love Timon feels in the first act is closer to universal hate than it is to modest, realistic love.

DISGUST AT ALL PEOPLE *Timon of Athens* is memorable for the remarkable curses Timon hurls again and again in the latter half of the play. He tells prostitutes to infect men with horrible diseases, thieves to rob and murder as much as they can, and a soldier to kill all the men, women, and children of Athens. He fervently hopes that plagues, misery, treachery, and death befall everyone. Timon's curses are so extreme that they cease to be terrifying and eventually turn amusing. Yet behind the ridiculous excess of Timon's rants lies deep disgust at everything that characterizes normal human behavior. Timon has decided that there is something so fundamentally wrong with life as it is lived in Athens that blind rage at all people is the only possible response.

Having been betrayed by his friends, Timon does not conclude that one can't always trust one's friends. Instead, he takes this betrayal as an indictment of humanity as a whole. This reaction might seem extreme, but Timon merely vocalizes the crushing disillusionment that many feel after a betrayal. Timon is emblematic of a world where real human connections have been replaced by money, where the only friends that exist are the ones you can buy. While neither our world nor Shakespeare's is quite as extreme as the one portrayed in the play, both worlds have been sufficiently distorted by consumerism and materialism that Timon's world is at least recognizable.

THE ABSENCE OF LOVE Almost all of Shakespeare's tragedies have to do with families and their difficulties. *Timon of Athens* is an exception: Timon has no family, and there are no women in the play apart from a couple of prostitutes. The absence of family and women marks a complete absence of love in Timon's life. Nobody in the play owes Timon love for the sake of love alone. Even his loyal servants are people he pays to be with him. Perhaps as a result of this lack of love, Timon believes that love can be bought like any other commodity.

Like King Lear, Timon wants a display of genuine love, but asks for a display of artificial love, and is outraged when he gets what he asks for rather than what he wants. In rewarding his friends with gifts and asking for nothing in return, Timon shows them that he thinks of them as a commodity he can buy. They see the friendship on the terms he sets up, and give him none of the love, loyalty, respect, and gratitude he desires.

MOTIFS

DOGS The word "dog" occurs twenty times in *Timon of Athens*, not counting other related utterances. Comparing people to dogs is a common form of insult, in Shakespeare's day and in ours, but the frequency of dog references in this play is unusual. Most often, "dog" is used as an insult: dogs are considered less intelligent and dirtier than humans. They are also stereotypically subservient. A dog is at the beck and call of its master and will eat scraps off the floor. In a play whose tragedy is precipitated by false flattery and groveling, "dog" is an accurate insult. Timon's false friends are dogs, as Apemantus and Timon say.

FRIENDSHIP Friendship is a central concern of *Timon*, a play in which unconditional, familial, and romantic love are conspicuously absent. Friendship is the only human relationship that is possible in the play, but even it never exists. Flavius is kind to Timon, and Apemantus is honest with him, but this is not the same as friendship. In neither case do two people on roughly equal footing respect each other. Shakespeare sketches friendship as a commodity with a fixed price, rather than as a priceless treasure. Timon thinks he can buy his friends with gifts, and those supposed friends value Timon's friendship only as they would a material object. They are willing to be Timon's companions as long as Timon showers them with gifts, but not when he starts asking them for loans in return. Friendship is central to the play, but only in that Shakespeare repeatedly points to its rarity or impossibility.

SYMBOLS

MEAT In Shakespeare's time, meat was a rare commodity, something people could only afford to eat on special occasions or if they were wealthy. Timon's willingness to serve meat to large groups symbolizes his great wealth and generosity. But meat also symbolizes Timon, who is the victim of his vampire-like friends. Timon eventually recognizes his friends' greed for what it is and sarcastically commands them to "[m]ake the meat be beloved more than the man that gives it."

THE SEA In literature in general, and in Shakespeare's later plays particularly, the sea symbolizes the vast emptiness of eternity. Because the fetus is suspended in liquid before birth, we associate the sea with birth, and because the sea stretches out from the point where the land ends, we associate it with death. The sea plays a subtle but increasingly important symbolic role in *Timon of Athens*. When Timon leaves Athens, he chooses to live in a cave by the sea. When he finally dies, he buries himself on the seashore so that the waves will wash over his body for all eternity. As Timon distances himself from humanity, he brings himself closer to the sea, and hence closer to eternity. Although Timon ends his life full of bitterness and hate, his approach to the sea injects a note of peace into his unhappiness.

IMPORTANT QUOTATIONS FROM *TIMON OF ATHENS*

---

1. *[H]e that loves to be flattered is worthy o'th' flatterer.*

Location: Act I, scene i, line 227
Speaker: Apemantus
Context: Apemantus chides Timon for accepting the flattery of a poet

In the first scene, Shakespeare uses Apemantus to expose the hypocrisy of Timon and his flatterers. Apemantus accuses the poet of being a liar, saying that in the poet's latest poem he called Timon a worthy man. The poet indignantly counters that Timon is a worthy man, to which Apemantus replies that Timon is worthy of the poet: Timon loves to be flattered by the poet, so he deserves this kind of shallow friendship. Apemantus is making a play on the word "worthy." When the poet calls Timon "worthy," he means it in an absolute sense: calling Timon a worthy gentleman is like calling him a good person. Apemantus intentionally misunderstands the poet to mean that Timon is worthy of something specific rather than simply worthy in a general sense. He says that calling Timon worthy of the poet is an insult, since neither are worthy at all.

Apemantus's claim that "he that loves to be flattered is worthy o' the flatterer" is one of the play's central points. Timon's downfall is his own fault, because he accepts the flattery of his supposed friends as genuine displays of friendship. Timon has no sense of what true friendship is. He thinks that he is being a friend by giving gifts, and that the gentlemen are being friends by praising him. Apemantus points out that Timon is no better than his shallow, selfish friends, because he enjoys their false flattery.

---

2. ALCIBIADES: *Why, fare thee well.*
    Here is some gold for thee.
    TIMON: *Keep it. I cannot eat it.*

Location: Act IV, scene iii, lines 98–100
Speaker: Alcibiades and Timon
Context: Alcibiades, seeing how futile conversation with Timon is, tries to leave

In the wild, Timon faces the irony of finding gold he once would have cherished, when all he wants now is a simple meal. When Timon tells Alcibiades, "keep it, I cannot eat it," he expresses his recognition of the true value of gold. Having abandoned the high society of Athens, he has gained a clearer sense of what a human being really needs: food and shelter. He sees the wealth of Athens as corrupt and wants only those bare necessities that will ensure his survival. In his new state, gold is as worthless to him as dirt, because neither of them provide food or shelter.

---

3.   APEMANTUS: *I love thee better now than e'er I did.*
     TIMON: *I hate thee worse.*
     APEMANTUS: *Why?*
     TIMON: *Thou flatter'st misery.*

Location: Act IV, scene iii, lines 233–234
Speakers: Timon and Apemantus
Context: Apemantus urges Timon to go back to Athens and find shelter and comfort

Apemantus dresses poorly, lives poorly, and expresses only contempt for human society. Seeing Timon wearing rags and cursing humanity, Apemantus observes that they are now quite similar. This similarity does not please him; he urges Timon not to imitate him, but rather to imitate his flatterers and try to profit from them as they profited from him in the past. Timon dismisses Apemantus's idea, and over the course of the scene repeatedly insults him, calling him a shallow, hateful man who curses humanity without having any reason for doing so.

Although Apemantus is extremely blunt, he has always treated Timon as a friend. Rather than flatter Timon like everyone else, Apemantus tells Timon what he really thinks, making plain his disgust at the flattery of Timon's friends and at Timon's grotesque displays of wealth. Now that Timon, too, has seen through his friends' flattery and the emptiness of his wealth, Apemantus feels he has found a kindred spirit. Timon, however, is disgusted by Apemantus's show of friendship. Timon's other friends were nice to him when he was rich, flattering his wealth because they were attracted to it. Apemantus is nice to Timon only now, when he is miserable, and Timon infers that this is because Apemantus is attracted to misery. Timon believes that Apemantus is not more honest than Timon's other friends, he is simply a sourpuss who enjoys unhappiness. Apemantus is a flatterer because his cynicism comes not from true suffering, like Timon's, but from an unpleasant disposition.

---

4.   *The middle of humanity thou never knewest, but the extremity of both ends. When thou wast in thy gilt and thy perfume, they mocked thee for too much curiosity; in thy rags thou know'st none, but art despised for the contrary.*

Location: Act IV, scene iii, lines 300–303
Speaker: Apemantus
Context: Apemantus reflects on how completely Timon's fortunes have reversed

Finding Timon in the woods, Apemantus engages him in a lengthy conversation that goes nowhere. Both men are so full of hate that they can only hurl insults at each other. At one point, Timon says he wishes he could poison Apemantus's food, to which Apemantus replies with the passage above.

Apemantus is right to characterize Timon as a bit of a caricature. Timon has no self-knowledge or sophistication, so when he discovers the falsity of his friends, he can do nothing but shut down, dispense with his good cheer entirely, and take to cursing all humanity. We see Timon in only two states: cheerful kindness or vehement rage. As Apemantus says, Timon never exists in "[t]he middle of humanity." Apemantus also observes that Timon's extremes of behavior have earned him disrespect. Timon's flatterers mocked him behind his back when he was extravagant, and now everyone mocks him for having nothing.

---

5.   *Lips, let four words go by and language end.*
     What is amiss, plague and infection mend.
     Graves only be men's works, and death their gain.

Sun, hide thy beams. Timon hath done his reign.

Location: Act V, scene ii, lines 105-108
Speaker: Timon
Context: Timon utters one last curse at the senators before retreating into his cave

These are the last words spoken by Timon in the last tragedy by Shakespeare. *Timon of Athens* is as lonely and bitter a play as exists in Shakespeare's canon, and Timon's final curse typifies the mood of the play. In telling his lips to "let sour words go by and language end," Timon acknowledges that his anger and suffering have surpassed the limits of language. His attempts to put his misery into words result in bitter, hollow curses. The language of tragedy is no longer sufficient to express Timon's predicament, so he lets language go. He hopes that disease can do what his words cannot: make people realize that their lives are valueless and that death is their only end.

TITUS ANDRONICUS

After the unjust executions of his sons and the rape and mutilation of his daughter Lavinia, Titus takes revenge by feeding the empress's sons to her in a pie.

TITUS ANDRONICUS IN CONTEXT

If not Shakespeare's worst, *Titus Andronicus* is easily his bloodiest, most perverse play. Shakespearean scholar S. Clark Hulse counts "fourteen killings, nine of them on stage, six severed members, one rape (or two or three, depending on how you count), one live burial, one case of insanity and one of cannibalism—an average of 5.2 atrocities per act, or one for every 97 lines." Reviewer Mike Gene Wallace adds, "This is a great play. We're talking fourteen dead bodies, kung-fu, sword-fu, spear-fu, dagger-fu, arrow-fu, pie-fu, animal screams on the soundtrack, heads roll, hands roll, tongues roll, nine and a half quarts of blood, and a record-breaking 94 on the vomit meter." Indeed, *Titus Andronicus* is a non-stop catalog of abominations.

In 1687, almost a hundred years after its first performance, the English playwright Edward Ravenscroft adapted *Titus Andronicus* for a more refined audience. In his introduction, he insists that Shakespeare was not the play's true author: "I have been told by some anciently conversant with the Stage, that it was not Originally his [Shakespeare's], but brought by a private Author to be Acted, and he only gave some Master-touches to one or two Principal Parts of Characters; this I am apt to believe, because 'tis the most incorrect and indigested piece in all his works; it seems rather a heap of Rubbish than a structure." Ravenscroft's determination to clear Shakespeare's good name from association with this "Rubbish" captures the essence of the play's history. The debate about its authorship has carried over into this century. If scholars acknowledge Shakespeare's hand at all, they usually point to his youth and inexperience as an explanation. Shakespeare would have been twenty-six at the time of writing, and *Titus* would have been his first attempt at tragedy.

One of the reasons *Titus Andronicus* has sparked such controversy rests in its resistance to easy categorization. It is a work of historical fiction, portraying entirely fictitious events set during the late Roman empire. It is a tragedy that fails to offer its audience catharsis. Its best description is revenge tragedy, which is a genre defined by a hero who doggedly pursues vengeance and perishes at his moment of success. Its bloodlusty excesses often make it seem a deliberate parody of the form.

Whether Rubbish or revenge, the play met with great public enthusiasm upon opening, and remained a favorite for over a decade. Though not one of Shakespeare's most compelling plays, *Titus Andronicus* features poetry and characters that look forward to Shakespeare's masterpieces.

TITUS ANDRONICUS: KEY FACTS

Full title: Titus Andronicus

Time and place written: 1592; London

Date of first publication: 1594 (in First Folio)

Genre: Tragedy

Setting (time): Fourth century A.D.

Setting (place): Rome

Protagonist: Titus Andronicus

Major conflict: After Titus sacrifices one of Tamora's sons, she becomes empress and, with her lover Aaron's help, rapes and mutilates Titus's daughter Lavinia and executes two of his sons.

TITUS ANDRONICUS: CHARACTER LIST

THE ANDRONICI

Lavinia Titus's daughter. Lavinia spurns Saturninus's proposal in favor of his brother Bassianus. After she is brutally raped and maimed by Tamora's sons, she becomes a mute and grotesque presence, an incapacitated heroine.

Lucius Titus's last surviving son by the end. Banished from Rome for trying to free his framed brothers, Lucius raises an army of Goth soliders and returns as the voice of reason to become the new emperor.

Marcus Andronicus Roman Tribune of the People and Titus's brother, who remains conspicuously separated from the bloodshed throughout the play.

Titus Andronicus Roman general and the play's tragic hero, and Lavinia and Lucius's father. His staunch reverence for tradition leads him to support an unbalanced emperor (Saturninus), kill his own son, and earn Tamora's hatred. He seeks vengeance and dies exacting it.

THE EMPERORS

Bassianus The late emperor's younger son, Saturninus's brother, and Lavinia's fiancé. A man of grace and virtue, his failure to secure the crown in Act I signals Rome's degeneracy. His elopement with Lavinia humiliates Saturninus and prompts Titus to kills his own son. Two more of Titus's sons are executed after being framed for Bassanius's murder by Aaron.

Saturninus The late Emperor's eldest son and Bassanius's brother. Saturninus is less deserving of the throne, but becomes emperor because he is the firstborn. His choice of Tamora for his empress allows her to wreak havoc on Rome and Titus's family.

THE GOTHS

Tamora Queen of the Goths, and Chiron and Demetrius' mother. Tamora is associated with barbarism and lasciviousness, the thematic opposite of innocent victim Lavinia.

Chiron and Demetrius Tamora's sons. Chiron and Demetrius murder Bassianus and brutally rape and maim Lavinia. Nothing more than engines of lust, destruction, and depravity, they lack the wit and intelligence that make Aaron a compelling villain. They are finally killed by Titus, who cooks them into a pie to feed to Tamora.

THE MOOR

Aaron Tamora's lover. By his own admission, Aaron is involved with all of *Titus*'s crimes. A simplistic evil incarnate, Aaron is a descendant of the Devil or Vice character of Elizabethan morality plays. Accordingly, we get little in the way of explanation of his motives, although his unconditional defense of his child contrasts with both Tamora's and Titus's attitudes toward parenthood.

TITUS ANDRONICUS: PLOT OVERVIEW

Roman general Titus Andronicus returns from ten years of war with only four out of twenty-five sons left. He has captured Tamora, queen of the Goths, her three sons, and Aaron the Moor. In obedience to Roman rituals, he sacrifices her eldest son to his own dead sons, which earns him Tamora's unending hatred and promise of revenge.

The new Emperor Saturninus wants to marry Titus's daughter Lavinia, but Lavinia is spirited away by her fiancé, Saturninus's brother Bassianus. Publicly humiliated, Saturninus makes Tamora empress instead. To get back at Titus, Tamora schemes with her lover Aaron to frame Titus's sons for the murder of Bassianus. Moreover, Aaron urges Tamora's sons to rape Lavinia, after which they cut off her hands and tongue to keep her mute. Titus's accused sons are beheaded, and Titus's last surviving son Lucius is banished from Rome. Lucius seeks alliance with the enemy Goths in order to attack Rome. Faced with so many misfortunes, Titus begins to see black humor in his situation, leading to the public assumption that he is crazy.

Tamora tries to capitalize on Titus's apparent madness by pretending to be the figure of Revenge, come to offer him justice if Titus will only convince Lucius to cease attacking Rome. Titus tricks Tamora, captures her sons, kills them, and makes pie out of them. He feeds this pie to Tamora, after which he kills both Tamora and Lavinia, his own daughter. After Saturninus kills Titus and Lucius kills Saturninus, the people of Rome elect Lucius emperor. Lucius orders the unrepentant Aaron buried alive, and Tamora's corpse thrown to the beasts.

TITUS ANDRONICUS: SCENE SUMMARY

ACT I

Saturninus becomes the new Roman emperor, but his brother Bassianus wins Titus's daughter Lavinia with the help of Titus's sons.

I.I Location: Rome. Near the capitol

Publicly humiliated by the Andronicus clan when general Titus's daughter Lavinia prefers his brother Bassanius, the new Roman Emperor Saturninus weds the sly captive Queen Tamora of the Goths.

The Roman emperor has died and his two sons, Saturninus and Bassianus, ask the people to choose one of them to succeed to the throne. Saturninus, the eldest son, invokes primogeniture. Bassianus calls upon his virtue and graciousness. They are silenced by Marcus Andronicus, the tribune of the people, who announces that the people of Rome have elected to the throne his brother Titus Andronicus, a general who has spent the last ten years vanquishing Rome's enemies, losing twenty-one sons in battle. Titus enters to great fanfare, trailed by his four remaining sons, as well as new captives: Queen Tamora of the Goths, her three sons, and Aaron the Moor. In spite of Tamora's desperate pleas, Titus orders Tamora's eldest son, Alarbus, sacrificed in exchange for Titus's own dead offspring, in accordance with Roman custom.

Marcus offers Titus the scepter of Rome on behalf of the people, but Titus refuses the throne because of his advanced age. Instead, Titus proclaims firstborn Saturninus rightful emperor. Saturninus returns the favor by declaring that Titus's daughter Lavinia will be his wife. Bassianus challenges Saturninus, the new emperor, claiming that Lavinia is betrothed to him, Bassanius. He spirits her away with the aid of Lavinia's brothers Lucius, Mutius, Quintus, and Martius. In the commotion, Mutius holds off Titus, and Titus kills him. It is only after his other sons plead with him that Titus allows Mutius to be interred in the family tomb.

Publicly humiliated by the loss of Lavinia, Saturninus declares that Tamora will be his empress instead. Tamora slyly advises Saturninus to accept the apologies of the Andronicus clan, secretly promising to help him exact revenge later. Saturninus invites everyone to the court to celebrate his coronation and wedding. In return, Titus promises to organize a hunt in Saturninus's honor the next day.

ACT II

At Aaron's instigation and with Tamora's help, Tamora's sons kill Bassianus and rape Lavinia; Titus's sons are framed for murder.

II.I Location: Rome. Near the capitol

Tamora's lover Aaron counsels Tamora's sons to catch and rape Lavinia during the hunt.

Aaron rejoices that Tamora, his lover, has become the new empress. Tamora's sons Chiron and Demetrius interrupt Aaron's thoughts with their argument over who better deserves Lavinia's love. Aaron counsels them to stop arguing. Instead, they should both catch her and rape her during the next day's hunt.

II.II Location: a forest near Rome

The hunt begins.

The next day, as everyone gathers for the hunt, Chiron and Demetrius reaffirm their intention to accost and have sex with Lavinia.

II.III Location: a forest near Rome

Tamora's sons kill Bassianus, and Aaron frames two of Titus's sons for the murder.

Away from the hunting party, Aaron buries a bag of gold under a tree. Tamora finds him and urges him to make love to her. Aaron says that he rather wants vengeance, and asks her to deliver a letter to Saturninus. Bassianus and Lavinia spot Aaron and Tamora together, and coarsely insult Tamora. Tamora's sons Chiron and Demetrius enter and stab Bassianus to death in defense of Tamora's honor. Tamora urges them to stab Lavinia too, but when they say that they want to satisfy their lust first, Tamora agrees, ignoring Lavinia's plea to die instead. Chiron and Demetrius dump Bassianus's body into a pit and drag Lavinia off.

Aaron leads Titus's sons Quintus and Martius, promising to show them a sleeping panther. Quintus and Martius both fall into the same pit. Aaron then brings Saturninus to the pit. Tamora hands him Aaron's letter incriminating Quintus and Martius in the murder of Bassianus. The bag of gold that Aaron buried is conveniently uncovered as proof that Quintus and Martius were planning to pay a huntsman to kill Bassianus. Titus pleads for his sons in vain. On Saturninus's orders, they are taken away to be executed.

II.IV Location: a forest near Rome

Marcus discovers Lavinia, who has been raped and whose hands and tongue have been cut off by Tamora's sons.

Chiron and Demetrius enter with a ravished Lavinia, whose hands and tongue they have cut off to prevent her from identifying them. They make fun of her and leave her alone in the wilderness. The wretched girl is discovered by her uncle Marcus in a poignant, poetic tirade. Lavinia tries to flee in shame, but Marcus stops her and takes her home to Titus.

ACT III

His sons executed and his daughter Lavinia raped and maimed, Titus loses his hand through Aaron's treachery and begins to see dark humor in his situation.

III.I Location: Rome. A street

Titus's two accused sons are executed and his remaining son Lucius is exiled; moreover Aaron tricks him into cutting off his hand.

Titus entreats the Roman judges to spare the lives of his arrested sons, in the name of his long service and his old age. Ignored, he prostrates himself upon the ground. His son Lucius unsuccessfully attempts to free Martius and Quintus. For his efforts, he is banished. Titus calls Lucius lucky for escaping the Roman "wilderness of tigers" (III.i.53). Marcus brings in the ravished Lavinia, and all break down in tears.

Aaron brings Titus a message from Saturninus: if Titus cuts off one of his own hands, Saturninus will spare Titus's sons. Marcus and Lucius leave to fetch an ax, arguing about which of them should sacrifice his hand. Left alone together, Titus persuades Aaron to help him cut off his hand, with the farcical line "Lend me thy hand, and I will give thee mine" (III.i.186). Aaron's deal turns out to be a trick: after Aaron leaves with Titus's hand, a messenger comes in with the severed heads of Quintus and Martius. Titus laughs, for he has cried all his tears (III.i.265). Titus sends Lucius to raise an army of Goths against Saturninus, and retires home with Marcus and Lavinia.

III.II Location: Rome. Titus's house

His sons dead, his hand cut off, and his daughter raped and maimed, Titus begins to unravel.

Titus, Marcus, Lavinia, and Young Lucius (Lucius's son) have a small banquet. Titus feeds Lavinia and tries to decipher her mimed gestures. She refuses to drink anything but her own tears. Marcus kills a fly, and Titus waxes poetic for the fly's poor parents. When Marcus says that the fly was black like Aaron, Titus is so delighted that Marcus begins to think that Titus is losing his mind. Titus takes Lavinia and Young Lucius away to read.

ACT IV

Titus learns that Tamora's sons raped and maimed Lavinia; his exiled son Lucius advances on Rome with a Goth army.

IV.I Location: Rome. Outside Titus's house

With the help of classical texts, Lavinia communicates that Chiron and Demetrius cut off her tongue to keep her silent after they raped her; Titus and Marcus promise to take revenge.

Young Lucius flees from his aunt Lavinia, fearing that she is insane. In fact, she merely wants his book, Ovid's *Metamorphoses*. To indicate what has happened to her, she shows Titus and Marcus the story of Philomela and Tereus. (Tereus cuts off his sister-in-law Philomela's tongue to keep her silent after raping her.) At Marcus's suggestion, she holds a staff in her mouth and writes "*Stuprum* [Latin for rape]—Chiron—Demetrius" in the sand. They all kneel and promise to take revenge.

IV.II Location: Rome. The emperor's palace

Aaron refuses to kill his and Tamora's bastard son.

On Titus's orders, Young Lucius brings Chiron and Demetrius weapons from Titus's armory, along with a scroll bearing a Latin quotation from Horace: "The man upright in life and free from crime, needs neither the Moorish javelin nor the bow." Aaron notes the insult.

A nurse comes in bearing Tamora and Aaron's bastard "blackamoor" child. She asks Aaron to kill it to protect Tamora's reputation, but Aaron roars to his son's defense, claiming that black is the best color for skin because it can never be altered: "Coal-black is better than another hue / In that it scorns to bear another hue" (IV.ii.98–99). He kills the nurse to keep the existence of the child a secret, then resolves to take him to be raised by the Goths to be a warrior.

IV.III Location: Rome. Outside the emperor's palace

Titus and his kinsmen shoot arrows to ask the gods for help and intimidate Saturninus.

Titus brings Young Lucius, Marcus, Marcus's son Publius and kinsmen Sempronius and Caius to shoot arrows bearing supplications to the gods into the sky. Marcus advises them all to ensure that the letters fall into the emperor's court in order to scare him. Along comes a clown carrying two pigeons on his way to the court to settle a personal dispute. Titus promises to pay the clown generously if he brings Saturninus a message with a knife wrapped in it.

IV.IV Location: Rome. The emperor's palace

Saturninus gets word that Lucius advances on Rome with an army of Goths.

Saturninus is furious about Titus's arrows, which have announced his crimes to all of Rome. The clown enters with the two pigeons and Titus's letter. Saturninus takes the letter with the knife enclosed and immediately orders the clown hanged. The messenger Aemilius enters with word that Lucius advances on Rome with an army of Goths. Saturninus panics, afraid that the people of Rome will support Lucius. Tamora calms him, and promises to persuade Titus to entreat Lucius to stop his war efforts. She sends Aemilius to the Goths to summon Lucius to a meeting at Titus's house.

ACT V

Titus cooks and serves Tamora's sons to her at a banquet; Lavinia, Tamora, Titus, and Saturninus die, and Lucius becomes the next emperor.

V.I Location: the Goth camp near Rome

Lucius captures Aaron, who confesses his role in all the misfortunes of the Andronicus family.

Lucius tells the Goths that he has word that the Romans hate Saturninus and eagerly await Lucius's arrival. The Goths, Lucius's onetime enemies, promise to follow his lead into battle. A Goth soldier brings in Aaron and his baby, whom he has discovered hiding out in an abandoned monastery. Lucius orders a ladder to hang first the baby and then Aaron. At the last moment, Aaron makes a bargain: Lucius will spare the baby if Aaron reveals everything he knows, admitting that Chiron and Demetrius killed Bassanius and raped Lavinia, Tamora gave birth to an illegitimate child, and Aaron tricked Titus into chopping off his hand. Proud of his role in all of the misfortunes of the Andronicus family, Aaron continues to list other crimes, and claims that his sole regret is that he cannot commit ten thousand more. Horrified, Lucius orders Aaron taken down because hanging is too nice a death. Aaron is gagged.

Aemilius enters with Saturninus's request for a meeting. Lucius agrees.

V.II Location: Rome. Outside Titus's house

Titus tricks Tamora and captures Chiron and Demetrius, whom he kills and plans to cook into pies.

Tamora, Demetrius, and Chiron appear to Titus in disguise, masquerading as Revenge and her attendants Rape and Murder. Believing Titus mad, Tamora-as-Revenge promises to punish all his enemies if he convinces Lucius to attend a banquet at Titus's house. She plans to wreak confusion among the Goths while Lucius, their new leader, is at the banquet. Titus agrees on the condition that she leaves Rape and Murder—Chiron and Demetrius in disguise—with him. Upon Tamora's departure, Titus gets his kinsmen to gag and bind Chiron and Demetrius. Lavinia holds the basin to catch their blood, and Titus "play[s] the cook" (V.ii.203) who slits their throats. He plans to grind their bones into flour, mix it with their blood, and make pie crust to serve Tamora her sons as pies at the banquet.

V.III Location: Rome. Outside Titus's house

After Titus feeds Tamora her sons in a pie, he, she, Lavinia, and Satuninus are slain, and Lucius becomes the next emperor.

Lucius asks Marcus to take custody of Aaron for the time being. Titus, dressed as a cook, welcomes Saturninus and Tamora to his banquet. Titus asks Saturninus about Virginius, a Roman general whose daughter was raped. Saturninus replies that a girl should not survive her shame, and Virginius should have killed his daughter. At this, Titus kills Lavinia. Saturninus is horrified, but Titus claims that her real killers are Chiron and Demetrius. Saturninus calls for them, and Titus answers that they are already present, in the pies Tamora has been eating. Titus stabs Tamora; Saturninus kills Titus; Lucius kills Saturninus.

Marcus and another nobleman speak out in grief against the barbarism in Rome. Lucius defends his actions by citing all the crimes that have been committed against the Andronici. Marcus asks the judgment of the Roman people. The people, led by Aemilius, call for Lucius to be emperor. Lucius accepts. He, Marcus, and Young Lucius pay tribute to Titus's corpse. Lucius orders Aaron buried breast-deep and left to starve to death. Aaron does not repent. Lucius orders Tamora's corpse thrown to wild beasts, since she led a beastly life.

THEMES, MOTIFS, & SYMBOLS IN *TITUS ANDRONICUS*

THEMES

CIVILIZED ROME VERSUS BARBARISM The world of *Titus Andronicus* is divided into civilized Rome and the barbaric world outside, populated by savage Goths and Moors. The play opens with civilized, quasi-democratic elections of a new emperor. This organized proceeding is interrupted and threatened by the arrival of Titus, fresh from the wars with Goths, who has lost twenty-one sons fighting barbarians. Later, when the barbaric outsiders Tamora and Aaron gain entrance into Rome, they wreak havoc on all order. Much of their destruction is violent and corporeal. They kill Bassianus, rape and mutilate Lavinia, manipulate Saturninus into executing Martius and Quintus, and trick Titus into cutting off his hand.

Of course, some of the laws of civilized Rome appear quite barbaric. Titus executes Tamora's son as a mandated sacrifice to his own dead sons. Soon after, he kills his own son Mutius in the name of honor. Barbarism lurks just under the surface, no matter how assiduously the Roman characters try to distance themselves from it. Marcus urges Titus to bury Mutius with "Thou art a Roman; be not barbarous" (I.i.375). Barbarism is seen as a continual threat, a dangerous natural urge that humans must guard against with reason and willpower. When Tamora and Aaron enter Roman society, the barbarism under the surface is unleashed. Rome becomes barbaric, and Titus imagines Rome as a beast preying on his family: "Why, foolish Lucius, dost thou not perceive / That Rome is but a wilderness of tigers? / Tigers must prey, and Rome affords no prey/ But me and mine" (III.i.52–55).

TRADITION IN CONFLICT WITH REASON *Titus* is set in the late years of the Roman Empire, well after the democratic golden age of the Roman Republic. The traditions that had guided the empire in its glory days had lost much of their meaning in this time. In this play, these stale traditions undermine and hurt Roman society. At the beginning of the play, the imperial throne is passed to Saturninus, the dead emperor's eldest son, in accordance with the laws of primogeniture. At the same time, Shakespeare portrays Bassianus as unquestionably the better, less volatile ruler. Bassianus is less hot-tempered than Saturninus. He gives in to Titus and shows that he respects the Roman people, telling them to "fight for freedom in your [election] choice" (I.i.17). His relationship with Lavinia seems genuine.

But it is the hot-headed firstborn to whom the Roman general abdicates. Crippled by petty jealousies, Saturninus allows himself to be manipulated by Tamora and, through her, by Aaron, which leads to an escalation of violence and misrule. When Titus sacrifices Tamora's sons in accordance with Roman tradition, he creates an enemy and becomes trapped in a vicious revenge cycle.

Even literary tradition is a force of destruction in the play. Tamora's sons rape Lavinia and cut out her tongue, mimicking Tereus, who rapes and maims Philomela in the Roman author Ovid's *Metamorphoses*. In Ovid's story, Philomela identifies her rapist by weaving a tapestry that depicts the crime. Familiar with Ovid, Lavinia's tormentors cut off her hands as well to prevent her from following Philomela's example.

TRAGEDY BECOMING FARCE *Titus*'s black humor and over-the-top gore and violence often pushes the play into farce, muddying the line between tragedy and comedy. The most openly comedic moment is Titus's request for help in cutting off his hand: "Lend me thy hand, and I will give thee mine" (III.i.186). The violence of the action is hugely exaggerated. In the very first scene of the play, Titus declares that he has lost twenty-one sons in the wars with the Goths. Lavinia is raped not once but twice, and both she and Titus lose their hands. Shakespeare amplifies the horror of the situations adapted from classical storylines. In Ovid's *Metamorphoses*, the heroine, Philomela, is raped by her brother-in-law and has her tongue cut out. Shakespeare's Lavinia is raped by two men, and loses her tongue and both hands. In *Metamorphoses*, Philomela's sister bakes one son for the villainous Tereus to eat. In *Titus*, Titus kills and bakes both of Tamora's sons. This amplification of disaster catapults Titus into farce. When Titus receives the heads of his dead sons after cutting off his own hand to save them, he begins to laugh, having shed all possible tears. At times, Shakespeare exaggerates, perhaps even mocks, his play and his genre. Tamora's appearance onstage disguised as Revenge reminds us that we are watching a revenge tragedy, but in a mocking, hyperliteral way. Titus throws arrows with appeals to the gods, but the clown who appears, pigeon basket in hand, deflates the nobility of Titus's speech and actions.

MOTIFS

BLOOD AND BLOODLINES Blood is a powerful motif in *Titus*, and the link between family bloodlines and violent bloodshed is crucial to the plot. Titus's loss of his sons in war prompts him to sacrifice Tamora's son, which in turn sets her bloody revenge in motion. Everyone in the play has strong family connections. Even the outsider Aaron ends up becoming a father. The important role of blood relationship evokes the Roman focus on continuity and traditions. Indeed, all citizens are described as "sons of Rome" (V.iii.66).

Many of the blood relationships in the play end with blood: Saturninus quarrels with Bassanius, Tamora wants to kill her illegitimate baby, Titus does kill two of his children and, finally, Tamora eats her sons, consuming what she has brought to life.

PIT, MOUTH, AND WOMB The pit into which Chiron and Demetrius hurl the dead Bassianus, and where Aaron traps Quintus and Martius, symbolizes evil, corruption, and deceit. It is literally lower than the rest of the earth, an "abhorrèd" (II.iii.98), "loathsome" (II.iii.176), "unhallowed and blood-stained" (II.iii.210) place. Tamora implicitly compares it to hell: "They told me here at dead time of the night / A thousand fiends, a thousand hissing snakes, / Ten thousand swelling toads, as many urchins / Would make such fearful and confusèd cries" (II.iii.99–102). It becomes a grave for Bassanius, Quintus, and Martius.

Throughout the play, the pit is associated with graves, mouths, and wombs. Its "bloodstained hole" evokes both Lavinia's genitalia after she has been raped and her mouth after her tongue has been cut off. At the end of the play, Tamora's mouth/womb becomes a grave for her children when she eats them, burying them in her body, from which they came. The perversity of this image, which unites pit, mouth, and womb, symbolizes the violent perversion of peace and natural order portrayed in the play.

SYMBOLS

THE MUTILATED HUMAN BODY Mutilated bodies—Lavinia's severed hands and tongue, Titus's severed hand, Chiron and Demetrius in a pie—symbolize the corruption of Roman society. During the Renaissance, the well-proportioned human body was often associated with cosmic order, as well as the political order of a state. Accordingly, ravaged bodies correspond to the political turmoil in the declining Roman empire. Indeed, at the play's end, Lucius uses body vocabulary to promise to restore order in the empire: "O, let me teach you how to knit again / This scattered corn into one mutual sheaf, / These broken limbs again into one body" (V.iii.69–71).

TITUS'S ARROWS In one of the play's most bizarre scenes, Titus, Marcus, and what's left of their circle write petitions to Roman gods, wrap them around the arrowheads, and shoot the arrows into the air, appealing to the gods for help. Help never comes, because humans have been abandoned by the gods. Instead of help, an absurd clown arrives on his way to the market carrying a basket of pigeons. Titus's attempt to accuse his enemies of injustice by literally covering them with words and texts fail: Saturninus notices the arrows as degraded "Sweet scrolls to fly about the streets of Rome!" (IV.iv.16).

IMPORTANT QUOTATIONS FROM *TITUS ANDRONICUS*

1. *She is a woman, therefore may be wooed;*
   She is a woman, therefore may be won;
   She is Lavinia, therefore must be loved.

Location: II.i.82–84
Speaker: Demetrius
Context: Demetrius and Chiron discuss with Aaron how Demetrius and Chiron can have Lavinia

Demetrius's cynical sentiment is the only snatch from *Titus* to enter popular culture. He suggests that any woman may be seduced. At the same time, in distinguishing between any woman who may be seduced and a Lavinia who must be loved, Demetrius separates her from the female masses. Ironically, after he and Chiron rape and maim her, they render her incapable of expressing herself, of distinguishing herself as a human being.

2. *What subtle hole is this,*
   Whose mouth is covered with rude-grown briers
   Upon whose leaves are drops of new-shed blood
   As fresh as morning dew distilled on flowers?
   A very fatal place it seems to me.

Location: II.iii.198–202
Speaker: Quintus
Context: Quintus notices the pit into which Martius has fallen

Quintus's description of the hole evokes the genitalia of a deflowered woman, just as Chiron and Demetrius rape Lavinia offstage. Quintus's image of the pit as a "mouth" sprinkled with blood draws a comparison between the ravished Lavinia's genitalia and her maimed tongueless mouth. The image also foreshadows Tamora's ingesting of her children's bodies. He describes the pit as "fatal," which in Elizabethan times meant not only deadly, but also ominous, tinged with bad fate.

3. *Coal-black is better than another hue,*
   In that it scorns to bear another hue;
   For all the water in the ocean
   Can never turn the swan's black legs to white,
   Although she lave them hourly in the flood.

Location: IV.ii.98–102
Speaker: Aaron
Context: Aaron refuses to let Tamora's sons kill his and Tamora's half-black baby

In Shakespeare's time, blackness was associated with evil and also with strength. Here, Aaron describes black as a strong color, because it eclipses all others. Unlike lighter shades, black does not fade or bleed. He associates blackness with fortitude and self-reliance. Aaron's speech is not refined, as evidenced, for example, by his awkward repetition of "hue." Still, his speech is plain and direct. Ironically, although Aaron is the self-acknowledged villain of the play, he is also the most empathetic parent. Tamora wishes to kill her love child, and Titus kills both his son Mutius and his daughter Lavinia.

4. *Why, there they are, both baked in this pie,*
   Whereof their mother daintily hath fed,
   Eating the flesh that she herself hath bred.
   'Tis true, 'tis true, witness my knife's sharp point.

Location: V.iii.59–62
Speaker: Titus
Context: Titus reveals that he has tricked Tamora into eating her sons Chiron and Demetrius

Titus's matter-of-fact revelation that Tamora has eaten her sons is both comic and horrifying. His description of her eating habits as "dainty" contrasts ironically with the barbarism of cannibalism. Titus's "Why, there they are" is studiedly casual. His pun as he makes his point with his "knife's sharp point" demonstrates that he is in complete control of his reason. Unlike Hamlet, Titus is completely certain of his moral right. His revenge is cool and calculating.

5. *Ah, why should wrath be mute and fury dumb?*
   I am no baby, I, that with base prayers
   I should repent the evils I have done.
   Ten thousand worse than ever yet I did
   Would I perform if I might have my will.
   If one good deed in all my life I did
   I do repent it from my very soul.

Location: V.iii.183–189
Speaker: Aaron
Context: Sentenced to death by exposure and starvation, Aaron refuses to repent

Like many of Shakespeare's villains, Aaron earnestly identifies himself as evil from the beginning. Unlike Titus, who struggles to contain his base instincts under a civilized appearance, Aaron makes no such efforts. Instead, he rejoices in his amorality. Here, Aaron mocks religious language to reject religion: he refuses to repent his evil deeds with "base prayers" and repent his rare good deeds. His eight "I's" in seven short lines proclaim him as independent and powerful, even when sentenced to death. Lavinia is rendered mute when her tongue is cut out, and Titus's impotent arrows never reach their destination, but Aaron refuses to be "mute" and "dumb." He defines himself in opposition to the Roman "civilization," and dies as a beast from starvation, trapped in the earth.

TROILUS AND CRESSIDA

Troilus persuades Cressida to be his lover, but she betrays him when she moves to the Greek camp.

TROILUS AND CRESSIDA IN CONTEXT

Shakespeare wrote *Troilus and Cressida* around 1602, shortly after *Hamlet* but before his other great tragedies. The play was likely first performed in the winter of 1602–1603, but no performance record survives. Moreover, the play was not published in a collection until 1609. Consequently, a number of critics have suggested that *Troilus and Cressida* was performed only once or not at all during Shakespeare's lifetime, possibly because some of the characters caricatured his contemporaries, either other playwrights or members of King James I's court.

The genre classification of *Troilus and Cressida* has been in dispute from the beginning. Labeled a history play in an early folio, it bears superficial similarities to the tragedies, but lacks the typical tragic plot structure. Today, *Troilus and Cressida* is often grouped with the so-called problem comedies *Measure for Measure* and *All's Well That Ends Well*. All three share a dark, bitter wit and a pessimistic view of human relations that contrast sharply with earlier, sunnier comedies such as *Twelfth Night* and *As You Like It*.

Sources for the play include Homer's *Iliad*, which provides the Achilles-Hector story arc. The romance of Troilus and Cressida is derived from pseudo-Homeric medieval sources, as well as from Chaucer's great fourteenth-century epic, *Troilus and Criseyde*. True to form, Shakespeare used only the bare bones of these stories for his play. Unlike Chaucer, he emphasized Cressida's frivolity and unfaithfulness. In reading *Troilus and Cressida*, it is important to remember the popularity of Trojan War stories in Shakespeare's time. Audiences would have expected the denouement of Cressida's treachery and Hector's death from the beginning of the play.

TROILUS AND CRESSIDA: KEY FACTS

Full title: Troilus and Cressida

Time and place written: 1601–1602; London, England

Date of first publication: 1609

Genre: Problem play; satire; comedy

Setting (time): Mid-thirteenth century B.C.; seven years into the Trojan War

Setting (place): Troy

Protagonist: Troilus; Hector; Ulysses

Major conflict: Cressida is traded to the Greek camp after she and Troilus consummate their love; the moody Achilles refuses to participate in the war.

TROILUS AND CRESSIDA: CHARACTER LIST

GREEKS

Achilles The greatest of the Greek warriors. Achilles is an arrogant, vicious thug who refuses to fight whenever his pride is injured.

Agamemnon The Greek general, and Menelaus's elder brother.

Ajax A Greek warrior. Ajax is as proud as Achilles, but less intelligent and less skilled in battle.

Diomedes A Greek commander who seduces Cressida.

Helen Menelaus's wife. She elopes with Paris, which begins the Trojan War.

Menelaus A Greek commander, Agamemnon's brother, and Helen's abandoned husband.

Nestor The oldest of the Greek commanders.

Patroclus A Greek warrior. Achilles' close friend and lover.

Thersites A cynical Greek soldier who has a vicious, abusive tongue. Thersites rails against both war and warriors.

Ulysses A Greek commander. A highly intelligent, even philosophical man, Ulysses is renowned for his cunning.

TROJANS

Aeneas A Trojan commander.

Andromache Hector's wife.

Antenor A Trojan commander who is captured by the Greeks and exchanged for Cressida.

Calchas Cressida's father, and a Trojan priest. Calchas defected to the Greeks in the early days of the war.

Cassandra A Trojan princess and prophetess, often considered mad.

Cressida A beautiful young Trojan woman who becomes Troilus's lover. Cressida's father Calchas defected to the Greeks. The Trojans send Cressida to the Greeks to join him in exchange for the return of Antenor.

Hector A Trojan prince and hero. Hector is the greatest Trojan warrior. Matched in might only by Achilles himself, Hector is respected even by his enemies.

Helenus A Trojan prince.

Pandarus Cressida's uncle. He serves as a go-between for Troilus and Cressida, acting as a cheerful, bawdy pimp for his niece.

Paris A Trojan prince who steals Menelaus's wife Helen, precipitating the Trojan War.

Priam The King of Troy, and the father of Hector, Paris, Helenus, Troilus, and Cassandra, among others.

Troilus A Trojan prince, and Hector and Paris's younger brother. An honorable and valiant warrior, Troilus is desperately in love with Cressida.

TROILUS AND CRESSIDA: PLOT OVERVIEW

Seven years into the siege of Troy, the Trojan Prince Troilus falls in love with Cressida, the daughter of a Trojan priest who has defected to the Greek side. Cressida's uncle Pandarus has been helping Troilus woo her. In the Greek camp, the general Agamemnon wonders why Greek morale is low. The crafty Ulysses informs him that the army's troubles spring from a lack of respect for authority brought about by the behavior of Achilles. Achilles, the greatest Greek warrior, refuses to fight and instead spends his time sitting in his tent with his comrade and lover Patroclus, mocking his superiors. A challenge to single combat arrives from Prince Hector, the greatest Trojan warrior. Ulysses decides to have Ajax, a headstrong fool, fight Hector instead of Achilles, in the hope that this gesture will wound Achilles' pride and bring him back into the war.

Pandarus brings Troilus and Cressida together to consummate their love. The next morning, the Trojans agree to trade Cressida to the Greeks in exchange for a prisoner. Troilus gives Cressida his sleeve as a gift of remembrance before Cressida is led away by the Greek lord Diomedes. That afternoon, Ajax and Hector fight to a draw, and after Hector and Achilles exchange insults, Hector and Troilus feast with the Greeks under a truce flag. As the camp goes to bed, Ulysses leads Troilus to Cressida's tent. There, Troilus watches from hiding as Cressida agrees to become Diomedes' lover and gives him Troilus's sleeve as a keepsake.

The next day, Hector and Troilus return to the battlefield and drive the Greeks back, but Patroclus is killed, which brings a vengeful Achilles back into the war. Achilles catches Hector unarmed, orders his followers to kill Hector, then drags Hector's body around the walls of Troy.

TROILUS AND CRESSIDA: SCENE SUMMARY

PROLOGUE

The play opens seven years into the Trojan War, as the Greeks besiege Troy.

The Prologue, dressed as a soldier, gives some background to the story. The Trojan War began when the Trojan Prince Paris stole Helen, the wife of the Greek King Menelaus of Sparta. In response, Menelaus gathered his fellow Greek warriors and sailed to Troy to pillage the city and reclaim Helen. The play opens seven years into the Siege of Troy.

ACT I

Pandarus woos his niece Cressida on behalf of Trojan Prince Troilus; the Greeks discuss their hero Achilles' recent refusal to fight.

I.I Location: Troy. Within the city walls

Heartsick with love for Pandarus's niece Cressida, Troilus heads to war when his brother Paris is wounded on the battlefield.

Prince Troilus complains to Pandarus that he is unable to fight because of the heartache of being desperately in love with Pandarus's beautiful niece Cressida. (Cressida's father, a Trojan priest, has betrayed his city and defected to the Greeks.) Pandarus complains that he has been doing his best to help Troilus woo Cressida, but has received little thanks for his labors from Troilus. Alone, Troilus notes that even though Pandarus has been growing irritable, he is still his best hope for winning Cressida. The Trojan commander Aeneas dashes in, bringing word that Troilus's brother Paris has been wounded in combat with the Greek King Menelaus. As battle sounds waft in from offstage, Troilus leaves to join his Trojan comrades on the field.

I.II Location: Troy. Another part of the city

Pandarus praises Troilus highly in front of Cressida.

Cressida's servant Alexander tells Cressida about how the Greek warrior Ajax, a valiant but stupid man, managed to overcome the great Trojan Prince Hector the previous day. Embarrassed by his defeat, Hector fights furiously today. Cressida is joined by Pandarus, and they discuss the Trojan princes. Pandarus unexpectedly argues that Troilus is a greater man than Hector. As they converse, several Trojan commanders—Antenor, Aeneas, Hector, Paris, and Helenus—pass by on the way back from battle. Pandarus praises each one, but tells Cressida that none of them can match Troilus. Finally, Troilus passes, and Pandarus crows that even a goddess would be a fair match for Troilus. He leaves Cressida, promising to bring a token from Troilus. Alone, Cressida remarks that she finds Troilus very attractive, but enjoys playing hard-to-get.

I.III Location: outside Troy. The Greek camp

The Greek commanders Ulysses and Nestor plot to have Ajax, instead of the capricious Achilles, accept the Trojan Prince Hector's challenge of single combat.

Agamemnon, the great general and king, asks his lieutenants and fellow kings why they seem so glum and downcast. It is true that their seven-year siege of Troy has been unsuccessful, but adversity is the only thing that can bring out true greatness. Nestor, the oldest commander, agrees with Agamemnon and cites examples of heroism emerging from hardship. In response, Ulysses points out that the Greek army faces a crisis not because of the duration of the war, but because of a breakdown in unity and authority within the camp. The root of the problem is Achilles, the greatest of the Greek warriors, who refuses to fight and instead sits in his tent while his friend (and lover, it is later implied) Patroclus makes fun of the Greek commanders. Others, like Ajax and his foul-mouthed slave Thersites, follow Achilles' example, and so the entire army is corrupted.

The other Greeks agree that Achilles is a problem. As they discuss possible solutions, the Trojan commander Aeneas appears with a white flag and a challenge from Hector, who offers to fight any Greek in single combat for the honor of their wives. The Greeks offer Aeneas hospitality and agree to find a champion to accept Hector's challenge. Ulysses privately tells Nestor that the challenge is clearly meant for Achilles, the only true match for Hector. However, if Achilles lost, the morale of the whole Greek army would suffer. Therefore, Ulysses suggests, Ajax should fight Hector instead. That way, if Ajax loses, they can claim that Achilles would have won. Moreover, choosing Ajax to represent the Greek army will infuriate Achilles, and perhaps goad him into rejoining the war. Nestor, impressed with Ulysses' intelligence, agrees to the plan.

ACT II

The Greek commanders decide that Ajax, rather than the moody Achilles, will answer Hector's challenge to fight in single combat.

II.I   Location: outside Troy. The Greek camp

Achilles tells Ajax that a lottery will decide the Greek warrior who will accept Hector's challenge.

Ajax sends Thersites to find out the nature of the recently posted proclamation. A foul-mouthed ruffian, Thersites refuses to obey and curses Ajax and the rest of the Greeks until Ajax beats him. Achilles and Patroclus arrive and send Thersites away. Achilles tells Ajax that Hector has sent an open challenge to any brave Greek warrior. The warrior will be decided by lottery. Otherwise, Achilles says as he leaves, he would have been the only possible choice. Ajax sneers in response.

II.II   Location: the Trojan palace

King Priam and Hector want to end the war, but Troilus and Paris convince them to keep fighting.

King Priam and his sons, Hector, Helenus, Troilus, and Paris, debate whether to end the war now by returning Helen to the Greeks. Hector and Helenus argue that even through capturing Helen was a brave act, she is not worth the great and bloody price of continuing the war. Their sister Cassandra, a prophetess who is considered mad, dashes in and cries that Troy will burn unless they send Helen back. Troilus dismisses her warning as ravings, and argues that keeping Helen is a matter of honor. Paris agrees, but Hector retorts that young men like Troilus are too easily swayed by "the hot passion of distempered blood" (II.ii.168). Eventually, Hector yields and agrees to continue the war. He announces that he has sent the challenge to the Greeks, and hopes that Achilles will accept it.

II.III   Location: outside Achilles' tent, in the Greek camp

Achilles refuses to fight the Trojans, and the Greek commanders decide that Ajax will answer Hector's challenge.

Alone, Thersites sneers at the pretensions of both Ajax and Achilles. When Patroclus and Achilles appear, he calls them fools. Patroclus moves to strike him, but Achilles holds Patroclus off. They see the Greek commanders—Agamemnon, Ulysses, Nestor, and Diomedes—approaching, accompanied by Ajax. Achilles quickly retires to his tent. To Agamemnon's request to see Achilles, Patroclus responds that Achilles is ill. Agamemnon grows angry, but Achilles refuses to emerge. He tells Ulysses, who goes in to see him, that he refuses to fight the Trojans. Agamemnon suggests that Ajax should go in and plead with Achilles, but Ulysses declares that doing so would be insulting to Ajax. The Greek commanders praise

Ajax profusely, saying that he is the best of their warriors. They agree to leave Achilles in his tent, and decide that Ajax will be their champion against Hector the next day.

ACT III

In Troy, Troilus and Cressida pledge and consummate their love, but the Greeks plan to ask for her at the next prisoner-of-war exchange.

III.I   Location: the Trojan palace

Pandarus starts a conversation about Troilus and Cressida with Paris and Helen.

Pandarus converses with a servant while waiting to speak with Paris and Helen. They come in, and he compliments Helen profusely. He tells her that Troilus may not come to dinner that night, but refuses to say why. Both Paris and Helen guess that he will be courting Cressida and make bawdy jokes as they depart to greet the returning warriors.

III.II   Location: Troy. Cressida's orchard

Brought together by Pandarus, Troilus and Cressida pledge their undying love and fidelity to each other.

Pandarus finds Troilus pacing about impatiently, and assures him that his desire for Cressida will soon be satisfied. Pandarus goes out, leaving Troilus giddy with expectation, and brings in Cressida. After urging them to embrace, he departs. Left alone, Troilus and Cressida profess their love and pledge to be faithful to each other. Pandarus returns, and Cressida is nervous and considers leaving, but Troilus reassures her and again pledges to be faithful, declaring that thereafter history will say of all lovers that they were as "true as Troilus" (III.ii.169). Cressida replies that if she ever strays from him, she hopes that people will say of false lovers that they were as "false as Cressid" (III.ii.183). Pandarus observes the compact, and then leads them off to a secluded bedchamber to consummate their love.

III.III   Location: the Greek camp

The Greeks decide to ask for Cressida at the next prisoner-of-war exchange and work to make Achilles believe that they think his heroic days are past.

Cressida's father Calchas, who has betrayed Troy in order to join the Greeks, asks Agamemnon to trade the recently captured Trojan commander Antenor for Cressida. Agamemnon agrees, and orders Diomedes to supervise the exchange. On Ulysses' advice, the Greek commanders file past Achilles' tent and conspicuously ignore his greetings. Achilles asks Ulysses why they treat him with such scorn, and Ulysses responds that Achilles is no longer a hero. Ajax is the man of the hour, and Achilles will be forgotten quickly. That, says Ulysses, is the way of the world. Good deeds are quickly forgotten, and only the present is remembered: " … things in motion sooner catch the eye / Than what not stirs" (III.iii.177-8). Ulysses then tells Achilles that he should spend less time dallying with enemy women (specifically Polyxena, the Trojan princess) and more time in battle if he wants his peers' respect.

   Ulysses leaves and Patroclus tells Achilles to follow Ulysses' advice. Achilles agrees. Thersites enters to report that Ajax has grown self-important as he struts about the camp. Patroclus persuades Thersites to talk Ajax into bringing Hector to see Achilles after their fight the next day.

ACT IV

Cressida is sent to the Greek camp; Hector and Ajax agree to end their duel in a draw.

IV.I   Location: Troy. A street

The Greek commander Diomedes comes to Troy to exchange Antenor for Cressida.

Diomedes has arrived to oversee the exchange of Antenor for Cressida. He is greeted heartily by Aeneas and Paris. Aeneas goes to fetch Cressida, remarking that Troilus will be upset. When asked who deserves Helen more, Paris or Menelaus, Diomedes bitterly answers that both are fools who are willing to pay a great price in blood for a "whore."

IV.II   Location: Troy. Cressida's house

The morning after their night together, Troilus finds that Cressida is going to the Greek camp.

As morning breaks, Troilus takes regretful leave of Cressida. She pleads with him to stay a little longer. Pandarus comes in and makes several bawdy jokes about their night together. Suddenly there is a knock at the door, and Cressida hides Troilus in her bedroom. Aeneas enters and demands that Pandarus bring out Troilus. Troilus emerges, and Aeneas tells him that Cressida must go to her father Calchas in the Greek camp. Distraught, Troilus leaves with Aeneas to see their father, King Priam.

IV.III   Location: Troy. Cressida's house

Pandarus tells Cressida that she must go to the Greek camp.

Pandarus tells Cressida that she will be sent to her father in the Greek camp. She begins to weep, swearing her love for Troilus.

IV.IV   Location: Troy. In front of Cressida's house

Troilus resigns himself to taking Cressida to the Greek camp.

Paris sympathizes with Troilus, but tells him he must send Cressida away. Troilus, who has grimly accepted the fact that his beloved must be sent to the Greeks, offers to escort her to Diomedes.

IV.V   Location: Troy. Cressida's house

Troilus and Cressida say goodbye and promise to remain faithful to each other.

Troilus pledges to be faithful to Cressida. She too promises to remain true to him, even in the Greek camp. They exchange gifts of remembrance: Troilus gives Cressida his sleeve, and she gives him her glove. Diomedes enters, and Troilus demands that he promise to treat Cressida with respect. Diomedes retorts that he will make no promises. He will treat Cressida as she deserves, but not because a Trojan such as Troilus orders him to. A trumpet sounds, calling them all to see the duel between Hector and Ajax.

IV.VI   Location: a battlefield

Cressida joins the Greeks; Hector and Ajax prepare to duel.

Cressida arrives and is greeted by all the Greek commanders. Ulysses insists that everyone kiss her, but refuses to kiss her himself. After she leaves, he declares that she is a loose woman. The Trojan lords arrive. Aeneas introduces the duel and remarks that since Ajax and Hector are related (they are cousins), Hector will not be able to fight with his whole heart. As Hector and Ajax prepare to fight, Agamemnon asks Ulysses about the downcast Troilus. Ulysses identifies Troilus and praises him, saying that Troilus may even be a greater man than Hector.

IV.VII   Location: a battlefield

Hector and Ajax agree to end their duel in a draw; Achilles challenges Hector to fight the next day.

Ajax and Hector have been dueling but break off, agreeing to embrace as kinsmen and call the duel a draw. Then Hector is invited to come unarmed to the Greek tents; Achilles desires to see him. Hector agrees to come, accompanied by Troilus. Hector meets the Greek commanders and greets them one by one, exchanging compliments down the line until he reaches Achilles, with whom he trades insults. Achilles promises to meet Hector on the field of battle the following day and kill him, and Hector accepts the challenge. The Greeks lead Hector and Troilus to the feast. Troilus asks Ulysses about Calchas's tent, planning to find Cressida there later that night. Ulysses promises to lead him there, but also notes that Diomedes has been looking at Cressida with lust.

ACT V

Cressida cheats on Troilus with a Greek warrior; enraged by the death of his close companion, Achilles joins the fight and slays Hector.

V.I Location: the Greek camp. Outside Achilles' tent

At his sweetheart's request, Achilles decides not to fight the next day; Troilus follows Diomedes to Cressida's tent.

After the feast, Achilles boasts to Patroclus that he will kill Hector the next day. They encounter Thersites, who delivers a letter to Achilles and insults their campaign as usual. The letter is from Queen Hecuba's daughter, Polyxena, the Trojan princess whom Achilles loves. In the letter, she begs him not to fight the next day. Sadly, Achilles tells Patroclus that he must obey her wishes. Thersites remains alone and watches from the shadows as the feast breaks up. Most of the lords go to bed, but Diomedes slips off to see Cressida, and Ulysses and Troilus follow him. Noting that Diomedes is an untrustworthy, lustful rogue, Thersites follows him as well.

V.II Location: the Greek camp. Near Calchas's tent

Troilus watches as Cressida allows Diomedes to woo her.

Diomedes calls to Cressida. Calchas fetches her while Troilus and Ulysses watch from one hiding place and Thersites from another. With Thersites' profanities and Troilus's shock providing a counterpoint, Diomedes woos Cressida, who is reluctant yet coy. Eventually, she gives him the sleeve that Troilus had given her as a token of his love. She takes it back, then gives it to him once more and promises to see and sleep with him later. After Cressida and Diomedes part and leave, Troilus is in agony. He pledges to kill Diomedes on the field of battle. As morning nears, Troilus's brother Aeneas arrives to lead him back to Troy.

V.III Location: Troy. Priam's palace

Despite the premonitions of his relatives, Hector resolves to fight today; Troilus will fight too.

Hector girds for battle as his wife Andromache and his sister Cassandra plead with him not to go. Both have had dreams that prophesy his death, but he dismisses their warnings. Troilus comes in and announces that he will fight too. He chides Hector for having been too merciful in the past and plans to slay as many Greeks as he can today. Cassandra leads in King Priam, who pleads with Hector not to fight. Priam too has felt foreboding about this day. Hector refuses to listen and goes out to the battlefield. Pandarus brings Troilus a letter from Cressida. He reads the letter, then tears it up and follows Hector out to the field.

V.IV Location: the battlefield

The battle rages.

As the battle rages, Thersites wanders the field, escaping death by brazen cowardice, even admitting to Hector that he is "a rascal, a scurvy railing knave, a very filthy rogue" (V.iv.24–25).

V.V   Location: the battlefield

Moved to rage by Patroclus's death, Achilles joins the fray.

Diomedes orders Troilus's horse stolen and presented to Cressida as proof of Diomedes' mettle. Overall, however, the Trojans are winning, and Patroclus is killed. Agamemnon orders Patroclus's body brought to Achilles, who is roused to fury and joins the battle. Achilles demands to meet Hector on the battle-field, and Diomedes and Ajax search for Troilus.

V.VI   Location: the battlefield

Achilles briefly fights Hector.

Diomedes and Ajax fight with Troilus while Achilles duels with Hector. Achilles, who is out of practice, tires and retreats. Hector continues slaying.

V.VII   Location: the battlefield

Achilles sets out to fight Hector.

Achilles finds his soldiers, the Myrmidons, and sets out to find Hector again.

V.VIII   Location: the battlefield

Thersites escapes death with cowardice.

Pursued by a bastard son of Priam's, Thersites runs away from battle.

V.IX   Location: the battlefield

Achilles and his men slay the unarmed Hector.

As the day nears its close, Achilles and the Myrmidons find Hector, who has finished fighting and taken off his armor. Achilles and the Myrmidons surround him and stab him to death, planning to tie his body to a chariot and drag it around the walls of Troy.

V.X   Location: the battlefield

The Greek commanders are overjoyed to hear that Achilles has slain Hector.

Agamemnon and Nestor hear that Achilles has slain Hector. Agamemnon sees the fact that Achilles joined them in battle again as a good sign for the Greeks.

V.XI   Location: the battlefield

Saddened by Hector's death, Troilus curses Pandarus on the way back to Troy.

The Trojan soldiers are grief-stricken to hear that Hector is dead. On the way back to Troy, Troilus encounters Pandarus and curses him. Alone, Pandarus wonders why he should be so abused when his services were so eagerly desired only a little while before.

THEMES, MOTIFS, & SYMBOLS IN *TROILUS AND CRESSIDA*

THEMES

HEROIC AND ROMANTIC IDEALS DEBUNKED   Contrary to tradition, Shakespeare depicts the heroes of the Trojan War as confused, shiftless men driven by petty concerns and desires. Troilus, supposedly one of the finest Trojan warriors, opens the play by refusing to fight out of lovesickness: "I'll unarm again. / Why should I war without the walls of Troy / That find such cruel battle here within?" (I.i.1–3). Ajax and Hector, great warriors, call off their duel of honor instead of fighting. Thersites sums up the play's cynicism by describing the whole war as conflict between a "whore" (Helen of Troy) and a "cuckold" (Menelaus) (II.iii.65).

Shakespeare similarly debunks the ideals of romantic love. Troilus describes Cressida in poetic terms in Act I, but by the end of the play both he and we recognize her as a frivolous flirt. Troilus and Cressida may be united and separated as swiftly and unexpectedly and Romeo and Juliet, but their romance is cynically presented as contrived and insincere.

SELF-INTEREST VS. STATE INTEREST   *Troilus and Cressida* cynically points to a tension between the best interests of a state or community and the selfish interests of private individuals. In Act I, scene iii, Ulysses argues for a system of universal order, whose every element "observe[s] degree, priority, and place" (I.iii.86). Humans too must find their proper place within their society. Without balance, Ulysses argues, "hark, what discord follows. Each thing meets / In mere oppugnancy" (I.iii.110–11). On the other end of the spectrum is the self-interested Thersites, who sees the Greek military chain of command as a joke: "Agamemnon is a fool to offer to command Achilles; Achilles is a fool to be commanded of Agamemnon, Thersites is a fool to serve such a fool, and Patroclus is a fool positive" (II.iii.56–58). As Thersites deflates the Greek warriors from without, so the moody Achilles and the "self-willed" Ajax (I.iii.188) threaten the Greek war effort from within. Ulysses believes that Ajax and Achilles are responsible for the continual failure to take Troy.

OBJECTIVE VS. SUBJECTIVE VALUES   *Troilus and Cressida* is one of Shakespeare's most talky and philosophical plays. This philosophizing contrasts with relatively little action, as well as with the foolish behavior of the philosophers. In particular, the play's characters debate the origin and nature of values such as goodness and beauty. Are things good because they possess some inherent goodness, or because people value them as good? In Act II, scene ii, for example, Hector argues that objectively, Helen is not worth the trouble of continuing the war. Troilus counters with a rhetorical question, "What's aught but as 'tis valued?" (II.ii.51). This line sums up Troilus's personal dilemma as well: he values the objectively cheap Cressida.

MOTIFS

PROSTITUTION   Prostitution, or love tainted by the desire for personal gain, is frequently mentioned in this dark and cynical play. Many of the play's characters, some of them male, are accused of being whores. Thersites describes the Trojan War as a squabble between a whore (Helen) and a cuckold (Menelaus) (II.iii.65). The unfaithful Cressida is called a whore several times. Patroclus is referred to as Achilles' "masculine whore" (V.i.16). Thersites freely admits that he is the son of a whore, which becomes his excuse for not participating in this foolish war (V.viii.12). By the end of the play, prostitution has come to include any small, ignoble, selfish act.

EFFEMINATE MEN   The warriors in *Troilus and Cressida* frequently compare each other and themselves to women. Often these comparisons are pejorative. Thersites sneers when he calls Patroclus Achilles' whore (V.i.16), and Ajax derogatively calls Thersites "mistress" (II.i.34). At other times, they are simply acknowledgements of traits traditionally associated with women. Achilles contemplates that he would like to reconcile with Hector: "I have a woman's longing, / An appetite that I am sick withal, / To see great Hector in his weeds of peace" (III.iii.230–32). Hector describes his fear of battle with "There is no lady of more softer bowels … Than Hector is" (II.ii.10–13). Troilus opens the play by declaring himself "less valiant than the virgin in the night" (I.i.11). With these comparisons, Shakespeare casts doubt on the image of the fearless warrior and the traditional association of militarism with masculinity. At the same time, femaleness in the play is unquestionably associated with cowardice and failure to do one's duty. Critics have called *Troilus and Cressida* one of Shakespeare's most misogynistic plays.

SYMBOLS

TROILUS'S SLEEVE Troilus gives Cressida his sleeve as a token of his love in Act IV, scene v. In Act V, scene ii, Cressida gives this same sleeve to Diomedes when he asks her for a token of her commitment to have sex with him later. The sleeve thus symbolizes Cressida's sexual infidelity. Cressida herself realizes the sleeve's symbolic importance, and tries to take it back from Diomedes.

THE ARMOR OF THE UNKNOWN WARRIOR In Act V, scene vi, Hector admires the armor of an unidentified warrior. By Act V, scene ix, this warrior is dead, killed by Hector. As Hector drags the corpse off the battlefield, he addresses it: "Most putrefyèd core, so fair without, / Thy goodly armor thus hath cost thy life" (V.ix.1–2). The warrior proves less valiant than he looks. "[P]utrefied" may refer to moral degeneration as well as to physical decomposition of the body. The attractive armor that hides a less attractive core represents the depravity and moral compromises of all the so-called noble heroes of the play. Mere lines after Hector drags the "putrefyèd core" onstage, Achilles and his Myrmidons, skilled and honorable warriors, kill the unarmed Hector in vengeance.

IMPORTANT QUOTATIONS FROM *TROILUS AND CRESSIDA*

1. *O brave Troilus! Look well upon him, niece. Look you how his sword is bloodied and his helm more hacked than Hector's, and how he looks and how he goes. O admirable youth! … O admirable man! Paris? Paris is dirt to him, and I warrant Helen to change would give eye to boot.*

Location: I.ii.213–220
Speaker: Pandarus to Cressida
Context: Pandarus praises Troilus to his niece Cressida

In this passage, Pandarus combines high and low styles of speech. On one hand, he echoes epic praises in "O brave Troilus!" and "O admirable youth!" On the other hand, he uses colloquial vocabulary when he describes Troilus's helmet as "hacked" and calls Paris "dirt" next to Troilus. This mix of registers throughout *Troilus and Cressida* deflates the heroic ideal. Mythical figures from Homer are portrayed as petty humans.

2. *The heavens themselves, the planets, and this centre*
   Observe degree, priority, and place,
   Infixture, course, proportion, season, form,
   Office and custom, in all line of order.
   And therefore is the glorious planet Sol
   In noble eminence enthroned and sphered
   Amidst the other, whose med'cinable eye
   Corrects the ill aspects of planets evil
   And posts like the commandment of a king,
   Sans check, to good and bad.

Location: I.iii.85–94
Speaker: Ulysses to Agamemnon and the Greek leaders
Context: Ulysses suggests that the Greeks have not been able to break the siege of Troy because Achilles has disrupted the natural order in the Greek camp

In these famous lines, Ulysses explains that there is a natural cosmic order in the universe, that everything has its own proper degree and location. The macrocosm of space is mirrored by the microcosm of human society. The sun ("Sol") acts as the king of space, correcting the errors of the planets as the king corrects the errors of his subjects. At the same time, the careful order described by Ulysses is little present in the world of *Troilus and Cressida*. According to Thersites, Menelaus, a Greek king, behaves like a foolish ass. Ulysses himself carries out deceptions in the play: in Act III, scene iii, for example, he attempts to lure Achilles back to battle by telling him that the other Greek captains think his days of heroism are past.

---

3. *Troilus: What's aught but as 'tis valued?*
   Hector: But value dwells not in particular will.
   It holds his estimate and dignity
   As well wherein 'tis precious of itself
   As in the prizer. 'Tis mad idolatry
   To make the service greater than the god;
   And the will dotes that is inclinable
   To what infectiously itself affects
   Without some image of th' affected merit.

Location: II.ii.51–59
Speakers: Troilus and Hector
Context: Hector cautions Troilus that placing too much value on something (Helen, in this case) is wrong

Troilus and Cressida discuss whether Helen is worth the war that they are leading. Hector believes that people and objects have an objective value. Troilus suggests that this value is subjective, and depends only on the evaluator. In the play, Troilus's subjectivism is undercut by his too-strong affection for the frivolous Cressida.

---

4. *Troilus: But I can tell that in each grace of these [virtues]*
   There lurks a still and dumb-discoursive devil
   That tempts most cunningly. But be not tempted.
   Cressida: Do you think I will?
   Troilus:No, but something may be done that we will not,
   And sometimes we are devils to ourselves . . .

Location: IV.v.90–95
Speakers: Troilus and Cressida
Context: Troilus warns Cressida not to be unfaithful to him

Troilus and Cressida's vows of love are complicated by this passage, which dwells too long on Cressida's potential infidelity, foreshadowing her scene with Diomedes in Act V, scene ii. Often described as a "problem play," *Troilus and Cressida* never forgets the darker, destructive undercurrents of life. At times "we are devils to ourselves" and do things that we may not want or intend to do.

---

5. *With too much blood and too little brain these two may run mad, but if with too much brain and too*
   little blood they do, I'll be a curer of madmen. Here's Agamemnon: an honest fellow enough, and one
   that loves quails, but he has not so much brain as earwax. And the goodly transformation of Jupiter
   there, his brother the bull, the primitive statue and oblique memorial of cuckolds, a thrifty shoeing-horn
   in a chain, hanging at his brother's leg: to what form but that he is should wit larded with malice and

malice farced with wit turn him to? To an ass were nothing: he is both ass and ox. To an ox were nothing: he is both ox and ass.

Location: V.i.43–53
Speaker: Thersites
Context: Thersites mocks Agamemnon and Menelaus

Throughout the play, Shakespeare slyly forces us to sympathize with the unsavory Thersites who, like many of Shakespeare's pragmatic and ignoble clowns, dares to speak the impolite truth. Here, Thersites deflates Agamemnon and Menelaus, two supposedly great Greek heroes. Agamemnon is a thug with more earwax than brains, and Menelaus is both an ass (an idiot) and an ox (a cuckold).

TWELFTH NIGHT

Viola dresses as a man to find employment with Orsino, but she falls in love with her employer.

TWELFTH NIGHT IN CONTEXT

Shakespeare wrote *Twelfth Night* near the middle of his career, probably in 1601. Most critics consider it one of his greatest comedies, along with plays such as *As You Like It, Much Ado About Nothing*, and *A Midsummer Night's Dream*. Scholars generally accept the "Twelfth Night" of the title as a reference to Epiphany, or the twelfth night of the Christmas celebration (January 6). In Shakespeare's day, Epiphany was a festival day on which everything was turned upside-down.

Twelfth Night is one of Shakespeare's so-called transvestite comedies, a category that also includes *As You Like It* and *The Merchant of Venice*. These plays feature female protagonists who disguise themselves as young men. In Shakespeare's day, men played all roles, so Viola would have been a male actor pretending to be a female pretending to be a male.

As is the case with most of Shakespeare's plays, the story of *Twelfth Night* comes from other sources. In particular, Shakespeare seems to have consulted an Italian play from the 1530s entitled *Gl'Ingannati*, which features twins who are mistaken for each other and contains a version of the Viola-Olivia-Orsino love triangle in *Twelfth Night*. He also seems to have used a 1581 English story entitled "Apollonius and Silla," by Barnabe Riche, which contains many of *Twelfth Night*'s plot elements, including a shipwreck, a pair of twins, and a woman disguised as a man. A number of sources have been suggested for the Malvolio subplot, none of them very convincing.

TWELFTH NIGHT: KEY FACTS

Full Title: Twelfth Night, or What You Will

Time and place written: Between 1600 and 1602; England

Date of first publication: 1623, in the First Folio

Genre: Comedy

Setting (time): Unknown

Setting (place): The mythical land of Illyria (Illyria is a real place, corresponding to the coast of present-day Albania, but *Twelfth Night* is clearly set in a fictional kingdom)

Protagonist: Viola

Major conflict: Viola is in love with Orsino, who is in love with Olivia, who is in love with Viola's male persona, Cesario.

TWELFTH NIGHT: CHARACTER LIST

Sir Andrew Aguecheek   A friend of Sir Toby's. Sir Andrew Aguecheek attempts to court Olivia. He is an idiot, but he fancies himself witty, brave, youthful, and good at languages and dancing.

Antonio   A man who rescues Sebastian after his shipwreck. Antonio cares for Sebastian with a love that might be romantic.

Feste   The clown, or fool, of Olivia's household. Feste earns his living by making pointed jokes, singing old songs, offering witticisms, and offering good advice cloaked by foolishness.

Malvolio   The straight-laced steward (head servant) in Olivia's household. Malvolio is efficient and self-righteous. He has a poor opinion of drinking, singing, and fun. His priggishness earns him the enmity of Sir Toby, Sir Andrew, and Maria. In his fantasies about marrying his mistress, Malvolio reveals a powerful ambition to rise above his social class.

Maria   Olivia's clever, daring young serving-woman. Like Malvolio, Maria aspires to rise in the world through marriage. She succeeds where Malvolio fails, perhaps because she is in tune with the anarchic, topsy-turvy spirit that animates the play.

Olivia   A wealthy, beautiful, and noble Illyrian lady. Like Orsino, Olivia enjoys wallowing in misery. Her romantic feelings do not run deep.

Orsino   A powerful nobleman in the country of Illyria. A supreme egotist, Orsino mopes around complaining that he is heartsick over Olivia, but he loves the idea of being in love and enjoys making a spectacle of himself.

Sebastian   Viola's lost twin brother. Sebastian's character seems to exist mainly to take over Viola's male persona and become Olivia's mate.

Sir Toby   Olivia's uncle. Olivia lets Sir Toby Belch live with her, but she does not approve of his rowdy behavior, practical jokes, heavy drinking, late-night carousing, or silly friends.

Viola (Cesario)   The play's protagonist. Viola, a young woman of aristocratic birth, must make her own way in the world after she is shipwrecked. She disguises herself as a young man, calling herself Cesario, and becomes a page to Duke Orsino.

TWELFTH NIGHT: PLOT OVERVIEW

Viola, a young noblewoman, is shipwrecked and separated from her twin brother, Sebastian. After washing ashore in the kingdom of Illyria, Viola disguises herself as a man and calls herself Cesario so she can gain employment. She finds work in the household of Count Orsino, who makes her his page boy. When Orsino sends Viola to deliver love messages to Lady Olivia, Olivia falls in love with Viola, who strikes her as a beautiful young man. Viola falls in love with her master, Orsino.

Olivia's uncle, Toby, her clown, Feste, and her serving-woman, Maria, play a practical joke on the steward of the house, Malvolio, making him think that Olivia loves him and inspiring him to act strangely to win Olivia's affection. Then they convince Olivia that Malvolio is mad and lock him in a dark room for treatment. Toby's friend, Sir Andrew Aguecheek, tries to woo Olivia, without success. Perceiving that Olivia loves Cesario (Viola in disguise), Sir Andrew challenges Cesario to a duel.

Sebastian arrives in Illyria accompanied by Antonio, a man from a neighboring country who has cared for Sebastian since the shipwreck. Mistaking Sebastian for Cesario, Sir Andrew and Sir Toby attack him. Olivia also mistakes Sebastian for Cesario and marries him. Orsino's officers arrest Antonio, who is not supposed to be in Illyria. He vainly calls for help from Viola, mistaking her for Sebastian. Viola and Sebastian finally encounter each other at Olivia's house, and the misunderstandings are resolved. Orsino marries Viola, and Malvolio is released.

TWELFTH NIGHT: SCENE SUMMARY

ACT I

After being saved from a shipwreck, Viola disguises herself as a young man named Cesario, finds work in Duke Orsino's house, and inadvertently causes Lady Olivia to fall in love with her.

I.I   Location: Duke Orsino's house

Duke Orsino pines for Lady Olivia.

Duke Orsino enters, attended by his lords. Orsino is hopelessly in love with the beautiful Lady Olivia. He refuses to hunt and orders musicians to entertain him while he thinks about his desire for Olivia. His servant Valentine reminds him that Olivia does not return his love or even listen to the messages he sends her. We learn from Valentine that Olivia is in mourning for her brother, who has recently died. She wears a dark veil and has vowed that no one will see her face for another seven years. She refuses to marry anyone until then. Orsino wants only to lie around on beds of flowers, listening to sweet music and dreaming of Olivia.

I.II   Location: the Illyrian sea coast

Viola is rescued from a shipwreck and decides to disguise herself as a man and seek employment.

On the Illyrian sea coast, a young noblewoman named Viola speaks with the captain whose crew has just rescued her from a shipwreck. Although Viola was found and rescued, her brother, Sebastian, seems to have vanished in the storm. The captain tells Viola that Sebastian may still be alive. He says he saw Sebastian trying to keep afloat by tying himself to a broken mast.

Viola needs to find a way to support herself in this strange land. The ship's captain tells her about Duke Orsino, who rules Illyria. Viola says she has heard of this duke and mentions that he used to be a bachelor. The captain says that Orsino still is a bachelor, although he is courting the Lady Olivia, whose brother recently died. Viola says she wishes she could become a servant in Olivia's house and hide herself away from the world. The captain says this is unlikely, because Olivia refuses to see any visitors. Viola decides to disguise herself as a young man and seek service with Duke Orsino. When she promises to pay him well, the captain agrees to help her, and they go off together in order to find a disguise for her.

I.III   Location: Lady Olivia's house

Sir Toby comforts Sir Andrew.

Sir Toby Belch, Olivia's uncle, lives with Olivia. He is cheerful, amusing, and usually tipsy. Maria, Olivia's handmaiden, warns Sir Toby that his drinking annoys Olivia, but Sir Toby does not care. Maria says she heard that he has brought a foolish friend to court Olivia: Sir Andrew Aguecheek, who shares Sir Toby's disreputable habits. Sir Toby protests that Sir Andrew is a perfect match for his niece, because he is very rich and accomplished in music and languages. Maria thinks Sir Andrew is a fool, a brawler, and a drunk.

Sir Andrew enters and acts like a bumbling idiot. After Maria leaves, Sir Andrew and Sir Toby talk and joke. But Sir Andrew tells Sir Toby that he is discouraged and that he does not think Olivia likes him. He plans to leave the next morning. He remarks that Olivia will probably choose Orsino over him. Sir Toby persuades him to stay by flattering him. He says that Olivia will never marry "above her degree, neither in estate, years, nor wit," so Sir Andrew has a good chance with her (I.iii.90–91). Sir Toby compliments his friend's dancing and gets the vain and weak-minded—but good-hearted—Sir Andrew to show off his dancing skills.

I.IV   Location: Duke Orsino's house

Violat-as-Cesario agrees to carry Orsino's message of love to Olivia.

At Duke Orsino's house, Viola has adopted a new name—Cesario—to go with her new persona as a teenage boy. After only three days in Orsino's service, Cesario has already become a favorite of Orsino's. Orsino picks Cesario to go on a most important errand, carrying his messages of love to Olivia.

Viola-as-Cesario says that Olivia, who has ignored Orsino for a long time, is not likely to start listening to his love messages now. But Orsino points out that Cesario is extremely young and handsome—so beautiful, in his lips and features, that he resembles a woman—and that Olivia is sure to be impressed by his attractiveness. Orsino tells Cesario to "act my woes" when he goes to see Olivia—to behave as if he shares Orsino's adoration for the noblewoman (I.iv.25). Cesario reluctantly agrees to carry the message, telling the audience in a quick aside that she (Viola) herself has fallen in love with Orsino.

I.V   Location: Lady Olivia's house

Viola-as-Cesario delivers Orsino's message of love to Olivia, and Olivia falls in love with Viola-as-Cesario.

Maria talks with Feste, Olivia's clown. Feste has been away for some time, and nobody knew where he was. Maria tells Feste that Olivia will probably fire him. Feste refuses to tell Maria where he has been. Olivia arrives with Malvolio, the steward of her household, and orders her servants to turn Feste out of the house. But Feste, summoning up all his wit and skill, manages to put Olivia into a better mood. He asks her why she is mourning, and she answers that she is mourning for her brother. He says her brother's soul must be in hell, and she replies that he is in heaven. "The more fool, madonna, to mourn for your brother's soul, being in heaven," he says, and she responds approvingly (I.v.61–62). Malvolio does not like Feste and coldly asks why Olivia wants him around. Olivia rebukes Malvolio for his "self-love" and says that Feste's insults are only "birdbolts" that do no damage (I.v.77–79).

Maria announces there is a young man at the gate to see Olivia. Sir Toby comes in, obviously drunk although it is early in the morning. Olivia criticizes him for his alcoholism. Sir Toby goes out, and Olivia sends Feste to look after him. Malvolio comes back, reporting that the young man refuses to leave the house until he has spoken with Olivia. Olivia asks Malvolio what the young man is like and receives the report that he is very young, handsome, and delicate-looking. Intrigued, Olivia decides to let the boy speak with her.

Viola, disguised as Cesario, comes in and begins to deliver the love speech that Orsino gave her. Olivia refuses to hear the memorized speech, so Cesario adlibs praise for Olivia's great beauty and virtues. Olivia, increasingly fascinated by the messenger, begins asking Cesario about himself and learns that he comes from an aristocratic family.

Olivia sends Cesario back to tell Orsino that Olivia does not love him and never will. But she tells Cesario to come back, if he wishes, and speak to her again about "how he [Orsino] takes it" (I.v.252). After Cesario leaves, she sends Malvolio after him with a ring that she pretends Cesario left with her. Olivia finds that she has fallen passionately in love with young Cesario.

ACT II

Sebastian heads to Orsino's court, Viola realizes that Olivia has fallen in love with her male persona, and Maria and her friends trick Malvolio into thinking that Olivia loves him.

II.I   Location: the Illyrian sea coast

Antonio follows Sebastian, despite the danger.

A man called Antonio has been hosting Sebastian, Viola's twin brother, in his home. Antonio has been caring for Sebastian ever since he washed up after the shipwreck. Antonio does not know Sebastian's real name, but now that Sebastian plans to leave Antonio and go wandering, he decides to tell his benefactor his true identity and the tale of his sister, whom he assumes drowned in the shipwreck. We learn that Sebastian and Viola's father is long dead. Sebastian is devastated by the loss of his sister and does not care much what the future holds.

Antonio urges Sebastian to let him come with him on his journey. It is clear that Antonio has become very fond of Sebastian and does not want to lose him. But Sebastian is afraid that his travels will be dangerous and he urges Antonio to let him go alone. After Sebastian leaves to go to Orsino's court, Antonio ponders the situation. He wants to follow his friend and help him, but he has many enemies in Orsino's court and is afraid to go there. He cares about Sebastian so much, however, that he decides to follow him to Orsino's court despite the danger.

II.II   Location: outside Lady Olivia's house

Viola receives the ring from Olivia and realizes that Olivia has fallen in love with her as Cesario.

Malvolio has caught up with Violet-as-Cesario. He gives Cesario the ring from Olivia, rebuking him for leaving it behind. Viola understands Olivia's deception and plays along with it, pretending that she did give the ring to Olivia. She tells Malvolio that Olivia took the ring, and insists that Olivia must keep it.

Malvolio throws the ring onto the ground and exits. Alone, Viola picks up the ring and wonders why Olivia has given it to her. She wonders if it means that Olivia has fallen in love with Cesario. "Poor lady, she were better love a dream," Viola says to herself (II.ii.24). Apparently loved by Olivia and in love with Orsino, who loves Olivia, Viola hopes that time will untangle these problems, since she certainly cannot figure out how to solve them.

II.III   Location: Lady Olivia's house

Annoyed by Malvolio, Maria concocts a plan to make him think that Olivia loves him.

Sir Toby and Sir Andrew stay up late drinking in Olivia's house. Feste appears, and Sir Andrew compliments him on his singing. While Feste sings, Maria enters, warning them to keep their voices down or Olivia will call Malvolio and tell him to kick them out. The tipsy Sir Toby and Sir Andrew cheerfully ignore her.

Malvolio comes into the room and criticizes the men for being drunk at all hours of the night and for singing so loudly. He warns Sir Toby that his behavior is intolerably rude and that, while Olivia is willing to let him be her guest, she will ask him to leave if he does not change his behavior. Sir Toby, along with Sir Andrew and Feste, responds with jokes and insults. After making a final threat, this one directed at Maria, Malvolio leaves, warning them all that he will let Olivia know about their behavior.

Sir Andrew suggests challenging Malvolio to a duel, but Maria has a better idea: they should play a practical joke on him. She tells Sir Toby and Sir Andrew that Malvolio is a puritan, but he has an enormous ego and believes that everybody loves him. Maria will use that weakness to get her revenge on him for spoiling their fun. Since Maria's handwriting is almost identical to Olivia's, Maria plans to leave letters lying around that seem to have been written by Olivia. These letters will make Malvolio think that Olivia is in love with him.

Sir Toby and Sir Andrew are amazed by Maria's cleverness. Maria goes off to bed, planning to get started on her joke the next day. Sir Toby and Sir Andrew, deciding that it is now too late to go to sleep, head off to warm up more wine.

II.IV   Location: Duke Orsino's house

Orsino and Viola-as-Cesario talk about love.

The next day, Orsino discusses love with Viola-as-Cesario. He accuses Cesario of being in love. Cesario is really in love with Orsino, so he admits that Orsino is right. When Orsino asks what the woman is like, Cesario says she is very much like Orsino in age and features. Orsino, not picking up on his page's meaning, remarks that Cesario would be better off loving a younger woman, because men are naturally fickle, and only a younger woman can keep them satisfied for a long time.

Orsino has sent for Feste, who apparently moves back and forth between the houses of Olivia and Orsino. Feste sings a very sad love song. Afterward, Orsino orders Cesario to go to Olivia again and make Orsino's case. Cesario reminds Orsino that Olivia has denied his advances many times before, suggesting that Orsino accept Olivia's lack of interest just as a woman Orsino did not love would have to accept *his* lack of interest in her. But Orsino says no woman can love with the same kind of passion as a man. Cesario disagrees and tells the story of a woman he knew who died for love of a man. Cesario refers to this girl as her father's daughter, leading Orsino to think that it must be Cesario's sister. Orsino gives Cesario a jewel to present to Olivia on his behalf, and Cesario departs.

II.V   Location: Lady Olivia's garden

Maria's forgery tricks Malvolio into believing that Olivia loves him.

Sir Toby, Sir Andrew, Maria, and Fabian, one of Olivia's servants, prepare to play their practical joke on Malvolio. Maria drops the letter in the garden path, where Malvolio will see it, and exits, while the three men hide among the trees and shrubbery. Malvolio approaches on the path, talking to himself. He speaks of Olivia. It seems he already thinks it possible that she might be in love with him. He fantasizes about Olivia's husband and the master of her house, wielding power over all the other servants and even over Sir Toby. Sir Toby and the others jeer quietly from their hiding place.

Malvolio spots the letter lying in the garden path. As Maria predicted, he mistakes Maria's handwriting for Olivia's. Maria sealed the letter with Olivia's sealing ring to make it look even more authentic. Malvolio decides to read the letter aloud. The letter, which is addressed to "the unknown beloved," suggests that the writer is in love with somebody but must keep her love a secret from the world, though she wants her beloved to know about it. The first part of the letter concludes by saying that the beloved's identity is represented by the letters M.O.A.I. Malvolio concludes that he is the beloved. Sir Toby and the others laugh at him from behind the bush.

Once he has convinced himself that Olivia is in love with him, Malvolio reads the second half of the letter. The mysterious message implies that the writer wants to raise Malvolio up from his position of servitude to one of power. The letter also asks him to show the writer that he returns her love through certain signs. The letter orders him to wear yellow stockings, "go cross-gartered" (that is, wear the straps of his stockings crossed around his knees), be sharp-tempered with Sir Toby, be rude to the servants, behave strangely, and smile all the time. Jubilantly, Malvolio vows to do all of these things in order to show Olivia that he loves her.

After Malvolio leaves, Sir Toby says he "could marry this wench [Maria] for this device. … And ask no other dowry with her but such another jest" (II.v.158–160). Maria rejoins the men and laughs with them, anticipating Malvolio's behavior. They know he will bewilder Olivia, who hates the color yellow, can't stand crossed garters, and does not want anybody smiling because she is still in mourning.

ACT III

Olivia makes an unsuccessful declaration of love to Viola-as-Cesario, Sebastian and Antonio arrive in Illyria, and Antonio mistakes Cesario for Sebastian.

III.I Location: Lady Olivia's garden

Olivia declares her love to Viola-as-Cesario and is rejected.

Viola, still disguised as Cesario, has returned to Lady Olivia's house to bring her another message of love from Orsino. Outside Olivia's house, Cesario meets Feste, who jokes and makes puns. Cesario jokes with comparable skill and gives Feste some coins for his trouble. Feste goes inside to announce Cesario's arrival.

Sir Toby and Sir Andrew arrive in the garden and, meeting Cesario for the first time, make rather awkward conversation with him. Sir Andrew behaves foolishly, as usual, and both men are slightly drunk. Olivia comes down to the garden accompanied by Maria. She sends everyone else away in order to listen to what Cesario has to say.

Once alone with Cesario, Olivia begs him not to give her any more love messages from Orsino. She tells Cesario that she is deeply in love with him. Cesario tells Olivia that he cannot love her. Olivia seems to accept this rejection, but privately she realizes that she cannot easily stop loving this beautiful young man, even if he scorns her. Cesario swears to Olivia that no woman shall ever be mistress of his heart and turns to go. Olivia begs him to come back again, desperately suggesting that maybe Cesario can convince her to love Orsino after all.

III.II Location: Lady Olivia's house

Sir Andrew considers leaving, but Sir Toby and Fabian dissuade him.

Sir Andrew tells Sir Toby that he has decided to leave. He has seen Olivia fawning over Viola-as-Cesario in the orchard and seems to realize at last that Olivia is not likely to marry him. Sir Toby wants to keep Andrew around because he has been spending Sir Andrew's money, so he tells Sir Andrew that he ought to stay and show off his manliness. Fabian suggests that Olivia might have been teasing Sir Andrew and trying to make him jealous. Sir Andrew agrees, and Sir Toby encourages him to challenge Cesario to a duel in order to prove his love for Olivia.

Maria comes in and reports that Malvolio is behaving like an ass. He is wearing yellow stockings and crossed garters and will not stop smiling. Sir Toby and Fabian eagerly follow Maria to see what is going on.

III.III Location: a street in Illyria

Sebastian and Antonio arrive in Illyria.

Sebastian and Antonio arrive. Antonio is not safe in Illyria, because many years ago he was involved in a sea fight against Orsino. Antonio goes to find lodging for himself and Sebastian at an inn. Sebastian goes sightseeing. Antonio gives Sebastian his purse so that Sebastian can buy any trinkets he likes. They agree to meet in an hour at the inn.

III.IV   Location: Lady Olivia's house

Malvolio is locked in a dark room, Viola-as-Cesario and Sir Andrew nearly duel, and Antonio mistakes Cesario for Sebastian, giving Viola some hope that her brother is alive.

Olivia, who sent a servant after the departing Viola-as-Cesario to persuade him to return, tries to figure out how to make Cesario love her. Olivia sends for Malvolio because she wants someone solemn and sad to help with her strategy. Malvolio appears and behaves very strangely. He is wearing crossed garters and yellow stockings, smiling foolishly, and quoting from the letter. Olivia thinks Malvolio has gone mad. When the news arrives that Cesario has returned, she tells Maria and Sir Toby to take care of Malvolio, and goes off to see Cesario.

Malvolio is still convinced that Olivia is in love with him. But Sir Toby, Fabian, and Maria pretend to believe that Malvolio is possessed by the devil. Malvolio, remembering the letter's advice that he speak scornfully to the servants and Sir Toby, sneers at them and stalks out. Delighted, Sir Toby and the others decide to lock Malvolio in a dark room—a common treatment for madmen or people thought to be possessed by devils.

Sir Andrew enters with a letter challenging Cesario to a duel. Sir Toby privately decides he will not deliver the silly letter. Instead he will walk back and forth between Sir Andrew and Cesario, telling each that the other is fearsome and out for the other's blood. That, he decides, should make for a very funny duel.

Cesario comes back out of the house accompanied by Olivia, who insists that Cesario take a locket with her picture as a love token. She tells him to come again the next day and then goes back inside. Sir Toby approaches Cesario, delivering Sir Andrew's challenge and telling him what a fierce fighter Sir Andrew is. Cesario says that he does not wish to fight and prepares to leave. Sir Toby returns to Sir Andrew and tells him that Cesario is a tremendous swordsman spoiling for a fight. When Andrew and Cesario cross paths, Sir Toby tells each of them that the other has promised not to draw blood in the duel. Reluctantly, the two draw their swords and prepare for a fight.

Antonio enters. He sees Cesario, mistakes him for his beloved Sebastian, and volunteers to fight Sir Andrew in Sebastian's place. Several Illyrian officers burst onto the scene. They arrest Antonio, who is a wanted man in Illyria. Antonio needs bail money, so he asks Cesario, still thinking he is Sebastian, to return his purse. Cesario has no idea who Antonio is. Antonio thinks that Sebastian is betraying him by pretending not to know him. Shocked and heartbroken, he rebukes Sebastian. The officers assume that Antonio is insane and take him away. Antonio's mention of someone named "Sebastian" gives Viola some hope that her own brother is alive and nearby. She runs off to look for him, leaving Sir Andrew and Sir Toby confused.

ACT IV

Sir Toby and the others torture Malvolio by insisting he is insane, and Sebastian agrees to marry Olivia, who thinks she has proposed to Cesario.

IV.I   Location: near Lady Olivia's house

Sir Andrew, Sir Toby, and Olivia mistake Sebastian for Cesario.

Near Olivia's house, Feste comes across Sebastian, mistakes him for Cesario, and tries to bring him to Olivia's house. Sir Toby and Sir Andrew come along. Sir Andrew, mistaking Sebastian for Cesario, attacks him. Sebastian is a scrappy fighter and starts to beat Sir Andrew with his dagger. Bewildered by these events, Sebastian wonders if he is surrounded by madmen and tries to leave. But Sir Toby prevents him from going. The two exchange insults and draw their swords.

Olivia enters and angrily orders Sir Toby to put away his sword. She begs Sebastian, whom she also mistakes for Cesario, to come into her house with her. Sebastian is bewildered but agrees to follow her, saying, "If it be thus to dream, still let me sleep!" (IV.i.59).

IV.II Location: Lady Olivia's house

Feste, Maria, and Sir Toby torment Malvolio.

Maria asks Feste to put on the robes of a clergyman and visit Malvolio, pretending to be Sir Topas, a fictional priest. As Sir Toby and Maria listen in, Feste addresses Malvolio, who cannot see him inside his prison. Malvolio tells Feste that he is not insane and begs Feste to get him out of the locked room. Feste deliberately misunderstands and misleads the steward, telling Malvolio that the room is not dark, but full of windows and light. He says Malvolio must be mad or possessed if he cannot see the light. Malvolio urges Feste to question him in the hopes of proving his sanity. But Feste asks ridiculous questions and then contradicts the steward's answers. He tells Malvolio he is still mad.

Sir Toby and Maria are delighted by the joke but are also tiring of it. Sir Toby worries that Olivia, already offended by his drinking and carousing, might catch him in this prank. They send Feste back to Malvolio. Feste—now using both his own voice and that of Sir Topas, as if the two are having a conversation—speaks to Malvolio again. Malvolio swears he isn't crazy and begs for paper, ink, and light with which to write a letter to Olivia. Feste promises to fetch him the items.

IV.III Location: elsewhere in Lady Olivia's house

Sebastian agrees to marry Olivia, who thinks he is Cesario.

Sebastian wanders around, dazed but happy. He does not feel insane, but he cannot believe that Olivia is really giving him gifts and saying she wants to marry him. He wishes he could find Antonio to discuss the situation with him, but Antonio did not show up at the inn. Olivia comes in with a priest, asking Sebastian (whom she still thinks is Cesario) if he is still willing to marry her. Sebastian happily agrees, and they go off to get married.

ACT V

[A summary of act 5]

V.I Location: near Lady Olivia's house

Cesario's true identity emerges; Viola learns that Sebastian is truly alive; Orsino and Viola affirm their love; Malvolio leaves confinement and vows revenge.

Orsino approaches Olivia's house, accompanied by Viola (still disguised as Cesario) and his men. The Illyrian law officers come in looking for Orsino, dragging Antonio with them. Orsino, who fought against Antonio long ago, recognizes him as an honorable enemy. He asks Antonio what made him put himself in danger by coming into Orsino's territory. Antonio responds by telling the story of how he rescued, befriended, and protected Sebastian, traveling with him to this hostile land. He lashes out at Cesario, whom he continues to mistake for Sebastian, claiming that Sebastian stole his purse and denied knowing him. Cesario and Orsino are bewildered.

Olivia enters and speaks to Cesario, mistaking him for Sebastian, whom she has just married. Orsino, angry at Cesario's apparent betrayal of him, threatens to kill Cesario. Cesario prepares to die, telling Orsino she loves only him. Olivia is shocked, believing that her new spouse is betraying her. She calls in the priest, who, thinking that the young man in front of him is Sebastian, testifies that he just married Olivia to this young man. Orsino orders Olivia and Cesario to leave together and never to appear in his sight again.

Sir Andrew enters, injured and calling for a doctor. He says that he and Sir Toby have just been in a fight with Orsino's servant, Cesario. Seeing Cesario, Sir Andrew accuses him of the attack, but the confused Cesario answers that he is not responsible. Olivia orders Sir Andrew and Sir Toby to seek medical attention.

Sebastian appears, apologizing to Olivia for beating up Sir Toby and Sir Andrew. Seeing Antonio, and not yet seeing his sister, Sebastian cries out with happiness. Dazed, all the others stare at Sebastian and Viola, who finally see one another. They barrage each other with questions about their birth and family history. Finally, they believe that they are twins. Viola excitedly tells Sebastian to wait until she has put her woman's clothing back on. Everyone realizes that Cesario is really a woman.

Orsino, realizing that Olivia has married Sebastian, does not seem terribly unhappy at losing her. Turning back to Viola, he reminds her that, disguised as a boy, she often vowed her love to him. Viola reaffirms her love, and Orsino asks to see her in female garb. She tells him that her clothes were hidden with a sea captain who has taken service with Malvolio. Suddenly, everybody remembers what happened to Malvolio. Feste and Fabian come in with Malvolio's letter, delivered from his cell. At Olivia's order, Feste reads it aloud. Malvolio writes that the letter seemingly written to him by Olivia will explain his behavior and prove he is not insane.

Realizing that Malvolio's writing does not seem like that of a crazy man, Olivia orders him brought before her. Malvolio is brought in and angrily gives Olivia the letter that Maria forged, demanding to know why he has been so ill-treated. Olivia understands what must have happened. Fabian interrupts to explain to the trick. He mentions in passing that Sir Toby has just married Maria. Malvolio, still furious, vows revenge and leaves abruptly. Orsino sends someone after Malvolio to make peace and find Viola's female garments. He then announces that a double wedding will be celebrated shortly. Everyone exits except Feste, who sings one last song, a mournful melody about growing up and growing old.

ANALYSIS OF MAJOR CHARACTERS IN *TWELFTH NIGHT*

VIOLA

Viola is a very likable figure. Among all of the characters, she is the only one capable of pure love. The other characters are fickle: Orsino jumps from Olivia to Viola, Olivia jumps from Viola to Sebastian, and Sir Toby and Maria's marriage seems more a matter of whim than an expression of deep passion. Only Viola seems capable of truly, passionately loving as opposed to enjoying the feeling of lovesickness, as the others do. Viola's disguise forces her to be herself in private and Cesario in public. This dual identity leads to complexities that culminate in the final scene, when Viola finds herself surrounded by people with different and clashing assumptions about her. Sebastian's appearance saves Viola by allowing her to put aside her male identity in favor of her female one. Sebastian's most important role in the play is to take over the aspects of Viola's disguise that she no longer wishes to maintain.

ORSINO AND OLIVIA

Orsino and Olivia have similar personalities. Both claim to be buffeted by strong emotions, but are actually self-indulgent people who relish melodrama. When we first meet them, Orsino pines away for Olivia, while Olivia pines away for her dead brother. They show no interest in the outside world, preferring to lock themselves up with their sorrows and mope around their houses. Viola's arrival begins to interest both characters in something outside themselves, but neither undergoes a drastic change. Orsino's interest in Cesario (Viola) diminishes his self-involvement and makes him more likable, but he persists in his belief that he is in love with Olivia until the final scene, in spite of the fact that he never once speaks to her during the course of the play. Olivia sets aside her grief when Cesario comes to see her, but she also enjoys the melodrama and self-indulgence of pining away for someone who does not want her. The similarity between Orsino and Olivia increases at the end of the play, when Orsino and Olivia essentially marry female and male versions of the same person.

MALVOLIO

Most critics judge Malvolio the most complex and fascinating character in *Twelfth Night*. At first, Malvolio seems to be a simple puritan, a stiff and proper servant who likes nothing better than to spoil other people's fun. But Sir Toby and Maria engineer his downfall by playing on a side of Malvolio that is not immediately obvious: his self-regard and his remarkable ambitions, which extend to marrying Olivia and becoming, as he puts it, "Count Malvolio" (II.v.30). When he finds the forged letter, Malvolio transforms from a prig into a happy, if deluded, lover. He is ridiculous as he capers around in the yellow stockings and crossed garters, but only because we know he has been fooled. His behavior is what we expect of a lovesick hero, so the fact that it is a mistake makes him pitiable. Malvolio ceases being a figure of fun when the vindictive Maria and Toby confine him to a dark room in Act IV. Malvolio, the embodiment of order and sobriety, is sacrificed so that the rest of the characters can indulge in the madcap spirit that suffuses *Twelfth Night*. Over the course of this sacrifice, Malvolio wins our sympathy. It is too much to call him a tragic figure, but there is some nobility in the way he stubbornly clings to his sanity, even in the face of overwhelming insistence that he is mad. As Malvolio desperately protests that he is not mad, Maria and Toby seem not like merry pranksters, but like sadistic beasts. The play allows Malvolio no real recompense for his sufferings. He is brought out of the darkness into a celebration in which he has no part, and where no one will apologize to him. "I'll be revenged on the whole pack of you," he snarls, striking a dark chord in an otherwise harmonious ending.

THEMES, MOTIFS & SYMBOLS IN *TWELFTH NIGHT*

THEMES

LOVE AS A CAUSE OF SUFFERING *Twelfth Night* is a romantic comedy, and romantic love is the play's main focus. Although the play ends happily, its general contention is that love causes great pain. Many of the characters view love as a curse that attacks its victims suddenly and disruptively. Many claim that love, or the pangs of unrequited love, cause them to suffer. Orsino speaks of love as an "appetite" that he wants to satisfy and cannot (I.i.1–3). At another point, he calls his desires "fell and cruel hounds" (I.i.21). Olivia more bluntly describes love as a "plague" from which she suffers terribly (I.v.265). These metaphors suggest random violence. Even the less melodramatic Viola says, "My state is desperate for my master's love" (II.ii.35). The desperation caused by love sometimes result in violence—as in Act V, scene i, when Orsino threatens to kill Viola-as-Cesario because he thinks Cesario has left him. The incomplete happiness of the play's ending emphasizes the pain of love. As the story draws to a close and happy lovers rejoice, Malvolio and Antonio are shut out. Malvolio must face the fact that he is a fool and socially unworthy of his noble mistress. Antonio is also hampered by society, unable to act on his love for Sebastian because homosexual love is not accepted. For those who eventually find happiness, the pain love once caused makes fulfillment all the more satisfying, but for people like Malvolio and Antonio, love means a lifetime of pain.

THE UNCERTAINTY OF GENDER Viola's cross-dressing creates a sexual mess: Viola falls in love with Orsino but cannot tell him because he thinks she is a man, while Olivia, the object of Orsino's affection, falls for Viola because she thinks Viola is a man. The subtext is clearly homoerotic. Olivia is in love with a woman, even though she thinks Viola is a man, and Orsino often remarks on Cesario's beauty, suggesting that he is attracted to Viola even before she drops her male disguise. This latent homoeroticism is made explicit with Antonio's love for his male friend, Sebastian. Antonio, whose homosexual desires are more than mere urges, never finds satisfaction, and his unhappiness keeps the homosexual subtext in view. And although Orsino's and Olivia's eventual heterosexual gratification largely glosses over their homoerotic urges, Shakespeare never comes down firmly on the side of unambiguous heterosexuality. Orsino's declaration of love for Viola suggests that he enjoys prolonging the pretense of her masculinity. Although he now knows that Viola is a woman, Orsino says, "Boy, thou hast said to me a thousand times / Thou never should'st love woman like to me" (V.i.260–261). In his last lines, Orsino declares, "Cesario, come— / For so you shall be while you are a man; / But when in other habits you are seen, / Orsino's mistress, and his fancy's queen" (V.i.372–375). Orsino continues to address Viola as a boy, using her male name, as if her masculinity is an important part of his attraction to her.

THE FOLLY OF AMBITION Malvolio seems to be a competent servant, if prudish and dour, but it turns out that he is also a supreme egotist with tremendous social ambitions. Maria plays on these ambitions when she forges a letter purporting to be from Olivia. Sir Toby and the others find the fantasy of Olivia's love for Malvolio hysterically funny, not only because of Malvolio's unattractive personality but also because Malvolio is not of noble blood. In the class system of Shakespeare's time, most noblewomen would not sully their reputations and shame their families by marrying a man of lower social status. Yet the atmosphere of the play makes Malvolio's aspirations less unreasonable than Sir Toby and the rest think them. The feast of Twelfth Night, from which the play takes its name, was a time when social hier-archies were turned upside-down. That subversive spirit animates Illyria, where Maria moves up in the world by marrying Sir Toby. Still, Malvolio fails to embrace subversiveness. He refuses to understand that his own social ambitions are subversive and is priggish and uptight about other people's behavior and desires. He wants to blur class lines for himself alone, while making sure that everyone else behaves dec-orously. Maria's success may be due to her willingness to accept and promote the anarchy that Sir Toby and the others embrace.

MOTIFS

MADNESS No one is truly insane in *Twelfth Night*, yet a number of characters are accused of being mad, and a current of insanity runs through the action of the play. After Sir Toby and Maria dupe Malvo-lio into believing that Olivia loves him, Malvolio behaves so bizarrely that people assume he is mad. Malvolio himself knows that he is sane and accuses everyone around him of being mad. When Antonio encounters Viola (disguised as Cesario), he mistakes her for Sebastian, and his angry insistence that she recognizes him leads people to assume that he is mad.

DISGUISES Many characters in *Twelfth Night* assume disguises, beginning with Viola, who dresses as a man. Other characters in disguise include Malvolio, who puts on crossed garters and yellow stockings in the hope of winning Olivia, and Feste, who dresses up as a priest when he speaks to Malvolio. Feste puts on the disguise even though Malvolio will not be able to see him from his dark cell, which suggests that clothing is important not just to signal identity to observers, but to give the wearer a sense of identity. In order to act like Sir Topas, Feste must look like Sir Topas.

SYMBOLS

OLIVIA'S GIFTS When Olivia wants to let Viola-as-Cesario know that she loves him, she sends him a ring. Later, when she mistakes Sebastian for Cesario, she gives him a precious pearl. In each case, the gift is a physical symbol of Olivia's romantic attachment to a man who is really a woman. The gifts are also bribes. Olivia says, "Youth is bought more oft than begged or borrowed," suggesting that if she can-not inspire Cesario's love, she will buy it.

THE DARKNESS OF MALVOLIO'S PRISON Sir Toby and Maria pretend that Malvolio is mad and confine him in a pitch-black chamber. Darkness becomes a symbol of his supposed insanity, as they tell him that the room is filled with light and his inability to see is a sign of his madness. Malvolio reverses the symbolism: "I say this house is as dark as ignorance, though ignorance were as dark as hell; and I say there was never man thus abused" (IV.ii.40–42). He insists that the darkness—meaning madness—is not in the room with him, but outside, with Sir Toby and Feste and Maria, who have unjustly imprisoned him.

IMPORTANT QUOTATIONS FROM *TWELFTH NIGHT*

1. *If music be the food of love, play on,*
   Give me excess of it that, surfeiting,
   The appetite may sicken and so die.
   That strain again, it had a dying fall.
   O, it came o'er my ear like the sweet sound
   That breathes upon a bank of violets,
   Stealing and giving odour. Enough, no more,
   'Tis not so sweet now as it was before.
   [Music ceases]
   O spirit of love, how quick and fresh art thou
   That, notwithstanding thy capacity
   Receiveth as the sea, naught enters there,

Of what validity and pitch so e'er,
But falls into abatement and low price
Even in a minute! So full of shapes is fancy
That it alone is high fantastical.

Location: I.i.1–15
Speaker: Orsino to his servants and musicians
Context: Orsino tries to amuse himself

The play's opening speech includes one of its most famous lines, as the unhappy, lovesick Orsino tells his servants and musicians, "If music be the food of love, play on." In the speech that follows, Orsino asks for the musicians to give him so much musical love-food that he will overdose ("surfeit") and cease to desire love any longer. This request introduces the idea of love as something unwanted, something that comes upon people unexpectedly. This image is complicated by Orsino's comment about the relationship between romance and imagination: "So full of shapes is fancy / That it alone is high fantastical," he says, relating overpowering love ("fancy") to imagination (that which is "fantastical"). Through this connection, the play asks whether romantic love has more to do with the person who is loved or with the lover's own imagination. For Orsino and Olivia, both of whom are willing to switch lovers at a moment's notice, imagination often seems more powerful than reality.

---

2. *Make me a willow cabin at your gate*
   And call upon my soul within the house,
   Write loyal cantons of contemn_d love,
   And sing them loud even in the dead of night;
   Hallow your name to the reverberate hills,
   And make the babbling gossip of the air
   Cry out 'Olivia!' O, you should not rest
   Between the elements of air and earth
   But you should pity me.

Location: I.v.237–245
Speaker: Viola (as Cesario) to Olivia
Context: Orsino has sent Viola, disguised as Cesario, to carry his message of love to Olivia

In this speech, Viola-as-Cesario sets aside the prepared messages from Orsino and instead tells Olivia what he would do if he were in love with her. Instead of helping win Olivia for Orsino, which he could not have done using Orsino's words, Cesario's passionate words make Olivia fall in love with him. Cesario's idea of love, which involves standing outside Olivia's gate night and day until Olivia takes "pity" on him, contrasts with the way Orsino actually pursues Olivia. Instead of planting himself outside her door and demonstrating his devotion, he prefers to remain at home, lolling on couches, complaining of his broken heart, and sending someone else to do the hard work of wooing for him.

---

3. *There is no woman's sides*
   Can bide the beating of so strong a passion
   As love doth give my heart; no woman's heart
   So big, to hold so much. They lack retention.
   Alas, their love may be called appetite,
   No motion of the liver, but the palate,
   That suffer surfeit, cloyment, and revolt.
   But mine is all as hungry as the sea,
   And can digest as much. Make no compare
   Between that love a woman can bear me

And that I owe Olivia.

Location: II.iv.91–101
Speaker: Orsino to Violet-as-Cesario
Context: Orsino describes manly love

Orsino argues that there can be no comparison between the kind of love that men feel for women and the kind of love that women feel for men. Women, he suggests, love only superficially—in the "palate," not the "liver." Men love more deeply and less changeably than women, whose love is characterized by "surfeit, cloyment, and revolt." Self-involved Orsino demonstrates that he cares only about his own emotions. He belittles Olivia, the woman he purports to love, assuring Violet-as-Cesario that whatever she feels pales in comparison to what he feels. Ironically, the qualities Orsino ascribes to women's love actually apply to his own infatuations. He claims that women love superficially and change their feelings easily. Later in the play, Orsino happily transfers his affections from Olivia to Viola. It is a woman, Viola, whose love for Orsino remains constant.

---

4. *Daylight and champaign discovers not more. This is open. I will be proud, I will read politic authors, I will baffle Sir Toby, I will wash off gross acquaintance, I will be point-device the very man. I do not now fool myself, to let imagination jade me; for every reason excites to this, that my lady loves me. She did commend my yellow stockings of late, she did praise my leg, being cross-gartered, and in this she manifests herself to my love, and with a kind of injunction drives to these habits of her liking. I thank my stars, I am happy. I will be strange, stout, in yellow stockings, and cross-gartered, even with the swiftness of putting on. Jove and my stars be praised.*

Location: II.v.140–150
Speaker: Malvolio
Context: Malvolio has found the letter Maria forged and thinks Olivia is in love with him

Until this point, Malvolio has seemed like a straight-laced prig with no enthusiasms or desires beyond decorum and an orderly house. Here he reveals that his puritanical exterior is only a veneer covering powerful feelings. Malvolio dreams of winning Olivia's love and of rising in the world to become a nobleman. For the audience, Malvolio's excitement is comic, since we know that he will make a fool of himself by following the letter's instructions and wearing yellow stockings and crossed garters. But there is also pathos in Malvolio's situation, since Maria and the others are making a fool of him, and his grand ambitions will certainly come crashing down. Malvolio is too absurd to be a tragic figure, but his vanity and excitement make him a pitiable one.

---

5. *Orsino: If this be so, as yet the glass seems true,*
   I shall have share in this most happy wrack.
   [To Viola] Boy, thou hast said to me a
   thousand times
   Thou never shouldst love woman like to me.
   Viola: And all those sayings will I overswear,
   And all those swearings keep as true in soul
   As doth that orb_d continent the fire
   That severs day from night.
   Orsino: Give me thy hand,
   And let me see thee in thy woman's weeds.

Location: V.i.258–266
Speaker: Orsino and Viola
Context: Sebastian and Viola have reunited, and all the misunderstandings have resolved themselves

Orsino ushers in a happy ending for his long-suffering Viola by declaring his willingness to wed her. This interchange sets the stage for general rejoicing, although even here, gender ambiguities persist. Orsino knows that Viola is a woman, and it seems he is attracted to her. Yet he addresses her as "Boy" in this speech, even as he accepts her vows of love. This incident is not isolated: later, Orsino continues to call his new betrothed "Cesario," using her male name. This odd mode of address raises the question of whether Orsino is in love with Cesario, the beautiful young man, or with Viola, the beautiful young woman.

THE TWO GENTLEMEN OF VERONA

Proteus forsakes his betrothed Julia and betrays his best friend Valentine in pursuit of Valentine's beloved Silvia, but then repents.

THE TWO GENTLEMEN OF VERONA IN CONTEXT

The year of composition of *The Two Gentlemen of Verona* is uncertain. One popular theory is that the play was written in two stages, first begun in 1592 then hastily finished in 1593 for a specific performance date. This theory explains the characters Launce and Crab, who are not very well integrated into the storyline, as well as the inconsistent references to the duke/emperor of Milan/Verona. Although the play is not first mentioned until 1598, its themes and theatrical techniques suggest that it was written before the other early comedies, *As You Like It* and *Twelfth Night*. Some critics go so far as to insist that *The Two Gentlemen of Verona* is Shakespeare's first play. At any rate, it is one of his least accomplished.

Shakespeare may have looked to works by authors such as Geoffrey Chaucer, Francis Bacon, John Lyly, and George Peele to inform the *Two Gentlemen of Verona* debate on the conflicts between male friendships and romantic love. However, the main source for *The Two Gentlemen of Verona* is the story of Felix and Felismena as told in *Diana*, a novel by the Portuguese writer Jorge de Montemayor in the sixteenth century. Shakespeare may have read *Diana* in a French translation. Alternatively, he may have seen it performed at the court in 1585. In his retelling of the story, Shakespeare made plot changes that allowed for a happier, more symmetrical ending. He kept Silvia alive until the end and added the character of Valentine, allowing for the double betrothal at the end.

THE TWO GENTLEMEN OF VERONA: KEY FACTS

Full title: The Two Gentlemen of Verona

Time and place written: 1592–1593; London, England

Date of first publication: 1623 (First Folio)

Genre: Comedy; romance; satire

Setting (time): Sixteenth century

Setting (place): Italy: Verona, Milan, and a forest

Protagonist: Proteus; Valentine

Major conflict: Even though he is engaged to Julia, Proteus falls in love with Valentine's beloved Silvia.

THE TWO GENTLEMEN OF VERONA: CHARACTER LIST

Antonio Proteus's father, and Panthino's master.

Crab Launce's dog. Crab plays the straight man in the Launce-Crab comic pairing. Launce berates Crab for not showing more sorrow on leaving his family; Crab sits still and pants. Launce berates Crab for peeing at the duke's table; Crab sits still and pants. Launce tells Crab he would make any sacrifice on his behalf; Crab sits still and pants. By juxtaposing scenes, the play draws parallels between Crab and the female lovers.

Sir Eglamour Silvia's cowardly escort as she flees the imperial palace in search of the banished Valentine.

Host Julia-as-Sebastian's landlord in Milan.

Julia (a.k.a. Sebastian) Proteus's beloved, and Lucetta's mistress. After Proteus leaves, Julia disguises herself as a page named Sebastian and follows Proteus to Milan.

Launce Proteus's comical servant. Launce is Crab's devoted owner. Launce falls in love with an ugly, wealthy girl.

Lucetta Julia's servant. Unlike Julia, Lucetta has a practical view of love.

Emperor of Milan Silvia's father. The emperor wants to marry Silvia to the boorish but wealthy Thurio. After Proteus tells the emperor that Valentine plans to elope with Silvia, the emperor cleverly manages to "discover" Valentine's plan without letting Valentine know that Proteus denounced him.

Panthino Antonio's servant.

Proteus Valentine's ignoble best friend, Julia's suitor, and one of the title gentlemen of Verona. Proteus behaves in a most ungentlemanly fashion when he falls in love with Valentine's sweetheart Silvia, and betrays both Julia and Valentine in pursuit of her.

Silvia Daughter to the emperor of Milan, and Valentine's beloved. Proteus, too, falls in love with Silvia, unrequitedly. Silvia commiserates with Julia-as-Sebastian about Proteus's mistreatment of Julia. When the emperor banishes Valentine, she escapes to seek him with the help of Sir Eglamour.

Speed Valentine's page.

Sir Thurio Silvia's wealthy yet boorish suitor. Sir Thurio is the emperor's favorite for Silvia's hand.

Valentine Proteus's noble best friend, Silvia's sweetheart, and one of the title gentlemen of Verona. Banished from Milan after Proteus betrays him by revealing his plan to elope with Silvia to the emperor, Valentine becomes king of the outlaws.

THE TWO GENTLEMEN OF VERONA: PLOT OVERVIEW

In Verona, two friends, Valentine and Proteus, bid farewell to each other. Valentine is off to Milan to see the world, while Proteus stays behind to woo Julia, the woman he loves. Proteus sends Julia a letter, and though she tears it up impulsively, she immediately regrets doing so, because she loves Proteus too. Proteus's father forces Proteus to go to Milan so that he too can find out about life at court. Proteus and Julia exchange rings and vows of love before Proteus leaves.

In Milan, Valentine has fallen in love with the emperor's daughter, Silvia. When Proteus arrives, he also falls in love with Silvia and betrays Valentine by warning the emperor that Valentine and Silvia plan to elope. The emperor banishes Valentine.

Julia disguises herself as a young man (Sebastian) and follows Proteus to Milan, where she sees Proteus wooing Silvia. Proteus, thinking that Julia is a page, sends her to deliver a ring to Silvia.

Valentine is stopped by a band of outlaws who make him their leader. To avoid marrying Thurio, her father's choice for her, Silvia runs away from home and is captured by outlaws. Proteus frees Silvia from the outlaws and then tries to rape her. Valentine intercedes, Proteus repents, and Valentine offers Silvia to Proteus. Julia reveals herself, and Proteus rejects the offer and marries Julia instead. Valentine marries Silvia.

THE TWO GENTLEMEN OF VERONA: SCENE SUMMARY

ACT I

Proteus woos his beloved Julia, but his father sends him to Milan to rejoin Proteus's friend Valentine.

I.I Location: Verona. A street

Valentine heads to Milan to see the world while Proteus stays in Verona to be near his love, Julia.

Valentine bids an emotional farewell to his dearest friend, Proteus. Valentine explains that he must leave Verona for Milan to gain worldly experience. Proteus responds that it's his passion for Julia that keeps him at home in Verona. Valentine chides Proteus for being so consumed with love, hinting that Proteus's devotion to love will ultimately make him a fool. Proteus promises to pray for Valentine, and Valentine departs. Proteus muses that Valentine has set out to find honor, honoring his friends by becoming more dignified. With a hint of melancholy, Proteus notes that he has abandoned his friends, his studies, and reason, all for his love of Julia.

Proteus's mournful thoughts are interrupted by Speed, Valentine's punning page. After a long, silly discussion about whether Speed is a sheep and Valentine his shepherd, Proteus asks Speed whether he has delivered Proteus's love letter to Julia. More punning ensues, until Speed finally confesses that he did indeed deliver the letter, but could discern no particular response from Julia: she simply nodded her head. Because Julia did not tip him for delivering the letter, Speed suggests that Julia will be hard and withholding toward Proteus as well. Proteus angrily sends Speed to Valentine's ship, worrying about Julia's cold reception to his love letter.

I.II Location: Verona. Julia's garden

In a silly fight with her maid Lucetta, Julia tears up Proteus's love letter without reading it.

Julia asks her maid Lucetta about how to fall in love. Lucetta replies that she should fall in love carefully, so as not to be caught by surprise. Julia lists all of her suitors, and asks Lucetta to pick out the one most worthy of her love. Lucetta tells Julia that her womanly instincts suggest Proteus more than anyone else. Lucetta's choice surprises Julia, because Proteus has never told Julia that he loves her. Lucetta replies that the "[f]ire that's closest kept burns most of all," meaning that secret loves are the most passionate (I.ii.30).

Lucetta confesses to Julia that Speed brought a letter from Proteus, which she, Lucetta, accepted, pretending to be Julia. Julia's temper flares not because Lucetta pretended to be her, but because Lucetta harbors such a scandalous letter. Julia says that modest, proper girls would refuse to read such a letter. She angrily sends Lucetta away, but then quickly changes her mind and calls Lucetta back with silly questions about dinner. Julia asks Lucetta to sing her Proteus's letter. But after another squabble with Lucetta, Julia is so irked that she tears up the letter. Lucetta exits, and Julia mourns the torn pieces of paper, reading words of love on separate scraps.

I.III Location: Verona. Antonio's house

Proteus's father Antonio sends Proteus to join Valentine at the emperor's court in Milan.

Proteus's father Antonio and his manservant Panthino discuss Proteus's future. Antonio asks Panthino whether he should sent Proteus to the emperor's court in Milan to stay with Valentine. Panthino advises Antonio to do this, so that Proteus can partake in life at court. Antonio likes Panthino's advice so much that he resolves to send Proteus to Milan the next day.

Antonio seeks out Proteus to tell him the good news, and discovers him reading a letter. The letter is from Julia, confessing her love for Proteus and her desire to marry him. Proteus lies to Antonio and tells him that the letter is from Valentine: an invitation for Proteus to join him in Milan. Antonio announces that Proteus will depart the next day for the emperor's court in Milan. Proteus is devastated by this development, but Antonio will not be dissuaded. Proteus laments about not having been brave enough to show Antonio the real letter, and agonizes over leaving his beloved Julia.

ACT II

Upon arrival in Milan, Proteus falls in love with Silvia, the emperor's daughter and Valentine's beloved.

II.I Location: Milan. The emperor's palace

Valentine's beloved, the emperor's daughter Silvia, shows some interest in him too.

Speed helps Valentine put on his gloves, only to realize that there is one glove too many. The third glove, we quickly realize, belongs to the emperor's daughter Silvia, the object of Valentine's affection. Valentine, however, is surprised to hear that Speed knows that Silvia is his beloved. Valentine asks Speed how he knows. Speed humorously rattles off a long list of Valentine's lovesick behavior: he adores love songs, sighs, weeps, has no appetite, and crosses his arms discontentedly. Speed says that these love-struck traits point to the truth as clear as "water in a urinal" (II.i.39–40). Valentine confesses that Silvia has entreated him to write a love letter to an unnamed recipient.

Silvia enters. When Valentine gives her the letter, she coldly replies that it is written in a too scholarly a fashion. She insists that he take the letter back, and wants Valentine to write another love letter, to *her*. Valentine is disappointed, but Speed says that he should be happy to be receiving a letter from Silvia (meaning the very letter that Valentine wrote and she just returned). Valentine tries to convince Speed that Silvia is the fairest maid of all, but Speed refuses to be swayed, saying that Valentine's love has blinded his ability to judge rationally.

II.II Location: Verona. Julia's house

Proteus and Julia say goodbye.

Proteus and Julia bid a tearful goodbye and exchange rings as a pledge of their devotion to one another. Proteus vows that the ring Julia has given him will remind him eternally of her, his true love. Julia departs wordlessly and Panthino arrives to hasten Proteus aboard the ship to Milan.

II.III Location: Verona. A street

Proteus's servant Launce clowns around on the way to the ship.

Proteus's servant Launce dilly-dallies en route to the Milan-bound ship, dragging his dog Crab. He complains that Crab is the surliest dog that ever lived. His family cried bitterly when he bade them farewell, while Crab neither said a word of sorrow nor shed a tear of sympathy. Launce enacts the entire farewell scene with his shoes and apparel: the shoe with the hole in the toe stands in for his mother, and the shoe without the hole for his father. His staff stands in for his sister, and his hat for the family maid. Confusion ensues as Launce debates whether he or Crab should play Launce himself. Panthino arrives to fetch Launce, interrupting his production.

II.IV Location: Milan. The emperor's palace

Proteus arrives in Milan and falls in love with Silvia at first sight.

Valentine and Thurio, a boorish admirer of Silvia's, show off in front of Silvia. Speed stands by, trying to start a fight between the rivals by encouraging Valentine to punch Thurio. Silvia commends the men for their witty dialogue as the emperor enters.

The emperor marvels at the number of admirers clustering around Silvia, and asks Valentine about his friend Proteus. Valentine praises Proteus, calling him a perfect gentleman. The emperor announces that Proteus will arrive momentarily. When Proteus arrives, Valentine introduces him to Silvia. Silvia and Thurio exit promptly.

Valentine admits to Proteus that he has fallen in love, despite his past criticism of Proteus for succumbing to a woman's sweet ways. Valentine presses Proteus to admit that Silvia's beauty is divine and exceeds that of any living woman, but Proteus refuses to concede. Valentine confesses that he and Silvia are betrothed and that they plan to elope that night. He has a ladder made of cords and plans to climb to Silvia's window and ferry her away. Valentine asks Proteus to advise him about the plan, but Proteus weakly invents some pressing business. After Valentine exits, Proteus admits that he, too, has fallen in love with Silvia, having all but forgotten Julia in the face of this more beautiful competitor. Proteus ominously says that because he loves Silvia so much, he cannot love Valentine at all.

II.V Location: Milan. A street

Speed and Launce discuss their masters Valentine and Proteus with bawdy humor.

Speed welcomes Launce to Milan. Launce replies that no one can truly feel welcome in a town until someone buys him a shot of liquor at the local tavern. Speed offers to do so, but first inquires about Proteus and Julia. By way of answer, Launce confuses Speed, implying through a series of puns that Proteus and Julia have simultaneously parted and become engaged. The exchange ends with Launce's traditional dirty joke: when Proteus "stands" well, Julia is happy too. Speed, not so speedy at comprehending Launce's jokes, calls Launce an ass and complains that he does not understand what Launce means. Launce tells Speed to ask Crab whether Julia and Proteus are engaged: if Crab talks or wags his tail, that means they are. Speed boasts that his master Valentine has become a "notable lover" (II.v.36). Launce, feigning to have misheard him, replies that he has always known that Valentine was a "notable lubber" (II.v.39). Launce finally convinces Speed to buy him a drink, like a good Christian.

II.VI Location: Milan. The emperor's palace

For love of Silvia, Proteus plans to betray Valentine's trust and tell the emperor that Valentine and Silvia plan to elope that night.

Proteus debates whether or not to pursue his infatuation with Silvia. To stay true to his love impulses, he would worship Silvia and betray both Julia and Valentine. Prizing his amorous desires over friendship, Proteus devises a plot to snatch Silvia from Valentine's arms while simultaneously gaining favor with the emperor: he plans to tell the emperor that Valentine plans to elope with Silvia. The emperor will then banish Valentine and encourage Thurio, his preferred suitor, to continue courting Silvia. Proteus plans to trick both Thurio and Silvia with a ruse involving musicians and leave Silvia with no choice but to love him, Proteus. His soliloquy ends with a couplet: "Love, lend me wings to make my purpose swift, / As thou hast lent me wit to plot this drift" (II.vi.42–43).

II.VII Location: Verona. Julia's house

Julia plans to dress up as a boy and travel to Milan to see Proteus.

Julia asks Lucetta to help her devise a plan to travel to Milan to visit Proteus. Lucetta warns Julia that it is a long and dangerous journey, and counsels Julia to wait for his return. Julia insists that a "true-devoted pilgrim is not weary" (II.vii.9). Lucetta responds that she wants only to ensure that Julia's love does not exceed the bounds of rationality.

Julia reveals that she plans to disguise herself as a boy for the journey, to avoid the unwanted advances of lecherous men. She asks Lucetta to design a costume befitting a high-class page. Julia fears that her reputation will be tarnished if her unladylike behavior is discovered. She believes, however, that Proteus is so pure, sincere, and immaculate that seeing him is worth any risk. Lucetta is skeptical of Proteus's alleged faultlessness, but Julia chides Lucetta, instructing her to love Proteus just as Julia herself does.

ACT III

After Proteus betrays Valentine by telling the emperor that Valentine plans to elope with Silvia, the emperor banishes Valentine.

III.I Location: Milan. The emperor's palace

Tipped off by Proteus, the emperor exposes Valentine's plan to elope with Silvia and banishes Valentine.

Proteus alerts the emperor that Valentine plans to elope with his daughter Silvia. Proteus explains that were it not his "duty" to notify the emperor of this development, he would not betray his friend in such a manner. (Proteus is lying. His true motivation is his desire for Silvia.) The emperor admits that he has known for some while that Valentine has been visiting Silvia in her room by means of a ladder, but that he did not want to challenge Valentine and appear ungentlemanly. Proteus begs the emperor to foil Valentine's plot without revealing that Proteus betrayed Valentine's trust.

Valentine rushes through the courtyard, past the emperor, who asks him to stop a while and chat. Valentine is perturbed by this request, but nonetheless stays patiently. The emperor confesses to Valentine that he is frustrated with Silvia for not wanting to marry Thurio. The emperor, a widower, makes up a story about searching for a new wife to replace the love he once felt for his disobedient daughter Silvia.

He plans to "turn [Silvia] out to who will take her in. / Then let her beauty be her wedding dower, / For me and my possessions she esteems not" (III.i.77–79). He asks Valentine for advice on how to woo a coy lady from Milan to marry him. Valentine embarks on a love lesson befitting his name: he explains that all women love jewels and that when a woman frowns upon a suitor, it is not out of hatred but out of a desire to make him love her even more. Valentine advises the emperor to visit his ladylove by night, using a "ladder made of cords" to enter her locked chamber. At the emperor's request, Valentine promises to procure such a ladder.

Valentine begins to lose patience as the emperor pesters him with more questions. He asks Valentine how he should convey the ladder to the scene. Exasperated, Valentine says that the emperor could hide it under any cloak. The emperor insists on trying on Valentine's cloak, claiming that he needs to get used to wearing one. While trying on Valentine's cloak, the emperor discovers a letter in the pocket that outlines Valentine's plans to escape with Silvia. The enraged emperor banishes Valentine from his court, leaving Valentine distraught. Proteus comforts Valentine with an exaggerated description of Silvia's mourning and kindly accompanies him out of the emperor's palace.

Launce tells the audience that his master Proteus is a knave. Launce then announces that he himself is in love, though no one knows about it, and shows a letter to Speed describing his beloved: she can fetch, carry, milk, sew, brew good ale, knit, wash, and scour. She is not without her detriments: she is toothless, overly fond of liquor, has illegitimate children, and "... more hair than wit, and more faults than hairs, and more wealth than faults" (III.i.339–340).

III.II Location: Milan. The emperor's palace

The emperor asks Proteus to get Silvia to marry the boorish Thurio.

The emperor asks Proteus to convince Silvia to fall in love with Thurio. Proteus feigns unwillingness to slander Valentine, but the emperor tells him that since nothing Proteus can say will help Valentine, no words can hurt him either. Proteus asks, "But say this [slandering] weed her love from Valentine, / It follows not that she will love Sir Thurio," hatching his plot to divert Silvia's affections directly to himself (III.ii.49–50). Proteus advises Thurio to gather musicians to sing a sonnet under Silvia's balcony that evening.

ACT IV

Julia, dressed as a page, arrives in Milan and overhears Proteus wooing Silvia.

IV.I Location: a forest

A group of banished outlaws elects Valentine to be their leader.

A group of outlaws overtakes the recently banished Valentine and Speed, who are traveling in the forest between Milan and Mantua. Instead of robbing Valentine on the spot, the outlaws listen to his tale of woe. Valentine wisely adds a few spicy details about slaying a man in a fierce confrontation. The outlaws are much impressed. They ask Valentine if he is fluent in many languages, to which he replies affirmatively. The outlaws, who, like Valentine, are banished gentlemen, tell Valentine that if he refuses to become their leader, they will kill him. Valentine commits himself to leading the outlaws, but only on the condition that the bands do "no outrages / On silly women or poor passengers" (IV.i.69–70).

IV.II Location: Milan. Outside Silvia's window

Julia, disguised as a page, overhears Proteus wooing an indignant Silvia.

Proteus lays his plans to double-cross Thurio. He meets up with Thurio and a band of musicians under Silvia's window. As the musicians begin to play an ode to Silvia, Julia arrives dressed as a page and calling herself Sebastian. Her host asks her why she appears sad, and she replies that the musicians are out of tune. The host informs her that Proteus is so smitten with Silvia that he has ordered Launce to give Crab to her. As the music stops, Proteus shoos Thurio away from the scene, telling Thurio to leave him to plead Thurio's case with Silvia. When Silvia appears at her window, she believes that Proteus has been the one wooing her.

Silvia rebuffs all of Proteus's loving advances, calling him a "perjured, false, disloyal man" (IV.ii.89). She warns him that she will not be swayed by the lies that tricked Valentine and Julia. Proteus tells Silvia that Julia is dead. Julia, in the shadows, is quite surprised to hear this, but does not speak out. Proteus begs Silvia to give him the picture of her that hangs in her bedchamber (perhaps he knows this from Valentine). Silvia is loath to give it to him, although she stingingly adds that since Proteus worships shadows and false shapes, the falsest version of a person (i.e., a picture) would be a fitting idol for him. She agrees to send it in the morning. Having heard the entire exchange, Julia returns with a heavy heart to her host's lodgings.

IV.III Location: Milan. The emperor's court

Silvia asks an elderly friend to escort her to Mantua to find Valentine.

Silvia calls upon Sir Eglamour, a friend, to help her escape her "most unholy match" to the detested Thurio (IV.iii.30). She yearns to reunite with Valentine but knows she cannot travel to Mantua alone. Eglamour is a safe chaperone for Silvia, as he has taken a vow of chastity since the death of his beloved wife. Silvia and Eglamour make plans to meet the following day at Friar Patrick's cell.

IV.IV Location: Milan. The emperor's court

Proteus sends Julia-as-Sebastian on an errand to visit Silvia.

Launce describes his visit to the emperor's dining chamber to deliver Crab as a gift to Silvia. Launce and Crab are in the room not longer than a "pissing while" when Crab urinates on the floor (IV.iv.16–17). The emperor calls his servants to beat Crab, but because Launce loves Crab so dearly, he claims that he himself urinated on the floor, and takes the beating in place of Crab.

Proteus meets Julia, who is disguised as Sebastian, and takes an immediate liking to him. He asks him to deliver to Silvia the ring that Julia gave Proteus at his departure. Greatly vexed at Proteus's infidelity, Julia sighs that she "cannot be true servant to my master [Proteus] / Unless I prove false traitor to myself" (IV.iv.97–98).

Julia, as Sebastian, goes to Silvia's chamber to deliver the ring and collect Silvia's portrait. Silvia expresses her dislike for Proteus, especially when she realizes that the ring originally belonged to Julia. Julia thanks Silvia for being sympathetic to Julia's plight. Intrigued, Silvia asks Julia-as-Sebastian whether he knew Julia. Julia-as-Sebastian replies that he was very close to Julia, and even once wore one of her dresses for a pageant at Pentecost. Silvia departs, and Julia compares herself to Silvia's picture, thinking that she herself is prettier.

ACT V

Everyone meets in the forest after Silvia flees to look for Valentine; Proteus changes his mind and marries Julia, and Valentine marries Silvia.

V.I Location: Milan. Friar Patrick's cell

Silvia sets out to look for Valentine.

Eglamour and Silvia rendezvous at Friar Patrick's cell.

V.II Location: Milan. The emperor's palace

The emperor's court discovers that Silvia has fled.

Proteus interrogates Julia-as-Sebastian about her interaction with Silvia. The emperor interrupts them and announces that Silvia has disappeared. Proteus, Sebastian, and the emperor form a search party with Thurio and ride off to find Silvia.

V.III Location: the forest

Silvia is captured by a band of outlaws.

A band of outlaws captures Silvia on her ride through the forest. Her chaperone Eglamour flees, too fearful for his own safety to protect her. As the outlaws bring Silvia to their captain, she wails, "O Valentine! This I endure for thee" (V.iii.15).

V.IV Location: another part of the forest

Summary

Valentine sits alone in the forest, extolling the virtues of life in the middle of nature. He hears shouts in the distance and hides. Proteus, Silvia, and Julia, disguised as Sebastian, enter. Proteus has rescued Silvia from the outlaws, and pleads with her to give him one kind glance as recompense. Valentine overhears their conversation, but decides to wait to reveal himself. Silvia tells Proteus that she would have preferred being eaten by a lion to being saved by him. She emphasizes that she loves Valentine and hates Proteus for betraying him. "In love / Who respects friend?" he asks her. "All men but Proteus," she replies (V.iv.53–55).

Proteus grows enraged at Silvia and moves to rape her. When Silvia cries out, Valentine angrily leaps out of the bushes and curses Proteus for betraying him. Proteus begs Valentine's forgiveness. Valentine immediately pardons Proteus and offers Silvia to him, at which point Julia (as Sebastian) faints. When she regains consciousness, she explains that she fainted because she forgot to give Proteus's ring to Silvia. Julia-as-Sebastian then produces two rings: the one that Julia had given to Proteus (and which he later intended for Silvia) and the one that Proteus had given to Julia. When Proteus asks Julia-as-Sebastian how she obtained Julia's ring, Julia reveals who she is. Proteus immediately decides that Julia is more beautiful after all and decides to marry her instead of Silvia.

Thurio, the emperor, and the outlaws arrive. Thurio claims Silvia as his, but Valentine threatens to kill him if he touches her. Thurio confesses that he doesn't really love Silvia, and that it would be stupid to be killed for someone he doesn't love. The emperor tells Thurio that he is a "degenerate," and applauds Valentine's noble behavior: " … by the honour of my ancestry / I do applaud thy spirit. … Sir Valentine, / Thou art a gentleman, and well derived" (V.iv.136–43). The emperor grants Valentine's request to pardon his band of gentlemanly outlaws and Valentine decrees that both couples—he and Silvia, Proteus and Julia—should be married on the same day.

THEMES, MOTIFS, & SYMBOLS IN *THE TWO GENTLEMEN OF VERONA*

THEMES

THE CONFLICTING DEMANDS OF FRIENDSHIP AND LOVE At the heart of the play lies Proteus and Valentine's friendship. The play explores what they will and will not do for each other out of their friendship. In Milan, Proteus is forced to choose between his friendship with Valentine and his love for Silvia. Proteus chooses love and betrays Valentine to the emperor. The rest of the play focuses on restoring the balance between the conflicting demands of friendship and love.

The astute modern reader will find homoerotic overtones to Valentine and Proteus's relationship, but in Elizabethan England, loyalty in friendship was valued deeply, generally more deeply than romantic love. (Indeed, critics often speak of a "Renaissance cult of friendship.") In the play, the proper love relationships cannot be restored until the friendship of the two gentlemen has been mended. The final scene does just that, however awkwardly and implausibly. For Valentine and Proteus to be reconciled, Proteus must apologize to Valentine and Valentine must accept the apology. To seal the bonds of friendship, one of the friends must make a sacrifice that demonstrates that friendship is indeed more important than love. This need for a sacrifice results in Valentine's offer of Silvia to Proteus. At the same time, to prevent both from breaking their vows to their sweethearts, Valentine must end up with Silvia and Proteus with Julia.

ROMANTIC IDEALS DEBUNKED *The Two Gentlemen of Verona* is roughly structured as a romance, a medieval genre that details the quest of a chivalrous knight, devoted to a beautiful and chaste woman, who travels the world in search of adventure. Like the medieval knight, Valentine and Proteus leave home to see the world in Milan. However, Shakespeare uses them to expose the hollowness of romantic ideals by showing how the complexities of the modern world often demand more than steadfast adherence to a code of honor. In the last scene, Valentine gallantly offers Silvia to Proteus by way of accepting Proteus's apology. Though the offer is meant to cement their friendship, it strikes us as perverse. Silvia has many a time explained that she loves Valentine and hates Proteus (who incidentally had just tried to rape her). Shakespeare's female heroines are fuller and more developed than the bland damsels in distress of medieval romances, so treating them as objects of barter is absurd.

THE CLOWN AS MICROCOSM The play's clowns, Speed and Launce, play only peripheral roles in the development of the main plot. Instead, they provide comic relief, counterbalancing the earnestness of the main storyline. In particular, Launce's scenes are juxtaposed with and comment on scenes in the main plot. He first appears in II.iii, after Proteus and Julia's parting scene, in which Proteus tells Julia neither to speak nor cry. In their scene, Launce curses his dog Crab for not speaking or crying as they follow Proteus to Milan. The obvious parallel between Launce and his dog and Proteus and Julia makes a dig at the sincerity of Proteus's love. Proteus is content if Julia is silent and dry-eyed, while Launce is hurt for Crab to be so. The implication is that Launce cares for Crab more than Proteus cares for Julia.

The play explores three types of relationships: master and servant, friend and friend, and lover and lover. Launce participates in all three types. He is both master and friend to Crab. In III.i, Launce describes his milkmaid sweetheart, showing more faith, loyalty, and acceptance than either Proteus or Valentine. Launce makes excuses for his milkmaid's shortcomings and praises her for simple talents such as knowing how to milk cows. Like many of Shakespeare's clowns, Launce exhibits more warmth and compassion than the gentlemen and noblemen of his play.

MOTIFS

METAMORPHOSIS Change takes many forms in *The Two Gentlemen of Verona*. On a literal level, Julia disguises herself as a boy and reveals herself as a woman at the end, while Valentine is transformed first into an outlaw and then back into a well-regarded gentleman. Proteus changes when he falls in love with Silvia, then again when he returns to Julia. Proteus is named for a shape-changing Greek god, and his change of heart sets the plot in motion and motivates both Julia's and Valentine's transformations. Valentine becomes an outlaw when he is banished through Proteus's machinations. Julia pretends to be a boy to seek Proteus after he goes away. Figuratively, she turns into a boy when Proteus spurns her love, upon which she stakes her womanhood.

PLOT PARALLELS Structurally, the play jumps back and forth between many subplots, developing each gradually. Act I deals with the burgeoning romance between Proteus and Julia. Act II abruptly jumps to Milan to examine Valentine's love for Silvia. After Valentine is banished, Proteus's storyline is interlaced with Valentine's. In this way, the scene in which Silvia rejects Proteus is followed by the scene in which the outlaws accept Valentine. Emotionally climactic scenes are frequently followed by comedic scenes featuring Launce or Speed, which both deflate the tension of the play and comment on the developments of the main storyline.

SYMBOLS

VERONA, MILAN, AND THE FOREST The play is set in three separate locations: Verona, Valentine's and Proteus's home town; the imperial court in Milan; and the forest. These locations define a trajectory in the coming of age of the two protagonists. Verona is home; the site of innocence, comfort, and youthful love. Both Proteus and Valentine must leave Verona and go on a journey to become men. Cosmopolitan Milan and the court represent the more complicated world of adulthood. Valentine falls in love, and Proteus falls out of love with his own sweetheart and in love with Valentine's. As in other

Shakespearean comedies such as *As You Like It* and *A Midsummer Night's Dream*, the forest is a mysterious, magical place where the ordinary rules of conduct are suspended. Here, the play becomes a fairy tale in which the complications of maturity may be resolved easily. Unconstrained by the bonds of society, the characters reveal their true nature in the forest: Julia throws off her disguise, and Valentine confronts Proteus and his hypocrisy.

VALENTINE AND PROTEUS The names of the two protagonists are hardly accidental. Valentine, the play's true lover, is named after St. Valentine, the patron saint of lovers. He falls in love with Silvia and remains devoted to her until the end of the play. The fickle Proteus, on the other hand, is named after a Greek god famous for his ability to change his shape. The classical Proteus is the son of Poseidon, the god of the sea. Proteus must predict the future for anyone who can tie him down. He shirks his responsibilities by changing his shape. Julia wants to "tie down" Proteus by marrying him, thus ending his bachelor life and making his future all too predictable. Like his namesake, Proteus "changes shape" by falling in love with Silvia, thus dodging his responsibility to make a solid commitment to the future.

IMPORTANT QUOTATIONS FROM *THE TWO GENTLEMEN OF VERONA*

---

1. *He after honor hunts, I after love;*
   He leaves his friends, to dignify them more;
   I leave myself, my friends, and all, for love:
   Thou, Julia, thou hast metamorphosed me.

Location: I.i.63–66
Speaker: Proteus
Context: Valentine has left for Milan, but Proteus remains in Verona to woo Julia

The play opens on a friendly argument between Valentine and Proteus. Valentine believes that coming of age by seeing the world is the most important thing, while Proteus argues that love is more important. Once Valentine leaves, Proteus acknowledges that his decision to stay behind and woo Julia is a poor one. On his journey, Valentine will grow into an honorable man, which will reflect well on his friends. Proteus, on the other hand, has forsaken his friends in favor of Julia. He has been changed ("metamorphosed") by her into a less honorable person. The opening scene thus sets up the play's crucial contrast. Valentine does the "right" thing: he goes to court to find honor, falls in love, and remains constant to his love. Proteus, named after a Greek god who changes his shape (i.e., metamorphoses), has been persuaded (changed) by love for Julia to stay home. Then he goes to court, where he betrays Julia by falling in love with Silvia and betrays Valentine by denouncing him to the emperor. The play's conflict derives from Proteus's changing fancies, so it is fitting that he acknowledges himself as subject to change (metamorphosis) in his first soliloquy.

---

2. *Nay, 'twill be this hour ere I have done weeping. All the kind of the Launces have this very fault. I have received my proportion, like the prodigious son, and am going with Sir Proteus to the Imperial's court. I think Crab my dog be the sourest-natured dog that lives: my mother weeping; my father wailing; my sister crying; our maid howling; our cat wringing her hands, and all our house in a great perplexity; yet did not this cruel-hearted cur shed one tear.*

Location: II.iii.1–8
Speaker: Launce
Context: Proteus's servant Launce prepares to follow Proteus to Milan

Launce and his dog Crab, the play's comic relief characters, are often cited as the play's most memorable elements. Launce's speech follows and mocks the solemn farewell between Proteus and Julia, during which Proteus instructs Julia not to speak and not to cry. Launce relates his own tearful farewell from his family, which progresses from the normal (his mother weeping) to the absurd (the maid "howling" and the cat "wringing her hands"). Launce turns the tragedy of Proteus and Julia's sorrowful parting into a farce. Where Proteus asks Julia not to cry, Launce is outraged that his crabby dog Crab didn't shed a tear. The implicit comic parallel between Julia and Crab further undercuts the solemnity of the previous scene.

---

3. *To leave my Julia, shall I be forsworn;*
   To love fair Silvia, shall I be forsworn;
   To wrong my friend, I shall be much forsworn.
   And ev'n that power which gave me first my oath
   Provokes me to this threefold perjury.
   Love bade me swear, and Love bids me forswear.

Location: II.vi.1–6
Speaker: Proteus
Context: Proteus struggles to decide what to do now that he has fallen in love with Silvia

Proteus, who has sworn to love Julia, acknowledges that if he pursues Silvia, he will commit "threefold perjury." He will betray Julia, break his vow to love only her (II.ii), and stab Valentine in the back. Love is the culprit: his former love for Julia and for Valentine is at odds with his current love for Silvia. In typical fashion, Proteus refuses to take responsibility for his actions and blames love for his misfortune.

---

4. *Then I am paid;*
   And once again I do receive thee honest.
   Who by repentance is not satisfied,
   Is nor of heaven, nor earth; for these are pleased:
   By penitence th' Eternal's wrath's appeased.
   And that my love may appear plain and free,
   All that was mine in Silvia I give thee.

Location: V.iv.77–83
Speaker: Valentine
Context: Valentine forgives Proteus for betraying him and threatening to rape Silvia

Valentine forgiving Proteus is one of the more shocking speeches in Shakespeare. Proteus has betrayed Valentine's trust by revealing his elopement plan, and has threatened to rape Silvia. After Valentine reveals who he is, Proteus delivers a five-line speech of apology. In response, Valentine not only forgives Proteus but, as a show of friendship, offers Silvia to Proteus. (Typically enough, Silvia is not consulted.) We could choose to dismiss this scene as a weak attempt by an inexperienced Shakespeare. Alternatively, the scene satirizes gentlemanly behavior. Courtesy demands that Valentine offer Proteus something in accepting his apology, so Valentine offers Silvia. This conclusion shows upper-class manners impeding, rather than encouraging, correct behavior.

---

5. *It is the lesser blot modesty finds,*
   Women to change their shapes, than men their minds.

Location: V.iv.106–107
Speaker: Julia
Context: Julia-as-Sebastian has revealed who she is to Proteus, and chastises him for his bad behavior, which has forced her to dress as a boy

In the Middle Ages (before Shakespeare's time) cross-dressing was considered sinful, and the sense that cross-dressing is debasing remained in Shakespeare's day. Julia insists, however, that her disguise was less sinful than Proteus's change of heart. Where Valentine forgives Proteus, Julia has the sense to scold him for his irresponsibility. Julia's disguise as a boy prefigures a number of Shakespearean comic heroines, most notably Viola in *Twelfth Night* and Rosaline in *As You Like It*. Cross-dressing is a common device in Shakespearean comedies, in which a woman often enters a man's world to effect a happy resolution. Feminist readings of these plays, including *The Two Gentleman of Verona*, emphasize how women are denied success and happiness so that they are forced to take on disguises to fully realize themselves.

THE TWO NOBLE KINSMEN

*When Arcite and Palamon, two equally worthy cousins, compete for Emilia's hand, Arcite beats
Palamon in battle but Palamon wins Emilia anyway.*

THE TWO NOBLE KINSMEN IN CONTEXT

The Two Noble Kinsmen is one of a few plays spuriously attributed to Shakespeare. The play was first
printed in 1634, almost twenty years after Shakespeare's death, and some have suggested that the attribution to Shakespeare (as well as his contemporary John Fletcher) on the title page was an attempt to raise
revenue by the publisher. Most scholars agree that the play was a collaboration between Shakespeare and
Fletcher, who succeeded Shakespeare as the primary playwright for the King's Men. Stylistically, the
play resembles other late Shakespeare works, such as *Henry VIII* (a.k.a. *All Is True*), *The Tempest*, and
Cymbeline, so we have reason to believe that Shakespeare did indeed play a part in the composition of
The Two Noble Kinsmen.

John Fletcher began working as a playwright around 1605, first in collaboration with the playwright
Francis Beaumont and later with Shakespeare, Ben Jonson, and others. He and Shakespeare likely col-
laborated on *Henry VIII*, the lost *Cardenio*, and *The Two Noble Kinsmen* before Shakespeare retired and
Fletcher took over. Critics believe that Shakespeare wrote Acts I and V (except for V.ii and the first thirty-
three lines of V.i) as well as II.i and III.i. Shakespeare's scenes are relatively undramatic, whereas
Fletcher's, which strive to imitate Shakespeare's earlier works, range in quality from touching to absurd.
The play is inspired by Chaucer's *The Knight's Tale*, which in turn is drawn from Boccaccio's *Theseid*.
Boccaccio's tale favors Arcite, and Chaucer's favors Palamon, but Shakespeare and Fletcher's version
makes it difficult to prefer one to the other. Shakespeare's version also downplays the role of the gods in
Arcite's death. The subplot surrounding the jailer's daughter appears to be Shakespeare and Fletcher's
original contribution.

Scholars have suggested that *The Two Noble Kinsmen* is Shakespeare's commentary on the openly
homosexual court of King James I (reigned 1603–1625). Some have even suggested fully allegorical readings of the play wherein the characters represent members of the royal family. Whatever the motivations
for its creation, the play has been revived with great success in the late twentieth century, largely because
it touches on themes salient to feminist criticism. In many ways as complex as the great works of the
Shakespearean canon, *The Two Noble Kinsmen* is becoming more and more resonant to modern audiences.

THE TWO NOBLE KINSMEN: KEY FACTS

Full title: The Two Noble Kinsmen	
Authors: William Shakespeare, John Fletcher	
Time and place written: 1613 or 1614; England	
Date of first performance: 1613 or 1614	
Genre: Romance; tragicomedy; comedy	
Setting (time): Ancient or mythological	
Setting (place): Greece: Athens, Thebes, and environs	
Protagonist: Palamon, Arcite	
Major conflict: Palamon and Arcite compete for Emilia	

THE TWO NOBLE KINSMEN: CHARACTER LIST

THE NOBLES

Arcite Palamon's cousin and Creon's nephew. A powerful fighter, Arcite remains concerned with his honor, his moral innocence, and his love for Palamon throughout the conflict over Emilia.

Hippolyta The Queen of the Amazons. Recently captured by Theseus, Hippolyta is about to be wed to him, and approaches her fate complacently. She frequently opposes Theseus's decisions and persuades him to change his mind.

Emilia Hippolyta's sister. Emilia is the unwitting cause of Palamon and Arcite's feud. She privileges same-sex relationships over heterosexual ones, and some modern critics have suggested that she is a lesbian. Emilia wants to stay a virgin.

Palamon Arcite's cousin and Creon's nephew. Sullen and proud, Palamon is a formidable warrior. Governed by a strong sense of honor, he fights with Creon against Theseus even though he hates Creon. Palamon quickly becomes enraged with Arcite when Arcite declares his love for Emilia.

Pirithous Theseus's close friend. Together, Pirithous and Theseus have gone on many heroic quests.

Three Queens The widows of the three kings who died in the war of the Seven Against Thebes, a civil war between the sons of Oedipus. Their complaint that King Creon of Thebes did not let them bury their dead husbands spurs the battle between Athens and Thebes in which Palamon and Arcite are captured.

Theseus The duke of Athens. A warrior of mythical strength, Theseus has recently subdued the Amazons and won their queen, Hippolyta, for his bride. Theseus is related to Hercules and is a close quest companion of Pirithous. Theseus is responsive to the pleas of those close to him.

THE COMMONERS

Doctor A cynical man, he values psychological well-being over conventional moral standards.

Jailer The guard of the prison where Palamon and Arcite are held in Act II. He is attached to both his daughter and the wooer, and reluctantly acquiesces to cure her by encouraging her to have sex.

Jailer's Brother A tender uncle to the jailer's daughter.

Jailer's Daughter The protagonist of the subplot. The jailor's daughter is a young and very foolish girl who falls madly in love with Palamon. The jailer's daughter is ready to sacrifice her father and her wooer to be with Palamon. She goes mad when he rejects her, but is cured when she has sex with the wooer.

Wooer The jailer's daughter's fiancé. He loves her, but remains calm when she falls in love with Palamon.

Schoolmaster A pretentious man who organizes the morris dance. He is mocked by the countrymen and gently ridiculed by Theseus.

Four Countrymen Jolly men who plan to dance before Theseus and hope to sleep with the female dancers.

Timothy the Taborer The tabor player for the morris dance.

Boy The singer in Theseus and Hippolyta's wedding procession.

Valerius A messenger from Creon to Palamon and Arcite in I.ii.

THE TWO NOBLE KINSMEN: PLOT OVERVIEW

As Theseus, duke of Athens, returns to Athens to celebrate his wedding to Hippolyta, the newly conquered queen of the Amazons, he is accosted by three widowed queens who beg for his help. The husbands of the three queens were all killed by Creon, the ruler of Thebes, who has left their bodies to rot, denying them burial. Theseus goes to Thebes and defeats Creon, restoring the dead kings' remains to their spouses. He takes prisoner two of Creon's noblemen, Palamon and Arcite, cousins who performed nobly in the battle. From their prison, Palamon sees Hippolyta's sister Emilia in a garden and falls in love with her. Arcite glimpses her moments later and falls in love with her too, for which Palamon accuses him of treachery. At the entreaty of Theseus's friend Pirithous, Arcite is freed from jail, but banished from Athens.

Arcite returns to Athens in disguise and wins a competition of wrestling and running, gaining the attention of Theseus and Emilia. Theseus promotes Arcite to be Emilia's servant, and the Athenians treat him as a gentleman. Meanwhile, the daughter of the jailer who keeps Palamon prisoner falls in love with Palamon and helps him escape into the woods, hoping that Palamon will have sex with her. When Palamon runs away from her, she goes insane. Arcite encounters Palamon in the woods and the two agree to fight one another after Arcite brings Palamon files for his shackles, food, and armor. They begin to fight, but Theseus finds them and is about to have them executed until Hippolyta, Emilia, and Pirithous convince him otherwise. Theseus decrees that Palamon and Arcite will return in a month with three friends apiece and fight a tournament for Emilia. At the suggestion of a doctor, the jailer's daughter has sex with her former wooer and is cured of her madness. Before the tournament, Arcite prays to Mars, god of war, and Palamon prays to Venus, goddess of love. The gods help them both: Arcite wins the tournament, but is crushed by his horse, so Palamon wins Emilia.

THE TWO NOBLE KINSMEN: SCENE SUMMARY

PROLOGUE

The prologue compares the play to a virgin on her wedding night and asks for the audience's support.

The prologue compares the play that the audience is about to see to a virgin on her wedding night. He asks the audience not to boo the play too loudly so as not to offend Chaucer (whose *Knight's Tale* was Shakespeare's primary source) in his grave. He also asks for applause, and mentions that the theatrical troupe depends on financial support for its existence.

ACT I

Duke Theseus of Athens defeats the Theban King Creon and takes his nephews Palamon and Arcite prisoner.

I.I Location: Athens

Duke Theseus of Athens defers his marriage to the Amazon Queen Hippolyta to make war on the Theban King Creon.

Theseus, duke of Athens, has conquered the Amazons and is about to marry their queen, Hippolyta. A boy performs a song about flowers and birds. The song and the wedding procession are interrupted by the entrance of three queens, widows of three kings who died in a recent war with Thebes. They ask Theseus to declare war on King Creon of Thebes, who refused to bury their dead husbands. Theseus is sympathetic to their plight, but wants to marry Hippolyta first. However, the queens, joined by Hippolyta and Emilia, beg Theseus to defer the marriage until after defeating Creon. Theseus reluctantly assents and begins preparation for war. His friend Pirithous wants to help him in the war, but Theseus tells him to stay behind. The queens praise Theseus for the self-control he will exhibit by abstaining from sex with Hippolyta until after the war is over.

I.II Location: Thebes

Palamon and Arcite pledge to support Creon in the war against Theseus even though they think Creon corrupt.

Creon's nephews Palamon and Arcite discuss mortality. Arcite recommends that they should leave Thebes because the city is too corrupt. Palamon agrees, and complains about the treatment of the city soldiers who fought in the recent war. The soldiers were never paid and are not respected by the citizens for their service. Arcite reminds Palamon that they were discussing how the corruption in the city will lead to their own moral corruption, not the plight of the common soldiers. Palamon replies that he cannot be corrupted by a corrupt city. He does not blindly follow others. In religious language, he condemns Creon's villainous behavior. Arcite suggests again that they abandon Thebes and Creon's court.

Valerius enters to tell the cousins that Creon has called for them. They have just received word that Theseus will attack Thebes. Palamon and Arcite pledge to fight for Thebes against Theseus. In wartime it would be dishonorable to oppose Creon, even though Theseus is the more honorable man. Arcite suggests that they let the outcome of the war decide whether their decision to support Creon is morally good or bad.

I.III Location: near Athens

Emilia suggests that same-sex friendships are deeper than heterosexual love, but Hippolyta disagrees.

Hippolyta and Emilia have accompanied Pirithous on his journey from Athens to Thebes to help Theseus in the war against Creon. Pirithous leaves them, and commands them to go no further.

Emilia and Hippolyta discuss the intimate friendship between Theseus and Pirithous. Emilia reminisces about Flavina, a dear, close friend who died young. She adds that she could never love a man as much as she loved Flavina. Hippolyta claims that Emilia wants a man even if she claims not to. Indeed, if she, Hippolyta, believed Emilia's claim that same-sex relationships are deeper than heterosexual relationships, she would not marry Theseus for fear that he loved Pirithous. Emilia continues to disagree.

I.IV Location: near Athens

Theseus has defeated Creon and takes Palamon and Arcite prisoner.

Theseus enters victorious. The three queens praise and thank him. As they leave, Theseus notices Palamon and Arcite lying unconscious. He learns from a herald that they are Creon's nephews, and remembers their valor in combat. Theseus sends for a doctor to resuscitate them in order to take them prisoner. He plans to take Thebes and return to Athens to marry Hippolyta.

I.V Location: near Athens

The three dead kings are buried.

A funeral dirge begins the burial of the three dead kings. The three queens bid adieu to their husbands.

ACT II

Arcite and Palamon fall in love with Emilia; Arcite, disguised, becomes Emilia's servant; the jailer's daughter falls in love with Palamon and frees him from jail.

II.I Location: Athens. Garden outside the jail

The jailer's daughter, who is engaged to the wooer, is quite taken with the imprisoned Palamon and Arcite.

The jailer and the wooer discuss the financial arrangements of the wooer's upcoming marriage to the jailer's daughter. She comes in with fresh rushes for Palamon and Arcite's cell. She praises Palamon and Arcite's friendship, patience, and noble character. They see the two above (on a balcony), and the jailer and his daughter debate which one is which.

II.II Location: Athens. The jail

In jail, Palamon and Arcite both glimpse and fall in love with Emilia; Arcite is freed from jail but banished from Athens.

Palamon laments his and Arcite's imprisonment. He misses hunting and battles. Arcite thinks it is a shame that they will never be able to marry and reproduce, and encourages Palamon to enjoy their togetherness patiently. If they were free, life might separate them. Palamon agrees that the outside world is often petty.

Emilia enters the garden below. Palamon notices her and stops speaking. Emilia asks her maid about the narcissus (a flower named after the mythological figure who loved himself) she has picked. Palamon has fallen in love with Emilia, and tells Arcite that he wishes to be free to be with her. Arcite looks at her and also falls in love with her. Emilia and her waiting woman banter with sexual puns and go back inside (to sleep together, some critics suggest).

When Arcite confesses to Palamon that he is in love with Emilia, Palamon commands him not to be because he, Palamon, saw her first. Arcite says that he and Palamon are so close that it makes sense that they have fallen in love with the same woman. Palamon threatens to kill him, but Arcite scorns his threat.

The jailer comes in and sends Arcite to see Theseus, who frees him from prison but banishes him from Athens. Palamon worries that Arcite will marry Emilia. The jailer announces that Palamon will be moved to another cell, one that does not overlook the garden.

II.III   Location: outside Athens

Arcite resolves to compete in a sporting competition to win Emilia's admiration.

Arcite laments his freedom, which has separated him from Emilia. He resolves to disguise himself as a beggar and sneak back into Athens.

Four Theban countrymen enter, passing on their way to games (sporting competitions). The first countryman says that his wife will be angry at him for skipping work, but he'll appease her with a good night of sex. A series of racy double entendres ensues. The countrymen also discuss plans for a morris dance (a traditional English folk dance) in the forest after the games. The stuffy schoolmaster will direct the dance.

Arcite asks the countrymen about the games and they explain: they are in honor of Theseus and will include wrestling and running. They leave, and Arcite resolves to compete in the games to make Emilia admire him.

II.IV   Location: Athens. The jail

The jailer's daughter is in love with Palamon, and decides to break him out of jail in order to sleep with him.

The jailer's daughter speaks about her "infinite" love for Palamon. Though she is too poor to marry him, and though she should not have sex with him without marrying him, she decides to free him, despite her father's wrath, so that she can sleep with him.

II.V   Location: Athens

Disguised, Arcite wins the tournament and Theseus's favor, and becomes Emilia's servant.

Arcite, disguised, has won the tournament. Theseus commends him, and Arcite asks for a place in his court. He is made a servant to Emilia. Pirithous offers Arcite a horse, which Arcite says that he will like all the more because it is rough.

II.VI   Location: Athens. Near the jail

The jailer's daughter has freed Palamon and returned to fetch food and a metal file.

In a monologue, the jailer's daughter reveals that she has set Palamon free and left him in the forest, promising to return with food and a metal file to remove his shackles. Palamon did not want her to free him because he did not want her or the jailer to be punished. He has not even kissed her, but she believes that he will come to love her. She knows that because of her behavior her father will be punished with imprisonment at the very least.

ACT III

Theseus, Palamon, and Arcite decide that Palamon and Arcite will duel for Emilia's hand; the loser will be put to death.

III.I Location: the forest near Athens

Arcite runs into the shackled Palamon in the forest, and they plan to duel that night.

Arcite feels lucky to have become Emilia's servant. Suddenly Palamon, in shackles, breaks out of a bush and yells that he would kill Arcite if he were free and had a weapon. Arcite responds in a friendly way, but Palamon insults Arcite's honor and goads him into agreeing to a duel. The duel will be fought on fair terms, after Arcite frees Palamon from his shackles, feeds him, and brings him a sword. Arcite agrees to bring him a metal file, a meal, and a sword that night. Arcite embraces Palamon, but Palamon is still hostile. Hearing Theseus approach, Arcite urges Palamon to hide in the bushes. Arcite agrees to the duel.

III.II Location: another part of the forest

The jailer's daughter cannot find Palamon and resolves to kill herself.

The jailer's daughter has come for Palamon, but cannot find him. She worries that he has been eaten by wolves, and realizes that by freeing Palamon she has doomed her father to be hanged. She decides to kill herself.

III.III Location: the forest near Athens

Arcite frees and feeds Palamon, who picks another fight over Emilia.

In the middle of the night, Arcite brings food, drink, and metal files for Palamon. Arcite suggests that they speak of something other than Emilia. Palamon reminds Arcite about a girl whom Arcite got pregnant. Arcite remembers a sexual tryst of Palamon's. Palamon hears Arcite sigh, thinks that the sigh is for Emilia, and accuses Arcite of breaking their agreement not to mention her. Arcite says that Palamon is too worked up, and promises to return the next day with armor and a sword.

III.IV Location: another part of the forest

Unable to find Palamon, the jailer's daughter has gone mad.

The jailer's daughter has become insane, believing Palamon dead. She imagines that she sees a sinking ship. She remembers that her father will be hanged the next day. She breaks into song and leaves.

III.V Location: a third part of the forest

Led by the schoolmaster, the countrymen, including the jailer's daughter, perform a morris dance for Theseus.

The schoolmaster leads the preparations for the morris dance. One of the female dancers is missing. The jailer's daughter enters, singing, and the countrymen decide to incorporate her into morris dance. The schoolmaster hears Theseus's hunting horns and tells the dancers to hide.

Theseus, Pirithous, Hippolyta, Emilia, and Arcite enter, hunting a wild stag. The schoolmaster asks Theseus, very pretentiously, to watch their dance. The countrymen pair up into a lord and lady of May, a servingman and a chambermaid, a host and his spouse, a clown and the fool (likely played by the jailer's daughter), and a man dressed as a baboon with a long tail and penis. The pairs dance.

The schoolmaster asks Theseus for compensation, and Theseus promises to reward them.

III.VI Location: the forest near Athens

To punish Palamon and Arcite for dueling in the forest, Theseus plans another combat, whose winner will marry Emilia and whose loser will be put to death.

Palamon awaits Arcite, whom he deems a fair foe. Arcite arrives. The two cordially arm each other, but plan to fight in earnest. They remember each other's bravery in the recent battle against Theseus. They ceremoniously prepare to fight, but the duel is interrupted by Theseus's approach. Theseus, Pirithous, Hippolyta, and Emilia enter the stage, still hunting for the stag. Theseus sees the combatants and immediately sentences them to death.

Palamon explains that he and Arcite are battling because of Emilia, and asks Theseus to let them finish the duel and sentence the winner to death. Hippolyta urges Emilia to beg for Palamon's and Arcite's lives, and Emilia reluctantly agrees. Together with Pirithous, Hippolyta and Emilia plead with Theseus to spare Palamon and Arcite. Emilia appeals to his kindness and virtue; Hippolyta to their marriage; and Pirithous to the things that Theseus loves.

Emilia says that it is absurd for men to die for her love, and asks Theses to banish them if they swear to stop loving her. Palamon and Arcite refuse, and Theseus asks Emilia to choose one to marry, and the other to be put to death. Emilia says that she cannot choose. Theseus devises a solution: Palamon and Arcite will fight each other (each is allowed three allies). The winner will marry Emilia and the loser will be put to death. They will be Theseus's guests until the combat.

ACT IV

Theseus and his court prepare for the duel; the doctor says that the wooer should court the jailer's daughter as Palamon in order to cure her from her madness.

IV.I Location: Athens. Outside the jail

The jailer has been pardoned for allowing Palamon to escape, but the jailer's daughter is mad.

The jailer's first friend tells him the story of the meeting between Theseus, Palamon, and Arcite in the forest. The jailer's second friend comes in to tell the jailer that Palamon has procured a pardon for both the jailer and the jailer's daughter. The wooer comes in, and tells the jailer that he was out fishing and heard the daughter singing near the lake. She tried to drown herself and although he managed to save her, she ran away. The jailer's brother caught her and is on his way to bring her home.

The jailer's brother comes in with the jailer's daughter. She sings, and acknowledges neither the jailer (her father) nor the jailer's brother (her uncle). She says that she must lose her virginity by dawn, and talks about Palamon having sex with twenty women a night. Saddened, the jailer and his friends bring the jailer's mad daughter inside.

IV.II Location: Athens. Theseus's palace

Theseus eagerly awaits Palamon and Arcite's duel, but Emilia feels guilty.

Emilia considers Palamon's and Arcite's relative merits. Arcite is more manly and handsome, but Palamon is melancholy like the heavenly Narcissus (the young man who fell in love with his own image, from Greek mythology). Emilia realizes that she cannot choose between them.

A gentleman announces that Arcite and Palamon are ready to begin their combat. Emilia wishes herself dead. That way, she would keep her chastity and neither Palamon nor Arcite would die. Theseus, Hippolyta, and Pirithous enter. Theseus is eager to see the match, but Emilia is troubled.

A messenger comes in and praises one of Arcite's ally knights. Pirithous counters with a long description of one of Palamons's allies. The messenger tells of a third knight who combines the best attributes of the first two, but is quite short. Theseus is eager to see the match, but Hippolyta notices Emilia weeping.

Theseus leads the way to the forest to see the fight. Left alone, Emilia blames herself for the upcoming battle.

IV.III Location: Athens. The jail

The doctor suggests that the wooer pretend to be Palamon and court the jailer's daughter in order to cure her.

The doctor examines the jailer's daughter. Raving mad, she incessantly talks about death: chaste women scorned by their lovers die and pick flowers in the underworld, but promiscuous women go to hellish places. The doctor concludes that she is profoundly lovesick for Palamon. To cure her, the wooer whom the jailer's daughter once loved should pretend to be Palamon and love her in return.

ACT V

Arcite wins the duel, but is crushed by his horse, so Palamon wins Emilia.

V.I Location: Athens. The altar to Mars

Palamon and Arcite embrace before their duel, and Arcite prays to Mars, god of war.

Theseus summons Palamon and Arcite to pray before their duel. Palamon and Arcite steel themselves for battle, and embrace with a final farewell. After Palamon and his knights leave, Arcite prays to Mars, the god of war, and asks for victory. He and his knights prostrate themselves. They hear a "clanging of armor" (V.i.62–63 SD) and the beginning of battle, and interpret the sounds as a favorable sign from Mars.

V.II Location: Athens. The altar to Venus

Palamon prays to Venus, goddess of love, before the duel.

Palamon enters with his knights to pray to Venus, the goddess of love. He praises Venus's hot flames and claims to have been always faithful to the laws of love and honor. He keeps confidence, has never committed adultery, and does not keep company with braggarts who do not respect women. He asks Venus for victory. Doves flutter across the stage and music sounds, which are favorable signs from Venus.

V.III Location: Athens. The altar to Diana

Emilia prays to Diana, goddess of chastity.

Emilia prays to Diana, goddess of chastity and the hunt. Emilia wears white, and her attendant carries a vessel for incense in the shape of a silver doe to offer as a sacrifice to Diana. She says that Palamon and Arcite are equally worthy in her eyes, and she cannot choose between them. Emilia asks Diana to let the one who loves her more win, or rather to let her stay chaste. The hind, burning at the altar, disappears, and is replaced with a bush with a single rose, which is a sign that Emilia interprets to mean that both Palamon and Arcite will be killed and that Emilia will be able to stay a virgin. The rose falls from the tree and Emilia realizes that she will lose her virginity after all, although she wonders to whom she will lose it.

V.IV Location: Athens. The jail

At the doctor's instigation, the jailer's daughter and the wooer leave to have sex in order to cure her.

The wooer tells the doctor and the jailer that he has partially convinced the jailer's daughter that he is Palamon, and has kissed her twice. The doctor replies that the more kisses, the better the cure. Indeed, the wooer should have sex with the jailer's daughter if she is willing because sex will cure her. The jailer has his doubts, but the doctor insists that sex is the only cure.

V.V Location: the forest near Athens

From near the jousting field, Emilia hears that Arcite has won.

On the way to the tournament, Emilia stops and refuses to go further: she does not want to watch anyone die. Theseus insists that as the prize, she must be present at the duel. Emilia holds her ground and Theseus acquiesces. Everyone but Emilia leaves.

Alone, Emilia hears the trumpets that signal the beginning of the duel. She says that Palamon and Arcite appear menacing as well as noble to her. She hears a cry, which means that Palamon has won. A servant arrives to announce the news, but Emilia sends him back to make sure. The servant returns to say that the duel is not over yet. Another cry sounds, meaning that Arcite has won. Theseus, Hippolyta, and Arcite come in. Theseus announces that Arcite will marry Emilia. Emilia asks Arcite whether she is worth losing his closest friend, a man more worthy than any woman. Hippolyta and Theseus both agree that it is a shame that Palamon must die.

V.VI Location: the forest near Athens

Arcite has been crushed by his horse; instead of being executed, Palamon will marry Emilia.

Palamon and his three knights await execution, which is supervised by the jailer. Palamon expresses regret to his three knights. Palamon sees the jailer and remembers hearing about the jailer's daughter's illness. The jailer says that she has been healed and will be married. Palamon and the knights decide to give their wealth to the jailer's daughter for her dowry.

EPILOGUE

The epilogue hopes that the audience enjoyed the play.

The epilogue asks the audience whether they liked the play. If they did, the company will put on more plays.

THEMES, MOTIFS, & SYMBOLS IN *THE TWO NOBLE KINSMEN*

THEMES

LIFE'S JUXTAPOSITION OF HAPPINESS AND SORROW The play opens with Theseus and Hippolyta's wedding ceremony, where a singer urges us to banish thoughts of suffering and death. Soon after, however, the three queens mourn their husbands and banish everything happy and light. Throughout, the play stresses that life's events are complex and cannot be interpreted as simply happy or tragic. The end of the play unites Arcite's death and Palamon's marriage. The two are inseparable in Theseus's final speech. Shakespeare suggests that like his play, human life is neither a tragedy nor a comedy: it is both and therefore neither.

HOMOSOCIAL VERSUS ROMANTIC RELATIONSHIPS Emilia believes that love between two people of the same sex is deeper than heterosexual love. Hippolyta argues that heterosexual relationships are inevitable. Both the Sonnets and this play suggest that Shakespeare agrees with both of his heroines. Some critics see Theseus as the sole example of a man who has found a delicate balance between his love for Pirithous and his love for Hippolyta.

COMPULSORY SEX Hippolyta, Emilia, and the jailer's daughter are all compelled into sexual relationships without choice. Hippolyta must marry Theseus after he defeats the Amazons. Emilia must marry either Palamon or Arcite, although she would have preferred to stay chaste. The jailer's daughter sleeps with the wooer thinking that he is Palamon. The heterosexual relationships in the play are neither romantic not mutually decided. This pessimistic view of human relationships contributes to the darkness of the play.

MOTIFS

HONOR   Both Palamon and Arcite are deeply concerned with their honor. They fight for Creon and Thebes even though they think both corrupt. Later they fight each other to defend their honor. Their code of honor is constricting, but it allows them to act without getting mired in considerations and thought.

RITUALISTIC CEREMONIES   Theseus's wedding procession in the first act is juxtaposed with the funeral of the three kings. Both begin with songs. The wedding song banishes ill omens, pain, and thoughts of death, and the funeral dirge banishes happiness. These ceremonies allow characters to react in simple, prescribed ways to complicated situations in life.

SYMBOLS

SHIPS   As in other late romances such as *The Tempest* and *Pericles*, Shakespeare uses maritime imagery in *The Two Noble Kinsmen* as a metaphor for the precarious nature of human life. The jailer's daughter has a vision of a sinking ship as she goes mad. When Arcite is close to death, Pirithous describes him as a ship about to be overturned by the next wave. Ships also suggest loneliness and isolation within the imperfect relationships of the play.

IMPORTANT QUOTATIONS FROM *THE TWO NOBLE KINSMEN*

---

1. *King Capaneus was your lord: the day*
   That he should marry you—at such a season
   As now it is with me—I met your groom
   By Mars's altar. You were that time fair,
   Not Juno's mantle fairer than your tresses,
   Nor in more bounty spread her. Your wheaten wreath
   Was then nor threshed nor blasted; fortune at you
   Dimpled her cheek with smiles; Hercules our kinsman—
   Then weaker than your eyes—laid by his club.
   He tumbled down upon his Nemean hide
   And swore his sinews thawed. O grief and time,
   Fearful consumers, you will all devour.

Location: I.i.59–70
Speaker: Theseus to the first queen
Context: In response to the first queen's request that Theseus attack Creon, Theseus remarks how much the first queen has changed since her wedding day.

Theseus's wedding ceremony has been attempting to banish all grief. For example, the boy singer sings about roses without thorns. The queens who interrupt the wedding remind Theseus that life has a darker side: their dead husbands lie unburied, fodder for birds.

   In this passage, Theseus also comments on the power of love: Hercules was subdued by the queen's beauty on her wedding day. Similarly, Emilia's beauty destroys Palamon and Arcite's friendship, and Palamon's beauty drives the jailer's daughter mad. These lines remind us that beauty, however powerful, is fleeting, and inevitably gives way to grief.

---

2. *'Tis in our power,*
   Unless we fear that apes can tutor's, to
   Be masters of our manners. What need I
   Affect another's gait, which is not catching
   Where there is faith? Or be fond upon

Another's way of speech, when by mine own
I may be reasonably conceived—saved, too—
Speaking it truly? . . .
Either I am
The fore-horse in the team or I am none
That draw i'th' sequent trace.

Location: I.ii.42–60
Speaker: Palamon to Arcite
Context: Arcite is concerned that Thebes will corrupt him and Palamon, but Palamon responds that he is unaffected by others' behavior

Palamon exhibits both his deep pride and his scorn for others. To justify himself, he finds recourse in the vocabulary of Protestant Christians: one's moral character is determined by "faith" and not by "works" (the classic Protestant dichotomy). He believes that he himself is "saved." Palamon's religious language here foreshadows his veneration of Emilia as goddess. Palamon's self-righteousness resurfaces throughout the play, although in the end he prays to Venus and seeks to justify himself by "works" (the tournament with Arcite) rather than by faith.

---

3. *This world's a city full of straying streets,*
   And death's the market-place where each one meets.

Location: I.v.15–16
Speaker: Third queen
Context: The queens bury their dead husbands

These lines, like Theseus's comment that "grief and time . . . will all devour" (I.i.69–70; see Quote 1), cast a long shadow over the play. Death hangs over all lives, and despite the characters' petty struggles to find love, they will all eventually die. Any happiness is tempered by the knowledge that all happiness is ephemeral.

---

4. *I knew a man*
   Of eighty winters, this I told them, who
   A lass of fourteen brided—'twas thy power
   To put life into dust. The agèd cramp
   Had screwed his square foot round,
   The gout had knit his fingers into knots,
   Torturing convulsions from his globy eyes
   Had almost drawn their spheres, that what was life
   In him seemed torture. This anatomy
   Had by his young fair fere a boy, and I
   Believed it was his, for she swore it was,
   And who would not believe her?

Location: V.ii.39–50
Speaker: Palamon
Context: Palamon prays to Venus before his tournament with Arcite

Palamon tells the story of an old man whose fourteen-year-old child bride had borne him a son to suggest that the power of love, which is Venus's domain, can give life the most abject of creatures.

---

5. *O you heavenly charmers,*

What things you make of us! For what we lack
We laugh, for what we have, are sorry; still
Are children in some kind. Let us be thankful
For that which is, and with you leave dispute
That are above our question. Let's go off
And bear us like the time.

Location: V.vi.131–37
Speaker: Theseus
Context: At the play's conclusion, Theseus remarks how powerless people are before the gods

Theseus suggests that the gods routinely toy with humans in shaping their destinies. Humans are unable to see themselves objectively and human judgment is always inadequate. (This point has been made several times in the play. For example, as soon as Theseus and Hippolyta resolve to banish death for their wedding, three queens appear to bemoan their unburied dead husbands.) The gods will always thwart human attempts to understand their lives. Because humans cannot understand their lives, events are ambiguous. After the duel, Arcite prepares to marry Emilia and Palamon prepares to die, but both judge incorrectly. Theseus urges people to stop trying to control their lives.

THE WINTER'S TALE

King Leontes' insane jealousy causes him to lose his friend Polixenes, his wife Hermione, and his daughter Perdita, but when Perdita grows up and marries Polixenes' son Florizel, Hermione comes to life and all are reconciled.

THE WINTER'S TALE IN CONTEXT

The Winter's Tale is one of Shakespeare's final plays. Composed and performed around 1609–1611, it joins *Pericles, Cymbeline*, and *The Tempest* on the roster of later plays that scholars usually refer to as romances, or tragicomedies. These plays have happy endings that set them apart from earlier histories and tragedies, but each emphasizes the imminence of death and the danger of evil in the world. *The Winter's Tale* ends with joy and reconciliation, but we must endure Leontes' savage madness as well as the deaths of three innocent people—Mamillius, Hermione, and Antigonus—on the way to the happy resolution.

There is no single source for *The Winter's Tale*, although Shakespeare relies heavily on *Pandosto*, a 1588 prose romance by the London writer Robert Greene. Greene, who was dead by 1592, was likely the author of a pamphlet attacking Shakespeare, which makes Shakespeare's appropriation of his work particularly ironic. Shakespeare borrowed most of the characters and events of the first three acts from *Pandosto*, but created several characters, such as Autolycus and Paulina. The story of the abandoned royal baby raised by peasants owes much to contemporary popular folklore, and the seasonal themes touched upon in Act IV echo Ovid's *Metamorphoses*. Perdita is associated with Proserpina (or Persephone), the goddess whose emergence from the underworld in Greek mythology was supposed to herald the return of spring. The resurrection of Hermione in Act V owes an obvious debt to Ovid's story of Pygmalion, in which a sculptor's work comes to life through divine intervention.

In terms of strength of character, unity of plot, and audience satisfaction, *The Winter's Tale* may be the best of the later romances, and has been a favorite of directors and audiences to the present day.

THE WINTER'S TALE: KEY FACTS

Full title: The Winter's Tale

Time and place written: Between 1609–1611; London

Date of first performance: Likely 1611

Genre: Romance

Setting (time): Fairy-tale past

Setting (place): Sicilia and Bohemia

Protagonists: Hermione, Leontes, Perdita

Major conflict: Leontes loses his wife Hermione and daughter Perdita because of his jealousy.

THE WINTER'S TALE: CHARACTER LIST

Antigonus Paulina's husband and Hermione's loyal supporter. He is given the unfortunate task of abandoning the baby Perdita on the Bohemian coast.

Archidamus A lord of Bohemia.

Autolycus A roguish peddler, vagabond, and pickpocket. Autolycus steals the clown's purse and does a great deal of pilfering at the shepherd's sheepshearing, but at the end helps Perdita and Florizel elope.

Camillo An honest Sicilian nobleman. Camillo refuses to follow Leontes' order to poison Polixenes, deciding instead to flee Sicily and serve Polixenes instead.

Cleomenes A lord of Sicilia, sent to Delphi to ask the oracle about Hermione's guilt.

Clown The shepherd's buffoonish son, and Perdita's adopted brother.

Dion A Sicilian lord. Dion accompanies Cleomenes to Delphi.

Emilia One of Hermione's ladies-in-waiting.

Florizel Polixenes' only son and heir. Florizel falls in love with Perdita unaware of her royal ancestry, and defies his father by eloping with her.

Hermione The virtuous and beautiful queen of Sicilia. Falsely accused of infidelity by her husband Leontes, she is announced dead of grief just after being vindicated by the oracle of Delphi, but is restored to life at the play's close.

Leontes The king of Sicilia, Hermione's husband, and Polixenes' childhood friend. He is gripped by jealous fantasies that convince him that Polixenes has been having an affair with Hermione. Leontes' jealousy leads to the destruction of his family.

Mamillius The young prince of Sicilia, and Leontes' and Hermione's son. Mamillius dies of grief after his father wrongly imprisons his mother.

Paulina A noblewoman of Sicilia. Paulina fiercely defends Hermione's virtue, and unrelentingly condemns Leontes after Hermione's death. She brings about the (apparently) dead Hermione's resurrection.

Perdita The daughter of Leontes and Hermione. Because her father believes her to be illegitimate, she is abandoned as a baby on the coast of Bohemia and brought up by a shepherd. Unaware of her royal lineage, she falls in love with the Bohemian Prince Florizel.

Polixenes The king of Bohemia and Leontes' boyhood friend. He is falsely accused of having an affair with Leontes' wife, and barely escapes Sicilia with his life. Much later in life, he sees his only son fall in love with Perdita, whom he believes a lowly shepherd's daughter but is, in fact, a Sicilian princess.

Shepherd An old and honorable sheep-tender. The shepherd finds Perdita as a baby and raises her as his own daughter.

THE WINTER'S TALE: PLOT OVERVIEW

While King Polixenes of Bohemia is on an extended visit to his childhood friend King Leontes of Sicilia, Leontes becomes convinced that his pregnant wife Hermione is cheating on him with Polixenes, and that the baby she is carrying is illegitimate. Driven insane by his jealousy, Leontes plots to poison Polixenes, but Polixenes manages to escape. Further enraged by Polixenes' flight, Leontes throws Hermione into prison. To mollify his outraged court, he sends messengers to the oracle of Delphi to confirm his suspicions. When Hermione gives birth to a baby girl, Leontes gives the baby to a lord named Antigonus to abandon in some desolate place. The oracle sends word that Hermione is innocent, and that Leontes will have no heir until his daughter is found. Word arrives that Mamillius, Leontes' and Hermione's young son, has died. Hermione too dies of grief. Leontes realizes that he has made a terrible mistake and pledges to spend the rest of his life in penance for his sins.

Antigonus, following the instructions given to him in a dream by Hermione, names the baby Perdita and leaves her on the coast of Bohemia, after which he is killed by a bear. Perdita is found and raised by a shepherd. Sixteen years later, Polixenes' son Florizel falls in love with Perdita. When Polixenes refuses to let Florizel marry her, they elope and flee to Sicilia. There, the shepherd who raised Perdita reveals her story, and Leontes is reunited with his daughter and reconciled with Polixenes. Paulina, a lady in Leontes' court, brings a lifelike statue of Hermione to life, and the Sicilian royal family is reunited.

THE WINTER'S TALE: SCENE SUMMARY

ACT I

Convinced that his friend King Polixenes of Bohemia is sleeping with his wife Hermione, King Leontes of Sicilia plots to poison Polixenes, but Polixenes manages to escape.

I.I Location: Sicilia. Leontes' palace

Two lords discuss the friendship between King Leontes of Sicilia and King Polixenes of Bohemia, who is visiting Leontes.

King Polixenes of Bohemia has been visiting his childhood friend, King Leontes of Sicilia. Camillo, one of Leontes' lords, discusses the striking differences between the two kingdoms with Archidamus, a Bohemian nobleman. The conversation turns to the great and enduring friendship between Leontes and Polixenes, and the beauty and promise of Leontes' young son Mamillius.

I.II   Location: Sicilia. Leontes' palace

Jealous of his wife Hermione and Polixenes' bond, Leontes schemes to have Polixenes poisoned, but Polixenes escapes to Bohemia.

Polixenes prepares to depart for home. Leontes pleads with him to stay a little longer in Sicilia, but Polixenes refuses: he has been away from Bohemia for nine months, which is long enough. But when Hermione asks Polixenes to extend his stay a little while longer, he yields to her entreaties. Polixenes reminisces about his wonderful childhood with Leontes, when they were "[t]wo lads that thought there was no more behind / But such a day tomorrow as today, / And to be boy eternal" (I.ii.64–66).

Leontes tells Hermione her supplication to Polixenes, which convinced Polixenes to extend his stay, is the best thing she has ever said besides agreeing to marry Leontes. But as Hermione and Polixenes walk together, apart from him, Leontes feels stirrings of jealousy and tells us that he suspects that they are lovers. He turns to his son Mamillius and notes that the boy resembles him, and this reassures him that Mamillius is, in fact, *his* son and not someone else's. His suspicion of Hermione remains, however, and escalates until he is certain that she is sleeping with Polixenes. He sends the two of them to walk in the garden together, promising to join them later, and then calls Camillo over, asking if he has noticed anything peculiar about Polixenes' behavior lately. Camillo says that he has not. Leontes accuses him of being negligent, and then declares that Hermione and Polixenes have made him a cuckold). Appalled, Camillo refuses to believe it, but Leontes insists that it is true, and orders Camillo to be Polixenes' cupbearer and to poison Polixenes at the first opportunity.

Camillo promises to obey, but his conscience is greatly troubled. When Leontes leaves and Polixenes reappears, Polixenes has realized that something is amiss. He tells Camillo that Leontes just gave him a peculiar and threatening look, and demands to know what is going on. After some hesitation, Camillo tells Polixenes about Leontes' jealousy and order to poison Polixenes. He begs Polixenes for protection, and Polixenes accepts him into his service. They resolve to flee Sicilia immediately by sneaking out of the castle and taking a ship for Bohemia. Camillo promises to use his authority in Sicilia to help them escape.

ACT II

Leontes arrests Hermione for infidelity and orders her newborn baby girl abandoned in the wilderness, over his court's protests.

II.I   Location: Sicilia. Leontes' palace

Leontes arrests Hermione on charges of treasonous adultery, but promises his shocked lords to consult the oracle at Delphi.

Hermione asks her little son Mamillius to tell her a story. Leontes storms in, having just learned of Camillo's betrayal and Polixenes' escape. Now he is convinced that his suspicions of Hermione and Polixenes were correct. He orders Mamillius taken away from Hermione and then accuses Hermione, who is pregnant, of carrying Polixenes' child. Hermione, astonished, denies it vigorously, but to no avail. Leontes orders her taken away to jail. She is taken off, accompanied by her ladies-in-waiting. After she has been dragged off, the lords of Sicilia plead with Leontes, declaring that Hermione is innocent. Her most vocal defender is a lord named Antigonus. Leontes will have none of it. He self-righteously insists that the matter is none of their concern. Nonetheless, he promises to ask the celebrated oracle of Apollo at Delphi for a verdict before proceeding against his wife.

II.II   Location: a prison in Sicilia

Hermione's companion Paulina is not allowed to visit Hermione in prison, but manages to take Hermione's newborn baby away to Leontes.

Antigonus's wife Paulina attempts to visit Hermione in prison, but is rebuffed by the guards. She is allowed to speak to Emilia, one of Hermione's ladies, who reports that Hermione has given birth to a beautiful daughter. Over the uncertain jailer's protests, Paulina decides to take the baby and bring her to Leontes in the hopes that the sight of his newborn daughter will mollify his rage.

II.III   Location: Sicilia. Leontes' palace

Leontes orders Antigonus to abandon Hermione's baby girl in the wilderness.

Mamillius has fallen sick since Hermione's imprisonment. Leontes attributes Mamillius's illness to shame over his mother's infidelity. At the same time, he angrily wishes that Polixenes had not managed to escape his wrath. Paulina arrives with Hermione's baby, but Leontes grows furious and demands Antigonus why he cannot manage to control his wife Paulina. Paulina defends Hermione's honor, lays the baby before Leontes, and then departs. Leontes orders Antigonus to take the child away and throw it into the fire, so that he will never have to see another man's bastard call him father. His lords are horrified and beg Leontes to reconsider. He relents after a moment, but only slightly. Instead of burning the infant, he tells Antigonus to carry it into the wilderness and leave it there. After Antigonus unhappily departs with the child, word arrives that the messengers to the oracle of Delphi have returned with the divine verdict.

ACT III

Hermione is announced to be dead of grief just after the oracle at Delphi pronounces her innocent; a Bohemian shepherd discovers her baby, Perdita.

III.I   Location: Sicilia. A road

Two messengers return to the palace with the oracle's verdict.

On the way back from the oracle at Delphi, Sicilian lords Dion and Cleomenes discuss recent events and hope that the message they bring from the oracle will vindicate the unfortunate Hermione.

III.II   Location: Sicilia. A court of law

After Leontes sentences Hermione to death, the messengers from the oracle arrive to vindicate her, but she is announced dead of grief.

Leontes convenes a court, with himself as judge, to try Hermione for treasonous adultery. She is brought in from prison, and the indictment, charging her with adultery and conspiracy in Polixenes' and Camillo's escape, is read to the entire court. Hermione defends herself eloquently, saying that she loved Polixenes "as in honor he required" (III.ii.61), but no more; that she is ignorant of any conspiracy; and that Camillo is an honest man. Leontes pays little heed to her words, declares that she is guilty, and sentences her to death. Hermione bitterly retorts that given her sufferings so far, death would be a blessed release.

Dion and Cleomenes arrive with the message from the oracle. The seal is broken and the message is read aloud. "Hermione is chaste," it reports, "Polixenes blameless, Camillo a true subject, Leontes a jealous tyrant, his innocent babe truly begotten, and the King shall live without an heir if that which is lost be not found" (III.ii.131–34). The court rejoices, but Leontes refuses to believe the oracle's words.

A servant rushes in and announced that Mamillius has died. The enormity of Leontes' mistake comes crashing down on him. Hermione faints, and is quickly carried away by her ladies and Paulina, who frantically attempt to revive her. Leontes, now grief-stricken, pours curses upon his own head. Paulina reenters and announces that Hermione too has died, and that it is he who has murdered her. One of the lords rebukes her, but Leontes accepts her accusation as no more than his due. He orders a single grave for Hemione's and Mamillius's bodies, and pledges to spend the rest of his life doing penance for his sin.

III.III   Location: the Bohemian coast

Antigonus leaves Hermione's baby, Perdita, on the Bohemian coast, where a shepherd and his son discover her.

Unaware of what has happened in the Sicilian court, Antigonus has arrived on the desolate Bohemian coast bearing the infant princess. He says that Hermione appeared to him in a dream, told him to name the baby Perdita, and declared that he would never again see his wife Paulina. He lays the infant down in the woods. Next to her he places gold and jewels, as well as a note about her history and family. As he prepares to depart, a storm arises, and a bear appears and chases Antigonus away.

A shepherd comes in and finds Perdita. He is joined by his son, a clown, who reports seeing a bear kill a man (Antigonus), and a ship (Antigonus's vessel) go down in the storm. The shepherd and the clown discover the treasure left by Antigonus. They rejoice in their good fortune and vow to raise the baby themselves.

ACT IV

Sixteen years later, Polixenes' son Florizel wants to marry Perdita, and elopes with her to Sicilia when Polixenes forbids the marriage.

IV.I   Sixteen years pass.

Time passes.

The character Time appears and announces that sixteen years have passed.

IV.II   Location: Bohemia. Polixenes' palace

Polixenes refuses to let Camillo to return to Sicilia; instead, they plan to spy on Polixenes' son Florizel, who has been spending time with a shepherd's daughter.

In conversation with Polixenes, Camillo asks him for leave to return to his native Sicilia. His years away have made him homesick, and the still-grieving Leontes has asked him to return. Polixenes replies that he cannot manage the kingdom without Camillo's assistance. They discuss Polixines' son Florizel, who has been spending a great deal of time away from court at the house of a wealthy shepherd whose daughter (Perdita) is reputed to be a great beauty. Somewhat worried, Polixenes decides that they will visit this shepherd's house, but in disguise, and see what Florizel is up to.

IV.III   Location: Bohemia. Near the shepherd's cottage

The pickpocket Autolycus steals the clown's money and plans to come to the local sheepshearing festival.

Autolycus, a jovial vagabond, peddler, and thief, sings loudly as he wanders along a road. He encounters the clown counting a substantial sum of money with which he plans to go to the market to buy supplies for the country sheepshearing festivities. Autolycus accosts him and pretends to be the victim of a robbery. As the clown commiserates with him, the crafty Autolycus picks his pocket. After the clown leaves, Autolycus resolves to make an appearance at the sheepshearing in a different disguise.

IV.IV   Location: Bohemia. In front of the shepherd's cottage

At the sheepshearing festival, Polixenes catches Florizel courting Perdita and forbids their union; counseled by Camillo, Florizel and Perdita decide to flee to Sicilia.

On the day of the sheepshearing festival, Perdita meets her beau Florizel. She is decked out in flowers, and he compliments her on her grace and beauty. Perdita is concerned whether they could ever marry, given that Florizel's father Polixenes will oppose their union. Florizel reassures her: "I'll be thine, my fair, / Or not my father's" (IV.iv.42–43). The shepherd comes in with a large crowd, including the clown, a group of shepherdesses, and the disguised Polixenes and Camillo. The shepherd tells Perdita to be the hostess, as is proper, and so she busies herself distributing flowers to the new arrivals and becomes involved in a discussion of horticulture with Polixenes. Watching her, Florizel effusively declares his love. Polixenes remarks to Camillo that Perdita is too pretty and gracious to be a shepherd's daughter. He asks the shepherd about Florizel, whom Perdita and the shepherd know as Doricles. The shepherd says that Doricles is a gentleman, and that he and Perdita are deeply in love.

Meanwhile, a peddler—Autolycus in disguise—arrives, promising to entertain the party with songs. He sells ballads to the clown and the shepherdesses, and then begins to sing. Polixenes asks Florizel (who does not recognize Polixenes) why Florizel has bought nothing for Perdita. Florizel answers that Perdita does not care about the peddler's trifles. Florizel asks the shepherd for Perdita's hand. The shepherd is about to agree when Polixenes asks Florizel why he has not consulted Florizel's father. Florizel says he has his reasons.

Polixenes throws off his disguise and forbids the betrothal. He sentences the shepherd to death and Perdita to disfigurement, threatens to disinherit Florizel if he ever speaks of Perdita again, and orders Florizel to follow him to court. He soon relents, however, and spares the shepherd's life and Perdita's face, but tells them that they cannot see Florizel again on pain of death. Polixenes departs. Everyone is horrified.

The shepherd curses Florizel for deceiving them and storms off. Florizel assures Perdita that he is willing to give up his throne and his country to be with her. Camillo suggests that Florizel and Perdita flee to Sicilia, while he, Camillo, will try to persuade Polixenes to allow Florizel to marry a commoner. Secretly, Camillo hopes that Polixenes and Camillo, as his adviser, will follow Florizel to Sicilia. This way Camillo can see his native land.

Florizel agrees to Camillo's plan, but asks for Camillo's help in securing attendants and letters of introduction appropriate to a king's son. Autolycus comes in, bragging to himself about the cheap goods he has sold and all the purses he has stolen during the sheepshearing. Camillo asks Autolycus to exchange his peddler's rags for Florizel's clothes. Autolycus, baffled, agrees. Florizel hopes that this peddler's disguise will enable him to reach a ship for Sicilia undetected by Polixenes. Left alone, Autolycus declares that he has figured out what they are plotting, but will not reveal their plans to Polixenes. That would be a good deed, which is against his nature.

The clown and the shepherd return. The clown advises the shepherd to tell Polixenes that Perdita is not his real daughter, and therefore he should not be responsible for her actions. Autolycus, dressed in Florizel's garb, overhears them and decides to make a little mischief. Pretending to be a nobleman, he sends them to the ship that Florizel and Perdita are taking to Sicilia to look for Polixenes.

ACT V

Polixenes follows Perdita and Florizel to Sicilia, where Leontes watches Hermione's statue come to life and all are reunited.

V.I   Location: Sicilia. Leontes' palace

Florizel and Perdita are welcomed in Sicilia, but word comes that Polixenes and Camillo have arrived in pursuit.

Leontes is still in mourning for Hermione and Mamillius, although some of his lords urge him to forget the past, forgive himself, and marry again. Paulina, however, encourages his continued contrition, and extracts from him a promise that he will never take another wife until she gives him leave.

Prince Florizel and his new wife Perdita, recently arrived from Bohemia, are announced. Leontes greets them eagerly. He has had no word from Bohemia for years. Florizel pretends to be on a diplomatic mission from Polixenes. Everyone remarks on Perdita's beauty and grace. A lord brings news that Polixenes himself, along with Camillo, have arrived in pursuit of Florizel and that they have the shepherd and the clown (who arrived on Florizel's ship) in their custody. Leontes, stunned, leaves to see his former friend Polixenes immediately, bringing along the despairing Florizel and Perdita.

V.II   Location: Sicilia. Leontes' palace

Leontes and Polixenes have figured out that Perdita is Leontes' daughter, much to everyone's joy.

Several of Leontes' lords tell the newly-arrived Autolycus what has happened. After the shepherd recounted how he found Perdita and showed the tokens that were with her, Leontes realized that she is his daughter. Both kings, but especially Leontes, were overcome with joy. Perdita wanted to see the statue of her mother Hermione, recently erected at Paulina's country house, so the whole party has gone there.

The clown and the shepherd enter. They are now gentlemen, and Autolycus pledges to amend his life and become their loyal servant.

V.III   Location: Sicilia. Paulina's house

At Paulina's house, the new statue of Hermione comes to life; all rejoice.

Paulina unveils Hermione's statue, which impresses everyone with its realism and attention to detail, as well as with the fact that the sculptor made Hermione look older, the age she would have been now if she had lived. Leontes tries to touch the statue's hand, but Paulina keeps him back. She offers to draw the curtain, saying that she did not expect it to move him to such grief, but he refuses to allow it. Paulina offers to make the statue come down from the pedestal and, to everyone's amazement, music sounds and Hermione's statue moves. Hermione, alive, steps down and embraces Leontes. She blesses Perdita. Leontes betrothes Paulina and Camillo, and leads the company out. All rejoice in the apparent miracle.

THEMES, MOTIFS, & SYMBOLS IN *THE WINTER'S TALE*

THEMES

ART VS. NATURE   The natural world is a powerful presence throughout *The Winter's Tale*, from the sheep-shearing festival in Act IV, to the bear that kills Antigonus, to the seasonal reference of the title. Moreover, Shakespeare portrays the play's human relationships in a psychologically realistic fashion. At the same time, the plot of the play frequently incorporates artificial, artistic elements. Perdita dresses up as queen of the feast. Mamillius wants to tell a story of sprites and goblins. Deception and confusion, a kind of artifice, plays a key role: Florizel deceives both his father and the shepherd; Perdita grows up not knowing who she is; and Leontes deceives himself into a jealous rage. Art and artfulness become devices for propelling the realistic exploration of human relationships.

The animation of Hermione's statue, which is the play's most famous device, illustrates this subtle interplay of naturalism and artifice. Shakespeare leaves open two possible interpretations, both an artful, miraculous one and a realistic one: either Paulina uses her craft to bring Hermione's statue to life, or Paulina has kept Hermione hidden for sixteen years. The very fact that both interpretations are possible demonstrates that, as Polixenes remarks, in this play "The art itself is nature" (IV.iv.97).

DESTRUCTION TO REBIRTH AS A NATURAL PROGRESSION   The title situates the play in a natural world of changing seasons. The tragedy and destruction of the first three acts gives way to the rebirth and renewal of the last two, as naturally as winter gives way to spring. Shakespeare alludes to the Greek myth of the seasons. In Ovid's *Metamorphoses*, Persephone (or Proserpina, with whom Perdita is identified) is the daughter of Demeter (or Ceres), who controls the seasons. Persephone is doomed to spend half of every year with her husband Dis (also known as Hades or Pluto), the ruler of the under-world. During this time, Demeter grieves, and winter reigns in the world. When Persephone emerges, Demeter rejoices and spring comes again. Indeed, historically, Sicilia (or Sicily) is associated with the cult of Persephone.

QUALIFIED REDEMPTION   In the last two acts, the first three resolve their mistakes: Leontes achieves redemption, Perdita finds her parents, and the family reunites. At the same time, the redemption is not complete: Mamillius and Antigonus are dead, Hermione has aged and wrinkled, and all have lost sixteen years. Though the play uses artful, miraculous elements, it never veers off into fairy-tale. The story is firmly grounded in the difficult, imperfect real world where people must pay for their mistakes.

MOTIFS

FLOWERS   Flowers, which symbolize spring, freshness, and renewal, abound in Act IV. Autolycus uses flowers to tell the seasons in his song: "When daffodils begin to peer, / … / Why then comes in the sweet o'the year" (IV.iii.1–3). Florizel compares Perdita to the Roman goddess of flowers, Flora (IV.iv.2–3). Florizel's name is derived from the same root. During the sheepshearing, Perdita bestows rue and rosemary on Camillo and Polixenes (IV.iv.73–74). Rue and rosemary are flowers that keep their color and fragrance throughout the winter. Similarly, the play's characters, especially Leontes and Hermione, retain their capacity to love and be human through years of hardship and depression.

JUXTAPOSITION OF OPPOSITES   Shakespeare constructs *The Winter's Tale* around many pairs of opposites. The wintry gloom of Acts I–III in the Sicilian court contrasts with the spring and renewal of Act I in the Bohemian countryside. The older generation—Leontes, Hermione, and Polixenes—give way to the youth of Florizel and Perdita. Antigonus's death is coupled with Perdita's birth. Leontes' guilt is redeemed by Perdita's innocence. The naturalism of the psychological family drama contrasts with fantastical elements such as the bear on the seacoast and a statue coming to life. These pairs of contrasting elements add dynamism to the play and suggest that radical change is possible at any point.

SYMBOLS

HERMIONE'S STATUE   Hermione's frozen statue symbolizes the frozen hearts of the unjustly accused Hermione and the grieving Leontes, both of whom have suffered in suspended animation for the sixteen years between Acts III and IV. Paulina's command, "Be stone no more" (V.iii.99), heralds the un-stony, life-embracing reunion of Leontes with Hermione. As the cold stone of the statue becomes the warmth of human flesh, Sicilia thaws from frozen winter to spring and renewal.

THE STORM   The storm in Act III, scene iii is a physical manifestation of the emotional turmoil of the first three acts, brought about by Leontes' stormy jealousy. The mariner who notices the gray skies remarks as much, interpreting the storm as a symbolic condemnation of Antigonus's assignment to abandon Perdita. Indeed, the storm breaks just when Antigonus sets down the gold and jewels with the baby. Similarly, the turmoil brewing in the play breaks in this scene, as Antigonus exits "pursued by a bear" and the shepherd and clown come on to save Perdita.

IMPORTANT QUOTATIONS FROM *THE WINTER'S TALE*

---

1. *Go play, boy, play. Thy mother plays, and I*
   Play too; but so disgraced a part, whose issue
   Will hiss me to my grave … Go play, boy, play. There have been,
   Or I am much deceived, cuckolds ere now,
   And many a man there is, even at this present,
   Now, while I speak this, holds his wife by th'arm,
   That little thinks she has been sluiced in's absence,
   And his pond fished by his next neighbor, by
   Sir Smile, his neighbor Nay, there's comfort in't,
   Whiles other men have gates, and those gates opened,
   As mine, against their will.

Location: I.ii.188–99
Speaker: Leontes to Mamillius
Context: Watching Hermione walking with Polixenes, Leontes' jealousy grows

In Leontes' phrase "Or I am much deceived"—meaning, "unless I am mistaken"—Shakespeare draws a connection between a troubled marriage (Hermione's alleged sexual deception) and a troubled mind (Leontes' self-deception). Leontes describes sexual intercourse in vulgar terms, as "fishing" in a "pond" that has been "sluiced." He misuses innocent, natural words to describe adultery in a vivid fashion. Psychoanalytic critics have argued that Leontes' jealous madness stems from nostalgia for the innocent of childhood and a resentment of adult sexuality, which he directs toward Hermione.

---

2. *A sad tale's best for winter. I have one*
   Of sprites and goblins.

Location: II.i.27-28
Speaker: Mamillius to Hermione
Context: Hermione asks Mamillius to tell her a story

With Mamillius's phrase "a sad tale," Shakespeare describes the story of the first three acts: Leontes' jealousy, Hermione's imprisonment, his own and Hermione's death, sixteen years of grief. The "sprites and goblins" that haunt Mamillius's sad tale evoke Leontes' jealousy, which haunts the first three acts. At the same time, Shakespeare foreshadows that change is possible. As winter leads to spring, thus sad tales lead to happy ones.

---

3. Exit, pursued by a bear.

Location: III.iii.57 SD
Speaker: [stage direction]
Context: Antigonus has left the baby Perdita on the Bohemian coast, and a bear attacks him.

The most famous stage direction in Shakespeare, "Exit, pursued by bear" visually underscores some of the play's central themes. *The Winter's Tale* is a complex story of human relationships, but it is self-consciously a story, one that relies on fairy-tale elements such as a bear on a seacoast. Moreover, the pursuit of a man by a bear introduces us to a new world: in Bohemia, nature has the upper hand. Most importantly, this point marks the break of tragedy into farce. Perdita has been abandoned in the wilderness, and Antigonus is about to die, but his death is comical. From this point, the wintry sadness and destruction of the first thee acts gives way to the springy rebirth and renewal of the fourth act.

---

4. *Though I am not naturally honest, I am so sometimes by chance.*

Location: IV.iv.692–93
Speaker: Autolycus
Context: Sensing potential personal gain, Autolycus decides to point the clown and the shepherd, who are looking for Polixenes, in the right direction.

In *The Winter's Tale*, reality is never divorced from trickery and artifice. Here, Autolycus, who prides himself on being a cheat and a liar, demonstrates that trickery twice can sometimes lead to honesty. Autolycus's desire for mischief leads him to be unfaithful to his principles of deceitfulness and tell the truth. He unwittingly enables the shepherd to reach Sicilia with evidence that Perdita is Leontes' daughter.

---

5. *O, she's warm!*
   If this be magic, let it be an art
   Lawful as eating.

Location: V.iii.109–11
Speaker: Leontes
Context: Leontes watches Hermione's statue come to life

Leontes touches Hermione's statue, and is surprised to discover it warm and living. Hermione's rebirth completes the cycle of destruction to renewal, coldness to warmth. Nature and artistry are closely linked through a living woman and her statue, and quotidian eating and miraculous rebirth.

THE HISTORY PLAYS

Shakespeare's oeuvre includes ten plays that chronicle real events in English history. Each of these ten plays, which are usually called the history plays, chronicles the major events in the reign of a particular monarch and strives to teach history flavored with patriotism.

The history plays are often separated into smaller groups: two tetralogies and two outliers. The first tetralogy, also called the Henriad, consists of *Richard II*, *1 Henry IV*, *2 Henry IV*, and *Henry V*. This tetralogy opens with the future Henry IV overthrowing Richard II, continues with Henry IV's troubled reign, and concludes with the military triumphs of Henry IV's prodigal son Prince Hal, who rejects his lowly comrades and leads England to its greatest glory. The second tetralogy—*1 Henry VI*, *2 Henry VI*, *3 Henry VI*, and *Richard III*—portrays England spinning into turmoil, torn apart by the Wars of the Roses and petty infighting among the nobility after the death of King Henry V. Edward IV, the heir of Richard II, seizes the throne from the weak King Henry VI. This seizure provides a brief respite from violent conflict, but Edward's brother Richard III turns increasingly evil and steals the throne. The two tetralogies end with a marriage between Henry Tudor, a prominent relative of Henry IV, and Elizabeth, daughter of Edward IV. They will be the parents of Henry VIII and the grandparents of Queen Elizabeth I, who ruled during the early part of Shakespeare's career. Two more history plays round out the cycle: *King John* and *Henry VIII*. *King John* takes place two hundred years before the Wars of the Roses and deals with the problematic and haphazard reign of a medieval king. *Henry VIII*, which takes place a hundred years later, recounts how history miraculously conspires to bring about the birth of Queen Elizabeth.

"The Wars of the Roses" refers to the long dynastic struggle for control of the English throne between the Yorkists (whose emblem was a white rose) and the Lancastrians (red rose). The power struggle involved many people, and much of the English nobility died violent deaths during it. The conflict can be traced to the death of King Edward III, who ruled for much of the fourteenth century and left seven powerful sons. His fourth son, John (of Gaunt), Duke of Lancaster, and his fifth son, Edmund (of Langley), Duke of York, fathered the two dynasties that clashed for power. When Edward III died in 1377, the crown passed to his first son's son, Richard II, who was still a child. Richard's reign was challenged by power-hungry nobles, many of them his uncles and cousins. Eventually, in 1399, John of Gaunt's son Henry Bolingbroke overthrew his cousin Richard and became King Henry IV, the first of three kings of the House of Lancaster. Richard died in captivity in 1400, possibly murdered by Henry IV's henchmen (Shakespeare depicts his death as a murder).

Henry IV ruled until 1413. During his difficult reign, he tried to consolidate his power and quell rebellions in Wales and at home. He was succeeded by his son Henry V (known as Prince Hal before his accession to the throne), whose youth was probably a little bit dissolute. Henry V reopened England's wars with France and led a number of very successful campaigns, including the victory at Agincourt in 1415. By 1420, Henry V had negotiated a treaty that made him heir to the French throne. His health broken by his military campaigns, he died in 1422, leaving behind an infant son who was crowned King Henry VI.

During Henry VI's youth, the government again engaged in clashes between powerful ministers. In particular, Henry VI's claim to the throne was challenged by Richard Plantagenet, the head of the House of York, who, through a complicated intermarriage, was both the grandson of Edward III's fifth son (and so Duke of York) and the great-grandson of Edward III's third son. Richard of York based his claim to the throne on the fact that Henry VI descended from Edward III's fourth son, who was younger than Richard of York's ancestor.

In 1455, fighting between the Lancastrians and the Yorkists broke out in earnest. After several bloody confrontations, Henry VI was deposed in 1461. Richard of York died in battle, and his eldest son took the throne as King Edward IV. Henry, himself a weak and disinterested ruler, was briefly reinstated in 1470–71, but Edward IV definitively recaptured control of government at the Battle of Tewksbury (1471). After Edward IV's death in 1483, the throne went to his young son, proclaimed Edward V, but Edward IV's brother Richard took command of both Edward V and his younger brother in the Tower of London, effectively imprisoning them there. Richard then claimed that the boys were illegitimate because Edward IV's marriage to their mother had been invalid. The two little princes never left the Tower; presumably they were murdered either by Richard or by one of the other factions vying for the throne. Little

Edward V was deposed and his uncle was crowned Richard III in his place. Richard—who was probably not as villainous or as hunchbacked as Shakespeare suggests—ruled until 1485, when Henry Tudor, the great-great-grandson of the Lancastrian John of Gaunt through his third wife, supported by both the Lancastrians and the Yorkists, who were dissatisfied by Richard III's usurpation of the throne, defeated and killed Richard at the Battle of Bosworth Field in 1485. To mollify all sides, Henry married a Yorkist heiress, the eldest daughter of Edward IV. Henry VII became the first Tudor king, the father of Henry VIII, and the grandfather of Queen Elizabeth I.

RICHARD II

Bolingbroke (King Henry IV) seizes the throne from the poetic and ineffectual King Richard II, but his reign is troubled.

RICHARD II IN CONTEXT

Richard II is the first play in Shakespeare's second tetralogy of history plays, which details the rise of the royal House of Lancaster (reigned 1399–1461 and briefly 1470–1471). The second tetralogy continues in the two *Henry IV* plays and concludes with *Henry V*. (The first tetralogy—the three *Henry VI* plays and *Richard III*—chronicle the Wars of the Roses.) *Richard II* was likely composed around 1595, and certainly no later than 1597.

The play has been no stranger to censorship: in many editions and performances over the last four hundred years, Act IV, scene i, in which Richard ceremoniously cedes his crown, has been heavily edited. In 1601, however, the earl of Essex paid Shakespeare's company to perform the play uncut in an attempt to gather support for his upcoming rebellion (the Essex Rebellion) against Queen Elizabeth. When she heard about the production, Queen Elizabeth allegedly made an astute comment: "I am Richard II, know ye not that?" Essex and his hundred men marched through London the following day, but were captured within hours. Essex was put to death two weeks later. The historical precedent did not hold: Elizabeth, unlike Richard, retained her crown.

The play has fascinated critics down through the centuries, although it has long been less popular with directors and audiences than some of Shakespeare's other history plays. Richard's deeply poetic musings on the metaphysical nature of kingship and identity mark a new direction for Shakespeare. Indeed, many see *Richard II* as practice for the more fully developed intellectual angst of *Hamlet*. Linguistically, the play is highly stylized. Unlike the *Henry* plays that follow, it contains virtually no prose. The text makes good use of grand metaphors, most notably comparing England to a garden and the king to the sun.

RICHARD II: KEY FACTS

Full title: The Tragedy of King Richard the Second

Time and place written: probably 1595–1596; London, England

Date of first publication: 1597

Genre: History play

Setting (time): Late fourteenth century (from Bolingbroke's exile in 1397 to Richard's death in 1400)

Setting (place): England

Protagonist: Richard II; Bolingbroke

Major conflict: Bolingbroke, a man of action, pressures the poetic King Richard II to abdicate.

RICHARD II: CHARACTER LIST

Duke of Aumerle, Earl of Rutland   York's son, and Richard and Bolingbroke's cousin. Aumerle remains loyal to Richard throughout the play. Toward the end, he is involved in a failed scheme to assassinate the newly crowned King Henry Bolingbroke.

Bagot, Bushy, Green, and Wiltshire   King Richard's favorites and loyal supporters. Bushy and Green are captured and executed in II.ii. Bagot is captured too and turns informer in IV.i. Wiltshire never appears in the play.

Lord Berkeley   A nobleman loyal to Richard. York's army meets Bolingbroke's army at Berkeley Castle in II.iii.

Henry Bolingbroke, Duke of Hereford; later, King Henry IV   Richard's cousin and John of Gaunt's son. Pragmatic and capable, Bolingbroke is loved by the people and respected by English noblemen. Despite concerns that God is on Richard's side, Bolingbroke stages a nearly bloodless coup and is crowned King Henry IV.

Bishop of Carlisle A clergyman loyal to Richard. Carlisle is arrested for supporting Richard in IV.i. Later, he is indicted but pardoned for conspiring to assassinate Bolingbroke.

Sir Piers Exton A nobleman who assassinates the imprisoned Richard as a favor to Bolingbroke.

Lord Fitzwalter A nobleman who supports Bolingbroke.

John of Gaunt, Duke of Lancaster Richard's uncle, Bolingbroke's father, and York's and Gloucester's brother. A respected elderly nobleman, Gaunt dies in II.i, condemning Richard for mismanaging the country.

Thomas of Woodstock, Duke of Gloucester Richard's uncle, and Gaunt's and York's brother. Gloucester is dead at the start of the play, killed in a conspiracy that involved Mowbray and Richard.

Duchess of Gloucester Gloucester's widow, and John of Gaunt's and York's sister-in-law. The duchess of Gloucester is dead by II.ii.

Thomas Mowbray, Duke of Norfolk A nobleman accused by Bolingbroke of conspiring to kill Gloucester. Banished by Richard, Mowbray dies in exile.

Henry Percy, Earl of Northumberland An early supporter of Bolingbroke's.

Henry ("Harry") Percy Northumberland's son.

Queen Isabella King Richard's wife, and a French princess.

Lord Ross An early supporter of Bolingbroke's.

King Richard II of England The ruler of England at the start of the play. Poetic but wasteful and ineffectual, Richard is disconnected from England and her people. He is overthrown by Bolingbroke, imprisoned, and eventually assassinated by Exton.

Lord Salisbury Richard's loyal supporter. Salisbury unsuccessfully manages Richard's Welsh army. Later, he is beheaded for conspiring to kill the new King Henry IV (Bolingbroke).

Sir Stephen Scrope Richard's supporter.

Edmund of Langley, Duke of York Richard's uncle, Gaunt's brother, and Aumerle's father. York is left lord governor of England while Richard leads an army to Ireland, but effectively helps Bolingbroke usurp the crown. York is a traditionalist who supports the monarchy.

Duchess of York York's wife and Aumerle's mother.

Abbot of Westminster A clergyman loyal to Richard. He is beheaded for conspiring against the new King Henry Bolingbroke.

Lord Willoughby An early supporter of Bolingbroke.

Thomas Percy, Earl of Worcester Northumberland's brother, and the lord steward of Richard's household. Worcester never appears in the play, but defects to support Bolingbroke at a key moment in the play.

RICHARD II: PLOT OVERVIEW

King Richard II of England makes himself unpopular by spending money irresponsibly and giving too much power to his close friends. He exiles his cousin Henry Bolingbroke for six years after Bolingbroke makes accusations about the assassination of one of the royal uncles. (Richard himself was involved in that murder.) While Bolingbroke is away, Bolingbroke's father, John of Gaunt, dies. Richard seizes Gaunt's property to finance a war in Ireland.

Bolingbroke returns from exile with an army, bent on reclaiming his inheritance. Outraged by Richard's abuses, commoners and noblemen flock to Bolingbroke's cause. Richard loses the kingdom without even a battle. He is put in prison. Bolingbroke is crowned King Henry IV. Sir Piers Exton, acting on Henry IV's suggestion, assassinates the deposed Richard. Henry IV repudiates Exton's actions and vows to go on a pilgrimage to Jerusalem as penance for usurping the throne. His reign continues to be troubled by conspiracies and insurrections.

RICHARD II: SCENE SUMMARY

ACT I

Richard II banishes his cousin Bolingbroke after Bolingbroke makes accusations that could expose Richard's role in a political assassination.

I.I Location: near London. Windsor Castle

Richard II's cousin Bolingbroke has accused Mowbray of conspiring in the murder of Richard's uncle Gloucester; the matter will be settled in a formal duel.

The young King Richard II has just arrived to arbitrate a dispute between two prominent noblemen. Richard's cousin Henry Bolingbroke, duke of Hereford, has accused Thomas Mowbray, Duke of Norfolk, of several treasonous crimes: embezzlement, conspiracy, and—by far the most heinous—involvement in the recent murder of Richard's (and Bolingbroke's) uncle, the late Thomas of Woodstock, Duke of Gloucester. Mowbray denies all of Bolingbroke's charges. At the same time, Mowbray admits that he knew about the plot to kill Gloucester. He also confesses that he had been involved in an unsuccessful plot to kill John of Gaunt, Richard's elderly and distinguished uncle (and Bolingbroke's father). Mowbray denies any actual responsibility for Gloucester's death, and claims to have repented for all of his intentions. Mowbray and Bolingbroke insult each other in increasingly angry, heated, and creative terms. As Richard comments before the argument starts, "High-stomached are they both and full of ire; / In rage, deaf as the sea, hasty as fire" (I.i.18–19). That is, both Mowbray and Bolingbroke are rash, hot-tempered, and unwilling to listen to reason.

Mowbray and Bolingbroke call each other liars and traitors, and throw down their "gages" (gloves or hoods), challenging each other to a duel. Richard and John of Gaunt try to reconcile them, but both Mowbray and Bolingbroke refuse to be mollified as a point of honor. Richard sets St. Lambert's Day (September 17) in Coventry as the time and place for a formal, traditional tournament, in order to settle the matter.

I.II Location: John of Gaunt's house

Gloucester's widow asks John of Gaunt to avenge Gloucester's death, but Gaunt refuses.

John of Gaunt, Bolingbroke's father, receives the old duchess of Gloucester, his sister-in-law and the widow of the murdered Gloucester. The duchess urges Gaunt to take revenge for Gloucester's death. She suggests that if the murder goes unavenged, Gaunt himself will become an easy target for political assassination. Gaunt refuses, saying that punishment should be left up to God. He also reveals to us what Shakespeare's audience already knew: King Richard himself was involved in the conspiracy to kill his uncle Gloucester. Gaunt refuses to take action because he believes that the king of England is appointed divinely, that Richard is God's representative on earth. Treason against Richard would be blasphemy against God, Gaunt argues.

Disappointed, the duchess bids Gaunt farewell as he departs to watch Bolingbroke and Mowbray's tournament. She prays for a victory for Bolingbroke, especially since Mowbray, she believes, also played a role in her husband Gloucester's death. As Gaunt leaves, she asks him to send her greetings to his brother Edmund, Duke of York (another of Richard's uncles) and to ask York to visit her in her estate at Pleshey.

I.III Location: Coventry. The tournament field

Richard interrupts the duel between Bolingbroke and Mowbray to exile both from England.

Bolingbroke and Mowbray enter fully armed into the lists (the field of ritual combat). Richard formally questions them and asks them to repeat their accusations. Both Bolingbroke and Mowbray make dramatic speeches. Each asserts his innocence, the guilt of his opponent, his pleasure in the fight, and his certainty of victory. John of Gaunt blesses his son Bolingbroke and King Richard wishes good luck to both. Heralds and trumpets announce the beginning of the fight, but King Richard interrupts the proceedings by ritually throwing down his warder (i.e., umpire's baton). He orders the duel to stop.

After consulting his advisors, King Richard determines that the duel will not take place: "our kingdom's earth should not be soiled / With that dear blood which it hath fosterèd" (I.iii.124–5). Instead, he exiles Bolingbroke for ten years and Mowbray for life. Both appeal for clemency, but to no avail. Richard forces them to swear never to contact each other, even in exile. Mowbray departs in grief. Richard relents and reduces Bolingbroke's sentence to six years, saying that he takes pity upon the saddened John of Gaunt, Bolingbroke's father. Gaunt thanks Richard, but notes that he will likely die before Bolingbroke can return in any case. After Richard departs with his retinue, Bolingbroke continues to lament his sentence. Gaunt philosophically counsels him to bear his punishment like a man and try to take it lightly. Bolingbroke answers that misery cannot be vanquished by imagination.

I.IV   Location: King Richard's court

Richard tries to improvise ways to raise money to quell a rebellion in Ireland.

At court, Richard and his favorites Bagot and Green greet his cousin, the Duke of Aumerle (son of the Duke of York), who has returned from escorting Bolingbroke to a ship bound for Europe. Aumerle reports that they parted coolly. Richard describes in detail Bolingbroke's departure from London. Richard saw how much the people love Bolingbroke. He feels that Bolingbroke behaved as though he were the heir to the throne.

Green reminds Richard about the Irish rebellion that must be quelled soon. Richard announces that he will sail to Ireland in person to oversee the suppression of the uprising. Since the treasury is low on funds, he will "rent out" the realm of England. That is, he will reinstate a complicated medieval tax, both borrowing and taking money from the wealthy citizens.

Bushy, another of Richard's favorites, enters with important news: old John of Gaunt lies on his deathbed. Richard rejoices at the news: as soon as Gaunt is dead, he will seize his property to fund the war in England (instead of allowing Gaunt's heir, the exiled Bolingbroke, to inherit). Everyone heads off to see John of Gaunt at the bishop of Ely's castle.

ACT II

After Richard seizes Bolingbroke's dead father's lands to finance the Irish war, Bolingbroke returns to England supported by an army and many English noblemen.

II.I   Location: bishop of Ely's castle

Gaunt dies, cursing Richard's profligacy; Richard seizes Gaunt's estate to finance the Irish wars; meanwhile, exiled Bolingbroke plans a royal coup.

John of Gaunt, on his deathbed, speaks with York while awaiting Richard's arrival. Gaunt hopes to have time to give the foolhardy Richard some useful advice before his dies. York replies that Richard is too surrounded by flatterers, and too interested in the follies and fashions of the world, to take Gaunt's advice. In response, Gaunt prophesies Richard's doom: "His rash, fierce blaze of riot cannot last, / For violent fires soon burn out themselves" (II.i.33–34). In one of the play's most well-known speeches, Gaunt laments that England has been rented out (as a form of taxation):

> This royal throne of kings, this sceptred isle,
> This earth of majesty, this seat of Mars,
> This other Eden, demi-paradise
> This blessèd plot, this earth, this realm, this England
> …
> Is now leased out—I die pronouncing it—
> Like to a tenement or pelting farm.
> (II.i.40–60)

King Richard arrives with a large train of followers, including Queen Isabella, Aumerle, Bushy, Bagot, Green, Ross, and Willoughby. When Richard casually inquires after Gaunt's health, Gaunt bitterly rebukes Richard for exiling his son Bolingbroke. He then accuses Richard of mismanaging the kingdom: wasting money, taxing the people excessively, and letting himself be swayed by his selfish and power-hungry advisors. Infuriated, Richard interrupts Gaunt and says that he would kill Gaunt were Gaunt not his uncle. Gaunt, emboldened by his nearing death, reminds Richard that Richard had no qualms about causing the death of his uncle Gloucester. Gaunt curses Richard and is escorted out on a chair. York tries to make excuses for Gaunt's behavior. The earl of Northumberland comes and announces that Gaunt is dead.

Richard promptly proclaims his intention to seize all of Gaunt's estate to finance the Irish war. York (Gaunt's brother and Richard's uncle) protests vehemently: Gaunt's estate should go to Gaunt's son, the exiled Bolingbroke. Richard refuses to listen to him and York departs. Richard announces that he will set sail for Ireland tomorrow, leaving York as lord governor of England in his absence. Richard departs with Bushy, Bagot, and Green.

The earl of Northumberland, Lord Ross, and Lord Willoughby remain. Outraged by Richard's antics, they agree that Richard is bringing England to ruin. Northumberland confides to Ross and Willoughby that Bolingbroke has many English allies and plans to sail for England on the king of Brittany's ships as soon as Richard leaves for Ireland. Bolingbroke will land in Ravenspurgh, a northeastern port in England, and stage a royal coup. The three decide to join Bolingbroke.

II.II Location: Windsor Castle

With Richard in Ireland, Bolingbroke has landed in northeastern England; he is supported by the people and many noblemen.

Richard has left for Ireland to suppress the rebellion. Queen Isabella despairs in his absence, haunted by presentiment of disaster: "Some unborn sorrow, ripe in Fortune's womb, / Is coming towards me; and my inward soul / At nothing trembles. With some thing it grieves" (II.ii.10–12). Bushy tries to console her, but the queen will not be assuaged.

Green enters with bad news: Henry Bolingbroke has landed at Ravenspurgh with his army. Since Richard and the royal army have left for Ireland, there is no one to stop Bolingbroke. Moreover, many English lords have defected to Bolingbroke's side: Northumberland, his young son Henry Percy, Lord Ross, Lord Beaumont, Lord Willoughby. Worst of all, the earl of Worcester, Northumberland's brother and the lord steward of the royal household, has defected, and all the royal servants with him.

York, the acting head of government, enters. He is fearful about the impending war: King Richard is gone, York himself is "weak with age" (II.ii.83), and the commoners may join Bolingbroke. A servant informs him moreover that York's son Aumerle has already left to join Richard in Ireland. His sister-in-law, the duchess of Gloucester, has died and therefore cannot help him finance an army to repel Boling-broke's attack. York departs for Berkeley Castle in Gloucestershire (in south central England) to try to raise an army there, taking Queen Isabella along.

Left alone, Bushy, Bagot, and Green all agree that as Richard's favorites, they are in serious danger: it is unlikely that York will be able to raise an army large enough to deflect Bolingbroke's. The people of England have turned against Richard, and so may menace the three of them. All three decide to flee: Bushy and Green to Bristol Castle in the west, Bagot to Ireland to find Richard. They bid one other fare-well.

II.III Location: Gloucestershire (south central England). Near Berkeley Castle

Though technically loyal to Richard, York sympathizes with and helps Bolingbroke.

On the way to meet Ross and Willoughby in Berkeley Castle, Bolingbroke and Northumberland encounter Harry Percy, Northumberland's young son. Percy tells them that Worcester (Northumber-land's brother) has joined Bolingbroke's side (which we already know from II.ii) because Northumber-land and the other defectors have been declared traitors. Worcester has sent Percy on a reconnaissance mission to scout out Berkeley Castle and York's army. Northumberland introduces Percy to Bolingbroke. Percy swears allegiance to him.

Percy has found out that York's army is small: three hundred men and only three noblemen—York, Berkeley, and Seymour. Ross and Willoughby arrive to join Bolingbroke.

Berkeley and York emerge from the castle. Bolingbroke greets him respectfully, but York angrily chides him for disturbing the peace with his invasion. In an eloquent speech, Bolingbroke declares that he had no other choice after Richard took his estate and titles. York is sympathetic but cannot condone a rebellion against the lawful king. However, because he does not have an army to repel Bolingbroke, he plans to be neutral. He invites Bolingbroke and his allies to spend the night in Berkeley Castle. Bolingbroke accepts, planning to head to Bristol Castle to destroy Bushy and Bagot the next day.

II.IV Location: the coast of Wales. A camp

Richard's Welsh army disperses.

Lord Salisbury has been waiting with a large Welsh army for Richard to return from Ireland. After ten days of waiting with no news, the army has seen bad omens in the surrounding landscape and in the sky. The Welsh captain and his men, convinced that Richard is dead, disperse. Salisbury declares that he can see Richard's star falling, like one of the Welshmen's bad omens.

ACT III

Having lost his army and most of his supporters, Richard surrenders to Bolingbroke without a fight.

III.I Location: Western England. Outside Bristol Castle

Bolingbroke apprehends and executes two of Richard's favorites.

Henry Bolingbroke and his men have apprehended Richard's favorites Bushy and Green. Bolingbroke accuses them of having "misled a prince" (III.i.8)—that is, of having deliberately given Richard bad advice—and condemns them to death. Bushy and Green are defiant but resigned. Northumberland leads them away to be executed. Bolingbroke sends York with courteous greetings to Queen Isabella, who is staying at York's house, and gathers his army to fight rebellious Welshmen before facing Richard.

III.II Location: Wales. Outside Barkloughly Castle

Richard returns to England to find that all of his allies have defected or been executed.

King Richard has landed on the coast of Wales, accompanied by Aumerle, the bishop of Carlisle, and a small army. Richard greets the earth and air of England in poetic terms. Aumerle points out that while they delay, Bolingbroke grows stronger in power. Richard replies that since he is the rightful king, no rebel stands a chance. God is on their side, and they will easily sweep Bolingbroke out of England.

Salisbury enters and delivers bad news: the day before, the twelve-thousand-strong Welsh army dispersed and defected to Bolingbroke. Richard now has no army. Richard momentarily succumbs to despair, but then recovers his self-assurance. Lord Scrope arrives with more news: as Bolingbroke makes his way through England, all the people swear allegiance to him. Richard asks Scrope about Bagot, Bushy, Green, and Wiltshire. (Wiltshire never appears in the play.) Scrope tells him that they have made "peace" with Bolingbroke (III.ii.124), meaning that they have been executed. (Actually, Bagot is still alive.)

Richard gives a long, eloquent, and despairing monologue, but Carlisle urges him not to give up hope. Richard agrees and decides to face Bolingbroke in combat despite his losses. Scrope delivers more bad news: York too has joined Bolingbroke. All the royal castles in the north are in Bolingbroke's possession. Richard loses all hope, and resolves to go to Flint Castle (in northeastern Wales) to "pine away" (III.ii.205).

III.III Location: Wales. Outside Flint Castle

Bolingbroke confronts Richard, who is resigned to losing his crown.

Bolingbroke, York, and Northumberland have arrived to seek Richard. York is concerned about possible divine retribution for the overthrow of the lawful king. Bolingbroke acknowledges his concerns. Young Harry Percy arrives with news that Richard is holed up inside the castle with several allies—Aumerle, Salisbury, Scrope, and Carlisle. Bolingbroke sends Northumberland forth with a message: he, Bolingbroke, is prepared to surrender his army if Richard returns to him the lands seized from his late father John of Gaunt.

Before Northumberland has entered the castle, Richard and his allies appear upon the castle walls. Richard thunderingly tells Northumberland to relay a message to Bolingbroke: if Bolingbroke dares try to usurp the throne, both the heavens and King Richard will rain vengeance upon him. Bolingbroke will not take his crown until the fields of England are stained with blood.

Bolingbroke denies that he has come to seize the throne, claiming that he seeks only his rightful inheritance. Richard agrees to Bolingbroke's demands, but then tells his attendants, in highly dramatic and despairing language, that his reign as king has ended because Bolingbroke will not let him stay on the throne. Bolingbroke asks Richard to come down from the castle and parley with him. Richard and his attendants obediently descend. Though Bolingbroke never mentions that he intends to take the crown, Richard asks Bolingbroke whether he must go with Bolingbroke to London. Bolingbroke says yes. Richard agrees, saying that he has no choice.

III.IV Location: Langley. York's garden

Queen Isabella finds out that Richard is in Bolingbroke's custody in London.

Queen Isabella, who has been staying at York's house, is in the garden with her waiting-women. They suggest games, singing, dancing, and storytelling to distract her, but Isabella says that any attempt to forget her grief would only add to it.

An aged gardener and his assistant enter the garden to tend to some of the plants. At the queen's suggestion, she and her ladies conceal themselves to eavesdrop. The queen has noticed that even the commoners have been discussing affairs of state, as if something important were about to happen.

The gardener and his assistant speak about the state of the country, using the garden as a metaphor. Why, the assistant asks, should the two of them bother to take care of their garden when the country outside has been allowed to sprout weeds and be infested by insects (a reference to Richard's mismanagement and unpopular advisors)? The gardener shushes his assistant, since the person who caused the country's disorder has "met with the fall of leaf" (III.iv.50)—that is, King Richard has been overthrown. The gardener also tells his assistant that a friend of York's received letters with more news: the "weeds"— Richard's allies Wiltshire, Bushy, and Green—have been "plucked up" by Bolingbroke. King Richard himself has been captured too.

Queen Isabella bursts out from her hiding place to confront the gardener about what he has just said. The gardener apologetically confirms that King Richard is in Bolingbroke's custody. It has moreover become apparent that the noblemen of England support Bolingbroke.

The queen, lamenting her misfortune, summons her ladies to go with her to London to meet the captured Richard. She casts upon the gardener a half-hearted curse as she departs: "[F]or telling me these news of woe, / Pray God the plants thou graft'st may never grow" (III.iv.101–02). The good-natured gardener decides to plant a bed of rue (the herb of sorrow) in the place where her tears fell.

ACT IV

Richard publicly abdicates his crown to Bolingbroke, who will become King Henry IV.

IV.I Location: London. Westminster Hall

Richard formally abdicates his crown to Bolingbroke, although he still has a few supporters.

Having returned to London, Bolingbroke and his allies interrogate Bagot, demanding that he reveal who conspired with Richard to kill Gloucester. Bagot claims that Aumerle (York's son) was a key conspirator. Aumerle heatedly denies Bagot's accusations and throws down his gage as a challenge to a duel. Three of Bolingbroke's allies, including Fitzwalter and Percy, then throw down their gages to challenge Aumerle.

Surrey throws down his gage in support of Aumerle. Fitzwalter throws down his gage again. Aumerle, out of gages, is forced to borrow someone else's just to throw it down again.

Bolingbroke puts an end to the gage-throwing, announcing that he will find out the truth of the conspiracy from Mowbray. However, Carlisle informs everyone that Mowbray has died fighting in the Crusades.

York enters with news that King Richard has agreed to "adopt" Bolingbroke as his "heir" (IV.i.100) and yield the throne to him immediately. The bishop of Carlisle prophesies that if Bolingbroke takes the crown from the true king, generations yet to come will pay for his usurpation with suffering until the earth is soaked in English blood. (The reference is to the civil Wars of the Roses, which ended the reign of Bolingbroke's grandson Henry VI in the mid-fifteenth century.) Northumberland promptly arrests Carlisle on charges of high treason.

Bolingbroke summons Richard so that Richard can abdicate in public. Richard enters, helpless and despairing. He delivers a long, grief-stricken monologue in which he surrenders his land, his crown, and his right to rule. Northumberland asks Richard to publicly confess his crimes, so that the people "may deem that you are worthily deposed" (IV.i.217). Richard resists. He calls for a mirror and, after staring into it and wondering aloud about his own identity now that he is no longer king, smashes it to the floor.

Richard asks Bolingbroke to be allowed to leave in peace. Bolingbroke commands that Richard be taken to the Tower of London (the traditional holding place for political prisoners). Richard departs under guard. Bolingbroke sets the date of his coronation as the following Wednesday. Left alone, Carlisle, Aumerle, and the abbot of Westminster confer, presumably conspiring against Bolingbroke.

ACT V

Richard is assassinated as a favor to the new king, Henry IV (Bolingbroke), whose reign continues to be troubled.

V.I Location: London. A street near the tower

Queen Isabella bids farewell to Richard, who is to be imprisoned.

Queen Isabella has arrived in London and waits for Richard to pass by on his way to the tower. Richard and his guard ride into view. Isabella laments how much he has changed. Richard comforts her: he tells her that she must learn to live with grief, counsels her to focus on the afterlife, and instructs her to return to France (her native country) and enter a convent. Isabella asks Richard why he is so resigned: has Bolingbroke taken his courage and indignation as well as his crown? Richard replies that there is no point in fighting his fate. Isabella should think of him as dead.

Northumberland arrives to tell Richard that Bolingbroke has changed his mind: Richard is to be sent to Pomfret Castle, in the north, instead of the tower. Richard prophesies—or curses—that Northumberland and the new king, Henry Bolingbroke, will not stay allies for long (portending the conflict between Northumberland and Bolingbroke—and between their sons, Percy (Hotspur) and Price Hal—dramatized in *1 Henry VI*). Northumberland replies curtly. Richard and Isabella bid each other a long farewell, in highly stylized language, and part. He goes to Pomfret Castle, she goes to France.

V.II Location: Langley. York's house

Bolingbroke has been crowned King Henry IV; York discovers that his son Aumerle has conspired to assassinate Bolingbroke.

York tells his wife, the duchess of York, about Bolingbroke's coronation: as Bolingbroke rode into London, leading Richard in captivity, the people dumped rubbish onto Richard's head and cheered wildly for Bolingbroke. Though upset about how they treated Richard, York vows to be loyal to the new King Henry IV (Bolingbroke).

Aumerle, son to the duke and duchess of York, enters. (Technically, he has lost the duchy of Aumerle and is now known as the Earl of Rutland.) York notices a letter tucked into his shirt. Aumerle tries to conceal it, but York seizes and reads it. Agitated, York calls Aumerle a traitor. The letter reveals that Aumerle has conspired with a dozen noblemen who plan to assassinate the new King Henry IV during the coronation celebrations at Oxford.

The duchess pleads with York not to reveal Aumerle's treason. She is too old to bear more children if they lose him. York refuses to listen, and rides off to see Bolingbroke. The duchess sends Aumerle to try to reach Bolingbroke first and beg for forgiveness. She herself will follow too, to plead for Aumerle's life.

V.III   Location: Windsor Castle

York denounces Aumerle to Bolingbroke, who agrees to spare Aumerle's life.

Bolingbroke complains to young Harry Percy about his son's wild ways. The young prince (the future King Henry V) has been spending his time in taverns and whorehouses.

Aumerle enters and begs Bolingbroke for a private audience. Bolingbroke dismisses his companions. Aumerle falls to his knees and says that he will not rise until Bolingbroke forgives him for his crime, nor will he name the crime until he has been pardoned. He also begs Bolingbroke to lock the door. Bolingbroke complies.

York bangs on the door from the outside and cries out that Aumerle is a traitor. Bolingbroke lets York in, and York shows Bolingbroke Aumerle's letter. The duchess is heard outside. She too enters to beg Bolingbroke to spare Aumerle's life. In highly formal language, York begs Bolingbroke to execute Aumerle as a traitor. The duchess begs Bolingbroke to spare Aumerle's life. At last, Bolingbroke pardons Aumerle, but promises to execute all the other conspirators immediately.

V.IV   Location: Windsor Castle

Sir Piers Exton believes that Bolingbroke has asked him to assassinate the imprisoned Richard.

Sir Piers Exton, a nobleman, tells his servants that King Henry Bolingbroke has asked his companions, "'Have I no friend will rid me of this living fear?'" (V.iv.2). Exton guesses that the "living fear" refers to the still-living Richard, imprisoned at Pomfret Castle. Exton thinks that Bolingbroke meant this comment for him, and resolves to be Bolingbroke's "friend" (V.iv.11) and kill Richard.

V.V   Location: Yorkshire. Pomfret Castle

Sir Piers Exton kills Richard.

Alone in prison, Richard is trying to come to terms with his isolation from the world. He tries several metaphorical and metaphysical tricks to convince himself that he is still a part of the outside world. A former groom of Richard's stables enters and tries to comfort him. The keeper of the castle enters with food. Wary, Richard asks the keeper to taste the food first (to prove that it is not poisoned), but the keeper tells Richard that one Sir Piers Exton has forbidden him to taste it. Richard strikes the keeper in anger. The keeper cries out and Exton rushes in with his accomplices. After a brief scuffle in which Richard kills two of the accomplices, Exton stabs Richard. Richard dies, cursing Exton. Troubled by doubt and guilt, Exton plans to convey Richard's body to Bolingbroke at Windsor.

V.VI   Location: Windsor Castle

His reign still troubled, Bolingbroke banishes Exton for killing Richard.

Bolingbroke is discussing affairs of state with his advisors. Rebels are setting fire to a town in Gloucestershire in the northwest. On the other hand, the main conspirators, including Salisbury and the abbot of Westminster, have been executed. The bishop of Carlisle has been spared, and presents himself to Bolingbroke for sentencing. Bolingbroke orders Carlisle to find a "secret place" (V.vi.25) and live the rest of his life under a low profile.

Suddenly, Exton enters with the coffin containing Richard's body, and tells Bolingbroke that he has done Bolingbroke's bidding and assassinated Richard. Bolingbroke replies that while he cannot help but rejoice at Richard's death, he never ordered Richard killed. Bolingbroke declares that he loathes Exton and banishes Exton from court. Bolingbroke himself vows to take a pilgrimage to Jerusalem to cleanse himself from the guilt of Richard's death.

THEMES, MOTIFS, & SYMBOLS IN *RICHARD II*

THEMES

THE DIVINE RIGHT OF KINGS   The divine right of kings is the belief, originating in the Middle Ages, that a king is God's anointed ruler on earth, and so rules with a "divine right." At the beginning of the play, for example, everyone knows that Richard II was involved in the assassination of his uncle Thomas of Woodstock, Duke of Gloucester, but his guilt is never mentioned in public, even as Bolingbroke accuses Mowbray of the same crime. Richard is "God's substitute, / His deputy anointed in his sight" (I.ii.37–38), so even the respected John of Gaunt refuses to accuse Richard—however much he disapproves of Richard's policies. Bolingbroke never dares to directly demand Richard's crown; Richard is pressured to abdicate instead. As Richard gives his crown to Bolingbroke, he makes explicit the fact that he is committing blasphemy against God: "With mine own tongue [I] deny my sacred state" (IV.i.199). Bolingbroke may be portrayed as a much more popular and effective ruler than Richard, but the enormity of usurpation presses over everyone in the play, including York, Richard, and Bolingbroke himself. Bolingbroke's usurpation troubles all the Lancaster kings in *Henry IV*, *Henry V*, and *Henry VI*. According to a traditional interpretation of Shakespeare's history play cycle, the civil wars of the mid-fifteenth century are divine punishment for Bolingbroke's usurpation. Peace is not restored until much of the English nobility is wiped out and the heir of Richard II (Elizabeth of the House of York) marries the heir of Bolingbroke (Henry of the House of Lancaster), who is crowned Henry VII at the end of *Richard III*.

ARTISTIC INTROSPECTION VERSUS DECISIVE ACTION   Shakespeare sets up a contrast between the dreamy, intellectual Richard II and the decisive Henry Bolingbroke. Richard is a poet, a philosopher-king. He contemplates his roles both as a man and a king in the world imaginatively. Alone and isolated in prison, Richard comforts himself by casting his thoughts as characters in a play created by his mind and his soul: "My brain I'll prove the female to my soul, / My soul the father, and these two beget / A generation of still-breeding thoughts; / And these same thoughts people this little world" (V.v.6–9). Though Richard's powers of imagination are impressive, his creative temperament proves useless in controlling a country. His rival Bolingbroke is represented as a practical man of action for whom words alone are meaningless: "What my tongue speaks my right-drawn sword may prove" (I.i.46). Bolingbroke's effortless coup shows him as the better king. Shakespeare further explores the tension between thought and action in *Hamlet*.

THE MIDDLE AGES GIVING WAY TO THE RENAISSANCE   In *Richard II*, Shakespeare, writing during the Renaissance, depicted a changing world. John of Gaunt stands in for the medieval system of values. He piously trusts in God to right all wrongs and resolve all conflicts. He refuses the duchess of Gloucester's plea to avenge her husband's death because it was sanctioned by King Richard—God's representative on earth. After his son Bolingbroke is exiled in Act I, Gaunt urges Bolingbroke to find the hidden benefits of exile visible with the "eye of heaven" (I.iii.264). Gaunt's death marks the end of an era, a philosophy of English government. Bolingbroke's reign ushers in a new era of personal responsibility.

Gages (gloves or hoods thrown down to challenge an opponent to a duel) are another relic from medieval traditions. Mowbray and Bolingbroke throw down their gages to formally challenge each other in the opening scene. Richard initially allows them to resolve their conflict with a duel. The idea was that God would ensure that the just competitor won. By Shakespeare's day, justice-by-tournament had become outdated. Richard prevents Mowbray and Bolingbroke's duel from taking place, invalidating the medieval gage. In Act IV, Shakespeare slyly ridicules gage-throwing when Aumerle runs out of his own gages and is forced to borrow more.

MOTIFS

HONOR   Honor is an important value in Shakespeare's history plays, and *Richard II* is no exception. With characteristic subtlety, Shakespeare makes distinctions between an idealistic belief in personal honor and the more complicated problem of reputation in the real world. In the first scene, for example, Mowbray speaks about the importance of personal honor:

> The purest treasure mortal times afford
> Is spotless reputation; that away,
> Men are but gilded loam, or painted clay.
> . . .
> Mine honor is my life. Both grow in one.
> Take honor from me, and my life is done.
> Then, dear my liege, mine honor let me try.
> In that I live, and for that will I die.
> I.i.177–85

Explicitly, Mowbray asks Richard to allow him to defend himself, since his honor is more important to him than his life. However, Mowbray, like everyone else gathered, knows that Richard was involved in Gloucester's assassination, for which Mowbray now stands accused. His impassioned declaration is also a subtle, ironic dig at Richard. Richard's official reputation may be intact, but his personal honor is compromised.

CONSPIRACIES AND INSURRECTIONS King Richard II and King Henry IV (Bolingbroke) are both troubled by political unrest in *Richard II*. The opening conflict of the play, between Mowbray and Bolingbroke, is spillover from earlier political turmoil brought about by the many royal uncles surrounding a young and inexperienced Richard II. During the play, Richard goes to Ireland to quell a political uprising. In Act V, Henry IV finds out about a conspiracy against his life and executes the perpetrators. In the last scene, he is troubled by new insurrections in Gloucestershire. Neither of the kings is particularly powerful, and neither reign is trouble-free. In his old age, as portrayed in *2 Henry IV*, Henry Bolingbroke philosophically notes, "Uneasy lies the head that wears a crown" (2HIV III.i.31). Shakespeare's history plays portray a troubled century in English history.

SYMBOLS

THE GARDEN OF LANGLEY In III.iv, in York's garden at Langley, Queen Isabella overhears a conversation between York's gardener and his assistant. In this allegorical conversation, the garden is a stand-in for England. A healthy country corresponds to a well-weeded and orderly garden, a country in turmoil to a garden that has been let go. The gardener's figurative vocabulary cements the allegory. He tells his assistant to cut off the "heads" of fast-growing twigs on the apricot trees "like an executioner" (III.iv.34–35). He tells his assistant to work hard because "all must be even in our government" (III.iv.37). The assistant makes the allegory explicit when he compares the garden to the whole land: "our sea-wallèd garden, the whole land, / Is full of weeds, her fairest flowers choked up, / Her fruit trees all unpruned, her hedges ruined" (III.iv.44–46). Unlike Richard, Bolingbroke is a good manager for the country. He has "plucked up, root and all" Richard's weed-like supporters (III.iv.51–53). The correspondence between the garden and the country is furthered by the comparison of the king to the sun (see also Quotation 3).

THE KING'S BODY Throughout *Richard II*, Richard's body is associated with the kingdom of England. This conceit is deeply rooted in the medieval view that the king is God's representative on earth, an embodiment of the cosmic order of the country. The king's health and sickness is then indicative of the well-being of the nation. Richard makes explicit this connection several times in the play. Mourning the crown he is about to lose, he laments, "We'll make foul weather with despisèd tears. / Our sighs and they shall lodge the summer corn, / And make a dearth in this revolting land" (III.iii.160–62). His tears are associated with literal storms, and his grief with a famine ("dearth") in the land. At the end of the play, fatally wounded, he accuses his killer Exton of "stain[ing] the king's own land" with "the king's blood." (V.v.110). Shakespeare's cycle of history plays often cast Henry IV's usurpation of the throne and Richard's death as the original cause of the mid–fifteenth-century civil wars.

IMPORTANT QUOTATIONS FROM *RICHARD II*

1. *O, who can hold a fire in his hand*
   By thinking on the frosty Caucasus,
   Or cloy the hungry edge of appetite
   By bare imagination of a feast,
   Or wallow naked in December snow
   By thinking on fantastic summer's heat?
   O no, the apprehension of the good
   Gives but the greater feeling to the worse.
   Fell sorrow's tooth doth never rankle more
   Than when he bites, but lanceth not the sore.

Location: I.iii.257–66
Speaker: Bolingbroke to his father John of Gaunt
Context: Richard has exiled Bolingbroke, and John of Gaunt urges Bolingbroke to think positively

In these lines, Bolingbroke rejects John of Gaunt's idea that sorrow is alleviated when it is perceived lightly, arguing that thought alone does not change a miserable situation. Their philosophical disagreement is a manifestation of a larger generational gap within the play, between Gaunt's pious medieval perspective and Bolingbroke's more practical approach. Gaunt believes that events on earth always evolve according to God's will, and the appropriate response is to take life in stride. Bolingbroke values the immediate experience of the material world. Thinking of cold ("the frosty Caucasus") does not change the physical reality of a fire. Thinking of food does not alleviate real hunger. Bolingbroke is a man of literalism and action whose speeches set up a clear contrast between him and the more philosophical and dreamy Richard. The play suggests that the more self-reflective thinker is not always the better king.

2. *...Of comfort no man speak.*
   Let's talk of graves, of worms and epitaphs,
   Make dust our paper, and with rainy eyes
   Write sorrow on the bosom of the earth.
   Let's choose executors and talk of wills—
   And yet not so, for what can we bequeath
   Save our deposèd bodies to the ground?
   Our lands, our lives, and all are Bolingbroke's;
   And nothing can we call our own but death,
   And that small model of the barren earth
   Which serves as paste and cover to our bones.
   For God's sake, let us sit upon the ground,
   And tell sad stories of the death of kings—
   How some have been deposed, some slain in war,
   Some haunted by the ghosts they have deposed,
   Some poisoned by their wives, some sleeping killed,
   All murdered. For within the hollow crown
   That rounds the mortal temples of a king
   Keeps Death his court; and there the antic sits,
   Scoffing his state and grinning at his pomp,
   Allowing him a breath, a little scene,
   To monarchize, be feared, and kill with looks,
   Infusing him with self and vain conceit,
   As if this flesh which walls about our life
   Were brass impregnable; and humoured thus
   Comes at the last, and with a little pin

Bores through his castle wall; and farewell, king.
Cover your heads, and mock not flesh and blood
With solemn reverence. Throw away respect,
Tradition, form, and ceremonious duty,
For you have but mistook me all this while.
I live with bread, like you; feel want,
Taste grief, need friends. Subjected thus,
How can you say to me I am a king?

Location: III.ii.140–73
Speaker: Richard
Context: Richard waxes poetic and philosophical as he resigns himself to the idea that Bolingbroke has usurped his throne

Richard's speech, effectively his concession of his crown to Bolingbroke, highlights a key difference between the two men. For Bolingbroke, the coup is a struggle between men and rulers. He rebels because he is outraged at Richard's actions and believes that he could be a better king. For Richard, the coup is a travesty of the natural, God-ordained order of the universe. As a result, Richard sees Death, rather than Bolingbroke, as his opponent. Indeed, he does not even mention Bolingbroke by name after the eighth line. Robbed of his crown, Richard becomes merely a human being, "subject" to the needs and limitations of his human body.

---

3. *See, see, King Richard doth himself appear,*
As doth the blushing discontented sun
From out the fiery portal of the east,
When he perceives the envious clouds are bent
To dim his glory and to stain the track
Of his bright passage to the occident.

Location: III.iii.61–66
Speaker: Bolingbroke
Context: Bolingbroke notices Richard on the walls of Flint Castle

In this passage, Bolingbroke compares King Richard to the sun, which is a metaphor with a long history (for example, Louis XIV of France was known as the Sun King). The implication is that the country completely depends on the king, just as the earth depends on the sun for nourishment. Although Richard's sun is setting (passing to "the occident"), Bolingbroke describes himself, the obstacle to the Richard's glory, as unsubstantial "envious clouds," a temporary obstruction. Although he is about to overthrow the king, Bolingbroke demonstrates, with his strong imagery, that he believes in the divine right of the king. The *Henry IV* plays further explore his anxiety about his unlawful assumption of the throne. Surprisingly, the poetic imagination displayed in these lines is more characteristic of Richard than of Bolingbroke.

---

4. *Ay, no; no, ay; for I must nothing be.*
Therefore no, "no," for I resign to thee.
Now mark me how I will undo myself.
I give this heavy weight from off my head,
And this unwieldy sceptre from my hand,
The pride of kingly sway from out my heart.
With mine own tears I wash away my balm,
With mine own hands I give away my crown,
With mine own tongue deny my sacred state,
With mine own breath release all duteous oaths.
All pomp and majesty I do forswear.

My manors, rents, revenues I forego.
My acts, decrees, and statutes I deny.
God pardon all oaths that are broke to me.
God keep all vows unbroke are made to thee.

Location: IV.i.191–205
Speaker: Richard to Bolingbroke
Context: Richard formally abdicates his crown to Bolingbroke

Richard's ambivalent "Ay, no; no, ay" is a response to Bolingbroke's question about whether he is "content to resign the crown" (IV.i.190). Richard has difficulty answering the question because he both does not want to give up his crown and thinks that he has no choice. Alternatively, we may argue that unlike Bolingbroke, Richard does not see the crown as something to resign, as it is divinely conferred. Giving up the crown, for Richard, is self-annihilation. He "undo[es]" himself and becomes "nothing."

   In language and rhythm, Richard's speech mimics the divine coronation ritual. Richard emphasizes the sanctity of kingship even as he gives it up, forcing Bolingbroke to acknowledge the gravity of the situation. This speech was seen as a scandalous perversion of a sacred ceremony, and was often eliminated in early editions of the play.

---

5. *A brittle glory shineth in this face.*
   As brittle as the glory is the face,
   [He shatters the glass]
   For there it is, cracked in an hundred shivers.
   Mark, silent king, the moral of this sport
   How soon my sorrow hath destroyed my face.

Location: IV.i.277–81
Speaker: Richard
Context: Richard smashes a mirror as he abdicates his throne

Richard believes in symbols. Here, he smashes a hand-mirror to physically demonstrate that the abdication of the crown is tantamount to his annihilation. For Richard, his identity as a man is inextricable from his identity as a king. When he shatters the mirror, he metaphorically commits ritual suicide, foreshadowing his death. Richard's perspective contrasts sharply with Bolingbroke's. For Bolingbroke, tangible deeds trump words and symbols. After Richard breaks the mirror, Bolingbroke reminds Richard that Richard is still alive.

1 HENRY IV

Prince Hal rises above his criminal youth to become a military hero.

1 HENRY IV IN CONTEXT

Henry IV, Part 1, often referred to as *1 Henry IV*, is a history play. It is the second part of tetralogy that deals with the historical rise of the English royal House of Lancaster. (The tetralogy proceeds in the following order: *Richard II*; *Henry IV, Part 1*; *Henry IV, Part 2*; and *Henry V*.) Shakespeare probably wrote *1 Henry IV* in the years 1596–1597.

Although the events he writes about occurred some two centuries before his own time, Shakespeare expected his audience to be familiar with the characters and events he was describing. The battles among houses and the rise and fall of kings were woven into the cultural fabric of England and formed an integral part of the country's patriotic legends and national mythology. One might compare this knowledge to the American public's general awareness of the events and figures of the American Revolution, which occurred more than two centuries ago. As it did for the English commoners of Shakespeare's era, the passage of time has obscured many of the specific details of important historical events, and thus the heroes and battles of an event like the American Revolution are, to some degree, cloaked in myth. Similarly, Shakespearean history is often inaccurate in its details, although it reflects popular conceptions of history.

Shakespeare drew on a number of sources in writing his history plays, as he did in nearly all his work. Scholars generally agree that his primary source for historical material is the second edition of Raphael Holinshed's massive work *The Chronicles of England, Scotland and Ireland*, published in 1587. Holinshed's account provides the fundamental chronology of events that Shakespeare follows, alters, or conveniently ignores to suit his dramatic purposes.

An important question that preoccupies the characters in the history plays, including *Henry IV, Part 1*, is whether God appointed the king of England. If the king is divinely appointed, then the overthrow, deposition, or, worst of all, murder of a king is an affront to God. In Shakespeare's works, as in the classical Greek tragedies (such as Aeschylus's *Oresteia*), a king who deposes or murders his predecessor may suffer for it, and so may his descendants. In the play that bears his name, Richard II is haunted by a politically motivated murder—not that of an actual king but that of his uncle, Thomas of Woodstock, Duke of Gloucester. In *Henry IV, Part I*, Henry IV is haunted by his own responsibility for Richard's overthrow and eventual murder. Only after Henry IV's death does his own son, Henry V, symbolically prove himself worthy to rule as king of England.

1 Henry IV blends history with comedy, moving from lofty scenes involving kings and battles to sordid scenes involving ruffians and drunkards. Set in 1402–1403, the play generally concerns historical events and figures, although Shakespeare significantly alters or invents history where it suits him. For instance, Hotspur was not the same age as Prince Hal, and the character Mortimer is a conflation of two people. Falstaff, a character in *1 Henry IV* and one of Shakespeare's most famous creations, was likely influenced by archetypes like Vice from medieval morality plays and Gluttony from medieval pageants about the seven deadly sins. His character also draws on both the *miles gloriosus* figure, an arrogant soldier from classical Greek and Roman comedy, and the Lord of Misrule, the title given to an individual appointed to reign over folk festivities in medieval England.

1 HENRY IV: KEY FACTS

Full Title: The History of Henry the Fourth (1 Henry IV)

Time and place written: Probably 1596–1597; London

Date of first publication: 1598 (in quarto), 1623 (in folio)

Genre: Historical drama, military drama

Setting (time): Around 1402–1403

Setting (place): London, especially the royal palace and the Boar's Head Tavern; various other locales places in England

Protagonist: Prince Hal

Major conflict: The Percy family, encouraged by the young nobleman Hotspur, seeks to overthrow the reigning king of England, Henry IV. Hal, the crown prince of England, must work to win back his honor after squandering it.

1 HENRY IV: CHARACTER LIST

The Archbishop of York The archbishop, whose given name is Richard Scrope, has a grievance against King Henry and conspires with the Percys.

Archibald, Earl of Douglas The leader of the large army of Scottish rebels. Usually called "The Douglas" (a traditional title for a Scottish clan chief), the deadly and fearless Douglas fights on the side of the Percys.

Sir Walter Blunt A loyal and trusted ally of King Henry's and a valuable warrior.

Sir John Falstaff Hal's closest friend. Falstaff is a fat man between the ages of about fifty and sixty-five who hangs around in taverns on the wrong side of London and makes his living as a thief, highwayman, and mooch. Falstaff mentors Hal, instructing him in the practices of criminals and vagabonds. He is the only one who can match Hal's quick wit.

Gadshill A highwayman friend of Hal, Falstaff, and the rest. Gadshill seems to be nicknamed after a place on the London road called Gad's Hill, where he has set up many robberies.

Owain Glendower The leader of the Welsh rebels and the father of Lady Mortimer. Glendower joins the Percys in their insurrection against King Henry. Well-read, educated in England, and highly capable in battle, Glendower is also steeped in the traditional lore of Wales and claims to be a magician. He is mysterious and superstitious.

Prince Hal The protagonist of the play and King Henry IV's son. Hal, Prince of Wales, goes by Hal among his friends. He is also sometimes called Hal Monmouth. Though Hal spends all his time hanging around highwaymen, robbers, and whores, he secretly plans to transform himself into a noble prince, and his regal qualities emerge as the play unfolds.

King Henry IV The ruling king of England. Worries have worn down Henry, who feels guilty that he won his throne through a civil war that deposed the former king, Richard II. Henry also worries about the internal strife that dogs England, and about the irresponsible antics of his eldest son, Prince Hal. King Henry is regal, proud, and somewhat aloof.

Hotspur The son and heir of the Earl of Northumberland and the nephew of the Earl of Worcester. Hotspur's real name is Henry Percy (he is also called Hal or Percy), but he has earned his nickname from his fierceness in battle. Hotspur is a member of the powerful Percy family of the North, which helped bring King Henry IV to power but now feels that the king is ungrateful. In Shakespeare's account, Hotspur is the same age as Prince Hal and becomes his archrival. Quick-tempered and impatient, Hotspur is obsessed with honor and glory.

Lord John of Lancaster The younger son of King Henry and the younger brother of Prince Hal. Despite his youth, John is wise and valiant in battle.

Edmund Mortimer, called the Earl of March The son-in-law of Welsh rebel Owain Glendower. Mortimer is a conflation of two historical figures: Mortimer and the Earl of March. Mortimer had a strong claim to the throne of England before King Henry overthrew Richard II.

Henry Percy, Earl of Northumberland Hotspur's father. Northumberland conspires with the Percys, but he claims to be sick before the Battle of Shrewsbury and does not bring his troops into the fray.

Thomas Percy, Earl of Worcester Hotspur's uncle. Shrewd and manipulative, Worcester is the mastermind behind the Percy rebellion.

Ned Poins, Bardolph, and Peto Criminals and highwaymen. Poins, Bardolph, and Peto drink with Falstaff and Hal in the Boar's Head Tavern, accompany them in highway robbery, and go with them to war.

Mistress Quickly The hostess of the Boar's Head Tavern, a seedy dive.

Sir Richard Vernon A relative and ally of the Earl of Worcester.

Earl of Westmoreland A nobleman and military leader who is a close companion and valuable ally of King Henry IV.

1 HENRY IV: PLOT OVERVIEW

King Henry IV has recently seized the throne from Richard II, but the allies who helped him become king now turn against him. The powerful lords Worcester, Hotspur (Hal Percy), and Northumberland join forces with the rebel Mortimer and the feared Welsh leader, Owain Glendower. King Henry's son Prince Hal spends his time drinking, thieving, and whoring with assorted scoundrels, in particular an obese, debauched knight named Sir John Falstaff. Because of his wild ways, Hal has earned a bad reputation with his father and the rest of the kingdom, but he plans to exploit this reputation to make himself look spectacularly noble when he reforms. When King Henry has to lead his forces against the rebels, Hal reconciles with his father and performs heroically in battle, saving his father's life and killing the renowned Hotspur in single combat at the Battle of Shrewsbury. Falstaff abuses the command Hal gives him and behaves like a coward in the battle, but Hal backs up Falstaff's lie that Falstaff killed Hotspur.

1 HENRY IV: SCENE SUMMARY

ACT 1

Hotspur performs valiantly in battle but begins to turn against King Henry, encouraged by the Earl of Worcester; Prince Hal hangs out with his low-rent friends.

I.I Location: Royal Palace of London

Hotspur performs valiantly in battle, defeating thousands of Scottish rebels, but he disloyally refuses to turn over all of the prisoners of war to King Henry IV.

King Henry IV speaks with his counselors. Worn out by the recent civil wars that have wracked his country, he looks forward to a project he has been planning for a long time: joining in the Crusades. He plans to lead a military expedition to Jerusalem, the Holy Land, to join in the battle between the Islamic peoples who currently occupy it and the European armies who are trying to seize it.

News from two separate borders of Henry's kingdom almost immediately changes his plans. Skirmishes have broken out between the English forces on one side and the Scottish and Welsh rebels on the other. The king's trusted advisor, the Earl of Westmoreland, relays the bad news that Edmund Mortimer, an English military leader, has lost a battle against a band of guerrilla fighters in Wales, who are led by the powerful and mysterious Welsh rebel Owain Glendower. Glendower has captured Mortimer, and the rebels have slaughtered one thousand of Mortimer's soldiers. The Welsh women, following their traditions, have mutilated the soldiers' corpses.

Young Hal Percy, nicknamed Hotspur, another of the king's best military men, has defeated Archibald, also known as the Douglas, the leader of ten thousand Scottish rebels. Hotspur has taken several important Scotsmen prisoners, including the Douglas's own son, Mordake, Earl of Fife. King Henry cannot help comparing Hotspur's stellar behavior with the idleness of his own son, Prince Hal. Hal is the same age as Hotspur, but he has not won any military glory and behaves dishonorably. King Henry wishes that Hotspur were his son.

Hotspur has sent word to King Henry that he plans to send only one of his prisoners, Mordake, to the king and retain the rest. This strange action flouts standard procedure, as the king has an automatic right to all noble prisoners captured in battle. Westmoreland suggests that Hotspur's uncle, the Earl of Worcester, has prompted this rebellious act. The Earl is known to be hostile to the king. Angered, Henry agrees and says that he has demanded that Hotspur come and explain himself. Henry decides that the Crusades project will have to be put off and that he will hold court the next Wednesday at Windsor Castle to hear what Hotspur has to say.

I.II Location: Prince Hal's house in London

> *Hal hangs out with his sleazy, jovial friends, admitting to the audience that he does so because he wants to shock everyone by one day cleaning up and behaving like a prince should.*

Prince Hal passes the time with his friend Sir John Falstaff. Falstaff is an old, fat criminal who loves to drink sack (sweet wine), eat, and sleep away the day. He makes his living as a highwayman and robber and sponges off Hal and his other friends. But Falstaff is clever and entertaining, and he and Hal exchange familiar banter and quick-witted puns.

Hal and Falstaff are joined by their acquaintance Edward ("Ned") Poins, another highwayman. Poins tells them that a robbery has been set up for early the following morning. He and Gadshill, a thief, have learned that some rich pilgrims and prosperous traders will be passing Gad's Hill at around four o'clock in the morning. Falstaff says he will participate in the robbery and urges Hal to come along too. Hal refuses, saying that he is not a thief, but Poins asks Falstaff to leave him alone with Hal, suggesting that he will be able to persuade the prince to go with them.

When they are alone, Poins explains to Hal that he has a marvelous practical joke planned: Poins and Hal will ride out to Gad's Hill with their four friends during the night, but they will pretend to get lost and fail to show up at the meeting place. Instead, they will hide and watch as the robbery occurs. Then Poins and Hal will rob Falstaff and the others, taking the money that their friends have just stolen. Poins assures Hal that he has masks to hide their faces and suits of rough cloth ("buckram") to hide their clothes (I.ii.159). He also points out that since Falstaff and the others are complete cowards, they are sure to run away as soon as Poins and Hal attack them. The best part of the trick will be listening to the enormous lies that Falstaff is sure to tell about the encounter. At this point, Poins and Hal will be able to cut him down when they reveal that they themselves were the thieves. Amused, Hal agrees to play along.

As soon as Poins leaves the room, Hal begins to muse aloud to himself. He reveals that he hangs around with these low-class friends as part of a clever psychological plan: he is deliberately trying to make his father and the English people think poorly of him so that he can surprise and impress them all when he decides to grow up and start behaving like a royal prince. Hal feels that if he lowers people's expectations, it will be much easier to awe and please them later on than it would be if people expected great things of him. Hal concludes by suggesting that sometime very soon he plans to reveal his true nature to those around him.

I.III Location: Windsor Castle

> *Hotspur's appearance before King Henry goes badly, and King Henry orders him to return the prisoners or face retribution; Hotspur's uncle, the Earl of Worcester, explains his plan to stir up rebellion against King Henry.*

Hotspur comes to tell King Henry why he refused to hand over the prisoners he captured in Scotland. Hotspur's father, the Earl of Northumberland, and his uncle, the Earl of Worcester, accompany him. Henry speaks to Hotspur in threatening language. When Worcester, already hostile toward Henry, reacts rudely, Henry orders him out of the room. Hotspur and Northumberland now try to explain that Hotspur's refusal to return the captives was not meant as an act of rebellion. Just as Hotspur's battle against the Scots ended, a prissy and effeminate courtier arrived with Henry's demands for the prisoners. Wounded, tired, and angry, Hotspur refused and insulted the foolish messenger in the heat of the moment.

Henry is not pacified. Hotspur still refuses to hand over the prisoners unless the king pays the ransom that the Welsh rebels demand for the release of Hotspur's brother-in-law, Lord Mortimer, who became a prisoner after the Welsh defeated his army. Henry refuses, calling Mortimer a traitor. He has learned that Mortimer recently married the daughter of the Welsh rebel Glendower. Henry believes that Mortimer lost his battle with Glendower on purpose. Hotspur denies this charge against his kinsman, but Henry calls him a liar. He forbids Hotspur to mention Mortimer's name ever again and demands he return the prisoners instantly or face retribution.

After Henry and his attendants leave the room, Worcester returns to his brother and nephew, and Hotspur makes an enraged speech. He thinks Henry may have ulterior motives for refusing to ransom Mortimer: before he was deposed, Richard II, Henry's predecessor, had named Mortimer heir to the throne. Since Henry obtained his crown by deposing Richard illegally, Mortimer's claim to the kingdom might be better than Henry's own. Hotspur is also bitter because his family helped Henry overthrow Richard in the first place, and Henry seems to have forgotten the debt he owes to the Percy family.

Worcester and Northumberland have some trouble calming Hotspur, but finally Worcester succeeds in explaining that he has already formulated a cunning plan. He says that the Percys must seek an alliance with the rebel forces in both Scotland and Wales and with the many powerful English nobles who are dissatisfied with Henry. For now, Hotspur should return to Scotland, release his prisoners without demanding ransom, and establish an alliance with the Douglas, the leader of the Scottish rebellion. Northumberland must seek the support of the Archbishop of York, who is unhappy because Henry executed his brother for conspiring against the king's life. Worcester will go to Wales to discuss strategy with Mortimer and Glendower.

ACT II

Hal and Poins play a prank on Falstaff and the others by robbing them in disguise; Hotspur quarrels with his wife and leaves to begin the rebellion.

II.I Location: an inn yard in Rochester

Gadshill learns that a group of rich travelers will soon be ripe for robbing.

It is early morning. Beside the main highway about twenty-five miles outside of London, two carriers— middlemen who deliver goods from one merchant to another—are readying their horses to depart. The stable boy is slow in coming out to help, and the carriers are annoyed. Gadshill, the highwayman friend of Falstaff and Hal, appears from the darkness and asks the carriers if he may borrow a lantern. They are suspicious of Gadshill and refuse.

As soon as the carriers have gone on their way, a chamberlain of the inn comes out to talk to Gadshill. The chamberlain, Gadshill's informer, tells him that some very wealthy travelers are currently having their breakfast at the inn and will be on the road soon. Gadshill offers him a cut of the profits, which the chamberlain refuses. Gadshill calls for his horse and rides off to set his ambush.

II.II Location: Gad's Hill

Falstaff and his cronies rob the travelers.

Falstaff searches for his horse, which Poins has secretly concealed in the woods. Peto, Bardolph, and Hal stand by. The fat Falstaff is very uncomfortable on foot. He puffs, pants, and complains loudly. Hal soothes Falstaff by telling him he will look for his horse (which he does not intend to do). Gadshill shows up with news that the wealthy travelers are approaching. Hal suggests that Falstaff, Peto, Bardolph, and Gadshill confront the travelers on the highway. He and Poins will then flank them on either side of the road to catch any who try to escape. The men put on their masks, and Poins and Hal hide. When the travelers appear, Falstaff, Peto, Bardolph, and Gadshill rob them and tie them up.

II.III Location: Gad's Hill

In disguise, Poins and Hal rob Falstaff and the others.

As the four split up the gold, Poins and Hal, in their buckram disguises and new masks, charge the thieves and demand their money. The four flee in terror without putting up a fight. Only Falstaff even tries to get in a punch or two. Laden with gold and mightily entertained, Poins and Hal go to their horses, laughing to think of how angry Falstaff will be when he finds out that they have gotten rid of his horse and he will have to walk back to London.

II.IV Location: Warkworth Castle

Hotspur decides to start the rebellion and quarrels with his wife.

Hotspur has asked a nobleman for support in the rebellion that the Percy family is planning against Henry. He reads a letter from the nobleman in which the nobleman refuses help, saying that the Percy plot is not well planned and their allies are not strong or reliable enough to face so great a foe as Henry. Hotspur angrily criticizes the writer's cowardice. He is concerned that the writer will reveal the plot to Henry, so he decides to set out that night to join his allies and start the rebellion.

Hotspur's wife, Lady Percy (also called Kate), comes in to speak to her husband. When Hotspur tells her that he will be leaving the castle within two hours, she becomes upset. She points out that for the past two weeks Hotspur has not eaten properly, slept well, or made love to her. Furthermore, he has been breaking out into a sweat in the middle of the night and babbling in his sleep about guns, cannons, prisoners, and soldiers. Lady Percy thinks Hotspur should tell her what he has been planning.

Hotspur ignores his wife and instructs his servant to get his horse ready. Enraged, Lady Percy stops pleading and starts demanding answers. She suspects that Hotspur's machinations have something to do with her brother, Lord Mortimer, and his claim to the throne. She threatens to break Hotspur's "little finger" (a euphemism for his penis) if he does not tell her what is going on (II.iv.79).

Hotspur turns on Lady Percy and angrily insults her, saying that he does not love her and that this is no world for womanly thoughts or for love, but for war and fighting. He will not tell her what he is doing because he believes that women cannot be trusted. He says only that she may follow him on horseback the next day. Lady Percy cannot get any more information out of her belligerent husband.

II.V   Location: Boar's Head Tavern

Hal admits that it was he and Poins who robbed Falstaff and the others and hides Falstaff when the police come looking for him.

Prince Hal, who has been drinking and making friends with the bartenders, emerges from the wine cellar. He is pleased that he has learned the bartenders' names and their slang. "Dyeing scarlet," for example, refers to chugging a mug of wine (II.v.13). Hal announces that these men, who like him, have called him "the king of courtesy, and . . . a good boy" (II.v.8–13). Hal meets Poins upstairs, and together they tease a young apprentice bartender named Francis.

Falstaff and his friends arrive, and Falstaff launches into the tale of how he and his friends were robbed just after they had committed their own robbery. Falstaff tells outrageous lies, claiming that a hundred men attacked him and that he himself fought a dozen. Eventually Hal tells Falstaff that he and Poins were the robbers. Falstaff promptly bluffs, saying he recognized Hal immediately when he and Poins attacked the party and that he only ran away to avoid having to hurt Hal. But he is glad to hear that Hal and Poins have the money, since now they can pay for everyone to get drunk.

The tavern's hostess, Mistress Quickly, comes in to tell Hal a nobleman has arrived with a message for Hal from his father. Falstaff goes to the door to get rid of the nobleman and returns with heavy news: civil war is brewing in England, and Hal must go to the court to see his father in the morning. The rebellious Percys and their many allies have joined together to attack King Henry, and the king's beard has "turned white" with worry (II.v.328).

Hal and Falstaff decide to engage in a role-playing game so that Hal can prepare for his interview with his father the following morning. Falstaff will pretend to be King Henry and scold Hal, who will practice his answers. In the role of the king, Falstaff bombastically defends himself to Hal, suggesting that even if Hal drops all his other rascally companions, he should keep the virtuous old Falstaff around. Hal, objecting that his father would not speak in this manner, suggests that he and Falstaff switch places. Now playing the role of King Henry, Hal rebukes Falstaff, who now plays the role of Hal, for hanging around with such a disreputable old man. Falstaff tries to defend himself, but he has trouble holding his own in the face of Hal's sharp intelligence and regal bearing.

The sheriff and his night watch arrive at the tavern looking for Falstaff and the others in connection with the robbery. Hal tells Falstaff to hide and misdirects the sheriff by swearing that Falstaff is not there and that he himself will be responsible for finding the thief and turning him over. The sheriff leaves, and Hal finds Falstaff asleep in his hiding place. After picking Falstaff's pockets out of curiosity, Hal tells Peto that he will see his father in the morning and that all of them must go off to war. He adds that he will secure places in the army for all of his companions and jokes that he will place Falstaff in charge of a brigade of foot soldiers.

ACT III

The rebel leaders meet, and King Henry rebukes Prince Hal, who promises to change.

III.I Location: Owain Glendower's castle

The rebel leaders meet and decide how to divide Britain among themselves.

In Wales, at the castle of Owain Glendower, the leaders of the rebel armies have gathered to discuss strategy. The two most important members of the Percy family, Hotspur and Worcester, are there, along with Lord Mortimer, Hotspur's brother-in-law, referred to in the play as his cousin. Their host, Glendower, is Mortimer's father-in-law and the leader of the Welsh rebels. He has a strong belief in ancient Welsh pagan prophecies, omens, magic, and demons. He claims to be able to call spirits from hell and says that at his birth the earth shook and the sky filled with fire. Hotspur makes fun of Glendower's claims. Mortimer tries to shut Hotspur up, but Hotspur mocks Glendower's claim that he can command the devil. Glendower says he has repelled Henry's invasions three times. By the time the four get down to discussing strategy, Glendower is annoyed with Hotspur.

The men take out a large map of Britain and divide it up. After they defeat King Henry, Glendower will get the western part of Britain, western England and all of Wales, Mortimer will get the southeast part of England, including London, and Hotspur will get the northern part. Hotspur complains about the way a river curves through his land and says he will have the river straightened out. Irritated, Glendower tells Hotspur he should not do this. The two bicker again.

After Glendower leaves the room, Mortimer chides Hotspur. Hotspur says he is bored and annoyed with Glendower's talk of prophecies and magic. Mortimer reminds him that Glendower is a powerful, courageous, and well-read man, and also possibly a dangerous magician. He points out that Glendower has been very tolerant of Hotspur's youthful obnoxiousness. Anyone else would have felt the force of Glendower's anger already. Worcester agrees and urges Hotspur to mind his manners and show respect. Hotspur claims he has learned his lesson.

Glendower comes in with Mortimer's and Hotspur's wives. The four must say goodbye, for the men must ride off to meet their allies that night. Mortimer cannot speak to his wife, who is Glendower's daughter, because she cannot speak English, and Mortimer knows no Welsh. Lady Mortimer weeps for her husband, who speaks lovingly to her, and Glendower translates for them. Mortimer lays his head in her lap, and she sings a song in Welsh. Hotspur and his wife, Lady Percy, bid each other farewell in a half-affectionate, half-quarrelsome manner. The men sign their formal contracts of agreement, and Mortimer, Hotspur, and Worcester set forth. They are heading to Shrewsbury, near the English border with Wales, to meet the Earl of Northumberland (Hotspur's father) and his ally, the Douglas of Scotland, who will bring with him a thousand soldiers. Glendower will gather his army, which he plans to lead into England within two weeks.

III.II Location: the royal palace in London

King Henry reprimands his son, who swears he will do better; Henry says he can prove himself in the war.

After a long absence, Prince Hal arrives to answer his father's summons. Henry, sad and angry, rebukes his son in stinging terms. He says he would like to be able to forgive Hal but he cannot tolerate his recent behavior. He says that if Hal continues to hang around with commoners, he will never command the respect a king must have. Henry believes that only that which is rare and unusual is well-respected. When he himself was waging the war that made him a king, he says, he did not slum around London the way Hal does. Rather, he was courteous and regal when he made his occasional appearances. The common people respected and loved him in a way that they do not respect or love Hal.

Henry tells Hal that he is behaving just like Richard II, who indulged himself and had fools for friends and counselors, earning the scorn and hatred of the common people. In Henry's opinion, Hal's dissolute behavior will make the people hate him. Henry says Hotspur currently has more real right than Hal to inherit the throne. Hal might claim blood inheritance, but Hotspur is the one who demonstrates his courage in warfare, winning honor in battle and daring to take on the king himself. Hotspur reminds

Henry of himself when he was young. In fact, Henry believes that Hal acts like such a scoundrel because he hates his father. Henry is sure that Hal will soon go over to Hotspur's side, joining forces with Henry's deadly enemies.

Hal breaks out into an emotional speech, asserting that Henry is wrong. He swears he will take revenge on Hotspur for everything that Hotspur has ever done to Henry. He says that when he finally defeats Hotspur in combat, all of Hotspur's honor, glory, and achievements will pass to him. He vows to begin acting as the heir to the throne should and solemnly declares that he will carry out what he has sworn or die in the attempt. Pleased but wary, Henry tells Hal that he may have the command of soldiers in the upcoming war, to prove himself sincere and carry out his vow.

Sir Walter Blunt, one of Henry's trusted allies, enters with news that the Douglas, the leader of the Scottish rebels, met the English rebels several days earlier at Shrewsbury, in the west of England. The combined force will soon be ready to attack. Henry says that he already knows about this development and has sent out his younger son, Prince John (Lord of Lancaster), and the Earl of Westmoreland to meet them. Next Wednesday, he adds, Hal will set out. On Thursday, Henry and his forces will follow. All will meet at Bridgnorth, not far from the rebels' camp at Shrewsbury, in twelve days.

III.III Location: Boar's Head Tavern

After settling a quarrel between Falstaff and Mistress Quickly, Hal gives his friends war commissions.

Falstaff complains to Bardolph about how thin and weak he has gotten of late. The hostess of the tavern, Mistress Quickly, demands payment from Falstaff for the food and drink he has consumed, as well as for some clothing she has recently bought for him. Falstaff says his pocket was picked the previous night while he was asleep and accuses her of having done it. He says he had money and a valuable ring in his pocket. The hostess accuses Falstaff of trying to get out of paying his bill. The entrance of Prince Hal and Peto interrupts their argument.

Hal announces that war is at hand, and all must go off to fight. After some bawdy teasing at the expense of the dim-witted hostess, Hal reveals that he himself emptied Falstaff's pockets the night before and found nothing in them but tavern bills, receipts from whorehouses, and a handful of candy. Falstaff weasels out of admitting wrongdoing, tells the hostess he forgives her, and orders breakfast.

Hal tells Falstaff he has bailed him out again. He paid back the money that Falstaff and the others stole the day before. Hal assigns war commissions to his friends and sends Bardolph off to deliver letters on horseback to King Henry's troops, who are already on their way—one letter to Hal's younger brother, John, Lord of Lancaster, and another to the Earl of Westmoreland. He orders Peto to come on a different errand with him and tells Falstaff that he is in charge of a brigade of foot soldiers. Hal departs on his military errand with Peto. Falstaff does not plan to let the war effort come between him and a good breakfast.

ACT IV

The rebels' chance of victory begins to look grim.

IV.I Location: the rebels' camp in Shrewsbury

The rebels receive bad news.

Hotspur, Worcester, and the Douglas are discussing their strategy when a messenger arrives bearing bad news. Hotspur's father, Northumberland, is very sick and has decided not to lead his troops to Hotspur or to send them at all. Worcester is deeply disturbed by this news, since not only will Northumberland's absence seriously weaken the rebel forces, but it will also betray to the world that the rebels are divided among themselves. Hotspur quickly manages to convince himself that all is well.

Sir Richard Vernon, a relative of the Percys, arrives with a message. Henry's forces, commanded by the Earl of Westmoreland and Henry's younger son, Prince John, are marching toward Shrewsbury with seven thousand men. King Henry and Prince Hal are also approaching with still more forces. Vernon has seen Hal bearing himself regally in his armor. All who see him perceive him as an excellent horseman and an awe-inspiring young soldier. Hotspur says he wants to meet Hal in single combat to the death.

Vernon also announces that Glendower has sent word from Wales that he will not be able to assemble his forces within the allotted fourteen days. This development alarms Worcester and the Douglas, since the battle will occur before Glendower can arrive. But Hotspur refuses to let anything sway his confidence. The Douglas says he does not fear death at all, and the men continue to plan their battle.

IV.II Location: a road near Coventry

Falstaff explains his corrupt methods for finding foot soldiers.

In southeastern England, east of London, Falstaff and his men march west toward their rendezvous with Henry at Bridgnorth. Falstaff sends Bardolph to buy some wine. Once Bardolph is gone, Falstaff talks aloud about his corrupt methods for finding foot soldiers. Instead of using his power of impressment (the power to draft soldiers) to get the best fighters available, he targets wealthy merchants and farmers who want to stay home and are willing to bribe Falstaff in order to get out of the service. Falstaff has made a good deal of money for himself, but his troops are ragtag souls willing to fight for pay—kleptomaniac house servants, youngest sons with no inheritance, and bankrupt laborers. They are mostly undernourished, untrustworthy, and unimpressive.

Henry's ally, the Earl of Westmoreland, comes down the road with Hal, taking Falstaff by surprise. Westmoreland casts a dubious eye upon Falstaff's conscripts, but Falstaff cheerfully tells him that they are good enough for cannon fodder. Hal tells Falstaff he must hurry, for Hotspur and the Percy allies are preparing to fight, and Henry has already made camp at Bridgnorth. The group hurries westward to meet Henry.

IV.III Location: the rebels' camp in Shrewsbury

Sir Walter Blunt brings an offer of peace from King Henry, and Hotspur explains his family's grievances against Henry.

Hotspur and the Douglas argue with Worcester about whether they should attack Henry's forces right away or hold off for a while. Worcester and Vernon urge them to wait. Not all of Vernon's forces have arrived yet, and since Worcester's band of knights on horseback has just arrived that day, the horses are still worn out. But Hotspur and the Douglas are impatient to attack.

Sir Walter Blunt arrives in their camp bearing an offer of peace from Henry. If Hotspur and his allies will state their grievances against Henry and disband, he says, Henry promises to satisfy their desires and grant full amnesty to the rebels. Hotspur makes a long speech about his family's dissatisfaction with Henry, saying that when Henry was the underdog several years before, the Percy family gave him invaluable help in his bid to seize the throne from Richard II. Henry, then known as Henry Bolingbroke, was a mere cousin of Richard II. Henry was exiled for flimsy reasons and snuck back into England while King Richard was away fighting in Ireland. He originally claimed that he had only come to reclaim the title and inheritance that were due to him from his father, Richard's recently deceased uncle, whose lands Richard had seized upon his death. But Henry stayed to fight for the crown of England. Partly swayed by the influence and power of the Percy family, the common people of England and the nobles of Richard's court joined Henry's faction, allowing him to take over power from Richard in a bloodless coup—although Richard was later assassinated in mysterious circumstances.

Now, Hotspur says, King Henry seems to have forgotten the gratitude he owes the Percy family. Most recently, he refused to pay a ransom for Mortimer after Mortimer was captured in Wales. Blunt asks if he should take Hotspur's words as a declaration of war. Hotspur tells Blunt he should return to Henry and await Worcester, who will come in the morning with the rebels' decision. Hotspur suggests they may decide to accept Henry's offer of amnesty after all.

IV.IV Location: York

The Archbishop of York frets over the rebels' poor chance of defeating the king's forces.

The Archbishop of York, an ally of Hotspur and the other rebels, speaks with a friend of his named Sir Michael. The archbishop gives Sir Michael urgent letters, including one to the archbishop's cousin

Scrope and another to the Lord Marshal. He tells Sir Michael that the next day will be very important, saying the "fortune of ten thousand men" depends on the outcome of the battle that will occur at Shrewsbury (IV.iv.9). He is very concerned, for he has heard that Henry's forces are powerful and that the absence of Northumberland, Glendower, and Mortimer has weakened the Percy forces.

Sir Michael urges the archbishop to be optimistic, since the rebellion does have on its side powerful warriors like the Douglas, his son Mordake, Vernon, Hotspur, Worcester, and others. But the archbishop says the king has all the other finest warriors in the land, including the Prince of Wales (Hal), his younger brother, Prince John, Westmoreland, Blunt, and many more. The archbishop urges Sir Michael to make haste with the letters. Apparently, the archbishop wants to set up a contingency plan in case Henry wins at Shrewsbury. He knows that Henry is aware of his involvement in the uprising.

ACT V

In part because of Worcester's dishonesty, the rebels insist on fighting and lose badly to King Henry's forces.

V.I Location: the rebels' camp in Shrewsbury

Worcester refuses to make peace, and Hal offers to fight Hotspur to settle the conflict.

Henry and Hal watch the sun rise, red and dim, on the morning of the battle. Worcester and Vernon arrive as messengers from the rebel camp. Henry asks Worcester if he is willing to avoid the conflict, which will surely be destructive. Worcester says that Henry's behavior has made it impossible to avoid conflict. He reminds Henry that the Percy family gave him assistance when Henry was still the underdog and that, without their help, Henry never could have overthrown Richard II. He says that Henry has become so forgetful of his debts and so hostile toward the Percys that the family feels it has no choice but to flee from court and raise an army to bring about justice.

Henry dismisses these charges as mere excuses, declaring that those who are discontented for petty reasons and who are driven by the lust for power can always find some reason to attempt an overthrow of those currently in power. Hal offers a solution: he tells Worcester to tell Hotspur that, since the whole world knows what a valiant knight Hotspur is, Hal himself will meet Hotspur in single combat to decide the conflict. This way, he says, the many men who would die in a full-fledged battle will be spared.

Worcester departs, and Hal and Henry agree that the rebels probably will not accept the offer—Hotspur and the Douglas are both too confident of their chances in pitched battle. Henry departs to prepare his troops, and Hal and Falstaff say goodbye before the fight. After Hal leaves, Falstaff muses about the worthlessness of honor, saying that only dead men can keep it, although they get no benefit from it, while the living suffer on honor's behalf.

V.II Location: the rebels' camp in Shrewsbury

Worcester lies to Hotspur, who rushes his men into battle.

Worcester has decided not to tell Hotspur about Henry's respectful offer of amnesty or Hal's challenge to single combat. He is afraid that Hotspur would accept the offer of peace and worries that if that happened, he and Northumberland would never be left in peace. Even if Henry forgave Hotspur because of his youth, Worcester reasons, he and Northumberland would eventually be accused of treachery.

Worcester lies to Hotspur, telling him that Henry insulted the Percys and mocked their grievances. The rash Hotspur immediately sends off a messenger to demand that Henry meet the Percys on the battlefield. Worcester tells him about Hal's offer to meet him in single combat, and Hotspur declares that he will seek Hal out on the battlefield and engage him one-on-one. A messenger arrives with urgent letters for Hotspur, but Hotspur decides that he does not have time to read them. He and the other leaders withdraw to prepare their troops for battle.

V.III Location: the battlefield of Shrewsbury

The Douglas kills Sir Walter Blunt, and Falstaff refuses to lend Hal his sword.

The army of King Henry and the forces of the Percy rebellion clash. The Douglas, the fearless leader of the Scotsmen, searches the battlefield for Henry. He meets Sir Walter Blunt, dressed like the king and acting as a decoy. The two fight, and the Douglas kills Blunt. Hotspur enters and identifies the dead Blunt as an impostor. The two leave in search of the real Henry. Falstaff appears, trying to avoid the heat of the battle. He encounters a breathless Hal, who has lost his sword. Hal asks Falstaff if he can borrow his sword, but Falstaff does not want to give it up and go unarmed. Disgusted, Hal leaves, and Falstaff goes off in a different direction.

V.IV Location: the battlefield of Shrewsbury

Hal protects his father from the Douglas and kills Hotspur; Falstaff avoids dangerous combat and pretends it was he who killed Hotspur.

Hal reenters with his father, his brother John, and Westmoreland. He is wounded but refuses to stop fighting and seek medical attention. He heads off with John and Westmoreland to fight, leaving Henry alone. The Douglas reenters, still seeking the king. Henry bravely meets the Douglas in single combat, although he knows that he can hardly hope to win. Hal reappears and challenges the Douglas, whom he beats back so ferociously that the Douglas flees the field. Henry thanks his son with warmth and pride, saying he respects him once again. Hal heads back into battle.

Hotspur enters and finds Hal alone. They identify one another and agree to fight to the death. In the heat of their battle, Falstaff wanders in. The fighters do not notice him, but Falstaff cheers Hal on. The Douglas returns again and attacks Falstaff. Falstaff falls down, pretending to be dead, and the Douglas leaves him where he lies.

Hal kills Hotspur. Spying Falstaff lying on the ground as if dead, Hal eulogizes both and leaves after vowing to come back and bury them. As soon as Hal is gone, Falstaff springs up and stabs the dead Hotspur in the leg. When Hal and John reenter, Falstaff claims that he fought a bloody battle with the wounded Hotspur after Hal left and finally finished him off. John and the dumbfounded Hal decide to settle the matter later. They hear trumpets sounding retreat and all return together to the base camp.

V.V Location: the battlefield of Shrewsbury

Hal orders the Douglas set free, and Henry makes plans for dealing with the remaining rebel leaders.

Henry's forces have won the battle. The rebel leaders are all dead or captured. Henry, who has discovered that Worcester did not deliver his offer of peace to Hotspur, orders Worcester and Vernon executed. News arrives that the Douglas has been captured. Hal asks his father for permission to handle the case and then commands that the Douglas be set free in recognition of his valor and integrity. Henry, realizing that there are still powerful rebels left alive, makes plans to deal with them. He will send John and Westmoreland to York to contend with Northumberland and the archbishop, whom he knows are up in arms against him. Meanwhile, he will take Prince Hal with him to Wales to see to Mortimer and Owain Glendower.

ANALYSIS OF MAJOR CHARACTERS IN *1 HENRY IV*

PRINCE HAL

Prince Hal, the only character to move between the grave, serious world of King Henry and Hotspur and the rollicking, comical world of Falstaff and the Boar's Head Tavern, bridges the play's two major plotlines. An initially disreputable prince who eventually wins back his honor and the king's esteem, Hal undergoes the greatest dramatic development in the play, deliberately transforming himself from the wastrel he pretends to be into a noble leader. Additionally, as the character whose sense of honor and leadership Shakespeare most directly endorses, Hal is the moral focus of the play. He is also a complicated character whose real nature is difficult to pin down. As a young man, he is capable of sly psychological machinations, idling away his time with Falstaff and earning the displeasure of his father and England, and then announcing that his dissolute lifestyle is all an act: he is simply trying to lower expectations so that he can emerge as his true, heroic self and win the people's love and his father's admiration.

The plan is wily, but the deceit it involves calls his honor into question. His treatment of Falstaff further muddies his character. There is real affection between the prince and the roguish knight, but Hal also torments and humiliates his friend. Whatever his merit as an individual, Hal's complexity and self-control make him an ideal leader.

SIR JOHN FALSTAFF

Old, fat, lazy, selfish, dishonest, corrupt, thieving, manipulative, boastful, and lecherous, Falstaff is perhaps the most popular of all of Shakespeare's comic characters. Though he is a knight, Falstaff has nothing to do with ideals of courtly chivalry. As Falstaff notes, honor is useless to him: "Can honour set-to a leg? No. Or an arm? No. Or take away the grief of a wound? No. . . . What is honour? A word" (V.i.130–133). He perceives honor as a mere "word," an abstract concept that has no relevance to practical matters. Falstaff scorns morality largely because he has such a hearty appetite for life and finds the niceties of courtesy and honor useless when there are jokes to be told and feasts to be eaten. A creature of words, Falstaff constantly creates a myth of himself, a myth that defines his identity even when it is revealed as false. A master of punning and wordplay, Falstaff provides most of the comedy in the play.

KING HENRY IV

King Henry IV, the title character of this play, is not yet an old man in *1 Henry IV*, but concern over his crumbling kingdom, guilt over his uprising against Richard II, and concern about his son's behavior have diluted his earlier energy and strength. Henry remains stern, aloof, and resolute, but he is no longer the force of nature he was in *Richard II*, in which, as the ambitious, energetic, and capable Bolingbroke, he seized the throne from the inept Richard II after likely arranging his murder. Henry's trouble stems from his own uneasy conscience and his uncertainty about the legitimacy of his rule. He is a murderer who has illegally usurped the throne from Richard II, so it is difficult to blame Hotspur and the Percys for wanting to usurp his throne for themselves. Furthermore, it is unclear whether Henry's kingship is any more legitimate than that of Richard II. Henry maintains a tight, tenuous hold on the throne and never loses his majesty. But with a lack of moral legitimacy and a sense of compromised honor, Henry is not a great king.

THEMES, MOTIFS & SYMBOLS IN *1 HENRY IV*

THEMES

THE NATURE OF HONOR   Shakespeare depicts honor not as a constant set of guidelines, but as a series of values and goals that varies from individual to individual. Hotspur, a quick-tempered and military-minded young man, believes that honor is achieving glory on the battlefield and defending one's reputation and good name from any perceived insult. For the troubled and contemplative King Henry IV, on the other hand, honor has to do with the well-being of the nation and the legitimacy of its ruler. Henry is troubled in part because he views his rebellion against Richard II, which won him the crown, as a dishonorable act. For Prince Hal, honor is a flexible concept that can be dropped and regained at will. Hal also conceives of honor almost as a physical possession. He believes that when he kills Hotspur, Hotspur's honor becomes his own. For the amoral rogue Falstaff, honor is nothing but hot air and wasted effort that does no one any good.

THE LEGITIMACY OF RULE   *1 Henry IV*, a tale of political instability and violent rebellion, is preoccupied with questions of rule. It investigates what makes a ruler legitimate, which qualities are desirable in a ruler, when it is acceptable to usurp a ruler's authority, and what consequences come of rebelling against a ruler. King Henry agrees that if a ruler is illegitimate, then it is acceptable to usurp his power. His own fears come from this belief, since he worries that his illegal usurpation of the crown makes his own rule illegitimate. Scenes depicting violent lawlessness and rebellion sweeping England illustrate the consequences of failed leadership. Shakespeare contrasts his major characters to explore desirable qualities in a ruler. Each man has a different leadership style: Henry is stern and aloof, Hal is unpredictable and intelligent, and Hotspur is decisive and hot-tempered. Hal's ability to think his way through a situation and to manipulate others without straying too far from the dictates of conscience seem to be the most successful kingly abilities.

HIGH AND LOW LANGUAGE   *1 Henry IV* easily switches back and forth between noble and lowly people. Because of the scope of its cast of characters, the play includes many different languages and manners of expression, from the Welsh and Irish the English characters cannot understand, to the coarse language Hal picks up and uses to insinuate himself in lower class society. Knowledge of these languages and the ability to shift between them is an invaluable tool for Hal. He makes fast friends with the bartenders precisely because, unlike his father, he is able to emulate them and speak their language. Hal is also a master of noble diction, as he proves when he eloquently declares his loyalty to his father. In addition to high speech and low speech, the play is full of the various accents of Britain's various locales.

MOTIFS

DOUBLES   *1 Henry IV* uses a number of doubles, contrasting pairs of characters, actions, and scenes. The differences between Hal and Hotspur illustrate different perceptions of honor, and the differences between the Boar's Head Tavern and the royal palace reveal the breadth of England's class differences. Falstaff and the king act are both father figures for Hal. Hal and Hotspur are both potential successors to Henry IV. Falstaff's comical robbery in Act II, scene ii is a double of the nobles' Battle of Shrewsbury.

MAGIC   Magic has very little to do with the plot of the play, but characters mention it with uncommon frequency. As with the subject of honor, a character's opinion about the existence of magic reveals more about the character than it does about magic itself. The pragmatic and overconfident Hotspur, for instance, expresses contempt for belief in the black arts, repeatedly mocking Glendower for claiming to have magical powers. The sensuous and narcissistic Glendower, by contrast, believes in magic and the idea that he is a magician.

SYMBOLS

REPRESENTATIVE CHARACTERS   Most characters in *1 Henry IV* represent the set of ideas and traits with which they are involved. Glendower represents both the Welsh motif and the magic motif. Hotspur represents rebellion and the idea that honor is won and lost in battle.

THE SUN   The sun represents the king and his reign. Both Hal and his father, Henry, use an image of the sun obscured by clouds to describe themselves. For King Henry, the clouds that blur his light are his own doubts about the legitimacy of his reign. For Hal, these clouds are his immaturity and initial refusal to accept his noble responsibilities. After accepting his royal duties, Hal can anticipate radiating regal glory.

IMPORTANT QUOTATIONS FROM *1 HENRY IV*

1. *Yea, there thou mak'st me sad and mak'st me sin*
   In envy that my Lord Northumberland
   Should be the father to so blest a son—
   A son who is the theme of honour's tongue,
   Amongst a grove the very straightest plant,
   Who is sweet Fortune's minion and her pride—
   Whilst I, by looking on the praise of him
   See riot and dishonor stain the brow
   Of my young Hal. O, that it could be proved
   That some night-tripping fairy had exchanged
   In cradle clothes our children where they lay,

And called mine Percy, his Plantagenet!

Location: I.i.77–88
Speaker: King Henry IV to Westmorland
Context: Henry contrasts Hotspur to his own wayward son

Henry praises the fame and fortune of young Hotspur, the son of Lord Northumberland, calling him "the theme of honour's tongue," and laments that his own son, Prince Hal, has been sullied by "riot and dishonour." Henry refers to an old English folk superstition—one of the many references to folk culture and magic in the play—that sometimes fairies switch young children at birth. Henry says he wishes a fairy had switched Hal and Hotspur at birth, so that he could claim Hotspur as his son. This quotation reveals the common view that Hal is a disappointment and introduces the doubles motif by describing Hal and Hotspur as son figures for Henry. It also foreshadows the rivalry of Hal and Hotspur and establishes Henry's careworn, worried condition.

---

2. *I know you all, and will awhile uphold*
   The unyoked humour of your idleness.
   Yet herein will I imitate the sun,
   Who doth permit the base contagious clouds
   To smother up his beauty from the world,
   That when he please again to be himself,
   Being wanted, he may be more wondered at
   By breaking through the foul and ugly mists
   Of vapours that did seem to strangle him.
   If all the year were playing holidays,
   To sport would be as tedious as to work;
   But when they seldom come, they wished-for come,
   And nothing pleaseth but rare accidents.
   So, when this loose behaviour I throw off
   And pay the debt I never promisèd,
   By how much better than my word I am,
   By so much shall I falsify men's hopes;
   And like bright metal on a sullen ground,
   My reformation, glitt'ring o'er my fault,
   Shall show more goodly and attract more eyes
   Than that which hath no foil to set it off.
   I'll so offend to make offence a skill,
   Redeeming time when men think least I will.

Location: I.ii.173–195
Speaker: Prince Hal
Context: Hal speaks of his deception

Prince Hal nominally addresses this monologue to Falstaff and his friends, who have just left the room. It is in this speech that Hal first reveals his deception, saying his idling with the Boar's Head company is all an act. When the need arises, he will cast off the deception and reveal his true, noble nature. Hal tells the departed Falstaff that he "will a while uphold / The unyoked humour of your idleness," but that, just as the sun permits the clouds to cover is so that the people who miss its light will be all the happier when it reappears, he too will hide behind the cloud cover of his lower-class friends and then emerge in a blaze of glory. Hal says people quickly tire of anything familiar. If every day were a holiday, he says, then holidays would soon seem as tiresome as work. Hal concludes that by earning the people's disapproval with his current behavior, he will appear all the more glorious when he finally decides to behave well. This quotation exposes the complexities and ambiguities of an apparently virtuous young man who willingly lies to achieve his somewhat selfish goals.

3. *When I was dry with rage and extreme toil,*

   . . .

   Came there a certain lord, neat and trimly dressed,
   Fresh as a bridegroom, and his chin, new-reaped
   Showed like a stubble-land at harvest-home.
   He was perfumèd like a milliner,

   . . .

   With many holiday and lady terms
   He questioned me; amongst the rest demanded
   My prisoners in your majesty's behalf.
   I then, all smarting with my wounds being cold —
   To be so pestered with a popinjay! —
   Out of my grief and my impatience
   Answered neglectingly, I know not what —
   He should, or should not — for he made me mad
   To see him shine so brisk, and smell so sweet,
   And talk so like a waiting gentlewoman

   . . .

   So cowardly, and but for these vile guns
   He would himself have been a soldier.

Location: I.iii.28–68
Speaker: Hotspur to Henry
Context: Hotspur explains why he did not release a group of prisoners when Henry's messenger ordered him to do so

Hotspur tells Henry that the messenger, who confronted him immediately after a pitched battle, disgusted him with his simpering and effeminate behavior. Hotspur's explanation reveals him to be a soldierly man with no patience for weakness, fashion, cowardice, manners, or the niceties of courtly behavior. Although Hotspur takes pains to portray himself as a man of action rather than words, his speech about the messenger is long, eloquent, and vivid. He describes the "neat and trimly dressed" courtier who reminds him of a "waiting gentlewoman."

---

4. Falstaff: *But to say I know more harm in him than in myself were to say more than I know. That he is*
   old, the more the pity, his white hairs do witness it. But that he is, saving your reverence, a
   whoremaster, that I utterly deny. If sack and sugar be a fault, God help the wicked. If to be old and
   merry be a sin, then many an old host that I know is damned. If to be fat be to be hated, then
   Pharaoh's lean kine are to be loved. No, my good lord, banish Peto, banish Bardolph, banish Poins,
   but for sweet Jack Falstaff, kind Jack Falstaff, true Jack Falstaff, valiant Jack Falstaff, and therefore
   more valiant being, as he is, old Jack Falstaff,
   Banish not him thy Hal's company,
   Banish not him thy Hal's company.
   Banish plump Jack, and banish all the world.
   Prince: *I do; I will.*

Location: II.v.425–439
Speaker: Sir John Falstaff and Prince Hal
Context: Falstaff pretends to be Hal so that Hal can prepare for his upcoming meeting with his father

Falstaff uses his time in the role of King Henry mainly to praise himself, urging Hal to keep Falstaff near him. The real king would never make this recommendation, of course. Playing Hal, Falstaff lists his own faults and then mitigates each of them—"If sack and sugar be a fault, God help the wicked. If to be old and merry be a sin, then many and old host that I know is damned." Then, in a burst of self-praise, he

393

lists his own supposed virtues, calling himself "sweet," "kind," "true," and "valiant." Falstaff is not sweet, kind, true, or valiant, but his constant claims to be these things are part of what makes him endearing. As he reveals in this speech, Falstaff understands that he is undesirable company for Hal and worries that Hal will one day break his ties with him. Hal's icy reply that he will banish Falstaff foreshadows his actual break with him in the next play.

---

5. *Well, 'tis no matter; honour pricks me on. Yea, but how if honour prick me off when I come on? How then? Can honour set-to a leg? No. Or an arm? No. Or take away the grief of a wound? No. Honour hath no skill in surgery, then? No. What is honour? A word. What is in that word "honour"? What is that "honour"? Air. A trim reckoning! Who hath it? He that died o' Wednesday. Doth he feel it? No. Doth he hear it? No. 'Tis insensible then? Yea, to the dead. But will it not live with the living? No. Why? Detraction will not suffer it. Therefore I'll none of it. Honour is a mere scutcheon. And so ends my catechism.*

Location: V.i.129–139
Speaker: Sir John Falstaff
Context: Falstaff is about to go into battle

Falstaff delivers this diatribe against honor just before the climax of the play. Linking honor to violence, Falstaff says that honor "pricks him on" to fight, meaning that honor motivates him. Changing the meaning of the word, he then asks what he will do if honor "pricks him off"—that is, kills or injures him. He says that honor is useless when one is wounded: it cannot set an arm or a leg, or take away the "grief of a wound," or operate on you. In fact, being merely a word, honor is nothing but thin air—the breath that one exhales in saying a word. Falstaff says that the only people who have honor are the dead, and it does them no good because they cannot feel or hear it. He therefore concludes that honor is worthless, "a mere scutcheon," and that he wants nothing to do with it. In a play obsessed with the idea of honor, this speech calls into question the moral system on which most of the characters base their lives.

2 HENRY IV

King Henry IV's weakness makes England vulnerable to ambitious nobles and rebellious commoners.

2 HENRY IV IN CONTEXT

2 Henry IV is the third part of tetralogy, or four-part series, that deals with the historical rise of the English royal House of Lancaster. (*Richard II* and *Henry IV, Part 1* precede it, and *Henry V* follows it.) Shakespeare probably wrote the play around the year 1598.

Although the events he writes about occurred some two centuries before his own time, Shakespeare expected his audience to be familiar with the characters and events he was describing. The battles among houses and the rise and fall of kings were woven into the cultural fabric of England and formed an integral part of the country's patriotic legends and national mythology. One might compare this knowledge to the American public's general awareness of the events and figures of the American Revolution, which occurred more than two centuries ago. As it did for the English commoners of Shakespeare's era, the passage of time has obscured many of the specific details of important historical events, and thus the heroes and battles of an event like the American Revolution are, to some degree, cloaked in myth. Similarly, Shakespearean history is often inaccurate in its details, although it reflects popular conceptions of history.

Shakespeare drew on a number of sources in writing his history plays, as he did in nearly all his work. Scholars generally agree that the primary source for historical material is the second edition of Raphael Holinshed's massive work *The Chronicles of England, Scotland and Ireland*, published in 1587. Holinshed's account provides the fundamental chronology of events that Shakespeare follows, alters, or conveniently ignores to suit his dramatic purposes.

An important question that preoccupies the characters in the history plays, including *2 Henry IV*, is whether or not God appointed the king of England. If he is divinely appointed, then the overthrow, deposition, or, worst of all, murder of a king is an affront to God. In Shakespeare's works, as in the classical Greek tragedies (such as Aeschylus's *Oresteia*), a king who deposes or murders his predecessor may suffer for it, and so may his descendants. In the play that bears his name, Richard II is haunted by a politically motivated murder — not that of an actual king but that of his uncle, Thomas of Woodstock, Duke of Gloucester. In *Henry IV, Part I*, Henry IV is haunted by his own responsibility for Richard's overthrow and eventual murder by a hired assassin. Only after Henry IV's death does his own son, Henry V, symbolically prove himself worthy to rule as king of England.

2 HENRY IV: KEY FACTS

Full title: The Second Part of Henry IV (2 Henry IV)

Time and place written: Probably 1598; London

Date of first publication: Around 1598-1600

Genre: Historical drama, military drama

Setting (time): Early fifteenth century

Setting (place): England

Protagonist: Henry IV

Major conflict: The ailing King Henry IV worries that his son, Hal, is too reckless and irresponsible to be a good king.

2 HENRY IV: CHARACTER LIST

Ensign Pistol An extremely aggressive army ensign who serves under Falstaff. Ensign Pistol is also known as "Ancient Pistol" ("ancient" meant "ensign" in Elizabethan English).

Lord Bardolph An ally of Northumberland's. Lord Bardolph brings Northumberland the false news of Hotspur's success in I.i. (He is not to be confused with Falstaff's friend Bardolph.)

Davy One of Justice Shallow's household servants. Davy is honest, industrious, and talkative.

Sir John Falstaff Prince Hal's mentor and close friend. A fat, cheerful, witty, aging criminal, Falstaff pretended to kill Hotspur at the Battle of Shrewsbury, and Prince Hal—the real killer—agreed to go along with the lie. Everyone respects Falstaff because they think he killed Hotspur.

Fang and Snare Incompetent officers of the law. Mistress Quickly calls Fang and Snare to arrest Falstaff in II.i.

Owen Glendower A mysterious and influential leader of a group of rebel guerrilla fighters in Wales. Glendower never appears onstage.

Prince Hal (later King Henry V) Called "Hal" by Falstaff and his friends, the prince is also called Prince Henry, Harry, Prince Harry, Harry Monmouth, the Prince of Wales, and, after his father's death, King Henry V. Hal, the play's protagonist, changes from a youthful hell-raiser into a dignified king.

King Henry IV The ruling king of England at the beginning of the play. Henry's health declines throughout the play, in part due to his anxiety about civil insurrection and the fate of his son, Hal. He dies before the end of the play, never having fulfilled his dream of leading a company of soldiers to fight in the Crusades in Jerusalem.

Hotspur Northumberland's deceased son and a leader of the rebellion against the king. Hotspur was also called Percy or Harry Percy. Prince Hal killed him at the Battle of Shrewsbury.

Prince John, Duke of Lancaster; Humphrey, Duke of Gloucester; Thomas, Duke of Clarence Sons of King Henry IV and younger brothers of Prince Hal.

The Lord Chief Justice The most powerful official of the law in England. Level-headed, calm, perceptive, and intelligent, the Lord Chief Justice is a close advisor to King Henry IV. He also becomes an advisor and father figure for Prince Hal after Henry IV's death.

Mouldy, Shadow, Wart, Feeble, and Bullcalf Army recruits. Falstaff inspects the recruits in Gloucestershire, and all but Shadow, Wart, and Feeble bribe their way out of service.

Mowbray and Hastings Two lords. Mowbray and Hastings conspire with the Archbishop of York to overthrow King Henry IV.

Page The boy who carries Falstaff's sword and runs his errands.

Henry Percy, Earl of Northumberland A powerful northern nobleman. The earl, usually called Northumberland but sometimes called Percy, lost his brother, Worcester, and son, Hotspur, in battle against King Henry IV.

Poins, Peto, Bardolph Friends of Falstaff's and Prince Hal's. Formerly highwaymen and robbers, they have, like Falstaff, gotten richer and gained prestige since the Battle of Shrewsbury. Poins is the smartest of the bunch and the closest to Hal. Bardolph, an insatiable drinker, has a famously bright red nose.

Mistress Quickly The proprietress of the seedy Boar's Head Tavern in Eastcheap, London. Mistress Quickly has a dim wit but a good heart.

Justice Shallow and Justice Silence Middle-class country landowners and justices of the peace (minor local law officers). Shallow and Silence, who are cousins, live up to their names: Justice Shallow talks endlessly about trivial topics, while Justice Silence opens his mouth only to sing raunchy songs when he gets drunk.

Doll Tearsheet Falstaff's favorite prostitute and a good friend of Mistress Quickly's. Doll has a bottomless repertoire of insults and is fiercer and smarter than most of the law officers hanging around Eastcheap. She may be in love with Falstaff.

Travers Northumberland's servant.

Earl of Warwick, Earl of Surrey, Earl of Westmorland, Gower, Harcourt, Sir John Blunt Noblemen, and allies and advisors to King Henry IV.

Archbishop of York   A powerful northern clergyman. The Archbishop of York leads the rebellion against King Henry IV.

2 HENRY IV: PLOT OVERVIEW

At the end of *Henry IV, Part 1*, King Henry and Prince Hal (also known as Prince Harry) defeated part of the rebel forces at the battle of Shrewsbury, and Hal became a military hero. In *2 Henry IV*, they must face the rebel forces of the Archbishop of York, Lord Mowbray, and Lord Hastings. Hal's younger brother, Prince John, tricks the rebels into dismissing their troops by promising to negotiate with them. He then has the leaders executed for treason.

The central question in *2 Henry IV* is whether Henry will become a responsible ruler or abuse his position by indulging the criminals he befriended in his youth. Falstaff, Hal's low-class friend and mentor, is now a captain. He and Hal's other no-account friends think they will have the run of the kingdom when Hal is king. King Henry, concerned about the rebels and his wayward son, falls ill. Hal repents his former behavior and vows to be a responsible king, and Henry forgives him before dying. Hal is crowned King Henry V. When Falstaff comes to greet him in London, Hal banishes him and goes into court to plan an invasion of France.

2 HENRY IV: SCENE SUMMARY

ACT 1

Northumberland and his rebel forces suffer serious defeats at the hands of the forces of King Henry IV, including the death of Hotspur, but they maintain hope and plan new attacks.

PROLOGUE   Location: Warkworth, near Northumberland's castle

Rumor explains its job and describes the conflict between Northumberland and King Henry IV.

Rumor, a semi-mythological personification of gossip, presents a prologue to the play. It tells us that its job is to carry messages across the world as fast as the wind. Its messages are usually false and often trick people into making bad mistakes. Rumor causes nations to ready for war when no war is coming and makes people think that all is peaceful despite danger and conspiracy. Since crowds are always quick to believe gossip, it never has any trouble doing its job.

Rumor is now in northern England visiting the castle of the Earl of Northumberland, a powerful nobleman. Northumberland is part of a dangerous conspiracy to overthrow King Henry IV. The rebel army, led by Northumberland's son, young Hotspur, has just been defeated by the king's forces at Shrewsbury, but Rumor has come to misinform Northumberland, telling him that his side has won and that his son, Hotspur, is still safe—both lies.

I.I   Location: outside Northumberland's castle

Northumberland receives bad news: most of the rebel forces have been defeated, and Prince Hal has killed his son, Hotspur.

Lord Bardolph, a messenger from the battle, arrives at Northumberland's house with news from Shrewsbury, where the great battle is taking place. He tells Northumberland that the rebels are victorious: King Henry has suffered wounds, his allies are hostages or are dead, and Prince Hal has killed the king's own son, Hotspur. Another messenger, Travers, arrives with more recent news: the rebels have lost badly. Lord Bardolph does not believe him, but a third messenger, Morton, confirms Travers's news. He also reports Hotspur's death. When the rebel army saw that their leader, Hotspur, was dead, they turned and ran. The king's forces have taken Northumberland's brother and the co-leader of the rebellion, the Earl of Worcester, prisoner, and have done the same with the Douglas, a Scottish leader who has been aiding the rebels.

Heartbroken, Northumberland vows to take a terrible revenge. Lord Bardolph and Morton calm him, reminding him that everyone knew the risks of war. Morton also reminds Northumberland that there are still some rebel allies who have not been defeated. The Archbishop of York, who did not fight at Shrewsbury, is mustering up forces to continue opposing King Henry. Northumberland says he will get a grip on himself. He sends letters to his allies in order to get things moving as quickly as possible.

I.II Location: a London street

Falstaff talks with his page and the Lord Chief Justice.

Sir John Falstaff, a friend of Prince Hal's, is an old, fat, rowdy and witty scoundrel who has gained fame and importance since the Battle of Shrewsbury by pretending that he killed the courageous rebel leader Hotspur. Actually, the deed was done by Prince Hal was the murderer, who willingly let Falstaff take credit for it.

Falstaff now has a page to carry his sword. He asks his page what the doctor said about Falstaff's urine sample, and the page says the doctor thought the urine was possibly diseased. Falstaff asks what the merchant said about the fancy new suit he ordered, and the page admits that the merchant refused Falstaff's order because of his shady credit. Falstaff bursts into a stream of witty insults against the absent merchant.

The Lord Chief Justice, the top legal official in the court of England, approaches Falstaff to speak with him about a criminal charge regarding the robbery at Gads Hill. It seems that Falstaff was ordered into court several weeks ago in connection with the highway robbery, but he did not appear because he was suddenly called away to fight on the king's side in the recent civil war that had culminated at the Battle of Shrewsbury. The Justice, who is not fooled by Falstaff's new rank and importance, calmly ignores Falstaff's insults and tells Falstaff that he (the Justice) will be forgiving this time, since there is no need to reopen old wounds. We learn that Falstaff is being called away to fight the Earl of Northumberland and the Archbishop of York, as part of an army led by Prince John, the younger son of King Henry. After the justice leaves, Falstaff sends his page off with letters to the military leaders and goes to prepare to leave for the war.

I.III Location: the palace of the Archbishop of York

The Archbishop and three of his allies agree to maintain their rebellion against King Henry IV, even though they are not sure whether Northumberland can be counted on to send troops to their aid.

The Archbishop and three of his allies—Thomas Mowbray, the Earl Marshal; Lord Hastings; and Lord Bardolph—are planning their next move against King Henry's forces. The critical question is whether or not the Earl of Northumberland will support them. If he sends his army, the rebels will have enough men to stand a good chance against the king, but if he does not, their numbers may be too few. Hastings argues that Northumberland is sure to send his troops because he is angry about the death of his son Hotspur, but Lord Bardolph and the Archbishop point out that Hotspur lost, in part, because at the last minute his father decided against sending his troops. Hastings reminds them that the king must now divide his forces into three separate parts—one to fight them, one to fight the guerrilla rebels, led by Owen Glendower, in Wales, and one to maintain the fight in a current dispute with the French. The three conspirators agree to move ahead with their challenge of the king, whether or not Northumberland supports them.

ACT II

Prince Hal plays a practical joke on Falstaff, who insults him; Northumberland decides not to send his troops to aid the rebels.

II.I Location: near the Boar's Head Tavern in Eastcheap, London

Falstaff manages to avoid paying Mistress Quickly the money he owes her; the Lord Chief Justice urges him to head toward the battle.

Mistress Quickly, the dim-witted but good-hearted hostess of the Boar's Head Tavern, one of Falstaff's favorite dives, talks to two officers of the law. She has called them to arrest Falstaff for the large unpaid bar tab he owes her. The officers, Fang and Snare, try to arrest Falstaff when he walks in, but Falstaff attacks the officers with the help of his page and his friend Bardolph. The Lord Chief Justice unexpectedly enters with his men, breaking up the fight. The justice orders Falstaff to compensate Mistress Quickly both for the money he owes her and for a false promise he made to marry her—the first by paying her the money he owes, the second by apologizing. Falstaff takes Mistress Quickly aside and, instead of paying her, convinces her to pawn her silver plates and tapestries in order to lend him ten pounds. Falstaff also makes arrangements to have supper that night at the Boar's Head Tavern with a favorite prostitute of his named Doll Tearsheet.

Gower, one of King Henry IV's courtiers, enters with messages for the Lord Chief Justice. The king, who has been fighting native rebels in Wales, is returning to London. A portion of his forces has gone to the north of England to face the rebelling Earl of Northumberland and Archbishop of York. The justice sends Falstaff on his way, telling him he should start his journey. He will have to draft men along the way in order to have a company of soldiers to command when he reaches the battle.

II.II Location: Hal's house

Prince Hal expresses regret about his youthful carousing with Falstaff and others, and plans to play a practical joke on Falstaff.

Prince Hal, who has recently come back from the Battle of Shrewsbury, is with Poins, one of the smarter, quieter, and more dangerous members of Falstaff's crowd. Hal says he is tired and could use some beer, but he will not drink any because he has started to have mixed feelings about the days when he used to drink and carouse with Falstaff, Poins, Bardolph, and the rest. Implying that he regrets these gatherings, he subtly insults Poins. Hal says he feels terrible about his father, King Henry IV, who is very sick. Poins thinks Hal is being a hypocrite, but Hal swears he is not.

Bardolph comes in with Falstaff's page, who bears a letter to Hal from Falstaff. The letter is brief and ridiculous. Using silly, high-flown language, it says nothing but hello and good-bye. Prince Hal suddenly decides to play a practical joke. Learning from Falstaff's page that Falstaff plans to eat at the Boar's Head with Doll Tearsheet tonight, Hal agrees to Poins's suggestion that the two of them dress up as servingmen and spy on Falstaff. Bardolph and the page agree to keep their mouths shut, and everyone heads off to get ready.

II.III Location: the Earl of Northumberland's castle

Lady Percy convinces Northumberland not to send troops to aid the rebels.

Northumberland talks with his wife, Lady Northumberland, and his daughter-in-law, Lady Percy—the widow of his son Hotspur. Northumberland has been saying that he plans to go back to war against the king, and both women have been trying to persuade him not to go. Lady Percy is angry. She reminds Northumberland that his son—her husband—is dead because Northumberland refused to send his troops to help him at Shrewsbury. She argues that there is little point in going back to war now. Northumberland decides that she is right and that he will leave the Archbishop of York and Mowbray, the Earl Marshal, to fight alone against the king.

II.IV Location: the Boar's Head Tavern

Falstaff insults Hal and Poins, angering Hal; army captains come for Falstaff, and he leaves for war.

Falstaff has dinner with Bardolph, Mistress Quickly, and Doll Tearsheet. An old acquaintance, Ancient Pistol—an ensign in the army who serves under Falstaff—pays a visit. Pistol is prone to fighting and nearly gets into a brawl with Doll Tearsheet. Falstaff and Bardolph drive him out, and Doll sits in Falstaff's lap and flirts with him. Musicians enter and play music. Prince Hal and Poins come in, disguised as barmen in order to spy on Falstaff, and serve dinner. Doll questions Falstaff about his friends, and Falstaff jovially insults Hal and Poins. Hal and Poins reveal themselves, and Hal angrily accuses Falstaff of hypocrisy. Falstaff is flustered, and they get into an argument.

Peto, another of Falstaff's men, enters with news. King Henry IV has returned to Westminster Palace, his castle outside London, and the officers of the army are seeking Falstaff. Hal and Poins leave for the castle. Army captains come to the tavern asking for Falstaff. The Hostess and Doll bid Falstaff a touching good-bye, and he goes off to war.

ACT III

King Henry philosophizes and plans for the war; Falstaff visits an old friend and drums up three recruits.

III.I   Location: King Henry's Westminster Palace

King Henry thinks about power, time, betrayal, and thwarted dreams, and talks to the Earl of Warwick and the Earl of Surrey about the war.

It is the middle of the night. King Henry is making war plans. He talks to himself and the audience, saying he suffers from bad insomnia and these days cannot sleep at all. He addresses a personified sleep, bemoaning the way sleep visits even the poorest of his subjects, but he, the wealthy king, is kept awake by worry and remorse. He concludes that people in positions of power are usually unhappier than poor people, saying, "Uneasy lies the head that wears the crown."

The Earl of Warwick and the Earl of Surrey enter and discuss the nation's current state of affairs with the king. They know that the Earl of Northumberland is considering waging war against them. (They do not yet know what Shakespeare revealed in II.iii: that Northumberland has decided against supporting the rebellion.) The king comments on how swiftly time flows, how the years turn, and how people change. Less than ten years ago, Northumberland was a good friend of King Richard II, the king who reigned before Henry IV and was Henry IV's cousin. Eight years ago, Northumberland turned against Richard and helped Henry take the throne from him. Now Northumberland has turned against Henry himself. King Richard prophesied this, and King Henry is now disturbed at the realization that Richard was right.

Warwick says Richard simply guessed that Northumberland would turn on Henry because he had already betrayed Richard. King Henry agrees, and the conversation turns to the course of the war. Warwick does not believe the rumor that the rebels have fifty thousand men. He thinks they probably have no more than half that number. He has good new from the west: Owen Glendower, the leader of the rebellious Welsh guerrilla fighters, is dead, so the king will be able to focus his efforts on the English rebels. The lords urge Henry, who is in bad health, to go to bed. Henry agrees to their council, but before going to bed he expresses regret that this war has prevented him from joining the Crusades in Jerusalem.

III.II   Location: rural Gloucestershire

Falstaff visits Justice Shallow and Justice Silence and picks out three recruits.

Cousins Justice Shallow and Justice Silence are two prosperous farmers and justices of the peace, or minor law officials. They are getting ready for Falstaff's arrival. Falstaff will be coming through Gloucestershire looking for recruits to draft into the king's war. Both men live up to their names. Shallow talks jovially and abundantly, and Silence answers Shallow but seldom begins a conversation. Shallow talks about farming, neighbors, and fond memories of his school days. He and Falstaff went to college together at the Inns of Court, the elite law school in London. Shallow fondly recalls their visits with the "bona-robas" (high-class prostitutes) of London. He remembers watching Falstaff beat up a man named Scoggin at the very gate of the court when Falstaff was a mere "crack," or boy.

Falstaff and Bardolph arrive, and the two justices present the recruits they have rounded up. The recruits are country men named Mouldy, Shadow, Wart, Feeble, and Bullcalf. They are mostly ragged and skinny, but Falstaff chooses all of them except Wart, ordering Bardolph to write down their names in the book of draftees. Bullcalf and Mouldy bribe Bardolph to let them off the hook, and when Bardolph quietly passes on the word to Falstaff, he tells them they can go. Justice Shallow is confused and protests loudly that Falstaff has not chosen the best men. Falstaff bewilders him with a grandiose speech about how a soldier's physical strength is not always the best measure of his valor. He declares that he will take only Shadow, Feeble, and Wart.

Shallow presses Falstaff to stay for dinner, but Falstaff says he must march on toward the war. They exchange fond good-byes. Once alone, Falstaff recalls in a vindictive soliloquy that Shallow has always been a fool. Now that Shallow is also rich, Falstaff decides that if he returns from the war he will come back and steal money from Shallow.

ACT IV

Prince John defeats the rebels by deceiving them, and the dying King Henry reconciles with Hal.

IV.I Location: Gaultree Forest in Yorkshire

Prince John tricks the rebel leaders into disbanding their army and then orders them executed.

The leaders of the rebel army—the Archbishop of York, Mowbray, and Hastings—have arrived with their army. The Archbishop tells his allies he has received a letter from Northumberland saying he will not come to their aid. A soldier returning to the camp from a scouting mission reports that King Henry's army is barely a mile away. Prince John, the king's younger son, leads the army. The king is in bad health at Westminster.

The Earl of Westmoreland, an ally of King Henry's, enters and accuses the Archbishop of improperly using his religious authority to support rebellion. The Archbishop says he did not want to, but he felt he had no choice, since King Henry was leading the country into ruin and refusing to address the rebels' complaints. Westmoreland tells the rebels that Prince John has been given full authority to act in the king's name and is willing to grant their demands if they seem reasonable. The Archbishop gives Westmoreland a list of the rebels' demands, and Westmoreland leaves to show it to Prince John.

While the rebels wait for Westmoreland to return, Mowbray says he fears that the royal family will have them killed even if they do make peace. Hastings and the Archbishop assure him that his fears are groundless. Westmoreland returns and leads the rebels to speak with Prince John. John says the rebels' demands look reasonable, so he will grant all of them. The rebels should discharge their army and let the soldiers go home.

Very pleased, the rebel leaders send word that their soldiers can go home. They drink with Prince John and discuss the upcoming peace. As soon as word comes from the rebels' messengers that their army has scattered, Prince John orders Hastings, Mowbray, and the Archbishop arrested as traitors. When they ask how he can be so dishonorable, Prince John says he is not breaking his word. He promised to address their complaints, and he will, but he never promised not to kill the rebels themselves. He gives orders for the rebels to be taken away and executed.

IV.II Location: Gaultree Forest in Yorkshire

Falstaff takes a captive, turns him over for execution, and heads to Gloucestershire.

Sir John Coleville of the Dale, one of the departing rebels, runs into Falstaff, who has finally made it to the field of battle. Recognizing Falstaff and believing him to be the man who killed Hotspur, Coleville surrenders to him. Prince John enters and Falstaff presents his captive to him. Westmoreland appears and tells John that the army is withdrawing. John sends Coleville off with the other rebels to execution and then he says he will return to the court in London because he hears that his father is very sick. Falstaff heads off to Gloucestershire, intending to extort money from Justice Shallow.

IV.III Location: the Jerusalem chamber in Westminster Palace

King Henry, dying, rages at Hal for his irresponsible ways; Hal weeps, apologizes, and professes his love for his father.

King Henry talks with his advisors and his younger sons, Thomas, Duke of Clarence and Humphrey, Duke of Gloucester. He says that as soon as the present civil war is resolved, he wants to lead an army to join the Crusades in Jerusalem. The king is very sick and may not last long. Learning that Hal is in London this evening with his rascally friends, the king laments Hal's waywardness. Westmoreland enters with news that the three rebel leaders—Mowbray, Hastings, and the Archbishop of York—have been executed. Harcourt, another lord, enters and announces that the rebellious Northumberland has been overthrown. The king rejoices. He suddenly feels much worse, and goes to lie quietly on a bed in another chamber.

Prince Hal enters, and his brothers tell him of their father's illness. Hal goes to sit by Henry's side. Contemplating the crown that lies beside him on the pillow, he criticizes it for imposing its heavy weight on his father. Henry seems to stop breathing, and Hal, thinking he is dead, reverentially lifts the crown onto his own head and goes into another room to think alone. King Henry wakes up and, calling his attendants, learns that Hal was with him a moment ago. Finding his crown gone, he grows angry and bitter, convinced that Hal has revealed his own greediness and lack of love for his father. Warwick spies Hal weeping in the next room, and King Henry sends the others away so that he can speak with Hal alone.

The king angrily rebukes Hal for being so quick to seize the crown. He condemns him for his careless, violent, freewheeling life and paints a vivid picture of the horrors he thinks England can expect when Hal becomes king. Hal kneels before his father, weeping, and swears that he loves his father and was full of grief when he thought he had died. He says he views the crown as an enemy to fight with, not as a treasure. King Henry, moved by the speech, lets Hal sit next to him. He tells Hal that he hopes he will find more peace as king than he did himself.

The younger princes return, and King Henry is pleased to see them. He asks the name of the chamber where he first collapsed and learns that it is called "Jerusalem." The king realizes that he will never see the real Jerusalem. There was a prophecy that he would die there, but now he realizes he will die in the room named "Jerusalem." The others carry him away to this room.

ACT V

V.I Location: Shallow's house in Gloucestershire

Falstaff goes to Shallow's house for dinner.

Justice Shallow welcomes Falstaff and Bardolph back to Gloucestershire and orders his servant, Davy, to prepare a fine dinner for the guests. Davy continually interrupts him, asking questions about the household management and requesting favors for servants and local peasants. Falstaff, left alone, laughs about Shallow's friendly foolishness and declares he will get enough stories out of Shallow to make Prince Hal laugh for a year.

V.II Location: Westminster Palace

King Henry IV has died, and Hal promises to be a just leader and listen to the council of the Lord Chief Justice.

King Henry IV has died and everyone in the castle is frightened of what will happen to them, and to the rule of law, now that Prince Hal is in charge. The Lord Chief Justice expects to be punished severely, since he always scolded Hal for his violations of the law. He also briefly imprisoned Hal after Hal struck him during a dispute, and he is the most despised enemy of Hal's lawless friends, particularly Falstaff. The young princes urge the justice to flatter Falstaff now, but the Justice says he has always done what he believes is right and he will not compromise now.

The former Prince Hal enters dressed in the royal robes of the king: he is now King Henry V. He tells his brothers and the courtiers not to worry and promises not to harm them. They continue looking at him strangely, especially the justice. King Henry V reminds the justice that he rebuked him and punished him for breaking the law when he was still a prince. The justice says that he was only maintaining the laws and order of Henry IV, the new king's own father. He asks Henry V to imagine himself in a similar situation and decide whether the justice was wrong.

King Henry V agrees with the justice. He tells the justice he has always been wise and just and thanks the justice for punishing him when he was a wild young prince. He asks the Justice to serve as a father figure to him, teaching him how to keep order honorably and help him keep his own future sons in line.

V.III Location: Shallow's house in Gloucestershire

Falstaff learns of Henry IV's death and assumes Hal will now give him a position of great prominence.

Falstaff eats a merry dinner with Justice Shallow and Justice Silence, as well as Bardolph, Davy, and Falstaff's page. The group eats good country fruit and meat, drinks wine, and laughs. Justice Silence surprises Falstaff by getting drunk and becoming very noisy, singing snatches of hearty, old-fashioned songs throughout the meal. When Falstaff comments on this approvingly, Silence tells him that there is nothing to be surprised at—he has been cheerful three times already in his life.

Ancient Pistol arrives unexpectedly with news from the court in London. Old King Henry IV is dead, and Prince Hal is now King Henry V. Falstaff and his friends assume that Falstaff will now be in a position of great comfort and power, since he is Hal's closest friend. Falstaff generously offers all his friends high positions in the court and calls for his horse, saying that they must all leave for London. Justice Silence, who seems to have succumbed to the effects of the wine, makes his drunken way to bed.

V.IV Location: a London street

Beadles drag Doll Tearsheet and Mistress Quickly off to see a justice.

Two beadles (minor law officers) drag Doll Tearsheet and Mistress Quickly from the Boar's Head Tavern. The hostess and Doll struggle and curse. Doll's insults are especially impressive and nearly unman the beadles. It seems that a man whom Pistol beat up while in their company has died, so the beadles are dragging the women off to jail, probably for a whipping, but possibly for execution. Doll claims to be pregnant, but the beadle accuses her of lying and says she has merely padded her belly with a cushion. The hostess wishes that Falstaff were there. The beadles take the indignant women to see a justice.

V.V Location: near Westminster Abbey

King Henry V renounces Hal and the others, forbidding them to come within ten miles of him.

Falstaff and his companions have ridden hard from Gloucestershire and wait to greet the newly crowned King Henry V and his attendants. Falstaff happily anticipates the warm welcome he will receive from the new king. But when he hails King Henry V (whom he still calls "Hal"), the king first ignores him and then tells him, "I know thee not, old man." He tells the bewildered Falstaff that he remembers dreaming about a foolish old man such as Falstaff is—fat, obscene, ridiculous—but now he has woken up and despises his former dream. The king says he has left behind the wild days he had as Prince Hal, and he will also leave behind the people he knew in those days. He says that Falstaff and the rest cannot come within ten miles of him. He will give Falstaff and his friends adequate income so that poverty does not drive them back into crime, and will provide them with advancement if they reform themselves.

The king sweeps onward without a backward look. Falstaff, astonished and confused, still retains some hope. He suggests to the others that Hal's speech was a formality performed for the sake of the public, and that later, in private, Hal will call for his old friend Falstaff. But that hope is dashed when the Lord Chief Justice returns accompanied by Prince John and several police officers. They have orders to take Falstaff and the others away to a prison, where they will stay until their exile from London. The officers lead Falstaff away.

Left alone with the Lord Chief Justice, Prince John comments admiringly on the way his older brother, the new King Henry V, handled his former friends. Prince John says he hears that the king has summoned his Parliament, and he expects they will discuss invading France. The Lord Chief Justice agrees, and the two depart together toward the court.

EPILOGUE

Epilogue apologizes and promises a sequel to the play.

A character called Epilogue offers an exaggeratedly humble apology for the "badness" of the play and requests applause from the audience. It also promises the audience a sequel to the play they have just seen—one that will feature Falstaff as well as the lovely Katherine of France. The epilogue concludes with a prayer for the Queen.

THEMES, MOTIFS & SYMBOLS IN *2 HENRY IV*

THEMES

THE PRICE OF POWER Henry IV, who seized the crown from Richard II and endured an attempted overthrow, is an amazing political success story. But Henry's success also leads to a lifetime of anxiety and guilt. No matter how wisely and effectively he reigns, he will never escape the fact that his regime—not only in other people's eyes, but in his own—is unlawful. The constant stress of illegitimacy causes Henry's premature aging and illness. He is king of the realm, but he cannot sleep at night. He admits that poor beggars sleep better than he does. To his great distress, he realizes that his political success may not have been worth the psychological anguish it entailed. Henry's realization that power carries a price pains him not only on his own behalf, but on his son's. He knows Hal will suffer the burden of kingship. Henry speaks his most famous line in the play—"Uneasy lies the head that wears the crown"(III.i.31)—in the third person, emphasizing that not only Henry himself, but every king, including Hal, is made uneasy by the monarchy. Although eventually Henry tries to believe that things will be easier for Hal, since Hal did not steal the kingship as Henry did, we suspect this is partly wishful thinking.

THE MEETING OF HIGH AND LOW *Henry IV* investigates many diverse aspects of social life, ranging from kings and nobles to prostitutes and innkeepers, and zigzagging from noble palaces to taverns and back again. The spectrum of social portraits provides a rich impression of England, juxtaposing the large-scale battles of the nobles with the network of ordinary people from upper and lower classes. Shakespeare reminds us that Doll Tearsheet and Mistress Quickly are just as much a part of England as Lady Percy. Hal, a man of lofty birth who associates with thugs and prostitutes, must reconcile his high status with his lowly tastes. He worries that his fondness for beer makes him vulgar, and frets over his association with low-born men like Falstaff and Poins. He says to Poins: "What a disgrace is it to me to remember thy name! Or to know thy face tomorrow!"(II.ii.12–13). Although he rejects these friends in the end, he will maintain a fondness for the lower classes, and a natural affinity for them, that will make him a better ruler.

The interrelation of high and low also characterizes the play's structure and language. More than half of the play is in prose, the traditional language of the lower classes in Shakespearean drama. Structurally, elements from the high-class stories of Henry and Hal often parallel the lower-class characters' stories, as when Justice Shallow's comments on mortality reflect the king's musings on death. These echoes of the high in the low suggest that the two are part of the same social fabric and the same human condition.

THE STRUGGLE BETWEEN LAWLESSNESS AND ORDER The forces of lawlessness always threaten to upset the social order in *Henry IV, Part II*. The Yorkist rebels are the clearest embodiment of this threat; they are associated throughout the Henry plays with "wild" parts of Britain like Scotland and Wales. The rebels' planned coup would overthrow the reigning monarch and turn his regime upside down. Other chaotic forces lurk everywhere. Falstaff, who repeatedly thumbs his nose at English law officers and the social order, is a comic figure, but he represents a serious form of disorder that threatens to engulf Hal. Hal vacillates between unruliness and sobriety, carousing in taverns and then feeling pangs of regret.

The political triumph of the law comes with the final squelching of the rebels. The personal triumph of the law comes when Hal, now Henry V, announces that he is a new man, rejects the company of Falstaff, and submits to the Lord Chief Justice who earlier punished Hal for disrespect. The Justice reminds Hal that the law is higher even than princes, and chastises him for striking a man who embodies order and justice: "Your highness pleased to forget my place, / The majesty and power of law and justice, / The image of the King whom I presented"(V.ii.76–78). The Justice's exalted vision of the "majesty and power of law" ends *2 Henry IV* with the sense that social order has been newly restored under the valiant and reformed Henry V.

MOTIFS

MATURITY *2 Henry IV* concerns the maturation of two royals. Hal undergoes the shift from carefree adolescence to responsible adulthood, and King Henry the shift from vigorous middle age to weakened old age. Both shifts call for reflection on the aims of human life, since Hal is approaching his heyday while Henry is growing old and disillusioned with his successes. For Hal, the question is what he will attain, while for Henry the question is whether his attainments have been worthwhile.

For Hal, maturation means self-reform. He vows that he will renounce not just his seedy friends, but his whole former self: "For God doth know, so shall the world perceive, / That I have turned away my former self; / So will I those that kept me company"(V.v.55–57). The totality of Hal's maturation is symbolized by the change of his name from Hal to Henry V. Shakespeare presents both men's processes as natural, but also as sad. As Henry ages, he contemplates his insomnia, his anxieties, and his weakening powers. Hal must cast off, regretfully, the boisterous adventures and friends of his youth.

TRICKERY Tricks, deceptions, and manipulations fill 2 Henry IV. The most objectionable use of deception is Prince John's deception of the rebels at Gaultree. When John appears to renege on a promise of asylum for the rebels, the Archbishop of York asks him, "Will you thus break your faith?"(IV.i.337). Prince John responds that he vowed he would listen to the rebels' grievances seriously, and he assures them he will do so "with a most Christian care" (341). But John carefully avoids promising not to kill the rebels. His cleverness is impressive, but the cruelty of his deception is unsettling. Another instance of trickery is Hal's disguise as a waiter, which tricks Falstaff into mildly slandering Hal. Even if Falstaff deserves what he gets, his abuse at Hal's hands is uncomfortable.

SYMBOLS

JERUSALEM Jerusalem symbolizes both the high and sacred aspirations of King Henry IV, and his disillusionment when he realizes how far short of his ideals he has fallen. Henry dreamed of fighting a holy Crusade in Jerusalem in 1 Henry IV, and talks about it again in 2 Henry IV, although now his longing is tinged with regret. He realizes that because of the rebellions at home, he will likely never make it to Jerusalem or attain the heights of heroism that Jerusalem symbolizes for him. Shakespeare underscores the shift in Jerusalem's symbolism from idealism to disillusionment in Act V, when King Henry asks whether the room where he first fell ill has a particular name. Warwick says, "'Tis called Jerusalem, my noble lord" (V.i.362). Jerusalem, which one symbolized heroism, now symbolizes King Henry's humble, human weakness. Henry recalls a prophecy: "I should not die but in Jerusalem, / Which vainly I supposed the Holy Land"(V.i.365–56). He now realizes that the prophecy referred not to a noble and exotic place, but to a humdrum bit of real estate.

SMALL BEER "Small beer," the watered-down beer that was considered a comforting, homey drink in Elizabethan England, symbolizes the lower-class tastes and interests that characterize Hal. Hal worries about his fondness for such a beverage, wondering whether it reflects badly on his royal blood: "Doth it not show vilely in me to desire small beer?"(II.ii.5–6). Just as he worries about his taste in alcohol, he worries about his taste in friends, who are not fitting companions for a crown prince. Hal frets to Poins about his own readiness "to take note how many pair of silk stocking thou hast"(II.ii.13–14). He worries that he should be thinking about more important matters than Poins's underwear.

Though Hal worries about his lower-class tastes, his concerns may be misplaced. People may like and respect a ruler all the more if he is not only wise and effective, as Hal turns out to be, but intimately familiar with the commoners. Hal's humble tastes make him seem like one of the people at heart, even if he must eventually renounce his lower-class associates to assume the dignity of the kingship.

IMPORTANT QUOTATIONS FROM 2 HENRY IV

1. Uneasy lies the head that wears the crown.

Location: III.i.31
Speaker: Henry IV to the audience
Context: Henry describes the difficulties of being king

Henry IV's famous aside to the audience, spoken in a moment of solitude in Westminster Palace, expresses the high price of kingship and worldly power in general. Henry expresses this sentiment in an impersonal proverb form, referring to "the head" rather than "my head" and emphasizing the universality of the tradeoff between power and peace of mind. It is not Henry in particular who has trouble maintaining tranquility while he reigns, but anyone who has fought hard and compromised his principles to seize power.

Henry devoted his whole career to the project of winning and keeping the crown, but once his power seems safe, he ceases worrying about the uneasy fit of his crown and starts worrying about the uneasy feel of his head. Psychological worries have replaced political difficulties, and the man who once craved ultimate power now envies his own beggarly subjects, who can sleep better at night than he can. Instead of describing the uneasiness of an upright head, Henry describes the uneasiness of a head that lies, calling up an image of himself lying in bed, worried and unable to sleep.

---

2. *God knows, my son,*
   By what bypaths and indirect crook'd ways
   I met this crown; and I myself know well
   How troublesome it sat upon my head.
   To thee it shall descend with better quiet,
   Better opinion, better confirmation;
   For all the soil of the achievement goes
   With me into the earth.

Location: IV.iii.311-318
Speaker: Henry IV
Context: Henry addresses his son while on his deathbed

As he lies dying, Henry wishes for a happier reign for his son than the one he enjoyed. During his life, Henry insisted on the legitimacy of his kingship, but before death, he admits the "crook'd ways" he has followed in pursuit of the crown. Henry says he "met this crown" instead of saying he won it or took it, perhaps revealing his belief that power is an accident, or perhaps revealing his desire to downplay his own aggression and hunger for power. Henry hopes that things will go more easily for Hal. A self-sacrificing parent, he says he will take the "soil of the achievement," the dark byproducts of his success, to the grave with him, and Hal can enjoy the fruits of kingship without worrying. As Shakespeare's audience knew, this is wishful thinking: civil wars would erupt again and dispute the legitimacy of the Lancastrian line.

---

3. *I would you had but the wit; 'twere better than your dukedom. Good faith, this same young sober-blooded boy doth not love me, nor a man cannot make him laugh. But that's no marvel; he drinks no wine. There's never none of these demure boys come to any proof; for thin drunk doth so overcool their blood, and making many fish meals, that they fall into a kind of male green-sickness; and then when they marry, then get wenches. They are generally fools and cowards—which some of us should be too, but for inflammation.*

Location: IV.ii.78–86
Speaker: Falstaff
Context: Prince John has promised to say good things about Falstaff at court

Falstaff tells John that he wishes John had "the wit" to praise Falstaff satisfactorily. This is a proud reference to Falstaff's verbal skills, which are evident throughout the *Henry IV* plays, but it also implies a serious skepticism about the assumption that noble birth is better than wit. A dukedom is an external possession that may be won or lost. Wit, once attained, is almost impossible to lose or steal. In its bond to its owner, wit is superior to wealth and social status.

This speech brims with Falstaff's jovial vitality. Still, a dark current runs underneath his constant high spirits. He says that men like John who do not drink a lot are generally "fools and cowards," but he adds that "some of us" would be fools and cowards too if not for alcohol. Falstaff blusters and brags, but he also worries about his own worth.

---

4. *O yet, for God's sake, go not to these wars!*
   The time was, father, that you broke your word
   When you were more endeared to it than now —
   When your own Percy, when my heart's dear Harry,
   Threw many a northward look to see his father
   Bring up his powers; but he did long in vain.
   Who then persuaded you to stay at home?
   There were two honours lost, yours and your son's.

Location: II.iii.9–16
Speaker: Lady Percy to Northumberland
Context: Lady Percy chastises her father-in-law

Lady Percy lashes out at Northumberland, whose failure to send troops to support Hotspur in the battle at Tewkesbury may have indirectly caused Hotspur's death. The possibility that he will send troops now, when it is too late to save his son, worsens the disgrace, as Lady Percy suggests. Northumberland's behavior stands for the demise of the age of chivalric honor in Britain. Hotspur assumed his father would take his side, but in the new world fathers can no longer be counted on to back up their sons. Hotspur was the incarnation of medieval honor in *1 Henry IV*, so his transformation emphasizes how quickly the old-fashioned code of honor has given way to modern practical concerns and realistic motivations. With the passing of the idealistic knight Hotspur, pragmatism encroaches on the world of *2 Henry IV*.

---

5. *I know thee not, old man. Fall to thy prayers.*
   How ill white hairs becomes a fool and jester!
   I have long dreamt of such a kind of man,
   So surfeit-swelled, so old, and so profane;
   But being awake, I do despise my dream.

Location: V.v.45–49
Speaker: Hal to Falstaff
Context: Hal renounces Falstaff

Hal renounces his former mentor and drinking companion with thoroughness and coldness. He does not even respect Falstaff enough to call him by his name, instead addressing him condescendingly and carelessly as "old man." In a priggish, judgmental fashion, Hal orders his former cohort to start praying, as if he has forgotten that he himself caroused and robbed at Falstaff's side and has equal need to atone for his sins. Hal has embraced his responsibilities suddenly and completely, as this total break with his past proves. In psychological terms it is true that Hal no longer knows Falstaff, since Hal is no longer Hal, but Henry V. The transformation is so complete that the new king cannot afford to recognize his old friend. Yet as much as Henry V claims to "despise" Falstaff, he does call the knight "my dream," as if Falstaff remains an impractical ideal for Hal.

HENRY V

Prince Harry rises above his criminal youth to become a military hero.

HENRY V IN CONTEXT

Henry V is one of Shakespeare's history plays. It forms the fourth part of a tetralogy (a four-part series) dealing with the historical rise of the English royal House of Lancaster. *Henry V*, which Shakespeare probably wrote in 1599, is one of his most popular history plays. It contains a host of entertaining characters who speak in many accents and languages. The play is full of noble speeches, heroic battles, and valiant English underdogs who fight their way to victory against all odds. Additionally, King Henry seems to be a perfect leader—brave, modest, fiercely focused, and possessed of a sense of humor.

The play's treatment of King Henry V, however, is more complicated than it comes across at first glance. Henry is a model of traditional heroism, but his choices can be troubling. His sense of honor leads him to invade a nonaggressive country and slaughter thousands of people. He sentences to death former friends and prisoners of war while claiming to value mercy, and he never acknowledges any responsibility for the bloodshed he has caused. Whether or not he is an admirable man, Henry is presented as a nearly ideal king, with a diamond-hard focus, an intractable resolve, and the willpower to subordinate his own personal feelings to the needs of his nation and his throne. The brilliance of Henry's speeches and his careful cultivation of his image make him an effective and inspiring leader. Whether he emerges from the play as an heroic figure or merely a king as cold as he is brilliant depends largely on each individual's interpretation.

HENRY V: KEY FACTS

Full title: The Life of King Henry the Fifth

Time and place written: Probably 1599, London

Date of first publication: 1600 (in quarto), 1623 (in folio)

Genre: History play

Setting (time): Around 1414–1415

Setting (place): London, at the royal palace and the Boar's Head Tavern; various locales in France, including the battlefields of Harfleur and Agincourt and Charles VI's court

Protagonist: Henry V

Major conflict: Henry leads an English army to invade and conquer France, and tries to prove his moral authority as king.

HENRY V: CHARACTER LIST

Alice   The maid of the French princess Catherine. Alice has spent time in England and teaches Catherine some English.

Bardolph   A commoner from London. Bardolph serves in the war with Henry, who was his friend as a wild youth. He is a friend of Pistol and Nim.

Boy   Formerly in the service of Falstaff, the nameless boy leaves London after his master's death and goes with Pistol, Nim, and Bardolph to the war in France. The boy is somewhat embarrassed that his companions are cowardly thieves.

Cambridge, Scrope, and Grey   Three men bribed by French agents to kill Henry before he sets sail for France. Scrope is one of Henry's good friends.

The Archbishop of Canterbury and the Bishop of Ely   Wealthy and powerful English clergymen. The Archbishop of Canterbury and the Bishop of Ely do not go to fight in the war, but their urging and fundraising are important factors in Henry's decision to invade France.

Chorus   A single character who introduces each of the play's five acts. Like choruses in Greek drama, the Chorus in Henry V comments on the play's plot and themes.

The Dukes of Clarence, Bedford, and Gloucester   Henry's three younger brothers. Clarence, Bedford, and Gloucester are noblemen and fighters.

Sir Thomas Erpingham   A wise, aged veteran of many wars who serves with Henry's campaign.

The Dukes of Exeter, Westmorland, Salisbury, and Warwick   Trusted advisors to King Henry and the leaders of his military. The Duke of Exeter, who is also Henry's uncle, is entrusted with carrying important messages to the French king.

Sir John Falstaff   Henry's former friend and mentor. Falstaff does not appear in Henry V, but he the characters mention him.

Captain Fluellen, Captain MacMorris, and Captain Jamy   The captains of King Henry's troops from Wales, Ireland, and Scotland, respectively. All of the captains have heavy accents reflecting their countries of origin. Fluellen, a close friend of Captain Gower, is the most prominent of the three. His wordiness provides comic relief, and he is likable and intelligent.

Captain Gower   An army captain and capable fighter who serves with Henry's campaign.

King Henry V   The young king of England. Henry is brilliant, focused, fearless, and committed to the responsibilities of kingship. These responsibilities often force him to subordinate his personal feelings to the needs of the country. Henry is a brilliant orator who uses his skill to justify his claims and to motivate his troops. Once Henry has resolved to conquer France, he pursues his goal relentlessly.

Hostess   The keeper of the Boar's Head Tavern in London. Mistress Quickly, as she is also known, is married to Pistol.

Nim   A commoner from London. Nim serves in the war with Henry. He is a friend of Pistol and Bardolph.

Ancient Pistol   A commoner from London. Pistol serves in the war with Henry. He is a friend to Nim and Bardolph. Pistol speaks in blustery, melodramatic language. He is married to the hostess of the Boar's Head Tavern in London.

Michael Williams, John Bates, and Alexander Court   Common soldiers. The night before the Battle of Agincourt, Henry disguises himself and argues with them. Though he disagrees heatedly with Williams, Henry is generally impressed with these men's intelligence and courage.

York and Suffolk   Two noble cousins who die together at the Battle of Agincourt.

FRENCHMEN

Catherine   The daughter of the King of France. Catherine is eventually married off to King Henry in order to cement the peace between England and France. She speaks little English.

Charles VI   The King of France. A capable leader, Charles does not underestimate King Henry.

The Dauphin   The son of the king of France and heir to the throne (until Henry takes this privilege from him). The dauphin is a headstrong and overconfident young man, more inclined to mock the English than to think of them as an enemy worthy of respect. The dauphin also mocks Henry, making frequent mention of the king's irresponsible youth.

Monsieur le Fer   A French soldier and gentleman whom Pistol captures at the Battle of Agincourt.

French Noblemen and Military Leaders   The Constable of France, the Duke of Orléans, the Duke of Britain, the Duke of Bourbon, the Earl of Grandpré, Lord Rambures, the Duke of Burgundy, and the Governor of Harfleur are French noblemen and military leaders. Like the dauphin, most of these leaders do not take the English seriously. The English capture or kill most of them at the Battle of Agincourt, though the Duke of Burgundy survives and helps with the peace negotiations between France and England.

Isabel The queen of France, the wife of Charles VI, and the mother of Catherine. Isabel does not
appear until the final scene.

Montjoy The French herald, or messenger.

HENRY V: PLOT OVERVIEW

The recently crowned King Henry V must convince his unsettled nation that he is a competent and worthy king. Citing a legal argument that he has a right to the French throne, he decides to invade France.
The lower-class characters he used to associate with prepare to leave their homes and families to go to
war. Three of Henry's noble friends are convicted of treason, and he has them executed to show that he
has abandoned his old ways. Henry inspires his troops with an impassioned speech, and they conquer the
town of Harfleur against incredible odds. After Henry gives another powerful speech, his forces rout the
French at the Battle of Agincourt, even though the French outnumber them five to one. Henry marries
Catherine, the daughter of the King of France, and forces the king to appoint Henry his heir.

HENRY V: SCENE SUMMARY

ACT I

*Canterbury and Ely agree to support Henry's invasion of France for their own selfish reasons; French
ambassadors insult Henry, who decides to invade France.*

I. PROLOGUE Location:

The Chorus urges the audience to use its imagination as it watches the play.

The Chorus—a single character whose speeches open each of the play's five acts—announces that we
are about to watch a story that will include huge fields, grand battles, and fighting kings. The Chorus
notes that we will have to use our imaginations to make the story come to life: we must imagine that the
small wooden stage is actually the fields of France and that the few actors who will appear onstage are
actually huge armies that fight to the death in those fields.

I.I Location: Henry's court

*Canterbury and Ely discuss holding on to their wealth, and agree that Henry is a surprisingly wonderful
king.*

The Archbishop of Canterbury and the Bishop of Ely, two powerful English churchmen, confer with
one another. They are concerned about a bill that has been brought up for the consideration of the king
of England, Henry V. Canterbury and Ely don't want the king to pass this bill into law, because it would
authorize the government to take away a great deal of the church's land and money. The money would
be used to maintain the army, support the poor, and supplement the king's treasury. The clergymen, who
have grown wealthy and powerful with this land and money, want to keep it for themselves.

The Archbishop of Canterbury has come up with a plan. The young King Henry V has been thinking
about invading France, because he believes he has a claim to the French throne. Canterbury thinks a
war would distract Henry from the bill, so he wants to encourage Henry to concentrate on the invasion.
Canterbury has promised Henry to raise a very large donation from the clergymen of the church to help
fund the war effort.

Canterbury and Ely express admiration for Henry's virtue and intelligence. They note that "[t]he
courses of his youth promised it not" (I.i.25)—in other words, no one thought Henry would turn out so
well, considering he wasted his adolescence on "riots, banquets, sports," (I.i.57) and lowlifes. His reformation has been nothing short of miraculous. The new, improved Henry is about to meet with the delegation of French ambassadors who have come to England. Ely and Canterbury head for the throne room
to participate in the meeting.

I.II Location: the throne room

Canterbury explains Henry's claim to the French throne; the French dauphin mocks Henry via his ambassadors, and Henry decides to invade France.

Henry prepares to speak with a delegation of ambassadors from France. Several of his advisors and two of his younger brothers (Humphrey, Duke of Gloucester, and Thomas, Duke of Clarence) accompany him. Before speaking to the ambassadors, Henry wants to talk to the representatives of the English church.

Henry asks Canterbury to explain to him, in clear and educated terms, why the King of England has a rightful claim to the throne of France. This logic is complicated, going back several generations, and Henry wants to be able to justify a potentially bloody invasion. He reminds Canterbury of the responsibility that Canterbury himself will bear for the death toll of the war if he tells anything less than the truth, and he orders Canterbury to give him an honest opinion and faithful advice.

Canterbury gives a lengthy explanation of why Henry has a valid claim to France. In France, Canterbury explains, a law called the Salic law stipulates that the throne cannot be inherited through a mother. That is, if a king has a daughter, the daughter's son has no claim to the throne. But England has no such law, and kings can inherit the throne through the female line. Because King Henry's great-great-grandmother was a daughter of the King of France, English law says that Henry is the rightful heir to the throne of France. The French don't agree with this assessment, and they believe that their king, Charles VI, is the rightful monarch. If Henry wants to claim France, or even part of it, Canterbury concludes, he will have to invade and fight the French for it.

Both clergymen urge Henry to invade, as do his advisors, Exeter and Westmorland. Canterbury promises to raise from the clergymen a large war chest to finance the project. Henry expresses concern that the Scottish rebels on his northern border will invade while he is away, so Canterbury suggests that Henry take only one-quarter of his army with him to France, leaving the rest behind to defend England. Henry resolves to proceed with the invasion.

Henry calls in the French ambassadors. The ambassadors represent the dauphin, the son of the King of France and, in the eyes of the French, the heir to the throne. The ambassadors report that the dauphin laughs at Henry's claim to any part of France and says that Henry is still too young to be responsible. The ambassadors present Henry with a gift from the dauphin: a container of tennis balls, a mocking reference to Henry's sportive and idle youth. Enraged, Henry gives the ambassadors a dark reply, warning them that the dauphin has made a serious error in judgment, for Henry is not the foolish boy the dauphin thinks he is. Henry declares his intent to invade and conquer France. The dauphin will regret his mockery of the English king, he says, "[w]hen thousands weep more than did laugh at it" (I.ii.296).

ACT II

Henry orders three traitorous noblemen executed; Falstaff dies; Henry arrives in France and demands that Charles hand over the crown.

II. PROLOGUE

The Chorus names the English noblemen who are acting as secret agents for France.

The Chorus says all of England is fired up and arming for the war, and King Henry is almost ready to invade France. But French agents have found some corrupt noblemen within the English ranks, and they have bribed them into acting as secret agents. These noblemen are Richard, Earl of Cambridge; Henry Lord Scrope of Masham; and Sir Thomas Grey of Northumberland. This trio has agreed to kill Henry in Southampton, just before he sets sail for France.

II.I Location: A tavern in Eastcheap, London

Bardolph and Nim put aside their quarrel to visit Falstaff, who is dying.

Lieutenant Bardolph and Corporal Nim prepare to head off for the war. Both of these men are commoners, and Bardolph was once a criminal. Nim is angry with a fellow soldier, Ancient Pistol, who has married Mistress Quickly, the hostess of the Boar's Head Tavern in London. Quickly had previously promised to marry Nim. Pistol and Nim want to fight and must be quieted several times by the hostess and Bardolph.

A boy, the page of a knight named Sir John Falstaff, appears. Falstaff, a close friend of everyone present, is old and very sick in bed, and the boy reports that he is getting worse. The hostess goes to see Falstaff and comes back to tell the others that he is dying. The men put aside their quarrel to go to visit him. Nim and Pistol speak of something that King Henry has done to Falstaff. Apparently, it is somehow the king's fault that Falstaff is on his deathbed.

II.II Location: the port of Southhampton

Henry orders the three traitors executed.

King Henry prepares his armies to sail for France. The conversation between Gloucester, Exeter, and Westmorland reveals that Henry has discovered the treachery of Cambridge, Scrope, and Grey, but the traitors don't know it yet. Henry enters with these traitors, asking their advice on a case: a drunken man was arrested the previous day for speaking against Henry in public. Henry plans to free the man, but Cambridge, Scrope, and Grey advise Henry to punish him instead.

Henry decides to free the man anyway. He lets Cambridge, Scrope, and Grey know that he has discovered their intended betrayal, handing them the incriminating evidence on paper. The three beg for mercy, but Henry is inflexible. He asks how they can possibly seek mercy for themselves when they think an ordinary drunkard deserves no mercy. Henry can hardly believe they would sell his life for money—especially Scrope, who has been a close friend. He orders them all executed. Taking the discovery of the traitors as a sign that God is on the side of the English, Henry orders his fleet to sail for France.

II.III Location: Eastcheap

Pistol, Bardolph, Nim, and the hostess grieve over Falstaff's death.

Pistol, Bardolph, Nim, and the hostess grieve over the death of Sir John Falstaff. The hostess describes his final moments. Falstaff was happy but also delirious at the very end. He said bad things about wine, and possibly about women. Despite their sadness, the men must finally go off to the war, so Pistol kisses his wife and gives her advice and instructions. He heads off with the others, including Falstaff's newly masterless boy.

II.IV Location: the king's court in France

Charles tells the dauphin that Henry is a serious threat; Exeter delivers a warning from Henry to Charles.

Charles VI, the King of France, and his nobles and advisors discuss the approach of King Henry V's English forces. Charles's eldest son, the dauphin, believes that Henry is the foolish and idle boy he once was. The dauphin is eager to fight, but Charles and the Constable of France do not share his enthusiasm. They have spoken with the ambassadors who recently returned from England and are convinced of Henry's might. Charles also reminds the dauphin that Henry's forebears have been fierce and victorious fighters against the French—especially Henry's great-grandfather, Edward III of England, and his son, Edward, Black Prince of Wales, who conquered the French at the Battle of Crécy (or Cressy).

The English nobleman Exeter arrives bearing a message from Henry. Henry has landed in France and formally demands that Charles yield the crown of France and all the honors and land that go with it. If Charles refuses, Henry will invade France and take it by force. Exeter tells Charles to consider carefully and return an answer quickly. Charles says he will send Exeter back to his king with an answer in the morning.

ACT III

Henry rallies his soldiers and captures Harfleur; Catherine learns some English; Charles and his men come up with a plan to defeat Henry.

III. PROLOGUE

The Chorus describes Henry's siege of France.

The Chorus describes Henry's magnificent sail from England to France. It says that Henry lands with a large fleet of warships at Harfleur, a port city on the northern coast of France. There, the English army attacks the city with terrifying force. The alarmed King Charles offers Henry a compromise: he will not give him the crown of France, but he will give him some small dukedoms—that is, small sub-regions within France—as well as the hand of his daughter, Catherine, in marriage. But Henry rejects the offer, and the siege continues.

III.I Location: outside Harfleur

Henry rallies his soldiers with a stirring speech.

In the midst of the siege, Henry rallies his soldiers. He delivers a powerful speech, invoking the memory of the Englishmen's warlike ancestors and appealing to soldiers, noblemen, and commoners alike.

III.II Location: outside Harfleur

Nim, Bardolph, Pistol, and the boy talk about the speech and avoid the battle until an officer sends them back into it; the boy reflects on his companions' dishonesty.

Nim, Bardolph, Pistol, and the boy talk. Their conversation reveals that reaction to the king's speech is rather mixed. Bardolph appears eager for the fight, but Nim, Pistol, and the boy are less than happy about facing death. They wish they were safely back in London, drinking ale.

A superior officer, a Welsh captain named Fluellen, notices the men loitering and beats them with a sword until they rush back into the fight. The boy remains behind for a few moments to muse on the folly and hypocrisy of Nim, Bardolph, and Pistol. He declares that they are all cowards. He says they want him to start learning to pick pockets, but that such an idea is an affront to his manhood. He decides he must leave them and start looking for a better job.

III.III Location: outside Harfleur

Fluellen quarrels with some other officers; Henry threatens to destroy Harfleur, rape its women, and kill its children, so the overmatched governor surrenders.

Captain Fluellen enters with Captain Gower, his fellow officer and friend. Gower and Fluellen discuss the "mines," or tunnels, that the English side has dug in order to get under the walls of Harfleur (III.iii.4). Fluellen, who is well informed about ancient Roman tactics of war, thinks the mines are being dug incorrectly. In an amusing and wordy manner typical of him, Fluellen expresses scorn for Captain MacMorris, the Irish officer in charge of digging the mines, and admiration for Captain Jamy, the officer in charge of the Scottish troops.

MacMorris and Jamy enter, and Fluellen offers MacMorris some advice about digging the tunnels. The hotheaded MacMorris takes offense, and they begin to quarrel. But they are all responsible officers, and there is much work to be done, so after some philosophizing about the hazards of war and the inevitability of death, all four head back into the battle.

With a flourish of trumpets, Henry appears before the gates of Harfleur. The town has sounded a parley—in other words, its inhabitants have asked for a cease-fire in order to negotiate. The governor of Harfleur stands on the town walls. Henry addresses him, advising him to surrender immediately. Henry declares that if the governor surrenders, the people of the town will be allowed to live, but if he does not, the English will destroy the town, rape the women, and kill the children. The governor replies that although he would rather not surrender, he has just received word from the dauphin that no army can be raised in time to rescue Harfleur. He declares that he will therefore open the gates. Henry orders Exeter to fortify Harfleur as a citadel from which the English can fight the French. He says he himself will take his forces onward to Calais the next day.

III.IV Location: Charles VI's palace

Catherine learns some English from her maid, Alice.

Charles's daughter, Catherine, speaks with her maid, Alice. Catherine speaks no English, and this scene takes place almost entirely in French. Alice has spent some time in England and knows some English, and so Catherine asks Alice to teach her the language. Catherine seems to suspect that she may need to communicate with the King of England. They begin by learning the names of parts of the body. Catherine mispronounces them, but she is eager to learn until they get to the final two words, "foot" and "cown" (gown), which sound like the words for "fuck" and "cunt."

III.V Location: the French court

Charles and his men, outraged by Henry's success, decide to raise an army and defeat Henry.

Charles, the dauphin, and his advisors—including the Constable of France and the Duke of Bourbon— have an urgent meeting to discuss Henry's swift advance through France. French exclamations pepper their English conversation. They cannot figure out how the English got to be so courageous, since they come from such a damp, gloomy climate. They feel that France's national honor has been outraged by the British successes, and they are determined to turn the tables. Worst of all, their wives and mistresses have started to make fun of them for being beaten by Henry's forces.

Charles, more sensible and decisive than his followers, orders his noblemen to raise troops for the army. Charles and his men are confident that with this great number of troops raised, they can intimidate Henry, conquer his army, and bring him back as a defeated prisoner.

III.VI Location: the English camp

Bardolph is sentenced to death for stealing from Harfleur, a sentence Henry supports; Charles sends a menacing message to Henry.

After the English take Harfleur, the Welsh Captain Fluellen talks with the English Captain Gower about the battle for a bridge that is currently taking place. Ancient Pistol enters to ask a favor of Fluellen. Pistol's good friend and fellow soldier Bardolph has been found guilty of stealing from the conquered French town. He has stolen a "pax," a tablet made out of valuable material and used in religious rites (III.vi.35), and has been sentenced to death by hanging, the punishment Henry has decreed for looters. Pistol begs Fluellen to intercede with the Duke of Exeter to save Bardolph's life, but Fluellen politely refuses, saying that discipline must be maintained. Despairing, Pistol curses Fluellen, makes an obscene gesture at him, and stalks away.

Gower, who watched the exchange, realizes that he recognizes Pistol. He tells Fluellen that Pistol is the kind of man who only goes off to war now and then but pretends to be a full-time soldier when he is back home. Fluellen says he will keep an eye on Pistol.

With a drumroll and fanfare, Henry enters. He questions Fluellen about the battle for the bridge and about how many soldiers the English side lost in the last skirmish. Fluellen says that thanks to the smart fighting of the Duke of Exeter, the English have won the bridge. Amazingly, no English soldiers have been lost in combat. Henry hears that Bardolph has been sentenced to hang for stealing. He displays no visible emotion (even though Bardolph was a friend when Henry was a prince) and says he approves of the punishment, stressing how important it is that the conquered French and their property be treated with the utmost respect.

Montjoy, a French messenger, arrives with a menacing message from Charles, who sends word that the time has come for him to punish the overly proud King Henry. He suggests that Henry start thinking about his "ransom"—the recompense that the French will demand for their losses when they defeat the English king (III.vi.113).

King Henry sends back an even-tempered reply. He admits that his army has tired and that he would rather not fight the French if he can avoid it. However, he will continue to march because he believes he is in the right and will eventually be victorious. Montjoy departs, and the English camp goes to sleep for the night.

III.VII   Location: the French camp

The French talk and make fun of Henry.

Several French noblemen—including the Duke of Orléans, the Constable of France, and Lord Rambures—discuss the upcoming battle. The Duke of Orléans brags about his horse, and the others tease him. A messenger enters to say that the English army is camped nearby. The French nobles make fun of Henry and the Englishmen.

ACT IV

On the eve of battle, Henry disguises himself as a common soldier and talks to his men; after Henry gives an inspiring speech, the English rout the French and Henry orders his men to kill all the prisoners of war; Henry plays a joke on Michael Williams.

IV. PROLOGUE

On the eve of battle, the French swagger and Henry cheers his men.

The Chorus describes the scene in the French and English camps the night before the battle: the quiet night, the burning watch fires, the clank of the knights being suited up in their armor. In the French camp, the overly confident officers have already decided how to divide up the loot, for they outnumber the English by five to one. In the English camp, the soldiers believe that they will die the next morning and wait patiently for their fate. During the night, Henry visits his soldiers, calling them brothers and cheering them up. This visit raises morale greatly. Every soldier is pleased to see "[a] little touch of Harry in the night" (IV.Prologue.47).

IV.I   Location: the English camp

Henry disguises himself as a common soldier and talks to his men.

Henry talks briefly with his brothers, Gloucester and Clarence, and with old Sir Thomas Erpingham. He asks to borrow Erpingham's dirty cloak, then sends his advisors off to confer with the other noblemen in his royal tent, saying he wants to be alone for a while. Disguised by the borrowed cloak, Henry sits by the common campfire pretending to be an ordinary soldier and talking with whoever wanders by. The first person to come by is Pistol. When Henry brings up the subject of the king, Pistol praises Henry. Pistol then insults Fluellen. Henry, going under the name Harry le roi (le roi is French for "the king"), pretends to be Fluellen's relative. Pistol makes an obscene gesture at Henry and leaves.

Fluellen and Gower walk by. They are so busy talking to each other that neither of them sees Henry. Fluellen tells Gower to talk more softly while they are so close to the enemy. Henry silently admires Fluellen's prudence and intelligence. Three common soldiers—John Bates, Alexander Court, and Michael Williams—join Henry at the campfire. Henry talks to them about the English troops' odds in the coming battle and finds that they doubt the motives and the courage of the king. Henry defends himself, but Williams will not back down, so they agree to establish a quarrel. They exchange gloves, signaling their intent to find each other later and fight if they both survive the battle.

The three soldiers leave, and Henry thinks. He laments the lonely isolation and eternal vigilance required by power. The only consolation Henry can see in being king is the elaborate ceremony and costuming that accompanies the position. Yet he thinks this ceremony is empty. He would rather be a slave, who is at least able to rest easy and not worry about the safety of his country.

It is nearly dawn and almost time for the battle. Henry, still alone, prays to God to strengthen the hearts of his soldiers. He also entreats God not to punish him for the bloody manner in which his own father took the English crown.

IV.II   Location: the French camp

The French forces prepare for battle, which they feel sure they will win.

415

The French prepare for the battle. The constable, Lord Rambures, the Earl of Grandpré, and others put on their armor and mount their horses. The constable and Grandpré give speeches full of confidence and cheerfulness. Seeing the English army's ragged appearance and small numbers, the French look forward to an easy victory.

IV.III Location: the English camp

Henry gives an inspiring speech, and the English march into battle.

The English noblemen, gathering before the Battle of Agincourt, realize that the French outnumber them five to one. Westmorland wishes they were accompanied by some of the men who sit idle in England. Henry overhears him and disagrees. In a speech known at the St. Crispin's Day speech (so called because he addresses his troops on October 25, St. Crispin's Day), King Henry tells his men that they should be happy that there are so few of them present, for that way each can earn a greater share of honor.

Henry says he does not want to fight alongside any man who does not wish to fight with the English. He tells the soldiers that anyone who wants to leave can and will be given some money to head for home. But anyone who stays to fight will have something to boast about for the rest of his life and will always remember this battle with pride. He adds that every commoner who fights today with the king will become his brother, and all the Englishmen who have stayed at home will regret not being in France to gain honor on this famous day of battle. The soldiers and noblemen are greatly inspired.

The French are ready for the battle. Montjoy, the French messenger, comes to the English camp one more time, asking King Henry if he wants to take the last opportunity for peace and surrender himself for ransom instead of facing certain defeat in battle. Henry rejects the offer in strong but courteous terms, and the English organize and march into battle.

IV.IV Location: the battlefield

Pistol takes a French prisoner and talks to him with the boy working as translator; the boy reveals that Nim has been hanged for stealing.

As the battle rages, Pistol takes a French prisoner. The scene is comic: Pistol, who cannot speak French, tries to communicate with the Frenchman, who cannot speak English. Fortunately, the boy is present and speaks very good French. Still, hotheaded Pistol makes communication difficult. The terrified soldier is convinced that Pistol is a nobleman and a ferocious fighter.

The French soldier, who gives his name as Monsieur le Fer, says he is from a respected house and family and his relatives will give Pistol a rich ransom if Pistol lets him live. Pistol accepts this bargain, and the grateful Frenchman surrenders as a willing captive. As the boy follows them offstage, he complains about Pistol's empty boasting, saying that Bardolph and Nim had ten times as much real courage as Pistol. The boy reveals that Nim, like Bardolph, has been hanged for stealing.

IV.V Location: the French camp

The English forces rout the French.

The French camp is in disarray. The French soldiers' cries reveal that, against all expectations, the English are winning the day. The French troops have been routed and scattered. Astonished and dismayed, the French nobles speak of their great shame and contemplate suicide. But they decide that rather than surrender in shame and defeat, they will go down fighting and return to the field for one final attempt.

IV.VI Location: the battlefield

Exeter reports that the Duke of York and the Earl of Suffolk have died; suspecting that the French are rallying, Henry orders his men to kill their French prisoners.

The French continue to fight. Exeter tells Henry that two noble cousins, the Duke of York and the Earl of Suffolk, have been killed. Exeter describes the way the wounded York lay down to die beside the body of his beloved cousin Suffolk. Henry, like Exeter, is moved to tears by the story. A noise sounds. King Henry, interpreting the commotion as a rally by the French, orders every English soldier to kill his French prisoners.

IV.VII Location: the battlefield

Fluellen and Gower talk about the French, who have murdered the English pages and looted the camp; Montjoy tells Henry that the English have won; Henry plans to trick Michael Williams.

Fluellen talks with Gower. A small group of French soldiers, fleeing the main crush of the battle, have attacked the English camp, looting it and murdering the young pages, mere children. Fluellen is outraged that the French have violated the chivalrous codes of battle. He agrees with Gower that Henry was right to order the slaughter of the French prisoners. He compares the valiant Henry to Alexander the Great.

Henry appears with the Duke of Bourbon as a prisoner. Having learned about the slaughter of the boys, he says he is angrier than he has ever been before and repeats the order to kill the French prisoners. Montjoy, the now-humbled French messenger, reappears. He brings a request from the king of France that the French be allowed to go safely into the battlefield to identify, recover, and bury their dead. Henry demands to know whether the English won. Montjoy says they have, and Henry praises God for the victory.

Henry spots the soldier Michael Williams, with whom he argued and exchanged gloves the night before. Henry decides to play a practical joke: he gives Williams's glove to Fluellen and tells him to wear it publicly, saying it came from a noble Frenchman in the field and anyone who attacks Fluellen over it must be a traitor to the English. Henry then follows them to see the fun.

IV.VIII Location: the battlefield

Henry rewards Michael Williams's bravery with a glove full of coins; Exeter reports that ten thousand French soldiers and twenty-nine English soldiers have died.

When Williams sees Fluellen, he recognizes his own glove and thinks Fluellen was the man with whom he quarreled the night before. He strikes Fluellen, and Fluellen, believing that Williams is a French traitor, orders him arrested. Henry arrives, innocently asking what is going on, and then he reveals to Williams that his quarrel is really with Henry himself. Williams says he cannot be held responsible for picking a quarrel with the king because Henry was in disguise. Henry approves of Williams's courage and rewards him by filling his glove with coins.

Exeter and a herald return to report the total number of casualties. Ten thousand French soldiers are dead, but the English have lost only twenty-nine men. Recognizing their extraordinary good luck, the Englishmen praise God. Henry orders his men to proceed to the captured village without bragging.

V. PROLOGUE

The Chorus tells of England's happiness and Henry's modesty.

The Chorus relates that King Henry has returned to the port city of Calais in France and, from there, has sailed back to England. The women and children of England are overjoyed to have their men returned to them. When Henry returns to London, the people flock to see him and to celebrate. Henry is humble and forbids a triumphal procession to celebrate his victory. He returns to France, and the Chorus orders the audience to return its imagination to France, with the understanding that some time has passed.

V.I Location: the English camp

Fluellen humiliates Pistol, who has made fun of him; Pistol says his wife is dead, and decides to become a pimp and a thief.

Gower asks Fluellen why he still wears a leek in his hat, since St. Davy's Day was the previous day. (St. Davy is the patron saint of Wales, and on St. Davy's Day, March 1, Welsh people traditionally wear a leek in their hats as a sign of patriotism.) Fluellen explains that, the day before, the obnoxious soldier Pistol insulted him by sending him bread and salt and suggesting that Fluellen eat his leek.

When Pistol appears, Fluellen beats him with his cudgel until Pistol agrees to eat the leek that Fluellen has been carrying in his hat. Pistol obliges, and Fluellen gives him some money to ease the pain of his cudgel wounds. After Fluellen leaves, Pistol vows to revenge himself, but Gower says it was Pistol's own fault for making fun of Fluellen and for underestimating him simply because he speaks with a funny (Welsh) accent.

When he is left alone, Pistol grows serious. He says that his wife, the hostess, has died of venereal disease (presumably syphilis) and that Pistol no longer has a home. He decides to become a pimp and a thief back in England.

V.II Location: Charles's palace

Catherine agrees to marry Henry.

Henry has come to meet with Charles and his queen, Isabel and negotiate a lasting peace between France and England. Despite his military victory, Henry will allow Charles to retain his throne. However, Henry has a list of demands. He wants to marry his distant cousin and Charles's daughter, Princess Catherine of France. That way, Henry and his heirs will inherit France as well as England.

The others discreetly retire from the room, leaving Henry and Catherine alone together. Catherine's maid, Alice, stays to help translate. In a comic scene, Henry courts Catherine, trying to persuade her to marry him. Understanding the gist of his English words and occasional French ones, Catherine agrees, pointing out that the decision is actually up to her father.

The rest of the noblemen come back in, and Henry and the Duke of Burgundy trade some manly innuendoes about what Catherine will be like in bed. Everyone signs the treaties that will make Henry and his sons heirs to the throne of France after Charles dies.

V. EPILOGUE

The Chorus speaks of Henry's son and asks for the audience's indulgence.

The Chorus says that Catherine and Henry have a son, King Henry VI of England, who went on to lose France and bring England into war. The Chorus asks the audience to tolerate the play it has seen.

ANALYSIS OF MAJOR CHARACTERS IN *HENRY V*

KING HENRY V

Henry, the play's protagonist and hero, is an extraordinary figure who possesses a degree of intelligence and charisma that set him apart from his younger self, the pleasure-seeking hellion depicted in Shakespeare's two *Henry IV* plays.

One of Henry V's most remarkable qualities is his resolve. Once he has decided to accomplish a goal, he uses every resource at his disposal to see that it is accomplished. He also takes pains to present himself as an unstoppable force—a valuable psychological maneuver that Henry uses to pressure his enemies into doing what he wants them to do. Again and again, Henry acts in a manner that would be deplorable for a common citizen but that makes him an exemplary king. For example, Henry refuses to take responsibility for the war in France. He even tells the French governor at Harfleur that if the French do not surrender, they will be responsible for the carnage that Henry will unleash.

Another of Henry's extraordinary qualities is facility with language. Henry's rhetorical skill is a forceful weapon, the strength of which nearly equals that of his army's swords. With words, Henry can inspire and rouse his followers and intimidate his enemies. His rhetoric is, as he is, at once candidly frank and extremely sophisticated. Henry can be cold and menacing, as when he speaks to the dauphin's messenger; he can be passionate and uplifting, as in his St. Crispin's Day speech, and he can be gruesome, as in his diatribe against the Governor of Harfleur. In each case, Henry's words suggest that he is merely speaking his mind without editing himself, even though he is actually making a careful, brilliantly crafted speech. Henry presents himself honestly while manipulating his audience.

Although we do not know precisely why Henry invades France, his speeches suggest that his motivation is not lust for power or land. Henry often speaks about the weight of responsibility. He mourns his inability to sleep the untroubled sleep of the common man. It also seems clear from Henry's undeniably uplifting speeches that Shakespeare intends for us to see him as a hero, or, at the very least, as an estimable king. If Henry is a hero, it is because of his commitment to his responsibilities above his own feelings.

CATHERINE

The young, pretty princess of France does not play a very active role in the play, but she is a significant figure because she typifies the role played by women in this masculine play. The scenes that center on Catherine and her tutor, Alice, depict a female world that contrasts with the grim, violent world in which the play's men exist. While the men fight bloody battles, Catherine lives a gentle, quiet existence, generally ignorant of the larger struggle going on around her. She fills her days mainly with laughing and teasing Alice.

While Catherine's life may be more pleasant than the men's, the scope of her existence is extremely limited and is not of her choosing. She has been raised to be pleasant, yielding, graceful, and charming because those qualities will make her desirable to a future husband. Shakespeare uses Catherine's English lessons with Alice to highlight her role as a tool of negotiation among the men. As the English conquer more and more of France, Catherine's potential husband seems likely to be English, and Catherine begins to study English because her father wants her to be attractive to his enemy, Henry V.

FLUELLEN

Fluellen, Jamy, and MacMorris broadly represent their respective nationalities. Fluellen, a Welshman, embodies many of the comical stereotypes associated with the Welsh in Shakespeare's day: he is wordy, overly serious, and possessed of a ludicrous pseudo-Welsh accent that principally involves replacing the letter "b" with the letter "p." However, Fluellen is also a well-defined and likable individual who tends to work against the limitations of stereotype. Though he is clownish in his early scenes, he is also extremely well-informed and appears to be quite competent, especially compared to the cowardly commoners from England whom he orders into battle at Harfleur. Like Bottom in *A Midsummer Night's Dream* or Falstaff in the *Henry IV* plays, Fluellen tends to steal the scenes he is in and to win the affection of the audience. The fact that Shakespeare wrote such a role for a Welsh character, a typical figure of ridicule, is a strong sign that Fluellen is intended to be more than a comic compendium of ethnic stereotypes.

THEMES, MOTIFS & SYMBOLS IN *HENRY V*

THEMES

THE RUTHLESSNESS OF THE GOOD KING   *Henry V* explores the nature of leadership and its relationship to morality. The play proposes that the qualities that define a good ruler are not necessarily the same qualities that define a good person. Henry is an extraordinarily good leader: he is intelligent, focused, and inspiring to his men. He uses all resources at his disposal to ensure that he achieves his goals. Shakespeare presents the ability to connect with and motivate subjects as the fundamental skill of good leaders, and it is this skill that Henry has in spades. It is this skill that allows him to win the Battle of Agincourt despite overwhelming odds.

But in becoming a great king, Henry acts in a way that, were he a common man, might seem immoral and even unforgivable. In order to stabilize his throne, Henry betrays friends such as Falstaff and puts other friends to death in order to uphold the law. While it is difficult to fault Henry for having Scrope killed, since Scrope was plotting to assassinate him, Henry's cruel punishment of Bardolph is less understandable, as is his willingness to threaten the gruesome murder of the children of Harfleur in order to persuade the governor to surrender. Henry talks of favoring peace, but once his mind is settled on a course of action, he is willing to condone and even create massive and unprovoked violence in order to achieve his goal.

Shakespeare's portrayal of the king shows that power complicates the traditional distinctions between heroism and villainy, so that to call Henry one or the other would be an oversimplification. As Henry himself comments, the massive responsibilities of a king make him different from all other people, and those judging a king must take that difference into account. A king, in Shakespeare's portrayal, is responsible for the well-being and stability of his entire nation. He must subordinate his feelings, desires, dislikes, and even conscience wholly to this responsibility. Perhaps the very nature of power is morally ambiguous, which would account for the implicit critique of Henry's actions that many contemporary readers find in the play.

THE DIVERSITY OF THE ENGLISH   *Henry V*'s interest in the breadth of humanity is apparent from its first lines, in which the Chorus reminds the audience that the few actors who will appear onstage represent thousands of their countrymen. The characters in *Henry V* encompass the range of social classes and nationalities united under the English crown during Henry's reign. The catalog of characters from different countries emphasizes the diversity of medieval England. The play is largely about the nature of absolute political power, but there is something remarkably democratic in its enlivening portrayal of rich and poor, English and Welsh, Scottish and Irish, as their roles intertwine in the war effort and as the king attempts to give them direction and momentum.

This disparate group of characters is not unanimous in supporting Henry. Many of them do admire the king, but other intelligent and courageous men, such as Michael Williams, distrust his motives. Henry tolerates Williams's type of dissent with magnanimity, but it would be a waste of energy for him to seek the approval of the many different groups of people he leads.

MOTIFS

PARALLELS BETWEEN RULERS AND COMMONERS   *Henry V* portrays a wide range of common citizens. Some scenes portray the king's interactions with his subjects, most notably in Act IV, scene i, when Henry moves among his soldiers in disguise. The play also presents a number of mirror scenes, in which the actions of commoners either parallel or parody the actions of Henry and the nobles. Examples of mirror scenes include the commoners' participation at Harfleur in Act III, scene ii, which echoes Henry's battle speech in Act III, scene i, as well as Act II, scene i, in which the commoners plan their futures, mirroring the graver councils of the French and English nobles.

WAR IMAGERY   *Henry V* uses a number of recurring metaphors for the violence of war, including images of eating and devouring, images of fire and combustion, and, oddly, the image of a tennis match. All of this imagery is rooted in aggression: in his rousing speech before the Battle of Harfleur, for example, Henry urges his men to be savage and predatory like tigers. Even the tennis balls, the gift from the dauphin to Henry, play into Henry's aggressive war rhetoric. He states that the dauphin's mocking renders the tennis balls "gunstones," or cannonballs, thus transforming them from frivolous objects of play into deadly weapons of war (I.ii.282).

SYMBOLS

THE TUN OF TENNIS BALLS   The dauphin knows that Henry was an idler before becoming king, so he sends Henry a tun, or chest, of tennis balls to remind Henry of his reputation for being a careless pleasure-seeker. This gift symbolizes the dauphin's scorn for Henry. The tennis balls enrage Henry, and he uses the dauphin's scorn to motivate himself. The tennis balls thus come to symbolize Henry's burning desire to conquer France. As he tells the French ambassador, the dauphin's jests have initiated a deadly match, and the tennis balls have become cannonballs.

CHARACTERS AS CULTURAL TYPES   As the Chorus tells the audience, it is impossible for a stage to hold the vast numbers of soldiers that actually participated in Henry V's war with France. As a result, many of the characters represent large groups or cultures: Fluellen represents the Welsh, Pistol represents the underclass, Jamy represents the Scottish, and MacMorris represents the Irish. These characters are often given the stereotypical traits thought to characterize each group in Shakespeare's day— MacMorris, for instance, has a fiery temper, a trait thought to be common to the Irish.

IMPORTANT QUOTATIONS FROM *HENRY V*

1. And tell the pleasant Prince this mock of his
Hath turned his balls to gunstones, and his soul
Shall stand sore charg_d for the wasteful vengeance
That shall fly from them—for many a thousand widows
Shall this his mock mock out of their dear husbands,
Mock mothers from their sons, mock castles down;
. . .
But this lies all within the will of God,
To whom I do appeal, and in whose name
Tell you the dauphin I am coming on
To venge me as I may, and to put forth
My rightful hand in a well-hallowed cause.

Location: I.ii.281–293
Speaker: Henry V to the dauphin's messanger
Context: The dauphin has given Henry a mocking gift of tennis balls

Henry responds to the dauphin's gift with wrath, turning the jest on its head and threatening to treat the fields of France like a tennis court and play a game for the dauphin's father's crown. In his repeated insistence that the dauphin's jest will be responsible for the terrible carnage that he will bring to France (the dauphin will "[m]ock mothers from their sons"), Henry starts what will become a pattern of putting responsibility for his actions on his enemies. By saying he will go to France in the name of God and by blaming the dauphin for the consequences, Henry presents himself as an unappeasable, unstoppable force. Henry tempers the appearance of arrogance by appealing to God rather than to his own power. This speech is an early blueprint for almost all of Henry's future self-characterizations: he claims that his enemies' wickedness is to blame for the violence brought by his own army, then depicts himself as an instrument of God whose desire to further God's will dictates his actions.

2. Then imitate the action of the tiger.
Stiffen the sinews, summon up the blood,
Disguise fair nature with hard-favoured rage.
Then lend the eye a terrible aspect,
. . .
Now set the teeth and stretch the nostril wide,
Hold hard the breath, and bend up every spirit
To his full height. On, on, you noblest English,
Whose blood is fet from fathers of war-proof,
Fathers that like so many Alexanders
Have in these parts from morn till even fought,
And sheathed their swords for lack of argument.
Dishonour not your mothers; now attest
That those whom you called fathers did beget you.
Be copy now to men of grosser blood,
And teach them how to war. And you, good yeomen,
Whose limbs were made in England, show us here
The mettle of your pasture.

Location: III.i.6–27
Speaker: Henry V to his soldiers
Context: Henry rouses his troops

This passage is from Henry's famous speech, which begins with the line, "Once more unto the breach, dear friends" and ends with the battle cry, "God for Harry! England, and St. George!" Rallying his men to charge once more into the fray at the Battle of Harfleur (the "breach" refers to the hole in the town wall created by the bombardment of Henry's cannons), Henry employs two separate strategies for psychological motivation, each of which has its own language and rhetoric. First, Henry attempts to tap into a primal inclination toward violence in his men, hoping to rouse them into a killing frenzy. To this end, he tells his men they should resemble angry tigers, urging them toward a mindless fury represented by snarling teeth and flared nostrils.

Henry employs a second strategy, trying to inflame the men's patriotism by urging them to do honor to their country and prove that they are worthy of being called English. This strategy is somewhat more sophisticated than the urging to primal violence, and Henry turns away from the blunt physical description of the early part of his speech to a more complex rhetoric that combines historical reference ("so many Alexanders"), sentimental appeals to family pride ("[d]ishonour not your mothers"), and reminders of birthplace ("you, good yeomen, / Whose limbs were made in England"). At the end of his speech, Henry links St. George, the patron saint of England, to his battle cry, providing his men with a treasured and familiar symbol of patriotic ideals.

---

3. 'Tis not the balm, the sceptre, and the ball,
The sword, the mace, the crown imperial,
The intertissued robe of gold and pearl,
The farc_d title running fore the king,
The throne he sits on, nor the tide of pomp
That beats upon the high shore of this world—
No, not all these, thrice-gorgeous ceremony,
Not all these, laid in bed majestical,
Can sleep so soundly as the wretched slave
Who with a body filled and vacant mind
Gets him to rest, crammed with distressful bread;

. . .

And but for ceremony such a wretch,
Winding up days with toil and nights with sleep,
Had the forehand and vantage of a king.
The slave, a member of the country's peace,
Enjoys it, but in gross brain little wots
What watch the King keeps to maintain the peace,
Whose hours the peasant best advantages.

Location: IV.i.242–266
Speaker: Henry V
Context: Disguised as a commoner, Henry muses privately about kingship

This soliloquy is the only time Henry speaks privately to himself, without needing to appear kingly in front of others. Sitting alone in his camp, disguised as a commoner, Henry reveals the envy he feels for commoners not weighed down by the responsibilities of a ruler. Kings are pampered with in pomp and "ceremony"—Henry's word for the opulent trappings of royalty—but Henry considers ceremony a waste, no more than a "tide of pomp" beating on a shore. Henry says that he would trade all that ceremony for the peaceful sleep of the slave, who can go to bed happy as long as his stomach is full and who has no idea "[w]hat watch the King keeps to maintain the peace."

Henry's speech is somewhat self-pitying. As a royal, he can have no idea of the worry and sadness that afflict slaves and commoners. Still, the disdain he feels for the trappings of power speak well for him. He is such a good ruler precisely because he rules for the good of the country, not because he loves power and riches.

4. If we are marked to die, we are enough
To do our country loss; and if to live,
The fewer men, the greater share of honour.
God's will, I pray thee wish not one man more.
By Jove, I am not covetous for gold,

. . .

But if it be a sin to covet honour
I am the most offending soul alive.
No, faith, my coz, wish not a man from England.
God's peace, I would not lose so great an honour
As one man more methinks would share from me
For the best hope I have. O do not wish one more.
Rather proclaim it presently through my host
That he which hath no stomach to this fight,
Let him depart. His passport shall be made
And crowns for convoy put into his purse.
We would not die in that man's company
That fears his fellowship to die with us.

Location: IV.iii.20–39
Speaker: Henry V to his men
Context: Henry rallies his troops before the Battle of Agincourt

This quotation, from Henry's St. Crispin's Day speech, presumably inspires his soldiers to route a French force that outnumbers them five to one. Henry's opening lines, in which he says he does not want more men to fight with him, because the fewer the men the greater the share of honor each will get, showcase his ability to make abstract moral concepts, such as honor, tangible and urgent.

In most battles, soldiers are compelled to fight and deserters are killed, but Henry backs up his claim that he wants a small army by offering to dismiss any man who does not desire to fight with him. Henry implies that the man who chooses to leave is a sorry creature not worthy of belonging to the fraternity of worthy soldiers.

---

5. I think it is e'en Macedon where Alexander is porn. I tell you, captain, if you look in the maps of the world I warrant you sall find, in the comparisons between Macedon and Monmouth, that the situations, look you, is both alike. There is a river in Macedon, and there is also moreover a river at Monmouth. . . .
If you mark Alexander's life well, Harry of Monmouth's life is come after it indifferent well. For there is figures in all things. Alexander, God knows, and you know, in his rages and his furies and his wraths and his cholers and his moods and his displeasures and his indignations, and also being a little intoxicates in his prains, did in his ales and his angers, look you, kill his best friend Cleitus —

Location: IV.vii.18–32
Speaker: Captain Fluellen to Gower
Context: Henry has commanded the English soldiers to kill all of their French prisoners

In this amusing and ominous speech, Fluellen compares Henry to Alexander the Great, whom he initially calls "Alexander the Pig," meaning "Alexander the Big" (IV.vii.10). Fluellen bases his comparison on the irrelevant fact that Henry and Alexander were both born in towns that had rivers. Fluellen ends his speech by noting that Alexander killed his best friend, a crime of which the audience might also accuse Henry, who indirectly or directly causes the deaths of Falstaff, Scrope, and Bardolph. Fluellen's humor is a moment of comic relief, but it also probes some of the moral anxiety lurking beneath Shakespeare's heroic portrait of Henry. Fluellen's comparison of Henry to Alexander is highly flattering to Henry, but it is also unintentionally troubling.

1 HENRY VI

With the great King Henry V dead, personal rivalries and political factions lead England to lose control of France, whose spirit is revived by Joan of Arc's victories.

1 HENRY VI IN CONTEXT

1 Henry VI is an approximate historical chronicle of the English monarchy from Henry V's death in 1422 to just before Henry VI's marriage in 1445. It covers the emergence of the conflict that developed into the Wars of the Roses (1455–1485) and the loss of England's brief control over France. History plays as a genre held a particular fascination for the English public of the late sixteenth century. Patriotic sentiments ran high in the years following the defeat of the Spanish Armada in 1588. 1 Henry VI appears to reference the English campaigns in France of the 1590s. In particular, the play's battle near Rouen suggests the Duke of Essex's 1592 efforts to aid the French in squashing a Protestant uprising in Rouen.

1 Henry VI is the first part of a trilogy, but most critics believe that 2 Henry VI and 3 Henry VI were written first. The trilogy represents one of Shakespeare's first forays into the genre of history. They were followed by Richard III, in which the Wars of the Roses finally come to an end and a relative calm returns to England. The Henriad (those plays surrounding the reign of Henry VI's father and grandfather, Henry V and Henry IV) are believed to have been written later in Shakespeare's career. The story is based on contemporary chronicles including, most notably, Raphael Holinshed's *Chronicles of England, Scotland, and Ireland.*

1 HENRY VI: KEY FACTS

Full title: The First Part of Henry the Sixth

Time and place written: 1592; London

Date of first performance: 1592

Genre: History play

Setting (time): First half of the fifteenth century

Setting (place): England; France

Protagonist: Talbot; Richard Plantagenet (Duke of York); England

Major conflict: Split into rival factions in the power vacuum left by Henry V's death, the English government cannot cope with resistance from France led by Joan la Pucelle (Joan of Arc).

1 HENRY VI: CHARACTER LIST

THE ENGLISH IN ENGLAND

Basset Somerset's follower. Basset's fight with York's follower Vernon shows the noblemen's disagreement trickling down to their supporters.

Duke of Exeter King Henry's great-uncle. Exeter comments on the action of several public scenes, predicting (correctly) that the squabbles in the English command will develop into great strife.

Duke of Gloucester King Henry's uncle and Lord Protector of the Realm until Henry comes of age. Gloucester and his kinsman Winchester struggle for control of the government.

King Henry VI King of England and France, and son of the great King Henry V, who conquered France. Young and inexperienced, Henry faces great difficulty with his squabbling advisors. At the end he agrees to marry Margaret, a French noblewoman, on Suffolk's advice.

Mayor of London He struggles to keep peace between Winchester and Gloucester's men on the streets of London. When he orders them to cease fighting with weapons, they revert to throwing rocks.

Mortimer Plantagenet's uncle and the Duke of York. Mortimer has been imprisoned in the Tower of London for years because he tried to claim his right to the English throne. He dies in the tower, passing his claim and his titles to Plantagenet.

Richard Plantagenet, later Duke of York An English nobleman and Mortimer's nephew. York inherits Mortimer's claim to the throne after Mortimer's death. York's quarrel with Somerset in the Temple Garden leads to the Wars of the Roses. York's symbol is the white rose. His dispute with Somerset leads to Talbot's death and the English defeat in France.

Duke of Somerset King Henry VI's cousin. Somerset's disagreement with Richard Plantagenet, later Duke of York, at the Temple Garden eventually leads to the Wars of the Roses. Somerset chooses the red rose to represent his side, the House of Lancaster. His dispute with York leads to Talbot's death and the English defeat in France.

Earl of Suffolk An English nobleman who captures Margaret at Anjou and, taken with her, woos her on behalf of King Henry. Suffolk plans to use his connection to the future Queen of England to control King Henry and the government.

Vernon York's follower. Vernon's fight with Somerset's follower Basset shows the noblemen's disagreement trickling down to their supporters.

Earl of Warwick An English nobleman. Warwick judges several issues, including Somerset and York's dispute in the garden and, later, Joan's trial.

Bishop of Winchester, later cardinal Head of the Catholic Church in England and Gloucester's nemesis. Winchester accuses Gloucester of trying to take too much power from King Henry. Eventually, he purchases the title of cardinal from the Pope in hopes of acquiring more power.

Woodville Lieutenant of the Tower of London, who bars Gloucester from entering the tower on Winchester's orders.

THE ENGLISH MILITARY IN FRANCE

Duke of Bedford King Henry VI's uncle, and regent of the English territories in France. Too old and ill to lead the English forces at Rouen, Bedford directs his soldiers from his chair. He dies content after the English win.

Sir John Fastolf A coward, Fastolf is an English soldier who repeatedly flees the scene of battle when he fears for his life. Talbot curses Fastolf for lacking the valor and honor of the old generation of knights.

Gargrave An English soldier who dies at the siege of Orléans.

Glasdale An English soldier who fights at the siege of Orléans.

Sir William Lucy A messenger who asks York and Somerset for reinforcements for Talbot at Bordeaux, and scolds them when they cannot cooperate to help Talbot.

Earl of Salisbury An English nobleman killed during the siege of Orléans.

Lord Talbot General of the English troops in France. Talbot has a fearsome reputation, and recaptures several towns taken by Joan and the French forces. At Bordeaux, Talbot is trapped between two armies. Because of York and Somerset's personal quarrel, reinforcements do not come in time. His son John dies in battle, and Talbot dies of grief. Talbot represents a dying breed of chivalrous soldiers fighting for the honor of king and country.

John Talbot Talbot's son. John arrives at the battlefield of Bordeaux to experience war firsthand. When Talbot realizes that their army is doomed, he urges John to flee. John refuses because flight would disgrace the family name. He fights bravely and dies in battle.

THE FRENCH

Duke of Alençon A French lord.

Countess of Auvergne A French noblewoman who lures Talbot to her castle in the hopes of capturing him and saving France from the English. Talbot out-tricks her.

Bastard of Orléans A French commander who introduces Charles to Joan la Pucelle.

Duke of Burgundy A French nobleman who fights with the English. Joan convinces him to return to the French side. His departure leaves Talbot weakened.

Charles, Dauphin of France The heir to the French throne. Charles gathers enough support in France to crown himself king and sets about recapturing France from England. Charles is enchanted by Joan when he meets her. He loses to her in single combat. With Joan's help, Charles regains half of France. At the end, he agrees to make peace with the English and becomes viceroy of France under King Henry VI.

Joan la Pucelle A French girl who comes to see Charles, claiming that she has visions that direct her to fight for France. She leads French troops to victory at Orléans and Rouen, only to see both cities recaptured by the English. She is ultimately defeated and captured at Bordeaux. At the end of the play, we learn that her spirits are demons. York puts her on trial and burns her at the stake as a witch.

Margaret of Anjou René's daughter. Margaret is captured by Suffolk, who is so taken with her that he convinces Henry to wed her in what is a politically disadvantageous marriage. Suffolk hopes to use Margaret to control King Henry.

Master Gunner and Boy A French soldier and his son who help Joan bring down the English siege at Orléans.

René Charles's ally; Duke of Anjou; the impoverished King of Naples and Sicily; and Margaret's father.

Shepherd Joan's alleged father, although she denies a connection to him at her trial.

1 HENRY VI: PLOT OVERVIEW

The play opens with the funeral of King Henry V, the great English king who conquered France. Under the new king, the young Henry VI, both England's hegemony over France and her internal affairs begin to unravel. In France, England's military hero, Lord Talbot, meets increasing opposition from forces led by Charles, the heir to the French throne, and Joan la Pucelle (Joan of Arc), a French peasant who claims to have received divine instructions to free her people. Joan manages to lift the siege of Orléans against great odds, but Talbot and his men sneak in and retake the city while the French celebrate. Later, Joan retakes and loses the city of Rouen in the same day.

In England, the Duke of Gloucester, Henry's uncle and the lord protector of the realm until Henry comes of age, clashes violently with the bishop of Winchester in a struggle for control of the government. In a garden in England, a quarrel begins between Richard Plantagenet (who later becomes Duke of York) and the Duke of Somerset. The other English noblemen choose sides by plucking white and red roses. Over the course of the *Henry VI* trilogy, this quarrel will develop into the Wars of the Roses, in which the houses of York and Lancaster fight for the throne. In this play, York inherits a tenuous claim to the throne from his dying uncle.

When the English court moves to France for King Henry VI's coronation, the conflict between York and Somerset leads to Talbot's death and an English defeat when York and Somerset cannot cooperate to send Talbot reinforcements. At the battle of Bordeaux, York captures Joan, whose "divine" voices are revealed as demons, and burns her at the stake as a witch. Under pressure from the Pope, the English and French sign a peace treaty, and Charles becomes viceroy of France under the English crown. Finally, the Earl of Suffolk persuades King Henry to marry Margaret, a French noblewoman with close ties to Suffolk. This marriage is a politically unfortunate match that leaves the king under Margaret and Suffolk's control.

1 HENRY VI: SCENE SUMMARY

ACT I

With the great King Henry V dead, the English lords struggle for power as the French, led by Joan la Pucelle, revolt against English rule.

I.I Location: England. Westminster Abbey

At King Henry V's funeral, his relatives and nobles of the country learn that some of the English possessions in France are lost and that their general, Talbot, has been taken prisoner by the French.

At King Henry V's funeral, his relatives Bedford, Gloucester, Exeter, Warwick, Winchester, and Somerset mourn the dead king, who had ruled England so well and conquered his enemies so bravely. Henry V's son, now crowned King Henry VI, is still too young to rule in his own right, so Gloucester has been named lord protector of the realm, the temporary ruler of the kingdom. Gloucester accuses the bishop of Winchester of not praying enough for Henry V while he was still alive. Perhaps if Winchester had tried harder, Henry V would have lived. But Bedford urges Gloucester and Winchester to stop their quarreling. As the coffin is carried out, Bedford asks Henry V's spirit to watch over them and help England prosper.

A messenger enters with bad news from France: the French have recaptured eight towns that Henry V took for England during his reign. The effect of the news is all the more bitter because the words are spoken over the late king's coffin. Exeter asks about possible treachery, but the messenger attributes the defeat to a lack of men and money. The English lords express concern that at this time when solidarity is most needed, England's leadership is splintering into factions. The messenger calls to the lords to wake up, not to rest complacently on their past laurels.

Bedford, who is Regent of the English dominions in France, resolves to leave for France immediately to remedy the situation. A second messenger enters to announce that the dauphin Charles has been crowned king in Rheims, one of the towns recaptured by the French. Bedford again prepares to depart when a third messenger enters to report that the English general Talbot has been captured. Retreating from a battle at Orléans, Talbot was surrounded by French troops. Though he battled valiantly for three hours, he was undone when one of the English commanders, the cowardly Sir John Fastolf, fled, leaving Talbot exposed. Talbot was captured.

Shocked by the tale, Bedford makes plans to pay the ransom to free Talbot. He leaves for France. The other lords set off to prepare for the imminent war: Gloucester heads to the tower to check on the weapons stored there, and Exeter goes to attend to the safety of the young Henry VI. Left alone, Winchester reveals his plot to ingratiate himself with the young Henry, so that he (Winchester) can emerge as the most powerful man in the war.

I.II Location: France. Near Orléans

With Talbot taken prisoner, the French dauphin Charles hopes that the siege of Orléans will soon be over.

The French dauphin Charles and his nobles Alençon and René express their pleasure: they have captured Talbot and the English troops remain leaderless outside the city walls. The Frenchmen agree that the English look pitifully weak. Perhaps, the Frenchmen think, they may be able to break their siege and travel outside the city again.

I.III Location: France. Near Orléans

Charles meets Joan la Pucelle, a shepherdess who promises to lift the siege of Orléans.

The English nevertheless continue their siege on the French, killing many. Charles and his lords gather again, astonished that the English have held out. Then, the Bastard of Orléans enters with news for Charles. He announces that he may have found the key to their salvation: "A holy maid hither with me I bring / Which, by a vision sent to her from heaven, / Ordainèd is to raise this tedious siege / And drive the English forth the bounds of France" (I.iii.30–34). Charles calls for the "holy maid" to be brought in, but wants to test her ostensible clairvoyance: he changes places with René before Joan enters to see if she will see through the ruse. Joan la Pucelle approaches, and indeed immediately recognizes Charles, though she has never seen him before. She asks the other lords to leave her and Charles alone.

Joan explains that she is only a shepherd's daughter. One day when she was tending her sheep, the Virgin Mary appeared to her in a vision and told her to leave her sheep and help free her country. She tells Charles that he may ask her anything or test her in any way he wants, through questions or even combat, assuring him that she has the power to succeed in any undertaking. Charles, astonished at her audacity, agrees to a trial of single combat, saying he fears no woman. She responds that she fears no man, and soundly beats him. He calls her an Amazon (a mythological race of women warriors) who fights with the sword of Deborah, an Old Testament prophet. He asks her to become his lover, but she refuses: her sacred task requires her to remain a virgin.

The other French lords return and ask whether they should abandon Orléans to the English. Joan replies that they will fight for the city, and Charles agrees. Joan proclaims that she will raise the siege that very day. She remarks that "Glory is like a circle in the water" (I.iii.12), expanding infinitely until something stops it. With the death of Henry V, the English circle of glory has ceased to spread. Charles and his lords urge Joan to do what she can to end the siege.

I.IV Location: England. In front of the Tower of London

A disagreement between Winchester and Gloucester escalates into violence.

Gloucester arrives at the Tower of London with his blue-clad servants. When the warders inside refuse to let him in, Gloucester orders his men to storm the gates. Before they can break down the door, the lieutenant of the tower, Woodville, speaks from within, explaining that Winchester has ordered him to forbid Gloucester from entering.

Winchester and his men enter, distinguished by their tawny-colored coats. He confirms that he gave the order and refuses to submit to Gloucester in his role of protector. Winchester and Gloucester curse each other and order their men to draw their swords. Gloucester's soldiers defeat Winchester's men.

The mayor of London enters with his officers, temporarily halting the skirmish. After Winchester publicly accuses Gloucester of trying to steal the artillery housed there in order to overthrow the young king Henry VI and usurp the throne, Winchester's and Gloucester's men fight again. The mayor stops the battle and orders them to refrain from using their weapons under penalty of death. Winchester and Gloucester agree to obey the law and to continue their argument elsewhere. The mayor expresses amazement at Winchester's and Gloucester's appetite for conflict and violence.

I.V Location: France. Orléans

The French in Orléans prepare to defend themselves against the English.

The master gunner orders his boy to watch a nearby tower while he goes to see the governor. He has heard that the English lords use the tower as a lookout over Orléans to plan their assault. The gunner tells his boy he has aimed a piece of artillery at the tower in case the lords reappear there.

I.VI Location: France. A tower outside Orléans

Talbot has been ransomed; the French counterattack, led by Joan la Pucelle, begins.

Salisbury, Talbot, Gargrave, and Glasdale stand on turrets overlooking Orléans. Salisbury asks how Talbot escaped the French jail, and Talbot explains that Bedford ransomed him with a French prisoner. Talbot tells about his French guards, who were so frightened of him that they had a watch of marksmen aim their arrows at him even while he slept.

The soldiers look out over the roofs of Orléans and plan their attack. Just then the tower convulses in explosions, killing Gargrave and seriously wounding Salisbury. Talbot rushes to Salisbury, and a messenger enters to tell of a French attack led by Joan la Pucelle. Talbot orders the injured Salisbury conveyed to his tent while he deals with the French.

I.VII Location: France. Orléans

Talbot fights Joan la Pucelle, then orders a retreat.

Talbot attacks the French and drives them back, then Joan's forces drive back Talbot's army. Talbot cannot understand how a woman could be defeating his troops. Talbot and Joan come face-to-face. He challenges her to a fight, accusing her of being a witch. They fight, and her strength amazes him. Joan tells Talbot that his time to die has not yet come. She says she must return to Orléans, and he should go cheer on his troops.

Talbot cannot understand Joan's power: she drives the English forces away as effortlessly as smoke drives away bees. Talbot urges his troops to another skirmish but orders their retreat when it becomes obvious that they cannot win. He accuses his soldiers of consenting willingly to Salisbury's death, since none managed to effect a revenge. Talbot exits in shame.

I.VIII Location: France. Orléans

Joan la Pucelle has lifted the siege of Orléans.

Joan calls for French flags to be flown from Orléans's towers: as promised, she has freed the city from the English siege. Charles wants to honor Joan for her remarkable leadership. Alençon and René suggest they should celebrate the successes of all the warriors, including themselves, but Charles says it was Joan, not they, who won the day. He offers to divide the crown with her, to order all the religious men in his realm to sing her praises, and to honor her ashes highly when she dies. He declares Joan la Pucelle France's new saint and leads them off to a banquet.

ACT II

Talbot and the English forces retake Orléans; meanwhile, the English lords choose sides for the internal Wars of the Roses.

II.I Location: France. Orléans

The English mount a surprise attack on Orléans.

A French soldier instructs several sentinels to keep watch on the walls. Talbot enters with Bedford, Burgundy (a French lord fighting on the English side), and other soldiers, equipped with ladders. Talbot says that they have chosen the best time to launch a surprise attack, for the French have tired themselves out in celebrations. Bedford and Burgundy criticize Charles for thinking so little of his troops that he would turn to a witch (Joan) for aid. The English lords split up and enter the city from three different directions. Talbot and his men scale the wall and the sentinels call the alarm.

Alençon and René emerge, half-equipped for battle, followed by Charles and Joan. Charles asks Joan if she has been treacherous and helped the British mount this surprise attack. But she tells him he is just being impatient with her, unfairly expecting her to prevail both while awake and while sleeping. She says the blame is not hers but that of Charles's bad watchmen. Charles condemns Alençon, as it was his men who were on the watch that night. The lords bicker and blame each other for weak fortifications, but Joan stops them and tells them to gather up their troops to launch a counter-attack. The French leaders flee when an English soldier enters with the war-cry "A Talbot! A Talbot!" (II.i.79).

II.II Location: France. Orléans

The English have retaken and sacked Orléans.

The next morning Bedford and Talbot walk through Orléans, noting that the French have fled. Talbot calls for the body of Salisbury to be brought into the city. Talbot intends to bury him in the center of Orléans to immortalize Salisbury's death and the sack of Orléans.

A messenger arrives and tells Talbot that the countess of Auvergne has summoned him to her castle so she may behold the man who has achieved such fame. Burgundy thinks her request trivializes war and tells Talbot to ignore it. Talbot, however, decides to visit her and sends the messenger back to the countess to announce his acceptance.

II.III   Location: France. The castle of the countess of Auvergne

The countess of Auvergne tries, in vain, to trick and defeat Talbot.

The countess prepares for Talbot's visit, remarking that if everything works out as planned, she will be famous. The messenger announces Talbot's arrival. Seeing him, the countess wonders aloud if Talbot can be the same man so feared throughout France. She thinks reports of him must be false, because he does not present an imposing figure. Hearing her expressions of doubt, he turns to leave. She calls him back, and when he confirms that he is indeed Talbot, she tells him that he is now her prisoner.

The countess states that she has lured Talbot to her home to make him pay for the deaths of her countrymen. Talbot laughs, remarking that she sees before him not the whole Talbot, but a small piece of him. Her castle could never obtain all of him. The countess thinks he speaks in riddles, so he shows her his meaning by blowing his trumpet. Instantly, English soldiers arrive. Talbot explains that they are the substance and arms of the greater Talbot, who still holds power over the towns of France.

The countess asks Talbot to forgive her for misunderstanding his power. Talbot replies that he is not offended and asks her to host his soldiers for dinner.

II.IV   Location: England. The Temple Garden of the London law courts

The Wars of the Roses begin as Plantagenet and Somerset urge their supporters to choose white and red roses to symbolize their allegiance.

Several lords, including Richard Plantagenet, Warwick, Somerset, Suffolk, and Vernon, enter the garden from the courts to continue their angry dispute. Somerset asks Warwick to settle the argument, the topic of which may be the succession to the throne. Warwick says that such a choice is too difficult. Both Plantagenet and Somerset are outraged at his hesitation.

Plantagenet has presented a case for his noble birth. He now says that those who are on his side should pluck a white rose off the briar to show their allegiance. Somerset asks those who support him against Plantagenet to pluck a red rose. Warwick says he "love[s] no colours" (II.iv.34) and plucks a white rose with Plantagenet. Suffolk says he believes Somerset and picks a red rose. Vernon urges them to stop plucking until they discover which side has more people on it, and both Somerset and Plantagenet agree to yield if they have fewer supporters. And with that, Vernon picks a white rose. Then, a lawyer picks a white rose, too, saying that he believes Plantagenet's case is more correct in the law.

Plantagenet and Somerset trade insults about their flowers and scorn each other. Somerset criticizes Plantagenet's father, who was executed by King Henry V for treason. Plantagenet says that his father's guilt was never proven. He promises to remember this offense for a long time. Somerset welcomes future strife, and promises that his allies will wear a red rose to remind Plantagenet of this disagreement. Plantagenet too promises that his faction will wear a white rose as a marker of his continued hatred for Somerset. Somerset departs.

Warwick tells Plantagenet that he believes that the next Parliament will restore Plantagenet to his father's title. Meanwhile, he will continue to support Plantagenet, though he foresees that this small brawl in the garden will send thousands of people to their deaths, all in the name of the white and the red rose.

II.V   Location: England. The Tower of London

Plantagenet inherits a claim to the English crown from his dying uncle.

Plantagenet's elderly uncle Mortimer is close to death. He speaks of his declining strength and wonders when Plantagenet will come. He speaks about the misfortunes he has suffered since Henry V first came to power. Plantagenet has suffered under the same fate. Plantagenet arrives at the cell. Mortimer asks him about his recent argument with Somerset.

Plantagenet explains that Somerset insulted his dead father, and asks Mortimer to explain why his father was executed. Mortimer says that Plantagenet's father was condemned for the same crime for which he, Mortimer, has been imprisoned all these years. Mortimer explains that his family was supposed to inherit the throne after Richard II, but because Henry IV (the dead Henry V's father) deposed

Richard, Mortimer's family lost their right to the throne. When Mortimer attempted to reassert his right, he was thrown in jail. Later, Plantagenet's father raised an army in Mortimer's support, but was executed for treason.

Mortimer, who is childless, names Plantagenet as his heir. Plantagenet says that his father was the victim of the whims of bloody tyranny, and did not deserve to die. Mortimer insists that the house of Lancaster (the dynasty of Henry IV, V, and VI) now has a firm hold on the throne.

Mortimer dies, asking Plantagenet not to mourn his passing. Plantagenet promises to keep Mortimer's words to himself, but also wants to right the wrongs Somerset has done to his family. He hurries off to the Parliament, seeking to gain some power.

ACT III

The English lose and retake Rouen in France, while the Plantagenet-Somerset factions solidify.

III.I   Location: London. The Parliament house

In public, Gloucester and Winchester put their disagreement on hold; King Henry VI officially makes Plantagenet his uncle's heir.

Young King Henry VI enters, followed by many lords, including Exeter, Gloucester, Winchester, Somerset, Suffolk, Warwick, and Plantagenet. Gloucester tries to post a prewritten bill, but Winchester seizes it, tears it up, and mocks Gloucester for not being able to speak extemporaneously. Gloucester accuses Winchester of behaving with underhanded treachery in a plot to kill him at London Bridge as well as at the tower. The two bicker, each proclaiming himself superior to the other.

Other nobles step in and stop the argument. Henry pleads for peace between the two factions. The mayor of London enters and reports that Winchester's and Gloucester's men, forbidden to use weapons in their conflict (in I.iv), now chase each other around the city, hurling rocks at each other. The battling servants enter the court and continue fighting, despite Henry's and Gloucester's orders for them to cease. Henry asks Winchester to order his men to yield, but Winchester says he will never yield until Gloucester submits. Gloucester offers Winchester his hand in conciliation, and after some urging by Henry, Winchester agrees. Gloucester and Winchester shake hands, muttering to themselves that the argument is not yet over.

Warwick then presents Plantagenet's request: Plantagenet wants to be restored to his hereditary rights. Henry grants him both the earldom of Cambridge (inherited from his father) and the dukedom of York (inherited from his uncle Mortimer). Plantagenet thanks Henry. Everyone cheers for him, except Somerset, who curses him under his breath.

Gloucester urges Henry to be crowned king in France to help establish English control over France. Henry agrees. Everyone except Exeter departs.

Exeter comments on the scene. The nobles do not see that this disagreement between the lords will someday "break out into a flame" (III.i.195). Just as a dead body rots little by little, so this discord will slowly destroy the kingdom. He remembers a prophecy, once well known: Henry V would win everything and Henry VI would lose it all. Exeter hopes that he will die before this happens.

III.II   Location: France. Rouen

Joan infiltrates English-controlled Rouen in disguise.

Disguised as peasants, Joan and several of her soldiers gather outside the gates of Rouen, which has come back under English control. She tells them to wander around quietly and look for ways to attack the city.

III.III   Location: France. Rouen

At Joan's signal, Charles attacks Rouen with his forces.

Charles and his lords Alençon, René, and the Bastard of Orléans wait outside the city. Charles wonders how they will know when to attack, when Joan appears with a torch on the city walls. The lords immediately launch their forces.

III.IV   Location: France. Rouen

Talbot learns that Joan has attacked Rouen.

Talbot learns that the attack is in progress and curses Joan. He blames his soldiers' weaknesses on her sorcery.

III.V   Location: France. Rouen

The French have taken Rouen, but the English recapture it in the same evening.

Burgundy and Talbot sit with Bedford, who is ill and propped up in a chair. Meanwhile, Charles, Joan, and the French army taunt the English from atop the city walls, signifying that they are close to regaining Rouen. Talbot curses Joan for mocking the valiant-but-weak Bedford. He asks the French if they will dare meet in the field to fight an honest battle. Joan and the rest refuse, departing to prepare for battle, as Talbot scorns them.

Talbot is angered by their insults. He swears by King Henry VI and by the dead King Henry V that he will retake Rouen or die trying. Talbot asks Burgundy to help him move the ill and aged Bedford to a safer place, but Bedford says he would be ashamed to be anywhere but here, near his men. Talbot is impressed by Bedford's indomitable spirit and lets him stay near the fight. The English lords exit, and Sir John Fastolf runs onstage. A soldier asks him where he is going, and he says that he is fleeing for his life because the English are about to be defeated.

Meanwhile, offstage, the British troops chase away Joan and her French forces, to Bedford's great satisfaction. Now, he says, he can die, having seen the enemy overthrown.

III.VI   Location: France. Rouen

Talbot surveys the reconquered Rouen.

Talbot and Burgundy enter, congratulating themselves on having both lost and recovered their positions in the same day. Talbot wonders whether Joan and her forces have fled. They plan to restore order in Rouen and then depart for Paris to see King Henry VI. Before they go, they will bury and honor the dead Bedford.

III.VII   Location: France. Near Rouen

Joan lures Burgundy, a French lord who has been fighting with the English, back to the French side.

Joan tells Charles and his lords Alençon and the Bastard of Orléans not to despair after losing to Talbot, because she foresees crushing him later. Charles says that he does not doubt her skill. One small setback will not make him distrust her. Alençon and the bastard assure her that they will make her famous throughout the world, placing her statue in a prominent location and treating it like a sacred relic if she continues her work. She announces her plan to lure Burgundy back to the French side. Charles and his lords are delighted, sure that her plan will rid France of the English soldiers forever.

Glimpsing Talbot and Burgundy approaching with their troops, Joan orders a messenger to summon Burgundy. When Burgundy arrives, Charles asks Joan to enchant Burgundy with her words. Joan tells Burgundy to listen to her, a humble handmaiden. She calls to him to look on the fields of France and to see the destruction wrought by the English, and the wounds he has caused his country by siding with its foe. She urges him to turn against those who have hurt his country. Burgundy remarks to himself that either she has a very good point or her words bewitch him.

Joan goes on to say that the French now doubt whether he is truly French. She suggests that the English will reject him if they win. She accuses him of fighting against his countrymen and slaughtering his kinsmen. Burgundy admits he is vanquished. Joan's words have battered him. He asks the French lords to forgive him and accept his embrace, as he intends to hand over his forces to them and break with Talbot. Charles welcomes him.

III.VIII Location: Paris. The palace

King Henry arrives in Paris for his coronation, but the rift among the English lords remains.

In Paris, King Henry and his lords Gloucester, Winchester, Exeter, Warwick, Suffolk, Somerset, York (formerly Richard Plantagenet), Vernon, and Basset welcome the arrival of Talbot. Talbot announces that he has reclaimed fifty fortresses, twelve cities, and seven walled towns, along with many prisoners. King Henry thanks him and rewards him with an earldom in gratitude for his long service to the crown and to England.

The lords all exit, leaving Vernon and Basset alone. Vernon wears a white rose and Basset a red one. Vernon asks Basset if he meant the disparaging things he said at sea about his lord, York. Basset says he did and wonders if Vernon stands by his comments about Somerset. The two argue, and Vernon strikes Basset. Basset reminds him that they have been forbidden to draw weapons upon pain of death. Basset concedes that the time is not right for a fight, but another time will come when he will revenge the wrongs against him. Vernon agrees, and the two depart.

ACT IV

Because of York's (Plantagenet) and Somerset's quarrel, Talbot is trapped by the French and dies, losing the Battle of Bordeaux.

IV.I Location: Paris. The palace

During Henry's French coronation ceremony, Somerset and York (Plantagenet) have another ugly argument.

On behalf of the church, the bishop of Winchester crowns Henry king of both England and France. The governor of Paris is about to swear allegiance to Henry when Sir John Fastolf enters with a letter from Burgundy. Talbot is enraged to see the cowardly knight and rips off Fastolf's garter, which symbolizes Fastolf's membership in the Order of the Garter (the top rank of English knighthood). Talbot reminds Henry of Fastolf's craven flight during the siege of Orléans (see I.i) and says that Fastolf's knighthood sullies the title of knight. Henry calls Fastolf a stain to his countrymen and banishes him.

Gloucester reads Burgundy's letter, in which he announces his intention of abandoning the English and fighting for Charles. Henry asks Talbot to seek out Burgundy and find out what has caused his change of heart. Talbot departs.

Vernon and Basset enter to ask Henry for the right to duel. When asked why they want to duel, Basset and Vernon explain that, as they were crossing the channel, each ridiculed the other's rose. Henry marvels at the madness that drives men to develop such decisive splits for frivolous causes. He asks York and Somerset to overlook their differences and reconcile. York and Somerset argue about settling their disagreements with a duel.

Gloucester scolds the lords, saying they should be ashamed for so troubling the king with this ridiculous argument. Exeter urges them to be friends. Henry orders York and Somerset to forget their quarrel. They should make peace especially here, in France, "amongst a fickle and wavering nation"(IV.i.138), the English lords must present an appearance of unity lest the French dare rebel. It would be embarrassing to lose France over such a small matter. Henry proclaims that he favors neither Somerset nor York: "Both are my kinsmen, and I love them both" (IV.i.155). He offers them important positions in the French campaign: York is made leader of the troops in the English-controlled French regions; and Somerset is ordered to unite the horsemen and the infantry. As he exits, he urges them to direct their anger at the French rather than at each other.

York, Warwick, Vernon, and Exeter remain. York is wary because Henry chose Somerset's red rose to use as an example. Warwick thinks that Henry meant nothing by it.

Alone, Exeter notes that York did well not to voice his wariness and anger toward Somerset in public. Exeter is sure that these small arguments among the nobility "presage[s] some ill event" (IV.i.191). England faces enough of a challenge with its young and inexperienced King Henry. When the lords are divided by envy and malice, the country faces doom. What begins in confusion will end in ruin, he predicts.

IV.II Location: France. Outside Bordeaux

Talbot's army is trapped between Bordeaux and Charles's French forces.

Talbot arrives outside the gates of Bordeaux, in search of Burgundy. Talbot tells the French general to open the city gates and acknowledge King Henry VI, or face a violent attack on his city. The general replies that they are well fortified and strong enough to resist his attack. Moreover, he announces, Charles's armies now plan to attack Talbot from behind, so the English forces will be unable to retreat. Death faces Talbot from both sides, he declares, as thousands of Frenchmen have no other destination in mind for their arrows and swords than Talbot himself. This is Talbot's last moment of glory, says the general, for he will soon fall.

Talbot hears the sound of Charles's approach and sends some of his men to reconnoiter their forces. He compares his forces to deer trapped in a kennel and surrounded by savage dogs. But the English will not die without a fight, he says. They will turn on the French forces that surround them. He prays that England may prosper in the coming fight.

IV.III Location: France. A field

York blames Somerset for Talbot's situation.

York asks his messenger where Charles's troops are, and the messenger announces that they have gone to Bordeaux to fight with Talbot. Charles's troops outnumber Talbot's, the messenger adds. York curses Somerset, who has delayed the promised supply of horsemen that he had expected to send to join Talbot. Talbot was relying on York's aid, but he can do nothing alone.

Another messenger, Sir William Lucy, enters. He says that Talbot badly needs troops, for he is encircled by French troops. Lucy urges York to send troops or Talbot will be doomed. York wishes Somerset were in Talbot's place, so a coward could die in place of a valiant warrior. York says he can't do anything, sadly aware that if Talbot dies, then France will fall to Charles. Lucy says that Talbot's son John had just traveled to be with his father at Bordeaux, which means he will die with his father. York is even more upset, cursing the cause that stops him from helping Talbot. He exits, leaving Lucy alone to ruminate on the fact that dissention among the nobles will lead to the loss of France, the greatest conquest of their recently dead King Henry V.

IV.IV Location: France. A field

Somerset blames York for Talbot's impending doom.

Somerset enters with his army, commenting that it is too late to send the army to help Talbot. He says he is sure that York has, in fact, planned the impending defeat, having sent a too-daring Talbot into battle in order to bring about his death so York might figure as the preeminent hero in coming battles. Lucy arrives at Somerset's camp. Somerset asks him who sent him, and Lucy says he was sent by the betrayed Talbot, who will now die while awaiting rescue from other English forces. Lucy urges him not to let his private disagreements keep aid from reaching Talbot in time.

Somerset blames York for the whole situation. York sent Talbot to Bordeaux, and York should help him. Lucy says that York had said he was awaiting Somerset's horsemen before he could help Talbot. Somerset says that York is lying, and York could have sent the horsemen but simply didn't want to. And besides, says Somerset, he dislikes York and doesn't take well to the idea of sending him his horsemen. Lucy charges Somerset with causing the death of Talbot with his petty dispute. Somerset says he'll send his horsemen now, but Lucy says it's too late. Lucy declares that Talbot's fame lies in his deeds in the world, but his final shame and death are attributable to the warring lords.

IV.V Location: France. Outside Bordeaux

After much discussion, Talbot and his son resolve to stay and face death together.

Talbot and his son John stand on the battlefield near Bordeaux. Talbot says he had sent for his son to teach him the strategies of war so that the name of Talbot might be carried on into future wars. But John has arrived in a situation of too much danger, and Talbot tells his son to escape. John refuses, however, explaining that to flee now would be to disgrace the name of Talbot. Talbot tells John to flee so that he may avenge his father's death, but John says anyone who flees will never again be taken seriously in a fight.

Talbot says they can't both stay, as they will both die. So John tells Talbot to flee, offering to stay himself. John argues that Talbot's death would be a greater blow to England than his own. Moreover, Talbot has done so many great deeds that a retreat now would not blemish Talbot's reputation the way it would John's. Talbot asks him if he wants his mother's heart to be broken when her only son and husband both die, but John says he prefers that his mother grieve for his death rather than for his honor. Talbot repeats that if John flees the Talbot legacy will live on, but John insists that that legacy will be worthless if he sullies it by fleeing. Finally, Talbot relents and sadly welcomes his son to fight and probably die with him.

IV.VI Location: France. Outside Bordeaux

Talbot and his son again argue about which one should flee and save himself.

In the ensuing battle, John becomes surrounded by French soldiers, and Talbot rescues him. Talbot sees that John has been wounded—his first battle wound—by the Bastard of Orléans. This first penetration by a sword has deflowered this young soldier, Talbot says. He asks if John is tired, urging him again to leave the battlefield. Hasn't he achieved enough glory now to escape with honor and live on to avenge Talbot's death? Why endanger both their lives on the same bloody field? Talbot is old, and if he dies he loses only a few years, but if John dies, then the Talbot name in English leadership will die too.

John understands Talbot's arguments, but insists that if he flees he will no longer deserve the name of Talbot's son. As a Talbot, John's duty is to die at his father's side. Talbot compares John to Icarus, the mythological youth who flew out of prison using wings his father Daedalus created, but drowned in the sea when the sun melted the wax in his wings because he flew too high. Talbot and John return to battle.

IV.VII Location: France. Outside Bordeaux

Talbot and his son die, and the French win the battle of Bordeaux.

A little later Talbot reappears, mourning John's death. He says that John fought valiantly and saved his life several times. Yet, like Icarus, John aimed too high and fell, brought down by the French. John's body is borne in and Talbot weeps over it. Talbot says that his spirit cannot survive this blow. Talbot dies. Soldiers depart with the bodies.

Charles and his men, including Alençon, Burgundy, the Bastard of Orléans, and Joan, enter. Charles is happy that York and Somerset's troops never arrived, because otherwise the French would not have won. The lords discuss what a valiant warrior John Talbot proved to be before he fell. Joan says that she encountered him in the field but he refused to fight with her because she is a woman. Burgundy says he would have made a noble knight.

Lucy enters, asking to know the names of prisoners and to view the bodies of the English dead. He recites a long, eloquent list of men lost in the battle and asks where they are now. Joan makes fun of Lucy's style: "Him that thou magnifi'st with all these titles / Stinking and flyblown lies here at our feet" (IV.vii.75–76). These noble-sounding people are all dead and rotting. Lucy inquires after Talbot, and asks to bury the bodies with fitting honor. Joan, bored with Lucy's elevated speech, urges Charles to give him the bodies and send Lucy on his way.

ACT V

The English capture Joan and burn her at the stake; the French and English negotiate peace; Suffolk persuades Henry to marry a French noblewoman under his control.

V.I Location: London. The royal palace

At the Pope's urging, the English agree to seek peace with the French.

King Henry enters with Gloucester, Exeter, and other lords. He asks Gloucester about the letters from the Pope. Gloucester replies that the Pope urges England and France to negotiate peace. At Henry's request for advice, Gloucester says that a peace treaty will probably be the only thing that will stop the bloodshed. He suggests that Henry marry the daughter of the earl of Armagnac, Charles's close relative, to cement the peace. Henry replies that he may be better suited to study than to marriage, but promises to take Gloucester's advice.

Winchester enters, dressed as a cardinal, with several messengers from the Pope. Exeter wonders to himself how Winchester came to be a cardinal, a position that will give him more influence over the king. Henry tells the Pope's messengers that he agrees to seek friendly peace with France. Gloucester tells the messengers that Henry has also agreed to marry the earl of Armagnac's daughter. The court departs, except for Winchester and the Pope's first messenger. Winchester tells the messenger that he owes the Pope money for his cardinalship. Now he won't have to submit to anyone, Winchester declares, especially not to Gloucester.

V.II Location: France. Anjou

Charles and Joan hear that a large English army plans to attack their troops.

Charles and his nobles, including Burgundy, Alençon, the Bastard of Orléans, René, and Joan, ponder news from Paris, which has sworn allegiance to England. Alençon urges Charles to march to Paris and clear up the situation. Then, a messenger enters to announce that the two segments of the English army have merged and are preparing to attack the French troops. Joan urges Charles to lead the battle, and declares that he will win.

V.III Location: France. Angiers

Afraid of defeat in battle, Joan summons her demonic spirits, but they refuse to help her.

In the midst of battle, Joan alone realizes that the English, led by York, are winning. She calls on the fiendish spirits that help her see the future and asks them to come to her. The spirits arrive. She asks them to help her win the fight for France, but they refuse to speak to her. She reminds them that she has always offered her blood to them in exchange for their help, yet the demonic spirits show no interest in her offerings. Desperate, she offers them first her body, then her soul, but they depart. Forsaken by her former powers, Joan declares that France will now surely fall to the English.

V.IV Location: France. Outside Angiers

The English win the battle; York takes Joan prisoner.

York prevails in battle over Burgundy as the French begin to flee. York seizes Joan and tauntingly asks her if her demons can help her now. Calling her a "[f]ell banning hag, enchantress" (V.iv.13), he drags her off.

V.V Location: France. Outside Angiers

Enthralled with his prisoner Margaret, the daughter of one of Charles's allies, Suffolk resolves to marry her to King Henry.

Suffolk has taken prisoner the lovely young Margaret. Her beauty enthralls him. She says that she is René's daughter. (René is Duke of Anjou and king of Naples and Sicily.) Suffolk wants to free her but cannot bear to part with her.

Margaret asks Suffolk what ransom she must pay before she can leave. Suffolk mutters to himself that she must submit to being wooed, since "she is a woman, therefore to be won" (V.v.35). While Margaret keeps asking him whether she can go, Suffolk thinks to himself that he cannot woo her because he is already married. At the same time, he cannot resist the delightful challenge of winning her. Finally, he decides to woo her on behalf of King Henry. He thinks he can cleverly legitimate such a move: after all, Margaret is the daughter of the king of Naples, even if Naples isn't much of a kingdom and her father has no money.

Meanwhile, Margaret grows annoyed that Suffolk, lost in his schemes, is ignoring her questions. Finally Suffolk speaks to her and asks if she would marry King Henry. She says she would prefer to be a queen in bondage than a servant, so she agrees if Henry and her father also desire the match.

The French generals enter, and Suffolk calls to René. René is upset to learn that his daughter has been captured, since he has no money to ransom her. But Suffolk offers him an alternative: his daughter will be married to the king of England. René says that he will give his consent to the marriage in exchange for control of the French territories Maine and Anjou. Suffolk agrees and prepares to go to England to complete the deal. René and Margaret prepare to depart, but Suffolk asks Margaret for a kiss first. She consents.

When they are gone, Suffolk expresses the wish that he could woo Margaret for himself. But he determines to go to Henry and speak of Margaret's virtues and convince him to marry her.

V.VI   Location: France. York's camp

York orders Joan burned at the stake as a witch and a whore; peace is negotiated: Charles agrees to become viceroy of France under the English crown.

York has arranged a trial for Joan, attended by Warwick and Joan's father, a shepherd. She refuses to acknowledge her relation to the shepherd. Warwick asks her if she denies her parentage, which York sees as a sign of her wickedness. The shepherd begs her to admit that he is her father, but Joan insists that the English have merely brought him in to suggest her birth was low. Distraught, the shepherd says he wishes some wolf had eaten her when she tended his sheep. He urges the English to burn her, as hanging would be too good a death, and departs.

York orders her to be taken away, but Joan insists on telling her story. She announces that she is the descendant of kings, chosen by the heavens to be virtuous and holy and to bring miracles to the earth. She declares that York and Warwick do not see her innocence because they are polluted by their own lusts and stained by the blood of the innocents they have killed before. She declares she has always been a chaste virgin. If the English spill her blood, they will only be sending her to heaven, where she can call upon God to reap revenge. Unconvinced, York orders the guards to take her away. Warwick orders a large bonfire to burn her at the stake.

Joan asks them to spare her life because she is pregnant. York is startled and wonders who fathered her baby. They suggest Charles, but she denies it. She says it was Alençon, then she names René. The English think all these names suggest she has been promiscuous with the French lords, all the while claiming to be a virgin. York tells her to cease her efforts, for they are in vain. She will be burned no matter what she says. Joan then curses England, and she is led away.

Winchester enters with letters from Henry. York reads of the plan to negotiate peace. He is frustrated to think that so many died and were captured for their country, only to now be dishonored by what he considers "effeminate peace" (V.vi.107). He foresees the loss of the rest of the French kingdom.

Charles enters with his lords Alençon, René, and the Bastard of Orléans to discuss the terms of the treaty. York asks Winchester to negotiate because he is too angry. Winchester announces that Henry consents to cease the war and to let Charles's men become feudal lords, loyal to the crown of England. Moreover, Charles will become a viceroy under King Henry. But Alençon doesn't want Charles to become a shadow of his former powerful self, and Charles himself reminds Winchester that he possesses more than half the French territories and is already reverenced as king in those regions. He would rather be king of half a kingdom than viceroy of a whole one. York sneers at Charles's quibbling.

René urges Charles to accept the offer because another is not likely to come again. Alençon agrees. Charles should accept and, thus, stop the massacre of his people. He can always go back on his word when conditions are favorable. Charles agrees to the truce, on the condition that the English leave him all his fortified towns. York insists that they swear allegiance to the English throne, and they do. Then, York tells them to dismiss their armies.

V.VII Location: London. The royal palace

Suffolk persuades Henry to marry Margaret and looks forward to controlling Henry through her.

Suffolk arrives to confer with Henry, Gloucester, and Exeter. Henry tells Suffolk that his account of the lovely Margaret has convinced him that she would be a good bride for him. Suffolk speaks further of her virtue and loveliness, and Henry asks Gloucester (as protector of the realm) to give him consent to marry Margaret. Gloucester reminds him that he is already engaged to the daughter of the earl of Armagnac, and it would damage his honor to break that contract.

Suffolk says that a daughter of a poor earl such as Armagnac is nothing special, so it's okay to break the engagement. Gloucester points out that Margaret, too, is no more than an earl's daughter, but Suffolk insists she is the child of the king of Naples, a man who has such authority in France that to marry her would mean continued French allegiance. Gloucester says that such a plan was exactly what he had in mind with his suggestion of the earl of Armagnac's daughter, except his plan will work better since the earl of Armagnac is actually related to Charles. Exeter adds that Margaret's father René has no dowry to offer, but Suffolk notes that the Henry is rich enough not to need a dowry.

Suffolk tells the lords that the choice of wife is Henry's, not theirs. Henry says that he cannot tell if he's just inexperienced or if he's charmed by Suffolk's description, but he wants to marry Margaret. He tells Suffolk to bring her from France to crown her queen. He asks Gloucester to forgive him, and the lords depart. Suffolk remains, saying that he has prevailed: after the wedding, Margaret will rule Henry, and because Suffolk rules Margaret, he will have control over King Henry and the kingdom.

THEMES, MOTIFS, & SYMBOLS IN *1 HENRY VI*

THEMES

NATIONAL SECURITY THREATENED BY CIVIL DISCORD   One of the major themes of Shakespeare's history plays, articulated by the bastard at the end of *King John*, is that England always defeats its enemies unless its strength is undermined by weak leadership resulting from domestic conflict. In *1 Henry VI* this theory is played out in the most explicit of ways: the animosity between Somerset and York renders them incapable of working together to send Talbot reinforcements, which results in French victory and Talbot's death. King Henry VI calls Somerset and York's conflict "a viperous worm / That gnaws at the bowels of the commonwealth" (III.i.73–74). With the death of the strong Henry V, the rotting English state caves in, resulting in war, first abroad and then at home.

WOMEN AS UNNATURAL AND THREATENING   The three female characters in *1 Henry VI*—Joan la Pucelle, the countess of Auvergne, and Margaret of Anjou—all represent a threat to England and its male leaders. Joan represents a very real military threat to English hegemony over France. The countess of Auvergne tries to use her feminine charms to lure and trap Talbot after his early victories quelling the French resistance. Margaret becomes Suffolk's tool in gaining more power in English government when he persuades King Henry to marry her, thus making a less strategically and financially lucrative match. All of these women are foreign and French, and their nationality represents a very real threat to English prosperity. Moreover, in this play Shakespeare implicitly links femaleness with foreignness: none of the play's female characters are English, so women are necessarily against England by virtue of their gender alone.

Both the countess and Margaret threaten England, using their sexuality as a tool. Joan, the play's most important female character, does too; she is presented as unnatural and monstrous. Both virgin and whore, she undermines female humility and religious devotion by using them both as a cover for military prowess. By Act V, her religious devotion is revealed as a scam as she contacts the demonic spirits that have been fueling her visions all along. The women in the play are strong and admirable, but also dangerous to English society.

THE END OF CHIVALRY   In writing about the mid-fifteenth century from the perspective of the end of the sixteenth, Shakespeare distinguished between the dying feudal codes of chivalry and honor and the emerging culture of pragmatism. Talbot and his son function as romantic representations of the old order. Their talent and skill is for battle, and their mission is protecting their country. They both hold honor dearer than life, family continuity, and the practical needs of their country. After much discussion, both stay to their certain doom when their army is trapped between two French forces at Bordeaux. The death of their line represents the end of medieval chivalry, the beginning of the modern era.

At the same time, the characters that represent this more pragmatic, bureaucratic modern era are portrayed as self-serving, petty, and sometimes even corrupt. Church and state, as symbolized by the bishop of Winchester and Lord Protector Gloucester, jockey for political power. The bishop of Winchester even buys the title of cardinal from the Pope in order to consolidate his authority. Somerset and York's inconsequential squabble develops into an all-out war. Indeed, it is because they fail to rise above their personal disagreement that they betray Talbot in battle. Chivalry dies because it is squashed by emerging self-interest.

MOTIFS

HISTORY AS MAN-MADE VS. HISTORY AS FATE   Shakespeare's history plays demonstrate a tension between conflicting perspectives on history. They raise the question of whether the course of events is predetermined by God or determined by human decisions. On the one hand, small human decisions such as Somerset's and York's quarrel in the Temple Garden evolve to take on more and more significance, as Talbot's army perishes when the two fail to cooperate to send reinforcements. On the other hand, Exeter continually suggests that these little struggles are part of a grander design, evil omens that will lead, he hints, to the Wars of the Roses. The conflict between these two historical perspectives is best illuminated in the opposition between Joan and Talbot. Talbot relies on valor and strength to secure his victories, while Joan claims to be guided by divine (or satanic) inspiration. Both perish, and the tension between free will and determinism remains unresolved.

ABSURD CONFLICTS   The play portrays and ridicules two major disagreements among English nobles. Gloucester, the lord protector, clashes with the bishop of Winchester in a bid for power. Somerset and York's petty disagreement escalates into full-blown animosity. Both conflicts solidify in childish ways. In front of the London Tower, Winchester tears up Gloucester's official announcement without reading it. Their servants resort to throwing rocks at each other after the mayor of London forbids them to fight with weapons. York and Somerset demand that English nobles choose sides, then and there, by plucking roses. Shakespeare portrays fifteenth-century English nobles as squabbling children playing with the fire that is the government of a nation.

SYMBOLS

ROSES   Fifteenth-century England devolved into a series of domestic conflicts collectively entitled the Wars of the Roses. The two roses represented the symbols of the two major factions. The white rose represented the House of York, which claimed the throne in the name of descendants of Edward III, whose grandson Richard II had been deposed in 1399 by Henry IV (Henry VI's grandfather). The red rose represented the House of Lancaster, which supported the Henry IV-V-VI line. The rose selection scene in the Temple Garden is Shakespeare's evocative invention; roses were ready-made symbols for his history plays. Though roses often represent fragility and love, they also have thorns, which are draw blood and represent the threat of war. Somerset's warning to Vernon as Vernon chooses his red rose, "Prick not your finger as you pluck it off" (II.iv.49) serves as a reminder of the bloodshed that this conflict will bring.

THE SIEGE OF ORLÉANS   The siege of Orléans embodies the struggle between conflicting views of history. At the beginning of the play, the bickering English noblemen who direct their actions contrast with the divinely inspired Joan. Her initial success in lifting the siege of Orléans against great odds symbolizes a victory for divine nobility over petty man. When the assault begins, Salisbury and Talbot hear thunderous explosions, as if Joan were an agent of God's punishing judgment.

IMPORTANT QUOTATIONS FROM *1 HENRY VI*

1. *King Henry the Fifth, too famous to live long.*
   England ne'er lost a king of so much worth.

Location: I.i.6–7
Speaker: Bedford
Context: The duke of Bedford laments the death of King Henry V.

1 Henry VI opens the play on a dark note: the funeral of King Henry V, the greatest English king, according to Bedford. Indeed, the play depicts the loss of French possessions and internal strife that comes after Henry V's death. Bedford's lines focus on England's loss—the loss of a king that precipitates the loss of France and the loss of unity. Bedford calls Henry V "too famous to live long," opposing glory and permanence. Indeed, Joan and Talbot, the most glorious characters of this play, die before the end.

2. *No, no, I am but shadow of myself.*
   You are deceived, my substance is not here.
   For what you see is but the smallest part
   And least proportion of my humanity.

Location: II.iii.50–53
Speaker: Talbot to the countess of Auvergne
Context: The countess thinks that she has tricked and trapped Talbot, unaware that his whole army is just behind him.

Talbot's response to the countess of Auvergne demonstrates both his wit and his honor. He has come prepared for a trap, and has the presence of mind to confuse her with his lofty rhetoric. The main substance of Talbot is his army, and he is but a little part of the English power. His retort is medieval in sentiment. He minimizes his own glory and gives credit to his soldiers. His emphasis on honor contrasts with the newer culture of Englishmen, as exemplified by the cowardly Sir John Fastolf, who put themselves first.

3. *O what a scandal is it to our crown*
   That two such noble peers as ye should jar!
   Believe me, lords, my tender years can tell
   Civil dissention is a viperous worm
   That gnaws at the bowels of the commonwealth.

Location: III.i.70–73
Speaker: Henry VI
Context: Henry pleads with Winchester and Gloucester to make peace for the good of the country.

Henry VI's plea for peace foreshadows his simpleminded and ineffectual desire for peace as the Wars of the Roses escalates. He compares internal strife to a "viperous worm," building on the frequent comparison of a healthy state to a healthy body, as embodied in the body of the king.

4. *O young John Talbot! I did send for thee*
   To tutor thee in stratagems of war,

That Talbot's name might be in thee revived
When sapless age and weak unable limbs
Should bring thy father to his drooping chair.
But, O—malignant and ill-boding stars!—
Now thou art come unto a feast of death,
A terrible and unavoided danger.

Location: IV.v.1–8
Speaker: Talbot to John
Context: Trapped between two French armies, Talbot laments his son John's imminent death.

Within the play, the character of Talbot represents the age of chivalry. His speech both emphasizes the honor code that guides his life and heralds the end of chivalry. Talbot and his son engage in a lofty discussion about which one of them should stay to fight and die. Ultimately they resolve that honor commands both of them to remain. That Talbot blames his downfall on "ill-boding stars" rather than the French, or the failure of the English to send reinforcements, suggests that he himself is aware that he and his chivalric code are relics that have outlived their time. The danger that he and John face is "unavoided," and their end has come.

---

5. *First, let me tell you whom you have condemned:*
 Not one begotten of a shepherd swain,
 But issued from the progeny of kings;
 Virtuous and holy, chosen from above
 By inspiration of celestial grace
 To work exceeding miracles on earth.

Location: V.vi.36–41
Speaker: Joan la Pucelle
Context: At her trial, Joan claims that she is the descendant of kings and has been divinely inspired to work miracles.

Over the course of the play, our perception of Joan as a character evolves dramatically. In the beginning, she presents herself as a shepherd's daughter, a virtuous and courageous girl who fights for her God and her country. As she summons her demons in V.iii, she turns into a sorceress with connections to evil spirits. Here, she announces that she is the daughter of kings, chosen by God to perform miracles on earth. Shakespeare's portrayal of Joan is both confusing and problematic. She turns from a virgin into a whore and from a girl guided by heaven to a hag guided by hell.

2 HENRY VI

The Duke of York instigates a popular rebellion, makes a claim to the throne, and wins the first battle of the Wars of the Roses against King Henry VI's forces.

2 HENRY VI IN CONTEXT

Shakespeare composed 2 *Henry VI*, one of his first plays, in the early 1590s. Its full title ("The First Part of the Contention of the Two Famous Houses of York and Lancaster") suggests that it was the first play of the *Henry VI* trilogy. 3 *Henry VI* ("The Second Part . . .") followed soon after, and *1 Henry VI* became a prequel later on. *1 Henry VI* depicts the beginning of factionalism at the English court after the death of the great King Henry V. In particular, the Duke of Somerset and the Duke of York start a quarrel that leads to the defeat of Lord Talbot, the great English military hero, and precipitates the loss of the English dominions in France. At the end of *1 Henry VI*, the Earl of Suffolk (promoted to marquess in this play) captures Margaret of Anjou, the daughter of a bankrupt French lord. Infatuated with Margaret, Suffolk resolves to marry her to Henry.

2 *Henry VI* covers the period roughly from Henry VI's marriage to Margaret of Anjou in 1445 through the Battle of St. Albans, the first open conflict of the Wars of the Roses, in 1455. It portrays the continuing intrigues at the English court: first the conflict between the Duke of Gloucester and Cardinal Beaufort, then between York's faction and Henry's supporters. In Act IV, Jack Cade leads a popular uprising against the government. The absence of a strong ruler on the throne leads to chaos.

For his historical details, Shakespeare likely relied on contemporary chronicle histories of fifteenth-century England. Raphael Holinshed's *Chronicles of England, Scotland, and Ireland* probably furnished the inspiration for Cade's rebellion, modeled on the revolt by Wat Tyler in the Peasant's Rebellion of 1381. Two versions of 2 *Henry VI* exist—a shorter one published in 1594 and a longer one that first appeared in the First Folio of 1623. Scholars suspect that the first version was a reconstruction prepared by actors. The second version came from a promptbook.

2 HENRY VI: KEY FACTS

Full Title: The First Part of the Contention of the Two Famous Houses of York and Lancaster

Time and place written: 1591; London

Date of first publication: 1594

Genre: History play

Setting (time): Mid-fifteenth century (historically, from Henry VI's marriage in 1445 to the First Battle of St. Albans in 1455)

Setting (place): England

Protagonist: Gloucester; York

Major conflict: After Gloucester, the Protector of the Realm, is assassinated, York makes a public claim to King Henry VI's throne.

2 HENRY VI: CHARACTER LIST

LANCASTRIANS

Cardinal Beaufort, Bishop of Winchester Henry's great-uncle and the head of the Catholic Church in England. The long-standing mutual animosity between Beaufort and Gloucester (see also *1 Henry VI*) comes to a head when Gloucester is arrested and assassinated. Crippled by guilt because of his role in Gloucester's death, Beaufort falls ill and dies miserably soon after.

Duke of Buckingham An English nobleman who joins Somerset, Suffolk, Beaufort and Margaret in their plot against Gloucester. Buckingham supports and represents King Henry in Jack Cade's and York's rebellions.

Lord Clifford Henry's elderly supporter. Clifford convinces Jack Cade's Rebels to lay down their arms. York kills him at the Battle of St. Albans. Lord of the court, Clifford helps convince Jack Cade's troops to lay down their arms. Later, Clifford must judge York when he makes his claim to the throne. In battle, York kills Clifford, and Clifford's son decides he is finished with pity for any Yorkist after he finds his father's body.

Young Clifford Clifford's son. After seeing his elderly father Clifford dead, Young Clifford resolves to be ruthless in battle with Yorkists.

Duke of Gloucester Henry's uncle. Gloucester is Lord Protector of the Realm until Henry comes of age. The people love Gloucester, but other noblemen who think that he has too much power hate him. An honorable figure, Gloucester is arrested for treason and assassinated by Suffolk and Beaufort's hit men.

Eleanor, Duchess of Gloucester Gloucester's ambitious wife. Eleanor wants to be queen and hires conjurers (Bolingbroke and the Witch) to predict her future. She is arrested and paraded through the streets of London in shame. Her disgrace complicates Gloucester's situation and precipitates his downfall.

King Henry VI The King of England, crowned in infancy. A good man but an ineffectual king, Henry allows ambitious nobles, foreign opposition, and popular rebellions to erode his kingdom. Henry is the son of the great King Henry V, who conquered France for England. During Henry VI's reign, the French lands are lost. Henry makes a politically unadvisable marriage to the manipulative Margaret of Anjou (see *1 Henry VI*). Henry's weakness as a ruler leads to civil war—the Wars of the Roses—as York asserts his claim to the throne and attacks the royal troops.

Queen Margaret Daughter of an impoverished French duke, Henry's wife, and Suffolk's lover. Conniving and manipulative, Margaret plots with Suffolk and Beaufort against Gloucester to secure more control of the government.

Duke of Somerset York's long-standing enemy (see *1 Henry VI*) and Henry's supporter.

Stafford, Stafford's brother Noblemen who lead the effort to suppress Jack Cade's rebellion in Kent. Both die in battle.

Marquess of Suffolk Margaret's lover. Suffolk works with Beaufort to arrest and assassinate Gloucester. He is banished when the people demand accountability for Gloucester's death. Pirates at sea kill him on his way to France.

YORKISTS

Earl of Salisbur, Earl of Warwick Lords who support York's claim to the thone.

Duke of York (Richard Plantagenet) A distant relative of Henry VI's. York has a complicated claim to the throne. Both he and Henry VI are descendants of King Edward III, but York's ancestor was an older son of Edward III's than Henry VI's ancestor. York has been involved in a long-standing dispute with Somerset (see *1 Henry VI*). Here, he allies himself with Salisbury and Warwick to bide his time until he can make his claim known. York hires Jack Cade to stir up a rebellion by making a similar claim to the throne as York's, in order to test how the York claim to the throne will be received by the people. After he quells an Irish rebellion, York returns and uses his army to announce his claim to King Henry and begin the Wars of the Roses with the Battle of St. Albans.

Edward York's eldest son, who fights with York in the Battle of St. Albans. Edward will become King Edward IV of England after York deposes Henry VI but dies in battle.

Richard York's younger hunchback son, who fights with York in the battle of St. Albans. After Edward's death, Richard will become King Richard III of England, one of Shakespeare's great villains.

MINOR NOBLES

Sir John Hume A man Beaufort bribes to encourage Eleanor to dabble in the occult in order to make trouble for Gloucester. Eleanor hires Hume to arrange for her to speak to conjurers.

Alexander Iden A small-property owner who prefers his peaceful garden to the intrigues of the court. Iden kills Jack Cade and presents his head to King Henry.

Lord Saye A nobleman blamed by Jack Cade's rebels for the loss of France.

COMMONERS

Bolingbroke A conjurer Eleanor hires.

Butcher Jack Cade's supporter.

Jack Cade A fierce commoner hired by York to raise a popular rebellion. Cade manages to defeat the Stafford brothers and King Henry's army at Kent and reach London. When his fickle rebels, swayed by Clifford's rhetoric, turn against him, Cade escapes to the countryside. Alexander Iden kills Cade in a duel in Iden's garden.

Captain The captain of the pirate ship that captures Suffolk's ship, headed to France.

Thomas Horner Peter's master. Accused by Peter of supporting York, Horner must fight Peter in single combat. Horner fights drunk and dies. His death marks the beginning of a public Yorkist threat to King Henry's throne.

Peter Thump Horner's servant, who accuses Horner of treason. Sentenced by Gloucester to fight Horner in single combat, Peter unexpectedly wins.

Saunder Simpcox A peasant who pretends that he regained his sight through a miracle. Gloucester's ability to see through Simpcox's lie points both to his wisdom and to his ability to understand the common people.

Weaver Jack Cade's supporter.

Walter Whitmore A pirate who, with his captain, attacks Suffolk's ship. Whitmore beheads Suffolk.

Witch (Margery Jourdain) A woman hired by Eleanor to contact evil spirits.

2 HENRY VI: PLOT OVERVIEW

King Henry VI of England has little authority. Gloucester, the Lord Protector, has ruled the kingdom since Henry was a child. Henry is poised to marry the manipulative Margaret of Anjou, a politically unhelpful match, and the English nobles are angry that England is losing control of the French territories won by Henry's father, King Henry V.

Gloucester's wife Eleanor, who wants to be queen, is arrested for participating in witchcraft and forced to parade through the streets in shame. Gloucester is framed for treason and assassinated by Cardinal Beaufort and Margaret's lover Suffolk. Henry banishes Suffolk, who is beheaded by pirates aboard a ship to France. Queen Margaret carries around Suffolk's severed head as she laments his death.

The Duke of York, who plans to make a claim to the throne, takes an army to Ireland to quell a rebellion. In his absence, he pays a commoner named Jack Cade to lead a people's rebellion against King Henry. Cade and his army reach London, where they wreak havoc until the lords Buckingham and Clifford talk the fickle rebels into supporting the monarchy again. Cade flees, but is killed five days later as he steals food from the garden of Alexander Iden.

York returns from Ireland with his army and confronts King Henry with his claim to the throne. With the help of his sons and his supporters Salisbury and Warwick, York defeats Henry's army at the Battle of St. Albans, which is the first armed conflict of the Wars of the Roses between the House of York and the royalist House of Lancaster. Henry flees to London. York follows him.

2 HENRY VI: SCENE SUMMARY

ACT I

The English court is splitting into factions; Cardinal Beaufort arranges to disgrace Gloucester, the Protector of the Realm.

I.I Location: London. The palace

The English court is splitting in factions: Salisbury, Warwick, and York support Gloucester; Beaufort and Suffolk oppose them; Buckingham and Somerset want more power; York wants the throne.

King Henry VI is at court with the Duke of Gloucester, the Duke of Somerset, the Duke of Buckingham, and Cardinal Beaufort (formerly the Bishop of Winchester). The Duke of York, the Marquess of Suffolk, the Earl of Salisbury, the Earl of Warwick, and Margaret enter. Suffolk bows before the king, relating how he captured Margaret during the French wars and negotiated for her to become Henry's wife. He presents Margaret to the king, andHenry welcomes her. Margaret greets him, saying her only desire is for him to love her. Henry asks his lords to welcome her. Suffolk presents the king with a copy of the peace treaty with the French. Gloucester reads it aloud, growing faint at the passages about the lands of Anjou and Maine being returned to the French in exchange for Margaret's hand. Henry is pleased and so promotes Suffolk to the rank of duke. Henry then thanks all his lords. Suffolk, Henry, and Margaret depart to prepare for her coronation.

Gloucester reminds the other lords that the late King Henry V, as well as the lords present at court, had fought hard in the French wars to win the very lands that Henry has so easily given back to the French. He further argues that a marriage between Margaret and Henry would be a fatal pairing, one that would eradicate from history the names of all those who have fought for France. Beaufort rebukes Gloucester, reminding the court that the rest of France is still in English hands. But Salisbury and Warwick agree that Anjou and Maine are the key regions of Normandy (in northern France), and that their loss heralds the loss of the rest of France. York too condemns the marriage: English kings have traditionally received large dowries from their wives, but Henry is receives nothing as is content to give away. Beaufort says that Gloucester is too hasty in his predictions, and Gloucester explodes, claiming that Beaufort criticizes him because he hates him, not because he disagrees with his words. Gloucester walks out, reminding the court that he has prophesied the loss of all French lands.

Beaufort, Somerset, Buckingham, Salisbury, Warwick, and York remain. Beaufort reminds the other lords that Gloucester represents a danger to the government: as Lord Protector of the Realm (the acting ruler until Henry comes of age), Gloucester is the current heir to the throne. Beaufort urges the court not to be swayed by Gloucester's words. Gloucester may be popular, but he surely wants to amass power and become king. Buckingham agrees that Henry is old enough to rule for himself and suggests that he, Beaufort, Somerset, and Suffolk join together to remove him from office. Beaufort departs.

Somerset advises Buckingham not to help Beaufort unseat Gloucester because, Somerset thinks, Beaufort wants to become Protector in Gloucester's place. Buckingham suggests that either he or Somerset should be the next Protector. Buckingham and Somerset depart.

Salisbury, York, and Warwick remain. Salisbury remarks how ambitious Beaufort, Buckingham and Somerset are. He notes that he has always known Gloucester to be an honorable man. Salisbury suggests to Warwick and York that they band together for the public good, to try to save Gloucester and suppress Suffolk's and Beaufort's pride as well as Somerset's and Buckingham's ambition. All agree. Salisbury and Warwick exit.

Alone, York speaks about his own claim to the throne. He is angry about the loss of Anjou and Maine (French lands under York's control). Someday he will claim his birthright, but until then, he will ally himself with Salisbury and Warwick. He must remain calm even though the kingdom is in turmoil, for soon the House of York will topple the reign of the House of Lancaster (i.e., the family of Henry IV, V, and VI).

I.II Location: London. Gloucester's house

Gloucester tries to squelch Eleanor's treasonous thoughts; Hume plans to ruin Gloucester by ruining Eleanor.

Cardinal Beaufort has arranged to catch Gloucester's wife Eleanor, who wants to be queen, contacting evil spirits. Gloucester's wife Eleanor (the Duchess of Gloucester) asks him why he is so gloomy. Does he dream of Henry's throne, she asks. Gloucester tells her to banish such ambitious thoughts. He is moody because he had an unsettling dream: he saw his staff, the badge of his office, broken in two, with the heads of Somerset and Suffolk impaled on the two halves. Eleanor too has had dreams: she saw herself in Westminster Abbey, about to be crowned queen, with Henry and Margaret at her feet. Gloucester, astonished, chides her and reminds her that she is the second woman in the realm, second to Margaret only. He warns her not to hatch any treacherous plans.

A messenger enters to summon Gloucester to join Henry on a hunt at Saint Albans. Gloucester leaves. Alone, Eleanor thinks about how much more easily she could reach the throne if she were a man. As a woman, she will do what she can. She calls in her counselor Sir John Hume and asks him whether he has asked the Witch and the conjurer (Bolingbroke) to advise her about the future. Hume says that they have promised to raise a spirit to answer all her questions. She gives him money to complete the deal and leaves.

Alone, Hume ponders the fact that Eleanor has given him money to hire a witch, while Beaufort and Suffolk have also given him money to get her to dabble in the occult, so as to ruin her. He's playing both sides, he realizes. He will ruin Gloucester by ruining Eleanor.

I.III Location: London. The palace

Working together, the ambitious Margaret and Suffolk ensure that York comes under suspicion for pretensions to the throne.

Several petitioners, including Peter, enter the palace in search of Gloucester, who they hope will help them. Suffolk and Margaret enter. The petitioners are confused about who he is. At Suffolk's request, one of the petitioners offers his complaint. Margaret realizes that the complaints are addressed to Gloucester, and eagerly reads the papers. The second petitioner's complaint is against Suffolk, but Suffolk reacts only at Peter's complaint against his master Thomas Horner. Peter claims that Horner said that York is the rightful heir to the crown. Suffolk sends Peter to make his complaint formally. Margaret rips up the other petitioner's papers.

Margaret asks Suffolk whether she, as queen, must follow Gloucester's decisions like Henry does. She is disappointed that Henry, contrary to her expectations, is not as valorous or attractive as Suffolk. Instead, Henry is more concerned with piety and prayer. Suffolk tells her to be patient: just as he arranged for her to become queen, so will he arrange her life in England. Suffolk and Margaret discuss all their enemies, from Beaufort and Gloucester to Somerset, Buckingham, and York, and finally to Salisbury and Warwick. Additionally, Margaret adds that she cannot stand Gloucester's wife Eleanor and her haughty demeanor. Suffolk replies that he has already set a trap for Eleanor. Moreover, even though they don't like Beaufort, they must side with him until Gloucester is out of the way. As for York, Peter's complaint may help bring him down. Little by little, they will weed out their enemies.

Henry arrives with York and Somerset, followed by Gloucester, Eleanor, Buckingham, Salisbury, Warwick, and Beaufort. York and Somerset disagree about who should become Regent of France. Henry does not have an opinion. The other lords join in, suggesting their preferred candidate. Gloucester says that Henry should decide, but Margaret demands to establish Gloucester's role in government, now that Henry is of age. Gloucester says that he would willingly resign from the post of Protector if Henry wishes. Suffolk, Beaufort, Buckingham, and Margaret accuse Gloucester of having made a mess of the kingdom. Gloucester, insulted, leaves.

Margaret drops her fan and asks Eleanor to pick it up. As Eleanor leans over, Margaret strikes Eleanor's ear. Enraged, Eleanor promises revenge and storms out.

Gloucester returns, calmed, and recommends making York Regent of France. York demurs at the suggestion: he could not cooperate effectively with Somerset, who is in charge of supplies for the English troops in France, so England would lose France to Charles (the viceroy of France).

Horner and his servant Peter enter. Suffolk explains that Peter has accused Horner of saying that York should be on the throne. Horner denies Peter's accusations, and suggests that Peter is just angry because he, Horner, criticized Peter's work. Gloucester suggests that, now that York is under suspicion, Somerset should become Regent of France. Moreover, Gloucester recommends that Horner and Peter settle their differences in armed single combat. Henry agrees. Horner is satisfied, but Peter is hysterical: he doesn't know how to fight and worries he will die. Horner and Peter are taken to prison to await their battle.

I.IV Location: London. Gloucester's garden

Eleanor is arrested for witchcraft.

The conjurer Bolingbroke and the witch Margery Jourdain arrive with Hume and John Southwell, another priest. They decide that Eleanor and Hume will watch Bolingbroke, Southwell, and the Witch work from above. Eleanor enters, above, and greets them. The conjuring ceremony begins with Bolingbroke's incantations. A spirit appears and promises to answer their questions. Bolingbroke reads a list of questions. First, he asks about what will become of Henry. The spirit responds, "The Duke yet lives that Henry shall depose, / But him outlive, and die a violent death" (I.iv.29–30). The spirit also predicts that Suffolk will die "by water" (I.iv.32) and that Somerset should avoid castles. Then, the spirit sinks into the ground as thunder crashes.

York and Buckingham enter with soldiers. York orders Bolingbroke, Southwell, and the Witch arrested. Buckingham finds the list of questions and orders Eleanor and Hume arrested too. All are led away. Buckingham asks York for permission to ride to Saint Albans and tell Henry and Gloucester that Eleanor has been arrested.

ACT II

York gathers supporters to make a claim for the throne.

II.I Location: St. Albans

On a hunt, Gloucester defrauds a peasant claiming to be blind and lame, then receives news of Eleanor's arrest.

Henry, Margaret, Gloucester, Beaufort, and Suffolk are on a hunt. Beaufort and Gloucester bicker, and Henry asks them to try to get along. Beaufort and Gloucester speak privately and challenge each other to a duel later that evening. They pretend to be discussing the hunt as they threaten each other under their breath.

A man enters and announces that there has been a miracle: a blind man named Simpcox has regained his vision at the shrine in St. Albans. Simpcox is brought in. Simpcox explains that he was born blind but now can see. Beaufort notices that Simpcox is lame, and Simpcox explains that he fell while climbing a tree as a child. To test Simpcox, Gloucester asks him to describe some robes. Simpcox correctly identifies them by color—red and black. Gloucester then accuses Simpcox of lying: a man born blind would not know how to name colors even if he could suddenly see them. Gloucester calls for a whip, saying that he will heal Simpcox's lameness. Simpcox says that he cannot stand up without help, but after the first blow falls, he runs off. Gloucester orders him caught, paraded through town, and whipped.

Buckingham arrives and reports that Gloucester's wife Eleanor has been arrested for associating with conjurers. Buckingham presents a record of the questions and answers. Suffolk learns that the spirit has predicted that he will die at sea. In private, Beaufort tells Gloucester that their duel is off, now that Gloucester has his own problems. Gloucester grudgingly agrees. Gloucester tells Henry that he is sorry for Eleanor's actions and says that he has always done his best. He pledges to banish Eleanor from his life for dishonoring him. Henry decrees that they will return to London the next day to deal with these developments.

II.II Location: London. York's garden

York explains his (complicated) claim to the throne.

York tells Salisbury and Warwick about his claim to the throne. Edward III had seven sons. The eldest son died, leaving his son, Richard II, as heir. Richard II ruled until the Duke of Lancaster, son of the fourth son of Edward III, deposed him and was crowned Henry IV. The current king, Henry VI is Henry IV's grandson. Thus the House of Lancaster now holds the throne illegally. York himself is the heir of the third son of Edward III. Legally, the descendant of the third son should rule before the descendants of a fourth son. Thus, York should be king instead of Henry VI.

Convinced, Salisbury and Warwick bow to York as England's true king. But York reminds them that he is not king yet. They must wait until the others' schemes bring down the honest and decent Gloucester. Eventually, their foolery will bring about their own ends, too.

II.III Location: London. The Hall of Justice

Eleanor is sentenced to public penance and banishment.

Henry and Margaret, Gloucester, Suffolk, Buckingham, and Beaufort enter the court of justice, followed by Eleanor, the Witch, Hume, and Bolingbroke. York enters with Salisbury and Warwick. Henry condemns the Witch, Bolingbroke, and Hume to death. He sentences Eleanor to three days of penance in the streets of the city followed by banishment to the Isle of Man. Gloucester seconds Henry's decrees, and Eleanor is led out of the court.

Saddened, Gloucester asks to leave the court. Henry asks for Gloucester's staff (the emblem of Gloucester's official position as Lord Protector) and tells him to go in peace. Margaret too demands Gloucester's staff, less kindly, and reminds him that there is no need for Gloucester to be Protector now that Henry is old enough to rule. Gloucester lays the staff at Henry's feet, wishes for peace for the throne, and exits. Margaret picks up Gloucester's staff and gives it to Henry.

York announces that Peter and Horner's combat is today, adding that he has never seen anyone less prepared to fight than Peter. Peter and Horner enter, carrying their weapons, which are staffs with sandbags tied to the ends. Horner is drunk, and continues drinking. Peter refuses alcohol. Peter and Horner fight, and Peter kills Horner. Henry declares that Horner's death proves that he was a traitor (which casts suspicion that York aspires to the throne).

II.IV Location: London. A street

Gloucester bids farewell to Eleanor, who warns him that he is in danger.

Gloucester and his men, in mourning clothes, wait for Eleanor to pass by performing her public penance. She enters, barefoot, with a candle. She has papers announcing her crimes pinned to her back. Eleanor tells Gloucester that the people have been staring at her with eyes full of hate. Gloucester tells her that she must be patient. Eleanor thinks that she, as wife of the Protector, does not deserve such shameful punishment.

Eleanor warns Gloucester that he is in danger too. Suffolk, Beaufort, and York have all been making plans to trap him. Gloucester tells her that she must be mistaken—he has done no wrong and been loyal. Even her scandal can't harm him, for he is beyond reproach. A herald enters to summon Gloucester to a parliament at Bury St. Edmunds. Gloucester bids Eleanor farewell, so teary he can barely speak. Eleanor says that death is her only joy now. An attendant escorts her away to the Isle of Man.

ACT III

Gloucester is arrested for treason and assassinated.

III.I Location: Bury St. Edmunds. Parliament hall

Gloucester is arrested for treason; York is sent to Ireland to quell a rebellion, and has hired Jack Cade as a first step toward seizing the throne.

Buckingham, Suffolk, York, Beaufort, King Henry, Margaret, Salisbury and Warwick meet in the hall. Margaret remarks that Gloucester's demeanor has changed dramatically. He has become insolent and angry. She reminds Henry that Gloucester is the heir to the throne and thus a danger to him. Moreover, Gloucester has won the support of the common people and could instigate a revolt if he chose. She asks Suffolk, Buckingham, and York to back her up. Suffolk agrees that Eleanor's actions demonstrate that Gloucester has considered treason. Beaufort reminds Henry that Gloucester has been unjustly harsh in punishing small criminals. York suggests that Gloucester misused funds from taxes levied during the wars with France.

Henry disagrees with them all and supports Gloucester as a good, loyal man. Margaret says that Gloucester's seeming goodness is what makes him all the more dangerous. Somerset enters to report that all the English possessions in France have been lost.

Gloucester enters. Suffolk arrests him for treason. Gloucester says that he has done nothing wrong and demands to know the charge. York accuses him of not paying the English soldiers fighting in France. Gloucester answers that he, in fact, sent much of his own money because he did not want to raise taxes. York accuses Gloucester of inflicting unusual punishments, but Gloucester says that he only tortured the worst criminals. Suffolk insists there are more charges.

Henry says he hopes that Gloucester will prove his innocence. Gloucester says that he realizes that the other noblemen want him dead. He would gladly die if his death would end their tyranny and ambition, but he suspects that his death is but a prologue to much violence. He mentions Beaufort's malice, Suffolk's hate, Buckingham's envy, York's ambition. He accuses Margaret of slander. He realizes that he will not be able to prove his innocence because the others will support their false accusations with false witnesses. Beaufort orders Gloucester taken away. Gloucester ominously says that in bringing him down, Henry throws away his crutch (i.e., Gloucester's help) before he has learned to walk alone (i.e., rule the kingdom).

Distraught, Henry realizes that even though Gloucester is innocent, he will be powerless to save Gloucester. Gloucester's enemies—the other nobles and Queen Margaret—are too powerful. Henry exits with Salisbury and Warwick.

Buckingham, Suffolk, York, Beaufort, and Margaret remain. Beaufort wonders how they can bring about Gloucester's death. Suffolk says that because they have no hard evidence against him, they should simply assassinate him. All agree.

A messenger arrives with news of a new rebellion in Ireland (which is under English control). York sarcastically suggests sending Somerset, since he has been so successful in France. York and Somerset bicker. Beaufort sends York to Ireland with soldiers. York agrees. Everyone leaves.

Alone, York says that the time has come for him to act. He now has an army. He has hired Jack Cade, a fierce commoner, to pretend to be the now-dead John Mortimer, who had a claim to the throne. With Cade's help, York will find out what the populace thinks of the Yorkist claim to the throne. Cade will not reveal that York hired him, even under torture. If Cade is successful, York will return to England with an army and seize the throne.

III.II Location: Bury St. Edmunds

Suffolk's hit men kill Gloucester; when people find out about it, Suffolk is banished to France; Margaret promises to arrange for his return.

Two murderers have smothered Gloucester in his bed. Suffolk enters to check on them and sends them to be paid. Henry, Margaret, Beaufort, and Somerset enter the adjoining room. Henry tells Suffolk to summon Gloucester for his trial. Suffolk returns to report that Gloucester is dead. Henry faints. Suffolk tries to help him up, but Henry curses him and calls him a murderous tyrant. Margaret asks Henry why he is so cruel to Suffolk. Like Suffolk, she didn't like Gloucester, but like Suffolk, she cries for his death. She laments the fact that people will now suspect that she plotted to kill Gloucester. Henry continues to weep for Gloucester, and Margaret accuses him of being heard-hearted. Why did she come to England, she asks, for such bad treatment? She says that Suffolk bewitches her with false tales of Henry's greatness. She feels unloved and calls for death.

Warwick and Salisbury enter with a crowd of commoners. The commoners have heard that Beaufort and Suffolk have murdered Gloucester. Henry says Gloucester is dead, but no one knows why. Warwick and Salisbury lead the commoners to look at the body. Henry says he suspects that Gloucester was murdered. Warwick brings out Gloucester's body. He too thinks that Gloucester was killed: Gloucester's face is contorted in pain. Suffolk says that murderers could not get in because he, Suffolk, and Beaufort were protecting Gloucester, but Warwick points out that Gloucester was their enemy. Suffolk dares Warwick to accuse him properly. Beaufort falls down, and Somerset helps him out. Warwick accuses Suffolk of murder. They argue and depart. Henry and Margaret remain.

Then, Suffolk and Warwick reenter with swords drawn. Suffolk complains that Warwick has set the commoners against him. Salisbury enters and reports that the commoners believe that Suffolk killed Gloucester and are clamoring for Suffolk's death or banishment, because they fear that he may kill Henry. Henry sends Salisbury to thank the commoners and tell them that he will banish Suffolk, as they wish. Margaret pleads for Suffolk, but Henry tells Suffolk to be gone within three days. Henry departs with Warwick.

Margaret and Suffolk remain. Margaret wails about their misfortune. Suffolk curses his enemies. She kisses his palm, and tells him that she will devise a way for him to return, or else be banished herself so that she can be with him. Suffolk tells her that being parted from her is the worst part of the banishment. A messenger passes through with news that Beaufort is delirious and keeps talking to Gloucester's ghost in his madness. Suffolk asks Margaret for permission to stay with her and die rather than leave. She sends him away to France and promises to be in touch.

III.III Location: London. Beaufort's chamber

Beaufort dies, confessing that he too had a role in Gloucester's death.

Henry, Salisbury, and Warwick, enter to see Beaufort, who raves about Gloucester's ravaged body. Close to death, Beaufort promises to confess. He dies. Warwick notes that such a troubled death ends only a terrible life. Henry tells him not to judge others, for all people are sinners.

ACT IV

York hires Jack Cade to stir up a large populist rebellion, which defeats royal forces but dissipates when the people recall the glory of the monarchy.

IV.I Location: Off the coast of Kent. Aboard an English ship

Pirates behead Suffolk aboard a ship taking him to France.

Pirates have attacked the ship carrying Suffolk to France. The enemy captain has taken Suffolk and two gentlemen prisoner, and distributes the prisoners among his crew. He gives Suffolk, who is in disguise, to a sailor named Walter Whitmore. Suffolk is taken aback. Not only had Eleanor's conjurers predicted that he would die "by water" (which is how "Walter" was pronounced), but he also once heard from an astrologer that he would die with a man named Whitmore.

Suffolk reveals who he is, expecting to be set free. The captain, annoyed, orders Suffolk taken away and beheaded. The captain accuses Suffolk of bringing about the loss of Anjou and Maine (by pressuring King Henry to marry Margaret, daughter to the Duke of Anjou and Maine) and of encouraging the House of York to rise up against King Henry. Suffolk insists that he cannot die at the hands of someone as lowly as Whitmore. One of the other prisoners recommends that Suffolk beg for his life, but Suffolk responds that begging is beneath him. Whitmore leads Suffolk off, beheads him, and returns with his head. Released by the Captain, the prisoner decides to carry Suffolk's body to King Henry.

IV.II Location: Kent

Jack Cade has organized a populist rebellion, which the brothers Stafford have arrived to quell.

English rebels discuss what their leader Jack Cade plans to do after he takes control of the kingdom. Workmen, not artisans, will be honored, they agree. Cade enters with the butcher and the weaver. Cade, pretending to be York's (dead) kinsman Mortimer, explains his claim to the throne. During Cade's speech, the butcher makes fun of him. Cade promises, once he is king, to deliver much beer, outlaw money, kill the lawyers, and punish all those who are literate. Just then, a Clerk comes in, and Cade orders him lynched for knowing how to read and write.

A messenger enters to announce that Stafford and his brother have attacked the rebels. Cade brushes off the threat. Stafford enters and commands the rebels to lay down their arms. Cade and Stafford debate Cade's alleged claim to the throne. Stafford's brother (correctly) suggests that Cade has been set on by York, but Cade denies it. Cade and the butcher announce that they plan to kill Lord Saye, who, they claim, sold Maine to the French.

Stafford and his brother agree that there is no point in negotiating with Cade. They proclaim Cade's followers traitors and prepare to attack. As the royal army approaches, the butcher is frightened by its orderly rows, but Cade claims that his army of rebels is most effective when they are most disorderly.

IV.III Location: Kent

Cade's rebels kill the Stafford brothers and head to London.

IV.IV Location: London. The palace

Henry and Margaret leave London as Cade's rebel army approaches.

Henry is reading the rebels' statement when Margaret enters with Suffolk's head. Buckingham and Lord Saye enter as well. Margaret tries to focus on revenge rather than sadness. Henry tells Saye that the rebels want him dead. Noticing Margaret distraught, Henry remarks that she would not have mourned as much for him as for Suffolk.

A messenger enters and announces that Cade's rebel army approaches. Cade has been calling himself Mortimer and claiming that he is the rightful king. Buckingham advises Henry to leave London. Henry suggests that Saye come, too, but Saye decides to stay in London so as not to endanger Henry with his presence. A second messenger announces that Cade is approaching London Bridge, and Londoners have joined his march. Henry and Margaret depart. Saye and Buckingham exchange words of encouragement.

IV.V Location: London. Outside the tower

Cade's army advances.

From the tower above, a lord asks several citizens whether Cade is dead. They report that the mayor of London has called for reinforcements. The lord sends more troops.

IV.VI Location: London. Cannon Street

Cade and the rebels have taken London.

Cade and his rebels have taken London. Cade kills a messenger who arrives to announce that there is an army gathering to oppose Cade (the troops from the tower). Cade and the rebels head out to fight.

IV.VII Location: London. Smithfield

Reminded of the glory of the monarchy, the rebels disperse; Cade runs away.

Jack Cade has killed the leaders of the tower army. Cade declares that all written records will be burned and all laws will be oral. A messenger announces that Saye has been captured. Saye enters.

In a long prose speech affecting courtly language, Cade accuses Saye of giving up Normandy to the French, of corrupting children by sending them to school, of using printing presses and a paper mill, and of imprisoning illiterate men. In his response, Saye flatters Kent (the region where the rebellion began) and denies any role in losing Normandy. He defends knowledge as godly. Cade orders Saye beheaded.

A sergeant enters and accuses the butcher of raping his wife. Cade declares that all women in his realm shall be available to all men. He orders the butcher to cut out the sergeant's tongue and then kill him. Cade's rebels return with pikes bearing the heads of Saye and Saye's son-in-law. Cade orders them to parade the streets.

Buckingham and Clifford enter as ambassadors from King Henry. They offer to pardon the rebels if they put down their weapons and leave. Clifford appeals to the rebels, reminding them of the glory of King Henry V. The rebels support Clifford and King Henry VI. Then Cade appeals to the rebels and reminds them that he has won their freedom. The rebels change their minds and support Cade. Clifford speaks, warning that this civil brawl will make England vulnerable to attacks by the French. Again the rebels support Clifford and King Henry.

Cade notes to himself how easily the mob changes its mind. He curses the rebels and runs away. Buckingham sends soldiers to capture Cade.

IV.VIII Location: Kenilworth Castle

York has returned from Ireland with an army, and demands to fight Somerset.

Buckingham and Clifford arrive to see Henry and Margaret. They announce that Cade has fled, and his former rebels are below, and await his clemency. Henry addressed the people, thanks them, and promises to be kind.

A messenger enters with news that York has returned from Ireland and approaches with a powerful army, demanding to fight Somerset, whom York deems a traitor. Henry compares his kingdom to a ship, reeling as if in a storm from the assault by Cade and York. He sends Buckingham to greet York and sends Somerset to the tower, for safety.

IV.IX Location: Kent. Alexander Iden's garden

Weak from hunger, Cade picks a fight with Alexander Iden, who kills him.

Cade has been in hiding, weak from five days without food. He jumps into Iden's vegetable patch and starts eating his herbs. Iden enters with his men and mentions that he has inherited his garden from his father and enjoys spending time there in peace. Iden notices Cade, and Cade threatens to kill Iden. Though Iden does not want to fight a man as weak as Cade, Cade insists. They fight, and Iden kills Cade. Dying, Cade tells Iden his name. Iden is amazed, but Cade insists that he was vanquished by hunger, not Iden's valor. Iden tells his men to leave Cade's body in a dunghill, and takes Cade's head to King Henry.

ACT V

York makes public his claim to the throne and wins the Battle of St. Albans against King Henry's army.

V.I Location: St. Albans. A field

The Wars of the Roses begin in earnest as York publicly announces his claim to the throne and other noblemen take sides.

York enters with his army and tells of his journey from Ireland to claim the throne from the weak King Henry. He sees Buckingham and plans to lie to him. On behalf of King Henry, Buckingham asks York why he marches on London. Privately, York is furious and frustrated that he must bend to someone as weak and undeserving of the crown as King Henry, but aloud he announces that he has come to accuse Somerset of treason and take him away from the court. Buckingham tells York that Somerset has been imprisoned in the Tower. York dismisses his troops until the next day.

Henry enters and asks York about his army. York repeats that he comes to unseat Somerset, adding that his troops may also help defend London from Jack Cade. Alexander Iden arrives with Cade's head. Pleased, King Henry knights Iden.

Margaret and Somerset arrive. Furious to see Somerset free, York demands an explanation from Henry. York accuses Henry of usurping the throne and being unfit to rule. On the other hand, York claims, he (York) deserves the throne both on both legal grounds and merit. Somerset orders York arrested for treason. York calls for his sons Edward and Richard (the future Edward IV and Richard III). They come in, along with Clifford. York insists that he is the rightful king and calls for Salisbury and Warwick to come and stand up for him. Richard and Clifford trade insults. Salisbury tells King Henry that he indeed believes that York is the rightful holder of the crown. York and Henry prepare to gather their allies and armies.

V.II Location: St. Albans. Near an alehouse

York kills Somerset in battle.

Somerset and York's son Richard enter, fighting. Richard kills Somerset under the sign of a castle on an alehouse, remarking that the conjurer who predicted that Somerset would die near castles proved right.

V.III Location: St. Albans. The battlefield

York kills Clifford, which steels Clifford's son against the Yorkists.

Warwick enters, chasing Clifford. York asks Warwick to let him fight Clifford. Warwick concedes and leaves. York and Clifford fight, and York kills Clifford. York exits. Young Clifford (Clifford's son) enters and sees Clifford's body. He notes the irony: Clifford lived long in peacetime but died in battle in his old age. Since York did not spare Clifford's old life, Young Clifford plans not to spare the young lives of Yorkists.

V.IV Location: St. Albans. The Lancaster camp

The Lancastrians have lost the Battle of St. Albans.

Buckingham, wounded, is carried to his tent. Henry and Margaret enter. Margaret tells Henry that he should flee, but Henry does not want to. Margaret is astonished at Henry's cowardice, but Henry is too scared to fight or to flee. Both she and Young Clifford urge him to save his throne and flee to London, where he has popular support.

V.V Location: St. Albans. The battlefield

The Yorkists have won the Battle of St. Albans, but not yet the crown.

York enters with his sons Edward and Richard. It has been a good day, he says. They have won the fight. He asks about Salisbury, and Richard reports that he helped Salisbury three times after Salisbury fell from his horse. Salisbury thanks Richard for saving him. They have won the battle, but not yet the war. York says he has heard that King Henry has fled to London to summon Parliament. They agree to go to London too and, with luck, overtake Henry. Warwick predicts that the York victory at the Battle of St. Albans will be immortalized in history.

THEMES, MOTIFS, & SYMBOLS IN *2 HENRY VI*

THEMES

MORAL GOODNESS AS INCOMPATIBLE WITH EFFECTIVE LEADERSHIP Shakespeare presents Henry as a good, moral man, but a disastrous king. A devout Christian, Henry cares deeply for those close to him, such as Gloucester. At the same time, his political naïveté renders him helpless and ineffectual. His reproach to Salisbury and Warwick stems from sense of personal affront, not political betrayal. He becomes susceptible to Margaret and Suffolk's manipulations. His lack of interest in France leads to England losing her French dominions, and his inability to relate to his subjects leads to the popular uprising instigated by Jack Cade. Shakespeare's *Henry VI* trilogy suggests that a good Christian cannot be a good king.

WOMEN AS HUNGRY FOR POWER Both of the major female characters of 2 *Henry VI* are uncontrollably ambitious. Margaret involves herself in an adulterous affair and schemes to gain control of government. Gloucester's wife Eleanor prefigures Lady Macbeth in her lust for power and associations with evil spirits. Both are married to gentle and humane men who remain largely unaware of their machinations, and both contribute to their husbands' downfalls. Eleanor's desire for power is presented as wanton and unbridled. She hires conjurers because she cannot help herself. The implication is that women cannot control their impulses and bring their men down with them.

WEAK RULE LEADS TO CHAOS *2 Henry VI* shows England in the hands of a weak king, threatened from every possible angle. Queen Margaret schemes behind his back with her lover Suffolk. The Duke of York bides his time until he can make a viable claim for the throne. His other advisers are too busy bringing down Lord Protector Gloucester to be trusted. The English subjects are rebelling against his government, and the French territories are falling back into the hands of viceroy Charles. The play closes with the start of a full-blown civil war.

MOTIFS

MASS UPRISING *2 Henry VI* mentions two populist rebellions. The first one happens offstage in Ireland. To quell it, York receives the army that he uses to challenge King Henry at the Battle of St. Albans in Act V. The second one is, of course, Jack Cade's uprising, which takes up most of Act IV. Additionally, the threat of uprising is constantly in the background as Suffolk and Beaufort consider what to do with Gloucester, given how popular he is with the people. Indeed, it is the masses that demand Suffolk's banishment after Gloucester's death. These mass uprisings present a threat to the welfare of the state. They are one of many problems besieging an England that lacks a strong ruler. They are prompted by the very real grievances of the people, which are often forgotten amid the squabbles of the nobility. At the same time, Shakespeare does not present his rebels as noble or wise: they shun knowledge and follow Jack Cade, a disorganized brute and aspiring tyrant. Most importantly, they are easily swayed: in IV.vii, they switch sides three times in response to rhetoric. In his dramatization of the Jack Cade rebellion, Shakespeare suggests that the uneducated masses need a strong and wise leader.

SUPERNATURAL FORCES AND PROPHECIES Shakespeare raises the stakes of the squabbles among the English noblemen by including supernatural forces that care and comment on their behavior. The spirit of Asnath, summoned by the conjurer Bolingbroke, makes predictions about the fates of Suffolk and Somerset, as well as foretelling that Henry VI will be deposed by a duke (the Duke of York), but will outlive that duke. All of the prophecies come true: Suffolk dies at sea and Somerset dies in battle under a sign with a picture of a castle. In *3 Henry VI*, York deposes Henry VI, then dies a violent death in battle.

SYMBOLS

IDEN'S GARDEN In IV.ix, the hungry Jack Cade steals from the garden of small-property holder Alexander Iden. Cade dies in a duel with Iden that Cade himself instigates. The garden is Alexander Iden's idyllic refuge from the turmoil of the court: similar in sound to the biblical Garden of Eden, it represents an Edenic, ideal place of peace and contentment. Like the biblical Adam and Eve, Cade takes forbidden food from a garden. Also like Adam and Eve, Cade is punished (he dies where they are banished).

MARGARET'S FAN In I.iii, Margaret drops a fan in public, asks Eleanor to pick it up, and then hits Eleanor on the ear as she bends over. The fan symbolizes the empty power plays that infect the English court. Margaret's petty scheming is a manifestation of the divisive tactics of all the dissenters, from Cardinal Beaufort, the head of the Church in England, to the lower-class followers of Jack Cade.

IMPORTANT QUOTATIONS FROM *2 HENRY VI*

1. *Ay, uncle, we will keep it if we can—*
   But now it is impossible we should.
   Suffolk, the new-made duke that rules the roast,

Hath given the duchy of Anjou and Maine
Unto the poor King René, whose large style
Agrees not with the leanness of his purse.

Location: I.i.103–108
Speaker: Gloucester to Cardinal Beaufort
Context: Gloucester predicts that England will lose control of all of France

Here, Gloucester is frustrated that Suffolk has persuaded Henry VI to marry Margaret, in return for which Henry must return the French duchy of Anjou and Maine back to Margaret's father René. (René, King of Naples and Duke of Anjou and Maine, is too poor to give Margaret a dowry.) Gloucester's tone is pessimistic. His prediction foreshadows and sets up the loss of France.

---

2. *Now, lords, my choler being overblown*
With walking once about the quadrangle,
I come to talk of commonwealth affairs.
As for your spiteful false objections,
Prove them, and I lie open to the law.
But God in mercy so deal with my soul
As I in duty love my King and country.

Location: I.iii.156–162
Speaker: Gloucester
Context: Gloucester returns to court after storming out after Suffolk and Beaufort blame him, as Lord Protector, for England's sorry state

In returning to the court, Gloucester shows strength of character and a devotion to his country. He has the poise and presence of mind to distinguish between private emotions (his "choler," or anger) and public policy. Though he is angry about "your spiteful false objections," he is able to respond coolly and objectively ("Prove them"). His clean, direct style identifies him as a good, noble character and contrasts with the courtly bombast of other lords such as Beaufort and Suffolk. Gloucester's death heralds the spread of corruption in the court.

---

3. *Ah, Gloucester, teach me to forget myself;*
For whilst I think I am thy married wife,
And thou a prince, Protector of this land,
Methinks I should not thus be led along,
Mailed up in shame, with papers on my back,
And followed with a rabble that rejoice
To see my tears and hear my deep-fet groans.

Location: II.iv.28–34
Speaker: Eleanor, Duchess of Gloucester
Context: Eleanor does public penance and laments her fate

Eleanor pleads for help "forget[ting]" herself (meaning her plight). Ironically, she has been forgetting herself and imagining herself queen all along. Like many of the play's noblemen, Eleanor is ambitious and hungry for power. Her derogatory "rabble" (commoners) contrasts with Gloucester's respect for the people. The class conflicts in England are indeed simmering close to the surface, ready to explode in Cade's rebellion in Act IV.

---

4. *Seems he a dove? His feathers are but borrowed,*

For he's disposèd as the hateful raven.
Is he a lamb? His skin is surely lent him,
For he's inclined as is the ravenous wolf.
Who cannot steal a shape that means deceit?

Location: III.i.75–79
Speaker: Margaret to Henry
Context: Margaret urges Henry to be more suspicious of Gloucester

Queen Margaret says that Gloucester may seem as peaceful as a dove and as gentle as a lamb, but is really as voracious as a raven and as cruel as a wolf. Her fancy rhetoric, which is exemplified by two complex metaphors in four lines, suggests that she cannot speak directly and prefers to play mind games and dissimulate. On the one hand, Margaret is justified in accusing Henry of naïveté. Henry is too pious and well-meaning to be effective in uncovering the many plots of his advisors. He may be a good person, but he is not a good king. Ironically, Margaret's accusations of Gloucester apply better to her than to him. She is the one who "means deceit" and knows how to pretend to be decent.

---

5. *Lord, who would live turmoilèd in the court*
And may enjoy such quiet walks as these?
This small inheritance my father left me
Contenteth me, and worth a monarchy.
I seek not to wax great by others' waning,
Or gather wealth I care not with what envy.

Location: IV.ix.14–19
Speaker: Iden
Context: Alexander Iden is pleased to have inherited his father's garden, where he can relax in peace

Though only a minor character, Alexander Iden serves as a foil to the ambitious and scheming movers and shakers at court. A small property owner, Iden appears apart from both the vicious courtiers and from Jack Cade. Unlike them, Iden is neither greedy nor power-hungry. He "seek[s] not to wax by others' waning, / Or gather wealth." Instead, he is content with "quiet walks" in his garden, which to him are "worth a monarchy"—the throne. Ironically, Jack Cade and most of the play's noblemen spend the play fighting for control of this "monarchy." Critics have suggested that the sympathetic portrayal of Iden in this scene points to Shakespeare's belief that it is the middle classes, not the upper-class nobility or the lower-class Jack Cade, that represent England's strength and future.

3 HENRY VI

The Duke of York's son takes up the struggle and deposes Henry VI to become King Edward IV, but his brothers and other alienated supporters threaten his reign.

3 HENRY VI IN CONTEXT

One of Shakespeare's earliest plays, 3 *Henry VI* continues the story of the Wars of the Roses begun in *1 Henry VI* and 2 *Henry VI*. The sequence depicts the struggle of the House of Lancaster (red rose) with the House of York (white rose) for control of the throne. Both houses are descendants of Edward III, Richard II's grandfather. 3 *Henry VI* ambitiously depicts many of the civil war's most significant battles and events, from York's death at the Battle of Wakefield in 1460 to Edward IV's final victory over the Lancastrians at the Battle of Tewkesbury in 1471.

Some readers have harshly criticized 3 *Henry VI*, attributing its flaws to Shakespeare's weariness with Wars of the Roses or to the difficulty of portraying so much historical matter on the stage. Yet contemporary productions have enjoyed success, particularly through their depiction of the ruthless Margaret and the increasingly alienated and enraged Richard, who emerges as the play's real anti-hero. Post- World War II productions have emphasized the play's representation of a once-calm world spiraling toward chaos.

3 *Henry VI* was first published in 1595 in an octavo volume under the title *The True Tragedie of Richard Duke of Yorke and the Death of Good King Henrie the Sixt*. In 1623, another version, a thousand lines longer than the original, appeared in the First Folio with the title *The Third Part of Henry the Sixth*. Scholars are conflicted about the circumstances of publication, but most believe that the 1595 edition, which includes more stage directions, was based on an actors' promptbook, whereas the 1623 copy represents Shakespeare's official written version. The play's historical information likely comes from contemporary chronicle histories such as Raphael Holinshed's *Chronicles of England, Scotland, and Ireland* (1587) and Edward Hall's *Union of the Two Noble and Illustre Families of Lancaster and York* (1548).

3 HENRY VI: KEY FACTS

Full Title: The True Tragedy of Richard Duke of York and the Death of Good King Henry the Sixth, with the whole Contention between the two houses of Lancaster and York

Time and place written: 1591–92; London

Date of first publication: 1595

Genre: History play

Setting (time): Mid-fifteenth century (from after the First St. Albans battle in 1455 to Edward IV return to the throne in 1471)

Setting (place): England

Protagonist: Edward of York

Major conflict: Edward struggles first to depose Henry VI, then to maintain control of the throne.

3 HENRY VI: CHARACTER LIST

LANCASTRIANS

Lord Clifford Known as "Young Clifford" in 2 *Henry VI*. Clifford kills York's son Rutland to avenge his father, whom York killed in 2 *Henry VI*. After York's death, Richard takes up the feud, but Clifford dies before Richard can kill him.

Duke of Exeter Henry's supporter.

King Henry VI The weak ruler of England at the beginning of the play. Henry is dominated by his wife Margaret and her allies. Pious and meek, Henry wishes he could be a shepherd. He is twice deposed and twice imprisoned. Henry prophesies further bloodshed in England before Richard kills him in the tower.

Queen Margaret Henry's French wife. A strong, resourceful, ambitious woman, Margaret raises and leads an army to defend her husband's and her son's throne. After Edward takes the throne, she goes to France to seek military aid. Henry's staunchest supporter, Margaret is repeatedly denounced as an unnatural woman.

Earl of Northumberland Margaret's ally.

Earl of Oxford Margaret's ally.

Prince Edward Margaret and Henry's teenage son. Courageous and spirited, Prince Edward gives hope to Henry's supporters. Edward, Richard, and George capture and publicly stab him to death.

Henry Tudor, Earl of Richmond Henry VI's distant cousin and the future King Henry VII. Henry gets good vibes from Richmond. Indeed, in *Richard III*, Richmond will marry Edward's daughter, thereby uniting the Houses of York and Lancaster, and found the Tudor dynasty.

Earl of Westmorland Henry's supporter.

YORKISTS

Edward, later Duke of York, later King Edward IV York's eldest son, and the brother of George, Richard, and Rutland. Edward inherits York's claim to the throne and continues York's struggle after York's death. Once king, Edward manages to alienate both his brothers and his advisors, especially after he marries Lady Grey. Edward loses the crown, but regains it by the end with Richard's help.

George, later Duke of Clarence York's second son, and the brother of Edward, Richard, and Rutland. George begins the play in France, and returns with reinforcements after York's death. He joins Edward's struggle for the throne, but follows Warwick in deserting Edward. By the end, he returns to support Edward. Richard marks George as his next target.

Elizabeth Woodville, Lady Grey, later Queen Elizabeth A widow who becomes Edward's wife and queen. Lady Grey approaches Edward seeking to regain her husband's lands. Edward proposes to her after she refuses to become his mistress.

Lord Hastings Edward's supporter.

Marquess of Montague Warwick's brother and York's supporter. Montague follows Warwick in deserting Edward and fighting for the Lancastrian side. Montague and Warwick die in the same battle.

Montgomery Edward's supporter.

Richard, later Duke of Gloucester York's third son, and the brother of Edward, George, and Rutland. A fierce supporter of the York cause, Richard is physically deformed: he has a hump back, a lame leg, and a shriveled arm. Richard takes his physical deformities as manifestations of his spiritual deformities, decides that there is no hope for him in human relationships, and determines to pursue power and become king, depending on no one and eliminating his competition little by little. He begins by killing Henry, and sets his sights on George next.

Lord Rivers Lady Grey's brother, and Edward's supporter.

Earl of Rutland York's youngest son, and the younger brother of Edward, George, and Richard. Rutland is killed by Clifford in revenge for York killing Clifford's father in *2 Henry VI*.

Duke of Somerset Edward's supporter, who follows Warwick in deserting Edward.

Earl of Warwick York's relative and chief supporter, and Montague's brother. Warwick puts Edward on the throne, but then, feeling betrayed and underappreciated when Edward marries Lady Grey while Warwick is on a marriage-arranging diplomatic mission in France, he deserts Edward, allies himself with Margaret, and fights to put Henry back on the throne. (The historical Warwick was known as the Kingmaker.) He dies in battle.

Richard Plantagenet, Duke of York The patriarch of the York clan, father to Edward, George, Richard, Rutland, and kinsman to Warwick and Montague. In *2 Henry VI*, York makes public his claim to the throne of England (he is a descendant of an older son of King Edward III than Henry is). York dies in battle in Act I.

FRENCHMEN

Lady Bona   Louis's sister, whom Louis and Warwick agreed to marry to Edward.

King Louis XI of France   The ruler of France, who gives military aid to Margaret in Warwick after Edward insults Lady Bona by marrying someone else (Lady Grey) instead.

3 HENRY VI: PLOT OVERVIEW

Having won the Battle of St. Albans (end of *2 Henry VI*), York arrives in London and, after much argument, makes a deal with King Henry VI: Henry will remain king, but the kingdom will pass to York and his heirs after Henry's death. Queen Margaret bitterly rebukes Henry for disinheriting their son.

York's sons Edward and Richard convince York to make a bid for the throne now instead of waiting for Henry to die. Angered by Henry's weakness, Margaret leads an army against York. She captures York and taunts him with a handkerchief dipped in the blood of York's young son. Margaret and her ally Clifford stab York to death. With York dead, his eldest son Edward inherits his claim to the throne. United with his brothers Richard and George, Edward continues to pursue the crown.

King Henry watches from afar as Edward's and Margaret's armies battle again. Edward wins the battle and is crowned King Edward IV. Henry flees, but is arrested by gamekeepers in a forest. The Earl of Warwick, Edward's most powerful supporter, goes to France to ask for the hand of the French king's sister for Edward. When Warwick finds out that Edward has married Lady Grey, a little-known widow, Warwick feels publicly humiliated. Warwick and George join forces with Margaret and march against Edward with French troops. Richard, outwardly loyal to Edward, begins plotting secretly to seize the crown for himself.

Edward regains his brother George's allegiance, kills Warwick, and defeats Henry's forces for good. He imprisons Margaret and kills her and Henry's son. Richard murders Henry in the Tower of London. Before dying, Henry predicts that thousands will suffer from Richard's deeds. Lady Grey gives birth to a son, and Edward's reign seems at last secure, though Richard continues to plot against him.

3 HENRY VI: SCENE SUMMARY

ACT I

York makes and breaks a peace agreement with King Henry VI, and dies in battle against forces led by Queen Margaret, Henry's powerful wife.

I.I   Location: London. Parliament House

Pressured by York and Warwick, King Henry VI names York successor to the throne, which outrages both Queen Margaret and Henry's supporters.

The Duke of York has publicly announced his claim to the throne, and has won the Battle of St. Albans against King Henry VI's forces. York enters with two of his sons, Edward and Richard, and his supporters the Duke of Norfolk, the Marquess of Montague, and the Earl of Warwick. They wonder where Henry VI is. Warwick points out that they are near the royal throne. At his urging, the lords help York ascend and sit on the throne.

Henry enters with his supporters: Lord Clifford, the Earl of Westmorland, the Earl of Northumberland, the Duke of Exeter. Henry notices York on the throne, and reminds his supporters that York, who has killed both Clifford's and Northumberland's fathers, wants to seize his throne. Henry's supporters move to attack, but Henry holds them off, since York's troops are nearby.

Henry demands to know York's claim to the throne, especially since Henry himself is the son of the great King Henry V. York accuses Henry of losing French lands. Henry blames the loss on the Lord Protector of the Realm (Henry's late uncle, Humphrey, Duke of Gloucester, who was arrested and assassinated in *2 Henry VI*). Richard and Edward urge their father York to seize the crown, but Henry's supporters quiet them. Henry tells York that he has no intention of giving up his throne, inherited from his father (Henry V) and his grandfather (Henry IV). York reminds Henry that his grandfather Henry IV deposed the rightful King Richard II. Henry acknowledges that his claim to the throne is a little shaky.

Confronted with this new information, Exeter switches sides to support York. Henry worries that all of his lords will abandon him. Clifford vows to fight on Henry's behalf regardless of the righteousness of Henry's claim. Warwick threatens to let his troops come in unless Henry abdicates. At Henry's suggestion, York and Henry agree that Henry will continue ruling, but on his death the throne will pass to York and his heirs. Clifford is appalled that Henry has disinherited his own son. Disgusted, Clifford, Northumberland, and Westmorland leave to report to Queen Margaret what has happened. York swears allegiance to Henry and descends from the throne. They embrace. York and his men depart, leaving Henry and Exeter alone.

Queen Margaret and Prince Edward enter. Margaret upbraids Henry for disinheriting their son (Prince Edward). Henry makes feeble excuses, but Margaret shames him for allowing York and Warwick to bully him around. She announces that she will distance herself from Henry until he annuls his agreement to disinherit their son: "I here divorce myself / Both from thy table, Henry, and thy bed" (I.i.247–48). She leaves with Prince Edward.

Henry asks Exeter to help him reconcile with his angered supporters.

I.II Location: Yorkshire. York's castle

York decides to break his agreement with Henry and try to seize the throne.

York enters and asks Richard, Edward, and Montague about their discussion. Edward and Richard ask York about the crown, and he tells them that they will inherit it after Henry's death. They urge him to take the throne now, especially since Henry is likely to outlive York. York protests that they took an oath of loyalty, but Richard replies that the oath is not legally binding, because it was not sworn before a magistrate. Convinced, York sends Montague to see Warwick and other supporters in London.

A messenger arrives with news that Queen Margaret's army approaches the castle. York urges Montague to hurry. Two of York's uncles arrive with reinforcements.

I.III Location: Yorkshire. A battlefield

Clifford, whose father was killed by York, kills York's youngest son Rutland.

The Earl of Rutland, York's youngest son, accompanied by his tutor, encounters Clifford on his way back to York's castle. Rutland begs Clifford to quarrel with his father York, not with him. But Clifford reminds Rutland that York killed Clifford's father (see *2 Henry VI*). Clifford will kill Rutland to begin to avenge Clifford's father's death. Rutland begs for his life, but Clifford kills him.

I.IV Location: Yorkshire. A battlefield

In battle, Margaret and Clifford capture, taunt, and kill York.

York's army has been unable to beat back Margaret's forces. York surveys the field and predicts that he is done for. Margaret enters with Clifford, Northumberland, and Prince Edward. Clifford wants to kill York, but Margaret holds him back. Northumberland and Clifford capture York. Once he is tied up, Margaret mocks him for wanting to be king. She tells him that his son Rutland is dead and offers him Rutland's bloodstained handkerchief to wipe his tears. York does not react, and she calls him a madman. She has her soldiers fashion a paper crown, and puts it on York's head, mocking his claim to the throne. She reminds him that he has broken his oath to Henry (see I.i and I.ii), and knocks the crown from his head.

York verbally attacks Margaret with bitterness. He calls her evil and unnatural because she (as a woman) leads an army. She is an abomination of a woman, not beautiful, virtuous, or restrained. What kind of a woman would offer a handkerchief stained with the blood of a child to his father? He can weep and rage well enough, if that's what she wants.

Northumberland observes that he sympathizes with York's grief. Clifford and Margaret stab York to death. Margaret orders York's head hung along the gates of the town of York.

ACT II

York's eldest son Edward inherits York's claim to the throne, and wins a decisive battle of this bloody civil war against Henry's forces.

II.I Location: Yorkshire. Another part of the battlefield

York's sons Edward and Richard see and interpret three rising suns; with York dead, Edward has inherited York's claim to the throne.

Edward and Richard meet, seeking their father York. Richard tells Edward that he saw York fighting fiercely, which made him proud. Edward and Richard notice light on the horizon, and look on as three suns rise. Richard remarks that the suns look as though they are embracing after having made a pact. Edward suggests that the suns represent the three York brothers—Edward, Richard, and George—who together will shine on the world.

A messenger arrives and tells Edward and Richard about York's death. York was captured with great difficulty, tormented by Margaret armed with Rutland's bloody handkerchief, and killed by Clifford and Margaret. Though capturing York was extremely difficult, Margaret tormented him with Rutland's bloody handkerchief and ultimately, she and Clifford killed him. Edward is deeply grieved, and Richard, consumed with rage, vows to avenge York's death. Edward (the eldest son), Richard says, has inherited not only the dukedom of York, but the claim to the throne as well.

Warwick and Montague enter. Warwick, who already knows that York is dead, has sent his troops to intercept Margaret's army on its way to London to force Parliament to repeal York's agreement with Henry and officially reinstate Prince Edward as the heir to the throne. Warwick's army has lost that battle, but on the bright side, George—Edward and Richard's middle brother—has returned from France. At Warwick's urging, Richard and Edward prepare to march to London to protect York's agreement with Henry. A messenger announces that Margaret's army approaches.

II.II Location: York

An attempted parley between Edward's and Henry's supporters ends in insults that lead to battle.

Henry, Margaret, Clifford, Northumberland, and Prince Edward have arrived at York. They see York's head, and Henry asks Margaret to restrain her bloodthirsty glee. Clifford argues that, just as animals naturally protect their young from threats, so Henry should ensure that his son Prince Edward inherits his throne. Henry replies that sons are not always happy with their inheritance. For example, he himself would have preferred to inherit the legacy of virtuous deeds from his father (Henry V) rather than the throne. Margaret interrupts him. At her prompting, Henry knights Prince Edward.

A messenger arrives to announce that Warwick's army approaches. Clifford asks Henry to leave, since Margaret is a better commander without him. Edward and his supporters—Richard, George, Warwick, Norfolk, and Montague—arrive. Edward accuses Henry of going back on his oath to York (the oath that ensures that York will inherit the throne after Henry). Richard and Clifford get involved in a shouting match. Warwick interrupts and asks Henry to yield his crown to Edward, York's heir, which prompts more arguments. Henry tries to interrupt, and Margaret tells him that he must either speak more forcefully or shut up.

Clifford and Richard continue to trade insults; Edward and Warwick demand the crown, and Prince Edward urges Henry not to yield. Edward insults Margaret's station (she is the daughter of a minor French nobleman) and blames all conflicts on her ambition. If she had not been so power-hungry, Yorkists would not have publicly demanded the throne. Edward calls for battle and walks out.

II.III Location: Yorkshire. Another battlefield

The Yorkists are losing the battle.

Warwick, joined by Edward and later by George and Richard, realize that they are losing the battle. Richard tells Warwick that Warwick's half-brother (not Montague) is dead. Warwick and Edward both swear revenge. All return to battle.

II.IV Location: Yorkshire. Another part of the same battlefield

Richard seeks to kill Clifford.

Richard finds Clifford, seeking to avenge the deaths of York (his father) and Rutland (his brother). Richard and Clifford fight. Warwick arrives to aid Richard, and Clifford flees. Richard asks Warwick to let him kill Clifford by himself.

II.V Location: Yorkshire. Another part of the same battlefield

As he observes the battle of the civil war—father against son, son against father—Henry wishes he could have been born a shepherd.

Henry watches the battle. He compares the motion of the two opposing sides to the back-and-forth motion of ocean waves. Observing that the opposing sides sway like the ocean, he sits down on a hill and thinks about his sad life. He would have been happier, he supposes, as a shepherd than as a king. He would have spent lovely hours with his flock, resting and thinking. Henry concludes that a shepherd's life is much happier than a king's.

A soldier enters, carrying another dead soldier. Henry watches from the side as the soldier searches the dead body, looking for money or loot. As he takes off the helmet, the soldier realizes that he has killed his own father. His father served Warwick while he himself was drafted into the royal army. As the soldier weeps, Henry muses that these times of conflict in the upper classes are truly terrible for the common people.

Another second soldier enters with another dead body. He too searches the dead body for valuables. Removing the helmet, this second soldier discovers that he has killed his own son. He cries out against this miserable, unnatural era, when atrocities happen because of strife among the nobility.

Henry wants to die, hoping that his death will end the wars. The first soldier wonders what he will tell his mother, and the second soldier wonders what he will tell his wife. The soldiers exit, leaving Henry with his woe.

Prince Edward enters and tells Henry to flee, for Warwick's army is winning. Margaret and Exeter enter to corroborate.

II.VI Location: Yorkshire. Another part of the same battlefield

Clifford dies; the Yorkists have won the battle and plan to claim the throne in London.

Clifford enters, an arrow in his neck. He knows that he is dying, and grieves for how much his death will weaken Henry's side. If Henry had been a stronger king, he remarks, it would have prevented this bloodshed.

Edward, Richard, and George enter, followed by Warwick and Montague. They have won the battle. Clifford groans as he dies, and Richard notices him. Warwick orders that York's head, currently on the town wall, be replaced by Clifford's head. The lords make fun of Clifford, who is already dead.

Warwick urges Edward, George, and Richard to go to London to claim the crown. Warwick himself plans to go to France and arrange for Edward's marriage to Lady Bona, the sister of the King of France. With France as an ally, Edward will be able to resist Margaret's force, should her supporters regroup. Edward makes Richard the Duke of Gloucester and George the Duke of Clarence. Richard remembers that previous Gloucesters died violently, and asks to switch with George. (Edward III's son Thomas of Woodstock, first Duke of Gloucester and one of Henry VI's great-great-uncles, was assassinated on Richard II's request before the start of *Richard II*. Humphrey, second Duke of Gloucester and one of Henry VI's uncles, was assassinated in *2 Henry VI*.) Edward dismisses Richard's request as silly.

ACT III

Edward deposes Henry and becomes King Edward IV, but inadvertently alienates his main supporter Warwick by marrying Lady Grey, a little-known widow.

III.I Location: Northern England. A forest

Gamekeepers discover and arrest Henry, who has fled to Scotland in disguise.

Two gamekeepers traveling through a Scottish forest notice a man approaching and hide. The man is King Henry in disguise: he has escaped to Scotland to flee the wars. Margaret and Prince Edward have traveled to France to ask King Louis for aid, and Warwick is in France to ask Louis for his sister Lady Bona's hand for Edward. Henry fears that Warwick, a subtle orator, will sway Louis.

The gamekeepers, who have overheard Henry's musings, come forward and ask Henry where his crown is. He replies that his crown is in his heart. They arrest him in Edward's name. Henry remarks that commoners are fickle. Edward has easily replaced him as their liege. They lead him away.

III.II Location: London. The palace

The new King Edward IV proposed to the widowed Lady Grey (even as Warwick works to secure French support by marrying Edward to the French king's sister); Richard resolves to use trickery and murder to become king himself.

Lady Grey, a widow who lost all her lands when her husband was killed, has approached King Edward IV, Richard, and George. Richard and George have noticed that Edward is attracted to her, and chuckle to each other that Edward plans to restore her lands in exchange for sleeping with her. Indeed, King Edward tells her that she can have her lands if she loves the king. She replies that as a subject, she does love him. He clarifies, saying he wants her to make love to him. She refuses. Nonplussed, Edward asks her to marry him. She thinks that he mocks her, but he insists that she will be queen.

Edward announces his decision to Richard and George. They are surprised, but soon distracted by news: Henry has been captured and is imprisoned in the tower. Everyone except Richard leaves to see Henry.

Alone, Richard delivers a long monologue. He hopes that Lady Grey will not bear Edward any children. He enumerates the people in line for the throne before him: Edward, George, Henry, Prince Edward, and any of their offspring. He dreams of the crown like one would dream of a far-off land. He ponders the options in his life. He could lead a life filled with pleasure and women, but he is a hunchback with a shriveled arm, so no one will love him. Since he cannot get pleasure from his body, his only other option is pleasure from dominating those around him. He wants the crown! But how? So many people stand in his way. He is confused about what to do like one lost in a thorny forest. He plans to be devious:

> Why, I can smile, and murder whiles I smile,
> And cry "Content!" to that which grieves my heart,
> And wet my cheeks with artificial tears,
> And frame my face to all occasions.

and deceitful:

> I can add colors to the chameleon
> Change shapes with Proteus for advantages,
> And set the murderous Machiavel to school.
> Can I do this, and cannot get a crown?"
> (III.ii.182–85, 191–94)

(Proteus is a Greek shape-changing God; see also Symbols in *The Two Gentleman of Verona*. Niccolò Machiavelli was a sixteenth-century Italian statesman who argued that government leaders should be guided by pragmatism, not morals.)

III.III Location: France. King Louis's palace

Publicly humiliated by Edward's marriage to Lady Grey, Warwick reconciles with Margaret and secures military aid from the French King to overthrow Edward.

King Louis of France, accompanied by his sister Lady Bona, meets with Margaret, Prince Edward, Margaret, and the Earl of Oxford. Margaret relates their misfortunes. Edward, Duke of York, has taken the throne and Henry has fled to Scotland. She and Prince Edward beg for Louis's aid.

Warwick arrives with greetings from Edward IV, and asks Louis for Lady Bona's hand for Edward. Margaret interrupts, calling Edward a tyrant usurper. Warwick reminds everyone that Henry's grandfather, Henry IV, illegally deposed Richard II to become king. Warwick and Oxford argue. Louis asks to speak to Warwick alone.

In private, Louis asks Warwick whether Edward has been legally crowned king and whether Edward genuinely loves Lady Bona. Warwick assures him of both. Louis announces that he has decided to support Edward and give him Lady Bona as wife.

A messenger brings letters for Warwick, Louis, and Margaret. All announce the same news: Edward has married Lady Grey. Warwick announces that Edward has dishonored him by marrying while he, Warwick, has been negotiating a marriage with Lady Bona. He renounces Edward and asks Margaret's forgiveness. She welcomes him. Warwick asks Louis for military support to oust Edward from the throne. He mentions that George too has been thinking about breaking with Edward, which will help their cause. Louis agrees to help. They send messages to Edward. To seal their alliance, Warwick offers to marry his daughter to Prince Edward.

Left alone, Warwick muses that he left England as Edward's chief ally and ambassador, and now returns as Edward's chief enemy.

ACT IV

Having joined forces with Margaret, Warwick deposes Edward and reinstates King Henry VI; Edward escapes to France, gathers an army, and returns to challenge Warwick.

IV.I Location: London. The palace

When the English court learns that Warwick has changed sides to support Henry, Edward's brother George and Somerset abandon Edward as well.

Richard, George, Montague, and the Duke of Somerset agree that Edward should have waited until Warwick returned from France before marrying Lady Grey. Edward and Lady Grey—now Queen Elizabeth—enter, accompanied by the Earl of Pembroke, Lord Stafford, and Lord Hastings. Edward asks Richard and George their opinion of his marriage. They ironically reply that they are as pleased as Louis or Warwick (i.e., not at all). Edward insists that he can do as he pleases. George reminds Edward that the marriage has angered Louis and dishonored and alienated Warwick. Montague points out that an alliance with France through marriage would have strengthened Edward's reign. Hastings retorts that England does need France. Richard blames Edward for marrying Lady Grey's brother—rather than Richard or George—to an heiress.

A messenger arrives to announce that Warwick has abandoned Edward and joined Henry's supporters, that Margaret has prepared her troops, and that both King Louis and Lady Bona are insulted that Edward has jilted Lady Bona. Upon hearing that Warwick has married one of his daughters to Prince Edward to seal his new alliance, George announces that he will marry Warwick's second daughter, and walks out. Somerset follows. Richard remarks to himself that he will stay with Edward not for Edward's sake, but for the sake of the crown. Hastings and Montague too still support Edward.

IV.II Location: near Warwick. A field

George and Somerset join Warwick, who has landed in England with French forces.

Warwick and Oxford have landed in England, leading French soldiers. George and Somerset join them. Pleased, Warwick suggests a plan to capture Edward.

IV.III Location: near Warwick. Outside King Edward's tent

Warwick leads an attack on Edward's tent.

Edward has arrived in the town of Warwick to meet Warwick's army. Three watchmen guard Edward's tent. Warwick, George, Oxford, and Somerset, arrive and attack the tent.

IV.IV Location: near Warwick. Outside King Edward's tent

Warwick takes Edward prisoner and takes the crown.

Richard and Hastings flee, but Warwick captures Edward. Warwick tells Edward that he is incompetent and unfit to rule. He does not know how to deal with ambassadors properly, nor how to treat his brothers well. When Edward sees that George supports Warwick, he surrenders. Warwick removes Edward's crown and sends Somerset to imprison Edward on the estate of the Archbishop of York. Warwick's troops prepare to march to London and reinstall Henry on the throne.

IV.V Location: London. The palace

Edward's supporters as well as his pregnant wife Lady Grey flee London.

Lady Grey tells her brother Lord Rivers that Edward has been taken prisoner. She urges Rivers and Edward's other supporters to flee, while she takes sanctuary (in a nearby abbey) to protect her unborn baby, the heir to the crown.

IV.VI Location: Yorkshire. The Archbishop of York's estate

Richard breaks Edward out of prison.

Richard and Hastings have arrived near the Archbishop of York's estate and await Edward. Though Edward is under house arrest, he is allowed to go hunting. Richard has sent him a message to meet them here on his hunt. Edward arrives, and Richard and Hastings whisk him away.

IV.VII Location: London. The tower

Newly reinstated, King Henry VI leaves Warwick and George to rule the country; Edward has fled to France to seek aid.

Warwick and George arrive with the crown. Henry, who has been imprisoned in the tower while Edward was king, enters with Oxford, Montague, Somerset, and the young Earl of Richmond (Henry VI's distant cousin and the future King Henry VII. He is currently Somerset's ward). Henry thanks Warwick for freeing him, and mentions that he received fair treatment in prison. Intending to live a quiet, private life, Henry makes both Warwick and George protectors of the realm. George and Warwick agree to work together to run the country and ensure that Prince Edward inherits the crown.

Impressed by the young Richmond, Henry remarks that he seems made for the crown. Henry predicts that Richmond will bring the country peace. (Indeed, Richmond will marry Edward's daughter, thereby uniting the Houses of York and Lancaster. As king, he will usher in the Tudor dynasty, which will spawn both Henry VIII and Elizabeth I, Shakespeare's patron. See *Richard III*.)

A messenger arrives with news that Edward has escaped and fled to Burgundy, in France. Oxford and Somerset guess that the Duke of Burgundy will likely give Edward military aid, which will lead to more war. Somerset plans to send Richmond to Brittany, France, for safety in the meantime.

IV.VIII Location: outside York

Edward has returned from France to reclaim the Duchy of York; he plans to make another bid for the crown soon.

Edward, Richard, and Hastings have returned to England with an army provided by the Duke of Burgundy. They knock at the doors of the town of York (in the domain of Edward, who is Duke of York). The mayor reluctantly lets them in when Edward promises that he supports King Henry VI. Sir John Montgomery arrives and offers himself as an ally to King Edward. Edward replies that first, he just wants to reclaim his Duchy of York. Montgomery announces that he will only support Edward if Edward plans to retake the throne. Edward wants to wait and gather supporters, but Hastings urges Edward to strike immediately. Edward is convinced.

IV.IX Location: London. The Bishop of London's palace

Warwick urges Henry's supporters to prepare for war with Edward.

Warwick reports to Henry VI, Warwick, Montague, George (Duke of Clarence) and Oxford that Edward has returned from Burgundy with an army. He urges them to raise their armies.

IV.X Location: London. The Bishop of London's palace

Edward takes Henry prisoner again.

Henry tells Exeter that Warwick's army will probably beat Edward's army. Henry wonders why some people prefer Edward to him, considering what a gentle and compassionate king he has been. Edward and Richard arrive with their army. Edward takes Henry prisoner, sends him to back to the tower, and sets off to meet Warwick on the battlefield.

ACT V

Edward defeats and kills Warwick, captures Margaret prisoner, and retakes the throne; Richard kills Henry and plots to eventually make his way to the throne.

V.I Location: Coventry

Edward and supporters meet Warwick and supporters before battle; George returns to Edward's side.

Warwick learns that his allies Montague and George have arrived with their troops. Edward and Richard arrive with their army. Warwick points out that he has put Edward on the throne, and he has deposed Edward. Edward tells Warwick that Henry has been captured. Warwick's supporters arrive—Oxford, Montague, Somerset, and George (Edward's brother). Edward asks George whether George really intends to fight against him. After Richard speaks to George privately, George repents and asks Edward and Richard to forgive him for his betrayal. Edward and Warwick prepare to begin the battle.

V.II Location: Barnet. a battlefield

Warwick dies in battle just as Margaret arrives with reinforcements from France.

The battle has begun. Edward drags in a wounded Warwick, and leaves him to die. On the brink of death, Warwick compares himself to a giant tree that has been sheltering the monarchy under its branches. The only thing that belongs to him now is the bit of earth under him. Somerset and Oxford enter and announce that Margaret has arrived from France with a powerful army. Somerset reports that Montague (Warwick's brother) is dead. Warwick dies.

V.III Location: Barnet. a battlefield

Edward's forces have defeated Warwick's troops and prepare to face Margaret's.

Edward, Richard, and George rejoice in their victory over Warwick's forces. Margaret's troops approach, so they discuss their armies and prepare for another battle.

V.IV   Location: Tewkesbury

Margaret rouses her troops in preparation for battle.

Margaret gives her commanders—Prince Edward, Somerset, and Oxford—an inspirational talk before battle. She compares them all to the crew of a ship: they have lost their captain (Henry has been taken prisoner); many sailors have drowned (Warwick and Montague are dead); the masts are damaged, but still they (Edward and his supporters) persevere over rough seas and sharp rocks. Inspired, Prince Edward urges those who are frightened to leave. Oxford marvels that a woman (Margaret) and a young man (Prince Edward) are more courageous than soldiers. A messenger enters to announce that Edward's troops approach.

   Edward enters, rousing his own troops. Margaret reminds her followers that they fight for King Henry's freedom. All prepare for battle.

V.V   Location: Tewkesbury

Edward, Richard, and George have won the battle and taken Margaret and her commanders prisoner; they slaughter Prince Edward.

Edward's troops have won the battle, and Margaret, Oxford, Somerset, and Prince Edward have been taken prisoner. Edward sentences Oxford to prison and Somerset to death. Prince Edward comes in under guard. He demands that Edward relinquish the throne. Richard and Prince Edward trade insults. Edward, Richard, and George take turns stabbing Prince Edward to death. Margaret faints. Richard slips off to see Henry in the tower.

   Margaret revives. Lamenting Prince Edward's death, she calls Edward, Richard, and George butchers. She asks George and Richard to kill her. She is escorted away.

V.VI   Location: The Tower of London. Henry's cell

Richard kills Henry and plots to take the throne, allowing his mind to as crooked as his deformed body.

Richard comes in to see Henry, who has heard of Prince Edward's death and suspects that Richard has come to kill him. Henry compares himself and Prince Edward to Dædalus and Icarus. In Greek mythology, Dædalus is a master craftsman who fashions wings for himself and his son Icarus to fly out of prison. When Icarus flies too close to the sun, the wax in his wings melts and he plummets to his death in the sea. Edward is the sun that has melted Prince Edward's wings, and Richard is the sea in which Prince Edward has drowned. Henry predicts that Richard will make thousands weep for their dead relatives: "The owl shrieked at thy birth—an evil sign / . . . / Teeth hadst thou in thy head when thou wast born, / To signify thou cam'st to bite the world" V.vi.44–54).

   Richard interrupts Henry's speech and stabs Henry to death. He muses over Henry's body. Indeed, his mother had told him that he was a breech baby (positioned upside-down in the womb), born with fully grown teeth. Since he is a deformed hunchback with a crooked body, his mind will be similarly crooked. He will not love others and will depend only on himself. Now that Henry and Prince Edward are out of the way, Richard plans to continue working toward the throne and bring about George's downfall.

V.VII   Location: London. The palace

Edward has retaken the throne; his reign is strengthened by the birth of an heir but weakened by Richard's plotting.

King Edward IV sits on the throne again, as Lady Grey (now Queen Elizabeth), their infant son Edward, George, Richard, and Hastings look on. Edward presents his son, the heir to the throne, to George and Richard, and asks them to kiss the baby. Richard privately compares himself to Judas Iscariot, who kissed his master Jesus in order to identify him to his executioners. George asks Edward about Margaret, whom the French have been trying to ransom, and Edward agrees to send her back. Edward calls for revelry and celebration.

THEMES, MOTIFS, & SYMBOLS IN *3 HENRY VI*

THEMES

CIVIL WAR AS UNNATURAL The Wars of the Roses, the conflicts portrayed in the Henry VI trilogy, were civil wars. Shakespeare shows these wars as "unnatural," against nature because countrymen fight one another, and points out many markers of the unnatural that surround them. The conflict begins with an unnatural act: the future Henry IV deposes and eliminates his cousin Richard II. This crime upsets the cosmic order and unleashes a multigenerational curse upon the House of Lancaster, which includes Henry IV, Henry V, and Henry VI. In 3 *Henry VI*, Margaret becomes a commander of troops, an unusual and "unnatural" occupation for a woman. To seal her image as a woman who flouts nature, Margaret taunts York with a handkerchief dipped in his son Rutland's blood. Clifford accuses Henry of unnatural behavior when Henry agrees to pass his crown to York, disinheriting his son Prince Edward. Both excessive bloodthirstiness and excessive meekness are denounced as unnatural over the course of the play.

THE RISE OF THE SELF-EMPOWERED INDIVIDUAL Against the backdrop of the Wars of the Roses between the Lancastrians and the Yorkists, where alliances and family membership define individuals, 3 *Henry VI* puts forth a new model of power: the independent individual who relies on no one else. Margaret and Richard, the two most powerful characters in 3 *Henry VI*, depend least on allegiances and alliances. They both persevere through cunning and survive into *Richard III*.

BETRAYAL When social bonds and family ties unravel as England approaches chaos, many characters betray others, whether personally or politically. Margaret perceives Henry's agreement with York, which disinherits her son, as a betrayal. York betrays his agreement with Henry and gathers and army to make a bid for the throne. Warwick feels betrayed by Edward when Edward marries the little-known widow against Warwick's advice. Warwick then betrays Edward and joins forces with Margaret to bring about his downfall. George too betrays Edward by joining Warwick, then betrays Warwick by returning to support Edward. Richard plots to betray both George and Edward's baby (the future Prince Edward, imprisoned and killed by Richard in *Richard III*). He compares himself to Judas Iscariot, the ultimate traitor of Christian lore.

MOTIFS

THE PAST REVISITED The major events of 3 *Henry VI* all recall other events of the history plays. Through this repetition, the past continually recurs in the present. Richard, Duke of York, works to depose Henry IV because Henry VI (Henry's grandfather) deposed Richard II in *Richard II*. Captured by Margaret and Clifford, York predicts that even though he may die, his heirs will rise up out of his ashes and avenge his death. Indeed, his son, another Richard, will wreak havoc on England in *Richard III*. As a female general, Margaret recalls Joan la Pucelle of 1 *Henry VI*. Edward's ill-advised marriage to Lady Grey behind Warwick's back recalls Henry's decision to marry Margaret of Anjou against his advisor's suggestions at the end of 1 *Henry VI*.

THE BREAK-UP OF FAMILIES 3 *Henry VI* shows many families threatened from within. Henry gives in to pressure from York and Warwick and agrees to disinherit his son Prince Edward. Richard schemes to become a much more dangerous threat to his brothers Edward and George than their enemy Lancastrians. The breakup of families from internal forces is starkly dramatized in II.iv, in which Henry observes a father who has killed his son and a son who has killed his father.

SYMBOLS

YORK'S PAPER CROWN The paper crown that York briefly wears before his death symbolizes the instability of royal power in Shakespeare's history plays. Margaret places it on York's head to taunt and ridicule him for having designs on the throne. The crown is made of paper, which is flimsy material, and Margaret crowns and uncrowns York with ease. The real crown, a symbol of royal authority, is a similarly fragile possession. Henry VI loses, regains, and loses his crown again within the scope of the play. The paper crown also subtly suggests that royal power may be worthless. Henry VI has been a king all of his life, but has less power than his wife and his many uncles. Henry himself says that, for him, being happy is more valuable than reigning over a country (III.i.62–5).

THE THREE SUNS In II.i, meeting on the battlefield, Edward and Richard see an omen: three suns rise in the sky and merge together into one. These suns symbolize an unattainable ideal of family unity. Edward guesses that the suns prophesy the glorious rise and harmonious reign of the three adult York brothers, Edward, George, and Richard. Richard takes the visions less seriously and mocks Edward's plan to make the suns a family emblem. Fittingly, it is Richard who, in *Richard III*, eliminates both George and Edward's little sons on his way to the throne, leaving only one sun shining. Richard's rise to power heralds a new age that shuns medieval traditions such as interpreting celestial events as predictions of humans affairs.

IMPORTANT QUOTATIONS FROM *3 HENRY VI*

---

1. *I here divorce myself*
   Both from thy table, Henry, and thy bed,
   Until that act of Parliament be repealed
   Whereby my son is disinherited.

Location: I.i.248–51
Speaker: Margaret to King Henry
Context: Outraged that Henry has agreed to pass his throne to York after his death, Margaret refuses to be a wife to Henry

Margaret conveys her fury bluntly and directly. The imperiousness of her words—"I here divorce myself"—is associated with masculine power, and foreshadows her command of the royal troops. She calls Prince Edward "my son," not "our." She has claimed Henry's son as hers as well as Henry's royal authority. Her words tear apart the family unit and signal more violent troubles. In emphasizing that the family tension is caused by an "act of Parliament," she situates the private drama within a larger public sphere. In *Henry VI* as in *Richard II*, the welfare of the king corresponds to the well-being of the country, and the rift within the family mirrors civil war.

---

2. *My ashes, as the phoenix, may bring forth*
   A bird that will revenge upon you all,
   And in that hope I throw mine eyes to heaven,
   Scorning whate'er you can afflict me with.

Location: I.iv.36–39
Speaker: York to Northumberland and Clifford
Context: Surrounded by Margaret's troops, York predicts both his death and the rise of his heirs to power

The phoenix is a glorious mythological bird that dies in flames and is reborn anew from its own ashes. Aware that his downfall is near, York predicts that his legacy will live on and avenge his death. Indeed, York's sons Edward and Richard will both rule England, and Edward's daughter Elizabeth will marry Henry VII and engender the Tudor dynasty, which will include Henry VIII and Queen Elizabeth I.

Shakespeare allows York to predict both his demise and the continuation of his line in one image. York's allusion to classical mythology echoes Clifford's allusion to Phaëton, the Greek god associated with the sun (I.iv.34). Both York and Clifford are literate, classically educated noblemen who value their honor and their families. (Clifford's grudge against York stems from the fact that York killed Clifford's father at the battle of St. Albans in *2 Henry VI*.) York's son is symbolized by the phoenix reborn from York's demise. He will rise from the ashes to become the future Richard III. Ironically, Shakespeare portrays York's son as a villain who assassinates both his brother and his two young nephews, destroying his family in his quest for power. Richard's ambition is more ruthless and less constrained by concerns for honor than his father York's. This brand of ambition marks a transition away from medieval chivalry to new, pragmatic values explored in Shakespeare's history plays.

---

3. *My gracious liege, this too much lenity*
   And harmful pity must be laid aside.
   To whom do lions cast their gentle looks?
   Not to the beast that would usurp their den.
   Whose hand is that the forest bear doth lick?
   Not his that spoils her young before her face.

Location: II.ii.9–14
Speaker: Clifford to Henry
Context: Clifford uses examples from animal life to argue that Henry should leave his kingdom to Prince Edward

Clifford strongly disapproves of Henry's agreement with York to bequeath the throne to York's heirs. Clifford accuses Henry "too much lenity"—a trait that makes Henry a decent human being but a terrible king. Clifford's elaborate animal metaphors contrast natural with unnatural behavior. As lions and bears do not show gentleness to the enemies of their cubs, so Henry should not give his kingdom to York and disinherit Prince Edward. Clifford urges Henry to let his animal instincts triumph. Henry remains gentle, but the rest of the nobles engage in a wild and bloody civil war. Shakespeare attributes both natural and unnatural aspects to this war: it is human nature to seek power and protect one's heir, but it is against nature for fathers and sons to kill one another, as we see in II.v.

---

4. *My crown is in my heart, not on my head;*
   Not decked with diamonds and Indian stones,
   Nor to be seen. My crown is called content—
   A crown it is that seldom kings enjoy.

Location: III.i.62–65
Speaker: Henry to the two gamekeepers
Context: Henry explains that his true crown, the keystone of his joy, is his personal contentment: the physical headdress of a crown does not bring him true joy or contentment

Two gamekeepers stumble upon the exiled and disguised Henry. Overhearing that he is King Henry VI, they mock him and ask him about his crown. Henry responds that his crown is not the one that marks him as a king, the one encrusted with diamonds and jewels. Rather, his true crown is his personal sense of well-being, which is a feeling kings enjoy only rarely. Henry thus prefers psychological satisfaction to political power. He is neither a good ruler nor a happy one.

---

5. *Then, since the heavens have shaped my body so,*
   Let hell make crooked my mind to answer it.
   I had no father, I am like no father;
   I have no brother, I am like no brother;

And this word "love," which greybeards call divine,
Be resident in men like one another
And not in me—I am myself alone.

Location: V.vi.78–84
Speaker: Richard
Context: Having killed Henry, Richard acknowledges his physical deformities and resolves to be dependent on no one

Richard's speech here and in III.ii foreshadows his villainous actions in *Richard III*. Whereas most of the characters in Shakespeare's history plays have deep connections to their families, Richard declares his independence from his dead father (York) and his brothers (Edward and George). Because he was born deformed, he fundamentally differs from other human beings. Richard forces his physical deformities to embody his action, and resolves to be cruel and ruthless. In rejecting "divine" love, Richard turns his back on religion and morality, the guiding principles of the Middle Ages. In resolving to stand alone, he embraces the pragmatic politics of a new modern era, one that Shakespeare's audience associated with Niccolò Machiavelli, the political theorist that Richard purports to follows.

RICHARD III

After resolving to steal the crown from his brother Edward, Richard becomes increasingly evil, murdering everyone who stands in his way.

RICHARD III IN CONTEXT

Richard III, a history play that is often viewed as a sequel to three of Shakespeare's earlier history plays—*Henry VI, Part 1*; *Henry VI, Part 2*; and *Henry VI, Part 3*—chronicles the bloody deeds of the murderous and tyrannical King Richard III. Richard, a brilliant wordsmith and a skilled manipulator, is both repellent and fascinating. The motivation for his malevolent hatred is hard to pinpoint. Some critics believe that Richard is not as fully conceived as some of Shakespeare's later characters, such as Macbeth or Hamlet. Such critics argue that Richard is less a complex human than a figure who recalls stock characters like "Vice" from early medieval drama.

The historical King Richard III was not necessarily more murderous than the kings who preceded or succeeded him. Nor is it likely that he was deformed, as Shakespeare portrays him. Current events likely influenced Shakespeare's version of events: Queen Elizabeth I, a descendent of the king who overthrew Richard, was on the throne. Thus, the official party line of the Elizabethan era was that Richard was a monster who was not a legitimate ruler of England.

RICHARD III: KEY FACTS

Full title: The Tragedy of King Richard the Third

Time and place written: Around 1592; London

Date of first publication: 1597

Genre: History play

Setting (time): Around 1485, though the actual historical events of the play took place over a much longer period, around 1471–1485

Setting (place): England

Protagonist: Richard III

Major conflict: Richard, the power-hungry younger brother of the king of England, longs to seize control of the throne.

RICHARD III: CHARACTER LIST

Anne   Prince Edward's young widow. Prince Edward was the son of the former king, Henry VI. Lady Anne hates Richard, but Richard persuades her to marry him for political reasons and for his own sadistic pleasure.

Buckingham   Richard's right-hand man. The duke of Buckingham is almost as amoral and ambitious as Richard.

Clarence   The gentle, trusting brother of Edward and Richard. To get Clarence out of the way, Richard has him murdered.

Duchess of York   The widowed mother of Richard, Clarence, and King Edward IV. The duchess of York is very protective of Elizabeth, her daughter-in-law, and Elizabeth's children. She curses Richard's evil acts.

King Edward IV   The older brother of Richard and Clarence, and the king of England at the beginning of the play. Edward was deeply involved in the Yorkists' brutal overthrow of the Lancaster regime, but as king he is devoted to reconciling the conflicting political factions. He does not realize that Richard attempts to thwart him at every turn.

Queen Elizabeth The wife of King Edward IV and the mother of two young boys and a girl: young Elizabeth. After Edward's death, Queen Elizabeth (also called Lady Gray) is at Richard's mercy. Richard views her as an enemy because she opposes his rise to power, and because she is intelligent and fairly strong-willed. Elizabeth is part of the Woodeville family. Her kinsmen—Dorset, Rivers, and Gray—are her allies in the court.

Young Elizabeth Queen Elizabeth's daughter. Young Elizabeth is a pawn in political power-brokering. Her engagement to Richmond, the Lancastrian rebel leader, is meant to unite the warring houses of York and Lancaster.

Hastings A lord. Hastings maintains his integrity, remaining loyal to the family of King Edward IV. He makes the mistake of trusting Richard, which leads to his death.

Lord Mayor of London A gullible, suggestible fellow. Richard and Buckingham use the lord mayor of London as a pawn.

Margaret The widow of the deceased King Henry VI, and the mother of Prince Edward. Before she married Prince Edward, Margaret was married to Henry VI, who was deposed and murdered by the family of King Edward IV and Richard. She hates both Richard and the people he is trying to get rid of, all of whom were complicit in the destruction of the Lancasters.

The Princes The two young sons of King Edward IV and his wife, Elizabeth. Their names are Prince Edward and the young duke of York. These boys, Richard's nephews, are murdered by Richard's agents in the Tower of London. Young Prince Edward, the rightful heir to the throne, should not be confused with the elder Edward, prince of Wales (the first husband of Lady Anne, and the son of the former king, Henry VI), who was killed before the play begins.

Ratcliffe and Catesby Two of Richard's flunkies.

Richard The protagonist and villain of the play. Richard, also called the duke of Gloucester, is eventually crowned King Richard III. Deformed in body and mind, Richard is evil, corrupt, sadistic, manipulative, and intensely ambitious. He is also brilliant and gifted at politics.

Richmond A member of the Lancaster royal family. Richmond gathers a force of rebels to challenge Richard for the throne. Richmond represents goodness, justice, and fairness. He founded the Tudor dynasty, which still ruled England in Shakespeare's day.

Rivers, Dorset, and Gray The kinsmen and allies of Queen Elizabeth. Rivers is Elizabeth's brother, and Gray and Dorset are her sons from her first marriage. Richard eventually executes Rivers and Gray, but Dorset flees and survives.

Lord Stanley Richmond's stepfather. Lord Stanley, earl of Derby, secretly helps Richmond.

Tyrrell A murderer whom Richard hires to kill his young cousins, the princes.

Vaughan A friend of Elizabeth's. Richard has Vaughan executed along with Rivers and Grey.

RICHARD III: PLOT OVERVIEW

After a long civil war between the houses of York and Lancaster, England enjoys peace under King Edward IV. Edward's younger brother, Richard, resents Edward's powerful yet peaceful rule. Malicious, power-hungry, and bitter about his physical deformity, Richard plots to seize the throne, resolving to kill anyone who stands in his way. He manipulates a noblewoman, Lady Anne, into marrying him. He has his older brother Clarence executed and blames his sick brother King Edward for the crime in order to accelerate Edward's illness and death. After King Edward dies, Richard becomes lord protector of England, a position he is meant to hold onto until Edward's eldest son comes of age.

Richard kills the noblemen loyal to the princes and has the princes' relatives on their mother's side arrested and executed. Richard's allies, led by Lord Buckingham, campaign to have Richard crowned king. Richard imprisons the young princes in the Tower of London and sends hired murderers to kill them.

Richard's reign of terror makes the common people of England fear and loathe him, and alienates nearly all the noblemen. When rumors begin to circulate that the earl of Richmond is gathering forces in France in preparation to invade England and overthrow Richard, noblemen defect in droves to join his forces. Richard has his wife murdered so he can marry young Elizabeth, the daughter of the former

Queen Elizabeth and the deceased King Edward. Queen Elizabeth manages to stop the marriage and secretly promises to marry young Elizabeth to Richmond.

Richmond invades England. The night before the battle, Richard has a terrible dream in which the ghosts of the people he has murdered appear and curse him. Richard is killed in the battle, and Richmond is crowned King Henry VII. Promising a new era of peace for England, the new king is betrothed to young Elizabeth in order to unite the warring houses of Lancaster and York.

RICHARD III: SCENE SUMMARY

ACT I

In his quest for the throne, Richard woos Anne and has his brother Clarence killed.

I.I Location: the palace

Richard admits his ambitions to the throne and delights that his scheming has caused his brother, Clarence, to be imprisoned.

Richard, the duke of Gloucester, addresses himself and the audience. After a lengthy civil war, he says, peace has returned to the royal house of England. Richard's older brother, King Edward IV, now sits on the throne, and everyone is celebrating. But Richard himself will not join in the festivities. He complains that he was born deformed and ugly, and bitterly laments his bad luck. He vows to make everybody around him miserable. Richard says he is power-hungry and wants control of the entire court. He implies that his ultimate goal is to make himself king.

To achieve this goal, Richard is scheming against the other noblemen of the court. Richard says that he has planted rumors to make Edward suspicious of Clarence, their brother. Edward IV is very ill and highly suggestible at the moment.

Clarence enters under armed guard. Richard's plan has worked, and Clarence is being led to the Tower of London (where English political prisoners were traditionally imprisoned and often executed). Richard, feigning distress, says King Edward must have been influenced by his wife, Queen Elizabeth, or by his mistress, Lady Shore. Richard promises that he will try to have Clarence set free. After Clarence is led offstage toward the tower, Richard gleefully says to himself that he will make sure Clarence never returns.

Lord Hastings, the lord chamberlain of the court, enters. He was earlier imprisoned in the tower by the suspicious King Edward, but has now been freed. Richard, pretending ignorance, asks Hastings for the latest news, and Hastings tells him that Edward is very sick. After Hastings leaves, Richard gloats over Edward's illness. Edward's death would bring Richard one step closer to the throne. Richard wants Clarence to die first, however, so that Richard will be the legal heir to power. Richard's planned next step is to try to marry a noblewoman named Lady Anne Neville. An alliance with her would help Richard take the throne. Lady Anne has recently been widowed—she was married to the son of the previous king, Henry VI, who was deposed and murdered, along with his son, by Richard's family, the House of York. Richard is amused by the idea of persuading a woman in mourning to marry him.

I.II Location: the palace

Richard woos Anne.

Lady Anne enters the palace with a group of men bearing the coffin of Henry VI. She curses Richard for killing Henry, her father-in-law, and Edward, her husband. She prays that Richard's future children will be deformed and sick, and that he will make any woman he marries as miserable as Anne is.

Richard enters the room. Anne reacts with horror and spite, but Richard orders the attendants to stop the procession so that he can speak with her. He addresses Anne gently, but she curses him as the murderer of her husband and father-in-law. Anne points to the bloody wounds on the corpse of Henry VI, saying that they have started to bleed. (According to Renaissance tradition, the wounds of a murdered person begin to bleed again if the killer comes close to the corpse.)

Richard courts Anne, praising her gentleness and beauty. Horrified, Anne repeatedly reminds Richard that she knows he killed her husband and King Henry. He tells Anne she should forgive him his crime out of Christian charity, and then denies that he killed her husband at all. Anne remains angry, but her fierceness gradually dwindles in the face of Richard's eloquence and apparent sincerity. Finally, Richard kneels before Anne and hands her his sword, telling her to kill him if she will not forgive him. Anne begins to bring the sword toward his chest, but Richard keeps speaking, saying he killed Henry IV and Edward out of passion for Anne herself—Anne's beauty drove him to it. Anne lowers the sword.

Richard slips his ring onto her finger, telling her she can make him happy only by forgiving him and becoming his wife. Anne says she may take the ring, but she will not give him her hand. Richard persists, and Anne agrees to meet him later. As soon as Richard is alone, he gleefully celebrates his conquest of Anne. He scornfully asks whether she has already forgotten her husband, murdered by Richard's hand. He delights in winning Anne even while her eyes were still filled with tears of mourning.

I.III Location: the palace

Queen Elizabeth fights with Richard, and Margaret curses everyone.

Queen Elizabeth, the wife of the sickly King Edward IV, enters with members of her family: her brother, Lord Rivers, and her two sons from a previous marriage, Lord Gray and the marquis of Dorset. The queen tells her relatives that her husband is growing sicker and seems unlikely to survive his illness. The king and queen have two sons, but the princes are still too young to rule. If King Edward dies, control of the throne will go to Richard until the oldest son comes of age. Elizabeth tells her kinsmen that Richard is hostile to her and that she fears for her own and her sons' safety.

The duke of Buckingham and Stanley, the earl of Derby, enter. They report that King Edward is improving, and that he wants to make peace between Richard and Elizabeth's kinsmen, who are hostile to each other. Richard enters, complaining loudly. He says that people at court slander him because he is such an honest and plainspoken man, pretending that he has said hostile things about Elizabeth's kins-men. He accuses Elizabeth and her kinsmen of hoping Edward will die soon. Elizabeth, forced to defend herself, tells Richard that Edward simply wants to make peace among all of them. But Richard accuses Elizabeth of engineering the imprisonment of Clarence.

As Elizabeth and Richard argue, old Queen Margaret enters unobserved. Margaret comments to herself that power is temporary and condemns Richard for his part in the death of her husband, Henry VI, and his son, Prince Edward. Margaret steps forward and accuses Elizabeth and Richard of causing her downfall. She tells them they do not know what sorrow is. She adds that Elizabeth enjoys the privileges of being queen, which should be Margaret's, and that Richard is to blame for the murders of her family members. The others thought Margaret had been banished from the kingdom, and join together against her.

Margaret curses all those present. She prays that Elizabeth will outlive her glory and see her husband and children die before her, just as Margaret has. She curses Hastings, Rivers, and Dorset to die early deaths, since they were all bystanders when the York family murdered her son, Edward. Finally, she curses Richard, praying that he will mistake his friends for enemies, and his enemies for friends, and that he will never sleep peacefully.

Margaret leaves. Catesby, a nobleman, enters to say that King Edward wants to see his family and speak with them. The others leave, but Richard stays behind. He announces that he has set all his plans in motion and is tricking everybody into thinking that he is a good person. Two men enter. They are murderers whom Richard has hired to kill his brother Clarence.

I.IV Location: the Tower of London

Richard's hired murderers kill Clarence.

Clarence tells Brackenbury, the lieutenant of the tower, about the strange dream he had the night before. Clarence says he dreamed that he was outside of the tower and about to set sail for France along with his brother, Richard. But as they walked along the deck of the ship, Richard stumbled, and when Clarence tried to help him, Richard accidentally pushed him into the ocean. Clarence saw all the treasures of the deep laid out before him. He struggled to die, but felt the terrible pain of drowning over and over again.

Clarence then dreamed that he visited the underworld, where he saw the ghosts of those for whose deaths he was partly responsible in the recent overthrow of the monarchy. In particular, Clarence dreamed that he saw the ghost of Prince Edward—the son of Henry VI and Lady Anne's first husband— whom Clarence himself helped to kill. Prince Edward cried out aloud, cursing Clarence, and the Furies seized Clarence to drag him down to hell. Clarence woke from the dream trembling and terrified.

Clarence asks Brackenbury to stay with him while he sleeps. Brackenbury agrees, and Clarence falls asleep. Richard's hired murderers enter unannounced. They rudely hand Brackenbury the warrant that Richard gave them—a legal document that orders Brackenbury to leave them alone with Clarence. Brackenbury leaves quickly.

The two murderers, left alone with the sleeping Clarence, debate how best to kill him. Both suffer some pangs of conscience, but the memory of the reward Richard offered them overcomes their qualms. Eventually they decide to beat Clarence with their swords and then drown him in the keg of wine in the next room. Clarence wakes and pleads with them for his life. The murderers waver in their resolve, and Clarence finally asks them to go to his brother Richard who, Clarence says, will reward them for sparing his life. One of the murderers hesitates, but the other, after revealing to the unbelieving Clarence that it is Richard who has sent them to kill him, stabs Clarence and puts his body in the keg. The murderers flee the scene before anyone comes to investigate.

ACT II

Edward deteriorates and dies after learning of Clarence's death; Prince Edward makes his way to London; Richard orders the arrest of Rivers and Gray, Elizabeth's allies.

II.I Location: the palace

Edward forces the conflicting factions at court to make peace, but his health suffers after he hears of Clarence's death.

A flourish of trumpets sounds, and the sickly King Edward IV enters with his family, his wife's family, and his advisors. Edward says there has been too much quarreling among these factions and insists that everybody apologize and make peace. He also announces that he has sent a letter of forgiveness to the Tower of London, where his brother Clarence has been imprisoned and sentenced to death. (At this point, King Edward does not know that Richard has intercepted his message and had Clarence murdered.)

After a great deal of urging, King Edward finally gets the noblemen Buckingham and Hastings to make peace with Queen Elizabeth and her kinsmen, Rivers, Dorset, and Gray. Richard enters and, at the king's request, gives a very noble-sounding speech in which he apologizes for any previous hostility toward Buckingham, Hastings, or the queen's family, and presents himself as a friend to all. Peace seems to have been restored.

But when Elizabeth asks King Edward to forgive Clarence and summon him to the palace, Richard reacts as if Elizabeth is deliberately making fun of him. He announces Clarence's death to the group. He reminds Edward of his guilt in condemning Clarence to death and says that the cancellation of the sentence was delivered too slowly. The grieving, guilty Edward blames himself for his brother's death. Stanley, the earl of Derby, rushes in to beg the king to spare the life of a servant condemned to death. Edward angrily blasts his noblemen for not interceding to save Clarence when the king let his anger run away with him. Edward suddenly seems to grow sicker. He has to be helped to his bed.

II.II Location: elsewhere in the palace

The duchess of York mourns with her grandchildren and Elizabeth; Richard and Buckingham volunteer to bring the heir to the throne, Elizabeth's eldest son, to London.

The duchess of York—the mother of Richard, Clarence, and King Edward—comforts Clarence's two young children. The boy and girl ask their grandmother if their father is dead, and she lies and says he is not, in an attempt to spare their feelings. But the duchess knows that her evil son Richard killed his brother, and she grieves that she ever gave birth to him.

Elizabeth enters, lamenting out loud. She tells the duchess that King Edward has died, and the duchess joins her in mourning. The two children cry for their dead father, Clarence; Elizabeth cries for her dead husband, Edward; and the duchess cries for both of her dead sons, Edward and Clarence.

Elizabeth's kinsmen, Rivers and Dorset, remind Elizabeth that she must think of her eldest son, the prince. Young Prince Edward, named after his father, is the heir to the throne. He must be called to London and crowned. Richard enters, along with Buckingham, Hastings, Stanley, and Ratcliffe. Buckingham and Richard agree that the prince should be brought to London, and decide the two of them will go together to fetch him. All the others depart to discuss who should go to get the prince, but Richard and Buckingham linger behind. It is clear that Buckingham has become Richard's ally and accomplice. He says he has further ideas about how to separate the prince from Elizabeth and her family. Richard happily addresses Buckingham as his friend, right-hand man, and soulmate, and quickly agrees with Buckingham's plans.

II.III Location: a street in London

Three citizens discuss the worrisome state of the nation.

Three citizens discuss the state of national affairs and King Edward's death. Although one of them is optimistic about the future, saying Edward's son will rule, the others are very worried. Prince Edward, the oldest of the king's sons, is still too young to reign, and the two sides of his family—the kinsmen of Queen Elizabeth on one side (Rivers, Dorset, and Gray) and his uncle Richard on the other—are locked in a power struggle. The citizens see that Richard is dangerous, cunning, and thirsty for power. They say it would be better for the prince to have no uncles than to have uncles struggling over control of him and the country. They dread what the future will bring.

II.IV Location: the palace

Elizabeth and her allies learn that Rivers and Gray have been arrested on the order of Richard and Buckingham.

The cardinal, an ally of Elizabeth's family, tells Elizabeth, the duchess of York, and Elizabeth's youngest son that Prince Edward has nearly reached London and should arrive within two days. The marquis of Dorset arrives with terrible news. He says that Elizabeth's kinsmen, Rivers and Gray, have been arrested along with an ally of theirs named Sir Thomas Vaughan. They have been sent to Pomfret, a castle where prisoners are held and often killed. The order to arrest them came from Richard and Buckingham. Elizabeth and the duchess realize that this news probably means the beginning of the end for their family. They weep for their loss and for what is to come. Elizabeth decides to take her youngest son and flee to a place where, she hopes, Richard cannot come after them. The cardinal promises his support and gives Elizabeth the Great Seal of England.

ACT III

Hastings ignores the warnings of Stanley and is executed; Rivers, Gray, and Vaughan are executed; Richard tries and fails to convince the citizens that Hastings was a traitor; he agrees to become king after a show of reluctance.

III.I Location: a street in London

Prince Edward arrives and is brought to the Tower of London, along with his brother; Richard continues plotting his power grab with Buckingham and Catesby.

With a flourish of trumpets, Prince Edward, heir to the throne, rides into London with his retinue. His uncle Richard is there to greet him, accompanied by several noblemen, including Richard's close allies, the lords Buckingham and Catesby. The intelligent Edward is suspicious of his uncle and parries Richard's flattering language with wordplay as clever as Richard's own. The prince wants to know what has happened to his relatives on his mother's side—Rivers, Gray, and Dorset. (Although he does not tell

Prince Edward, Richard has had Rivers and Gray arrested and imprisoned in the castle of Pomfret. Dorset is presumably in hiding.)

Lord Hastings enters and announces that Elizabeth and her younger son, the duke of York, have taken sanctuary (that is, retreated to a church or other holy ground where, by ancient English tradition, it was blasphemous for enemies to pursue a fugitive). Buckingham is very irritated by this news. He asks the lord cardinal to go to Elizabeth and take young York from her, and he orders Hastings to accompany the cardinal and forcibly remove the young prince if Elizabeth refuses to yield him. The cardinal refuses, but Buckingham says a young child is not self-determining enough to claim sanctuary. The cardinal gives in and goes with Lord Hastings to fetch young York. By the time they return, Richard has told Prince Edward that he and his brother will stay in the Tower of London until the young prince's coronation, even though neither of the princes want to be shut up in the tower.

After the princes leave, Richard holds a private conference with Buckingham and Catesby to discuss the progress of his master plan. Buckingham asks Catesby whether he thinks Lord Hastings and Lord Stanley can be counted on to help Richard seize the throne. Although Lord Hastings is an enemy of Elizabeth and her family, Catesby believes that Hastings's loyalty to the dead King Edward IV would prevent him from supporting Richard's bid for the crown. Catesby believes that Lord Stanley will follow whatever Lord Hastings does.

Buckingham suggests that Richard hold a council in the palace on the following day, supposedly to discuss when to crown young Prince Edward. To determine which of the noblemen they can count on as allies, they will have "divided counsels" the following day, strategizing at a secret council and then holding a public counsel.

Buckingham and Richard order Catesby to go to Lord Hastings and find out if he might be willing to go along with Richard's plans. Richard says Hastings should be told that Queen Elizabeth's kinsmen, who are currently imprisoned in Pomfret Castle, will be executed the next day. He thinks this news will please Hastings, who has long been their enemy. After Catesby leaves, Buckingham asks Richard what they will do if Hastings remains loyal to Prince Edward. Richard says they will chop off Hastings's head. Buoyed by his plans, Richard promises Buckingham the title of earl of Hereford when he (Richard) is made king.

III.II   Location: Lord Hastings's home

Despite the ominous dream of his friend Stanley, Hastings refuses to fear Richard.

Early in the morning, a messenger knocks at the door of Lord Hastings's house. The messenger, who comes from Hastings's friend Lord Stanley, tells Hastings that Stanley has learned about the "divided counsels" that Richard plans to hold (III.i.176). The messenger says that Stanley had a nightmare in which a boar attacked and killed him. The boar is Richard's heraldic symbol, and Stanley is afraid for his own and Hastings's safety. He urges Hastings to flee with him on horseback before the sun rises.

Hastings tells the messenger to assure Stanley that there is nothing to fear. Catesby arrives at Hastings's house. When Catesby brings up the idea that Richard should take the crown instead of Prince Edward, Hastings recoils in horror. Seeing that Hastings will not change his mind, Catesby seems to drop the issue.

Stanley arrives, complaining of his forebodings, but Hastings cheerfully reassures him of their safety. Hastings goes off to the council meeting along with Buckingham, celebrating the news that Elizabeth's kinsmen will be executed.

III.III   Location: the prison at Pomfret Castle

Rivers, Gray, and Vaughan prepare for death.

Guarded by the armed Sir Richard Ratcliffe, the queen's kinsmen Rivers and Gray, along with their friend Sir Thomas Vaughan, enter their prison at Pomfret Castle. Rivers laments their impending execution. He tells Ratcliffe that they are being killed for nothing but their loyalty, and that their killers will eventually pay for their crimes. Gray says Margaret's curse has finally descended on them, and that their fate is punishment for complying in the Yorks' murder of Henry VI and his son. Rivers reminds Gray that Margaret also cursed Richard and his allies. He prays for God to remember these curses but to forgive the one Margaret swore against Elizabeth and her two young sons. The three embrace and prepare for their deaths.

III.IV   Location: the Tower of London

Richard accuses Hastings of treachery and condemns him to death.

At Richard's council session in the Tower of London, Hastings grows suspicious and asks the councilors why they are meeting. He says they are supposed to be discussing when to crown Prince Edward king. Derby affirms that this is the purpose of the meeting. Richard arrives, smiling and pleasant, and asks the bishop of Ely to send for a bowl of strawberries. Buckingham takes Richard aside to tell him that Hastings is loyal to the young princes and is unlikely to go along with Richard's plans to seize power.

When Richard reenters the council room, he pretends to be enraged and displays his arm, which everyone knows has been deformed since his birth. He says that Queen Elizabeth, conspiring with Hastings's mistress, Shore, must have cast a spell on him that withered his arms. When Hastings hesitates before accepting this speculation as fact, Richard accuses Hastings of treachery, orders his execution, and tells his men that he will not eat until he has been presented with Hastings's head. Left alone with his executioners, the stunned Hastings slowly realizes that Stanley was right. Richard is a manipulative, power-hungry traitor, and Hastings has been dangerously overconfident. Hastings cries out that Margaret's curse has descended on him.

III.V   Location: the palace

Richard makes plans to convince the people of London that Hastings was a traitor and turn them against the princes.

Richard questions Buckingham about his loyalty and his capabilities. Buckingham says he can lie, cheat, and kill, and is willing to do all of the above to help Richard. Now that Lord Hastings and Elizabeth's family have been killed, and the court is under Richard's control, Richard and Buckingham need to manipulate the common people of England so that Richard will be crowned king. First, they must make the lord mayor of London believe that Hastings was a traitor. Buckingham assures Richard that he is a good enough actor to pull off this feat.

The lord mayor enters the castle, followed by Catesby, who has Hastings's head. Buckingham tells the mayor about Hastings's alleged betrayal. He says that Hastings was plotting to kill him and Richard. Richard tells the lord mayor that Hastings confessed everything before his death. The mayor says he believes Richard and Buckingham just as if he heard Hastings's confession himself. He says he will tell all the people of London what a dangerous traitor Hastings was.

After the mayor departs, Richard, very pleased with their progress, tells Buckingham the next part of the plan: Buckingham is to make speeches to the people of London in which he will try to stir up bad feelings against the dead King Edward IV and the young princes, implying that the princes are not Edward's legitimate heirs. The goal is to make the people turn against the princes and demand that Richard be crowned king instead. While Buckingham is on this errand, Richard sends his other henchmen to recruit more allies. He himself makes arrangements to get rid of Clarence's children and ensure that no one can visit the young princes imprisoned in the tower.

III.VI   Location: a street in London

A scrivener says that he, like all of London, knows that Richard is lying about Hastings's guilt.

A scrivener (someone who writes and copies letters and documents for a living) says he has just finished copying the paper that will be read aloud to all of London later that day. The paper says that Hastings was a traitor. The scrivener condemns the hypocrisy of the world, for he, like everybody else, knows that the claim in the paper is a lie invented by Richard to justify killing his political rival.

III.VII   Location: the palace

Londoners react with horror to the idea of Richard as their king; after pretending he does not want the honor, Richard accepts the kingship at Buckingham's request.

Buckingham returns to Richard and reports that his speech to the Londoners was received very badly. Buckingham says he tried to stir up bad feelings about King Edward and his sons and then proposed that Richard should be king instead. Instead of cheering, the crowd just stared at him in terrified silence. Only a few of Buckingham's own men threw their hats in the air and cheered for the idea of King Richard. Buckingham had to end his speech quickly and leave.

Richard is furious to hear that the people do not like him, but he and Buckingham decide to go ahead with their plan anyway. Their strategy is to press the suggestible lord mayor to ask Richard to be king. They will pretend that this request represents the will of the people. Instead of seeming to desire the crown, Richard will pretend to accept it only for the good of the country.

Richard shuts himself up with two priests so that the lord mayor will believe that he spends a great deal of time in prayer. In a long and elaborately structured speech, Buckingham makes a show of pleading with Richard to accept the crown, which Richard finally does. Buckingham suggests that Richard be crowned the very next day, to which Richard consents.

ACT IV

Richard is crowned king and soon has Anne and the princes killed; Richmond and Buckingham amass forces to fight Richard.

IV.I Location: outside the Tower of London

While trying to visit the princes, Elizabeth and Anne learn that Richard is about to be crowned king.

Elizabeth, her son Dorset, and the duchess of York meet Lady Anne, who is now Richard's wife, and Clarence's young daughter. Lady Anne tells Elizabeth that they have come to visit the princes who are imprisoned in the tower, and Elizabeth says her group is there for the same reason. But the women learn from the guardian of the tower that Richard has forbidden anyone to see the princes.

Stanley, earl of Derby, arrives with the news that Richard is about to be crowned king. Anne must go to the coronation to be crowned queen. Anne fears that Richard's coronation will mean ruin for England, and says that she should have resisted marrying Richard, the man she cursed for killing her first husband. Her own curses have come true: Richard's wife, Anne herself, has no peace; and Richard is continually haunted by bad dreams. The duchess of York instructs Dorset to flee to France and join the forces of the earl of Richmond, a nobleman with a claim to the royal throne.

IV.II Location: the palace

Richard orders the princes killed and the rumor spread that Anne is sick.

Richard, now king of England, enters in triumph with Buckingham and Catesby. He says he does not yet feel secure in his position of power. He tells Buckingham that he wants the two young princes, the rightful heirs to the throne, to be murdered in the tower. For the first time, Buckingham does not obey Richard immediately, saying that he needs more time to think about the request. Richard murmurs to himself that Buckingham is too weak to be his right-hand man. He summons a lowlife named Tyrrell who is willing to accept the mission. Immediately, Richard instructs Catesby to spread a rumor that Queen Anne is sick and likely to die, and gives orders to keep the queen confined. He then announces his intention to marry the late King Edward's daughter, Elizabeth of York.

Buckingham, uneasy about his future, asks Richard to give him what Richard promised him earlier: the earldom of Hereford. Richard angrily rejects Buckingham's demands and walks out. Buckingham realizes he has fallen out of Richard's favor and decides to flee to his family home in Wales before he meets the fate of Richard's other enemies.

IV.III Location: the palace

Richard ruminates on his success with satisfaction; Ratcliffe announces that some of Richard's noblemen are fleeing to join Richmond's forces, and that Buckingham is amassing an army in Wales.

Tyrrell returns to the palace and tells Richard that the princes are dead. He says he has been deeply shaken by the deed and that the two men he commissioned to perform the murders are also full of regret after smothering the two children to death in their sleep. But Richard is delighted to hear the news and offers Tyrrell a rich reward. After Tyrrell leaves, Richard summarizes the development of his plots to get rid of everyone who might threaten his grasp on power. The two young princes are dead. Richard has married Clarence's daughter to an unimportant man and locked up Clarence's son, who is not very smart and does not present a real threat. Queen Anne is now dead (Richard presumably has had her murdered). He plans to woo and marry young Elizabeth, the daughter of the former King Edward and Queen Elizabeth. He believes that this alliance with her family will cement his hold on the throne.

Ratcliffe enters with the bad news that some of Richard's noblemen are fleeing to join Richmond in France, and that Buckingham has returned to Wales and is now leading a large army against Richard. Richard decides he must gather his own army and head out to face battle.

IV.IV   Location: the palace

Margaret advises Elizabeth on cursing; Richard tells Elizabeth he wants to marry her daughter.

Elizabeth and the duchess of York lament the deaths of the princes. Old Queen Margaret enters and says the duchess is the mother of a monster. Richard, she says, will not stop his campaign of terror until they are all dead. Margaret rejoices. She is glad to see her curses against the York and Woodeville families come true. She is still bitter about the deaths of her husband, Henry VI, and her son, Prince Edward, and says that the York deaths are fair payment.

Elizabeth asks Margaret to teach her how to curse, and Margaret advises her to experience as much bitterness and pain as Margaret herself has. Margaret then departs for France. When Richard enters with his noblemen and the commanders of his army, the duchess curses him, condemning him for the bloody murder of his extended family and telling him that she regrets giving birth to him. Enraged, Richard orders his men to strike up loud music to try to drown out the women's curses, but it does not work, and the duchess curses him to die a bloody death.

Although shaken, Richard recovers and pulls Elizabeth aside. He tells her he wants to marry her daughter, the young Elizabeth. Elizabeth is horrified and sarcastically tells Richard he should send her daughter the bloody hearts of her two little brothers as a gift to win her love. Richard, using all his gifts of persuasion and insistence, pursues Elizabeth, insisting that this way he can make amends to what remains of her family for all he has done before. He argues that the marriage is also the only way the kingdom can avoid civil war. Elizabeth seems to be swayed by his words and tells him she will speak with her daughter about it. As soon as Elizabeth leaves the stage, Richard calls her a foolish and weak-willed woman.

Richard's soldiers and army commanders bring him reports about Richmond's invasion. As bad news piles up, Richard gets panicky for the first time. Richmond is reported to be approaching England with a fleet of ships. Richard's allies are half-hearted and unwilling to fight the invader. All over Britain, noblemen have taken up arms against Richard. The only good news for Richard is that his forces have dispersed Buckingham's army and captured Buckingham. Richard learns that Richmond has landed with a mighty force. He leads out his army to meet Richmond in battle.

IV.V   Location: a house

Stanley tells a nobleman that he would desert Richard's side, but Richard has taken his son hostage.

Stanley, earl of Derby, meets a lord from Richmond's forces for a secret conversation. Richard is suspicious of Stanley and has insisted that Stanley give his son to him as a hostage so that Stanley will not desert. Stanley explains that this situation is all that prevents him from joining Richmond. But he sends his regards to the rebel leader, as well as the message that the former Queen Elizabeth has agreed that Richmond should marry her daughter, young Elizabeth. The other nobleman gives Stanley information about the whereabouts of Richmond and about the vast number of English noblemen who have flocked to his side. All are marching toward London to engage Richard in battle.

ACT V

Richmond defeats Richard.

V.I Location: Salisbury

Buckingham decides his execution is just punishment for all his folly.

An armed sheriff leads Buckingham to his execution. Buckingham asks to speak to King Richard, but the sheriff denies his request. Upon discovering that it is All-Souls Day, Buckingham's thoughts turn to repentance and judgment. He recalls promising King Edward IV that he would always stand by Edward's children and his wife's family. He remembers how certain he was that Richard would never betray him, and recalls Margaret's prophecy: "[R]emember this another day, / When he [Richard] shall split thy very heart with sorrow" (I.iii.297–298). Buckingham concludes that Margaret was right and that he deserves to suffer for his wrongdoing—for breaking his vows, for being an accomplice to foul play and murder, and for trusting Richard, who has broken his heart. He tells the officers to bring him to "the block of shame," and is led away to die (V.i.28).

V.II Location: the camp of Richmond's army

Richmond and his men eagerly prepare to fight Richard.

Richmond tells his men that he has just received a letter from his relative Stanley, telling him about Richard's camp and movements. Richard's army is only a day's march away. The men recall the crimes that Richard has perpetrated and the darkness he has brought to the land. A nobleman points out that none of Richard's allies are with him because they believe in his cause. They stay with him only out of fear and will flee when Richard most needs them. Eager to do battle, Richmond and his men march toward Richard's camp.

V.III Location: the camp of Richard's army

Richard tries to stir up some enthusiasm in his men.

Richard orders his men to pitch their tents for the night. He says that they will engage in battle in the morning. Richard tries to stir up some enthusiasm in his noblemen, but they are all subdued. Richard says he has learned that Richmond has only one-third as many fighting men as he does himself. He says he is confident that he can easily win.

V.IV Location: the camp of Richmond's army

Richmond sends a letter to his stepfather, Lord Stanley.

Richmond tells a messenger to deliver a secret letter to his stepfather, Lord Stanley, who is in an outlying camp. Stanley is forced to fight on Richard's side, but Richmond hopes to get some help from him nonetheless.

V.V Location: Richard's tent

Ghosts visit Richard to condemn him, and Richmond to prophecy success.

Richard issues commands to his lieutenants. He has an order sent to Lord Stanley telling him to bring his troops to the main camp before dawn, or else he will kill George, Lord Stanley's son. Declaring that he will eat no supper, Richard prepares to go to sleep.

Stanley pays a secret visit to Richmond in his tent. He explains the situation and promises to help Richmond however he can. Richmond thanks him and prepares for sleep.

As both leaders sleep, they begin to dream. A parade of the ghosts of everyone Richard has murdered—Prince Edward, King Henry VI, Clarence, Rivers, Gray, Vaughan, the two young princes, Hastings, Anne, and Buckingham—comes across the stage. Each ghost stops to speak to Richard, condemning him bitterly for his or her death and telling him he will be killed in battle the next morning. Each orders him to despair and die. The ghosts then speak to the sleeping Richmond, telling him that they are on Richmond's side and that Richmond will rule England and father a race of kings.

Richard wakes up sweating and gasping. In an impassioned soliloquy, he searches his soul to find the cause of such a terrible dream. Realizing that he is a murderer, Richard tries to figure out what he fears. He asks himself whether he is afraid of himself or whether he loves himself. He realizes that he does not have any reason to love himself and asks whether he doesn't hate himself, instead.

Ratcliffe comes to Richard's tent to let him know that the rooster has crowed and it is time to prepare for battle. Richard tells Ratcliffe of his terrifying dream, but Ratcliffe dismisses it, telling Richard not to be afraid of shadows and superstition.

In his camp, Richmond wakes and tells his advisers about his dream, which was full of good omens. Richmond gives a stirring oration to his soldiers, reminding them that they are defending their native country from a fearsome tyrant and murderer. Richmond's men cheer and head off to battle.

V.VI Location: the camp of King Richard's army

Richard learns that Stanley hhas mutinied.

Richard tells his army about the raggedness of the rebel forces and their opposition to himself, the rightful king. A messenger brings the bad news that Stanley has mutinied and refused to bring his army. There is not enough time even to execute young Stanley, for the enemy is already upon them. Richard and his forces head out to war.

V.VII Location: a battlefield

Richard loses his horse and looks for Richmond on foot.

The two armies fight a pitched battle. Catesby appears onstage and calls to Richard's ally Norfolk, asking for help for Richard. Catesby reports that the king's horse has been killed and the king is fighting on foot like a madman, challenging everyone he sees in the field as he attempts to track down Richmond himself.

Richard appears, calling out for a horse. But he refuses Catesby's offer of help, saying that he has prepared to face the fortunes of battle and will not run from them now. He says that Richmond seems to have filled the field with decoys, common soldiers dressed like Richmond. Richard has already killed five of them. He departs, seeking Richmond.

V.VIII Location: a battlefield

Richmond kills Richard, wins the battle, is crowned king, and announces his plans to marry young Elizabeth.

Richmond and Richard fight a bloody duel. Richmond kills Richard with his sword and runs back into battle. The noise of battle dies down and Richmond returns, accompanied by his noblemen. Richmond's side has won the battle. Stanley, swearing his loyalty to the new king, presents Richmond with the crown, which has been taken from Richard's body. Richmond accepts the crown and puts it on.

Relatively few noblemen have been killed, and Stanley's son, George, is still safe. Richmond, now King Henry VII, orders that the bodies of the dead be buried and that Richard's soldiers be given amnesty. He then announces his intention of marrying young Elizabeth, daughter of the former Queen Elizabeth and the late King Edward IV. The houses of Lancaster and York will be united at last, and the bloodshed will end. The new king asks for God's blessing for England and the marriage, and for a lasting peace.

ANALYSIS OF MAJOR CHARACTERS IN *RICHARD III*

RICHARD III

Richard is both the protagonist of the play and its major villain. Critics sometimes compare Richard to the medieval morality character Vice, who was a flat and one-sided embodiment of evil. But while Richard may cultivate this image of himself—he says "like the formal Vice, Iniquity, / I moralize two meanings in one word" (III.i.82–83)—he is highly self-reflective and complicated in a way that Vice could never be.

Richard is clearly a villain: he declares outright in his first speech that he intends to stop at nothing to achieve his nefarious designs. But despite his open allegiance to evil, he is such a charismatic and fascinating figure that he is almost sympathetic, or at least impressive. The audience's shifting perception of Richard mimics the characters' relationships with him. Lady Anne, for example, has an explicit knowledge of Richard's wickedness, but finds herself seduced by his brilliant wordplay and his relentless pursuit of his selfish desires.

Shakespeare uses monologues to control the audience's impression of Richard. In Act I, scene i, Richard claims that no one loves him because he is deformed, and that this lack of love has made him malicious. This claim, which casts the other characters as villains who cruelly scorn a cripple, makes it easy to sympathize with Richard during the first scenes of the play. But, it becomes clear that Richard's monologue was a manipulation. Richard uses his deformity as a tool to gain the sympathy of others and win their trust. He dupes us just as he dupes the people around him. After Richard's manipulations have won him the crown, his monologues end, he stops making an effort to win sympathy, and his monstrous nature becomes more apparent.

THE PRINCES

The most infamous crime of the historical Richard III was his murder of the two young princes in the Tower of London. For centuries after the death of Edward IV, the fate of the princes was a mystery—all that was known was that they had disappeared. People speculated that Richard had them killed, or that they had spent their entire lives as prisoners in the tower, or that they had escaped and lived abroad. The English author Sir Thomas More wrote that they were killed and buried at the foot of a staircase in the White Tower. Many years later, in 1674, workers in the Tower of London discovered two tiny skeletons in a chest buried beneath a staircase of the tower. The skeletons, which date from approximately the late fifteenth century, are the best evidence that the princes were murdered in the tower. There is no conclusive proof that it was Richard who had them murdered; some scholars think Richmond might have given the order. In Shakespeare's play, Richard orders the murder of the princes, highly intelligent boys who are the only characters to see through Richard's scheme entirely. The princes are courageous, standing up fearlessly to the powerful Richard. They are charismatic, outdoing Richard in games of wordplay. However, they are utterly helpless because they are so young. Shakespeare suggests that the princes, had they lived, would have grown up to be more than a match for their wicked uncle.

MARGARET

Though she plays a very minor role in the play's plot, mostly prowling around the castle and cursing to herself, Margaret is one of the most important and memorable characters in *Richard III*. The impotent, overpowering rage that she directs at Richard and his family stands for the helpless, righteous anger of all of Richard's victims. The curses she levels at the royals in Act I, which are among the most startling and memorable in all of Shakespeare's works, foreshadow future events. As the wife of the dead and vanquished King Henry VI, Margaret also represents the plight of women in patriarchal England. Without a husband to give her status and security, Margaret is reduced to depending on the charity of her family's murderers to survive.

THEMES, MOTIFS, & SYMBOLS IN RICHARD III

THEMES

THE ALLURE OF EVIL *Richard III* does not explore the cause of evil so much as it explores evil's operation. It shows Richard manipulating us and others, depicting the methods he uses to control, trick, and injure for his own gain. Richard is so skillful that he makes his victims complicit in their own destruction. Lady Anne allows Richard to seduce her even though she knows that he will kill her. Other characters allow themselves to be taken in by Richard's charisma, turning a blind eye to his dishonesty and violence. The audience likely has a similar reaction to Richard, shuddering at his actions but liking him because of his gleeful, brilliant, revealing monologues and perhaps even rooting for his success.

THE CONNECTION BETWEEN RULER AND STATE Several scenes, often called window scenes, suggest the way the drama in the royal palace affects the lives of the common people outside its walls. These scenes are the conversation of the common people in Act II, scene iii; Buckingham's speech to the masses and Richard's acceptance of the crown in Act III; and the scene of the scrivener in Act III, scene iv. As a history play, *Richard III* is at least briefly concerned with the consequences of the behavior of those in power, and with ideas of good leadership and governance. The common people are portrayed as savvy and important as a group. They come to fear and distrust Richard long before most of the nobles in the palace do, and their opposition to Richard is one of the main forces enabling Richmond to overthrow him. *Richard III* explores a theme Shakespeare revisits in *Hamlet* and *Macbeth*: the idea that the moral righteousness of a political ruler has a direct bearing on the health of the state. A state with a moral ruler will flourish, as Denmark does under King Hamlet, while a state with an immoral ruler will suffer, as Scotland does under Macbeth.

THE POWER OF LANGUAGE In *Richard III*, language is useful for achieving political power. Richard's extraordinary facility with words enables him to manipulate, confuse, and control those around him. Richard's skill with language and argument is what allows him to woo Lady Anne, have Clarence thrown in prison, keep the Woodevilles off his track, blame the king for Clarence's death, and achieve Hastings's execution—all at very little risk to himself. Language, Richard's most effective weapon, is also the defense his enemies use against him. When the princes match his skill at wordplay, they prove that they see through his schemes.

MOTIFS

THE SUPERNATURAL *Richard III* includes a great number of supernatural elements, including Margaret's prophetic curses, Clarence and Stanley's prophetic dreams, the allegations of witchcraft Richard levels at Elizabeth and Lady Shore, the continual association of Richard with devils and demons, Richard's comparison of himself to the shape-shifting Proteus, the princes' discussion of the ghosts of their dead uncles, and the parade of eleven ghosts that visits Richard and Richmond on the night before the battle. These supernatural elements create an atmosphere of dread and heighten the sense that Richard's evil reign transforms England into a Gothic netherworld.

DREAMS Clarence and Stanley have dreams that predict the future and contain important symbolism. Clarence dreams that Richard will make him drown at sea. Immediately after the dream, murderers hired by Richard drown Clarence in a cask of wine. Stanley dreams that Hastings will be gored by a boar—Richard's heraldic symbol. Immediately after the dream, Richard orders Hastings's execution.

SYMBOLS

THE BOAR The boar, Richard's heraldic symbol, symbolizes Richard. The boar, an ugly animal, suggests Richard's deformity. The duchess curses Richard as an "abortive, rooting hog" (I.iii.225). The boar was one of the most dangerous animals that people hunted in the Middle Ages and Renaissance, and Shakespeare's audience would have associated it with untamed aggression and uncontrollable violence.

IMPORTANT QUOTATIONS FROM RICHARD III

1. *Now is the winter of our discontent*
   Made glorious summer by this son of York;
   And all the clouds that loured upon our house
   In the deep bosom of the ocean buried.
   Now are our brows bound with victorious wreaths,
   Our bruisèd arms hung up for monuments,
   Our stern alarums changed to merry meetings,
   Our dreadful marches to delightful measures.
   Grim-visaged war hath smoothed his wrinkled front,
   . . .
   He capers nimbly in a lady's chamber
   To the lascivious pleasing of a lute.
   But I, that am not shaped for sportive tricks
   Nor made to court an amorous looking-glass;
   . . .
   Why, I in this weak piping time of peace
   Have no delight to pass away the time,
   Unless to spy my shadow in the sun
   And descant on mine own deformity.
   And therefore since I cannot prove a lover
   To entertain these fair well-spoken days,
   I am determined to prove a villain
   And hate the idle pleasures of these days.

Location: I.i.1–40
Speaker: Richard
Context: Richard addresses the audience

In these lines, Richard sets the scene, informing the audience that the play begins shortly after the death of Henry VI and the restoration of King Edward IV to the throne of England. Richard speaks of recent fighting, saying that "All the clouds that loured upon our house"—that is, the house of York—have been dispelled by the "son of York," King Edward, whose symbol is the sun. Richard paints a picture of the English people putting aside their arms and armor and celebrating in peace and happiness, of the god of war smoothing his rough appearance and playing the part of a lover in a woman's chamber. By using these images, Richard freely admits that England is an idyllic place under his brother, King Edward, and that he himself has no justification for seizing the throne. He goes on to admit that he intends to upset the kingdom by seizing power for himself. Richard offers an explanation for his villainy: he is deformed. He says that since he was not made to be a lover, he has no use for peace and will happily destroy it. This explanation may not convince us of anything other than Richard's villainy, but its stark honesty is fascinating.

2. *Thy friends suspect for traitors while thou liv'st,*
   And take deep traitors for thy dearest friends.
   No sleep close up that deadly eye of thine,
   Unless it be while some tormenting dream
   Affrights thee with a hell of ugly devils.
   Thou elvish-marked, abortive, rooting hog,
   Thou that wast sealed in thy nativity
   The slave of nature and the son of hell.
   Thou slander of thy heavy mother's womb.
   Thou loathèd issue of thy father's loins.

Thou rag of honour, thou detested—

Location: I.iii.220–230
Speaker: Margaret to Richard
Context: Margaret concludes her long diatribe against the Yorks and the Woodevilles

Margaret's speech and the scene that accompanies it foreshadow the ends of nearly all the major characters, including the deaths of the queen's kinsmen and Elizabeth's fall from grace. Here, Margaret foreshadows Richard's end by cursing him to mistake his friends for enemies and his enemies for friends. Her wish comes true: Richard eventually mistakes Buckingham for an enemy and Stanley for a friend. She also curses him to sleeplessness, which plagues him the night before the Battle of Bosworth Field, when the ghosts of his victims visit him.

---

3. *Methoughts that I had broken from the Tower,*
   And was embarked to cross to Burgundy,
   And in my company my brother Gloucester,

   . . .

   Methought that Gloucester stumbled, and in falling
   Struck me—that thought to stay him—overboard
   Into the tumbling billows of the main.

Location: I.iv.9–20
Speaker: Clarence to Brackenbury
Context: Brackenbury has asked Clarence to describe his dream

Clarence delivers this speech shortly before the murderers come to kill him in the tower. Clarence says that he dreamed he escaped from the tower and fled with Richard (Gloucester) to France, but on the ship, Richard betrayed him and cast him overboard. This, the first of several prophetic dreams in the play, contributes to the sense that supernatural forces are driving the plot. Clarence's dream foreshadows the closeness and the manner of his death. Clarence's speech reveals the depth of his trust in Richard. He refuses to contemplate the idea that Richard wishes him dead, even after dreaming that Richard will betray and kill him. Clarence's disbelief in his own dream suggests that Richard's evil is too monstrous for those around him to accept or imagine.

---

4. *Forbear to sleep the nights, and fast the days;*
   Compare dead happiness with living woe;
   Think that thy babes were sweeter than they were,
   And he that slew them fouler than he is.
   Bett'ring thy loss makes the bad causer worse.
   Revolving this will teach thee how to curse.

Location: IV.iv.118–123
Speaker: Margaret to the duchess and Elizabeth
Context: Margaret teaches the duchess and Elizabeth how to curse

Margaret tells the duchess and Elizabeth that in order to wrench the full power of anguish from language, one must wallow in misery, staying awake at night, going hungry during the day, and even remembering one's children as sweeter than they actually were. By giving this advice, Margaret reveals herself as a woman who has refused to forget her loss, try to feel better, or forgive the man who harmed her. Like the other women in the play, Margaret has little recourse beyond language. To use language as an effective weapon, she must continually inflict psychological violence on herself. When Richard appears in the middle of this scene, the women, one of whom is his own mother, turn on him with ferocious insults, indicating that they have internalized Margaret's advice and learned how to transform their pain into curses.

---

5. *The lights burn blue. It is now dead midnight.*
   Cold fearful drops stand on my trembling flesh.
   What do I fear? Myself? There's none else by.
   Richard loves Richard; that is, I am I.
   Is there a murderer here? No. Yes, I am.
   Then fly! What, from myself? Great reason. Why:
   Lest I revenge. Myself upon myself?
   Alack, I love myself. Wherefore? For any good
   That I myself have done unto myself?
   O no, alas, I rather hate myself
   For hateful deeds committed by myself.
   I am a villain.

Location: V.v.134–145
Speaker: Richard
Context: Ghosts of those he murdered have visited Richard

This speech is one of the only moments in the play in which Richard betrays any self-doubt, conscience, or regret for his brutal actions. "Cold fearful drops" of sweat cover him, and he realizes that fear fills him. To regain calm, Richard reminds himself that he is alone and therefore safe. But then he realizes that to be alone is to be alone with a murderer. He wonders if he should run from himself and worries that he will take revenge on himself. He asserts that he could not hurt himself because he loves himself. He realizes that he does not love himself, because he has never done anything good for himself. He admits that he "rather hate[s]" himself for his evil deeds. In the first speech of the play, Richard declared his determination "to prove a villain" (I.i.30). He now declares that he has become one ("I am a villain"). But rather than taking satisfaction in the achievement of his goal, Richard is suddenly afflicted with moral loathing and self-doubt, a development that may contribute to his downfall during the battle.

HENRY VIII

During the reign of Henry VIII, a series of powerful men and women of the kingdom fall from grace so that history can bring about the birth of Henry's daughter, Elizabeth.

HENRY VIII IN CONTEXT

Henry VIII is both a history play and a tragicomic romance, a genre that was gaining popularity in the early seventeenth century. The play focuses on the instabilities of the royal court in the late fifteenth and early sixteenth centuries. The most important event of *Henry VIII*, the occasion toward which all of the action moves, is the birth of Elizabeth, the future queen of England. Shakespeare suggests that fate or providence was guiding English history toward this moment, putting a complex series of events into motion and getting rid of anyone who stood in the way of Elizabeth's birth.

Henry VIII also depicts another significant moment in English history: England's religious break with Rome and the Catholic Church. In 1531, King Henry VIII, disappointed that his wife Catherine (spelled "Katherine" in this play) had borne him no male heirs, decided to divorce her. His advisors argued that the marriage was invalid, but the pope ruled against the divorce. Defying the pope's views, Henry divorced his wife and married Anne Boleyn in 1533. The Pope promptly excommunicated Henry. In response, Henry declared himself the head of the Church of England and seized the wealth of the monasteries. The rest of Henry's reign was beset by rebellions both small and large by groups who wanted to restore Catholicism or strengthen various religious reformation movements. *Henry VIII* does not depict the actual break with the pope, but it does show Henry's advisors discussing ways to negotiate a legal divorce and Cardinal Wolsey urging the pope to refuse Henry's request for a divorce.

After Henry's death, religious disagreement and rebellions wracked the country. His daughter, Queen Mary, reinstituted Catholicism as the official religion of England and ordered many bloody religious persecutions. When Queen Elizabeth came to the throne, she reversed Mary's orders and returned the kingdom to Protestant rule. But religious unrest continued. The frequent publi executions that took place following Henry's break with Rome and during the reigns of Mary and Elizabeth are prefigured in the execution of Buckingham.

Henry VIII contains a mild critique of its title character. At first Henry seems to be an inattentive king, content to let his aides takecare of business. But when he steps in to stop the trial of his friendCranmer, it seems possible that he always knew what was going on, and merely feigned inattention. Henry's divorce also comes in for criticism. No one believes he truly wants to divorce Katherine because he is worried about the legality of the marriage. Everyone thinks he merely wants to marry Anne Boleyn. Despite a compliment to James I, a descendent of Elizabeth's who was king at the time Shakespeare wrote *Henry VIII*, the criticism of Henry was probably also an indirect criticism of King James, who was known to neglect affairs of state.

While this play is now called *Henry VIII*, comments on early performances suggest it was originally titled *All Is True*. Early editors may have adapted the title to conform to Shakespeare's history plays, which are titled after English kings. The text is based not on an authorial manuscript but on a scribe's copy, which may have been later revised for performance. In the eighteenth century, some scholars made a case that Shakespeare collaborated on this play with John Fletcher, who succeeded Shakespeare as the principal author of Shakespeare's theater group. Scholars disagree on the details, but they agree that Shakespeare probably wrote most of the big scenes, while Fletcher may have had a hand in some of the minor ones. The language is consistent throughout, suggesting that Fletcher's role was small. Several long stage directions appear in scenes II.i and IV.i—characteristic of Fletcher's style rather than Shakespeare's—but there is no other conclusive evidence of collaboration.

During the June 29, 1613 performance of *Henry VIII*, the Globe Theater burned to the ground. Several small cannons were shot off during various scenes, and the thatch roof of the theater ignited. No one was hurt, but the theater was destroyed.

HENRY VIII: KEY FACTS

Full Title: The Famous History of the Life of King Henry the Eighth (All Is True)

Time and place written: 1611–1613, London (uncertain)

Date of first publication: 1623 (in First Folio)

Genre: History play; tragicomic romance

Setting (time): Sixteenth century

Setting (place): England

Protagonist: Henry VIII, Katherine

Major conflict: Internal conflict dogs Henry's court

HENRY VIII: CHARACTER LIST

Abergavenny   Buckingham's friend. Abergavenny is taken to the tower at the same time Buckingham is arrested.

Anne Boleyn   Henry's wife after Katherine. Aside from giving birth to Elizabeth, Anne has little to do as Henry's wife.

Brandon   A sergeant at arms. Brandon is sent to arrest Buckingham.

Buckingham   A powerful duke. Buckingham rails against Cardinal Wolsey, whom he believes unfairly influences the king. Buckingham is accused of plotting to gain the throne and is executed.

Buckingham's surveyor   A surveyor. He has a grudge against Buckingham, whose land he managed and who recently fired him because of complaints from the tenants. Cardinal Wolsey brings in the surveyor to speak against Buckingham at Buckingham's trial.

Butts   Henry's doctor. Butts knows the council is up to no good. He and Henry watch Cranmer's trial from a hidden spot.

Cardinal Campeius   An emissary from the pope. Campeius comes to assess the legality of Henry's divorce. It is not clear whether Campeius supports or opposes the divorce or whether he is a pawn of the pope's or of Wolsey's.

Capucius   An ambassador from the king of Spain. Henry sends Capucius to talk to Katherine, the daughter of the king of Spain. Katherine gives Capucius a letter asking Henry to care for their child and her servants.

Cardinal Wolsey   Henry's right-hand man. Wolsey is a scheming man who controls England's relationships with other countries and steals from fallen lords. After Henry learns of Wolsey's betrayal, he fires him, removes his royal protection, and takes his possessions. Eventually Wolsey decides his own arrogance and secret plotting were wrong.

Lord Chamberlain   A lord of the court. Lord Chamberlain is a member of the council that tries Cranmer.

Lord Chancellor   A lord of the court. Lord Chancellor presides over the council that tries Cranmer.

Cranmer   The Archbishop of Canterbury. As Cranmer travels, asking scholars what they think about the legality of Henry's divorce, Gardiner spreads rumors about him and plots his demise. Henry discovers Gardiner's scheming and gives Cranmer his protection. Cranmer baptizes Elizabeth.

Cromwell   A friend of Cardinal Wolsey's. Cromwell is devastated by Wolsey's fall from favor, but Wolsey encourages him to go back to Henry and to serve the state with honor and humility.

Denny   A lord of the court.

Elizabeth   Henry and Anne's daughter. Elizabeth will later be queen.

Gardiner   Cardinal Wolsey's secretary. Wolsey assigns Gardiner to Henry with the understanding that Gardiner will remain loyal to Wolsey. When Wolsey falls from grace, Gardiner receives a promotion and becomes a member of the council. Out of personal dislike and lingering loyalty to Wolsey, Gardiner tries to bring Cranmer down.

Gentleman   One of the many regular people who eagerly attends every significant event in the play, from Buckingham's sentencing to the Anne's coronation and the child's baptism.

Griffith   Queen Katherine's attendant. Griffith's kind elegy is filled with forgiveness and pity.

Guildford   A lord of the court.

King Henry VIII   The King of England. At the beginning of the play, Henry is under the powerful influence of Cardinal Wolsey, who manipulates him into doing away with Buckingham and divorcing Katherine. Henry eventually discovers Wolsey's manipulations and punishes him. Henry takes a more active role when his friend Cranmer is threatened. Henry fathers Elizabeth.

Lovell   A lord of the court.

Queen Katherine   The ex-wife of King Henry VIII's brother and Henry's wife as the play opens. Queen Katherine is the only one who suspects wrongdoing in Buckingham's trial. She refuses to let Cardinal Wolsey judge her and will not agree to divorce Henry. Despite Wolsey's pretended kindness to her, she charges him with being a traitor and plotting to bring her down. After hearing her attendants speak well of Wolsey, Katherine forgives him.

Norfolk   A lord of the court. Although at first Norfolk does not believe Buckingham's criticism of Cardinal Wolsey, eventually he turns against Wolsey. After Wolsey's demise, Norfolk receives a promotion. He takes part in a plot to bring down Cranmer.

Old Lady   Anne Boleyn's attendant.

Sands   A lord of the court.

Suffolk   A lord of the court. Suffolk is a member of the council that tries Cranmer.

Surrey   Buckingham's son-in-law and a lord of the court. Because of Buckingham's demise, Surrey turns against Cardinal Wolsey.

Vaux   A lord of the court.

HENRY VIII: PLOT OVERVIEW

The powerful Duke of Buckingham publicly criticizes the influence that the church leader, Cardinal Wolsey, has on King Henry, and is imprisoned for speaking out. After Wolsey produces a witness accusing Buckingham of disloyalty, Henry has Buckingham executed, despite Buckingham's eloquent defense. Henry falls in love with Anne Boleyn and petitions the pope for a divorce from his wife, Katherine. Katherine beseeches Henry not to divorce her after her years of faithful devotion, but Henry presses ahead. He discovers that Wolsey has betrayed him by urging the pope not to grant the divorce and by enriching himself with possessions seized from fallen lords. Henry strips Wolsey of his title and possessions and has him killed. Henry marries Anne Boleyn, who soon becomes pregnant. Henry's friend Cranmer, the Archbishop of Canterbury, is falsely accused by Henry's council and almost executed, but Henry rescues him. Cranmer is godparent at the christening of Henry's daughter, Elizabeth.

HENRY VIII: SCENE SUMMARY

PROLOGUE

Prologue tells the audience what to expect.

The character Prologue comes on stage and explains that what follows is a serious play. The events to come will inspire the audience's pity, bringing some members to tears. The play will also tell the truth. Those hoping for a bawdy, humorous play will be disappointed. The Prologue asks the audience to imagine that the noble characters of the play are alive and urges them to watch as mightiness leads to misery.

ACT I

Buckingham, who has criticized Wolsey, is arrested and accused of plotting against Henry's life; Henry meets Anne Boleyn at a party at Wolsey's house.

I.I Location: the court in London

Buckingham, who has criticized Wolsey, is arrested, as is Abergavenny.

The Duke of Norfolk, the Duke of Buckingham, and the Lord Abergavenny enter. Buckingham greets Norfolk and asks him how he has been since they met in France. Buckingham was confined to his tent with an illness, but Norfolk witnessed grandiose displays by the king of France and the king of England, who met on a field with forces to show off. Buckingham asks who had planned the glamorous scene, and Norfolk says Cardinal Wolsey organized it.

Buckingham rails against Wolsey's ambitious nature. Norfolk weakly defends him, but Abergavenny agrees that Wolsey displays undue pride. Buckingham says Wolsey gave the least honor to those who spent the most—the nobles who paid for the trip to France. Abergavenny speaks of nobles forced to sell off their property to afford to keep up with the court. Norfolk agrees that the peace between England and France may be more costly than is reasonable. But he warns Buckingham that Wolsey is a powerful man, prone to revenging himself on those who speak badly of him.

Wolsey enters with his aides. Glaring at Buckingham, he asks if one of Buckingham's estate overseers has arrived to give testimony against Buckingham. His aides say the man has arrived, and Wolsey and his train depart. Buckingham says he believes Wolsey is plotting against him. He thinks Wolsey is on his way to gossip to Henry about him, so he determines to rush to Henry's quarters first. Norfolk urges Buckingham to calm down and keep his anger from injuring his own case. Buckingham agrees to calm himself but repeats that he thinks Wolsey is corrupt and treasonous. Buckingham lists the charges against Wolsey to Henry: he is prone to mischief, he engineered the entire arrangement with France to benefit himself, he secretly deals with Charles V, the Holy Roman Emperor and king of Spain, and he buys and sells his honor to his own advantage. Norfolk is sorry to hear these charges and wonders if there could be a mistake, but Buckingham says there is none.

Brandon, the sergeant-at-arms, enters and announces he has arrived to arrest Buckingham in the name of the king and to take him to the Tower. Buckingham says goodbye to Abergavenny, but Brandon says he must arrest Abergavenny, too, along with several other men. Both submit to arrest. Buckingham sees he is done for and bids farewell to Norfolk.

I.II Location: a chamber in the court

The evidence of the surveyor convinces King Henry VIII that Buckingham was plotting to kill him.

King Henry VIII enters with Cardinal Wolsey and Sir Thomas Lovell. Henry ascends to his throne, thanks Wolsey for stopping the plots against him, and asks that Buckingham's estate manager be called in to speak. Queen Katherine enters with Norfolk and the Duke of Suffolk. She kneels before Henry and says she has been asked to speak on behalf of Henry's subjects, who are upset about the levying of new taxes. While the people complain mostly about Wolsey, the originator of the taxes, they also speak against Henry. Katherine warns there is a threat of rebellion. Henry says he has not heard about this tax, but Katherine reminds him that whether he created it or not, the people will hold him responsible for it.

Henry asks for more information, and Katherine explains that the tax is said to help pay for campaigns in France, which angers the people. Henry says this tax displeases him. Wolsey claims he only set it up because the judges told him to, but he urges Henry not to make changes just to please naysayers. Wolsey says that the public often views our best act as our worst one, and our worst as our best. Henry still thinks the tax is too much, so he undoes it and orders anyone who has been imprisoned for resisting payment released. Wolsey quietly instructs his secretary to let it be known that the tax was reduced through the encouragement of Wolsey himself.

Buckingham's surveyor, who ran Buckingham's estates, enters. Katherine tells Henry that she thinks it is a pity that Buckingham is out of favor. Henry agrees, but he thinks that advantageous positions sometimes lead to corruption, even in the seemingly wonderful Buckingham. Wolsey orders the surveyor to recount what he knows of Buckingham.

The surveyor says that he heard Buckingham say he wanted to succeed Henry should Henry die without a male heir. Apparently, a friar had led Buckingham to believe that he could be in line to the throne, and Buckingham shared this information with his friends. Katherine notes that Buckingham fired the surveyor because of complaints from the tenants, and the surveyor may be trying to get revenge on Buckingham. But Henry urges the surveyor to continue. The surveyor says Buckingham declared he would have Wolsey and Lovell killed if Henry died and then gain the throne himself. He also says that Buckingham contrasted himself to his father, who refrained from stabbing Richard III to death, saying he will appear loyal but kill Henry. Henry, now convinced that Buckingham is a traitor who intends to assassinate him, calls for a trial.

I.III Location: the court

Chamberlain and Sands discuss French fashion and then head to Wolsey's house with Lovell.

Chamberlain and Sands discuss the oddity of the nobles' behavior since they returned from France. The nobles have taken up ridiculous continental fashions and manners. Lovell enters and speaks of proposed reformations urging the returned nobles to give up French-influenced styles. The three agree that such reformations are the right idea. Lovell says he is on his way to a great dinner celebration at Wolsey's house, to which the lords Chamberlain and Sands are also invited. They agree that Wolsey is generous and set out for his house.

I.IV Location: a hall in Westminster

King Henry and some of his men go to Wolsey's party in disguise; Henry meets Anne Boleyn.

Guildford makes a dedication to begin the events at Wolsey's house, welcoming the guests. Chamberlain, Lovell, and Sands arrive. Sands flirts with Anne Boleyn, Wolsey enters the party and strangers arrive. They are shepherds from France who heard talk of Wolsey's party and were so impressed that they had to attend. Wolsey invites them in. The shepherds are really King Henry and some of his men in disguise. The shepherds dance with the ladies, and Henry dances with Anne. He is very taken with her beauty. Wolsey strolls among the shepherds and sees through Henry's disguise, unmasking him. Henry asks Chamberlain about Anne. Telling Anne it is bad manners to dance with her without kissing her, Henry kisses her. He goes to a private banquet room with his men, promising Anne that he will not forget her.

ACT II

The Duke of Buckingham is condemned to death; King Henry decides to divorce Queen Katherine, who objects strongly and suspects the influence of Wolsey.

II.I Location: a street in Westminster

Buckingham, who has been condemned to death, makes a humble, moving speech in front of some citizens.

Two gentlemen meet. One reports that he has been to the trial of the Duke of Buckingham. Buckingham has been found guilty and sentenced to death, even though he pleaded not guilty and spoke eloquently in his own defense. The gentlemen agree that Cardinal Wolsey is behind the fall of Buckingham and has been busy sending any lords favored by Henry to distant parts or to jail. Apparently, "All the commons / Hate [Wolsey] perniciously and, o' my conscience, / Wish him ten fathom deep" (II.i.50–52).

Buckingham enters guarded by soldiers and accompanied by Lovell, Sands, Vaux, and a crowd of commoners. He addresses the people, saying a traitor has condemned him, but he bears the law no ill will. He forgives those who have done him wrong and asks those who have loved him to weep for his death, then forget him. Lovell asks Buckingham to forgive him, which he does.

Vaux must accompany Buckingham to the river, where a barge waits to take him to his death. He offers to make the barge fit for a duke, but Buckingham stops him. He says he came to the court with a high position and now leaves it as a poor man stripped of titles. Buckingham speaks of his father, who was killed by the king he stayed loyal to, Richard III. The father of King Henry VIII, who came to the throne after deposing Richard III, pitied Buckingham and restored his title and nobility, but now King Henry VIII has taken it all back. Both Buckingham and his father were brought down by men they served loyally.

Buckingham counsels the audience to be careful with their loyalty and love, saying people you befriend will leave you at the slightest provocation: "those you make friends / And give your hearts to, when they perceive / The least rub in your fortunes, fall away / Like water from ye, never found again / But where they mean to sink ye" (II.i.128–132). Officers lead him away.

The gentlemen agree that Buckingham's fate is very sad. They have heard that Henry wishes to separate from Queen Katherine and suspect Wolsey has urged Henry to this, perhaps because he wants Henry to marry someone else. Cardinal Campeius has arrived from Rome to discuss the matter, which suggests that the rumor is true. The gentlemen speculate that Wolsey wants to get back at Katherine's father, the Holy Roman Emperor and king of Spain, who failed to give him a job in the past.

II.II Location: the court

After speaking to an emissary from the pope, King Henry says he must leave Katherine because his conscience demands it.

Chamberlain enters, reading a letter from one of his employees. The letter says that Cardinal Wolsey's men seized several of Chamberlain's horses, claiming they must be given to Henry. Chamberlain says he thinks Wolsey will end up taking everything from the nobles. Norfolk and Suffolk enter, asking after Henry. Chamberlain notes that Henry is brooding about his marriage to Katherine, perhaps worrying that it was illegal. Suffolk thinks it is more likely that Henry is thinking about another woman. Norfolk says Wolsey planted the idea that Henry's marriage could be annulled. Norfolk is astonished that Wolsey has managed to engineer a break with the king of Spain and convinced Henry to cast off his loyal wife of twenty years. Chamberlain hopes one day Henry's eyes will be opened to Wolsey's scheming.

Chamberlain exits, and Suffolk and Norfolk go to speak to Henry. Henry is not pleased to see them and ignores them as soon as Wolsey and Cardinal Campeius enter. Henry dismisses Suffolk and Norfolk, who leave muttering that they do not trust Campeius, an envoy from the pope.

Wolsey says that no one could be angry with Henry for leaving Katherine, because the pope has been asked to arbitrate Henry's decision. Campeius embraces Henry and gives him papers that detail his judgment of the situation. Henry sends for his new secretary, Gardiner, to plan for a reading of the decision. Gardiner was formerly Wolsey's secretary, which Wolsey reminds Gardiner as he enters. Gardiner whispers back that his first loyalties are still to Wolsey. Henry and Gardiner go off to talk, and the two cardinals discuss the downfall of the previous secretary.

Henry announces that they will go to Blackfriars to make the announcement about his decision to leave Katherine. He is grieved to leave such a good wife, but he says his conscience demands the move.

II.III Location: Katherine's apartments in London

Anne Boleyn discusses Queen Katherine's plight with her attendant; Chamberlain announces that Henry has given Anne a new title and a larger annual income.

Outside Queen Katherine's quarters, Anne Boleyn and her attendant, an old lady, discuss the downfall of Katherine. Anne is saddened that Katherine lived for so long without reproach and is nonetheless about to fall from grace. Anne thinks Katherine's demise will be all the more bitter because she has known such heights. She suggests it may be better to be poor and happy than rich and miserable.

Anne says she herself would never want to be a queen. The old lady assures her that she would, since all women desire wealth, eminence, and sovereignty. The old lady says she would consent to be a queen for mere pocket change, but Anne insists that nothing could convince her.

The Chamberlain enters with a message from Henry, who has such a high opinion of Anne that he wants to honor her with a new title and an increased annual income. Anne says the only thing she can give in return is thanks. On his way out, Chamberlain notes to himself that Anne has such a wonderful mix of beauty and honor that she could not help but attract Henry's eye. He suspects that "from this lady may proceed a gem / To lighten all this isle" (II.iii.78–79).

The old lady exclaims that she has been working at the court for sixteen years without improving her situation, whereas Anne has received these blessings almost without effort. She believes that Anne's new title, given merely as a sign of respect and without requiring any obligation, promises more gifts in the future. Anne quiets the old lady and worries about what will happen next. Before returning to comfort Katherine, she asks the old lady not to mention her new title to Katherine.

II.IV   Location: a hall at Blackfriars

The divorce proceedings begin, but Katherine appeals to Henry, criticizes Wolsey, and refuses to stay.

Many official types enter a hall at Blackfriars, including bishops, dukes, and scribes. Cardinal Wolsey, Cardinal Campeius, and Henry and Katherine enter. Wolsey calls for silence while the report from Rome is read, but Henry says it has already been read and there is no need to read it again. Queen Katherine kneels at Henry's feet and asks him to have pity on her, a stranger in a foreign kingdom. She asks how she has offended Henry, what she has done to make him want to cast her off. She says she has been a true and loyal wife, always obeying him in every matter for twenty years, and bearing many children by him. She reminds him that Henry's father and her father, Henry of Spain, were wise men who agreed that their marriage was lawful. She begs Henry to allow her time to receive counsel from Spain before submitting to a trial.

Wolsey declares that the many learned men on hand cannot sway Henry from his course, so there is no point in delaying the proceedings. Campeius agrees that they should proceed. Katherine addresses Wolsey, saying she believes he is her enemy, but she will not allow him to be her judge. She believes he has arranged this divorce. Wolsey says she wrongs him. He claims to have nothing against her and says the divorce has been discussed by many people other than himself. He denies stirring up trouble and says he hopes Henry will defend him against Katherine's assault.

Katherine says she is unable to defend herself against Wolsey's cunning. She accuses him of being arrogant and proud and of going beyond the power of his office to influence Henry. She repeats that she will not be judged by him and starts to leave. Campeius and Henry call her back, but she insists that she will not appear during the rest of the proceeding and leaves.

Henry lets her go, saying that no man has had a better wife than the noble and obedient Katherine. Wolsey asks Henry to say whether he has influenced him unduly with regard to Katherine, and Henry clears him of wrongdoing. Henry explains how he came to doubt his marriage to Katherine. An ambassador from France, in the process of negotiating for the hand of Henry's daughter, asked if she was legitimate. His question set Henry thinking. He thought he must not be doing right in the eyes of heaven, since all of his children by Katherine were either born dead or died soon after birth or were girls. Believing this to be a sign that Katherine was unfit to be queen, he started the divorce process, despite his feelings for her. Henry says he first spoke to some of his nobles about his plans, later asking the opinion of all his men.

Campeius says they must adjourn until another day when Katherine is present to complete the divorce. Henry notes to himself that he does not like the tricks of these cardinals and has no respect for Rome. He looks forward to the return of Cranmer, his trustworthy religious advisor.

ACT III

Katherine continues to resent her accusers; Wolsey falls from Henry's favor.

III.I   Location: Katherine's apartments in London

Cardinals Wolsey and Campeius speak to Katherine but fail to convince her that they mean well.

Cardinal Wolsey and Cardinal Campeius arrive at Katherine's apartments and ask to speak to her in private. Katherine's conscience is clear, so she is content to converse in a public room. Wolsey says he has come not to accuse her, but to learn her thoughts on the dissolution of her marriage and to offer advice. Katherine does not believe Wolsey and Campeius have come on an honorable errand, but nevertheless she voices thanks for their efforts. She says she is alone, without friends or hope. Wolsey insists that she does have friends in England, but Katherine disagrees. Campeius advises Katherine to put her hope in Henry and believe that he will protect her when they are divorced. Katherine accuses them of corruption and reminds them that God will judge them.

Katherine tells the cardinals that she thought they were holy men and is shocked to see their apparent pleasure in making her life wretched. She cannot believe they would advise her to put her future in the hands of one who has already rejected her. The cardinals tell her she is mistaken. Katherine says her obedience and honor have been rewarded with dishonorable divorce, and moreover that only death will take the title of queen from her. She wishes she had never come to England, a place full of flattery and untruth.

Wolsey breaks in to insist that their goals are honorable, that they want to ease her sorrow, and that she misunderstands them. As peacemakers, they suggest that she try to stay in Henry's good favor. Campeius assures her that Henry loves her, and he promises they will try to help her. Katherine tells them to do whatever they want, saying sarcastically that if she has misunderstood their intentions, it is because she is a woman, lacking understanding.

III.II Location: the court

Wolsey falls from grace.

Norfolk, Suffolk, Chamberlain, and Surrey enter. Norfolk says they should combine their complaints against Cardinal Wolsey, who would not be able to withstand a united front. Chamberlain says the only way to get at Wolsey is to keep him away from Henry. Norfolk says Henry is already displeased with Wolsey, because Wolsey's double-dealing in the divorce proceedings has come to light. Suffolk explains that Henry intercepted Wolsey's letters to the pope in which Wolsey urged the pope to deny Henry the right to divorce until Henry had gotten over his infatuation with Anne Boleyn. Chamberlain reveals that Henry has already married Anne. Suffolk compliments Anne, whom he thinks will bring blessings to the land. Suffolk says that Cranmer will soon return from consulting scholars about the legality of Henry's remarriage, and thereafter the new marriage will be publicized and Katherine will be demoted to "Princess Dowager."

Wolsey and Cromwell enter, and the other lords stand aside to observe them. Wolsey asks about the delivery of his letters. Cromwell leaves, Wolsey comments to himself that Henry will marry the French king's sister, not Anne Boleyn, who is a Lutheran and will make Henry hard to control. He also talks to himself about Cranmer, who is now in favor with Henry. The lords cannot hear Wolsey speak, but they can tell he is angry about something.

Henry enters with Lovell, muttering to himself about the wealth Wolsey has accumulated. He asks the lords if they have seen Wolsey, and they tell him Wolsey is nearby and strangely upset. Henry says it may be because of some papers Henry just saw that detail Wolsey's surprisingly large fortune. Henry tells Wolsey he must be too busy contemplating spiritual matters to consider the earthly world, but Wolsey says he has time for both. Henry reminds Wolsey that he served under Henry's father and has been a right-hand man throughout Henry's own reign. Wolsey says that the praise Henry has showered on him has been more than enough reward for his efforts and that all his work has been aimed at the good of Henry and the profit of the country. Wolsey declares his loyalty, and Henry says he sounds like a loyal servant. He comments that loyalty and obedience reward the servant with honor, and disloyalty and corruption reward the servant with dishonor. Wolsey repeats that he has always worked for good and honorable ends.

Henry gives Wolsey the papers he has intercepted and exits with the nobles. Wolsey looks at the papers and immediately realizes his career is over. The first paper is the inventory of the wealth Wolsey has accumulated for his own ends. The second paper is his letter to the pope. Norfolk, Suffolk, Surrey, and Chamberlain reenter and announce that Henry has ordered Wolsey to give over the seal of his office and stay in his house. Wolsey, unwilling to step down before these lesser lords, accuses them of envy. He says they are too eager to watch Wolsey's disgrace and fall and says he prefers to give the seal directly to Henry.

Surrey accuses Wolsey of ambitiously and heartlessly bringing about the death of Surrey's father-in-law, Buckingham, and sending Surrey away to Ireland so he could not protest the death. Wolsey says he did not have any private malice toward Buckingham and reminds Surrey that a jury sent Buckingham to his death. Surrey, angered by Wolsey's arrogant speech, reminds Wolsey of his efforts to take the lands and holdings of other nobles and the scheme he had been cooking up with the pope against Henry. Norfolk tells Wolsey that he has a set of articles Henry wrote listing Wolsey's faults. Wolsey says his innocence will be found when Henry knows of his loyalty.

The lords begin to read the articles against Wolsey. The first accuses him of scheming to become a papal representative without Henry's assent or knowledge. The next accuses him of writing to the pope without Henry's knowledge or permission. Wolsey is declared guilty of other, smaller political schemes, including sending bribes to the pope. Chamberlain stops the proceedings, saying they should not pile on Wolsey. Surrey says he forgives Wolsey, and Suffolk finishes Henry's articles with the announcement that all Wolsey's goods shall be forfeited and he shall lose Henry's protection. The lords depart to tell Henry of Wolsey's refusal to give up the seal.

Alone, Wolsey considers the fate of men. One sprouts like a tender plant, then blooms. Then a frost comes and brings death just when one was on the verge of ripening into greatness. "I have ventured," he says, "far beyond my depth" (III.ii.359, 362). His pride was not enough to support him, and now he must fall prey to opinion. He curses the pomp and glory of the world and his own efforts to win Henry's favor.

Cromwell enters and weeps at Wolsey's misfortunes. Wolsey tells him not to weep, saying he knows himself now and is at peace. He has been cured by Henry and is glad to be unburdened. Now, he says, he can bear more misfortunes than his enemies could bear.

Cromwell says Henry has appointed Sir Thomas More to Wolsey's position, Cranmer has returned, and Anne is officially the new queen. Wolsey says his sun has set and sends Cromwell to Henry, whose sun he prays will never go down. He assures Cromwell that Henry will promote him. Cromwell is saddened and says that while Henry may have his service, Wolsey will have his prayers. Wolsey weeps and tells Cromwell to remind the world, once Wolsey has been forgotten, that Wolsey taught Cromwell how to avoid the pitfalls of honor and dishonor. He advises Cromwell to forget his ambition, to love himself last, and to cherish those who hate him. "Corruption wins not more than honesty," he says, and urges Cromwell to be just (III.ii.445). Wolsey exhorts Cromwell to serve Henry above all.

ACT IV

Anne receives the crown and becomes queen, and Katherine prepares to die.

IV.I Location: a street in Westminster

Three gentlemen discuss Anne's coronation ceremony.

One gentleman meets another in the city street. They wait to see Anne, the new queen, pass on the way to her coronation. The last time they met in the street was for the sad event of Buckingham's trial, so they are glad for a return to the more usual pomp of the royalty. They discuss all those who are to be promoted today, including Suffolk and Norfolk, and note that Katherine has been renamed "Princess Dowager."

Suffolk, Norfolk, Anne, Surrey, and other important state officials pass by. The gentlemen are impressed with Anne. A third gentleman arrives and describes the coronation ceremony, which he just saw. He says everyone was amazed by Anne's beauty. The Archbishop of Canterbury, Cranmer, performed the ceremony, the choir sang, and the procession went to the court to celebrate. The third gentlemen notes that Gardiner was there. Gardiner is not fond of Cranmer, but the gentlemen agree that nothing can come of this rivalry, since Cranmer has one friend who will not abandon him—Cromwell, who is in favor with Henry and just got a promotion.

IV.II Location: Katherine's apartments in Kimbolton

Katherine prepares to die.

Katherine asks her attendants to tell her about the death of Cardinal Wolsey. Her attendant Griffith explains that after his arrest, Wolsey grew ill and died a broken man. Katherine says she will speak of him with charity but says his enormous ambition shackled Henry's kingdom. He used bribes for ecclesiastical favors, he lied, and he set a bad example for the clergy.

But Griffith speaks well of Wolsey, calling him a good scholar, a kind and generous friend, and a patron of education. After Henry found him out, Wolsey discovered humility and died fearing God. Katherine says she hopes Griffith will eulogize her when she dies, since he speaks so well. Griffith's words have made her want to honor the man she hated most. She wishes Wolsey peace in death.

Katherine goes to sleep with her attendants by her. She sees a vision of six people in white robes with garlands around their heads. They dance around Katherine, offering her a garland, and then dance away. Katherine wakes and calls to her attendants, asking if they have seen anything. She tells them about the vision, saying it promised her eternal happiness. The attendants tell each other Katherine has not long to live if she is seeing such visions.

A messenger enters, announcing the arrival of Capucius, an ambassador from Katherine's father, Charles V of Spain. Capucius says Henry sent him to ask after her health, but Katherine says he is too late—she is already dying. She gives Capucius a letter for Henry, in which she asks Henry to care for their daughter and to provide for her servants. Katherine says she will soon die and not be a trouble to Henry. Calling to her servants, she prepares for bed.

ACT V

Henry prevents Cranmer's imprisonment; Elizabeth is baptized.

V.I Location: a gallery in London

As Anne gives birth, Henry reassures his recently accused friend Cranmer.

Late at night, Gardiner and Lovell meet. Gardiner asks why Lovell is in such a rush. Lovell reports that Queen Anne is in labor. Gardiner says he wishes her well, but he thinks she may not be of the best stock to mother the heir to the throne. Gardiner thinks the kingdom will not be safe until Anne is dead, along with Cranmer and Cromwell. Lovell reminds him that those two men are in the highest favor with Henry. But Gardiner says he has already denounced Cranmer as a heretic, and Cranmer will appear before a council in the morning for examination. They must root out bad weeds, Gardiner declares. He departs.

Henry and Suffolk enter and ask Lovell for a report on Anne's labor. Henry says he has to think and sends Suffolk away. Denny enters with Archbishop Cranmer. Henry sends Lovell and Denny away. Henry tells Cranmer that he has heard many bad complaints about him, and he will have to appear before the council about them. Cranmer must be imprisoned while the complaints are investigated, and Henry asks him to be patient. Cranmer thanks Henry for his warning, saying he knows how he is subject to rumors. Cranmer says he fears nothing that can be said against him, but Henry reminds Cranmer that he has many enemies. He asks if corrupt men may be convinced to testify against Cranmer, which would ruin his case for innocence. Cranmer thinks he will inevitably fall into a trap set for him.

Henry tells Cranmer that if the council decides to imprison him, he should argue forcefully against the decision. Henry gives Cranmer his ring and tells him to show it to the council if they try to cart him away, and then Henry himself will be authorized to hear Cranmer's appeal. Cranmer weeps in thanks, and Henry says Cranmer is the best soul in his kingdom. Cranmer departs.

The old lady and Lovell enter to tell Henry of the birth of his child. He asks her to tell him it is a boy, so she does, even though it is actually a girl. The old lady says the baby resembles him, and Lovell and Henry rush out to see it.

V.II Location: a chamber at court

The council moves to imprison Cranmer, but Henry prevents them.

Cranmer enters, hoping he is not late for the council meeting. The doorkeeper says he must wait until he is called. Doctor Butts crosses the stage, saying malice is afoot if the council members are requiring Cranmer, himself a member of the council, to wait outside. Henry and Butts go to observe the council from a window, and Butts tells Henry how Cranmer has been forced to wait at the door. Henry is surprised that the council would be so rude. He says there is one above them who will judge them.

The council enters, consisting of Chancellor, Suffolk, Norfolk, Surrey, Chamberlain, Gardiner, and Cromwell. They allow Cranmer to enter. The Chancellor says he has heard complaints that Cranmer has been teaching heretical new opinions and ideas around the kingdom. Gardiner speaks more harshly, saying they must swiftly deal with such bad behavior or the state will fall.

Cranmer says he has always taught correct teachings and has never tried to disturb the public peace. He says he would like to hear what his accusers have to say. Because Cranmer is a council member himself, no one can bring complaints against him, so they plan to imprison Cranmer in the tower. This will return him to the status of a common man and allow people to accuse him openly. Cranmer responds kindly to Gardiner, saying that love and humility serve churchmen more than ambition. Cranmer doubts that Gardiner is acting ethically, but he will submit to his decision. Gardiner accuses Cranmer of being a Protestant, but Cromwell tells Gardiner to hold his tongue. Gardiner lashes out against Cromwell and accuses him of favoring Protestants. The two men argue viciously until Chancellor stops them.

Chancellor tells Cranmer that he will be conveyed to the Tower. A guard enters to take him away, and Cranmer reveals that he is wearing Henry's ring. The members of the council realize they have made a mistake in targeting Cranmer, not realizing how much he was in favor with Henry. Henry and Butts come down to the council.

Gardiner addresses Henry and gives thanks for having a king who wants to strengthen the church. Henry says that Gardiner is a master flatterer, but he isn't interested in flattery now, and he believes Gardiner has bloody plots in mind. Henry tells the council that he thought they were men of understanding and wisdom, but he sees he was wrong. He says it was cruel to make Cranmer, their equal, wait outside the council door. He had given them the authority to try Cranmer, but some would simply send him to the Tower to rot. Chancellor disagrees, saying they really did want to imprison Cranmer in the Tower simply to allow for full investigation of the charges against him. Henry urges them to trust Cranmer, since he himself does, and tells them all to embrace and be friends.

Henry asks the council to baptize his young daughter. Gardiner is slow to embrace Cranmer, so Henry urges him again. Cranmer weeps, and Henry recalls an old saying: even if you do wrong by the Archbishop of Canterbury, he will still be your friend.

V.III Location: the palace courtyard

A large crowd waits for Elizabeth's baptism.

A porter and a large group of men enter. The crowd has arrived to see Elizabeth's christening. The porter thinks the crowd is made up of the same louts who go to public executions and cheer loudly at the playhouse. Chamberlain enters and yells at the porter for letting the crowd block so much space. Chamberlain thinks the crowd is made up of people from the suburbs. The royals arrive, and the porter shouts at the crowd to make way.

V.IV Location: the court

Elizabeth is baptized.

Cranmer, Norfolk, Suffolk, and other noblemen enter the scene with the baby Elizabeth. Henry enters. Cranmer baptizes Elizabeth and makes a speech about her future greatness. He says she holds great promise for England, and few can imagine the great things she will accomplish. She will know truth, she will be loved and feared, and she will be a great ruler. When she dies, she will be reborn like a phoenix in her heir, and all her good attributes will carry on in the next ruler. Henry is amazed at the wonders of which Cranmer speaks. Cranmer goes on to announce that Elizabeth will bring happiness to England, and when she dies a virgin, the world will mourn her. Henry is pleased with Cranmer's words and says that with this child he finally feels he has accomplished something great. He looks forward to seeing what she will do from his future home in heaven.

EPILOGUE

Summary

Epilogue enters, saying it is likely that the play did not please its audience. Some may have dozed for a few acts, only to be woken by the trumpets. Others may have come to hear the court ridiculed and been disappointed. The only praise Epilogue anticipates will come from good women, who likely enjoyed the characterization of Katherine. If the ladies clap, their men will surely follow.

THEMES, MOTIFS, & SYMBOLS IN *HENRY VIII*

THEMES

THE DANGEROUS ALLURE OF POWER   Power seduces almost everyone in *Henry VIII*, with tragic results. Every character who falls from grace, except the saintly Katherine, has at least some aspiration to power. Buckingham may have had designs on the throne. Wolsey longs for wealth and power. Anne Boleyn, who swears that "By my troth and maidenhead, / I would not be a queen" (II.iii.23–24), may have a hidden interest in marrying a king. But power itself, not character flaws, corrupts these characters, none of whom are evil at heart. Even the scheming Wolsey receives such high praise from Griffith after his fall that his archenemy, Katherine, is moved to forgive him. The downfall of these characters demonstrates not an inner propensity for wickedness that must be punished, but rather the corrupting power of success.

THE FALL OF THE MIGHTY   Many tragedies feature the downfall of one central character. *Henry VIII* features the downfall of three: first Buckingham is ruined, then Katherine, then Wolsey. Anne's ruination is implied, although the play does not show it happening. The very number of these falls makes disgrace seem like not just the fault of scheming enemies, but an inevitable component of life. During the Renaissance, many people conceived of life as a "wheel of fortune," in which those who lived at the top for a while would eventually fall to the bottom as the wheel turned. Like the wheel of fortune rubric, *Henry VIII* suggests that shifts in power are natural and inescapable.

The great number of failures also makes Henry's stability look impressive by comparison. He seems almost unnaturally invincible, maintaining a firm hold on power while everyone around him crumbles. Henry VIII's reign, and that of his daughter Elizabeth, was recent enough when Shakespeare was writing to influence Shakespeare's depiction of him. But his invincibility also concludes Shakespeare's history plays on a comforting, stabilizing note. After the violent usurpation of Richard II's crown by Henry IV and the bloody rebellions and wars of the Henry VI tetralogy, *Henry VIII* ends with an optimistic picture of England ruled by competent, confident monarchs.

THE OPPOSITION OF CUNNING AND SIMPLICITY   Deceitful cleverness continually opposes simplicity and truth in *Henry VIII*. But the two are not always easy to distinguish. It is unclear, for example, whether the noble Buckingham is an honest plain-dealer calmly defending his innocence, or a supremely tricky would-be assassin who covers up his plans for a power-grab with a patina of sincerity. Shakespeare plays on stereotypes about the deceitfulness of court life, suggesting that nobles hardly ever speak openly or with complete honesty. The play is set almost entirely at court, without rustic or lower-class scenes, like those in earlier Henry plays, in which characters drunkenly speak their minds. At court in *Henry VIII*, nobody speaks his or her mind fully, except perhaps for Katherine. Anne Boleyn, for example, seems trustworthy enough when she tells her attendant that she would never want to be queen, but her assertion looks deceitful when, in the next act, she becomes queen. Even the scheming Wolsey is skilled at putting on the appearance of humility and honesty. Katherine's accusation of Wolsey suggests that in court, cunning runs so deep that even the appearance of honesty is suspect: "I am a simple woman, much too weak / To oppose your cunning. You're meek and humble-mouthed"(II.iv.104–105).

MOTIFS

THE PANGS OF CONSCIENCE   Conscience is a constant but mostly ineffective presence in *Henry VIII*. Henry VIII often claims to act according to the dictates of his conscience, but privately he knows that he is actually ignoring his conscience. In Act II, scene ii, Henry VIII discusses his anguishing decision to divorce Katherine and refers to Cardinal Wolsey as the "quiet of my wounded conscience"(II.ii.74), as if Wolsey's function is not to urge Henry to do the right thing, but to silence moral doubt and make sinners feel that their actions are justified.

SYMBOLS

THE BIRTH OF ELIZABETH   Elizabeth's birth in Act V symbolizes the beginning of political stability and national glory after long years of discord. The birth of the girl who will become Queen Elizabeth of England, Shakespeare's first patron, also marks the resolution of Shakespeare's history plays. With Elizabeth's appearance, the decades of civil strife depicted in plays from *Richard II* to *3 Henry VI* come to a symbolic end, and a new age of prosperity and legitimacy begins.

Cranmer imagines Elizabeth at the end of her reign as "[a] most unspotted lily"(V.iv.61), an allusion to her lifelong virginity and to her mostly peaceful reign. Elizabeth symbolically brings divine sanction to Henry VIII, who says that when he goes to heaven he will look down to see what Elizabeth accomplishes during her reign.

TAXES   The heavy taxes imposed on the common folk by Wolsey, without the knowledge or approval of Henry VIII, symbolize the unlawful, deceitful power Wolsey wields over Henry and the English people. Wolsey perverts the relationship between Henry and his subjects and cheats everyone by keeping the tax revenue for himself. Henry's outraged reaction when he finds out about these taxes shows his concern for the people, and Katherine's concern about the sufferings of the commoners—she is the one who brings the matter to Henry's attention—demonstrates her natural goodness.

IMPORTANT QUOTATIONS FROM *HENRY VIII*

---

1. Go with me, like good angels, to my end;
   And, as the long divorce of steel falls on me,
   Make of your prayers one sweet sacrifice,
   And lift my soul to heaven.

Location: II.i.76–79
Speaker: Buckingham to the crowd
Context: Buckingham prepares for his execution

Buckingham's farewell address, in its simplicity and directness, contrasts with Wolsey's many complex, bombastic speeches. Buckingham speaks in a straightforward way that even the uneducated members of the crowd can understand. The simple grammatical structure of his speech, and his uncomplicated vocabulary, reflect his own trustworthiness. In what is perhaps a subtler brand of honesty, Buckingham does not assert his innocence. He calls the onlookers "good angels," but does not imply that he has been an angel in his own life. He may have had designs on the throne, as Wolsey claimed. He asks for the prayers of his listeners, as if he could not reach heaven on his merits. That Wolsey is such a likable, noble character despite his possible treason suggests that all people are flawed, and their flaws do not damn them and should not make them victims of their enemies.

---

2. I swear 'tis better to be lowly born,
   And range with humble livers in content
   Than to be perked up in a glist'ring grief
   And wear a golden sorrow.

Location: II.iii.19–22
Speaker: Anne to the old woman
Context: Anne discusses Queen Katherine's sad situation with her attendant

In these lines, Anne suggests it is better to be poor and happy than powerful and miserable, a theme that runs through all of Shakespeare's history plays. From observing Katherine and other royals, Anne knows that a golden crown brings "a golden sorrow." Just as Henry IV envied the common people who could sleep well at night, Anne says it is better to be "humble livers in content" than sad royalty. The events of the next act, in which Anne becomes queen, call into question her sincerity in these lines. Perhaps Anne was deceiving herself or her attendant in asserting her preference for happy anonymity, or perhaps the allure of great power changed her mind.

3. *Oh, good my lord, no Latin.*
   I am not such a truant since my coming
   As not to know the language I have lived in.
   A strange tongue makes my cause more strange suspicious.
   Pray, speak in English.

Location: III.i.41–45
Speaker: Katherine to Wolsey
Context: Katherine has been demoted to Princess Dowager

Katherine has lost her patience for courtly pomposity and deceitfulness, typified by Cardinal Wolsey's attempt to speak in Latin. Katherine's abrupt interruption of his speech with her blunt Anglo-Saxon simplicity ("Oh, good my lord, no Latin") shows her new insistence on speaking the truth openly. The sort of back-stabbing that has defeated her makes her distrustful of all sly words and actions. Katherine is Spanish, but her refusal to speak Latin makes her seem more English than the Englishman she is talking to. Many Protestant Englishmen in Shakespeare's day distrusted the pope as a tricky foreigner, so Wolsey's secret correspondence with the pope and his Latin-speaking intensify his characterization as a tricky, secretive man. Similarly, Shakespeare stresses Katherine's innocence by associating her with the English language and English values of simplicity and openness.

4. *I have touched the highest point of all my greatness,*
   And from that full meridian of my glory
   I haste now to my setting. I shall fall
   Like a bright exhalation in the evening,
   And no man see me more.

Location: III.ii.224–228
Speaker: Wolsey
Context: Wolsey realizes that Henry has found him out

Wolsey's acceptance of his ruin is strangely impersonal. He compares his career to the sun rising to its highest point in the sky and then "setting" until night falls and it disappears entirely. In comparing his fall to the natural, inevitable passage of the sun, Wolsey refuses to express guilt or regret. He implies that he could not help what he did any more than the sun can help setting in the evening.

5. *Nor shall this peace sleep with her, but, as when*
   The bird of wonder dies—the maiden phoenix—
   Her ashes new create another heir
   As great in admiration as herself.

Location: V.iv.39–42
Speaker: Cranmer
Context: The archbishop speaks at Elizabeth's christening

With this speech, Shakespeare closes his series of history plays and stresses the legitimacy of the king who ruled in his day. Referring to James as Elizabeth's "heir," despite his distant familial connection to her, suggests that questions of inheritance, which once dogged England, will cease to create conflict.

A VERY BRIEF INTRODUCTION TO SHAKESPEARE'S SONNETS

Shakespeare's sonnets first appeared in 1609. A series of alternatively loving, chiding, dark, and humorous poems, Shakespeare's sonnets do not tell a particular story. This contrasts with the sonnets of such poets as Edmund Spenser and Sir Philip Sidney, who created a narrative with their sonnet sequences. Some critics argue that Shakespeare intended an order that has been lost to us, perhaps because the original printer rearranged the sonnets. Other critics suggest that the sonnets were never meant to tell a story.

Sonnets 1 through 17 are addressed to a young man. The narrator of the sonnets urges the young man to have babies and assures him that he will live on forever in these sonnets. In Sonnets 18 through 126, the poet again addresses a young man, probably the same one as the subject of the first seventeen sonnets, again assuring him of his immortality through verse and sometimes scolding him. Because many of the first 126 sonnets are romantic and have sexual overtones, critics who believe Shakespeare was homosexual or bisexual often cite them.

Sonnets 127 through 152 address a "dark lady" with whom the poet is in love. In these sonnets, the poet expresses his admiration for the lady, admits her faults, and speaks of his sadness when the lady betrays him. The last two sonnets are about Cupid.

The sonnets analyzed in this book have been selected because they are the ones scholars most frequently study. For an explanation of puzzling poetic terms used on the following pages, turn to the Glossary.

SONNET 1

You cheat the world and yourself by refusing to have children.

From fairest creatures we desire increase*,	*Offspring*
That thereby beauty's rose¹ might never die,	
But as the riper* should by time decease,	*Older, more mature*
His tender heir* might bear his memory;	*A child*
But thou, contracted to* thine own bright eyes,	*Engaged to, loving only, reduced to*
Feed'st thy light's flame with self-substantial fuel²,	
Making a famine where abundance lies,	
Thyself thy foe, to thy sweet self too cruel.	
Thou that art now the world's fresh ornament*	*New thing of beauty*
And only herald to the gaudy* spring	*Brightly colored, brilliant*
Within thine own bud* buriest thy content³,	*Happiness, substance, children, semen*
And, tender churl*, mak'st waste in niggarding*:	*Young miser / Hoarding, accumulating*
Pity the world, or else this glutton be:	
To eat the world's due, by the grave and thee⁴.	

SUMMARY

The poet writes that we want beautiful people to reproduce, because then their beauty won't die with them, but will live on in their children. When old people—"the riper"—die (3), their children will keep their memories alive. The poet turns to the young man he is addressing, saying that the young man is in love with himself alone. Instead of coming together with another and reproducing his beauty, the young man is "self-substantial" (6). Like a fire, he feeds on himself. The poet says that the young man undercuts himself by failing to have children. The young man who is now a carefree, youthful decoration in the world will eventually die, and with him will die the children he did not have. The poet calls the young man a miser for wasting his capacity to procreate. He entreats the young man to "[p]ity the world" (13) by bestowing beautiful children upon it. If he does not, the young man will be a glutton who gobbles up his offspring, which should belong to the world.

ANALYSIS

Sonnet 1 introduces a theme that Shakespeare will develop over the subsequent sixteen sonnets: the urgent need for the young man to sustain his beauty by producing an heir. Shakespeare uses the image of a rose to suggest that man's life is as beautiful and ephemeral as flowers, which bloom gloriously and wither quickly. The poet urges the young man to imitate the flowers, who replace themselves with buds. The poet chastises the young man for cutting off his own line, consigning to the grave both himself and the countless future generations that could spring from him.

In the Elizabethan Age, nature had a quasi-divine status as the "Ordering Principle." Nature represented the world as it should be: orderly and truthful. Metaphors drawn from nature, such as the ones Shakespeare uses in Sonnet 1, suggest a world unburdened by human error. Shakespeare uses images of roses and fire to illustrate the young man's crime, which is his abuse of nature. Nature wants the young man to reproduce as roses do, but instead the young man consumes himself like a fire. When a fire's "fuel"(6) is exhausted, the fire dies and cannot be revived, just as the young man will die forever if he

---

1. *beauty's rose:* The rose was a traditional symbol of female beauty and female genitalia. Shakespeare invokes it here to contrast his addressee, a young man with no children, to those who reproduce.
2. *Feed'st thy light's flame with self-substantial fuel:* The poet accuses the young man of loving only himself and of wasting his life just as a candle burns itself up.
3. *Content:* happiness or substance. The poet is suggesting that the young man is denying himself the pleasure of reproducing. Another meaning is that the young man is giving himself pleasure by masturbating, which does not lead to reproduction.
4. *To eat the world's due, by the grave and thee:* The poet calls the young man a "glutton" (13) because, by not reproducing, the young man metaphorically eats his own young, taking them to the grave with him when he dies

does not have children. The rose represents cyclical life, reproductive life, and the fire suggests the inevitability and irreversibility of death.

The preoccupation with immortality that characterizes Shakespeare's first seventeen sonnets reflects historical concerns. The bubonic plague (or "Black Death") had killed three-quarters of Europe's and Asia's populations in the 1300s. Shakespeare himself lived through several plague outbreaks in London. In Sonnet 1, the poet compares the young man to "glutton[ous]" (13) death, a serious charge that has echoes of the grossly overfed reaper of plague times. When death is not only inevitable but likely to happen soon and to overtake even young men, it becomes even more important to reproduce and thus gain some measure of immortality. Shakespeare attaches a strong moral imperative to reproductive duties. He calls children "the world's due" (14), as if one's life were merely a loan from nature that must be repaid through the production of more life.

LANGUAGE NOTES

Tone	gentle criticism and exhortation
Themes	the immortality of beauty; the wastefulness and sin of refusing to procreate
Symbol	the young man as rose; the young man, in his choice to be childless, as flame (5–6)
Metaphors	beauty and youth (and by extension, the beautiful young man) as rose; the life force as fire or flame; childlessness as famine; a childless person as enemy of himself; the young man as decoration on the world; the young man as paragon of youth and beauty; spring as the height of youth and beauty; the childless young man as miser ; death as a glutton
Pattern	repetition of language associated with the natural world

LANGUAGE

Shakespeare uses highly sensual language in the service of a persuasive rhetorical point. Dense internal rhymes combine with alliteration ("self-substantial," (6) "sweet self," (8) "bud buriest," (11)) and alternating end-rhymes to create a thicket of rich sounds. The numerous, vivid metaphors drawn from the natural world paint a colorful picture. Shakespeare's use of the word "tender" (4, 12) suggests both the warm familiarity the poet shares with the young man and the gentle nature of the poet's criticism. But the fact that he repeats the word suggests that while he is urging his friend kindly, he is also urging him insistently. Although Shakespeare devotes more lines to narration and lament than to direct commands, the overall structure is that of an exhortation. The alternation of the ideal example and imperfect reality creates the effect of a sonnet-long indirect command.

FORM

Sonnet 1 uses many of the formal innovations developed by Wyatt and Surrey. In his three quatrains, Shakespeare develops three sections: first, the narrative explanation of the perfection of reproduction; second, the contrasting lament that the young man is squandering his life by refusing to produce an heir; and third, the thesis that refusal to procreate ruins not one life, but two or more (those of the young man and his potential heir[s]). The couplet condenses the sonnet's point in a punchy unit, demanding pity and condemning the man who doesn't have children as a glutton.

SONNET 12[1]

When I notice signs of aging in the world, I remember that your beauty too will fade and die.

When I do count* the clock that tells the time,	*keep track of*
And see the brave* day sunk[2] in hideous night;	*glorious*
When I behold* the violet past prime,	*observe*
And sable* curls all silvered o'er with white;	*black*
When lofty* trees I see barren of leaves,	*stately*
Which erst* from heat* did canopy* the herd,	*formerly / i.e., from the sun / shelter*
And summer's green* all girded up* in sheaves,	*i.e., crops / tied up*
Borne on the bier* with white and bristly beard:[3]	*cart*
Then of thy beauty do I question make*	*wonder (about)*
That thou among the wastes of time must go[4],	
Since sweets and beauties do themselves forsake,[5]	
And die as fast as they see others grow[6];	
And nothing 'gainst Time's scythe[7] can make defense*	*protect*
Save breed* to brave* him* when he takes thee hence.	*i.e., having children / defy / i.e., time*

SUMMARY

The poet notes myriad signs of aging in the world around him, which remind him that his beautiful young man too will inevitably age and die. The poet lists markers of the passage of time: the chiming of a clock, the sunset at the end of the day, a drooping violet, a head of curly black hair turning white. Tall trees, which create shade for sheep and cattle in the summer, lose their leaves in the fall. Wheat and barley, crops of the summer, are harvested, tied up, and carried away on a wagon like an old man carried away on a funeral cart. All these images prompt the poet to wonder about his young friend's beauty, which is also subject to the ravages of time. All sweet and beautiful things must die while news ones grow to take their place. The poet concludes that children, who live on to bear their parents' likeness, are the only measure of defense against time and death.

ANALYSIS

The first seventeen sonnets revolve around a single goal: convincing the poet's young friend to procreate, and soon. The sonnets employ a wide range of tactics and tones to make their argument, alternately flattering, wheedling, nagging, and rebuking. Time is the eternal enemy, an incessant threat to the young man's beauty. The poet argues that the only way to preserve the young man's magnificence and defeat time's ravages is through children, who will serve as replicas of the young man when he himself is old and withered.

Sonnet 12 differs significantly from the rest of the first seventeen sonnets in tone, content, and execution. It lacks sprawling conceits and fanciful rhetoric. The metaphors are simple and linear, their purpose less puzzling wordplay than evocative imagery. The sonnet is a mood piece. Instead of cajoling and

---

1. The placing of the sonnet within the sequence matches the number of minutes (60) in an hour.
2. *sunk*: Recalling the setting of the sun (the "brave day").
3. *And summer's green all girded up in sheaves, /Borne on the bier with white and bristly beard*: And the sheaves of grain all tied up and carried off on the cart. Harvested wheat has a whiskery growth around the grain (i.e., a "white and bristly beard"). Line 8 also suggests an old man ("with white and bristly beard") being carried away to his funeral; biers were also used to carry coffins to gravesites.
4. *That thou among the wastes of time must go*: That you, like all things, will atrophy and waste away into oblivion.
5. *Since sweets and beauties do themselves forsake*: Since all beautiful things age and turn unbeautiful ("forsake" themselves).
6. *as fast as they see others grow*: as quickly as children grow up. Things at their prime ("sweets and beauties") decline as new things bloom towards their prime.
7. *And nothing 'gainst Time's scythe can make defense / Save breed, to brave him when he takes thee hence.*: And nothing can protect one from time and prevent one's eventual death—except children, in whom one lives on. Time and Death were often portrayed as a Grim Reaper carrying a scythe, a curved blade used to claim their victims.

harassing, it creates an atmosphere of anxiety about aging, decay, and death. The poet defers the main argument until the couplet (compare to Sonnet 1 "From fairest creatures we desire increase" (1)), and does not even mention the young man until line 9.

While the rest of this group of seventeen sonnets focuses on the young man, Sonnet 12 foregrounds the poet and his engagement with the outside world. Though thoughts of the young man inform his observations in lines 1–8, it is the poet's perspective and the poet's emotional life that we observe. Examining the images in the first eight lines may give some insight into that emotional life. A withered flower (3) or a head of gray hair (4) easily suggest the decay of youth and beauty. However, other images that are less obvious metaphors for aging and death establish a heightened preoccupation with death. For example, the image of bundled-up wheat on a farmer's cart may more readily recall bounty and the earth's fertility than a funeral hearse. The sonnets have repeatedly prompted speculation into Shakespeare's biographical details. This sonnet in particular poses delicious questions. What might have prompted Shakespeare to look at the world and see nothing but signs of death? Why did he write seventeen sonnets urging a friend, however beloved, with increasing desperation to have children? Though efforts to answer these questions have been, for the most part, exercises in futility, many critics and scholars remain undeterred.

LANGUAGE NOTES

Tone	elegiac, contemplative
Themes	the inescapability of death; time conquers all; offspring as way of securing a measure of immortality
Symbol	the young man stands as a representative of perfect youth and beauty; the images portraying the passage of time in 1–8 all symbolically represent the young man's decline and death
Metaphors	a ticking clock as a metonym for the passage of time (1); day and night reified to enact the passage of time (2); the passage of time embodied by a "violet past prime" (3) and by trees bereft of leaves (5–6); the sheaved, harvested wheat implicitly compared to a dead old man being carried away to his burial (8); time is personified as a scythe-wielding force of death (13–14)
Pattern	opposites—youth and beauty declining: "brave day" and "hideous night" (2), "sable" and "white" (4), "lofty" and "barren" (5), "green" and "white and bristly beard" (7–8), "die" and "grow" (12).

LANGUAGE

Within its language and its rhythms, Sonnet 12 consistently reflects its anxieties about the passage of time. The poem opens with the word "when," a temporal signifier that, when used to pose a question, expresses uncertainty. Fittingly, the sonnet's first image is a clock. The use of the definite article ("the clock" as opposed to "a clock," with the indefinite article "a") suggests that the clock in question is no ordinary instrument, but rather a metaphorical divine clock, a clock that keeps track of the progression of human lives. Rhythmically, the language of the first line echoes these concerns. The consonance of the repeated *k* and *t* sounds mimics the ticking of a clock: "When I do count the clock that tells the time" (1). The line's extraordinarily regular iambic pentameter approximates the tempo of a clock. This steady beat drums out in one-syllable words. The sonnet maintains its regular meter throughout with few exceptions. "Barren" (5) is one of the only words to disrupt the meter—a significant choice, given that it is the youth's "barrenness" that is (allegedly) the source of the poet's distress.

FORM

The rhyme scheme of Sonnet 12 is typically Elizabethan, with the requisite three quatrains in an *abab* rhyme pattern and a concluding heroic couplet. The quatrains delineate three distinct stages in the poet's thought process. In the first quatrain, he describes four brief images of aging. The two images of the second quatrain each take up two lines, and the poet explores them in greater depth. In the third quatrain, he turns his attention to the young man. Over the course of the sonnet, Shakespeare progressively broadens the metaphors he uses to describe aging, moving from clock to flower to hair to trees to fields in order to suggest the way aging becomes increasingly prominent in people's lives. The epigrammatic couplet is self-contained and easily extractable from the rest of the poem. It's also the only part of the sonnet that makes an explicit argument. At the same time, Sonnet 12 fits neatly into the Petrarchan octave-sestet configuration, with the octave concerning the abstract, external world, and the sestet focusing on the poet's young friend.

SONNET 18

Your beauty is more constant than summer's, and will be immortalized in my poetry.

Shall I compare thee to a summer's day?	
Thou art more lovely and more temperate*.	*moderate, pleasant*
Rough winds do shake the darling* buds of May,	*young and lovely*
And summer's lease* hath all too short a date*[1].	*i.e., reign / i.e., duration*
Sometime too hot the eye of heaven* shines,	*i.e., the sun*
And often is his* gold complexion dimmed,	*i.e., the sun's*
And every fair from fair sometime declines,	
By chance or nature's changing course untrimmed*[2];	*shorn of beauty*
But thy eternal summer shall not fade[3]	
Nor lose possession of that fair* thou ow'st*,	*i.e., your beauty / possess*
Nor shall Death brag thou wander'st in his shade[4]	
When in eternal lines* to* time thou grow'st*[5].	*poetry (e.g., this sonnet) / i.e., with / keep pace, endure*
So long as men can breathe or eyes can see,	
So long lives this*, and this gives life to thee.	*i.e., this sonnet*

SUMMARY

The poet wonders about an appropriate metaphor to describe the young man. Summer is not as consistently beautiful and balanced; more constant and beautiful than summer weather, the young man will be immortalized in the poet's verses for eternity.

ANALYSIS

Sonnet 18 is unquestionably the most famous in Shakespeare's sequence; it may be the most famous lyric poem in the language. It continues the theme explored in the first seventeen sonnets: the young man's beauty must be preserved. Whereas in previous sonnets, the poet proposed procreation as a way of ensuring immortality, here he declares that the young man's beauty will live on eternally in these verses.

The shift in emphasis, from procreation to poetry, of the solution to the ravages of time happens gradually. Sonnet 15 marks the beginning of the poet's assumption of personal responsibility for preserving the young man's beauty. Sonnet 16 recants that assumption and laments that the poet's "pupil pen" (16:10) cannot guard the young man from death. Sonnet 17 comes back to assert the transformative and youth-sustaining power of the poet's poetry. In the couplet at the end of Sonnet 18, the poet finally swears that his poetry guarantees the youth immortality.

The sonnet is a self-conscious literary exercise. The project is clear from the first line: "Shall I compare thee to a summer's day?" (1). Shakespeare chooses summer to stand for youth and beauty, both because summer is a season of full and fruitful bloom and because summer is always followed by fall and withering. At the same time, the cyclical nature of the seasons promises that summer will come again. Just as the seasons progress, new generations of people will enter their prime. Alternatively, through Shakespeare's verse, the youth is able to cycle through and live again.

---

1. *And summer's lease hath all too short a date*: Summer is too short.
2. *every fair from fair sometime declines / By chance or nature's changing course untrimmed*: Everything beautiful (such as beautiful people) becomes not beautiful, whether by accident or because of the natural progression of things (such as old age).
3. *thy eternal summer shall not fade*: you will remain beautiful forever
4. *his shade*: Death's shade is the antithesis of the sunny summer day. From the times of classical antiquity, "shade" has also meant "ghost," which here refers, ominously, to the haunting figure of Death.
5. *Nor shall Death brag thou wander'st in his shade / When in eternal lines to time thou growest*: Immortalized in my poetry ("eternal lines") you will progress ("grow") in step with time ("to time"). Shakespeare's young man will, as he lives on in the poetry, "grow" (12) or progress alongside eternal Time and thus prove Immortal.

LANGUAGE NOTES

Tone	rapturously contemplative (1–12); assured, epic (13–14)
Themes	human beauty as greater than any metaphor ; poetry as guarantee of immortality
Symbol	summer as a symbol of perfect youth
Metaphors	the sun as "the eye of heaven" (5); death personified as shadowy creature (11)
Pattern	repetition of temporal qualifiers: "sometime" (5, 7), "often"(6) in opposition to "eternal" (9, 12)

LANGUAGE

The language of Sonnet 18 carefully leads us through a detailed explanation of a conceit. Shakespeare makes his point through quiet repetition—of sounds (alliteration), of structures (anaphora), and of categories of words. Instances of alliteration and assonance are either local, as in "*fair from fair*" (7) or "by *chance* or nature's *changing* course" (8), or interweave, as in "So *long lives this* and *this* gives *life* to *thee*" (14). The anaphora come in pairs—"And often is his gold complexion dimmed / And every fair from fair sometime declines" (6–7). These pairs emphasize the fact that the sonnet is organized around a comparison of two things. By repeating temporal qualifiers ("sometime" (5, 7), "often" (6)), Shakespeare underscores the constancy of his beloved in the face of time and change. Finally, Shakespeare makes extensive use of personification, describing heaven as a person with the sun as its eye, the sun as a creature with a complexion, and death as a shady wanderer. These are the agents of change that haunt the world in which the young man stays unchanging.

FORM

Sonnet 18 resembles the Petrarchan sonnet in structure. Lines 1–8 form an octet that discusses all the ways in which summer is a fickle season. Lines 6–14 form a sestet "answer" to the octet's dilemma: the metaphorical "summer" of the youth's beauty will retain its perfection for eternity. The autonomy of the epigrammatic couplet, however, is an innovation of the Elizabethan sonnet.

SONNET 19

Let time devastate all things except my beloved's beauty, which is immortalized in my poetry in any case.

Devouring Time, blunt thou the lion's paws,
And make the earth devour her own sweet brood*[1];　　　　　　　　*children*
Pluck the keen teeth from the fierce tiger's jaws,
And burn the long-lived phoenix[2] in her blood*[3].　　　　　　　*in its prime of life*
Make glad and sorry seasons as thou* fleet'st,　　　　　　　　　　*i.e., time*
And do whate'er thou wilt, swift-footed Time,
To the wide world and all her fading sweets.
But I forbid thee one most heinous crime:
O, carve* not with thy hours my love's fair brow,　　　　　　　*i.e., make wrinkled*
Nor draw no lines there with thine antique[4] pen.
Him in thy course* untainted* do allow[5]　　　　　　　　　*progress / undefiled*
For Beauty's pattern to succeeding men[6].
　　Yet do thy worst*, old Time; despite thy wrong　　　　*i.e., in aging my beloved*
　　My love shall in my verse ever live young.

SUMMARY

The poet addresses a cruel and all-devastating ("devouring") time (1). Time may devastate all things, including the virile power of a lion or a tiger, or the immortality of the mythical phoenix. Time may bring about its cycles of good and bad things, and cause the whole world to atrophy. Age the world, the poet commands, yet spare my love and his beauty. But even if his beloved ages, his beauty will live on in the poet's verses.

ANALYSIS

In the first two quatrains, the poet issues a series of commands, ordering time to devastate and ruin the world with age—as time will anyway, with or without his will. He commands time to return all living things to the earth (i.e., in death and decomposition), to change the seasons, to corrode the young and powerful with marks of age. Because the poet lacks any actual authority over time, his irrelevant commands only highlight his impotence. The poet finally acknowledges his powerlessness in the third quatrain, as his commands slip into pleas.

---

1. *make the earth devour her sweet brood*: The earth devours her own children ("brood") in the sense that her creatures all return to die and decompose into the earth.
2. *the long-lived phoenix*: The phoenix, a traditional symbol of immortality, is a glorious mythical bird that lives for 500 years, then self-immolates, and rises again from its own ashes.
3. "in blood" is a hunting expression meaning "vigorous," "in the prime of life."
4. *Draw no lines there with thy antique pen*: Do not age my beloved (by giving him facial wrinkles). In Shakespeare's time, *antique* sounded like *antic*, or "crazy."
5. More hunting vocabulary: *course* meant "pursuit"; *untainted* meant "untouched by a weapon."
6. *For beauty's pattern to succeeding men*: So that my beloved can serve as a paradigm of a beautiful person in the future.

LANGUAGE NOTES

Tone:	vehement (1–4); elegiac (5–8); beseeching (9–12); determined (13–14)
Themes	the relentless, devastating passage of time; immortality through poetry
Symbol:	The phoenix is a traditional symbol of immortality (4); The lion and the tiger symbolize nature at its most virile (1, 3)
Metaphor	time as a carnivorous, all-devouring beast (1–4); earth as a mother (2); time as a swift runner (5); time as an artist (9–10); hours as carving tools (9); wrinkles as drawn lines (10)
Pattern	hunting vocabulary: "in her blood" (4), "course" (11), "untainted" (11); repetition of images of destruction: "devour" (1, 2), "blunt" (1), "pluck" (3), "burn" (4), "fading" (7), "heinous crime" (8), "do thy worst" (13), "thy wrong" (13); artistic imagery: "carve" (9), "draw no lines … with thy antique pen" (10)

LANGUAGE

In the first quatrain, the poet personifies time as a callous beast that perverts nature. Time robs the lion of claws, the tiger of teeth, the earth of maternal instincts, and the phoenix of immortality. The poet's diction mirrors the unforgiving nature of time's actions. He chooses harsh, heavy, single-syllable words: "blunt" (1), "make" (2), "pluck" (3), and "burn" (4). The bitterness is crystallized in the assonance of long *e* sounds of "sweet" (2), "keen teeth" (3), and "phoenix" (4).

The poet's commands to time are less vitriolic in the second quatrain. Time is "swift-footed" (6) and "fleet[ing]" (5) rather than "devouring" (1); it is a runner leaving a trail of change in his wake. In this quatrain, the changes time enacts—the "glad and sorry seasons" (5), the world's "fading sweets" (7)—are all natural developments. The tone has subsided from angry bitterness to elegiac resignation.

In the third quatrain, as the poet asks time not to make his beloved grow old, his attempts to "forbid" (8) quickly give way to pleas: "O, carve not" (9), "do allow" (11). Time becomes an artist who can "carve" (9) and "draw" (10). The resolution of the couplet is weary and resigned. "Old Time" (13) will do his "worst" (13). The change in meter reflects this weariness. Lines 1–13 are encumbered and heavy with certainty: the iambs are often replaced by spondees and trochees: "blunt thou" (1) "sweet brood" (2), "pluck the" (3), "keen teeth" (3), "fierce tiger's" (3), "lived phoenix" (4), "wide world" (7), "fair brow" (9). The last line is, as the scholar Stephen Booth notes, metrically limp, and belies the poet's claim that his verse will save his beloved from death.

Shakespeare subtly indicates the poet's attitude toward time through internal rhyme. The phonetic similarity between "devour" (1) and "hour" (9) suggests that time's destructive force is due to the relentless passage of the hours. Similarly, the rhyme of "time" (1, 6) and "crime" (8) is an open accusation. Later, the similar end rhyme of "men" (12) and "pen" (10) creates collusion between the poet (a man) and time (the wielder of the "antique pen"). Both the poet and time are artists who will potentially use the beloved as a "pattern" (12) for beauty.

FORM

The three quatrains of Sonnet 19 vary in emotional intensity. The sonnet opens on an intense quatrain; time is vilified as a ravenous, unnatural force. In the second quatrain, time is portrayed more evenly as a force that does both bad and good ("glad and sorry" (5)) as it takes its toll. In the third quatrain, the poet shifts from command to prayer, and begs time not to age his beloved. Finally, in the couplet, the poet changes tactics; he recognizes that prayer is useless and proposes another solution.

SONNET 20

Love me, even though I cannot have sex with you because you are a man.

A woman's face with Nature's own hand painted*   *without makeup*
Hast thou, the master-mistress of my passion[1];
A woman's gentle heart, but not acquainted
With shifting change, as is false women's fashion;[2]
An eye more bright than theirs, less false in rolling*,   *wandering (as in "a wandering eye")*
Gilding* the object whereupon* it gazeth;   *making more beautiful / on which*
A man in hue*, all hues in his controlling[3],   *appearance, features*
Which* steals men's eyes and women's souls amazeth.   *i.e., his hue (7) or appearance*

And for a woman[4] wert thou first created,
Till Nature as she wrought thee fell a-doting,
And by addition* me of thee defeated   *i.e., by adding a penis (see also 12)*
By adding one thing to my purpose nothing[5].

    But since she* pricked thee out for women's pleasure[6],   *i.e. Nature*
    Mine be thy love, and thy love's use* their* treasure[7].   *i.e., sexual pleasure / i.e., women's*

SUMMARY

The poet addresses the young man, telling him that he is as lovely as a woman, but has none of women's bad qualities, such as deceitfulness and unfaithfulness. As nature was creating you, the poet tells the young man, she fell in love with you and gave you the body of a man so that she could have sex with you herself. The poet says that the young man's additional organ (his penis) means that the poet, as a man, cannot have sex with him. Women may enjoy the young man's physical love—sexual intercourse—but the young man's true, spiritual love is reserved for the poet.

ANALYSIS

Shakespeare addresses many of his sonnets to a beloved, handsome young man whose identity remains unknown. Sonnet 20 may contain certain clues. The poetry scholar Helen Vendler has noted the frequency of the letters *H, E, W,* and *S* throughout the sonnet. These letters come together in line 7, the middle of the sonnet, where the word "hue" (or "hew" in original Quarto) appears twice. Vendler suggests that the poet went to great lengths to ensure the appearance of the four letters in every line (except for the eleventh). For example, she argues that ending –*eth* of "gazeth" (6) and "amazeth" (8) is awkward. The lines could have ended much more naturally in –*es*. Similarly, the Quarto spellings of "rowling" (5) and "controwling" (7) are somewhat jarring. Vendler argues the alternate spellings were chosen to add instances of *H* and *W*, respectively, and that these added instances suggest that HEWS may be an anagram that combines the initials of the young man (H. E.) with Shakespeare's (W. S.).

    Sonnet 20 establishes a clear opposition between physical, sexual love and a more authentic spiritual love. Though many readers have suggested on the basis of the sonnets addressed to the young man that Shakespeare was bisexual, Sonnet 20 may offer a counterargument. The sonnet is very sexual in subtext, but it's a traditional love sonnet in form and content. Both this distinction and the final couplet suggest

---

1. *my passion:* (1) my love; (2) my heartfelt utterance—i.e., the poem itself; (3) my suffering (referring to Jesus' passion on the cross)
2. *[thou art] not acquainted / With shifting change, as is false women's fashion:* you, unlike women, are not fickle. There is a pun in "not acquainted"—i.e., not having a quaint (Elizabethan slang for "cunt").
3. *all hues in his controlling:* who captivates and dominates all others
4. *for a woman:* to satisfy women [sexually]
5. *one thing to my purpose nothing:* a penis, which to me is useless
6. *pricked thee out for women's pleasure* chose you to be male (i.e., to please women sexually). "Pricked thee out" also means "gave you a prick," or penis.
7. *Mine be thy love, and thy love's use their treasure:* Give sexual pleasure ("thy love's use") to women, but give me your love.

that the poet perceives a schism between love and sexual intercourse. Within the sonnet, Shakespeare argues that his body is sexually incompatible with the body of his beloved. While undoubtedly homo-erotic, Sonnet 20 may be read as an explicit resistance to homosexual intercourse.

Sonnet 20 presents a pre-Christian, primitive view of creation. Nature is a female mother-creator, not a male creator God. Some critics have also pointed out that Shakespeare may have chosen the number 20 for its associations with the human anatomy: each person has twenty digits (fingers and toes). Twenty was an important number in the evolution of Western culture, as evidenced, for example, by the English word "score" and by the French word for "eighty"—*quatre-vingts*, or, literally, "four twenties."

LANGUAGE NOTES

Tone	light-hearted, impish (1–8); bitter (9–12); defiant (13–14)
Themes	the separation of physical love from spiritual love
Metaphor	nature is personified as a woman; nature is portrayed as an artist (1, 10)

LANGUAGE

Sonnet 20 makes plenty of sexual puns and references to genitalia, which ultimately establish an opposi-tion between physical and spiritual love. The comparisons of the young man to women throughout the first two quatrains are impishly enhanced with sexual puns. Explicitly "but not acquainted / With shifting change" (3–4) means roughly "but not fickle." At the same time, "quaint" was Elizabethan slang for "cunt." To "change" a "shift" (4) meant to change clothes, which women had to do frequently during menstruation. The lines, then, acquire additional meanings: the young man is not "a-quaint-ed"—that is, he lacks female genitalia—and is not familiar with the tedium of menstruation.

In line 11, the poet makes reference to the "addition" to the young man's body that distinguishes him from women—a penis. Some readers have suggested that in line 12, Shakespeare makes a homoerotic pun on the slang meaning of "nothing," which is vagina. Explicitly, the penis, the presence of which pre-vents the poet from having sex with the young man, is, for the poet, "nothing," or useless. The poet may be implying that the young man's penis is, for him, like a vagina in that it is a sexual organ with which to copulate. Such a secondary reading reverses the literal meaning of the sonnet: that the poet is prevented from engaging in sexual intercourse with the addressee because he is a man.

In the sonnet, as elsewhere in Western tradition, nature is portrayed as a woman, the mother creator. However, throughout the sonnet women are described as false and deceitful, and this misogynist under-tone extends to the depiction of nature. A selfish woman, nature has created the beautiful beloved as a man so that he could be a potential sexual partner to her.

FORM

Shakespeare gives the first two quatrains equal weight, as they describe the young man to whom the son-net is addressed. The third quatrain looks back on nature creating the young man's beauty, at which point she made him a man rather than a woman. The couplet responds to the end result of the creative process described in the third quatrain. The young man's physical love may be unattainable, but his spir-itual love remains fully the poet's.

Sonnet 20 is Shakespeare's only sonnet with all feminine rhymes, meaning that the penultimate sylla-ble is stressed, and both it and the final syllable of the appropriate lines rhyme together: "*pain*-ted" / "a-*cquain*-ted" (1, 3) or "*ro*-lling" / "con-*tro*-lling" (5, 7). (As a result, the last foot of each line has three beats instead of two—an amphibrach rather than an iamb.) The feminine rhymes suggest the feminine quality of the young man's beauty. Most rhymes in Shakespeare's sonnets are masculine: "Shall I compare thee to a summer's *day* / ... / Rough winds do shake the darling buds of *May*" (Sonnet 18, lines 1 & 3).

Critics such as Helen Vendler have noted that the letters of the word "hews" (or "hues") occur in every line, and have conjectured that they encode a message. Perhaps H.E. are the initials of the beloved young man. *The Norton Shakespeare* points out that the youth "has most often been identified with Henry Wriothesley, Earl of Southhampton, and William Herbert, Earl of Pembroke." W.S., in that case, would stand for William Shakespeare.

SONNET 23

I feel too much to express my love in words; read my feelings in my poetry instead.

As an unperfect actor on the stage
Who with his fear is put besides his part,*   *i.e., forgets his lines*
Or some fierce thing[1] replete with too much rage
Whose strength's abundance weakens his own heart,
So I, for fear of trust[2], forget to say
The perfect ceremony of love's rite[3],
And in my own love's strength seem to decay,
O'ercharged* with burden of my own love's might[4].   *overladen*
O let my books[5] be then the eloquence
And dumb* presagers* of my speaking breast,   *mute / prophets, indicators*
Who* plead for love, and look for recompense   *i.e. the dumb presagers (acting for the "books")*
More than that tongue that more hath more expressed.[6]
   O learn to read what silent love hath writ;
   To hear with eyes belongs to love's fine wit[7].

SUMMARY

The poet compares himself both to an actor who has forgotten his lines in stage fright and to a beast undone by his excessive anger. As the actor is paralyzed by fear or the beast is rendered impotent by his rage, so the poet is overcome by the force of his love to the extent that he cannot articulate his feeling to his beloved. He prays that his writing ("books") might express that which he cannot say, and scorns others who can speak glibly but do not feel as much. He appeals to his beloved to discern his true feelings from his written words. In some editions of the sonnet, "books" is replaced with "looks." In this version, the poet urges his beloved to perceive the strength of his love from his face, eyes, and body language.

ANALYSIS

Sonnet 23 explores the psychology of power and expression. The actor's "fear" (2) leaves him incapable of delivering his lines. The beast's excessive rage ("strength's abundance" [4]) "weakens" (4) him. The poet is rendered similarly powerless, overcome both by the strength of his feeling, like the beast, and by his "fear" (5) of trust, like the actor. The third quatrain suggests that the "fear of trust" is caused by the unnamed rival or rivals ("that tongue" [12]) who can express themselves with ease.

    The sexual puns in the first eight lines belie the poet's claim of inarticulateness. "Some fierce thing" (3) may be a reference to the penis. "[R]age" (3) can also mean "lust." "Love's rite" puns on "love's right"—sexual intercourse. "Mine own love's might" (8), then, can refer to sexual power, either to the poet's overwhelming sexual desire, whose strength renders him impotent, or to the power of his beloved (i.e., the sexual "might" of "mine own love"), who "o'ercharge[s]" the poet with the "burden" of his lust or his body. By embedding this sexual reading within the sonnet, Shakespeare (and the poet) subtly flexes

---

1. *some fierce thing*: some wild beast; *thing* can also mean "penis," in which case lines 3–4 convey a fear of impotence.
2. *for fear of trust*: either "afraid to trust myself" or "afraid of the trust you have given me"
3. *The perfect ceremony of love's rite*: the traditional exchange of love vows. The "perfect ceremony" recalls the marriage ceremony. *Love's rite* also suggests *love's right* (some editors prefer this spelling), in the sense of "what is due, owed to love." This is potentially a reference to sexual intercourse.
4. *love's might*: the power of my love. Continuing the sexual readings from 3–4 and 6, *love's might* could refer to sexual power (see also Analysis).
5. *books*: Some editors give *looks* here. Either works within the sonnet.
6. *that tongue that more hath more expressed*: those (or that one) who have glibly spoken words of love. The repetition in "more hath more" is emphatic or evocative, not grammatical.
7. *To hear with eyes belongs to love's fine wit*: Love knows how to pick up on what is unspoken. Cupid, the cherubic god of love, who is traditionally portrayed as blind (by association with the saying "Love is blind") can hear even if he cannot see.

his literary muscle, proving that, at least in writing, the poet is eloquent indeed. This opposition, which is proof of articulateness hidden by protests of inarticulateness, is echoed by the imagery in the text: the actor, the beast, and the poet, are strong and weak at once.

LANGUAGE NOTES

Tone   contemplative (1–8); anguished (9–12); beseeching (13); resolute (14)

Theme   intensity of feelings renders them inexpressible; true emotion expressed though writing ("books") or appearance ("looks")

Metaphor   the poet as an under-rehearsed and nervous actor (1–2); implicitly, fear of rejection compared to stage fright; the poet overcome by love as a beast undone by excessive rage (3–4); implicitly, love compared to rage; strong emotion as a burden (8); books as prophets (10) who can "plead" (11) and seek ("look for") (11); blind love can "hear with eyes" (14)

Pattern   language associated with strength and weakness: "fierce" (3), "strength" (4, 7), "weakens" (4); language of communication: "say" (5), "eloquence" (9), "dumb" (10), "presagers" (10), "speaking" (10), "plead" (11), "look for" (11), "tongue" (12), "expressed" (12), "silent" (13), "writ" (13), "hear" (14); language of excess: "too much rage" (3), "abundance" (4), "o'ercharged" (8), "more than … that more hath more" (12); sexual puns: "some fierce thing" (3), "love's rite/right" (6), "love's strength" (7), "love's might" (8)

LANGUAGE

The repetition of the language of excess—"too much" (3), "abundance" (4), "o'ercharged" (8)—throughout the first three quatrains supports the strength of emotion claimed in these lines. The opposition between strength and weakness—the beast and the poet rendered powerless through excess of power—is echoed in the diction: words connoting strength interlace with words connoting weakness ("strength" (4, 7), "weaken" (4), "decay" (7), "might" (8)).

In the third quatrain, the triple repetition of "more" in "More than that tongue that more hath more expressed" (12) suggests that verbal expressions of love are easy and cheap. Love is best expressed in "books" or "looks."

FORM

The first quatrain summons up the images of a terrified actor and raging beast as analogues of the tongue-tied poet. The poet's own surfeit of emotion and inability to articulate it are described in the second quatrain. The first six lines form an imagistic tricolon (three-phrase) crescendo, with emphasis on the final description of the poet, which continues in lines 7–8. The first quatrain gives two models in two images for the second quatrain. The third quatrain responds to the situation described in the first two. In it, the poet prays that his writing will speak for him. The epigrammatic couplet summarizes and resolves. Its first line is personal, an appeal to the young man, but its second line is an abstract saw: "To hear with eyes belongs to love's fine wit" (14). In its resolute tone, the couplet contradicts the anxiety and uncertainty of the first three quatrains.

SONNET 27

I work hard by day, and think about you all night.

Weary with toil, I haste me to my bed,
The dear repose for limbs with travel tired;
But then begins a journey in my head
To work my mind when body's work's expired*;   *done*
For then my thoughts, from far where I abide*,   *i.e. from far away, where I currently am*
Intend* a zealous pilgrimage to thee,   *undertake*
And keep my drooping eyelids open wide,
Looking on darkness which the blind do see:
Save* that my soul's imaginary sight*   *except that / i.e., inner vision*
Presents thy shadow* to my sightless* view,   *i.e., image / blind, unseeing*
Which like a jewel hung in ghastly night
Makes black night beauteous, and her* old face[1] new.   *i.e., night's*
    Lo, thus by day my limbs, by night my mind,
    For thee, and for myself, no quiet find[2].

SUMMARY

After a tiring day of work and travel, the poet goes home to bed. But as soon as he lies down, his mind begins to wander to thoughts of his beloved, who is far away. The poet stares into the darkness of night, and has a vision of his beloved, like "a jewel ... in ghastly night." By day, the poet is exhausted by his physical work. By night, he restlessly thinks about his beloved.

ANALYSIS

Three conceptual oppositions mark Sonnet 27: between sight (day) and blindness (night), between body and mind, and between lover and absent beloved. The sonnet opens to introduce day and body: at the close of the day, the poet is weary from work and travel. The poet then enters night and the life of his mind. "Darkness" (8) and "shadow[s]" (10) dominate. "[B]ody's work" (4) is over, and weary "limbs" (2) have settled into "dear repose" (2). Just as the blinding darkness begins as daylight wanes, so mental "work" (4) begins as the physical variety ends. The day's physical "travel" (2) fades into the night's mental "journey" (3) toward the beloved. He is far away, so the poet must journey away from himself, "from far where I abide" (5) to join him. The vision of the beloved breaks through the blinding night, resolving oppositions: the poet begins to see even though he is "sightless" (10); "black night" becomes "beauteous" (12); its "old face" becomes "new" (12). The couplet affirms this resolution of oppositions: day and night, body and mind, are united in wearying the poet. He has no peace "for thee, and for myself" (14). In this formulation, the poet and his beloved are reunited. "For thee" may be read either as "because of you" or "for your benefit." There is some suggestion that, just as the poet journeys to join his beloved, the beloved too journeys to appear to him as a vision. In the middle of the night, in the realm of the mind, the impossible can happen: lover and absent beloved are reunited.

The possibility of reunion of the lover with his absent beloved, implied in the couplet, is a frequent theme of Shakespeare's sonnets. In Sonnet 22, the beloved's head lodges in the poet's own chest. In 25, the poet suggests that love prevents fate from separating him from his beloved. The complicated syntax of Sonnet 27's couplet, with its embedded clauses and ambiguous phrases, enacts the entanglement of the poet and his beloved explored in the sonnets.

---

1. *her old face:* Night and darkness are considered older than the world itself, according to Genesis I.4–5, 10.
2. *Lo, thus by day my limbs, by night my mind, / For thee, and for myself, no quiet find:* In this way I am always restless. During the day I do physical work, at night I think about you.

LANGUAGE NOTES

Tone   weary (1–8, 13–14); full of wonder (9–12)

Theme   lover and beloved as inseparable; longing for lover as exhausting ; travel as metaphor for thinking of a person; night as terrifying, blinding

Symbol   night and blindness symbolize existence without the beloved

Metaphor   travel and "pilgrimage" (6) as metaphor for thoughts; image of beloved as "jewel hung in ghastly night" (11); not seeing at night as blindness (8, 10)

Pattern   imagery of blindness: "drooping eyelids" (7), "looking" (8), "blind" (8), "see" (8), "imaginary sight" (9), "sightless view" (10), ; blackness of night: "darkness" (8), "shadow" (10), "ghastly night" (11), "black night" (12). ; imagery of travel: "travel" (1), "journey" (3), "pilgrimage" (6)

LANGUAGE

The opening word, "weary" (1), sets the tone for the sonnet. His mental "journey" (27), a word that recalls the French *jour* ("day"), embodies the sonnet's paradox of day continuing into night. The physical travel of the day has become the mental journey of the night. The nighttime landscape of the second quatrain is a place of darkness and blindness: "eyelids" (7) "drooping" (7); the poet likens "darkness" (8) to the darkness of "the blind" (8); "night" (12) is "black" (12); the poet's "view" (8) is "sightless" (8). Indeed, the only "sight" (9), the vision of his beloved, is "imaginary." The beloved sheds light on night and blindness. Shakespeare compares her to a "jewel." At the time, people thought precious stones could emit light, and the beloved illuminates the poet's darkness, uniting dark and light, the poet and his beloved.

FORM

The first two quatrains plod along in a loping iambic pentameter—the listless rhythm imitates the poet's fatigue. Nearly every line is contained with end-stop punctuation, as though the exertion of reaching the end of the line has sapped all of the phrase's energy. The third quatrain mollifies the frustration of the previous quatrains. The insomnia conjures up an image of the beloved, which breaks through the exhausting, blinding darkness. This is the climax of the sonnet. The couplet is neither a contradiction nor a resolution of the conflict of the quatrains. Rather, it meditates on the consequences of the story in the quatrains. The abundance of mid-line punctuation slows down the couplet to make time for peaceful reflection, evoking the soothing calm brought by the image of the beloved.

SONNET 29

When I feel wretched, I remember your love and feel better.

When, in disgrace with fortune* and men's eyes,	*luck, fate*
I all alone beweep* my outcast state,	*cry over*
And trouble deaf heaven with my bootless* cries,	*hopeless*
And look upon myself and curse my fate,	
Wishing me like to one more rich in hope,	
Featured like him, like him with friends possessed,	
Desiring this man's art* and that man's scope*¹,	*skill / range, capability*
With what I most enjoy* contented least;	*(1) what I like most (2) what I have the most of*
Yet in these thoughts myself almost despising,	
Haply² I think on thee, and then my state*,	*mood, fortune*
Like to the lark at break of day arising	
From sullen earth, sings* hymns at heaven's gate.	*i.e., "my state, like the lark, sings"*
For thy sweet love remembered such wealth brings	
That then I scorn to change my state with kings.	

SUMMARY

The poet begins in a state of "disgrace," scorned by "fortune" and rejected by other people. He prays to God, who ignores him, so he curses his bad luck. He compares himself to the men around him and finds each of them superior to him in his own way. Even that (unnamed) thing which he enjoys the most fails to satisfy him. At this low point, when he almost begins to hate himself, the poet remembers his good friend, at which point his mood changes, brightening like the morning after a particularly dark night. Like a lark, he sings God's praises. For when he remembers his friend's love, the poet realizes that he is rich indeed, and that he has no desire to trade places with anyone, not even a king.

ANALYSIS

Sonnet 29 resembles a classical Petrarchan love sonnet in several ways. The speaker is a self-absorbed figure, pining away in a state of acute and exquisite suffering. Unlike the speaker in Petrarchan sonnets, this poet does not suffer out of love. Rather, love relieves his misery. Love also helps the poet reorient his outlook. In the opening lines, the poet refers to himself only: he "look[s] upon [him]self" (4) and can't see beyond his own "state" (2) except to rail at an indifferent God or to compare himself unfavorably to other men. But after turning his thoughts to his beloved, he is able to open up and see beyond himself. It is no coincidence that this is where the poet allows himself the luxury of the poem's single extended metaphor.

In the courtly poetic tradition, love was frequently portrayed as a religion, with the loved one depicted as a deity to be worshipped. In this sonnet, devotion to the loved one doesn't necessarily *replace* devotion to God. Rather, the two forms of love are unambiguously linked. Adoration for his beloved leads the speaker out of his state of lonely despair. Similarly, Christianity maintains that love for the deity will lead a believer out of solipsism. Within the lark imagery of lines 10–12, the poem blurs the boundary between the speaker and the bird: both rise together from the "sullen earth" and "sing hymns" to the Lord. The speaker's love for the youth has metaphorically led him to God's door.

Sonnet 29, which is one of Shakespeare's most famous, falls within a sequence of poems that introduce dark, discordant notes into the collection. It follows two linked sonnets that, like 29, hinge on distinctions made between night and day. In 27 and 28, the poet is kept awake after a long day of hard work by thoughts of his distant beloved: both day and night are distressing spaces. In 28, day and night (though inherently opposed to one another) join forces to torment the lover. In 29, however, the traditional sym-

---

1. In 5–8, the poet compares himself to five different men and wishes he had their attributes. The first has better prospects ("more rich in hope"), the second better looks ("features"), the third more friends, the fourth more skill ("art"), the fifth better range of abilities ("scope").
2. *Haply:* accidentally, with residual meaning of "happily."

bolic meanings of "night" and "day" are restored: the dawn, accompanied by the sweet singing of the lark, marks the end of suffering and the renewal of hope.

The lover in 29, however, remains distant. The (presumably) geographic distance of the earlier poems replaced by a temporal one. Here, the beloved is "remembered," though possibly not currently enjoyed. The beloved as a pleasant figure of memory anticipates Sonnet 30, when the poet, deep in contemplation, remembers a host of "things past," (30:2) all of which sadden and demoralize him until he thinks of his lover, which "restore[s]" (30:14) his spirits. In Sonnets 33–36, the lover grows even more distant, perhaps even estranged. Though the reason for the rift is never explained, it is clear that either the youth or the poet has committed an offense that threatens to destroy the relationship.

Considerable critical energy has been spent on attempts to uncover this poem's biographical background, though little concrete evidence exists to suggest one reading over another. It remains unclear why the speaker is "outcast," what kind of "disgrace" he suffers, and whether this disgrace stems from his relationship with the youth.

LANGUAGE NOTES

Tone   bitter and despairing (1–8); hopeful (9–14)

Themes   love as remedy for despair; friendship and love as sentiments comparable to religious devotion

Symbol   the lark and the dawn (11) as symbols of hope and rejuvenation

Metaphors   "fortune" is attributed human sentiment (disdain) and implicitly personified (1) ; "heaven" personified as God; love for the addressee implicitly compared to religious devotion; the rising and singing of the lark (11) is a metaphor for the poet's rising spirits

Pattern: repetition of phrase associated with material wealth: "fortune" (1) "rich in hope" (5), "wealth" (13); anaphora: "And trouble deaf heaven … / And look upon myself and curse my fate" (3–4), "this man's art and that man's scope" (7).

LANGUAGE

The narrative arc of this poem—the poet's descent into despair and his eventual release—is mirrored and echoed in its rhythms. In the opening octave the speaker is overwhelmed by his own anguish, and this feeling is borne out by the verse's insistent repetitions. Parallel structure (anaphora) is used to great effect, particularly in "and trouble" / "and look" / "and curse" of lines 3–4 and "this man's art" / "that man's scope" of line 7. The syntactical repetition suggests that the poet is stuck on a single idea and unable to break out of a vicious pattern. Phrases come at a quick clip, particularly in lines 5–8: at each comma, the poet's attention is turned to yet another man and yet another reason for depression. In the lexical chiasmus in line 6 ("featured like him, like him with friends") the speaker's free-associative rant ricochets off the phrase "like him." The result is an oppressive litany of complaints that allows no space to step back and contemplate the situation rationally. The urgency of the diction and the syntax propels the poet forward to seemingly inevitable destruction, which throws into relief the joy at the end. The poet not only lifts himself out of depression, but also releases himself from the heated repetitions and anxious phrasing. The multiple instances of alliteration in the second half—"*l*ike to the *l*ark" (11) "*s*ullen earth, *s*ings" (12) "*h*ymns at *h*eaven['s gate]" (12)—lend these lines of relief a pleasing, soothing lilt.

FORM

Like several other sonnets, (such as 18 and 129) Sonnet 29 combines elements of both the Petrarchan and the Elizabethan sonnet. The rhyme scheme is typically Elizabethan, with three quatrains of an alternating *abab* pattern followed by a heroic couplet. Thematically, however, the poem can be charted in both forms. Within the Petrarchan model, the octave describes the poets' abject misery, and the sextet "answers" the problem. The poet is soothed and exalted when reminded of his beloved friend. Although the first eight lines have a cumulative force when taken as a whole octave, the sonnet may also be divided into three distinct Elizabethan quatrains. In the first quatrain, the poet looks at himself and realizes how solitary his condition is, how singular his anguish. In the second quatrain, he looks out and compares himself unfavorably to others. In the third quatrain, he looks back in time to remember his friend, which brings him out of despair. The final couplet is autonomous and epigrammatic in the Elizabeth style, and provides resolution for the entire poem.

SONNET 40

Go ahead and steal my mistress; I forgive you, even though you have hurt me greatly.

Take all my loves, my love, yea, take them all:
What hast thou then more than thy hadst before?
No love, my love, that thou mayst true love call—
All mine was thine before thou hadst this more.
Then if for my love thou my love receivest[1],
I cannot blame thee for my love thou usest*;   *exploit / have sex with*
But yet be blamed if thou this self* deceivest   *the poet*
By wilful taste* of what thyself[2] refusest.   *stubborn lust*
I do forgive thy robb'ry, gentle thief,
Although thou steal thee all my poverty*;   *my meager possessions*
And yet love knows it is a greater grief
To bear love's wrong than hate's known injury.
    Lascivious grace*, in whom all ill well shows[3],   *lustful charmer*
    Kill me with spites*, yet we must not be foes.   *injuries*

SUMMARY

The poet addresses this sonnet to the young man who has stolen the poet's mistress. He urges the young man to take all of his loves, meaning both the poet's love for others and the poet's mistress. He suggests that the young man gained nothing by stealing the poet's mistress—everything the poet owned was already his. The poet says he can forgive the young man if he stole the mistress out of love for the poet. The young man is to blame, however, if he is allowing lust to overshadow what he knows is right. The poet says he will forgive the young man for stealing his mistress, even though the theft has robbed the poet of everything he owns. He remarks that it is more painful to endure the hurtful behavior of a loved one than the open attacks of an enemy. The poet concludes on a note of reconciliation, saying that the young man makes misconduct look good. He decides that even if the young man kills him with his wrongdoing, he cannot make an enemy of him.

ANALYSIS

Sonnet 40, the cry of a betrayed man, is alternately weary, bitter, loving, and forgiving. Like Sonnets 41 and 42, it concerns the triangle made up of the poet, the young man, and the mistress. The repetition and multiple meanings of the word "love" suggest the confusion of the poet's relationship with the young man, and give rise to several readings of each line. In Sonnet 40, the definition of "love" shifts, sometimes several times per line, and often sustains several definitions simultaneously, referring to the young man, the poet's devotion, and the poet's lovers.

Although the couplet moves toward forgiveness, it does not achieve a resolution. The poet retreats from his criticisms, saying that the young man's loveliness makes even his wicked deeds seem appealing. He sounds defeated and masochistic when he orders the young man to "[k]ill me with spites," and pleading when he says "we must not be foes" (14).

---

1. *if for my love thou my love receivest*: if you love her because I love her
2. *of what thyself refusest*: the editors of the Norton Shakespeare (1997) suggest that the phrase means the young man is to blame if he deceives his own "better nature" ("thyself"), which does not want to steal the poet's mistress.
3. *In whom all ill well shows*: who makes every vice look good

LANGUAGE NOTES

Tone	introspective, critical, anguished, forgiving, rueful
Theme	the debasement of the subordinate lover; the selfishness of the dominant lover; the mystery of other people's motivations; the impossibility of holding a grudge against one's true love
Metaphor	the young man's affair with the mistress as "robb'ry" (9); the young man as "thief" (9); the poet's possessions and mistress as "poverty" (10) (that is, unimportant or small)
Pattern	oxymoronic concepts such as "gentle thief" (9), "[l]ascivious grace" (13), and "ill well" (13)

LANGUAGE

Repetition and multiple meanings make Sonnet 40 a difficult poem to decipher. In contrast to Sonnet 39, in which the poet describes love's unity and disunity in clear and almost colloquial language, Sonnet 40 plays with language to create a sense of confusion and ambiguity. The syncopated repetition of the word "love" ("Take all my loves, my love" (1), "No love, my love" (3), "if for my love thou my love" (5)) emphasizes the poet's preoccupation with defining love, and the shifting definition of the word suggests that the concept of love is flexible, variable, unstable. "Love" can refer to a young man, a woman, an emotion, or all three at once. The complexity of the poem's language also suggests the poet's grief and confusion.

Shakespeare uses imperatives, exclamations, and interjections to create a sense of drama in Sonnet 40. He also suggests the passion of the poet with violent words such as "deceivest' (7), "wilful" (8), "robb'ry" (9), "grief" (11), "hate" (12), "[l]ascivious" (13), "[k]ill" (14), "spites" (14), and "foes" (14).

FORM

In Sonnet 40, Shakespeare uses the three quatrains to develop three different ideas. In the first, the poet almost sarcastically urges his beloved young man to "take all [his] loves" (1) since "all [his love]" (1) already belongs to the young man. In the second quatrain, the poet says he will forgive the young man if he transgressed out of love for the poet and not out of senseless lust. In the third quatrain, the poet says he will pardon the young man, even though the injuries done to us by loved ones are the most painful injuries of all. In the couplet, Shakespeare summarizes the movement of the sonnet and shifts in a slightly new direction. The violence of the couplet's diction ("ill" (13), "[k]ill" (14), "spites" (14), "foes" (14)) suggests the poet's righteousness and hurt feelings, while the sentiment Shakespeare expresses suggests the poet's masochistic longing for the young man, and his willingness to make peaceful overtures to him even when it is the poet, not the young man, who deserves an apology.

SONNET 55

Because I have written poetry about you, you will outlast statues, wars, and death.

Not marble nor the gilded* monuments	*decorated*
Of princes shall outlive this powerful rhyme[1],	
But you shall shine more bright in these contents	
Than unswept stone besmeared with sluttish* time.	*messy*
When wasteful war shall statues overturn,	
And broils* root out the work of masonry*,	*battles / stone-carving*
Nor Mars[2] his sword nor war's quick fire shall burn	
The living record of your memory.	
'Gainst death and all oblivious enmity*	*hostility*
Shall you pace forth*; your praise shall still find room	*go forward*
Even in the eyes of all posterity	
That wear this world out to the ending doom[3].	
So, till the judgment that yourself arise,	
You live in this, and dwell in lovers' eyes.	

SUMMARY

In Sonnet 55, the poet promises the young man immortality through poetry. The poet says that his sonnet will outlast even statues. The young man, he writes, is more dazzling than stone dulled by the passage of time. War will topple and destroy statues, which are physical things, but nothing can touch or harm poetry, a "living record" of the young man. The young man will march forth in defiance of death and everything hateful. His memory will persist until the end of time. The poet says that until Judgment Day, the young man will live in this sonnet and in lovers who will read it.

ANALYSIS

The thesis of Sonnet 55—the ability of poetry to confer immortality—is a frequent theme in the sonnet sequence. Shakespeare introduces it in Sonnet 15, recants it in 16, reiterates it in 17, gives it full backing in 18, and then continues to refer to it throughout the sequence. This vacillation maps the process of a writer developing his idea, hesitating, thinking as he writes, testing the idea, and finally fleshing it out fully.

Sonnet 55 draws on an ode by the Roman poet Horace. Classical works such as those by Horace were a staple in sixteenth-century study and had a wide influence on literature. Latin was culturally prominent, and vernacular (colloquial) Latin was gaining respect. In Shakespeare's day, translations from Latin into English were important texts that were consumed and criticized with enthusiasm, and emulation of the classicists was commended. Shakespeare frequently used classical works as inspiration and source material. *Comedy of Errors*, for example, borrows heavily from the Latin dramatist Plautus.

---

1. An allusion to the first line of the Roman poet Horace's *Ode* 3.30, which begins,

   I have built a monument more lasting than bronze,
   And more lofty than the regal structure of the Pyramids,
   A monument which neither the eroding rain, nor the raging North Wind,
   Nor the endless procession of the years, nor fleeting Time
   Is able to destroy.
   I will not entirely die, but a great part of me will escape Death:
   And endlessly I will be new, born again in future praise...

2. Mars was the Roman God of War.
3. *the ending doom*: Doomsday or Judgment Day. According to Christian doctrine, on Judgment Day the dead arise to rejoin their souls and Christ passes final judgment on everyone, saving some from the apocalypse

Horace's *Ode 3.30* informs Sonnet 55. In the ode, Horace catalogues regal memorials and says his art will outlast all of them. Shakespeare echoes this idea, writing that neither "marble nor gilded monuments" (1) will last longer than the young man. Just as Horace defies the elements and time itself to challenge his art, Shakespeare says that the young man will outlive memorials, civilizations, and death itself.

To compare poetry favorably to a monument is to convey a deep, almost religious appreciation of literature. Monuments are grand, public objects meant to be permanent appreciations of civilization's heroes. But, Shakespeare suggests, we are wrong to imagine that our heroes and ideals, as symbolized by the statues we put up, will maintain their power forever. It is literature, he says, that is the grand, lasting achievement of civilization.

LANGUAGE NOTES

Tone	majestic, elevated
Theme	poetry's ability to defy death and destruction and bestow immortality
Symbol	poetry as a monument
Pattern:	repetition of language associated with war and ruins

LANGUAGE

Sonnet 55 unfolds in a majestic, firm, prayerful tone. The diction is lush—"unswept stone besmeared with sluttish time" (4) is extravagant, and the four-fold repetition of "s" suggests the sweep and messiness of time's passage. Although sprinklings of assonance and alliteration bolster the urgent tone, the poem is otherwise unusually unadorned for a sonnet. There is the allusion to the mythical Mars and the personification of war, but there are no grand or extended metaphors or similes.

FORM

Over the course of three quatrains, Shakespeare defies heroes, civilization, and finally time itself. In the first quatrain, the poet states that the young man will outlive the proud "monuments" (1) that history erects to honor its heroes. By virtue of his immortalization in verse, the young man is greater than history's heroes, kings, and "princes" (2). In the second quatrain, the poet says the young man will outlive the terrors of "war" (7), which suggests that the young man will transcend the rise and fall of entire civilizations. In the third quatrain, the poet says that the young man will persist "'Gainst death and all oblivious enmity" (9). By beating death, the young man undoes time's power to obliterate. In the couplet, the poet says that the young man will live on in verse until God puts an end to time.

SONNET 60[1]

Time is a relentless, natural force that destroys all living things.

Like as* the waves make* towards the pebbled shore,	*just as / move, make their way*
So do our minutes[2] hasten to their end,	
Each* changing place with that which goes before;	*i.e., wave*
In sequent* toil all forwards do contend[3].	*successive*
Nativity*, once in the main of light,	*birth, a newborn baby*
Crawls to maturity[4], wherewith* being crowned	*i.e., with maturity*
Crookèd* eclipses* 'gainst his* glory fight,[5]	*pernicious / i.e., portents / i.e., nativity-cum-maturity's*
And Time that gave doth now his gift confound*.[6]	*ruin, destroy*
Time doth transfix* the flourish* set on youth,[7]	*destroy / beauty, bloom*
And delves* the parallels[8] in beauty's brow;	*digs / i.e., wrinkle lines*
Feeds* on the rarities* of nature's truth*,	*i.e., devours / extraordinary things / nature in its perfection*
And nothing stands but for his* scythe to mow[9].	*i.e., Time's*
And yet to* times in hope* my verse shall stand,	*until / of the future*
Praising thy worth despite his* cruèl hand.	*i.e., Time's*

SUMMARY

The poet compares the progress of time to the continual cycle of waves reaching the shore. Men are born with great potential, but as they progress to old age, they are thwarted by fate and eventually die. Time relentlessly erodes youth and beauty, devours even the most precious natural things. Eventually, it mows down everything. The poet hopes that his poetic praise of the young man will survive into the future, despite the ravages of time.

ANALYSIS

Sonnet 60 is preoccupied with topics that are popular within the sonnet sequence, such as the relentlessness of time, the inevitability of death, and the power of poetry to immortalize. Sonnets 15–18, first cautiously, then with increasing confidence, propose poetry as a solution for the young man's inevitable decline and death.

As the sequence progresses, the emphasis shifts from the young man's mortality to the poet's. Poetry remains the answer.

The second quatrain presents time as the primary force in human life, for good and for ill. Time brings humans into existence, nurtures them into adulthood, and then destroys them in death. The imagery suggests that the force of time is natural, however melancholy and sinister. In the first quatrain, Shakespeare casts time as the faceless, unchanging sea, relentlessly eroding life's shore. In the third, the poet compares wrinkles to lines of crops and death to harvesting (10–12). The scythe is a particularly rich

---

1. The placing of the sonnet within the sequence matches the number of minutes (60) in an hour.
2. *our minutes*: Puns on "hour minutes."
3. *In sequent toil all forwards do contend*: Each one (wave or minute) strives to move forward, competing with others.
4. *Nativity, once in the main of light, / Crawls to maturity*: Newborn children, initially gloriously illuminated, slowly progress ("crawls") to old age. "Crawls" suggests the gait of both babies and of old men.
5. *wherewith being crowned, / Crookèd eclipses 'gainst his glory fight*: As humans grow toward (are "crowned" with) maturity, their efforts and potential for greatness ("glory") are thwarted by fate. Eclipses of the sun or the moon, caused by the ("crooked") misalignment of the planets, were seen as dangerous omens. An eclipse is an instance of darkness (i.e., death) triumphing over light.
6. *Time that gave doth now his gift confound*: Time, which gave life, takes life away (i.e., brings death). Recalls "The Lord giveth and the Lord taketh away" (Job 1:21).
7. *Time doth transfix the flourish set on youth*: Time destroys the beauty of youth.
8. *delves the parallels in beauty's brow*: [time] creates wrinkles ("parallels") in beauty's forehead. In other words, time ages beautiful things.
9. *nothing stands but for his scythe to mow*: Everything that grows will be mowed down by time's scythe — i.e., everything that lives will die.

image: it is both a natural tool and an attribute of death (see, for example, images of the grim reaper). Here, as in Sonnet 19, time is closely associated with death.

LANGUAGE NOTES

Tone   solemn, pessimistic (1–12); quietly defiant (13–14)

Theme   the relentless progression of time; aging and death as inevitable; life as ephemeral; poetry as a way of achieving immortality

Symbol   the seashore (border of the sea) symbolizes an end (1); time's scythe symbolizes death (13); light as a symbol of glorious youth (5); darkness (of "eclipse") as a symbol of destructive force (7) ; eclipses symbolize fateful portents, the triumph of darkness over light; standing as marker of immortality (12, 13)

Metaphor   the relentless progress of time as like waves hitting the shore, perpetually (1–2); time as a scythe-wielding, all-devouring force of destruction, mowing down life (8–12); ephemeral beauty personified as an aging woman (10); living creatures compared to growing crops, to be mowed down by death (12)

Pattern   language associated with harvesting or agriculture: "scythe," "mow" (12), "delve" (10); language associated with progress, usually slow but relentless: "make towards" (1), "hasten" (2), "sequent toil" (4), "forwards" (4), "contend" (4), "crawls" (6)

LANGUAGE

Shakespeare illustrates his thesis through three distinct images of time. First, time is a natural, inevitable force, like the tides. Next, time becomes a divine force that first gives life and then takes it away. Finally, Shakespeare portrays time as an aggressive, destructive assailant. The force of the images is rooted in the strong verbs: "crawls" (6), "transfix" (9), "delves" (10). Indeed, the sonnet portrays its elements in perpetual motion: the waves "make towards" (1) the shore, the minutes "hasten" (2), the baby "crawls" toward death. The personification of time blurs the line between the force of time and its human victims.

FORM

Sonnet 60 is an Elizabethan sonnet, divided neatly into three quatrains and an autonomous, defiant couplet. Each of the quatrains develops a separate idea: the first compares time to the continual process of waves crashing upon the shore, the second charts mankind's journey through life, and the third personifies time as a devouring, scythe-wielding force of destruction. The couplet, which presents poetry as a way of achieving immortality, stands apart from the rest of the sonnet: its rhyme is self-contained, its focus is personal, and its tone is defiant.

SONNET 65

Youth and beauty can survive the ravages of time only if they live on in print.

Since[1] brass, nor stone, nor earth, nor boundless sea[2],	
But sad mortality* o'ersways* their power,	*inevitable death / vanquishes*
How with this rage shall beauty hold a plea*,	*sue*
Whose action* is no stronger than a flower?	*power*
O how shall summer's honey breath hold out	
Against the wrackful* siege of battering days	*destructive*
When rocks impregnable* are not so stout,	*unconquerable*
Nor gates of steel so strong, but time decays[3]?	
O fearful meditation*! Where, alack,	*thought*
Shall time's best jewel from time's chest lie hid[4],	
Or what strong hand can hold his swift foot back,	
Or who his spoil* of beauty can forbid?	*ruin*
O none, unless this miracle have might:	
That in black ink my love may still shine bright.	

SUMMARY

The poet points out that death destroys everything solid, including earth and sea. If this is so, he asks, how can beauty, which has no power, hold its own against death? How can gentle summer days resist the passage of time when even rocks and steel cannot? Calling this a frightening thought, the poet wonders how youthful beauty can escape death, or what person could prevent time from ruining youth and beauty. He concludes that only by living on in print can the young man retain his youth.

ANALYSIS

Sonnet 65 combines two of the sonnet sequence's main themes: the desperate need to resist all-powerful, destructive time, and the importance of preserving and cultivating beauty. Shakespeare says that time erodes everything, including seemingly invulnerable elements of nature like rocks and oceans. He portrays time as a malevolent force, reifying it as a "wrackful siege," a force that means to attack and destroy.

In several of the sonnets in Shakespeare's cycle, time is portrayed as destructive, but also necessary, balancing, and natural. This perception of time is symbolized by the scythe (sickle), which, in literature, personifications of death and time often carry. In Sonnet 116, for example, Shakespeare refers to "Time's ... bending sickle" (9–10). Although it cuts, a scythe is not necessarily a frightening weapon. It is an instrument for mowing wheat or other crops, so associating death with a scythe suggests that death harvests souls as naturally as farmers harvest their crops.

In Sonnet 65, however, Shakespeare abandons any implication of time's naturalness, necessity, or nobility. Instead he conceives of time and death as sinister, violent, and unthinking. Although the couplet suggests that "black ink" (14)—that is, the written word—offers hope for immortality, the suggestion is a tentative one. The poet writes "unless this miracle have might," (13) using "unless" to convey his uncertainty. The doubtful efficacy of poetry to preserve youth emphasizes death's power.

---

1. *Since*: since neither
2. The first line of Sonnet 65 recalls Sonnet 55, the first line of which is: "Not marble nor the gilded monuments / Of princes shall outlive this powerful rhyme" (1–2). Sonnet 55 and 65 share the themes of immortality through art and the ravages of time
3. *decays*: makes them decay
4. *Where...shall time's best jewel from time's chest hid*: How shall the young man escape the grave (that is, death's coffin, or "chest")?

LANGUAGE NOTES

Tone   dramatic, urgent, anxious

Themes   the corrosive power of time ; the aggression and violence of death; the urgent need to protect beauty and youth; the possible power of poetry to defeat time and death

Symbol   time as a hostile enemy at war with life and beauty

Metaphors   love as a matter of law (2, 3, 4); beauty as a flower; summer's warmth and ease as "honey breath" (5); time as a besieging force; the young man as "Time's best jewel" (10); coffins as "Time's chest" (10); time's onslaught as a "swift foot" (11)

Pattern   repetition of language associated with warfare ("siege … battering" (6), "impregnable" (7), "spoils" (12))

LANGUAGE

Sonnet 65, like Sonnet 146, utilizes emotional and exclamatory language to convey urgency. The exclamation "O fearful meditation!" and the constant questions give the lines a forceful, staccato rhythm. As they pile up, the questions convey a sensation of motion, urgency, and fear. Alliteration ("steel so strong" (8)) and repetition ("brass, nor stone, nor earth, nor boundless sea" (1)) also convey movement. Shakespeare's diction in Sonnet 65 is dramatic and exuberant: words such as "boundless" (1), "wrackful" (6), "impregnable" (7), and "miracle" (13) suggest the vastness of death and the potential power of literature.

FORM

In the first quatrain, the poet describes the ill-fated "suit" or "plea" (3) of frail beauty against all-powerful "mortality" (2). In quatrain two, he describes time as an aggressor who wages war against the natural world and damages even the sturdiest objects, such as "rocks impregnable" (7) and "gates of steel" (8). Quatrain three emphasizes the necessity of preserving the young man in the face of time's onslaught. In the couplet, the poet says that the only "miracle" (13) that could possibly preserve youth is poetry.

SONNET 73

Love me more now, for I am on the cusp of old age and death.

That time of year thou mayst in me behold
When yellow leaves, or none, or few, do hang
Upon those boughs which shake against the cold,
Bare ruined choirs*[1] where late* the sweet birds sang.   *i.e., tree branches / recently*
In me thou seest the twilight of such day
As after sunset fadeth in the west,
Which by and by black night doth take away,
Death's second self*, that seals up all in rest.   *i.e., night (sleep = Death's younger brother)*
In me thou seest the glowing of such fire
That* on the ashes of his* youth doth lie[2]   *as / its (i.e., the fire's)*
As the death-bed whereon it must expire,
Consumed with that which* it was nourished by[3]:   *i.e., the ashes*

    This* thou perceiv'st, which makes thy love more strong[4],   *i.e., that the poet will die soon*
    To love that* well which thou must leave ere long.   *i.e., the poet*

SUMMARY

The poet invokes a series of metaphors to describe what he perceives as his old age. In the first quatrain, he compares his age to autumn, a season of gentle, natural decline and creeping cold. In the second quatrain, the poet's old age is like twilight, a time of dwindling light and gradual loss of focus. In the third quatrain, the poet compares his stage of life to the last gasps of a fire as it smolders and is smothered under its ashes. Since the young man continues to love the poet even though he knows that the poet will soon die of old age, the young man must love the poet a great deal indeed.

ANALYSIS

Sonnet 73, like many of the first 126 sonnets, expresses anxiety about the relentless passage of time and the proximity of death. Sonnet 73 develops this theme through a carefully constructed sequence of metaphors, all of which portray liminal (or threshold) states: autumn hovering on the treacherous cusp of winter, twilight dwindling into blackness, and embers snuffing out into lifeless ash. These images derive their emotional force from their liminality. Their closeness to death lends them a sinister hue.

    The order of the metaphors too is carefully chosen to reflect increasing urgency. The first metaphor—late middle age as autumn—depends on the cycle of seasons of the year. By the second metaphor—late middle age as twilight—the cycle is radically shorter, and a year has become a day. The final metaphor—late middle age as dying embers—not only shrinks the time scale even more, but breaks with the cyclical aspect of the other metaphors. A fire burns out forever. The phoenix may rise from the ashes, but the poet will not. By the end of the sonnet, death arrives with an unapologetic finality.

---

1. *choir*: (1)The heart of a church, from which the church choir sings. (2) Alternate spelling of "quire," which is a stack of sheets (a twentieth of a ream) of a manuscript. Some critics have suggested that "bare ruined choirs" is a reference to the Catholic monasteries plundered by Henry VIII after 1538, when he split off from the church. In *Seven Types of Ambiguity*, William Empson writes: "the comparison holds for many reasons; because ruined monastery choirs are places in which to sing, because they involve sitting in a row, because they are made of wood, are carved into knots and so forth. . ."
2. A possible allusion to the phoenix, a glorious mythological bird that dies in flames and is reborn new from its own ashes.
3. *Consumed with that which it was nourished by*: smothered ("consumed") by the ashes, byproduct of the fuel that fed ("nourished") the fire. This self-smothering fire is the image from Sonnet 1 of extreme selfishness and wastefulness. As an image, it drips with irony.
4. *This thou perceiv'st, which makes thy love more strong*: (1) Because you understand that I will die soon, you love me more. (2) Because, as you know, I will die soon, please love me more now. (3) Because you continue to love me even though you know that I will die soon, I conclude that you must love me a lot indeed.

LANGUAGE NOTES

Tone   mournful and contemplative (1–12); gently didactic (13–14)

Themes   the poignant proximity of old age to inevitable death; the cold finality of death; the especial urgency of love in the face of impending death

Symbol   old age approaching death symbolized by liminal states: autumn on the cusp of winter, twilight about to dissolve into night, fire close to dying (1–12)

Metaphor   old age as rural autumn (1–4); leafless branches as "bare ruined choirs" (4); old age as twilight (5–8); night as "Death's second self" (8); old age as the final embers of a fire (9–12); ashes as the "death-bed" of a fire (11)

Pattern   repetition of words associated with vision: "behold" (1), "seest" (5, 9), and "perceiv'st" (13)

LANGUAGE

Sonnet 73 is one of Shakespeare's most accessible. The vocabulary is straightforward, the sentiments are relatively concrete, and the allusions remain in check. The sonnet's focus is on describing its sophisticated metaphors in uncomplicated terms. Shakespeare devotes each quatrain to a single extended metaphor, which allows him to set the scene and provide context carefully. If the purpose of the poem is to persuade the young man to "love more strong" (13), the meticulous attention to detail makes the argument more persuasive.

The progression of the metaphors (see Analysis) moves the sonnet along. Shakespeare personifies time, night, and death as sinister agents who pose a very real threat to humans. The reification of the trappings of the poet's age—yellow leaves, bare branches, ashes—emphasizes the ways in which time and decay reduces human beings to dust. These markers of decay create an unsettled mood and sense of urgency to inspire the young man to action and appreciation.

FORM

Sonnet 73 is a classic Elizabethan sonnet. The three quatrains present three distinct thoughts: old age is like autumn; old age is like twilight; old age is like a dying fire. The couplet is an autonomous declaration that concludes the thrust of the argument: because life is short and death inevitable, the young man should "love more strong" (13) while he is alive.

SONNET 94

Beautiful people should exercise self-control.

They that have the power to hurt and will do none*,[1]	*i.e., no harm*
That* do not do the thing they most do show[2],	*i.e., who*
Who moving* others are themselves as stone*,	*i.e., eliciting emotion, prompting to action / umoved*
Unmovèd, cold*, and to temptation slow* —	*composed, cold / not wont to succumb to temptation*
They rightly* do inherit* heaven's graces*,	*justly / receive / divine blessings*
And husband* nature's riches from expense*[3];	*preserve, use sparingly / waste*
They are the lords and owners of their faces,	
Others but stewards* of their* excellence*.[4]	*managers / i.e., their own / beauty*
The summer's flower is to the summer sweet	
Though to itself it only live and die[5],	
But if that flower with base infection* meet*	*disease, corruption / be afflicted*
The basest weed outbraves* his* dignity*[6]:	*surpasses / i.e., the flower's / virtues*

    For sweetest things turn sourest by their deeds:

    Lilies that fester smell far worse than weeds[7].

SUMMARY

In the first eight lines, the poet praises beautiful people who exercise restraint. Although, because of their beauty, these people have power over others, they refrain from hurting others—presumably, by not leading them on. Such people are truly in control of their lives and their beauty, and deserve blessing. In the sestet, the poet constructs an elaborate allegory. However self-centered, flowers are beautiful and so contribute to the goodness of the world. At the same time, a diseased flower is much worse than any weed. The implication is that beautiful people who are corrupted by their own power over others are uglier and more despicable than people who are born unattractive.

ANALYSIS

Sonnet 94 is one of the most ambiguous and difficult of the sequence. Its neighboring sonnets, especially 95, suggest that the poet is obliquely chiding his young man for ignoble behavior. The young man is the "summer's flower" (9) in danger of "base infection" (11)—presumably, sexual or romantic indiscretions. Most critics agree that the "power to hurt" (1) refers to emotional, rather than, say, physical or political, damage. The young man is beautiful and attractive. He has power to hurt the poet because the poet is emotionally attached to him. His beauty is his "nature's riches" (6) that, the poet insists, he should not squander—presumably, through sexual promiscuity.

    Many of the sonnet's lines are problematic. For example, many critics interpret the "faces" in lines 7–8 ("They are the lords and stewards of their faces, / Others, but stewards of their excellence") as meaning

---

1. The "hurt" mentioned here is likely emotional. Those who are beautiful have power to hurt because their beauty makes others vulnerable.
2. *That do not do the thing they most do show*: Who do not behave as we would expect from their (beautiful) appearance—i.e., beautiful people who do not hurt others despite the fact that their beauty has given them "power to hurt."
3. *Husband nature's riches from expense*: use their beauty (their "nature's riches") prudently and sparingly—likely, refrain from sleeping around. *Expense* can also mean "ejaculation."
4. *They are the lords and owners of their faces / Others but stewards of their excellence*: They—i.e., those who exercise self-control—justly possess (are "lords and owners" of) their beauty; other people (i.e., those who do not always have perfect self-control) only manage (are "stewards" of) their beauty without truly possessing it.
5. *The summer's flower is to the summer sweet, / Though to itself it only life and die*: (perhaps) Those who are beautiful and self-controlled contribute to the goodness of the world, even if their lives are focused on themselves.
6. *But if that flower with base infection meet, / The basest weed outbraves his dignity*: (perhaps) But if such a beautiful person is corrupted, he becomes more despicable that the lowliest and ugliest person alive.
7. *Lilies that fester smell far worse than weeds*: Noble, pure, and lovely things (or people) that are corrupt are much worse than lowly and common things. Lilies were associated with purity, so "lilies that fester" represent the ultimate floral fall from grace. Line 14 appears also in the 1596 anonymous play *The Reign of King Edward III*, contributing to speculation that Shakespeare had a hand in writing the play.

"personality," "willpower." From this interpretation of "faces" comes this reading: "They exercise complete self-control; others only manage their virtues and desires without controlling them." Some critics, however, suggest that "faces" (7) and "excellence" (8) refer to beauty only, not all personal attributes more generally. This is the reading suggested in our glosses. Still other critics suggest that "their excellence" (8) refers not to the virtues of the steward-like people, but rather to the virtues of the lord-like people. Lines 7–8 would then mean, "They exercise complete control over themselves; others are subservient to them."

LANGUAGE NOTES

Tone	philosophical, didactic (1–12); indignant, moralizing (13–14)
Theme	the virtue of restraint; moral corruption as an ever-present threat; virtue corrupted as worse than lack of virtue
Symbols	the flower (in particular, the lily) symbolizes a beautiful nobleman; the diseased flower represents that man corrupted; the weed represents an ugly and lowly commoner; one's life as an estate
Metaphor	restraint described as being like "stone" (3); personal beauty and goodness compared to an estate whose "nature's riches" must be "husband[ed]" (6) ; those in control are "lords and owners" (7); others are mere "stewards" (8)
Pattern	vague third-person generalities throughout; repetition of words: three "do"s (2), two "summer"'s (9)

LANGUAGE

Like the literal meaning, the syntax and the sounds of Sonnet 94 are often convoluted. The first sentence lasts the whole octave. The pronoun referents are always obscure and often ambiguous. The octet in particular skirts the issues rather than addressing them directly. "[They] do not do the thing they most do show" (2) is a typically vague line. We never learn what the "thing" is (sexual promiscuity?). The relatively content-free word "do" appears three times, weaving through the line as though to obscure its meaning.

The noisome, sickly sweet long *e* sound dominates the sestet. Both the quatrain and the couplet use it as an end rhyme—"sweet" (9) / "meet" (11) and "deeds" (13) / "weeds" (14). Internal "weed" (12) and "sweetest" (13) contribute to the impression of insidious poison.

FORM

Sonnet 94 fits the Petrarchan sonnet model better than the Elizabethan. The octave does not lend itself to being broken up into two quatrains. Rather, it develops a single, continuous idea about people who exercise self-control. The sextet develops an allegorical argument through flower imagery. The couplet stands somewhat apart and epigrammatically concludes the floral argument, suggesting Elizabethan sonnet influences.

SONNET 116

True love weathers any obstacle and does not waver with time or hardships.

Let me not to the marriage of true minds
Admit impediments*[1]. Love is not love   *obstacles*
Which alters when it alteration finds,
Or bends with the remover to remove[2].
O no, it is an ever-fixèd mark[3]
That looks on tempests and is never shaken;
It is the star[4] to every wandering barque*,   *ship*
Whose* worth's unknown, although his* height be taken[5].   *i.e., the star's / i.e., the star's*
Love's not time's fool, though rosy lips and cheeks[6]
Within his* bending sickle's compass* come[7];   *i.e., time's / reach*
Love alters not with his* brief hours and weeks,   *i.e., time's*
But bears it out* even to the edge of doom*.   *endures / beginning of doomsday*
   If this be error and upon me proved,
   I never writ, nor no man ever loved.

SUMMARY

Sonnet 116 attempts to define love by distinguishing what it is from what it is not. Shakespeare opens by describing true love as a cerebral "marriage of true minds" (1), untainted by lust. True love admits no obstacles, and will not change under any circumstance, come what may. Like a beacon in the tempest of life's problems, true love is dependable. Like the North Star (which sailors used to navigate), love is always visible and guides people through life. Moreover, true love is immortal. Though beauty may fade with time, love cannot be reached by death's grim, all-destroying "sickle" (10). True love endures past the end of time, until doomsday. The poet ends with a vow: if he is mistaken, he is no poet, and there is no love in the world.

ANALYSIS

Sonnet 116 is one of the most famous sonnets, and its opening definition of love one of the most frequently quoted and anthologized in the poetic canon. In essence, Sonnet 116 is one long exercise in hyperbole that explores an unattainable ideal of love. At the same time, its earnestness and force of conviction, from the emphatic "O no" (5) opening the second quatrain to the epic assertion in the couplet, is contagious and impossible to deny.

    Thematically, Sonnet 116 is very simple: true love is constant. This constancy is particularly valuable in a fickle world subject to time's ravages. The relentless passage of time is a key concern in Shakespeare's sonnets. Elsewhere, the poet prescribes procreation or poesy. For example, Sonnet 12 offers this

---

1. *Let me not to the marriage of true minds admit impediments*: This introductory declaration recalls the Christian marriage ceremony, in which the officiator gives anyone present who may know of any "just impediment" to the marriage a last chance to speak.
2. *which alters when it alteration finds / Or bends with the remover to remove*: which changes when the relationship alters, by hardship, separation, infidelity, death, etc.
3. A mark is an unmoving object or point of focus, as seen from ships at sea, such as a lighthouse or beacon. Such unmoving objects were important in navigation for their ability to provide reference points to sailors as they navigated.
4. *the star*: i.e. the North Star, which sailors in the northern hemisphere use to navigate.
5. *Whose worth's unknown, although his height be taken*: the star's value may be unknown or immeasurable, but its position ("height") is a constant guide. By tracing the metaphor, true love may be immeasurable but constant and dependable.
6. *rosy lips and cheeks* were conventional markers of beauty in love poetry from Petrarch to Sidney.
7. *Love's not Time's fool, though rosy lips and cheeks / Within his bending sickle's compass come*: love does not waver with time, even if physical beauty—traditionally associated with love—fades as time passes. In lines 10–12, time is portrayed as a scythe-wielding figure of Death, which destroys everything in its reach. The scythe ("bending sickle") is a traditional a symbol of Death's destructive force, as evidenced by the grim reaper.

reason for bearing children: "And nothing 'gainst time's scythe can make defence / Save breed to brave him when he takes thee hence." (12:13–14). His recommendations are compelling: both progeny and poetry have lived on. How does immortal love fit in? Most readers agree that the love that Shakespeare advocates here is lifelong, devoted partnership—the "marriage" of the opening. Marriage provided stability in an era troubled by outbreaks of the plague and foreign invasions (such as the Spanish Armada of 1588). Shakespeare evokes the uncertainty of life in difficult times by describing mankind as a fleet of "wandering barque[s]" (7) for whom love provides the necessary "mark" (5) or beacon. Sea voyages were (and still are) a dangerous mode of transportation, made perilous by storms and confused by poor navigation technology. The language has preserved some of these worries: someone "at sea" or "adrift" is uncertain or lost. As an allegorical space for life's journey, the sea fits well with Shakespeare's fixation on the passage of time: like time, the sea is vast and endlessly cyclical. In the sonnet, love does not conquer time, and there are no martial absolutes. Instead, as a beacon, love helps guide individuals on their passage though time. Love endures time's ravages rather than combating them.

LANGUAGE NOTES

Tone	philosophical; impassioned, righteous (5–14); defiant, epic (13–14)
Theme	love is a paragon of constancy in a fickle world eroded by time.
Symbol	lines 5–8 develop an extended symbolization: life is a sea journey, people are "barques," life's troubles are tempests, love is the North Star, a dependable guide; the "true minds" married in line 1 symbolize the non-physical aspects of love; "[r]osy lips and cheeks" (9) stand in for physical beauty (synechdoche)
Metaphor	extended metaphor in 5–8: people are "barques," life's troubles are tempests, love is the North Star (a dependable guide); implicitly, life is a sea journey; love as a beacon or lighthouse, a dependable guide in the tempest-turmoils of life (5–6); time personified as a scythe-wielding Grim Reaper, a harbinger of death (10–12)
Pattern	repetition of words associated with duration: "ever" (5, 14), "never" (6, 14), "Time" (9), and "brief" (11); repetition of roots in different structure: "*alters* when it *alter*ation finds" (3) and "bends with the *remover* to *remove*" (4)

LANGUAGE

Sonnet 116 is renowned for its sentiment and forceful conviction rather than for linguistic or imagistic innovation. Many of the images and metaphors are old tropes: time's "bending sickle" (10) and a beauty's "rosy lips and cheeks" (9) were already poetic staples by Shakespeare's time. Moreover, it is their very familiarity that drives the rhetoric. The images are mere vehicles to drive the force of conviction. Earnest and philosophical, Sonnet 116 is a serious mini-treatise on idealized love. To concretize his abstract ideas, Shakespeare reifies love in the second quatrain, then personifies both time and love in the third. The sonnet first phrase delivers the ceremonial drumming of extended alliteration, a foretaste of love's constancy: "Let me not to the marriage of true minds / Admit impediments" (1–2). The absolute modifiers "ever" (5, 14), "every" (7), and "never" (6, 14) similarly echo that same constancy and give the sonnet an epic flavor.

FORM

Like other English sonnets, Shakespeare composed 116 with three quatrains that develop the argument followed by an autonomous couplet that sums up and makes a final twist. The three quatrains develop three separate ideas: love as constant in the face of hardship in the first, love as a dependable beacon on the sea journey of life in the second, and love constant through time in the third. The epigrammatic couplet makes a claim of epic certainty and stands apart from the rest of the sonnet.

SONNET 129

Lust is a hellish, maddening trap to which all people succumb.

Th' expense of spirit* in a waste of shame	*energy, semen*
Is lust in action*¹; and till action*, lust	*sexual intercourse / until consummation*
Is perjured*, murd'rous, bloody, full of blame,	*deceitful*
Savage, extreme, rude*, cruel, not to trust*,	*coarse, unrefined / untrustworthy*
Enjoyed no sooner but despisèd straight*,	*immediately*
Past reason* hunted, and no sooner had*,	*irrationally / consummated*
Past reason* hated as a swallowed bait*	*irrationally / trap*
On purpose laid to make the taker mad²;	
Mad in pursuit and in possession so*,	*also (i.e., mad)*
Had*, having, and in quest to have*, extreme;	*consummated / in attempting to consummate*
A bliss in proof* and proved*, a very woe*;	*experience (i.e., orgasm) / experienced / true regret*
Before, a joy proposed; behind, a dream*.	*nightmare, illusion*
All this the world well knows, yet none knows well	
To shun the heaven* that leads men to this hell³.	*bliss of orgasm*

SUMMARY

Sonnet 129 grapples with the idea of lust (sexual desire) in anticipation, consummation, and memory. The first quatrain discusses lust prior to consummation as violent and irrational in the extreme. The second quatrain describes the change of state once the threshold of consummation is crossed, and impulsive desire crumples to crippling disgust. Lust is like a piece of bait: tempting before one has entered the trap, but cursed once the ruse is played out. The third quatrain debunks sexual desire as miserable in all three aspects: anticipation, consummation, and retrospection. The couplet concludes that although everyone knows that lust is a dangerous trap, no one is able to avoid it.

ANALYSIS

In this moralizing, indignant sonnet, Shakespeare rails against lust with the carnality and fervor of a pimp who has found the pulpit. The viciousness of emotions described belies the distancing, third-person narration (a rarity in the sonnets), suggesting that that Shakespeare has indeed experienced the disorienting dervish of lust personally.

The sonnet argues that lust is all-consuming and disorienting, and enacts this disorientation through the savagery of its verse. The goal is to shock a public that has grown too complacent: they know that lust is dangerous, "yet none knows well / To shun the heaven that leads men to this hell" (13–14). The "well" here distinguishes theory from application, hypocrisy from true understanding. People know that lust is evil, but not "well" enough to avoid it. This unsettling poem is an evocative cautionary tale.

The sonnet's key metaphor of lust as "bait" (7) most cleanly symbolizes lust in its three stages, which are anticipation, consummation, and retrospection. For its victim, bait first represents a treat, then, once consumed, a moment of horrible realization, and finally shame and regret. Similarly, lust first appears like "bliss" (11), but once achieved proves to be "a very woe" (11).

---

1. *Th' expense of spirit in a waste of shame / Is lust in action*: consummated lust ("lust in action") is a shameful waste of energy and/or semen ("spirit").
2. *a swallowed bait on purpose laid to make the taker mad*: lust is an intentional, maddening trap, with orgasm (lust "had") as the bait.
3. *this hell*: this shame of sex; also, the vagina

LANGUAGE NOTES

Tone	disgusted; dramatic; indignant

Themes   lust is disorienting, violent, and maddening (8) in all its stages: anticipation, consummation, and retrospection; despite their better judgment, humans continue to indulge their lust

Symbol   in lines 7–8, the object of lust takes the form of "bait" (7) in a trap

Metaphors   the poet describes lust prior to consummation as prey, something "hunted" (6); Lust prior to consummation is "a joy" (12); lust after consummation is a "dream" (12) or nightmare; lust is a trap, with the promise of orgasm as the "bait" (7)

Pattern   extensive use of catalogues: e.g., "perjured, murderous, bloody, full of blame / Savage, extreme, rude, cruel, not to trust" (3–4) ; several tenses of a verb referring to the various stages of lust: e.g., "had, having, and in quest to have" (10)

LANGUAGE

The language of Sonnet 129 seeks to mirror the frenzy and disorientation that lust wreaks on the human psyche. The tone of the sonnet is dramatically indignant, its word choices are extreme, and its syntax is fragmentary and explosive. The poem is littered with assonance of vague, unclear sounds: the murk of "perjured, murd'rous" (3) and the diphthongs of "hated as a swallowed bait / On purpose lgd to make the taker" (11). The instances of alliteration and consonance are dense and tangled. The most relentless sounds are the hiss of the sibilants, such as in "Savage, extreme … not to trust, / Enjoyed no sooner but despisèd straight / Past reason … " (4–6), and the accusatory bilabial pops of "A bliss in proof, and proved, a very woe, / Before, a joy progosed, behind, a dream" (10–12). Lust is both personified as a treacherous thug (3–4) and reified as prey and bait for a trap (6–14). The long, asyndeton lists ("perjured, murderous, bloody, full of blame / Savage, extreme, rude, cruel, not to trust" [3–4]) present a relentless assault of incantatory repetition. Both these lists and the repetitions of variously inflected verbs—"had, having, and in quest to have" (10), "proof … proved" (11)—not only contribute to the disorientation but also give the piece a violent staccato rhythm. All of these devices add up to a raw, anguished poem that overwhelms the reader with its urgent confusion of figurations. Shakespeare's techniques suggest that inflammation of passion disorders the usually smooth musicality of poetry. Because the main effects come from the linguistic and syntactic rhythms, the metaphors are few and fleeting, which is unusual for a sonnet of Shakespeare's. Buried in the linguistic avalanche, they participate in the cumulative onslaught of the verse.

FORM

Sonnet 129 is a curious beast: it does not decisively identify itself as either a Petrarchan sonnet or an English sonnet until the couplet. The couplet summarizes and concludes the argument in an autonomous epigrammatic form, placing Sonnet 129 firmly within the English model. We could categorize the quatrains as follows: the first introduces lust prior to consummation; the second explores the change brought about by consummation, swinging desire to disgust; the third completes the cycle by categorizing lust as mad before, during, and after consummation. At the same time, the three quatrains together derive their force from the continuity of onslaught. The turns and pauses at the quatrain breaks are not as decisive here as in other sonnets. Rather, the relentless forward motion of the lines strives to capture the frenzy of lust described in the poem.

SONNET 130

I see my beloved as she really is, not in exaggerated metaphors, and still find her extraordinary.

My mistress' eyes are nothing like the sun;
Coral is far more red than her lips' red;
If snow be white, why then her breasts are dun*;   *grayish brown*
If hair be wires, black wires grow on her head.[1]
I have seen roses damasked*, red and white,   *dappled, patterned*
But no such roses see I in her cheeks;
And in some perfumes is there more delight
Than in the breath that from my mistress reeks*.   *issues, stinks*
I love to hear her speak, yet well I know
That music hath a far more pleasing sound;
I grant I never saw a goddess go*:   *move*
My mistress when she walks treads on the ground.
    And yet, by heaven, I think my love as rare*   *extraordinary*
    As any she* belied* with false compare*.[2]   *woman / misrepresented / comparisons*

SUMMARY

The poet contrasts his beloved with exaggerated descriptions of women in poetic convention. His lady's eyes, lips, hair, and breasts all fall short of traditional grand metaphors. Her cheeks and her breath too miss the poetic ideal. Finally, both her speech and her gait are banal. However, he still finds her more extraordinary than any imaginary ideal.

ANALYSIS

This sonnet, one of Shakespeare's better-known, plays an elaborate joke on the conventions of Elizabethan love poetry, and readers are still laughing today. The sonnet mocks the traditional conceits of love poetry. These traditions take their root in the work of Petrarch, the Italian Renaissance poet whose sonnet sequence *Canzoniere* proved highly influential in the development of poetry. In his poetry, Petrarch described his beloved Laura with lists of comparisons of her features to natural phenomena: lips red as rubies, skin clear as snow, hair like spun flax, etc. After the Sir Philip Sidney popularized the sonnet form with his successful collection *Astrophil and Stella*, these Petrarchan conceits evolved into to the clichés they have been to this day.

Shakespeare's sonnets subvert their Petrarchan origins in many ways. He addresses most of the sonnets not to an idealized woman, but to a flawed, if beautiful, young man. Sonnet 18, for example, asks "Shall I compare thee to a summer's day?" In contrast, Sonnet 130 pokes fun at Petrarchan conceits by taking them too literally and then countering their dramatic hyperbole with refreshing authenticity. Poetic figuration, the sonnet suggests, creates standards that are idealized and guaranteed to disappoint. These standards can be replaced by a more realistic, human perspective on beauty.

---

1. *If hair be wires*: blond hair was often described as golden wires in Elizabethan poetry. The poet's mistress is dark-haired, not a conventional blond beauty. Sonnet 127 offers further insight into a beloved's dark complexion.
2. *any she belied with false compare*: any girl wrongly praised in misleading poetic conceits.

LANGUAGE NOTES

Tone   humorous (1–12); quietly defiant (13–14)

Theme   poetic conceits of beauty are unrealistic, hyperbolized, and silly; real women do not fit idealized standards of beauty, but are worthy of love nonetheless

Metaphor   eyes implicitly compared to the sun (1) ; the poet's beloved hair is "black wires" (4); the poet describes flush facial skin as "roses" (6)

Pattern   sequence of near-miss metaphors and similes: "My mistress' eyes are nothing like the sun" (1), "but no such roses see I in her cheeks" (6), etc.

LANGUAGE

Sonnet 130 derives its punch from a conscious departure from poetic commonplaces. The language of the poem similarly avoids traditionally poetic language. The verse is sparse and straightforward, with only one minor alliterative indulgence: "I grant I never saw a goddess go" (11). The constraints of Shakespeare's project lead to monotonous syntax: most of the phrases follow the basic pattern "she is not this way, but that way." The structure of lines 3 and 4 is so similar as to be anaphoric: "If snow be white, why then her breasts are dun; / If hair be wires, black wires grow on her head." The rejection of stylistic poetic conventions echoes the rejection of poetic conceits. The sonnet advocates acceptance of flawed authenticity in straightforward, authentic language.

FORM

Sonnet 130 fits into both the Elizabethan and the Petrarchan sonnet models. According to the Petrarchan model, the octave of the sonnet focuses on the beloved's appearance, while the sestet describes her speech, gait, and stature. Within the Elizabethan model, the first quatrain proceeds through its negative comparisons line by line, whereas the second and third spread their comparisons over two lines, expanding and developing their argument. The change of pace adds variety to what is essentially a one-trick poem. The couplet, as customary, stands apart and comments on the preceding lines.

SONNET 138

My beloved and I lie to each other in order to maintain a balanced relationship.

When my love swears that she is made of truth[1]
I do believe her though I know she lies,
That* she might think me some untutored* youth   *so that / uneducated*
Unlearnèd in the world's false subtleties.
Thus vainly* thinking that she thinks me young,   *(1) in vain (2) with vanity*
Although she knows my days are past the best,
Simply* I credit her false-speaking* tongue;   *like a simpleton / lying*

On both sides thus is simple truth suppressed[2].
But wherefore* says she not she is unjust*,   *why / untruthful*
And wherefore say not I that I am old?
O, love's best habit* is in seeming trust,[3]   *outfit (here meaning "usual practice")*
And age in love* loves not to have years told.[4]   *old lovers*

     Therefore I lie with her, and she with me[5],
     And in our faults by lies we flattered be.

SUMMARY

In this tongue-in-cheek sonnet, the poet describes why he and his lover willingly fool each other. Even though he knows that she lies to him (about being faithful), he chooses to believe her in order to seem unworldly and unsophisticated and therefore to seem younger than he really is. So why doesn't she admit that she's cheating? And why doesn't the poet admit to being old? Because lovers are supposed to appear to trust each other. Besides, old people in love don't like revealing how old they really are. So both the poet and his beloved lie to each other, and let themselves go on being flattered and deceived.

ANALYSIS

Like many other pieces in Shakespeare's sequence of sonnets, 138 mocks and discredits the traditional Petrarchan love sonnet. In Sonnet 130, for example, the poet goes to great lengths to debunk all sorts of poetic lies about his beloved: her eyes are nothing like the sun, she has no corals in her lips, her breath is not as sweet as perfume. The beloved is resolutely human and flawed, and yet the speaker finds her as "rare" as any other woman about whom poets have written beautiful lies. Ultimately, Sonnet 130 suggests truth and reality, as opposed to fanciful notions, form a good basis for a romantic relationship.

     Sonnet 138 continues 130's project of rendering romance more realistically. This work depicts a relationship far from the ideal. Traditional Petrarchan character archetypes are inverted and recast: the passionate, anguished poet has been replaced by a smug, glib cad and the distant, idealized beloved is traded for a lying adulteress. This aging poet and his dishonest lover are more recognizably human than the near-mythic characters found in traditional love poetry, and their relationship, while it is flawed in many ways, is nonetheless a real one. The beloved is not a distant, untouchable figure. She comes down to earth and actively engages with the poet. Pronouns referring to the poet (I, me, my) alternate continually with pronouns referring to the beloved (she, her). The attention shifts equally between the two, suggesting that the two are equal partners in this game of lies. "Both sides" (8) participate in the project of mutual deception.

---

1. *is made of truth*: tells the truth, with a pun on *maid of truth*, or "virgin."
2. *On both sides thus is simple truth suppressed*: so both of us lie—she by saying untruths, and I by pretending to believe her.
3. *Love's best habit is in seeming trust*: love works best (is best dressed in) when the lovers pretend to trust each other.
4. *Age in love loves not to have years told*: old lovers (i.e., the poet) don't like revealing their true ages.
5. *I lie with her, and she with me*: (1) She and I lie to each other. (2) She and I have sex with ("lie with") each other.

However, where Sonnet 130 criticizes those who dress their love up in lies, Sonnet 138 embraces the need for dishonesty in love. The beloved needs to believe that the poet is still young, and the poet needs to believe that his beloved is chaste and faithful. The speaker's situation is inherently paradoxical: because of his need to believe that his beloved is truthful, he chooses to ignore the fact that she's lying. The scholar Stephen Booth points out that we as readers experience the same dilemma as the poet when we read his glib claim "I do believe her though I know she lies" (2): although we understand what he says (and so believe him), we know that there is a logical contradiction in his statement (i.e., we know he lies). The lovers' blatant, forthright hypocrisy, and the poem's sly, winking tone, pokes fun at those who believe in the classical ideal of romantic love, with its virtuous ladies, tortured poets, and grand passion.

Sonnets 138 and 144 are the only ones in the sequence that appear in an edition other than the 1609 Quarto. In 1599, William Jaggard published a collection of twenty poems entitled "The Passionate Pilgrim." Though the poems were advertised as the work of "W. Shakespeare," only five of the twenty are Shakespeare's, including Sonnets 138 and 144.

LANGUAGE NOTES

Tone	arch, amused, flippant
Themes	the necessary compromises of love; love as a game
Metaphors	the lover swears that she is "made of truth" (1); good practices described as habitual outfits: "love's best habit" (11)
Pattern	repetition of personal pronouns: I, my, she, her; lexical chiasmus: "she not she is" (9), "I that I" (10) "age in love loves not" (11)

LANGUAGE

In its language, Sonnet 138 distinguishes itself from traditional courtly love poetry. It is relatively free of complex metaphors and imagery (a notable exception is the gruesome synecdoche "false-speaking tongue" (7)). No extended conceits describe the beloved's beauty, youth, or virtue. Instead of figuration, a fairly complicated linguistic play mirrors the lovers' emotional games. Each line is end-stopped (i.e., no enjambment), creating an even, back-and-forth rhythm between the lines. In the first six lines, the personal pronouns alternate from "she" (1) to "I" (2), and back to "she" (5–6) again. Together these rhythmic exchanges create the effect of a tennis match: we watch as the two lovers volley their lies back and forth. This feeling of play is further enhanced by other poetic devices that imitate a back-and-forth game. For example, in the tripping, sing-song consonance of "On both sides thus is simple truth suppressed" (8, an unfortunate doozy for the lisping reader), the ss and ths playfully alternate. Another poetic device used to great effect in this poem is the chiasmus. In lines 9, 10, and 11, phrases that reflect and wrap around each other—"she not she," "I that I," and "age in love loves not"—enhance the bouncy, alternating rhythm of the verse. The use of chiasmus also suggests that the two lovers, like the criss-crossing chiasmus, reflect each other, mirroring each other's actions and maintaining an equal balance.

FORM

Sonnet 138 follows the Elizabethan model, with three quatrains of alternating *abab* rhyme and a final heroic couplet. The epigrammatic couplet here makes for particularly successful conclusion. In accordance with the Shakespearean model, the couplet is autonomous and provides a pithy summary of the lovers' relationship. Its cleverness and quip-like structure are the perfect cap to this witty, comical piece. The couplet also resolves several of the poem's linguistic threads. For example, throughout the poem a string of pronouns bounces back and forth between the speaker's "I" and the lover's "she." This focuses the attention first on one partner, then the other. We experience the sonnet as if we are watching a tennis match, in which the lovers remain distinct and separate on their respective sides of the court. In the first line of the couplet, this separation of the lovers is taken to an extreme: "I lie with her, and she with me" (13) gives the impression that there are two sets of lovers in the bed. In the final lines, the lovers finally join under the plural pronouns "our" and "we," suggesting that, ultimately, the two are indeed a real couple. At the same time, the poet maintains the playful, back-and-forth rhythm in the final line within the teasing, flirting consonance: "in our *f*aults by *l*ies we *f*lattered be" (14). Finally, the concluding couplet makes obvious the double entendre that has been lurking under the word "lie" from the beginning. The lovers not only "tell lies" together, but also "lie" together sexually.

SONNET 146

Instead of satisfying the mortal body, focus resources on the immortal soul.

Poor soul, the center of my sinful earth*,	*i.e., my body*
[Feeding]¹ these rebel powers* that thee array*²;	*physical desires (lust, hunger) / i.e., my soul / adorn*
Why dost thou pine* within and suffer dearth*,	*languish / starvation*
Painting thy outward walls* so costly gay*?	*i.e., the body / extravagantly flashy*
Why so large cost, having so short a lease,	
Dost thou upon thy fading mansion* spend? ³	*i.e., the body*
Shall worms, inheritors of this excess,	
Eat up thy charge*?⁴ Is this thy body's end*?	*i.e., the body / (1) final state (2) purpose*
Then, soul, live thou upon thy servant's* loss,	*i.e., the body's*
And let that* pine to aggravate* thy store*. ⁵	*i.e., the body / increase / resources*
Buy terms divine* in selling hours of dross*⁶;	*i.e., eternity / worthlessness*
Within* be fed, without* be rich no more.	*internally / externally*
So shalt thou* feed on Death, that feeds on men,	*i.e., my soul*
And Death once dead, there's no more dying then⁷.	

SUMMARY

The poet laments spending time on satisfying the desires of the mortal body at the expense of enriching the immortal soul. His soul is a prisoner of the body and its needs. Why has he allowed his soul to languish while worrying about his appearance? Since his body will die and fall prey to worms, he should put his energy into his soul and let his body languish instead. Once the body is dead, the soul will live on, immortal.

ANALYSIS

A rare ascetic in an aesthetic project, Sonnet 146 takes up the themes of other sonnets and presents them in a religious light. The sonnets explore several oppositions, including age and youth, dark and light, despair and solace, and the body and the soul. The poet often pursues this last in tirades against artifice and makeup, obstacles to nature and truth: "Truth needs no color with his color fixed" (101:6). In Sonnet 146, excessive attention to the mortal body diverts resources away from the true immortal soul within. The body is portrayed as a temporary house, with the implication that the permanent home is the heavenly afterlife. Shakespeare uses financial vocabulary, implying that Jesus Christ "bought" salvation for all men and "paid" with his life. This vocabulary is part of everyday speech, not poetic.

---

1. The first foot of line 2 has not been recovered. "Feeding" has been suggested by the scholar Helen Vendler. Other editorial suggestions include prey to", "ruled by", "slave of", "vexed by", and "hiding."
2. *Poor soul, the center of my sinful earth / [Feeding] these rebel powers that thee array*; My poor soul—the core of my body and being—you have been taken over by greedy physical yearnings (hunger and lust).
3. *Why so large cost, having so short a lease / Dost thou upon thy fading mansion spend?*: Why do you (my soul) spend so much energy on the atrophying physical body, which will die soon anyway?
4. *Shall worms, inheritors of this excess, / Eat up thy charge?*: Won't worms devour the body, and the energy you have put into it, after death anyway?
5. *Then, soul, live thou upon thy servant's loss, / And let that pine to aggravate thy store.* Therefore (i.e., because the body will die and be consumed by worms) put your financial and spiritual energy into the soul, letting the body (the soul's "servant") languish.
6. *Buy terms divine in selling hours of dross*: Rather than spending time on worthless earthly pursuits, invest your energy into your eternal afterlife. Buy" and "sell" may poke at the Catholic Church's practice of literally selling indulgences (forgiveness for sins), which was popularly considered one of the Catholic Church's vices.
7. *So shalt thou feed on Death, that feeds on men, / And Death once dead, there's no more dying then*: In taking away from the body to give to the soul, the soul will grow (be fed) at the expense of the body, which will be consumed by Death. Once the body (i.e., "Death") is dead, the soul will enjoy eternal life.

LANGUAGE NOTES

Tone   Mournful, contemplative (1–8); inspiring (9–12); resolved (13–14)

Themes   The attention to the body and its needs as excessive and unwarranted; prioritizing the needs of the mind over the desires of the body

Symbols   Physical center as the core (1); feeding as symbol for "focusing on," "enriching"

Metaphors   The body as a "sinful earth," with the soul at its core (1)
The desires of the body as hungry "rebel powers" holding the soul hostage (2)
The implementations of the desires of the body (such as nice clothes) as decorative garments that "array" the soul (2)
The body as a decrepit house, whose outer walls are too well taken care of, and on which the soul has only a temporary lease (4, 5, 6)
Worms of the grave personified as the body's heirs (7)
The body as the soul's "servant" (9)
The riches of the soul are reified as a supply, or "store" (10), as something that can be bought (11), as food (13)
Death as metonym for the mortal body (13–14)
Soul personified as something that can "feed" and grow at the expense of the body (13).
Death personifies as a creature that feeds on the body (13)

Patterns   Military language: "rebel powers" (2), "array"—i.e., outfit for battle (2
Language of financial transactions: "poor" (1), "costly" (4), "large cost" (5), "lease" (5), "spend" (6), "inheritors" (7), "buy" (11), "selling" (11), "rich" (12)
Language of feeding, growing, consuming: "feed" etc. ([2], 12, 13, 13), "eat up" (8), "aggravate" (10), "store" (10),
Language of languishing: "poor" (1), "pine" (3, 10), "suffer" (3), "dearth" (3), "loss" (9), "dross" (11), "death," "dying" (13–14)

LANGUAGE

Sonnet 146 is dense with metaphoric figuration. The house, a physical object vulnerable to decay, stands in to represent the physical body. In contrast, Shakespeare personifies both death and the soul. Both are important forces, in life and within the Christian doctrine. The immortal contract of the soul with God is represented as a physical, financial contract.

FORM

Sonnet 146 shows the influences of both Petrarchan and English sonnets. The first eight lines introduce and develop the conceit of the soul trapped inside a decrepit house of a body. The sestet "answers" the octave and presents a solution. At the same time, the couplet follows the English model, summarizing and concluding the sonnet in a pat epigram.

GLOSSARY

ALLEGORY (Genre): A narrative whose literal elements, both characters and events, correspond clearly and directly to abstract ideas and theories.

Ex: *The narrator's journey in Dante's* Inferno *is an allegory for his—and all humankind's—search for meaning and divine grace.* Animal Farm *allegorically depicts the rise of Soviet communism and oppression.*

ALLITERATION (Figurative Language/sound): The repetition of initial consonant sounds in nearby words for poetic effect.

Ex: *Beowulf bode in the burg*

ALLUSION (Literary Technique): An implicit reference to a historical, literary, or biblical character, event, or element. The title of Faulkner's *The Sound and the Fury* alludes to a line from Shakespeare's *Macbeth*: "[Life] is a tale told by an idiot / Full of sound and fury signifying nothing." Allusions add symbolic weight by making subtle connections with other works. Captain Ahab's name in Melville's *Moby-Dick* is a running allusion to the wicked and idolatrous biblical king Ahab—a connection that adds depth to Ahab's character.

AMPHIBRACH (Poetry/meter: foot type): A trisyllabic foot: one stressed syllable in between two unstressed ones.

Ex: *horrendous*

ANAPEST (Poetry/meter: foot type): A trisyllabic foot: two unstressed syllable and one stressed syllable.

Ex: *far away*

ANAPHORA (Figurative Language/phrase structure): Deliberate repetition of the phrase structure for effect.

ANTAGONIST (Story Elements/character): The entity that acts to frustrate the goals of the protagonist. The antagonist is usually another character but may also be a non-human force.

Ex: *The antagonist to Hamlet is Claudius; the antagonist to Yossarian in Joseph Heller's* Catch-22 *is the military bureaucracy.*

ANTHROPOMORPHISM (Figurative Language/imagery): The attribution of human characteristics to animals, things, or ideas.

ANTITHESIS (Figurative Language/phrase structure): The juxtaposition of two contradictory ideas in similar grammatical structures. Also used to refer to the second of such ideas.

ANTONYM (Words): A word that means the opposite of another word.

Ex: "High" and "low" are antonyms.

APOSTROPHE (Literary Technique/narration): A direct address to an object, to an idea, or to an absent or dead person.

Ex: *Shakespeare uses apostrophe in Juliet's soliloquy as she impatiently awaits her wedding night and addresses the night directly: "Come, civil night, / Thou sober-suited matron, all in black, / And learn me how to lose a winning match, / Played for a pair of stainless maidenhoods"* (R&J, III.ii).

ASSONANCE (Figurative Language/sound): The repetition of similar vowel sounds in a sequence of nearby words, especially in stressed syllables.

ASYNDETON (Figurative Language/phrase structure): The omission of conjunctions for a cumulative, list-like effect. The opposite of **asyndeton** is **polysyndeton**.
Ex: *"I came, I saw, I conquered."*

BLANK VERSE (Poetry/poetic form): Unrhymed iambic pentameter. Most of Shakespeare's verse work is in iambic pentameter.

CAESURA (Poetry/rhythm & meaning): In verse, a pronounced pause between feet caused by the meaning of the text (rather than by its metrical structure). In analysis, a caesura is often marked with ||.
Ex: Sonnet 116: *"Let me | not to | the mar|riage of | true minds / Admit | impe|diments. || Love is | not love . . ."*

CHARACTER (Story Elements): Any person, animal, or other being who plays a role in a story.

CHIASMUS (Figurative Language/phrase structure): A criss-crossing effect, whether lexical or syntactical.
Ex: Lexical: *"The spectacle of power and the power of spectacle."* Syntactical: *"I love too much and too little hate."*

CHORUS (Drama/stock character): In Greek drama, a group of singers and dancers who filled in plot points or provided commentary on the action. A solitary chorus figure sometimes recited the prologue, epilogue, and inter-act commentary in Elizabethan drama, including some of Shakespeare's plays.
Ex: Shakespeare's Romeo and Juliet *begins with summary of the action delivered by a chorus: "Two houses, both alike in dignity . . ."*

CLIMAX (Story Elements/plot): In a narrative, the moment at which the conflict comes to a head. This moment usually coincides with the *dramatic climax*, the moment of highest dramatic tension, when the reader is most emotionally invested in the story.

COMEDY (Genre/drama): A play written to amuse the audience. In the middle ages, the term "comedy" referred to a poetic work with a happy ending, like Dante's *Divine Comedy*. Later it extended to dramatic works as well. Shakespearean comedies are light in tone and end in marriage. There are many types of comedy, including the **comedies of manners**.

COMEDY OF MANNERS (Genre/drama): A comedy, often satirical, that revolves around the social customs of sophisticated society. Common character types of this genre include clandestine lovers, jealous husbands, foolish dandies, and witty observers.
Ex: Oscar Wilde's The Importance of Being Earnest *and other works; works by Moliere; works by Noel Coward.*

CONCEIT (Figurative Language/imagery): An elaborate parallel between two seemingly dissimilar objects or ideas.

CONNOTATION (Words): The figurative meanings and associations of a word. Contrasted with **denotation**.

CONSONANCE (Figurative Language/sound): The repetition of consonant sounds in nearby words, especially of final sounds.

COUPLET (Poetry/stanza form): Two consecutive rhyming lines of verse. *See also* **heroic couplet**.

DACTYL (Poetry/meter: foot type): A trisyllabic foot: one stressed syllable followed by two unstressed syllables.
Ex: **difficult**

DENOTATION (Words): The literal, dictionary meaning of a word. Contrasted with **connotation**, the figurative and associative meanings.

Ex: *The denotation of the word "diamond" is "an extremely hard carbon compound"; the connotations of "diamond" range from engagement rings to love to two months' salary.*

DEUX EX MACHINA (Literary Technique/plot): The use of a forced, unexpected event to resolve the conflicts in a story.

Ex: *Fortinbras's appearance at the end of* Hamlet *is a* deux ex machina *that assures the succession to the Danish thone.*

DIMETER (Poetry/Meter: Length): Two feet per line of verse.

DOPPELGANGER (Literary Technique/stock character): A mysterious figure, often haunting, who is in some way the double of another character.

DRAMATIC IRONY (Literary Technique/plot): Any situation in which the audience understands more about the characters' words or actions than the characters do themselves.

ELIZABETHAN SONNET (Poetry/poetic form): *See **Shakespearean sonnet**.*

END RHYME (Poetry/rhyme): Rhyme between the ends of two lines. When thinking about whether a poem rhymes, most people think of end rhyme first.

END-STOP (Poetry/rhythm & meaning): The completion of the thought and the grammatical construction (sentence or clause) at the end of a line of verse. An end-stopped line usually ends in a comma, a semicolon, or a period.

ENGLISH SONNET (Poetry/poetic form): *See **Shakespearean sonnet**.*

ENJAMBMENT (Poetry/Rhythm & Meaning): The continuation of a grammatical construction (sentence or clause) of a line of verse into the next line. Enjambment stands in opposition to an **end-stop**. It creates a sense of suspense and excitement, and emphasizes the last word of the enjambed line. It also adds emphasis to the word at the end of the line.

Ex: *John Keats's "Ode to a Nightingale": "Thy plaintive anthem fades / Past the near meadows, over the still stream."*

EPIGRAPH (Publishing): A short quotation that introduces a novel or a chapter.

Ex: *"No man is an island... therefore ask not for whom the bell tolls. It tolls for thee."* For Whom the Bell Tolls, *Hemingway*

EPIPHANY (Literary Technique): A sudden, powerful, and often spiritual or life-changing realization that a character reaches in an otherwise ordinary or everyday moment.

Ex: *Many of the short stories in James Joyce's* Dubliners *involve moments of epiphany.*

FEMININE ENDING (Poetry/meter): An extrametrical unstressed syllable added to an **iamb** or an **anapest**.

FEMININE RHYME (Poetry/rhyme): A rhyme consisting of a stressed syllable followed by an unstressed syllable.

FIGURE OF SPEECH (Figurative Language): Any expression that stretches the meaning of words beyond their literal meanings.

FIRST FOLIO (Publishing/Shakespeare; 1623): The first (almost complete) publication of Shakespeare's collected works, and the major primary source for many of his plays.

FLASHBACK (Literary Technique/plot): Any presentation of material that happens before the opening scene. Flashbacks are most often narrated as memories or stories told by characters.

FOIL (Story Elements/character): A character who, by comparison, brings the characteristics of another character (often, a major character) into relief.
Ex: Laertes, quick to act and slow to think, is a foil for Hamlet. In The Awakening, *Adele, a committed mother, is a foil for Edna.*

FOLIO (Publishing): A standard sheet of paper folded in half; also, a book made up of folio sheets. Most of Shakespeare's plays appear in the 1623 First Folio publication.

FOOT (Poetry/meter): In verse, a unit of rhythm, usually with at least one accented syllable. Iamb, trochee, anapest, dactyl, amphibrach, and spondee are all types of feet.

FORESHADOWING (Literary Technique/plot): Any clue or hint of future events in a literary work.
Ex: The yellow fever is mentioned several times in Daisy Miller *before the title character becomes sick.*

FRAME STORY (Genre): A narrative that consists of or connects several otherwise unrelated stories. The term "frame story," or sometimes "**framework story**" can also refer to any story-within-a-story narrative.
Ex: Geoffrey Chaucer's Canterbury Tales; *Bocaccio's* The Decameron; *Shakespeare's* The Taming of the Shrew; *Joseph Conrad's* Heart of Darkness; *Emily Bontë's* Wuthering Heights

FRAMEWORK STORY (Genre): See *frame story.*

FREE VERSE (Poetry/poetic form): Verse that does not conform to any fixed meter or rhyme scheme. Less evident rhythmic patterns are present to give the poem shape.
Ex: Walt Whitman's "Leaves of Grass" is a seminal work of free verse.

GENRE: A catergory of literary works, determined based on themes, literary techniques, or, sometimes, era of composition.

GREEK CHORUS (Drama/stock character): See *chorus.*

HERO, HEROINE (Story Elements/character type): The main character of a literary work. The terms "hero" and "heroine" are often synonymous with **protagonist**, but sometimes they are reserved for admirable protagonists and contrasted with **antihero**.

HEROIC COUPLET (Poetry/stanza form): Two rhyming lines of iambic pentameter. A **Shakespearean sonnet** ends with a heroic couplet.
Ex: "The time is out of joint: O cursed spite, / That ever I was born to set it right!" (Hamlet)

HEXAMETER (Poetry/meter: length): Six feet per line of verse.

HISTORY PLAY (Genre/drama; late 16th century; England): A genre of Elizabethan drama that loosely depicts historical events, often surrounding the reign of a single king. These plays were based on contemporary historical chronicles, which were sometimes tweaked to suit the dramatic structure. Patriotic in spirit and massive in cast size, they featured sensational scenes such as coronations and battles.
Ex: Shakespeare wrote ten history plays, from the forgettable 1 Henry VI *to the iconic* Richard III.

HOMONYM (Words): A word that sounds the same as another word but has a different meaning.
Ex: "Know" and "no" are homonyms, as are "leaves" (form of "to leave") and "leaves" (plural of "leaf").

HUBRIS (Literary Technique/character): Excessive pride that leads to the **protagonist**'s downfall.

HYPERBOLE (Figurative Language/degree): Any kind of exaggeration, including for humor or effect.

IAMB (Poetry/meter: foot type): A disyllabic foot: one unstressed syllable and one stressed syllable.
Ex: *behold*

IAMBIC PENTAMETER (Poetry/meter): Each line of verse has five **iambic** feet (unstressed syllable followed by stressed syllable). Iambic pentameter is one of the most popular metrical schemes in English poetry. Most of Shakespeare's work is in iambic pentameter.
Ex: *The meter of "When **I** | do **count** | the **clock** | that **tells** | the **time**" (Sonnet 12) is perfect iambic pentameter.*

INTERIOR MONOLOGUE (Literary Technique/narration): A record of a character's thoughts and impressions; a technique for presenting the character's **stream of consciousness**. The term "interior monologue" may be used as a synonym for "stream of consciousness," but is often restricted to refer to a more structured sequence of rational thoughts.

INTERNAL RHYME (Poetry/rhyme): Rhyme between two or more words within a single line of verse.
Ex: *"And all is seared with trade; bleared, smeared with toil."*

IRONY (Literary Technnique): The use of detachment to draw awareness to the discrepancy between the apparent literal meaning of words and their intended implication, between the stated and the actual. *See also **dramatic irony.***

ITALIAN SONNET (Poetry/poetic form): *See **Petrarchan sonnet.***

LITOTES (Figurative Language/degree): Understatement expressed through negating the opposite.
Ex: *"She's no fool."*

LYRIC POETRY (Poetry/genre): A short poetic composition that describes the thoughts of a single speaker. Most modern poetry is lyrical (as opposed to dramatic or narrative). The **ode** and the **sonnet** are types of lyric poetry.
Ex: *Shakespeare's sonnets; John Keats' "Ode on a Grecian Urn"*

MASCULINE RHYME (Poetry/rhyme): End rhyme of stressed syllables.

MEDIEVAL ROMANCE (Genre; Middle Ages): A tale about knights and ladies incorporating courtly love themes. Standard narrative elements include knights rescuing maidens, embarking on quests, and forming bonds with kings, queens, and other knights.
Ex: *Stories of King Arthur, his queen Guinevere, and his "knights of the round table," including Launcelot. The Knight's Tale, the Miller's Tale, and the Wife of Bath's Tale of the* Canterbury Tales *all include elements of medieval romance. Don Quixote looks back on medieval romances with both ridicule and homage.*

MEIOSIS (Figurative Language/degree): Intentional understatement used for ironic effect. **Litotes** is a type of meiosis.
Ex: *In Act III of* Romeo and Juliet, *the mortally wounded Mercutio insists that his wound is merely "a scratch" (R&J III.i.98).*

METAPHOR (Figurative Language/imagery): A comparison of two things that does not use the words "like" or "as." Colloquially, the word "metaphor" is often used to refer to any kind of imaginative comparison, including **simile**.

Ex: *"Life is but a walking shadow; a poor player / That struts and frets his hour upon the stage / And then is heard no more"* (Macbeth, V.v.23–25).

METONYMY (Figurative Language/imagery): The substitution of one term for another closely associated term; for example, calling businessmen "suits." **Synecdoche** is a type of metonymy.

Ex: In *"Uneasy lies the head that wears the crown"* (2 Henry IV, III.i.31), *"wear[ing] the crown"* implies *"being a king."*

MIXED METAPHOR (Figurative Language/imagery): A combination of metaphors that produces a confused or contradictory image.

Ex: *"The collapse of the movie studio left mountains of debt in its wake."*

MONOLOGUE (Drama): A speech of a single character. If the character is alone on stage, the monologue is often called a **soliloquy**, although the term "monologue" is usually reserved to represent words spoken to a listener, even if none is present. In contrast, a **soliloquy** is meant to represent a character's thoughts.

Ex: Mark Antony's *"Friends, Romans, countrymen, lend me your ears; / I come to bury Caesar, not to praise him"* (Julius Caesar, III.ii) is a monologue.

MORALITY PLAY (Genre/drama; 15th–16th centuries): A play that presents an **allegory** of the Christian struggle for salvation.

MOTIF (Thematic Meaning): A recurring object, phrase, idea, emotion, or other device that develops or informs a work's major themes.

NARRATIVE (Story Elements): A sequence of events told by a **narrator** in story form.

NARRATOR (Story Elements): Anyone who tells the story. The narrator may or may not be a **character** in the narrative. In careful speech or writing, the narrator is always present, explicitly or implicitly; the narrator is a presence distinct from the author.

OBLIQUE RHYME (Poetry/rhyme): Imperfect rhyme of similar but not identical syllables, as between "port" and "heart." Also known as **off rhyme** and **slant rhyme**. Modern poets often use oblique rhyme as a subtler alternative to perfect rhyme.

OCTAVE (Poetry/stanza form): An eight-line stanza, especially in a **Petrarchan sonnet**.

ODE (Poetry/poetic form): A serious lyric poem, often of significant length, that usually conforms to an elaborate metrical structure.

Ex: William Wordsworth's *"Ode: Intimations of Immortality."*

OEDIPUS COMPLEX (Literary Technique/character): In psychoanalysis, the subconsciously sexual attachment of a young boy to his mother.

OFF RHYME (Poetry/rhyme): *See oblique rhyme.*

ONOMATOPOEIA (Figurative Language/sound & sense): The effect produced by a word whose sound evokes its meaning.

Ex: *"Meow," "buzz," "murmur,"* and *"moan"* are onomatopoeic.

OXYMORON (Figurative Language/imagery): The association of two conflicting terms, as in the word "bittersweet" or the expression "same difference."

Ex: *In* Romeo and Juliet, *Romeo's melodramatic outburst:* "O brawling love, O loving hate, / O anything of nothing first create! / O heavy lightness, serious vanity, / Misshapen chaos of well-seeming forms! / Feather of lead, bright smoke, cold fire, sick health, / Still-waking sleep, that is not what it is." (R&J, I.i.169-174)

PASTORAL (Genre): A celebration of the simple, rustic life of shepherds and farmers, often written by a sophisticated urban author. The lonely farmer or shepherd who longs to wed, like Farmer Oak from *Far From the Madding Crowd*, is a typical hero of the genre.

Ex: Far from the Madding Crowd; As You Like It *contains pastoral elements.*

PENTAMETER (Poetry/meter: length): Five feet per line of verse.

PERSONIFICATION (Figurative Language/imagery): The attribution of personal characteristics to animals, things, or ideas. **Anthropomorphism**—attribution of specifically human emotions and characteristics—is a type of personification.

Ex: *In Sonnet 65, Shakespeare personifies death as an attacking enemy.*

PETRARCHAN SONNET (Poetry/poetic form): A sonnet composed of an eight-line **octave** with the rhyme scheme *abbaabba* followed by a six-line **sestet** rhyming *cdecde* or *cdccdc*. The octave poses a problem that the sestet answers. This form was developed by the Italian Renaissance poet Petrarch; it is also known as the Italian sonnet.

PLOT (Story Elements): The arrangement of events in a narrative, including their order, their relative emphasis, and the implied causal connections between them.

POLYSYNDETON (Figurative Language/phrase structure): The repetition of conjunctions where they would not normally be used. The opposite of polysyndeton is **asyndeton**.

PROBLEM PLAY (Genre/drama): A term sometimes used to refer to three or four of Shakespeare's plays that do not comfortably fit into a traditional genre—plays that present a classification problem. Like the comedies, they end in or revolve around marriage, but the circumstances and the dark tone leave audiences uneasy. At the same time, the characters are not treated with enough dignity for tragedy. The three problem plays are *All's Well that Ends Well*, *Troilus and Cressida*, and *Measure for Measure*; *The Merchant of Venice* is occasionally cited as well. The term is also used to describe modern plays that confront a contemporary social problem with the intent of influencing public opinion. Problem plays in this sense were developed and popularized by Henrik Ibsen in works such as *A Doll's House* and *Hedda Gabler*. George Bernard Shaw continued the tradition.

PROTAGONIST (Story Elements/character): The main character in a literary work. Typically, the protagonist undergoes some kind of change or development over the course of the story. *See also* **antagonist.**

QUARTO (Publishing): A standard sheet of paper folded into quarters; also a book made up of quarto sheets. Eighteen of Shakespeare's plays appeared in one or more quarto editions before the publication of the *First Folio* in 1623.

QUATRAIN (Poetry/Stanza Form): A four-line stanza. The most common form of English verse. The quatrain has many variants, including staples such as the heroic quatrain, which is four lines of iambic pentameter rhyming *abab*.

REIFICATION (Figurative Language/imagery): Referring to an abstract concept as a concrete thing.

Ex: *In Sonnet 65, Shakespeare reifies coffins as "Time's chest."*

RENAISSANCE (Movement; 14th–16th centuries; Western Europe): The revival of the art and learning of antiquity that accompanied the transition between the Middle Ages and the modern world. The Renaissance spread throughout Europe after beginning in Italy in the fourteenth century.
Ex: Dante, Shakespeare, Marlowe

RHYME (Poetry): Similarity of endings of stressed syllables in words, often in corresponding positions of lines of verse. "Summer" and "drummer" rhyme, as do "say" and "away." *See also* **end rhyme, internal rhyme, masculine rhyme, feminine rhyme, oblique rhyme**.

RHYME SCHEME (Poetry): The pattern of **end rhymes** in a **stanza**. Rhyme scheme is usually notated with a letter of the alphabet for each similar end sound.
Ex: *"Roses are red; / Violets are blue. / You are so sweet / That I love you"* has the rhyme scheme abcb.

RHYTHM (Poetry): The recurring pattern of stressed and unstressed syllables, especially in verse.

ROMANCE (Genre): A nonrealistic story, in verse or prose, that features idealized characters, improbable adventures, and exotic settings. Although love often plays a significant role, the association of the word "romance" with love is a modern phenomenon. Romances were particularly popular in the Middle Ages and during the Renaissance. *See also* **medieval romance**.
Ex: The Winter's Tale, The Tempest, Pericles, Cymbeline, *Edmund Spenser's* The Faerie Queene

SATIRE (Genre): A work that exposes to ridicule the shortcomings of individuals, institutions, or society, often to make a political point.
Ex: *Jonathan Swift's* Gulliver's Travels *is one of the most famous satires in English literature.*

SESTET (Poetry/stanza form): A six-line stanza, especially in a **Petrarchan sonnet.**

SETTING (Story Elements): The time and place of a narrative. Setting may be very specific historically or geographically, as in the ancient Rome of Robert Graves's I, *Claudius*; or it may be vague and imaginary, as in the Neverland of J.M. Barrie's *Peter Pan.*

SHAKESPEAREAN SONNET (Poetry/poetic form): A sonnet composed of three rhyming quatrains and a heroic couplet; the usual rhyme scheme is *abab cdcd efef gg.* This form was popularized by Shakespeare durring the rule of Queen Elizabeth. It is also known as the Elizabethan sonnet or the English sonnet.

SIMILE (Figurative Language/imagery): A comparison of two things using "like" or "as."
Ex: *The expressions "cool as a cucumber," "happy as a clam," "sick as a dog" are all similes.*

SLANT RHYME (Poetry/rhyme): *See* **oblique rhyme**.

SOLILOQUY (Drama): A speech, often in verse, delivered by a character alone on stage. A soliloquy is a type of **monologue**, although the term soliloquy is usually reserved for representations of the character's inner thoughts.
Ex: *Hamlet's "To be or not to be" speech is the most famous soliloquy in English drama.*

SONNET (Poetry/poetic form): A single-stanza **lyric poem** of fourteen lines of equal length. In English, sonnets are in **iambic pentameter**. There are two major sonnet types: the **Petrarchan sonnet** (also known as Italian sonnet), and the **Shakespearean sonnet** (also known as English sonnet or Elizabethan sonnet). The Italian sonnet is divided into a problem-posing **octave** and a resolving **sestet**. The Shakespearean sonnet is divided into three **quatrains** and a **couplet.**

SPEECH ACT (Theory & Criticism): An utterance that performs an action in a particular context. For example, the words "I promise" perform the act of promising when they are spoken.

Ex: *"Hail!" is a speech act that appears frequently in Shakespeare's plays but has no adequate modern equivalent.*

SPONDEE (Poetry/meter: foot type): A disyllabic foot of two stressed syllables.

Ex: *men's eyes, Mozart*

STANZA (Poetry): A group of two or more lines of verse whose metrical form and rhyme scheme may be repeated in other stanzas of a poem.

STOCK CHARACTER (Story Elements/character): A character type that recurs throughout literature, or throughout a literary genre. Notable examples include the witty servant, the scheming villain, and the femme fatale. The fairy godmother is a stock character of fairy tales.

SUBPLOT (Story Elements/plot): A secondary plot. A subplot serves as a point of contrast or comparison to the main plot.

Ex: *In* King Lear, *Gloucester's conflicts with his sons form a subplot that comments on the main plot about Lear and his daughters.*

SYMBOL (Thematic Meaning/object): An object, character, image or another element that represents an abstract idea or concept. Symbols may be universal or take on different meanings in different contexts.

Ex: *A red rose is associated with romantic love. The fork in the road in Robert Frost's poem "The Road Not Taken" symbolizes the choice between two paths in life.*

SYNECDOCHE (Figurative Language/imagery): A form of **metonymy** in which a part is used to refer to the whole (as in "my wheels" instead of "my car"), or the whole is used to refer to a part (as in "the U.S. won the cup" instead of "the U.S. sailing team won the cup").

Ex: *In "Uneasy lies the head that wears the crown" (*2 Henry IV, *III.i.31), having a head implies being a person.*

SYNONYM (Words): A word that has the same or a similar meaning as a different word.

Ex: *"Raise" and "elevate" are synonyms.*

TERCET (Poetry/stanza form): A three-line stanza, often rhyming *aaa*.

TETRALOGY (Publishing): Four works grouped together.

Ex: *Eight of Shakespeare's history plays form two tetralogies:* Richard II, 1 Henry IV, 2 Henry IV, *and* Henry V; *and* 1 Henry VI, 2 Henry VI, 3 Henry VI, *and* Richard III.

TETRAMETER (Poetry/meter: length): Four feet per line of verse.

Ex: *Robert Frost sometimes uses tetrameter. From "The Road Not Taken": "Two roads diverged in a yellow wood / And sorry I could not travel both / And be one traveler, long I stood . . ."*

THEME (Thematic Meaning/story): A fundamental and universal idea explored in a literary work.

TRAGEDY (Genre/drama): A serious play that ends unhappily for the protagonist.

Ex: *Euripedes'* Medea; *Shakespeare's* King Lear

TRAGIC FLAW (Literary Technique/character): In critical theory, the flaw that leads to the downfall of a tragic hero. In *Othello*, jealousy is Othello's tragic flaw.

TRILOGY (Publishing): Three works grouped together.

Ex: *Shakespeare's* Henry VI *is a trilogy. Jules Verne's adventure tales* The Children of Captain Grant, The Mysterious Island, *and* Twenty Thousand Leagues Under the Sea *form a trilogy, although they do not happen consecutively.*

TRIMETER (Poetry/meter: length): Three feet per line of verse.

Ex: *Emily Dickinson often uses trimeter: "Success is counted sweetest / By those who ne'er succeed. / To comprehend a nectar / Requires sorest need"*

TROCHEE (Poetry/meter: foot type): A disyllabic foot: one stressed syllable followed by a stressed syllable.

Ex: *stupid*

TROPE (Figurative Language): A category of figures of speech that extend the literal meanings of words by inviting a comparison to other words, things, or ideas. **Metaphor**, **metonymy**, and **simile** are three common tropes.

VILLAIN (Story Elements/character type): The evil character who opposes the **hero**. A villain is an **antagonist** who has been judged as evil.